20th Edition

Principles of Financial Accounting

John J. Wild
University of Wisconsin at Madison

Ken W. Shaw
University of Missouri at Columbia

Barbara Chiappetta
Nassau Community College

With Working Papers

Learning Solutions

Boston Burr Ridge, IL Dubuque, IA New York San Francisco St. Louis
Bangkok Bogotá Caracas Lisbon London Madrid
Mexico City Milan New Delhi Seoul Singapore Sydney Taipei Toronto

The McGraw-Hill Companies

HM1030
PRINCIPLES OF FINANCIAL ACCOUNTING, Twentieth Edition
with Working Papers

7 8 9 10 11 12 QVS/QVS 19 18 17 16 15

ISBN-13: 978-0-697-80974-2
ISBN-10: 0-697-80974-9

Learning Solutions Consultant: Melani Theis
Learning Solutions Representative: Nada Mraovic
Production Editor: Carrie Braun
Printer/Binder: Quad/Graphics
Cover Images: Mountains © 2012 JupiterImages Corporation

dual pagination contents

Brief Contents

Contents

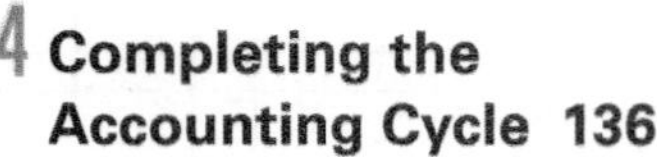

4 Completing the Accounting Cycle 136

7 Accounting Information Systems 270

12 Accounting for Partnerships 478

13 Accounting for Corporations 506

14 Long-Term Liabilities 550

16 Reporting the Statement of Cash Flows 630

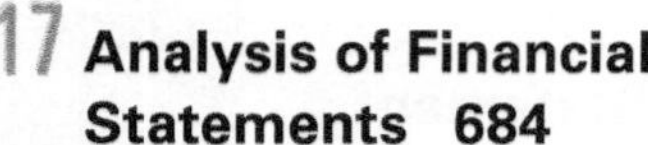

Principles of Financial Accounting

1 Accounting in Business

A Look at This Chapter

Accounting is crucial in our information age. In this chapter, we discuss the importance of accounting to different types of organizations and describe its many users and uses. We explain that ethics are essential to accounting. We also explain business transactions and how they are reflected in financial statements.

A Look Ahead

Chapter 2 describes and analyzes business transactions. We explain the analysis and recording of transactions, the ledger and trial balance, and the double-entry system. More generally, Chapters 2 through 4 show (via the accounting cycle) how financial statements reflect business activities.

Learning Objectives

Learning Objectives are classified as conceptual, analytical, or procedural.

CONCEPTUAL

C1 Explain the purpose and importance of accounting. (p. 4)

C2 Identify users and uses of, and opportunities in, accounting. (p. 5)

C3 Explain why ethics are crucial to accounting. (p. 8)

C4 Explain generally accepted accounting principles and define and apply several accounting principles. (p. 9)

C5 *Appendix 1B*—Identify and describe the three major activities of organizations. (p. 26)

ANALYTICAL

A1 Define and interpret the accounting equation and each of its components. (p. 14)

A2 Compute and interpret return on assets. (p. 22)

A3 *Appendix 1A*—Explain the relation between return and risk. (p. 26)

LP1

PROCEDURAL

P1 Analyze business transactions using the accounting equation. (p. 15)

P2 Identify and prepare basic financial statements and explain how they interrelate. (p. 19)

Decision Insight

*A **Decision Feature** launches each chapter showing the relevance of accounting for a real entrepreneur. An **Entrepreneurial Decision** problem at the end of the assignments returns to this feature with a mini-case.*

Accounting for Facebook

"We are focused on . . . helping people share information"

—MARK ZUCKERBERG

PALO ALTO, CA—"Open Society" conjures up philosophical thoughts and political ideologies. However, for Mark Zuckerberg, his vision of an open society "is to give people the power to share and make the world more open and connected." That vision led Mark to create Facebook **(Facebook.com)** from his college dorm. Today, Facebook is the highest-profile social networking site. Along the way, Mark had to learn accounting and the details of preparing and interpreting financial statements.

"It's all been very interesting," says Mark. Important questions involving business formation, transaction analysis, and financial reporting arose. Mark answered them and in the process has set his company apart. "I'm here to build something for the long term," declares Mark. "Anything else is a distraction."

Information is the focus—both within Facebook and within its accounting records. Mark recalls that when he launched his business, there were "all these reasons why they could not aggregate this [personal] information." He took a similar tactic in addressing accounting information. "There's an intense focus on . . . information, as both an ideal and a practical strategy to get things done," insists Mark. This includes using accounting information to make key business decisions.

While Facebook is the language of social networking, accounting is the language of business networking. "As a company we are very focused on what we are building," says Mark. "We are adding a certain amount of value to people's lives if we build a very good product." That value is reflected in its financial statements, which are based on transaction analysis and accounting concepts.

Facebook's success is reflected in its revenues, which continue to grow and exhibit what people call the monetizing of social networking. "Social Ads are doing pretty well," asserts Mark. "We are happy with how we are doing in terms of numbers of advertisers and revenue." Facebook also tracks its expenses and asset purchases. "We expect to achieve . . . profitability next year," states Mark. "It means we will be able to fund all of our operations and server purchases from the cash we generate." This is saying a lot as Facebook's operating expenditures must support nearly 1 billion photo uploads and 8 million video uploads per day.

Mark emphasizes that his financial house must be in order for Facebook to realize its full potential—and that potential is in his sights. "We believe really deeply that if people are sharing more, then the world will be a more open place where people can understand what is going on with the people around them."

[Sources: *Facebook Website,* January 2011; *CNN,* October 2008; *Mercury News,* April 2009; *VentureBeat,* March 2008; *FastCompany.com,* May 2007; *Wired,* June 2009]

Chapter Preview

*A **Preview** opens each chapter with a summary of topics covered.*

Today's world is one of information—its preparation, communication, analysis, and use. Accounting is at the core of this information age. Knowledge of accounting gives us career opportunities and the insight to take advantage of them. This book introduces concepts, procedures, and analyses that help us make better decisions, including career choices. In this chapter we describe accounting, the users and uses of accounting information, the forms and activities of organizations, and several accounting principles. We also introduce transaction analysis and financial statements.

Accounting in Business

Importance of Accounting
- Accounting information users
- Opportunities in accounting

Fundamentals of Accounting
- Ethics—key concept
- Generally accepted accounting principles
- International standards

Transaction Analysis
- Accounting equation
- Transaction analysis—illustrated

Financial Statements
- Income statement
- Statement of owner's equity
- Balance sheet
- Statement of cash flows

IMPORTANCE OF ACCOUNTING

C1 Explain the purpose and importance of accounting.

Why is accounting so popular on campuses? Why are there so many accounting jobs for graduates? Why is accounting so important to companies? Why do politicians and business leaders focus on accounting regulations? The answer is that we live in an information age, where that information, and its reliability, impacts the financial well-being of us all.

Accounting is an information and measurement system that identifies, records, and communicates relevant, reliable, and comparable information about an organization's business activities. *Identifying* business activities requires selecting transactions and events relevant to an organization. Examples are the sale of iPhones by **Apple** and the receipt of ticket money by **TicketMaster**. *Recording* business activities requires keeping a chronological log of transactions and events measured in dollars and classified and summarized in a useful format. *Communicating* business activities requires preparing accounting reports such as financial statements. It also requires analyzing and interpreting such reports. (The financial statements and notes of **Research In Motion**, the maker of *BlackBerry*, are shown in Appendix A near the end of this book. This appendix also shows the financial statements of **Apple**, **Palm**, and **Nokia**.) Exhibit 1.1 summarizes accounting activities.

Real company names are printed in bold magenta.

We must guard against a narrow view of accounting. Our most common contact with accounting is through credit approvals, checking accounts, tax forms, and payroll. These experiences are limited and tend to focus on the recordkeeping parts of accounting. **Recordkeeping,** or **bookkeeping,** is the recording of transactions and events, either manually or electronically. This is just one part of accounting. Accounting also identifies and communicates information on transactions and events, and it includes the crucial processes of analysis and interpretation.

EXHIBIT 1.1
Accounting Activities

Identifying → Recording → Communicating

Select transactions and events

Input, measure, and classify

Prepare, analyze, and interpret

Technology is a key part of modern business and plays a major role in accounting. Technology reduces the time, effort, and cost of recordkeeping while improving clerical accuracy. Some small organizations continue to perform various accounting tasks manually, but even they are impacted by technology. As technology has changed the way we store, process, and summarize masses of data, accounting has been freed to expand. Consulting, planning, and other financial services are now closely linked to accounting. These services require sorting through data, interpreting their meaning, identifying key factors, and analyzing their implications.

Point: Technology is only as useful as the accounting data available, and users' decisions are only as good as their understanding of accounting. The best software and recordkeeping cannot make up for lack of accounting knowledge.

Margin notes further enhance the textual material.

Users of Accounting Information

Accounting is often called the *language of business* because all organizations set up an accounting information system to communicate data to help people make better decisions. Exhibit 1.2 shows that the accounting information system serves many kinds of users (this is a partial listing) who can be divided into two groups: external users and internal users.

EXHIBIT 1.2

Users of Accounting Information

External users

- Lenders
- Shareholders
- Governments
- Consumer groups
- External auditors
- Customers

Internal users

- Officers
- Managers
- Internal auditors
- Sales staff
- Budget officers
- Controllers

Infographics reinforce key concepts through visual learning.

C2 Identify users and uses of, and opportunities in, accounting.

External Information Users **External users** of accounting information are *not* directly involved in running the organization. They include shareholders (investors), lenders, directors, customers, suppliers, regulators, lawyers, brokers, and the press. External users have limited access to an organization's information. Yet their business decisions depend on information that is reliable, relevant, and comparable.

Financial accounting is the area of accounting aimed at serving external users by providing them with *general-purpose financial statements*. The term *general-purpose* refers to the broad range of purposes for which external users rely on these statements.

Each external user has special information needs depending on the types of decisions to be made. *Lenders* (creditors) loan money or other resources to an organization. Banks, savings and loans, co-ops, and mortgage and finance companies are lenders. Lenders look for information to help them assess whether an organization is likely to repay its loans with interest. *Shareholders* (investors) are the owners of a corporation. They use accounting reports in deciding whether to buy, hold, or sell stock. Shareholders typically elect a *board of directors* to oversee their interests in an organization. Since directors are responsible to shareholders, their information needs are similar. *External* (independent) *auditors* examine financial statements to verify that they are prepared according to generally accepted accounting principles. *Nonexecutive employees* and *labor unions* use financial statements to judge the fairness of wages, assess job prospects, and bargain for better wages. *Regulators* often have legal authority over certain activities of organizations. For example, the Internal Revenue Service (IRS) and other tax authorities require organizations to file accounting reports in computing taxes. Other regulators include utility boards that use accounting information to set utility rates and securities regulators that require reports for companies that sell their stock to the public.

Accounting serves the needs of many other external users. *Voters, legislators,* and *government officials* use accounting information to monitor and evaluate government receipts and expenses. *Contributors* to nonprofit organizations use accounting information to evaluate the use and impact of their donations. *Suppliers* use accounting information to judge the soundness of a customer before making sales on credit, and *customers* use financial reports to assess the staying power of potential suppliers.

Internal Information Users **Internal users** of accounting information are those directly involved in managing and operating an organization. They use the information to help improve the efficiency and effectiveness of an organization. **Managerial accounting** is the area of accounting that serves the decision-making needs of internal users. Internal reports are not subject to the same rules as external reports and instead are designed with the special needs of internal users in mind.

There are several types of internal users, and many are managers of key operating activities. *Research and development managers* need information about projected costs and revenues of any proposed changes in products and services. *Purchasing managers* need to know what, when, and how much to purchase. *Human resource managers* need information about employees' payroll, benefits, performance, and compensation. *Production managers* depend on information to monitor costs and ensure quality. *Distribution managers* need reports for timely, accurate, and efficient delivery of products and services. *Marketing managers* use reports about sales and costs to target consumers, set prices, and monitor consumer needs, tastes, and price concerns. *Service managers* require information on the costs and benefits of looking after products and services. Decisions of these and other internal users depend on accounting reports.

Both internal and external users rely on internal controls to monitor and control company activities. *Internal controls* are procedures set up to protect company property and equipment, ensure reliable accounting reports, promote efficiency, and encourage adherence to company policies. Examples are good records, physical controls (locks, passwords, guards), and independent reviews.

Decision Insight boxes highlight relevant items from practice.

Decision Insight

Virtuous Returns Virtue is not always its own reward. Compare the S&P 500 with the Domini Social Index (DSI), which covers 400 companies that have especially good records of social responsibility. We see that returns for companies with socially responsible behavior are at least as high as those of the S&P 500. ■

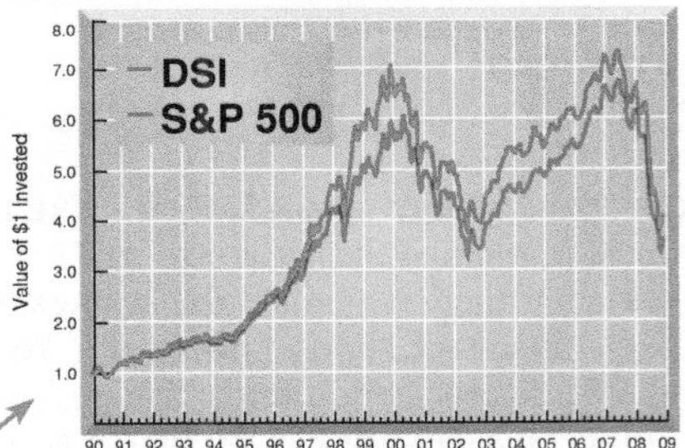

Graphical displays are often used to illustrate key points.

Opportunities in Accounting

Accounting information affects many aspects of our lives. When we earn money, pay taxes, invest savings, budget earnings, and plan for the future, we are influenced by accounting. Accounting has four broad areas of opportunities: financial, managerial, taxation, and accounting-related. Exhibit 1.3 lists selected opportunities in each area.

EXHIBIT 1.3

Accounting Opportunities

Opportunities in accounting

Financial	Managerial	Taxation	Accounting-related	
• Preparation	• General accounting	• Preparation	• Lenders	• FBI investigators
• Analysis	• Cost accounting	• Planning	• Consultants	• Market researchers
• Auditing	• Budgeting	• Regulatory	• Analysts	• Systems designers
• Regulatory	• Internal auditing	• Investigations	• Traders	• Merger services
• Consulting	• Consulting	• Consulting	• Directors	• Business valuation
• Planning	• Controller	• Enforcement	• Underwriters	• Forensic accounting
• Criminal investigation	• Treasurer	• Legal services	• Planners	• Litigation support
	• Strategy	• Estate plans	• Appraisers	• Entrepreneurs

The majority of accounting opportunities are in *private accounting,* which are employees working for businesses, as shown in Exhibit 1.4. *Public accounting* offers the next largest number of opportunities, which involve services such as auditing and tax advice to a vast range of businesses. Still other opportunities exist in government and not-for-profit agencies, including business regulation and investigation of law violations.

EXHIBIT 1.4

Accounting Jobs by Area

Private accounting 60%
Government, not-for-profit and education 16%
Public accounting 24%

Accounting specialists are highly regarded. Their professional standing often is denoted by a certificate. Certified public accountants (CPAs) must meet education and experience requirements, pass an examination, and exhibit ethical character. Many accounting specialists hold certificates in addition to or instead of the CPA. Two of the most common are the certificate in management accounting (CMA) and the certified internal auditor (CIA). Employers also look for specialists with designations such as certified bookkeeper (CB), certified payroll professional (CPP), personal financial specialist (PFS), certified fraud examiner (CFE), and certified forensic accountant (CrFA).

Point: The largest accounting firms are Deloitte, Ernst & Young, KPMG, and PricewaterhouseCoopers.

Individuals with accounting knowledge are always in demand as they can help with financial analysis, strategic planning, e-commerce, product feasibility analysis, information technology, and financial management. Benefit packages can include flexible work schedules, telecommuting options, career path alternatives, casual work environments, extended vacation time, and child and elder care.

Demand for accounting specialists is strong. Exhibit 1.5 reports average annual salaries for several accounting positions. Salary variation depends on location, company size, professional designation, experience, and other factors. For example, salaries for chief financial officers (CFO) range from under $75,000 to more than $1 million per year. Likewise, salaries for bookkeepers range from under $30,000 to more than $80,000.

Point: Census Bureau (2009) reports that for workers 18 and over, higher education yields higher average pay:

Advanced degree	$80,977
Bachelor's degree	57,181
High school degree	31,286
No high school degree	21,484

EXHIBIT 1.5

Accounting Salaries for Selected Fields

Field	Title (experience)	2009 Salary	2014 Estimate*
Public Accounting	Partner	$191,000	$211,000
	Manager (6–8 years)	94,500	104,000
	Senior (3–5 years)	72,000	79,500
	Junior (0–2 years)	51,500	57,000
Private Accounting	CFO	232,000	256,000
	Controller/Treasurer	147,500	163,000
	Manager (6–8 years)	87,500	96,500
	Senior (3–5 years)	72,500	80,000
	Junior (0–2 years)	49,000	54,000
Recordkeeping	Full-charge bookkeeper	57,500	63,500
	Accounts manager	51,000	56,500
	Payroll manager	54,500	60,000
	Accounting clerk (0–2 years)	37,500	41,500

* Estimates assume a 2% compounded annual increase over current levels (rounded to nearest $500).

Point: For updated salary information:
Abbott-Langer.com
www.AICPA.org
Kforce.com

Quick Check Answers — p. 28

Quick Check is a chance to stop and reflect on key points.

1. What is the purpose of accounting?
2. What is the relation between accounting and recordkeeping?
3. Identify some advantages of technology for accounting.
4. Who are the internal and external users of accounting information?
5. Identify at least five types of managers who are internal users of accounting information.
6. What are internal controls and why are they important?

FUNDAMENTALS OF ACCOUNTING

Accounting is guided by principles, standards, concepts, and assumptions. This section describes several of these key fundamentals of accounting.

Ethics—A Key Concept

C3 Explain why ethics are crucial to accounting.

The goal of accounting is to provide useful information for decisions. For information to be useful, it must be trusted. This demands ethics in accounting. **Ethics** are beliefs that distinguish right from wrong. They are accepted standards of good and bad behavior.

Identifying the ethical path is sometimes difficult. The preferred path is a course of action that avoids casting doubt on one's decisions. For example, accounting users are less likely to trust an auditor's report if the auditor's pay depends on the success of the client's business. To avoid such concerns, ethics rules are often set. For example, auditors are banned from direct investment in their client and cannot accept pay that depends on figures in the client's reports. Exhibit 1.6 gives guidelines for making ethical decisions.

Point: Sarbanes-Oxley Act requires each issuer of securities to disclose whether it has adopted a code of ethics for its senior financial officers and the contents of that code.

EXHIBIT 1.6

Guidelines for Ethical Decision Making

Identify ethical concerns → **Analyze options** → **Make ethical decision**

Use personal ethics to recognize an ethical concern.

Consider all good and bad consequences.

Choose best option after weighing all consequences.

Providers of accounting information often face ethical choices as they prepare financial reports. These choices can affect the price a buyer pays and the wages paid to workers. They can even affect the success of products and services. Misleading information can lead to a wrongful closing of a division that harms workers, customers, and suppliers. There is an old saying: *Good ethics are good business.*

Some people extend ethics to *social responsibility,* which refers to a concern for the impact of actions on society. An organization's social responsibility can include donations to hospitals, colleges, community programs, and law enforcement. It also can include programs to reduce pollution, increase product safety, improve worker conditions, and support continuing education. These programs are not limited to large companies. For example, many small businesses offer discounts to students and senior citizens. Still others help sponsor events such as the Special Olympics and summer reading programs.

Point: The American Institute of Certified Public Accountants' *Code of Professional Conduct* is available at www.AICPA.org.

Decision Insight

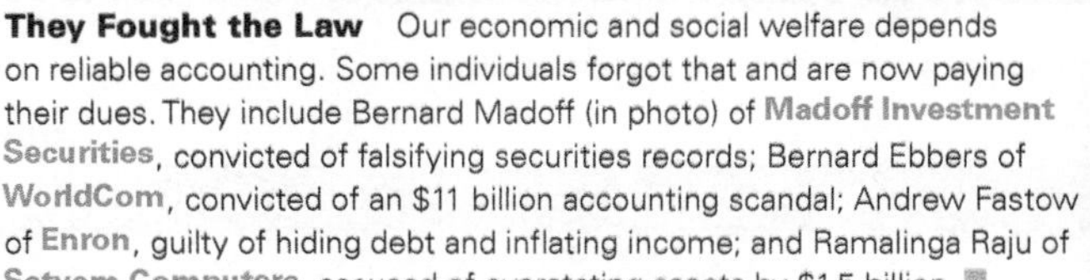

They Fought the Law Our economic and social welfare depends on reliable accounting. Some individuals forgot that and are now paying their dues. They include Bernard Madoff (in photo) of **Madoff Investment Securities**, convicted of falsifying securities records; Bernard Ebbers of **WorldCom**, convicted of an $11 billion accounting scandal; Andrew Fastow of **Enron**, guilty of hiding debt and inflating income; and Ramalinga Raju of **Satyam Computers**, accused of overstating assets by $1.5 billion. ■

Generally Accepted Accounting Principles

Financial accounting practice is governed by concepts and rules known as **generally accepted accounting principles (GAAP).** To use and interpret financial statements effectively, we need to understand these principles, which can change over time in response to the demands of users.

GAAP aims to make information in financial statements *relevant, reliable,* and *comparable.* Relevant information affects the decisions of its users. Reliable information is trusted by users. Comparable information is helpful in contrasting organizations.

C4 Explain generally accepted accounting principles and define and apply several accounting principles.

In the United States, the **Securities and Exchange Commission (SEC),** a government agency, has the legal authority to set GAAP. The SEC also oversees proper use of GAAP by companies that raise money from the public through issuances of their stock and debt. Those companies that issue their stock on U.S. exchanges include both *U.S. SEC registrants* (companies incorporated in the United States) and *non-U.S. SEC registrants* (companies incorporated under non-U.S. laws). The SEC has largely delegated the task of setting U.S. GAAP to the **Financial Accounting Standards Board (FASB),** which is a private-sector group that sets both broad and specific principles.

Point: State ethics codes require CPAs who audit financial statements to disclose areas where those statements fail to comply with GAAP. If CPAs fail to report noncompliance, they can lose their licenses and be subject to criminal and civil actions and fines.

International Standards

In today's global economy, there is increased demand by external users for comparability in accounting reports. This demand often arises when companies wish to raise money from lenders and investors in different countries. To that end, the **International Accounting Standards Board (IASB),** an independent group (consisting of individuals from many countries), issues **International Financial Reporting Standards (IFRS)** that identify preferred accounting practices.

If standards are harmonized, one company can potentially use a single set of financial statements in all financial markets. Differences between U.S. GAAP and IFRS are slowly fading as the FASB and IASB pursue a *convergence* process aimed to achieve a single set of accounting standards for global use. More than 115 countries now require or permit companies to prepare financial reports following IFRS. Further, non-U.S. SEC registrants can use IFRS in financial reports filed with the SEC (with no reconciliation to U.S. GAAP). This means there are *two* sets of accepted accounting principles in the United States: (1) U.S. GAAP for U.S. SEC registrants and (2) either IFRS or U.S. GAAP for non-U.S. SEC registrants.

The convergence process continues and, in late 2008, the SEC set a roadmap for use of IFRS by publicly traded U.S. companies. This roadmap proposes that large U.S. companies adopt IFRS by 2014, with midsize and small companies following in 2015 and 2016, respectively. Early adoption is permitted for large multinationals that meet certain criteria. For updates on this roadmap, we can check with the AICPA (IFRS.com), FASB (FASB.org), and IASB (IASB.org.uk).

 **IFRS**

Like the FASB, the IASB uses a conceptual framework to aid in revising or drafting new standards. However, unlike the FASB, the IASB's conceptual framework is used as a reference when specific guidance is lacking. The IASB also requires that transactions be accounted for according to their substance (not only their legal form), and that financial statements give a fair presentation, whereas the FASB narrows that scope to fair presentation *in accordance with U.S. GAAP.* ■

Conceptual Framework and Convergence

The FASB and IASB are attempting to converge and enhance the **conceptual framework** that guides standard setting. The framework consists broadly of the following:

- **Objectives**—to provide information useful to investors, creditors, and others.
- **Qualitative Characteristics**—to require information that is relevant, reliable, and comparable.
- **Elements**—to define items that financial statements can contain.
- **Recognition and Measurement**—to set criteria that an item must meet for it to be recognized as an element; and how to measure that element.

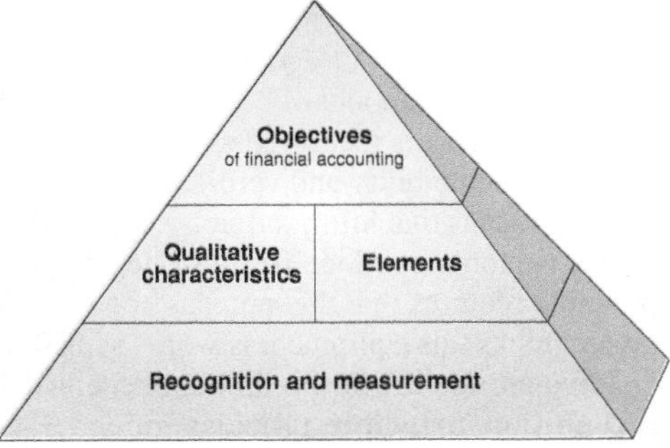

For updates on this joint FASB and IASB conceptual framework convergence we can check with FASB.org or IASB.org.uk Websites. We must remember that U.S. GAAP and IFRS are two similar, but not identical, systems. However, their similarities greatly outweigh any differences. The remainder of this section describes key principles and assumptions of accounting.

Decision Insight

Principles and Scruples Auditors, directors, and lawyers are using principles to improve accounting reports. Examples include accounting restatements at Navistar, financial restatements at Nortel, accounting reviews at Echostar, and expense adjustments at Electronic Data Systems. Principles-based accounting has led accounting firms to drop clients deemed too risky. Examples include Grant Thornton's resignation as auditor of Fremont General due to alleged failures in providing information when promised, and Ernst and Young's resignation as auditor of Catalina Marketing due to alleged accounting errors. ■

Principles and Assumptions of Accounting Accounting principles (and assumptions) are of two types. *General principles* are the basic assumptions, concepts, and guidelines for preparing financial statements. *Specific principles* are detailed rules used in reporting business transactions and events. General principles stem from long-used accounting practices. Specific principles arise more often from the rulings of authoritative groups.

EXHIBIT 1.7
Building Blocks for GAAP

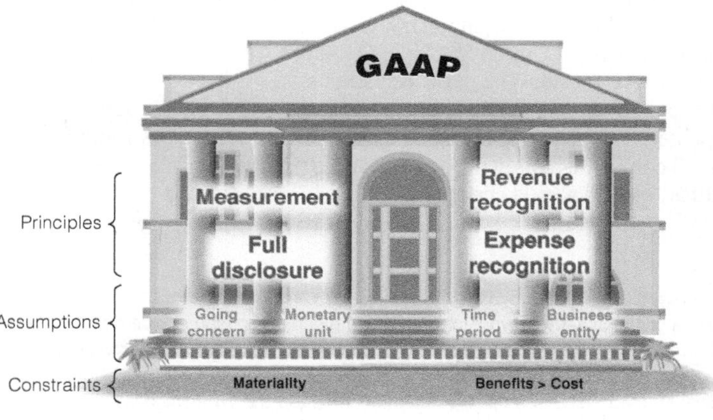

We need to understand both general and specific principles to effectively use accounting information. Several general principles are described in this section that are relied on in later chapters. General principles (in purple font with white shading) and assumptions (in red font with yellow shading) are portrayed as building blocks of GAAP in Exhibit 1.7. The specific principles are described as we encounter them in the book.

Accounting Principles General principles consist of at least four basic principles, four assumptions, and two constraints.

Point: The cost principle is also called the *historical cost principle*.

The **measurement principle,** also called the **cost principle,** usually means that accounting information is based on actual cost (with a potential for subsequent adjustments to market). Cost is measured on a cash or equal-to-cash basis. This means if cash is given for a service, its cost is measured as the amount of cash paid. If something besides cash is exchanged (such as a car traded for a truck), cost is measured as the cash value of what is given up or received. The cost principle emphasizes reliability and verifiability, and information based on cost is considered objective. *Objectivity* means that information is supported by independent, unbiased evidence; it demands more than a person's opinion. To illustrate, suppose a company pays $5,000 for equipment. The cost principle requires that this purchase be recorded at a cost of $5,000. It makes no difference if the owner thinks this equipment is worth $7,000. Later in the book we introduce *fair value* measures.

Revenue (sales) is the amount received from selling products and services. The **revenue recognition principle** provides guidance on when a company must recognize revenue. To *recognize* means to record it. If revenue is recognized too early, a company would look more profitable than it is. If revenue is recognized too late, a company would look less profitable than it is.

Three concepts are important to revenue recognition. (1) *Revenue is recognized when earned.* The earnings process is normally complete when services are performed or a seller transfers ownership of products to the buyer. (2) *Proceeds from selling products and services need not be in cash.* A common noncash proceed received by a seller is a customer's promise to pay at a future date, called *credit sales.* (3) *Revenue is measured by the cash received plus the cash value of any other items received.*

Example: When a bookstore sells a textbook on credit is its earnings process complete? *Answer:* A bookstore can record sales for these books minus an amount expected for returns.

The **expense recognition principle,** also called the **matching principle,** prescribes that a company record the expenses it incurred to generate the revenue reported. The principles of matching and revenue recognition are key to modern accounting.

The **full disclosure principle** prescribes that a company report the details behind financial statements that would impact users' decisions. Those disclosures are often in footnotes to the statements.

Decision Insight

Revenues for the **Green Bay Packers** and **Dallas Cowboys** football teams include ticket sales, television and cable broadcasts, radio rights, concessions, and advertising. Revenues from ticket sales are earned when the NFL team plays each game. Advance ticket sales are not revenues; instead, they represent a liability until the NFL team plays the game for which the ticket was sold. At that point, the liability is removed and revenues are reported. ■

Accounting Assumptions There are four accounting assumptions: the going concern assumption, the monetary unit assumption, the time period assumption, and the business entity assumption.

The **going-concern assumption** means that accounting information reflects a presumption that the business will continue operating instead of being closed or sold. This implies, for example, that property is reported at cost instead of, say, liquidation values that assume closure.

The **monetary unit assumption** means that we can express transactions and events in monetary, or money, units. Money is the common denominator in business. Examples of monetary units are the dollar in the United States, Canada, Australia, and Singapore; and the peso in Mexico, the Philippines, and Chile. The monetary unit a company uses in its accounting reports usually depends on the country where it operates, but many companies today are expressing reports in more than one monetary unit.

Point: For currency conversion: xe.com

The **time period assumption** presumes that the life of a company can be divided into time periods, such as months and years, and that useful reports can be prepared for those periods.

The **business entity assumption** means that a business is accounted for separately from other business entities, including its owner. The reason for this assumption is that separate information about each business is necessary for good decisions. A business entity can take one of three legal forms: *proprietorship, partnership,* or *corporation.*

Point: Abuse of the entity assumption was a main culprit in **Enron**'s collapse.

1. A **sole proprietorship,** or simply **proprietorship,** is a business owned by one person. No special legal requirements must be met to start a proprietorship. It is a separate entity for accounting purposes, but it is *not* a separate legal entity from its owner. This means, for example, that a court can order an owner to sell personal belongings to pay a proprietorship's debt. This *unlimited liability* of a proprietorship is a disadvantage. However, an advantage is that a proprietorship's income is not subject to a business income tax but is instead reported and taxed on the owner's personal income tax return. Proprietorship attributes are summarized in Exhibit 1.8, including those for partnerships and corporations.
2. A **partnership** is a business owned by two or more people, called *partners.* Like a proprietorship, no special legal requirements must be met in starting a partnership. The only

EXHIBIT 1.8
Attributes of Businesses

Attribute Present	Proprietorship	Partnership	Corporation
One owner allowed	yes	no	yes
Business taxed	no	no	yes
Limited liability	no*	no*	yes
Business entity	yes	yes	yes
Legal entity	no	no	yes
Unlimited life	no	no	yes

* Proprietorships and partnerships that are set up as LLCs provide limited liability.

requirement is an agreement between partners to run a business together. The agreement can be either oral or written and usually indicates how income and losses are to be shared. A partnership, like a proprietorship, is *not* legally separate from its owners. This means that each partner's share of profits is reported and taxed on that partner's tax return. It also means *unlimited liability* for its partners. However, at least three types of partnerships limit liability. A *limited partnership* (*LP*) includes a general partner(s) with unlimited liability and a limited partner(s) with liability restricted to the amount invested. A *limited liability partnership* (*LLP*) restricts partners' liabilities to their own acts and the acts of individuals under their control. This protects an innocent partner from the negligence of another partner, yet all partners remain responsible for partnership debts. A *limited liability company* (*LLC*) offers the limited liability of a corporation and the tax treatment of a partnership (and proprietorship). Most proprietorships and partnerships are now organized as LLCs.

Point: Proprietorships and partnerships are usually managed by their owners. In a corporation, the owners (shareholders) elect a board of directors who appoint managers to run the business.

3. A **corporation** is a business legally separate from its owners, meaning it is responsible for its own acts and its own debts. Separate legal status means that a corporation can conduct business with the rights, duties, and responsibilities of a person. A corporation acts through its managers, who are its legal agents. Separate legal status also means that its owners, who are called **shareholders** (or **stockholders**), are not personally liable for corporate acts and debts. This limited liability is its main advantage. A main disadvantage is what's called *double taxation*—meaning that (1) the corporation income is taxed and (2) any distribution of income to its owners through dividends is taxed as part of the owners' personal income, usually at the 15% rate. (For lower income taxpayers, the dividend tax is less than 15%, and in some cases zero.) An *S corporation,* a corporation with special attributes, does not owe corporate income tax. Owners of S corporations report their share of corporate income with their personal income. Ownership of all corporations is divided into units called **shares** or **stock.** When a corporation issues only one class of stock, we call it **common stock** (or *capital stock*).

Decision Ethics boxes are role-playing exercises that stress ethics in accounting and business.

Decision Ethics Answer — p. 27

Entrepreneur You and a friend develop a new design for in-line skates that improves speed by 25% to 30%. You plan to form a business to manufacture and market those skates. You and your friend want to minimize taxes, but your prime concern is potential lawsuits from individuals who might be injured on these skates. What form of organization do you set up? ■

Accounting Constraints There are two basic constraints on financial reporting. The **materiality constraint** prescribes that only information that would influence the decisions of a reasonable person need be disclosed. This constraint looks at both the importance and relative size of an amount. The **cost-benefit constraint** prescribes that only information with benefits of disclosure greater than the costs of providing it need be disclosed.

Sarbanes–Oxley (SOX)

Point: An audit examines whether financial statements are prepared using GAAP. It does *not* attest to absolute accuracy of the statements.

Congress passed the **Sarbanes–Oxley Act,** also called *SOX,* to help curb financial abuses at companies that issue their stock to the public. SOX requires that these public companies apply both accounting oversight and stringent internal controls. The desired results include more transparency, accountability, and truthfulness in reporting transactions.

Compliance with SOX requires documentation and verification of internal controls and increased emphasis on internal control effectiveness. Failure to comply can yield financial penalties, stock market delisting, and criminal prosecution of executives. Management must issue a report stating that internal controls are effective. CEOs and CFOs who knowingly sign off on bogus accounting reports risk millions of dollars in fines and years in prison. **Auditors** also must verify the effectiveness of internal controls.

Point: *BusinessWeek* reports that external audit costs run about $35,000 for start-ups, up from $15,000 pre-SOX.

A listing of some of the more publicized accounting scandals in recent years follows.

Company	Alleged Accounting Abuses
Enron	Inflated income, hid debt, and bribed officials
WorldCom	Understated expenses to inflate income and hid debt
Fannie Mae	Inflated income
Adelphia Communications	Understated expenses to inflate income and hid debt
AOL Time Warner	Inflated revenues and income
Xerox	Inflated income
Bristol-Myers Squibb	Inflated revenues and income
Nortel Networks	Understated expenses to inflate income
Global Crossing	Inflated revenues and income
Tyco	Hid debt, and CEO evaded taxes
Halliburton	Inflated revenues and income
Qwest Communications	Inflated revenues and income

To reduce the risk of accounting fraud, companies set up *governance systems*. A company's governance system includes its owners, managers, employees, board of directors, and other important stakeholders, who work together to reduce the risk of accounting fraud and increase confidence in accounting reports.

The impact of SOX regulations for accounting and business is discussed throughout this book. Ethics and investor confidence are key to company success. Lack of confidence in accounting numbers impacts company value as evidenced by huge stock price declines for Enron, WorldCom, Tyco, and ImClone after accounting misconduct was uncovered.

Decision Insight

Economic Downturn, Fraud Uptum? Executives polled show that 80% believe that the economic downturn has or will have a significant impact on fraud control in their companies (Deloitte 2009). The top three responses to the question "What activity would best counter this increased fraud risk?" are tallied in the graphic to the right.

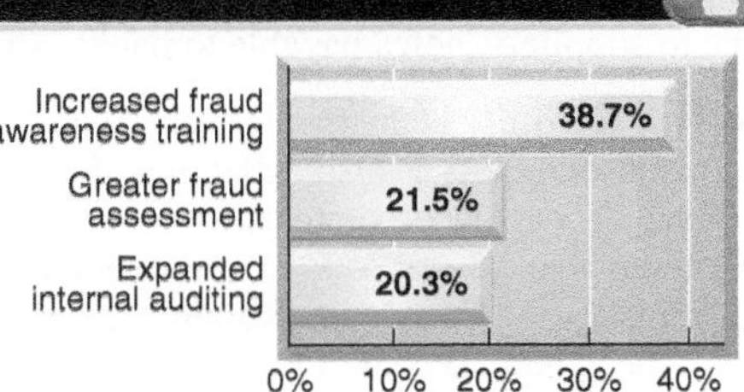

Quick Check

Answers — p. 28

7. What three-step guidelines can help people make ethical decisions?
8. Why are ethics and social responsibility valuable to organizations?
9. Why are ethics crucial in accounting?
10. Who sets U.S. accounting rules?
11. How are U.S. companies affected by international accounting standards?
12. How are the objectivity concept and cost principle related?
13. Why is the business entity assumption important?
14. Why is the revenue recognition principle important?
15. What are the three basic forms of business organization?
16. Identify the owners of corporations and the terminology for ownership units.

TRANSACTION ANALYSIS AND THE ACCOUNTING EQUATION

To understand accounting information, we need to know how an accounting system captures relevant data about transactions, and then classifies, records, and reports data.

Accounting Equation

A1 Define and interpret the accounting equation and each of its components.

The accounting system reflects two basic aspects of a company: what it owns and what it owes. *Assets* are resources a company owns or controls. Examples are cash, supplies, equipment, and land, where each carries expected benefits. The claims on a company's assets—what it owes—are separated into owner and nonowner claims. *Liabilities* are what a company owes its nonowners (creditors) in future payments, products, or services. *Equity* (also called owner's equity or capital) refers to the claims of its owner(s). Together, liabilities and equity are the source of funds to acquire assets. The relation of assets, liabilities, and equity is reflected in the following **accounting equation:**

Assets = Liabilities + Equity

Liabilities are usually shown before equity in this equation because creditors' claims must be paid before the claims of owners. (The terms in this equation can be rearranged; for example, Assets − Liabilities = Equity.) The accounting equation applies to all transactions and events, to all companies and forms of organization, and to all points in time. For example, Research In Motion's assets equal $10,204,409, its liabilities equal $2,601,746, and its equity equals $7,602,663 ($ in thousands). Let's now look at the accounting equation in more detail.

Assets **Assets** are resources a company owns or controls. These resources are expected to yield future benefits. Examples are Web servers for an online services company, musical instruments for a rock band, and land for a vegetable grower. The term *receivable* is used to refer to an asset that promises a future inflow of resources. A company that provides a service or product on credit is said to have an account receivable from that customer.

Point: The phrases "on credit" and "on account" imply that cash payment will occur at a future date.

Liabilities **Liabilities** are creditors' claims on assets. These claims reflect company obligations to provide assets, products or services to others. The term *payable* refers to a liability that promises a future outflow of resources. Examples are wages payable to workers, accounts payable to suppliers, notes payable to banks, and taxes payable to the government.

Equity **Equity** is the owner's claim on assets. Equity is equal to assets minus liabilities. This is the reason equity is also called *net assets* or *residual equity*.

Equity for a noncorporate entity—commonly called owner's equity—increases and decreases as follows: owner investments and revenues *increase* equity, whereas owner withdrawals and expenses *decrease* equity. **Owner investments** are assets an owner puts into the company and are included under the generic account **Owner, Capital. Revenues** are sales of products or services to customers. Revenues increase equity (via net income) and result from a company's earnings activities. Examples are consulting services provided, sales of products, facilities rented to others, and commissions from services. **Owner withdrawals** are assets an owner takes from the company for personal use. **Expenses** are the costs necessary to earn revenues. Expenses decrease equity. Examples are costs of employee time, use of supplies, and advertising, utilities, and insurance services from others. In sum, equity is the accumulated revenues and owner investments less the accumulated expenses and withdrawals since the company began. This breakdown of equity yields the following **expanded accounting equation.**

*Key **terms** are printed in bold and defined again in the end-of-book **glossary.***

Equity

Assets = Liabilities + Owner, Capital − Owner, Withdrawals + Revenues − Expenses

Net income occurs when revenues exceed expenses. Net income increases equity. A **net loss** occurs when expenses exceed revenues, which decreases equity.

Decision Insight

Web Info Most organizations maintain Websites that include accounting data—see Research in Motion (RIM.com) as an example. The SEC keeps an online database called EDGAR (www.SEC.gov/edgar.shtml), which has accounting information for thousands of companies that issue stock to the public (EDGAR is being upgraded and renamed IDEA). Information services such as Finance.Google.com and Finance.Yahoo.com offer additional online data and analysis.

Transaction Analysis

P1 Analyze business transactions using the accounting equation.

Business activities can be described in terms of transactions and events. **External transactions** are exchanges of value between two entities, which yield changes in the accounting equation. An example is the sale of ad space by Facebook. **Internal transactions** are exchanges within an entity, which may or may not affect the accounting equation. An example is Facebook's use of its supplies, which are reported as expenses when used. **Events** refer to happenings that affect the accounting equation *and* are reliably measured. They include business events such as changes in the market value of certain assets and liabilities and natural events such as floods and fires that destroy assets and create losses. They do not include, for example, the signing of service or product contracts, which by themselves do not impact the accounting equation.

This section uses the accounting equation to analyze 11 selected transactions and events of FastForward, a start-up consulting (service) business, in its first month of operations. Remember that each transaction and event leaves the equation in balance and that assets *always* equal the sum of liabilities and equity.

Transaction 1: Investment by Owner On December 1, Chas Taylor forms a consulting business, named FastForward and set up as a proprietorship, that focuses on assessing the performance of footwear and accessories. Taylor owns and manages the business. The marketing plan for the business is to focus primarily on publishing online reviews and consulting with clubs, athletes, and others who place orders for footwear and accessories with manufacturers. Taylor personally invests $30,000 cash in the new company and deposits the cash in a bank account opened under the name of FastForward. After this transaction, the cash (an asset) and the owner's equity each equal $30,000. The source of increase in equity is the owner's investment, which is included in the column titled C. Taylor, Capital. (Owner investments are always included under the title *'Owner name,' Capital.*) The effect of this transaction on FastForward is reflected in the accounting equation as follows:

Point: There are 3 basic types of company operations: (1) **Services**—providing customer services for profit, (2) **Merchandisers**—buying products and re-selling them for profit, and (3) **Manufacturers**—creating products and selling them for profit.

	Assets	=	Liabilities	+	Equity
	Cash	=			**C. Taylor, Capital**
(1)	+$30,000	=			+$30,000

Transaction 2: Purchase Supplies for Cash FastForward uses $2,500 of its cash to buy supplies of brand name footwear for performance testing over the next few months. This transaction is an exchange of cash, an asset, for another kind of asset, supplies. It merely changes the form of assets from cash to supplies. The decrease in cash is exactly equal to the increase in supplies. The supplies of footwear are assets because of the expected future benefits from the test results of their performance. This transaction is reflected in the accounting equation as follows:

	Assets			=	Liabilities	+	Equity
	Cash	+	**Supplies**	=			**C. Taylor, Capital**
Old Bal.	$30,000			=			$30,000
(2)	−2,500	+	$2,500				
New Bal.	$27,500	+	$ 2,500	=			$30,000
	$30,000				$30,000		

Transaction 3: Purchase Equipment for Cash FastForward spends $26,000 to acquire equipment for testing footwear. Like transaction 2, transaction 3 is an exchange of one asset, cash, for another asset, equipment. The equipment is an asset because of its expected future benefits from testing footwear. This purchase changes the makeup of assets but does not change the asset total. The accounting equation remains in balance.

	Assets					=	Liabilities	+	Equity
	Cash	+	Supplies	+	Equipment	=			C. Taylor, Capital
Old Bal.	$27,500	+	$2,500			=			$30,000
(3)	−26,000			+	$26,000				
New Bal.	$ 1,500	+	$2,500	+	$ 26,000	=			$30,000
			$30,000					$30,000	

Example: If FastForward pays $500 cash in transaction 4, how does this partial payment affect the liability to CalTech? What would be FastForward's cash balance? *Answers:* The liability to CalTech would be reduced to $6,600 and the cash balance would be reduced to $1,000.

Transaction 4: Purchase Supplies on Credit Taylor decides more supplies of footwear and accessories are needed. These additional supplies total $7,100, but as we see from the accounting equation in transaction 3, FastForward has only $1,500 in cash. Taylor arranges to purchase them on credit from CalTech Supply Company. Thus, FastForward acquires supplies in exchange for a promise to pay for them later. This purchase increases assets by $7,100 in supplies, and liabilities (called *accounts payable* to CalTech Supply) increase by the same amount. The effects of this purchase follow:

	Assets					=	Liabilities	+	Equity
	Cash	+	Supplies	+	Equipment	=	Accounts Payable	+	C. Taylor, Capital
Old Bal.	$1,500	+	$2,500	+	$26,000	=			$30,000
(4)		+	7,100				+$7,100		
New Bal.	$1,500	+	$9,600	+	$26,000	=	$ 7,100	+	$30,000
			$37,100					$37,100	

Transaction 5: Provide Services for Cash FastForward earns revenues by selling online ad space to manufacturers and by consulting with clients about test results on footwear and accessories. It earns net income only if its revenues are greater than its expenses incurred in earning them. In one of its first jobs, FastForward provides consulting services to a powerwalking club and immediately collects $4,200 cash. The accounting equation reflects this increase in cash of $4,200 and in equity of $4,200. This increase in equity is identified in the far right column under Revenues because the cash received is earned by providing consulting services.

	Assets					=	Liabilities	+	Equity		
	Cash	+	Supplies	+	Equipment	=	Accounts Payable	+	C. Taylor, Capital	+	Revenues
Old Bal.	$1,500	+	$9,600	+	$26,000	=	$7,100	+	$30,000		
(5)	+4,200									+	$4,200
New Bal.	$5,700	+	$9,600	+	$26,000	=	$7,100	+	$30,000	+	$ 4,200
			$41,300						$41,300		

Transactions 6 and 7: Payment of Expenses in Cash FastForward pays $1,000 rent to the landlord of the building where its facilities are located. Paying this amount allows FastForward to occupy the space for the month of December. The rental payment is reflected in the following accounting equation as transaction 6. FastForward also pays the biweekly $700 salary of the company's only employee. This is reflected in the accounting equation as transaction 7. Both transactions 6 and 7 are December expenses for FastForward. The costs of both rent and salary are expenses, as opposed to assets, because their benefits are used in December (they have no future benefits after December). These transactions also use up an asset (cash) in carrying out FastForward's operations. The accounting equation shows that both transactions reduce cash and equity. The far right column identifies these decreases as Expenses.

By definition, increases in expenses yield decreases in equity.

	Assets					=	Liabilities	+	Equity				
	Cash	+	**Supplies**	+	**Equipment**	=	**Accounts Payable**	+	**C. Taylor, Capital**	+	**Revenues**	−	**Expenses**
Old Bal.	$5,700	+	$9,600	+	$26,000	=	$7,100	+	$30,000	+	$4,200		
(6)	−1,000											−	$1,000
Bal.	4,700	+	9,600	+	26,000	=	7,100	+	30,000	+	4,200	−	1,000
(7)	− 700											−	700
New Bal.	$4,000	+	$9,600	+	$26,000	=	$7,100	+	$30,000	+	$4,200	−	$ 1,700
			$39,600							$39,600			

Transaction 8: Provide Services and Facilities for Credit FastForward provides consulting services of $1,600 and rents its test facilities for $300 to a podiatric services center. The rental involves allowing members to try recommended footwear and accessories at FastForward's testing area. The center is billed for the $1,900 total. This transaction results in a new asset, called *accounts receivable,* from this client. It also yields an increase in equity from the two revenue components reflected in the Revenues column of the accounting equation:

	Assets							=	Liabilities	+	Equity				
	Cash	+	**Accounts Receivable**	+	**Supplies**	+	**Equipment**	=	**Accounts Payable**	+	**C. Taylor, Capital**	+	**Revenues**	−	**Expenses**
Old Bal.	$4,000	+		+	$9,600	+	$26,000	=	$7,100	+	$30,000	+	$4,200	−	$1,700
(8)		+	$1,900									+	1,600		
												+	300		
New Bal.	$4,000	+	$ 1,900	+	$9,600	+	$26,000	=	$7,100	+	$30,000	+	$6,100	−	$1,700
					$41,500							$41,500			

Transaction 9: Receipt of Cash from Accounts Receivable The client in transaction 8 (the podiatric center) pays $1,900 to FastForward 10 days after it is billed for consulting services. This transaction 9 does not change the total amount of assets and does not affect liabilities or equity. It converts the receivable (an asset) to cash (another asset). It does not create new revenue. Revenue was recognized when FastForward rendered the services in transaction 8, not when the cash is now collected. This emphasis on the earnings process instead of cash flows is a goal of the revenue recognition principle and yields useful information to users. The new balances follow:

Point: Receipt of cash is not always a revenue.

	Assets							=	Liabilities	+	Equity				
	Cash	+	**Accounts Receivable**	+	**Supplies**	+	**Equipment**	=	**Accounts Payable**	+	**C. Taylor, Capital**	+	**Revenues**	−	**Expenses**
Old Bal.	$4,000	+	$1,900	+	$9,600	+	$26,000	=	$7,100	+	$30,000	+	$6,100	−	$1,700
(9)	+1,900	−	1,900												
New Bal.	$5,900	+	$ 0	+	$9,600	+	$26,000	=	$7,100	+	$30,000	+	$6,100	−	$1,700
					$41,500							$41,500			

Transaction 10: Payment of Accounts Payable FastForward pays CalTech Supply $900 cash as partial payment for its earlier $7,100 purchase of supplies (transaction 4), leaving $6,200 unpaid. The accounting equation shows that this transaction decreases FastForward's cash by $900 and decreases its liability to CalTech Supply by $900. Equity does not change. This event does not create an expense even though cash flows out of FastForward (instead the expense is recorded when FastForward derives the benefits from these supplies).

	Assets				= Liabilities	+ Equity		
	Cash	+ Accounts Receivable	+ Supplies	+ Equipment	= Accounts Payable	+ C. Taylor, Capital	+ Revenues	− Expenses
Old Bal.	$5,900	+ $ 0	+ $9,600	+ $26,000	= $7,100	+ $30,000	+ $6,100	− $1,700
(10)	− 900				− 900			
New Bal.	$5,000	+ $ 0	+ $9,600	+ $26,000	= $6,200	+ $30,000	+ $6,100	− $1,700
	$40,600				$40,600			

Transaction 11: Withdrawal of Cash by Owner The owner of FastForward withdraws $200 cash for personal use. Withdrawals (decreases in equity) are not reported as expenses because they are not part of the company's earnings process. Since withdrawals are not company expenses, they are not used in computing net income.

By definition, increases in withdrawals yield decreases in equity.

	Assets				= Liabilities	+ Equity			
	Cash	+ Accounts Receivable	+ Supplies	+ Equipment	= Accounts Payable	+ C. Taylor, Capital	− C. Taylor, Withdrawals	+ Revenues	− Expenses
Old Bal.	$5,000	+ $ 0	+ $9,600	+ $26,000	= $6,200	+ $30,000		+ $6,100	− $1,700
(11)	− 200						− $200		
New Bal.	$4,800	+ $ 0	+ $9,600	+ $26,000	= $6,200	+ $30,000	− $200	+ $6,100	− $1,700
	$40,400				$40,400				

Summary of Transactions

We summarize in Exhibit 1.9 the effects of these 11 transactions of FastForward using the accounting equation. First, we see that the accounting equation remains in balance after each transaction. Second, transactions can be analyzed by their effects on components of the

EXHIBIT 1.9

Summary of Transactions Using the Accounting Equation

	Assets				= Liabilities	+ Equity			
	Cash	+ Accounts Receivable	+ Supplies	+ Equipment	= Accounts Payable	+ C. Taylor, Capital	− C. Taylor, Withdrawals	+ Revenues	− Expenses
(1)	$30,000				=	$30,000			
(2)	− 2,500		+ $2,500						
Bal.	27,500		+ 2,500		=	30,000			
(3)	−26,000			+ $26,000					
Bal.	1,500		+ 2,500	+ 26,000	=	30,000			
(4)			+ 7,100		+$7,100				
Bal.	1,500		+ 9,600	+ 26,000	= 7,100	+ 30,000			
(5)	+ 4,200							+ $4,200	
Bal.	5,700		+ 9,600	+ 26,000	= 7,100	+ 30,000		+ 4,200	
(6)	− 1,000								− $1,000
Bal.	4,700		+ 9,600	+ 26,000	= 7,100	+ 30,000		+ 4,200	− 1,000
(7)	− 700								− 700
Bal.	4,000		+ 9,600	+ 26,000	= 7,100	+ 30,000		+ 4,200	− 1,700
(8)		+ $1,900						+ 1,600 + 300	
Bal.	4,000	+ 1,900	+ 9,600	+ 26,000	= 7,100	+ 30,000		+ 6,100	− 1,700
(9)	+ 1,900	− 1,900							
Bal.	5,900	+ 0	+ 9,600	+ 26,000	= 7,100	+ 30,000		+ 6,100	− 1,700
(10)	− 900				− 900				
Bal.	5,000	+ 0	+ 9,600	+ 26,000	= 6,200	+ 30,000		+ 6,100	− 1,700
(11)	− 200						− $200		
Bal.	$ 4,800	+ $ 0	+ $ 9,600	+ $ 26,000	= $ 6,200	+ $ 30,000	− $ 200	+ $6,100	− $ 1,700

accounting equation. For example, in transactions 2, 3, and 9, one asset increased while another asset decreased by equal amounts.

Point: Knowing how financial statements are prepared improves our analysis of them. We develop the skills for analysis of financial statements throughout the book. Chapter 17 focuses on financial statement analysis.

Quick Check Answers — p. 28 

17. When is the accounting equation in balance, and what does that mean?
18. How can a transaction not affect any liability and equity accounts?
19. Describe a transaction increasing equity and one decreasing it.
20. Identify a transaction that decreases both assets and liabilities.

FINANCIAL STATEMENTS

P2 Identify and prepare basic financial statements and explain how they interrelate.

This section introduces us to how financial statements are prepared from the analysis of business transactions. The four financial statements and their purposes are:

1. **Income statement**—describes a company's revenues and expenses along with the resulting net income or loss over a period of time due to earnings activities.
2. **Statement of owner's equity**—explains changes in equity from net income (or loss) and from any owner investments and withdrawals over a period of time.
3. **Balance sheet**—describes a company's financial position (types and amounts of assets, liabilities, and equity) at a point in time.
4. **Statement of cash flows**—identifies cash inflows (receipts) and cash outflows (payments) over a period of time.

We prepare these financial statements, in this order, using the 11 selected transactions of FastForward. (These statements are technically called *unadjusted*—we explain this in Chapters 2 and 3.)

Income Statement

FastForward's income statement for December is shown at the top of Exhibit 1.10. Information about revenues and expenses is conveniently taken from the Equity columns of Exhibit 1.9. Revenues are reported first on the income statement. They include consulting revenues of $5,800 from transactions 5 and 8 and rental revenue of $300 from transaction 8. Expenses are reported after revenues. (For convenience in this chapter, we list larger amounts first, but we can sort expenses in different ways.) Rent and salary expenses are from transactions 6 and 7. Expenses reflect the costs to generate the revenues reported. Net income (or loss) is reported at the bottom of the statement and is the amount earned in December. Owner's investments and withdrawals are *not* part of income.

Point: Net income is sometimes called *earnings* or *profit*.

Statement of Owner's Equity

The statement of owner's equity reports information about how equity changes over the reporting period. This statement shows beginning capital, events that increase it (owner investments and net income), and events that decrease it (withdrawals and net loss). Ending capital is computed in this statement and is carried over and reported on the balance sheet. FastForward's statement of owner's equity is the second report in Exhibit 1.10. The beginning capital balance is measured as of the start of business on December 1. It is zero because FastForward did not exist before then. An existing business reports a beginning balance equal to that as of the end of the prior reporting period (such as from November 30). FastForward's statement of owner's equity shows that Taylor's initial investment created $30,000 of equity. It also shows the $4,400 of net income earned during the period. This links the income statement to the statement of owner's equity (see line ①). The statement also reports Taylor's $200 cash withdrawal and FastForward's end-of-period capital balance.

Point: The statement of owner's equity is also called the *statement of changes in owner's equity.* Note: Beg. Capital + Net Income − Withdrawals = Ending Capital

EXHIBIT 1.10

Financial Statements and Their Links

Point: A statement's heading identifies the company, the statement title, and the date or time period.

Point: Arrow lines show how the statements are linked. ① Net income is used to compute equity. ② Owner capital is used to prepare the balance sheet. ③ Cash from the balance sheet is used to reconcile the statement of cash flows.

Point: The income statement, the statement of owner's equity, and the statement of cash flows are prepared for a *period* of time. The balance sheet is prepared as of a *point* in time.

Point: A single ruled line denotes an addition or subtraction. Final totals are double underlined. Negative amounts are often in parentheses.

FASTFORWARD
Income Statement
For Month Ended December 31, 2011

Revenues		
Consulting revenue ($4,200 + $1,600)	$ 5,800	
Rental revenue	300	
Total revenues		$ 6,100
Expenses		
Rent expense	1,000	
Salaries expense	700	
Total expenses		1,700
Net income		$ 4,400

FASTFORWARD
Statement of Owner's Equity
For Month Ended December 31, 2011

C. Taylor, Capital, December 1, 2011		$ 0
Plus: Investments by owner	$30,000	
Net income	4,400	34,400
		34,400
Less: Withdrawals by owner		200
C. Taylor, Capital, December 31, 2011		$34,200

FASTFORWARD
Balance Sheet
December 31, 2011

Assets		Liabilities	
Cash	$ 4,800	Accounts payable	$ 6,200
Supplies	9,600	Total liabilities	6,200
Equipment	26,000		
		Equity	
		C. Taylor, Capital	34,200
Total assets	$40,400	Total liabilities and equity	$40,400

FASTFORWARD
Statement of Cash Flows
For Month Ended December 31, 2011

Cash flows from operating activities		
Cash received from clients ($4,200 + $1,900)	$ 6,100	
Cash paid for supplies ($2,500 + $900)	(3,400)	
Cash paid for rent	(1,000)	
Cash paid to employee	(700)	
Net cash provided by operating activities		$ 1,000
Cash flows from investing activities		
Purchase of equipment	(26,000)	
Net cash used by investing activities		(26,000)
Cash flows from financing activities		
Investments by owner	30,000	
Withdrawals by owner	(200)	
Net cash provided by financing activities		29,800
Net increase in cash		$ 4,800
Cash balance, December 1, 2011		0
Cash balance, December 31, 2011		$ 4,800

Balance Sheet

FastForward's balance sheet is the third report in Exhibit 1.10. This statement refers to FastForward's financial condition at the close of business on December 31. The left side of the balance sheet lists FastForward's assets: cash, supplies, and equipment. The upper right side of the balance sheet shows that FastForward owes $6,200 to creditors. Any other liabilities (such as a bank loan) would be listed here. The equity (capital) balance is $34,200. Line ② shows the link between the ending balance of the statement of owner's equity and the equity balance on the balance sheet. (This presentation of the balance sheet is called the *account form:* assets on the left and liabilities and equity on the right. Another presentation is the *report form:* assets on top, followed by liabilities and then equity at the bottom. Either presentation is acceptable.) As always, we see the accounting equation applies: Assets of $40,400 = Liabilities of $6,200 + Equity of $34,200.

Decision Maker boxes are role-playing exercises that stress the relevance of accounting.

Decision Maker Answer — p. 28

Retailer You open a wholesale business selling entertainment equipment to retail outlets. You find that most of your customers demand to buy on credit. How can you use the balance sheets of these customers to help you decide which ones to extend credit to? ■

Statement of Cash Flows

FastForward's statement of cash flows is the final report in Exhibit 1.10. The first section reports cash flows from *operating activities*. It shows the $6,100 cash received from clients and the $5,100 cash paid for supplies, rent, and employee salaries. Outflows are in parentheses to denote subtraction. Net cash provided by operating activities for December is $1,000. If cash paid exceeded the $5,100 cash received, we would call it "cash used by operating activities." The second section reports *investing activities,* which involve buying and selling assets such as land and equipment that are held for *long-term use* (typically more than one year). The only investing activity is the $26,000 purchase of equipment. The third section shows cash flows from *financing activities,* which include the *long-term* borrowing and repaying of cash from lenders and the cash investments from, and withdrawals by, the owner. FastForward reports $30,000 from the owner's initial investment and the $200 cash withdrawal. The net cash effect of all financing transactions is a $29,800 cash inflow. The final part of the statement shows FastForward increased its cash balance by $4,800 in December. Since it started with no cash, the ending balance is also $4,800—see line ③. We see that cash flow numbers are different from income statement (*accrual*) numbers, which is common.

Point: Statement of cash flows has three main sections: operating, investing, and financing.

Point: Payment for supplies is an operating activity because supplies are expected to be used up in short-term operations (typically less than one year).

Point: Investing activities refer to long-term asset investments by the company, *not* to owner investments.

Quick Check Answers — p. 28

21. Explain the link between the income statement and the statement of owner's equity.
22. Describe the link between the balance sheet and the statement of owner's equity.
23. Discuss the three major sections of the statement of cash flows.

GLOBAL VIEW

Accounting according to U.S. GAAP is similar, but not identical, to IFRS. Throughout the book we use this last section to identify major similarities and differences between IFRS and U.S. GAAP for the materials in each chapter.

Basic Principles Both U.S. GAAP and IFRS include broad and similar guidance for accounting. However, neither system specifies particular account names nor the detail required. (A typical *chart of accounts* is shown near the end of this book.) IFRS does require certain minimum line items be reported in the balance sheet along with other minimum disclosures that U.S. GAAP does not. On the other hand, U.S. GAAP requires disclosures for the current and prior two years for the income statement, statement of cash flows, and statement of retained earnings (equity), while IFRS requires disclosures for the current and prior year. Still, the basic principles behind these two systems are similar.

Transaction Analysis Both U.S. GAAP and IFRS apply transaction analysis identically as shown in this chapter. Although some variations exist in revenue and expense recognition and other principles, all of the transactions in this chapter are accounted for identically under these two systems. It is often said that U.S. GAAP is more *rules-based* whereas IFRS is more *principles-based*. The main difference on the rules versus principles focus is with the approach in deciding how to account for certain transactions. Under U.S. GAAP, the approach is more focused on strictly following the accounting rules; under IFRS, the approach is more focused on a review of the situation and how accounting can best reflect it. This difference typically impacts advanced topics beyond the introductory course.

NOKIA

Financial Statements Both U.S. GAAP and IFRS prepare the same four basic financial statements. To illustrate, a condensed version of Nokia's income statement follows (numbers are in Euros millions). Nokia is a leader in mobile technology, from smartphones to mobile computers. Similar condensed versions can be prepared for the other three statements.

NOKIA
Income Statement (in € millions)
For Year Ended December 31, 2009

Net sales	40,984
Cost of sales	27,720
Research, selling, administrative, and other expenses	12,302
Taxes	702
Net income (profit)	260

***Decision Analysis** (a section at the end of each chapter) introduces and explains ratios helpful in decision making using real company data. Instructors can skip this section and cover all ratios in Chapter 17.*

Decision Analysis

Return on Assets

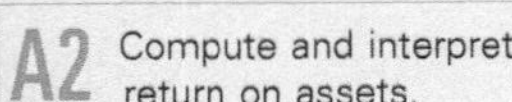

A *Decision Analysis* section at the end of each chapter is devoted to financial statement analysis. We organize financial statement analysis into four areas: (1) liquidity and efficiency, (2) solvency, (3) profitability, and (4) market prospects—Chapter 17 has a ratio listing with definitions and groupings by area. When analyzing ratios, we need benchmarks to identify good, bad, or average levels. Common benchmarks include the company's prior levels and those of its competitors.

This chapter presents a profitability measure: return on assets. Return on assets is useful in evaluating management, analyzing and forecasting profits, and planning activities. Dell has its marketing department compute return on assets for *every* order. **Return on assets (ROA),** also called *return on investment (ROI)*, is defined in Exhibit 1.11.

EXHIBIT 1.11

Return on Assets

$$\textbf{Return on assets} = \frac{\textbf{Net income}}{\textbf{Average total assets}}$$

Net income is from the annual income statement, and average total assets is computed by adding the beginning and ending amounts for that same period and dividing by 2. To illustrate, Best Buy reports net income of $1,317 million for fiscal year 2010. At the beginning of fiscal 2010, its total assets are $15,826 million and at the end of fiscal 2010, they total $18,302 million. Best Buy's return on assets for fiscal 2010 is:

$$\text{Return on assets} = \frac{\$1{,}317 \text{ million}}{(\$15{,}826 \text{ million} + \$18{,}302 \text{ million})/2} = 7.7\%$$

Is a 7.7% return on assets good or bad for Best Buy? To help answer this question, we compare (benchmark) Best Buy's return with its prior performance, the returns of competitors (such as RadioShack, Conn's, and Rex Stores), and the returns from alternative investments. Best Buy's return for each of the prior five years is in the second column of Exhibit 1.12, which ranges from 7.0% to 10.8%.

Fiscal Year	Return on Assets	
	Best Buy	Industry
2010	7.7%	2.9%
2009	7.0	2.5
2008	10.7	3.4
2007	10.8	3.5
2006	10.3	3.3

EXHIBIT 1.12

Best Buy and Industry Returns

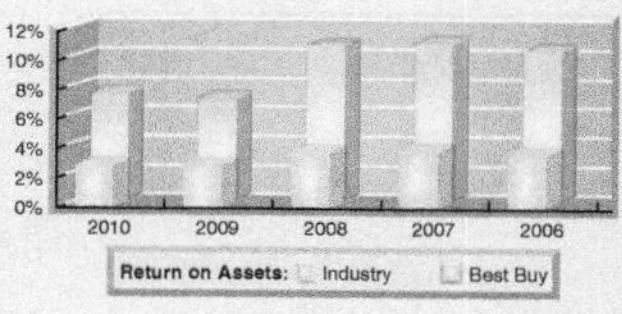

Best Buy shows a fairly stable pattern of good returns that reflect its productive use of assets. There is a decline in its 2009 return reflecting the recessionary period. We compare Best Buy's return to the normal return for similar merchandisers of electronic products (third column). Industry averages are available from services such as **Dun & Bradstreet**'s *Industry Norms and Key Ratios* and **The Risk Management Association**'s *Annual Statement Studies*. When compared to the industry, Best Buy performs well.

*Each **Decision Analysis** section ends with a role-playing scenario to show the usefulness of ratios.*

Decision Maker Answer — p. 28

Business Owner You own a small winter ski resort that earns a 21% return on its assets. An opportunity to purchase a winter ski equipment manufacturer is offered to you. This manufacturer earns a 19% return on its assets. The industry return for this manufacturer is 14%. Do you purchase this manufacturer? ■

*The **Demonstration Problem** is a review of key chapter content. The Planning the Solution offers strategies in solving the problem.*

DEMONSTRATION PROBLEM

After several months of planning, Jasmine Worthy started a haircutting business called Expressions. The following events occurred during its first month of business.

a. On August 1, Worthy invested $3,000 cash and $15,000 of equipment in Expressions.
b. On August 2, Expressions paid $600 cash for furniture for the shop.
c. On August 3, Expressions paid $500 cash to rent space in a strip mall for August.
d. On August 4, it purchased $1,200 of equipment on credit for the shop (using a long-term note payable).
e. On August 5, Expressions opened for business. Cash received from haircutting services in the first week and a half of business (ended August 15) was $825.
f. On August 15, it provided $100 of haircutting services on account.
g. On August 17, it received a $100 check for services previously rendered on account.
h. On August 17, it paid $125 cash to an assistant for hours worked during the grand opening.
i. Cash received from services provided during the second half of August was $930.
j. On August 31, it paid a $400 installment toward principal on the note payable entered into on August 4.
k. On August 31, Worthy made a $900 cash withdrawal from the company for personal use.

Required

1. Arrange the following asset, liability, and equity titles in a table similar to the one in Exhibit 1.9: Cash; Accounts Receivable; Furniture; Store Equipment; Note Payable; J. Worthy, Capital; J. Worthy, Withdrawals; Revenues; and Expenses. Show the effects of each transaction using the accounting equation.
2. Prepare an income statement for August.
3. Prepare a statement of owner's equity for August.
4. Prepare a balance sheet as of August 31.
5. Prepare a statement of cash flows for August.
6. Determine the return on assets ratio for August.

PLANNING THE SOLUTION

- Set up a table like Exhibit 1.9 with the appropriate columns for accounts.
- Analyze each transaction and show its effects as increases or decreases in the appropriate columns. Be sure the accounting equation remains in balance after each transaction.
- Prepare the income statement, and identify revenues and expenses. List those items on the statement, compute the difference, and label the result as *net income* or *net loss*.
- Use information in the Equity columns to prepare the statement of owner's equity.
- Use information in the last row of the transactions table to prepare the balance sheet.
- Prepare the statement of cash flows; include all events listed in the Cash column of the transactions table. Classify each cash flow as operating, investing, or financing.
- Calculate return on assets by dividing net income by average assets.

SOLUTION TO DEMONSTRATION PROBLEM

1.

	Assets							=	Liabilities	+	Equity						
	Cash	**+**	**Accounts Receivable**	**+**	**Furniture**	**+**	**Store Equipment**	**=**	**Note Payable**	**+**	**J.Worthy, Capital**	**−**	**J.Worthy, Withdrawals**	**+**	**Revenues**	**−**	**Expenses**
a.	$3,000						$15,000				$18,000						
b.	− 600			+	$600												
Bal.	2,400	+		+	600	+	15,000	=			18,000						
c.	− 500															−	$500
Bal.	1,900	+		+	600	+	15,000	=			18,000					−	500
d.						+	1,200		+$1,200								
Bal.	1,900	+		+	600	+	16,200	=	1,200	+	18,000					−	500
e.	+ 825													+	$ 825		
Bal.	2,725	+		+	600	+	16,200	=	1,200	+	18,000			+	825	−	500
f.		+	$100											+	100		
Bal.	2,725	+	100	+	600	+	16,200	=	1,200	+	18,000			+	925	−	500
g.	+ 100	−	100														
Bal.	2,825	+	0	+	600	+	16,200	=	1,200	+	18,000			+	925	−	500
h.	− 125															−	125
Bal.	2,700	+	0	+	600	+	16,200	=	1,200	+	18,000			+	925	−	625
i.	+ 930													+	930		
Bal.	3,630	+	0	+	600	+	16,200	=	1,200	+	18,000			+	1,855	−	625
j.	− 400								− 400								
Bal.	3,230	+	0	+	600	+	16,200	=	800	+	18,000			+	1,855	−	625
k.	− 900											−	$900				
Bal.	$ 2,330	+	0	+	$600	+	$ 16,200	=	$ 800	+	$ 18,000	−	$900	+	$1,855	−	$625

2.

EXPRESSIONS Income Statement For Month Ended August 31		
Revenues		
Haircutting services revenue		$1,855
Expenses		
Rent expense	$500	
Wages expense	125	
Total expenses		625
Net Income		$1,230

3.

EXPRESSIONS
Statement of Owner's Equity
For Month Ended August 31

J. Worthy, Capital, August 1*			$ 0
Plus:	Investments by owner	$18,000	
	Net income	1,230	19,230
			19,230
Less:	Withdrawals by owner		900
J. Worthy, Capital, August 31			$18,330

* If Expressions had been an existing business from a prior period, the beginning capital balance would equal the Capital account balance from the end of the prior period.

4.

EXPRESSIONS
Balance Sheet
August 31

Assets		Liabilities	
Cash	$ 2,330	Note payable	$ 800
Furniture	600	**Equity**	
Store equipment	16,200	J. Worthy, Capital	18,330
Total assets	$19,130	Total liabilities and equity	$19,130

5.

EXPRESSIONS
Statement of Cash Flows
For Month Ended August 31

Cash flows from operating activities		
Cash received from customers	$1,855	
Cash paid for rent	(500)	
Cash paid for wages	(125)	
Net cash provided by operating activities		$1,230
Cash flows from investing activities		
Cash paid for furniture		(600)
Cash flows from financing activities		
Cash investments by owner	3,000	
Cash withdrawals by owner	(900)	
Partial repayment of (long-term) note payable	(400)	
Net cash provided by financing activities		1,700
Net increase in cash		$2,330
Cash balance, August 1		0
Cash balance, August 31		$2,330

6. Return on assets $= \frac{\text{Net income}}{\text{Average assets}} = \frac{\$1,230}{(\$18,000^{*} + \$19,130)/2} = \frac{\$1,230}{\$18,565} = \mathbf{6.63\%}$

* Uses the initial $18,000 investment as the beginning balance for the *start-up period only.*

APPENDIX

1A Return and Risk Analysis

A3 Explain the relation between return and risk.

This appendix explains return and risk analysis and its role in business and accounting.

Net income is often linked to **return.** Return on assets (ROA) is stated in ratio form as income divided by assets invested. For example, banks report return from a savings account in the form of an interest return such as 4%. If we invest in a savings account or in U.S. Treasury bills, we expect a return of around 2% to 7%. We could also invest in a company's stock, or even start our own business. How do we decide among these investment options? The answer depends on our trade-off between return and risk.

Risk is the uncertainty about the return we will earn. All business investments involve risk, but some investments involve more risk than others. The lower the risk of an investment, the lower is our expected return. The reason that savings accounts pay such a low return is the low risk of not being repaid with interest (the government guarantees most savings accounts from default). If we buy a share of eBay or any other company, we might obtain a large return. However, we have no guarantee of any return; there is even the risk of loss.

EXHIBIT 1A.1

Average Returns for Bonds with Different Risks

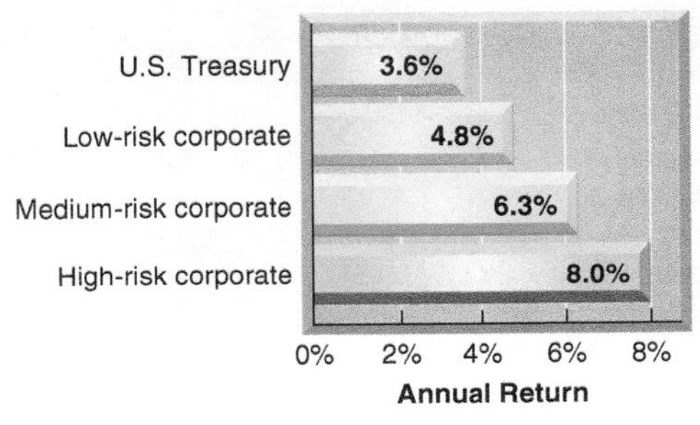

The bar graph in Exhibit 1A.1 shows recent returns for 10-year bonds with different risks. *Bonds* are written promises by organizations to repay amounts loaned with interest. U.S. Treasury bonds provide a low expected return, but they also offer low risk since they are backed by the U.S. government. High-risk corporate bonds offer a much larger potential return but with much higher risk.

The trade-off between return and risk is a normal part of business. Higher risk implies higher, but riskier, expected returns. To help us make better decisions, we use accounting information to assess both return and risk.

APPENDIX

1B Business Activities and the Accounting Equation

C5 Identify and describe the three major activities of organizations.

This appendix explains how the accounting equation is derived from business activities.

There are three major types of business activities: financing, investing, and operating. Each of these requires planning. *Planning* involves defining an organization's ideas, goals, and actions. Most public corporations use the *Management Discussion and Analysis* section in their annual reports to communicate plans. However, planning is not cast in stone. This adds *risk* to both setting plans and analyzing them.

Financing *Financing activities* provide the means organizations use to pay for resources such as land, buildings, and equipment to carry out plans. Organizations are careful in acquiring and managing financing activities because they can determine success or failure. The two sources of financing are owner and nonowner. *Owner financing* refers to resources contributed by the owner along with any income the owner leaves in the organization. *Nonowner* (or *creditor*) *financing* refers to resources contributed by creditors (lenders). *Financial management* is the task of planning how to obtain these resources and to set the right mix between owner and creditor financing.

Point: Management must understand accounting data to set financial goals, make financing and investing decisions, and evaluate operating performance.

Investing *Investing activities* are the acquiring and disposing of resources (assets) that an organization uses to acquire and sell its products or services. Assets are funded by an organization's financing. Organizations differ on the amount and makeup of assets. Some require land and factories to operate. Others need only an office. Determining the amount and type of assets for operations is called *asset management*. Invested amounts are referred to as *assets*. Financing is made up of creditor and owner financing, which hold claims on assets. Creditors' claims are called *liabilities,* and the owner's claim is called *equity.* This basic equality is called the *accounting equation* and can be written as: Assets = Liabilities + Equity.

Point: Investing (assets) and financing (liabilities plus equity) totals are *always* equal.

Operating *Operating activities* involve using resources to research, develop, purchase, produce, distribute, and market products and services. Sales and revenues are the inflow of assets from selling products and services. Costs and expenses are the outflow of assets to support operating activities. *Strategic management* is the process of determining the right mix of operating activities for the type of organization, its plans, and its market.

Exhibit 1B.1 summarizes business activities. Planning is part of each activity and gives them meaning and focus. Investing (assets) and financing (liabilities and equity) are set opposite each other to stress their balance. Operating activities are below investing and financing activities to show that operating activities are the result of investing and financing.

EXHIBIT 1B.1
Activities of Organizations

*A **Summary** organized by learning objectives concludes each chapter.*

C1 Explain the purpose and importance of accounting. Accounting is an information and measurement system that aims to identify, record, and communicate relevant, reliable, and comparable information about business activities. It helps assess opportunities, products, investments, and social and community responsibilities.

C2 Identify users and uses of, and opportunities in, accounting. Users of accounting are both internal and external. Some users and uses of accounting include (a) managers in controlling, monitoring, and planning; (b) lenders for measuring the risk and return of loans; (c) shareholders for assessing the return and risk of stock; (d) directors for overseeing management; and (e) employees for judging employment opportunities. Opportunities in accounting include financial, managerial, and tax accounting. They also include accounting-related fields such as lending, consulting, managing, and planning.

C3 Explain why ethics are crucial to accounting. The goal of accounting is to provide useful information for decision making. For information to be useful, it must be trusted. This demands ethical behavior in accounting.

C4 Explain generally accepted accounting principles and define and apply several accounting principles. Generally accepted accounting principles are a common set of standards applied by accountants. Accounting principles aid in producing relevant, reliable, and comparable information. Four principles underlying financial statements were introduced: cost, revenue recognition, matching, and full disclosure. Financial statements also reflect four assumptions: going-concern, monetary unit, time period, and business entity.

C5B Identify and describe the three major activities of organizations. Organizations carry out three major activities: financing, investing, and operating. Financing is the means used to pay for resources such as land, buildings, and machines. Investing refers to the buying and selling of resources used in acquiring and selling products and services. Operating activities are those necessary for carrying out the organization's plans.

A1 Define and interpret the accounting equation and each of its components. The accounting equation is: Assets = Liabilities + Equity. Assets are resources owned by a company. Liabilities are creditors' claims on assets. Equity is the owner's claim on assets (*the residual*). The expanded accounting equation is: Assets = Liabilities + [Owner Capital − Owner Withdrawals + Revenues − Expenses].

A2 Compute and interpret return on assets. Return on assets is computed as net income divided by average assets. For example, if we have an average balance of $100 in a savings account and it earns $5 interest for the year, the return on assets is $5/$100, or 5%.

A3A Explain the relation between return and risk. *Return* refers to income, and *risk* is the uncertainty about the return we hope to make. All investments involve risk. The lower the risk of an investment, the lower is its expected return. Higher risk implies higher, but riskier, expected return.

P1 Analyze business transactions using the accounting equation. A *transaction* is an exchange of economic consideration between two parties. Examples include exchanges of products, services, money, and rights to collect money. Transactions always have at least two effects on one or more components of the accounting equation. This equation is always in balance.

P2 Identify and prepare basic financial statements and explain how they interrelate. Four financial statements report on an organization's activities: balance sheet, income statement, statement of owner's equity, and statement of cash flows.

Guidance Answers to Decision Maker and Decision Ethics

Entrepreneur (p. 12) You should probably form the business as a corporation if potential lawsuits are of prime concern. The corporate form of organization protects your personal property from lawsuits directed at the business and places only the corporation's resources at risk. A downside of the corporate form is double taxation: The corporation must pay taxes on its income, and you normally must pay taxes on any money distributed to you from the business (even though the corporation already paid taxes on this money). You should also examine the ethical and socially responsible aspects of starting a business in which you anticipate injuries to others. Formation as an LLC or S corp. should also be explored.

Retailer (p. 21) You can use the accounting equation (Assets = Liabilities + Equity) to help identify risky customers to whom you would likely not want to extend credit. A balance sheet provides amounts for each of these key components. The lower a customer's equity is relative to liabilities, the less likely you would be to extend credit. A low equity means the business has little value that does not already have creditor claims to it.

Business Owner (p. 23) The 19% return on assets for the manufacturer exceeds the 14% industry return (and many others). This is a positive factor for a potential purchase. Also, the purchase of this manufacturer is an opportunity to spread your risk over two businesses as opposed to one. Still, you should hesitate to purchase a business whose return of 19% is lower than your current resort's return of 21%. You are probably better off directing efforts to increase investment in your resort, assuming you can continue to earn a 21% return.

Guidance Answers to Quick Checks

1. Accounting is an information and measurement system that identifies, records, and communicates relevant information to help people make better decisions.
2. Recordkeeping, also called *bookkeeping,* is the recording of financial transactions and events, either manually or electronically. Recordkeeping is essential to data reliability; but accounting is this and much more. Accounting includes identifying, measuring, recording, reporting, and analyzing business events and transactions.
3. Technology offers increased accuracy, speed, efficiency, and convenience in accounting.
4. External users of accounting include lenders, shareholders, directors, customers, suppliers, regulators, lawyers, brokers, and the press. Internal users of accounting include managers, officers, and other internal decision makers involved with strategic and operating decisions.
5. Internal users (managers) include those from research and development, purchasing, human resources, production, distribution, marketing, and servicing.
6. Internal controls are procedures set up to protect assets, ensure reliable accounting reports, promote efficiency, and encourage adherence to company policies. Internal controls are crucial for relevant and reliable information.
7. Ethical guidelines are threefold: (1) identify ethical concerns using personal ethics, (2) analyze options considering all good and bad consequences, and (3) make ethical decisions after weighing all consequences.
8. Ethics and social responsibility yield good behavior, and they often result in higher income and a better working environment.
9. For accounting to provide useful information for decisions, it must be trusted. Trust requires ethics in accounting.
10. Two major participants in setting rules include the SEC and the FASB. (*Note:* Accounting rules reflect society's needs, not those of accountants or any other single constituency.)
11. Most U.S. companies are not directly affected by international accounting standards. International standards are put forth as preferred accounting practices. However, stock exchanges and other parties are increasing the pressure to narrow differences in worldwide accounting practices. International accounting standards are playing an important role in that process.
12. The objectivity concept and cost principle are related in that most users consider information based on cost as objective. Information prepared using both is considered highly reliable and often relevant.
13. Users desire information about the performance of a specific entity. If information is mixed between two or more entities, its usefulness decreases.
14. The revenue recognition principle gives preparers guidelines on when to recognize (record) revenue. This is important; for example, if revenue is recognized too early, the statements report revenue sooner than it should and the business looks more profitable than it is. The reverse is also true.
15. The three basic forms of business organization are sole proprietorships, partnerships, and corporations.
16. Owners of corporations are called *shareholders* (or *stockholders*). Corporate ownership is divided into units called *shares* (or *stock*). The most basic of corporate shares is common stock (or capital stock).
17. The accounting equation is: Assets = Liabilities + Equity. This equation is always in balance, both before and after each transaction.
18. A transaction that changes the makeup of assets would not affect liability and equity accounts. FastForward's transactions 2 and 3 are examples. Each exchanges one asset for another.
19. Earning revenue by performing services, as in FastForward's transaction 5, increases equity (and assets). Incurring expenses while servicing clients, such as in transactions 6 and 7, decreases equity (and assets). Other examples include owner investments that increase equity and withdrawals that decrease equity.
20. Paying a liability with an asset reduces both asset and liability totals. One example is FastForward's transaction 10 that reduces a payable by paying cash.
21. An income statement reports a company's revenues and expenses along with the resulting net income or loss. A statement of owner's equity shows changes in equity, including that from net income or loss. Both statements report transactions occurring over a period of time.
22. The balance sheet describes a company's financial position (assets, liabilities, and equity) at a point in time. The equity amount in the balance sheet is obtained from the statement of owner's equity.
23. Cash flows from operating activities report cash receipts and payments from the primary business the company engages in. Cash flows from investing activities involve cash transactions from buying and selling long-term assets. Cash flows from financing activities include long-term cash borrowings and repayments to lenders and the cash investments from and withdrawals by the owner.

A list of key terms with page references concludes each chapter (a complete glossary is at the end of the book and also on the book's Website).

Key Terms

mhhe.com/wildFAP20e

Accounting (p. 4)
Accounting equation (p. 14)
Assets (p. 14)
Audit (p. 12)
Auditors (p. 13)
Balance sheet (p. 19)
Bookkeeping (p. 4)
Business entity assumption (p. 11)
Common stock (p. 12)
Conceptual framework (p. 9)
Corporation (p. 12)
Cost-benefit constraint (p. 12)
Cost principle (p. 10)
Equity (p. 14)
Ethics (p. 8)
Events (p. 15)
Expanded accounting equation (p. 14)
Expense recognition principle (p. 11)
Expenses (p. 14)
External transactions (p. 15)
External users (p. 5)
Financial accounting (p. 5)
Financial Accounting Standards Board (FASB) (p. 9)
Full disclosure principle (p. 11)
Generally accepted accounting principles (GAAP) (p. 8)
Going-concern assumption (p. 11)
Income statement (p. 19)
Internal transactions (p. 15)
Internal users (p. 6)
International Accounting Standards Board (IASB) (p. 9)
International Financial Reporting Standards (IFRS) (p. 9)
Liabilities (p. 14)
Managerial accounting (p. 6)
Matching principle (p. 11)
Materiality constraint (p. 12)
Measurement principle (p. 10)
Monetary unit assumption (p. 11)
Net income (p. 14)
Net loss (p. 14)
Owner, Capital (p. 14)
Owner investment (p. 14)
Owner withdrawals (p. 14)
Partnership (p. 11)
Proprietorship (p. 11)
Recordkeeping (p. 4)
Return (p. 26)
Return on assets (p. 22)
Revenue recognition principle (p. 10)
Revenues (p. 14)
Risk (p. 26)
Sarbanes–Oxley Act (p. 12)
Securities and Exchange Commission (SEC) (p. 9)
Shareholders (p. 12)
Shares (p. 12)
Sole proprietorship (p. 11)
Statement of cash flows (p. 19)
Statement of owner's equity (p. 19)
Stock (p. 12)
Stockholders (p. 12)
Time period assumption (p. 11)
Withdrawals (p. 14)

Multiple Choice Quiz

Answers on p. 47

mhhe.com/wildFAP20e

Additional Quiz Questions are available at the book's Website.

1. A building is offered for sale at $500,000 but is currently assessed at $400,000. The purchaser of the building believes the building is worth $475,000, but ultimately purchases the building for $450,000. The purchaser records the building at:
a. $50,000
b. $400,000
c. $450,000
d. $475,000
e. $500,000

2. On December 30, 2010, KPMG signs a $150,000 contract to provide accounting services to one of its clients in 2011. KPMG has a December 31 year-end. Which accounting principle or assumption requires KPMG to record the accounting services revenue from this client in 2011 and not 2010?
a. Business entity assumption
b. Revenue recognition principle
c. Monetary unit assumption
d. Cost principle
e. Going-concern assumption

3. If the assets of a company increase by $100,000 during the year and its liabilities increase by $35,000 during the same year, then the change in equity of the company during the year must have been:
a. An increase of $135,000.
b. A decrease of $135,000.
c. A decrease of $65,000.
d. An increase of $65,000.
e. An increase of $100,000.

4. Brunswick borrows $50,000 cash from Third National Bank. How does this transaction affect the accounting equation for Brunswick?
a. Assets increase by $50,000; liabilities increase by $50,000; no effect on equity.
b. Assets increase by $50,000; no effect on liabilities; equity increases by $50,000.
c. Assets increase by $50,000; liabilities decrease by $50,000; no effect on equity.
d. No effect on assets; liabilities increase by $50,000; equity increases by $50,000.
e. No effect on assets; liabilities increase by $50,000; equity decreases by $50,000.

5. Geek Squad performs services for a customer and bills the customer for $500. How would Geek Squad record this transaction?
   a. Accounts receivable increase by $500; revenues increase by $500.
   b. Cash increases by $500; revenues increase by $500.
   c. Accounts receivable increase by $500; revenues decrease by $500.
   d. Accounts receivable increase by $500; accounts payable increase by $500.
   e. Accounts payable increase by $500; revenues increase by $500.

A(B) *Superscript letter A (B) denotes assignments based on Appendix 1A (1B).*
Icon denotes assignments that involve decision making.

Discussion Questions

1. What is the purpose of accounting in society?
2. Technology is increasingly used to process accounting data. Why then must we study and understand accounting?
3. Identify four kinds of external users and describe how they use accounting information.
4. What are at least three questions business owners and managers might be able to answer by looking at accounting information?
5. Identify three actual businesses that offer services and three actual businesses that offer products.
6. Describe the internal role of accounting for organizations.
7. Identify three types of services typically offered by accounting professionals.
8. What type of accounting information might be useful to the marketing managers of a business?
9. Why is accounting described as a service activity?
10. What are some accounting-related professions?
11. How do ethics rules affect auditors' choice of clients?
12. What work do tax accounting professionals perform in addition to preparing tax returns?
13. What does the concept of *objectivity* imply for information reported in financial statements? Why?
14. A business reports its own office stationery on the balance sheet at its $400 cost, although it cannot be sold for more than $10 as scrap paper. Which accounting principle and/or assumption justifies this treatment?
15. Why is the revenue recognition principle needed? What does it demand?
16. Describe the three basic forms of business organization and their key attributes.
17. Define (*a*) *assets,* (*b*) *liabilities,* (*c*) *equity,* and (*d*) *net assets.*
18. What events or transactions change equity?
19. Identify the two main categories of accounting principles.
20. What do accountants mean by the term *revenue?*
21. Define *net income* and explain its computation.
22. Identify the four basic financial statements of a business.
23. What information is reported in an income statement?
24. Give two examples of expenses a business might incur.
25. What is the purpose of the statement of owner's equity?
26. What information is reported in a balance sheet?
27. The statement of cash flows reports on what major activities?
28. Define and explain return on assets.
29.A Define return and risk. Discuss the trade-off between them.
30.B Describe the three major business activities in organizations.
31.B Explain why investing (assets) and financing (liabilities and equity) totals are always equal.
32. Refer to the financial statements of Research In Motion in Appendix A near the end of the book. To what level of significance are dollar amounts rounded? What time period does its income statement cover? RIM
33. Identify the dollar amounts of Apple's 2009 assets, liabilities, and equity as reported in its statements in Appendix A near the end of the book. Apple
34. Refer to Nokia's balance sheet in Appendix A near the end of the book. Confirm that its total assets equal its total liabilities plus total equity. NOKIA
35. Access the SEC EDGAR database (www.SEC.gov) and retrieve Palm's 2009 10-K (filed July 24, 2009). Identify its auditor. What responsibility does its independent auditor claim regarding Palm's financial statements? Palm

Connect reproduces assignments online, in static or algorithmic mode, which allows instructors to monitor, promote, and assess student learning. It can be used for practice, homework, or exams.

Quick Study exercises give readers a brief test of key elements.

connect

QUICK STUDY

QS 1-1
Identifying accounting terms C1

Reading and interpreting accounting reports requires some knowledge of accounting terminology. (*a*) Identify the meaning of these accounting-related acronyms: GAAP, SEC, FASB, IASB and IFRS. (*b*) Briefly explain the importance of the knowledge base or organization that is referred to for each of the accounting-related acronyms.

QS 1-2
Explaining internal control
C1

An important responsibility of many accounting professionals is to design and implement internal control procedures for organizations. Explain the purpose of internal control procedures. Provide two examples of internal controls applied by companies.

QS 1-3
Identifying accounting users
C2

Identify the following users as either external users (E) or internal users (I).

a. Lenders	**d.** Sales staff	**g.** Brokers	**j.** Managers
b. Controllers	**e.** FBI and IRS	**h.** Suppliers	**k.** Business press
c. Shareholders	**f.** Consumer group	**i.** Customers	**l.** District attorney

QS 1-4
Accounting opportunities C2

There are many job opportunities for those with accounting knowledge. Identify at least three main areas of opportunities for accounting professionals. For each area, identify at least three job possibilities linked to accounting.

QS 1-5
Identifying ethical concerns C3

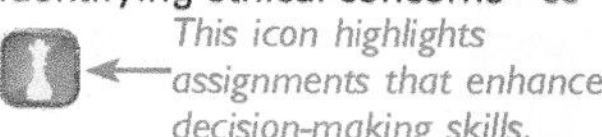

Accounting professionals must sometimes choose between two or more acceptable methods of accounting for business transactions and events. Explain why these situations can involve difficult matters of ethical concern.

QS 1-6
Identifying accounting principles
C4 

Identify which accounting principle or assumption best describes each of the following practices:

a. If $51,000 cash is paid to buy land, the land is reported on the buyer's balance sheet at $51,000.

b. Alissa Kees owns both Sailing Passions and Dockside Supplies. In preparing financial statements for Dockside Supplies, Kees makes sure that the expense transactions of Sailing Passions are kept separate from Dockside's transactions and financial statements.

c. In December 2010, Ace Landscaping received a customer's order and cash prepayment to install sod at a new house that would not be ready for installation until March 2011. Ace should record the revenue from the customer order in March 2011, not in December 2010.

QS 1-7
Applying the accounting equation
A1 

a. Total assets of Caldwell Company equal $40,000 and its equity is $10,000. What is the amount of its liabilities?

b. Total assets of Waterworld equal $55,000 and its liabilities and equity amounts are equal to each other. What is the amount of its liabilities? What is the amount of its equity?

QS 1-8
Applying the accounting equation
A1

Use the accounting equation to compute the missing financial statement amounts (*a*), (*b*), and (*c*).

Company	Assets	=	Liabilities	+	Equity
1	$ 30,000		$ (a)		$ 20,000
2	(b)		50,000		30,000
3	90,000		10,000		(c)

QS 1-9
Identifying transactions and events P1

Accounting provides information about an organization's business transactions and events that both affect the accounting equation and can be reliably measured. Identify at least two examples of both (*a*) business transactions and (*b*) business events that meet these requirements.

QS 1-10
Identifying and computing assets, liabilities, and equity
P1 

Use Apple's September 26, 2009, financial statements, in Appendix A near the end of the book, to answer the following:

a. Identify the dollar amounts of Apple's 2009 (1) assets, (2) liabilities, and (3) equity.

b. Using Apple's amounts from part *a*, verify that Assets = Liabilities + Equity.

32

QS 1-11
Computing and interpreting return on assets
A2

In a recent year's financial statements, Home Depot reported the following results. Compute and interpret Home Depot's return on assets (assume competitors average a 5% return on assets).

Sales	$71,288 million
Net income	2,260 million
Average total assets	42,744 million

QS 1-12
Identifying items with financial statements
P2

Indicate in which financial statement each item would most likely appear: income statement (I), balance sheet (B), statement of owner's equity (OE), or statement of cash flows (CF).

a. Assets
b. Revenues
c. Liabilities
d. Equipment
e. Withdrawals
f. Expenses
g. Total liabilities and equity
h. Cash from operating activities
i. Net decrease (or increase) in cash

QS 1-13
International accounting standards C4

This icon highlights assignments that focus on IFRS-related content.

Answer each of the following questions related to international accounting standards.

a. The International Accounting Standards Board (IASB) issues preferred accounting practices that are referred to as what?

b. The FASB and IASB are working on a convergence process for what purpose?

c. The SEC has proposed a roadmap for use of IFRS by U.S. companies. What is the proposed adoption date for large U.S. companies to adopt IFRS?

connect

EXERCISES

Exercise 1-1
Classifying activities reflected in the accounting system
C1

Accounting is an information and measurement system that identifies, records, and communicates relevant, reliable, and comparable information about an organization's business activities. Classify the following activities as part of the identifying (I), recording (R), or communicating (C) aspects of accounting.

_____ **1.** Determining employee tasks behind a service.
_____ **2.** Establishing revenues generated from a product.
_____ **3.** Maintaining a log of service costs.
_____ **4.** Measuring the costs of a product.
_____ **5.** Preparing financial statements.
_____ **6.** Analyzing and interpreting reports.
_____ **7.** Presenting financial information.

Exercise 1-2
Identifying accounting users and uses
C2

Part A. Identify the following users of accounting information as either an internal (I) or an external (E) user.

_____ **1.** Shareholders
_____ **2.** Creditors
_____ **3.** Nonexecutive employee
_____ **4.** Research and development director
_____ **5.** Purchasing manager
_____ **6.** Human resources director
_____ **7.** Production supervisors
_____ **8.** Distribution managers

Part B. Identify the following questions as most likely to be asked by an internal (I) or an external (E) user of accounting information.

_____ **1.** What are the costs of our service to customers?
_____ **2.** Should we make a five-year loan to that business?
_____ **3.** Should we spend further research on our product?
_____ **4.** Do income levels justify the current stock price?
_____ **5.** What are reasonable payroll benefits and wages?
_____ **6.** Which firm reports the highest sales and income?
_____ **7.** What are the costs of our product's ingredients?

Exercise 1-3
Describing accounting responsibilities
C2

Many accounting professionals work in one of the following three areas:

A. Managerial accounting **B.** Financial accounting **C.** Tax accounting

Identify the area of accounting that is most involved in each of the following responsibilities:

_____ **1.** Reviewing reports for SEC compliance.
_____ **2.** Planning transactions to minimize taxes.
_____ **3.** Investigating violations of tax laws.
_____ **4.** Preparing external financial statements.
_____ **5.** Budgeting.
_____ **6.** Cost accounting.
_____ **7.** External auditing.
_____ **8.** Internal auditing.

Exercise 1-4
Identifying ethical concerns
C3 

Assume the following role and describe a situation in which ethical considerations play an important part in guiding your decisions and actions:

a. You are a student in an introductory accounting course.
b. You are an accounting professional with audit clients that are competitors in business.
c. You are an accounting professional preparing tax returns for clients.
d. You are a manager with responsibility for several employees.

Exercise 1-5
Learning the language of business
C1–C3

Match each of the numbered descriptions with the term or phrase it best reflects. Indicate your answer by writing the letter for the term or phrase in the blank provided.

A. Audit **C.** Ethics **E.** SEC **G.** Net income
B. GAAP **D.** Tax accounting **F.** Public accountants **H.** IASB

_______ **1.** Amount a business earns after paying all expenses and costs associated with its sales and revenues.
_______ **2.** An examination of an organization's accounting system and records that adds credibility to financial statements.
_______ **3.** Principles that determine whether an action is right or wrong.
_______ **4.** Accounting professionals who provide services to many clients.
_______ **5.** An accounting area that includes planning future transactions to minimize taxes paid.

Exercise 1-6
Identifying accounting principles and assumptions
C4

Match each of the numbered descriptions with the principle or assumption it best reflects. Enter the letter for the appropriate principle or assumption in the blank space next to each description.

A. Cost principle **E.** General accounting principle
B. Matching principle **F.** Business entity assumption
C. Specific accounting principle **G.** Revenue recognition principle
D. Full disclosure principle **H.** Going-concern assumption

_______ **1.** Revenue is recorded only when the earnings process is complete.
_______ **2.** Information is based on actual costs incurred in transactions.
_______ **3.** Usually created by a pronouncement from an authoritative body.
_______ **4.** Financial statements reflect the assumption that the business continues operating.
_______ **5.** A company reports details behind financial statements that would impact users' decisions.
_______ **6.** A company records the expenses incurred to generate the revenues reported.
_______ **7.** Derived from long-used and generally accepted accounting practices.
_______ **8.** Every business is accounted for separately from its owner or owners.

Exercise 1-7
Distinguishing business organizations
C4

The following describe several different business organizations. Determine whether the description refers to a sole proprietorship, partnership, or corporation.

a. A-1 pays its own income taxes and has two owners.
b. Ownership of Zeller Company is divided into 1,000 shares of stock.
c. Waldron is owned by Mary Malone, who is personally liable for the company's debts.
d. Micah Douglas and Nathan Logan own Financial Services, a financial services provider. Neither Douglas nor Logan has personal responsibility for the debts of Financial Services.
e. Bailey and Kay own Squeaky Clean, a cleaning service. Both are personally liable for the debts of the business.
f. Plasto Products does not pay income taxes and has one owner.
g. Ian LLC does not have separate legal existence apart from the one person who owns it.

Exercise 1-8
Using the accounting equation
A1 P1 

Answer the following questions. (*Hint:* Use the accounting equation.)

a. Office Mart has assets equal to $123,000 and liabilities equal to $53,000 at year-end. What is the total equity for Office Mart at year-end?
b. At the beginning of the year, Logan Company's assets are $200,000 and its equity is $150,000. During the year, assets increase $70,000 and liabilities increase $30,000. What is the equity at the end of the year?
c. At the beginning of the year, Keller Company's liabilities equal $60,000. During the year, assets increase by $80,000, and at year-end assets equal $180,000. Liabilities decrease $10,000 during the year. What are the beginning and ending amounts of equity?

Check (c) Beg. equity, $40,000

Exercise 1-9
Using the accounting equation
A1

Determine the missing amount from each of the separate situations *a*, *b*, and *c* below.

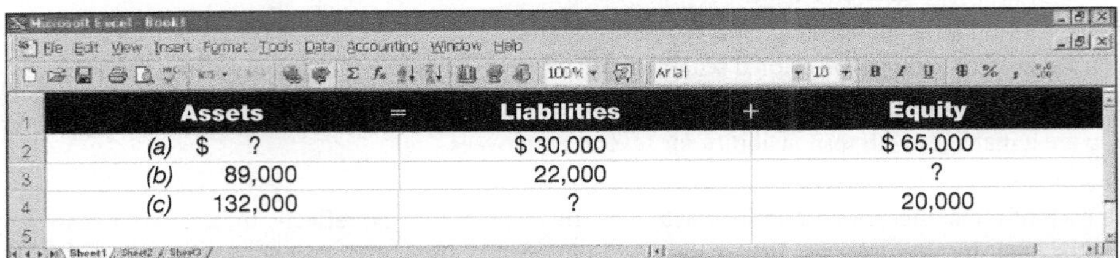

	Assets	=	Liabilities	+	Equity
(a)	$?		$ 30,000		$ 65,000
(b)	89,000		22,000		?
(c)	132,000		?		20,000

Exercise 1-10
Identifying effects of transactions on the accounting equation
P1 

Provide an example of a transaction that creates the described effects for the separate cases *a* through *g*.

a. Increases an asset and decreases an asset.
b. Decreases an asset and decreases a liability.
c. Decreases a liability and increases a liability.
d. Increases an asset and increases a liability.
e. Decreases an asset and decreases equity.
f. Increases a liability and decreases equity.
g. Increases an asset and increases equity.

Exercise 1-11
Identifying effects of transactions using the accounting equation
P1 

Lena Gold began a professional practice on June 1 and plans to prepare financial statements at the end of each month. During June, Gold (the owner) completed these transactions:

a. Owner invested $50,000 cash in the company along with equipment that had a $10,000 market value.
b. The company paid $1,600 cash for rent of office space for the month.
c. The company purchased $12,000 of additional equipment on credit (payment due within 30 days).
d. The company completed work for a client and immediately collected the $2,000 cash earned.
e. The company completed work for a client and sent a bill for $7,000 to be received within 30 days.
f. The company purchased additional equipment for $8,000 cash.
g. The company paid an assistant $2,400 cash as wages for the month.
h. The company collected $5,000 cash as a partial payment for the amount owed by the client in transaction *e*.
i. The company paid $12,000 cash to settle the liability created in transaction *c*.
j. Owner withdrew $500 cash from the company for personal use.

Required

Create a table like the one in Exhibit 1.9, using the following headings for columns: Cash; Accounts Receivable; Equipment; Accounts Payable; L. Gold, Capital; L. Gold, Withdrawals; Revenues; and Expenses. Then use additions and subtractions to show the effects of the transactions on individual items of the accounting equation. Show new balances after each transaction.

Check Net income, $5,000

Exercise 1-12
Analysis using the accounting equation

Zelda began a new consulting firm on January 5. The accounting equation showed the following balances after each of the company's first five transactions. Analyze the accounting equation for each transaction and describe each of the five transactions with their amounts.

	Assets							=	Liabilities	+	Equity		
Transaction	Cash	+	Accounts Receivable	+	Office Supplies	+	Office Furniture	=	Accounts Payable	+	Zelda, Capital	+	Revenues
a.	$20,000	+	$ 0	+	$ 0	+	$ 0	=	$ 0	+	$20,000	+	$ 0
b.	19,000	+	0	+	1,500	+	0	=	500	+	20,000	+	0
c.	11,000	+	0	+	1,500	+	8,000	=	500	+	20,000	+	0
d.	11,000	+	3,000	+	1,500	+	8,000	=	500	+	20,000	+	3,000
e.	11,500	+	3,000	+	1,500	+	8,000	=	500	+	20,000	+	3,500

Exercise 1-13
Identifying effects of transactions on accounting equation
P1 

The following table shows the effects of five transactions (*a* through *e*) on the assets, liabilities, and equity of Vera's Boutique. Write short descriptions of the probable nature of each transaction.

	Assets				=	Liabilities +	Equity	
	Cash	+ Accounts Receivable	+ Office Supplies	+ Land	=	Accounts Payable	+ Vera, Capital	+ Revenues
	$ 10,500	+ $ 0	+ $1,500	+ $ 9,500	=	$ 0	+ $21,500	+ $ 0
a.	− 2,000			+ 2,000				
b.			+ 500			+500		
c.		+ 950						+ 950
d.	− 500					−500		
e.	+ 950	− 950						
	$ 8,950	+ $ 0	+ $2,000	+ $11,500	=	$ 0	+ $21,500	+ $950

Exercise 1-14
Preparing an income statement
P2

On October 1, Natalie King organized Real Solutions, a new consulting firm. On October 31, the company's records show the following items and amounts. Use this information to prepare an October income statement for the business.

Cash	$ 2,000	Cash withdrawals by owner	$ 3,360
Accounts receivable	13,000	Consulting fees earned	15,000
Office supplies	4,250	Rent expense	2,550
Land	36,000	Salaries expense	6,000
Office equipment	28,000	Telephone expense	660
Accounts payable	7,500	Miscellaneous expenses	680
Owner investments	74,000		

Check Net income, $5,110

Exercise 1-15
Preparing a statement of owner's equity P2

Use the information in Exercise 1-14 to prepare an October statement of owner's equity for Real Solutions.

Exercise 1-16
Preparing a balance sheet P2

Use the information in Exercise 1-14 (if completed, you can also use your solution to Exercise 1-15) to prepare an October 31 balance sheet for Real Solutions.

Exercise 1-17
Preparing a statement of cash flows
P2

Use the information in Exercise 1-14 to prepare an October 31 statement of cash flows for Real Solutions. Also assume the following:

a. The owner's initial investment consists of $38,000 cash and $36,000 in land.
b. The company's $28,000 equipment purchase is paid in cash.
c. The accounts payable balance of $7,500 consists of the $4,250 office supplies purchase and $3,250 in employee salaries yet to be paid.
d. The company's rent, telephone, and miscellaneous expenses are paid in cash.
e. $2,000 has been collected on the $15,000 consulting fees earned.

Check Net increase in cash, $2,000

Exercise 1-18
Analysis of return on assets
A2 

Geneva Group reports net income of $20,000 for 2011. At the beginning of 2011, Geneva Group had $100,000 in assets. By the end of 2011, assets had grown to $150,000. What is Geneva Group's 2011 return on assets? How would you assess its performance if competitors average a 10% return on assets?

Exercise 1-19
Identifying sections of the statement of cash flows
P2

Indicate the section where each of the following would appear on the statement of cash flows.

A. Cash flows from operating activity
B. Cash flows from investing activity
C. Cash flows from financing activity

_____ **1.** Cash paid for wages
_____ **2.** Cash withdrawal by owner
_____ **3.** Cash purchase of equipment
_____ **4.** Cash paid for advertising
_____ **5.** Cash paid on an account payable
_____ **6.** Cash investment by owner
_____ **7.** Cash received from clients
_____ **8.** Cash paid for rent

36 Chapter 1 Accounting in Business

Exercise 1-20[B]
Identifying business activities
C5

Match each transaction or event to one of the following activities of an organization: financing activities (F), investing activities (I), or operating activities (O).

1. ______ An owner contributes resources to the business.
2. ______ An organization purchases equipment.
3. ______ An organization advertises a new product.
4. ______ The organization borrows money from a bank.
5. ______ An organization sells some of its land.

Exercise 1-21
Preparing an income statement for a global company
P2 

Nintendo Company reports the following income statement accounts for the year ended March 31, 2009. (Japanese yen in millions.)

Net sales	¥1,838,622
Cost of sales	1,044,981
Selling, general and administrative expenses	238,378
Other expenses	276,174

Use this information to prepare Nintendo's income statement for the year ended March 31, 2009.

Problem Set B located at the end of Problem Set A is provided for each problem to reinforce the learning process.

PROBLEM SET A

Problem 1-1A
Identifying effects of transactions on financial statements
A1 P1 

Identify how each of the following separate transactions affects financial statements. For the balance sheet, identify how each transaction affects total assets, total liabilities, and total equity. For the income statement, identify how each transaction affects net income. For the statement of cash flows, identify how each transaction affects cash flows from operating activities, cash flows from financing activities, and cash flows from investing activities. For increases, place a "+" in the column or columns. For decreases, place a "−" in the column or columns. If both an increase and a decrease occur, place a "+/−" in the column or columns. The first transaction is completed as an example.

		Balance Sheet			Income Statement	Statement of Cash Flows		
	Transaction	Total Assets	Total Liab.	Total Equity	Net Income	Operating Activities	Financing Activities	Investing Activities
1	Owner invests cash in business	+		+			+	
2	Incurs legal costs on credit							
3	Pays cash for employee wages							
4	Borrows cash by signing long-term note payable							
5	Receives cash for services provided							
6	Buys land by signing note payable							
7	Buys office equipment for cash							
8	Provides services on credit							
9	Collects cash on receivable from (8)							
10	Owner withdraws cash							

Problem 1-2A
Computing missing information using accounting knowledge
A1 P1 

The following financial statement information is from five separate companies:

	Company A	Company B	Company C	Company D	Company E
December 31, 2010					
Assets	$45,000	$35,000	$29,000	$80,000	$123,000
Liabilities	23,500	22,500	14,000	38,000	?
December 31, 2011					
Assets	48,000	41,000	?	125,000	112,500
Liabilities	?	27,500	19,000	64,000	75,000
During year 2011					
Owner investments	5,000	1,500	7,750	?	4,500
Net income (loss)	7,500	?	9,000	12,000	18,000
Owner cash withdrawals	2,500	3,000	3,875	0	9,000

Required

1. Answer the following questions about Company A:
   a. What is the amount of equity on December 31, 2010?
   b. What is the amount of equity on December 31, 2011?
   c. What is the amount of liabilities on December 31, 2011?
2. Answer the following questions about Company B:
   a. What is the amount of equity on December 31, 2010?
   b. What is the amount of equity on December 31, 2011?
   c. What is net income for year 2011?
3. Calculate the amount of assets for Company C on December 31, 2011.
4. Calculate the amount of owner investments for Company D during year 2011.
5. Calculate the amount of liabilities for Company E on December 31, 2010.

Check (1*b*) $31,500

(2*c*) $2,500

(3) $46,875

Problem 1-3A
Preparing a balance sheet
P2

The following is selected financial information for Affiliated Company as of December 31, 2011: liabilities, $34,000; equity, $56,000; assets, $90,000.

Required

Prepare the balance sheet for Affiliated Company as of December 31, 2011.

Problem 1-4A
Preparing an income statement
P2

The following is selected financial information for Sun Energy Company for the year ended December 31, 2011: revenues, $65,000; expenses, $50,000; net income, $15,000.

Required

Prepare the 2011 calendar-year income statement for Sun Energy Company.

Problem 1-5A
Preparing a statement of owner's equity
P2

Following is selected financial information for Boardwalk for the year ended December 31, 2011.

B. Walk, Capital, Dec. 31, 2011	$15,000	B. Walk, Withdrawals	$2,000
Net income	9,000	B. Walk, Capital, Dec. 31, 2010	8,000

Required

Prepare the 2011 statement of owner's equity for Boardwalk.

Problem 1-6A
Preparing a statement of cash flows
P2

Following is selected financial information of Trimark for the year ended December 31, 2011.

Cash used by investing activities	$(3,000)
Net increase in cash	200
Cash used by financing activities	(3,800)
Cash from operating activities	7,000
Cash, December 31, 2010	3,300

Check Cash balance, Dec. 31, 2011, $3,500

Required

Prepare the 2011 statement of cash flows for Trimark Company.

Problem 1-7A
Analyzing effects of transactions
C4 P1 P2 A1

Miranda Right started Right Consulting, a new business, and completed the following transactions during its first year of operations.

a. M. Right invests $60,000 cash and office equipment valued at $30,000 in the company.
b. The company purchased a $300,000 building to use as an office. Right paid $50,000 in cash and signed a note payable promising to pay the $250,000 balance over the next ten years.
c. The company purchased office equipment for $6,000 cash.
d. The company purchased $4,000 of office supplies and $1,000 of office equipment on credit.
e. The company paid a local newspaper $1,000 cash for printing an announcement of the office's opening.
f. The company completed a financial plan for a client and billed that client $4,000 for the service.
g. The company designed a financial plan for another client and immediately collected an $8,000 cash fee.
h. M. Right withdrew $1,800 cash from the company for personal use.
i. The company received $3,000 cash as partial payment from the client described in transaction *f.*
j. The company made a partial payment of $500 cash on the equipment purchased in transaction *d.*
k. The company paid $2,500 cash for the office secretary's wages for this period.

Required

1. Create a table like the one in Exhibit 1.9, using the following headings for the columns: Cash; Accounts Receivable; Office Supplies; Office Equipment; Building; Accounts Payable; Notes Payable; M. Right, Capital; M. Right, Withdrawals; Revenues; and Expenses.
2. Use additions and subtractions within the table created in part *1* to show the dollar effects of each transaction on individual items of the accounting equation. Show new balances after each transaction.
3. Once you have completed the table, determine the company's net income.

Check (2) Ending balances: Cash, $9,200; Expenses, $3,500; Notes Payable, $250,000
(3) Net income, $8,500

Problem 1-8A
Analyzing transactions and preparing financial statements
C4 P1 P2

mhhe.com/wildFAP20e

J. D. Simpson started The Simpson Co., a new business that began operations on May 1. The Simpson Co. completed the following transactions during its first month of operations.

May 1 J. D. Simpson invested $60,000 cash in the company.
1 The company rented a furnished office and paid $3,200 cash for May's rent.
3 The company purchased $1,680 of office equipment on credit.
5 The company paid $800 cash for this month's cleaning services.
8 The company provided consulting services for a client and immediately collected $4,600 cash.
12 The company provided $3,000 of consulting services for a client on credit.
15 The company paid $850 cash for an assistant's salary for the first half of this month.
20 The company received $3,000 cash payment for the services provided on May 12.
22 The company provided $2,800 of consulting services on credit.
25 The company received $2,800 cash payment for the services provided on May 22.
26 The company paid $1,680 cash for the office equipment purchased on May 3.
27 The company purchased $60 of advertising in this month's (May) local paper on credit; cash payment is due June 1.
28 The company paid $850 cash for an assistant's salary for the second half of this month.
30 The company paid $200 cash for this month's telephone bill.
30 The company paid $480 cash for this month's utilities.
31 J. D. Simpson withdrew $1,200 cash from the company for personal use.

Required

1. Arrange the following asset, liability, and equity titles in a table like Exhibit 1.9: Cash; Accounts Receivable; Office Equipment; Accounts Payable; J. D. Simpson, Capital; J. D. Simpson, Withdrawals; Revenues; and Expenses.

2. Show effects of the transactions on the accounts of the accounting equation by recording increases and decreases in the appropriate columns. Do not determine new account balances after each transaction. Determine the final total for each account and verify that the equation is in balance.
3. Prepare an income statement for May, a statement of owner's equity for May, a May 31 balance sheet, and a statement of cash flows for May.

Check (2) Ending balances: Cash, $61,140; Expenses, $6,440

(3) Net income, $3,960; Total assets, $62,820

Problem 1-9A
Analyzing transactions and preparing financial statements
C4 P1 P2 

mhhe.com/wildFAP20e

Curtis Hamilton started a new business and completed these transactions during December.

Dec. 1 Curtis Hamilton transferred $56,000 cash from a personal savings account to a checking account in the name of Hamilton Electric.
2 The company rented office space and paid $800 cash for the December rent.
3 The company purchased $14,000 of electrical equipment by paying $3,200 cash and agreeing to pay the $10,800 balance in 30 days.
5 The company purchased office supplies by paying $900 cash.
6 The company completed electrical work and immediately collected $1,000 cash for these services.
8 The company purchased $3,800 of office equipment on credit.
15 The company completed electrical work on credit in the amount of $4,000.
18 The company purchased $500 of office supplies on credit.
20 The company paid $3,800 cash for the office equipment purchased on December 8.
24 The company billed a client $600 for electrical work completed; the balance is due in 30 days.
28 The company received $4,000 cash for the work completed on December 15.
29 The company paid the assistant's salary of $1,200 cash for this month.
30 The company paid $440 cash for this month's utility bill.
31 C. Hamilton withdrew $700 cash from the company for personal use.

Required

1. Arrange the following asset, liability, and equity titles in a table like Exhibit 1.9: Cash; Accounts Receivable; Office Supplies; Office Equipment; Electrical Equipment; Accounts Payable; C. Hamilton, Capital; C. Hamilton, Withdrawals; Revenues; and Expenses.
2. Use additions and subtractions to show the effects of each transaction on the accounts in the accounting equation. Show new balances after each transaction.
3. Use the increases and decreases in the columns of the table from part 2 to prepare an income statement, a statement of owner's equity, and a statement of cash flows—each of these for the current month. Also prepare a balance sheet as of the end of the month.

Check (2) Ending balances: Cash, $49,960, Accounts Payable, $11,300

(3) Net income, $3,160; Total assets, $69,760

Analysis Component

4. Assume that the owner investment transaction on December 1 was $40,000 cash instead of $56,000 and that Hamilton Electric obtained another $16,000 in cash by borrowing it from a bank. Explain the effect of this change on total assets, total liabilities, and total equity.

Problem 1-10A
Determining expenses, liabilities, equity, and return on assets
A1 A2 

Nolan manufactures, markets, and sells cellular telephones. The average total assets for Nolan is $250,000. In its most recent year, Nolan reported net income of $55,000 on revenues of $455,000.

Required

1. What is Nolan's return on assets?
2. Does return on assets seem satisfactory for Nolan given that its competitors average a 12% return on assets?
3. What are total expenses for Nolan in its most recent year?
4. What is the average total amount of liabilities plus equity for Nolan?

Check (3) $400,000
(4) $250,000

Problem 1-11A
Computing and interpreting return on assets
A2  

Coca-Cola and PepsiCo both produce and market beverages that are direct competitors. Key financial figures (in $ millions) for these businesses over the past year follow.

Key Figures ($ millions)	Coca-Cola	PepsiCo
Sales	$30,990	$43,232
Net income	6,906	5,979
Average assets	44,595	37,921

Required

Check (1*a*) 15.5%; (1*b*) 15.8%

1. Compute return on assets for (*a*) Coca-Cola and (*b*) PepsiCo.
2. Which company is more successful in its total amount of sales to consumers?
3. Which company is more successful in returning net income from its assets invested?

Analysis Component

4. Write a one-paragraph memorandum explaining which company you would invest your money in and why. (Limit your explanation to the information provided.)

Problem 1-12A[A]
Identifying risk and return
A3 

All business decisions involve aspects of risk and return.

Required

Identify both the risk and the return in each of the following activities:

1. Investing $1,000 in a 4% savings account.
2. Placing a $1,000 bet on your favorite sports team.
3. Investing $10,000 in Yahoo! stock.
4. Taking out a $10,000 college loan to earn an accounting degree.

Problem 1-13A[B]
Describing organizational activities C5

An organization undertakes various activities in pursuit of business success. Identify an organization's three major business activities, and describe each activity.

Problem 1-14A[B]
Describing organizational activities
C5

A start-up company often engages in the following transactions in its first year of operations. Classify those transactions in one of the three major categories of an organization's business activities.

F. Financing **I.** Investing **O.** Operating

______	**1.** Owner investing land in business.	______	**5.** Purchasing equipment.
______	**2.** Purchasing a building.	______	**6.** Selling and distributing products.
______	**3.** Purchasing land.	______	**7.** Paying for advertising.
______	**4.** Borrowing cash from a bank.	______	**8.** Paying employee wages.

PROBLEM SET B

Problem 1-1B
Identifying effects of transactions on financial statements A1 P1

Identify how each of the following separate transactions affects financial statements. For the balance sheet, identify how each transaction affects total assets, total liabilities, and total equity. For the income statement, identify how each transaction affects net income. For the statement of cash flows, identify how each transaction affects cash flows from operating activities, cash flows from financing activities, and cash flows from investing activities. For increases, place a "+" in the column or columns. For decreases, place a "−" in the column or columns. If both an increase and a decrease occur, place "+/−" in the column or columns. The first transaction is completed as an example.

		Balance Sheet			Income Statement	Statement of Cash Flows		
	Transaction	**Total Assets**	**Total Liab.**	**Total Equity**	**Net Income**	**Operating Activities**	**Financing Activities**	**Investing Activities**
1	Owner invests cash in business	+		+			+	
2	Buys building by signing note payable							
3	Pays cash for salaries incurred							
4	Provides services for cash							
5	Pays cash for rent incurred							
6	Incurs utilities costs on credit							
7	Buys store equipment for cash							
8	Owner withdraws cash							
9	Provides services on credit							
10	Collects cash on receivable from (9)							

Problem 1-2B
Computing missing information using accounting knowledge
A1 P1 

The following financial statement information is from five separate companies.

	Company V	Company W	Company X	Company Y	Company Z
December 31, 2010					
Assets	$45,000	$70,000	$121,500	$82,500	$124,000
Liabilities	30,000	50,000	58,500	61,500	?
December 31, 2011					
Assets	49,000	90,000	136,500	?	160,000
Liabilities	26,000	?	55,500	72,000	52,000
During year 2011					
Owner investments	6,000	10,000	?	38,100	40,000
Net income or (loss)	?	30,000	16,500	24,000	32,000
Owner cash withdrawals	4,500	2,000	0	18,000	6,000

Required

1. Answer the following questions about Company V:
   a. What is the amount of equity on December 31, 2010?
   b. What is the amount of equity on December 31, 2011?
   c. What is the net income or loss for the year 2011?
2. Answer the following questions about Company W:
   a. What is the amount of equity on December 31, 2010?
   b. What is the amount of equity on December 31, 2011?
   c. What is the amount of liabilities on December 31, 2011?
3. Calculate the amount of owner investments for Company X during 2011.
4. Calculate the amount of assets for Company Y on December 31, 2011.
5. Calculate the amount of liabilities for Company Z on December 31, 2010.

Check (1*b*) $23,000

(2*c*) $32,000

(4) $137,100

Problem 1-3B
Preparing a balance sheet
P2

The following is selected financial information for RWB Company as of December 31, 2011.

Liabilities	$74,000	Equity	$40,000	Assets	$114,000

Required

Prepare the balance sheet for RWB Company as of December 31, 2011.

Problem 1-4B
Preparing an income statement
P2

Selected financial information for Online Co. for the year ended December 31, 2011, follows.

Revenues	$58,000	Expenses	$30,000	Net income	$28,000

Required

Prepare the 2011 income statement for Online Company.

Problem 1-5B
Preparing a statement of owner's equity
P2

Following is selected financial information of ComEx for the year ended December 31, 2011.

C. Tex, Capital, Dec. 31, 2011	$47,000	C. Tex, Withdrawals	$ 8,000
Net income	6,000	C. Tex, Capital, Dec. 31, 2010	49,000

Required

Prepare the 2011 statement of owner's equity for ComEx.

Problem 1-6B
Preparing a statement of cash flows
P2

Selected financial information of BuyRight Co. for the year ended December 31, 2011, follows.

Cash from investing activities	$2,600
Net increase in cash	1,400
Cash from financing activities	2,800
Cash used by operating activities	(4,000)
Cash, December 31, 2010	1,300

Required

Prepare the 2011 statement of cash flows for BuyRight Company.

Problem 1-7B
Analyzing effects of transactions
C4 P1 P2 A1

Tiana Moore started a new business, Tiana's Solutions, and completed the following transactions during its first year of operations.

a. T. Moore invests $95,000 cash and office equipment valued at $20,000 in the company.
b. The company purchased a $120,000 building to use as an office. It paid $20,000 in cash and signed a note payable promising to pay the $100,000 balance over the next ten years.
c. The company purchased office equipment for $20,000 cash.
d. The company purchased $1,400 of office supplies and $3,000 of office equipment on credit.
e. The company paid a local newspaper $400 cash for printing an announcement of the office's opening.
f. The company completed a financial plan for a client and billed that client $1,800 for the service.
g. The company designed a financial plan for another client and immediately collected a $2,000 cash fee.
h. T. Moore withdrew $5,000 cash from the company for personal use.
i. The company received $1,800 cash from the client described in transaction *f*.
j. The company made a payment of $2,000 cash on the equipment purchased in transaction *d*.
k. The company paid $2,000 cash for the office secretary's wages.

Required

1. Create a table like the one in Exhibit 1.9, using the following headings for the columns: Cash; Accounts Receivable; Office Supplies; Office Equipment; Building; Accounts Payable; Notes Payable; T. Moore, Capital; T. Moore, Withdrawals; Revenues; and Expenses.
2. Use additions and subtractions within the table created in part *1* to show the dollar effects of each transaction on individual items of the accounting equation. Show new balances after each transaction.
3. Once you have completed the table, determine the company's net income.

Check (2) Ending balances: Cash, $49,400; Expenses, $2,400; Notes Payable, $100,000
(3) Net income, $1,400

Problem 1-8B
Analyzing transactions and preparing financial statements
C4 P1 P2

Ken Stone launched a new business, Ken's Maintenance Co., that began operations on June 1. The following transactions were completed by the company during that first month.

June	1	K. Stone invested $120,000 cash in the company.
	2	The company rented a furnished office and paid $4,500 cash for June's rent.
	4	The company purchased $2,400 of equipment on credit.
	6	The company paid $1,125 cash for this month's advertising of the opening of the business.
	8	The company completed maintenance services for a customer and immediately collected $750 cash.
	14	The company completed $6,300 of maintenance services for City Center on credit.
	16	The company paid $900 cash for an assistant's salary for the first half of the month.
	20	The company received $6,300 cash payment for services completed for City Center on June 14.
	21	The company completed $3,500 of maintenance services for Skyway Co. on credit.
	24	The company completed $825 of maintenance services for Comfort Motel on credit.
	25	The company received $3,500 cash payment from Skyway Co. for the work completed on June 21.
	26	The company made payment of $2,400 cash for equipment purchased on June 4.
	28	The company paid $900 cash for an assistant's salary for the second half of this month.
	29	K. Stone withdrew $2,000 cash from the company for personal use.
	30	The company paid $120 cash for this month's telephone bill.
	30	The company paid $525 cash for this month's utilities.

Required

1. Arrange the following asset, liability, and equity titles in a table like Exhibit 1.9: Cash; Accounts Receivable; Equipment; Accounts Payable; K. Stone, Capital; K. Stone, Withdrawals; Revenues; and Expenses.

2. Show the effects of the transactions on the accounts of the accounting equation by recording increases and decreases in the appropriate columns. Do not determine new account balances after each transaction. Determine the final total for each account and verify that the equation is in balance.
3. Prepare a June income statement, a June statement of owner's equity, a June 30 balance sheet, and a June statement of cash flows.

Check (2) Ending balances: Cash, $118,080; Expenses, $8,070

(3) Net income, $3,305; Total assets, $121,305

Problem 1-9B
Analyzing transactions and preparing financial statements
C4 P1 P2 

Swender Excavating Co., owned by Patrick Swender, began operations in July and completed these transactions during that first month of operations.

July 1 P. Swender invested $60,000 cash in the company.
2 The company rented office space and paid $500 cash for the July rent.
3 The company purchased excavating equipment for $4,000 by paying $800 cash and agreeing to pay the $3,200 balance in 30 days.
6 The company purchased office supplies for $500 cash.
8 The company completed work for a customer and immediately collected $2,200 cash for the work.
10 The company purchased $3,800 of office equipment on credit.
15 The company completed work for a customer on credit in the amount of $2,400.
17 The company purchased $1,920 of office supplies on credit.
23 The company paid $3,800 cash for the office equipment purchased on July 10.
25 The company billed a customer $5,000 for work completed; the balance is due in 30 days.
28 The company received $2,400 cash for the work completed on July 15.
30 The company paid an assistant's salary of $1,260 cash for this month.
31 The company paid $260 cash for this month's utility bill.
31 P. Swender withdrew $1,200 cash from the company for personal use.

Required

1. Arrange the following asset, liability, and equity titles in a table like Exhibit 1.9: Cash; Accounts Receivable; Office Supplies; Office Equipment; Excavating Equipment; Accounts Payable; P. Swender, Capital; P. Swender, Withdrawals; Revenues; and Expenses.
2. Use additions and subtractions to show the effects of each transaction on the accounts in the accounting equation. Show new balances after each transaction.
3. Use the increases and decreases in the columns of the table from part 2 to prepare an income statement, a statement of owner's equity, and a statement of cash flows—each of these for the current month. Also prepare a balance sheet as of the end of the month.

Check (2) Ending balances: Cash, $56,280; Accounts Payable, $5,120

(3) Net income, $7,580; Total assets, $71,500

Analysis Component

4. Assume that the $4,000 purchase of excavating equipment on July 3 was financed from an owner investment of another $4,000 cash in the business (instead of the purchase conditions described in the transaction). Explain the effect of this change on total assets, total liabilities, and total equity.

Problem 1-10B
Determining expenses, liabilities, equity, and return on assets
A1 A2 

Aspen Company manufactures, markets, and sells ATV and snowmobile equipment and accessories. The average total assets for Aspen is $2,000,000. In its most recent year, Aspen reported net income of $100,000 on revenues of $1,200,000.

Required

1. What is Aspen Company's return on assets?
2. Does return on assets seem satisfactory for Aspen given that its competitors average a 9.5% return on assets?
3. What are the total expenses for Aspen Company in its most recent year?
4. What is the average total amount of liabilities plus equity for Aspen Company?

Check (3) $1,100,000

(4) $2,000,000

Problem 1-11B
Computing and interpreting return on assets
A2 

AT&T and Verizon produce and market telecommunications products and are competitors. Key financial figures (in $ millions) for these businesses over the past year follow.

Key Figures ($ millions)	AT&T	Verizon
Sales	$123,018	$107,808
Net income	12,535	10,358
Average assets	266,999	214,937

Required

Check (1*a*) 4.7%; (1*b*) 4.8%

1. Compute return on assets for (*a*) AT&T and (*b*) Verizon.
2. Which company is more successful in the total amount of sales to consumers?
3. Which company is more successful in returning net income from its assets invested?

Analysis Component

4. Write a one-paragraph memorandum explaining which company you would invest your money in and why. (Limit your explanation to the information provided.)

Problem 1-12B[A]
Identifying risk and return
A3

All business decisions involve aspects of risk and return.

Required

Identify both the risk and the return in each of the following activities:

1. Stashing $1,000 cash under your mattress.
2. Placing a $500 bet on a horse running in the Kentucky Derby.
3. Investing $10,000 in Nike stock.
4. Investing $10,000 in U.S. Savings Bonds.

Problem 1-13B[B]
Describing organizational activities C5

Identify in outline format the three major business activities of an organization. For each of these activities, identify at least two specific transactions or events normally undertaken by the business's owners or its managers.

Problem 1-14B[B]
Describing organizational activities
C5

A start-up company often engages in the following activities during its first year of operations. Classify each of the following activities into one of the three major activities of an organization.

A. Financing **B.** Investing **C.** Operating

_____	**1.** Providing client services.	_____	**5.** Supervising workers.
_____	**2.** Obtaining a bank loan.	_____	**6.** Owner investing money in business.
_____	**3.** Purchasing machinery.	_____	**7.** Renting office space.
_____	**4.** Research for its products.	_____	**8.** Paying utilities expenses.

This serial problem starts in this chapter and continues throughout most chapters of the book. It is most readily solved if you use the Working Papers that accompany this book (but working papers are not required).

SERIAL PROBLEM

Business Solutions
C4 P1

SP 1 On October 1, 2011, Santana Rey launched a computer services company, **Business Solutions,** that is organized as a proprietorship and provides consulting services, computer system installations, and custom program development. Rey adopts the calendar year for reporting purposes and expects to prepare the company's first set of financial statements on December 31, 2011.

Required

Create a table like the one in Exhibit 1.9 using the following headings for columns: Cash; Accounts Receivable; Computer Supplies; Computer System; Office Equipment; Accounts Payable; S. Rey, Capital; S. Rey, Withdrawals; Revenues; and Expenses. Then use additions and subtractions within the table created to show the dollar effects for each of the following October transactions for Business Solutions on the individual items of the accounting equation. Show new balances after each transaction.

Oct.	1	S. Rey invested $45,000 cash, a $20,000 computer system, and $8,000 of office equipment in the company.
	3	The company purchased $1,420 of computer supplies on credit from Harris Office Products.
	6	The company billed Easy Leasing $4,800 for services performed in installing a new Web server.
	8	The company paid $1,420 cash for the computer supplies purchased from Harris Office Products on October 3.
	10	The company hired Lyn Addie as a part-time assistant for $125 per day, as needed.
	12	The company billed Easy Leasing another $1,400 for services performed.
	15	The company received $4,800 cash from Easy Leasing as partial payment toward its account.
	17	The company paid $805 cash to repair computer equipment damaged when moving it.
	20	The company paid $1,728 cash for advertisements published in the local newspaper.
	22	The company received $1,400 cash from Easy Leasing toward its account.
	28	The company billed IFM Company $5,208 for services performed.
	31	The company paid $875 cash for Lyn Addie's wages for seven days of work this month.
	31	S. Rey withdrew $3,600 cash from the company for personal use.

Check Ending balances: Cash, $42,772; Revenues, $11,408; Expenses, $3,408

Beyond the Numbers (BTN) is a special problem section aimed to refine communication, conceptual, analysis, and research skills. It includes many activities helpful in developing an active learning environment.

Beyond the Numbers

REPORTING IN ACTION
A1 A2 A3 
RIM

BTN 1-1 Key financial figures for Research In Motion's fiscal year ended February 27, 2010, follow.

Key Figure	In Millions
Liabilities + Equity	$10,204
Net income	2,457
Revenues	14,953

Required

1. What is the total amount of assets invested in Research In Motion?
2. What is Research In Motion's return on assets? Its assets at February 28, 2009, equal $8,101 (in millions).
3. How much are total expenses for Research In Motion for the year ended February 27, 2010?
4. Does Research In Motion's return on assets seem satisfactory if competitors average an 18% return?

Check (2) 26.8%

Fast Forward

5. Access Research In Motion's financial statements (Form 10-K) for fiscal years ending after February 27, 2010, from its Website (RIM.com) or from the SEC Website (www.SEC.gov) and compute its return on assets for those fiscal years. Compare the February 27, 2010, fiscal year-end return on assets to any subsequent years' returns you are able to compute, and interpret the results.

COMPARATIVE ANALYSIS
A1 A2 A3 
RIM
Apple

BTN 1-2 Key comparative figures ($ millions) for both Research In Motion and Apple follow.

Key Figure	Research In Motion	Apple
Liabilities + Equity	$10,204	$47,501
Net income	2,457	8,235
Revenues and sales	14,953	42,905

Required

1. What is the total amount of assets invested in (*a*) Research In Motion and (*b*) Apple?
2. What is the return on assets for (*a*) Research In Motion and (*b*) Apple? Research In Motion's beginning-year assets equal $8,101 (in millions) and Apple's beginning-year assets equal $36,171 (in millions).
3. How much are expenses for (*a*) Research In Motion and (*b*) Apple?
4. Is return on assets satisfactory for (*a*) Research In Motion and (*b*) Apple? (Assume competitors average an 18% return.)
5. What can you conclude about Research In Motion and Apple from these computations?

Check (2b) 19.7%

ETHICS CHALLENGE
C3 C4

BTN 1-3 Madison Thorne works in a public accounting firm and hopes to eventually be a partner. The management of Allnet Company invites Thorne to prepare a bid to audit Allnet's financial statements. In discussing the audit fee, Allnet's management suggests a fee range in which the amount depends on the reported profit of Allnet. The higher its profit, the higher will be the audit fee paid to Thorne's firm.

Required

1. Identify the parties potentially affected by this audit and the fee plan proposed.
2. What are the ethical factors in this situation? Explain.
3. Would you recommend that Thorne accept this audit fee arrangement? Why or why not?
4. Describe some ethical considerations guiding your recommendation.

COMMUNICATING IN PRACTICE

A1 C2  

BTN 1-4 Refer to this chapter's opening feature about Facebook.® Assume that Mark Zuckerberg desires to expand his online services to meet people's demands. He decides to meet with his banker to discuss a loan to allow Facebook to expand.

Required

1. Prepare a half-page report outlining the information you would request from Mark Zuckerberg if you were the loan officer.
2. Indicate whether the information you request and your loan decision are affected by the form of business organization for Facebook.

TAKING IT TO THE NET

A2

BTN 1-5 Visit the EDGAR database at (www.SEC.gov). Access the Form 10-K report of Rocky Mountain Chocolate Factory (ticker RMCF) filed on May 26, 2009, covering its 2009 fiscal year.

Required

1. Item 6 of the 10-K report provides comparative financial highlights of RMCF for the years 2005–2009. How would you describe the revenue trend for RMCF over this five-year period?
2. Has RMCF been profitable (see net income) over this five-year period? Support your answer.

TEAMWORK IN ACTION

C1

BTN 1-6 Teamwork is important in today's business world. Successful teams schedule convenient meetings, maintain regular communications, and cooperate with and support their members. This assignment aims to establish support/learning teams, initiate discussions, and set meeting times.

Required

1. Form teams and open a team discussion to determine a regular time and place for your team to meet between each scheduled class meeting. Notify your instructor via a memorandum or e-mail message as to when and where your team will hold regularly scheduled meetings.
2. Develop a list of telephone numbers and/or e-mail addresses of your teammates.

ENTREPRENEURIAL DECISION

A1 P1  

BTN 1-7 Refer to this chapter's opening feature about Facebook. Assume that Mark Zuckerberg decides to open a new Website devoted to social networking for accountants and those studying accounting. This new company will be called AccountBook.

Required

1. AccountBook obtains a $500,000 loan and Mark Zuckerberg contributes $250,000 of his own assets in exchange for common stock in the new company.
   a. What is the new company's total amount of liabilities plus equity?
   b. What is the new company's total amount of assets?
2. If the new company earns $80,000 in net income in the first year of operation, compute its return on asset (assume average assets equal $750,000). Assess its performance if competitors average a 10% return.

Check (2) 10.7%

HITTING THE ROAD

C2  

BTN 1-8 You are to interview a local business owner. (This can be a friend or relative.) Opening lines of communication with members of the business community can provide personal benefits of business networking. If you do not know the owner, you should call ahead to introduce yourself and explain your position as a student and your assignment requirements. You should request a thirty minute appointment for a face-to-face or phone interview to discuss the form of organization and operations of the business. Be prepared to make a good impression.

Required

1. Identify and describe the main operating activities and the form of organization for this business.
2. Determine and explain why the owner(s) chose this particular form of organization.
3. Identify any special advantages and/or disadvantages the owner(s) experiences in operating with this form of business organization.

BTN 1-9 Nokia (www.Nokia.com) is a leading manufacturer of mobile devices and services, and it competes to some extent with both Research In Motion and Apple. Key financial figures for Nokia follow.

GLOBAL DECISION

A1 A2 A3

NOKIA

RIM

Apple

Key Figure*	Euro (EUR) in Millions
Average assets	37,660
Net income	260
Revenue	40,984
Return on assets	0.7%

* Figures prepared in accordance with International Financial Reporting Standards.

Required

1. Identify any concerns you have in comparing Nokia's income and revenue figures to those of Research In Motion and Apple (in BTN 1-2) for purposes of making business decisions.
2. Identify any concerns you have in comparing Nokia's return on assets ratio to those of Research In Motion and Apple (computed for BTN 1-2) for purposes of making business decisions.

ANSWERS TO MULTIPLE CHOICE QUIZ

1. c; $450,000 is the actual cost incurred.
2. b; revenue is recorded when earned.
3. d;

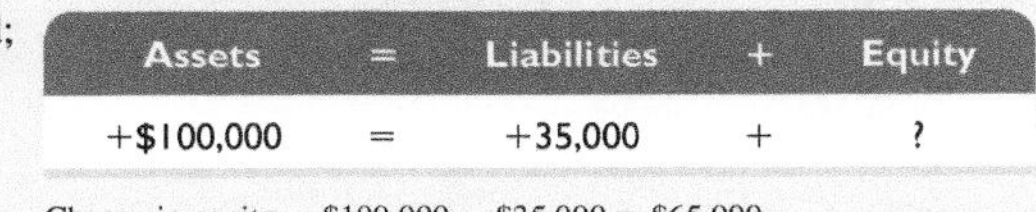

Assets	=	Liabilities	+	Equity
+$100,000	=	+35,000	+	?

Change in equity = $100,000 − $35,000 = $65,000

4. a
5. a

2 Analyzing and Recording Transactions

A Look Back

Chapter 1 defined accounting and introduced financial statements. We described forms of organizations and identified users and uses of accounting. We defined the accounting equation and applied it to transaction analysis.

A Look at This Chapter

This chapter focuses on the accounting process. We describe transactions and source documents, and we explain the analysis and recording of transactions. The accounting equation, T-account, general ledger, trial balance, and debits and credits are key tools in the accounting process.

A Look Ahead

Chapter 3 extends our focus on processing information. We explain the importance of adjusting accounts and the procedures in preparing financial statements.

Learning Objectives

CAP

CONCEPTUAL

C1 Explain the steps in processing transactions and the role of source documents. (p. 50)

C2 Describe an account and its use in recording transactions. (p. 51)

C3 Describe a ledger and a chart of accounts. (p. 54)

C4 Define *debits* and *credits* and explain double-entry accounting. (p. 55)

ANALYTICAL

A1 Analyze the impact of transactions on accounts and financial statements. (p. 59)

A2 Compute the debt ratio and describe its use in analyzing financial condition. (p. 69)

LP2

PROCEDURAL

P1 Record transactions in a journal and post entries to a ledger. (p. 56)

P2 Prepare and explain the use of a trial balance. (p. 65)

P3 Prepare financial statements from business transactions. (p. 66)

Decision Insight

Sole Sisters

"Every way we can cut costs, we do!"

—**SUSIE LEVITT** (on right)

NEW YORK—"High heels were killing our feet, but we didn't want to give them up because we aren't the tallest people out there," insists Susie Levitt, who stands no taller than 5′2″. "So we came up with the idea of emergency footwear." Susie, along with Katie Shea, designed a stylish, foldable slip-on ballet flat with a pouch that is readily tucked into a handbag and pulled out when their feet cry for mercy. The empty pouch then expands into a tote bag to hold their "killer" heels for carrying home. Launched from their college apartment, Susie and Katie invested "less than $10,000" for the cost of their first order of 1,000 pairs, including Website design, to launch **CitySlips** **(www.cityslips.com).**

To pursue their business ambitions, Susie and Katie took business courses, including accounting. They learned and applied recordkeeping processes, transaction analysis, inventory accounting, and financial statement reporting. We were careful to get a handle on our financial situation, says Katie. Today, the two are running a profitable business and have a reliable accounting system to help them make good business decisions.

We had to account for product costs, design expenses, supplier payments, patent fees, and other expenses, says Susie. At the same time, the two have grown sales and expanded their product line. "It was all done online," says Susie. "We became nocturnal!"

The two insist that it is crucial to track and account for all revenues and expenses, and what is invested in the business. They maintain that success requires proper accounting for and analysis of the financial side. Susie also suggests that young entrepreneurs "network with your professors and other staff members. They have years of experience and can often help you, or introduce you to people who can help you, with your business."

The bigger message of our company, says Susie, is promoting comfort and confidence for women. Adds Katie, "Regardless of what your business is, the story of starting while in college, differentiates you from the beginning!"

[Sources: *CitySlips Website,* January 2011; *Entrepreneur,* December 2009; *Examiner.com,* December 2009; *CNN.com,* August 2009; *Daily News,* May 2009.]

Chapter Preview

Financial statements report on the financial performance and condition of an organization. Knowledge of their preparation, organization, and analysis is important. A main goal of this chapter is to illustrate how transactions are recorded, how they are reflected in financial statements, and how they impact analysis of financial statements. Debits and credits are introduced and identified as a tool in helping analyze and process transactions.

Analyzing and Recording Transactions

Analyzing and Recording Process
- Source documents
- The account and its analysis
- Types of accounts

Analyzing and Processing Transactions
- General ledger
- Double-entry accounting
- Journalizing and posting
- An illustration

Trial Balance
- Trial balance preparation
- Search for and correction of errors
- Trial balance use

ANALYZING AND RECORDING PROCESS

The accounting process identifies business transactions and events, analyzes and records their effects, and summarizes and presents information in reports and financial statements. These reports and statements are used for making investing, lending, and other business decisions. The steps in the accounting process that focus on *analyzing and recording* transactions and events are shown in Exhibit 2.1.

EXHIBIT 2.1

The Analyzing and Recording Process

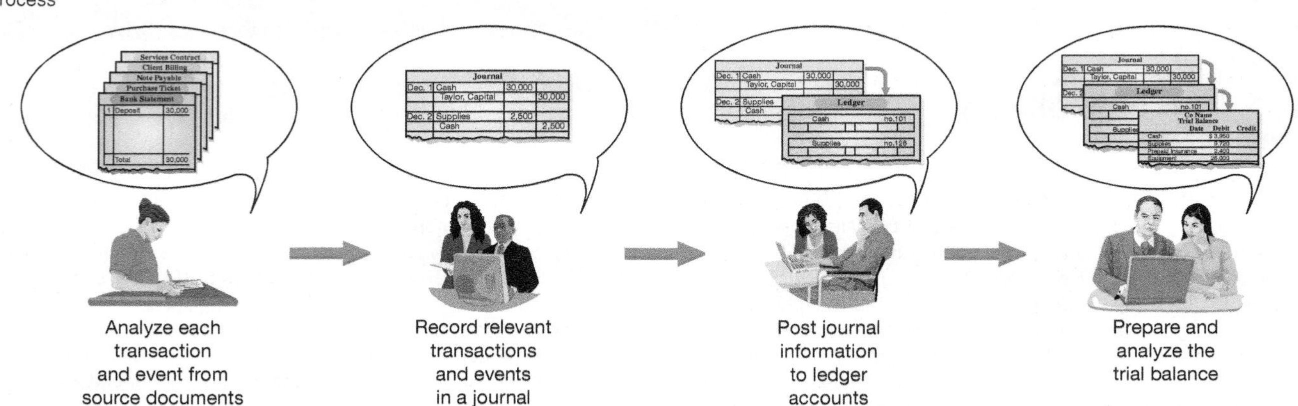

C1 Explain the steps in processing transactions and the role of source documents.

Business transactions and events are the starting points. Relying on source documents, the transactions and events are analyzed using the accounting equation to understand how they affect company performance and financial position. These effects are recorded in accounting records, informally referred to as the *accounting books,* or simply the *books.* Additional steps such as posting and then preparing a trial balance help summarize and classify the effects of transactions and events. Ultimately, the accounting process provides information in useful reports or financial statements to decision makers.

Source Documents

Source documents identify and describe transactions and events entering the accounting process. They are the sources of accounting information and can be in either hard copy or electronic form. Examples are sales tickets, checks, purchase orders, bills from suppliers, employee earnings records, and bank statements. To illustrate, when an item is purchased on credit, the seller usually prepares at least two copies of a sales invoice. One copy is given to the buyer. Another copy, often sent electronically, results in an entry in the seller's information system to record the sale. Sellers use invoices for recording sales and for control; buyers use them for recording purchases and for monitoring purchasing activity. Many cash registers record information for each sale on a tape or electronic file locked inside the register. This record can be used as a source document for recording sales in the accounting records. Source documents, especially if obtained from outside the organization, provide objective and reliable evidence about transactions and events and their amounts.

Point: To ensure that all sales are rung up on the register, most sellers require customers to have their receipts to exchange or return purchased items.

Decision Ethics Answer — p. 74

Cashier Your manager requires that you, as cashier, immediately enter each sale. Recently, lunch hour traffic has increased and the assistant manager asks you to avoid delays by taking customers' cash and making change without entering sales. The assistant manager says she will add up cash and enter sales after lunch. She says that, in this way, the register will always match the cash amount when the manager arrives at three o'clock. What do you do? ■

The Account and Its Analysis

C2 Describe an account and its use in recording transactions.

An **account** is a record of increases and decreases in a specific asset, liability, equity, revenue, or expense item. Information from an account is analyzed, summarized, and presented in reports and financial statements. The **general ledger,** or simply **ledger,** is a record containing all accounts used by a company. The ledger is often in electronic form. While most companies' ledgers contain similar accounts, a company often uses one or more unique accounts because of its type of operations. As shown in Exhibit 2.2, accounts are classified into three general categories based on the accounting equation: asset, liability, or equity.

EXHIBIT 2.2

Accounts Organized by the Accounting Equation

Asset Accounts Assets are resources owned or controlled by a company and that have expected future benefits. Most accounting systems include (at a minimum) separate accounts for the assets described here.

A *Cash* account reflects a company's cash balance. All increases and decreases in cash are recorded in the Cash account. It includes money and any medium of exchange that a bank accepts for deposit (coins, checks, money orders, and checking account balances).

Accounts receivable are held by a seller and refer to promises of payment from customers to sellers. These transactions are often called *credit sales* or *sales on account* (or *on credit*). Accounts receivable are increased by credit sales and are decreased by customer payments. A company needs a separate record for each customer, but for now, we use the simpler practice of recording all increases and decreases in receivables in a single account called Accounts Receivable.

Point: Customers and others who owe a company are called its **debtors.**

A *note receivable,* or promissory note, is a written promise of another entity to pay a definite sum of money on a specified future date to the holder of the note. A company holding a promissory note signed by another entity has an asset that is recorded in a Note (or Notes) Receivable account.

Prepaid accounts (also called *prepaid expenses*) are assets that represent prepayments of future expenses (*not* current expenses). When the expenses are later incurred, the amounts in prepaid accounts are transferred to expense accounts. Common examples of prepaid accounts include prepaid insurance, prepaid rent, and prepaid services (such as club memberships). Prepaid accounts expire with the passage of time (such as with rent) or through use (such as with prepaid meal tickets). When financial statements are prepared, prepaid accounts are adjusted so that (1) all expired and used prepaid accounts are recorded as regular expenses and (2) all unexpired and unused prepaid accounts are recorded as assets (reflecting future use in

Point: A college parking fee is a prepaid account from the student's standpoint. At the beginning of the term, it represents an asset that entitles a student to park on or near campus. The benefits of the parking fee expire as the term progresses. At term-end, prepaid parking (asset) equals zero as it has been entirely recorded as parking expense.

Point: Prepaid accounts that apply to current and future periods are assets. These assets are adjusted at the end of each period to reflect only those amounts that have not yet expired, and to record as expenses those amounts that have expired.

future periods). To illustrate, when an insurance fee, called a *premium,* is paid in advance, the cost is typically recorded in the asset account Prepaid Insurance. Over time, the expiring portion of the insurance cost is removed from this asset account and reported in expenses on the income statement. Any unexpired portion remains in Prepaid Insurance and is reported on the balance sheet as an asset. (An exception exists for prepaid accounts that will expire or be used before the end of the current accounting period when financial statements are prepared. In this case, the prepayments *can* be recorded immediately as expenses.)

Supplies are assets until they are used. When they are used up, their costs are reported as expenses. The costs of unused supplies are recorded in a Supplies asset account. Supplies are often grouped by purpose—for example, office supplies and store supplies. *Office supplies* include stationery, paper, toner, and pens. *Store supplies* include packaging materials, plastic and paper bags, gift boxes and cartons, and cleaning materials. The costs of these unused supplies can be recorded in an Office Supplies or a Store Supplies asset account. When supplies are used, their costs are transferred from the asset accounts to expense accounts.

Point: Some assets are described as *intangible* because they do not have physical existence or their benefits are highly uncertain. A recent balance sheet for **Coca-Cola Company** shows nearly $1 billion in intangible assets.

Equipment is an asset. When equipment is used and gets worn down, its cost is gradually reported as an expense (called depreciation). Equipment is often grouped by its purpose—for example, office equipment and store equipment. *Office equipment* includes computers, printers, desks, chairs, and shelves. Costs incurred for these items are recorded in an Office Equipment asset account. The Store Equipment account includes the costs of assets used in a store, such as counters, showcases, ladders, hoists, and cash registers.

Buildings such as stores, offices, warehouses, and factories are assets because they provide expected future benefits to those who control or own them. Their costs are recorded in a Buildings asset account. When several buildings are owned, separate accounts are sometimes kept for each of them.

The cost of *land* owned by a business is recorded in a Land account. The cost of buildings located on the land is separately recorded in one or more building accounts.

Decision Insight

Women Entrepreneurs The Center for Women's Business Research reports that women-owned businesses, such as **CitySlips**, are growing and that they:

- Total approximately 11 million and employ nearly 20 million workers.
- Generate $2.5 trillion in annual sales and tend to embrace technology.
- Are philanthropic—70% of owners volunteer at least once per month.
- Are more likely funded by individual investors (73%) than venture firms (15%).

Liability Accounts Liabilities are claims (by creditors) against assets, which means they are obligations to transfer assets or provide products or services to others. **Creditors** are individuals and organizations that have rights to receive payments from a company. If a company fails to pay its obligations, the law gives creditors a right to force the sale of that company's assets to obtain the money to meet creditors' claims. When assets are sold under these conditions, creditors are paid first, but only up to the amount of their claims. Any remaining money, the residual, goes to the owners of the company. Creditors often use a balance sheet to help decide whether to loan money to a company. A loan is less risky if the borrower's liabilities are small in comparison to assets because this means there are more resources than claims on resources. Common liability accounts are described here.

Point: Accounts payable are also called *trade payables.*

Accounts payable refer to oral or implied promises to pay later, which usually arise from purchases of merchandise. Payables can also arise from purchases of supplies, equipment, and services. Accounting systems keep separate records about each creditor. We describe these individual records in Chapter 5.

A *note payable* refers to a formal promise, usually denoted by the signing of a promissory note, to pay a future amount. It is recorded in either a short-term Note Payable account or a long-term Note Payable account, depending on when it must be repaid. We explain details of short- and long-term classification in Chapter 3.

Unearned revenue refers to a liability that is settled in the future when a company delivers its products or services. When customers pay in advance for products or services (before revenue is earned), the revenue recognition principle requires that the seller consider this payment as unearned revenue. Examples of unearned revenue include magazine subscriptions collected in advance by a publisher, sales of gift certificates by stores, and season ticket sales by sports teams. The seller would record these in liability accounts such as Unearned Subscriptions, Unearned Store Sales, and Unearned Ticket Revenue. When products and services are later delivered, the earned portion of the unearned revenue is transferred to revenue accounts such as Subscription Fees, Store Sales, and Ticket Sales.[1]

Point: If a subscription is canceled, the publisher is expected to refund the unused portion to the subscriber.

Accrued liabilities are amounts owed that are not yet paid. Examples are wages payable, taxes payable, and interest payable. These are often recorded in separate liability accounts by the same title. If they are not large in amount, one or more ledger accounts can be added and reported as a single amount on the balance sheet. (Financial statements often have amounts reported that are a summation of several ledger accounts.)

Decision Insight

Revenue Spread The New Orleans Saints have *Unearned Revenues* of about $60 million in advance ticket sales. When the team plays its home games, it settles this liability to its ticket holders and then transfers the amount earned to *Ticket Revenues.* ■

Equity Accounts The owner's claim on a company's assets is called *equity* or *owner's equity.* Equity is the owner's *residual interest* in the assets of a business after deducting liabilities. Equity is impacted by four types of accounts: owner's capital, owner's withdrawals, revenues, and expenses. We show this visually in Exhibit 2.3 by expanding the accounting equation.

Point: Equity is also called *net assets.*

EXHIBIT 2.3

Expanded Accounting Equation

Asset Accounts = Liability Accounts + Equity Accounts

+ Owner's Capital − Owner's Withdrawals + Revenues − Expenses

When an owner invests in a company, the invested amount is recorded in an account titled Owner, Capital (where the owner's name is inserted in place of "owner"). The account titled *C. Taylor, Capital* is used for FastForward. Any further owner investments are recorded in this account. When an owner withdraws assets for personal use it decreases both company assets and total equity. Withdrawals are not expenses of the business; they are simply the opposite of owner investments. The Owner, Withdrawals account is used to record asset distributions to the owner. The account titled *C. Taylor, Withdrawals* is used for FastForward. (Owners of proprietorships cannot receive company salaries because they are not legally separate from their companies; and they cannot enter into company contracts with themselves.)

Point: The Owner's Withdrawals account is a *contra equity* account because it reduces the normal balance of equity.

Point: The withdrawal of assets by the owners of a corporation is called a *dividend.*

Revenues and expenses also impact equity. Examples of revenue accounts are Sales, Commissions Earned, Professional Fees Earned, Rent Revenue, and Interest Revenue. *Revenues increase equity* and result from products and services provided to customers. Examples of expense accounts are Advertising Expense, Store Supplies Expense, Office Salaries Expense, Office Supplies Expense, Rent Expense, Utilities Expense, and Insurance Expense. *Expenses decrease equity* and result from assets and services used in a company's operations. The variety of revenues and expenses can be seen by looking at the *chart of accounts* that follows the index at the

[1] In practice, account titles vary. As one example, Subscription Fees is sometimes called Subscription Fees Revenue, Subscription Fees Earned, or Earned Subscription Fees. As another example, Rent Earned is sometimes called Rent Revenue, Rental Revenue, or Earned Rent Revenue. We must use good judgment when reading financial statements because titles can differ even within the same industry. For example, product sales are called *revenue* at Research In Motion, but *net sales* at Apple. Generally, the term *revenues* or *fees* is more commonly used with service businesses, and *net sales* or *sales* with product businesses.

back of this book. (Different companies sometimes use different account titles than those in this book's chart of accounts. For example, some might use Interest Revenue instead of Interest Earned, or Rental Expense instead of Rent Expense. It is important only that an account title describe the item it represents.)

Decision Insight

Sporting Accounts The Los Angeles Lakers and the other NBA teams have the following major revenue and expense accounts:

Revenues	Expenses
Basketball ticket sales	Team salaries
TV & radio broadcast fees	Game costs
Advertising revenues	NBA franchise costs
Basketball playoff receipts	Promotional costs

ANALYZING AND PROCESSING TRANSACTIONS

This section explains several tools and processes that comprise an accounting system. These include a ledger, T-account, debits and credits, double-entry accounting, journalizing, and posting.

Ledger and Chart of Accounts

C3 Describe a ledger and a chart of accounts.

The collection of all accounts and their balances for an information system is called a *ledger* (or *general ledger*). If accounts are in files on a hard drive, the sum of those files is the ledger. If the accounts are pages in a file, that file is the ledger. A company's size and diversity of operations affect the number of accounts needed. A small company can get by with as few as 20 or 30 accounts; a large company can require several thousand. The **chart of accounts** is a list of all ledger accounts and includes an identification number assigned to each account. A small business might use the following numbering system for its accounts:

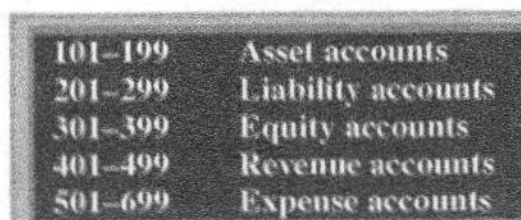

101–199	Asset accounts
201–299	Liability accounts
301–399	Equity accounts
401–499	Revenue accounts
501–699	Expense accounts

These numbers provide a three-digit code that is useful in recordkeeping. In this case, the first digit assigned to asset accounts is a 1, the first digit assigned to liability accounts is a 2, and so on. The second and third digits relate to the accounts' subcategories. Exhibit 2.4 shows a partial chart of accounts for FastForward, the focus company of Chapter 1. (Please review the more complete chart of accounts that follows the index at the back of this book.)

EXHIBIT 2.4

Partial Chart of Accounts for FastForward

Acct. No.	Account Name	Acct. No.	Account Name	Acct. No.	Account Name
101	Cash	236	Unearned consulting revenue	622	Salaries expense
106	Accounts receivable	301	C. Taylor, Capital	637	Insurance expense
126	Supplies	302	C. Taylor, Withdrawals	640	Rent expense
128	Prepaid insurance	403	Consulting revenue	652	Supplies expense
167	Equipment	406	Rental revenue	690	Utilities expense
201	Accounts payable				

Debits and Credits

C4 Define *debits* and *credits* and explain double-entry accounting.

A **T-account** represents a ledger account and is a tool used to understand the effects of one or more transactions. Its name comes from its shape like the letter T. The layout of a T-account, shown in Exhibit 2.5, is (1) the account title on top, (2) a left, or debit side, and (3) a right, or credit, side.

EXHIBIT 2.5

The T-Account

Account Title	
(Left side) *Debit*	(Right side) *Credit*

The left side of an account is called the **debit** side, often abbreviated *Dr*. The right side is called the **credit** side, abbreviated *Cr*.[2] To enter amounts on the left side of an account is to *debit* the account. To enter amounts on the right side is to *credit* the account. Do not make the error of thinking that the terms *debit* and *credit* mean increase or decrease. Whether a debit or a credit is an increase or decrease depends on the account. For an account where a debit is an increase, the credit is a decrease; for an account where a debit is a decrease, the credit is an increase. The difference between total debits and total credits for an account, including any beginning balance, is the **account balance.** When the sum of debits exceeds the sum of credits, the account has a *debit balance*. It has a *credit balance* when the sum of credits exceeds the sum of debits. When the sum of debits equals the sum of credits, the account has a *zero balance*.

Point: Think of *debit* and *credit* as accounting directions for left and right.

Double-Entry Accounting

Double-entry accounting requires that for each transaction:

- At least two accounts are involved, with at least one debit and one credit.
- The total amount debited must equal the total amount credited.
- The accounting equation must not be violated.

This means the sum of the debits for all entries must equal the sum of the credits for all entries, and the sum of debit account balances in the ledger must equal the sum of credit account balances.

The system for recording debits and credits follows from the usual accounting equation—see Exhibit 2.6. Two points are important here. First, like any simple mathematical relation, net increases or decreases on one side have equal net effects on the other side. For example, a net increase in assets must be accompanied by an identical net increase on the liabilities and equity side. Recall that some transactions affect only one side of the equation, meaning that two or more accounts on one side are affected, but their net effect on this one side is zero. Second, the left side is the *normal balance* side for assets, and the right side is the *normal balance* side for liabilities and equity. This matches their layout in the accounting equation where assets are on the left side of this equation, and liabilities and equity are on the right.

EXHIBIT 2.6

Debits and Credits in the Accounting Equation

Assets		=	Liabilities		+	Equity	
Debit for increases	Credit for decreases		Debit for decreases	Credit for increases		Debit for decreases	Credit for increases
+	−		−	+		−	+
Normal				Normal			Normal

Recall that equity increases from revenues and owner investments and it decreases from expenses and owner withdrawals. These important equity relations are conveyed by expanding the accounting equation to include debits and credits in double-entry form as shown in Exhibit 2.7.

Increases (credits) to owner's capital and revenues *increase* equity; increases (debits) to withdrawals and expenses *decrease* equity. The normal balance of each account (asset, liability, capital, withdrawals, revenue, or expense) refers to the left or right (debit or credit) side where

Point: Debits and credits do not mean favorable or unfavorable. A debit to an asset increases it, as does a debit to an expense. A credit to a liability increases it, as does a credit to a revenue.

[2] These abbreviations are remnants of 18th-century English recordkeeping practices where the terms *debitor* and *creditor* were used instead of *debit* and *credit*. The abbreviations use the first and last letters of these terms, just as we still do for Saint (St.) and Doctor (Dr.).

EXHIBIT 2.7

Debit and Credit Effects for Component Accounts

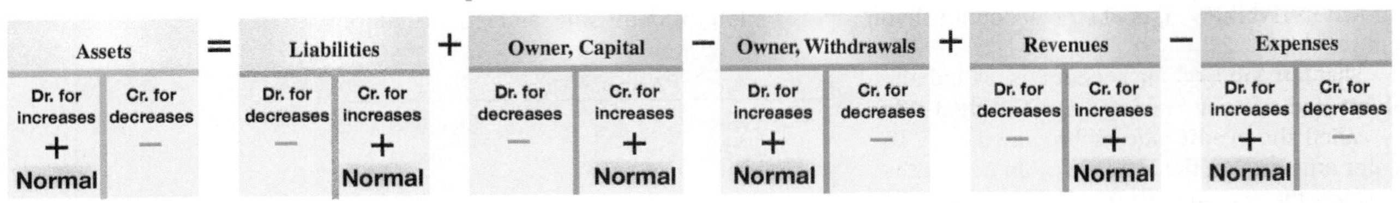

increases are recorded. Understanding these diagrams and rules is required to prepare, analyze, and interpret financial statements.

The T-account for FastForward's Cash account, reflecting its first 11 transactions (from Exhibit 1.9), is shown in Exhibit 2.8. The total increases in its Cash account are $36,100, the total decreases are $31,300, and the account's debit balance is $4,800. (We illustrate use of T-accounts later in this chapter.)

EXHIBIT 2.8

Computing the Balance for a T-Account

Cash			
Receive investment by owner	30,000	Purchase of supplies	2,500
Consulting services revenue earned	4,200	Purchase of equipment	26,000
Collection of account receivable	1,900	Payment of rent	1,000
		Payment of salary	700
		Payment of account payable	900
		Withdrawal by owner	200
Balance	4,800		

Point: The ending balance is on the side with the larger dollar amount. Also, a plus (+) and minus (−) are not used in a T-account.

Quick Check Answers — p. 75 

1. Identify examples of accounting source documents.
2. Explain the importance of source documents.
3. Identify each of the following as either an asset, a liability, or equity: (*a*) Prepaid Rent, (*b*) Unearned Fees, (*c*) Building, (*d*) Wages Payable, and (*e*) Office Supplies.
4. What is an account? What is a ledger?
5. What determines the number and types of accounts a company uses?
6. Does *debit* always mean increase and *credit* always mean decrease?
7. Describe a chart of accounts.

Journalizing and Posting Transactions

P1 Record transactions in a journal and post entries to a ledger.

Processing transactions is a crucial part of accounting. The four usual steps of this process are depicted in Exhibit 2.9. Steps 1 and 2—involving transaction analysis and the accounting equation—were introduced in prior sections. This section extends that discussion and focuses on steps 3 and 4 of the accounting process. Step 3 is to record each transaction chronologically in a journal. A **journal** gives a complete record of each transaction in one place. It also shows debits and credits for each transaction. The process of recording transactions in a journal is called **journalizing.** Step 4 is to transfer (or *post*) entries from the journal to the ledger. The process of transferring journal entry information to the ledger is called **posting.**

Journalizing Transactions The process of journalizing transactions requires an understanding of a journal. While companies can use various journals, every company uses a **general journal.** It can be used to record any transaction and includes the following information about each transaction: ⓐ date of transaction, ⓑ titles of affected accounts, ⓒ dollar amount of each

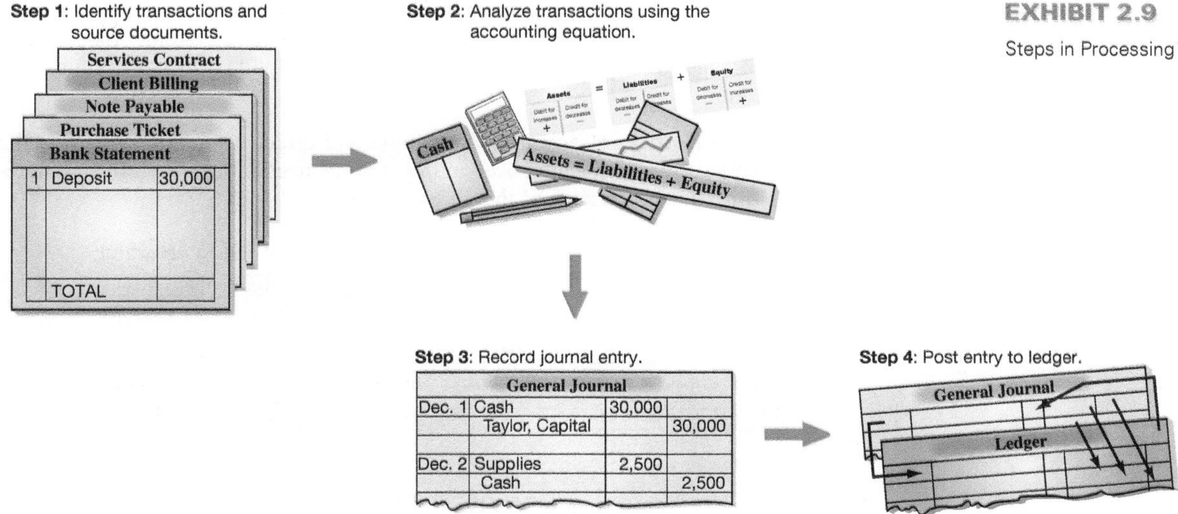

EXHIBIT 2.9

Steps in Processing Transactions

debit and credit, and ⓓ explanation of the transaction. Exhibit 2.10 shows how the first two transactions of FastForward are recorded in a general journal. This process is similar for manual and computerized systems. Computerized journals are often designed to look like a manual journal page, and also include error-checking routines that ensure debits equal credits for each entry. Shortcuts allow recordkeepers to select account names and numbers from pull-down menus.

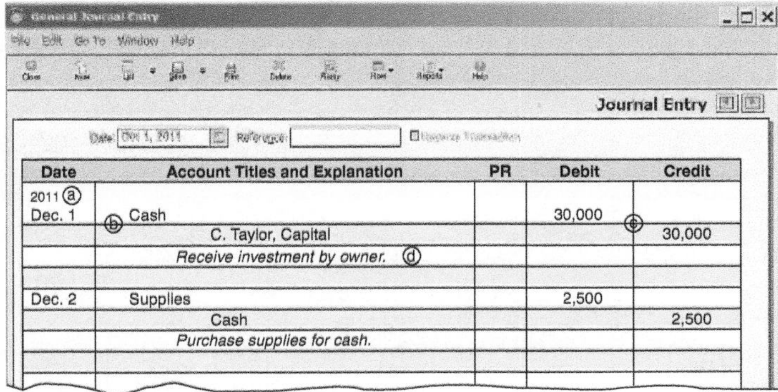

Date	Account Titles and Explanation	PR	Debit	Credit
2011 ⓐ				
Dec. 1	ⓑ Cash		30,000	ⓒ
	C. Taylor, Capital			30,000
	Receive investment by owner. ⓓ			
Dec. 2	Supplies		2,500	
	Cash			2,500
	Purchase supplies for cash.			

EXHIBIT 2.10

Partial General Journal for FastForward

To record entries in a general journal, apply these steps; refer to the entries in Exhibit 2.10 when reviewing these steps. (1) Date the transaction: Enter the year at the top of the first column and the month and day on the first line of each journal entry. (2) Enter titles of accounts debited and then enter amounts in the Debit column on the same line. Account titles are taken from the chart of accounts and are aligned with the left margin of the Account Titles and Explanation column. (3) Enter titles of accounts credited and then enter amounts in the Credit column on the same line. Account titles are from the chart of accounts and are indented from the left margin of the Account Titles and Explanation column to distinguish them from debited accounts. (4) Enter a brief explanation of the transaction on the line below the entry (it often references a source document). This explanation is indented about half as far as the credited account titles to avoid confusing it with accounts, and it is italicized.

Point: There are no exact rules for writing journal entry explanations. An explanation should be short yet describe why an entry is made.

IFRS

IFRS requires that companies report the following four basic financial statements with explanatory notes:

- Balance sheet
- Income statement
- Statement of changes in equity (or statement of recognized revenue and expense)
- Statement of cash flows

IFRS does not prescribe specific formats; and comparative information is required for the preceding period only. ■

A blank line is left between each journal entry for clarity. When a transaction is first recorded, the **posting reference (PR) column** is left blank (in a manual system). Later, when posting entries to the ledger, the identification numbers of the individual ledger accounts are entered in the PR column.

Balance Column Account T-accounts are simple and direct means to show how the accounting process works. However, actual accounting systems need more structure and therefore use **balance column accounts,** such as that in Exhibit 2.11.

EXHIBIT 2.11

Cash Account in Balance Column Format

		Cash			Account No. 101
Date	**Explanation**	**PR**	**Debit**	**Credit**	**Balance**
2011					
Dec. 1		G1	30,000		30,000
Dec. 2		G1		2,500	27,500
Dec. 3		G1		26,000	1,500
Dec. 10		G1	4,200		5,700

The balance column account format is similar to a T-account in having columns for debits and credits. It is different in including transaction date and explanation columns. It also has a column with the balance of the account after each entry is recorded. To illustrate, FastForward's Cash account in Exhibit 2.11 is debited on December 1 for the $30,000 owner investment, yielding a $30,000 debit balance. The account is credited on December 2 for $2,500, yielding a $27,500 debit balance. On December 3, it is credited again, this time for $26,000, and its debit balance is reduced to $1,500. The Cash account is debited for $4,200 on December 10, and its debit balance increases to $5,700; and so on.

Point: Explanations are typically included in ledger accounts only for unusual transactions or events.

The heading of the Balance column does not show whether it is a debit or credit balance. Instead, an account is assumed to have a *normal balance*. Unusual events can sometimes temporarily

EXHIBIT 2.12

Posting an Entry to the Ledger

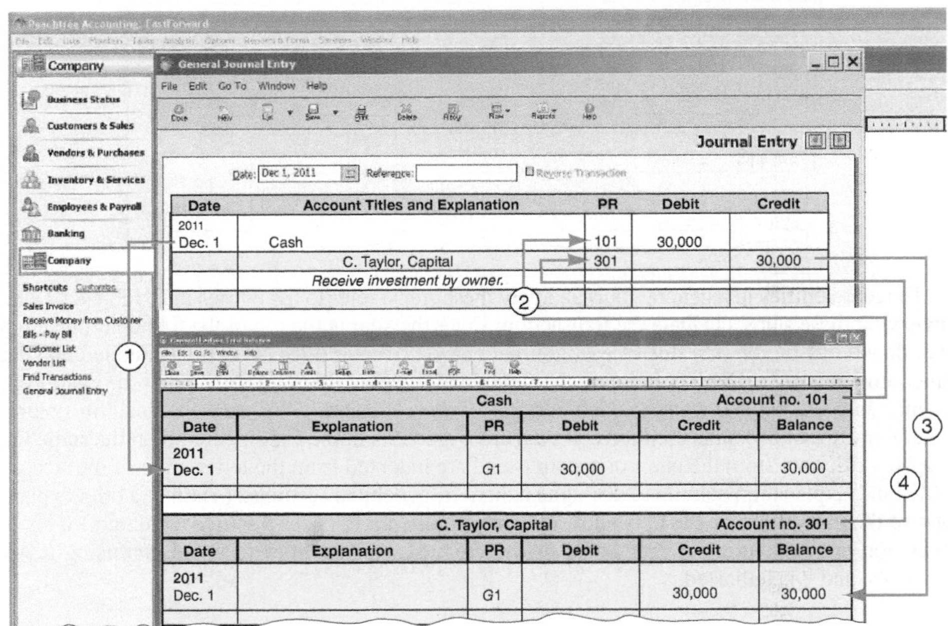

Key: ① Identify debit account in Ledger: enter date, journal page, amount, and balance.
② Enter the debit account number from the Ledger in the PR column of the journal.
③ Identify credit account in Ledger: enter date, journal page, amount, and balance.
④ Enter the credit account number from the Ledger in the PR column of the journal.

Point: The fundamental concepts of a manual (pencil-and-paper) system are identical to those of a computerized information system.

give an account an abnormal balance. An *abnormal balance* refers to a balance on the side where decreases are recorded. For example, a customer might mistakenly overpay a bill. This gives that customer's account receivable an abnormal (credit) balance. An abnormal balance is often identified by circling it or by entering it in red or some other unusual color. A zero balance for an account is usually shown by writing zeros or a dash in the Balance column to avoid confusion between a zero balance and one omitted in error.

Posting Journal Entries Step 4 of processing transactions is to post journal entries to ledger accounts (see Exhibit 2.9). To ensure that the ledger is up-to-date, entries are posted as soon as possible. This might be daily, weekly, or when time permits. All entries must be posted to the ledger before financial statements are prepared to ensure that account balances are up-to-date. When entries are posted to the ledger, the debits in journal entries are transferred into ledger accounts as debits, and credits are transferred into ledger accounts as credits. Exhibit 2.12 shows the *four steps to post a journal entry*. First, identify the ledger account that is debited in the entry; then, in the ledger, enter the entry date, the journal and page in its PR column, the debit amount, and the new balance of the ledger account. (The letter *G* shows it came from the General Journal.) Second, enter the ledger account number in the PR column of the journal. Steps 3 and 4 repeat the first two steps for credit entries and amounts. The posting process creates a link between the ledger and the journal entry. This link is a useful cross-reference for tracing an amount from one record to another.

Point: Computerized systems often provide a code beside a balance such as *dr.* or *cr.* to identify its balance. Posting is automatic and immediate with accounting software.

Point: A journal is often referred to as the *book of original entry.* The ledger is referred to as the *book of final entry* because financial statements are prepared from it.

Analyzing Transactions—An Illustration

We return to the activities of FastForward to show how double-entry accounting is useful in analyzing and processing transactions. Analysis of each transaction follows the four steps of Exhibit 2.9.

A1 Analyze the impact of transactions on accounts and financial statements.

Step 1 Identify the transaction and any source documents.

Step 2 Analyze the transaction using the accounting equation.

Step 3 Record the transaction in journal entry form applying double-entry accounting.

Step 4 Post the entry (for simplicity, we use T-accounts to represent ledger accounts).

Study each transaction thoroughly before proceeding to the next. The first 11 transactions are from Chapter 1, and we analyze five additional December transactions of FastForward (numbered 12 through 16) that were omitted earlier.

FAST*Forward*

1. Receive Investment by Owner

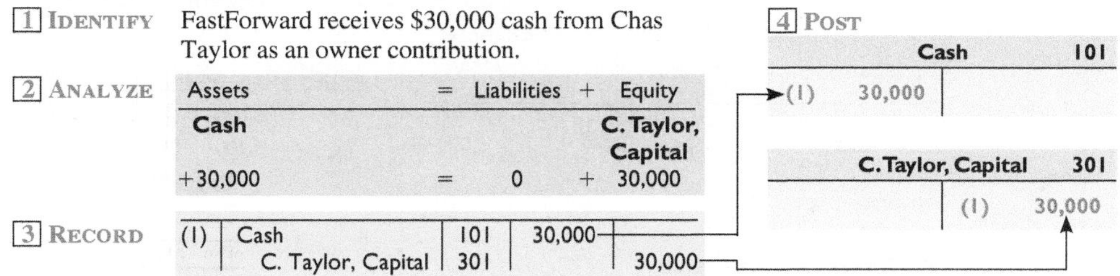

2. Purchase Supplies for Cash

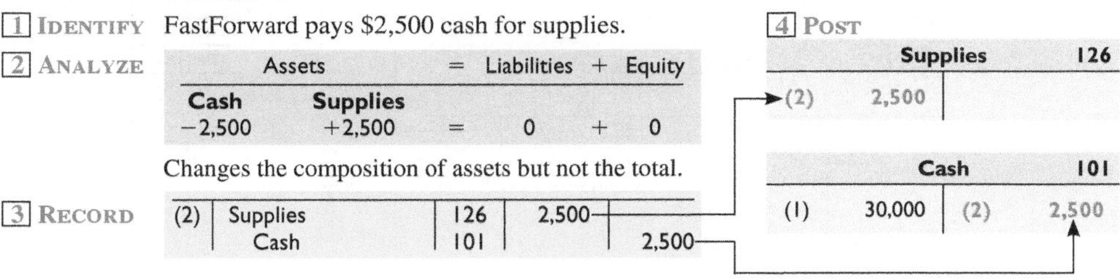

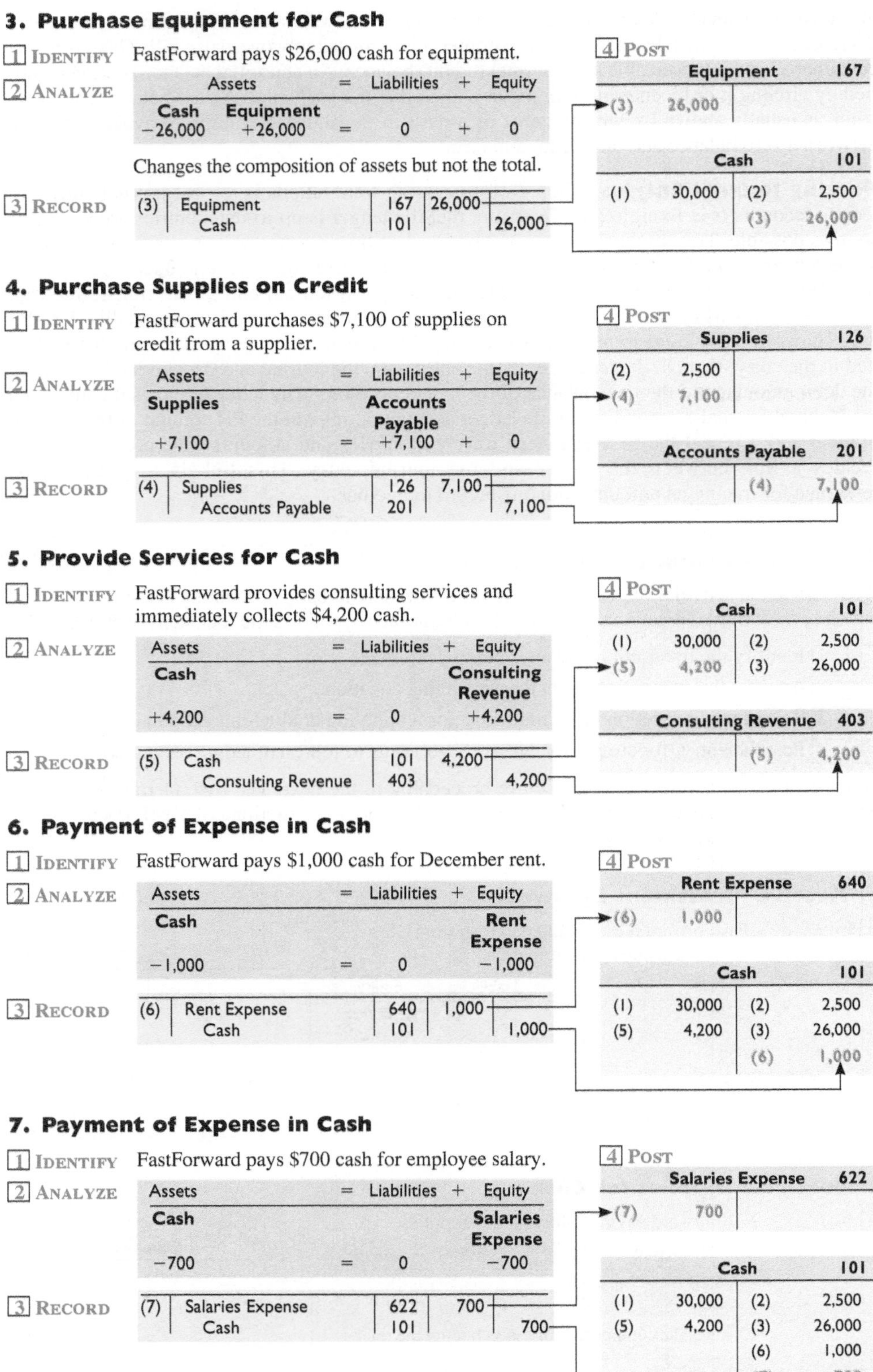

Point: *Salary* usually refers to compensation for an employee who receives a fixed amount for a given time period, whereas *wages* usually refers to compensation based on time worked.

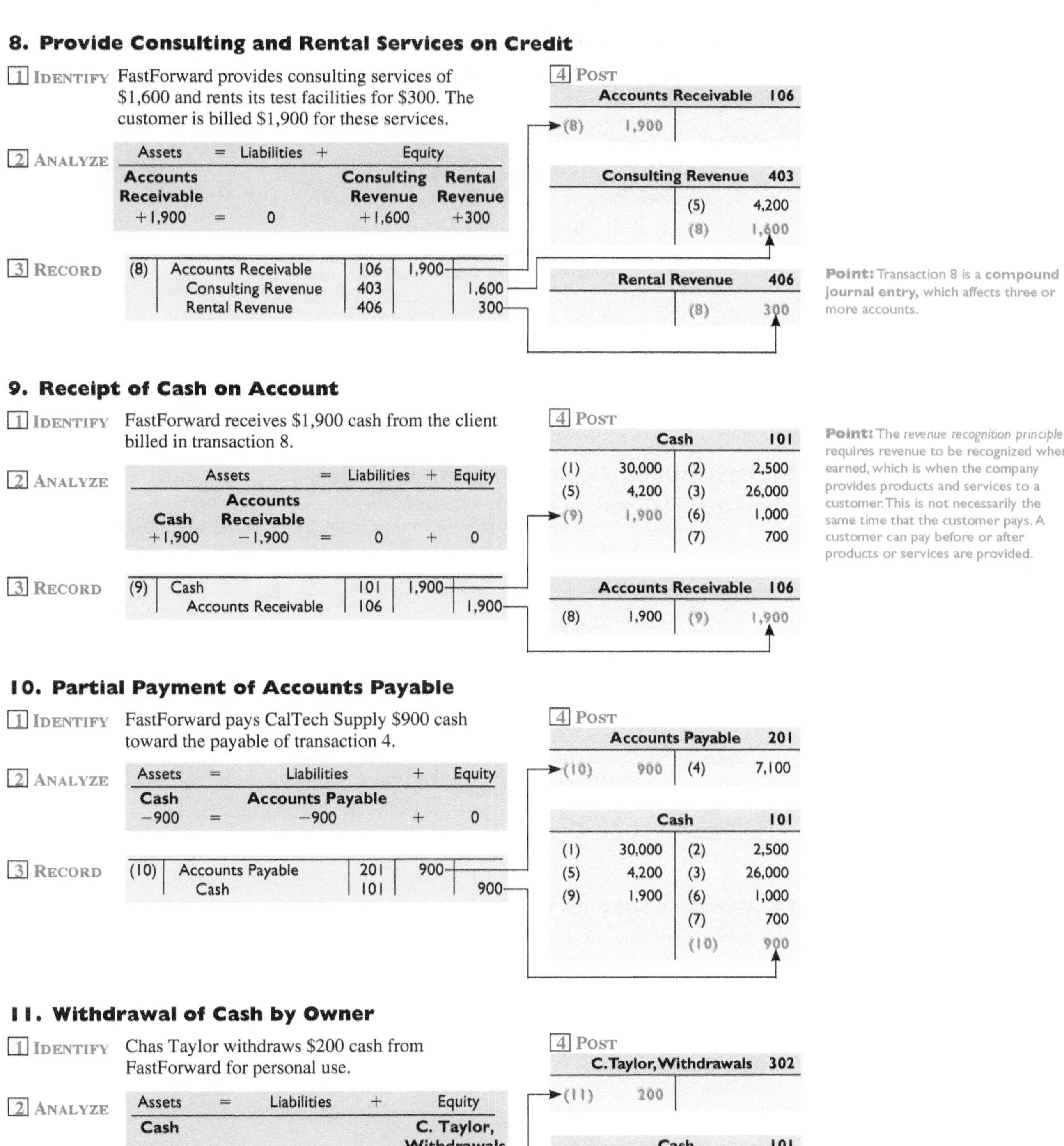

8. Provide Consulting and Rental Services on Credit

1 IDENTIFY FastForward provides consulting services of $1,600 and rents its test facilities for $300. The customer is billed $1,900 for these services.

2 ANALYZE

Assets	=	Liabilities	+	Equity	
Accounts Receivable				Consulting Revenue	Rental Revenue
+1,900	=	0		+1,600	+300

3 RECORD

(8)	Accounts Receivable	106	1,900	
	Consulting Revenue	403		1,600
	Rental Revenue	406		300

4 POST

Accounts Receivable			106
(8)	1,900		

Consulting Revenue			403
		(5)	4,200
		(8)	1,600

Rental Revenue			406
		(8)	300

Point: Transaction 8 is a **compound journal entry,** which affects three or more accounts.

9. Receipt of Cash on Account

1 IDENTIFY FastForward receives $1,900 cash from the client billed in transaction 8.

2 ANALYZE

Assets		=	Liabilities	+	Equity
Cash	Accounts Receivable				
+1,900	−1,900	=	0	+	0

3 RECORD

(9)	Cash	101	1,900	
	Accounts Receivable	106		1,900

4 POST

Cash			101
(1)	30,000	(2)	2,500
(5)	4,200	(3)	26,000
(9)	1,900	(6)	1,000
		(7)	700

Accounts Receivable			106
(8)	1,900	(9)	1,900

Point: The *revenue recognition principle* requires revenue to be recognized when earned, which is when the company provides products and services to a customer. This is not necessarily the same time that the customer pays. A customer can pay before or after products or services are provided.

10. Partial Payment of Accounts Payable

1 IDENTIFY FastForward pays CalTech Supply $900 cash toward the payable of transaction 4.

2 ANALYZE

Assets	=	Liabilities	+	Equity
Cash		Accounts Payable		
−900	=	−900	+	0

3 RECORD

(10)	Accounts Payable	201	900	
	Cash	101		900

4 POST

Accounts Payable			201
(10)	900	(4)	7,100

Cash			101
(1)	30,000	(2)	2,500
(5)	4,200	(3)	26,000
(9)	1,900	(6)	1,000
		(7)	700
		(10)	900

11. Withdrawal of Cash by Owner

1 IDENTIFY Chas Taylor withdraws $200 cash from FastForward for personal use.

2 ANALYZE

Assets	=	Liabilities	+	Equity
Cash				C. Taylor, Withdrawals
−200	=	0		−200

3 RECORD

(11)	C. Taylor, Withdrawals	302	200	
	Cash	101		200

4 POST

C. Taylor, Withdrawals			302
(11)	200		

Cash			101
(1)	30,000	(2)	2,500
(5)	4,200	(3)	26,000
(9)	1,900	(6)	1,000
		(7)	700
		(10)	900
		(11)	200

Point: Luca Pacioli, a 15th-century monk, is considered a pioneer in accounting and the first to devise double-entry accounting.

12. Receipt of Cash for Future Services

1 IDENTIFY FastForward receives $3,000 cash in advance of providing consulting services to a customer.

2 ANALYZE

Assets	=	Liabilities	+	Equity
Cash		**Unearned Consulting Revenue**		
+3,000	=	+3,000	+	0

Accepting $3,000 cash obligates FastForward to perform future services and is a liability. No revenue is earned until services are provided.

3 RECORD

(12)	Cash	101	3,000	
	Unearned Consulting Revenue	236		3,000

4 POST

Cash			101
(1)	30,000	(2)	2,500
(5)	4,200	(3)	26,000
(9)	1,900	(6)	1,000
(12)	3,000	(7)	700
		(10)	900
		(11)	200

Unearned Consulting Revenue			236
		(12)	3,000

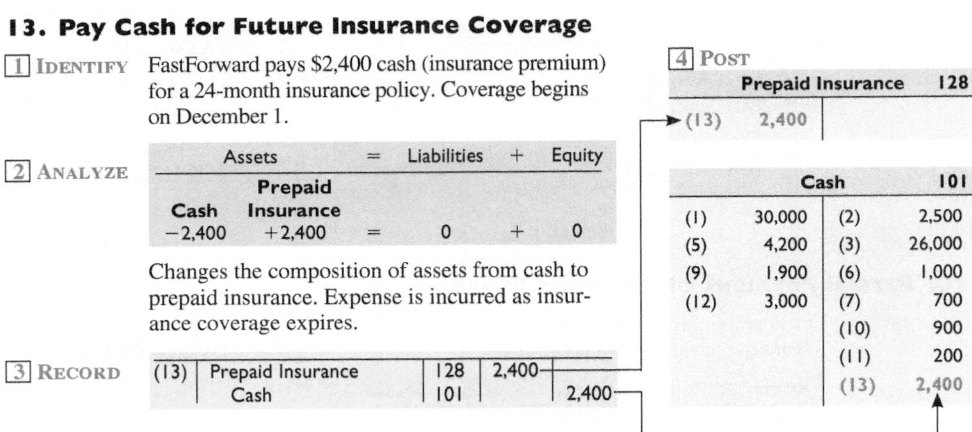

13. Pay Cash for Future Insurance Coverage

1 IDENTIFY FastForward pays $2,400 cash (insurance premium) for a 24-month insurance policy. Coverage begins on December 1.

2 ANALYZE

Assets		=	Liabilities	+	Equity
Cash	**Prepaid Insurance**				
−2,400	+2,400	=	0	+	0

Changes the composition of assets from cash to prepaid insurance. Expense is incurred as insurance coverage expires.

3 RECORD

(13)	Prepaid Insurance	128	2,400	
	Cash	101		2,400

4 POST

Prepaid Insurance			128
(13)	2,400		

Cash			101
(1)	30,000	(2)	2,500
(5)	4,200	(3)	26,000
(9)	1,900	(6)	1,000
(12)	3,000	(7)	700
		(10)	900
		(11)	200
		(13)	2,400

14. Purchase Supplies for Cash

1 IDENTIFY FastForward pays $120 cash for supplies.

2 ANALYZE

Assets		=	Liabilities	+	Equity
Cash	**Supplies**				
−120	+120	=	0	+	0

3 RECORD

(14)	Supplies	126	120	
	Cash	101		120

4 POST

Supplies			126
(2)	2,500		
(4)	7,100		
(14)	120		

Cash			101
(1)	30,000	(2)	2,500
(5)	4,200	(3)	26,000
(9)	1,900	(6)	1,000
(12)	3,000	(7)	700
		(10)	900
		(11)	200
		(13)	2,400
		(14)	120

15. Payment of Expense in Cash

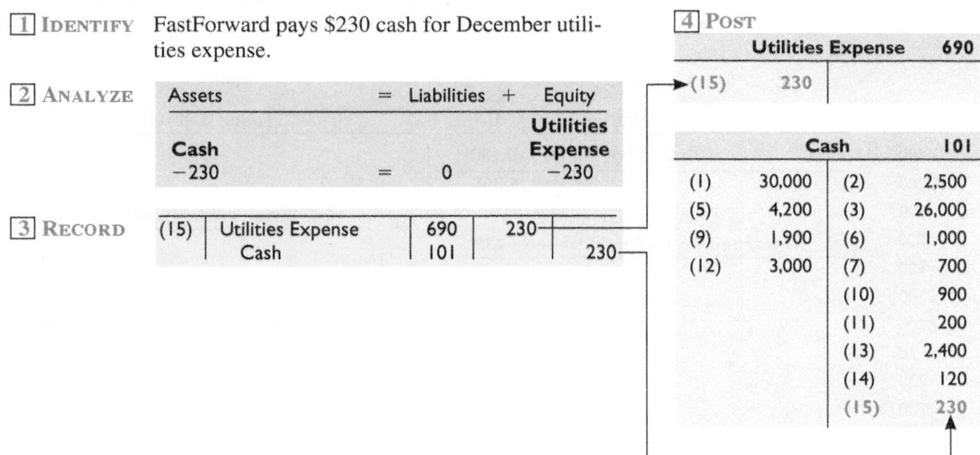

16. Payment of Expense in Cash

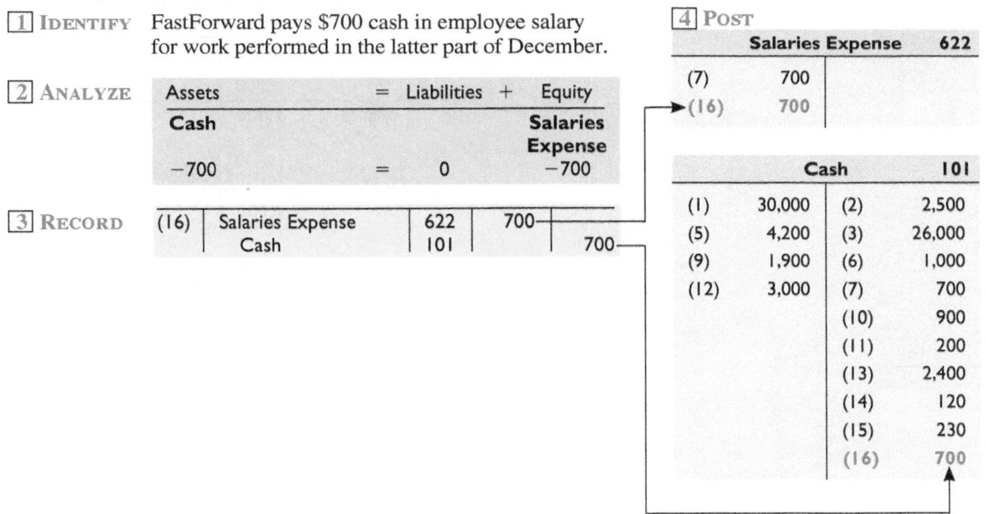

Point: We could merge transactions 15 and 16 into one *compound entry.*

Accounting Equation Analysis

Exhibit 2.13 shows the ledger accounts (in T-account form) of FastForward after all 16 transactions are recorded and posted and the balances computed. The accounts are grouped into three major columns corresponding to the accounting equation: assets, liabilities, and equity. Note several important points. First, as with each transaction, the totals for the three columns must obey the accounting equation. Specifically, assets equal $42,470 ($4,350 + $0 + $9,720 + $2,400 + $26,000); liabilities equal $9,200 ($6,200 + $3,000); and equity equals $33,270 ($30,000 − $200 + $5,800 + $300 − $1,400 − $1,000 − $230). These numbers prove the accounting equation: Assets of $42,470 = Liabilities of $9,200 + Equity of $33,270. Second, the capital, withdrawals, revenue, and expense accounts reflect the transactions that change equity. These account categories underlie the statement of owner's equity. Third, the revenue and expense account balances will be summarized and reported in the income statement. Fourth, increases and decreases in the cash account make up the elements reported in the statement of cash flows.

Debit and Credit Rules

Accounts	Increase (normal bal.)	Decrease
Asset	Debit	Credit
Liability	Credit	Debit
Capital	Credit	Debit
Withdrawals	Debit	Credit
Revenue	Credit	Debit
Expense	Debit	Credit

Point: Technology does not provide the judgment required to analyze most business transactions. Analysis requires the expertise of skilled and ethical professionals.

EXHIBIT 2.13

Ledger for FastForward (in T-Account Form)

Assets = **Liabilities** + **Equity**

Cash 101

	Debit		Credit
(1)	30,000	(2)	2,500
(5)	4,200	(3)	26,000
(9)	1,900	(6)	1,000
(12)	3,000	(7)	700
		(10)	900
		(11)	200
		(13)	2,400
		(14)	120
		(15)	230
		(16)	700
Balance	**4,350**		

Accounts Receivable 106

	Debit		Credit
(8)	1,900	(9)	1,900
Balance	**0**		

Supplies 126

	Debit		Credit
(2)	2,500		
(4)	7,100		
(14)	120		
Balance	**9,720**		

Prepaid Insurance 128

	Debit		Credit
(13)	**2,400**		

Equipment 167

	Debit		Credit
(3)	**26,000**		

Accounts Payable 201

	Debit		Credit
(10)	900	(4)	7,100
		Balance	**6,200**

Unearned Consulting Revenue 236

	Debit		Credit
		(12)	**3,000**

C. Taylor, Capital 301

	Debit		Credit
		(1)	**30,000**

C. Taylor, Withdrawals 302

	Debit		Credit
(11)	**200**		

Consulting Revenue 403

	Debit		Credit
		(5)	4,200
		(8)	1,600
		Balance	**5,800**

Rental Revenue 406

	Debit		Credit
		(8)	**300**

Salaries Expense 622

	Debit		Credit
(7)	700		
(16)	700		
Balance	**1,400**		

Rent Expense 640

	Debit		Credit
(6)	**1,000**		

Utilities Expense 690

	Debit		Credit
(15)	**230**		

Accounts in this white area reflect those reported on the income statement.

$42,470 = **$9,200** + **$33,270**

Quick Check Answers — p. 75 

8. What types of transactions increase equity? What types decrease equity?

9. Why are accounting systems called *double-entry?*

10. For each transaction, double-entry accounting requires which of the following? (*a*) Debits to asset accounts must create credits to liability or equity accounts, (*b*) a debit to a liability account must create a credit to an asset account, or (*c*) total debits must equal total credits.

11. An owner invests $15,000 cash along with equipment having a market value of $23,000 in a company. Prepare the necessary journal entry.

12. Explain what a compound journal entry is.

13. Why are posting reference numbers entered in the journal when entries are posted to ledger accounts?

TRIAL BALANCE

Double-entry accounting requires the sum of debit account balances to equal the sum of credit account balances. A trial balance is used to confirm this. A **trial balance** is a list of accounts and their balances at a point in time. Account balances are reported in their appropriate debit or credit columns of a trial balance. A trial balance can be used to confirm this and to follow up on any abnormal or unusual balances. Exhibit 2.14 shows the trial balance for FastForward after its 16 entries have been posted to the ledger. (This is an *unadjusted* trial balance—Chapter 3 explains the necessary adjustments.)

EXHIBIT 2.14

Trial Balance (Unadjusted)

FASTFORWARD
Trial Balance
December 31, 2011

	Debit	Credit
Cash	$ 4,350	
Accounts receivable	0	
Supplies	9,720	
Prepaid insurance	2,400	
Equipment	26,000	
Accounts payable		$ 6,200
Unearned consulting revenue		3,000
C. Taylor, Capital		30,000
C. Taylor, Withdrawals	200	
Consulting revenue		5,800
Rental revenue		300
Salaries expense	1,400	
Rent expense	1,000	
Utilities expense	230	
Totals	$ 45,300	$ 45,300

Point: The ordering of accounts in a trial balance typically follows their identification number from the chart of accounts.

Preparing a Trial Balance

P2 Prepare and explain the use of a trial balance.

Preparing a trial balance involves three steps:

1. List each account title and its amount (from ledger) in the trial balance. If an account has a zero balance, list it with a zero in its normal balance column (or omit it entirely).
2. Compute the total of debit balances and the total of credit balances.
3. Verify (*prove*) total debit balances equal total credit balances.

The total of debit balances equals the total of credit balances for the trial balance in Exhibit 2.14. Equality of these two totals does not guarantee that no errors were made. For example, the column totals still will be equal when a debit or credit of a correct amount is made to a wrong account. Another error that does not cause unequal column totals occurs when equal debits and credits of an incorrect amount are entered.

Point: A trial balance is *not* a financial statement but a mechanism for checking equality of debits and credits in the ledger. Financial statements do not have debit and credit columns.

Searching for and Correcting Errors If the trial balance does not balance (when its columns are not equal), the error (or errors) must be found and corrected. An efficient

Example: If a credit to Unearned Revenue was incorrectly posted from the journal as a credit to the Revenue ledger account, would the ledger still balance? Would the financial statements be correct? *Answers:* The ledger would balance, but liabilities would be understated, equity would be overstated, and income would be overstated (all because of overstated revenues).

way to search for an error is to check the journalizing, posting, and trial balance preparation in *reverse order.* Step 1 is to verify that the trial balance columns are correctly added. If step 1 fails to find the error, step 2 is to verify that account balances are accurately entered from the ledger. Step 3 is to see whether a debit (or credit) balance is mistakenly listed in the trial balance as a credit (or debit). A clue to this error is when the difference between total debits and total credits equals twice the amount of the incorrect account balance. If the error is still undiscovered, Step 4 is to recompute each account balance in the ledger. Step 5 is to verify that each journal entry is properly posted. Step 6 is to verify that the original journal entry has equal debits and credits. At this point, the errors should be uncovered.[3]

Point: The IRS requires companies to keep records that can be audited.

If an error in a journal entry is discovered before the error is posted, it can be corrected in a manual system by drawing a line through the incorrect information. The correct information is written above it to create a record of change for the auditor. Many computerized systems allow the operator to replace the incorrect information directly.

If an error in a journal entry is not discovered until after it is posted, we do not strike through both erroneous entries in the journal and ledger. Instead, we correct this error by creating a *correcting entry* that removes the amount from the wrong account and records it to the correct account. As an example, suppose a $100 purchase of supplies is journalized with an incorrect debit to Equipment, and then this incorrect entry is posted to the ledger. The Supplies ledger account balance is understated by $100, and the Equipment ledger account balance is overstated by $100. The correcting entry is: debit Supplies and credit Equipment (both for $100).

Using a Trial Balance to Prepare Financial Statements

P3 Prepare financial statements from business transactions.

This section shows how to prepare *financial statements* from the trial balance in Exhibit 2.14 and from information on the December transactions of FastForward. These statements differ from those in Chapter 1 because of several additional transactions. These statements are also more precisely called *unadjusted statements* because we need to make some further accounting adjustments (described in Chapter 3).

EXHIBIT 2.15

Links between Financial Statements across Time

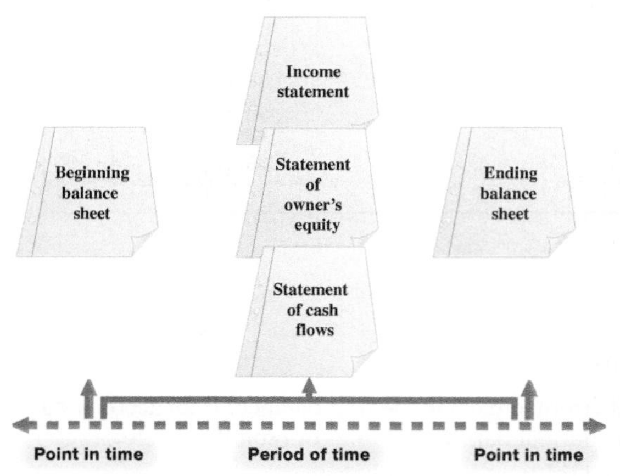

How financial statements are linked in time is illustrated in Exhibit 2.15. A balance sheet reports on an organization's financial position at a *point in time.* The income statement, statement of owner's equity, and statement of cash flows report on financial performance over a *period of time.* The three statements in the middle column of Exhibit 2.15 link balance sheets from the beginning to the end of a reporting period. They explain how financial position changes from one point to another.

Preparers and users (including regulatory agencies) determine the length of the reporting period. A one-year, or

[3] *Transposition* occurs when two digits are switched, or transposed, within a number. If transposition is the only error, it yields a difference between the two trial balance totals that is evenly divisible by 9. For example, assume that a $691 debit in an entry is incorrectly posted to the ledger as $619. Total credits in the trial balance are then larger than total debits by $72 ($691 − $619). The $72 error is *evenly* divisible by 9 (72/9 = 8). The first digit of the quotient (in our example it is 8) equals the difference between the digits of the two transposed numbers (the 9 and the 1). The number of digits in the quotient also tells the location of the transposition, starting from the right. The quotient in our example had only one digit (8), so it tells us the transposition is in the first digit. Consider another example where a transposition error involves posting $961 instead of the correct $691. The difference in these numbers is $270, and its quotient is 30 (270/9). The quotient has two digits, so it tells us to check the second digit from the right for a transposition of two numbers that have a difference of 3.

annual, reporting period is common, as are semiannual, quarterly, and monthly periods. The one-year reporting period is known as the *accounting,* or *fiscal, year.* Businesses whose accounting year begins on January 1 and ends on December 31 are known as *calendar-year* companies. Many companies choose a fiscal year ending on a date other than December 31. Research In Motion is a *noncalendar-year* company as reflected in the headings of its February 27 year-end financial statements in Appendix A near the end of the book.

Point: A statement's heading lists the 3 W's: **W**ho—name of organization, **W**hat—name of statement, **W**hen—statement's point in time or period of time.

Income Statement An income statement reports the revenues earned less the expenses incurred by a business over a period of time. FastForward's income statement for December is shown at the top of Exhibit 2.16. Information about revenues and expenses is conveniently taken from the trial balance in Exhibit 2.14. Net income of $3,470 is reported at the bottom of the statement. Owner investments and withdrawals are *not* part of income.

Statement of Owner's Equity The statement of owner's equity reports information about how equity changes over the reporting period. FastForward's statement of owner's equity is the second report in Exhibit 2.16. It shows the $30,000 owner investment, the $3,470 of net income, the $200 withdrawal, and the $33,270 end-of-period (capital) balance. (The beginning

EXHIBIT 2.16

Financial Statements and Their Links

FASTFORWARD
Income Statement
For Month Ended December 31, 2011

Revenues		
Consulting revenue ($4,200 + $1,600)	$ 5,800	
Rental revenue	300	
Total revenues		$ 6,100
Expenses		
Rent expense	1,000	
Salaries expense	1,400	
Utilities expense	230	
Total expenses		2,630
Net income		$ 3,470

Point: Arrow lines show how the statements are linked.

FASTFORWARD
Statement of Owner's Equity
For Month Ended December 31, 2011

C. Taylor, Capital, December 1, 2011		$ 0
Plus: Investments by owner	$30,000	
Net income	3,470	33,470
		33,470
Less: Withdrawals by owner		200
C. Taylor, Capital, December 31, 2011		$33,270

FASTFORWARD
Balance Sheet
December 31, 2011

Assets		Liabilities	
Cash	$ 4,350	Accounts payable	$ 6,200
Supplies	9,720	Unearned revenue	3,000
Prepaid insurance	2,400	Total liabilities	9,200
Equipment	26,000	**Equity**	
		C. Taylor, Capital	33,270
Total assets	$42,470	Total liabilities and equity	$ 42,470

Point: To *foot* a column of numbers is to add them.

balance in the statement of owner's equity is rarely zero; an exception is for the first period of operations. The beginning capital balance in January 2012 is $33,270, which is December's ending balance.)

Point: An income statement is also called an *earnings statement, a statement of operations*, or a *P&L* (profit and loss) *statement*. A balance sheet is also called a *statement of financial position*.

Point: While revenues increase equity, and expenses decrease equity, the amounts are not reported in detail in the statement of owner's equity. Instead, their effects are reflected through net income.

Balance Sheet The balance sheet reports the financial position of a company at a point in time, usually at the end of a month, quarter, or year. FastForward's balance sheet is the third report in Exhibit 2.16. This statement refers to financial condition at the close of business on December 31. The left side of the balance sheet lists its assets: cash, supplies, prepaid insurance, and equipment. The upper right side of the balance sheet shows that it owes $6,200 to creditors and $3,000 in services to customers who paid in advance. The equity section shows an ending balance of $33,270. Note the link between the ending balance of the statement of owner's equity and the capital balance. (Recall that this presentation of the balance sheet is called the *account form:* assets on the left and liabilities and equity on the right. Another presentation is the *report form:* assets on top, followed by liabilities and then equity. Either presentation is acceptable.)

Decision Maker Answer — p. 74

Entrepreneur You open a wholesale business selling entertainment equipment to retail outlets. You find that most of your customers demand to buy on credit. How can you use the balance sheets of these customers to decide which ones to extend credit to? ■

Point: Knowing how financial statements are prepared improves our analysis of them.

Presentation Issues Dollar signs are not used in journals and ledgers. They do appear in financial statements and other reports such as trial balances. The usual practice is to put dollar signs beside only the first and last numbers in a column. Research In Motion's financial statements in Appendix A show this. When amounts are entered in a journal, ledger, or trial balance, commas are optional to indicate thousands, millions, and so forth. However, commas are always used in financial statements. Companies also commonly round amounts in reports to the nearest dollar, or even to a higher level. Research In Motion is typical of many companies in that it rounds its financial statement amounts to the nearest thousand or million. This decision is based on the perceived impact of rounding for users' business decisions.

Quick Check Answers — p. 75

14. Where are dollar signs typically entered in financial statements?
15. If a $4,000 debit to Equipment in a journal entry is incorrectly posted to the ledger as a $4,000 credit, and the ledger account has a resulting debit balance of $20,000, what is the effect of this error on the Trial Balance column totals?
16. Describe the link between the income statement and the statement of owner's equity.
17. Explain the link between the balance sheet and the statement of owner's equity.
18. Define and describe revenues and expenses.
19. Define and describe assets, liabilities, and equity.

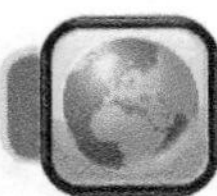

GLOBAL VIEW

Financial accounting according to U.S. GAAP is similar, but not identical, to IFRS. This section discusses differences in analyzing and recording transactions, and with the preparation of financial statements.

Analyzing and Recording Transactions Both U.S. GAAP and IFRS include broad and similar guidance for financial accounting. As the FASB and IASB work toward a common conceptual framework over the next few years, even those differences will fade. Further, both U.S. GAAP and IFRS apply transaction analysis and recording as shown in this chapter—using the same debit and credit system and accrual accounting. Although some variations exist in revenue and expense recognition and other accounting principles, all of the transactions in this chapter are accounted for identically under these two systems.

Financial Statements Both U.S. GAAP and IFRS prepare the same four basic financial statements. A few differences within each statement do exist and we will discuss those throughout the book. For example, both U.S. GAAP and IFRS require balance sheets to separate current items from noncurrent items. However, while U.S. GAAP balance sheets report current items first, IFRS balance sheets normally (but are not required to) present noncurrent items first, and equity before liabilities. To illustrate, a condensed version of Nokia's balance sheet follows (numbers using Euros in millions).

NOKIA

NOKIA
Balance Sheet (in EUR millions)
December 31, 2009

Assets		Equity and Liabilities	
Noncurrent assets	12,125	Total equity	14,749
Current assets	23,613	Noncurrent liabilities	5,801
		Current liabilities	15,188
Total assets	35,738	Total equity and liabilities	35,738

Accounting Controls and Assurance Accounting systems depend on control procedures that assure the proper principles were applied in processing accounting information. The passage of SOX legislation strengthened U.S. control procedures in recent years. However, global standards for control are diverse and so are enforcement activities. Consequently, while global accounting standards are converging, their application in different countries can yield different outcomes depending on the quality of their auditing standards and enforcement.

Decision Insight

Accounting Control Recording valid transactions, and not recording fraudulent transactions, enhances the quality of financial statements. The graph here shows the percentage of employees in information technology that report observing specific types of misconduct within the past year.

[Source: KPMG 2009]

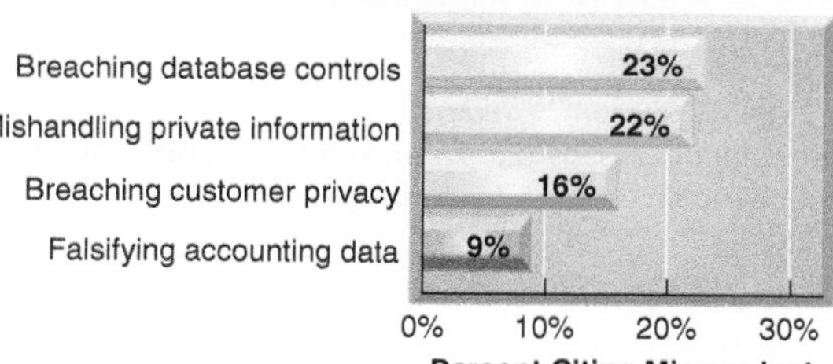

Debt Ratio — Decision Analysis

An important business objective is gathering information to help assess a company's risk of failing to pay its debts. Companies finance their assets with either liabilities or equity. A company that finances a relatively large portion of its assets with liabilities is said to have a high degree of *financial leverage*. Higher financial leverage involves greater risk because liabilities must be repaid and often require regular interest payments (equity financing does not). The risk that a company might not be able to meet such required payments is higher if it has more liabilities (is more highly leveraged). One way to assess the risk associated with a company's use of liabilities is to compute the **debt ratio** as in Exhibit 2.17.

A2 Compute the debt ratio and describe its use in analyzing financial condition.

EXHIBIT 2.17
Debt Ratio

$$\textbf{Debt ratio} = \frac{\textbf{Total liabilities}}{\textbf{Total assets}}$$

Point: Compare the equity amount to the liability amount to assess the extent of owner versus nonowner financing.

To see how to apply the debt ratio, let's look at Skechers's liabilities and assets. The company designs, markets, and sells footwear for men, women, and children under the Skechers brand. Exhibit 2.18 computes and reports its debt ratio at the end of each year from 2005 to 2009.

EXHIBIT 2.18

Computation and Analysis of Debt Ratio

$ in millions	2009	2008	2007	2006	2005
Total liabilities	$246	$204	$201	$288	$238
Total assets	$996	$876	$828	$737	$582
Debt ratio	0.25	0.23	0.24	0.39	0.41
Industry debt ratio	0.51	0.50	0.46	0.48	0.47

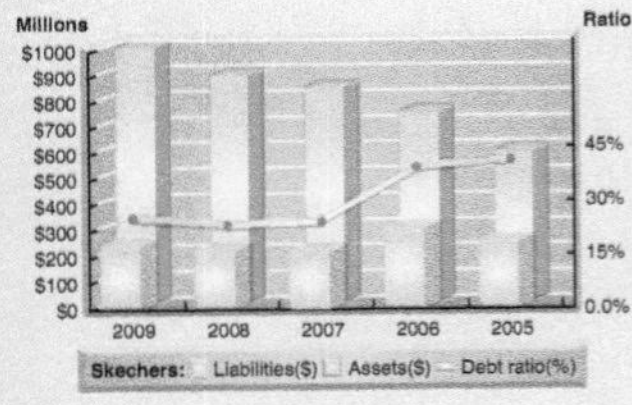

Skechers's debt ratio ranges from a low of 0.23 to a high of 0.41—also, see graph in margin. Its ratio is lower, and has been generally declining, compared with the industry ratio. This analysis implies a low risk from its financial leverage. Is financial leverage good or bad for Skechers? To answer that question we need to compare the company's return on the borrowed money to the rate it is paying creditors. If the company's return is higher, it is successfully borrowing money to make more money. A company's success with making money from borrowed money can quickly turn unprofitable if its own return drops below the rate it is paying creditors.

Decision Maker Answer — p. 74

Investor You consider buying stock in Converse. As part of your analysis, you compute its debt ratio for 2009, 2010, and 2011 as: 0.35, 0.74, and 0.94, respectively. Based on the debt ratio, is Converse a low-risk investment? Has the risk of buying Converse stock changed over this period? (The industry debt ratio averages 0.40.) ■

DEMONSTRATION PROBLEM

(This problem extends the demonstration problem of Chapter 1.) After several months of planning, Jasmine Worthy started a haircutting business called Expressions. The following events occurred during its first month.

a. On August 1, Worthy invested $3,000 cash and $15,000 of equipment in Expressions.
b. On August 2, Expressions paid $600 cash for furniture for the shop.
c. On August 3, Expressions paid $500 cash to rent space in a strip mall for August.
d. On August 4, it purchased $1,200 of equipment on credit for the shop (using a long-term note payable).
e. On August 5, Expressions opened for business. Cash received from haircutting services in the first week and a half of business (ended August 15) was $825.
f. On August 15, it provided $100 of haircutting services on account.
g. On August 17, it received a $100 check for services previously rendered on account.
h. On August 17, it paid $125 to an assistant for hours worked during the grand opening.
i. Cash received from services provided during the second half of August was $930.
j. On August 31, it paid a $400 installment toward principal on the note payable entered into on August 4.
k. On August 31, Worthy withdrew $900 cash for personal use.

Required

1. Open the following ledger accounts in balance column format (account numbers are in parentheses): Cash (101); Accounts Receivable (102); Furniture (161); Store Equipment (165); Note Payable (240); J. Worthy, Capital (301); J. Worthy, Withdrawals (302); Haircutting Services Revenue (403); Wages Expense (623); and Rent Expense (640). Prepare general journal entries for the transactions.
2. Post the journal entries from (1) to the ledger accounts.

3. Prepare a trial balance as of August 31.
4. Prepare an income statement for August.
5. Prepare a statement of owner's equity for August.
6. Prepare a balance sheet as of August 31.
7. Determine the debt ratio as of August 31.

Extended Analysis

8. In the coming months, Expressions will experience a greater variety of business transactions. Identify which accounts are debited and which are credited for the following transactions. (*Hint:* We must use some accounts not opened in part 1.)
   a. Purchase supplies with cash.
   b. Pay cash for future insurance coverage.
   c. Receive cash for services to be provided in the future.
   d. Purchase supplies on account.

PLANNING THE SOLUTION

- Analyze each transaction and use the debit and credit rules to prepare a journal entry for each.
- Post each debit and each credit from journal entries to their ledger accounts and cross-reference each amount in the posting reference (PR) columns of the journal and ledger.
- Calculate each account balance and list the accounts with their balances on a trial balance.
- Verify that total debits in the trial balance equal total credits.
- To prepare the income statement, identify revenues and expenses. List those items on the statement, compute the difference, and label the result as *net income* or *net loss*.
- Use information in the ledger to prepare the statement of owner's equity.
- Use information in the ledger to prepare the balance sheet.
- Calculate the debt ratio by dividing total liabilities by total assets.
- Analyze the future transactions to identify the accounts affected and apply debit and credit rules.

SOLUTION TO DEMONSTRATION PROBLEM

1. General journal entries:

General Journal Entry

Page 1

Date	Account Titles and Explanation	PR	Debit	Credit
Aug. 1	Cash	101	3,000	
	Store Equipment	165	15,000	
	J. Worthy, Capital	301		18,000
	Owner's investment.			
2	Furniture	161	600	
	Cash	101		600
	Purchased furniture for cash.			
3	Rent Expense	640	500	
	Cash	101		500
	Paid rent for August.			
4	Store Equipment	165	1,200	
	Note Payable	240		1,200
	Purchased additional equipment on credit.			
15	Cash	101	825	
	Haircutting Services Revenue	403		825
	Cash receipts from first half of August.			

[continued on next page]

[continued from previous page]

15	Accounts Receivable	102	100	
	Haircutting Services Revenue	403		100
	To record revenue for services provided on account.			
17	Cash	101	100	
	Accounts Receivable	102		100
	To record cash received as payment on account.			
17	Wages Expense	623	125	
	Cash	101		125
	Paid wages to assistant.			
31	Cash	101	930	
	Haircutting Services Revenue	403		930
	Cash receipts from second half of August.			
31	Note Payable	240	400	
	Cash	101		400
	Paid an installment on the note payable.			
31	J. Worthy, Withdrawals	302	900	
	Cash	101		900
	Cash withdrawal by owner.			

2. Post journal entries from part 1 to the ledger accounts:

General Ledger

Cash — **Account No. 101**

Date	PR	Debit	Credit	Balance
Aug. 1	G1	3,000		3,000
2	G1		600	2,400
3	G1		500	1,900
15	G1	825		2,725
17	G1	100		2,825
17	G1		125	2,700
31	G1	930		3,630
31	G1		400	3,230
31	G1		900	2,330

Accounts Receivable — **Account No. 102**

Date	PR	Debit	Credit	Balance
Aug. 15	G1	100		100
17	G1		100	0

Furniture — **Account No. 161**

Date	PR	Debit	Credit	Balance
Aug. 2	G1	600		600

Store Equipment — **Account No. 165**

Date	PR	Debit	Credit	Balance
Aug. 1	G1	15,000		15,000
4	G1	1,200		16,200

Note Payable — **Account No. 240**

Date	PR	Debit	Credit	Balance
Aug. 4	G1		1,200	1,200
31	G1	400		800

J. Worthy, Capital — **Account No. 301**

Date	PR	Debit	Credit	Balance
Aug. 1	G1		18,000	18,000

J. Worthy, Withdrawals — **Account No. 302**

Date	PR	Debit	Credit	Balance
Aug. 31	G1	900		900

Haircutting Services Revenue — **Account No. 403**

Date	PR	Debit	Credit	Balance
Aug. 15	G1		825	825
15	G1		100	925
31	G1		930	1,855

Wages Expense — **Account No. 623**

Date	PR	Debit	Credit	Balance
Aug. 17	G1	125		125

Rent Expense — **Account No. 640**

Date	PR	Debit	Credit	Balance
Aug. 3	G1	500		500

3. Prepare a trial balance from the ledger:

EXPRESSIONS
Trial Balance
August 31

	Debit	Credit
Cash	$ 2,330	
Accounts receivable	0	
Furniture	600	
Store equipment	16,200	
Note payable		$ 800
J. Worthy, Capital		18,000
J. Worthy, Withdrawals	900	
Haircutting services revenue		1,855
Wages expense	125	
Rent expense	500	
Totals	$20,655	$20,655

4.

EXPRESSIONS
Income Statement
For Month Ended August 31

Revenues		
Haircutting services revenue		$1,855
Operating expenses		
Rent expense	$500	
Wages expense	125	
Total operating expenses		625
Net income		$1,230

5.

EXPRESSIONS
Statement of Owner's Equity
For Month Ended August 31

J. Worthy, Capital, August 1		$ 0
Plus: Investments by owner	$18,000	
Net income	1,230	19,230
		19,230
Less: Withdrawals by owner		900
J. Worthy, Capital, August 31		$18,330

6.

EXPRESSIONS
Balance Sheet
August 31

Assets		**Liabilities**	
Cash	$ 2,330	Note payable	$ 800
Furniture	600	**Equity**	
Store equipment	16,200	J. Worthy, Capital	18,330
Total assets	$19,130	Total liabilities and equity	$19,130

7. Debt ratio $= \frac{\text{Total liabilities}}{\text{Total assets}} = \frac{\$800}{\$19,130} = \underline{\underline{\mathbf{4.18\%}}}$

8a. Supplies *debited*
Cash *credited*

8b. Prepaid Insurance *debited*
Cash *credited*

8c. Cash *debited*
Unearned Services Revenue *credited*

8d. Supplies *debited*
Accounts Payable *credited*

Summary

C1 Explain the steps in processing transactions and the role of source documents. The accounting process identifies business transactions and events, analyzes and records their effects, and summarizes and prepares information useful in making decisions. Transactions and events are the starting points in the accounting process. Source documents identify and describe transactions and events. Examples are sales tickets, checks, purchase orders, bills, and bank statements. Source documents provide objective and reliable evidence, making information more useful. The effects of transactions and events are recorded in journals. Posting along with a trial balance helps summarize and classify these effects.

C2 Describe an account and its use in recording transactions. An account is a detailed record of increases and decreases in a specific asset, liability, equity, revenue, or expense. Information from accounts is analyzed, summarized, and presented in reports and financial statements for decision makers.

C3 Describe a ledger and a chart of accounts. The ledger (or general ledger) is a record containing all accounts used by a company and their balances. It is referred to as the *books*. The chart of accounts is a list of all accounts and usually includes an identification number assigned to each account.

C4 Define *debits* and *credits* and explain double-entry accounting. *Debit* refers to left, and *credit* refers to right. Debits increase assets, expenses, and withdrawals while credits decrease them. Credits increase liabilities, owner capital, and revenues; debits decrease them. Double-entry accounting means each transaction affects at least two accounts and has at least one debit and one credit. The system for recording debits and credits follows from the accounting equation. The left side of an account is the normal balance for assets, withdrawals, and expenses, and the right side is the normal balance for liabilities, capital, and revenues.

A1 Analyze the impact of transactions on accounts and financial statements. We analyze transactions using concepts of double-entry accounting. This analysis is performed by determining a transaction's effects on accounts. These effects are recorded in journals and posted to ledgers.

A2 Compute the debt ratio and describe its use in analyzing financial condition. A company's debt ratio is computed as total liabilities divided by total assets. It reveals how much of the assets are financed by creditor (nonowner) financing. The higher this ratio, the more risk a company faces because liabilities must be repaid at specific dates.

P1 Record transactions in a journal and post entries to a ledger. Transactions are recorded in a journal. Each entry in a journal is posted to the accounts in the ledger. This provides information that is used to produce financial statements. Balance column accounts are widely used and include columns for debits, credits, and the account balance.

P2 Prepare and explain the use of a trial balance. A trial balance is a list of accounts from the ledger showing their debit or credit balances in separate columns. The trial balance is a summary of the ledger's contents and is useful in preparing financial statements and in revealing recordkeeping errors.

P3 Prepare financial statements from business transactions. The balance sheet, the statement of owner's equity, the income statement, and the statement of cash flows use data from the trial balance (and other financial statements) for their preparation.

Guidance Answers to Decision Maker and Decision Ethics

Cashier The advantages to the process proposed by the assistant manager include improved customer service, fewer delays, and less work for you. However, you should have serious concerns about internal control and the potential for fraud. In particular, the assistant manager could steal cash and simply enter fewer sales to match the remaining cash. You should reject her suggestion without the manager's approval. Moreover, you should have an ethical concern about the assistant manager's suggestion to ignore store policy.

Entrepreneur We can use the accounting equation (Assets = Liabilities + Equity) to help us identify risky customers to whom we would likely not want to extend credit. A balance sheet provides amounts for each of these key components. The lower a customer's equity is relative to liabilities, the less likely you would extend credit. A low equity means the business has little value that does not already have creditor claims to it.

Investor The debt ratio suggests the stock of Converse is of higher risk than normal and that this risk is rising. The average industry ratio of 0.40 further supports this conclusion. The 2011 debt ratio for Converse is twice the industry norm. Also, a debt ratio approaching 1.0 indicates little to no equity.

Guidance Answers to Quick Checks

1. Examples of source documents are sales tickets, checks, purchase orders, charges to customers, bills from suppliers, employee earnings records, and bank statements.
2. Source documents serve many purposes, including record-keeping and internal control. Source documents, especially if obtained from outside the organization, provide objective and reliable evidence about transactions and their amounts.
3.

Assets	Liabilities	Equity
a,c,e	b,d	—

4. An account is a record in an accounting system that records and stores the increases and decreases in a specific asset, liability, equity, revenue, or expense. The ledger is a collection of all the accounts of a company.
5. A company's size and diversity affect the number of accounts in its accounting system. The types of accounts depend on information the company needs to both effectively operate and report its activities in financial statements.
6. No. Debit and credit both can mean increase or decrease. The particular meaning in a circumstance depends on the *type of account*. For example, a debit increases the balance of asset, withdrawals, and expense accounts, but it decreases the balance of liability, capital, and revenue accounts.
7. A chart of accounts is a list of all of a company's accounts and their identification numbers.
8. Equity is increased by revenues and by owner investments. Equity is decreased by expenses and owner withdrawals.
9. The name *double-entry* is used because all transactions affect at least two accounts. There must be at least one debit in one account and at least one credit in another account.
10. The answer is (*c*).
11.

Cash	15,000	
Equipment	23,000	
Owner, Capital		38,000
Investment by owner of cash and equipment.		

12. A compound journal entry affects three or more accounts.
13. Posting reference numbers are entered in the journal when posting to the ledger as a cross-reference that allows the record-keeper or auditor to trace debits and credits from one record to another.
14. At a minimum, dollar signs are placed beside the first and last numbers in a column. It is also common to place dollar signs beside any amount that appears after a ruled line to indicate that an addition or subtraction has occurred.
15. The Equipment account balance is incorrectly reported at $20,000—it should be $28,000. The effect of this error understates the trial balance's Debit column total by $8,000. This results in an $8,000 difference between the column totals.
16. An income statement reports a company's revenues and expenses along with the resulting net income or loss. A statement of owner's equity reports changes in equity, including that from net income or loss. Both statements report transactions occurring over a period of time.
17. The balance sheet describes a company's financial position (assets, liabilities, and equity) at a point in time. The capital amount in the balance sheet is obtained from the statement of owner's equity.
18. Revenues are inflows of assets in exchange for products or services provided to customers as part of the main operations of a business. Expenses are outflows or the using up of assets that result from providing products or services to customers.
19. Assets are the resources a business owns or controls that carry expected future benefits. Liabilities are the obligations of a business, representing the claims of others against the assets of a business. Equity reflects the owner's claims on the assets of the business after deducting liabilities.

Key Terms

mhhe.com/wildFAP20e

Account (p. 51)
Account balance (p. 55)
Balance column account (p. 58)
Chart of accounts (p. 54)
Compound journal entry (p. 61)
Credit (p. 55)
Creditors (p. 52)
Debit (p. 55)
Debtors (p. 51)
Debt ratio (p. 69)
Double-entry accounting (p. 55)
General journal (p. 56)
General ledger (p. 51)
Journal (p. 56)
Journalizing (p. 56)
Ledger (p. 51)
Posting (p. 56)
Posting reference (PR) column (p. 58)
Source documents (p. 50)
T-account (p. 55)
Trial balance (p. 65)
Unearned revenue (p. 52)

Multiple Choice Quiz

Answers on p. 91 mhhe.com/wildFAP20e

Additional Quiz Questions are available at the book's Website.

1. Amalia Company received its utility bill for the current period of $700 and immediately paid it. Its journal entry to record this transaction includes a
   - **a.** Credit to Utility Expense for $700.
   - **b.** Debit to Utility Expense for $700.
   - **c.** Debit to Accounts Payable for $700.
   - **d.** Debit to Cash for $700.
   - **e.** Credit to capital for $700.
2. On May 1, Mattingly Lawn Service collected $2,500 cash from a customer in advance of five months of lawn service. Mattingly's journal entry to record this transaction includes a
   - **a.** Credit to Unearned Lawn Service Fees for $2,500.
   - **b.** Debit to Lawn Service Fees Earned for $2,500.
   - **c.** Credit to Cash for $2,500.
   - **d.** Debit to Unearned Lawn Service Fees for $2,500.
   - **e.** Credit to capital for $2,500.
3. Liang Shue contributed $250,000 cash and land worth $500,000 to open his new business, Shue Consulting. Which of the following journal entries does Shue Consulting make to record this transaction?

		Debit	Credit
a.	Cash Assets	750,000	
	L. Shue, Capital		750,000
b.	L. Shue, Capital	750,000	
	Assets		750,000
c.	Cash	250,000	
	Land	500,000	
	L. Shue, Capital		750,000
d.	L. Shue, Capital	750,000	
	Cash		250,000
	Land		500,000

4. A trial balance prepared at year-end shows total credits exceed total debits by $765. This discrepancy could have been caused by
   - **a.** An error in the general journal where a $765 increase in Accounts Payable was recorded as a $765 decrease in Accounts Payable.
   - **b.** The ledger balance for Accounts Payable of $7,650 being entered in the trial balance as $765.
   - **c.** A general journal error where a $765 increase in Accounts Receivable was recorded as a $765 increase in Cash.
   - **d.** The ledger balance of $850 in Accounts Receivable was entered in the trial balance as $85.
   - **e.** An error in recording a $765 increase in Cash as a credit.
5. Bonaventure Company has total assets of $1,000,000, liabilities of $400,000, and equity of $600,000. What is its debt ratio (rounded to a whole percent)?
   - **a.** 250%
   - **b.** 167%
   - **c.** 67%
   - **d.** 150%
   - **e.** 40%

[I] Icon denotes assignments that involve decision making.

Discussion Questions

1. Provide the names of two (*a*) asset accounts, (*b*) liability accounts, and (*c*) equity accounts.
2. What is the difference between a note payable and an account payable?
3. [I] Discuss the steps in processing business transactions.
4. What kinds of transactions can be recorded in a general journal?
5. Are debits or credits typically listed first in general journal entries? Are the debits or the credits indented?
6. If assets are valuable resources and asset accounts have debit balances, why do expense accounts also have debit balances?
7. Should a transaction be recorded first in a journal or the ledger? Why?
8. [I] Why does the recordkeeper prepare a trial balance?
9. If an incorrect amount is journalized and posted to the accounts, how should the error be corrected?
10. Identify the four financial statements of a business.
11. [I] What information is reported in an income statement?
12. [I] Why does the user of an income statement need to know the time period that it covers?
13. [I] What information is reported in a balance sheet?
14. Define (*a*) *assets,* (*b*) *liabilities,* (*c*) *equity,* and (*d*) *net assets.*
15. Which financial statement is sometimes called the *statement of financial position?*
16. [I] Review the **Research in Motion** balance sheet in Appendix A. Identify three accounts on its balance sheet that carry debit balances and three accounts on its balance sheet that carry credit balances. RIM
17. Review the **Apple** balance sheet in Appendix A. Identify an asset with the word *receivable* in its account title and a liability with the word *payable* in its account title. Apple
18. Locate **Palm**'s income statement in Appendix A. What is the title of its revenue account? Palm
19. Refer to **Nokia**'s balance sheet in Appendix A. What does Nokia title its current asset referring to merchandise available for sale? NOKIA

connect

QUICK STUDY

QS 2-1
Identifying financial statement items
C2 P3

Identify the financial statement(s) where each of the following items appears. Use I for income statement, E for statement of owner's equity, and B for balance sheet.

a. Accounts payable
b. Cash
c. Rent expense
d. Office supplies
e. Prepaid insurance
f. Revenue
g. Office equipment
h. Cash withdrawal by owner
i. Unearned rent revenue

QS 2-2
Identifying source documents
C1

Identify the items from the following list that are likely to serve as source documents.

a. Bank statement
b. Sales ticket
c. Income statement
d. Trial balance
e. Telephone bill
f. Invoice from supplier
g. Company revenue account
h. Balance sheet
i. Prepaid rent

QS 2-3
Analyzing debit or credit by account
A1

Identify whether a debit or credit yields the indicated change for each of the following accounts.

a. To increase Store Equipment
b. To increase Land
c. To decrease Cash
d. To increase Utilities Expense
e. To increase Fees Earned
f. To decrease Unearned Revenue
g. To decrease Prepaid Insurance
h. To increase Notes Payable
i. To decrease Accounts Receivable
j. To increase Owner Capital

QS 2-4
Identifying normal balance
C4

Identify the normal balance (debit or credit) for each of the following accounts.

a. Equipment
b. Wages Expense
c. Repair Services Revenue
d. Office Supplies
e. Owner Withdrawals
f. Accounts Receivable
g. Prepaid Insurance
h. Wages Payable
i. Owner Capital

QS 2-5
Linking debit or credit with normal balance
C4

Indicate whether a debit or credit *decreases* the normal balance of each of the following accounts.

a. Land
b. Service Revenue
c. Interest Payable
d. Accounts Receivable
e. Salaries Expense
f. Owner Capital
g. Prepaid Insurance
h. Buildings
i. Interest Revenue
j. Owner Withdrawals
k. Unearned Revenue
l. Accounts Payable

QS 2-6
Preparing journal entries
P1

Prepare journal entries for each of the following selected transactions.

a. On January 15, Kolby Anderson opens a remodeling company called Fancy Kitchens by investing $75,000 cash along with equipment having a $30,000 value.
b. On January 21, Fancy Kitchens purchases office supplies on credit for $650.
c. On January 25, Fancy Kitchens receives $8,700 cash for performing remodeling services.
d. On January 30, Fancy Kitchens receives $4,000 cash in advance of providing remodeling services to a customer.

QS 2-7
Identifying a posting error
P2  

A trial balance has total debits of $20,000 and total credits of $24,500. Which one of the following errors would create this imbalance? Explain.

a. A $2,250 debit posting to Accounts Receivable was posted mistakenly to Cash.
b. A $4,500 debit posting to Equipment was posted mistakenly to Supplies.
c. An entry debiting Cash and crediting Accounts Payable for $4,500 was mistakenly not posted.
d. A $2,250 credit to Revenue in a journal entry is incorrectly posted to the ledger as a $2,250 debit, leaving the Revenue account with a $6,300 credit balance.
e. A $4,500 debit to Rent Expense in a journal entry is incorrectly posted to the ledger as a $4,500 credit, leaving the Rent Expense account with a $750 debit balance.
f. A $2,250 debit to Utilities Expense in a journal entry is incorrectly posted to the ledger as a $2,250 credit, leaving the Utilities Expense account with a $3,000 debit balance.

QS 2-8
Classifying accounts in financial statements
P3

Indicate the financial statement on which each of the following items appears. Use I for income statement, E for statement of owner's equity, and B for balance sheet.

a. Buildings
b. Interest Expense
c. Owner Withdrawals
d. Office Supplies
e. Rental Revenue
f. Insurance Expense
g. Services Revenue
h. Interest Payable
i. Accounts Receivable
j. Salaries Expense
k. Equipment
l. Prepaid Insurance

QS 2-9
International accounting standards
C4

Answer each of the following questions related to international accounting standards.

a. What type of entry system is applied when accounting follows IFRS?
b. Identify the number and usual titles of the financial statements prepared under IFRS.
c. How do differences in accounting controls and enforcement impact accounting reports prepared across different countries?

connect

EXERCISES

Exercise 2-1
Steps in analyzing and recording transactions C1

Order the following steps in the accounting process that focus on analyzing and recording transactions.

_______ **a.** Record relevant transactions in a journal.
_______ **b.** Prepare and analyze the trial balance.
_______ **c.** Analyze each transaction from source documents.
_______ **d.** Post journal information to ledger accounts.

Exercise 2-2
Identifying and classifying accounts
C2

Enter the number for the item that best completes each of the descriptions below.

1. Account
2. Three
3. Asset
4. Liability
5. Equity

a. Owner, capital and owner, withdrawals are examples of _______ accounts.
b. Accounts payable, unearned revenue, and note payable are examples of _______ accounts.
c. Accounts receivable, prepaid accounts, supplies, and land are examples of _______ accounts.
d. Accounts are arranged into _______ general categories
e. An _______ is a record of increases and decreases in a specific asset, liability, equity, revenue, or expense item.

Exercise 2-3
Identifying a ledger and chart of accounts
C3

Enter the number for the item that best completes each of the descriptions below.

1. General ledger
2. Chart

a. The _______ is a record containing all accounts used by a company.
b. A _______ of accounts is a list of all accounts a company uses.

Exercise 2-4
Identifying type and normal balances of accounts
C4

For each of the following (1) identify the type of account as an asset, liability, equity, revenue, or expense, (2) identify the normal balance of the account, and (3) enter *debit* (*Dr.*) or *credit* (*Cr.*) to identify the kind of entry that would increase the account balance.

a. Fees Earned
b. Equipment
c. Notes Payable
d. Owner Capital
e. Cash
f. Legal Expense
g. Prepaid Insurance
h. Land
i. Accounts Receivable
j. Owner Withdrawals
k. License Fee Revenue
l. Unearned Revenue

Exercise 2-5
Analyzing effects of transactions on accounts
A1

Taylor Co. bills a client $48,000 for services provided and agrees to accept the following three items in full payment: (1) $7,500 cash, (2) computer equipment worth $75,000, and (3) to assume responsibility for a $34,500 note payable related to the computer equipment. The entry Taylor makes to record this transaction includes which one or more of the following?

a. $34,500 increase in a liability account
b. $7,500 increase in the Cash account
c. $7,500 increase in a revenue account
d. $48,000 increase in an asset account
e. $48,000 increase in a revenue account
f. $34,500 increase in an equity account

Exercise 2-6
Analyzing account entries and balances
A1 

Use the information in each of the following separate cases to calculate the unknown amount.

a. During October, Shandra Company had $97,500 of cash receipts and $101,250 of cash disbursements. The October 31 Cash balance was $16,800. Determine how much cash the company had at the close of business on September 30.

b. On September 30, Mordish Co. had a $97,500 balance in Accounts Receivable. During October, the company collected $88,950 from its credit customers. The October 31 balance in Accounts Receivable was $100,500. Determine the amount of sales on account that occurred in October.

c. Nasser Co. had $147,000 of accounts payable on September 30 and $136,500 on October 31. Total purchases on account during October were $270,000. Determine how much cash was paid on accounts payable during October.

Exercise 2-7
Preparing general journal entries
P1

Prepare general journal entries for the following transactions of a new company called Pose for Pics.

Aug.	1	Kasey Madison, the owner, invested $7,500 cash and $32,500 of photography equipment in the company.
	2	The company paid $3,000 cash for an insurance policy covering the next 24 months.
	5	The company purchased office supplies for $1,400 cash.
	20	The company received $2,650 cash in photography fees earned.
	31	The company paid $875 cash for August utilities.

Exercise 2-8
Preparing T-accounts (ledger) and a trial balance P2

Use the information in Exercise 2-7 to prepare an August 31 trial balance for Pose for Pics. Begin by opening these T-accounts: Cash; Office Supplies; Prepaid Insurance; Photography Equipment; K. Madison, Capital; Photography Fees Earned; and Utilities Expense. Then, post the general journal entries to these T-accounts (which will serve as the ledger), and prepare the trial balance.

Exercise 2-9
Recording effects of transactions in T-accounts
A1

Prepare general journal entries to record the transactions below for Dexter Company by using the following accounts: Cash; Accounts Receivable; Office Supplies; Office Equipment; Accounts Payable; M. Dexter, Capital; M. Dexter, Withdrawals; Fees Earned; and Rent Expense. Use the letters beside each transaction to identify entries. After recording the transactions, post them to T-accounts, which serves as the general ledger for this assignment. Determine the ending balance of each T-account.

a. Macy Dexter, owner, invested $12,750 cash in the company.

b. The company purchased office supplies for $375 cash.

c. The company purchased $7,050 of office equipment on credit.

d. The company received $1,500 cash as fees for services provided to a customer.

e. The company paid $7,050 cash to settle the payable for the office equipment purchased in transaction *c*.

f. The company billed a customer $2,700 as fees for services provided.

g. The company paid $525 cash for the monthly rent.

h. The company collected $1,125 cash as partial payment for the account receivable created in transaction *f*.

i. Macy Dexter withdrew $1,000 cash from the company for personal use.

Check Cash ending balance, $6,425

Exercise 2-10
Preparing a trial balance P2

After recording the transactions of Exercise 2-9 in T-accounts and calculating the balance of each account, prepare a trial balance. Use May 31, 2011, as its report date.

Exercise 2-11
Analyzing and journalizing revenue transactions
A1 P1 

Examine the following transactions and identify those that create revenues for Jade Services, a company owned by Mia Jade. Prepare general journal entries to record those revenue transactions and explain why the other transactions did not create revenues.

a. Mia Jade invests $38,250 cash in the company.

b. The company provided $1,350 of services on credit.

c. The company provided services to a client and immediately received $1,575 cash.

d. The company received $9,150 cash from a client in payment for services to be provided next year.

e. The company received $4,500 cash from a client in partial payment of an account receivable.

f. The company borrowed $150,000 cash from the bank by signing a promissory note.

Exercise 2-12
Analyzing and journalizing expense transactions
A1 P1 

Examine the following transactions and identify those that create expenses for Jade Services. Prepare general journal entries to record those expense transactions and explain why the other transactions did not create expenses.

a. The company paid $14,100 cash for payment on a 14-month old liability for office supplies.
b. The company paid $1,125 cash for the just completed two-week salary of the receptionist.
c. The company paid $45,000 cash for equipment purchased.
d. The company paid $930 cash for this month's utilities.
e. Owner (Jade) withdrew $5,000 cash from the company for personal use.

Exercise 2-13
Preparing an income statement
C3 P3

Dominick Lopez operates a consulting firm called Tech Today. On August 31, the company's records show the following accounts and amounts for the month of August. Use this information to prepare an August income statement for the business.

Cash	$ 8,360	D. Lopez, Withdrawals	$ 3,000
Accounts receivable	17,000	Consulting fees earned	17,000
Office supplies	3,250	Rent expense	4,550
Land	46,000	Salaries expense	8,000
Office equipment	18,000	Telephone expense	560
Accounts payable	8,000	Miscellaneous expenses	280
D. Lopez, Capital, July 31	4,000	Owner investments	80,000

Check Net income, $3,610

Exercise 2-14
Preparing a statement of owner's equity P3

Use the information in Exercise 2-13 to prepare an August statement of owner's equity for Tech Today. (The owner invested $84,000 cash in the company during the first week of August.)

Check End. Capital, $84,610

Exercise 2-15
Preparing a balance sheet P3

Use the information in Exercise 2-13 (if completed, you can also use your solution to Exercise 2-14) to prepare an August 31 balance sheet for Tech Today.

Exercise 2-16
Computing net income
A1 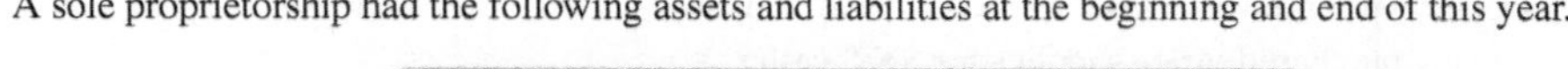

A sole proprietorship had the following assets and liabilities at the beginning and end of this year.

	Assets	Liabilities
Beginning of the year	$ 70,000	$30,000
End of the year	115,000	46,000

Determine the net income earned or net loss incurred by the business during the year for each of the following *separate* cases:

a. Owner made no investments in the business and no withdrawals were made during the year.
b. Owner made no investments in the business but withdrew $1,250 cash per month for personal use.
c. Owner made no withdrawals during the year but did invest an additional $45,000 cash.
d. Owner withdrew $1,250 cash per month for personal use and invested an additional $25,000 cash.

Exercise 2-17
Analyzing changes in a company's equity
P3 

Compute the missing amount for each of the following separate companies *a* through *d*.

	A	B	C	D	E
1		(a)	(b)	(c)	(d)
2	Equity, December 31, 2010	$ 0	$ 0	$ 0	$ 0
3	Owner investments during the year	120,000	?	87,000	210,000
4	Owner withdrawals during the year	?	54,000	10,000	55,000
5	Net income (loss) for the year	31,500	81,000	(4,000)	?
6	Equity, December 31, 2011	102,000	99,000	?	110,000
7					

Exercise 2-18
Interpreting and describing transactions from T-accounts
A1 

Assume the following T-accounts reflect Joy Co.'s general ledger and that seven transactions *a* through *g* are posted to them. Provide a short description of each transaction. Include the amounts in your descriptions.

Cash

	Debit		Credit
(a)	7,000	(b)	3,600
(e)	2,500	(c)	600
		(f)	2,400
		(g)	700

Automobiles

	Debit		Credit
(a)	11,000		

Accounts Payable

	Debit		Credit
(f)	2,400	(d)	9,600

Office Supplies

	Debit		Credit
(c)	600		
(d)	200		

D. Joy, Capital

	Debit		Credit
		(a)	23,600

Delivery Services Revenue

	Debit		Credit
		(e)	2,500

Prepaid Insurance

	Debit		Credit
(b)	3,600		

Gas and Oil Expense

	Debit		Credit
(g)	700		

Equipment

	Debit		Credit
(a)	5,600		
(d)	9,400		

Exercise 2-19
Preparing general journal entries
P1

Use information from the T-accounts in Exercise 2-18 to prepare general journal entries for each of the seven transactions *a* through *g*.

Exercise 2-20
Identifying effects of posting errors on the trial balance
A1 P2

Posting errors are identified in the following table. In column (1), enter the amount of the difference between the two trial balance columns (debit and credit) due to the error. In column (2), identify the trial balance column (debit or credit) with the larger amount if they are not equal. In column (3), identify the account(s) affected by the error. In column (4), indicate the amount by which the account(s) in column (3) is under- or overstated. Item (a) is completed as an example.

	Description of Posting Error	(1) Difference between Debit and Credit Columns	(2) Column with the Larger Total	(3) Identify Account(s) Incorrectly Stated	(4) Amount that Account(s) Is Over- or Understated
a.	$2,400 debit to Rent Expense is posted as a $1,590 debit.	$810	Credit	Rent Expense	Rent Expense understated $810
b.	$4,050 credit to Cash is posted twice as two credits to Cash.				
c.	$9,900 debit to the Withdrawals account is debited to Owner's Capital.				
d.	$2,250 debit to Prepaid Insurance is posted as a debit to Insurance Expense.				
e.	$42,000 debit to Machinery is posted as a debit to Accounts Payable.				
f.	$4,950 credit to Services Revenue is posted as a $495 credit.				
g.	$1,440 debit to Store Supplies is not posted.				

Exercise 2-21
Analyzing a trial balance error
A1 P2

You are told the column totals in a trial balance are not equal. After careful analysis, you discover only one error. Specifically, a correctly journalized credit purchase of a computer for $16,950 is posted from the journal to the ledger with a $16,950 debit to Office Equipment and another $16,950 debit to Accounts Payable. The Office Equipment account has a debit balance of $40,100 on the trial balance. Answer each of the following questions and compute the dollar amount of any misstatement.

a. Is the debit column total of the trial balance overstated, understated, or correctly stated?
b. Is the credit column total of the trial balance overstated, understated, or correctly stated?
c. Is the Office Equipment account balance overstated, understated, or correctly stated in the trial balance?
d. Is the Accounts Payable account balance overstated, understated, or correctly stated in the trial balance?
e. If the debit column total of the trial balance is $360,000 before correcting the error, what is the total of the credit column before correction?

Exercise 2-22
Interpreting the debt ratio and return on assets
A2 

a. Calculate the debt ratio and the return on assets using the year-end information for each of the following six separate companies ($ thousands).

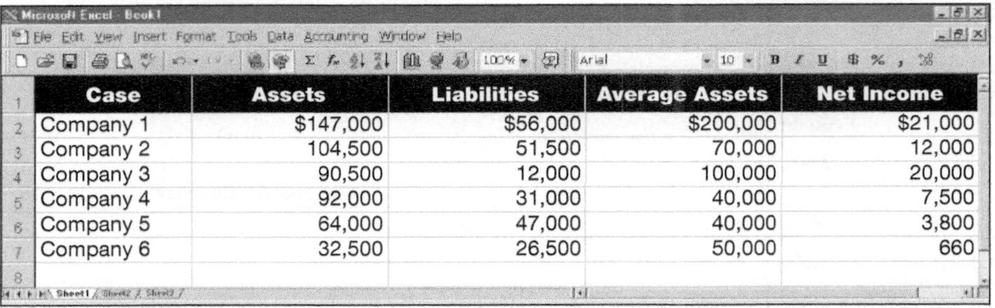

Case	Assets	Liabilities	Average Assets	Net Income
Company 1	$147,000	$56,000	$200,000	$21,000
Company 2	104,500	51,500	70,000	12,000
Company 3	90,500	12,000	100,000	20,000
Company 4	92,000	31,000	40,000	7,500
Company 5	64,000	47,000	40,000	3,800
Company 6	32,500	26,500	50,000	660

b. Of the six companies, which business relies most heavily on creditor financing?
c. Of the six companies, which business relies most heavily on equity financing?
d. Which two companies indicate the greatest risk?
e. Which two companies earn the highest return on assets?
f. Which one company would investors likely prefer based on the risk–return relation?

Exercise 2-23
Preparing a balance sheet following IFRS
P3 

BMW reports the following balance sheet accounts for the year ended December 31, 2009 (euro in millions). Prepare the balance sheet for this company as of December 31, 2009, following the usual IFRS formats.

Current liabilities	€ 8,350	Noncurrent liabilities	€10,943
Current assets	17,663	Noncurrent assets	6,984
Total equity	5,354		

connect

PROBLEM SET A

Problem 2-1A
Preparing and posting journal entries; preparing a trial balance
C3 C4 A1 P1 P2

mhhe.com/wildFAP20e

Gary Bauer opens a computer consulting business called Technology Consultants and completes the following transactions in April.

April	1	Bauer invested $100,000 cash along with $24,000 in office equipment in the company.
	2	The company prepaid $7,200 cash for twelve months' rent for an office. (*Hint:* Debit Prepaid Rent for $7,200.)
	3	The company made credit purchases of office equipment for $12,000 and office supplies for $2,400. Payment is due within 10 days.
	6	The company completed services for a client and immediately received $2,000 cash.
	9	The company completed an $8,000 project for a client, who must pay within 30 days.
	13	The company paid $14,400 cash to settle the account payable created on April 3.
	19	The company paid $6,000 cash for the premium on a 12-month insurance policy. (*Hint:* Debit Prepaid Insurance for $6,000.)
	22	The company received $6,400 cash as partial payment for the work completed on April 9.
	25	The company completed work for another client for $2,640 on credit.
	28	Bauer withdrew $6,200 cash from the company for personal use.
	29	The company purchased $800 of additional office supplies on credit.
	30	The company paid $700 cash for this month's utility bill.

Required

1. Prepare general journal entries to record these transactions (use the account titles listed in part 2).
2. Open the following ledger accounts—their account numbers are in parentheses (use the balance column format): Cash (101); Accounts Receivable (106); Office Supplies (124); Prepaid Insurance (128);

Prepaid Rent (131); Office Equipment (163); Accounts Payable (201); G. Bauer, Capital (301); G. Bauer, Withdrawals (302); Services Revenue (403); and Utilities Expense (690). Post the journal entries from part 1 to the ledger accounts and enter the balance after each posting.

3. Prepare a trial balance as of the end of April.

Check (2) Ending balances: Cash, $73,900; Accounts Receivable, $4,240; Accounts Payable, $800

(3) Total debits, $137,440

Problem 2-2A
Preparing and posting journal entries; preparing a trial balance
C3 C4 A1 P1 P2

Shelton Engineering completed the following transactions in the month of June.

a. Shana Shelton, the owner, invested $105,000 cash, office equipment with a value of $6,000, and $45,000 of drafting equipment to launch the company.
b. The company purchased land worth $54,000 for an office by paying $5,400 cash and signing a long-term note payable for $48,600.
c. The company purchased a portable building with $75,000 cash and moved it onto the land acquired in *b*.
d. The company paid $6,000 cash for the premium on an 18-month insurance policy.
e. The company completed and delivered a set of plans for a client and collected $5,700 cash.
f. The company purchased $22,500 of additional drafting equipment by paying $10,500 cash and signing a long-term note payable for $12,000.
g. The company completed $12,000 of engineering services for a client. This amount is to be received in 30 days.
h. The company purchased $2,250 of additional office equipment on credit.
i. The company completed engineering services for $18,000 on credit.
j. The company received a bill for rent of equipment that was used on a recently completed job. The $1,200 rent cost must be paid within 30 days.
k. The company collected $7,200 cash in partial payment from the client described in transaction *g*.
l. The company paid $1,500 cash for wages to a drafting assistant.
m. The company paid $2,250 cash to settle the account payable created in transaction *h*.
n. The company paid $675 cash for minor maintenance of its drafting equipment.
o. S. Shelton withdrew $9,360 cash from the company for personal use.
p. The company paid $1,500 cash for wages to a drafting assistant.
q. The company paid $3,000 cash for advertisements in the local newspaper during June.

Required

1. Prepare general journal entries to record these transactions (use the account titles listed in part 2).
2. Open the following ledger accounts—their account numbers are in parentheses (use the balance column format): Cash (101); Accounts Receivable (106); Prepaid Insurance (108); Office Equipment (163); Drafting Equipment (164); Building (170); Land (172); Accounts Payable (201); Notes Payable (250); S. Shelton, Capital (301); S. Shelton, Withdrawals (302); Engineering Fees Earned (402); Wages Expense (601); Equipment Rental Expense (602); Advertising Expense (603); and Repairs Expense (604). Post the journal entries from part 1 to the accounts and enter the balance after each posting.
3. Prepare a trial balance as of the end of June.

Check (2) Ending balances: Cash, $2,715; Accounts Receivable, $22,800; Accounts Payable, $1,200

(3) Trial balance totals, $253,500

Problem 2-3A
Computing net income from equity analysis, preparing a balance sheet, and computing the debt ratio
C2 A1 A2 P3 

mhhe.com/wildFAP20e

The accounting records of Fabiano Distribution show the following assets and liabilities as of December 31, 2010 and 2011.

December 31	2010	2011
Cash	$ 52,500	$ 18,750
Accounts receivable	28,500	22,350
Office supplies	4,500	3,300
Office equipment	138,000	147,000
Trucks	54,000	54,000
Building	0	180,000
Land	0	45,000
Accounts payable	7,500	37,500
Note payable	0	105,000

Late in December 2011, the business purchased a small office building and land for $225,000. It paid $120,000 cash toward the purchase and a $105,000 note payable was signed for the balance. Mr. Fabiano had to invest $35,000 cash in the business to enable it to pay the $120,000 cash. Mr. Fabiano withdraws $3,000 cash per month for personal use.

Required

1. Prepare balance sheets for the business as of December 31, 2010 and 2011. (*Hint:* Report only total equity on the balance sheet and remember that total equity equals the difference between assets and liabilities.)
2. By comparing equity amounts from the balance sheets and using the additional information presented in this problem, prepare a calculation to show how much net income was earned by the business during 2011.
3. Compute the 2011 year-end debt ratio for the business.

Check (2) Net income, $58,900

(3) Debt ratio, 30.29%

Problem 2-4A
Preparing and posting journal entries; preparing a trial balance
C3 C4 A1 P1 P2

Santo Birch opens a Web consulting business called Show-Me-the-Money and completes the following transactions in its first month of operations.

March 1 Birch invests $150,000 cash along with office equipment valued at $22,000 in the company.
2 The company prepaid $6,000 cash for twelve months' rent for office space. (*Hint:* Debit Prepaid Rent for $6,000.)
3 The company made credit purchases for $3,000 in office equipment and $1,200 in office supplies. Payment is due within 10 days.
6 The company completed services for a client and immediately received $4,000 cash.
9 The company completed a $7,500 project for a client, who must pay within 30 days.
13 The company paid $4,200 cash to settle the account payable created on March 3.
19 The company paid $5,000 cash for the premium on a 12-month insurance policy. (*Hint:* Debit Prepaid Insurance for $5,000.)
22 The company received $3,500 cash as partial payment for the work completed on March 9.
25 The company completed work for another client for $3,820 on credit.
29 Birch withdrew $5,100 cash from the company for personal use.
30 The company purchased $600 of additional office supplies on credit.
31 The company paid $200 cash for this month's utility bill.

Required

1. Prepare general journal entries to record these transactions (use account titles listed in part 2).
2. Open the following ledger accounts—their account numbers are in parentheses (use the balance column format): Cash (101); Accounts Receivable (106); Office Supplies (124); Prepaid Insurance (128); Prepaid Rent (131); Office Equipment (163); Accounts Payable (201); S. Birch, Capital (301); S. Birch, Withdrawals (302); Services Revenue (403); and Utilities Expense (690). Post journal entries from part 1 to the ledger accounts and enter the balance after each posting.
3. Prepare a trial balance as of April 30.

Check (2) Ending balances: Cash, $137,000; Accounts Receivable, $7,820; Accounts Payable, $600

(3) Total debits, $187,920

Problem 2-5A
Recording transactions; posting to ledger; preparing a trial balance
C3 A1 P1 P2

Business transactions completed by Eric Pense during the month of September are as follows.

a. Pense invested $23,000 cash along with office equipment valued at $12,000 in a new sole proprietorship named EP Consulting.
b. The company purchased land valued at $8,000 and a building valued at $33,000. The purchase is paid with $15,000 cash and a long-term note payable for $26,000.
c. The company purchased $600 of office supplies on credit.
d. Pense invested his personal automobile in the company. The automobile has a value of $7,000 and is to be used exclusively in the business.
e. The company purchased $1,100 of additional office equipment on credit.
f. The company paid $800 cash salary to an assistant.
g. The company provided services to a client and collected $2,700 cash.
h. The company paid $430 cash for this month's utilities.
i. The company paid $600 cash to settle the account payable created in transaction *c*.
j. The company purchased $4,000 of new office equipment by paying $4,000 cash.
k. The company completed $2,400 of services for a client, who must pay within 30 days.
l. The company paid $800 cash salary to an assistant.
m. The company received $1,000 cash in partial payment on the receivable created in transaction *k*.
n. Pense withdrew $1,050 cash from the company for personal use.

Required

1. Prepare general journal entries to record these transactions (use account titles listed in part 2).
2. Open the following ledger accounts—their account numbers are in parentheses (use the balance column format): Cash (101); Accounts Receivable (106); Office Supplies (108); Office Equipment (163); Automobiles (164); Building (170); Land (172); Accounts Payable (201); Notes Payable (250); E. Pense, Capital (301); E. Pense, Withdrawals (302); Fees Earned (402); Salaries Expense (601); and Utilities Expense (602). Post the journal entries from part 1 to the ledger accounts and enter the balance after each posting.
3. Prepare a trial balance as of the end of September.

Check (2) Ending balances: Cash, $4,020; Office Equipment, $17,100

(3) Trial balance totals, $74,200

Problem 2-6A
Analyzing account balances and reconstructing transactions
C1 C3 A1 P2 

Carlos Beltran started an engineering firm called Beltran Engineering. He began operations and completed seven transactions in May, which included his initial investment of $17,000 cash. After those seven transactions, the ledger included the following accounts with normal balances.

Cash	$26,660
Office supplies	660
Prepaid insurance	3,200
Office equipment	16,500
Accounts payable	16,500
C. Beltran, Capital	17,000
C. Beltran, Withdrawals	3,740
Engineering fees earned	24,000
Rent expense	6,740

Required

1. Prepare a trial balance for this business as of the end of May.

Check (1) Trial balance totals, $57,500

Analysis Components

2. Analyze the accounts and their balances and prepare a list that describes each of the seven most likely transactions and their amounts.
3. Prepare a report of cash received and cash paid showing how the seven transactions in part 2 yield the $26,660 ending Cash balance.

(3) Cash paid, $14,340

PROBLEM SET B

Problem 2-1B
Preparing and posting journal entries; preparing a trial balance
C3 C4 A1 P1 P2

Shaw Management Services opens for business and completes these transactions in November.

Nov. 1 Kita Shaw, the owner, invested $30,000 cash along with $15,000 of office equipment in the company.
2 The company prepaid $4,500 cash for six months' rent for an office. (*Hint:* Debit Prepaid Rent for $4,500.)
4 The company made credit purchases of office equipment for $2,500 and of office supplies for $600. Payment is due within 10 days.
8 The company completed work for a client and immediately received $3,400 cash.
12 The company completed a $10,200 project for a client, who must pay within 30 days.
13 The company paid $3,100 cash to settle the payable created on November 4.
19 The company paid $1,800 cash for the premium on a 24-month insurance policy.
22 The company received $5,200 cash as partial payment for the work completed on November 12.
24 The company completed work for another client for $1,750 on credit.
28 K. Shaw withdrew $5,300 cash from the company for personal use.
29 The company purchased $249 of additional office supplies on credit.
30 The company paid $531 cash for this month's utility bill.

Required

1. Prepare general journal entries to record these transactions (use account titles listed in part 2).
2. Open the following ledger accounts—their account numbers are in parentheses (use the balance column format): Cash (101); Accounts Receivable (106); Office Supplies (124); Prepaid Insurance (128); Prepaid Rent (131); Office Equipment (163); Accounts Payable (201); K. Shaw, Capital (301); K. Shaw, Withdrawals (302); Services Revenue (403); and Utilities Expense (690). Post the journal entries from part 1 to the ledger accounts and enter the balance after each posting.
3. Prepare a trial balance as of the end of November.

Check (2) Ending balances: Cash, $23,369; Accounts Receivable, $6,750; Accounts Payable, $249

(3) Total debits, $60,599

Problem 2-2B
Preparing and posting journal entries; preparing a trial balance
C3 C4 A1 P1 P2

At the beginning of April, Brooke Gable launched a custom computer solutions company called Softways. The company had the following transactions during April.

a. Brooke Gable invested $45,000 cash, office equipment with a value of $4,500, and $28,000 of computer equipment in the company.
b. The company purchased land worth $24,000 for an office by paying $4,800 cash and signing a long-term note payable for $19,200.
c. The company purchased a portable building with $21,000 cash and moved it onto the land acquired in *b*.
d. The company paid $6,600 cash for the premium on a two-year insurance policy.
e. The company provided services to a client and immediately collected $3,200 cash.
f. The company purchased $3,500 of additional computer equipment by paying $700 cash and signing a long-term note payable for $2,800.
g. The company completed $3,750 of services for a client. This amount is to be received within 30 days.
h. The company purchased $750 of additional office equipment on credit.
i. The company completed client services for $9,200 on credit.
j. The company received a bill for rent of a computer testing device that was used on a recently completed job. The $320 rent cost must be paid within 30 days.
k. The company collected $4,600 cash in partial payment from the client described in transaction *i*.
l. The company paid $1,600 cash for wages to an assistant.
m. The company paid $750 cash to settle the payable created in transaction *h*.
n. The company paid $425 cash for minor maintenance of the company's computer equipment.
o. B. Gable withdrew $3,875 cash from the company for personal use.
p. The company paid $1,600 cash for wages to an assistant.
q. The company paid $800 cash for advertisements in the local newspaper during April.

Required

Check (2) Ending balances: Cash, $10,650; Accounts Receivable, $8,350; Accounts Payable, $320

(3) Trial balance totals, $115,970

1. Prepare general journal entries to record these transactions (use account titles listed in part 2).
2. Open the following ledger accounts—their account numbers are in parentheses (use the balance column format): Cash (101); Accounts Receivable (106); Prepaid Insurance (108); Office Equipment (163); Computer Equipment (164); Building (170); Land (172); Accounts Payable (201); Notes Payable (250); B. Gable, Capital (301); B. Gable, Withdrawals (302); Fees Earned (402); Wages Expense (601); Computer Rental Expense (602); Advertising Expense (603); and Repairs Expense (604). Post the journal entries from part 1 to the accounts and enter the balance after each posting.
3. Prepare a trial balance as of the end of April.

Problem 2-3B
Computing net income from equity analysis, preparing a balance sheet, and computing the debt ratio
C2 A1 A2 P3 

The accounting records of Schmit Co. show the following assets and liabilities as of December 31, 2010 and 2011.

December 31	2010	2011
Cash	$14,000	$ 10,000
Accounts receivable	25,000	30,000
Office supplies	10,000	12,500
Office equipment	60,000	60,000
Machinery	30,500	30,500
Building	0	260,000
Land	0	65,000
Accounts payable	5,000	15,000
Note payable	0	260,000

Late in December 2011, the business purchased a small office building and land for $325,000. It paid $65,000 cash toward the purchase and a $260,000 note payable was signed for the balance. Janet Schmit, the owner, had to invest an additional $25,000 cash to enable it to pay the $65,000 cash toward the purchase. The owner withdraws $1,000 cash per month for personal use.

Required

1. Prepare balance sheets for the business as of December 31, 2010 and 2011. (*Hint:* Report only total equity on the balance sheet and remember that total equity equals the difference between assets and liabilities.)

2. By comparing equity amounts from the balance sheets and using the additional information presented in the problem, prepare a calculation to show how much net income was earned by the business during 2011.

3. Calculate the December 31, 2011, debt ratio for the business.

Check (2) Net income, $45,500

(3) Debt ratio, 58.76%

Problem 2-4B
Preparing and posting journal entries; preparing a trial balance
C3 C4 A1 P1 P2

Lummus Management Services opens for business and completes these transactions in September.

Sept. 1 Rhonda Lummus, the owner, invests $28,000 cash along with office equipment valued at $25,000 in the company.
2 The company prepaid $10,500 cash for 12 months' rent for office space. (*Hint:* Debit Prepaid Rent for $10,500.)
4 The company made credit purchases for $9,000 in office equipment and $1,200 in office supplies. Payment is due within 10 days.
8 The company completed work for a client and immediately received $2,600 cash.
12 The company completed a $13,400 project for a client, who must pay within 30 days.
13 The company paid $10,200 cash to settle the payable created on September 4.
19 The company paid $5,200 cash for the premium on an 18-month insurance policy. (*Hint:* Debit Prepaid Insurance for $5,200.)
22 The company received $7,800 cash as partial payment for the work completed on September 12.
24 The company completed work for another client for $1,900 on credit.
28 Lummus withdrew $5,300 cash from the company for personal use.
29 The company purchased $1,700 of additional office supplies on credit.
30 The company paid $460 cash for this month's utility bill.

Required

1. Prepare general journal entries to record these transactions (use account titles listed in part 2).

2. Open the following ledger accounts—their account numbers are in parentheses (use the balance column format): Cash (101); Accounts Receivable (106); Office Supplies (124); Prepaid Insurance (128); Prepaid Rent (131); Office Equipment (163); Accounts Payable (201); R. Lummus, Capital (301); R. Lummus, Withdrawals (302); Service Fees Earned (401); and Utilities Expense (690). Post journal entries from part 1 to the ledger accounts and enter the balance after each posting.

3. Prepare a trial balance as of the end of September.

Check (2) Ending balances: Cash, $6,740; Accounts Receivable, $7,500; Accounts Payable, $1,700

(3) Total debits, $72,600

Problem 2-5B
Recording transactions; posting to ledger; preparing a trial balance
C3 A1 P1 P2

Cooke Consulting completed the following transactions during June.

a. Chris Cooke, the owner, invested $80,000 cash along with office equipment valued at $30,000 in the new company.
b. The company purchased land valued at $30,000 and a building valued at $170,000. The purchase is paid with $40,000 cash and a long-term note payable for $160,000.
c. The company purchased $2,400 of office supplies on credit.
d. C. Cooke invested his personal automobile in the company. The automobile has a value of $18,000 and is to be used exclusively in the business.
e. The company purchased $6,000 of additional office equipment on credit.
f. The company paid $1,500 cash salary to an assistant.
g. The company provided services to a client and collected $6,000 cash.
h. The company paid $800 cash for this month's utilities.
i. The company paid $2,400 cash to settle the payable created in transaction *c*.
j. The company purchased $20,000 of new office equipment by paying $20,000 cash.
k. The company completed $5,200 of services for a client, who must pay within 30 days.
l. The company paid $1,500 cash salary to an assistant.
m. The company received $3,800 cash in partial payment on the receivable created in transaction *k*.
n. C. Cooke withdrew $6,400 cash from the company for personal use.

Required

1. Prepare general journal entries to record these transactions (use account titles listed in part 2).

2. Open the following ledger accounts—their account numbers are in parentheses (use the balance column format): Cash (101); Accounts Receivable (106); Office Supplies (108); Office Equipment (163); Automobiles (164); Building (170); Land (172); Accounts Payable (201); Notes Payable (250); C. Cooke, Capital (301); C. Cooke, Withdrawals (302); Fees Earned (402); Salaries Expense (601); and Utilities Expense (602). Post the journal entries from part 1 to the ledger accounts and enter the balance after each posting.

3. Prepare a trial balance as of the end of June.

Check (2) Ending balances: Cash, $17,200; Office Equipment, $56,000

(3) Trial balance totals, $305,200

Problem 2-6B
Analyzing account balances and reconstructing transactions
C1 C3 A1 P2 

Michael Gould started a Web consulting firm called Gould Solutions. He began operations and completed seven transactions in April that resulted in the following accounts, which all have normal balances.

Cash	$12,485
Office supplies	560
Prepaid rent	1,500
Office equipment	11,450
Accounts payable	11,450
M. Gould, Capital	10,000
M. Gould, Withdrawals	6,200
Consulting fees earned	16,400
Operating expenses	5,655

Required

Check (1) Trial balance total, $37,850

1. Prepare a trial balance for this business as of the end of April.

Analysis Component

2. Analyze the accounts and their balances and prepare a list that describes each of the seven most likely transactions and their amounts.

(3) Cash paid, $13,915

3. Prepare a report of cash received and cash paid showing how the seven transactions in part 2 yield the $12,485 ending Cash balance.

SERIAL PROBLEM

Business Solutions
A1 P1 P2

(This serial problem started in Chapter 1 and continues through most of the chapters. If the Chapter 1 segment was not completed, the problem can begin at this point. It is helpful, but not necessary, to use the Working Papers that accompany this book.)

SP 2 On October 1, 2011, Santana Rey launched a computer services company called **Business Solutions,** which provides consulting services, computer system installations, and custom program development. Rey adopts the calendar year for reporting purposes and expects to prepare the company's first set of financial statements on December 31, 2011. The company's initial chart of accounts follows.

Account	No.	Account	No.
Cash	101	S. Rey, Capital	301
Accounts Receivable	106	S. Rey, Withdrawals	302
Computer Supplies	126	Computer Services Revenue	403
Prepaid Insurance	128	Wages Expense	623
Prepaid Rent	131	Advertising Expense	655
Office Equipment	163	Mileage Expense	676
Computer Equipment	167	Miscellaneous Expenses	677
Accounts Payable	201	Repairs Expense—Computer	684

Required

1. Prepare journal entries to record each of the following transactions for Business Solutions.

Oct.	1	S. Rey invested $45,000 cash, a $20,000 computer system, and $8,000 of office equipment in the company.
	2	The company paid $3,300 cash for four months' rent. (*Hint:* Debit Prepaid Rent for $3,300.)
	3	The company purchased $1,420 of computer supplies on credit from Harris Office Products.
	5	The company paid $2,220 cash for one year's premium on a property and liability insurance policy. (*Hint:* Debit Prepaid Insurance for $2,220.)
	6	The company billed Easy Leasing $4,800 for services performed in installing a new Web server.
	8	The company paid $1,420 cash for the computer supplies purchased from Harris Office Products on October 3.
	10	The company hired Lyn Addie as a part-time assistant for $125 per day, as needed.
	12	The company billed Easy Leasing another $1,400 for services performed.

15 The company received $4,800 cash from Easy Leasing as partial payment on its account.
17 The company paid $805 cash to repair computer equipment that was damaged when moving it.
20 The company paid $1,728 cash for advertisements published in the local newspaper.
22 The company received $1,400 cash from Easy Leasing on its account.
28 The company billed IFM Company $5,208 for services performed.
31 The company paid $875 cash for Lyn Addie's wages for seven days' work.
31 S. Rey withdrew $3,600 cash from the company for personal use.
Nov. 1 The company reimbursed S. Rey in cash for business automobile mileage allowance (Rey logged 1,000 miles at $0.32 per mile).
2 The company received $4,633 cash from Liu Corporation for computer services performed.
5 The company purchased computer supplies for $1,125 cash from Harris Office Products.
8 The company billed Gomez Co. $5,668 for services performed.
13 The company received notification from Alex's Engineering Co. that Business Solutions' bid of $3,950 for an upcoming project is accepted.
18 The company received $2,208 cash from IFM Company as partial payment of the October 28 bill.
22 The company donated $250 cash to the United Way in the company's name.
24 The company completed work for Alex's Engineering Co. and sent it a bill for $3,950.
25 The company sent another bill to IFM Company for the past-due amount of $3,000.
28 The company reimbursed S. Rey in cash for business automobile mileage (1,200 miles at $0.32 per mile).
30 The company paid $1,750 cash for Lyn Addie's wages for 14 days' work.
30 S. Rey withdrew $2,000 cash from the company for personal use.

2. Open ledger accounts (in balance column format) and post the journal entries from part 1 to them.
3. Prepare a trial balance as of the end of November.

Check (2) Cash, Nov. 30 bal., $38,264
(3) Trial bal. totals, $98,659

Beyond the Numbers

REPORTING IN ACTION
A1 A2
RIM

BTN 2-1 Refer to Research In Motion's financial statements in Appendix A for the following questions.

Required

1. What amount of total liabilities does it report for each of the fiscal years ended February 28, 2009, and February 27, 2010?
2. What amount of total assets does it report for each of the fiscal years ended February 28, 2009, and February 27, 2010?
3. Compute its debt ratio for each of the fiscal years ended February 28, 2009, and February 27, 2010.
4. In which fiscal year did it employ more financial leverage (February 28, 2009, or February 27, 2010)? Explain.

Fast Forward

5. Access its financial statements (10-K report) for a fiscal year ending after February 27, 2010, from its Website (RIM.com) or the SEC's EDGAR database (www.SEC.gov). Recompute its debt ratio for any subsequent year's data and compare it with the debt ratio for 2009 and 2010.

COMPARATIVE ANALYSIS
A1 A2 
RIM
Apple

BTN 2-2 Key comparative figures for Research In Motion and Apple follow.

($ millions)	Research In Motion Current Year	Research In Motion Prior Year	Apple Current Year	Apple Prior Year
Total liabilities	$ 2,602	$ 2,227	$15,861	$13,874
Total assets	10,204	8,101	47,501	36,171

1. What is the debt ratio for Research In Motion in the current year and for the prior year?
2. What is the debt ratio for Apple in the current year and for the prior year?
3. Which of the two companies has the higher degree of financial leverage? What does this imply?

ETHICS CHALLENGE

C1 

BTN 2-3 Review the *Decision Ethics* case from the first part of this chapter involving the cashier. The guidance answer suggests that you should not comply with the assistant manager's request.

Required

Propose and evaluate two other courses of action you might consider, and explain why.

COMMUNICATING IN PRACTICE

C1 C2 A1 P3

BTN 2-4 Mora Stanley is an aspiring entrepreneur and your friend. She is having difficulty understanding the purposes of financial statements and how they fit together across time.

Required

Write a one-page memorandum to Stanley explaining the purposes of the four financial statements and how they are linked across time.

TAKING IT TO THE NET

A1 

BTN 2-5 Access EDGAR online (www.SEC.gov) and locate the 2009 year 10-K report of Amazon.com (ticker AMZN) filed on January 29, 2010. Review its financial statements reported for years ended 2009, 2008, and 2007 to answer the following questions.

Required

1. What are the amounts of its net income or net loss reported for each of these three years?
2. Does Amazon's operating activities provide cash or use cash for each of these three years?
3. If Amazon has a 2009 net income of more than $900 million and 2009 operating cash flows of more than $3,000 million, how is it possible that its cash balance at December 31, 2009, increases by less than $700 million relative to its balance at December 31, 2008?

TEAMWORK IN ACTION

C1 C2 C4 A1

BTN 2-6 The expanded accounting equation consists of assets, liabilities, capital, withdrawals, revenues, and expenses. It can be used to reveal insights into changes in a company's financial position.

Required

1. Form *learning teams* of six (or more) members. Each team member must select one of the six components and each team must have at least one expert on each component: (*a*) assets, (*b*) liabilities, (*c*) capital, (*d*) withdrawals, (*e*) revenues, and (*f*) expenses.
2. Form *expert teams* of individuals who selected the same component in part 1. Expert teams are to draft a report that each expert will present to his or her learning team addressing the following:
   a. Identify for its component the (i) increase and decrease side of the account and (ii) normal balance side of the account.
   b. Describe a transaction, with amounts, that increases its component.
   c. Using the transaction and amounts in (*b*), verify the equality of the accounting equation and then explain any effects on the income statement and statement of cash flows.
   d. Describe a transaction, with amounts, that decreases its component.
   e. Using the transaction and amounts in (*d*), verify the equality of the accounting equation and then explain any effects on the income statement and statement of cash flows.
3. Each expert should return to his/her learning team. In rotation, each member presents his/her expert team's report to the learning team. Team discussion is encouraged.

ENTREPRENEURIAL DECISION

A1 A2 P3  

BTN 2-7 Assume Susie Levitt and Katie Shea of CitySlips plan on expanding their business to accommodate more product lines. They are considering financing their expansion in one of two ways: (1) contributing more of their own funds to the business or (2) borrowing the funds from a bank.

Required

Identify at least two issues that Susie and Katie should consider when trying to decide on the method for financing their expansion.

ENTREPRENEURIAL DECISION

A1 A2 P3  

BTN 2-8 Lisa Langely is a young entrepreneur who operates Langely Music Services, offering singing lessons and instruction on musical instruments. Langely wishes to expand but needs a $15,000 loan. The bank requests Langely to prepare a balance sheet and key financial ratios. Langely has not kept formal records but is able to provide the following accounts and their amounts as of December 31, 2011.

Cash	$ 1,800	Accounts Receivable	$4,800	Prepaid Insurance	$ 750
Prepaid Rent	4,700	Store Supplies	3,300	Equipment	25,000
Accounts Payable	1,100	Unearned Lesson Fees	7,800	Total Equity*	31,450
Annual net income	20,000				

* The total equity amount reflects all owner investments, withdrawals, revenues, and expenses as of December 31, 2011.

Required

1. Prepare a balance sheet as of December 31, 2011, for Langely Music Services. (Report only the total equity amount on the balance sheet.)
2. Compute Langely's debt ratio and its return on assets (the latter ratio is defined in Chapter 1). Assume average assets equal its ending balance.
3. Do you believe the prospects of a $15,000 bank loan are good? Why or why not?

HITTING THE ROAD

C1

BTN 2-9 Obtain a recent copy of the most prominent newspaper distributed in your area. Research the classified section and prepare a report answering the following questions (attach relevant classified clippings to your report). Alternatively, you may want to search the Web for the required information. One suitable Website is CareerOneStop (www.CareerOneStop.org). For documentation, you should print copies of Websites accessed.

1. Identify the number of listings for accounting positions and the various accounting job titles.
2. Identify the number of listings for other job titles, with examples, that require or prefer accounting knowledge/experience but are not specifically accounting positions.
3. Specify the salary range for the accounting and accounting-related positions if provided.
4. Indicate the job that appeals to you, the reason for its appeal, and its requirements.

GLOBAL DECISION

A2  

NOKIA

RIM

Apple

BTN 2-10 Nokia (www.Nokia.com) is a leading global manufacturer of mobile devices and services, and it competes to some extent with both Research In Motion and Apple. Key financial ratios for the current fiscal year follow.

Key Figure	Nokia	Research In Motion	Apple
Return on assets	0.7%	26.8%	19.7%
Debt ratio	58.7%	25.5%	33.4%

Required

1. Which company is most profitable according to its return on assets?
2. Which company is most risky according to the debt ratio?
3. Which company deserves increased investment based on a joint analysis of return on assets and the debt ratio? Explain.

ANSWERS TO MULTIPLE CHOICE QUIZ

1. b; debit Utility Expense for $700, and credit Cash for $700.
2. a; debit Cash for $2,500, and credit Unearned Lawn Service Fees for $2,500.
3. c; debit Cash for $250,000, debit Land for $500,000, and credit L. Shue, Capital for $750,000.
4. d
5. e; Debt ratio = $400,000/$1,000,000 = 40%

Adjusting Accounts and Preparing Financial Statements

A Look Back

Chapter 2 explained the analysis and recording of transactions. We showed how to apply and interpret company accounts, T-accounts, double-entry accounting, ledgers, postings, and trial balances.

A Look at This Chapter

This chapter explains the timing of reports and the need to adjust accounts. Adjusting accounts is important for recognizing revenues and expenses in the proper period. We describe the adjusted trial balance and how it is used to prepare financial statements.

A Look Ahead

Chapter 4 highlights the completion of the accounting cycle. We explain the important final steps in the accounting process. These include closing procedures, the post-closing trial balance, and reversing entries.

Learning Objectives

CONCEPTUAL

C1 Explain the importance of periodic reporting and the time period assumption. (p. 94)

C2 Explain accrual accounting and how it improves financial statements. (p. 95)

C3 Identify the types of adjustments and their purpose. (p. 96)

ANALYTICAL

A1 Explain how accounting adjustments link to financial statements. (p. 105)

A2 Compute profit margin and describe its use in analyzing company performance. (p. 109)

LP3

PROCEDURAL

P1 Prepare and explain adjusting entries. (p. 97)

P2 Explain and prepare an adjusted trial balance. (p. 106)

P3 Prepare financial statements from an adjusted trial balance. (p. 106)

P4 *Appendix 3A*—Explain the alternatives in accounting for prepaids. (p. 113)

Decision Insight

Huh? Yes!

"Make sure that whatever commitment you make . . . you keep"
—BEN HUH

SEATTLE—"When we were starting this thing, people asked who was going to run it, and I said, 'I will, and my wife.' And they said, 'You're crazy.' And I said, 'Yes!' " Meet Ben Huh. His thing? **Cheezburger Network** **(Cheezburger.com/sites),** which controls over 30 Websites devoted to Internet memes. (Memes are running gags, usually in JPEG or video format, which spawn and spread on the Web.) His sites include ICanHasCheezburger?, FailBlog, IHasAHotdog!, ROFLrazzi, and TotallyLooksLike. Since launching his company just a few years ago, his network has nearly 200 million page views per month and annual revenue in the millions. Revenue comes from display ads, along with some merchandise sales.

Ben explains that he set up an accounting system early on to account for all business activities, including cash, revenues, receivables, and payables. He also had to learn about the deferral and accrual of revenues and expenses. Setting up a good accounting system is an important part of success, explains Ben. "I learned how to keep costs low."

In spite of his quirky business, Ben insists "it is very serious business." He also seriously monitors the adjusting of accounts so that revenues and expenses are properly reported so that good decisions are made. Adds Ben, "No matter how strange or ridiculous a business looks, those fundamentals still need to be there."

Financial statement preparation and analysis is a process that Ben emphasizes. Although he insists on timely and accurate accounting reports, Ben says "we're just having fun . . . we've always been very much counterculture." To achieve the fun part, Ben first took time to understand accounting adjustments and their effects. It is part of the larger picture. We "make people happy for five minutes every day." But, for Ben to do that, he insists that a reliable accounting system is necessary . . . otherwise his business would fail.

"We'd like to continue to do what we do . . . build bigger communities and just kind of evangelize the idea that the user is great at creating excellent content," says Ben. "The market is far more efficient than any one company . . . but we haven't applied that theory to [Web] content."

[Sources: *Cheezburger Website* and *BenHuh Website,* January 2011; *Entrepreneur,* August 2009; *Wired,* February 2010; *The New York Times,* April 2009; *Time,* August 2009]

Chapter Preview

Financial statements reflect revenues when earned and expenses when incurred. This is known as *accrual accounting,* which was the focus of Chapter 2. We showed how companies use accounting systems to collect information about *external* transactions and events. We also explained how journals, ledgers, and other tools are useful in preparing financial statements. This chapter describes the accounting process for producing useful information involving *internal* transactions and events. An important part of this process is adjusting the account balances so that financial statements at the end of a reporting period reflect the effects of all transactions. We then explain the important steps in preparing financial statements.

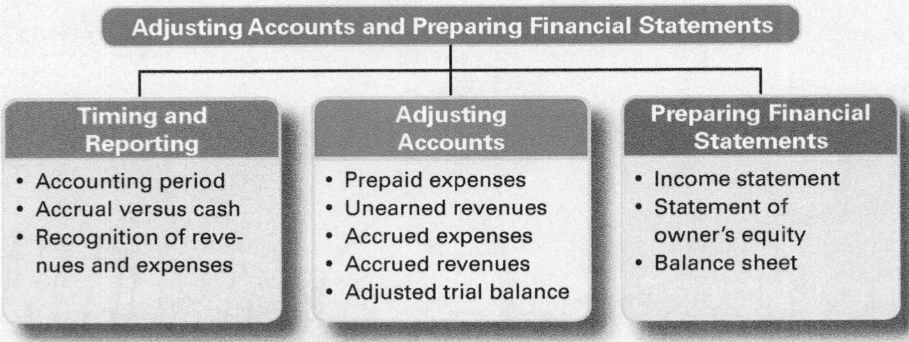

TIMING AND REPORTING

This section describes the importance of reporting accounting information at regular intervals and its impact for recording revenues and expenses.

The Accounting Period

C1 Explain the importance of periodic reporting and the time period assumption.

The value of information is often linked to its timeliness. Useful information must reach decision makers frequently and promptly. To provide timely information, accounting systems prepare reports at regular intervals. This results in an accounting process impacted by the time period (or periodicity) assumption. The **time period assumption** presumes that an organization's activities can be divided into specific time periods such as a month, a three-month quarter, a six-month interval, or a year. Exhibit 3.1 shows various **accounting,** or *reporting,* **periods.** Most organizations use a year as their primary accounting period. Reports covering a one-year period are known as **annual financial statements.** Many organizations also prepare **interim financial statements** covering one, three, or six months of activity.

"RIM announces annual income of . . ."

EXHIBIT 3.1
Accounting Periods

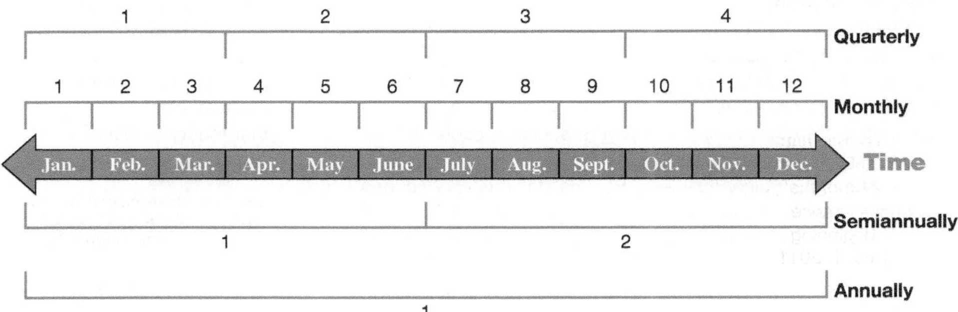

The annual reporting period is not always a calendar year ending on December 31. An organization can adopt a **fiscal year** consisting of any 12 consecutive months. It is also acceptable to adopt an annual reporting period of 52 weeks. For example, Gap's fiscal year consistently ends the final week of January or the first week of February each year.

Companies with little seasonal variation in sales often choose the calendar year as their fiscal year. The financial statements of The Kellogg Company (the company that controls characters such as Tony the Tiger, Snap! Crackle! Pop!, and Keebler Elf) reflect a fiscal year that ends on the Saturday nearest December 31. Companies experiencing seasonal variations in sales often choose a **natural business year** end, which is when sales activities are at their lowest level for the year. The natural business year for retailers such as Walmart, Target, and Macy's usually ends around January 31, after the holiday season.

Accrual Basis versus Cash Basis

C2 Explain accrual accounting and how it improves financial statements.

After external transactions and events are recorded, several accounts still need adjustments before their balances appear in financial statements. This need arises because internal transactions and events remain unrecorded. **Accrual basis accounting** uses the adjusting process to recognize revenues when earned and expenses when incurred (matched with revenues).

Cash basis accounting recognizes revenues when cash is received and records expenses when cash is paid. This means that cash basis net income for a period is the difference between cash receipts and cash payments. Cash basis accounting is not consistent with generally accepted accounting principles (neither U.S. GAAP nor IFRS).

It is commonly held that accrual accounting better reflects business performance than information about cash receipts and payments. Accrual accounting also increases the *comparability* of financial statements from one period to another. Yet cash basis accounting is useful for several business decisions—which is the reason companies must report a statement of cash flows.

To see the difference between these two accounting systems, let's consider FastForward's Prepaid Insurance account. FastForward paid $2,400 for 24 months of insurance coverage that began on December 1, 2011. Accrual accounting requires that $100 of insurance expense be reported on December 2011's income statement. Another $1,200 of expense is reported in year 2012, and the remaining $1,100 is reported as expense in the first 11 months of 2013. Exhibit 3.2 illustrates this allocation of insurance cost across these three years. Any unexpired premium is reported as a Prepaid Insurance asset on the accrual basis balance sheet.

EXHIBIT 3.2

Accrual Accounting for Allocating Prepaid Insurance to Expense

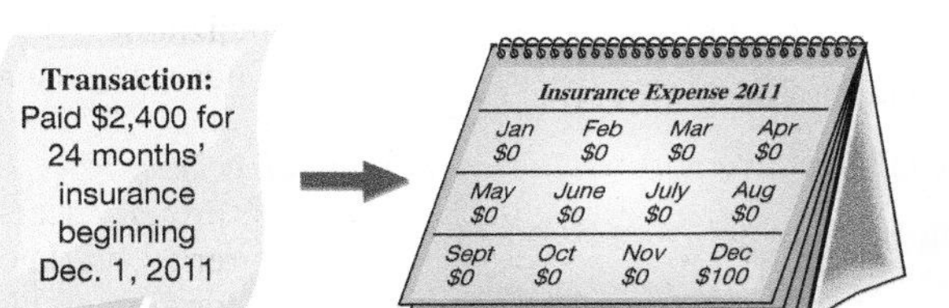

Alternatively, a cash basis income statement for December 2011 reports insurance expense of $2,400, as shown in Exhibit 3.3. The cash basis income statements for years 2012 and 2013 report no insurance expense. The cash basis balance sheet never reports an insurance asset because it is immediately expensed. This shows that cash basis income for 2011–2013 fails to match the cost of insurance with the insurance benefits received for those years and months.

EXHIBIT 3.3

Cash Accounting for Allocating Prepaid Insurance to Expense

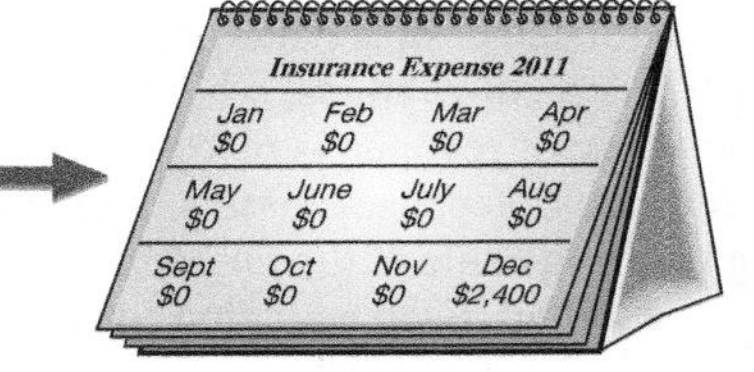

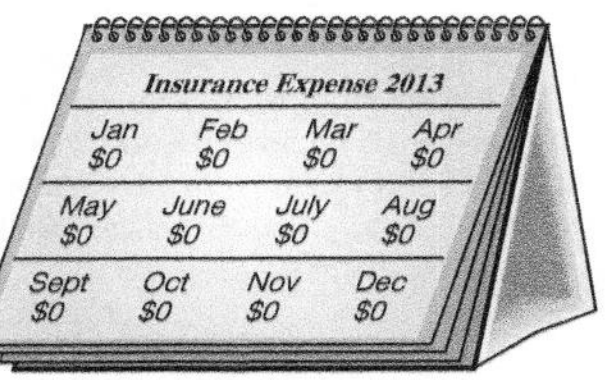

Recognizing Revenues and Expenses

Point: Recording revenue early overstates current-period revenue and income; recording it late understates current-period revenue and income.

Point: Recording expense early overstates current-period expense and understates current-period income; recording it late understates current-period expense and overstates current-period income.

We use the time period assumption to divide a company's activities into specific time periods, but not all activities are complete when financial statements are prepared. Thus, adjustments often are required to get correct account balances.

We rely on two principles in the adjusting process: revenue recognition and expense recognition (the latter is often referred to as matching). Chapter 1 explained that the *revenue recognition principle* requires that revenue be recorded when earned, not before and not after. Most companies earn revenue when they provide services and products to customers. A major goal of the adjusting process is to have revenue recognized (reported) in the time period when it is earned. The **expense recognition** (or **matching**) **principle** aims to record expenses in the same accounting period as the revenues that are earned as a result of those expenses. This matching of expenses with the revenue benefits is a major part of the adjusting process.

Matching expenses with revenues often requires us to predict certain events. When we use financial statements, we must understand that they require estimates and therefore include measures that are not precise. Walt Disney's annual report explains that its production costs from movies, such as *Alice in Wonderland,* are matched to revenues based on a ratio of current revenues from the movie divided by its predicted total revenues.

Quick Check Answers — p. 116 

1. Describe a company's annual reporting period.
2. Why do companies prepare interim financial statements?
3. What two accounting principles most directly drive the adjusting process?
4. Is cash basis accounting consistent with the matching principle? Why or why not?
5. If your company pays a $4,800 premium on April 1, 2011, for two years' insurance coverage, how much insurance expense is reported in 2012 using cash basis accounting?

ADJUSTING ACCOUNTS

Adjusting accounts is a 3-step process:

Step 1: **Determine what the current account balance *equals*.**

Step 2: **Determine what the current account balance *should equal*.**

Step 3: **Record an adjusting entry to get from step *1* to step *2*.**

Framework for Adjustments

C3 Identify the types of adjustments and their purpose.

Adjustments are necessary for transactions and events that extend over more than one period. It is helpful to group adjustments by the timing of cash receipt or cash payment in relation to the recognition of the related revenues or expenses. Exhibit 3.4 identifies four types of adjustments.

The upper half of this exhibit shows prepaid expenses (including depreciation) and unearned revenues, which reflect transactions when cash is paid or received *before* a related expense or revenue is recognized. They are also called *deferrals* because the recognition of an expense (or revenue) is *deferred* until after the related cash is paid (or received). The lower half of this exhibit shows accrued expenses and accrued revenues, which reflect transactions when cash is paid or received *after* a related expense or revenue is recognized. Adjusting entries are necessary for each of these so that revenues, expenses, assets, and liabilities are correctly reported. Specifically, an **adjusting entry** is made at the end of an accounting period to reflect a transaction or event that is not yet recorded. Each adjusting entry affects one or more income statement accounts *and* one or more balance sheet accounts (but never the Cash account).

Point: Source documents provide information for most daily transactions, and in many businesses the recordkeepers record them. Adjustments require more knowledge and are usually handled by senior accounting professionals.

EXHIBIT 3.4

Types of Adjustments

Adjustments

Paid (or received) cash before expense (or revenue) recognized
- Prepaid (Deferred) expenses*
- Unearned (Deferred) revenues

Paid (or received) cash after expense (or revenue) recognized
- Accrued expenses
- Accrued revenues

*Includes depreciation

Prepaid (Deferred) Expenses

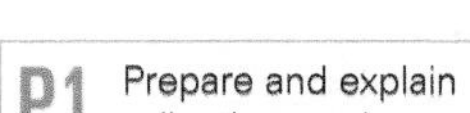

P1 Prepare and explain adjusting entries.

Prepaid expenses refer to items *paid for* in advance of receiving their benefits. Prepaid expenses are assets. When these assets are used, their costs become expenses. Adjusting entries for prepaids increase expenses and decrease assets as shown in the T-accounts of Exhibit 3.5. Such adjustments reflect transactions and events that use up prepaid expenses (including passage of time). To illustrate the accounting for prepaid expenses, we look at prepaid insurance, supplies, and depreciation.

EXHIBIT 3.5

Adjusting for Prepaid Expenses

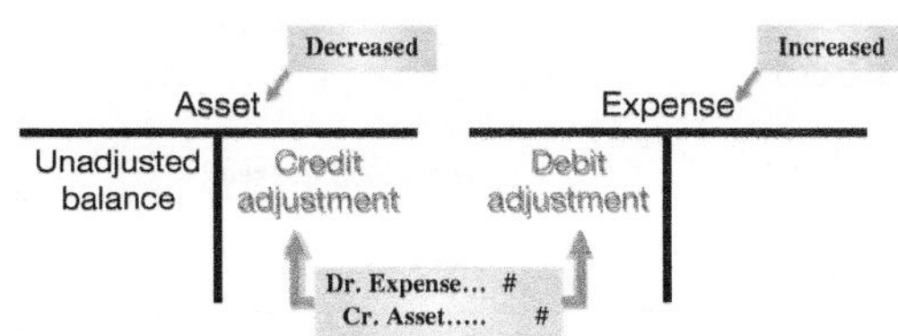

Prepaid Insurance We use our 3-step process for this and all accounting adjustments.

Step 1: We determine that the current balance of FastForward's prepaid insurance is equal to its $2,400 payment for 24 months of insurance benefits that began on December 1, 2011.

Step 2: With the passage of time, the benefits of the insurance gradually expire and a portion of the Prepaid Insurance asset becomes expense. For instance, one month's insurance coverage expires by December 31, 2011. This expense is $100, or 1/24 of $2,400, which leaves $2,300.

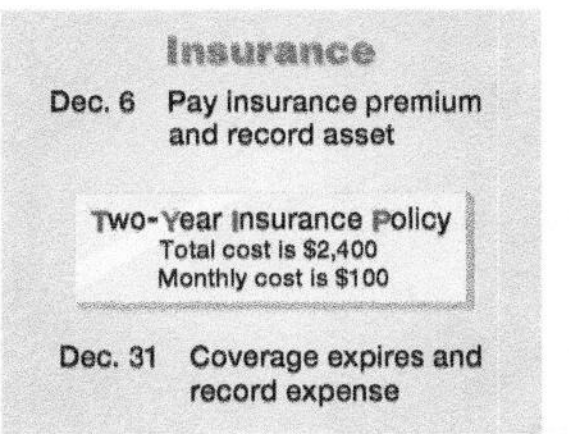

Step 3: The adjusting entry to record this expense and reduce the asset, along with T-account postings, follows:

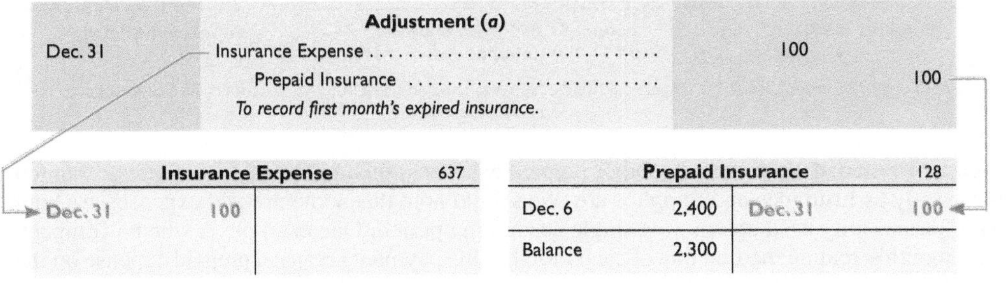

Adjustment (*a*)

Dec. 31	Insurance Expense	100	
	Prepaid Insurance		100
	To record first month's expired insurance.		

Insurance Expense 637

Dec. 31	100		

Prepaid Insurance 128

Dec. 6	2,400	Dec. 31	100
Balance	2,300		

Assets	=	Liabilities	+	Equity
−100				−100

Explanation After adjusting and posting, the $100 balance in Insurance Expense and the $2,300 balance in Prepaid Insurance are ready for reporting in financial statements. *Not* making the adjustment on or before December 31 would (1) understate expenses by $100 and overstate net income by $100 for the December income statement and (2) overstate both prepaid insurance (assets) and equity (because of net income) by $100 in the December 31 balance sheet. (Exhibit 3.2 showed that 2012's adjustments must transfer a total of $1,200 from Prepaid Insurance to Insurance Expense, and 2013's adjustments must transfer the remaining $1,100 to Insurance Expense.) The following table highlights the December 31, 2011, adjustment for prepaid insurance.

Point: Many companies record adjusting entries only at the end of each year because of the time and cost necessary.

Before Adjustment	Adjustment	After Adjustment
Prepaid Insurance = $2,400	**Deduct $100 from Prepaid Insurance Add $100 to Insurance Expense**	**Prepaid Insurance = $2,300**
Reports $2,400 policy for 24-months' coverage.	Record current month's $100 insurance expense and $100 reduction in prepaid amount.	Reports $2,300 in coverage for remaining 23 months.

Supplies Supplies are a prepaid expense requiring adjustment.

Step 1: FastForward purchased $9,720 of supplies in December and some of them were used during this month. When financial statements are prepared at December 31, the cost of supplies used during December must be recognized.

Step 2: When FastForward computes (takes physical count of) its remaining unused supplies at December 31, it finds $8,670 of supplies remaining of the $9,720 total supplies. The $1,050 difference between these two amounts is December's supplies expense.

Step 3: The adjusting entry to record this expense and reduce the Supplies asset account, along with T-account postings, follows:

Assets = Liabilities + Equity
−1,050 −1,050

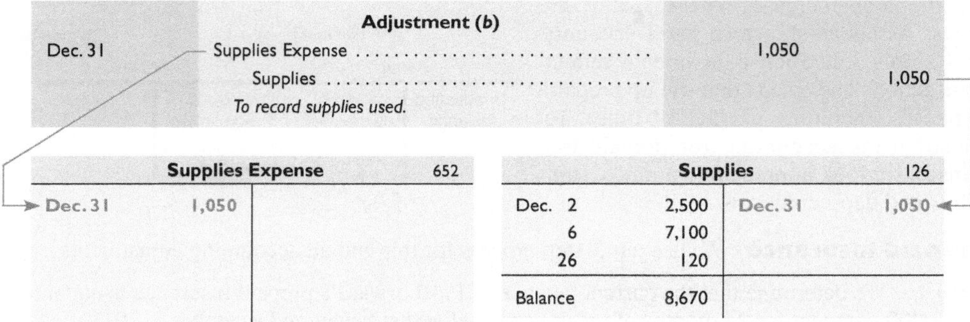

Adjustment (*b*)

		Debit	Credit
Dec. 31	Supplies Expense	1,050	
	Supplies		1,050
	To record supplies used.		

Supplies Expense 652

Debit		Credit	
Dec. 31	1,050		

Supplies 126

Debit		Credit	
Dec. 2	2,500	Dec. 31	1,050
6	7,100		
26	120		
Balance	8,670		

Explanation The balance of the Supplies account is $8,670 after posting—equaling the cost of the remaining supplies. *Not* making the adjustment on or before December 31 would (1) understate expenses by $1,050 and overstate net income by $1,050 for the December income statement and (2) overstate both supplies and equity (because of net income) by $1,050 in the December 31 balance sheet. The following table highlights the adjustment for supplies.

Before Adjustment	Adjustment	After Adjustment
Supplies = $9,720	**Deduct $1,050 from Supplies Add $1,050 to Supplies Expense**	**Supplies = $8,670**
Reports $9,720 in supplies.	Record $1,050 in supplies used and $1,050 as supplies expense.	Reports $8,670 in supplies.

Point: We assume that prepaid and unearned items are recorded in balance sheet accounts. An alternative is to record them in income statement accounts; Appendix 3A discusses this alternative. The adjusted financial statements are identical.

Other Prepaid Expenses Other prepaid expenses, such as Prepaid Rent, are accounted for exactly as Insurance and Supplies are. We should note that some prepaid expenses are both paid for and fully used up within a single accounting period. One example is when a company pays monthly rent on the first day of each month. This payment creates a prepaid expense on the first day of each month that fully expires by the end of the month. In these special cases, we can record the cash paid with a debit to an expense account instead of an asset account. This practice is described more completely later in the chapter.

Answer — p. 115

Investor A small publishing company signs a well-known athlete to write a book. The company pays the athlete $500,000 to sign plus future book royalties. A note to the company's financial statements says that "prepaid expenses include $500,000 in author signing fees to be matched against future expected sales." Is this accounting for the signing bonus acceptable? How does it affect your analysis? ■

Depreciation A special category of prepaid expenses is **plant assets,** which refers to long-term tangible assets used to produce and sell products and services. Plant assets are expected to provide benefits for more than one period. Examples of plant assets are buildings, machines, vehicles, and fixtures. All plant assets, with a general exception for land, eventually wear out or decline in usefulness. The costs of these assets are deferred but are gradually reported as expenses in the income statement over the assets' useful lives (benefit periods). **Depreciation** is the process of allocating the costs of these assets over their expected useful lives. Depreciation expense is recorded with an adjusting entry similar to that for other prepaid expenses.

Point: Plant assets are also called *Plant & Equipment*, or *Property, Plant & Equipment.*

Point: Depreciation does not necessarily measure decline in market value.

Point: An asset's expected value at the end of its useful life is called *salvage value*.

Step 1: Recall that FastForward purchased equipment for $26,000 in early December to use in earning revenue. This equipment's cost must be depreciated.

Step 2: The equipment is expected to have a useful life (benefit period) of four years and to be worth about $8,000 at the end of four years. This means the *net* cost of this equipment over its useful life is $18,000 ($26,000 − $8,000). We can use any of several methods to allocate this $18,000 net cost to expense. FastForward uses a method called **straight-line depreciation,** which allocates equal amounts of the asset's net cost to depreciation during its useful life. Dividing the $18,000 net cost by the 48 months in the asset's useful life gives a monthly cost of $375 ($18,000/48).

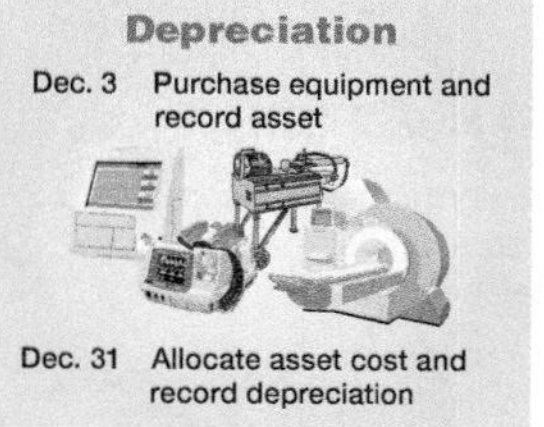

Step 3: The adjusting entry to record monthly depreciation expense, along with T-account postings, follows:

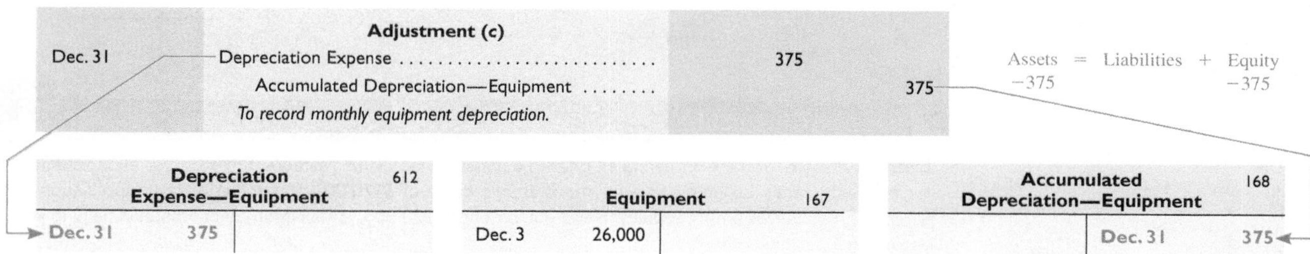

Assets = Liabilities + Equity
−375 −375

Explanation After posting the adjustment, the Equipment account ($26,000) less its Accumulated Depreciation ($375) account equals the $25,625 net cost (made up of $17,625 for the 47 remaining months in the benefit period plus the $8,000 value at the end of that time). The $375 balance in the Depreciation Expense account is reported in the December income statement. *Not* making the adjustment at December 31 would (1) understate expenses by $375 and overstate net income by $375 for the December income statement and (2) overstate both assets and equity (because of income) by $375 in the December 31 balance sheet. The following table highlights the adjustment for depreciation.

Before Adjustment	Adjustment	After Adjustment
Equipment, net = $26,000	**Deduct $375 from Equipment, net** **Add $375 to Depreciation Expense**	**Equipment, net = $25,625**
Reports $26,000 in equipment.	Record $375 in depreciation and $375 as accumulated depreciation, which is deducted from equipment.	Reports $25,625 in equipment, net of accumulated depreciation.

Accumulated depreciation is kept in a separate contra account. A **contra account** is an account linked with another account, it has an opposite normal balance, and it is reported as a subtraction from that other account's balance. For instance, FastForward's contra account of Accumulated Depreciation—Equipment is subtracted from the Equipment account in the balance sheet (see Exhibit 3.7). This contra account allows balance sheet readers to know both the full costs of assets and the total depreciation.

The title of the contra account, *Accumulated Depreciation,* reveals that this account includes total depreciation expense for all prior periods for which the asset was used. To illustrate, the Equipment and the Accumulated Depreciation accounts appear as in Exhibit 3.6 on February 28, 2012, after three months of adjusting entries. The $1,125 balance in the accumulated depreciation account can be subtracted from its related $26,000 asset cost. The difference ($24,875) between these two balances is the cost of the asset that has not yet been depreciated. This difference is

Point: The cost principle requires an asset to be initially recorded at acquisition cost. Depreciation causes the asset's book value (cost less accumulated depreciation) to decline over time.

EXHIBIT 3.6

Accounts after Three Months of Depreciation Adjustments

Equipment		167
Dec. 3	26,000	

Accumulated Depreciation—Equipment		168
	Dec. 31	375
	Jan. 31	375
	Feb. 28	375
	Balance	1,125

Point: The net cost of equipment is also called the *depreciable basis.*

called the **book value,** or the *net amount,* which equals the asset's costs less its accumulated depreciation.

These account balances are reported in the assets section of the February 28 balance sheet in Exhibit 3.7.

EXHIBIT 3.7

Equipment and Accumulated Depreciation on February 28 Balance Sheet

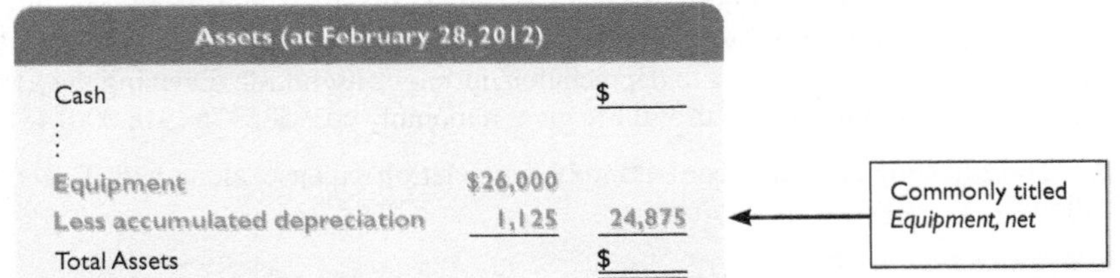

Assets (at February 28, 2012)		
Cash		$
⋮		
Equipment	$26,000	
Less accumulated depreciation	1,125	24,875
Total Assets		$

Decision Maker Answer — p. 116

Entrepreneur You are preparing an offer to purchase a family-run restaurant. The depreciation schedule for the restaurant's building and equipment shows costs of $175,000 and accumulated depreciation of $155,000. This leaves a net for building and equipment of $20,000. Is this information useful in helping you decide on a purchase offer? ■

Unearned (Deferred) Revenues

The term **unearned revenues** refers to cash received in advance of providing products and services. Unearned revenues, also called *deferred revenues,* are liabilities. When cash is accepted, an obligation to provide products or services is accepted. As products or services are provided, the unearned revenues become *earned* revenues. Adjusting entries for unearned revenues involve increasing revenues and decreasing unearned revenues, as shown in Exhibit 3.8.

EXHIBIT 3.8

Adjusting for Unearned Revenues

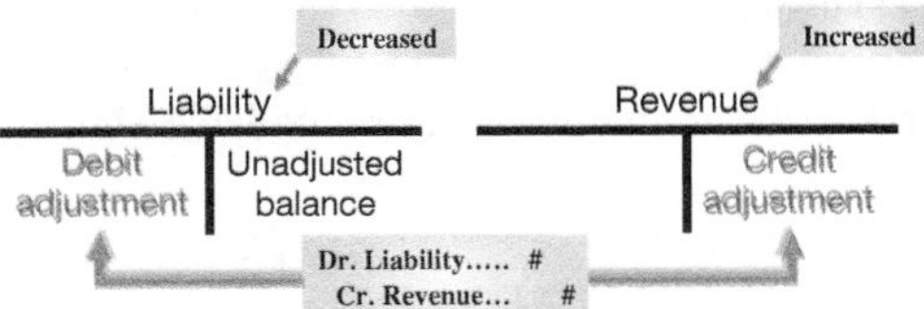

Point: To *defer* is to postpone. We postpone reporting amounts received as revenues until they are earned.

An example of unearned revenues is from The New York Times Company, which reports unexpired (unearned) subscriptions of $81 million: "Proceeds from ... subscriptions are deferred at the time of sale and are recognized in earnings on a pro rata basis over the terms of the subscriptions." Unearned revenues are nearly 10% of the current liabilities for the Times. Another example comes from the Boston Celtics. When the Celtics receive cash from advance ticket sales and broadcast fees, they record it in an unearned revenue account called *Deferred Game Revenues.* The Celtics recognize this unearned revenue with adjusting entries on a game-by-game basis. Since the NBA regular season begins in October and ends in April, revenue recognition is mainly limited to this period. For a recent season, the Celtics' quarterly revenues were $0 million for July–September; $34 million for October–December; $48 million for January–March; and $17 million for April–June.

Returning to FastForward, it also has unearned revenues. It agreed on December 26 to provide consulting services to a client for a fixed fee of $3,000 for 60 days.

Step 1: On December 26, the client paid the 60-day fee in advance, covering the period December 27 to February 24. The entry to record the cash received in advance is

Dec. 26	Cash	3,000	
	Unearned Consulting Revenue		3,000
	Received advance payment for services over the next 60 days.		

Assets = Liabilities + Equity
+3,000 +3,000

This advance payment increases cash and creates an obligation to do consulting work over the next 60 days.

Step 2: As time passes, FastForward earns this payment through consulting. By December 31, it has provided five days' service and earned 5/60 of the $3,000 unearned revenue. This amounts to $250 ($3,000 × 5/60). The *revenue recognition principle* implies that $250 of unearned revenue must be reported as revenue on the December income statement.

Step 3: The adjusting entry to reduce the liability account and recognize earned revenue, along with T-account postings, follows:

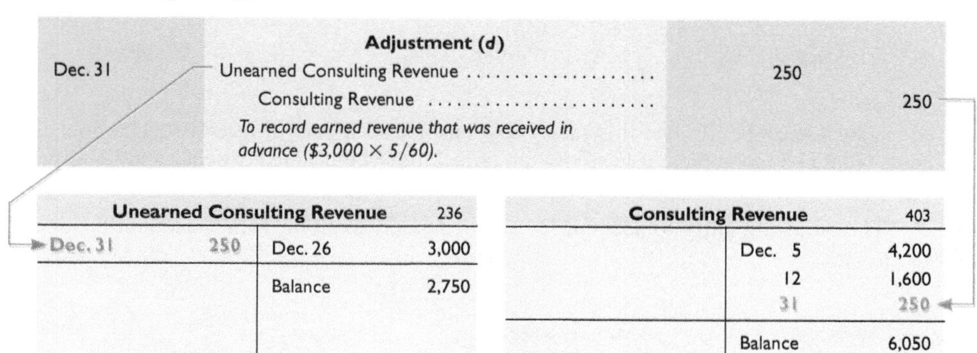

Assets = Liabilities + Equity
−250 +250

Explanation The adjusting entry transfers $250 from unearned revenue (a liability account) to a revenue account. *Not* making the adjustment (1) understates revenue and net income by $250 in the December income statement and (2) overstates unearned revenue and understates equity by $250 on the December 31 balance sheet. The following highlights the adjustment for unearned revenue.

Before Adjustment	Adjustment	After Adjustment
Unearned Consulting Revenue = $3,000	**Deduct $250 from Unearned Consulting Revenue Add $250 to Consulting Revenue**	**Unearned Consulting Revenue = $2,750**
Reports $3,000 in unearned revenue for consulting services promised for 60 days.	Record 5 days of earned consulting revenue, which is 5/60 of unearned amount.	Reports $2,750 in unearned revenue for consulting services owed over next 55 days.

Accounting for unearned revenues is crucial to many companies. For example, the National Retail Federation reports that gift card sales, which are unearned revenues for sellers, exceed $20 billion annually. Gift cards are now the top selling holiday gift.

Accrued Expenses

Accrued expenses refer to costs that are incurred in a period but are both unpaid and unrecorded. Accrued expenses must be reported on the income statement of the period when incurred. Adjusting entries for recording accrued expenses involve increasing expenses and increasing liabilities as shown in Exhibit 3.9. This adjustment recognizes expenses incurred in a period but not yet paid. Common examples of accrued expenses are salaries, interest, rent, and taxes. We use salaries and interest to show how to adjust accounts for accrued expenses.

Point: Accrued expenses are also called accrued liabilities.

EXHIBIT 3.9

Adjusting for Accrued Expenses

Increased
Expense
Debit adjustment
Increased
Liability
Credit adjustment
Dr. Expense..... #
Cr. Liability... #

Accrued Salaries Expense FastForward's employee earns $70 per day, or $350 for a five-day workweek beginning on Monday and ending on Friday.

Step 1: Its employee is paid every two weeks on Friday. On December 12 and 26, the wages are paid, recorded in the journal, and posted to the ledger.

Step 2: The calendar in Exhibit 3.10 shows three working days after the December 26 payday (29, 30, and 31). This means the employee has earned three days' salary by the close of business

EXHIBIT 3.10

Salary Accrual and Paydays

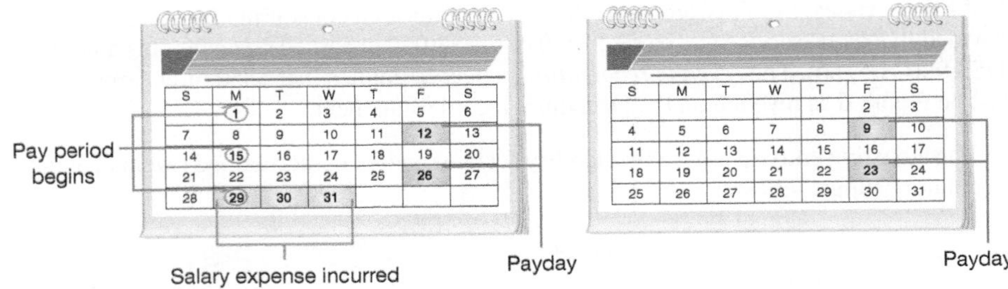

Point: An employer records salaries expense and a vacation pay liability when employees earn vacation pay.

on Wednesday, December 31, yet this salary cost has not been paid or recorded. The financial statements would be incomplete if FastForward fails to report the added expense and liability to the employee for unpaid salary from December 29, 30, and 31.

Step 3: The adjusting entry to account for accrued salaries, along with T-account postings, follows:

Assets = Liabilities + Equity
+210 −210

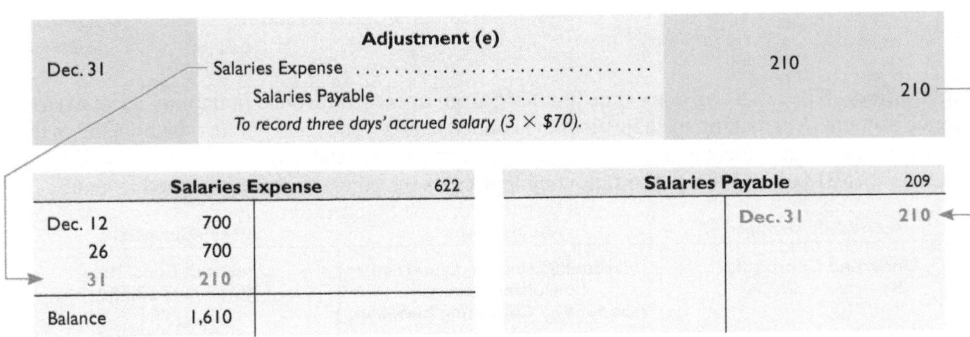

Adjustment (e)

Dec. 31	Salaries Expense	210	
	Salaries Payable		210
	To record three days' accrued salary (3 × $70).		

Salaries Expense 622

Debit		Credit
Dec. 12	700	
26	700	
31	210	
Balance	1,610	

Salaries Payable 209

Debit	Credit	
	Dec. 31	210

Explanation Salaries expense of $1,610 is reported on the December income statement and $210 of salaries payable (liability) is reported in the balance sheet. *Not* making the adjustment (1) understates salaries expense and overstates net income by $210 in the December income statement and (2) understates salaries payable (liabilities) and overstates equity by $210 on the December 31 balance sheet. The following highlights the adjustment for salaries incurred.

Before Adjustment	Adjustment	After Adjustment
Salaries Payable = $0	**Add $210 to Salaries Payable** **Add $210 to Salaries Expense**	**Salaries Payable = $210**
Reports $0 from employee salaries incurred but not yet paid in cash.	Record 3 days' salaries owed to employee, but not yet paid, at $70 per day.	Reports $210 salaries payable to employee but not yet paid.

Accrued Interest Expense Companies commonly have accrued interest expense on notes payable and other long-term liabilities at the end of a period. Interest expense is incurred with the passage of time. Unless interest is paid on the last day of an accounting period, we need to adjust for interest expense incurred but not yet paid. This means we must accrue interest cost from the most recent payment date up to the end of the period. The formula for computing accrued interest is:

Principal amount owed × Annual interest rate × Fraction of year since last payment date.

To illustrate, if a company has a $6,000 loan from a bank at 6% annual interest, then 30 days' accrued interest expense is $30—computed as $6,000 × 0.06 × 30/360. The adjusting entry would be to debit Interest Expense for $30 and credit Interest Payable for $30.

Point: Interest computations assume a 360-day year; known as the *bankers' rule*.

Future Payment of Accrued Expenses Adjusting entries for accrued expenses foretell cash transactions in future periods. Specifically, accrued expenses at the end of one accounting period result in *cash payment* in a *future period*(s). To illustrate, recall that FastForward recorded accrued salaries of $210. On January 9, the first payday of the next period, the following entry settles the accrued liability (salaries payable) and records salaries expense for seven days of work in January:

Jan. 9	Salaries Payable (3 days at $70 per day)	210	
	Salaries Expense (7 days at $70 per day)	490	
	Cash		700
	Paid two weeks' salary including three days accrued in December.		

Assets = Liabilities + Equity
−700 −210 −490

The $210 debit reflects the payment of the liability for the three days' salary accrued on December 31. The $490 debit records the salary for January's first seven working days (including the New Year's Day holiday) as an expense of the new accounting period. The $700 credit records the total amount of cash paid to the employee.

Accrued Revenues

The term **accrued revenues** refers to revenues earned in a period that are both unrecorded and not yet received in cash (or other assets). An example is a technician who bills customers only when the job is done. If one-third of a job is complete by the end of a period, then the technician must record one-third of the expected billing as revenue in that period—even though there is no billing or collection. The adjusting entries for accrued revenues increase assets and increase revenues as shown in Exhibit 3.11. Accrued revenues commonly arise from services, products, interest, and rent. We use service fees and interest to show how to adjust for accrued revenues.

Point: Accrued revenues are also called *accrued assets.*

EXHIBIT 3.11

Adjusting for Accrued Revenues

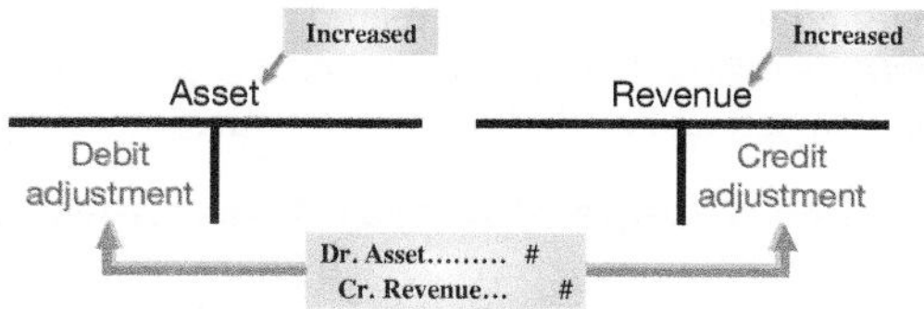

Accrued Services Revenue Accrued revenues are not recorded until adjusting entries are made at the end of the accounting period. These accrued revenues are earned but unrecorded because either the buyer has not yet paid for them or the seller has not yet billed the buyer. FastForward provides an example.

Step 1: In the second week of December, it agreed to provide 30 days of consulting services to a local fitness club for a fixed fee of $2,700. The terms of the initial agreement call for FastForward to provide services from December 12, 2011, through January 10, 2012, or 30 days of service. The club agrees to pay FastForward $2,700 on January 10, 2012, when the service period is complete.

Step 2: At December 31, 2011, 20 days of services have already been provided. Since the contracted services have not yet been entirely provided, FastForward has neither billed the club nor recorded the services already provided. Still, FastForward has earned two-thirds of the 30-day fee, or $1,800 ($2,700 × 20/30). The *revenue recognition principle* implies that it must report the $1,800 on the December income statement. The balance sheet also must report that the club owes FastForward $1,800.

Step 3: The year-end adjusting entry to account for accrued services revenue is

Assets = Liabilities + Equity
+1,800 +1,800

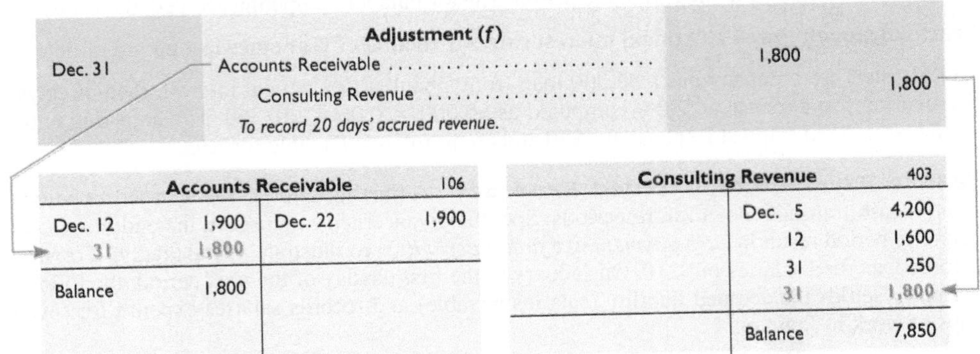

	Adjustment (f)		
Dec. 31	Accounts Receivable	1,800	
	Consulting Revenue		1,800
	To record 20 days' accrued revenue.		

Accounts Receivable 106

Dec. 12	1,900	Dec. 22	1,900
31	1,800		
Balance	1,800		

Consulting Revenue 403

		Dec. 5	4,200
		12	1,600
		31	250
		31	1,800
		Balance	7,850

Example: What is the adjusting entry if the 30-day consulting period began on December 22? *Answer:* One-third of the fee is earned:
Accounts Receivable 900
Consulting Revenue 900

Explanation Accounts receivable are reported on the balance sheet at $1,800, and the $7,850 total of consulting revenue is reported on the income statement. *Not* making the adjustment would understate (1) both consulting revenue and net income by $1,800 in the December income statement and (2) both accounts receivable (assets) and equity by $1,800 on the December 31 balance sheet. The following table highlights the adjustment for accrued revenue.

Before Adjustment	Adjustment	After Adjustment
Accounts Receivable = $0	**Add $1,800 to Accounts Receivable** **Add $1,800 to Consulting Revenue**	**Accounts Receivable = $1,800**
Reports $0 from revenue earned but not yet received in cash.	Record 20 days of earned consulting revenue, which is 20/30 of total contract amount.	Reports $1,800 in accounts receivable from consulting services provided.

Accrued Interest Revenue In addition to the accrued interest expense we described earlier, interest can yield an accrued revenue when a debtor owes money (or other assets) to a company. If a company is holding notes or accounts receivable that produce interest revenue, we must adjust the accounts to record any earned and yet uncollected interest revenue. The adjusting entry is similar to the one for accruing services revenue. Specifically, we debit Interest Receivable (asset) and credit Interest Revenue.

Future Receipt of Accrued Revenues Accrued revenues at the end of one accounting period result in *cash receipts* in a *future period*(s). To illustrate, recall that FastForward made an adjusting entry for $1,800 to record 20 days' accrued revenue earned from its consulting contract. When FastForward receives $2,700 cash on January 10 for the entire contract amount, it makes the following entry to remove the accrued asset (accounts receivable) and recognize the revenue earned in January. The $2,700 debit reflects the cash received. The $1,800 credit reflects the removal of the receivable, and the $900 credit records the revenue earned in January.

Assets = Liabilities + Equity
+2,700 +900
−1,800

Jan. 10	Cash	2,700	
	Accounts Receivable (20 days at $90 per day)		1,800
	Consulting Revenue (10 days at $90 per day)		900
	Received cash for the accrued asset and recorded earned consulting revenue for January.		

Decision Maker Answer — p. 116

Loan Officer The owner of an electronics store applies for a business loan. The store's financial statements reveal large increases in current-year revenues and income. Analysis shows that these increases are due to a promotion that let consumers buy now and pay nothing until January 1 of next year. The store recorded these sales as accrued revenue. Does your analysis raise any concerns? ■

Links to Financial Statements

A1 Explain how accounting adjustments link to financial statements.

The process of adjusting accounts is intended to bring an asset or liability account balance to its correct amount. It also updates a related expense or revenue account. These adjustments are necessary for transactions and events that extend over more than one period. (Adjusting entries are posted like any other entry.)

Exhibit 3.12 summarizes the four types of transactions requiring adjustment. Understanding this exhibit is important to understanding the adjusting process and its importance to financial statements. Remember that each adjusting entry affects one or more income statement accounts *and* one or more balance sheet accounts (but never cash).

EXHIBIT 3.12

Summary of Adjustments and Financial Statement Links

	BEFORE Adjusting		
Category	Balance Sheet	Income Statement	Adjusting Entry
Prepaid expenses†	Asset overstated Equity overstated	Expense understated	Dr. Expense Cr. Asset*
Unearned revenues†	Liability overstated Equity understated	Revenue understated	Dr. Liability Cr. Revenue
Accrued expenses	Liability understated Equity overstated	Expense understated	Dr. Expense Cr. Liability
Accrued revenues	Asset understated Equity understated	Revenue understated	Dr. Asset Cr. Revenue

* For depreciation, the credit is to Accumulated Depreciation (contra asset).

† Exhibit assumes that prepaid expenses are initially recorded as assets and that unearned revenues are initially recorded as liabilities.

Information about some adjustments is not always available until several days or even weeks after the period-end. This means that some adjusting and closing entries are recorded later than, but dated as of, the last day of the period. One example is a company that receives a utility bill on January 10 for costs incurred for the month of December. When it receives the bill, the company records the expense and the payable as of December 31. Other examples include long-distance phone usage and costs of many Web billings. The December income statement reflects these additional expenses incurred, and the December 31 balance sheet includes these payables, although the amounts were not actually known on December 31.

Decision Ethics

Answer — p. 116

Financial Officer At year-end, the president instructs you, the financial officer, not to record accrued expenses until next year because they will not be paid until then. The president also directs you to record in current-year sales a recent purchase order from a customer that requires merchandise to be delivered two weeks after the year-end. Your company would report a net income instead of a net loss if you carry out these instructions. What do you do?

Quick Check

Answers — p. 116

6. If an adjusting entry for accrued revenues of $200 at year-end is omitted, what is this error's effect on the year-end income statement and balance sheet?
7. What is a contra account? Explain its purpose.
8. What is an accrued expense? Give an example.
9. Describe how an unearned revenue arises. Give an example.

Adjusted Trial Balance

P2 Explain and prepare an adjusted trial balance.

An **unadjusted trial balance** is a list of accounts and balances prepared *before* adjustments are recorded. An **adjusted trial balance** is a list of accounts and balances prepared *after* adjusting entries have been recorded and posted to the ledger.

Exhibit 3.13 shows both the unadjusted and the adjusted trial balances for FastForward at December 31, 2011. The order of accounts in the trial balance is usually set up to match the order in the chart of accounts. Several new accounts arise from the adjusting entries.

EXHIBIT 3.13

Unadjusted and Adjusted Trial Balances

FASTFORWARD
Trial Balances
December 31, 2011

Acct. No.	Account Title	Unadjusted Trial Balance Dr.	Unadjusted Trial Balance Cr.	Adjustments Dr.	Adjustments Cr.	Adjusted Trial Balance Dr.	Adjusted Trial Balance Cr.
101	Cash	$ 4,350				$ 4,350	
106	Accounts receivable	0		*(f)* $1,800		1,800	
126	Supplies	9,720			*(b)* $1,050	8,670	
128	Prepaid insurance	2,400			*(a)* 100	2,300	
167	Equipment	26,000				26,000	
168	Accumulated depreciation—Equip.		$ 0		*(c)* 375		$ 375
201	Accounts payable		6,200				6,200
209	Salaries payable		0		*(e)* 210		210
236	Unearned consulting revenue		3,000	*(d)* 250			2,750
301	C. Taylor, Capital		30,000				30,000
302	C. Taylor, Withdrawals	200				200	
403	Consulting revenue		5,800		*(d)* 250		7,850
					(f) 1,800		
406	Rental revenue		300				300
612	Depreciation expense—Equip.	0		*(c)* 375		375	
622	Salaries expense	1,400		*(e)* 210		1,610	
637	Insurance expense	0		*(a)* 100		100	
640	Rent expense	1,000				1,000	
652	Supplies expense	0		*(b)* 1,050		1,050	
690	Utilities expense	230				230	
	Totals	$45,300	$45,300	$3,785	$3,785	$47,685	$47,685

Each adjustment (see middle columns) is identified by a letter in parentheses that links it to an adjusting entry explained earlier. Each amount in the Adjusted Trial Balance columns is computed by taking that account's amount from the Unadjusted Trial Balance columns and adding or subtracting any adjustment(s). To illustrate, Supplies has a $9,720 Dr. balance in the unadjusted columns. Subtracting the $1,050 Cr. amount shown in the adjustments columns yields an adjusted $8,670 Dr. balance for Supplies. An account can have more than one adjustment, such as for Consulting Revenue. Also, some accounts might not require adjustment for this period, such as Accounts Payable.

PREPARING FINANCIAL STATEMENTS

P3 Prepare financial statements from an adjusted trial balance.

Point: Sarbanes-Oxley Act requires that financial statements filed with the SEC be certified by the CEO and CFO, including a declaration that the statements fairly present the issuer's operations and financial condition. Violators can receive fines and/or prison terms.

We can prepare financial statements directly from information in the *adjusted* trial balance. An adjusted trial balance (see the right-most columns in Exhibit 3.13) includes all accounts and balances appearing in financial statements, and is easier to work from than the entire ledger when preparing financial statements.

Exhibit 3.14 shows how revenue and expense balances are transferred from the adjusted trial balance to the income statement (red lines). The net income and the withdrawals amount are then used to prepare the statement of owner's equity (black lines). Asset and liability balances on the adjusted trial balance are then transferred to the balance sheet (blue lines). The ending capital is determined on the statement of owner's equity and transferred to the balance sheet (green lines).

EXHIBIT 3.14

Preparing Financial Statements (Adjusted Trial Balance from Exhibit 3.13)

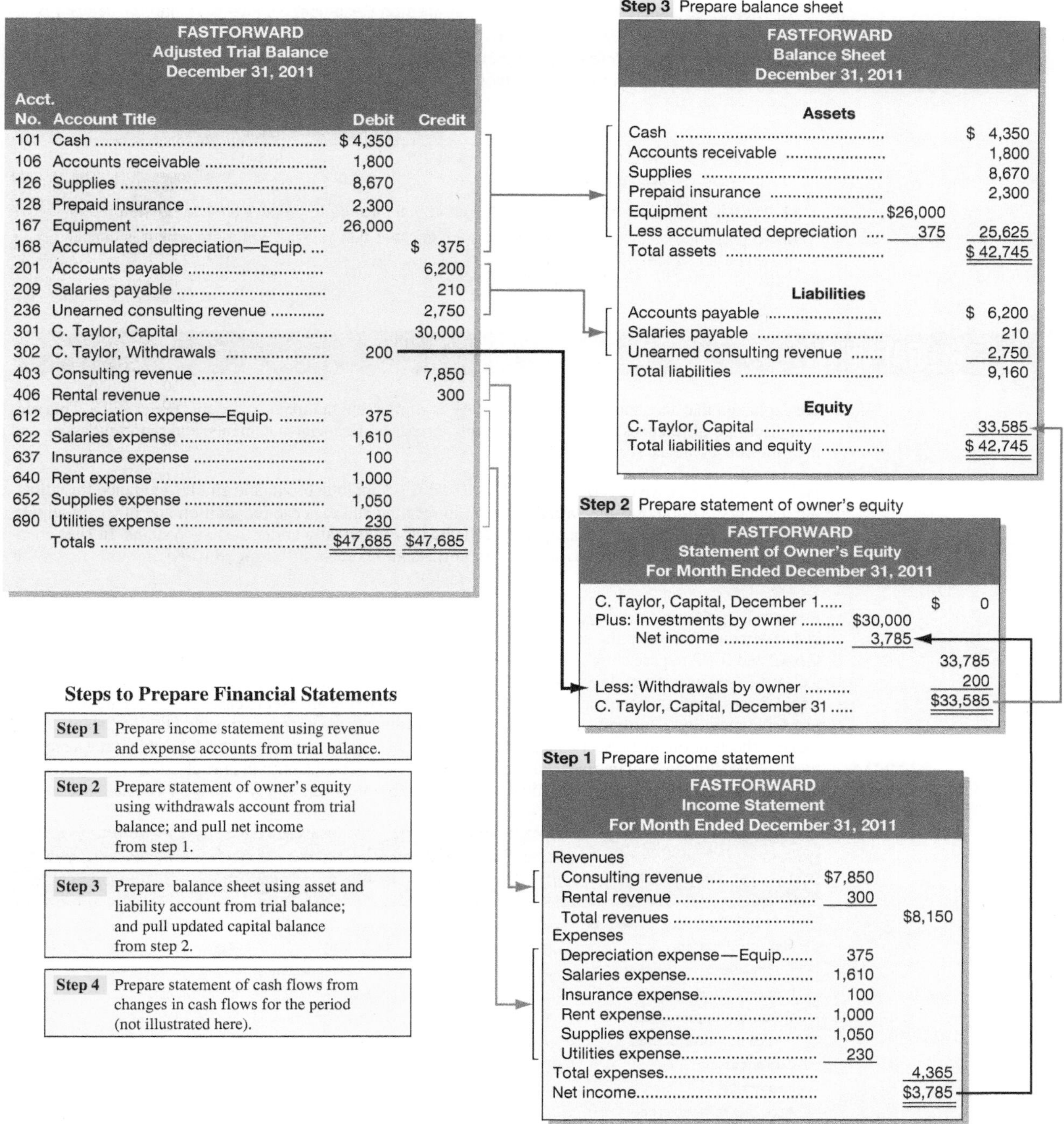

FASTFORWARD
Adjusted Trial Balance
December 31, 2011

Acct. No.	Account Title	Debit	Credit
101	Cash	$ 4,350	
106	Accounts receivable	1,800	
126	Supplies	8,670	
128	Prepaid insurance	2,300	
167	Equipment	26,000	
168	Accumulated depreciation—Equip.		$ 375
201	Accounts payable		6,200
209	Salaries payable		210
236	Unearned consulting revenue		2,750
301	C. Taylor, Capital		30,000
302	C. Taylor, Withdrawals	200	
403	Consulting revenue		7,850
406	Rental revenue		300
612	Depreciation expense—Equip.	375	
622	Salaries expense	1,610	
637	Insurance expense	100	
640	Rent expense	1,000	
652	Supplies expense	1,050	
690	Utilities expense	230	
	Totals	$47,685	$47,685

Step 3 Prepare balance sheet

FASTFORWARD
Balance Sheet
December 31, 2011

Assets		
Cash		$ 4,350
Accounts receivable		1,800
Supplies		8,670
Prepaid insurance		2,300
Equipment	$26,000	
Less accumulated depreciation	375	25,625
Total assets		$ 42,745
Liabilities		
Accounts payable		$ 6,200
Salaries payable		210
Unearned consulting revenue		2,750
Total liabilities		9,160
Equity		
C. Taylor, Capital		33,585
Total liabilities and equity		$ 42,745

Step 2 Prepare statement of owner's equity

FASTFORWARD
Statement of Owner's Equity
For Month Ended December 31, 2011

C. Taylor, Capital, December 1		$ 0
Plus: Investments by owner	$30,000	
Net income	3,785	
		33,785
Less: Withdrawals by owner		200
C. Taylor, Capital, December 31		$33,585

Step 1 Prepare income statement

FASTFORWARD
Income Statement
For Month Ended December 31, 2011

Revenues		
Consulting revenue	$7,850	
Rental revenue	300	
Total revenues		$8,150
Expenses		
Depreciation expense—Equip.	375	
Salaries expense	1,610	
Insurance expense	100	
Rent expense	1,000	
Supplies expense	1,050	
Utilities expense	230	
Total expenses		4,365
Net income		$3,785

Steps to Prepare Financial Statements

Step 1	Prepare income statement using revenue and expense accounts from trial balance.
Step 2	Prepare statement of owner's equity using withdrawals account from trial balance; and pull net income from step 1.
Step 3	Prepare balance sheet using asset and liability account from trial balance; and pull updated capital balance from step 2.
Step 4	Prepare statement of cash flows from changes in cash flows for the period (not illustrated here).

We prepare financial statements in the following order: income statement, statement of owner's equity, and balance sheet. This order makes sense because the balance sheet uses information from the statement of owner's equity, which in turn uses information from the income statement. The statement of cash flows is usually the final statement prepared.

Point: Each trial balance amount is used in only *one* financial statement and, when financial statements are completed, each account will have been used once.

Quick Check Answers – p. 116 

10. Music-Mart records $1,000 of accrued salaries on December 31. Five days later, on January 5 (the next payday), salaries of $7,000 are paid. What is the January 5 entry?
11. Jordan Air has the following information in its unadjusted and adjusted trial balances. What are the adjusting entries that Jordan Air likely recorded?

	Unadjusted		Adjusted	
	Debit	Credit	Debit	Credit
Prepaid insurance	$6,200		$5,900	
Salaries payable		$ 0		$1,400

12. What accounts are taken from the adjusted trial balance to prepare an income statement?
13. In preparing financial statements from an adjusted trial balance, what statement is usually prepared second?

GLOBAL VIEW

We explained that accounting under U.S. GAAP is similar, but not identical, to that under IFRS. This section discusses differences in adjusting accounts, preparing financial statements, and reporting assets and liabilities on a balance sheet.

Adjusting Accounts Both U.S. GAAP and IFRS include broad and similar guidance for adjusting accounts. Although some variations exist in revenue and expense recognition and other principles, all of the adjustments in this chapter are accounted for identically under the two systems. In later chapters we describe how certain assets and liabilities can result in different adjusted amounts using fair value measurements.

Preparing Financial Statements Both U.S. GAAP and IFRS prepare the same four basic financial statements following the same process discussed in this chapter. Chapter 2 explained how both U.S. GAAP and IFRS require current items to be separated from noncurrent items on the balance sheet (yielding a classified balance sheet). U.S. GAAP balance sheets report current items first. Assets are listed from most liquid to least liquid, where liquid refers to the ease of converting an asset to cash. Liabilities are listed from nearest to maturity to furthest from maturity, maturity refers to the nearness of paying off the liability. IFRS balance sheets normally present noncurrent items first (and equity before liabilities), but this is not a requirement. Other differences with financial statements exist, which we identify in later chapters. Nokia provides the following example of IFRS reporting for its assets, liabilities, and equity within the balance sheet:

NOKIA

NOKIA
Balance Sheet (in EUR millions)
December 31, 2009

Assets		Equity and Liabilities	
Noncurrent assets		Total equity	14,749
Goodwill and other intangibles	8,076	Noncurrent liabilities	
Property, plant and equipment	1,867	Long-term interest-bearing liabilities	4,432
Other noncurrent assets	2,182	Other long-term liabilities	1,369
Total noncurrent assets	12,125	Total noncurrent liabilities	5,801
Current assets		Current liabilities	
Inventories	1,865	Current portion of long-term loans........	44
Accounts receivable, net	7,981	Short-term borrowings and other liabilities ...	972
Prepaid expenses and accrued income	4,551	Accounts payable	4,950
Other current assets	8,074	Accrued expenses	6,504
Cash	1,142	Provisions	2,718
Total current assets	23,613	Total current liabilities	15,188
Total assets	35,738	Total equity and liabilities	35,738

IFRS

Revenue and expense recognition are key to recording accounting adjustments. IFRS tends to be more *principles-based* relative to U.S. GAAP, which is viewed as more *rules-based.* A principles-based system depends heavily on control procedures to reduce the potential for fraud or misconduct. Failure in judgment led to improper accounting adjustments at **Fannie Mae**, **Xerox**, **WorldCom**, and others. A KPMG 2009 survey of accounting and finance employees found that 13% of them had witnessed falsification or manipulation of accounting data within the past year. Internal controls and governance processes are directed at curtailing such behavior. ■

Profit Margin

Decision Analysis

A useful measure of a company's operating results is the ratio of its net income to net sales. This ratio is called **profit margin,** or *return on sales,* and is computed as in Exhibit 3.15.

A2 Compute profit margin and describe its use in analyzing company performance.

EXHIBIT 3.15
Profit Margin

$$\textbf{Profit margin} = \frac{\textbf{Net income}}{\textbf{Net sales}}$$

This ratio is interpreted as reflecting the percent of profit in each dollar of sales. To illustrate how we compute and use profit margin, let's look at the results of **Limited Brands, Inc.**, in Exhibit 3.16 for its fiscal years 2006 through 2010.

EXHIBIT 3.16
Limited Brands' Profit Margin

$ in millions	2010	2009	2008	2007	2006
Net income	$ 448	$ 220	$ 718	$ 676	$ 683
Net sales	$8,632	$9,043	$10,134	$10,671	$9,699
Profit margin	5.2%	2.4%	7.1%	6.3%	7.0%
Industry profit margin	0.9%	0.3%	1.1%	1.6%	1.5%

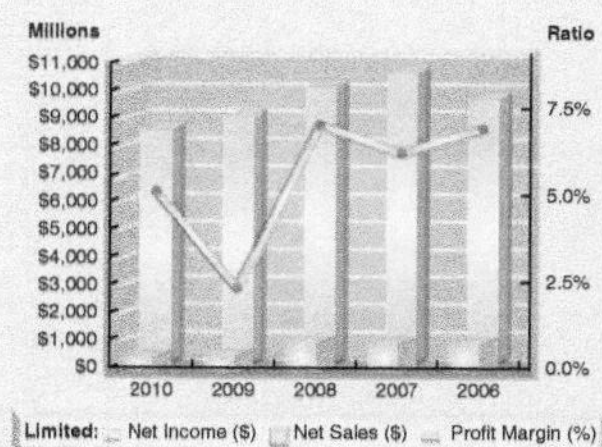

The Limited's average profit margin is 5.6% during this 5-year period. This favorably compares to the average industry profit margin of 1.1%. However, Limited's profit margin has declined in the most recent two years—from 7.1% in 2008 to 2.4% and 5.2% for the recent recessionary periods (see margin graph). Future success depends on Limited maintaining its market share and increasing its profit margin.

DEMONSTRATION PROBLEM 1

The following information relates to Fanning's Electronics on December 31, 2011. The company, which uses the calendar year as its annual reporting period, initially records prepaid and unearned items in balance sheet accounts (assets and liabilities, respectively).

a. The company's weekly payroll is $8,750, paid each Friday for a five-day workweek. Assume December 31, 2011, falls on a Monday, but the employees will not be paid their wages until Friday, January 4, 2012.

b. Eighteen months earlier, on July 1, 2010, the company purchased equipment that cost $20,000. Its useful life is predicted to be five years, at which time the equipment is expected to be worthless (zero salvage value).

c. On October 1, 2011, the company agreed to work on a new housing development. The company is paid $120,000 on October 1 in advance of future installation of similar alarm systems in 24 new homes. That amount was credited to the Unearned Services Revenue account. Between October 1 and December 31, work on 20 homes was completed.

d. On September 1, 2011, the company purchased a 12-month insurance policy for $1,800. The transaction was recorded with an $1,800 debit to Prepaid Insurance.

e. On December 29, 2011, the company completed a $7,000 service that has not been billed and not recorded as of December 31, 2011.

Required

1. Prepare any necessary adjusting entries on December 31, 2011, in relation to transactions and events *a* through *e*.
2. Prepare T-accounts for the accounts affected by adjusting entries, and post the adjusting entries. Determine the adjusted balances for the Unearned Revenue and the Prepaid Insurance accounts.
3. Complete the following table and determine the amounts and effects of your adjusting entries on the year 2011 income statement and the December 31, 2011, balance sheet. Use up (down) arrows to indicate an increase (decrease) in the Effect columns.

Entry	Amount in the Entry	Effect on Net Income	Effect on Total Assets	Effect on Total Liabilities	Effect on Total Equity

PLANNING THE SOLUTION

- Analyze each situation to determine which accounts need to be updated with an adjustment.
- Calculate the amount of each adjustment and prepare the necessary journal entries.
- Show the amount of each adjustment in the designated accounts, determine the adjusted balance, and identify the balance sheet classification of the account.
- Determine each entry's effect on net income for the year and on total assets, total liabilities, and total equity at the end of the year.

SOLUTION TO DEMONSTRATION PROBLEM 1

1. Adjusting journal entries.

(*a*) Dec. 31	Wages Expense	1,750	
	Wages Payable		1,750
	To accrue wages for the last day of the year ($8,750 × 1/5).		
(*b*) Dec. 31	Depreciation Expense—Equipment	4,000	
	Accumulated Depreciation—Equipment		4,000
	To record depreciation expense for the year ($20,000/5 years = $4,000 per year).		
(*c*) Dec. 31	Unearned Services Revenue	100,000	
	Services Revenue		100,000
	To recognize services revenue earned ($120,000 × 20/24).		
(*d*) Dec. 31	Insurance Expense	600	
	Prepaid Insurance		600
	To adjust for expired portion of insurance ($1,800 × 4/12).		
(*e*) Dec. 31	Accounts Receivable	7,000	
	Services Revenue		7,000
	To record services revenue earned.		

2. T-accounts for adjusting journal entries *a* through *e*.

Wages Expense			
(a)	1,750		

Wages Payable			
		(a)	1,750

Depreciation Expense—Equipment			
(b)	4,000		

Accumulated Depreciation—Equipment			
		(b)	4,000

Unearned Revenue			
		Unadj. Bal.	120,000
(c)	100,000		
		Adj. Bal.	20,000

Services Revenue			
		(c)	100,000
		(e)	7,000
		Adj. Bal.	107,000

Insurance Expense			
(d)	600		

Prepaid Insurance			
Unadj. Bal.	1,800		
		(d)	600
Adj. Bal.	1,200		

Accounts Receivable			
(e)	7,000		

3. Financial statement effects of adjusting journal entries.

Entry	Amount in the Entry	Effect on Net Income	Effect on Total Assets	Effect on Total Liabilities	Effect on Total Equity
a	$ 1,750	$ 1,750 ↓	No effect	$ 1,750 ↑	$ 1,750 ↓
b	4,000	4,000 ↓	$4,000 ↓	No effect	4,000 ↓
c	100,000	100,000 ↑	No effect	$100,000 ↓	100,000 ↑
d	600	600 ↓	$ 600 ↓	No effect	600 ↓
e	7,000	7,000 ↑	$7,000 ↑	No effect	7,000 ↑

DEMONSTRATION PROBLEM 2

Use the following adjusted trial balance to answer questions 1–3.

CHOI COMPANY
Adjusted Trial Balance
December 31

	Debit	Credit
Cash	$ 3,050	
Accounts receivable	400	
Prepaid insurance	830	
Supplies	80	
Equipment	217,200	
Accumulated depreciation—Equipment		$ 29,100
Wages payable		880

[continued on next page]

[continued from previous page]

Interest payable		3,600
Unearned rent		460
Long-term notes payable		150,000
M. Choi, Capital		40,340
M. Choi, Withdrawals	21,000	
Rent earned		57,500
Wages expense	25,000	
Utilities expense	1,900	
Insurance expense	3,200	
Supplies expense	250	
Depreciation expense—Equipment	5,970	
Interest expense	3,000	
Totals	$281,880	$281,880

1. Prepare the annual income statement from the adjusted trial balance of Choi Company.

Answer:

CHOI COMPANY
Income Statement
For Year Ended December 31

Revenues		
Rent earned		$57,500
Expenses		
Wages expense	$25,000	
Utilities expense	1,900	
Insurance expense	3,200	
Supplies expense	250	
Depreciation expense—Equipment	5,970	
Interest expense	3,000	
Total expenses		39,320
Net income		$18,180

2. Prepare a statement of owner's equity from the adjusted trial balance of Choi Company. Choi's capital account balance of $40,340 consists of a $30,340 balance from the prior year-end, plus a $10,000 owner investment during the current year.

Answer:

CHOI COMPANY
Statement of Owner's Equity
For Year Ended December 31

M. Choi, Capital, December 31 prior year-end		$30,340
Plus: Owner investments	$10,000	
Net income	18,180	28,180
		58,520
Less: Withdrawals by owner		21,000
M. Choi, Capital, December 31 current year-end		$37,520

3. Prepare a balance sheet from the adjusted trial balance of Choi Company.

Answer:

CHOI COMPANY Balance Sheet December 31		
Assets		
Cash		$ 3,050
Accounts receivable		400
Prepaid insurance		830
Supplies		80
Equipment	$217,200	
Less accumulated depreciation	29,100	188,100
Total assets		$192,460
Liabilities		
Wages payable		$ 880
Interest payable		3,600
Unearned rent		460
Long-term notes payable		150,000
Total liabilities		154,940
Equity		
M. Choi, Capital		37,520
Total liabilities and equity		$192,460

APPENDIX

Alternative Accounting for Prepayments 3A

This appendix explains an alternative in accounting for prepaid expenses and unearned revenues.

P4 Explain the alternatives in accounting for prepaids.

Recording Prepayment of Expenses in Expense Accounts An alternative method is to record *all* prepaid expenses with debits to expense accounts. If any prepaids remain unused or unexpired at the end of an accounting period, then adjusting entries must transfer the cost of the unused portions from expense accounts to prepaid expense (asset) accounts. This alternative method is acceptable. The financial statements are identical under either method, but the adjusting entries are different. To illustrate the differences between these two methods, let's look at FastForward's cash payment of December 6 for 24 months of insurance coverage beginning on December 1. FastForward recorded that payment with a debit to an asset account, but it could have recorded a debit to an expense account. These alternatives are shown in Exhibit 3A.1.

EXHIBIT 3A.1

Alternative Initial Entries for Prepaid Expenses

		Payment Recorded as Asset		Payment Recorded as Expense	
Dec. 6	Prepaid Insurance	2,400			
	Cash		2,400		
Dec. 6	Insurance Expense			2,400	
	Cash				2,400

At the end of its accounting period on December 31, insurance protection for one month has expired. This means $100 ($2,400/24) of insurance coverage expired and is an expense for December. The adjusting entry depends on how the original payment was recorded. This is shown in Exhibit 3A.2.

EXHIBIT 3A.2

Adjusting Entry for Prepaid Expenses for the Two Alternatives

		Payment Recorded as Asset		Payment Recorded as Expense	
Dec. 31	Insurance Expense	100			
	Prepaid Insurance		100		
Dec. 31	Prepaid Insurance			2,300	
	Insurance Expense				2,300

When these entries are posted to the accounts in the ledger, we can see that these two methods give identical results. The December 31 adjusted account balances in Exhibit 3A.3 show Prepaid Insurance of $2,300 and Insurance Expense of $100 for both methods.

EXHIBIT 3A.3

Account Balances under Two Alternatives for Recording Prepaid Expenses

Payment Recorded as Asset

Prepaid Insurance			128
Dec. 6	2,400	Dec. 31	100
Balance	2,300		

Insurance Expense			637
Dec. 31	100		

Payment Recorded as Expense

Prepaid Insurance			128
Dec. 31	2,300		

Insurance Expense			637
Dec. 6	2,400	Dec. 31	2,300
Balance	100		

Recording Prepayment of Revenues in Revenue Accounts As with prepaid expenses, an alternative method is to record *all* unearned revenues with credits to revenue accounts. If any revenues are unearned at the end of an accounting period, then adjusting entries must transfer the unearned portions from revenue accounts to unearned revenue (liability) accounts. This alternative method is acceptable. The adjusting entries are different for these two alternatives, but the financial statements are identical. To illustrate the accounting differences between these two methods, let's look at FastForward's December 26 receipt of $3,000 for consulting services covering the period December 27 to February 24. FastForward recorded this transaction with a credit to a liability account. The alternative is to record it with a credit to a revenue account, as shown in Exhibit 3A.4.

EXHIBIT 3A.4

Alternative Initial Entries for Unearned Revenues

		Receipt Recorded as Liability		Receipt Recorded as Revenue	
Dec. 26	Cash	3,000			
	Unearned Consulting Revenue		3,000		
Dec. 26	Cash			3,000	
	Consulting Revenue				3,000

By the end of its accounting period on December 31, FastForward has earned $250 of this revenue. This means $250 of the liability has been satisfied. Depending on how the initial receipt is recorded, the adjusting entry is as shown in Exhibit 3A.5.

EXHIBIT 3A.5

Adjusting Entry for Unearned Revenues for the Two Alternatives

		Receipt Recorded as Liability		Receipt Recorded as Revenue	
Dec. 31	Unearned Consulting Revenue	250			
	Consulting Revenue		250		
Dec. 31	Consulting Revenue			2,750	
	Unearned Consulting Revenue				2,750

After adjusting entries are posted, the two alternatives give identical results. The December 31 adjusted account balances in Exhibit 3A.6 show unearned consulting revenue of $2,750 and consulting revenue of $250 for both methods.

EXHIBIT 3A.6

Account Balances under Two Alternatives for Recording Unearned Revenues

Receipt Recorded as Liability

Unearned Consulting Revenue			236
Dec. 31	250	Dec. 26	3,000
		Balance	2,750

Consulting Revenue			403
		Dec. 31	250

Receipt Recorded as Revenue

Unearned Consulting Revenue			236
		Dec. 31	2,750

Consulting Revenue			403
Dec. 31	2,750	Dec. 26	3,000
		Balance	250

Summary

C1 Explain the importance of periodic reporting and the time period assumption. The value of information is often linked to its timeliness. To provide timely information, accounting systems prepare periodic reports at regular intervals. The time period assumption presumes that an organization's activities can be divided into specific time periods for periodic reporting.

C2 Explain accrual accounting and how it improves financial statements. Accrual accounting recognizes revenue when earned and expenses when incurred—not necessarily when cash inflows and outflows occur. This information is valuable in assessing a company's financial position and performance.

C3 Identify the types of adjustments and their purpose. Adjustments can be grouped according to the timing of cash receipts and cash payments relative to when they are recognized as revenues or expenses as follows: prepaid expenses, unearned revenues, accrued expenses, and accrued revenues. Adjusting entries are necessary so that revenues, expenses, assets, and liabilities are correctly reported.

A1 Explain how accounting adjustments link to financial statements. Accounting adjustments bring an asset or liability account balance to its correct amount. They also update related expense or revenue accounts. Every adjusting entry affects one or more income statement accounts *and* one or more balance sheet accounts. An adjusting entry never affects cash.

A2 Compute profit margin and describe its use in analyzing company performance. *Profit margin* is defined as the reporting period's net income divided by its net sales. Profit margin reflects on a company's earnings activities by showing how much income is in each dollar of sales.

P1 Prepare and explain adjusting entries. *Prepaid expenses* refer to items paid for in advance of receiving their benefits. Prepaid expenses are assets. Adjusting entries for prepaids involve increasing (debiting) expenses and decreasing (crediting) assets. *Unearned* (or *prepaid*) *revenues* refer to cash received in advance of providing products and services. Unearned revenues are liabilities. Adjusting entries for unearned revenues involve increasing (crediting) revenues and decreasing (debiting) unearned revenues. *Accrued expenses* refer to costs incurred in a period that are both unpaid and unrecorded. Adjusting entries for recording accrued expenses involve increasing (debiting) expenses and increasing (crediting) liabilities. *Accrued revenues* refer to revenues earned in a period that are both unrecorded and not yet received in cash. Adjusting entries for recording accrued revenues involve increasing (debiting) assets and increasing (crediting) revenues.

P2 Explain and prepare an adjusted trial balance. An adjusted trial balance is a list of accounts and balances prepared after recording and posting adjusting entries. Financial statements are often prepared from the adjusted trial balance.

P3 Prepare financial statements from an adjusted trial balance. Revenue and expense balances are reported on the income statement. Asset, liability, and equity balances are reported on the balance sheet. We usually prepare statements in the following order: income statement, statement of owner's equity, balance sheet, and statement of cash flows.

P4A Explain the alternatives in accounting for prepaids. Charging all prepaid expenses to expense accounts when they are purchased is acceptable. When this is done, adjusting entries must transfer any unexpired amounts from expense accounts to asset accounts. Crediting all unearned revenues to revenue accounts when cash is received is also acceptable. In this case, the adjusting entries must transfer any unearned amounts from revenue accounts to unearned revenue accounts.

Guidance Answers to Decision Maker and Decision Ethics

Investor Prepaid expenses are items paid for in advance of receiving their benefits. They are assets and are expensed as they are used up. The publishing company's treatment of the signing bonus is acceptable provided future book sales can at least match the $500,000 expense. As an investor, you are concerned about the risk of future book sales. The riskier the likelihood of future book sales is, the more likely your analysis is to treat the $500,000, or a portion of it, as an expense, not a prepaid expense (asset).

Entrepreneur Depreciation is a process of cost allocation, not asset valuation. Knowing the depreciation schedule is not especially useful in your estimation of what the building and equipment are currently worth. Your own assessment of the age, quality, and usefulness of the building and equipment is more important.

Loan Officer Your concern in lending to this store arises from analysis of current-year sales. While increased revenues and income are fine, your concern is with collectibility of these promotional sales. If the owner sold products to customers with poor records of paying bills, then collectibility of these sales is low. Your analysis must assess this possibility and recognize any expected losses.

Financial Officer Omitting accrued expenses and recognizing revenue early can mislead financial statement users. One action is to request a second meeting with the president so you can explain that accruing expenses when incurred and recognizing revenue when earned are required practices. If the president persists, you might discuss the situation with legal counsel and any auditors involved. Your ethical action might cost you this job, but the potential pitfalls for falsification of statements, reputation and personal integrity loss, and other costs are too great.

Guidance Answers to Quick Checks

1. An annual reporting (or accounting) period covers one year and refers to the preparation of annual financial statements. The annual reporting period is not always a calendar year that ends on December 31. An organization can adopt a fiscal year consisting of any consecutive 12 months or 52 weeks.
2. Interim financial statements (covering less than one year) are prepared to provide timely information to decision makers.
3. The revenue recognition principle and the matching principle lead most directly to the adjusting process.
4. No. Cash basis accounting is not consistent with the matching principle because it reports revenue when received, not necessarily when earned, and expenses when paid, not necessarily in the period when the expenses were incurred as a result of the revenues earned.
5. No expense is reported in 2012. Under cash basis accounting, the entire $4,800 is reported as an expense in April 2011 when the premium is paid.
6. If the accrued revenues adjustment of $200 is not made, then both revenues and net income are understated by $200 on the current year's income statement, and both assets and equity are understated by $200 on the balance sheet.
7. A contra account is an account that is subtracted from the balance of a related account. Use of a contra account provides more information than simply reporting a net amount.
8. An accrued expense is a cost incurred in a period that is both unpaid and unrecorded prior to adjusting entries. One example is salaries earned but not yet paid at period-end.
9. An unearned revenue arises when a firm receives cash (or other assets) from a customer before providing the services or products to the customer. A magazine subscription paid in advance is one example; season ticket sales is another.
10.

Salaries Payable	1,000	
Salaries Expense	6,000	
Cash		7,000
Paid salary including accrual from December.		

11. The probable adjusting entries of Jordan Air are:

Insurance Expense	300	
Prepaid Insurance		300
To record insurance expired.		
Salaries Expense	1,400	
Salaries Payable		1,400
To record accrued salaries.		

12. Revenue accounts and expense accounts.
13. Statement of owner's equity.

Key Terms

mhhe.com/wildFAP20e

Accounting period (p. 94)
Accrual basis accounting (p. 95)
Accrued expenses (p. 101)
Accrued revenues (p. 103)
Adjusted trial balance (p. 106)
Adjusting entry (p. 96)
Annual financial statements (p. 94)
Book value (p. 100)
Cash basis accounting (p. 95)
Contra account (p. 99)
Depreciation (p. 99)
Expense recognition (or **matching**) **principle** (p. 96)
Fiscal year (p. 95)
Interim financial statements (p. 94)
Natural business year (p. 95)
Plant assets (p. 99)
Prepaid expenses (p. 97)
Profit margin (p. 109)
Straight-line depreciation method (p. 99)
Time period assumption (p. 94)
Unadjusted trial balance (p. 106)
Unearned revenues (p. 100)

Multiple Choice Quiz

Answers on p. 135 mhhe.com/wildFAP20e

Additional Quiz Questions are available at the book's Website.

1. A company forgot to record accrued and unpaid employee wages of $350,000 at period-end. This oversight would
   a. Understate net income by $350,000.
   b. Overstate net income by $350,000.
   c. Have no effect on net income.
   d. Overstate assets by $350,000.
   e. Understate assets by $350,000.
2. Prior to recording adjusting entries, the Supplies account has a $450 debit balance. A physical count of supplies shows $125 of unused supplies still available. The required adjusting entry is:
   a. Debit Supplies $125; Credit Supplies Expense $125.
   b. Debit Supplies $325; Credit Supplies Expense $325.
   c. Debit Supplies Expense $325; Credit Supplies $325.
   d. Debit Supplies Expense $325; Credit Supplies $125.
   e. Debit Supplies Expense $125; Credit Supplies $125.
3. On May 1, 2011, a two-year insurance policy was purchased for $24,000 with coverage to begin immediately. What is the amount of insurance expense that appears on the company's income statement for the year ended December 31, 2011?
   a. $4,000
   b. $8,000
   c. $12,000
   d. $20,000
   e. $24,000
4. On November 1, 2011, Stockton Co. receives $3,600 cash from Hans Co. for consulting services to be provided evenly over the period November 1, 2011, to April 30, 2012—at which time Stockton credited $3,600 to Unearned Consulting Fees. The adjusting entry on December 31, 2011 (Stockton's year-end) would include a
   a. Debit to Unearned Consulting Fees for $1,200.
   b. Debit to Unearned Consulting Fees for $2,400.
   c. Credit to Consulting Fees Earned for $2,400.
   d. Debit to Consulting Fees Earned for $1,200.
   e. Credit to Cash for $3,600.
5. If a company had $15,000 in net income for the year, and its sales were $300,000 for the same year, what is its profit margin?
   a. 20%
   b. 2,000%
   c. $285,000
   d. $315,000
   e. 5%

A Superscript letter A denotes assignments based on Appendix 3A.
Icon denotes assignments that involve decision making.

Discussion Questions

1. What is the difference between the cash basis and the accrual basis of accounting?
2. Why is the accrual basis of accounting generally preferred over the cash basis?
3. What type of business is most likely to select a fiscal year that corresponds to its natural business year instead of the calendar year?
4. What is a prepaid expense and where is it reported in the financial statements?
5. What type of assets require adjusting entries to record depreciation?
6. What contra account is used when recording and reporting the effects of depreciation? Why is it used?
7. Apple has unearned revenue. What is unearned revenue and where is it reported in financial statements? Apple
8. What is an accrued revenue? Give an example.
9. [A] If a company initially records prepaid expenses with debits to expense accounts, what type of account is debited in the adjusting entries for those prepaid expenses?
10. Review the balance sheet of Research In Motion in Appendix A. Identify one asset account that requires adjustment before annual financial statements can be prepared. What would be the effect on the income statement if this asset account were not adjusted? RIM
11. Review the balance sheet of Nokia in Appendix A. Identify the amount for property, plant, and equipment. What adjusting entry is necessary (no numbers required) for this account when preparing financial statements? NOKIA
12. Refer to Palm's balance sheet in Appendix A. If it made an adjustment for unpaid wages at year-end, where would the accrued wages be reported on its balance sheet? Palm

connect

QUICK STUDY

QS 3-1
Identifying accounting adjustments
P1

Classify the following adjusting entries as involving prepaid expenses (PE), unearned revenues (UR), accrued expenses (AE), or accrued revenues (AR).

a. ______ To record revenue earned that was previously received as cash in advance.
b. ______ To record annual depreciation expense.
c. ______ To record wages expense incurred but not yet paid (nor recorded).
d. ______ To record revenue earned but not yet billed (nor recorded).
e. ______ To record expiration of prepaid insurance.

QS 3-2
Adjusting prepaid expenses
P1

a. On July 1, 2011, Baxter Company paid $1,800 for six months of insurance coverage. No adjustments have been made to the Prepaid Insurance account, and it is now December 31, 2011. Prepare the journal entry to reflect expiration of the insurance as of December 31, 2011.

b. Tyrell Company has a Supplies account balance of $1,000 on January 1, 2011. During 2011, it purchased $3,000 of supplies. As of December 31, 2011, a supplies inventory shows $1,300 of supplies available. Prepare the adjusting journal entry to correctly report the balance of the Supplies account and the Supplies Expense account as of December 31, 2011.

QS 3-3
Adjusting for depreciation
P1

a. Carlos Company purchases $30,000 of equipment on January 1, 2011. The equipment is expected to last five years and be worth $5,000 at the end of that time. Prepare the entry to record one year's depreciation expense of $5,000 for the equipment as of December 31, 2011.

b. Chaves Company purchases $40,000 of land on January 1, 2011. The land is expected to last indefinitely. What depreciation adjustment, if any, should be made with respect to the Land account as of December 31, 2011?

QS 3-4
Adjusting for unearned revenues
A1 P1 

a. Eager Co. receives $20,000 cash in advance for 4 months of legal services on October 1, 2011, and records it by debiting Cash and crediting Unearned Revenue both for $20,000. It is now December 31, 2011, and Eager has provided legal services as planned. What adjusting entry should Eager make to account for the work performed from October 1 through December 31, 2011?

b. Rutherford Co. started a new publication called *Contest News*. Its subscribers pay $48 to receive 12 issues. With every new subscriber, Rutherford debits Cash and credits Unearned Subscription Revenue for the amounts received. The company has 100 new subscribers as of July 1, 2011. It sends *Contest News* to each of these subscribers every month from July through December. Assuming no changes in subscribers, prepare the journal entry that Rutherford must make as of December 31, 2011, to adjust the Subscription Revenue account and the Unearned Subscription Revenue account.

QS 3-5
Accruing salaries
A1 P1

Marsha Moder employs one college student every summer in her coffee shop. The student works the five weekdays and is paid on the following Monday. (For example, a student who works Monday through Friday, June 1 through June 5, is paid for that work on Monday, June 8.) Moder adjusts her books monthly, if needed, to show salaries earned but unpaid at month-end. The student works the last week of July—Friday is August 1. If the student earns $100 per day, what adjusting entry must Moder make on July 31 to correctly record accrued salaries expense for July?

QS 3-6
Recording and analyzing adjusting entries
A1

Adjusting entries affect at least one balance sheet account and at least one income statement account. For the following entries, identify the account to be debited and the account to be credited. Indicate which of the accounts is the income statement account and which is the balance sheet account.

a. Entry to record revenue earned that was previously received as cash in advance.
b. Entry to record annual depreciation expense.
c. Entry to record wage expenses incurred but not yet paid (nor recorded).
d. Entry to record revenue earned but not yet billed (nor recorded).
e. Entry to record expiration of prepaid insurance.

QS 3-7
Computing accrual and cash income
P1 C2 

In its first year of operations, Harden Co. earned $39,000 in revenues and received $33,000 cash from these customers. The company incurred expenses of $22,500 but had not paid $2,250 of them at year-end. The company also prepaid $3,750 cash for expenses that would be incurred the next year. Calculate the first year's net income under both the cash basis and the accrual basis of accounting.

The following information is taken from Cruz Company's unadjusted and adjusted trial balances.

QS 3-8
Interpreting adjusting entries
C2 P2

	Unadjusted		Adjusted	
	Debit	Credit	Debit	Credit
Prepaid insurance.	$4,100		$3,700	
Interest payable		$ 0		$800

Given this information, which of the following is likely included among its adjusting entries?

a. A $400 credit to Prepaid Insurance and an $800 debit to Interest Payable.
b. A $400 debit to Insurance Expense and an $800 debit to Interest Payable.
c. A $400 debit to Insurance Expense and an $800 debit to Interest Expense.

In making adjusting entries at the end of its accounting period, Gomez Consulting failed to record $1,600 of insurance coverage that had expired. This $1,600 cost had been initially debited to the Prepaid Insurance account. The company also failed to record accrued salaries expense of $1,000. As a result of these two oversights, the financial statements for the reporting period will [choose one] (1) understate assets by $1,600; (2) understate expenses by $2,600; (3) understate net income by $1,000; or (4) overstate liabilities by $1,000.

QS 3-9
Determining effects of adjusting entries
C3 A1 

During the year, Lyle Co. recorded prepayments of expenses in asset accounts, and cash receipts of unearned revenues in liability accounts. At the end of its annual accounting period, the company must make three adjusting entries: (1) accrue salaries expense, (2) adjust the Unearned Services Revenue account to recognize earned revenue, and (3) record services revenue earned for which cash will be received the following period. For each of these adjusting entries (1), (2), and (3), indicate the account from *a* through *i* to be debited and the account to be credited.

QS 3-10
Preparing adjusting entries
C3 P1

a. Prepaid Salaries	**d.** Salaries Payable	**g.** Unearned Services Revenue
b. Salaries Expense	**e.** Equipment	**h.** Accounts Receivable
c. Services Revenue	**f.** Cash	**i.** Accounts Payable

Yang Company reported net income of $37,925 and net sales of $390,000 for the current year. Calculate the company's profit margin and interpret the result. Assume that its competitors earn an average profit margin of 15%.

QS 3-11
Analyzing profit margin
A2

Diego Consulting initially records prepaid and unearned items in income statement accounts. Given this company's accounting practices, which of the following applies to the preparation of adjusting entries at the end of its first accounting period?

QS 3-12[A]
Preparing adjusting entries
C3 P4

a. Earned but unbilled (and unrecorded) consulting fees are recorded with a debit to Unearned Consulting Fees and a credit to Consulting Fees Earned.
b. Unpaid salaries are recorded with a debit to Prepaid Salaries and a credit to Salaries Expense.
c. The cost of unused office supplies is recorded with a debit to Supplies Expense and a credit to Office Supplies.
d. Unearned fees (on which cash was received in advance earlier in the period) are recorded with a debit to Consulting Fees Earned and a credit to Unearned Consulting Fees.

Answer each of the following questions related to international accounting standards.

QS 3-13
International accounting standards
P3  

a. Do financial statements prepared under IFRS normally present assets from least liquid to most liquid or vice-versa?
b. Do financial statements prepared under IFRS normally present liabilities from furthest from maturity to nearest to maturity or vice-versa?

connect

EXERCISES

Exercise 3-1
Classifying adjusting entries
C3

In the blank space beside each adjusting entry, enter the letter of the explanation *A* through *F* that most closely describes the entry.

A. To record this period's depreciation expense.
B. To record accrued salaries expense.
C. To record this period's use of a prepaid expense.
D. To record accrued interest revenue.
E. To record accrued interest expense.
F. To record the earning of previously unearned income.

		Account	Debit	Credit
_____	1.	Salaries Expense	13,280	
		Salaries Payable		13,280
_____	2.	Interest Expense	2,208	
		Interest Payable		2,208
_____	3.	Insurance Expense	3,180	
		Prepaid Insurance		3,180
_____	4.	Unearned Professional Fees	19,250	
		Professional Fees Earned		19,250
_____	5.	Interest Receivable	3,300	
		Interest Revenue		3,300
_____	6.	Depreciation Expense	38,217	
		Accumulated Depreciation		38,217

Exercise 3-2
Preparing adjusting entries
P1

For each of the following separate cases, prepare adjusting entries required of financial statements for the year ended (date of) December 31, 2011. (Assume that prepaid expenses are initially recorded in asset accounts and that fees collected in advance of work are initially recorded as liabilities.)

a. One-third of the work related to $30,000 cash received in advance is performed this period.
b. Wages of $9,000 are earned by workers but not paid as of December 31, 2011.
c. Depreciation on the company's equipment for 2011 is $19,127.
d. The Office Supplies account had a $480 debit balance on December 31, 2010. During 2011, $5,349 of office supplies are purchased. A physical count of supplies at December 31, 2011, shows $587 of supplies available.
e. The Prepaid Insurance account had a $5,000 balance on December 31, 2010. An analysis of insurance policies shows that $2,200 of unexpired insurance benefits remain at December 31, 2011.
f. The company has earned (but not recorded) $750 of interest from investments in CDs for the year ended December 31, 2011. The interest revenue will be received on January 10, 2012.
g. The company has a bank loan and has incurred (but not recorded) interest expense of $3,500 for the year ended December 31, 2011. The company must pay the interest on January 2, 2012.

Check (*e*) Dr. Insurance Expense, $2,800; (*f*) Cr. Interest Revenue, $750

Exercise 3-3
Preparing adjusting entries
P1

Prepare adjusting journal entries for the year ended (date of) December 31, 2011, for each of these separate situations. Assume that prepaid expenses are initially recorded in asset accounts. Also assume that fees collected in advance of work are initially recorded as liabilities.

a. Depreciation on the company's equipment for 2011 is computed to be $16,000.
b. The Prepaid Insurance account had a $7,000 debit balance at December 31, 2011, before adjusting for the costs of any expired coverage. An analysis of the company's insurance policies showed that $1,040 of unexpired insurance coverage remains.
c. The Office Supplies account had a $300 debit balance on December 31, 2010; and $2,680 of office supplies were purchased during the year. The December 31, 2011, physical count showed $354 of supplies available.
d. One-half of the work related to $10,000 of cash received in advance was performed this period.
e. The Prepaid Insurance account had a $5,600 debit balance at December 31, 2011, before adjusting for the costs of any expired coverage. An analysis of insurance policies showed that $4,600 of coverage had expired.
f. Wage expenses of $4,000 have been incurred but are not paid as of December 31, 2011.

Check (*c*) Dr. Office Supplies Expense, $2,626; (*e*) Dr. Insurance Expense, $4,600

Exercise 3-4
Adjusting and paying accrued expenses
A1 P1

The following three separate situations require adjusting journal entries to prepare financial statements as of April 30. For each situation, present both the April 30 adjusting entry and the subsequent entry during May to record the payment of the accrued expenses.

a. On April 1, the company retained an attorney for a flat monthly fee of $2,500. This amount is paid to the attorney on the 12th day of the following month in which it was earned.

b. A $780,000 note payable requires 9.6% annual interest, or $6,240 to be paid at the 20th day of each month. The interest was last paid on April 20 and the next payment is due on May 20. As of April 30, $2,080 of interest expense has accrued.

c. Total weekly salaries expense for all employees is $9,000. This amount is paid at the end of the day on Friday of each five-day workweek. April 30 falls on Tuesday of this year, which means that the employees had worked two days since the last payday. The next payday is May 3.

Check (*b*) May 20 Dr. Interest Expense, $4,160

Exercise 3-5
Determining cost flows through accounts
C1 A1 P1

Determine the missing amounts in each of these four separate situations *a* through *d*.

	a	b	c	d
Supplies available—prior year-end	$ 300	$1,600	$1,360	?
Supplies purchased during the current year	2,100	5,400	?	$6,000
Supplies available—current year-end	750	?	1,840	800
Supplies expense for the current year	?	1,300	9,600	6,575

Exercise 3-6
Adjusting and paying accrued wages
C1 P1

Pablo Management has five part-time employees, each of whom earns $100 per day. They are normally paid on Fridays for work completed Monday through Friday of the same week. They were paid in full on Friday, December 28, 2011. The next week, the five employees worked only four days because New Year's Day was an unpaid holiday. Show (*a*) the adjusting entry that would be recorded on Monday, December 31, 2011, and (*b*) the journal entry that would be made to record payment of the employees' wages on Friday, January 4, 2012.

Exercise 3-7
Analyzing and preparing adjusting entries
A1 P1 P3 

Following are two income statements for Kendall Co. for the year ended December 31. The left column is prepared before any adjusting entries are recorded, and the right column includes the effects of adjusting entries. The company records cash receipts and payments related to unearned and prepaid items in balance sheet accounts. Analyze the statements and prepare the eight adjusting entries that likely were recorded. (*Note:* 30% of the $6,000 adjustment for Fees Earned has been earned but not billed, and the other 70% has been earned by performing services that were paid for in advance.)

KENDALL CO.
Income Statements
For Year Ended December 31

	Unadjusted	Adjusted
Revenues		
Fees earned	$24,000	$30,000
Commissions earned	42,500	42,500
Total revenues	66,500	72,500
Expenses		
Depreciation expense—Computers	0	1,500
Depreciation expense—Office furniture	0	1,750
Salaries expense	12,500	14,950
Insurance expense	0	1,300
Rent expense	4,500	4,500
Office supplies expense	0	480
Advertising expense	3,000	3,000
Utilities expense	1,250	1,320
Total expenses	21,250	28,800
Net income	$45,250	$43,700

Exercise 3-8
Determining assets and expenses for accrual and cash accounting
C2

On March 1, 2009, a company paid a $16,200 premium on a 36-month insurance policy for coverage beginning on that date. Refer to that policy and fill in the blanks in the following table.

Balance Sheet Prepaid Insurance Asset Using			Insurance Expense Using		
	Accrual Basis	Cash Basis		Accrual Basis	Cash Basis
Dec. 31, 2009	$_____	$_____	2009	$_____	$_____
Dec. 31, 2010	_____	_____	2010	_____	_____
Dec. 31, 2011	_____	_____	2011	_____	_____
Dec. 31, 2012	_____	_____	2012	_____	_____
			Total	$_____	$_____

Check 2011 insurance expense: Accrual, $5,400; Cash, $0. Dec. 31, 2011, asset: Accrual, $900; Cash, $0.

Exercise 3-9
Computing and interpreting profit margin
A2 

Use the following information to compute profit margin for each separate company *a* through *e*.

	Net Income	Net Sales		Net Income	Net Sales
a.	$ 5,390	$ 44,830	**d.**	$55,234	$1,458,999
b.	87,644	398,954	**e.**	70,158	435,925
c.	93,385	257,082			

Which of the five companies is the most profitable according to the profit margin ratio? Interpret that company's profit margin ratio.

Exercise 3-10^A
Recording and reporting revenues received in advance
P4

Corbel Company experienced the following events and transactions during July.

July 1 Received $2,000 cash in advance of performing work for Beth Oker.
6 Received $8,400 cash in advance of performing work for Lisa Poe.
12 Completed the job for Oker.
18 Received $7,500 cash in advance of performing work for Henry Coe.
27 Completed the job for Poe.
31 None of the work for Coe has been performed.

a. Prepare journal entries (including any adjusting entries as of the end of the month) to record these events using the procedure of initially crediting the Unearned Fees account when payment is received from a customer in advance of performing services.

b. Prepare journal entries (including any adjusting entries as of the end of the month) to record these events using the procedure of initially crediting the Fees Earned account when payment is received from a customer in advance of performing services.

c. Under each method, determine the amount of earned fees reported on the income statement for July and the amount of unearned fees reported on the balance sheet as of July 31.

Check (*c*) Fees Earned—using entries from part *b*, $10,400

Exercise 3-11^A
Adjusting for prepaids recorded as expenses and unearned revenues recorded as revenues
P4

On-The-Mark Construction began operations on December 1. In setting up its accounting procedures, the company decided to debit expense accounts when it prepays its expenses and to credit revenue accounts when customers pay for services in advance. Prepare journal entries for items *a* through *d* and the adjusting entries as of its December 31 period-end for items *e* through *g*.

a. Supplies are purchased on December 1 for $3,000 cash.

b. The company prepaid its insurance premiums for $1,440 cash on December 2.

c. On December 15, the company receives an advance payment of $12,000 cash from a customer for remodeling work.

d. On December 28, the company receives $3,600 cash from another customer for remodeling work to be performed in January.

e. A physical count on December 31 indicates that On-The-Mark has $1,920 of supplies available.

f. An analysis of the insurance policies in effect on December 31 shows that $240 of insurance coverage had expired.

g. As of December 31, only one remodeling project has been worked on and completed. The $6,300 fee for this project had been received in advance.

Check (*f*) Cr. Insurance Expense, $1,200; (*g*) Dr. Remodeling Fees Earned, $9,300

Exercise 3-12
Preparing a balance sheet following IFRS
P3

adidas AG reports the following balance sheet accounts for the year ended December 31, 2009 (euros in millions). Prepare the balance sheet for this company as of December 31, 2009, following usual IFRS practices.

Tangible and other assets	€1,410	Intangible assets	€2,980
Total equity	3,776	Total current liabilities	2,836
Receivables and financial assets	1,753	Inventories	1,471
Total noncurrent liabilities	2,263	Total liabilities	5,099
Cash and cash equivalents	775	Other current assets	486
Total current assets	4,485	Total noncurrent assets	4,390

connect

PROBLEM SET A

Problem 3-1A
Preparing adjusting and subsequent journal entries
C1 A1 P1

Meyer Co. follows the practice of recording prepaid expenses and unearned revenues in balance sheet accounts. The company's annual accounting period ends on December 31, 2011. The following information concerns the adjusting entries to be recorded as of that date.

a. The Office Supplies account started the year with a $3,000 balance. During 2011, the company purchased supplies for $12,400, which was added to the Office Supplies account. The inventory of supplies available at December 31, 2011, totaled $2,640.

b. An analysis of the company's insurance policies provided the following facts.

Policy	Date of Purchase	Months of Coverage	Cost
A	April 1, 2010	24	$15,840
B	April 1, 2011	36	13,068
C	August 1, 2011	12	2,700

The total premium for each policy was paid in full (for all months) at the purchase date, and the Prepaid Insurance account was debited for the full cost. (Year-end adjusting entries for Prepaid Insurance were properly recorded in all prior years.)

c. The company has 15 employees, who earn a total of $2,100 in salaries each working day. They are paid each Monday for their work in the five-day workweek ending on the previous Friday. Assume that December 31, 2011, is a Tuesday, and all 15 employees worked the first two days of that week. Because New Year's Day is a paid holiday, they will be paid salaries for five full days on Monday, January 6, 2012.

d. The company purchased a building on January 1, 2011. It cost $855,000 and is expected to have a $45,000 salvage value at the end of its predicted 30-year life. Annual depreciation is $27,000.

e. Since the company is not large enough to occupy the entire building it owns, it rented space to a tenant at $2,400 per month, starting on November 1, 2011. The rent was paid on time on November 1, and the amount received was credited to the Rent Earned account. However, the tenant has not paid the December rent. The company has worked out an agreement with the tenant, who has promised to pay both December and January rent in full on January 15. The tenant has agreed not to fall behind again.

f. On November 1, the company rented space to another tenant for $2,175 per month. The tenant paid five months' rent in advance on that date. The payment was recorded with a credit to the Unearned Rent account.

Check (1*b*) Dr. Insurance Expense, $12,312 (1*d*) Dr. Depreciation Expense, $27,000

Required

1. Use the information to prepare adjusting entries as of December 31, 2011.
2. Prepare journal entries to record the first subsequent cash transaction in 2012 for parts *c* and *e*.

Problem 3-2A
Identifying adjusting entries with explanations
C3 P1

For each of the following entries, enter the letter of the explanation that most closely describes it in the space beside each entry. (You can use letters more than once.)

A. To record receipt of unearned revenue.
B. To record this period's earning of prior unearned revenue.
C. To record payment of an accrued expense.
D. To record receipt of an accrued revenue.
E. To record an accrued expense.
F. To record an accrued revenue.
G. To record this period's use of a prepaid expense.
H. To record payment of a prepaid expense.
I. To record this period's depreciation expense.

		Account	Debit	Credit
____	1.	Rent Expense	2,000	
		Prepaid Rent		2,000
____	2.	Interest Expense	1,000	
		Interest Payable		1,000
____	3.	Depreciation Expense	4,000	
		Accumulated Depreciation		4,000
____	4.	Unearned Professional Fees	3,000	
		Professional Fees Earned		3,000
____	5.	Insurance Expense	4,200	
		Prepaid Insurance		4,200
____	6.	Salaries Payable	1,400	
		Cash		1,400
____	7.	Prepaid Rent	4,500	
		Cash		4,500
____	8.	Salaries Expense	6,000	
		Salaries Payable		6,000
____	9.	Interest Receivable	5,000	
		Interest Revenue		5,000
____	10.	Cash	9,000	
		Accounts Receivable (from consulting)		9,000
____	11.	Cash	7,500	
		Unearned Professional Fees		7,500
____	12.	Cash	2,000	
		Interest Receivable		2,000

Problem 3-3A
Preparing adjusting entries, adjusted trial balance, and financial statements
A1 P1 P2 P3

mhhe.com/wildFAP20e

Watson Technical Institute (WTI), a school owned by Tom Watson, provides training to individuals who pay tuition directly to the school. WTI also offers training to groups in off-site locations. Its unadjusted trial balance as of December 31, 2011, follows. WTI initially records prepaid expenses and unearned revenues in balance sheet accounts. Descriptions of items *a* through *h* that require adjusting entries on December 31, 2011, follow.

Additional Information Items

a. An analysis of WTI's insurance policies shows that $3,000 of coverage has expired.
b. An inventory count shows that teaching supplies costing $2,600 are available at year-end 2011.
c. Annual depreciation on the equipment is $12,000.
d. Annual depreciation on the professional library is $6,000.
e. On November 1, WTI agreed to do a special six-month course (starting immediately) for a client. The contract calls for a monthly fee of $2,200, and the client paid the first five months' fees in advance. When the cash was received, the Unearned Training Fees account was credited. The fee for the sixth month will be recorded when it is collected in 2012.

f. On October 15, WTI agreed to teach a four-month class (beginning immediately) for an individual for $3,000 tuition per month payable at the end of the class. The class started on October 15, but no payment has yet been received. (WTI's accruals are applied to the nearest half-month; for example, October recognizes one-half month accrual.)

g. WTI's two employees are paid weekly. As of the end of the year, two days' salaries have accrued at the rate of $100 per day for each employee.

h. The balance in the Prepaid Rent account represents rent for December.

WATSON TECHNICAL INSTITUTE Unadjusted Trial Balance December 31, 2011		
	Debit	**Credit**
Cash	$ 26,000	
Accounts receivable	0	
Teaching supplies	10,000	
Prepaid insurance	15,000	
Prepaid rent	2,000	
Professional library	30,000	
Accumulated depreciation—Professional library		$ 9,000
Equipment	70,000	
Accumulated depreciation—Equipment		16,000
Accounts payable		36,000
Salaries payable		0
Unearned training fees		11,000
T. Watson, Capital		63,600
T. Watson, Withdrawals	40,000	
Tuition fees earned		102,000
Training fees earned		38,000
Depreciation expense—Professional library	0	
Depreciation expense—Equipment	0	
Salaries expense	48,000	
Insurance expense	0	
Rent expense	22,000	
Teaching supplies expense	0	
Advertising expense	7,000	
Utilities expense	5,600	
Totals	$ 275,600	$ 275,600

Required

1. Prepare T-accounts (representing the ledger) with balances from the unadjusted trial balance.
2. Prepare the necessary adjusting journal entries for items *a* through *h* and post them to the T-accounts. Assume that adjusting entries are made only at year-end.
3. Update balances in the T-accounts for the adjusting entries and prepare an adjusted trial balance.
4. Prepare Watson Technical Institute's income statement and statement of owner's equity for the year 2011 and prepare its balance sheet as of December 31, 2011.

Check (2*e*) Cr. Training Fees Earned, $4,400; (2*f*) Cr. Tuition Fees Earned, $7,500; (3) Adj. Trial balance totals, $301,500; (4) Net income, $38,500; Ending T. Watson, Capital $62,100

Problem 3-4A
Interpreting unadjusted and adjusted trial balances, and preparing financial statements

C3 A1 P1 P2 P3 

mhhe.com/wildFAP20e

A six-column table for JJW Company follows. The first two columns contain the unadjusted trial balance for the company as of July 31, 2011. The last two columns contain the adjusted trial balance as of the same date.

Required

Analysis Component

1. Analyze the differences between the unadjusted and adjusted trial balances to determine the eight adjustments that likely were made. Show the results of your analysis by inserting these adjustment amounts in the table's two middle columns. Label each adjustment with a letter *a* through *h* and provide a short description of it at the bottom of the table.

Preparation Component

Check (2) Net income, $37,020; J. Winner, Capital (7/31/2011), $55,440; Total assets, $131,340

2. Use the information in the adjusted trial balance to prepare the company's (*a*) income statement and its statement of owner's equity for the year ended July 31, 2011 (*note:* J. Winner, Capital at July 31, 2010, was $28,420, and the current-year withdrawals were $10,000), and (*b*) the balance sheet as of July 31, 2011.

	Unadjusted Trial Balance		Adjustments		Adjusted Trial Balance	
Cash	$ 27,000				$ 27,000	
Accounts receivable	12,000				22,460	
Office supplies	18,000				3,000	
Prepaid insurance	7,320				4,880	
Office equipment	92,000				92,000	
Accum. depreciation—Office equip.		$ 12,000				$ 18,000
Accounts payable		9,300				10,200
Interest payable		0				800
Salaries payable		0				6,600
Unearned consulting fees		16,000				14,300
Long-term notes payable		44,000				44,000
J. Winner, Capital		28,420				28,420
J. Winner, Withdrawals	10,000				10,000	
Consulting fees earned		156,000				168,160
Depreciation expense—Office equip.	0				6,000	
Salaries expense	71,000				77,600	
Interest expense	1,400				2,200	
Insurance expense	0				2,440	
Rent expense	13,200				13,200	
Office supplies expense	0				15,000	
Advertising expense	13,800				14,700	
Totals	$265,720	$265,720			$290,480	$290,480

Problem 3-5A
Preparing financial statements from the adjusted trial balance and calculating profit margin
P3 A1 A2

The adjusted trial balance for Callahay Company as of December 31, 2011, follows.

	Debit	Credit
Cash	$ 22,000	
Accounts receivable	44,000	
Interest receivable	10,000	
Notes receivable (due in 90 days)	160,000	
Office supplies	8,000	
Automobiles	160,000	
Accumulated depreciation—Automobiles		$ 42,000
Equipment	130,000	
Accumulated depreciation—Equipment		10,000
Land	70,000	
Accounts payable		88,000
Interest payable		12,000
Salaries payable		11,000
Unearned fees		22,000
Long-term notes payable		130,000
J. Callahay, Capital		247,800
J. Callahay, Withdrawals	38,000	

[continued on next page]

[continued from previous page]

Fees earned		420,000
Interest earned		16,000
Depreciation expense—Automobiles	18,000	
Depreciation expense—Equipment	10,000	
Salaries expense	180,000	
Wages expense	32,000	
Interest expense	24,000	
Office supplies expense	26,000	
Advertising expense	50,000	
Repairs expense—Automobiles	16,800	
Totals	$998,800	$998,800

Required

1. Use the information in the adjusted trial balance to prepare (*a*) the income statement for the year ended December 31, 2011; (*b*) the statement of owner's equity for the year ended December 31, 2011; and (*c*) the balance sheet as of December 31, 2011.

2. Calculate the profit margin for year 2011.

Check (1) Total assets, $552,000

Problem 3-6A[A]
Recording prepaid expenses and unearned revenues
P1 P4

Quisp Co. had the following transactions in the last two months of its year ended December 31.

Nov.	1	Paid $1,500 cash for future newspaper advertising.
	1	Paid $2,160 cash for 12 months of insurance through October 31 of the next year.
	30	Received $3,300 cash for future services to be provided to a customer.
Dec.	1	Paid $2,700 cash for a consultant's services to be received over the next three months.
	15	Received $7,650 cash for future services to be provided to a customer.
	31	Of the advertising paid for on November 1, $900 worth is not yet used.
	31	A portion of the insurance paid for on November 1 has expired. No adjustment was made in November to Prepaid Insurance.
	31	Services worth $1,200 are not yet provided to the customer who paid on November 30.
	31	One-third of the consulting services paid for on December 1 have been received.
	31	The company has performed $3,000 of services that the customer paid for on December 15.

Required

1. Prepare entries for these transactions under the method that records prepaid expenses as assets and records unearned revenues as liabilities. Also prepare adjusting entries at the end of the year.

2. Prepare entries for these transactions under the method that records prepaid expenses as expenses and records unearned revenues as revenues. Also prepare adjusting entries at the end of the year.

Analysis Component

3. Explain why the alternative sets of entries in requirements 1 and 2 do not result in different financial statement amounts.

PROBLEM SET B

Problem 3-1B
Preparing adjusting and subsequent journal entries
C1 A1 P1

Nomo Co. follows the practice of recording prepaid expenses and unearned revenues in balance sheet accounts. The company's annual accounting period ends on October 31, 2011. The following information concerns the adjusting entries that need to be recorded as of that date.

a. The Office Supplies account started the fiscal year with a $500 balance. During the fiscal year, the company purchased supplies for $3,650, which was added to the Office Supplies account. The supplies available at October 31, 2011, totaled $700.

b. An analysis of the company's insurance policies provided the following facts.

Policy	Date of Purchase	Months of Coverage	Cost
A	April 1, 2010	24	$3,000
B	April 1, 2011	36	3,600
C	August 1, 2011	12	660

The total premium for each policy was paid in full (for all months) at the purchase date, and the Prepaid Insurance account was debited for the full cost. (Year-end adjusting entries for Prepaid Insurance were properly recorded in all prior fiscal years.)

c. The company has four employees, who earn a total of $800 for each workday. They are paid each Monday for their work in the five-day workweek ending on the previous Friday. Assume that October 31, 2011, is a Monday, and all four employees worked the first day of that week. They will be paid salaries for five full days on Monday, November 7, 2011.

d. The company purchased a building on November 1, 2010, that cost $155,000 and is expected to have a $20,000 salvage value at the end of its predicted 25-year life. Annual depreciation is $5,400.

e. Since the company does not occupy the entire building it owns, it rented space to a tenant at $600 per month, starting on September 1, 2011. The rent was paid on time on September 1, and the amount received was credited to the Rent Earned account. However, the October rent has not been paid. The company has worked out an agreement with the tenant, who has promised to pay both October and November rent in full on November 15. The tenant has agreed not to fall behind again.

f. On September 1, the company rented space to another tenant for $525 per month. The tenant paid five months' rent in advance on that date. The payment was recorded with a credit to the Unearned Rent account.

Required

Check (1*b*) Dr. Insurance Expense, $2,675; (1*d*) Dr. Depreciation Expense, $5,400.

1. Use the information to prepare adjusting entries as of October 31, 2011.

2. Prepare journal entries to record the first subsequent cash transaction in November 2011 for parts *c* and *e*.

Problem 3-2B
Identifying adjusting entries with explanations
C3 P1

For each of the following entries, enter the letter of the explanation that most closely describes it in the space beside each entry. (You can use letters more than once.)

A. To record payment of a prepaid expense.
B. To record this period's use of a prepaid expense.
C. To record this period's depreciation expense.
D. To record receipt of unearned revenue.
E. To record this period's earning of prior unearned revenue.
F. To record an accrued expense.
G. To record payment of an accrued expense.
H. To record an accrued revenue.
I. To record receipt of accrued revenue.

_____	1.	Unearned Professional Fees	6,000	
		Professional Fees Earned		6,000
_____	2.	Interest Receivable	3,500	
		Interest Revenue		3,500
_____	3.	Salaries Payable	9,000	
		Cash		9,000
_____	4.	Depreciation Expense	8,000	
		Accumulated Depreciation		8,000
_____	5.	Cash	9,000	
		Unearned Professional Fees		9,000
_____	6.	Insurance Expense	4,000	
		Prepaid Insurance		4,000
_____	7.	Interest Expense	5,000	
		Interest Payable		5,000
_____	8.	Cash	1,500	
		Accounts Receivable (from services)		1,500
_____	9.	Salaries Expense	7,000	
		Salaries Payable		7,000
_____	10.	Cash	1,000	
		Interest Receivable		1,000
_____	11.	Prepaid Rent	3,000	
		Cash		3,000
_____	12.	Rent Expense	7,500	
		Prepaid Rent		7,500

Problem 3-3B
Preparing adjusting entries, adjusted trial balance, and financial statements
A1 P1 P2 P3

Following is the unadjusted trial balance for Alcorn Institute as of December 31, 2011, which initially records prepaid expenses and unearned revenues in balance sheet accounts. The Institute provides one-on-one training to individuals who pay tuition directly to the business and offers extension training to groups in off-site locations. Shown after the trial balance are items *a* through *h* that require adjusting entries as of December 31, 2011.

ALCORN INSTITUTE
Unadjusted Trial Balance
December 31, 2011

	Debit	Credit
Cash	$ 50,000	
Accounts receivable	0	
Teaching supplies	60,000	
Prepaid insurance	18,000	
Prepaid rent	2,600	
Professional library	10,000	
Accumulated depreciation—Professional library		$ 1,500
Equipment	30,000	
Accumulated depreciation—Equipment		16,000
Accounts payable		12,200
Salaries payable		0
Unearned training fees		27,600
M. Alcorn, Capital		68,500
M. Alcorn, Withdrawals	20,000	
Tuition fees earned		105,000
Training fees earned		62,000
Depreciation expense—Professional library	0	
Depreciation expense—Equipment	0	
Salaries expense	43,200	
Insurance expense	0	
Rent expense	28,600	
Teaching supplies expense	0	
Advertising expense	18,000	
Utilities expense	12,400	
Totals	$ 292,800	$292,800

Additional Information Items

a. An analysis of the Institute's insurance policies shows that $6,400 of coverage has expired.

b. An inventory count shows that teaching supplies costing $2,500 are available at year-end 2011.

c. Annual depreciation on the equipment is $4,000.

d. Annual depreciation on the professional library is $2,000.

e. On November 1, the Institute agreed to do a special four-month course (starting immediately) for a client. The contract calls for a $4,600 monthly fee, and the client paid the first two months' fees in advance. When the cash was received, the Unearned Training Fees account was credited. The last two month's fees will be recorded when collected in 2012.

f. On October 15, the Institute agreed to teach a four-month class (beginning immediately) to an individual for $2,200 tuition per month payable at the end of the class. The class started on October 15, but no payment has yet been received. (Alcorn's accruals are applied to the nearest half-month; for example, October recognizes one-half month accrual.)

g. The Institute's only employee is paid weekly. As of the end of the year, three days' salaries have accrued at the rate of $180 per day.

h. The balance in the Prepaid Rent account represents rent for December.

Required

1. Prepare T-accounts (representing the ledger) with balances from the unadjusted trial balance.
2. Prepare the necessary adjusting journal entries for items *a* through *h*, and post them to the T-accounts. Assume that adjusting entries are made only at year-end.
3. Update balances in the T-accounts for the adjusting entries and prepare an adjusted trial balance.
4. Prepare the company's income statement and statement of owner's equity for the year 2011, and prepare its balance sheet as of December 31, 2011.

Check (2*e*) Cr. Training Fees Earned, $9,200; (2*f*) Cr. Tuition Fees Earned, $5,500; (3) Adj. trial balance totals, $304,840; (4) Net income, $6,460; Ending M. Alcorn, Capital, $54,960

Problem 3-4B
Interpreting unadjusted and adjusted trial balances, and preparing financial statements
C3 A1 P1 P2 P3 

A six-column table for Daxu Consulting Company follows. The first two columns contain the unadjusted trial balance for the company as of December 31, 2011, and the last two columns contain the adjusted trial balance as of the same date.

	Unadjusted Trial Balance		Adjustments		Adjusted Trial Balance	
Cash	$ 48,000				$ 48,000	
Accounts receivable	70,000				76,660	
Office supplies	30,000				7,000	
Prepaid insurance	13,200				8,600	
Office equipment	150,000				150,000	
Accumulated depreciation—Office equip.		$ 30,000				$ 40,000
Accounts payable		36,000				42,000
Interest payable		0				1,600
Salaries payable		0				11,200
Unearned consulting fees		30,000				17,800
Long-term notes payable		80,000				80,000
D. Chen, Capital		70,200				70,200
D. Chen, Withdrawals	10,000				10,000	
Consulting fees earned		264,000				282,860
Depreciation expense—Office equip.	0				10,000	
Salaries expense	115,600				126,800	
Interest expense	6,400				8,000	
Insurance expense	0				4,600	
Rent expense	24,000				24,000	
Office supplies expense	0				23,000	
Advertising expense	43,000				49,000	
Totals	$510,200	$510,200			$545,660	$545,660

Required

Analysis Component

1. Analyze the differences between the unadjusted and adjusted trial balances to determine the eight adjustments that likely were made. Show the results of your analysis by inserting these adjustment amounts in the table's two middle columns. Label each adjustment with a letter *a* through *h* and provide a short description of it at the bottom of the table.

Preparation Component

2. Use the information in the adjusted trial balance to prepare this company's (*a*) income statement and its statement of owner's equity for the year ended December 31, 2011 (*note:* D. Chen, Capital at December 31, 2010, was $70,200, and the current-year withdrawals were $10,000), and (*b*) the balance sheet as of December 31, 2011.

Check (2) Net income, $37,460; D. Chen, Capital (12/31/11), $97,660; Total assets, $250,260

Problem 3-5B
Preparing financial statements from the adjusted trial balance and calculating profit margin
P3 A1 A2

The adjusted trial balance for Lightning Courier as of December 31, 2011, follows.

	Debit	Credit
Cash	$ 48,000	
Accounts receivable	110,000	
Interest receivable	6,000	
Notes receivable (due in 90 days)	200,000	
Office supplies	12,000	
Trucks	124,000	
Accumulated depreciation—Trucks		$ 48,000
Equipment	260,000	
Accumulated depreciation—Equipment		190,000
Land	90,000	
Accounts payable		124,000
Interest payable		22,000
Salaries payable		30,000
Unearned delivery fees		110,000
Long-term notes payable		190,000
J. Hallam, Capital		115,000
J. Hallam, Withdrawals	40,000	
Delivery fees earned		580,000
Interest earned		24,000
Depreciation expense—Trucks	24,000	
Depreciation expense—Equipment	46,000	
Salaries expense	64,000	
Wages expense	290,000	
Interest expense	25,000	
Office supplies expense	33,000	
Advertising expense	26,400	
Repairs expense—Trucks	34,600	
Totals	$1,433,000	$1,433,000

Required

1. Use the information in the adjusted trial balance to prepare (*a*) the income statement for the year ended December 31, 2011, (*b*) the statement of owner's equity for the year ended December 31, 2011, and (*c*) the balance sheet as of December 31, 2011.

2. Calculate the profit margin for year 2011.

Check (1) Total assets, $612,000

Problem 3-6B[A]
Recording prepaid expenses and unearned revenues
P1 P4

Quake Co. had the following transactions in the last two months of its fiscal year ended May 31.

Apr.	1	Paid $3,450 cash to an accounting firm for future consulting services.
	1	Paid $2,700 cash for 12 months of insurance through March 31 of the next year.
	30	Received $7,500 cash for future services to be provided to a customer.
May	1	Paid $3,450 cash for future newspaper advertising.
	23	Received $9,450 cash for future services to be provided to a customer.
	31	Of the consulting services paid for on April 1, $1,500 worth has been received.
	31	A portion of the insurance paid for on April 1 has expired. No adjustment was made in April to Prepaid Insurance.
	31	Services worth $3,600 are not yet provided to the customer who paid on April 30.
	31	Of the advertising paid for on May 1, $1,050 worth is not yet used.
	31	The company has performed $4,500 of services that the customer paid for on May 23.

Required

1. Prepare entries for these transactions under the method that records prepaid expenses and unearned revenues in balance sheet accounts. Also prepare adjusting entries at the end of the year.

2. Prepare entries for these transactions under the method that records prepaid expenses and unearned revenues in income statement accounts. Also prepare adjusting entries at the end of the year.

Analysis Component

3. Explain why the alternative sets of entries in parts 1 and 2 do not result in different financial statement amounts.

SERIAL PROBLEM

Business Solutions

P1 P2 P3

This serial problem began in Chapter 1 and continues through most of the book. If previous chapter segments were not completed, the serial problem can still begin at this point. It is helpful, but not necessary, to use the Working Papers that accompany the book.

SP 3 After the success of the company's first two months, Santana Rey continues to operate Business Solutions. (Transactions for the first two months are described in the serial problem of Chapter 2.) The November 30, 2011, unadjusted trial balance of Business Solutions (reflecting its transactions for October and November of 2011) follows.

No.	Account Title	Debit	Credit
101	Cash	$38,264	
106	Accounts receivable	12,618	
126	Computer supplies	2,545	
128	Prepaid insurance	2,220	
131	Prepaid rent	3,300	
163	Office equipment	8,000	
164	Accumulated depreciation—Office equipment		$ 0
167	Computer equipment	20,000	
168	Accumulated depreciation—Computer equipment		0
201	Accounts payable		0
210	Wages payable		0
236	Unearned computer services revenue		0
301	S. Rey, Capital		73,000
302	S. Rey, Withdrawals	5,600	
403	Computer services revenue		25,659
612	Depreciation expense—Office equipment	0	
613	Depreciation expense—Computer equipment	0	
623	Wages expense	2,625	
637	Insurance expense	0	
640	Rent expense	0	
652	Computer supplies expense	0	
655	Advertising expense	1,728	
676	Mileage expense	704	
677	Miscellaneous expenses	250	
684	Repairs expense—Computer	805	
	Totals	$98,659	$98,659

Business Solutions had the following transactions and events in December 2011.

Dec.	2	Paid $1,025 cash to Hillside Mall for Business Solutions' share of mall advertising costs.
	3	Paid $500 cash for minor repairs to the company's computer.
	4	Received $3,950 cash from Alex's Engineering Co. for the receivable from November.
	10	Paid cash to Lyn Addie for six days of work at the rate of $125 per day.
	14	Notified by Alex's Engineering Co. that Business Solutions' bid of $7,000 on a proposed project has been accepted. Alex's paid a $1,500 cash advance to Business Solutions.
	15	Purchased $1,100 of computer supplies on credit from Harris Office Products.
	16	Sent a reminder to Gomez Co. to pay the fee for services recorded on November 8.
	20	Completed a project for Liu Corporation and received $5,625 cash.
	22–26	Took the week off for the holidays.
	28	Received $3,000 cash from Gomez Co. on its receivable.

29 Reimbursed S. Rey for business automobile mileage (600 miles at $0.32 per mile).
31 S. Rey withdrew $1,500 cash from the company for personal use.

The following additional facts are collected for use in making adjusting entries prior to preparing financial statements for the company's first three months:

a. The December 31 inventory count of computer supplies shows $580 still available.
b. Three months have expired since the 12-month insurance premium was paid in advance.
c. As of December 31, Lyn Addie has not been paid for four days of work at $125 per day.
d. The company's computer is expected to have a four-year life with no salvage value.
e. The office equipment is expected to have a five-year life with no salvage value.
f. Three of the four months' prepaid rent has expired.

Required

1. Prepare journal entries to record each of the December transactions and events for Business Solutions. Post those entries to the accounts in the ledger.
2. Prepare adjusting entries to reflect *a* through *f*. Post those entries to the accounts in the ledger.
3. Prepare an adjusted trial balance as of December 31, 2011.
4. Prepare an income statement for the three months ended December 31, 2011.
5. Prepare a statement of owner's equity for the three months ended December 31, 2011.
6. Prepare a balance sheet as of December 31, 2011.

Check (3) Adjusted trial balance totals, $109,034

(6) Total assets, $83,460

Beyond the Numbers

REPORTING IN ACTION
C1 C2 A1 A2

RIM

BTN 3-1 Refer to Research In Motion's financial statements in Appendix A to answer the following.

1. Identify and write down the revenue recognition principle as explained in the chapter.
2. Review Research In Motion's footnotes to discover how it applies the revenue recognition principle and when it recognizes revenue. Report what you discover.
3. What is Research In Motion's profit margin for fiscal years ended February 28, 2009, and February 27, 2010.

Fast Forward

4. Access RIM's annual report (10-K) for fiscal years ending after February 27, 2010, at its Website (RIM.com) or the SEC's EDGAR database (www.SEC.gov). Assess and compare the February 27, 2010, fiscal year profit margin to any subsequent year's profit margin that you compute.

COMPARATIVE ANALYSIS
A2

RIM
Apple

BTN 3-2 Key figures for the recent two years of both Research In Motion and Apple follow.

	Research In Motion		Apple	
($ millions)	Current Year	Prior Year	Current Year	Prior Year
Net income	$ 2,457	$ 1,893	$ 8,235	$ 6,119
Net sales	14,953	11,065	42,905	37,491
Current assets	5,813	4,842	31,555	30,006
Current liabilities	2,432	2,115	11,506	11,361

Required

1. Compute profit margins for (*a*) Research In Motion and (*b*) Apple for the two years of data shown.
2. Which company is more successful on the basis of profit margin? Explain.

ETHICS CHALLENGE
C1 C2 A1

BTN 3-3 Jackie Bergez works for Sea Biscuit Co. She and Bob Welch, her manager, are preparing adjusting entries for annual financial statements. Bergez computes depreciation and records it as

Depreciation Expense—Equipment	123,000	
Accumulated Depreciation—Equipment		123,000

Welch agrees with her computation but says the credit entry should be directly to the Equipment account. Welch argues that while accumulated depreciation is technically correct, "it is less hassle not to use a contra account and just credit the Equipment account directly. And besides, the balance sheet shows the same amount for total assets under either method."

Required

1. How should depreciation be recorded? Do you support Bergez or Welch?
2. Evaluate the strengths and weaknesses of Welch's reasons for preferring his method.
3. Indicate whether the situation Bergez faces is an ethical problem. Explain.

COMMUNICATING IN PRACTICE

C1 A2 

BTN 3-4 The class should be divided into teams. Teams are to select an industry (such as automobile manufacturing, airlines, defense contractors), and each team member is to select a different company in that industry. Each team member is to acquire the annual report of the company selected. Annual reports can be downloaded from company Websites or from the SEC's EDGAR database at (www.SEC.gov).

Required

1. Use the annual report to compute the return on assets, debt ratio, and profit margin.
2. Communicate with team members via a meeting, e-mail, or telephone to discuss the meaning of the ratios, how different companies compare to each other, and the industry norm. The team must prepare a single memo reporting the ratios for each company and identifying the conclusions or consensus of opinion reached during the team's discussion. The memo is to be copied and distributed to the instructor and all classmates.

TAKING IT TO THE NET

C1 A2  

BTN 3-5 Access EDGAR online (www.SEC.gov) and locate the 10-K report of **The Gap, Inc.**, (ticker GPS) filed on March 26, 2010. Review its financial statements reported for the year ended January 30, 2010, to answer the following questions.

Required

1. What are Gap's main brands?
2. What is Gap's fiscal year-end?
3. What is Gap's net sales for the period ended January 30, 2010?
4. What is Gap's net income for the period ended January 30, 2010?
5. Compute Gap's profit margin for the year ended January 30, 2010.
6. Do you believe Gap's decision to use a year-end of late January or early February relates to its natural business year? Explain.

TEAMWORK IN ACTION

C3 A1 P1 

BTN 3-6 Four types of adjustments are described in the chapter: (1) prepaid expenses, (2) unearned revenues, (3) accrued expenses, and (4) accrued revenues.

Required

1. Form *learning teams* of four (or more) members. Each team member must select one of the four adjustments as an area of expertise (each team must have at least one expert in each area).
2. Form *expert teams* from the individuals who have selected the same area of expertise. Expert teams are to discuss and write a report that each expert will present to his or her learning team addressing the following:
   a. Description of the adjustment and why it's necessary.
   b. Example of a transaction or event, with dates and amounts, that requires adjustment.
   c. Adjusting entry(ies) for the example in requirement *b*.
   d. Status of the affected account(s) before and after the adjustment in requirement *c*.
   e. Effects on financial statements of not making the adjustment.
3. Each expert should return to his or her learning team. In rotation, each member should present his or her expert team's report to the learning team. Team discussion is encouraged.

BTN 3-7 Review the opening feature of this chapter dealing with Cheezburger Network.

ENTREPRENEURIAL DECISION

A2  

Required

1. Assume that Cheezburger Network sells a $300 gift certificate to a customer, collecting the $300 cash in advance. Prepare the journal entry for the (*a*) collection of the cash for delivery of the gift certificate to the customer and (*b*) revenue from the subsequent delivery of merchandise when the gift certificate is used.
2. How can keeping less inventory help to improve Cheezburger Network's profit margin?
3. Ben Huh understands that many companies carry considerable inventory, and Ben is thinking of carrying additional inventory of merchandise for sale. Ben desires your advice on the pros and cons of carrying such inventory. Provide at least one reason for and one reason against carrying additional inventory.

BTN 3-8 Visit the Website of a major company that interests you. Use the Investor Relations link at the Website to obtain the toll-free telephone number of the Investor Relations Department. Call the company, ask to speak to Investor Relations, and request a copy of the company's most recent annual report. You should receive the requested report within one to two weeks. Once you have received your report, use it throughout the term to see that the principles you are learning in class are being applied in practice.

HITTING THE ROAD

C1

BTN 3-9 Nokia (www.Nokia.com) is a leading global manufacturer of mobile devices and services.

GLOBAL DECISION

A2 C1 C2  

NOKIA

Required

1. Locate the notes to its December 31, 2009, financial statements at the company's Website, and read note *1 Accounting Principles—Revenue Recognition,* first paragraph only. When is revenue recognized by Nokia?
2. Refer to Nokia's financials in Appendix A. What is Nokia's profit margin for the year ended December 31, 2009?

ANSWERS TO MULTIPLE CHOICE QUIZ

1. b; the forgotten adjusting entry is: *dr.* Wages Expense, *cr.* Wages Payable.
2. c; Supplies used = $450 − $125 = $325
3. b; Insurance expense = $24,000 × (8/24) = $8,000; adjusting entry is: *dr.* Insurance Expense for $8,000, *cr.* Prepaid Insurance for $8,000.
4. a; Consulting fees earned = $3,600 × (2/6) = $1,200; adjusting entry is: *dr.* Unearned Consulting Fee for $1,200, *cr.* Consulting Fees Earned for $1,200.
5. e; Profit margin = $15,000/$300,000 = 5%

Completing the Accounting Cycle

A Look Back

Chapter 3 explained the timing of reports. We described why adjusting accounts is key for recognizing revenues and expenses in the proper period. We prepared an adjusted trial balance and used it to prepare financial statements.

A Look at This Chapter

This chapter emphasizes the final steps in the accounting process and reviews the entire accounting cycle. We explain the closing process, including accounting procedures and the use of a post-closing trial balance. We show how a work sheet aids in preparing financial statements.

A Look Ahead

Chapter 5 looks at accounting for merchandising activities. We describe the sale and purchase of merchandise and their implications for preparing and analyzing financial statements.

Learning Objectives

CAP

CONCEPTUAL

C1 Explain why temporary accounts are closed each period. (p. 142)

C2 Identify steps in the accounting cycle. (p. 146)

C3 Explain and prepare a classified balance sheet. (p. 147)

ANALYTICAL

A1 Compute the current ratio and describe what it reveals about a company's financial condition. (p. 150)

LP4

PROCEDURAL

P1 Prepare a work sheet and explain its usefulness. (p. 138)

P2 Describe and prepare closing entries. (p. 143)

P3 Explain and prepare a post-closing trial balance. (p. 144)

P4 *Appendix 4A*—Prepare reversing entries and explain their purpose. (p. 154)

Decision Insight

Gamer Grub!

"Be in front of your customer . . . [and] have a little bit of an edge"
—**KEITH MULLIN** (far left)

SAN DIEGO—"I have been battling greasy fingers and keyboard crumbs," complained gamer Keith Mullin. "I thought '*there has to be a better way*!'" So, Keith-the-gamer morphed into Keith-the-entrepreneur. In 2008, Keith set up what he calls his "garage startup" and introduced **Gamer Grub®** **(GamerGrub.com),** which is performance snack food for gamers. "I got tired of wiping my hands on my jeans," laughs Keith. "And, I like to multi-task."

Success, however, requires Keith to monitor and minimize costs. "I made the first Gamer Grub prototypes in my mom's kitchen," explains Keith. He eventually set up an accounting system to track costs and match them with revenues. But, Keith says, it is a constant struggle as his business has been tripling in revenues each month. He explains that properly applying the accounting cycle, preparing classified financial statements, and acting on that information has helped in his success. However, admits Keith, "it is more of a collaborative effort."

To date, Keith has successfully controlled his costs while monitoring both revenues and customer needs. "You need to be in front of your customer, watch them taste it, watch them understand what you're doing," says Keith. "You have to be out there . . . we have given out at least 16,000 samples!" Keith adds that he applies the accounting cycle, including closing entries, to help identify and match costs with revenues for specific time periods. He also relies on classified balance sheets to plan payment schedules. But, what keeps him going, admits Keith, is knowing that he offers "different ways to snack while you're computer gaming or multi-tasking."

Keith is on a mission. What motivates him, explains Keith, is the "Wow! If you get that 'Wow' reaction, that's a really good thing." To make that happen, he tracks the accounting numbers to be sure his "Wow food" is a money-making venture. "Gamer Grub allows gamers to consume healthy, game-enhancing snacks," insists Keith. "Without greasy fingers or keyboard crumbs!"

[Sources: *GamerGrub* Website, January 2011; *Entrepreneur,* October 2009; *Business Wire,* September 2008; *MGC* Website, January 2010]

Chapter Preview

Many of the important steps leading to financial statements were explained in earlier chapters. We described how transactions and events are analyzed, journalized, and posted. This chapter explains the closing process that readies revenue, expense, and withdrawal accounts for the next reporting period and updates the capital account. A work sheet is shown to be a useful tool for these final steps and in preparing financial statements. It also explains how accounts are classified on a balance sheet to increase their usefulness to decision makers.

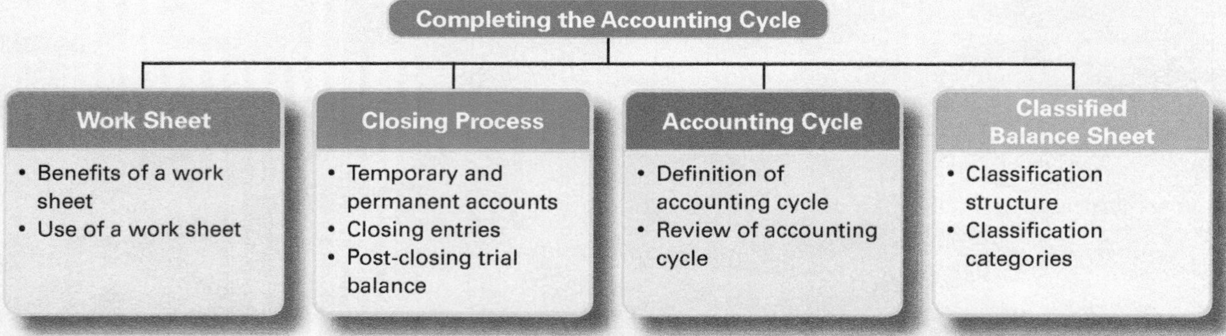

WORK SHEET AS A TOOL

Information preparers use various analyses and internal documents when organizing information for internal and external decision makers. Internal documents are often called **working papers.** One widely used working paper is the **work sheet,** which is a useful tool for preparers in working with accounting information. It is usually not available to external decision makers.

Benefits of a Work Sheet (Spreadsheet)

P1 Prepare a work sheet and explain its usefulness.

A work sheet is *not* a required report, yet using a manual or electronic work sheet has several potential benefits. Specifically, a work sheet

- Aids the preparation of financial statements.
- Reduces the possibility of errors when working with many accounts and adjustments.
- Links accounts and adjustments to their impacts in financial statements.
- Assists in planning and organizing an audit of financial statements—as it can be used to reflect any adjustments necessary.
- Helps in preparing interim (monthly and quarterly) financial statements when the journalizing and posting of adjusting entries are postponed until year-end.
- Shows the effects of proposed or "what-if" transactions.

Decision Insight

High-Tech Work Sheet An electronic work sheet using spreadsheet software such as Excel allows us to easily change numbers, assess the impact of alternative strategies, and quickly prepare financial statements at less cost. It can also increase the available time for analysis and interpretation. ■

Use of a Work Sheet

Point: Since a work sheet is *not* a required report or an accounting record, its format is flexible and can be modified by its user to fit his/her preferences.

When a work sheet is used to prepare financial statements, it is constructed at the end of a period before the adjusting process. The complete work sheet includes a list of the accounts, their balances and adjustments, and their sorting into financial statement columns. It provides two columns each for the unadjusted trial balance, the adjustments, the adjusted trial balance, the income statement, and the balance sheet (including the statement of owner's equity). To describe and interpret the work sheet, we use the information from FastForward. Preparing the work sheet has five important steps. Each step, 1 through 5, is color-coded and explained with reference to Exhibits 4.1 and 4.2.

1 Step 1. Enter Unadjusted Trial Balance

Refer to Exhibit 4.1. The first step in preparing a work sheet is to list the title of every account and its account number that is expected to appear on its financial statements. This includes all accounts in the ledger plus any new ones from adjusting entries. Most adjusting entries—including expenses from salaries, supplies, depreciation, and insurance—are predictable and recurring. The unadjusted balance for each account is then entered in the appropriate Debit or Credit column of the unadjusted trial balance columns. The totals of these two columns must be equal. Exhibit 4.1 shows FastForward's work sheet after completing this first step. Sometimes blank lines are left on the work sheet based on past experience to indicate where lines will be needed for adjustments to certain accounts. Exhibit 4.1 shows Consulting Revenue as one example. An alternative is to squeeze adjustments on one line or to combine the effects of two or more adjustments in one amount. In the unusual case when an account is not predicted, we can add a new line for such an account following the *Totals* line.

2 Step 2. Enter Adjustments

Refer to Exhibit 4.1a (turn over first transparency). The second step in preparing a work sheet is to enter adjustments in the Adjustments columns. The adjustments shown are the same ones shown in Exhibit 3.13. An identifying letter links the debit and credit of each adjusting entry. This is called *keying* the adjustments. After preparing a work sheet, adjusting entries must still be entered in the journal and posted to the ledger. The Adjustments columns provide the information for those entries.

Point: A recordkeeper often can complete the procedural task of journalizing and posting adjusting entries by using a work sheet and the guidance that *keying* provides.

3 Step 3. Prepare Adjusted Trial Balance

Refer to Exhibit 4.1b (turn over second transparency). The adjusted trial balance is prepared by combining the adjustments with the unadjusted balances for each account. As an example, the Prepaid Insurance account has a $2,400 debit balance in the Unadjusted Trial Balance columns. This $2,400 debit is combined with the $100 credit in the Adjustments columns to give Prepaid Insurance a $2,300 debit in the Adjusted Trial Balance columns. The totals of the Adjusted Trial Balance columns confirm the equality of debits and credits.

Point: To avoid omitting the transfer of an account balance, start with the first line (cash) and continue in account order.

4 Step 4. Sort Adjusted Trial Balance Amounts to Financial Statements

Refer to Exhibit 4.1c (turn over third transparency). This step involves sorting account balances from the adjusted trial balance to their proper financial statement columns. Expenses go to the Income Statement Debit column and revenues to the Income Statement Credit column. Assets and withdrawals go to the Balance Sheet & Statement of Owner's Equity Debit column. Liabilities and owner's capital go to the Balance Sheet & Statement of Owner's Equity Credit column.

5 Step 5. Total Statement Columns, Compute Income or Loss, and Balance Columns

Refer to Exhibit 4.1d (turn over fourth transparency). Each financial statement column (from Step 4) is totaled. The difference between the totals of the Income Statement columns is net income or net loss. This occurs because revenues are entered in the Credit column and expenses in the Debit column. If the Credit total exceeds the Debit total, there is net income. If the Debit total exceeds the Credit total, there is a net loss. For FastForward, the Credit total exceeds the Debit total, giving a $3,785 net income.

The net income from the Income Statement columns is then entered in the Balance Sheet & Statement of Owner's Equity Credit column. Adding net income to the last Credit column implies that it is to be added to owner's capital. If a loss occurs, it is added to the Debit column. This implies that it is to be subtracted from owner's capital. The ending balance of owner's capital does not appear in the last two columns as a single amount, but it is computed in the statement of owner's equity using these account balances. When net income or net loss is added

[continued on p. 142]

EXHIBIT 4.1

Work Sheet with Unadjusted Trial Balance

FastForward
Work Sheet
For Month Ended December 31, 2011

(1)

No.	Account	Unadjusted Trial Balance Dr.	Unadjusted Trial Balance Cr.	Adjustments Dr.	Adjustments Cr.	Adjusted Trial Balance Dr.	Adjusted Trial Balance Cr.	Income Statement Dr.	Income Statement Cr.	Balance Sheet & Statement of Owner's Equity Dr.	Balance Sheet & Statement of Owner's Equity Cr.
101	Cash	4,350									
126	Supplies	9,720									
128	Prepaid insurance	2,400									
167	Equipment	26,000									
201	Accounts payable		6,200								
236	Unearned consulting revenue		3,000								
301	C. Taylor, Capital		30,000								
302	C. Taylor, Withdrawals	200									
403	Consulting revenue		5,800								
406	Rental revenue		300								
622	Salaries expense	1,400									
640	Rent expense	1,000									
690	Utilities expense	230									
	Totals	45,300	45,300								

List all accounts from the ledger (can include those expected to arise from adjusting entries).

Enter all amounts available from ledger accounts. Column totals must be equal.

A work sheet collects and summarizes information used to prepare adjusting entries, financial statements, and closing entries.

EXHIBIT 4.1A

Enter Adjustments in the Work Sheet

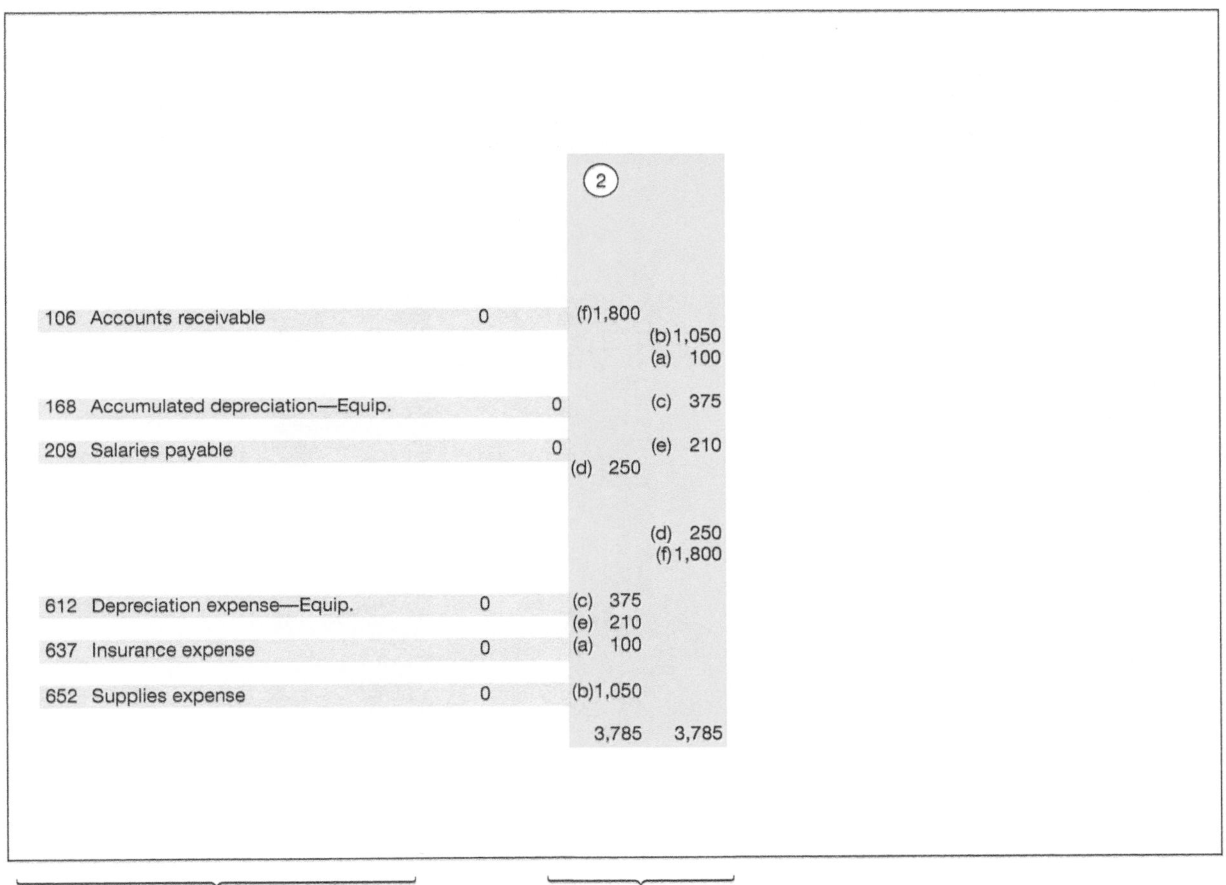

Add any accounts arising from adjusting entries.

Enter adjustment amounts and use letters to cross-reference debit and credit adjustments. Column totals must be equal.

EXHIBIT 4.1B

Compute and Enter Amounts for the Adjusted Trial Balance

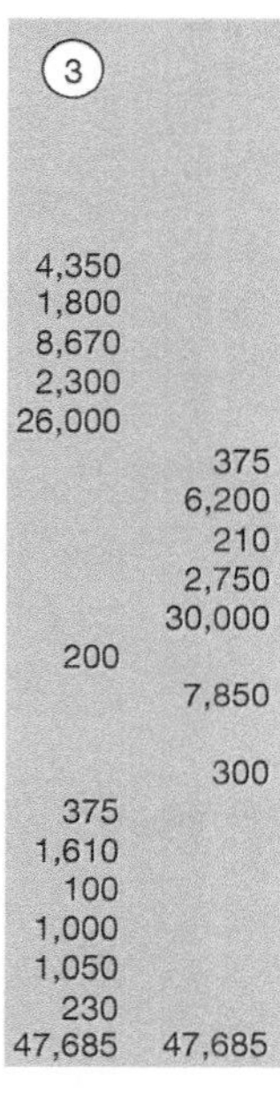

Combine unadjusted trial balance amounts with the adjustments to get the adjusted trial balance amounts. Column totals must be equal.

EXHIBIT 4.1C

Extend the Adjusted Trial Balance Amounts to the Financial Statement Columns

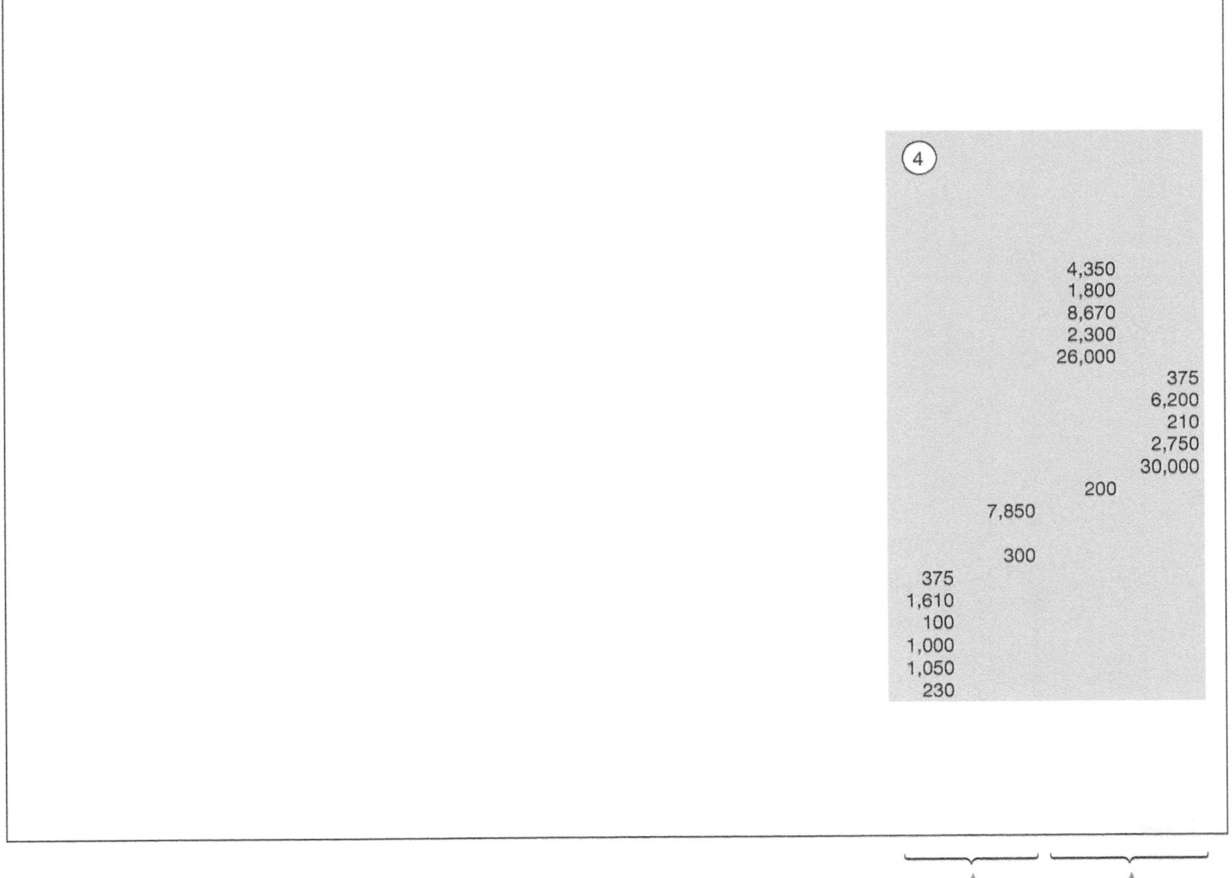

Extend all revenue and expense amounts to the income statement columns.

Extend all asset, liability, capital, and withdrawals amounts to these columns.

These column totals differ by the amount of net income or loss.

EXHIBIT 4.1D

Compute and Enter the Net Income or Loss and Complete the Work Sheet

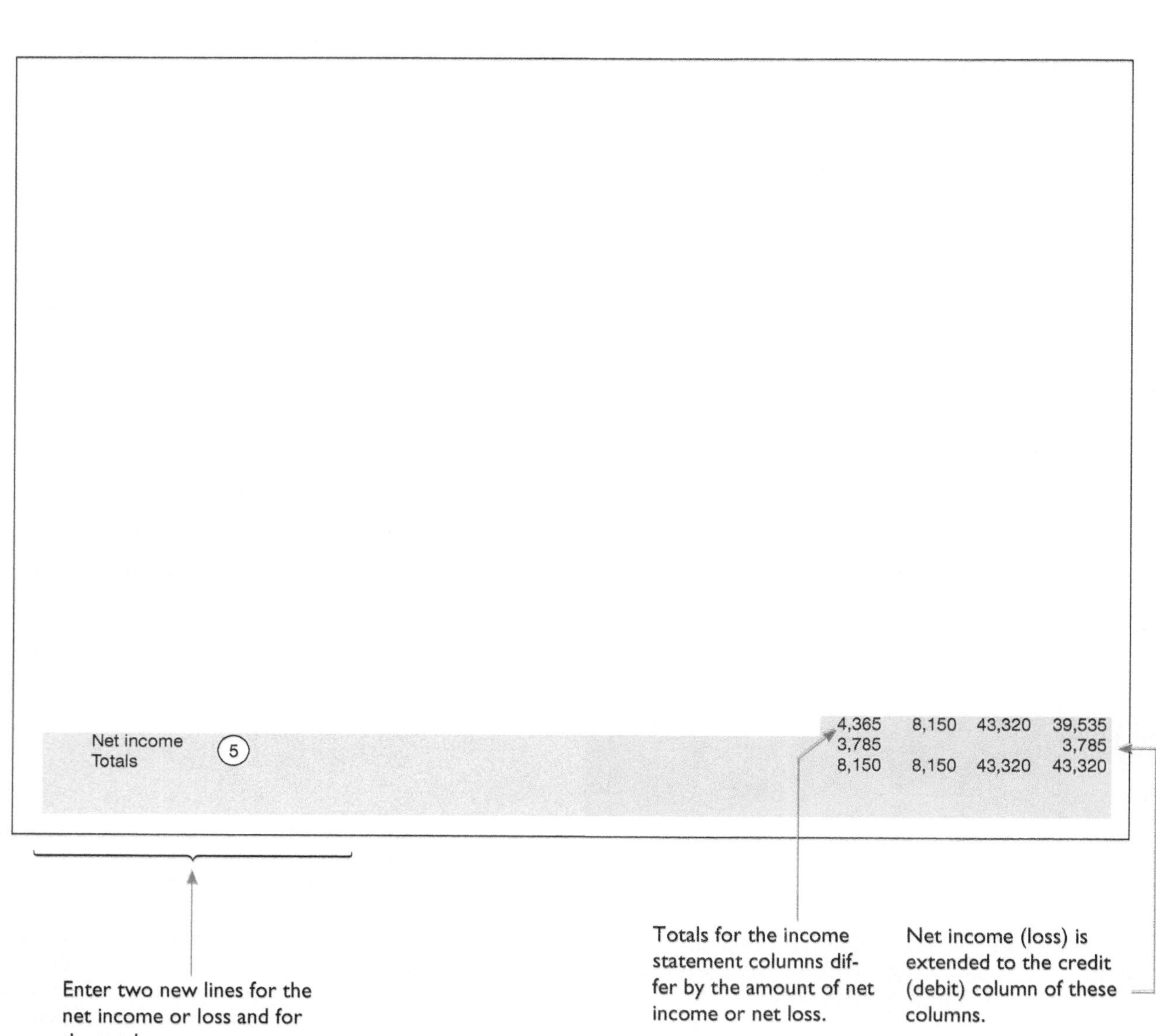

EXHIBIT 4.2

Financial Statements Prepared from the Work Sheet

FASTFORWARD
Income Statement
For Month Ended December 31, 2011

Revenues		
Consulting revenue	$ 7,850	
Rental revenue	300	
Total revenues		$ 8,150
Expenses		
Depreciation expense—Equipment	375	
Salaries expense	1,610	
Insurance expense	100	
Rent expense	1,000	
Supplies expense	1,050	
Utilities expense	230	
Total expenses		4,365
Net income		$ 3,785

FASTFORWARD
Statement of Owner's Equity
For Month Ended December 31, 2011

C. Taylor, Capital, December 1		$ 0
Add: Investment by owner	$30,000	
Net income	3,785	33,785
		33,785
Less: Withdrawals by owner		200
C. Taylor, Capital, December 31		$33,585

FASTFORWARD
Balance Sheet
December 31, 2011

Assets		
Cash		$ 4,350
Accounts receivable		1,800
Supplies		8,670
Prepaid insurance		2,300
Equipment	$26,000	
Accumulated depreciation—Equipment	(375)	25,625
Total assets		$42,745
Liabilities		
Accounts payable		$ 6,200
Salaries payable		210
Unearned consulting revenue		2,750
Total liabilities		9,160
Equity		
C. Taylor, Capital		33,585
Total liabilities and equity		$42,745

to the proper Balance Sheet & Statement of Owner's Equity column, the totals of the last two columns must balance. If they do not, one or more errors have been made. The error can either be mathematical or involve sorting one or more amounts to incorrect columns.

Decision Maker Answer — p. 156 

Entrepreneur You make a printout of the electronic work sheet used to prepare financial statements. There is no depreciation adjustment, yet you own a large amount of equipment. Does the absence of depreciation adjustment concern you? ■

Work Sheet Applications and Analysis

A work sheet does not substitute for financial statements. It is a tool we can use at the end of an accounting period to help organize data and prepare financial statements. FastForward's financial statements are shown in Exhibit 4.2. Its income statement amounts are taken from the Income Statement columns of the work sheet. Similarly, amounts for its balance sheet and its statement of owner's equity are taken from the Balance Sheet & Statement of Owner's Equity columns of the work sheet.

Information from the Adjustments columns of a work sheet can be used to journalize adjusting entries. It is important to remember that a work sheet is not a journal. This means that even when a work sheet is prepared, it is necessary to both journalize adjustments and post them to the ledger.

Work sheets are also useful in analyzing the effects of proposed, or what-if, transactions. This is done by entering financial statement amounts in the Unadjusted (what-if) columns. Proposed transactions are then entered in the Adjustments columns. We then compute "adjusted" amounts from these proposed transactions. The extended amounts in the financial statement columns show the effects of these proposed transactions. These financial statement columns yield **pro forma financial statements** because they show the statements *as if* the proposed transactions occurred.

Quick Check Answers — p. 156 

1. Where do we get the amounts to enter in the Unadjusted Trial Balance columns of a work sheet?
2. What are the advantages of using a work sheet to help prepare adjusting entries?
3. What are the overall benefits of a work sheet?

CLOSING PROCESS

C1 Explain why temporary accounts are closed each period.

Temporary Accounts
(closed at period-end)
Revenues
Expenses
Owner Withdrawals
Income Summary

Permanent Accounts
(not closed at period-end)
Assets
Liabilities
Owner Capital

The **closing process** is an important step at the end of an accounting period *after* financial statements have been completed. It prepares accounts for recording the transactions and the events of the *next* period. In the closing process we must (1) identify accounts for closing, (2) record and post the closing entries, and (3) prepare a post-closing trial balance. The purpose of the closing process is twofold. First, it resets revenue, expense, and withdrawals account balances to zero at the end of each period. This is done so that these accounts can properly measure income and withdrawals for the next period. Second, it helps in summarizing a period's revenues and expenses. This section explains the closing process.

Temporary and Permanent Accounts

Temporary (or *nominal*) **accounts** accumulate data related to one accounting period. They include all income statement accounts, the withdrawals account, and the Income Summary account. They are temporary because the accounts are opened at the beginning of a period, used to record transactions and events for that period, and then closed at the end of the period. *The closing process applies only to temporary accounts.* **Permanent** (or *real*) **accounts** report on activities related to one or more future accounting periods. They carry their ending balances into the next period and generally consist of all balance sheet accounts. These asset, liability, and equity accounts are not closed.

Recording Closing Entries

To record and post **closing entries** is to transfer the end-of-period balances in revenue, expense, and withdrawals accounts to the permanent capital account. Closing entries are necessary at the end of each period after financial statements are prepared because

- Revenue, expense, and withdrawals accounts must begin each period with zero balances.
- Owner's capital must reflect prior periods' revenues, expenses, and withdrawals.

An income statement aims to report revenues and expenses for a *specific accounting period.* The statement of owner's equity reports similar information, including withdrawals. Since revenue, expense, and withdrawals accounts must accumulate information separately for each period, they must start each period with zero balances. To close these accounts, we transfer their balances first to an account called *Income Summary.* **Income Summary** is a temporary account (only used for the closing process) that contains a credit for the sum of all revenues (and gains) and a debit for the sum of all expenses (and losses). Its balance equals net income or net loss and it is transferred to the capital account. Next the withdrawals account balance is transferred to the capital account. After these closing entries are posted, the revenue, expense, withdrawals, and Income Summary accounts have zero balances. These accounts are then said to be *closed* or *cleared.*

Point: To understand the closing process, focus on its *outcomes—updating* the capital account balance to its proper ending balance, and getting *temporary accounts* to show *zero balances* for purposes of accumulating data for the next period.

Exhibit 4.3 uses the adjusted account balances of FastForward (from the Adjusted Trial Balance columns of Exhibit 4.1 or from the left side of Exhibit 4.4) to show the four steps necessary to close its temporary accounts. We explain each step.

EXHIBIT 4.3

Four-Step Closing Process

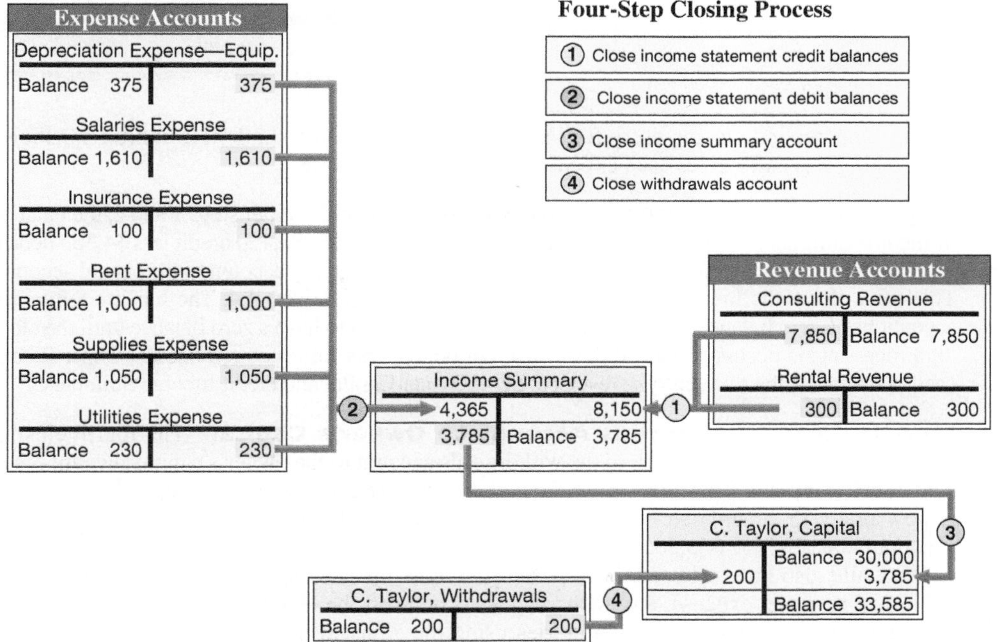

Point: C. Taylor, Capital is the only *permanent account* in Exhibit 4.3.

Step 1: Close Credit Balances in Revenue Accounts to Income Summary The first closing entry transfers credit balances in revenue (and gain) accounts to the Income Summary account. We bring accounts with credit balances to zero by debiting them. For FastForward, this journal entry is step 1 in Exhibit 4.4. This entry closes revenue accounts and leaves them with zero balances. The accounts are now ready to record revenues when they occur in the next period. The $8,150 credit entry to Income Summary equals total revenues for the period.

P2 Describe and prepare closing entries.

Step 2: Close Debit Balances in Expense Accounts to Income Summary The second closing entry transfers debit balances in expense (and loss) accounts to the Income Summary account. We bring expense accounts' debit balances to zero by crediting them. With a balance of zero, these accounts are ready to accumulate a record of expenses for the next

Point: It is possible to close revenue and expense accounts directly to owner's capital. Computerized accounting systems do this.

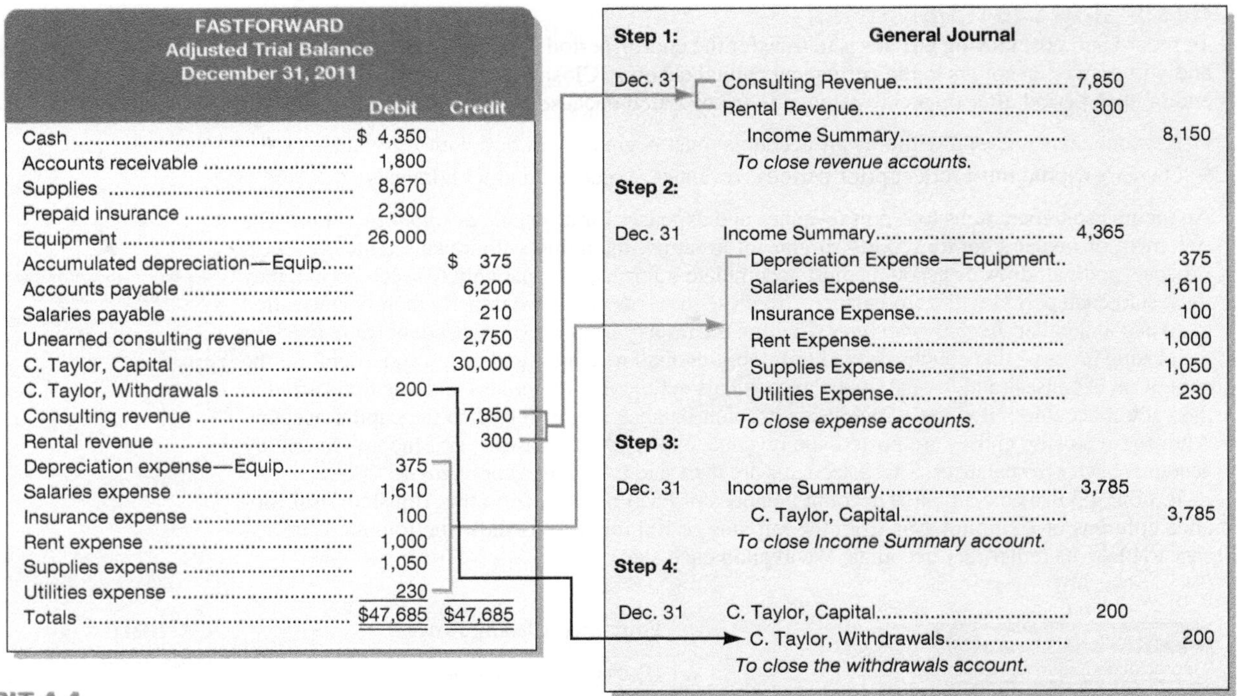

FASTFORWARD
Adjusted Trial Balance
December 31, 2011

	Debit	Credit
Cash	$ 4,350	
Accounts receivable	1,800	
Supplies	8,670	
Prepaid insurance	2,300	
Equipment	26,000	
Accumulated depreciation—Equip.		$ 375
Accounts payable		6,200
Salaries payable		210
Unearned consulting revenue		2,750
C. Taylor, Capital		30,000
C. Taylor, Withdrawals	200	
Consulting revenue		7,850
Rental revenue		300
Depreciation expense—Equip.	375	
Salaries expense	1,610	
Insurance expense	100	
Rent expense	1,000	
Supplies expense	1,050	
Utilities expense	230	
Totals	$47,685	$47,685

General Journal

Step 1:			
Dec. 31	Consulting Revenue	7,850	
	Rental Revenue	300	
	Income Summary		8,150
	To close revenue accounts.		
Step 2:			
Dec. 31	Income Summary	4,365	
	Depreciation Expense—Equipment		375
	Salaries Expense		1,610
	Insurance Expense		100
	Rent Expense		1,000
	Supplies Expense		1,050
	Utilities Expense		230
	To close expense accounts.		
Step 3:			
Dec. 31	Income Summary	3,785	
	C. Taylor, Capital		3,785
	To close Income Summary account.		
Step 4:			
Dec. 31	C. Taylor, Capital	200	
	C. Taylor, Withdrawals		200
	To close the withdrawals account.		

EXHIBIT 4.4

Preparing Closing Entries

period. This second closing entry for FastForward is step 2 in Exhibit 4.4. Exhibit 4.3 shows that posting this entry gives each expense account a zero balance.

Step 3: Close Income Summary to Owner's Capital After steps 1 and 2, the balance of Income Summary is equal to December's net income of $3,785 ($8,150 credit less $4,365 debit). The third closing entry transfers the balance of the Income Summary account to the capital account. This entry closes the Income Summary account–see step 3 in Exhibit 4.4. The Income Summary account has a zero balance after posting this entry. It continues to have a zero balance until the closing process again occurs at the end of the next period. (If a net loss occurred because expenses exceeded revenues, the third entry is reversed: debit Owner Capital and credit Income Summary.)

Step 4: Close Withdrawals Account to Owner's Capital The fourth closing entry transfers any debit balance in the withdrawals account to the owner's capital account—see step 4 in Exhibit 4.4. This entry gives the withdrawals account a zero balance, and the account is now ready to accumulate next period's withdrawals. This entry also reduces the capital account balance to the $33,585 amount reported on the balance sheet.

We could also have selected the accounts and amounts needing to be closed by identifying individual revenue, expense, and withdrawals accounts in the ledger. This is illustrated in Exhibit 4.4 where we prepare closing entries using the adjusted trial balance.[1] (Information for closing entries is also in the financial statement columns of a work sheet.)

Post-Closing Trial Balance

P3 Explain and prepare a post-closing trial balance.

Exhibit 4.5 shows the entire ledger of FastForward as of December 31 after adjusting and closing entries are posted. (The transaction and adjusting entries are in Chapters 2 and 3.) The temporary accounts (revenues, expenses, and withdrawals) have ending balances equal to zero.

[1] The closing process has focused on proprietorships. It is identical for partnerships with the exception that each owner has separate capital and withdrawals accounts (for steps 3 and 4). The closing process for a corporation is similar with the exception that it uses a Retained Earnings account instead of a Capital account, and a Dividend account instead of a Withdrawals account.

EXHIBIT 4.5

General Ledger after the Closing Process for FastForward

Asset Accounts

Cash — Acct. No. 101

Date	Explan.	PR	Debit	Credit	Balance
2011					
Dec. 1	(1)	G1	30,000		30,000
2	(2)	G1		2,500	27,500
3	(3)	G1		26,000	1,500
5	(5)	G1	4,200		5,700
6	(13)	G1		2,400	3,300
12	(6)	G1		1,000	2,300
12	(7)	G1		700	1,600
22	(9)	G1	1,900		3,500
24	(10)	G1		900	2,600
24	(11)	G1		200	2,400
26	(12)	G1	3,000		5,400
26	(14)	G1		120	5,280
26	(15)	G1		230	5,050
26	(16)	G1		700	**4,350**

Accounts Receivable — Acct. No. 106

Date	Explan.	PR	Debit	Credit	Balance
2011					
Dec. 12	(8)	G1	1,900		1,900
22	(9)	G1		1,900	0
31	Adj.(f)	G1	1,800		**1,800**

Supplies — Acct. No. 126

Date	Explan.	PR	Debit	Credit	Balance
2011					
Dec. 2	(2)	G1	2,500		2,500
6	(4)	G1	7,100		9,600
26	(14)	G1	120		9,720
31	Adj.(b)	G1		1,050	**8,670**

Prepaid Insurance — Acct. No. 128

Date	Explan.	PR	Debit	Credit	Balance
2011					
Dec. 6	(13)	G1	2,400		2,400
31	Adj.(a)	G1		100	**2,300**

Equipment — Acct. No. 167

Date	Explan.	PR	Debit	Credit	Balance
2011					
Dec. 3	(3)	G1	26,000		**26,000**

Accumulated Depreciation— Equipment — Acct. No. 168

Date	Explan.	PR	Debit	Credit	Balance
2011					
Dec. 31	Adj.(c)	G1		375	**375**

Liability and Equity Accounts

Accounts Payable — Acct. No. 201

Date	Explan.	PR	Debit	Credit	Balance
2011					
Dec. 6	(4)	G1		7,100	7,100
24	(10)	G1	900		**6,200**

Salaries Payable — Acct. No. 209

Date	Explan.	PR	Debit	Credit	Balance
2011					
Dec. 31	Adj.(e)	G1		210	**210**

Unearned Consulting Revenue — Acct. No. 236

Date	Explan.	PR	Debit	Credit	Balance
2011					
Dec. 26	(12)	G1		3,000	3,000
31	Adj.(d)	G1	250		**2,750**

C. Taylor, Capital — Acct. No. 301

Date	Explan.	PR	Debit	Credit	Balance
2011					
Dec. 1	(1)	G1		30,000	**30,000**
31	Clos.(3)	G1		3,785	33,785
31	Clos.(4)	G1	200		33,585

C. Taylor, Withdrawals — Acct. No. 302

Date	Explan.	PR	Debit	Credit	Balance
2011					
Dec. 24	(11)	G1	200		200
31	Clos.(4)	G1		200	0

Revenue and Expense Accounts (Including Income Summary)

Consulting Revenue — Acct. No. 403

Date	Explan.	PR	Debit	Credit	Balance
2011					
Dec. 5	(5)	G1		4,200	4,200
12	(8)	G1		1,600	5,800
31	Adj.(d)	G1		250	6,050
31	Adj.(f)	G1		1,800	**7,850**
31	Clos.(1)	G1	7,850		0

Rental Revenue — Acct. No. 406

Date	Explan.	PR	Debit	Credit	Balance
2011					
Dec. 12	(8)	G1		300	**300**
31	Clos.(1)	G1	300		0

Depreciation Expense— Equipment — Acct. No. 612

Date	Explan.	PR	Debit	Credit	Balance
2011					
Dec. 31	Adj.(c)	G1	375		**375**
31	Clos.(2)	G1		375	0

Salaries Expense — Acct. No. 622

Date	Explan.	PR	Debit	Credit	Balance
2011					
Dec. 12	(7)	G1	700		700
26	(16)	G1	700		1,400
31	Adj.(e)	G1	210		**1,610**
31	Clos.(2)	G1		1,610	0

Insurance Expense — Acct. No. 637

Date	Explan.	PR	Debit	Credit	Balance
2011					
Dec. 31	Adj.(a)	G1	100		**100**
31	Clos.(2)	G1		100	0

Rent Expense — Acct. No. 640

Date	Explan.	PR	Debit	Credit	Balance
2011					
Dec. 12	(6)	G1	1,000		**1,000**
31	Clos.(2)	G1		1,000	0

Supplies Expense — Acct. No. 652

Date	Explan.	PR	Debit	Credit	Balance
2011					
Dec. 31	Adj.(b)	G1	1,050		**1,050**
31	Clos.(2)	G1		1,050	0

Utilities Expense — Acct. No. 690

Date	Explan.	PR	Debit	Credit	Balance
2011					
Dec. 26	(15)	G1	230		**230**
31	Clos.(2)	G1		230	0

Income Summary — Acct. No. 901

Date	Explan.	PR	Debit	Credit	Balance
2011					
Dec. 31	Clos.(1)	G1		8,150	8,150
31	Clos.(2)	G1	4,365		3,785
31	Clos.(3)	G1	3,785		0

A **post-closing trial balance** is a list of permanent accounts and their balances from the ledger after all closing entries have been journalized and posted. It lists the balances for all accounts not closed. These accounts comprise a company's assets, liabilities, and equity, which are identical to those in the balance sheet. The aim of a post-closing trial balance is to verify that (1) total debits equal total credits for permanent accounts and (2) all temporary accounts have zero balances. FastForward's post-closing trial balance is shown in Exhibit 4.6. The post-closing trial balance usually is the last step in the accounting process.

EXHIBIT 4.6

Post-Closing Trial Balance

FASTFORWARD
Post-Closing Trial Balance
December 31, 2011

	Debit	Credit
Cash	$ 4,350	
Accounts receivable	1,800	
Supplies	8,670	
Prepaid insurance	2,300	
Equipment	26,000	
Accumulated depreciation—Equipment		$ 375
Accounts payable		6,200
Salaries payable		210
Unearned consulting revenue		2,750
C. Taylor, Capital		33,585
Totals	$43,120	$43,120

ACCOUNTING CYCLE

C2 Identify steps in the accounting cycle.

The term **accounting cycle** refers to the steps in preparing financial statements. It is called a *cycle* because the steps are repeated each reporting period. Exhibit 4.7 shows the 10 steps in the cycle, beginning with analyzing transactions and ending with a post-closing trial balance or

EXHIBIT 4.7

Steps in the Accounting Cycle*

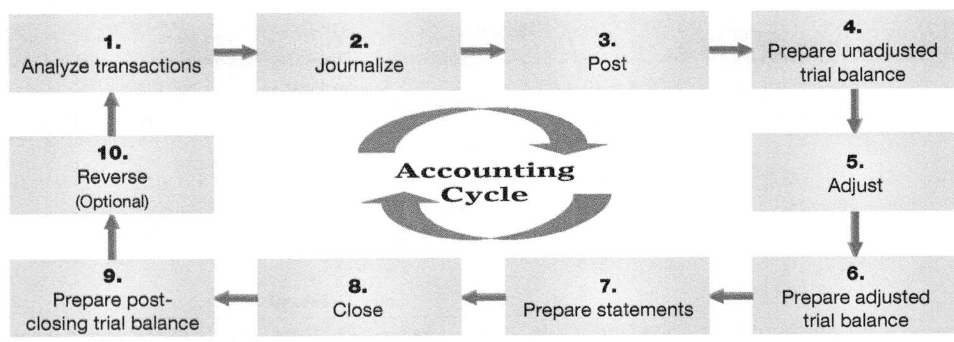

Explanations

1. Analyze transactions	Analyze transactions to prepare for journalizing.
2. Journalize	Record accounts, including debits and credits, in a journal.
3. Post	Transfer debits and credits from the journal to the ledger.
4. Prepare unadjusted trial balance	Summarize unadjusted ledger accounts and amounts.
5. Adjust	Record adjustments to bring account balances up to date; journalize and post adjustments.
6. Prepare adjusted trial balance	Summarize adjusted ledger accounts and amounts.
7. Prepare statements	Use adjusted trial balance to prepare financial statements.
8. Close	Journalize and post entries to close temporary accounts.
9. Prepare post-closing trial balance	Test clerical accuracy of the closing procedures.
10. Reverse (optional)	Reverse certain adjustments in the next period—optional step; see Appendix 4A.

* Steps 4, 6, and 9 can be done on a work sheet. A work sheet is useful in planning adjustments, but adjustments (step 5) must always be journalized and posted. Steps 3, 4, 6, and 9 are automatic with a computerized system.

reversing entries. Steps 1 through 3 usually occur regularly as a company enters into transactions. Steps 4 through 9 are done at the end of a period. *Reversing entries* in step 10 are optional and are explained in Appendix 4A.

Quick Check Answers – p. 156 

4. What are the major steps in preparing closing entries?
5. Why are revenue and expense accounts called *temporary?* Identify and list the types of temporary accounts.
6. What accounts are listed on the post-closing trial balance?

CLASSIFIED BALANCE SHEET

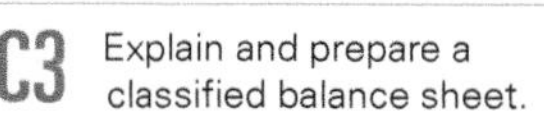

Our discussion to this point has been limited to unclassified financial statements. This section describes a classified balance sheet. The next chapter describes a classified income statement. An **unclassified balance sheet** is one whose items are broadly grouped into assets, liabilities, and equity. One example is FastForward's balance sheet in Exhibit 4.2. A **classified balance sheet** organizes assets and liabilities into important subgroups that provide more information to decision makers.

Classification Structure

A classified balance sheet has no required layout, but it usually contains the categories in Exhibit 4.8. One of the more important classifications is the separation between current and noncurrent items for both assets and liabilities. Current items are those expected to come due (either collected or owed) within one year or the company's operating cycle, whichever is longer. The **operating cycle** is the time span from when *cash is used* to acquire goods and services until *cash is received* from the sale of goods and services. "Operating" refers to company operations and "cycle" refers to the circular flow of cash used for company inputs and then cash received from its outputs. The length of a company's operating cycle depends on its activities. For a service company, the operating cycle is the time span between (1) paying employees who perform the services and (2) receiving cash from customers. For a merchandiser selling products, the operating cycle is the time span between (1) paying suppliers for merchandise and (2) receiving cash from customers.

EXHIBIT 4.8

Typical Categories in a Classified Balance Sheet

Assets	Liabilities and Equity
Current assets	Current liabilities
Noncurrent assets	Noncurrent liabilities
Long-term investments	Equity
Plant assets	
Intangible assets	

Most operating cycles are less than one year. This means most companies use a one-year period in deciding which assets and liabilities are current. A few companies have an operating cycle longer than one year. For instance, producers of certain beverages (wine) and products (ginseng) that require aging for several years have operating cycles longer than one year. A balance sheet lists current assets before noncurrent assets and current liabilities before noncurrent liabilities. This consistency in presentation allows users to quickly identify current assets that are most easily converted to cash and current liabilities that are shortly coming due. Items in current assets and current liabilities are listed in the order of how quickly they will be converted to, or paid in, cash.

EXHIBIT 4.9

Example of a Classified Balance Sheet

SNOWBOARDING COMPONENTS Balance Sheet January 31, 2011		
Assets		
Current assets		
Cash	$ 6,500	
Short-term investments	2,100	
Accounts receivable, net	4,400	
Merchandise inventory	27,500	
Prepaid expenses	2,400	
Total current assets		$ 42,900
Long-term investments		
Notes receivable	1,500	
Investments in stocks and bonds	18,000	
Land held for future expansion	48,000	
Total long-term investments		67,500
Plant assets		
Equipment and buildings	203,200	
Less accumulated depreciation	53,000	
Equipment and buildings, net		150,200
Land		73,200
Total plant assets		223,400
Intangible assets		10,000
Total assets		$343,800
Liabilities		
Current liabilities		
Accounts payable	$ 15,300	
Wages payable	3,200	
Notes payable	3,000	
Current portion of long-term liabilities	7,500	
Total current liabilities		$ 29,000
Long-term liabilities (net of current portion)		150,000
Total liabilities		179,000
Equity		
T. Hawk, Capital		164,800
Total liabilities and equity		$343,800

Classification Categories

This section describes the most common categories in a classified balance sheet. The balance sheet for Snowboarding Components in Exhibit 4.9 shows the typical categories. Its assets are classified as either current or noncurrent. Its noncurrent assets include three main categories: long-term investments, plant assets, and intangible assets. Its liabilities are classified as either current or long-term. Not all companies use the same categories of assets and liabilities for their balance sheets. K2 Inc., a manufacturer of snowboards, reported a balance sheet with only three asset classes: current assets; property, plant and equipment; and other assets.

Current Assets **Current assets** are cash and other resources that are expected to be sold, collected, or used within one year or the company's operating cycle, whichever is longer. Examples are cash, short-term investments, accounts receivable, short-term notes receivable, goods for sale (called *merchandise* or *inventory*), and prepaid expenses. The individual prepaid expenses of a company are usually small in amount compared to many other assets and are often combined and shown as a single item. The prepaid expenses in Exhibit 4.9 likely include items such as prepaid insurance, prepaid rent, office supplies, and store supplies. Prepaid expenses are usually listed last because they will not be converted to cash (instead, they are used).

Point: Current is also called *short-term*, and noncurrent is also called *long-term*.

Long-Term Investments A second major balance sheet classification is **long-term** (or *noncurrent*) **investments.** Notes receivable and investments in stocks and bonds are long-term assets when they are expected to be held for more than the longer of one year or the operating cycle. Land held for future expansion is a long-term investment because it is *not* used in operations.

Plant Assets Plant assets are tangible assets that are both *long-lived* and *used to produce* or *sell products and services*. Examples are equipment, machinery, buildings, and land that are used to produce or sell products and services. The order listing for plant assets is usually from most liquid to least liquid such as equipment and machinery to buildings and land.

Point: Plant assets are also called *fixed assets; property, plant and equipment;* or *long-lived assets.*

Intangible Assets **Intangible assets** are long-term resources that benefit business operations, usually lack physical form, and have uncertain benefits. Examples are patents, trademarks, copyrights, franchises, and goodwill. Their value comes from the privileges or rights granted to or held by the owner. K2, Inc., reported intangible assets of $228 million, which is nearly 20 percent of its total assets. Its intangibles included trademarks, patents, and licensing agreements.

Current Liabilities **Current liabilities** are obligations due to be paid or settled within one year or the operating cycle, whichever is longer. They are usually settled by paying out current assets such as cash. Current liabilities often include accounts payable, notes payable, wages payable, taxes payable, interest payable, and unearned revenues. Also, any portion of a long-term liability due to be paid within one year or the operating cycle, whichever is longer, is a current liability. Unearned revenues are current liabilities when they will be settled by delivering products or services within one year or the operating cycle, whichever is longer. Current liabilities are reported in the order of those to be settled first.

Point: Many financial ratios are distorted if accounts are not classified correctly.

Long-Term Liabilities **Long-term liabilities** are obligations *not* due within one year or the operating cycle, whichever is longer. Notes payable, mortgages payable, bonds payable, and lease obligations are common long-term liabilities. If a company has both short- and long-term items in each of these categories, they are commonly separated into two accounts in the ledger.

Point: Only assets and liabilities are classified as current or noncurrent.

Equity Equity is the owner's claim on assets. For a proprietorship, this claim is reported in the equity section with an owner's capital account. (For a partnership, the equity section reports a capital account for each partner. For a corporation, the equity section is divided into two main subsections, common stock and retained earnings.)

Quick Check Answers — p. 156 

7. Classify the following assets as (1) current assets, (2) plant assets, or (3) intangible assets: (*a*) land used in operations, (*b*) office supplies, (*c*) receivables from customers due in 10 months, (*d*) insurance protection for the next 9 months, (*e*) trucks used to provide services to customers, (*f*) trademarks.
8. Cite at least two examples of assets classified as investments on the balance sheet.
9. Explain the operating cycle for a service company.

GLOBAL VIEW

We explained that accounting under U.S. GAAP is similar, but not identical, to that under IFRS. This section discusses differences in the closing process and in reporting assets and liabilities on a balance sheet.

Closing Process The closing process is identical under U.S. GAAP and IFRS. Although unique accounts can arise under either system, the closing process remains the same.

Reporting Assets and Liabilities The definition of an asset is similar under U.S. GAAP and IFRS and involves three basic criteria: (1) the company owns or controls the right to use the item, (2) the right arises from a past transaction or event, and (3) the item can be reliably measured. Both systems define the initial asset value as historical cost for nearly all assets. After acquisition, one of two asset measurement systems is applied: historical cost or fair value. Generally, U.S. GAAP defines fair value as the amount to be received in an orderly sale. IFRS defines fair value as *exchange value*—either replacement cost or selling price. We describe these differences, and the assets to which they apply, in later chapters.

The definition of a liability is similar under U.S. GAAP and IFRS and involves three basic criteria: (1) the item is a *present* obligation requiring a probable future resource outlay, (2) the obligation arises from a past transaction or event, and (3) the obligation can be reliably measured. As with assets, both systems apply one of two measurement systems to liabilities: historical cost or fair value. Later chapters discuss specific differences.

Decision Analysis

Current Ratio

A1 Compute the current ratio and describe what it reveals about a company's financial condition.

An important use of financial statements is to help assess a company's ability to pay its debts in the near future. Such analysis affects decisions by suppliers when allowing a company to buy on credit. It also affects decisions by creditors when lending money to a company, including loan terms such as interest rate, due date, and collateral requirements. It can also affect a manager's decisions about using cash to pay debts when they come due. The **current ratio** is one measure of a company's ability to pay its short-term obligations. It is defined in Exhibit 4.10 as current assets divided by current liabilities.

EXHIBIT 4.10
Current Ratio

$$\textbf{Current ratio} = \frac{\textbf{Current assets}}{\textbf{Current liabilities}}$$

Using financial information from Limited Brands, Inc., we compute its current ratio for the recent four-year period. The results are in Exhibit 4.11.

EXHIBIT 4.11
Limited Brands' Current Ratio

$ in millions	2010	2009	2008	2007	2006
Current assets	$3,250	$2,867	$2,919	$2,771	$2,784
Current liabilities	$1,322	$1,255	$1,374	$1,709	$1,575
Current ratio	2.5	2.3	2.1	1.6	1.8
Industry current ratio	1.9	2.0	2.1	2.3	2.4

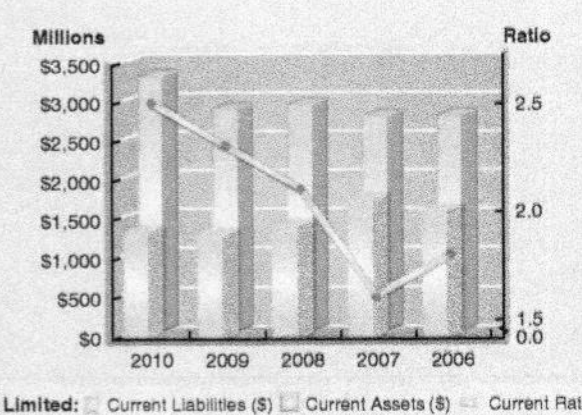

Limited Brands' current ratio averaged 2.1 for its fiscal years 2006 through 2010. The current ratio for each of these years suggests that the company's short-term obligations can be covered with its short-term assets. However, if its ratio would approach 1.0, Limited would expect to face challenges in covering liabilities. If the ratio were *less* than 1.0, current liabilities would exceed current assets, and the company's ability to pay short-term obligations could be in doubt.

Decision Maker Answer — p. 156

Analyst You are analyzing the financial condition of a company to assess its ability to meet upcoming loan payments. You compute its current ratio as 1.2. You also find that a major portion of accounts receivable is due from one client who has not made any payments in the past 12 months. Removing this receivable from current assets lowers the current ratio to 0.7. What do you conclude? ■

DEMONSTRATION PROBLEM

The partial work sheet of Midtown Repair Company at December 31, 2011, follows.

	Adjusted Trial Balance		Income Statement		Balance Sheet and Statement of Owner's Equity	
	Debit	Credit	Debit	Credit	Debit	Credit
Cash	95,600					
Notes receivable (current)	50,000					
Prepaid insurance	16,000					
Prepaid rent	4,000					
Equipment	170,000					
Accumulated depreciation—Equipment		57,000				
Accounts payable		52,000				
Long-term notes payable		63,000				
C. Trout, Capital		178,500				
C. Trout, Withdrawals	30,000					
Repair services revenue		180,800				
Interest revenue		7,500				
Depreciation expense—Equipment	28,500					
Wages expense	85,000					
Rent expense	48,000					
Insurance expense	6,000					
Interest expense	5,700					
Totals	538,800	538,800				

Required

1. Complete the work sheet by extending the adjusted trial balance totals to the appropriate financial statement columns.
2. Prepare closing entries for Midtown Repair Company.
3. Set up the Income Summary and the C. Trout, Capital account in the general ledger (in balance column format) and post the closing entries to these accounts.
4. Determine the balance of the C. Trout, Capital account to be reported on the December 31, 2011, balance sheet.
5. Prepare an income statement, statement of owner's equity, and classified balance sheet (in report form) as of December 31, 2011.

PLANNING THE SOLUTION

- Extend the adjusted trial balance account balances to the appropriate financial statement columns.
- Prepare entries to close the revenue accounts to Income Summary, to close the expense accounts to Income Summary, to close Income Summary to the capital account, and to close the withdrawals account to the capital account.

- Post the first and second closing entries to the Income Summary account. Examine the balance of income summary and verify that it agrees with the net income shown on the work sheet.
- Post the third and fourth closing entries to the capital account.
- Use the work sheet's two right-most columns and your answer in part 4 to prepare the classified balance sheet.

SOLUTION TO DEMONSTRATION PROBLEM

1. Completing the work sheet.

	Adjusted Trial Balance		Income Statement		Balance Sheet and Statement of Owner's Equity	
	Debit	Credit	Debit	Credit	Debit	Credit
Cash	95,600				95,600	
Notes receivable (current)	50,000				50,000	
Prepaid insurance	16,000				16,000	
Prepaid rent	4,000				4,000	
Equipment	170,000				170,000	
Accumulated depreciation—Equipment		57,000				57,000
Accounts payable		52,000				52,000
Long-term notes payable		63,000				63,000
C. Trout, Capital		178,500				178,500
C. Trout, Withdrawals	30,000				30,000	
Repair services revenue		180,800		180,800		
Interest revenue		7,500		7,500		
Depreciation expense—Equipment	28,500		28,500			
Wages expense	85,000		85,000			
Rent expense	48,000		48,000			
Insurance expense	6,000		6,000			
Interest expense	5,700		5,700			
Totals	538,800	538,800	173,200	188,300	365,600	350,500
Net income			15,100			15,100
Totals			188,300	188,300	365,600	365,600

2. Closing entries.

Dec. 31	Repair Services Revenue	180,800	
	Interest Revenue	7,500	
	Income Summary		188,300
	To close revenue accounts.		
Dec. 31	Income Summary	173,200	
	Depreciation Expense—Equipment		28,500
	Wages Expense		85,000
	Rent Expense		48,000
	Insurance Expense		6,000
	Interest Expense		5,700
	To close expense accounts.		
Dec. 31	Income Summary	15,100	
	C. Trout, Capital		15,100
	To close the Income Summary account.		
Dec. 31	C. Trout, Capital	30,000	
	C. Trout, Withdrawals		30,000
	To close the withdrawals account.		

3. Set up the Income Summary and the capital ledger accounts and post the closing entries.

Income Summary				Account No. 901	
Date	Explanation	PR	Debit	Credit	Balance
2011					
Jan. 1	Beginning balance				0
Dec. 31	Close revenue accounts			188,300	188,300
31	Close expense accounts		173,200		15,100
31	Close income summary		15,100		0

C. Trout, Capital				Account No. 301	
Date	Explanation	PR	Debit	Credit	Balance
2011					
Jan. 1	Beginning balance				178,500
Dec. 31	Close Income Summary			15,100	193,600
31	Close C. Trout, Withdrawals		30,000		163,600

4. The final capital balance of $163,600 (from part 3) will be reported on the December 31, 2011, balance sheet. The final capital balance reflects the increase due to the net income earned during the year and the decrease for the owner's withdrawals during the year.

5.

MIDTOWN REPAIR COMPANY
Income Statement
For Year Ended December 31, 2011

Revenues		
Repair services revenue	$180,800	
Interest revenue	7,500	
Total revenues		$188,300
Expenses		
Depreciation expense—Equipment	28,500	
Wages expense	85,000	
Rent expense	48,000	
Insurance expense	6,000	
Interest expense	5,700	
Total expenses		173,200
Net income		$ 15,100

MIDTOWN REPAIR COMPANY
Statement of Owner's Equity
For Year Ended December 31, 2011

C. Trout, Capital, December 31, 2010		$178,500
Add: Investment by owner	$ 0	
Net income	15,100	15,100
		193,600
Less: Withdrawals by owner		30,000
C. Trout, Capital, December 31, 2011		$163,600

MIDTOWN REPAIR COMPANY Balance Sheet December 31, 2011		
Assets		
Current assets		
Cash		$ 95,600
Notes receivable		50,000
Prepaid insurance		16,000
Prepaid rent		4,000
Total current assets		165,600
Plant assets		
Equipment	$170,000	
Less: Accumulated depreciation—Equipment	(57,000)	
Total plant assets		113,000
Total assets		$278,600
Liabilities		
Current liabilities		
Accounts payable		$ 52,000
Long-term liabilities		
Long-term notes payable		63,000
Total liabilities		115,000
Equity		
C. Trout, Capital		163,600
Total liabilities and equity		$278,600

APPENDIX

4A Reversing Entries

Reversing entries are optional. They are recorded in response to accrued assets and accrued liabilities that were created by adjusting entries at the end of a reporting period. The purpose of reversing entries is to simplify a company's recordkeeping. Exhibit 4A.1 shows an example of FastForward's reversing entries. The top of the exhibit shows the adjusting entry FastForward recorded on December 31 for its employee's earned but unpaid salary. The entry recorded three days' salary of $210, which increased December's total salary expense to $1,610. The entry also recognized a liability of $210. The expense is reported on December's income statement. The expense account is then closed. The ledger on January 1, 2012, shows a $210 liability and a zero balance in the Salaries Expense account. At this point, the choice is made between using or not using reversing entries.

Point: As a general rule, adjusting entries that create new asset or liability accounts are likely candidates for reversing.

Accounting *without* Reversing Entries The path down the left side of Exhibit 4A.1 is described in the chapter. To summarize here, when the next payday occurs on January 9, we record payment with a compound entry that debits both the expense and liability accounts and credits Cash. Posting that entry creates a $490 balance in the expense account and reduces the liability account balance to zero because the debt has been settled. The disadvantage of this approach is the slightly more complex entry required on January 9. Paying the accrued liability means that this entry differs from the routine entries made on all other paydays. To construct the proper entry on January 9, we must recall the effect of the December 31 adjusting entry. Reversing entries overcome this disadvantage.

P4 Prepare reversing entries and explain their purpose.

Accounting *with* Reversing Entries The right side of Exhibit 4A.1 shows how a reversing entry on January 1 overcomes the disadvantage of the January 9 entry when not using reversing entries. A reversing entry is the exact opposite of an adjusting entry. For FastForward, the Salaries Payable liability account is debited for $210, meaning that this account now has a zero balance after the entry is posted. The Salaries Payable account temporarily understates the liability, but this is not a problem since

EXHIBIT 4A.1

Reversing Entries for an Accrued Expense

Accrue salaries expense on December 31, 2011

Salaries Expense 210
  Salaries Payable 210

Salaries Expense

Date	Expl.	Debit	Credit	Balance
2011				
Dec. 12	(7)	700		700
26	(16)	700		1,400
31	*(e)*	210		1,610

Salaries Payable

Date	Expl.	Debit	Credit	Balance
2011				
Dec. 31	*(e)*		210	210

WITHOUT Reversing Entries — OR — **WITH Reversing Entries**

WITHOUT Reversing Entries

No reversing entry recorded on January 1, 2012

NO ENTRY

Salaries Expense

Date	Expl.	Debit	Credit	Balance
2012				

Salaries Payable

Date	Expl.	Debit	Credit	Balance
2011				
Dec. 31	*(e)*		210	210
2012				

WITH Reversing Entries

Reversing entry recorded on January 1, 2012

Salaries Payable 210
  Salaries Expense 210

Salaries Expense*

Date	Expl.	Debit	Credit	Balance
2012				
Jan. 1			210	(210)

Salaries Payable

Date	Expl.	Debit	Credit	Balance
2011				
Dec. 31	*(e)*		210	210
2012				
Jan. 1		210		0

Pay the accrued and current salaries on January 9, the first payday in 2012

WITHOUT Reversing Entries

Salaries Expense 490
Salaries Payable 210
  Cash 700

Salaries Expense

Date	Expl.	Debit	Credit	Balance
2012				
Jan. 9		490		490

Salaries Payable

Date	Expl.	Debit	Credit	Balance
2011				
Dec. 31	*(e)*		210	210
2012				
Jan. 9		210		0

WITH Reversing Entries

Salaries Expense 700
  Cash 700

Salaries Expense*

Date	Expl.	Debit	Credit	Balance
2012				
Jan. 1			210	(210)
Jan. 9		700		490

Salaries Payable

Date	Expl.	Debit	Credit	Balance
2011				
Dec. 31	*(e)*		210	210
2012				
Jan. 1		210		0

Under both approaches, the expense and liability accounts have identical balances after the cash payment on January 9.

Salaries Expense $490
Salaries Payable .... $ 0

*Circled numbers in the *Balance* column indicate abnormal balances.

financial statements are not prepared before the liability is settled on January 9. The credit to the Salaries Expense account is unusual because it gives the account an *abnormal credit balance.* We highlight an abnormal balance by circling it. Because of the reversing entry, the January 9 entry to record payment is straightforward. This entry debits the Salaries Expense account and credits Cash for the full $700 paid. It is the same as all other entries made to record 10 days' salary for the employee. Notice that after the payment entry is posted, the Salaries Expense account has a $490 balance that reflects seven days' salary of $70 per day (see the lower right side of Exhibit 4A.1). The zero balance in the Salaries Payable account is now correct. The lower section of Exhibit 4A.1 shows that the expense and liability accounts have exactly the same balances whether reversing entries are used or not. This means that both approaches yield identical results.

Summary

C1 Explain why temporary accounts are closed each period. Temporary accounts are closed at the end of each accounting period for two main reasons. First, the closing process updates the capital account to include the effects of all transactions and events recorded for the period. Second, it prepares revenue, expense, and withdrawals accounts for the next reporting period by giving them zero balances.

C2 Identify steps in the accounting cycle. The accounting cycle consists of 10 steps: (1) analyze transactions, (2) journalize, (3) post, (4) prepare an unadjusted trial balance, (5) adjust accounts, (6) prepare an adjusted trial balance, (7) prepare statements, (8) close, (9) prepare a post-closing trial balance, and (10) prepare (optional) reversing entries.

C3 Explain and prepare a classified balance sheet. Classified balance sheets report assets and liabilities in two categories: current and noncurrent. Noncurrent assets often include long-term investments, plant assets, and intangible assets. Owner's equity for proprietorships (and partnerships) report the capital account balance. A corporation separates equity into common stock and retained earnings.

A1 Compute the current ratio and describe what it reveals about a company's financial condition. A company's current ratio is defined as current assets divided by current liabilities. We use it to evaluate a company's ability to pay its current liabilities out of current assets.

P1 Prepare a work sheet and explain its usefulness. A work sheet can be a useful tool in preparing and analyzing financial statements. It is helpful at the end of a period in preparing adjusting entries, an adjusted trial balance, and financial statements. A work sheet usually contains five pairs of columns: Unadjusted Trial Balance, Adjustments, Adjusted Trial Balance, Income Statement, and Balance Sheet & Statement of Owner's Equity.

P2 Describe and prepare closing entries. Closing entries involve four steps: (1) close credit balances in revenue (and gain) accounts to Income Summary, (2) close debit balances in expense (and loss) accounts to Income Summary, (3) close Income Summary to the capital account, and (4) close withdrawals account to owner's capital.

P3 Explain and prepare a post-closing trial balance. A post-closing trial balance is a list of permanent accounts and their balances after all closing entries have been journalized and posted. Its purpose is to verify that (1) total debits equal total credits for permanent accounts and (2) all temporary accounts have zero balances.

P4A Prepare reversing entries and explain their purpose. Reversing entries are an optional step. They are applied to accrued expenses and revenues. The purpose of reversing entries is to simplify subsequent journal entries. Financial statements are unaffected by the choice to use or not use reversing entries.

Guidance Answers to Decision Maker and Decision Ethics

Entrepreneur Yes, you are concerned about the absence of a depreciation adjustment. Equipment does depreciate, and financial statements must recognize this occurrence. Its absence suggests an error or a misrepresentation (there is also the possibility that equipment is fully depreciated).

Analyst A current ratio of 1.2 suggests that current assets are sufficient to cover current liabilities, but it implies a minimal buffer in case of errors in measuring current assets or current liabilities. Removing the past due receivable reduces the current ratio to 0.7. Your assessment is that the company will have some difficulty meeting its loan payments.

Guidance Answers to Quick Checks

1. Amounts in the Unadjusted Trial Balance columns are taken from current account balances in the ledger. The balances for new accounts expected to arise from adjusted entries can be left blank or set at zero.
2. A work sheet offers the advantage of listing on one page all necessary information to make adjusting entries.
3. A work sheet can help in (a) accounting efficiency and avoiding errors, (b) linking transactions and events to their effects in financial statements, (c) showing adjustments for audit purposes, (d) preparing interim financial statements, and (e) showing effects from proposed, or what-if, transactions.
4. The major steps in preparing closing entries are to close (1) credit balances in revenue accounts to Income Summary, (2) debit balances in expense accounts to Income Summary, (3) Income Summary to owner's capital, and (4) any withdrawals account to owner's capital.
5. Revenue (and gain) and expense (and loss) accounts are called *temporary* because they are opened and closed each period. The Income Summary and owner's withdrawals accounts are also temporary.
6. Permanent accounts make up the post-closing trial balance, which consist of asset, liability, and equity accounts.
7. Current assets: (*b*), (*c*), (*d*). Plant assets: (*a*), (*e*). Item (*f*) is an intangible asset.
8. Investment in common stock, investment in bonds, and land held for future expansion.
9. For a service company, the operating cycle is the usual time between (1) paying employees who do the services and (2) receiving cash from customers for services provided.

Key Terms

mhhe.com/wildFAP20e

Accounting cycle (p. 146)
Classified balance sheet (p. 147)
Closing entries (p. 143)
Closing process (p. 142)
Current assets (p. 148)
Current liabilities (p. 149)
Current ratio (p. 150)
Income summary (p. 143)
Intangible assets (p. 149)
Long-term investments (p. 149)
Long-term liabilities (p. 149)
Operating cycle (p. 147)
Permanent accounts (p. 142)
Post-closing trial balance (p. 146)
Pro forma financial statements (p. 142)
Reversing entries (p. 154)
Temporary accounts (p. 142)
Unclassified balance sheet (p. 147)
Working papers (p. 138)
Work sheet (p. 138)

Multiple Choice Quiz

Answers on p. 177

mhhe.com/wildFAP20e

Additional Quiz Questions are available at the book's Website.

1. G. Venda, owner of Venda Services, withdrew $25,000 from the business during the current year. The entry to close the withdrawals account at the end of the year is:

		Debit	Credit
a.	G. Venda, Withdrawals	25,000	
	G. Venda, Capital		25,000
b.	Income Summary	25,000	
	G. Venda, Capital		25,000
c.	G. Venda, Withdrawals	25,000	
	Cash		25,000
d.	G. Venda, Capital	25,000	
	Salary Expense		25,000
e.	G. Venda, Capital	25,000	
	G. Venda, Withdrawals		25,000

2. The following information is available for the R. Kandamil Company before closing the accounts. After all of the closing entries are made, what will be the balance in the R. Kandamil, Capital account?

Total revenues	$300,000
Total expenses	195,000
R. Kandamil, Capital	100,000
R. Kandamil, Withdrawals	45,000

a. $360,000
b. $250,000
c. $160,000
d. $150,000
e. $60,000

3. Which of the following errors would cause the balance sheet and statement of owner's equity columns of a work sheet to be out of balance?

a. Entering a revenue amount in the balance sheet and statement of owner's equity debit column.
b. Entering a liability amount in the balance sheet and statement of owner's equity credit column.
c. Entering an expense account in the balance sheet and statement of owner's equity debit column.
d. Entering an asset account in the income statement debit column.
e. Entering a liability amount in the income statement credit column.

4. The temporary account used only in the closing process to hold the amounts of revenues and expenses before the net difference is added or subtracted from the owner's capital account is called the

a. Closing account.
b. Nominal account.
c. Income Summary account.
d. Balance Column account.
e. Contra account.

5. Based on the following information from Repicor Company's balance sheet, what is Repicor Company's current ratio?

Current assets	$ 75,000
Investments	30,000
Plant assets	300,000
Current liabilities	50,000
Long-term liabilities	60,000
D. Repicor, Capital	295,000

a. 2.10
b. 1.50
c. 1.00
d. 0.95
e. 0.67

A *Superscript letter A denotes assignments based on Appendix 4A.*
Icon denotes assignments that involve decision making.

Discussion Questions

1. What accounts are affected by closing entries? What accounts are not affected?
2. What two purposes are accomplished by recording closing entries?
3. What are the steps in recording closing entries?
4. What is the purpose of the Income Summary account?
5. Explain whether an error has occurred if a post-closing trial balance includes a Depreciation Expense account.
6. What tasks are aided by a work sheet?
7. Why are the debit and credit entries in the Adjustments columns of the work sheet identified with letters?
8. What is a company's operating cycle?
9. What classes of assets and liabilities are shown on a typical classified balance sheet?
10. How is unearned revenue classified on the balance sheet?
11. What are the characteristics of plant assets?
12.[A] How do reversing entries simplify recordkeeping?
13.[A] If a company recorded accrued salaries expense of $500 at the end of its fiscal year, what reversing entry could be made? When would it be made?
14. Refer to the balance sheet for **Research In Motion** in Appendix A. What five main noncurrent asset categories are used on its classified balance sheet? RIM
15. Refer to **Nokia**'s balance sheet in Appendix A. Identify and list its 9 current assets. NOKIA
16. Refer to **Apple**'s balance sheet in Appendix A. Identify the three accounts listed as current liabilities. Apple
17. Refer to **Palm**'s financial statements in Appendix A. What journal entry was likely recorded as of May 31, 2009, to close its Income Summary account? Palm

connect

QUICK STUDY

QS 4-1
Identifying the accounting cycle
C2

List the following steps of the accounting cycle in their proper order.

a. Preparing the post-closing trial balance.
b. Posting the journal entries.
c. Journalizing and posting adjusting entries.
d. Preparing the adjusted trial balance.
e. Journalizing and posting closing entries.
f. Analyzing transactions and events.
g. Preparing the financial statements.
h. Preparing the unadjusted trial balance.
i. Journalizing transactions and events.

QS 4-2
Explaining temporary and permanent accounts
C1

Complete the following descriptions related to temporary and permanent accounts.

1. Temporary accounts accumulate data related to ______ accounting period.
2. Permanent accounts report on activities related to ______ future accounting periods, and they carry their ending balances into the next period.
3. ______ accounts include all income statement accounts, the withdrawals account, and the Income Summary account.
4. ______ accounts generally consist of all balance sheet accounts, and these accounts are not closed.

QS 4-3
Identifying current accounts and computing the current ratio
A1

Compute Jamar Company's current ratio using the following information.

Accounts receivable	$15,000	Long-term notes payable	$20,000
Accounts payable	10,000	Office supplies	1,800
Buildings	42,000	Prepaid insurance	2,500
Cash	6,000	Unearned services revenue	4,000

QS 4-4
Classifying balance sheet items
C3

The following are common categories on a classified balance sheet.

A. Current assets
B. Long-term investments
C. Plant assets
D. Intangible assets
E. Current liabilities
F. Long-term liabilities

For each of the following items, select the letter that identifies the balance sheet category where the item typically would appear.

_____ **1.** Trademarks	_____ **5.** Cash
_____ **2.** Accounts receivable	_____ **6.** Wages payable
_____ **3.** Land not currently used in operations	_____ **7.** Store equipment
_____ **4.** Notes payable (due in three years)	_____ **8.** Accounts payable

QS 4-5
Applying a work sheet
P1

In preparing a work sheet, indicate the financial statement Debit column to which a normal balance in the following accounts should be extended. Use IS for the Income Statement Debit column and BS for the Balance Sheet and Statement of Owner's Equity Debit column.

_____ **a.** Insurance expense	_____ **d.** Depreciation expense—Equipment
_____ **b.** Equipment	_____ **e.** Prepaid rent
_____ **c.** Owner, Withdrawals	_____ **f.** Accounts receivable

QS 4-6
Ordering work sheet steps
P1

List the following steps in preparing a work sheet in their proper order by writing numbers 1–5 in the blank spaces provided.

a. _____ Prepare an adjusted trial balance on the work sheet.
b. _____ Prepare an unadjusted trial balance on the work sheet.
c. _____ Enter adjustments data on the work sheet.
d. _____ Extend adjusted balances to appropriate financial statement columns.
e. _____ Total the statement columns, compute net income (loss), and complete work sheet.

QS 4-7
Interpreting a work sheet
P1

The following selected information is taken from the work sheet for Wayman Company as of December 31, 2011. Using this information, determine the amount for K. Wayman, Capital, that should be reported on its December 31, 2011, balance sheet.

	Income Statement		Balance Sheet and Statement of Owner's Equity	
	Dr.	Cr.	Dr.	Cr.
⋮				
K. Wayman, Capital				65,000
K. Wayman, Withdrawals			32,000	
⋮				
Totals	115,000	174,000		

QS 4-8
Preparing a partial work sheet
P1

The ledger of Terrel Company includes the following unadjusted normal balances: Prepaid Rent $800, Services Revenue $11,600, and Wages Expense $5,000. Adjusting entries are required for **(a)** accrued rent expense $240; **(b)** accrued services revenue $180; and **(c)** accrued wages expense $160. Enter these unadjusted balances and the necessary adjustments on a work sheet and complete the work sheet for these accounts. *Note:* Also include the following accounts: Accounts Receivable, Wages Payable, and Rent Expense.

QS 4-9
Prepare closing entries from the ledger P2

The ledger of Avril Company includes the following accounts with normal balances: L. Avril, Capital $6,000; L. Avril, Withdrawals $400; Services Revenue $10,000; Wages Expense $5,200; and Rent Expense $800. Prepare the necessary closing entries from the available information at December 31.

QS 4-10
Identify post-closing accounts P3

Identify the accounts listed in QS 4-9 that would be included in a post-closing trial balance.

QS 4-11A
Reversing entries
P4

On December 31, 2010, Lester Co. prepared an adjusting entry for $6,700 of earned but unrecorded management fees. On January 16, 2011, Lester received $15,500 cash in management fees, which included the accrued fees earned in 2010. Assuming the company uses reversing entries, prepare the January 1, 2011, reversing entry and the January 16, 2011, cash receipt entry.

QS 4-12
International accounting standards P2

Answer each of the following questions related to international accounting standards.

a. Explain how the closing process is different between accounting under IFRS versus U.S. GAAP.

b. What basic principle do U.S. GAAP and IFRS rely upon in recording the initial acquisition value for nearly all assets?

connect

EXERCISES

Exercise 4-1
Preparing and posting closing entries
P2

Use the March 31 fiscal year-end information from the following ledger accounts (assume that all accounts have normal balances) to prepare closing journal entries and then post those entries to the appropriate ledger accounts.

Check M. Mallon, Capital (ending balance), $38,900

General Ledger

M. Mallon, Capital Acct. No. 301

Date	PR	Debit	Credit	Balance
Mar. 31	G2			42,000

M. Mallon, Withdrawals Acct. No. 302

Date	PR	Debit	Credit	Balance
Mar. 31	G2			25,000

Services Revenue Acct. No. 401

Date	PR	Debit	Credit	Balance
Mar. 31	G2			74,000

Depreciation Expense Acct. No. 603

Date	PR	Debit	Credit	Balance
Mar. 31	G2			17,000

Salaries Expense Acct. No. 622

Date	PR	Debit	Credit	Balance
Mar. 31	G2			21,000

Insurance Expense Acct. No. 637

Date	PR	Debit	Credit	Balance
Mar. 31	G2			4,500

Rent Expense Acct. No. 640

Date	PR	Debit	Credit	Balance
Mar. 31	G2			9,600

Income Summary Acct. No. 901

Date	PR	Debit	Credit	Balance

Exercise 4-2
Preparing closing entries and a post-closing trial balance
P2 P3

The adjusted trial balance for Sundance Marketing Co. follows. Complete the four right-most columns of the table by first entering information for the four closing entries (keyed *1* through *4*) and second by completing the post-closing trial balance.

No.	Account Title	Adjusted Trial Balance		Closing Entry Information		Post-Closing Trial Balance	
		Dr.	Cr.	Dr.	Cr.	Dr.	Cr.
101	Cash	$ 8,200					
106	Accounts receivable	24,000					
153	Equipment	41,000					
154	Accumulated depreciation—Equipment		$ 16,500				
193	Franchise	30,000					
201	Accounts payable		14,000				
209	Salaries payable		3,200				
233	Unearned fees		2,600				
301	H. Sundance, Capital		64,500				
302	H. Sundance, Withdrawals	14,400					
401	Marketing fees earned		79,000				
611	Depreciation expense—Equipment	11,000					
622	Salaries expense	31,500					
640	Rent expense	12,000					
677	Miscellaneous expenses	7,700					
901	Income summary						
	Totals	$179,800	$179,800				

Exercise 4-3
Preparing closing entries and a post-closing trial balance
P2 P3

The following adjusted trial balance contains the accounts and balances of Showers Company as of December 31, 2011, the end of its fiscal year. (1) Prepare the December 31, 2011, closing entries for Showers Company. (2) Prepare the December 31, 2011, post-closing trial balance for Showers Company.

No.	Account Title	Debit	Credit
101	Cash	$18,000	
126	Supplies	12,000	
128	Prepaid insurance	2,000	
167	Equipment	23,000	
168	Accumulated depreciation—Equipment		$ 6,500
301	R. Showers, Capital		46,600
302	R. Showers, Withdrawals	6,000	
404	Services revenue		36,000
612	Depreciation expense—Equipment	2,000	
622	Salaries expense	21,000	
637	Insurance expense	1,500	
640	Rent expense	2,400	
652	Supplies expense	1,200	
	Totals	$89,100	$89,100

Check (2) R. Showers, Capital (ending), $48,500; Total debits, $55,000

Exercise 4-4
Preparing the financial statements
C2

Use the following adjusted trial balance of Webb Trucking Company to prepare the (1) income statement and (2) statement of owner's equity, for the year ended December 31, 2011. The K. Webb, Capital, account balance is $161,000 at December 31, 2010.

Account Title	Debit	Credit
Cash	$ 7,000	
Accounts receivable	16,500	
Office supplies	2,000	
Trucks	170,000	
Accumulated depreciation—Trucks		$ 35,000
Land	75,000	
Accounts payable		11,000
Interest payable		3,000
Long-term notes payable		52,000
K. Webb, Capital		161,000
K. Webb, Withdrawals	19,000	
Trucking fees earned		128,000
Depreciation expense—Trucks	22,500	
Salaries expense	60,000	
Office supplies expense	7,000	
Repairs expense—Trucks	11,000	
Totals	$390,000	$390,000

Exercise 4-5
Preparing a classified balance sheet C3

Use the information in the adjusted trial balance reported in Exercise 4-4 to prepare Webb Trucking Company's classified balance sheet as of December 31, 2011.

Check Total assets, $235,500; K. Webb, Capital, $169,500

Exercise 4-6
Computing the current ratio
A1 

Use the information in the adjusted trial balance reported in Exercise 4-4 to compute the current ratio as of the balance sheet date (round the ratio to two decimals). Interpret the current ratio for the Webb Trucking Company. (Assume that the industry average for the current ratio is 1.5.)

Exercise 4-7
Computing and analyzing the current ratio

Calculate the current ratio in each of the following separate cases (round the ratio to two decimals). Identify the company case with the strongest liquidity position. (These cases represent competing companies in the same industry.)

	Current Assets	Current Liabilities
Case 1	$ 78,000	$31,000
Case 2	104,000	75,000
Case 3	44,000	48,000
Case 4	84,500	80,600
Case 5	60,000	99,000

Exercise 4-8
Extending adjusted account balances on a work sheet
P1

These 16 accounts are from the Adjusted Trial Balance columns of a company's 10-column work sheet. In the blank space beside each account, write the letter of the appropriate financial statement column (A, B, C, or D) to which a normal account balance is extended.

A. Debit column for the Income Statement columns.
B. Credit column for the Income Statement columns.
C. Debit column for the Balance Sheet and Statement of Owner's Equity columns.
D. Credit column for the Balance Sheet and Statement of Owner's Equity columns.

_____ **1.** Office Supplies
_____ **2.** Accounts Payable
_____ **3.** Owner, Capital
_____ **4.** Wages Payable
_____ **5.** Machinery
_____ **6.** Interest Receivable
_____ **7.** Interest Expense
_____ **8.** Owner, Withdrawals
_____ **9.** Service Fees Revenue
_____ **10.** Insurance Expense
_____ **11.** Accumulated Depreciation
_____ **12.** Interest Revenue
_____ **13.** Accounts Receivable
_____ **14.** Rent Expense
_____ **15.** Depreciation Expense
_____ **16.** Cash

Exercise 4-9
Preparing adjusting entries from a work sheet P1

Use the following information from the Adjustments columns of a 10-column work sheet to prepare the necessary adjusting journal entries (*a*) through (*e*).

	A	B	C	D	E	F	G	H	I	J	K	L
1											Balance Sheet	
2			Unadjusted				Adjusted		Income		and Statement of	
3			Trial Balance		Adjustments		Trial Balance		Statement		Owner's Equity	
4	No.	Account Title	Dr.	Cr.	Dr.	Cr.	Dr.	Cr.	Dr.	Cr.	Dr.	Cr.
5	109	Interest receivable					(d) $ 580					
6	124	Office supplies						(b) $1,650				
7	128	Prepaid insurance						(a) 900				
8	164	Accumulated depreciation—Office equipment						(c) 3,300				
9	209	Salaries payable						(e) 660				
10	409	Interest revenue						(d) 580				
11	612	Depreciation expense—Office equipment					(c) 3,300					
12	620	Office salaries expense					(e) 660					
13	636	Insurance expense—Office equipment					(a) 432					
14	637	Insurance expense—Store equipment					(a) 468					
15	650	Office supplies expense					(b) 1,650					
16		Totals					$7,090	$7,090				
17												

The Adjusted Trial Balance columns of a 10-column work sheet for Propel Company follow. Complete the work sheet by extending the account balances into the appropriate financial statement columns and by entering the amount of net income for the reporting period.

Exercise 4-10
Extending accounts in a work sheet P1

	A	B	C	D	E	F	G	H	I	J	K	L
1											Balance Sheet and	
2			Unadjusted				Adjusted		Income		Statement of	
3			Trial Balance		Adjustments		Trial Balance		Statement		Owner's Equity	
4	No.	Account Title	Dr.	Cr.	Dr.	Cr.	Dr.	Cr.	Dr.	Cr.	Dr.	Cr.
5	101	Cash					$ 6,000					
6	106	Accounts receivable					26,200					
7	153	Trucks					41,000					
8	154	Accumulated depreciation—Trucks						$ 16,500				
9	183	Land					30,000					
10	201	Accounts payable						14,000				
11	209	Salaries payable						3,200				
12	233	Unearned fees						2,600				
13	301	J. Propel, Capital						64,500				
14	302	J. Propel, Withdrawals					14,400					
15	401	Plumbing fees earned						79,000				
16	611	Depreciation expense—Trucks					5,500					
17	622	Salaries expense					37,000					
18	640	Rent expense					12,000					
19	677	Miscellaneous expenses					7,700					
20		Totals					$179,800	$179,800				
21												
22												

Check Net income, $16,800

These partially completed Income Statement columns from a 10-column work sheet are for Welch's Red Sail Rental Company. (1) Use the information to determine the amount that should be entered on the net income line of the work sheet. (2) Prepare the company's closing entries. The owner, L. Welch, did not make any withdrawals this period.

Exercise 4-11
Completing the income statement columns and preparing closing entries
P1 P2

Account Title	Debit	Credit
Rent earned		102,000
Salaries expense	45,300	
Insurance expense	6,400	
Dock rental expense	15,000	
Boat supplies expense	3,200	
Depreciation expense—Boats	19,500	____
Totals	____	____
Net income	____	____
Totals	____	____

Check Net income, $12,600

The following unadjusted trial balance contains the accounts and balances of Dalton Delivery Company as of December 31, 2011, its first year of operations.

Exercise 4-12
Preparing a work sheet and recording closing entries
P1 P2

(1) Use the following information about the company's adjustments to complete a 10-column work sheet.

a. Unrecorded depreciation on the trucks at the end of the year is $35,000.

b. The total amount of accrued interest expense at year-end is $8,000.

c. The cost of unused office supplies still available at the year-end is $1,000.

(2) Prepare the year-end closing entries for this company, and determine the capital amount to be reported on its year-end balance sheet.

	A	B	C
1		**Unadjusted Trial Balance**	
2	**Account Title**	**Debit**	**Credit**
3	Cash	$ 14,000	
4	Accounts receivable	33,000	
5	Office supplies	4,000	
6	Trucks	340,000	
7	Accumulated depreciation—Trucks		$70,000
8	Land	150,000	
9	Accounts payable		22,000
10	Interest payable		6,000
11	Long-term notes payable		104,000
12	V. Dalton, Capital		322,000
13	V. Dalton, Withdrawals	38,000	
14	Delivery fees earned		256,000
15	Depreciation expense—Truck	45,000	
16	Salaries expense	120,000	
17	Office supplies expense	14,000	
18	Interest expense	6,000	
19	Repairs expense—Trucks	16,000	
20	Totals	$780,000	$780,000
21			

Check Adj. trial balance totals, $817,000; Net income, $15,000

Exercise 4-13^{A}
Preparing reversing entries
P4

The following two events occurred for Tanger Co. on October 31, 2011, the end of its fiscal year.

a. Tanger rents a building from its owner for $3,200 per month. By a prearrangement, the company delayed paying October's rent until November 5. On this date, the company paid the rent for both October and November.

b. Tanger rents space in a building it owns to a tenant for $750 per month. By prearrangement, the tenant delayed paying the October rent until November 8. On this date, the tenant paid the rent for both October and November.

Required

1. Prepare adjusting entries that the company must record for these events as of October 31.

2. Assuming Tanger does *not* use reversing entries, prepare journal entries to record Tanger's payment of rent on November 5 and the collection of rent on November 8 from Tanger's tenant.

3. Assuming that the company uses reversing entries, prepare reversing entries on November 1 and the journal entries to record Tanger's payment of rent on November 5 and the collection of rent on November 8 from Tanger's tenant.

Exercise 4-14^{A}
Preparing reversing entries
P4

Hinson Company records prepaid assets and unearned revenues in balance sheet accounts. The following information was used to prepare adjusting entries for the company as of August 31, the end of the company's fiscal year.

a. The company has earned $5,000 in service fees that were not yet recorded at period-end.

b. The expired portion of prepaid insurance is $2,700.

c. The company has earned $1,900 of its Unearned Service Fees account balance.

d. Depreciation expense for office equipment is $2,300.

e. Employees have earned but have not been paid salaries of $2,400.

Prepare any necessary reversing entries for the accounting adjustments *a* through *e* assuming that the company uses reversing entries in its accounting system.

Exercise 4-15
Determining effects of closing entries
C1 

Argosy Company began the current period with a $14,000 credit balance in the D. Argosy, Capital account. At the end of the period, the company's adjusted account balances include the following temporary accounts with normal balances.

Service fees earned	$35,000	Interest revenue	$3,500
Salaries expense	19,000	D. Argosy, Withdrawals	6,000
Depreciation expense	4,000	Utilities expense	2,300

After closing the revenue and expense accounts, what will be the balance of the Income Summary account? After all closing entries are journalized and posted, what will be the balance of the D. Argosy, Capital account?

Exercise 4-16
Preparing closing entries
P2

Following are Nintendo's revenue and expense accounts for a recent calendar year (yen in millions). Prepare the company's closing entries for its revenues and its expenses.

Net sales	¥1,838,622
Cost of sales	1,044,981
Advertising expense	117,308
Other expense, net	397,244

Exercise 4-17
Completing a worksheet
P1

The following data are taken from the unadjusted trial balance of the Madison Company at December 31, 2011. Each account carries a normal balance and the accounts are shown here in alphabetical order.

Accounts Payable	$ 2	Prepaid Insurance	$ 6	T. Madison, Withdrawals	$2
Accounts Receivable	4	Revenue	25	Unearned Revenue	4
Accumulated Depreciation—Equip.	5	Salaries Expense	6	Utilities Expense	4
Cash	7	Supplies	8		
Equipment	13	T. Madison, Capital	14		

1. Use the data above to prepare a worksheet. Enter the accounts in proper order and enter their balances in the correct debit or credit column.

2. Use the following adjustment information to complete the worksheet.

a. Depreciation on equipment, $1
b. Accrued salaries, $2
c. The $4 of unearned revenue has been earned
d. Supplies available at December 31, 2011, $5
e. Expired insurance, $5

connect

PROBLEM SET A

Problem 4-1A
Determining balance sheet classifications
C3

In the blank space beside each numbered balance sheet item, enter the letter of its balance sheet classification. If the item should not appear on the balance sheet, enter a *Z* in the blank.

A. Current assets
B. Long-term investments
C. Plant assets
D. Intangible assets
E. Current liabilities
F. Long-term liabilities
G. Equity

_____ **1.** Office equipment
_____ **2.** Office supplies
_____ **3.** Buildings
_____ **4.** Store supplies
_____ **5.** Accumulated depreciation—Trucks
_____ **6.** Land (used in operations)
_____ **7.** Repairs expense
_____ **8.** Cash
_____ **9.** Current portion of long-term note payable
_____ **10.** Long-term investment in stock
_____ **11.** Depreciation expense—Building
_____ **12.** Prepaid rent
_____ **13.** Interest receivable
_____ **14.** Taxes payable
_____ **15.** Automobiles
_____ **16.** Notes payable (due in 3 years)
_____ **17.** Accounts payable
_____ **18.** Prepaid insurance
_____ **19.** Owner, Capital
_____ **20.** Unearned services revenue

Problem 4-2A
Applying the accounting cycle
C1 C2 P2 P3

excel
mhhe.com/wildFAP20e

On April 1, 2011, Jennifer Stafford created a new travel agency, See-It-Now Travel. The following transactions occurred during the company's first month.

April 1 Stafford invested $20,000 cash and computer equipment worth $40,000 in the company.
2 The company rented furnished office space by paying $1,700 cash for the first month's (April) rent.
3 The company purchased $1,100 of office supplies for cash.
10 The company paid $3,600 cash for the premium on a 12-month insurance policy. Coverage begins on April 11.
14 The company paid $1,800 cash for two weeks' salaries earned by employees.
24 The company collected $7,900 cash on commissions from airlines on tickets obtained for customers.
28 The company paid $1,800 cash for two weeks' salaries earned by employees.
29 The company paid $250 cash for minor repairs to the company's computer.
30 The company paid $650 cash for this month's telephone bill.
30 Stafford withdrew $1,500 cash from the company for personal use.

The company's chart of accounts follows:

101	Cash	405	Commissions Earned
106	Accounts Receivable	612	Depreciation Expense—Computer Equip.
124	Office Supplies	622	Salaries Expense
128	Prepaid Insurance	637	Insurance Expense
167	Computer Equipment	640	Rent Expense
168	Accumulated Depreciation—Computer Equip.	650	Office Supplies Expense
209	Salaries Payable	684	Repairs Expense
301	J. Stafford, Capital	688	Telephone Expense
302	J. Stafford, Withdrawals	901	Income Summary

Required

1. Use the balance column format to set up each ledger account listed in its chart of accounts.
2. Prepare journal entries to record the transactions for April and post them to the ledger accounts. The company records prepaid and unearned items in balance sheet accounts.
3. Prepare an unadjusted trial balance as of April 30.
4. Use the following information to journalize and post adjusting entries for the month:
   a. Two-thirds of one month's insurance coverage has expired.
   b. At the end of the month, $700 of office supplies are still available.
   c. This month's depreciation on the computer equipment is $600.
   d. Employees earned $320 of unpaid and unrecorded salaries as of month-end.
   e. The company earned $1,650 of commissions that are not yet billed at month-end.
5. Prepare the income statement and the statement of owner's equity for the month of April and the balance sheet at April 30, 2011.
6. Prepare journal entries to close the temporary accounts and post these entries to the ledger.
7. Prepare a post-closing trial balance.

Check (3) Unadj. trial balance totals, $67,900

(4*a*) Dr. Insurance Expense, $200

(5) Net income, $1,830; J. Stafford, Capital (4/30/2011), $60,330; Total assets, $60,650

(7) P-C trial balance totals, $61,250

Problem 4-3A
Preparing trial balances, closing entries, and financial statements
C3 P2 P3

mhhe.com/wildFAP20e

The adjusted trial balance of Kobe Repairs on December 31, 2011, follows.

KOBE REPAIRS
Adjusted Trial Balance
December 31, 2011

No.	Account Title	Debit	Credit
101	Cash	$ 13,000	
124	Office supplies	1,200	
128	Prepaid insurance	1,950	
167	Equipment	48,000	
168	Accumulated depreciation—Equipment		$ 4,000
201	Accounts payable		12,000
210	Wages payable		500
301	S. Kobe, Capital		40,000
302	S. Kobe, Withdrawals	15,000	
401	Repair fees earned		77,750
612	Depreciation expense—Equipment	4,000	
623	Wages expense	36,500	
637	Insurance expense	700	
640	Rent expense	9,600	
650	Office supplies expense	2,600	
690	Utilities expense	1,700	
	Totals	$134,250	$134,250

Required

1. Prepare an income statement and a statement of owner's equity for the year 2011, and a classified balance sheet at December 31, 2011. There are no owner investments in 2011.

Check (1) Ending capital balance, $47,650; net income, $22,650

2. Enter the adjusted trial balance in the first two columns of a six-column table. Use columns three and four for closing entry information and the last two columns for a post-closing trial balance. Insert an Income Summary account as the last item in the trial balance.
3. Enter closing entry information in the six-column table and prepare journal entries for it.

(2) P-C trial balance totals, $64,150

Analysis Component

4. Assume for this part only that
   a. None of the $700 insurance expense had expired during the year. Instead, assume it is a prepayment of the next period's insurance protection.
   b. There are no earned and unpaid wages at the end of the year. (*Hint:* Reverse the $500 wages payable accrual.)

   Describe the financial statement changes that would result from these two assumptions.

Problem 4-4A
Preparing closing entries, financial statements, and ratios
C3 A1 P2

The adjusted trial balance for Sharp Construction as of December 31, 2011, follows.

SHARP CONSTRUCTION Adjusted Trial Balance December 31, 2011			
No.	Account Title	Debit	Credit
101	Cash	$ 4,000	
104	Short-term investments	22,000	
126	Supplies	7,100	
128	Prepaid insurance	6,000	
167	Equipment	39,000	
168	Accumulated depreciation—Equipment		$ 20,000
173	Building	130,000	
174	Accumulated depreciation—Building		55,000
183	Land	45,000	
201	Accounts payable		15,500
203	Interest payable		1,500
208	Rent payable		2,500
210	Wages payable		1,500
213	Property taxes payable		800
233	Unearned professional fees		6,500
251	Long-term notes payable		66,000
301	J. Sharp, Capital		82,700
302	J. Sharp, Withdrawals	12,000	
401	Professional fees earned		96,000
406	Rent earned		13,000
407	Dividends earned		1,900
409	Interest earned		1,000
606	Depreciation expense—Building	10,000	
612	Depreciation expense—Equipment	5,000	
623	Wages expense	31,000	
633	Interest expense	4,100	
637	Insurance expense	9,000	
640	Rent expense	12,400	
652	Supplies expense	6,400	
682	Postage expense	3,200	
683	Property taxes expense	4,000	
684	Repairs expense	7,900	
688	Telephone expense	2,200	
690	Utilities expense	3,600	
	Totals	$363,900	$363,900

J. Sharp invested $50,000 cash in the business during year 2011 (the December 31, 2010, credit balance of the J. Sharp, Capital account was $32,700). Sharp Construction is required to make a $6,600 payment on its long-term notes payable during 2012.

Required

Check (1) Total assets (12/31/2011), $178,100; Net income, $13,100

1. Prepare the income statement and the statement of owner's equity for the calendar year 2011 and the classified balance sheet at December 31, 2011.
2. Prepare the necessary closing entries at December 31, 2011.
3. Use the information in the financial statements to compute these ratios: (*a*) return on assets (total assets at December 31, 2010, was $200,000), (*b*) debt ratio, (*c*) profit margin ratio (use total revenues as the denominator), and (*d*) current ratio.

Problem 4-5A
Preparing a work sheet, adjusting and closing entries, and financial statements

C3 P1 P2 

The following unadjusted trial balance is for Adams Construction Co. as of the end of its 2011 fiscal year. The June 30, 2010, credit balance of the owner's capital account was $52,660, and the owner invested $25,000 cash in the company during the 2011 fiscal year.

	A	B	C	D
1		**ADAMS CONSTRUCTION CO.**		
2		**Unadjusted Trial Balance**		
3		**June 30, 2011**		
4	**No.**	**Account Title**	**Debit**	**Credit**
5	101	Cash	$ 17,500	
6	126	Supplies	8,900	
7	128	Prepaid insurance	6,200	
8	167	Equipment	131,000	
9	168	Accumulated depreciation—Equipment		$ 25,250
10	201	Accounts payable		5,800
11	203	Interest payable		0
12	208	Rent payable		0
13	210	Wages payable		0
14	213	Property taxes payable		0
15	251	Long-term notes payable		24,000
16	301	S. Adams, Capital		77,660
17	302	S. Adams, Withdrawals	30,000	
18	401	Construction fees earned		134,000
19	612	Depreciation expense—Equipment	0	
20	623	Wages expense	45,860	
21	633	Interest expense	2,640	
22	637	Insurance expense	0	
23	640	Rent expense	13,200	
24	652	Supplies expense	0	
25	683	Property taxes expense	4,600	
26	684	Repairs expense	2,810	
27	690	Utilities expense	4,000	
28		Totals	$266,710	$266,710
29				

Required

1. Prepare a 10-column work sheet for fiscal year 2011, starting with the unadjusted trial balance and including adjustments based on these additional facts.
   a. The supplies available at the end of fiscal year 2011 had a cost of $3,200.
   b. The cost of expired insurance for the fiscal year is $3,900.
   c. Annual depreciation on equipment is $8,500.
   d. The June utilities expense of $550 is not included in the unadjusted trial balance because the bill arrived after the trial balance was prepared. The $550 amount owed needs to be recorded.
   e. The company's employees have earned $1,600 of accrued wages at fiscal year-end.
   f. The rent expense incurred and not yet paid or recorded at fiscal year-end is $200.
   g. Additional property taxes of $900 have been assessed for this fiscal year but have not been paid or recorded in the accounts.

h. The long-term note payable bears interest at 12% per year. The unadjusted Interest Expense account equals the amount paid for the first 11 months of the 2011 fiscal year. The $240 accrued interest for June has not yet been paid or recorded. (The company is required to make a $5,000 payment toward the note payable during the 2012 fiscal year.)

2. Enter adjusting and closing information in the work sheet; then journalize the adjusting and closing entries.

3. Prepare the income statement and the statement of owner's equity for the year ended June 30 and the classified balance sheet at June 30, 2011.

Check (3) Total assets, $120,250; Current liabilities, $14,290; Net income, $39,300

Analysis Component

4. Analyze the following separate errors and describe how each would affect the 10-column work sheet. Explain whether the error is likely to be discovered in completing the work sheet and, if not, the effect of the error on the financial statements.

a. Assume that the adjustment for supplies used consisted of a credit to Supplies and a debit to Supplies Expense for $3,200, when the correct amount was $5,700.

b. When the adjusted trial balance in the work sheet is completed, assume that the $17,500 Cash balance is incorrectly entered in the Credit column.

Problem 4-6A^A
Preparing adjusting, reversing, and next period entries
P4

The following six-column table for Bullseye Ranges includes the unadjusted trial balance as of December 31, 2011.

	A	B	C	D	E	F	G
1		BULLSEYE RANGES					
2		December 31, 2011					
3		Unadjusted				Adjusted	
4		Trial Balance		Adjustments		Trial Balance	
5	Account Title	Dr.	Cr.	Dr.	Cr.	Dr.	Cr.
6	Cash	$ 13,000					
7	Accounts receivable	0					
8	Supplies	5,500					
9	Equipment	130,000					
10	Accumulated depreciation—Equipment		$ 25,000				
11	Interest payable		0				
12	Salaries payable		0				
13	Unearned member fees		14,000				
14	Notes payable		50,000				
15	T. Allen, Capital		58,250				
16	T. Allen, Withdrawals	20,000					
17	Member fees earned		53,000				
18	Depreciation expense—Equipment	0					
19	Salaries expense	28,000					
20	Interest expense	3,750					
21	Supplies expense	0					
22	Totals	$200,250	$200,250				
23							

Required

1. Complete the six-column table by entering adjustments that reflect the following information.

a. As of December 31, 2011, employees had earned $900 of unpaid and unrecorded salaries. The next payday is January 4, at which time $1,600 of salaries will be paid.

b. The cost of supplies still available at December 31, 2011, is $2,700.

c. The notes payable requires an interest payment to be made every three months. The amount of unrecorded accrued interest at December 31, 2011, is $1,250. The next interest payment, at an amount of $1,500, is due on January 15, 2012.

d. Analysis of the unearned member fees account shows $5,600 remaining unearned at December 31, 2011.

e. In addition to the member fees included in the revenue account balance, the company has earned another $9,100 in unrecorded fees that will be collected on January 31, 2012. The company is also expected to collect $8,000 on that same day for new fees earned in January 2012.

f. Depreciation expense for the year is $12,500.

Check (1) Adjusted trial balance totals, $224,000

2. Prepare journal entries for the adjustments entered in the six-column table for part 1.
3. Prepare journal entries to reverse the effects of the adjusting entries that involve accruals.
4. Prepare journal entries to record the cash payments and cash collections described for January.

PROBLEM SET B

Problem 4-1B
Determining balance sheet classifications
C3

In the blank space beside each numbered balance sheet item, enter the letter of its balance sheet classification. If the item should not appear on the balance sheet, enter a *Z* in the blank.

A. Current assets
B. Long-term investments
C. Plant assets
D. Intangible assets
E. Current liabilities
F. Long-term liabilities
G. Equity

_____ **1.** Machinery
_____ **2.** Prepaid insurance
_____ **3.** Current portion of long-term note payable
_____ **4.** Interest receivable
_____ **5.** Rent receivable
_____ **6.** Land (used in operations)
_____ **7.** Copyrights
_____ **8.** Rent revenue
_____ **9.** Depreciation expense—Trucks
_____ **10.** Long-term investment in stock
_____ **11.** Office supplies
_____ **12.** Interest payable
_____ **13.** Owner, Capital
_____ **14.** Notes receivable (due in 120 days)
_____ **15.** Accumulated depreciation—Trucks
_____ **16.** Salaries payable
_____ **17.** Commissions earned
_____ **18.** Income taxes payable
_____ **19.** Office equipment
_____ **20.** Notes payable (due in 15 years)

Problem 4-2B
Applying the accounting cycle
C1 C2 P2 P3 

On July 1, 2011, Lucinda Fogle created a new self-storage business, KeepSafe Co. The following transactions occurred during the company's first month.

July 1 Fogle invested $20,000 cash and buildings worth $120,000 in the company.
2 The company rented equipment by paying $1,800 cash for the first month's (July) rent.
5 The company purchased $2,300 of office supplies for cash.
10 The company paid $5,400 cash for the premium on a 12-month insurance policy. Coverage begins on July 11.
14 The company paid an employee $900 cash for two weeks' salary earned.
24 The company collected $8,800 cash for storage fees from customers.
28 The company paid $900 cash for two weeks' salary earned by an employee.
29 The company paid $850 cash for minor repairs to a leaking roof.
30 The company paid $300 cash for this month's telephone bill.
31 Fogle withdrew $1,600 cash from the company for personal use.

The company's chart of accounts follows:

101	Cash	401	Storage Fees Earned
106	Accounts Receivable	606	Depreciation Expense—Buildings
124	Office Supplies	622	Salaries Expense
128	Prepaid Insurance	637	Insurance Expense
173	Buildings	640	Rent Expense
174	Accumulated Depreciation—Buildings	650	Office Supplies Expense
209	Salaries Payable	684	Repairs Expense
301	L. Fogle, Capital	688	Telephone Expense
302	L. Fogle, Withdrawals	901	Income Summary

Required

1. Use the balance column format to set up each ledger account listed in its chart of accounts.
2. Prepare journal entries to record the transactions for July and post them to the ledger accounts. Record prepaid and unearned items in balance sheet accounts.
3. Prepare an unadjusted trial balance as of July 31.

Check (3) Unadj. trial balance totals, $148,800

4. Use the following information to journalize and post adjusting entries for the month:
   a. Two-thirds of one month's insurance coverage has expired.
   b. At the end of the month, $1,550 of office supplies are still available.
   c. This month's depreciation on the buildings is $1,200.
   d. An employee earned $180 of unpaid and unrecorded salary as of month-end.
   e. The company earned $950 of storage fees that are not yet billed at month-end.
5. Prepare the income statement and the statement of owner's equity for the month of July and the balance sheet at July 31, 2011.
6. Prepare journal entries to close the temporary accounts and post these entries to the ledger.
7. Prepare a post-closing trial balance.

(4a) Dr. Insurance Expense, $300

(5) Net income, $2,570; L. Fogle, Capital (7/31/2011), $140,970; Total assets, $141,150

(7) P-C trial balance totals, $142,350

Problem 4-3B
Preparing trial balances, closing entries, and financial statements
C3 P2 P3 

Heel-To-Toe Shoes' adjusted trial balance on December 31, 2011, follows.

HEEL-TO-TOE SHOES
Adjusted Trial Balance
December 31, 2011

No.	Account Title	Debit	Credit
101	Cash	$ 13,450	
125	Store supplies	4,140	
128	Prepaid insurance	2,200	
167	Equipment	33,000	
168	Accumulated depreciation—Equipment		$ 9,000
201	Accounts payable		1,000
210	Wages payable		3,200
301	P. Holt, Capital		31,650
302	P. Holt, Withdrawals	16,000	
401	Repair fees earned		62,000
612	Depreciation expense—Equipment	3,000	
623	Wages expense	28,400	
637	Insurance expense	1,100	
640	Rent expense	2,400	
651	Store supplies expense	1,300	
690	Utilities expense	1,860	
	Totals	$106,850	$106,850

Required

1. Prepare an income statement and a statement of owner's equity for the year 2011, and a classified balance sheet at December 31, 2011. There are no owner investments in 2011.
2. Enter the adjusted trial balance in the first two columns of a six-column table. Use the middle two columns for closing entry information and the last two columns for a post-closing trial balance. Insert an Income Summary account (No. 901) as the last item in the trial balance.
3. Enter closing entry information in the six-column table and prepare journal entries for it.

Check (1) Ending capital balance, $39,590

(2) P-C trial balance totals, $52,790

Analysis Component

4. Assume for this part only that
   a. None of the $1,100 insurance expense had expired during the year. Instead, assume it is a prepayment of the next period's insurance protection.
   b. There are no earned and unpaid wages at the end of the year. (*Hint:* Reverse the $3,200 wages payable accrual.)

   Describe the financial statement changes that would result from these two assumptions.

Problem 4-4B
Preparing closing entries, financial statements, and ratios
C3 A1 P2

The adjusted trial balance for Giovanni Co. as of December 31, 2011, follows.

GIOVANNI COMPANY
Adjusted Trial Balance
December 31, 2011

No.	Account Title	Debit	Credit
101	Cash	$ 6,400	
104	Short-term investments	10,200	
126	Supplies	3,600	
128	Prepaid insurance	800	
167	Equipment	18,000	
168	Accumulated depreciation—Equipment		$ 3,000
173	Building	90,000	
174	Accumulated depreciation—Building		9,000
183	Land	28,500	
201	Accounts payable		2,500
203	Interest payable		1,400
208	Rent payable		200
210	Wages payable		1,180
213	Property taxes payable		2,330
233	Unearned professional fees		650
251	Long-term notes payable		32,000
301	J. Giovanni, Capital		91,800
302	J. Giovanni, Withdrawals	6,000	
401	Professional fees earned		47,000
406	Rent earned		3,600
407	Dividends earned		500
409	Interest earned		1,120
606	Depreciation expense—Building	2,000	
612	Depreciation expense—Equipment	1,000	
623	Wages expense	17,500	
633	Interest expense	1,200	
637	Insurance expense	1,425	
640	Rent expense	1,800	
652	Supplies expense	900	
682	Postage expense	310	
683	Property taxes expense	3,825	
684	Repairs expense	579	
688	Telephone expense	421	
690	Utilities expense	1,820	
	Totals	$196,280	$196,280

J. Giovanni invested $30,000 cash in the business during year 2011 (the December 31, 2010, credit balance of the J. Giovanni, Capital account was $61,800). Giovanni Company is required to make a $6,400 payment on its long-term notes payable during 2012.

Required

Check (1) Total assets (12/31/2011), $145,500; Net income, $19,440

1. Prepare the income statement and the statement of owner's equity for the calendar year 2011 and the classified balance sheet at December 31, 2011.
2. Prepare the necessary closing entries at December 31, 2011.
3. Use the information in the financial statements to calculate these ratios: *(a)* return on assets (total assets at December 31, 2010, were $150,000), *(b)* debt ratio, *(c)* profit margin ratio (use total revenues as the denominator), and *(d)* current ratio.

Problem 4-5B
Preparing a work sheet, adjusting and closing entries, and financial statements

The following unadjusted trial balance is for Crush Demolition Company as of the end of its April 30, 2011, fiscal year. The April 30, 2010, credit balance of the owner's capital account was $36,900, and the owner invested $30,000 cash in the company during the 2011 fiscal year.

	A	B		C
1		**CRUSH DEMOLITION COMPANY**		
2		**Unadjusted Trial Balance**		
3		**April 30, 2011**		
4	**No.**	**Account Title**	**Debit**	**Credit**
5	101	Cash	$ 9,000	
6	126	Supplies	18,000	
7	128	Prepaid insurance	14,600	
8	167	Equipment	140,000	
9	168	Accumulated depreciation—Equipment		$ 10,000
10	201	Accounts payable		16,000
11	203	Interest payable		0
12	208	Rent payable		0
13	210	Wages payable		0
14	213	Property taxes payable		0
15	251	Long-term notes payable		20,000
16	301	J. Bonair, Capital		66,900
17	302	J. Bonair, Withdrawals	24,000	
18	401	Demolition fees earned		177,000
19	612	Depreciation expense—Equipment	0	
20	623	Wages expense	51,400	
21	633	Interest expense	2,200	
22	637	Insurance expense	0	
23	640	Rent expense	8,800	
24	652	Supplies expense	0	
25	683	Property taxes expense	8,400	
26	684	Repairs expense	6,700	
27	690	Utilities expense	6,800	
28		Totals	$289,900	$289,900
29				

Required

1. Prepare a 10-column work sheet for fiscal year 2011, starting with the unadjusted trial balance and including adjustments based on these additional facts.

a. The supplies available at the end of fiscal year 2011 had a cost of $8,100.

b. The cost of expired insurance for the fiscal year is $11,500.

c. Annual depreciation on equipment is $18,000.

d. The April utilities expense of $700 is not included in the unadjusted trial balance because the bill arrived after the trial balance was prepared. The $700 amount owed needs to be recorded.

e. The company's employees have earned $2,200 of accrued wages at fiscal year-end.

f. The rent expense incurred and not yet paid or recorded at fiscal year-end is $5,360.

g. Additional property taxes of $450 have been assessed for this fiscal year but have not been paid or recorded in the accounts.

h. The long-term note payable bears interest at 12% per year. The unadjusted Interest Expense account equals the amount paid for the first 11 months of the 2011 fiscal year. The $200 accrued interest for April has not yet been paid or recorded. (Note that the company is required to make a $4,000 payment toward the note payable during the 2012 fiscal year.)

2. Enter adjusting and closing information in the work sheet; then journalize the adjusting and closing entries.

3. Prepare the income statement and the statement of owner's equity for the year ended April 30 and the classified balance sheet at April 30, 2011.

Check (3) Total assets, $132,200; current liabilities, $28,910; Net income, $44,390

Analysis Component

4. Analyze the following separate errors and describe how each would affect the 10-column work sheet. Explain whether the error is likely to be discovered in completing the work sheet and, if not, the effect of the error on the financial statements.

a. Assume the adjustment for expiration of the insurance coverage consisted of a credit to Prepaid Insurance and a debit to Insurance Expense for $3,100, when the correct amount was $11,500.

b. When the adjusted trial balance in the work sheet is completed, assume that the $6,700 Repairs Expense account balance is extended to the Debit column of the balance sheet columns.

Problem 4-6B^A
Preparing adjusting, reversing, and next period entries
P4

The following six-column table for Solutions Co. includes the unadjusted trial balance as of December 31, 2011.

	A	B	C	D	E	F	G
1		**SOLUTIONS COMPANY**					
2		**December 31, 2011**					
3		**Unadjusted**				**Adjusted**	
4		**Trial Balance**		**Adjustments**		**Trial Balance**	
5	**Account Title**	**Dr.**	**Cr.**	**Dr.**	**Cr.**	**Dr.**	**Cr.**
6	Cash	$ 9,000					
7	Accounts receivable	0					
8	Supplies	6,600					
9	Machinery	40,100					
10	Accumulated depreciation—Machinery		$15,800				
11	Interest payable		0				
12	Salaries payable		0				
13	Unearned rental fees		5,200				
14	Notes payable		20,000				
15	G. Clay, Capital		13,200				
16	G. Clay, Withdrawals	10,500					
17	Rental fees earned		37,000				
18	Depreciation expense—Machinery	0					
19	Salaries expense	23,500					
20	Interest expense	1,500					
21	Supplies expense	0					
22	Totals	$91,200	$91,200				
23							

Required

1. Complete the six-column table by entering adjustments that reflect the following information:

a. As of December 31, 2011, employees had earned $420 of unpaid and unrecorded wages. The next payday is January 4, at which time $1,250 in wages will be paid.

b. The cost of supplies still available at December 31, 2011, is $2,450.

c. The notes payable requires an interest payment to be made every three months. The amount of unrecorded accrued interest at December 31, 2011, is $500. The next interest payment, at an amount of $600, is due on January 15, 2012.

d. Analysis of the unearned rental fees shows that $3,100 remains unearned at December 31, 2011.

e. In addition to the machinery rental fees included in the revenue account balance, the company has earned another $2,350 in unrecorded fees that will be collected on January 31, 2012. The company is also expected to collect $4,400 on that same day for new fees earned in January 2012.

f. Depreciation expense for the year is $3,800.

Check (1) Adjusted trial balance totals, $98,270

2. Prepare journal entries for the adjustments entered in the six-column table for part 1.

3. Prepare journal entries to reverse the effects of the adjusting entries that involve accruals.

4. Prepare journal entries to record the cash payments and cash collections described for January.

SERIAL PROBLEM

Business Solutions
P2 P3

QB

(This serial problem began in Chapter 1 and continues through most of the book. If previous chapter segments were not completed, the serial problem can begin at this point. It is helpful, but not necessary, to use the Working Papers that accompany the book.)

SP 4 The December 31, 2011, adjusted trial balance of Business Solutions (reflecting its transactions from October through December of 2011) follows.

No.	Account Title	Debit	Credit
101	Cash	$ 48,372	
106	Accounts receivable	5,668	
126	Computer supplies	580	
128	Prepaid insurance	1,665	

[continued on next page]

[continued from previous page]

131	Prepaid rent	825	
163	Office equipment	8,000	
164	Accumulated depreciation—Office equipment		$ 400
167	Computer equipment	20,000	
168	Accumulated depreciation—Computer equipment		1,250
201	Accounts payable		1,100
210	Wages payable		500
236	Unearned computer services revenue		1,500
301	S. Rey, Capital		73,000
302	S. Rey, Withdrawals	7,100	
403	Computer services revenue		31,284
612	Depreciation expense—Office equipment	400	
613	Depreciation expense—Computer equipment	1,250	
623	Wages expense	3,875	
637	Insurance expense	555	
640	Rent expense	2,475	
652	Computer supplies expense	3,065	
655	Advertising expense	2,753	
676	Mileage expense	896	
677	Miscellaneous expenses	250	
684	Repairs expense—Computer	1,305	
901	Income summary		0
	Totals	$109,034	$109,034

Required

1. Record and post the necessary closing entries for Business Solutions.

2. Prepare a post-closing trial balance as of December 31, 2011.

Check Post-closing trial balance totals, $85,110

Beyond the Numbers

REPORTING IN ACTION

C1 P2 

RIM

BTN 4-1 Refer to Research In Motion's financial statements in Appendix A to answer the following.

Required

1. For the fiscal year ended February 27, 2010, what amount is credited to Income Summary to summarize its revenues earned?

2. For the fiscal year ended February 27, 2010, what amount is debited to Income Summary to summarize its expenses incurred?

3. For the fiscal year ended February 27, 2010, what is the balance of its Income Summary account before it is closed?

4. In its statement of cash flows for the year ended February 27, 2010, what amount of cash is paid in dividends to common stockholders?

Fast Forward

5. Access RIM's annual report for fiscal years ending after February 27, 2010, at its Website (RIM.com) or the SEC's EDGAR database (www.SEC.gov). How has the amount of net income closed to Income Summary changed in the fiscal years ending after February 27, 2010? How has the amount of cash paid as dividends changed in the fiscal years ending after February 27, 2010?

COMPARATIVE ANALYSIS

A1 

RIM

Apple

BTN 4-2 Key figures for the recent two years of Research In Motion and Apple follow.

Key Figures ($ millions)	Research In Motion		Apple	
	Current Year	Prior Year	Current Year	Prior Year
Current assets	$5,813	$4,842	$31,555	$30,006
Current liabilities	2,432	2,115	11,506	11,361

Required

1. Compute the current ratio for both years for both companies.
2. Which company has the better ability to pay short-term obligations according to the current ratio?
3. Analyze and comment on each company's current ratios for the past two years.
4. How do RIM's and Apple's current ratios compare to their industry (assumed) average ratio of 2.4?

ETHICS CHALLENGE

C2

BTN 4-3 On January 20, 2011, Tamira Nelson, the accountant for Picton Enterprises, is feeling pressure to complete the annual financial statements. The company president has said he needs up-to-date financial statements to share with the bank on January 21 at a dinner meeting that has been called to discuss Picton's obtaining loan financing for a special building project. Tamira knows that she will not be able to gather all the needed information in the next 24 hours to prepare the entire set of adjusting entries. Those entries must be posted before the financial statements accurately portray the company's performance and financial position for the fiscal period ended December 31, 2010. Tamira ultimately decides to estimate several expense accruals at the last minute. When deciding on estimates for the expenses, she uses low estimates because she does not want to make the financial statements look worse than they are. Tamira finishes the financial statements before the deadline and gives them to the president without mentioning that several account balances are estimates that she provided.

Required

1. Identify several courses of action that Tamira could have taken instead of the one she took.
2. If you were in Tamira's situation, what would you have done? Briefly justify your response.

COMMUNICATING IN PRACTICE

C1 P2

BTN 4-4 Assume that one of your classmates states that a company's books should be ongoing and therefore not closed until that business is terminated. Write a half-page memo to this classmate explaining the concept of the closing process by drawing analogies between (1) a scoreboard for an athletic event and the revenue and expense accounts of a business or (2) a sports team's record book and the capital account. (*Hint:* Think about what would happen if the scoreboard is not cleared before the start of a new game.)

TAKING IT TO THE NET

A1

BTN 4-5 Access Motley Fool's discussion of the current ratio at Fool.com/School/Valuation/CurrentAndQuickRatio.htm. (If the page changed, search that site for the *current ratio.*)

Required

1. What level for the current ratio is generally regarded as sufficient to meet near-term operating needs?
2. Once you have calculated the current ratio for a company, what should you compare it against?
3. What are the implications for a company that has a current ratio that is too high?

TEAMWORK IN ACTION

P1 P2 P3

BTN 4-6 The unadjusted trial balance and information for the accounting adjustments of Noseworthy Investigators follow. Each team member involved in this project is to assume one of the four responsibilities listed. After completing each of these responsibilities, the team should work together to prove the accounting equation utilizing information from teammates (1 and 4). If your equation does not balance, you are to work as a team to resolve the error. The team's goal is to complete the task as quickly and accurately as possible.

Unadjusted Trial Balance

Account Title	Debit	Credit
Cash	$15,000	
Supplies	11,000	
Prepaid insurance	2,000	
Equipment	24,000	
Accumulated depreciation—Equipment		$ 6,000
Accounts payable		2,000
D. Noseworthy, Capital		31,000
D. Noseworthy, Withdrawals	5,000	
Investigation fees earned		32,000
Rent expense	14,000	
Totals	$71,000	$71,000

Additional Year-End Information

a. Insurance that expired in the current period amounts to $1,200.
b. Equipment depreciation for the period is $3,000.
c. Unused supplies total $4,000 at period-end.
d. Services in the amount of $500 have been provided but have not been billed or collected.

Responsibilities for Individual Team Members

1. Determine the accounts and adjusted balances to be extended to the balance sheet columns of the work sheet for Noseworthy. Also determine total assets and total liabilities.
2. Determine the adjusted revenue account balance and prepare the entry to close this account.
3. Determine the adjusted account balances for expenses and prepare the entry to close these accounts.
4. Prepare T-accounts for both D. Noseworthy, Capital (reflecting the unadjusted trial balance amount) and Income Summary. Prepare the third and fourth closing entries. Ask teammates assigned to parts 2 and 3 for the postings for Income Summary. Obtain amounts to complete the third closing entry and post both the third and fourth closing entries. Provide the team with the ending capital account balance.
5. The entire team should prove the accounting equation using post-closing balances.

ENTREPRENEURIAL DECISION

BTN 4-7 Review this chapter's opening feature involving Keith Mullin and his Gamer Grub business.

1. Explain how a classified balance sheet can help Keith Mullin know what bills are due when, and whether he has the resources to pay those bills.
2. Why is it important for Keith Mullin to match costs and revenues in a specific time period? How do closing entries help him in this regard?
3. What objectives are met when Keith Mullin applies closing procedures each fiscal year-end?

HITTING THE ROAD

BTN 4-8 Select a company that you can visit in person or interview on the telephone. Call ahead to the company to arrange a time when you can interview an employee (preferably an accountant) who helps prepare the annual financial statements. Inquire about the following aspects of its *accounting cycle:*

1. Does the company prepare interim financial statements? What time period(s) is used for interim statements?
2. Does the company use the cash or accrual basis of accounting?
3. Does the company use a work sheet in preparing financial statements? Why or why not?
4. Does the company use a spreadsheet program? If so, which software program is used?
5. How long does it take after the end of its reporting period to complete annual statements?

NOKIA

BTN 4-9 Nokia (www.Nokia.com) is a leading global manufacturer of mobile devices and services. The following selected information is available from Nokia's financial statements.

(Euro millions)	Current Year	Prior Year
Current assets	23,613	24,470
Current liabilities	15,188	20,355

Required

1. Compute Nokia's current ratio for both the current year and the prior year.
2. Comment on any change from the prior year to the current year for the current ratio.

ANSWERS TO MULTIPLE CHOICE QUIZ

1. e
2. c
3. a
4. c
5. b

7 Accounting Information Systems

A Look Back

Chapters 5 and 6 focused on merchandising activities and accounting for inventory. We explained inventory systems, accounting for inventory transactions, and assigning costs to inventory.

A Look at This Chapter

This chapter emphasizes accounting information systems. We describe fundamental system principles, the system's components, use of special journals and subsidiary ledgers, and technology-based systems.

A Look Ahead

Chapter 8 focuses on internal controls and accounting for cash and cash equivalents. We explain good internal control procedures and their importance.

Learning Objectives

CAP

CONCEPTUAL

C1 Identify the principles and components of accounting information systems. (p. 272)

C2 Explain the goals and uses of special journals. (p. 275)

C3 Describe the use of controlling accounts and subsidiary ledgers. (p. 276)

ANALYTICAL

A1 Compute segment return on assets and use it to evaluate segment performance. (p. 288)

LP7

PROCEDURAL

P1 Journalize and post transactions using special journals. (p. 278)

P2 Prepare and prove the accuracy of subsidiary ledgers. (p. 279)

P3 *Appendix 7A*—Journalize and post transactions using special journals in a periodic inventory system. (p. 292)

Decision Insight

Successful Brew

"It's just following your instincts, knowing the basics, and sticking with what's important"

—KIM JORDAN

FORT COLLINS, CO—Kim Jordan's entrepreneurial roots were anything but frothy. "For about eight months, we didn't pay ourselves," explains Kim. "We borrowed money from parents and made payroll . . . looking at the bills, we had to decide which to pay." From those meager beginnings, Kim created **New Belgium Brewing Company** **(NewBelgium.com),** which is committed to the Belgian brewing tradition of delicious beers with loads of character.

"We did have a set of values, a purpose, and some outcomes that we wanted to achieve," says Kim. "Four things were important to us: to produce world class Belgium-style beers, to promote beer culture, to be environmental stewards, and to have fun!" To achieve those goals, Kim set up an accounting system to measure, track, summarize, and report on operations. "It is important to have the ability to read financial statements," insists Kim. "And, to understand ratios." Those expectations and priorities fundamentally shaped Kim's accounting system and controls.

"There has to be execution," explains Kim. That focus on execution includes applying internal controls, special journals, accounting ledgers, and systems technology. Kim maintains special journals for sales, cash receipts, purchases, and cash disbursements. Developing her accounting system to capture all aspects of her operations is no easy task, but well worth the effort. "Working hard and being dedicated or committed to an outcome are keys," asserts Kim. "Our co-workers [all employees] get to see all of our financials!" Kim explains that this in turn helps shape the special journals for her business, including the control procedures applied in the brewery.

Kim's company is riding high with the right accounting systems and controls for long-run success. "Stasis is not an option," says Kim. "If we're all in the same place today that we were five years ago, that wouldn't be very interesting." Kim smiles and adds, "There's something wrong if making beer can't be fun!"

[Sources: *NewBelgium Website,* January 2011; *Entrepreneur,* November 2009; *50entrepreneurs.com,* March 2010; *CNNMoney.com,* June 2009; *Beverage World,* September 2009]

Chapter Preview

With increases in the number and complexity of business activities, the demands placed on accounting information systems increase. Accounting information systems must meet this challenge in an efficient and effective manner. In this chapter, we learn about fundamental principles guiding information systems, and we study components making up these systems. We also explain procedures that use special journals and subsidiary ledgers to make accounting information systems more efficient. An understanding of the details of accounting reports makes us better decision makers when using financial information, and it improves our ability to analyze and interpret financial statements.

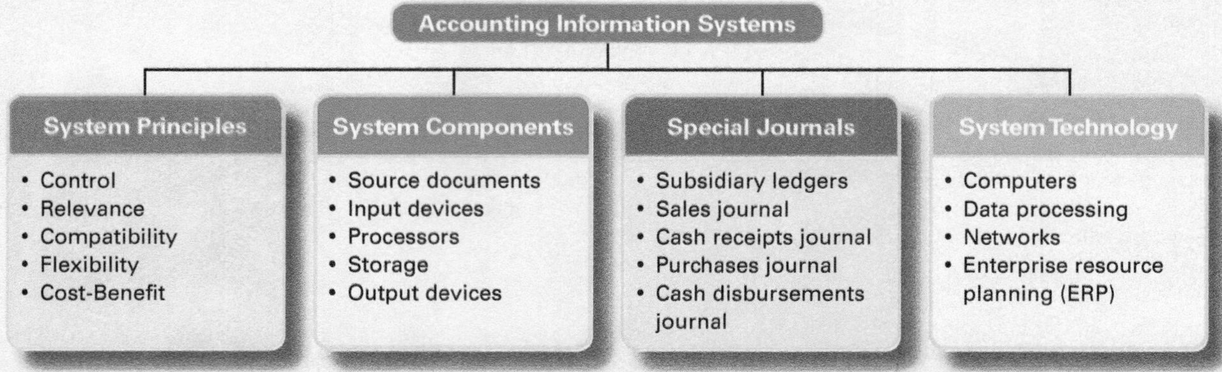

FUNDAMENTAL SYSTEM PRINCIPLES

C1 Identify the principles and components of accounting information systems.

Accounting information systems collect and process data from transactions and events, organize them in useful reports, and communicate results to decision makers. With the increasing complexity of business and the growing need for information, accounting information systems are more important than ever. All decision makers need to have a basic knowledge of how accounting information systems work. This knowledge gives decision makers a competitive edge as they gain a better understanding of information constraints, measurement limitations, and potential applications. It allows them to make more informed decisions and to better balance the risks and returns of different strategies. This section explains five basic principles of accounting information systems, shown in Exhibit 7.1.

EXHIBIT 7.1

System Principles

Control
Relevance
Compatibility
Flexibility
Cost-Benefit Principle
System Principles

Control Principle

Managers need to control and monitor business activities. The **control principle** prescribes that an accounting information system have internal controls. **Internal controls** are methods and procedures allowing managers to control and monitor business activities. They include policies to direct operations toward common goals, procedures to ensure reliable financial reports, safeguards to protect company assets, and methods to achieve compliance with laws and regulations.

Point: A hacker stole 300,000 credit card numbers from online music retailer CDUniverse due to internal control failure.

Relevance Principle

Decision makers need relevant information to make informed decisions. The **relevance principle** prescribes that an accounting information system report useful, understandable, timely, and pertinent information for effective decision making. The system must be designed to capture data that make a difference in decisions. To ensure this, we must consider all decision makers when identifying relevant information for disclosure.

Compatibility Principle

Accounting information systems must be consistent with the aims of a company. The **compatibility principle** prescribes that an accounting information system conform with a company's activities, personnel, and structure. It also must adapt to a company's unique characteristics. The system must not be intrusive but must work in harmony with and be driven by company goals. Most start-up entrepreneurs require only a simple information system. Harley-Davidson, on the other hand, demands both a merchandising and a manufacturing information system able to assemble data from its global operations.

Flexibility Principle

Accounting information systems must be able to adjust to changes. The **flexibility principle** prescribes that an accounting information system be able to adapt to changes in the company, business environment, and needs of decisions makers. Technological advances, competitive pressures, consumer tastes, regulations, and company activities constantly evolve. A system must be designed to adapt to these changes.

Cost-Benefit Principle

The **cost-benefit principle** prescribes that the benefits from an activity in an accounting information system outweigh the costs of that activity. The costs and benefits of an activity such as producing a specific report will impact the decisions of both external and internal users. Decisions regarding other systems principles (control, relevance, compatibility, and flexibility) are also affected by the cost-benefit principle.

Point: Law requires that *all* employers destroy credit-check and other employee records *before* tossing them. A cross-cut shredder is the tool of choice.

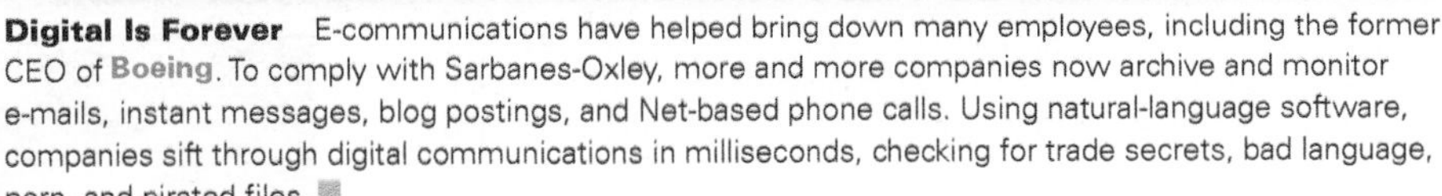

Digital Is Forever E-communications have helped bring down many employees, including the former CEO of Boeing. To comply with Sarbanes-Oxley, more and more companies now archive and monitor e-mails, instant messages, blog postings, and Net-based phone calls. Using natural-language software, companies sift through digital communications in milliseconds, checking for trade secrets, bad language, porn, and pirated files.

COMPONENTS OF ACCOUNTING SYSTEMS

Accounting information systems consist of people, records, methods, and equipment. The systems are designed to capture information about a company's transactions and to provide output including financial, managerial, and tax reports. All accounting information systems have these same goals, and thus share some basic components. These components apply whether or not a system is heavily computerized, yet the components of computerized systems usually provide more accuracy, speed, efficiency, and convenience than those of manual systems.

The five basic **components of accounting systems** are source documents, input devices, information processors, information storage, and output devices. Exhibit 7.2 shows these components as a series of steps, yet we know that much two-way communication occurs between many of these components. We briefly describe each of these key components in this section.

EXHIBIT 7.2

Accounting System Components

Source Documents

We introduced source documents in Chapters 1 and 2 and explained their importance for both business transactions and information collection. Source documents provide the basic information processed by an accounting system. Examples of source documents include bank statements and checks, invoices from suppliers, billings to customers, cash register files, and employee earnings records. Source documents can be paper, although they increasingly are taking the form of electronic files and Web communications. A growing number of companies are sending documents directly from their systems to their customers' and suppliers' systems. The Web is playing a major role in this transformation from paper-based to *paperless* systems.

Accurate source documents are crucial to accounting information systems. Input of faulty or incomplete information seriously impairs the reliability and relevance of the information system. We commonly refer to this as "garbage in, garbage out." Information systems are set up with attention on control procedures to limit the possibility of entering faulty data in the system.

Input Devices

Input devices capture information from source documents and enable its transfer to the system's information processing component. These devices often involve converting data on source documents from written or electronic form to a form usable for the system. Journal entries, both electronic and paper based, are a type of input device. Keyboards, scanners, and modems are some of the most common input devices in practice today. For example, bar code readers capture code numbers and transfer them to the organization's computer for processing. Moreover, a scanner can capture writing samples and other input directly from source documents.

Point: Understanding a manual accounting system is useful in understanding an electronic system.

Controls are used to ensure that only authorized individuals input data to the system. Controls increase the system's reliability and allow information to be traced back to its source.

Decision Insight

Geek Chic Cyberfashion pioneers are creating geek chic, a kind of wearable computer. Cyberfashion draws on digital cellular phones, lithium batteries, and miniature monitors. Special thread is woven into clothing to carry low-voltage signals from one part of the system to another, and fabric keyboards are sewn into clothes. These creations give new meaning to the term *software*. ■

Information Processors

Information processors are systems that interpret, transform, and summarize information for use in analysis and reporting. An important part of an information processor in accounting systems is professional judgment. Accounting principles are never so structured that they limit the need for professional judgment. Other parts of an information processor include journals, ledgers, working papers, and posting procedures. Each assists in transforming raw data to useful information.

Point: *BusinessWeek* reported that 75% of all e-mail traffic is spam.

Increasingly, computer technology (both computing hardware and software) is assisting manual information processors. This assistance is freeing accounting professionals to take on increased analysis, interpretive, and managerial roles. Web-based application service providers (ASPs) offer another type of information processor.

Information Storage

Information storage is the accounting system component that keeps data in a form accessible to information processors. After being input and processed, data are stored for use in future analyses and reports. The database must be accessible to preparers of periodic financial reports. Auditors rely on this database when they audit both financial statements and a company's controls. Companies also maintain files of source documents.

Point: A financial accounting database can be designed to support a wide range of internal reports for management.

Older systems consisted almost exclusively of paper documents, but most modern systems depend on electronic storage devices. Advances in information storage enable accounting systems to increasingly store more detailed data. This means managers have more data to access and work with in planning and controlling business activities. Information storage can be online, meaning that data can be accessed whenever, and from wherever, it is needed. Off-line storage means access often requires assistance and authorization. Information storage is increasingly augmented by Web sources such as SEC databases, benchmarking services, and financial and product markets.

Decision Insight

Direct Output A screenless computer display, called *virtual retinal display* (VRD), scans rows of pixels directly onto the user's retina by means of a laser. VRDs can simulate three-dimensional virtual worlds, including 3D financial graphics. ■

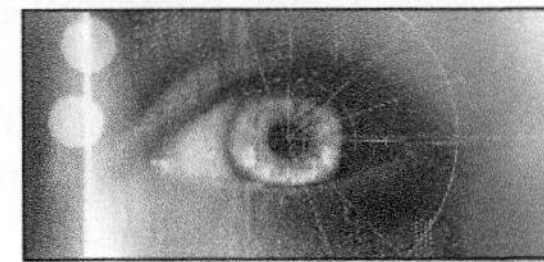

Output Devices

Output devices are the means to take information out of an accounting system and make it available to users. Common output devices are printers, monitors, projectors, and Web communications. Output devices provide users a variety of items including graphics, analysis reports, bills to customers, checks to suppliers, employee paychecks, financial statements, and internal reports. When requests for output occur, an information processor takes the needed data from a database and prepares the necessary report, which is then sent to an output device. A special type of output is an electronic funds transfer (EFT). One example is the transfer of payroll from the company's bank account to its employees' bank accounts. This requires an interface to allow a company's accounting system to send payroll data directly to the bank's accounting system. This interface can involve a company recording its payroll data in an encrypted zip file and forwarding it to the bank. The bank then uses this output to transfer wages earned to employees' accounts.

Decision Ethics

Answer — p. 296

Accountant Your client requests advice in purchasing software for its accounting system. You have been offered a 10% commission by a software company for each purchase of its system by one of your clients. Does this commission arrangement affect your evaluation of software? Do you tell your client about the commission arrangement? ■

Quick Check

Answers — p. 297

1. Identify the five primary components of an accounting information system.
2. What is the aim of information processors in an accounting system?
3. How are data in the information storage component of an accounting system used?

SPECIAL JOURNALS IN ACCOUNTING

C2 Explain the goals and uses of special journals.

This section describes the underlying records of accounting information systems. Designed correctly, these records support efficiency in processing transactions and events. They are part of all systems in various forms and are increasingly electronic. Even in technologically advanced systems, a basic understanding of the records we describe in this section aids in using, interpreting, and applying accounting information. It also improves our knowledge of computer-based systems. Remember that all accounting systems have common purposes and internal workings whether or not they depend on technology.

This section focuses on special journals and subsidiary ledgers that are an important part of accounting systems. We describe how special journals are used to capture transactions, and we explain how subsidiary ledgers are set up to capture details of accounts. This section uses a *perpetual* inventory system, and the special journals are set up using this system. Appendix 7A describes the change in special journals required for a *periodic* system. We also include a note at the bottom of each of the special journals explaining the change required if a company uses a periodic system.

Basics of Special Journals

A **general journal** is an all-purpose journal in which we can record any transaction. Use of a general journal for all transactions is usually more costly for a business *and* is a less effective control procedure. Moreover, for less technologically advanced systems, use of a general journal requires that each debit and each credit entered be individually posted to its respective ledger account. To enhance internal control and reduce costs, transactions are organized into common groups. A **special journal** is used to record and post transactions of similar type. Most transactions of a merchandiser, for instance, can be categorized into the journals shown in Exhibit 7.3. This section assumes the use of these four special journals along with the general journal. The general journal continues to be used for transactions not covered by special journals and for adjusting, closing, and correcting entries. We show in the following discussion that special journals are *efficient tools in helping journalize and post transactions.* This is done, for instance, by accumulating debits and credits of similar transactions, which allows posting of amounts as column *totals* rather than as individual amounts. The advantage of this system increases as the number of transactions increases. Special journals allow an *efficient division of labor,* which is also an effective control procedure.

Point: Companies can use as many special journals as necessary given their unique business activities.

Point: A specific transaction is recorded in only *one* journal.

EXHIBIT 7.3

Using Special Journals with a General Journal

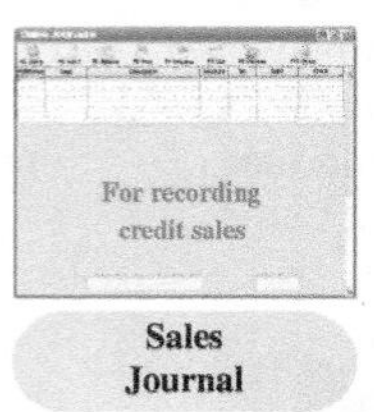

Sales Journal

Cash Receipts Journal

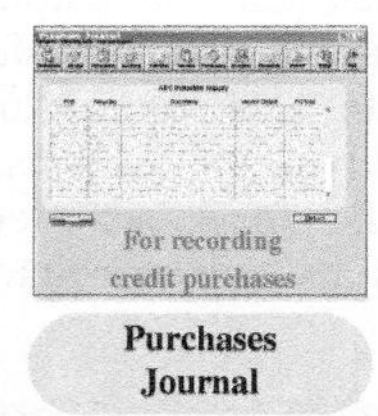

Purchases Journal

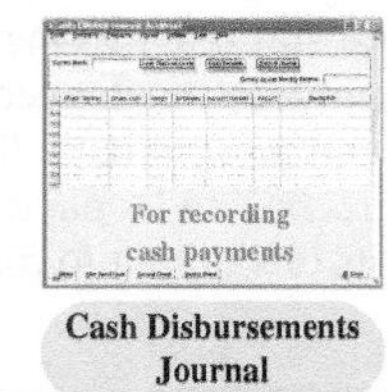

Cash Disbursements Journal

General Journal

It is important to note that special journals and subsidiary ledgers *are designed in a manner that is best suited for each business*. The most likely candidates for special journal status are recurring transactions—for many businesses those are sales, cash receipts, purchases, and cash disbursements. However, good systems design for a business could involve collapsing sales and cash receipts in one journal, or purchases and cash disbursements in another. It could also involve adding more special journals or additional subsidiary ledgers for other recurring transactions. This design decision extends to journal and ledger format. That is, the selection on number of columns, column headings, and so forth is based on what is best suited for each business. Thus, read the following sections as one example of a common systems design, but not the only design.

Subsidiary Ledgers

C3 Describe the use of controlling accounts and subsidiary ledgers.

To understand special journals, it is necessary to understand the workings of a **subsidiary ledger,** which is a list of individual accounts with a common characteristic. A subsidiary ledger contains detailed information on specific accounts in the general ledger. Information systems often include several subsidiary ledgers. Two of the most important are:

- *Accounts receivable ledger*—stores transaction data of individual customers.
- *Accounts payable ledger*—stores transaction data of individual suppliers.

Individual accounts in subsidiary ledgers are often arranged alphabetically, which is the approach taken here. We describe accounts receivable and accounts payable ledgers in this section. Our discussion of special journals uses these ledgers.

Accounts Receivable Ledger When we recorded credit sales in prior chapters, we debited (increased) Accounts Receivable. When a company has more than one credit customer, the accounts receivable records must show how much *each* customer purchased, paid, and has yet to pay. This information is collected by keeping a separate account receivable for each credit customer. A separate account for each customer *could* be kept in the general ledger with the other financial statement accounts, but this is uncommon. Instead, the general ledger usually has a single Accounts Receivable account, and a *subsidiary ledger* is set up to keep a separate account for each customer. This subsidiary ledger is called the **accounts receivable ledger** (also called *accounts receivable subsidiary ledger* or *customers ledger*), and it can exist in electronic or paper form.

Exhibit 7.4 shows the relation between the Accounts Receivable account and its individual accounts in the subsidiary ledger. After all items are posted, the balance in the Accounts Receivable account must equal the sum of all balances of its customers' accounts. The Accounts Receivable account is said to control the accounts receivable ledger and is called a **controlling account.** Since the accounts receivable ledger is a supplementary record controlled by an account in the general ledger, it is called a *subsidiary* ledger.

Point: When a general ledger account has a subsidiary ledger, any transaction that impacts one of them also impacts the other—some refer to this as *general and subsidiary ledgers kept in tandem.*

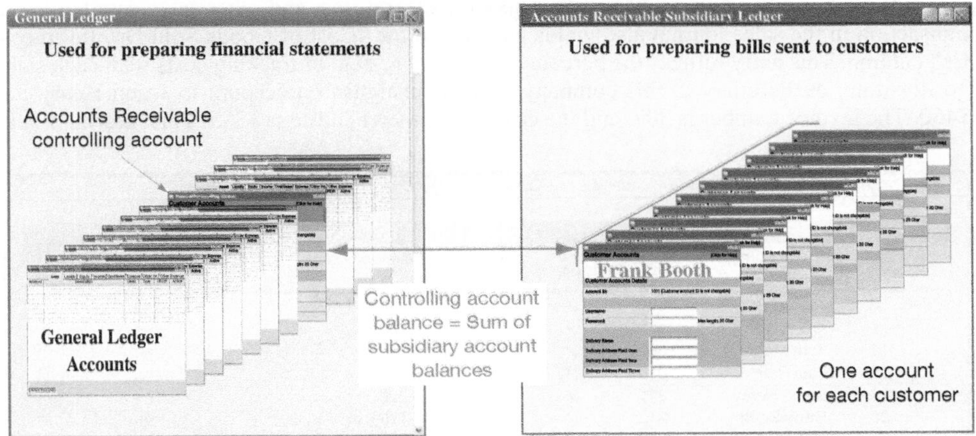

EXHIBIT 7.4

Accounts Receivable Controlling Account and Its Subsidiary Ledger

Point: A control account refers to any general ledger account that summarizes subsidiary ledger data.

Accounts Payable Ledger There are other controlling accounts and subsidiary ledgers. We know, for example, that many companies buy on credit from several suppliers. This means that companies must keep a separate account for each supplier by keeping an Accounts Payable controlling account in the general ledger and a separate account for each supplier (creditor) in an **accounts payable ledger** (also called *accounts payable subsidiary ledger* or *creditors ledger*).

Other Subsidiary Ledgers Subsidiary ledgers are common for several other accounts. A company with many classes of equipment, for example, might keep only one Equipment account in its general ledger, but its Equipment account would control a subsidiary ledger in which each class of equipment is recorded in a separate account. Similar treatment is common for investments, inventory, and any accounts needing separate detailed records. Genmar Holdings, which manufactures boats by Champion, Glastron, Four Winns, and Larson, reports sales information by product line in its report. Yet its accounting system keeps much more detailed sales records. Genmar Holdings, for instance, sells hundreds of different products and must be able to analyze the sales performance of each. This detail can be captured by many different general ledger sales accounts but is instead captured by using supplementary records that function like subsidiary ledgers. Overall, subsidiary ledgers are applied in many different ways to ensure that the accounting system captures sufficient details to support analyses that decision makers need. At least four benefits derive from subsidiary ledgers:

1. Removal of excessive details, and detailed accounts, from the general ledger.
2. Up-to-date information readily available on specific customers and suppliers.
3. Aid in error identification for specific accounts.
4. Potential efficiencies in recordkeeping through division of labor in posting.

Sales Journal

P1 Journalize and post transactions using special journals.

A typical **sales journal** is used to record sales of inventory *on credit.* Sales of inventory for cash are not recorded in a sales journal but in a cash receipts journal. Sales of noninventory assets on credit are recorded in the general journal.

Journalizing Credit sale transactions are recorded with information about each sale entered separately in a sales journal. This information is often taken from a copy of the sales ticket or invoice prepared at the time of sale. The top portion of Exhibit 7.5 shows a typical sales journal from a merchandiser. It has columns for recording the date, customer's name, invoice number, posting reference, and the retail and cost amounts of each credit sale. The sales journal in this exhibit is called a **columnar journal,** which is any journal with more than one column.

Point: Each transaction in the sales journal includes a debit to accounts receivable and a credit to sales.

Each transaction recorded in the sales journal yields an entry in the "Accounts Receivable Dr., Sales Cr." column. We usually need only one column for these two accounts. (An exception is when managers need more information about taxes, returns, and other sales details.) Each transaction in the sales journal also yields an entry in the "Cost of Goods Sold Dr., Inventory Cr." column. This entry reflects the perpetual inventory system of tracking costs with each sale. To illustrate, on February 2, this company sold merchandise on account to Jason Henry for $450. The invoice number is 307, and the cost of this merchandise is $315. This information is

EXHIBIT 7.5

Sales Journal with Posting*

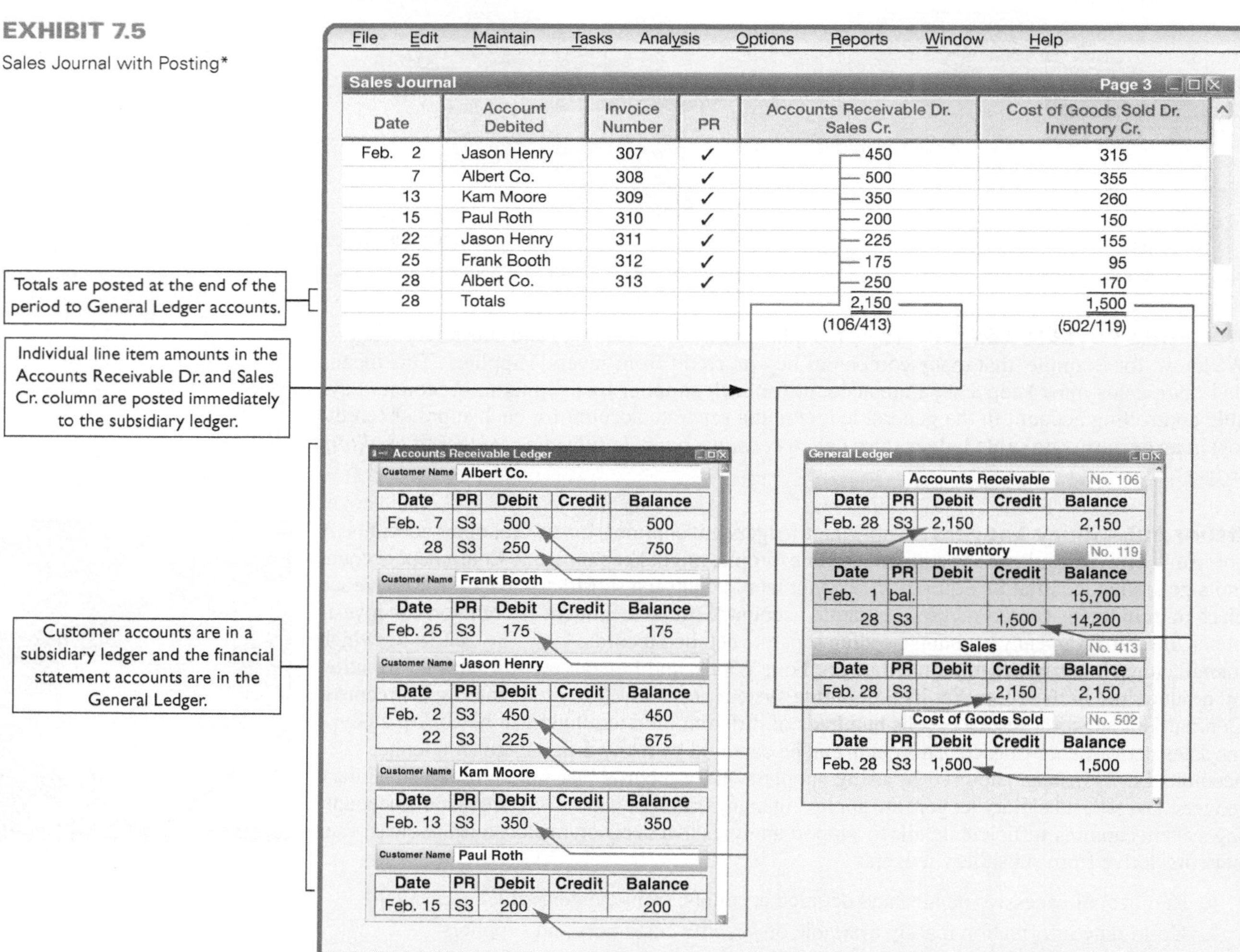

Date	Account Debited	Invoice Number	PR	Accounts Receivable Dr. Sales Cr.	Cost of Goods Sold Dr. Inventory Cr.
Feb. 2	Jason Henry	307	✓	450	315
7	Albert Co.	308	✓	500	355
13	Kam Moore	309	✓	350	260
15	Paul Roth	310	✓	200	150
22	Jason Henry	311	✓	225	155
25	Frank Booth	312	✓	175	95
28	Albert Co.	313	✓	250	170
28	Totals			2,150	1,500
				(106/413)	(502/119)

Accounts Receivable Ledger

Customer Name: Albert Co.

Date	PR	Debit	Credit	Balance
Feb. 7	S3	500		500
28	S3	250		750

Customer Name: Frank Booth

Date	PR	Debit	Credit	Balance
Feb. 25	S3	175		175

Customer Name: Jason Henry

Date	PR	Debit	Credit	Balance
Feb. 2	S3	450		450
22	S3	225		675

Customer Name: Kam Moore

Date	PR	Debit	Credit	Balance
Feb. 13	S3	350		350

Customer Name: Paul Roth

Date	PR	Debit	Credit	Balance
Feb. 15	S3	200		200

General Ledger

Accounts Receivable — No. 106

Date	PR	Debit	Credit	Balance
Feb. 28	S3	2,150		2,150

Inventory — No. 119

Date	PR	Debit	Credit	Balance
Feb. 1	bal.			15,700
28	S3		1,500	14,200

Sales — No. 413

Date	PR	Debit	Credit	Balance
Feb. 28	S3		2,150	2,150

Cost of Goods Sold — No. 502

Date	PR	Debit	Credit	Balance
Feb. 28	S3	1,500		1,500

*The Sales Journal in a *periodic* system would exclude the column on the far right titled "Cost of Goods Sold Dr., Inventory Cr." (see Exhibit 7A.1).

captured on one line in the sales journal. No further explanations or entries are necessary, saving time and effort. Moreover, this sales journal is consistent with most inventory systems that use bar codes to record both sales and costs with each sale transaction. Note that the Posting Reference (PR) column is not used when entering transactions but instead is used when posting.

Point: Continuously updated customer accounts provide timely information for customer inquiries on those accounts and on current amounts owed.

Posting A sales journal is posted as reflected in the arrow lines of Exhibit 7.5. Two types of posting can be identified: (1) posting to the subsidiary ledger(s) and (2) posting to the general ledger.

Posting to subsidiary ledger. Individual transactions in the sales journal are posted regularly (typically concurrently) to customer accounts in the accounts receivable ledger. These postings keep customer accounts up-to-date, which is important for the person granting credit to customers. When sales recorded in the sales journal are individually posted to customer accounts in the accounts receivable ledger, check marks are entered in the sales journal's PR column. Check marks are used rather than account numbers because customer accounts usually are arranged alphabetically in the accounts receivable ledger. Note that posting debits to Accounts Receivable twice—once to Accounts Receivable and once to the customer's subsidiary account—does not violate the accounting equation of debits equal credits. The equality of debits and credits is always maintained in the general ledger.

Point: PR column is only checked *after* the amount(s) is posted.

Posting to general ledger. The sales journal's account columns are totaled at the end of each period (the month of February in this case). For the "sales" column, the $2,150 total is debited to Accounts Receivable and credited to Sales in the general ledger (see Exhibit 7.5). For the "cost" column, the $1,500 total is debited to Cost of Goods Sold and credited to Inventory in the general ledger. When totals are posted to accounts in the general ledger, the account numbers are entered below the column total in the sales journal for tracking. For example, we enter (106/413) below the total in the sales column after this amount is posted to account number 106 (Accounts Receivable) and account number 413 (Sales).

Point: Postings are automatic in a computerized system.

A company identifies in the PR column of its subsidiary ledgers the journal and page number from which an amount is taken. We identify a journal by using an initial. Items posted from the sales journal carry the initial ***S*** before their journal page numbers in a PR column. Likewise, items from the cash receipts journal carry the initial ***R***; items from the cash disbursements journal carry the initial ***D***; items from the purchases journal carry the initial ***P***; and items from the general journal carry the initial ***G***.

P2 Prepare and prove the accuracy of subsidiary ledgers.

Proving the Ledgers Account balances in the general ledger and subsidiary ledgers are periodically proved (or reviewed) for accuracy after posting. To do this we first prepare a trial balance of the general ledger to confirm that debits equal credits. Second, we test a subsidiary ledger by preparing a *schedule* of individual accounts and amounts. A **schedule of accounts receivable** lists each customer and the balance owed. If this total equals the balance of the Accounts Receivable controlling account, the accounts in the accounts receivable ledger are assumed correct. Exhibit 7.6 shows a schedule of accounts receivable drawn from the accounts receivable ledger of Exhibit 7.5.

EXHIBIT 7.6

Schedule of Accounts Receivable

Schedule of Accounts Receivable February 28	
Albert Co.	$ 750
Frank Booth	175
Jason Henry	675
Kam Moore	350
Paul Roth	200
Total accounts receivable	$2,150

Additional Issues We consider three additional issues with the sales journal: (1) recording sales taxes, (2) recording sales returns and allowances, and (3) using actual sales invoices as a journal.

Point: In accounting, the word *schedule* generally means a list.

Sales taxes. Governmental agencies such as cities and states often require sellers to collect sales taxes from customers and to periodically send these taxes to the appropriate agency. When using a columnar sales journal, we can keep a record of taxes collected by adding a Sales Taxes Payable column as follows.

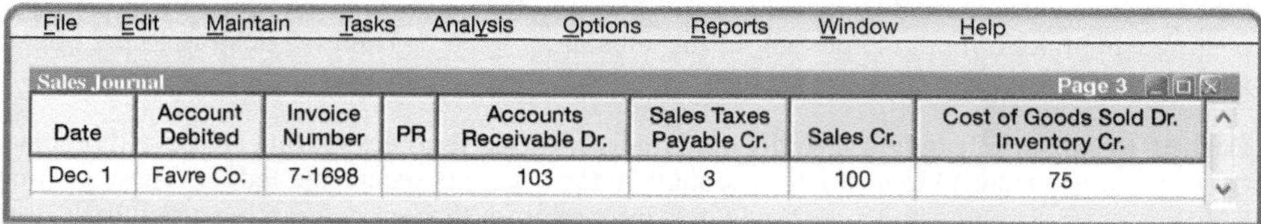

Date	Account Debited	Invoice Number	PR	Accounts Receivable Dr.	Sales Taxes Payable Cr.	Sales Cr.	Cost of Goods Sold Dr. Inventory Cr.
Dec. 1	Favre Co.	7-1698		103	3	100	75

Individual amounts in the Accounts Receivable column would continue to be posted immediately to customer accounts in the accounts receivable ledger. Individual amounts in the Sales Taxes Payable and Sales columns are not posted. Column totals would continue to be posted as usual. (A company that collects sales taxes on its cash sales can also use a Sales Taxes Payable column in its cash receipts journal.)

Sales returns and allowances. A company with only a few sales returns and allowances can record them in a general journal with an entry such as the following:

Assets = Liabilities + Equity
−175 −175

May 17	Sales Returns and Allowances	414	175	
	Accounts Receivable—Ray Ball	106/✓		175
	Customer returned merchandise.			

The debit in this entry is posted to the Sales Returns and Allowances account (no. 414). The credit is posted to both the Accounts Receivable controlling account (no. 106) and to the customer's account. When we enter the account number and the check mark, 106/✓, in the PR column on the credit line, this means both the Accounts Receivable controlling account in the general ledger and the Ray Ball account in the accounts receivable ledger are credited for $175. [*Note:* If the returned goods can be resold to another customer, the company would debit (increase) the Inventory account and credit (decrease) the Cost of Goods Sold account. If the returned goods are defective (worthless), the company could simply leave their costs in the Cost of Goods Sold account (see Chapter 5).] A company with a large number of sales returns and allowances can save time by recording them in a separate sales returns and allowances journal.

Sales invoices as a sales journal. To save costs, some small companies avoid using a sales journal for credit sales and instead post each sales invoice amount directly to the customer's account in the accounts receivable ledger. They then put copies of invoices in a file. At the end of the period, they total all invoices for that period and make a general journal entry to debit Accounts Receivable and credit Sales for the total amount. The file of invoice copies acts as a sales journal. This is called *direct posting of sales invoices.*

4. When special journals are used, where are cash payments by check recorded?
5. How does a columnar journal save posting time and effort?
6. How do debits and credits remain equal when credit sales are posted twice (once to Accounts Receivable and once to the customer's subsidiary account)?
7. How do we identify the journal from which an amount in a ledger account was posted?
8. How are sales taxes recorded in the context of special journals?
9. What is direct posting of sales invoices?

Cash Receipts Journal

A **cash receipts journal** is typically used to record all receipts of cash. Exhibit 7.7 shows one common form of the cash receipts journal.

Journalizing and Posting Cash receipts can be separated into one of three types: (1) cash from credit customers in payment of their accounts, (2) cash from cash sales, and (3) cash from other sources. The cash receipts journal in Exhibit 7.7 has a separate credit

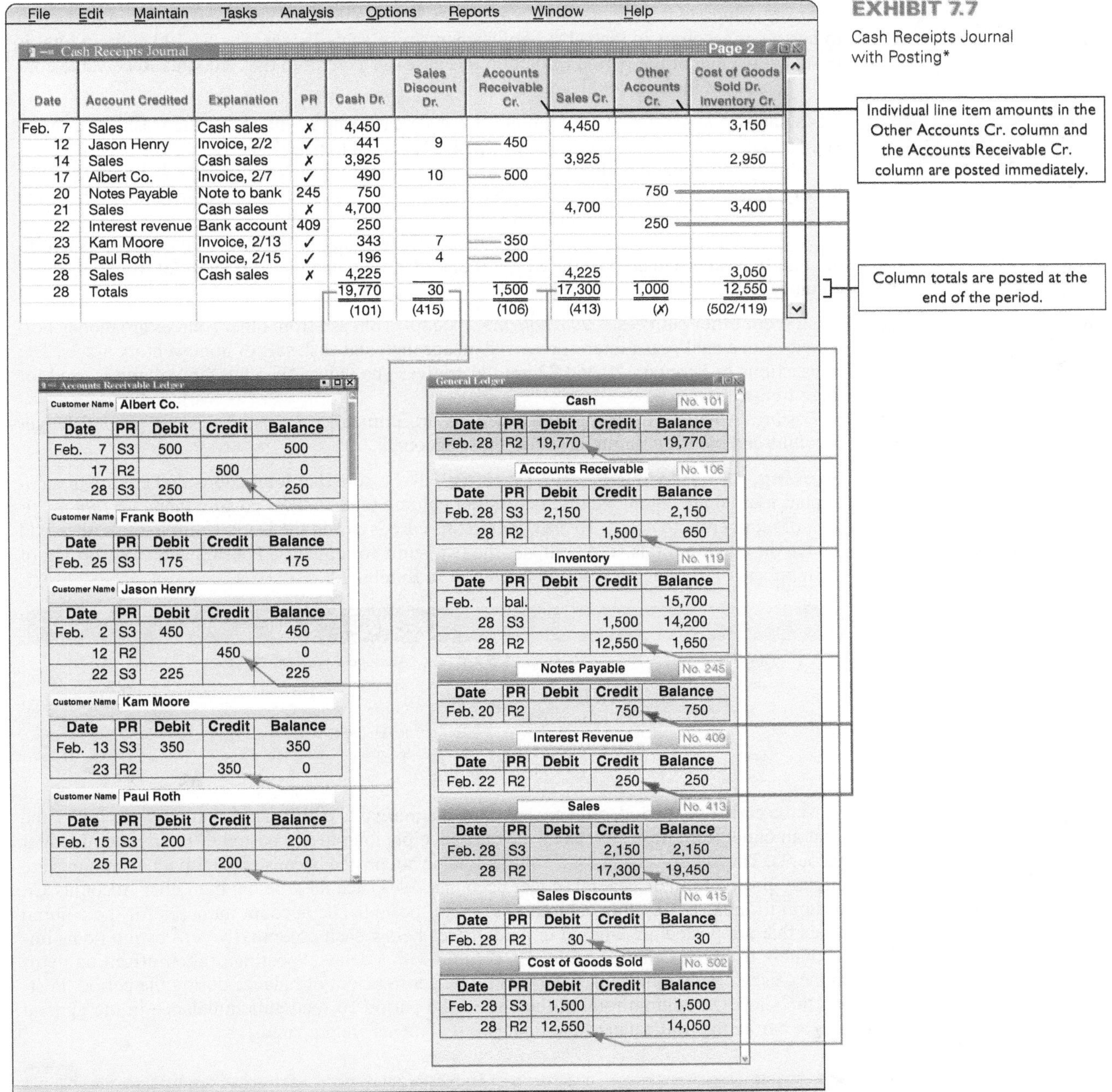

Date	Account Credited	Explanation	PR	Cash Dr.	Sales Discount Dr.	Accounts Receivable Cr.	Sales Cr.	Other Accounts Cr.	Cost of Goods Sold Dr. Inventory Cr.
Feb. 7	Sales	Cash sales	✗	4,450			4,450		3,150
12	Jason Henry	Invoice, 2/2	✓	441	9	450			
14	Sales	Cash sales	✗	3,925			3,925		2,950
17	Albert Co.	Invoice, 2/7	✓	490	10	500			
20	Notes Payable	Note to bank	245	750				750	
21	Sales	Cash sales	✗	4,700			4,700		3,400
22	Interest revenue	Bank account	409	250				250	
23	Kam Moore	Invoice, 2/13	✓	343	7	350			
25	Paul Roth	Invoice, 2/15	✓	196	4	200			
28	Sales	Cash sales	✗	4,225			4,225		3,050
28	Totals			19,770	30	1,500	17,300	1,000	12,550
				(101)	(415)	(106)	(413)	(✗)	(502/119)

Accounts Receivable Ledger

Customer Name: Albert Co.

Date	PR	Debit	Credit	Balance
Feb. 7	S3	500		500
17	R2		500	0
28	S3	250		250

Customer Name: Frank Booth

Date	PR	Debit	Credit	Balance
Feb. 25	S3	175		175

Customer Name: Jason Henry

Date	PR	Debit	Credit	Balance
Feb. 2	S3	450		450
12	R2		450	0
22	S3	225		225

Customer Name: Kam Moore

Date	PR	Debit	Credit	Balance
Feb. 13	S3	350		350
23	R2		350	0

Customer Name: Paul Roth

Date	PR	Debit	Credit	Balance
Feb. 15	S3	200		200
25	R2		200	0

General Ledger

Cash — No. 101

Date	PR	Debit	Credit	Balance
Feb. 28	R2	19,770		19,770

Accounts Receivable — No. 106

Date	PR	Debit	Credit	Balance
Feb. 28	S3	2,150		2,150
28	R2		1,500	650

Inventory — No. 119

Date	PR	Debit	Credit	Balance
Feb. 1	bal.			15,700
28	S3		1,500	14,200
28	R2		12,550	1,650

Notes Payable — No. 245

Date	PR	Debit	Credit	Balance
Feb. 20	R2		750	750

Interest Revenue — No. 409

Date	PR	Debit	Credit	Balance
Feb. 22	R2		250	250

Sales — No. 413

Date	PR	Debit	Credit	Balance
Feb. 28	S3		2,150	2,150
28	R2		17,300	19,450

Sales Discounts — No. 415

Date	PR	Debit	Credit	Balance
Feb. 28	R2	30		30

Cost of Goods Sold — No. 502

Date	PR	Debit	Credit	Balance
Feb. 28	S3	1,500		1,500
28	R2	12,550		14,050

EXHIBIT 7.7

Cash Receipts Journal with Posting*

*The Cash Receipts Journal in a *periodic* system would exclude the column on the far right titled "Cost of Goods Sold Dr., Inventory Cr." (see Exhibit 7A.2).

Point: Each transaction in the cash receipts journal involves a debit to Cash. Credit accounts will vary.

column for each of these three sources. We describe how to journalize transactions from each of these three sources. (An Explanation column is included in the cash receipts journal to identify the source.)

Cash from credit customers. *Journalizing.* To record cash received in payment of a customer's account, the customer's name is first entered in the Account Credited column—see transactions dated February 12, 17, 23, and 25. Then the amounts debited to both Cash and the Sales Discount (if any) are entered in their respective columns, and the amount credited to the customer's account is entered in the Accounts Receivable Cr. column.

Posting. Individual amounts in the Accounts Receivable Cr. column are posted immediately to customer accounts in the subsidiary accounts receivable ledger. The $1,500 column total is posted at the end of the period (month in this case) as a credit to the Accounts Receivable controlling account in the general ledger.

Cash sales. *Journalizing.* The amount for each cash sale is entered in the Cash Dr. column and the Sales Cr. column. The February 7, 14, 21, and 28 transactions are examples. (Cash sales are usually journalized daily or at point of sale, but are journalized weekly in Exhibit 7.7 for brevity.) Each cash sale also yields an entry to Cost of Goods Sold Dr. and Inventory Cr. for the cost of merchandise—see the far right column.

Point: Some software packages put cash sales in the sales journal.

Posting. For cash sales, we place an *x* in the PR column to indicate that its amount is not individually posted. We do post the $17,300 Sales Cr. total and the $12,550 total from the "cost" column.

Example: Record in the cash receipts journal a $700 cash sale of land when the land carries a $700 original cost. *Answer:* Debit the Cash column for $700, and credit the Other Accounts column for $700 (the account credited is Land).

Cash from other sources. *Journalizing.* Examples of cash from other sources are money borrowed from a bank, cash interest received on account, and cash sale of noninventory assets. The transactions of February 20 and 22 are illustrative. The Other Accounts Cr. column is used for these transactions.

Posting. Amounts from these transactions are immediately posted to their general ledger accounts and the PR column identifies those accounts.

Point: Subsidiary ledgers and their controlling accounts are *in balance* only after all posting is complete.

Footing, Crossfooting, and Posting To be sure that total debits and credits in a columnar journal are equal, we often crossfoot column totals before posting them. To *foot* a column of numbers is to add it. To *crossfoot* in this case is to add the Debit column totals, then add the Credit column totals, and compare the two sums for equality. Footing and crossfooting of the numbers in Exhibit 7.7 result in the report in Exhibit 7.8.

EXHIBIT 7.8

Footing and Crossfooting Journal Totals

Debit Columns		Credit Columns	
Cash Dr.	$19,770	Accounts Receivable Cr.	$ 1,500
Sales Discounts Dr.	30	Sales Cr.	17,300
Cost of Goods Sold Dr.	12,550	Other Accounts Cr.	1,000
		Inventory Cr.	12,550
Total	$32,350	Total	$32,350

At the end of the period, after crossfooting the journal to confirm that debits equal credits, the total amounts from the columns of the cash receipts journal are posted to their general ledger accounts. The Other Accounts Cr. column total is not posted because the individual amounts are directly posted to their general ledger accounts. We place an *x* below the Other Accounts Cr. column to indicate that this column total is not posted. The account numbers for the column totals that are posted are entered in parentheses below each column. (*Note:* Posting items immediately from the Other Accounts Cr. column with a delayed posting of their offsetting items in the Cash column total causes the general ledger to be out of balance during the period. Posting the Cash Dr. column total at the end of the period corrects this imbalance in the general ledger before the trial balance and financial statements are prepared.)

Decision Maker Answer — p. 297 

Entrepreneur You want to know how promptly customers are paying their bills. This information can help you decide whether to extend credit and to plan your cash payments. Where do you find this information? ■

Purchases Journal

A **purchases journal** is typically used to record all credit purchases, including those for inventory. Purchases for cash are recorded in the Cash Disbursements Journal.

Journalizing Entries in the purchases journal in Exhibit 7.9 reflect purchase invoices or other source documents. We use the invoice date and terms to compute the date when payment for each purchase is due. The Accounts Payable Cr. column is used to record the amounts owed to each creditor. Inventory purchases are recorded in the Inventory Dr. column.

Point: The number of special journals and the design of each are based on a company's specific needs.

To illustrate, inventory costing $200 is purchased from Ace Manufacturing on February 5. The creditor's name (Ace) is entered in the Account column, the invoice date is entered in the Date of Invoice column, the purchase terms are entered in the Terms column, and the $200 amount is entered in the Accounts Payable Cr. and the Inventory Dr. columns. When a purchase involves an amount recorded in the Other Accounts Dr. column, we use the Account column to identify the general ledger account debited. For example, the February 28 transaction involves purchases of inventory, office supplies, and store supplies from ITT. The journal has no column for store supplies, so the Other Accounts Dr. column is used. In this case, Store Supplies is entered in the Account column along with the creditor's name (ITT). This purchases journal also includes a separate column for credit purchases of office supplies. A separate column such as this is useful when several transactions involve debits to the same account. Each company uses its own judgment in deciding on the number of separate columns necessary.

Point: Each transaction in the purchases journal has a credit to Accounts Payable. Debit accounts will vary.

Point: The Other Accounts Dr. column allows the purchases journal to be used for any purchase on credit.

Posting The amounts in the Accounts Payable Cr. column are immediately posted to individual creditor accounts in the accounts payable subsidiary ledger. Individual amounts in the Other Accounts Dr. column are immediately posted to their general ledger accounts. At the end

EXHIBIT 7.9

Purchases Journal with Posting*

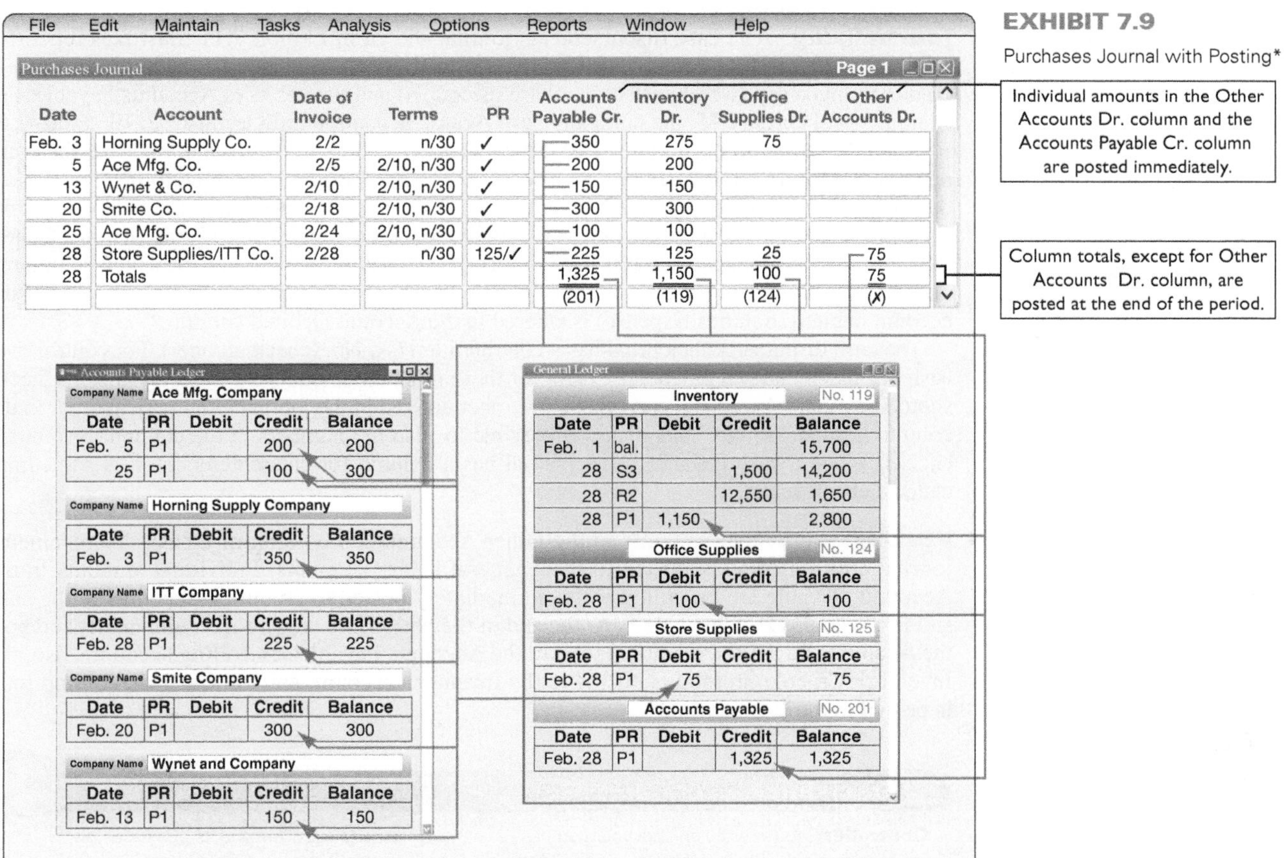

Date	Account	Date of Invoice	Terms	PR	Accounts Payable Cr.	Inventory Dr.	Office Supplies Dr.	Other Accounts Dr.
Feb. 3	Horning Supply Co.	2/2	n/30	✓	350	275	75	
5	Ace Mfg. Co.	2/5	2/10, n/30	✓	200	200		
13	Wynet & Co.	2/10	2/10, n/30	✓	150	150		
20	Smite Co.	2/18	2/10, n/30	✓	300	300		
25	Ace Mfg. Co.	2/24	2/10, n/30	✓	100	100		
28	Store Supplies/ITT Co.	2/28	n/30	125/✓	225	125	25	75
28	Totals				1,325	1,150	100	75
					(201)	(119)	(124)	(✗)

Accounts Payable Ledger

Company Name: Ace Mfg. Company

Date	PR	Debit	Credit	Balance
Feb. 5	P1		200	200
25	P1		100	300

Company Name: Horning Supply Company

Date	PR	Debit	Credit	Balance
Feb. 3	P1		350	350

Company Name: ITT Company

Date	PR	Debit	Credit	Balance
Feb. 28	P1		225	225

Company Name: Smite Company

Date	PR	Debit	Credit	Balance
Feb. 20	P1		300	300

Company Name: Wynet and Company

Date	PR	Debit	Credit	Balance
Feb. 13	P1		150	150

General Ledger

Inventory No. 119

Date	PR	Debit	Credit	Balance
Feb. 1	bal.			15,700
28	S3		1,500	14,200
28	R2		12,550	1,650
28	P1	1,150		2,800

Office Supplies No. 124

Date	PR	Debit	Credit	Balance
Feb. 28	P1	100		100

Store Supplies No. 125

Date	PR	Debit	Credit	Balance
Feb. 28	P1	75		75

Accounts Payable No. 201

Date	PR	Debit	Credit	Balance
Feb. 28	P1		1,325	1,325

*The Purchases Journal in a *periodic* system replaces "Inventory Dr." with "Purchases Dr." (see Exhibit 7A.3).

of the period, all column totals except the Other Accounts Dr. column are posted to their general ledger accounts.

Proving the Ledger Accounts payable balances in the subsidiary ledger can be periodically proved after posting. We prove the subsidiary ledger by preparing a **schedule of accounts payable,** which is a list of accounts from the accounts payable ledger with their balances and the total. If this total of the individual balances equals the balance of the Accounts Payable controlling account, the accounts in the accounts payable ledger are assumed correct. Exhibit 7.10 shows a schedule of accounts payable drawn from the accounts payable ledger of Exhibit 7.9. (This schedule can be done after any posting; for example, we could prepare another schedule of accounts payable after the postings in Exhibit 7.11.)

Point: The balance in the Accounts Payable controlling account must equal the sum of the individual account balances in the accounts payable subsidiary ledger after posting.

EXHIBIT 7.10

Schedule of Accounts Payable

Schedule of Accounts Payable February 28	
Ace Mfg. Company	$ 300
Horning Supply Company	350
ITT Company	225
Smite Company	300
Wynet & Company	150
Total accounts payable	$1,325

Cash Disbursements Journal

A **cash disbursements journal,** also called a *cash payments journal,* is typically used to record all cash payments.

Journalizing The cash disbursements journal shown in Exhibit 7.11 illustrates repetitive entries to the Cash Cr. column of this journal (reflecting cash payments). Also note the frequent credits to Inventory (which reflect purchase discounts) and the debits to Accounts Payable. For example, on February 15, the company pays Ace on account (credit terms of 2/10, n/30—see February 5 transaction in Exhibit 7.9). Since payment occurs in the discount period, the company pays $196 ($200 invoice less $4 discount). The $4 discount is credited to Inventory. Note that when this company purchases inventory for cash, it is recorded using the Other Accounts Dr. column and the Cash Cr. column as illustrated in the February 3 and 12 transactions. Generally, the Other Accounts column is used to record cash payments on items for which no column exists. For example, on February 15, the company pays salaries expense of $250. The title of the account debited (Salaries Expense) is entered in the Account Debited column.

Point: Each transaction in the cash disbursements journal involves a credit to Cash. The debit accounts will vary.

The cash disbursements journal has a column titled Ck. No. (check number). For control over cash disbursements, all payments except for those of small amounts are made by check. Checks should be prenumbered and each check's number entered in the journal in numerical order in the column headed Ck. No. This makes it possible to scan the numbers in the column for omitted checks. When a cash disbursements journal has a column for check numbers, it is sometimes called a **check register.**

Posting Individual amounts in the Other Accounts Dr. column of a cash disbursements journal are immediately posted to their general ledger accounts. Individual amounts in the Accounts Payable Dr. column are also immediately posted to creditors' accounts in the subsidiary Accounts Payable ledger. At the end of the period, we crossfoot column totals and post the Accounts Payable Dr. column total to the Accounts Payable controlling account. Also, the Inventory Cr. column total is posted to the Inventory account, and the Cash Cr. column total is posted to the Cash account.

Answer — p. 297

Controller You wish to analyze your company's cash payments to suppliers and its purchases discounts. Where do you find this information? ■

EXHIBIT 7.11

Cash Disbursements Journal with Posting*

File Edit Maintain Tasks Analysis Options Reports Window Help

Cash Disbursements Journal — Page 2

Date	Ck. No.	Payee	Account Debited	PR	Cash Cr.	Inventory Cr.	Other Accounts Dr.	Accounts Payable Dr.
Feb. 3	105	L. & N. Railroad	Inventory	119	15		15	
12	106	East Sales Co.	Inventory	119	25		25	
15	107	Ace Mfg. Co.	Ace Mfg. Co.	✓	196	4		200
15	108	Jerry Hale	Salaries Expense	622	250		250	
20	109	Wynet & Co.	Wynet & Co.	✓	147	3		150
28	110	Smite Co.	Smite Co.	✓	294	6		300
28		Totals			927	13	290	650
					(101)	(119)	(✗)	(201)

Individual amounts in the Other Accounts Dr. column and the Accounts Payable Dr. column are posted immediately.

Column totals, except for Other Accounts column, are posted at the end of the period.

General Ledger

Cash — No. 101

Date	PR	Debit	Credit	Balance
Feb. 28	R2	19,770		19,770
28	D2		927	18,843

Inventory — No. 119

Date	PR	Debit	Credit	Balance
Feb. 1	bal.			15,700
3	D2	15		15,715
12	D2	25		15,740
28	S3		1,500	14,240
28	R2		12,550	1,690
28	P1	1,150		2,840
28	D2		13	2,827

Accounts Payable — No. 201

Date	PR	Debit	Credit	Balance
Feb. 28	P1		1,325	1,325
28	D2	650		675

Salaries Expense — No. 622

Date	PR	Debit	Credit	Balance
Feb. 15	D2	250		250

Accounts Payable Ledger

Company Name: Ace Mfg. Company

Date	PR	Debit	Credit	Balance
Feb. 5	P1		200	200
15	D2	200		0
25	P1		100	100

Company Name: Horning Supply Company

Date	PR	Debit	Credit	Balance
Feb. 3	P1		350	350

Company Name: ITT Company

Date	PR	Debit	Credit	Balance
Feb. 28	P1		225	225

Company Name: Smite Company

Date	PR	Debit	Credit	Balance
Feb. 20	P1		300	300
28	D2	300		0

Company Name: Wynet & Company

Date	PR	Debit	Credit	Balance
Feb. 13	P1		150	150
20	D2	150		0

*The Cash Disbursements Journal in a *periodic* system replaces "Inventory Cr." with "Purchases Discounts Cr." (see Exhibit 7A.4).

General Journal Transactions

When special journals are used, we still need a general journal for adjusting, closing, and any other transactions for which no special journal has been set up. Examples of these other transactions might include purchases returns and allowances, purchases of plant assets by issuing a note payable, sales returns if a sales returns and allowances journal is not used, and receipt of a note receivable from a customer. We described the recording of transactions in a general journal in Chapters 2 and 3.

Quick Check

Answers — p. 297

10. What are the normal recording and posting procedures when using special journals and controlling accounts with subsidiary ledgers?
11. What is the process for posting to a subsidiary ledger and its controlling account?
12. How do we prove the accuracy of account balances in the general ledger and subsidiary ledgers after posting?
13. Why does a company need a general journal when using special journals for sales, purchases, cash receipts, and cash disbursements?

TECHNOLOGY-BASED ACCOUNTING SYSTEMS

Accounting information systems are supported with technology, which can range from simple calculators to advanced computerized systems. Since technology is increasingly important in accounting information systems, we discuss the impact of computer technology, how data processing works with accounting data, and the role of computer networks.

Computer Technology in Accounting

Computer technology provides accuracy, speed, efficiency, and convenience in performing accounting tasks. A program can be written, for instance, to process customers' merchandise orders. Multipurpose off-the-shelf software applications exist for a variety of business operations. These include familiar accounting programs such as Peachtree® and QuickBooks®. Off-the-shelf programs are designed to be user friendly and menu driven, and many operate more efficiently as *integrated* systems. In an integrated system, actions taken in one part of the system automatically affect related parts. When a credit sale is recorded in an integrated system, for instance, several parts of the system are automatically updated, such as posting.

Point: Companies that have reported missing or stolen employee data such as Social Security numbers include Time Warner, Polo Ralph Lauren, Lexis/Nexis, ChoicePoint, and DSW Shoes.

Computer technology can dramatically reduce the time and effort devoted to recordkeeping. Less effort spent on recordkeeping means more time for accounting professionals to concentrate on analysis and managerial decision making. These advances have created a greater demand for accounting professionals who understand financial reports and can draw insights and information from mountains of processed data. Accounting professionals have expertise in determining relevant and reliable information for decision making. They also can assess the effects of transactions and events on a company and its financial statements.

Decision Insight

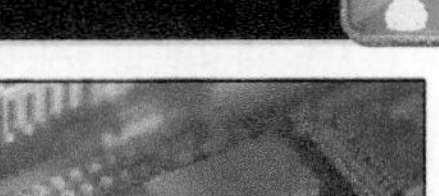

Middleware is software allowing different computer programs in a company or across companies to work together. It allows transfer of purchase orders, invoices, and other electronic documents between accounting systems. For example, suppliers can monitor inventory levels of their buyers for production and shipping purposes. ■

Data Processing in Accounting

Accounting systems differ with regard to how input is entered and processed. **Online processing** enters and processes data as soon as source documents are available. This means that databases are immediately updated. **Batch processing** accumulates source documents for a period of time and then processes them all at once such as daily, weekly, or monthly. The advantage of online processing is timeliness. This often requires additional costs related to both software and hardware requirements. Companies such as **Intuit** (Intuit.com) are making online processing of accounting data a reality for many businesses. The advantage of batch processing is that it requires only periodic updating of databases. Records used to send bills to customers, for instance, might require updating only once a month. The disadvantage of batch processing is the lack of updated databases for management to use when making business decisions.

Computer Networks in Accounting

Networking, or linking computers with each other, can create information advantages (and cost efficiencies). **Computer networks** are links among computers giving different users and different computers access to common databases, programs, and hardware. Many college computer labs, for instance, are networked. A small computer network is called a *local area network (LAN);* it links machines with *hard-wire* hookups. Large computer networks extending over long distances often rely on *modem* or *wireless* communication.

Demand for information sometimes requires advanced networks such as the systems **Federal Express** and **UPS** use to track packages and bill customers and the system **Walmart** uses to monitor inventory levels in its stores. These networks include many computers and satellite communications to gather information and to provide ready access to its databases from all locations.

Enterprise Resource Planning Software

Enterprise resource planning (ERP) software includes the programs that manage a company's vital operations. They extend from order taking to manufacturing to accounting. When working properly, these integrated programs can speed decision making, identify costs for reduction, and give managers control over operations with the click of a mouse. For many managers, ERP software allows them to scrutinize business, identify where inventories are piling up, and see what plants are most efficient. The software is designed to link every part of a company's operations. This software allowed Monsanto to slash production planning from six weeks to three, trim its inventories, and increase its bargaining power with suppliers. Monsanto estimates that this software saves the company $200 million per year.

ERP has several suppliers. SAP leads the market, with Oracle, which gobbled up PeopleSoft and J. D. Edwards, a distant second (*AMR Research*). SAP software is used by more than half of the world's 500 largest companies. It links ordering, inventory, production, purchasing, planning, tracking, and human resources. A transaction or event triggers an immediate chain reaction of events throughout the enterprise. It is making companies more efficient and profitable.

Total ERP Market: About $30 Billion

Other 23%
Infor (SSA) 7%
Microsoft Dynamics 6%
Sage Group 8%
Oracle Applications 21%
SAP 35%

ERP is pushing into cyberspace and customer relationship management (CRM). Now companies can share data with customers and suppliers. Applesauce maker Mott's is using SAP so that distributors can check the status of orders and place them over the Net, and the Coca-Cola Company uses it to ship soda on time. ERP is also increasingly used by small business. For example, NetSuite's accounting services to small and medium businesses are powered by Oracle's system.

Decision Insight

A new generation of accounting support is available. With the touch of a key, users can create real-time inventory reports showing all payments, charges, and credit limits at any point in the accounting cycle. Many services also include "alert signals" notifying the company when, for example, a large order exceeds a customer's credit limit or when purchases need to be made or when a bank balance is running low. These alerts occur via e-mail, fax, PDA, or phone. ■

Quick Check

Answers — p. 297

14. Identify an advantage of an integrated computer-based accounting system.
15. What advantages do computer systems offer over manual systems?
16. Identify an advantage of computer networks.
17. Describe ERP software and its potential advantages to businesses.

GLOBAL VIEW

This section discusses similarities and differences between U.S. GAAP and IFRS regarding system principles and components, and special journals.

System Principles and Components Both U.S. GAAP and IFRS aim for high-quality financial reporting. That aim implies that sound information system principles and components are applied worldwide.

However, while system principles and components are fundamentally similar across the globe, culture and other realities often mean different emphases are placed on the mix of system controls. Nokia provides the following description of its system controls:

> Nokia's disclosure controls and procedures . . . are designed to provide reasonable assurance regarding the quality and integrity of the company's financial statements and related disclosures.

Special Journals Accounting systems for recording sales, purchases, cash receipts, and cash disbursements are similar worldwide. Although the exact structure of special journals is unique to each company, the basic structure is identical. Companies desire to apply accounting in an efficient manner. Accordingly, systems that employ special journals are applied worldwide.

Decision Analysis — Segment Return on Assets

A1 Compute segment return on assets and use it to evaluate segment performance.

Good accounting information systems collect financial data for a company's various segments. A *segment* refers to a part of a company that is separately identified by its products or services, or by the geographic market it serves. Callaway Golf Company reports that it operates in two business segments: (1) golf clubs and (2) golf balls. Users of financial statements are especially interested in segment information to better understand a company's activities because segments often vary on profitability, risk, and growth.

Companies must report segment information, including their sales, operating income, identifiable assets, capital expenditures, and depreciation. However, managers are reluctant to release information that can harm competitive position. Exhibit 7.12 shows survey results on the number of companies with different (reported) segments.

EXHIBIT 7.12

Companies Reporting Operations by Types of Segments*

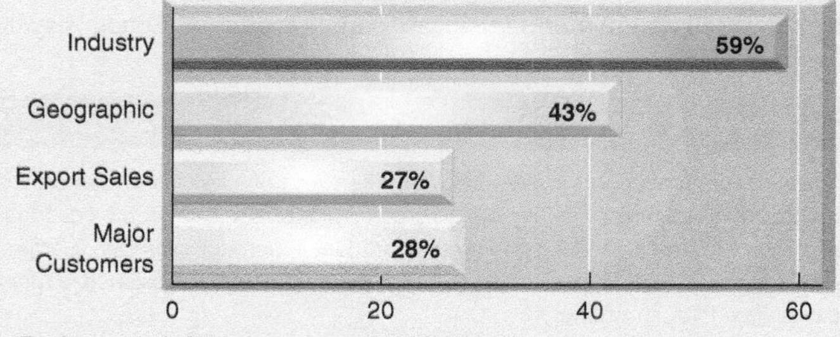

*Total exceeds 100% because companies can report more than one segment.

One measure of success for business segments is the **segment return on assets** ratio defined as follows.

$$\textbf{Segment return on assets} = \frac{\textbf{Segment operating income}}{\textbf{Segment average assets}}$$

EXHIBIT 7.13

Callaway Golf's Segment Return on Assets

This ratio reflects on the profitability of a segment. Exhibit 7.13 shows the segments' operating income, average assets, and return on assets for Callaway Golf Company.

Golf Segment* ($ thousands)	2009 Clubs	2009 Balls	2008 Clubs	2008 Balls	2007 Clubs	2007 Balls	2006 Clubs	2006 Balls
Operating income	$ 38,934	$(13,864)	$134,018	$ 6,903	$151,759	$ 902	$101,837	$ (6,396)
Average assets	$406,835	$129,796	$429,170	$146,855	$413,352	$140,730	$419,212	$152,282
Segment return on assets	10%	n.a.	31%	5%	37%	1%	24%	n.a.

* A segment's operating income is usually measured as pretax income, and assets is usually measured as identifiable assets.

The trend in Callaway's segment return on assets is up-and-down for its golf club segment, and similarly mixed for its golf balls segment. Importantly, its golf clubs segment makes up a much greater portion of its operations; for example, 2008 income of $134,018 from golf clubs make up 95% of its total income of $140,921 from both segments. Callaway should continue investments in its golf club segment vis-a-vis its golf balls segment given the greater returns and larger total income from that segment. Analysis can also be extended to geographical segments and any other segments that companies report.

Decision Maker Answer — p. 297

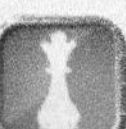

Banker A bicycle merchandiser requests a loan from you to expand operations. Its net income is $220,000, reflecting a 10% increase over the prior year. You ask about segment results. The owner reports that $160,000 of net income is from Cuban operations, reflecting a 60% increase over the prior year. The remaining $60,000 of net income is from U.S. operations, reflecting a 40% decrease. Does this segment information impact your loan decision? ■

DEMONSTRATION PROBLEM—PERPETUAL SYSTEM

Pepper Company completed the following selected transactions and events during March of this year. (Terms of all credit sales for the company are 2/10, n/30.)

Mar. 4 Sold merchandise on credit to Jennifer Nelson, Invoice No. 954, for $16,800 (cost is $12,200).
6 Purchased $1,220 of office supplies on credit from Mack Company. Invoice dated March 3, terms n/30.
6 Sold merchandise on credit to Dennie Hoskins, Invoice No. 955, for $10,200 (cost is $8,100).
11 Purchased $52,600 of merchandise, invoice dated March 6, terms 2/10, n/30, from Defore Industries.
12 Borrowed $26,000 cash by giving Commerce Bank a long-term promissory note payable.
14 Received cash payment from Jennifer Nelson for the March 4 sale less the discount (Invoice No. 954).
16 Received a $200 credit memorandum from Defore Industries for unsatisfactory merchandise Pepper purchased on March 11 and later returned.
16 Received cash payment from Dennie Hoskins for the March 6 sale less the discount (Invoice No. 955).
18 Purchased $22,850 of store equipment on credit from Schmidt Supply, invoice dated March 15, terms n/30.
20 Sold merchandise on credit to Marjorie Allen, Invoice No. 956, for $5,600 (cost is $3,800).
21 Sent Defore Industries Check No. 516 in payment of its March 6 dated invoice less the return and the discount.
22 Purchased $41,625 of merchandise, invoice dated March 18, terms 2/10, n/30, from Welch Company.
26 Issued a $600 credit memorandum to Marjorie Allen for defective merchandise Pepper sold on March 20 and Allen later returned.
31 Issued Check No. 517, payable to Payroll, in payment of $15,900 sales salaries for the month. Cashed the check and paid the employees.
31 Cash sales for the month are $134,680 (cost is $67,340). (Cash sales are recorded daily but are recorded only once here to reduce repetitive entries.)

Required

1. Open the following selected general ledger accounts: Cash (101), Accounts Receivable (106) Inventory (119), Office Supplies (124), Store Equipment (165), Accounts Payable (201), Long-Term Notes Payable (251), Sales (413), Sales Returns and Allowances (414), Sales Discounts (415), Cost of Goods Sold (502), and Sales Salaries Expense (621). Open the following accounts receivable ledger accounts: Marjorie Allen, Dennie Hoskins, and Jennifer Nelson. Open the following accounts payable ledger accounts: Defore Industries, Mack Company, Schmidt Supply, and Welch Company.
2. Enter the transactions using a sales journal, a purchases journal, a cash receipts journal, a cash disbursements journal, and a general journal similar to the ones illustrated in the chapter. Regularly post to the individual customer and creditor accounts. Also, post any amounts that should be posted as individual amounts to general ledger accounts. Foot and crossfoot the journals and make the month-end postings. *Pepper Co. uses the perpetual inventory system.*

3. Prepare a trial balance for the selected general ledger accounts in part 1 and prove the accuracy of subsidiary ledgers by preparing schedules of accounts receivable and accounts payable.

PLANNING THE SOLUTION

- Set up the required general ledger, the subsidiary ledger accounts, and the five required journals as illustrated in the chapter.
- Read and analyze each transaction and decide in which special journal (or general journal) the transaction is recorded.
- Record each transaction in the proper journal (and post the appropriate individual amounts).
- Once you have recorded all transactions, total the journal columns. Post from each journal to the appropriate ledger accounts.
- Prepare a trial balance to prove the equality of the debit and credit balances in your general ledger.
- Prepare schedules of accounts receivable and accounts payable. Compare the totals of these schedules to the Accounts Receivable and Accounts Payable controlling account balances, making sure that they agree.

SOLUTION TO DEMONSTRATION PROBLEM—PERPETUAL SYSTEM

Sales Journal — Page 2

Date	Account Debited	Invoice Number	PR	Accounts Receivable Dr. Sales Cr.	Cost of Goods Sold Dr. Inventory Cr.
Mar. 4	Jennifer Nelson	954	✓	16,800	12,200
6	Dennie Hoskins	955	✓	10,200	8,100
20	Marjorie Allen	956	✓	5,600	3,800
31	Totals			32,600	24,100
				(106/413)	(502/119)

Cash Receipts Journal — Page 3

Date	Account Credited	Explanation	PR	Cash Dr.	Sales Discount Dr.	Accounts Receivable Cr.	Sales Cr.	Other Accounts Cr.	Cost of Goods Sold Dr. Inventory Cr.
Mar. 12	L.T. Notes Payable	Note to bank	251	26,000				26,000	
14	Jennifer Nelson	Invoice 954, 3/4	✓	16,464	336	16,800			
16	Dennie Hoskins	Invoice 955, 3/6	✓	9,996	204	10,200			
31	Sales	Cash sales	x	134,680			134,680		67,340
31	Totals			187,140	540	27,000	134,680	26,000	67,340
				(101)	(415)	(106)	(413)	(x)	(502/119)

Purchases Journal — Page 3

Date	Account	Date of Invoice	Terms	PR	Accounts Payable Cr.	Inventory Dr.	Office Supplies Dr.	Other Accounts Dr.
Mar. 6	Office Supplies/Mack Co	3/3	n/30	✓	1,220		1,220	
11	Defore Industries	3/6	2/10, n/30	✓	52,600	52,600		
18	Store Equipment/Schmidt Supp	3/15	n/30	165/✓	22,850			22,850
22	Welch Company	3/18	2/10, n/30	✓	41,625	41,625		
31	Totals				118,295	94,225	1,220	22,850
					(201)	(119)	(124)	(x)

Cash Disbursements Journal — Page 3

Date	Ck. No.	Payee	Account Debited	PR	Cash Cr.	Inventory Cr.	Other Accounts Dr.	Accounts Payable Dr.
Mar. 21	516	Defore Industries	Defore Industries	✓	51,352	1,048		52,400
31	517	Payroll	Sales Salaries Expense	621	15,900		15,900	
31		Totals			67,252	1,048	15,900	52,400
					(101)	(119)	(x)	(201)

General Journal — Page 2

Date	Account	PR	Dr.	Cr.
Mar. 16	Accounts Payable—Defore Industries	201/✓	200	
	Inventory	119		200
	To record credit memorandum received.			
26	Sales Returns and Allowances	414	600	
	Accounts Receivable—Marjorie Allen	106/✓		600
	To record credit memorandum issued.			

Accounts Receivable Ledger

Marjorie Allen

Date	PR	Debit	Credit	Balance
Mar. 20	S2	5,600		5,600
26	G2		600	5,000

Dennie Hoskins

Date	PR	Debit	Credit	Balance
Mar. 6	S2	10,200		10,200
16	R3		10,200	0

Jennifer Nelson

Date	PR	Debit	Credit	Balance
Mar. 4	S2	16,800		16,800
14	R3		16,800	0

Accounts Payable Ledger

Defore Industries

Date	PR	Debit	Credit	Balance
Mar. 11	P3		52,600	52,600
16	G2	200		52,400
21	D3	52,400		0

Mack Company

Date	PR	Debit	Credit	Balance
Mar. 6	P3		1,220	1,220

Schmidt Supply

Date	PR	Debit	Credit	Balance
Mar. 18	P3		22,850	22,850

Welch Company

Date	PR	Debit	Credit	Balance
Mar. 22	P3		41,625	41,625

General Ledger (Partial Listing)

Cash Acct. No. 101

Date	PR	Debit	Credit	Balance
Mar. 31	R3	187,140		187,140
31	D3		67,252	119,888

Accounts Receivable Acct. No. 106

Date	PR	Debit	Credit	Balance
Mar. 26	G2		600	(600)
31	S2	32,600		32,000
31	R3		27,000	5,000

Inventory Acct. No. 119

Date	PR	Debit	Credit	Balance
Mar. 16	G2		200	(200)
21	D3		1,048	(1,248)
31	P3	94,225		92,977
31	S2		24,100	68,877
31	R3		67,340	1,537

Office Supplies Acct. No. 124

Date	PR	Debit	Credit	Balance
Mar. 31	P3	1,220		1,220

Store Equipment Acct. No. 165

Date	PR	Debit	Credit	Balance
Mar. 18	P3	22,850		22,850

Accounts Payable Acct. No. 201

Date	PR	Debit	Credit	Balance
Mar. 16	G2	200		(200)
31	P3		118,295	118,095
31	D3	52,400		65,695

Long-Term Notes Payable Acct. No. 251

Date	PR	Debit	Credit	Balance
Mar. 12	R3		26,000	26,000

Sales Acct. No. 413

Date	PR	Debit	Credit	Balance
Mar. 31	S2		32,600	32,600
31	R3		134,680	167,280

Sales Returns and Allowances Acct. No. 414

Date	PR	Debit	Credit	Balance
Mar. 26	G2	600		600

Sales Discounts Acct. No. 415

Date	PR	Debit	Credit	Balance
Mar. 31	R3	540		540

Cost of Goods Sold Acct. No. 502

Date	PR	Debit	Credit	Balance
Mar. 31	R3	67,340		67,340
31	S2	24,100		91,440

Sales Salaries Expense Acct. No. 621

Date	PR	Debit	Credit	Balance
Mar. 31	D3	15,900		15,900

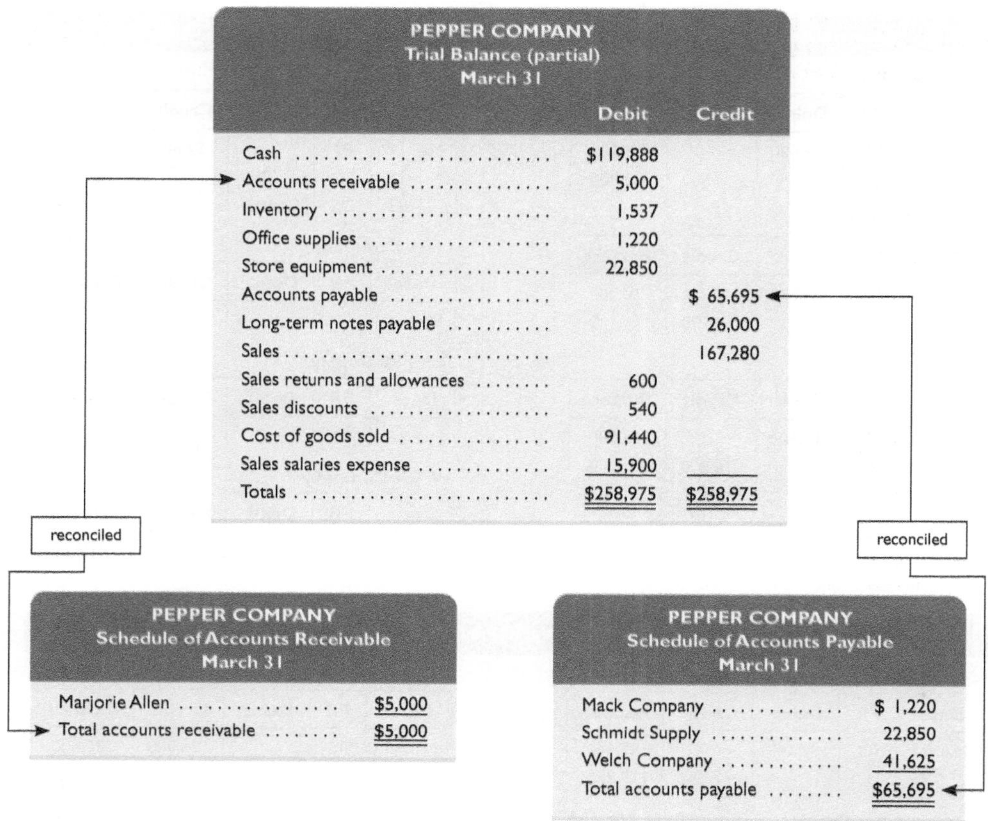

PEPPER COMPANY
Trial Balance (partial)
March 31

	Debit	Credit
Cash	$119,888	
Accounts receivable	5,000	
Inventory	1,537	
Office supplies	1,220	
Store equipment	22,850	
Accounts payable		$ 65,695
Long-term notes payable		26,000
Sales		167,280
Sales returns and allowances	600	
Sales discounts	540	
Cost of goods sold	91,440	
Sales salaries expense	15,900	
Totals	$258,975	$258,975

PEPPER COMPANY
Schedule of Accounts Receivable
March 31

Marjorie Allen	$5,000
Total accounts receivable	$5,000

PEPPER COMPANY
Schedule of Accounts Payable
March 31

Mack Company	$ 1,220
Schmidt Supply	22,850
Welch Company	41,625
Total accounts payable	$65,695

APPENDIX

7A Special Journals under a Periodic System

P3 Journalize and post transactions using special journals in a periodic inventory system.

This appendix describes special journals under a periodic inventory system. Each journal is slightly impacted. The sales journal and the cash receipts journal both require one less column (namely that of Cost of Goods Sold Dr., Inventory Cr.). The Purchases Journal replaces the Inventory Dr. column with a Purchases Dr. column in a periodic system. The cash disbursements journal replaces the Inventory Cr. column with a Purchases Discounts Cr. column in a periodic system. These changes are illustrated.

Sales Journal The sales journal using the periodic inventory system is shown in Exhibit 7A.1. The difference in the sales journal between the perpetual and periodic system is the exclusion of the column to record cost of goods sold and inventory amounts for each sale. The periodic system does *not* record the increase in cost of goods sold and the decrease in inventory at the time of each sale.

EXHIBIT 7A.1

Sales Journal—Periodic System

Sales Journal — Page 3

Date	Account Debited	Invoice Number	PR	Accounts Receivable Dr. Sales Cr.
Feb. 2	Jason Henry	307	✓	450
7	Albert Co.	308	✓	500
13	Kam Moore	309	✓	350
15	Paul Roth	310	✓	200
22	Jason Henry	311	✓	225
25	Frank Booth	312	✓	175
28	Albert Co.	313	✓	250
28	Total			2,150
				(106/413)

Cash Receipts Journal The cash receipts journal using the periodic system is shown in Exhibit 7A.2. Note the absence of the column on the far right side to record debits to Cost of Goods Sold and credits to Inventory for the cost of merchandise sold (seen under the perpetual system). Consistent with the cash receipts journal shown in Exhibit 7.7, we show only the weekly (summary) cash sale entries.

EXHIBIT 7A.2

Cash Receipts Journal—Periodic System

Cash Receipts Journal — Page 2

Date	Account Credited	Explanation	PR	Cash Dr.	Sales Discount Dr.	Accounts Receivable Cr.	Sales Cr.	Other Accounts Cr.
Feb. 7	Sales	Cash sales	x	4,450			4,450	
12	Jason Henry	Invoice 307, 2/2	✓	441	9	450		
14	Sales	Cash sales	x	3,925			3,925	
17	Albert Co.	Invoice 308, 2/7	✓	490	10	500		
20	Notes Payable	Note to bank	245	750				750
21	Sales	Cash sales	x	4,700			4,700	
22	Interest revenue	Bank account	409	250				250
23	Kam Moore	Invoice 309, 2/13	✓	343	7	350		
25	Paul Roth	Invoice 310, 2/15	✓	196	4	200		
28	Sales	Cash sales	x	4,225			4,225	
28	Totals			19,770	30	1,500	17,300	1,000
				(101)	(415)	(106)	(413)	(x)

Purchases Journal The purchases journal using the periodic system is shown in Exhibit 7A.3. This journal under a perpetual system included an Inventory column where the periodic system now has a Purchases column.

EXHIBIT 7A.3

Purchases Journal—Periodic System

Purchases Journal — Page 1

Date	Account	Date of Invoice	Terms	PR	Accounts Payable Cr.	Purchases Dr.	Office Supplies Dr.	Other Accounts Dr.
Feb. 3	Horning Supply Co.	2/2	n/30	✓	350	275	75	
5	Ace Mfg. Co.	2/5	2/10, n/30	✓	200	200		
13	Wynet and Co.	2/10	2/10, n/30	✓	150	150		
20	Smite Co.	2/18	2/10, n/30	✓	300	300		
25	Ace Mfg. Co.	2/24	2/10, n/30	✓	100	100		
28	Store Supplies/ITT Co.	2/28	n/30	125/✓	225	125	25	75
28	Totals				1,325	1,150	100	75
					(201)	(505)	(124)	(x)

Cash Disbursements Journal The cash disbursements journal using a periodic system is shown in Exhibit 7A.4. This journal under the perpetual system included an Inventory column where the periodic system now has the Purchases Discounts column.

EXHIBIT 7A.4

Cash Disbursements Journal—Periodic System

Cash Disbursements Journal — Page 2

Date	Ck. No.	Payee	Account Debited	PR	Cash Cr.	Purchases Discounts Cr.	Other Accounts Dr.	Accounts Payable Dr.
Feb. 3	105	L. and N. Railroad	Purchases	505	15		15	
12	106	East Sales Co.	Purchases	505	25		25	
15	107	Ace Mfg. Co.	Ace Mfg. Co.	✓	196	4		200
15	108	Jerry Hale	Salaries Expense	622	250		250	
20	109	Wynet and Co.	Wynet and Co.	✓	147	3		150
28	110	Smite Co.	Smite Co.	✓	294	6		300
28		Totals			927	13	290	650
					(101)	(507)	(x)	(201)

DEMONSTRATION PROBLEM—PERIODIC SYSTEM

Refer to Pepper Company's selected transactions described under the Demonstration Problem—Perpetual System to fulfill the following requirements.

Required

1. Open the following selected general ledger accounts: Cash (101), Accounts Receivable (106), Office Supplies (124), Store Equipment (165), Accounts Payable (201), Long-Term Notes Payable (251), Sales (413), Sales Returns and Allowances (414), Sales Discounts (415), Purchases (505), Purchases

Returns and Allowances (506), Purchases Discounts (507), and Sales Salaries Expense (621). Open the following accounts receivable ledger accounts: Marjorie Allen, Dennie Hoskins, and Jennifer Nelson. Open the following accounts payable ledger accounts: Defore Industries, Mack Company, Schmidt Supply, and Welch Company.

2. Enter the transactions using a sales journal, a purchases journal, a cash receipts journal, a cash disbursements journal, and a general journal similar to the ones illustrated in Appendix 7A. Regularly post to the individual customer and creditor accounts. Also, post any amounts that should be posted as individual amounts to general ledger accounts. Foot and crossfoot the journals and make the month-end postings. *Pepper Co. uses the periodic inventory system in this problem.*
3. Prepare a trial balance for the selected general ledger accounts in part 1 and prove the accuracy of subsidiary ledgers by preparing schedules of accounts receivable and accounts payable.

SOLUTION TO DEMONSTRATION PROBLEM—PERIODIC SYSTEM

Sales Journal Page 2

Date	Account Debited	Invoice Number	PR	Accounts Receivable Dr. Sales Cr.
Mar. 4	Jennifer Nelson	954	✓	16,800
6	Dennie Hoskins	955	✓	10,200
20	Marjorie Allen	956	✓	5,600
31	Totals			32,600
				(106/413)

Cash Receipts Journal Page 3

Date	Account Credited	Explanation	PR	Cash Dr.	Sales Discount Dr.	Accounts Receivable Cr.	Sales Cr.	Other Accounts Cr.
Mar. 12	L.T. Notes Payable	Note to bank	251	26,000				26,000
14	Jennifer Nelson	Invoice 954, 3/4	✓	16,464	336	16,800		
16	Dennie Hoskins	Invoice 955, 3/6	✓	9,996	204	10,200		
31	Sales	Cash sales	x	134,680			134,680	
31	Totals			187,140	540	27,000	134,680	26,000
				(101)	(415)	(106)	(413)	(x)

Purchases Journal Page 3

Date	Account	Date of Invoice	Terms	PR	Accounts Payable Cr.	Purchases Dr.	Office Supplies Dr.	Other Accounts Dr.
Mar. 6	Office Supplies/Mack Co	3/3	n/30	✓	1,220		1,220	
11	Defore Industries	3/6	2/10, n/30	✓	52,600	52,600		
18	Store Equipment/Schmidt Supp	3/15	n/30	165/✓	22,850			22,850
22	Welch Company	3/18	2/10, n/30	✓	41,625	41,625		
31	Totals				118,295	94,225	1,220	22,850
					(201)	(505)	(124)	(x)

Cash Disbursements Journal Page 3

Date	Ck. No.	Payee	Account Debited	PR	Cash Cr.	Purchases Discount Cr.	Other Accounts Dr.	Accounts Payable Dr.
Mar. 21	516	Defore Industries	Defore Industries	✓	51,352	1,048		52,400
31	517	Payroll	Sales Salaries Expense	621	15,900		15,900	
31		Totals			67,252	1,048	15,900	52,400
					(101)	(507)	(x)	(201)

General Journal Page 2

Date	Account	PR	Dr.	Cr.
Mar. 16	Accounts Payable—Defore Industries	201/✓	200	
	Purchases Returns and Allowances	506		200
	To record credit memorandum received.			
26	Sales Returns and Allowances	414	600	
	Accounts Receivable—Marjorie Allen	106/✓		600
	To record credit memorandum issued.			

Accounts Receivable Ledger

Marjorie Allen

Date	PR	Debit	Credit	Balance
Mar. 20	S2	5,600		5,600
26	G2		600	5,000

Dennie Hoskins

Date	PR	Debit	Credit	Balance
Mar. 6	S2	10,200		10,200
16	R3		10,200	0

Jennifer Nelson

Date	PR	Debit	Credit	Balance
Mar. 4	S2	16,800		16,800
14	R3		16,800	0

Accounts Payable Ledger

Defore Industries

Date	PR	Debit	Credit	Balance
Mar. 11	P3		52,600	52,600
16	G2	200		52,400
21	D3	52,400		0

Mack Company

Date	PR	Debit	Credit	Balance
Mar. 6	P3		1,220	1,220

Schmidt Supply

Date	PR	Debit	Credit	Balance
Mar. 18	P3		22,850	22,850

Welch Company

Date	PR	Debit	Credit	Balance
Mar. 22	P3		41,625	41,625

General Ledger (Partial Listing)

Cash Acct. No. 101

Date	PR	Debit	Credit	Balance
Mar. 31	R3	187,140		187,140
31	D3		67,252	119,888

Accounts Receivable Acct. No. 106

Date	PR	Debit	Credit	Balance
Mar. 26	G2		600	(600)
31	S2	32,600		32,000
31	R3		27,000	5,000

Office Supplies Acct. No. 124

Date	PR	Debit	Credit	Balance
Mar. 31	P3	1,220		1,220

Store Equipment Acct. No. 165

Date	PR	Debit	Credit	Balance
Mar. 18	P3	22,850		22,850

Accounts Payable Acct. No. 201

Date	PR	Debit	Credit	Balance
Mar. 16	G2	200		(200)
31	P3		118,295	118,095
31	D3	52,400		65,695

Long-Term Notes Payable Acct. No. 251

Date	PR	Debit	Credit	Balance
Mar. 12	R3		26,000	26,000

Sales Acct. No. 413

Date	PR	Debit	Credit	Balance
Mar. 31	S2		32,600	32,600
31	R3		134,680	167,280

Sales Returns and Allowances Acct. No. 414

Date	PR	Debit	Credit	Balance
Mar. 26	G2	600		600

Sales Discounts Acct. No. 415

Date	PR	Debit	Credit	Balance
Mar. 31	R3	540		540

Purchases Acct. No. 505

Date	PR	Debit	Credit	Balance
Mar. 31	P3	94,225		94,225

Purchases Returns and Allowances Acct. No. 506

Date	PR	Debit	Credit	Balance
Mar. 16	G2		200	200

Purchases Discounts Acct. No. 507

Date	PR	Debit	Credit	Balance
Mar. 31	D3		1,048	1,048

Sales Salaries Expense Acct. No. 621

Date	PR	Debit	Credit	Balance
Mar. 31	D3	15,900		15,900

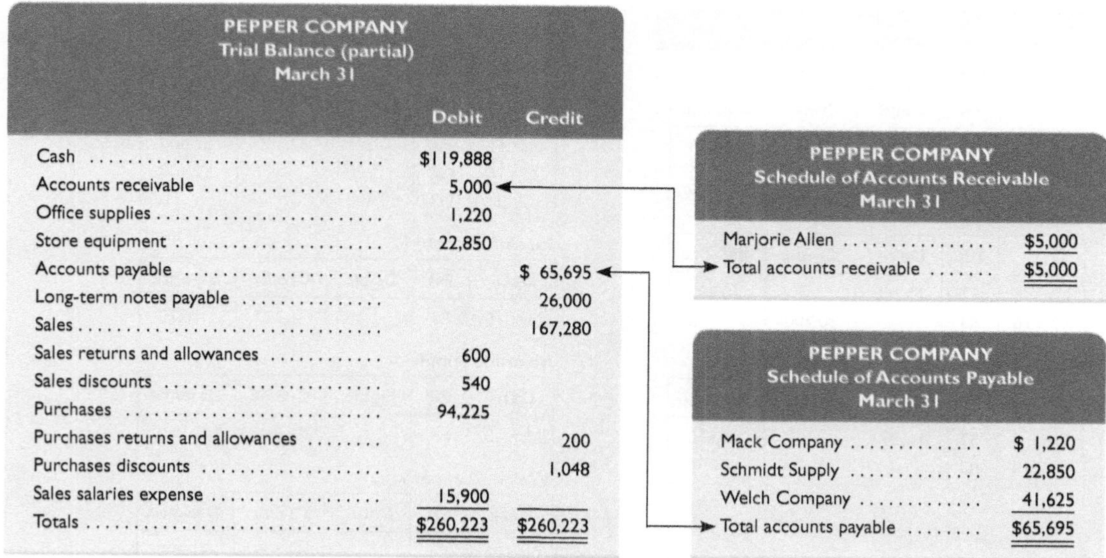

PEPPER COMPANY
Trial Balance (partial)
March 31

	Debit	Credit
Cash	$119,888	
Accounts receivable	5,000	
Office supplies	1,220	
Store equipment	22,850	
Accounts payable		$ 65,695
Long-term notes payable		26,000
Sales		167,280
Sales returns and allowances	600	
Sales discounts	540	
Purchases	94,225	
Purchases returns and allowances		200
Purchases discounts		1,048
Sales salaries expense	15,900	
Totals	$260,223	$260,223

PEPPER COMPANY
Schedule of Accounts Receivable
March 31

Marjorie Allen	$5,000
Total accounts receivable	$5,000

PEPPER COMPANY
Schedule of Accounts Payable
March 31

Mack Company	$ 1,220
Schmidt Supply	22,850
Welch Company	41,625
Total accounts payable	$65,695

Summary

C1 Identify the principles and components of accounting information systems. Accounting information systems are governed by five fundamental principles: control, relevance, compatibility, flexibility, and cost-benefit. The five basic components of an accounting information system are source documents, input devices, information processors, information storage, and output devices.

C2 Explain the goals and uses of special journals. Special journals are used for recording transactions of similar type, each meant to cover one kind of transaction. Four of the most common special journals are the sales journal, cash receipts journal, purchases journal, and cash disbursements journal. Special journals are efficient and cost-effective tools in the journalizing and posting processes.

C3 Describe the use of controlling accounts and subsidiary ledgers. A general ledger keeps controlling accounts such as Accounts Receivable and Accounts Payable, but details on individual accounts making up the controlling account are kept in subsidiary ledgers (such as an accounts receivable ledger). The balance in a controlling account must equal the sum of its subsidiary account balances after posting is complete.

A1 Compute segment return on assets and use it to evaluate segment performance. A business segment is a part of a company that is separately identified by its products or services or by the geographic market it serves. Analysis of a company's segments is aided by the segment return on assets (segment operating income divided by segment average assets).

P1 Journalize and post transactions using special journals. Each special journal is devoted to similar kinds of transactions. Transactions are journalized on one line of a special journal, with columns devoted to specific accounts, dates, names, posting references, explanations, and other necessary information. Posting is threefold: (1) individual amounts in the Other Accounts column are posted to their general ledger accounts on a regular (daily) basis, (2) individual amounts in a column whose total is *not* posted to a controlling account at the end of a period (month) are posted regularly (daily) to their general ledger accounts, and (3) total amounts for all columns except the Other Accounts column are posted at the end of a period (month) to their column's account title in the general ledger.

P2 Prepare and prove the accuracy of subsidiary ledgers. Account balances in the general ledger and its subsidiary ledgers are tested for accuracy after posting is complete. This procedure is twofold: (1) prepare a trial balance of the general ledger to confirm that debits equal credits and (2) prepare a schedule to confirm that the controlling account's balance equals the subsidiary ledger's balance.

P3A Journalize and post transactions using special journals in a periodic inventory system. Transactions are journalized and posted using special journals in a periodic system. The methods are similar to those in a perpetual system; the primary difference is that both cost of goods sold and inventory are not adjusted at the time of each sale. This usually results in the deletion (or renaming) of one or more columns devoted to these accounts in each special journal.

Guidance Answers to Decision Maker and Decision Ethics

Accountant The main issue is whether commissions have an actual or perceived impact on the integrity and objectivity of your advice. You probably should not accept a commission arrangement (the AICPA Code of Ethics prohibits it when you perform the audit or a review). In any event, you should tell the client of your commission arrangement. Also, you need to seriously examine the merits of agreeing to a commission arrangement when you are in a position to exploit it.

Entrepreneur The accounts receivable ledger has much of the information you need. It lists detailed information for each customer's account, including the amounts, dates for transactions, and dates of payments. It can be reorganized into an "aging schedule" to show how long customers wait before paying their bills.

Controller Much of the information you need is in the accounts payable ledger. It contains information for each supplier, the amounts due, and when payments are made. This subsidiary ledger along with information on credit terms should enable you to conduct your analyses.

Banker This merchandiser's segment information is likely to greatly impact your loan decision. The risks associated with the company's two sources of net income are quite different. While net income is up by 10%, U.S. operations are performing poorly and Cuban operations are subject to many uncertainties. These uncertainties depend on political events, legal issues, business relationships, Cuban economic conditions, and a host of other risks. Overall, net income results suggested a low-risk loan opportunity, but the segment information reveals a high-risk situation.

Guidance Answers to Quick Checks

1. The five components are source documents, input devices, information processors, information storage, and output devices.
2. Information processors interpret, transform, and summarize the recorded accounting information so that it can be used in analysis, interpretation, and decision making.
3. Data saved in information storage are used to prepare periodic financial reports and special-purpose internal reports as well as source documentation for auditors.
4. All cash payments by check are recorded in the cash disbursements journal.
5. Columnar journals allow us to accumulate repetitive debits and credits and post them as column totals rather than as individual amounts from each entry.
6. The equality of debits and credits is kept within the general ledger. The subsidiary ledger keeps the customer's individual account and is used only for supplementary information.
7. An initial and the page number of the journal from which the amount was posted are entered in the PR column next to the amount.
8. A separate column for Sales Taxes Payable can be included in both the cash receipts journal and the sales journal.
9. This refers to a procedure of using copies of sales invoices as a sales journal. Each invoice amount is posted directly to the customer's account. All invoices are totaled at period-end for posting to the general ledger accounts.
10. The normal recording and posting procedures are threefold. First, transactions are entered in a special journal if applicable. Second, individual amounts are posted to any subsidiary ledger accounts. Third, column totals are posted to general ledger accounts if not already individually posted.
11. Controlling accounts are debited periodically for an amount or amounts equal to the sum of their respective debits in the subsidiary ledgers (equals journal column totals), and they are credited periodically for an amount or amounts equal to the sum of their respective credits in the subsidiary ledgers (from journal column totals).
12. Tests for accuracy of account balances in the general ledger and subsidiary ledgers are twofold. First, we prepare a trial balance of the general ledger to confirm that debits equal credits. Second, we prove the subsidiary ledgers by preparing schedules of accounts receivable and accounts payable.
13. The general journal is still needed for adjusting, closing, and correcting entries and for special transactions such as sales returns, purchases returns, and certain asset purchases.
14. Integrated systems can save time and minimize errors. This is so because actions taken in one part of the system automatically affect and update related parts.
15. Computer systems offer increased accuracy, speed, efficiency, and convenience.
16. Computer networks can create advantages by linking computers, and giving different users and different computers access to common databases, programs, and hardware.
17. ERP software involves integrated programs, from order taking to manufacturing to accounting. It can speed decision making, help identify costs for reduction, and aid managers in controlling operations.

Key Terms

mhhe.com/wildFAP20e

Accounting information systems (p. 272)
Accounts payable ledger (p. 277)
Accounts receivable ledger (p. 277)
Batch processing (p. 286)
Cash disbursements journal (p. 284)
Cash receipts journal (p. 281)
Check register (p. 284)
Columnar journal (p. 278)
Compatibility principle (p. 273)
Components of accounting systems (p. 273)
Computer network (p. 286)
Control principle (p. 272)
Controlling account (p. 277)
Cost-benefit principle (p. 273)
Enterprise resource planning (ERP) software (p. 287)
Flexibility principle (p. 273)
General journal (p. 276)
Information processor (p. 274)
Information storage (p. 274)
Input device (p. 274)
Internal controls (p. 272)
Online processing (p. 286)
Output devices (p. 275)
Purchases journal (p. 283)
Relevance principle (p. 272)

Sales journal (p. 278)
Schedule of accounts payable (p. 284)
Schedule of accounts receivable (p. 279)
Segment return on assets (p. 288)
Special journal (p. 276)
Subsidiary ledger (p. 276)

Multiple Choice Quiz

Answers on p. 313 mhhe.com/wildFAP20e

Additional Quiz Questions are available at the book's Website.

1. The sales journal is used to record
   a. Credit sales
   b. Cash sales
   c. Cash receipts
   d. Cash purchases
   e. Credit purchases
2. The purchases journal is used to record
   a. Credit sales
   b. Cash sales
   c. Cash receipts
   d. Cash purchases
   e. Credit purchases
3. The ledger that contains the financial statement accounts of a company is the
   a. General journal
   b. Column balance journal
   c. Special ledger
   d. General ledger
   e. Special journal
4. A subsidiary ledger that contains a separate account for each supplier (creditor) to the company is the
   a. Controlling account
   b. Accounts payable ledger
   c. Accounts receivable ledger
   d. General ledger
   e. Special journal
5. Enterprise resource planning software
   a. Refers to programs that help manage company operations.
   b. Is another name for spreadsheet programs.
   c. Uses batch processing of business information.
   d. Is substantially declining in use.
   e. Is another name for database programs.

[A] *Superscript letter A denotes assignments based on Appendix 7A.*
Icon denotes assignments that involve decision making.

Discussion Questions

1. What are the five fundamental principles of accounting information systems?
2. What are five basic components of an accounting system?
3. What are source documents? Give two examples.
4. What is the purpose of an input device? Give examples of input devices for computer systems.
5. What is the difference between data that are stored off-line and data that are stored online?
6. What purpose is served by the output devices of an accounting system?
7. When special journals are used, they are usually used to record each of four different types of transactions. What are these four types of transactions?
8. What notations are entered into the Posting Reference column of a ledger account?
9. When a general journal entry is used to record sales returns, the credit of the entry must be posted twice. Does this cause the trial balance to be out of balance? Explain.
10. Describe the procedures involving the use of copies of a company's sales invoices as a sales journal.
11. Credits to customer accounts and credits to Other Accounts are individually posted from a cash receipts journal such as the one in Exhibit 7.7. Why not put both types of credits in the same column and save journal space?
12. Why should sales to and receipts of cash from credit customers be recorded and posted immediately?
13. Locate the note that discusses Research In Motion's operations by segments in Appendix A. In what segment does it predominantly operate? RIM
14. Does the income statement of Palm in Appendix A indicate the net income earned by its business segments? If so, list them. Palm
15. Locate the note that discusses Apple's segments from its 2009 annual report on its Website. What five reportable segments does Apple have? Apple
16. Does the balance sheet of Nokia in Appendix A indicate the identifiable assets owned by its business segments? If so, list them. NOKIA

connect

For account titles and numbers, use the Chart of Accounts at the end of the book.

QUICK STUDY

QS 7-1
Accounting information system components
C1

Identify the most likely role in an accounting system played by each of the numbered items 1 through 12 by assigning a letter from the list A through E on the left.

A. Source documents
B. Input devices
C. Information processors
D. Information storage
E. Output devices

_____ **1.** Bar code reader
_____ **2.** Filing cabinet
_____ **3.** Bank statement
_____ **4.** Computer scanner
_____ **5.** Computer keyboard
_____ **6.** Zip drive
_____ **7.** Computer monitor
_____ **8.** Invoice from a supplier
_____ **9.** Computer software
_____ **10.** Computer printer
_____ **11.** Digital camera
_____ **12.** MP3 player

QS 7-2
Accounting information system principles
C1

Enter the letter of each system principle in the blank next to its best description.

A. Control principle
B. Relevance principle
C. Compatibility principle
D. Flexibility principle
E. Cost-benefit principle

1. _____ The principle prescribes the accounting information system to change in response to technological advances and competitive pressures.
2. _____ The principle prescribes the accounting information system to help monitor activities.
3. _____ The principle prescribes the accounting information system to provide timely information for effective decision making.
4. _____ The principle prescribes the accounting information system to adapt to the unique characteristics of the company.
5. _____ The principle that affects all other accounting information system principles.

QS 7-3
Accounting information system
C1

Fill in the blanks to complete the following descriptions.

1. _____ _____ _____ software comprises programs that help manage a company's vital operations, from manufacturing to accounting.
2. A computer _____ allows different computer users to share access to data and programs.
3. A _____ is an input device that captures writing and other input directly from source documents.
4. With _____ processing, source documents are accumulated for a period and then processed all at the same time, such as once a day, week, or month.

QS 7-4
Identifying the special journal of entry
C2

General Electronics uses a sales journal, a purchases journal, a cash receipts journal, a cash disbursements journal, and a general journal as illustrated in this chapter. General recently completed the following transactions *a* through *h*. Identify the journal in which each transaction should be recorded.

a. Paid cash to a creditor.
b. Sold merchandise on credit.
c. Purchased shop supplies on credit.
d. Paid an employee's salary in cash.
e. Borrowed cash from the bank.
f. Sold merchandise for cash.
g. Purchased merchandise on credit.
h. Purchased inventory for cash.

QS 7-5
Entries in the general journal
C2

Lue Gifts uses a sales journal, a purchases journal, a cash receipts journal, a cash disbursements journal, and a general journal as illustrated in this chapter. Journalize its March transactions that should be recorded in the general journal. For those not recorded in the general journal, identify the special journal where each should be recorded.

Mar. 2 The company purchased $2,900 of merchandise on credit from the Elko Co., terms 2/10, n/30.
12 The owner, T. Lue, contributed an automobile worth $15,000 to the company.
16 The company sold $1,100 of merchandise (cost is $700) on credit to K. Gould, terms n/30.
19 K. Gould returned $150 of (worthless) merchandise to the company originally purchased on March 16 (assume the cost of this merchandise is left in cost of goods sold).

QS 7-6
Controlling accounts and subsidiary ledgers
C3

Following is information from Thompson Company for its initial month of business. (1) Identify the balances listed in the accounts receivable subsidiary ledger. (2) Identify the accounts receivable balance listed in the general ledger at month's end.

Credit Sales			Cash Collections		
Jan. 10	Boerman Company	$3,000	Jan. 20	Boerman Company	$2,000
19	Lehman Brothers	1,600	28	Lehman Brothers	1,600
23	Finger Company	2,200	31	Finger Company	1,300

QS 7-7
Purchases journal—perpetual
P1

Redmon Company uses a sales journal, a purchases journal, a cash receipts journal, a cash disbursements journal, and a general journal. The following transactions occur in the month of June.

June 1 Purchased $8,100 of merchandise on credit from Krause, Inc., terms n/30.
8 Sold merchandise costing $900 on credit to G. Seles for $1,500 subject to a $30 sales discount if paid by the end of the month.
14 Purchased $240 of store supplies from Chang Company on credit, terms n/30.
17 Purchased $260 of office supplies on credit from Monder Company, terms n/30.
24 Sold merchandise costing $400 to D. Lee for $630 cash.
28 Purchased store supplies from Porter's for $90 cash.
29 Paid Krause, Inc., $8,100 cash for the merchandise purchased on June 1.

Prepare headings for a purchases journal like the one in Exhibit 7.9. Journalize the June transactions that should be recorded in the purchases journal.

QS 7-8
Identifying journal of entry C2

Refer to QS 7-7 and for each of the June transactions identify the journal in which it would be recorded. Assume the company uses a sales journal, purchases journal, cash receipts journal, cash disbursements journal, and general journal as illustrated in this chapter.

QS 7-9A
Purchases journal—periodic P3

Prepare headings for a purchases journal like the one in Exhibit 7A.3. Journalize the June transactions from QS 7-7 that should be recorded in the purchases journal assuming the periodic inventory system is used.

QS 7-10
Accounts receivable ledger; posting from sales journal
P2

Winslow Company posts its sales invoices directly and then binds them into a Sales Journal. Winslow had the following credit sales to these customers during June.

June 2	Joe Mack	$ 3,600
8	Eric Horner	6,100
10	Tess Wilson	13,400
14	Hong Jiang	20,500
20	Tess Wilson	11,200
29	Joe Mack	7,300
	Total credit sales	$62,100

Required

1. Open an accounts receivable subsidiary ledger having a T-account for each customer. Post the invoices to the subsidiary ledger.
2. Open an Accounts Receivable controlling T-account and a Sales T-account to reflect general ledger accounts. Post the end-of-month total from the sales journal to these accounts.
3. Prepare a schedule of accounts receivable and prove that its total equals the Accounts Receivable controlling account balance.

QS 7-11
Analyzing segment reports
A1

Apple

Apple reports the following operating income (and average assets in parentheses) for each of its geographic segments—$ millions: Americas, $6,637 ($1,882); Europe, $4,296 ($1,352); and Japan, $961 ($483). Apple also reports the following sales (only) by product segments: iPhone, $13,033; iPod, $8,091; Desktops, $4,324; Portables, $9,535; Other, $7,922. Compute Apple's return on assets for each of its geographic segments, and assess the relative performance of these segments. Compute the percentage of total sales for each of its five product segments.

QS 7-12
International accounting and special journals
C2

Nestlé, a Switzerland-based company, uses a sales journal, a purchases journal, a cash receipts journal, a cash disbursements journal, and a general journal in a manner similar to that explained in this chapter. Journalize the following summary transactions of Nestlé transactions that should be recorded in the general journal. For those not recorded in the general journal, identify only the special journal where each should be recorded. (All amounts in millions of Swiss franc, CHF.)

1. Nestlé purchased CHF 8,000 of merchandise on credit from the suppliers.
2. Nestlé sold CHF 100,000 of merchandise (cost is CHF 44,000) on credit to customers.
3. A key customer returned CHF 900 of (worthless) merchandise to Nestlé (assume the cost of this merchandise is left in cost of goods sold).

connect

For account titles and numbers, use the Chart of Accounts at the end of the book.

EXERCISES

Exercise 7-1
Sales journal—perpetual
P1

Hutton Company uses a sales journal, a purchases journal, a cash receipts journal, a cash disbursements journal, and a general journal. The following transactions occur in the month of March.

Mar.	2	Sold merchandise costing $300 to B. Fager for $450 cash, invoice no. 5703.
	5	Purchased $2,300 of merchandise on credit from Marsh Corp.
	7	Sold merchandise costing $800 to J. Dryer for $1,150, terms 2/10, n/30, invoice no. 5704.
	8	Borrowed $8,000 cash by signing a note payable to the bank.
	12	Sold merchandise costing $200 to R. Land for $320, terms n/30, invoice no. 5705.
	16	Received $1,127 cash from J. Dryer to pay for the purchase of March 7.
	19	Sold used store equipment for $900 cash to Malone, Inc.
	25	Sold merchandise costing $350 to T. Burton for $550, terms n/30, invoice no. 5706.

Prepare headings for a sales journal like the one in Exhibit 7.5. Journalize the March transactions that should be recorded in this sales journal.

Exercise 7-2
Identifying journal of entry C2

Refer to Exercise 7-1 and for each of the March transactions identify the journal in which it would be recorded. Assume the company uses a sales journal, purchases journal, cash receipts journal, cash disbursements journal, and general journal as illustrated in this chapter.

Exercise 7-3A
Sales journal—periodic P3

Prepare headings for a sales journal like the one in Exhibit 7A.1. Journalize the March transactions shown in Exercise 7-1 that should be recorded in the sales journal assuming that the periodic inventory system is used.

Exercise 7-4
Cash receipts journal—perpetual
P1

Moeder Co. uses a sales journal, a purchases journal, a cash receipts journal, a cash disbursements journal, and a general journal. The following transactions occur in the month of November.

Nov.	3	The company purchased $3,100 of merchandise on credit from Hargrave Co., terms n/20.
	7	The company sold merchandise costing $840 on credit to J. York for $900, subject to an $18 sales discount if paid by the end of the month.
	9	The company borrowed $2,750 cash by signing a note payable to the bank.
	13	J. Emling, the owner, contributed $4,000 cash to the company.
	18	The company sold merchandise costing $130 to B. Box for $230 cash.
	22	The company paid Hargrave Co. $3,100 cash for the merchandise purchased on November 3.
	27	The company received $882 cash from J. York in payment of the November 7 purchase.
	30	The company paid salaries of $1,600 in cash.

Prepare headings for a cash receipts journal like the one in Exhibit 7.7. Journalize the November transactions that should be recorded in the cash receipts journal.

Exercise 7-5
Identifying journal of entry C2

Refer to Exercise 7-4 and for each of the November transactions identify the journal in which it would be recorded. Assume the company uses a sales journal, purchases journal, cash receipts journal, cash disbursements journal, and general journal as illustrated in this chapter.

Exercise 7-6A
Cash receipts journal—periodic
P3

Prepare headings for a cash receipts journal like the one in Exhibit 7A.2. Journalize the November transactions shown in Exercise 7-4 that should be recorded in the cash receipts journal assuming that the periodic inventory system is used.

Exercise 7-7
Controlling accounts and subsidiary ledgers
C3

Following is information from Ryan Company for its initial month of business. (1) Identify the balances listed in the accounts payable subsidiary ledger. (2) Identify the accounts payable balance listed in the general ledger at month's end.

Credit Purchases			Cash Paid		
Jan. 9	Boeder Company	$7,000	Jan. 19	Boeder Company	$5,100
18	Johnson Brothers	6,600	27	Johnson Brothers	6,600
22	Padley Company	4,200	31	Padley Company	3,400

Exercise 7-8
Cash disbursements journal—perpetual
P1

Pebblebrook Supply uses a sales journal, a purchases journal, a cash receipts journal, a cash disbursements journal, and a general journal. The following transactions occur in the month of April.

Apr. 3 Purchased merchandise for $2,750 on credit from Scott, Inc., terms 2/10, n/30.
9 Issued check no. 210 to Kidman Corp. to buy store supplies for $450.
12 Sold merchandise costing $400 on credit to C. Meyers for $670, terms n/30.
17 Issued check no. 211 for $1,500 to pay off a note payable to City Bank.
20 Purchased merchandise for $3,500 on credit from LeBron, terms 2/10, n/30.
28 Issued check no. 212 to LeBron to pay the amount due for the purchase of April 20, less the discount.
29 Paid salary of $1,700 to B. Decker by issuing check no. 213.
30 Issued check no. 214 to Scott, Inc., to pay the amount due for the purchase of April 3.

Prepare headings for a cash disbursements journal like the one in Exhibit 7.11. Journalize the April transactions that should be recorded in the cash disbursements journal.

Exercise 7-9
Identifying journal of entry C2

Refer to Exercise 7-8 and for each of the April transactions identify the journal in which it would be recorded. Assume the company uses a sales journal, purchases journal, cash receipts journal, cash disbursements journal, and general journal as illustrated in this chapter.

Exercise 7-10[A]
Cash disbursements journal—periodic P3

Prepare headings for a cash disbursements journal like the one in Exhibit 7A.4. Journalize the April transactions from Exercise 7-8 that should be recorded in the cash disbursements journal assuming that the periodic inventory system is used.

Exercise 7-11
Special journal transactions and error discovery
P1 

Porter Pharmacy uses the following journals: sales journal, purchases journal, cash receipts journal, cash disbursements journal, and general journal. On June 5, Porter purchased merchandise priced at $12,000, subject to credit terms of 2/10, n/30. On June 14, the pharmacy paid the net amount due for the merchandise. In journalizing the payment, the pharmacy debited Accounts Payable for $12,000 but failed to record the cash discount on the purchases. Cash was properly credited for the actual $11,760 paid. (*a*) In what journals would the June 5 and the June 14 transactions be recorded? (*b*) What procedure is likely to discover the error in journalizing the June 14 transaction?

Exercise 7-12
Posting to subsidiary ledger accounts; preparing a schedule of accounts receivable
P2

At the end of May, the sales journal of Clear View appears as follows.

Sales Journal — Page 2

Date	Account Debited	Invoice Number	PR	Accounts Receivable Dr. Sales Cr.	Cost of Goods Sold Dr. Inventory Cr.
May 6	Aaron Reckers	190		2,880	2,200
10	Sara Reed	191		1,940	1,600
17	Anna Page	192		850	500
25	Sara Reed	193		340	200
31	Totals			6,010	4,500

Clear View also recorded the return of defective merchandise with the following entry.

May 20	Sales Returns and Allowances	250	
	Accounts Receivable—Anna Page		250
	Customer returned (worthless) merchandise.		

Required

1. Open an accounts receivable subsidiary ledger that has a T-account for each customer listed in the sales journal. Post to the customer accounts the entries in the sales journal and any portion of the general journal entry that affects a customer's account.
2. Open a general ledger that has T-accounts for Accounts Receivable, Inventory, Sales, Sales Returns and Allowances, and Cost of Goods Sold. Post the sales journal and any portion of the general journal entry that affects these accounts.
3. Prepare a schedule of accounts receivable and prove that its total equals the balance in the Accounts Receivable controlling account.

Check (3) Ending Accounts Receivable, $5,760

Exercise 7-13
Purchases journal and error identification
P1 

A company that records credit purchases in a purchases journal and records purchases returns in a general journal made the following errors. Indicate when each error should be discovered.

1. Posted a purchases return to the Accounts Payable account and to the creditor's subsidiary account but did not post the purchases return to the Inventory account.
2. Posted a purchases return to the Inventory account and to the Accounts Payable account but did not post to the creditor's subsidiary account.
3. Correctly recorded a $4,000 purchase in the purchases journal but posted it to the creditor's subsidiary account as a $400 purchase.
4. Made an addition error in determining the balance of a creditor's subsidiary account.
5. Made an addition error in totaling the Office Supplies column of the purchases journal.

Exercise 7-14
Computing and analyzing segment return on assets
A1 

Refer to Exhibit 7.13 and complete the segment return on assets table for Wolfe Company. Analyze your findings and identify the segment with the highest, and that with the lowest, segment return on assets.

	Segment Operating Income (in $ mil.)		Segment Assets (in $ mil.)		Segment Return on Assets
Segment	2011	2010	2011	2010	2011
Specialty					
Skiing Group	$ 62	$ 58	$ 581	$440	
Skating Group	9	6	53	42	
Specialty Footwear	22	19	155	136	
Other Specialty	11	4	37	24	
Subtotal	104	87	826	642	
General Merchandise					
South America	32	36	305	274	
United States	7	8	52	35	
Europe	5	3	14	12	
Subtotal	44	47	371	321	
Total	$148	$134	$1197	$963	

Check Europe segment return, 38.5%

connect

For account titles and numbers, use the Chart of Accounts at the end of the book.

PROBLEM SET A

Problem 7-1A
Special journals, subsidiary ledgers, and schedule of accounts receivable—perpetual
C3 P1 P2 

Wise Company completes these transactions during April of the current year (the terms of all its credit sales are 2/10, n/30).

Apr. 2 Purchased $13,300 of merchandise on credit from Negi Company, invoice dated April 2, terms 2/10, n/60.
3 Sold merchandise on credit to Brooke Sledd, Invoice No. 760, for $3,000 (cost is $2,000).
3 Purchased $1,380 of office supplies on credit from Madison, Inc. Invoice dated April 2, terms n/10 EOM.
4 Issued Check No. 587 to *U.S. View* for advertising expense, $999.
5 Sold merchandise on credit to Paul Kohr, Invoice No. 761, for $8,000 (cost is $6,500).
6 Received an $85 credit memorandum from Madison, Inc., for the return of some of the office supplies received on April 3.
9 Purchased $11,125 of store equipment on credit from Ned's Supply, invoice dated April 9, terms n/10 EOM.

11 Sold merchandise on credit to Amy Nilson, Invoice No 762, for $9,500 (cost is $7,000).
12 Issued Check No. 588 to Negi Company in payment of its April 2 invoice, less the discount.
13 Received payment from Brooke Sledd for the April 3 sale, less the discount.
13 Sold $4,100 of merchandise on credit to Brooke Sledd (cost is $2,600), Invoice No. 763.
14 Received payment from Paul Kohr for the April 5 sale, less the discount.
16 Issued Check No. 589, payable to Payroll, in payment of sales salaries expense for the first half of the month, $9,750. Cashed the check and paid employees.
16 Cash sales for the first half of the month are $50,840 (cost is $33,880). (Cash sales are recorded daily from cash register data but are recorded only twice in this problem to reduce repetitive entries.)
17 Purchased $12,750 of merchandise on credit from Price Company, invoice dated April 17, terms 2/10, n/30.
18 Borrowed $50,000 cash from First State Bank by signing a long-term note payable.
20 Received payment from Amy Nilson for the April 11 sale, less the discount.
20 Purchased $730 of store supplies on credit from Ned's Supply, invoice dated April 19, terms n/10 EOM.
23 Received a $400 credit memorandum from Price Company for the return of defective merchandise received on April 17.
23 Received payment from Brooke Sledd for the April 13 sale, less the discount.
25 Purchased $10,375 of merchandise on credit from Negi Company, invoice dated April 24, terms 2/10, n/60.
26 Issued Check No. 590 to Price Company in payment of its April 17 invoice, less the return and the discount.
27 Sold $3,070 of merchandise on credit to Paul Kohr, Invoice No. 764 (cost is $2,420).
27 Sold $5,700 of merchandise on credit to Amy Nilson, Invoice No. 765 (cost is $3,305).
30 Issued Check No. 591, payable to Payroll, in payment of the sales salaries expense for the last half of the month, $9,750.
30 Cash sales for the last half of the month are $70,975 (cost is $55,900).

Required

1. Prepare a sales journal like that in Exhibit 7.5 and a cash receipts journal like that in Exhibit 7.7. Number both journal pages as page 3. Then review the transactions of Wise Company and enter those that should be journalized in the sales journal and those that should be journalized in the cash receipts journal. Ignore any transactions that should be journalized in a purchases journal, a cash disbursements journal, or a general journal.
2. Open the following general ledger accounts: Cash, Accounts Receivable, Inventory, Long-Term Notes Payable, B. Wise, Capital, Sales, Sales Discounts, and Cost of Goods Sold. Enter the March 31 balances for Cash ($85,000), Inventory ($125,000), Long-Term Notes Payable ($110,000), and B. Wise, Capital ($100,000). Also open accounts receivable subsidiary ledger accounts for Paul Kohr, Brooke Sledd, and Amy Nilson.
3. Verify that amounts that should be posted as individual amounts from the journals have been posted. (Such items are immediately posted.) Foot and crossfoot the journals and make the month-end postings.
4. Prepare a trial balance of the general ledger and prove the accuracy of the subsidiary ledger by preparing a schedule of accounts receivable.

Check Trial balance totals, $415,185

Analysis Component

5. Assume that the total for the schedule of Accounts Receivable does not equal the balance of the controlling account in the general ledger. Describe steps you would take to discover the error(s).

Problem 7-2A[A]
Special journals, subsidiary ledgers, and schedule of accounts receivable—periodic
C3 P2 P3

Assume that Wise Co. in Problem 7-1A uses the periodic inventory system.

Required

1. Prepare headings for a sales journal like the one in Exhibit 7A.1. Prepare headings for a cash receipts journal like the one in Exhibit 7A.2. Journalize the April transactions shown in Problem 7-1A that should be recorded in the sales journal and the cash receipts journal assuming the *periodic* inventory system is used.
2. Open the general ledger accounts with balances as shown in Problem 7-1A (do not open a Cost of Goods Sold ledger account). Also open accounts receivable subsidiary ledger accounts for

Brooke Sledd, Paul Kohr, and Amy Nilson. Under the periodic system, an Inventory account exists but is inactive until its balance is updated to the correct inventory balance at year-end. In this problem, the Inventory account remains inactive but must be included to correctly complete the trial balance.

3. Complete parts 3, 4, and 5 of Problem 7-1A using the results of parts 1 and 2 of this problem.

Check Trial balance totals, $415,185

Problem 7-3A
Special journals, subsidiary ledgers, and schedule of accounts payable—perpetual
C3 P1 P2

The April transactions of Wise Company are described in Problem 7-1A.

Required

1. Prepare a general journal, a purchases journal like that in Exhibit 7.9, and a cash disbursements journal like that in Exhibit 7.11. Number all journal pages as page 3. Review the April transactions of Wise Company and enter those transactions that should be journalized in the general journal, the purchases journal, or the cash disbursements journal. Ignore any transactions that should be journalized in a sales journal or cash receipts journal.

2. Open the following general ledger accounts: Cash, Inventory, Office Supplies, Store Supplies, Store Equipment, Accounts Payable, Long-Term Notes Payable, B. Wise, Capital, Sales Salaries Expense, and Advertising Expense. Enter the March 31 balances of Cash ($85,000), Inventory ($125,000), Long-Term Notes Payable ($110,000), and B. Wise, Capital ($100,000). Also open accounts payable subsidiary ledger accounts for Ned's Supply, Negi Company, Price Company, and Madison, Inc.

3. Verify that amounts that should be posted as individual amounts from the journals have been posted. (Such items are immediately posted.) Foot and crossfoot the journals and make the month-end postings.

4. Prepare a trial balance of the general ledger and a schedule of accounts payable.

Check Trial balance totals, $233,525

Problem 7-4A[A]
Special journals, subsidiary ledgers, and schedule of accounts payable—periodic
C3 P2 P3

Refer to Problem 7-1A and assume that Wise Co. uses the periodic inventory system.

Required

1. Prepare a general journal, a purchases journal like that in Exhibit 7A.3, and a cash disbursements journal like that in Exhibit 7A.4. Number all journal pages as page 3. Review the April transactions of Wise Company (Problem 7-1A) and enter those transactions that should be journalized in the general journal, the purchases journal, or the cash disbursements journal. Ignore any transaction that should be journalized in a sales journal or cash receipts journal.

2. Open the following general ledger accounts: Cash, Inventory, Office Supplies, Store Supplies, Store Equipment, Accounts Payable, Long-Term Notes Payable, B. Wise, Capital, Purchases, Purchases Returns and Allowances, Purchases Discounts, Sales Salaries Expense, and Advertising Expense. Enter the March 31 balances of Cash ($85,000), Inventory ($125,000), Long-Term Notes Payable ($110,000), and B. Wise, Capital ($100,000). Also open accounts payable subsidiary ledger accounts for Ned's Supply, Negi Company, Price Company, and Madison, Inc.

3. Complete parts 3 and 4 of Problem 7-3A using the results of parts 1 and 2 of this problem.

Check Trial balance totals, $234,438

Problem 7-5A
Special journals, subsidiary ledgers, trial balance—perpetual
C3 P1 P2

mhhe.com/wildFAP20e

Bishop Company completes these transactions and events during March of the current year (terms for all its credit sales are 2/10, n/30).

Mar. 1 Purchased $42,600 of merchandise from Soy Industries, invoice dated March 1, terms 2/15, n/30.
2 Sold merchandise on credit to Min Cho, Invoice No. 854, for $15,800 (cost is $7,900).
3 Purchased $1,120 of office supplies on credit from Stacy Company, invoice dated March 3, terms n/10 EOM.
3 Sold merchandise on credit to Lance Snow, Invoice No. 855, for $9,200 (cost is $4,600).
6 Borrowed $72,000 cash from Federal Bank by signing a long-term note payable.
9 Purchased $20,850 of office equipment on credit from Tells Supply, invoice dated March 9, terms n/10 EOM.
10 Sold merchandise on credit to Taylor Few, Invoice No. 856, for $4,600 (cost is $2,300).
12 Received payment from Min Cho for the March 2 sale less the discount.
13 Sent Soy Industries Check No. 416 in payment of the March 1 invoice less the discount.
13 Received payment from Lance Snow for the March 3 sale less the discount.
14 Purchased $31,625 of merchandise from the JW Company, invoice dated March 13, terms 2/10, n/30.
15 Issued Check No. 417, payable to Payroll, in payment of sales salaries expense for the first half of the month, $15,900. Cashed the check and paid the employees.

15 Cash sales for the first half of the month are $164,680 (cost is $138,000). (Cash sales are recorded daily, but are recorded only twice here to reduce repetitive entries.)
16 Purchased $1,670 of store supplies on credit from Stacy Company, invoice dated March 16, terms n/10 EOM.
17 Received a $2,425 credit memorandum from JW Company for the return of unsatisfactory merchandise purchased on March 14.
19 Received a $630 credit memorandum from Tells Supply for office equipment received on March 9 and returned for credit.
20 Received payment from Taylor Few for the sale of March 10 less the discount.
23 Issued Check No. 418 to JW Company in payment of the invoice of March 13 less the March 17 return and the discount.
27 Sold merchandise on credit to Taylor Few, Invoice No. 857, for $13,910 (cost is $6,220).
28 Sold merchandise on credit to Lance Snow, Invoice No. 858, for $5,315 (cost is $2,280).
31 Issued Check No. 419, payable to Payroll, in payment of sales salaries expense for the last half of the month, $15,900. Cashed the check and paid the employees.
31 Cash sales for the last half of the month are $174,590 (cost is $143,000).
31 Verify that amounts impacting customer and creditor accounts were posted and that any amounts that should have been posted as individual amounts to the general ledger accounts were posted. Foot and crossfoot the journals and make the month-end postings.

Required

1. Open the following general ledger accounts: Cash; Accounts Receivable; Inventory (March 1 beg. bal. is $300,000); Office Supplies; Store Supplies; Office Equipment; Accounts Payable; Long-Term Notes Payable; M. Bishop, Capital (March 1 beg. bal. is $300,000); Sales; Sales Discounts; Cost of Goods Sold; and Sales Salaries Expense. Open the following accounts receivable subsidiary ledger accounts: Taylor Few, Min Cho, and Lance Snow. Open the following accounts payable subsidiary ledger accounts: Stacy Company, Soy Industries, Tells Supply, and JW Company.

2. Enter these transactions in a sales journal like Exhibit 7.5, a purchases journal like Exhibit 7.9, a cash receipts journal like Exhibit 7.7, a cash disbursements journal like Exhibit 7.11, or a general journal. Number all journal pages as page 2.

Check Trial balance totals, $783,105

3. Prepare a trial balance of the general ledger and prove the accuracy of the subsidiary ledgers by preparing schedules of both accounts receivable and accounts payable.

Problem 7-6A[A]
Special journals, subsidiary ledgers, trial balance—periodic
C3 P2 P3

mhhe.com/wildFAP20e

Assume that Bishop Company in Problem 7-5A uses the periodic inventory system.

Required

1. Open the following general ledger accounts: Cash; Accounts Receivable; Inventory (March 1 beg. bal. is $300,000); Office Supplies; Store Supplies; Office Equipment; Accounts Payable; Long-Term Notes Payable; M. Bishop, Capital (March 1 beg. bal. is $300,000); Sales; Sales Discounts; Purchases; Purchases Returns and Allowances; Purchases Discounts; and Sales Salaries Expense. Open the following accounts receivable subsidiary ledger accounts: Taylor Few, Min Cho, and Lance Snow. Open the following accounts payable subsidiary ledger accounts: Stacy Company, Soy Industries, Tells Supply, and JW Company.

2. Enter the transactions from Problem 7-5A in a sales journal like that in Exhibit 7A.1, a purchases journal like that in Exhibit 7A.3, a cash receipts journal like that in Exhibit 7A.2, a cash disbursements journal like that in Exhibit 7A.4, or a general journal. Number journal pages as page 2.

Check Trial balance totals, $786,966

3. Prepare a trial balance of the general ledger and prove the accuracy of the subsidiary ledgers by preparing schedules of both accounts receivable and accounts payable.

PROBLEM SET B

For account titles and numbers, use the Chart of Accounts at the end of the book.

Problem 7-1B
Special journals, subsidiary ledgers, schedule of accounts receivable—perpetual
C3 P1 P2 

Alcorn Industries completes these transactions during July of the current year (the terms of all its credit sales are 2/10, n/30).

July 1 Purchased $6,300 of merchandise on credit from Tahoe Company, invoice dated June 30, terms 2/10, n/30.
3 Issued Check No. 300 to *The Weekly* for advertising expense, $575.
5 Sold merchandise on credit to Kim Newsom, Invoice No. 918, for $18,400 (cost is $9,700).

6 Sold merchandise on credit to Ruth Baker, Invoice No. 919, for $7,500 (cost is $4,300).
7 Purchased $1,050 of store supplies on credit from Pryor, Inc., invoice dated July 7, terms n/10 EOM.
8 Received a $150 credit memorandum from Pryor, Inc., for the return of store supplies received on July 7.
9 Purchased $37,710 of store equipment on credit from Caro's Supply, invoice dated July 8, terms n/10 EOM.
10 Issued Check No. 301 to Tahoe Company in payment of its June 30 invoice, less the discount.
13 Sold merchandise on credit to Stephanie Meyer, Invoice No. 920, for $8,350 (cost is $5,030).
14 Sold merchandise on credit to Kim Newsom, Invoice No. 921, for $4,100 (cost is $2,800).
15 Received payment from Kim Newsom for the July 5 sale, less the discount.
15 Issued Check No. 302, payable to Payroll, in payment of sales salaries expense for the first half of the month, $30,620. Cashed the check and paid employees.
15 Cash sales for the first half of the month are $121,370 (cost is $66,330). (Cash sales are recorded daily using data from the cash registers but are recorded only twice in this problem to reduce repetitive entries.)
16 Received payment from Ruth Baker for the July 6 sale, less the discount.
17 Purchased $8,200 of merchandise on credit from Dixon Company, invoice dated July 17, terms 2/10, n/30.
20 Purchased $750 of office supplies on credit from Caro's Supply, invoice dated July 19, terms n/10 EOM.
21 Borrowed $20,000 cash from College Bank by signing a long-term note payable.
23 Received payment from Stephanie Meyer for the July 13 sale, less the discount.
24 Received payment from Kim Newsom for the July 14 sale, less the discount.
24 Received a $2,400 credit memorandum from Dixon Company for the return of defective merchandise received on July 17.
26 Purchased $9,770 of merchandise on credit from Tahoe Company, invoice dated July 26, terms 2/10, n/30.
27 Issued Check No. 303 to Dixon Company in payment of its July 17 invoice, less the return and the discount.
29 Sold merchandise on credit to Ruth Baker, Invoice No. 922, for $28,090 (cost is $22,850).
30 Sold merchandise on credit to Stephanie Meyer, Invoice No. 923, for $15,750 (cost is $9,840).
31 Issued Check No. 304, payable to Payroll, in payment of the sales salaries expense for the last half of the month, $30,620.
31 Cash sales for the last half of the month are $79,020 (cost is $51,855).

Required

1. Prepare a sales journal like that in Exhibit 7.5 and a cash receipts journal like that in Exhibit 7.7. Number both journals as page 3. Then review the transactions of Alcorn Industries and enter those transactions that should be journalized in the sales journal and those that should be journalized in the cash receipts journal. Ignore any transactions that should be journalized in a purchases journal, a cash disbursements journal, or a general journal.

2. Open the following general ledger accounts: Cash, Accounts Receivable, Inventory, Long-Term Notes Payable, R. Alcorn, Capital, Sales, Sales Discounts, and Cost of Goods Sold. Enter the June 30 balances for Cash ($100,000), Inventory ($200,000), Long-Term Notes Payable ($200,000), and R. Alcorn, Capital ($100,000). Also open accounts receivable subsidiary ledger accounts for Kim Newsom, Stephanie Meyer, and Ruth Baker.

3. Verify that amounts that should be posted as individual amounts from the journals have been posted. (Such items are immediately posted.) Foot and crossfoot the journals and make the month-end postings.

4. Prepare a trial balance of the general ledger and prove the accuracy of the subsidiary ledger by preparing a schedule of accounts receivable.

Check Trial balance totals, $602,580

Analysis Component

5. Assume that the total for the schedule of Accounts Receivable does not equal the balance of the controlling account in the general ledger. Describe steps you would take to discover the error(s).

Problem 7-2B[A]
Special journals, subsidiary ledgers, and schedule of accounts receivable—periodic
C3 P2 P3

Assume that Alcorn Industries in Problem 7-1B uses the periodic inventory system.

Required

1. Prepare headings for a sales journal like the one in Exhibit 7A.1. Prepare headings for a cash receipts journal like the one in Exhibit 7A.2. Journalize the July transactions shown in Problem 7-1B that should be recorded in the sales journal and the cash receipts journal assuming the periodic inventory system is used.
2. Open the general ledger accounts with balances as shown in Problem 7-1B (do not open a Cost of Goods Sold ledger account). Also open accounts receivable subsidiary ledger accounts for Ruth Baker, Stephanie Meyer, and Kim Newsom. Under the periodic system, an Inventory account exists but is inactive until its balance is updated to the correct inventory balance at year-end. In this problem, the Inventory account remains inactive but must be included to correctly complete the trial balance.
3. Complete parts 3, 4, and 5 of Problem 7-1B using the results of parts 1 and 2 of this problem.

Check Trial balance totals, $602,580

Problem 7-3B
Special journals, subsidiary ledgers, and schedule of accounts payable—perpetual
C3 P1 P2

The July transactions of Alcorn Industries are described in Problem 7-1B.

Required

1. Prepare a general journal, a purchases journal like that in Exhibit 7.9, and a cash disbursements journal like that in Exhibit 7.11. Number all journal pages as page 3. Review the July transactions of Alcorn Industries and enter those transactions that should be journalized in the general journal, the purchases journal, or the cash disbursements journal. Ignore any transactions that should be journalized in a sales journal or cash receipts journal.
2. Open the following general ledger accounts: Cash, Inventory, Office Supplies, Store Supplies, Store Equipment, Accounts Payable, Long-Term Notes Payable, R. Alcorn, Capital, Sales Salaries Expense, and Advertising Expense. Enter the June 30 balances of Cash ($100,000), Inventory ($200,000), Long-Term Notes Payable ($200,000), and R. Alcorn, Capital ($100,000). Also open accounts payable subsidiary ledger accounts for Caro's Supply, Tahoe Company, Dixon Company, and Pryor, Inc.
3. Verify that amounts that should be posted as individual amounts from the journals have been posted. (Such items are immediately posted.) Foot and crossfoot the journals and make the month-end postings.
4. Prepare a trial balance of the general ledger and a schedule of accounts payable.

Check Trial balance totals, $349,130

Problem 7-4B[A]
Special journals, subsidiary ledgers, and schedule of accounts payable—periodic
C3 P2 P3

Refer to Problem 7-1B and assume that Alcorn uses the periodic inventory system.

Required

1. Prepare a general journal, a purchases journal like that in Exhibit 7A.3, and a cash disbursements journal like that in Exhibit 7A.4. Number all journal pages as page 3. Review the July transactions of Alcorn Company (Problem 7-1B) and enter those transactions that should be journalized in the general journal, the purchases journal, or the cash disbursements journal. Ignore any transaction that should be journalized in a sales journal or cash receipts journal.
2. Open the following general ledger accounts: Cash, Inventory, Office Supplies, Store Supplies, Store Equipment, Accounts Payable, Long-Term Notes Payable, R. Alcorn, Capital, Purchases, Purchases Returns and Allowances, Purchases Discounts, Sales Salaries Expense, and Advertising Expense. Enter the June 30 balances of Cash ($100,000), Inventory ($200,000), Long-Term Notes Payable ($200,000), and R. Alcorn, Capital ($100,000). Also open accounts payable subsidiary ledger accounts for Tahoe Company, Pryor, Inc., Caro's Supply, and Dixon Company.
3. Complete parts 3 and 4 of Problem 7-3B using the results of parts 1 and 2 of this problem.

Check Trial balance totals, $351,772

Problem 7-5B
Special journals, subsidiary ledgers, trial balance—perpetual
C3 P2 P3

Suppan Company completes these transactions during November of the current year (terms for all its credit sales are 2/10, n/30).

Nov. 1 Purchased $5,062 of office equipment on credit from Blix Supply, invoice dated November 1, terms n/10 EOM.

2 Borrowed $86,250 cash from Kansas Bank by signing a long-term note payable.

4 Purchased $11,400 of merchandise from ATM Industries, invoice dated November 3, terms 2/10, n/30.

5 Purchased $1,020 of store supplies on credit from Globe Company, invoice dated November 5, terms n/10 EOM.

8 Sold merchandise on credit to Sid Ragan, Invoice No. 439, for $6,350 (cost is $3,710).
10 Sold merchandise on credit to Carlos Mane, Invoice No. 440, for $12,500 (cost is $7,500).
11 Purchased $2,887 of merchandise from Xu Company, invoice dated November 10, terms 2/10, n/30.
12 Sent ATM Industries Check No. 633 in payment of its November 3 invoice less the discount.
15 Issued Check No. 634, payable to Payroll, in payment of sales salaries expense for the first half of the month, $8,435. Cashed the check and paid the employees.
15 Cash sales for the first half of the month are $27,170 (cost is $17,000). (Cash sales are recorded daily but are recorded only twice in this problem to reduce repetitive entries.)
15 Sold merchandise on credit to Tony Timmons, Invoice No. 441, for $4,250 (cost is $1,450).
16 Purchased $559 of office supplies on credit from Globe Company, invoice dated November 16, terms n/10 EOM.
17 Received a $487 credit memorandum from Xu Company for the return of unsatisfactory merchandise purchased on November 11.
18 Received payment from Sid Ragan for the November 8 sale less the discount.
19 Received payment from Carlos Mane for the November 10 sale less the discount.
19 Issued Check No. 635 to Xu Company in payment of its invoice of November 10 less the return and the discount.
22 Sold merchandise on credit to Carlos Mane, Invoice No. 442, for $2,595 (cost is $1,060).
24 Sold merchandise on credit to Tony Timmons, Invoice No. 443, for $3,240 (cost is $1,090).
25 Received payment from Tony Timmons for the sale of November 15 less the discount.
26 Received a $922 credit memorandum from Blix Supply for the return of office equipment purchased on November 1.
30 Issued Check No. 636, payable to Payroll, in payment of sales salaries expense for the last half of the month, $8,435. Cashed the check and paid the employees.
30 Cash sales for the last half of the month are $35,703 (cost is $20,400).
30 Verify that amounts impacting customer and creditor accounts were posted and that any amounts that should have been posted as individual amounts to the general ledger accounts were posted. Foot and crossfoot the journals and make the month-end postings.

Required

1. Open the following general ledger accounts: Cash; Accounts Receivable; Inventory (November 1 beg. bal. is $40,000); Office Supplies; Store Supplies; Office Equipment; Accounts Payable; Long-Term Notes Payable; J. Suppan, Capital (Nov. 1 beg. bal. is $40,000); Sales; Sales Discounts; Cost of Goods Sold; and Sales Salaries Expense. Open the following accounts receivable subsidiary ledger accounts: Carlos Mane, Tony Timmons, and Sid Ragan. Open the following accounts payable subsidiary ledger accounts: Globe Company, ATM Industries, Blix Supply, and Xu Company.
2. Enter these transactions in a sales journal like that in Exhibit 7.5, a purchases journal like that in Exhibit 7.9, a cash receipts journal like that in Exhibit 7.7, a cash disbursements journal like that in Exhibit 7.11, or a general journal. Number all journal pages as page 2.
3. Prepare a trial balance of the general ledger and prove the accuracy of the subsidiary ledgers by preparing schedules of both accounts receivable and accounts payable.

Check Trial balance totals, $223,777

Problem 7-6B[A]
Special journals, subsidiary ledgers, trial balance—periodic
C3 P2 P3

Assume that Suppan Company in Problem 7-5B uses the periodic inventory system.

Required

1. Open the following general ledger accounts: Cash; Accounts Receivable; Inventory (November 1 beg. bal. is $40,000); Office Supplies; Store Supplies; Office Equipment; Accounts Payable; Long-Term Notes Payable; J. Suppan, Capital (Nov. 1 beg. bal. is $40,000); Sales; Sales Discounts; Purchases; Purchases Returns and Allowances; Purchases Discounts; and Sales Salaries Expense. Open the following accounts receivable subsidiary ledger accounts: Carlos Mane, Tony Timmons, and Sid Ragan. Open the following accounts payable subsidiary ledger accounts: Globe Company, ATM Industries, Blix Supply, and Xu Company.
2. Enter the transactions from Problem 7-5B in a sales journal like that in Exhibit 7A.1, a purchases journal like that in Exhibit 7A.3, a cash receipts journal like that in Exhibit 7A.2, a cash disbursements journal like that in Exhibit 7A.4, or a general journal. Number journal pages as page 2.
3. Prepare a trial balance of the general ledger and prove the accuracy of the subsidiary ledgers by preparing schedules of both accounts receivable and accounts payable.

Check Trial balance totals, $224,540

SERIAL PROBLEM
Business Solutions P1

(This serial problem began in Chapter 1 and continues through most of the book. If previous chapter segments were not completed, the serial problem can begin at this point. It is helpful, but not necessary, to use the Working Papers that accompany the book.)

SP 7 Assume that Santana Rey expands Business Solutions' accounting system to include special journals.

Required

1. Locate the transactions related to January through March 2012 for Business Solutions in Chapter 5.
2. Enter the Business Solutions transactions for January through March in a sales journal like that in Exhibit 7.5 (insert "n/a" in the Invoice column), a cash receipts journal like that in Exhibit 7.7, a purchases journal like that in Exhibit 7.9 (use Computer Supplies heading instead of Office Supplies), and a cash disbursements journal like that in Exhibit 7.11 (insert "n/a" in the Check Number column), or a general journal. Number journal pages as page 2. If the transaction does not specify the name of the payee, state "not specified" in the Payee column of the cash disbursements journal.
3. The transactions on the following dates should be journalized in the general journal: January 5, 11, 20, 24, and 29 (no entry required) and March 24. Do not record and post the adjusting entries for the end of March.

COMPREHENSIVE PROBLEM
Colo Company

mhhe.com/wildFAP20e

(If the Working Papers that accompany this book are not available, omit this comprehensive problem.) Assume it is Monday, May 1, the first business day of the month, and you have just been hired as the accountant for Colo Company, which operates with monthly accounting periods. All of the company's accounting work is completed through the end of April and its ledgers show April 30 balances. During your first month on the job, the company experiences the following transactions and events (terms for all its credit sales are 2/10, n/30 unless stated differently):

May 1 Issued Check No. 3410 to S&P Management Co. in payment of the May rent, $3,710. (Use two lines to record the transaction. Charge 80% of the rent to Rent Expense—Selling Space and the balance to Rent Expense—Office Space.)

2 Sold merchandise on credit to Hensel Company, Invoice No. 8785, for $6,100 (cost is $4,100).

2 Issued a $175 credit memorandum to Knox Co., for defective (worthless) merchandise sold on April 28 and returned for credit. The total selling price (gross) was $4,725.

3 Received a $798 credit memorandum from Peyton Products for the return of merchandise purchased on April 29.

4 Purchased the following on credit from Gear Supply Co.: merchandise, $37,072; store supplies, $574; and office supplies, $83. Invoice dated May 4, terms n/10 EOM.

5 Received payment from Knox Co., for the balance from the April 28 sale less the May 2 return and the discount.

8 Issued Check No. 3411 to Peyton Products to pay for the $7,098 of merchandise purchased on April 29 less the May 3 return and a 2% discount.

9 Sold store supplies to the merchant next door at their cost of $350 cash.

10 Purchased $4,074 of office equipment on credit from Gear Supply Co., invoice dated May 10, terms n/10 EOM.

11 Received payment from Hensel Company for the May 2 sale less the discount.

11 Purchased $8,800 of merchandise from Garcia, Inc., invoice dated May 10, terms 2/10, n/30.

12 Received an $854 credit memorandum from Gear Supply Co. for the return of defective office equipment received on May 10.

15 Issued Check No. 3412, payable to Payroll, in payment of sales salaries, $5,320, and office salaries, $3,150. Cashed the check and paid the employees.

15 Cash sales for the first half of the month are $59,220 (cost is $38,200). (Cash sales are recorded daily but are recorded only twice here to reduce repetitive entries.)

15 Post to the customer and creditor accounts. Also post individual items that are not included in column totals at the end of the month to the general ledger accounts. (Such items are posted daily but are posted only twice each month because they are few in number.)

16 Sold merchandise on credit to Hensel Company, Invoice No. 8786, for $3,990 (cost is $1,890).

17 Purchased $13,650 of merchandise from Fink Corp., invoice dated May 14, terms 2/10, n/60.

19 Issued Check No. 3413 to Garcia, Inc., in payment of its May 10 invoice less the discount.

22 Sold merchandise to Lee Services, Invoice No. 8787, for $6,850 (cost is $4,990), terms 2/10, n/60.

23 Issued Check No. 3414 to Fink Corp. in payment of its May 14 invoice less the discount.

24 Purchased the following on credit from Gear Supply Co.: merchandise, $8,120; store supplies, $630; and office supplies, $280. Invoice dated May 24, terms n/10 EOM.

25 Purchased $3,080 of merchandise from Peyton Products, invoice dated May 23, terms 2/10, n/30.
26 Sold merchandise on credit to Crane Corp., Invoice No. 8788, for $14,210 (cost is $8,230).
26 Issued Check No. 3415 to Perennial Power in payment of the May electric bill, $1,283.
29 The owner of Colo Company, Jenny Colo, used Check No. 3416 to withdraw $7,000 cash from the business for personal use.
30 Received payment from Lee Services for the May 22 sale less the discount.
30 Issued Check No. 3417, payable to Payroll, in payment of sales salaries, $5,320, and office salaries, $3,150. Cashed the check and paid the employees.
31 Cash sales for the last half of the month are $66,052 (cost is $42,500).
31 Post to the customer and creditor accounts. Also post individual items that are not included in column totals at the end of the month to the general ledger accounts. Foot and crossfoot the journals and make the month-end postings.

Required

1. Enter these transactions in a sales journal, a purchases journal, a cash receipts journal, a cash disbursements journal, or a general journal as illustrated in this chapter (number all journal pages as page 2). Post when instructed to do so. Assume a perpetual inventory system.
2. Prepare a trial balance in the Trial Balance columns of the work sheet form provided with the working papers. Complete the work sheet using the following information for accounting adjustments.
   a. Expired insurance, $553.
   b. Ending store supplies inventory, $2,632.
   c. Ending office supplies inventory, $504.
   d. Depreciation of store equipment, $567.
   e. Depreciation of office equipment, $329.

   Prepare and post adjusting and closing entries.
3. Prepare a May 2011 multiple-step income statement, a May 2011 statement of owner's equity, and a May 31, 2011, classified balance sheet.
4. Prepare a post-closing trial balance. Also prove the accuracy of subsidiary ledgers by preparing schedules of both accounts receivable and accounts payable.

Check (2) Unadjusted trial balance totals, $545,020; Adjustments column totals, $2,407

(3) Net income, $31,647; Total assets, $385,791

Beyond the Numbers

REPORTING IN ACTION
A1

RIM

BTN 7-1 Refer to Research In Motion's financial statements in Appendix A to answer the following.

1. Identify the note that reports on Research In Motion's business segments.
2. Describe the focus and activities of each of Research In Motion's business segments.

Fast Forward

3. Access Research In Motion's annual report for fiscal years ending after February 27, 2010, from its Website (RIM.com) or the SEC's EDGAR database (www.SEC.gov). Has Research In Motion changed its reporting policy regarding segment information? Explain.

COMPARATIVE ANALYSIS
A1 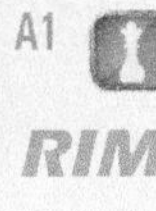

RIM
Apple

BTN 7-2 Key figures for Research In Motion and Apple follow ($ millions).

	Current Year		One Year Prior		Two Years Prior	
RIM Segment	Segment Revenue	Segment Assets	Segment Revenue	Segment Assets	Segment Revenue	Segment Assets
Domestic	$8,620	$4,059	$6,968	$2,647	$3,529	$1,739
International	6,333	6,145	4,097	5,454	2,480	3,772

	Current Year		One Year Prior		Two Years Prior	
Apple Segment	Segment Revenue	Segment Assets	Segment Revenue	Segment Assets	Segment Revenue	Segment Assets
Domestic	$22,325	$2,698	$20,893	$2,269	$14,683	$1,752
International	20,580	495	16,598	410	9,895	260

Required

1. Compute the ratio of segment revenue divided by segment assets for each of the segments of Research In Motion and Apple for each of the two most recent years shown. (We do not compute the segment return on assets as these companies did not report their segment income.)
2. Interpret and comment on your results of part 1.

ETHICS CHALLENGE

C1  

BTN 7-3 Erica Gray, CPA, is a sole practitioner. She has been practicing as an auditor for 10 years. Recently a long-standing audit client asked Gray to design and implement an integrated computer-based accounting information system. The fees associated with this additional engagement with the client are very attractive. However, Gray wonders if she can remain objective on subsequent audits in her evaluation of the client's accounting system and its records if she was responsible for its design and implementation. Gray knows that professional auditing standards require her to remain independent in fact and appearance from her auditing clients.

Required

1. What do you believe auditing standards are mainly concerned with when they require independence in fact? In appearance?
2. Why is it important that auditors remain independent of their clients?
3. Do you think Gray can accept this engagement and remain independent? Justify your response.

COMMUNICATING IN PRACTICE

C2 C3  

BTN 7-4 Your friend, Wendy Geiger, owns a small retail store that sells candies and nuts. Geiger acquires her goods from a few select vendors. She generally makes purchase orders by phone and on credit. Sales are primarily for cash. Geiger keeps her own manual accounting system using a general journal and a general ledger. At the end of each business day, she records one summary entry for cash sales. Geiger recently began offering items in creative gift packages. This has increased sales substantially, and she is now receiving orders from corporate and other clients who order large quantities and prefer to buy on credit. As a result of increased credit transactions in both purchases and sales, keeping the accounting records has become extremely time consuming. Geiger wants to continue to maintain her own manual system and calls you for advice. Write a memo to her advising how she might modify her current manual accounting system to accommodate the expanded business activities. Geiger is accustomed to checking her ledger by using a trial balance. Your memo should explain the advantages of what you propose and of any other verification techniques you recommend.

TAKING IT TO THE NET

A1  

BTN 7-5 Access the March 18, 2010, filing of the fiscal 2010 10-K report for **Dell** (ticker DELL) at www.SEC.gov. Read its Note 14 that details Dell's segment information and answer the following.

1. Dell's operations are divided among which four global business segments?
2. In fiscal year 2010, which segment had the largest dollar amount of operating income? Which had the largest amount of assets?
3. Compute the return on assets for each segment for fiscal year 2010. Use operating income and average total assets by segment for your calculation. Which segment has the highest return on assets?
4. For what product groups does Dell provide segment data? What percent of Dell's net revenue is earned by each product group?

TEAMWORK IN ACTION

C3 P1 P2

BTN 7-6 Each member of the team is to assume responsibility for one of the following tasks:

a. Journalizing in the purchases journal.
b. Journalizing in the cash disbursements journal.
c. Maintaining and verifying the Accounts Payable ledger.
d. Journalizing in the sales journal and the general journal.
e. Journalizing in the cash receipts journal.
f. Maintaining and verifying the Accounts Receivable ledger.

The team should abide by the following procedures in carrying out responsibilities.

Required

1. After tasks *a–f* are assigned, each team member is to quickly read the list of transactions in Problem 7-5A, identifying with initials the journal in which each transaction is to be recorded. Upon completion,

the team leader is to read transaction dates, and the appropriate team member is to vocalize responsibility. Any disagreement between teammates must be resolved.

2. Journalize and continually update subsidiary ledgers. Journal recorders should alert teammates assigned to subsidiary ledgers when an entry must be posted to their subsidiary.
3. Team members responsible for tasks *a*, *b*, *d*, and *e* are to summarize and prove journals; members responsible for tasks *c* and *f* are to prepare both payables and receivables schedules.
4. The team leader is to take charge of the general ledger, rotating team members to obtain amounts to be posted. The person responsible for a journal must complete posting references in that journal. Other team members should verify the accuracy of account balance computations. To avoid any abnormal account balances, post in the following order: P, S, G, R, D. (*Note:* Posting any necessary individual general ledger amounts is also done at this time.)
5. The team leader is to read out general ledger account balances while another team member fills in the trial balance form. Concurrently, one member should keep a running balance of debit account balance totals and another credit account balance totals. Verify the final total of the trial balance and the schedules. If necessary, the team must resolve any errors. Turn in the trial balance and schedules to the instructor.

ENTREPRENEURIAL DECISION

P1 

BTN 7-7 Refer to the chapter's opening feature about Kim Jordan and her company, New Belgium Brewing Company. Her manufacturing company deals with numerous suppliers and customers.

Required

1. Identify the special journals that New Belgium Brewing would be likely to use in its operations. Also identify any subsidiary ledgers that it would likely use.
2. New Belgium Brewing hopes to double yearly sales within five years hence from its current $100 million annual amount. Assume that its sales growth projections are as follows.

Year	One Year Hence	Two Years Hence	Three Years Hence	Four Years Hence	Five Years Hence
Projected growth in sales (from the preceding year)	0%	20%	15%	25%	20%

Estimate New Belgium Brewing's projected sales for each year (round to the nearest dollar). If this pattern of sales growth holds, will New Belgium Brewing achieve its goal of doubling sales in five years?

GLOBAL DECISION

A1  

NOKIA

BTN 7-8 Access and refer to the December 31, 2009, annual report for Nokia at www.Nokia.com.

Required

1. Identify its Note 2 (Segmental Information) to its financial statements and locate its information relating to Nokia's operating and reportable segments. Identify those three segments.
2. What financial figures does it disclose for each segment?
3. Does Nokia have a dominant segment? Explain.

ANSWERS TO MULTIPLE CHOICE QUIZ

1. a
2. e
3. d
4. b
5. a

Cash and Internal Controls

A Look Back

Chapter 7 focused on accounting information systems. We explained the principles and components of information systems, the use of special journals and subsidiary ledgers, and technology-based systems.

A Look at This Chapter

This chapter extends our study of accounting to internal control and the analysis of cash. We describe procedures that are good for internal control. We also explain the control of and the accounting for cash, including control features of banking activities.

A Look Ahead

Chapter 9 focuses on receivables. We explain how to account and report on receivables and their related accounts. This includes estimating uncollectible receivables and computing interest earned.

Learning Objectives

CONCEPTUAL

C1 Define internal control and identify its purpose and principles. (p. 316)

C2 Define cash and cash equivalents and explain how to report them. (p. 321)

ANALYTICAL

A1 Compute the days' sales uncollected ratio and use it to assess liquidity. (p. 335)

LP8

PROCEDURAL

P1 Apply internal control to cash receipts and disbursements. (p. 322)

P2 Explain and record petty cash fund transactions. (p. 326)

P3 Prepare a bank reconciliation. (p. 331)

P4 *Appendix 8A*—Describe the use of documentation and verification to control cash disbursements. (p. 338)

P5 *Appendix 8B—Apply the net method to control purchase discounts.* (p. 341)

Decision Insight

Candyland Biz

"It's a creative outlet for me . . . it doesn't feel like work"
—DYLAN LAUREN

NEW YORK—A 10-foot chocolate bunny greets you as you enter the store—that should be warning enough! This elite designer candy store, christened **Dylan's Candy Bar (DylansCandyBar.com),** is the brainchild of co-founder Dylan Lauren. Explains Dylan, "I got a business plan together and set out to make candy my livelihood."

This sweet-lovers' heaven offers more than 5,000 different choices of sweets from all over the world. It has become a hip hangout for locals and tourists—and it has made candy cool. Says Dylan, "Park Avenue women come in, and the first thing they ask for is Gummi bears. They love that it's very childhood, nostalgic."

Although marketing is an important part of its success, Dylan's management of internal controls and cash is equally impressive. Several control procedures monitor its business activities and safeguard its assets. An example is the biometric time and attendance control system using fingerprint characteristics. Says Dylan, "There's no fooling the system! It is going to help us remotely manage our employees while eliminating human error and dishonesty. [It] is a cost-effective and important business management tool." Similar controls are applied throughout the store. Dylan explains that such controls raise productivity and cut expenses.

The store's cash management practices are equally impressive, including controls over cash receipts, disbursements, and petty cash. The use of bank reconciliations further helps with the store's control and management of cash. Dylan explains that she takes advantage of available banking services to enhance controls over cash.

Internal controls are crucial when on a busy day its stores bring in thousands of customers, and their cash. They have already expanded to three stores in New York, and one each in Houston and Orlando. Through it all, Dylan says it is "totally fun."

[Sources: *Dylan's Candy Bar Website,* January 2011; *Entrepreneur,* June 2005; *NYC Official City Guide,* July 2009; *The New York Times,* June & March 2009; *Dolce Vita Magazine,* June 2009; *Luxury Insider,* March 2009.]

Chapter Preview

We all are aware of theft and fraud. They affect us in several ways: We lock doors, chain bikes, review sales receipts, and acquire alarm systems. A company also takes actions to safeguard, control, and manage what it owns. Experience tells us that small companies are most vulnerable, usually due to weak internal controls. It is management's responsibility to set up policies and procedures to safeguard a company's assets, especially cash. To do so, management *and* employees must understand and apply principles of internal control. This chapter describes these principles and how to apply them. It focuses special attention on cash because it is easily transferable and is often at high risk of loss.

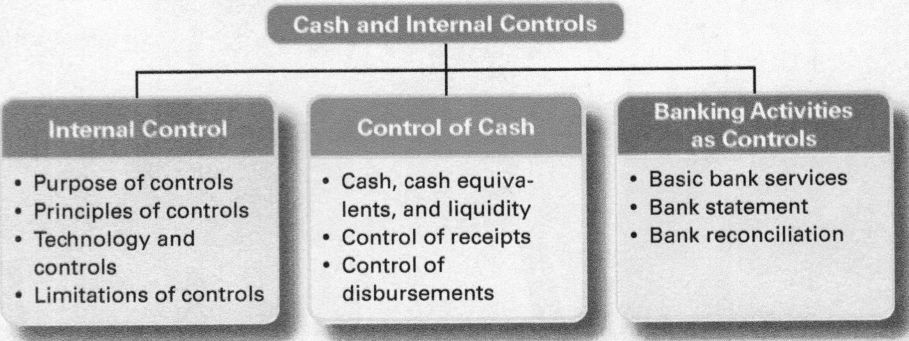

INTERNAL CONTROL

This section describes internal control and its fundamental principles. We also discuss the impact of technology on internal control and the limitations of control procedures.

Purpose of Internal Control

C1 Define internal control and identify its purpose and principles.

Managers (or owners) of small businesses often control the entire operation. These managers usually purchase all assets, hire and manage employees, negotiate all contracts, and sign all checks. They know from personal contact and observation whether the business is actually receiving the assets and services paid for. Most companies, however, cannot maintain this close personal supervision. They must delegate responsibilities and rely on formal procedures rather than personal contact in controlling business activities.

Internal Control System Managers use an internal control system to monitor and control business activities. An **internal control system** consists of the policies and procedures managers use to

- Protect assets.
- Ensure reliable accounting.
- Promote efficient operations.
- Urge adherence to company policies.

A properly designed internal control system is a key part of systems design, analysis, and performance. Managers place a high priority on internal control systems because they can prevent avoidable losses, help managers plan operations, and monitor company and employee performance. Internal controls do not provide guarantees, but they lower the company's risk of loss.

Sarbanes-Oxley Act (SOX) The **Sarbanes-Oxley Act (SOX)** requires the managers and auditors of companies whose stock is traded on an exchange (called *public companies*) to document and certify the system of internal controls. Following are some of the specific requirements:

- Auditors must evaluate internal controls and issue an internal control report.
- Auditors of a client are restricted as to what consulting services they can provide that client.
- The person leading an audit can serve no more than seven years without a two-year break.
- Auditors' work is overseen by the *Public Company Accounting Oversight Board* (PCAOB).
- Harsh penalties exist for violators—sentences up to 25 years in prison with severe fines.

SOX has markedly impacted companies, and the costs of its implementation are high. Importantly, **Section 404** of SOX requires that managers document and assess the effectiveness of all internal control processes that can impact financial reporting. The benefits include greater confidence in accounting systems and their related reports. However, the public continues to debate the costs versus the benefits of SOX as nearly all business activities of these companies are impacted by SOX. Section 404 of SOX requires that managers document and assess their internal controls *and* that auditors provide an opinion on managers' documentation and assessment. Costs of complying with Section 404 for companies is reported to average $4 million (source: Financial Executives Institute).

Principles of Internal Control

Internal control policies and procedures vary from company to company according to such factors as the nature of the business and its size. Certain fundamental internal control principles apply to all companies. The **principles of internal control** are to

1. Establish responsibilities.
2. Maintain adequate records.
3. Insure assets and bond key employees.
4. Separate recordkeeping from custody of assets.
5. Divide responsibility for related transactions.
6. Apply technological controls.
7. Perform regular and independent reviews.

This section explains these seven principles and describes how internal control procedures minimize the risk of fraud and theft. These procedures also increase the reliability and accuracy of accounting records. A framework for how these seven principles improve the quality of financial reporting is provided by the **Committee of Sponsoring Organizations (COSO)** (www.COSO.org). Specifically, these principles link to five aspects of internal control: control activities, control environment, risk assessment, monitoring, and communication.

Point: Sarbanes-Oxley Act (SOX) requires that each annual report contain an *internal control report*, which must: (1) state managers' responsibility for establishing and maintaining adequate internal controls for financial reporting; and (2) assess the effectiveness of those controls.

Establish Responsibilities Proper internal control means that responsibility for a task is clearly established and assigned to one person. When a problem occurs in a company where responsibility is not identified, determining who is at fault is difficult. For instance, if two salesclerks share the same cash register and there is a cash shortage, neither clerk can be held accountable. To prevent this problem, one clerk might be given responsibility for handling all cash sales. Alternately, a company can use a register with separate cash drawers for each clerk. Most of us have waited at a retail counter during a shift change while employees swap cash drawers.

Point: Many companies have a mandatory vacation policy for employees who handle cash. When another employee must cover for the one on vacation, it is more difficult to hide cash frauds.

Maintain Adequate Records Good recordkeeping is part of an internal control system. It helps protect assets and ensures that employees use prescribed procedures. Reliable records are also a source of information that managers use to monitor company activities. When detailed records of equipment are kept, for instance, items are unlikely to be lost or stolen without detection. Similarly, transactions are less likely to be entered in wrong accounts if a chart of accounts is set up and carefully used. Many preprinted forms and internal documents are also designed for use in a good internal control system. When sales slips are properly designed, for instance, sales personnel can record needed information efficiently with less chance of errors or delays to customers. When sales slips are prenumbered and controlled, each one issued is the responsibility of one salesperson, preventing the salesperson from pocketing cash by making a sale and destroying the sales slip. Computerized point-of-sale systems achieve the same control results.

Insure Assets and Bond Key Employees Good internal control means that assets are adequately insured against casualty and that employees handling large amounts of cash and easily transferable assets are bonded. An employee is *bonded* when a company purchases an insurance policy, or a bond, against losses from theft by that employee. Bonding reduces the risk of loss. It also discourages theft because bonded employees know an independent bonding company will be involved when theft is uncovered and is unlikely to be sympathetic with an employee involved in theft.

Point: The Association of Certified Fraud Examiners (cfenet.com) estimates that employee fraud costs small companies more than $100,000 per incident.

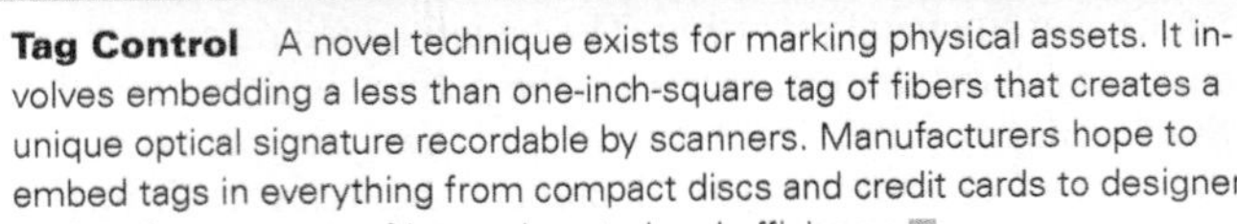

Decision Insight

Tag Control A novel technique exists for marking physical assets. It involves embedding a less than one-inch-square tag of fibers that creates a unique optical signature recordable by scanners. Manufacturers hope to embed tags in everything from compact discs and credit cards to designer clothes for purposes of internal control and efficiency. ■

Separate Recordkeeping from Custody of Assets A person who controls or has access to an asset must not keep that asset's accounting records. This principle reduces the risk of theft or waste of an asset because the person with control over it knows that another person keeps its records. Also, a recordkeeper who does not have access to the asset has no reason to falsify records. This means that to steal an asset and hide the theft from the records, two or more people must *collude*—or agree in secret to commit the fraud.

Divide Responsibility for Related Transactions Good internal control divides responsibility for a transaction or a series of related transactions between two or more individuals or departments. This is to ensure that the work of one individual acts as a check on the other. This principle, often called *separation of duties,* is not a call for duplication of work. Each employee or department should perform unduplicated effort. Examples of transactions with divided responsibility are placing purchase orders, receiving merchandise, and paying vendors. These tasks should not be given to one individual or department. Assigning responsibility for two or more of these tasks to one party increases mistakes and perhaps fraud. Having an independent person, for example, check incoming goods for quality and quantity encourages more care and attention to detail than having the person who placed the order do the checking. Added protection can result from identifying a third person to approve payment of the invoice. A company can even designate a fourth person with authority to write checks as another protective measure.

Point: There's a new security device—a person's ECG (electrocardiogram) reading—that is as unique as a fingerprint and a lot harder to lose or steal than a PIN. ECGs can be read through fingertip touches. An ECG also shows that a living person is actually there, whereas fingerprint and facial recognition software can be fooled.

Apply Technological Controls Cash registers, check protectors, time clocks, and personal identification scanners are examples of devices that can improve internal control. Technology often improves the effectiveness of controls. A cash register with a locked-in tape or electronic file makes a record of each cash sale. A check protector perforates the amount of a check into its face and makes it difficult to alter the amount. A time clock registers the exact time an employee both arrives at and departs from the job. Mechanical change and currency counters quickly and accurately count amounts, and personal scanners limit access to only authorized individuals. Each of these and other technological controls are an effective part of many internal control systems.

Decision Insight

About Face Face-recognition software snaps a digital picture of the face and converts key facial features—say, the distance between the eyes—into a series of numerical values. These can be stored on an ID or ATM card as a simple bar code to prohibit unauthorized access. ■

Perform Regular and Independent Reviews Changes in personnel, stress of time pressures, and technological advances present opportunities for shortcuts and lapses. To counter these factors, regular reviews of internal control systems are needed to ensure that procedures are followed. These reviews are preferably done by internal auditors not directly involved in the activities. Their impartial perspective encourages an evaluation of the efficiency as well as the effectiveness of the internal control system. Many companies also pay for audits by independent, external auditors. These external auditors test the company's financial records to give an opinion as to whether its financial statements are presented fairly. Before external auditors decide on how much testing is needed, they evaluate the effectiveness of the internal control system. This evaluation is often helpful to a client.

Decision Maker Answer — p. 343

Entrepreneur As owner of a start-up information services company, you hire a systems analyst. One of her first recommendations is to require all employees to take at least one week of vacation per year. Why would she recommend a "forced vacation" policy? ■

Technology and Internal Control

The fundamental principles of internal control are relevant no matter what the technological state of the accounting system, from purely manual to fully automated systems. Technology impacts an internal control system in several important ways. Perhaps the most obvious is that technology allows us quicker access to databases and information. Used effectively, technology greatly improves managers' abilities to monitor and control business activities. This section describes some technological impacts we must be alert to.

Point: Information on Internet fraud can be found at these Websites:
sec.gov/investor/pubs/cyberfraud.htm
ftc.gov/bcp/consumer.shtm
www.fraud.org

Reduced Processing Errors Technologically advanced systems reduce the number of errors in processing information. Provided the software and data entry are correct, the risk of mechanical and mathematical errors is nearly eliminated. However, we must remember that erroneous software or data entry does exist. Also, less human involvement in data processing can cause data entry errors to go undiscovered. Moreover, errors in software can produce consistent but erroneous processing of transactions. Continually checking and monitoring all types of systems are important.

Point: Evidence of any internal control failure for a company reduces user confidence in its financial statements.

More Extensive Testing of Records A company's review and audit of electronic records can include more extensive testing when information is easily and rapidly accessed. When accounting records are kept manually, auditors and others likely select only small samples of data to test. When data are accessible with computer technology, however, auditors can quickly analyze large samples or even the entire database.

Limited Evidence of Processing Many data processing steps are increasingly done by computer. Accordingly, fewer hard-copy items of documentary evidence are available for review. Yet technologically advanced systems can provide new evidence. They can, for instance, record who made the entries, the date and time, the source of the entry, and so on. Technology can also be designed to require the use of passwords or other identification before access to the system is granted. This means that internal control depends more on the design and operation of the information system and less on the analysis of its resulting documents.

Point: We look to several sources when assessing a company's internal controls. Sources include the auditor's report, management report on controls (if available), management discussion and analysis, and financial press.

Crucial Separation of Duties Technological advances in accounting information systems often yield some job eliminations or consolidations. While those who remain have the special skills necessary to operate advanced programs and equipment, a company with a reduced workforce risks losing its crucial separation of duties. The company must establish ways to control and monitor employees to minimize risk of error and fraud. For instance, the person who designs and programs the information system must not be the one who operates it. The company must also separate control over programs and files from the activities related to cash receipts and disbursements. For instance, a computer operator should not control check-writing activities. Achieving acceptable separation of duties can be especially difficult and costly in small companies with few employees.

Point: COSO organizes control components into five types:
- Control environment
- Control activities
- Risk assessment
- Monitoring
- Information and communication

Increased E-Commerce Technology has encouraged the growth of e-commerce. Amazon.com and eBay are examples of companies that have successfully exploited e-commerce. Most companies have some e-commerce transactions. All such transactions involve at least three risks. (1) *Credit card number theft* is a risk of using, transmitting, and storing such data online. This increases the cost of e-commerce. (2) *Computer viruses* are malicious programs that attach themselves to innocent files for purposes of infecting and harming other files and programs. (3) *Impersonation* online can result in charges of sales to bogus accounts, purchases of inappropriate materials, and the unknowing giving up of confidential information to hackers. Companies use both firewalls and encryption to

"Worst case of identity theft I've ever seen!"

combat some of these risks—firewalls are points of entry to a system that require passwords to continue, and encryption is a mathematical process to rearrange contents that cannot be read without the process code. Nearly 5% of Americans already report being victims of identity theft, and roughly 10 million say their privacy has been compromised.

Decision Insight

Cheery Fraud Victim Certified Fraud Examiners Website reports the following: Andrew Cameron stole Jacqueline Boanson's credit card. Cameron headed to the racetrack and promptly charged two bets for $150 on the credit card—winning $400. Unfortunately for Cameron the racetrack refused to pay him cash as its internal control policy is to credit winnings from bets made on a credit card to that same card. Cameron was later nabbed; and the racetrack let Ms. Boanson keep the winnings.

Limitations of Internal Control

All internal control policies and procedures have limitations that usually arise from either (1) the human element or (2) the cost–benefit principle.

Internal control policies and procedures are applied by people. This human element creates several potential limitations that we can categorize as either (1) human error or (2) human fraud. *Human error* can occur from negligence, fatigue, misjudgment, or confusion. *Human fraud* involves intent by people to defeat internal controls, such as *management override,* for personal gain. Fraud also includes collusion to thwart the separation of duties. The human element highlights the importance of establishing an *internal control environment* to convey management's commitment to internal control policies and procedures. Human fraud is driven by the *triple-threat* of fraud:

- **Opportunity**—refers to internal control deficiencies in the workplace.
- **Pressure**—refers to financial, family, society, and other stresses to succeed.
- **Rationalization**—refers to employees justifying fraudulent behavior.

The second major limitation on internal control is the *cost–benefit principle,* which dictates that the costs of internal controls must not exceed their benefits. Analysis of costs and benefits must consider all factors, including the impact on morale. Most companies, for instance, have a legal right to read employees' e-mails, yet companies seldom exercise that right unless they are confronted with evidence of potential harm to the company. The same holds for drug testing, phone tapping, and hidden cameras. The bottom line is that managers must establish internal control policies and procedures with a net benefit to the company.

Point: Cybercrime.gov pursues computer and intellectual property crimes, including that of e-commerce.

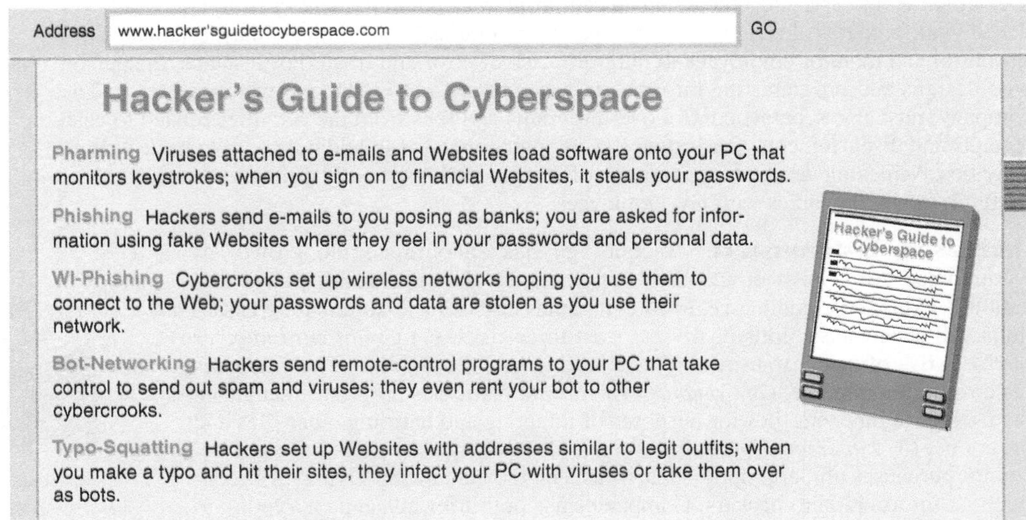

Quick Check Answers — p. 343 

1. Principles of internal control suggest that (choose one): (*a*) Responsibility for a series of related transactions (such as placing orders, receiving and paying for merchandise) should be assigned to one employee; (*b*) Responsibility for individual tasks should be shared by more than one employee so that one serves as a check on the other; or (*c*) Employees who handle considerable cash and easily transferable assets should be bonded.
2. What are some impacts of computing technology on internal control?

CONTROL OF CASH

Cash is a necessary asset of every company. Most companies also own *cash equivalents* (defined below), which are assets similar to cash. Cash and cash equivalents are the most liquid of all assets and are easily hidden and moved. An effective system of internal controls protects these assets and it should meet three basic guidelines:

1. Handling cash is separate from recordkeeping of cash.
2. Cash receipts are promptly deposited in a bank.
3. Cash disbursements are made by check.

The first guideline applies separation of duties to minimize errors and fraud. When duties are separated, two or more people must collude to steal cash and conceal this action in the accounting records. The second guideline uses immediate (say, daily) deposits of all cash receipts to produce a timely independent record of the cash received. It also reduces the likelihood of cash theft (or loss) and the risk that an employee could personally use the money before depositing it. The third guideline uses payments by check to develop an independent bank record of cash disbursements. This guideline also reduces the risk of cash theft (or loss).

This section begins with definitions of cash and cash equivalents. Discussion then focuses on controls and accounting for both cash receipts and disbursements. The exact procedures used to achieve control over cash vary across companies. They depend on factors such as company size, number of employees, volume of cash transactions, and sources of cash.

Cash, Cash Equivalents, and Liquidity

C2 Define cash and cash equivalents and explain how to report them.

Good accounting systems help in managing the amount of cash and controlling who has access to it. Cash is the usual means of payment when paying for assets, services, or liabilities. **Liquidity** refers to a company's ability to pay for its near-term obligations. Cash and similar assets are called **liquid assets** because they can be readily used to settle such obligations. A company needs liquid assets to effectively operate.

Cash includes currency and coins along with the amounts on deposit in bank accounts, checking accounts (called *demand deposits*), and many savings accounts (called *time deposits*). Cash also includes items that are acceptable for deposit in these accounts such as customer checks, cashier's checks, certified checks, and money orders. **Cash equivalents** are short-term, highly liquid investment assets meeting two criteria: (1) readily convertible to a known cash amount and (2) sufficiently close to their due date so that their market value is not sensitive to interest rate changes. Only investments purchased within three months of their due date usually satisfy these criteria. Examples of cash equivalents are short-term investments in assets such as U.S. Treasury bills and money market funds. To increase their return, many companies invest idle cash in cash equivalents. Most companies combine cash equivalents with cash as a single item on the balance sheet.

Point: The most liquid assets are usually reported first on a balance sheet; the least liquid assets are reported last.

Point: **Google** reports cash and cash equivalents of $10,198 million in its balance sheet. This amount makes up nearly 25% of its total assets.

Cash Management

When companies fail, one of the most common causes is their inability to manage cash. Companies must plan both cash receipts and cash payments. The goals of cash management are twofold:

1. Plan cash receipts to meet cash payments when due.
2. Keep a minimum level of cash necessary to operate.

The *treasurer* of the company is responsible for cash management. Effective cash management involves applying the following cash management principles.

- **Encourage collection of receivables.** The more quickly customers and others pay the company, the more quickly that company can use the money. Some companies have cash-only sales policies. Others might offer discounts for payments received early.
- **Delay payment of liabilities.** The more delayed a company is in paying others, the more time it has to use the money. Some companies regularly wait to pay their bills until the last possible day allowed—although, a company must take care not to hurt its credit standing.
- **Keep only necessary levels of assets.** The less money tied up in idle assets, the more money to invest in productive assets. Some companies maintain *just-in-time* inventory; meaning they plan inventory to be available at the same time orders are filled. Others might lease out excess warehouse space or rent equipment instead of buying it.
- **Plan expenditures.** Money should be spent only when it is available. Companies must look at seasonal and business cycles to plan expenditures.
- **Invest excess cash.** Excess cash earns no return and should be invested. Excess cash from seasonal cycles can be placed in a bank account or other short-term investment for income. Excess cash beyond what's needed for regular business should be invested in productive assets like factories and inventories.

Decision Insight

Days' Cash Expense Coverage The ratio of *cash (and cash equivalents) to average daily cash expenses* indicates the number of days a company can operate without additional cash inflows. It reflects on company liquidity and on the potential of excess cash.

Control of Cash Receipts

P1 Apply internal control to cash receipts and disbursements.

Internal control of cash receipts ensures that cash received is properly recorded and deposited. Cash receipts can arise from transactions such as cash sales, collections of customer accounts, receipts of interest earned, bank loans, sales of assets, and owner investments. This section explains internal control over two important types of cash receipts: over-the-counter and by mail.

Over-the-Counter Cash Receipts For purposes of internal control, over-the-counter cash receipts from sales should be recorded on a cash register at the time of each sale. To help ensure that correct amounts are entered, each register should be located so customers can read the amounts entered. Clerks also should be required to enter each sale before wrapping merchandise and to give the customer a receipt for each sale. The design of each cash register should provide a permanent, locked-in record of each transaction. In many systems, the register is directly linked with computing and accounting services. Less advanced registers simply print a record of each transaction on a paper tape or electronic file locked inside the register.

Proper internal control prescribes that custody over cash should be separate from its recordkeeping. For over-the-counter cash receipts, this separation begins with the cash sale. The clerk who has access to cash in the register should not have access to its locked-in record. At the end of the clerk's work period, the clerk should count the cash in the register, record the amount, and turn over the cash and a record of its amount to the company cashier. The cashier, like the clerk, has access to the cash but should not have access to accounting records (or the register tape or file). A third employee, often a supervisor, compares the record of total register transactions (or the register tape or file) with the cash receipts reported by the cashier. This record is the basis for a journal entry recording over-the-counter cash receipts. The third employee has access to the records for cash but not to the actual cash. The clerk and the cashier have access to cash but not to the accounting records. None of them can make a mistake or divert cash without the difference being revealed—see the following diagram.

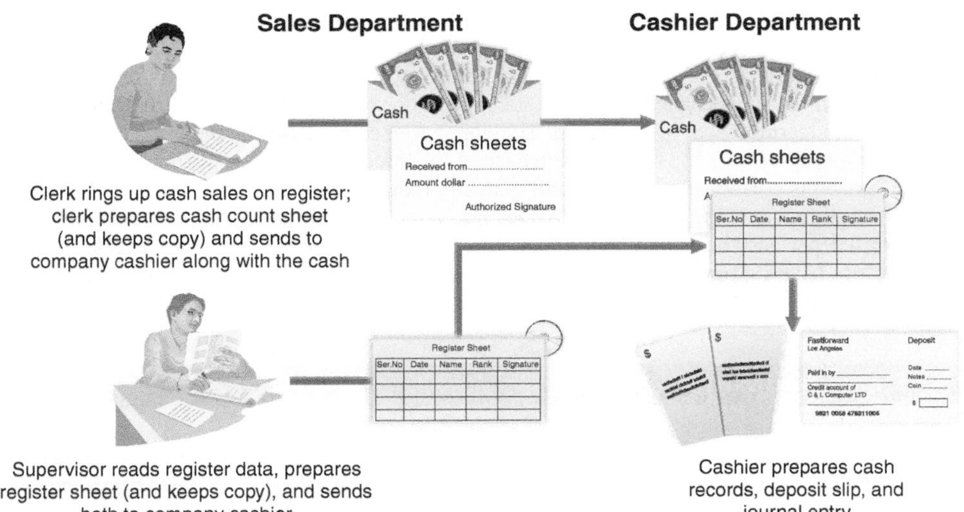

Cash over and short. Sometimes errors in making change are discovered from differences between the cash in a cash register and the record of the amount of cash receipts. Although a clerk is careful, one or more customers can be given too much or too little change. This means that at the end of a work period, the cash in a cash register might not equal the record of cash receipts. This difference is reported in the **Cash Over and Short** account, also called *Cash Short and Over,* which is an income statement account recording the income effects of cash overages and cash shortages. To illustrate, if a cash register's record shows $550 but the count of cash in the register is $555, the entry to record cash sales and its overage is

Point: Retailers often require cashiers to restrictively endorse checks immediately on receipt by stamping them "For deposit only."

Cash	555	
Cash Over and Short		5
Sales		550
To record cash sales and a cash overage.		

Assets = Liabilities + Equity
+555 + 5
+550

On the other hand, if a cash register's record shows $625 but the count of cash in the register is $621, the entry to record cash sales and its shortage is

Cash	621	
Cash Over and Short	4	
Sales		625
To record cash sales and a cash shortage.		

Assets = Liabilities + Equity
+621 − 4
+625

Since customers are more likely to dispute being shortchanged than being given too much change, the Cash Over and Short account usually has a debit balance at the end of an accounting period. A debit balance reflects an expense. It is reported on the income statement as part of general and administrative expenses. (Since the amount is usually small, it is often combined with other small expenses and reported as part of *miscellaneous expenses*—or as part of *miscellaneous revenues* if it has a credit balance.)

Point: Merchants begin a business day with a *change fund* in their cash register. The accounting for a change fund is similar to that for petty cash, including that for cash shortages or overages.

Cash Receipts by Mail Control of cash receipts that arrive through the mail starts with the person who opens the mail. Preferably, two people are assigned the task of, and are present for, opening the mail. In this case, theft of cash receipts by mail requires collusion between these two employees. Specifically, the person(s) opening the mail enters a list (in triplicate) of money received. This list should contain a record of each sender's name, the amount, and an explanation of why the money is sent. The first copy is sent with the money to the cashier. A second copy is sent to the recordkeeper in the accounting area. A third copy is kept by the

Point: Collusion implies that two or more individuals are knowledgeable or involved with the activities of the other(s).

clerk(s) who opened the mail. The cashier deposits the money in a bank, and the recordkeeper records the amounts received in the accounting records.

This process reflects good internal control. That is, when the bank balance is reconciled by another person (explained later in the chapter), errors or acts of fraud by the mail clerks, the cashier, or the recordkeeper are revealed. They are revealed because the bank's record of cash deposited must agree with the records from each of the three. Moreover, if the mail clerks do not report all receipts correctly, customers will question their account balances. If the cashier does not deposit all receipts, the bank balance does not agree with the recordkeeper's cash balance. The recordkeeper and the person who reconciles the bank balance do not have access to cash and therefore have no opportunity to divert cash to themselves. This system makes errors and fraud highly unlikely. The exception is employee collusion.

Decision Insight

Perpetual Accounting Walmart uses a network of information links with its point-of-sale cash registers to coordinate sales, purchases, and distribution. Its supercenters, for instance, ring up 15,000 separate sales on heavy days. By using cash register information, the company can fix pricing mistakes quickly and capitalize on sales trends. ■

Control of Cash Disbursements

Control of cash disbursements is especially important as most large thefts occur from payment of fictitious invoices. One key to controlling cash disbursements is to require all expenditures to be made by check. The only exception is small payments made from petty cash. Another key is to deny access to the accounting records to anyone other than the owner who has the authority to sign checks. A small business owner often signs checks and knows from personal contact that the items being paid for are actually received. This arrangement is impossible in large businesses. Instead, internal control procedures must be substituted for personal contact. Such procedures are designed to assure the check signer that the obligations recorded are properly incurred and should be paid. This section describes these and other internal control procedures, including the voucher system and petty cash system. A method for management of cash disbursements for purchases is described in Appendix 8B.

Decision Insight

Cash Budget Projected cash receipts and cash disbursements are often summarized in a *cash budget*. Provided that sufficient cash exists for effective operations, companies wish to minimize the cash they hold because of its risk of theft and its low return versus other investment opportunities. ■

Voucher System of Control A **voucher system** is a set of procedures and approvals designed to control cash disbursements and the acceptance of obligations. The voucher system of control establishes procedures for

- Verifying, approving, and recording obligations for eventual cash disbursement.
- Issuing checks for payment of verified, approved, and recorded obligations.

A reliable voucher system follows standard procedures for every transaction. This applies even when multiple purchases are made from the same supplier.

A voucher system's control over cash disbursements begins when a company incurs an obligation that will result in payment of cash. A key factor in this system is that only approved departments and individuals are authorized to incur such obligations. The system often limits the type of obligations that a department or individual can incur. In a large retail store, for instance, only a purchasing department should be authorized to incur obligations for merchandise inventory. Another key factor is that procedures for purchasing, receiving, and paying for merchandise are divided among several departments (or individuals). These departments include the one requesting the purchase, the purchasing department, the receiving department, and the accounting department. To coordinate and control responsibilities of these departments, a company uses

Point: MCI, formerly WorldCom, paid a whopping $500 million in SEC fines for accounting fraud. Among the charges were that it inflated earnings by as much as $10 billion. Its CEO, Bernard Ebbers, was sentenced to 25 years.

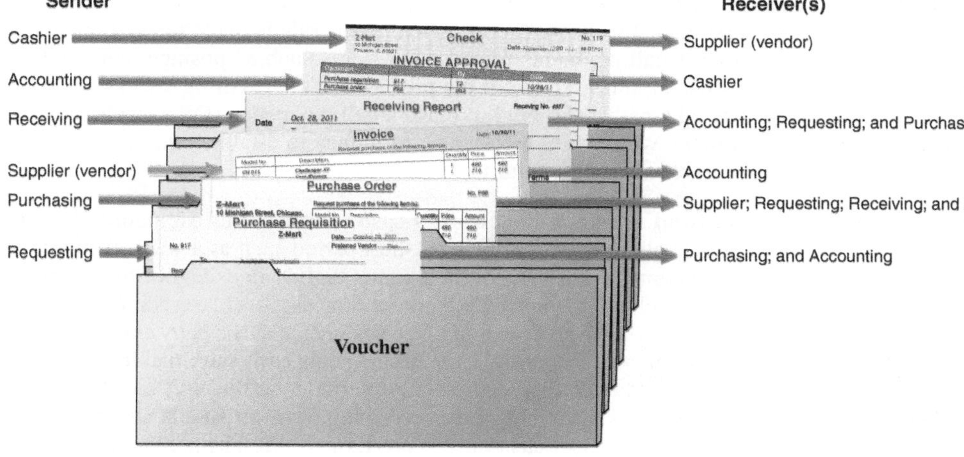

EXHIBIT 8.1

Document Flow in a Voucher System

several different business documents. Exhibit 8.1 shows how documents are accumulated in a **voucher,** which is an internal document (or file) used to accumulate information to control cash disbursements and to ensure that a transaction is properly recorded. This specific example begins with a *purchase requisition* and concludes with a *check* drawn against cash. Appendix 8A describes the documentation and verification necessary for a voucher system of control. It also describes the internal control objective served by each document.

A voucher system should be applied not only to purchases of inventory but to all expenditures. To illustrate, when a company receives a monthly telephone bill, it should review and verify the charges, prepare a voucher (file), and insert the bill. This transaction is then recorded with a journal entry. If the amount is currently due, a check is issued. If not, the voucher is filed for payment on its due date. If no voucher is prepared, verifying the invoice and its amount after several days or weeks can be difficult. Also, without records, a dishonest employee could collude with a dishonest supplier to get more than one payment for an obligation, payment for excessive amounts, or payment for goods and services not received. An effective voucher system helps prevent such frauds.

Point: A *voucher* is an internal document (or file).

Point: The basic purposes of paper and electronic documents are similar. However, the internal control system must change to reflect different risks, including confidential and competitive-sensitive information that is at greater risk in electronic systems.

Decision Insight

Cyber Setup The FTC is on the cutting edge of cyber-sleuthing. Opportunists in search of easy money are lured to WeMarket4U.net/SundaeStation and WeMarket4U.net/FatFoe. Take the bait and you get warned. The top 5 fraud complaints as compiled by the Bureau of Consumer Protection are shown to the right.

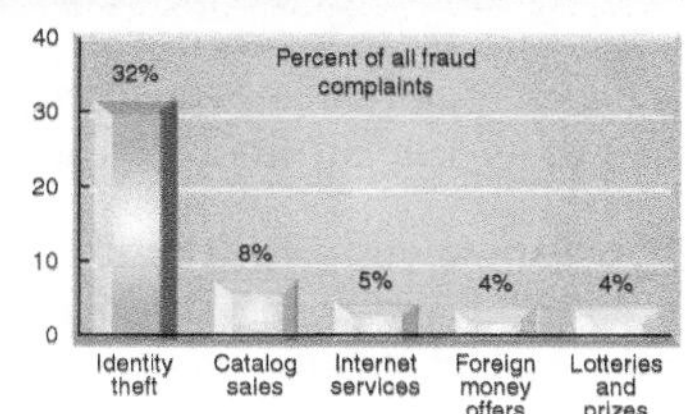

Quick Check

Answers — p. 343

3. Why must a company hold liquid assets?
4. Why does a company hold cash equivalent assets in addition to cash?
5. Identify at least two assets that are classified as cash equivalents.
6. Good internal control procedures for cash include which of the following? (*a*) All cash disbursements, other than those for very small amounts, are made by check; (*b*) One employee counts cash received from sales and promptly deposits cash receipts; or (*c*) Cash receipts by mail are opened by one employee who is then responsible for recording and depositing them.
7. Should all companies require a voucher system? At what point in a company's growth would you recommend a voucher system?

P2 Explain and record petty cash fund transactions.

Petty Cash System of Control A basic principle for controlling cash disbursements is that all payments must be made by check. An exception to this rule is made for *petty cash disbursements,* which are the small payments required for items such as postage, courier fees, minor repairs, and low-cost supplies. To avoid the time and cost of writing checks for small amounts, a company sets up a petty cash fund to make small payments. (**Petty cash** activities are part of an *imprest system,* which designates advance money to establish the fund, to withdraw from the fund, and to reimburse the fund.)

Operating a petty cash fund. Establishing a petty cash fund requires estimating the total amount of small payments likely to be made during a short period such as a week or month. A check is then drawn by the company cashier for an amount slightly in excess of this estimate. This check is recorded with a debit to the Petty Cash account (an asset) and a credit to Cash. The check is cashed, and the currency is given to an employee designated as the *petty cashier* or *petty cash custodian.* The petty cashier is responsible for keeping this cash safe, making payments from the fund, and keeping records of it in a secure place referred to as the *petty cashbox.*

Point: A petty cash fund is used only for business expenses.

When each cash disbursement is made, the person receiving payment should sign a prenumbered *petty cash receipt,* also called *petty cash ticket*—see Exhibit 8.2. The petty cash receipt is then placed in the petty cashbox with the remaining money. Under this system, the sum of all receipts plus the remaining cash equals the total fund amount. A $100 petty cash fund, for instance, contains any combination of cash and petty cash receipts that totals $100 (examples are $80 cash plus $20 in receipts, or $10 cash plus $90 in receipts). Each disbursement reduces cash and increases the amount of receipts in the petty cashbox.

EXHIBIT 8.2

Petty Cash Receipt

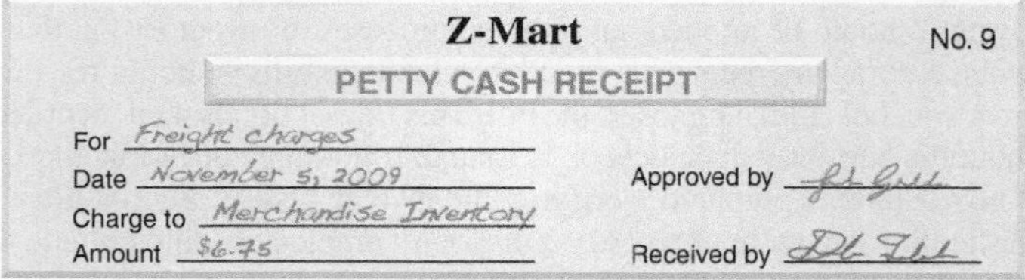

Z-Mart No. 9

PETTY CASH RECEIPT

For Freight charges
Date November 5, 2009
Charge to Merchandise Inventory
Amount $6.75
Approved by
Received by

Point: Petty cash receipts with either no signature or a forged signature usually indicate misuse of petty cash. Companies respond with surprise petty cash counts for verification.

The petty cash fund should be reimbursed when it is nearing zero and at the end of an accounting period when financial statements are prepared. For this purpose, the petty cashier sorts the paid receipts by the type of expense or account and then totals the receipts. The petty cashier presents all paid receipts to the company cashier, who stamps all receipts *paid* so they cannot be reused, files them for recordkeeping, and gives the petty cashier a check for their sum. When this check is cashed and the money placed in the cashbox, the total money in the cashbox is restored to its original amount. The fund is now ready for a new cycle of petty cash payments.

Illustrating a petty cash fund. To illustrate, assume Z-Mart establishes a petty cash fund on November 1 and designates one of its office employees as the petty cashier. A $75 check is drawn, cashed, and the proceeds given to the petty cashier. The entry to record the setup of this petty cash fund is

Assets	=	Liabilities	+	Equity
+75				
−75				

Date	Account	Debit	Credit
Nov. 1	Petty Cash	75	
	Cash		75
	To establish a petty cash fund.		

Point: Reducing or eliminating a petty cash fund requires a credit to Petty Cash.

Point: Although *individual* petty cash disbursements are not evidenced by a check, the initial petty cash fund is evidenced by a check, and later petty cash expenditures are evidenced by a check to replenish them *in total.*

After the petty cash fund is established, the Petty Cash account is not debited or credited again unless the amount of the fund is changed. (A fund should be increased if it requires reimbursement too frequently. On the other hand, if the fund is too large, some of its money should be redeposited in the Cash account.)

Next, assume that Z-Mart's petty cashier makes several November payments from petty cash. Each person who received payment is required to sign a receipt. On November 27, after making a $26.50 cash payment for tile cleaning, only $3.70 cash remains in the fund. The petty cashier then summarizes and totals the petty cash receipts as shown in Exhibit 8.3.

EXHIBIT 8.3
Petty Cash Payments Report

Z-MART Petty Cash Payments Report			
Miscellaneous Expenses			
Nov. 2	Cleaning of LCD panels	$20.00	
Nov. 27	Tile cleaning	26.50	$ 46.50
Merchandise Inventory (transportation-in)			
Nov. 5	Transport of merchandise purchased	6.75	
Nov. 20	Transport of merchandise purchased	8.30	15.05
Delivery Expense			
Nov. 18	Customer's package delivered		5.00
Office Supplies Expense			
Nov. 15	Purchase of office supplies immediately used		4.75
Total			$71.30

Point: This report can also include receipt number and names of those who approved and received cash payment (see Demo Problem 2).

The petty cash payments report and all receipts are given to the company cashier in exchange for a $71.30 check to reimburse the fund. The petty cashier cashes the check and puts the $71.30 cash in the petty cashbox. The company records this reimbursement as follows.

Nov. 27	Miscellaneous Expenses	46.50	
	Merchandise Inventory	15.05	
	Delivery Expense	5.00	
	Office Supplies Expense	4.75	
	Cash		71.30
	To reimburse petty cash.		

Assets	=	Liabilities	+	Equity
−71.30				−46.50
				−15.05
				−5.00
				−4.75

A petty cash fund is usually reimbursed at the end of an accounting period so that expenses are recorded in the proper period, even if the fund is not low on money. If the fund is not reimbursed at the end of a period, the financial statements would show both an overstated cash asset and understated expenses (or assets) that were paid out of petty cash. Some companies do not reimburse the petty cash fund at the end of each period under the notion that this amount is immaterial to users of financial statements.

Point: To avoid errors in recording petty cash reimbursement, follow these steps: (1) prepare payments report, (2) compute cash needed by subtracting cash remaining from total fund amount, (3) record entry, and (4) check "Dr. = Cr." in entry. Any difference is Cash Over and Short.

Increasing or decreasing a petty cash fund. A decision to increase or decrease a petty cash fund is often made when reimbursing it. To illustrate, assume Z-Mart decides to *increase* its petty cash fund from $75 to $100 on November 27 when it reimburses the fund. The entries required are to (1) reimburse the fund as usual (see the preceding November 27 entry) and (2) increase the fund amount as follows.

Nov. 27	Petty Cash	25	
	Cash		25
	To increase the petty cash fund amount.		

Alternatively, if Z-Mart *decreases* the petty cash fund from $75 to $55 on November 27, the entry is to (1) credit Petty Cash for $20 (decreasing the fund from $75 to $55) and (2) debit Cash for $20 (reflecting the $20 transfer from Petty Cash to Cash).

Cash over and short. Sometimes a petty cashier fails to get a receipt for payment or overpays for the amount due. When this occurs and the fund is later reimbursed, the petty cash payments report plus the cash remaining will not total to the fund balance. This mistake causes the fund to be *short*. This shortage is recorded as an expense in the reimbursing entry with a debit to the Cash Over and Short account. (An overage in the petty cash fund is recorded with a credit to Cash Over and Short in the reimbursing entry.) To illustrate, prepare the June 1 entry

Summary of Petty Cash Accounting

Event	Petty Cash	Cash	Expenses
Set up fund	Dr.	Cr.	—
Reimburse fund	—	Cr.	Dr.
Increase fund	Dr.	Cr.	—
Decrease fund	Cr.	Dr.	—

to reimburse a $200 petty cash fund when its payments report shows $178 in miscellaneous expenses and $15 cash remains.

$200 Petty Cash Fund

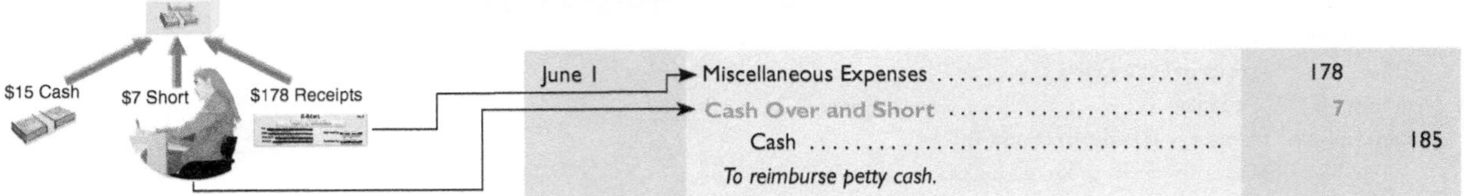

June 1	Miscellaneous Expenses	178	
	Cash Over and Short	7	
	Cash		185
	To reimburse petty cash.		

Decision Insight

Warning Signs There are clues to internal control violations. Warning signs from accounting include (1) an increase in customer refunds—could be fake, (2) missing documents—could be used for fraud, (3) differences between bank deposits and cash receipts—could be cash embezzled, and (4) delayed recording—could reflect fraudulent records. Warning signs from employees include (1) lifestyle change—could be embezzlement, (2) too close with suppliers—could signal fraudulent transactions, and (3) failure to leave job, even for vacations—could conceal fraudulent activities.

Quick Check

Answers — p. 343

8. Why are some cash payments made from a petty cash fund and not by check?
9. Why should a petty cash fund be reimbursed at the end of an accounting period?
10. Identify at least two results of reimbursing a petty cash fund.

BANKING ACTIVITIES AS CONTROLS

Banks (and other financial institutions) provide many services, including helping companies control cash. Banks safeguard cash, provide detailed and independent records of cash transactions, and are a source of cash financing. This section describes these services and the documents provided by banking activities that increase managers' control over cash.

Basic Bank Services

This section explains basic bank services—such as the bank account, the bank deposit, and checking—that contribute to the control of cash.

Bank Account, Deposit, and Check A *bank account* is a record set up by a bank for a customer. It permits a customer to deposit money for safekeeping and helps control withdrawals. To limit access to a bank account, all persons authorized to write checks on the account must sign a **signature card,** which bank employees use to verify signatures on checks. Many companies have more than one bank account to serve different needs and to handle special transactions such as payroll.

Point: Online banking services include the ability to stop payment on a check, move money between accounts, get up-to-date balances, and identify cleared checks and deposits.

Each bank deposit is supported by a **deposit ticket,** which lists items such as currency, coins, and checks deposited along with their corresponding dollar amounts. The bank gives the customer a copy of the deposit ticket or a deposit receipt as proof of the deposit. Exhibit 8.4 shows one type of deposit ticket.

To withdraw money from an account, the depositor can use a **check,** which is a document signed by the depositor instructing the bank to pay a specified amount of money to a designated recipient. A check involves three parties: a *maker* who signs the check, a *payee* who is the recipient, and a *bank* (or *payer*) on which the check is drawn. The bank provides a depositor the checks that are serially numbered and imprinted with the name and address of both the depositor and bank. Both checks and deposit tickets are imprinted with identification codes in magnetic ink

EXHIBIT 8.4

Deposit Ticket

Front

DEPOSIT TICKET — Date October 2 20 11

VideoBuster Company
901 Main Street
Hillcrest, NY 11749

CASH	CURRENCY	36	50
	COIN		
LIST CHECKS SINGLY			
TOTAL FROM OTHER SIDE		203	50
TOTAL		240	00
NET DEPOSIT		240	00

USE OTHER SIDE FOR ADDITIONAL LISTINGS. BE SURE EACH ITEM IS PROPERLY ENDORSED

Deposit checks
(Memo)

99-DT/101

FN First National
Hillcrest, New York 11750

Checks and other items are received for deposit subject to the provisions of the uniform commercial code or any applicable collection agreement

|:012410497||: 457923 • 02 75

Back

CHECKS LIST SINGLY		DOLLARS	CENTS
1	14-287/939	90	50
2	82-759/339	82	80
3	76-907/919	30	20
4			
5			
6			
7			
8			
9			
10			
11			
12			
13			
14			
15			
16			
17			
18			
19			
20			
21			
22			
TOTAL		203	50

ENTER TOTAL ON THE FRONT OF THIS TICKET

for computer processing. Exhibit 8.5 shows one type of check. It is accompanied with an optional *remittance advice* explaining the payment. When a remittance advice is unavailable, the *memo* line is often used for a brief explanation.

Electronic Funds Transfer **Electronic funds transfer (EFT)** is the electronic transfer of cash from one party to another. No paper documents are necessary. Banks simply transfer cash from one account to another with a journal entry. Companies are increasingly using EFT

EXHIBIT 8.5

Check with Remittance Advice

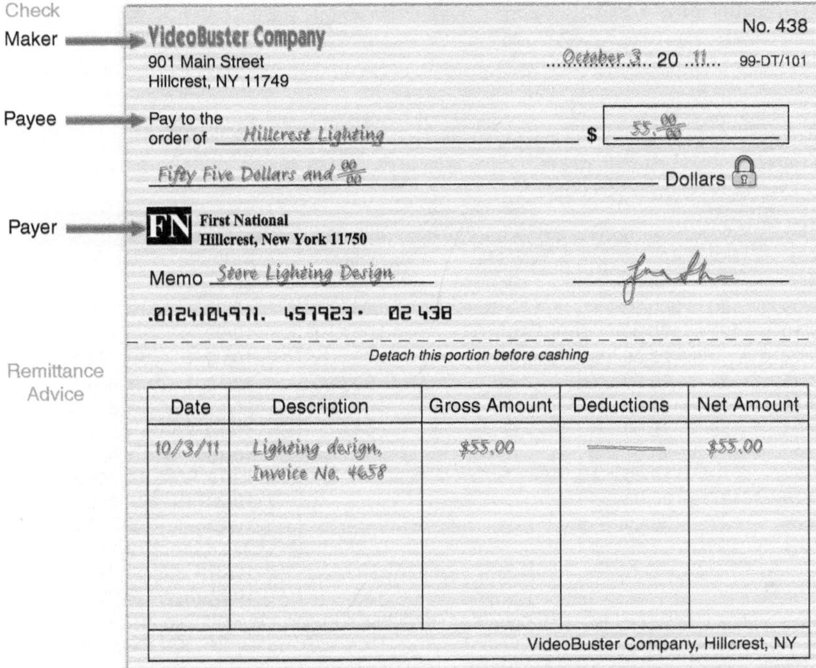

Check

Maker → VideoBuster Company
901 Main Street
Hillcrest, NY 11749

No. 438

October 3 20 11 99-DT/101

Payee → Pay to the order of Hillcrest Lighting $ 55.00

Fifty Five Dollars and 00/00 Dollars

Payer → FN First National
Hillcrest, New York 11750

Memo Store Lighting Design

.012410497|. 457923• 02 438

Detach this portion before cashing

Remittance Advice

Date	Description	Gross Amount	Deductions	Net Amount
10/3/11	Lighting design, Invoice No. 4658	$55.00	——	$55.00

VideoBuster Company, Hillcrest, NY

because of its convenience and low cost. For instance, it can cost up to 50 cents to process a check through the banking system, whereas EFT cost is near zero. We now commonly see items such as payroll, rent, utilities, insurance, and interest payments being handled by EFT. The bank statement lists cash withdrawals by EFT with the checks and other deductions. Cash receipts by EFT are listed with deposits and other additions. A bank statement is sometimes a depositor's only notice of an EFT. *Automated teller machines (ATMs)* are one form of EFT, which allows bank customers to deposit, withdraw, and transfer cash.

Bank Statement

Point: Good internal control is to deposit all cash receipts daily and make all payments for goods and services by check. This controls access to cash and creates an independent record of all cash activities.

Usually once a month, the bank sends each depositor a **bank statement** showing the activity in the account. Although a monthly statement is common, companies often regularly access information on their banking transactions. (Companies can choose to record any accounting adjustments required from the bank statement immediately or later, say, at the end of each day, week, month, or when reconciling a bank statement.) Different banks use different formats for their bank statements, but all of them include the following items of information:

1. Beginning-of-period balance of the depositor's account.
2. Checks and other debits decreasing the account during the period.
3. Deposits and other credits increasing the account during the period.
4. End-of-period balance of the depositor's account.

This information reflects the bank's records. Exhibit 8.6 shows one type of bank statement. Identify each of these four items in that statement. Part Ⓐ of Exhibit 8.6 summarizes changes in the account. Part Ⓑ lists paid checks along with other debits. Part Ⓒ lists deposits and credits to the account, and part Ⓓ shows the daily account balances.

In reading a bank statement note that a depositor's account is a liability on the bank's records. This is so because the money belongs to the depositor, not the bank. When a depositor increases

EXHIBIT 8.6

Bank Statement

FN First National
Hillcrest, New York 11750
Member FDIC

Bank Statement

VideoBuster Company
901 Main Street
Hillcrest, NY 11749

October 31, 2011
Statement Date

494 504 2
Account Number

Ⓐ

Previous Balance	Total Checks and Debits	Total Deposits and Credits	Current Balance
1,609.58	723.00	1,163.42	2,050.00

Ⓑ Checks and Debits

Date	No.	Amount
10/03	119	55.00
10/09	120	200.00
10/10	121	120.00
10/12		23.00 DM
10/14	122	70.00
10/16	123	25.00
10/23	125	15.00
10/25		20.00 NSF
		10.00 DM
10/26	127	50.00
10/29	128	135.00

Ⓒ Deposits and Credits

Date	Amount
10/02	240.00
10/09	180.00
10/15	100.00 EFT
10/16	150.00
10/23	485.00 CM
10/31	8.42 IN

Ⓓ Daily Balance

Date	Amount
10/01	1,609.58
10/02	1,849.58
10/03	1,794.58
10/09	1,774.58
10/10	1,654.58
10/12	1,631.58
10/14	1,561.58
10/15	1,661.58
10/16	1,786.58
10/23	2,256.58
10/25	2,226.58
10/26	2,176.58
10/29	2,041.58
10/31	2,050.00

Symbols: **CM**–Credit Memo **EC**–Error Correction **NSF**–Non-Sufficient Funds **SC**–Service Charge **DM**–Debit Memo **IN**–Interest Earned **EFT**–Electronic Funds Transfer **OD**–Overdraft

< Reconcile the account immediately. >

Point: Many banks separately report other debits and credits apart from checks and deposits.

the account balance, the bank records it with a *credit* to that liability account. This means that debit memos from the bank produce *credits* on the depositor's books, and credit memos from the bank produce *debits* on the depositor's books.

Enclosed with a bank statement is a list of the depositor's canceled checks (or the actual canceled checks) along with any debit or credit memoranda affecting the account. Increasingly, banks are showing canceled checks electronically via online access to accounts. **Canceled checks** are checks the bank has paid and deducted from the customer's account during the period. Other deductions that can appear on a bank statement include (1) service charges and fees assessed by the bank, (2) checks deposited that are uncollectible, (3) corrections of previous errors, (4) withdrawals through automated teller machines (ATMs), and (5) periodic payments arranged in advance by a depositor. (Most company checking accounts do not allow ATM withdrawals because of the company's desire to make all disbursements by check.) Except for service charges, the bank notifies the depositor of each deduction with a debit memorandum when the bank reduces the balance. A copy of each debit memorandum is usually sent with the statement (again, this information is often available earlier via online access and notifications).

Global: If cash is in more than one currency, a company usually translates these amounts into U.S. dollars using the exchange rate as of the balance sheet date. Also, a company must disclose any restrictions on cash accounts located outside the U.S.

Transactions that increase the depositor's account include amounts the bank collects on behalf of the depositor and the corrections of previous errors. Credit memoranda notify the depositor of all increases when they are recorded. A copy of each credit memorandum is often sent with the bank statement. Banks that pay interest on checking accounts often compute the amount of interest earned on the average cash balance and credit it to the depositor's account each period. In Exhibit 8.6, the bank credits $8.42 of interest to the account.

Bank Reconciliation

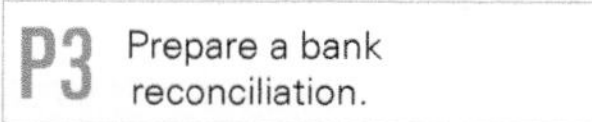

When a company deposits all cash receipts and makes all cash payments (except petty cash) by check, it can use the bank statement for proving the accuracy of its cash records. This is done using a **bank reconciliation,** which is a report explaining any differences between the checking account balance according to the depositor's records and the balance reported on the bank statement. The figure below reflects this process, which we describe in the following sections.

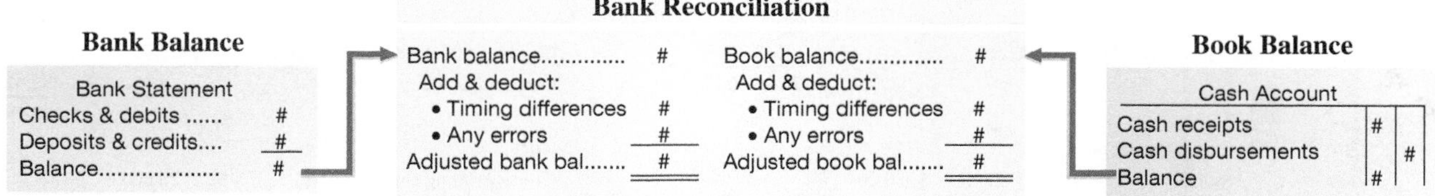

Purpose of Bank Reconciliation The balance of a checking account reported on the bank statement rarely equals the balance in the depositor's accounting records. This is usually due to information that one party has that the other does not. We must therefore prove the accuracy of both the depositor's records and those of the bank. This means we must *reconcile* the two balances and explain or account for any differences in them. Among the factors causing the bank statement balance to differ from the depositor's book balance are these:

- Outstanding checks. **Outstanding checks** are checks written (or drawn) by the depositor, deducted on the depositor's records, and sent to the payees but not yet received by the bank for payment at the bank statement date.
- Deposits in transit (also called outstanding deposits). **Deposits in transit** are deposits made and recorded by the depositor but not yet recorded on the bank statement. For example, companies can make deposits (in the night depository) at the end of a business day after the bank is closed. If such a deposit occurred on a bank statement date, it would not appear on this period's statement. The bank would record such a deposit on the next business day, and it would appear on the next period's bank statement. Deposits mailed to the bank near the end of a period also can be in transit and unrecorded when the statement is prepared.
- Deductions for uncollectible items and for services. A company sometimes deposits another party's check that is uncollectible (usually meaning the balance in that party's account is not large enough to cover the check). This check is called a *non-sufficient funds (NSF)* check. The bank would have initially credited the depositor's account for the amount of the

Forms of Check Fraud (CkFraud.org)

- Forged signatures—legitimate blank checks with fake payer signature
- Forged endorsements—stolen check that is endorsed and cashed by someone other than the payee
- Counterfeit checks—fraudulent checks with fake payer signature
- Altered checks—legitimate check altered (such as changed payee or amount) to benefit perpetrator
- Check kiting—deposit check from one bank account (without sufficient funds) into a second bank account

check. When the bank learns the check is uncollectible, it debits (reduces) the depositor's account for the amount of that check. The bank may also charge the depositor a fee for processing an uncollectible check and notify the depositor of the deduction by sending a debit memorandum. The depositor should record each deduction when a debit memorandum is received, but an entry is sometimes not made until the bank reconciliation is prepared. Other possible bank charges to a depositor's account that are first reported on a bank statement include printing new checks and service fees.

- **Additions for collections and for interest.** Banks sometimes act as collection agents for their depositors by collecting notes and other items. Banks can also receive electronic funds transfers to the depositor's account. When a bank collects an item, it is added to the depositor's account, less any service fee. The bank also sends a credit memorandum to notify the depositor of the transaction. When the memorandum is received, the depositor should record it; yet it sometimes remains unrecorded until the bank reconciliation is prepared. The bank statement also includes a credit for any interest earned.
- **Errors.** Both banks and depositors can make errors. Bank errors might not be discovered until the depositor prepares the bank reconciliation. Also, depositor errors are sometimes discovered when the bank balance is reconciled. Error testing includes: (a) comparing deposits on the bank statement with deposits in the accounting records and (b) comparing canceled checks on the bank statement with checks recorded in the accounting records.

Point: Small businesses with few employees often allow recordkeepers to both write checks and keep the general ledger. If this is done, it is essential that the owner do the bank reconciliation.

Point: The person preparing the bank reconciliation should not be responsible for processing cash receipts, managing checks, or maintaining cash records.

Illustration of a Bank Reconciliation We follow nine steps in preparing the bank reconciliation. It is helpful to refer to the bank reconciliation in Exhibit 8.7 when studying steps 1 through 9.

EXHIBIT 8.7

Bank Reconciliation

VIDEOBUSTER Bank Reconciliation October 31, 2011						
① Bank statement balance		$ 2,050.00		⑤ Book balance		$ 1,404.58
② Add				⑥ Add		
Deposit of Oct. 31 in transit		145.00		Collect $500 note less $15 fee	$485.00	
		2,195.00		Interest earned	8.42	493.42
③ Deduct						1,898.00
Outstanding checks				⑦ Deduct		
No. 124	$150.00			Check printing charge	23.00	
No. 126	200.00	350.00		NSF check plus service fee	30.00	53.00
④ Adjusted bank balance		$1,845.00		⑧ Adjusted book balance		$1,845.00

⑨ Balances are equal (reconciled)

1 Identify the bank statement balance of the cash account (*balance per bank*). VideoBuster's bank balance is $2,050.

2 Identify and list any unrecorded deposits and any bank errors understating the bank balance. Add them to the bank balance. VideoBuster's $145 deposit placed in the bank's night depository on October 31 is not recorded on its bank statement.

3 Identify and list any outstanding checks and any bank errors overstating the bank balance. Deduct them from the bank balance. VideoBuster's comparison of canceled checks with its books shows two checks outstanding: No. 124 for $150 and No. 126 for $200.

4 Compute the *adjusted bank balance,* also called the *corrected* or *reconciled balance.*

5 Identify the company's book balance of the cash account (*balance per book*). VideoBuster's book balance is $1,404.58.

6 Identify and list any unrecorded credit memoranda from the bank, any interest earned, and errors understating the book balance. Add them to the book balance. VideoBuster's bank statement includes a credit memorandum showing the bank collected a note receivable for the

Point: Outstanding checks are identified by comparing canceled checks on the bank statement with checks recorded. This includes identifying any outstanding checks listed on the *previous* period's bank reconciliation that are not included in the canceled checks on this period's bank statement.

company on October 23. The note's proceeds of $500 (minus a $15 collection fee) are credited to the company's account. VideoBuster's bank statement also shows a credit of $8.42 for interest earned on the average cash balance. There was no prior notification of this item, and it is not yet recorded.

7 Identify and list any unrecorded debit memoranda from the bank, any service charges, and errors overstating the book balance. Deduct them from the book balance. Debits on VideoBuster's bank statement that are not yet recorded include (a) a $23 charge for check printing and (b) an NSF check for $20 plus a related $10 processing fee. (The NSF check is dated October 16 and was included in the book balance.)

8 Compute the *adjusted book balance,* also called *corrected* or *reconciled balance.*

9 Verify that the two adjusted balances from steps 4 and 8 are equal. If so, they are reconciled. If not, check for accuracy and missing data to achieve reconciliation.

Point: Adjusting entries can be combined into one compound entry.

Adjusting Entries from a Bank Reconciliation A bank reconciliation often identifies unrecorded items that need recording by the company. In VideoBuster's reconciliation, the adjusted balance of $1,845 is the correct balance as of October 31. But the company's accounting records show a $1,404.58 balance. We must prepare journal entries to adjust the book balance to the correct balance. It is important to remember that only the items reconciling the *book balance* require adjustment. A review of Exhibit 8.7 indicates that four entries are required for VideoBuster.

Collection of note. The first entry is to record the proceeds of its note receivable collected by the bank less the expense of having the bank perform that service.

Oct. 31	Cash	485	
	Collection Expense	15	
	Notes Receivable		500
	To record the collection fee and proceeds for a note collected by the bank.		

Assets = Liabilities + Equity
+485 −15
−500

Interest earned. The second entry records interest credited to its account by the bank.

Oct. 31	Cash	8.42	
	Interest Revenue		8.42
	To record interest earned on the cash balance in the checking account.		

Assets = Liabilities + Equity
+8.42 +8.42

Check printing. The third entry records expenses for the check printing charge.

Oct. 31	Miscellaneous Expenses	23	
	Cash		23
	Check printing charge.		

Assets = Liabilities + Equity
−23 −23

NSF check. The fourth entry records the NSF check that is returned as uncollectible. The $20 check was originally received from T. Woods in payment of his account and then deposited. The bank charged $10 for handling the NSF check and deducted $30 total from VideoBuster's account. This means the entry must reverse the effects of the original entry made when the check was received and must record (add) the $10 bank fee.

Point: The company will try to collect the entire NSF amount of $30 from customer.

Oct. 31	Accounts Receivable—T. Woods	30	
	Cash		30
	To charge Woods' account for $20 NSF check and $10 bank fee.		

Assets = Liabilities + Equity
+30
−30

Point: The Demo Problem I shows an adjusting entry for an error correction.

Cash			
Unadj. bal.	1,404.58		
⑥	485.00	⑦	23.00
⑥	8.42	⑦	30.00
Adj. bal.	1,845.00		

After these four entries are recorded, the book balance of cash is adjusted to the correct amount of $1,845 (computed as $1,404.58 + $485 + $8.42 − $23 − $30). The Cash T-account to the side shows the same computation, where entries are keyed to the numerical codes in Exhibit 8.7.

Decision Insight

Fraud A survey reports that 74% of employees had 'personally seen' or had 'firsthand knowledge of' fraud or misconduct in their company within the past year. These employees also identified factors that would drive employees and managers to engage in misconduct. They cited pressures to meet targets, lack of standards, and other root causes—see graphic (KPMG 2009).

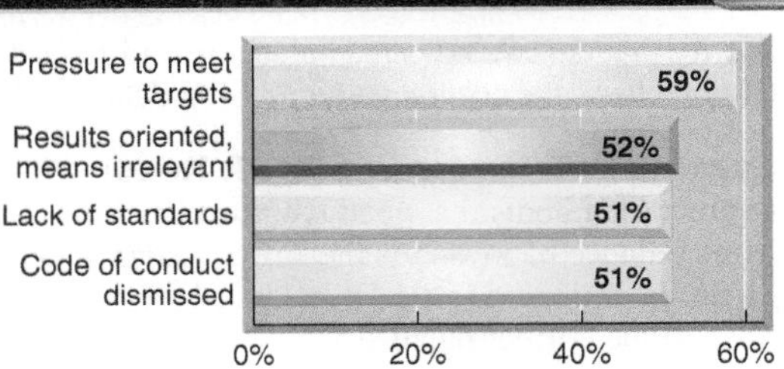

Quick Check

Answers – p. 344

11. What is a bank statement?

12. What is the meaning of the phrase *to reconcile a bank balance?*

13. Why do we reconcile the bank statement balance of cash and the depositor's book balance of cash?

14. List at least two items affecting the *bank balance* side of a bank reconciliation and indicate whether the items are added or subtracted.

15. List at least three items affecting the *book balance* side of a bank reconciliation and indicate whether the items are added or subtracted.

GLOBAL VIEW

This section discusses similarities and differences between U.S. GAAP and IFRS regarding internal controls and in the accounting and reporting of cash.

Internal Control Purposes, Principles, and Procedures Both U.S. GAAP and IFRS aim for high-quality financial reporting. That aim translates into enhanced internal controls worldwide. Specifically, the purposes and principles of internal control systems are fundamentally the same across the globe. However, culture and other realities suggest different emphases on the mix of control procedures, and some sensitivity to different customs and environments when establishing that mix. Nevertheless, the discussion in this chapter applies internationally. Nokia provides the following description of its control activities.

NOKIA

> Nokia has an internal audit function that acts as an independent appraisal function by examining and evaluating the adequacy and effectiveness of the company's system of internal control.

Control of Cash Accounting definitions for cash are similar for U.S. GAAP and IFRS. The need for control of cash is universal and applies globally. This means that companies worldwide desire to apply cash management procedures as explained in this chapter and aim to control both cash receipts and disbursements. Accordingly, systems that employ tools such as cash monitoring mechanisms, verification of documents, and petty cash processes are applied worldwide. The basic techniques explained in this chapter are part of those control procedures.

Banking Activities as Controls There is a global demand for banking services, bank statements, and bank reconciliations. To the extent feasible, companies utilize banking services as part of their effective control procedures. Further, bank statements are similarly used along with bank reconciliations to control and monitor cash.

 **IFRS**

Internal controls are crucial to companies that convert from U.S. GAAP to IFRS. Major risks include misstatement of financial information and fraud. Other risks are ineffective communication of the impact of this change for investors, creditors and others, and management's inability to certify the effectiveness of controls over financial reporting. ■

Days' Sales Uncollected  Decision Analysis 

A1 Compute the days' sales uncollected ratio and use it to assess liquidity.

An important part of cash management is monitoring the receipt of cash from receivables. If customers and others who owe money to a company are delayed in payment, then that company can find it difficult to pay its obligations when they are due. A company's customers are crucial partners in its cash management. Many companies attract customers by selling to them on credit. This means that cash receipts from customers are delayed until accounts receivable are collected.

One measure of how quickly a company can convert its accounts receivable into cash is the **days' sales uncollected,** also called *days' sales in receivables*. This measure is computed by dividing the current balance of receivables by net credit sales over the year just completed and then multiplying by 365 (number of days in a year). Since net credit sales usually are not reported to external users, the net sales (or revenues) figure is commonly used in the computation as in Exhibit 8.8.

EXHIBIT 8.8

Days' Sales Uncollected

$$\textbf{Days' sales uncollected} = \frac{\textbf{Accounts receivable}}{\textbf{Net sales}} \times 365$$

We use days' sales uncollected to estimate how much time is likely to pass before the current amount of accounts receivable is received in cash. For evaluation purposes, we need to compare this estimate to that for other companies in the same industry. We also make comparisons between current and prior periods.

To illustrate, we select data from the annual reports of two toy manufacturers, Hasbro and Mattel. Their days' sales uncollected figures are shown in Exhibit 8.9.

EXHIBIT 8.9

Analysis Using Days' Sales Uncollected

Company	Figure ($ millions)	2009	2008	2007	2006	2005
Hasbro	Accounts receivable	$1,039	$612	$655	$556	$523
	Net sales	$4,068	$4,022	$3,838	$3,151	$3,088
	Days' sales uncollected	93 days	56 days	62 days	64 days	62 days
Mattel	Accounts receivable	$749	$874	$991	$944	$761
	Net sales	$5,431	$5,918	$5,970	$5,650	$5,179
	Days' sales uncollected	50 days	54 days	61 days	61 days	54 days

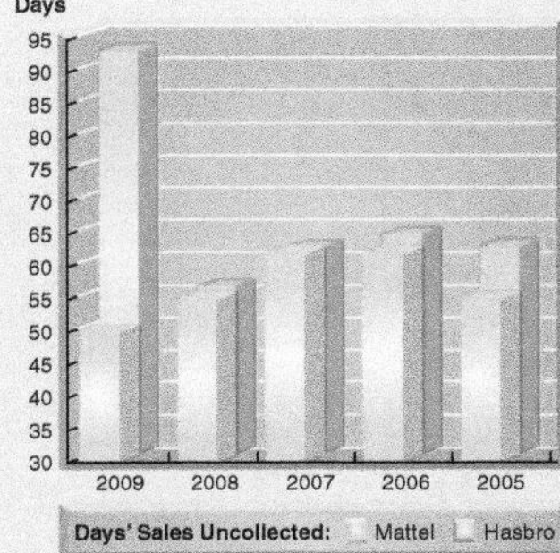

Days' sales uncollected for Hasbro in 2009 is computed as ($1,039/$4,068) × 365 days = 93 days. This means that it will take about 93 days to collect cash from ending accounts receivable. This number reflects one or more of the following factors: a company's ability to collect receivables, customer financial health, customer payment strategies, and discount terms. To further assess days' sales uncollected for Hasbro, we compare it to four prior years and to those of Mattel. We see that Hasbro's days' sales uncollected has worsened in 2009 as it takes much longer to collect its receivables relative to the prior four years. In comparison, Mattel fluctuated on days' sales uncollected for each of those years—from 54 days, to 61 days for two years, then back down to 54 days, and then down to the current 50 days. For all years, Mattel is superior to Hasbro on this measure of cash management. The less time that money is tied up in receivables often translates into increased profitability.

Decision Maker Answer — p. 343 

Sales Representative The sales staff is told to take action to help reduce days' sales uncollected for cash management purposes. What can you, a salesperson, do to reduce days' sales uncollected? ■

DEMONSTRATION PROBLEM 1

Prepare a bank reconciliation for Jamboree Enterprises for the month ended November 30, 2011. The following information is available to reconcile Jamboree Enterprises' book balance of cash with its bank statement balance as of November 30, 2011:

a. After all posting is complete on November 30, the company's book balance of Cash has a $16,380 debit balance, but its bank statement shows a $38,520 balance.

b. Checks No. 2024 for $4,810 and No. 2026 for $5,000 are outstanding.

c. In comparing the canceled checks on the bank statement with the entries in the accounting records, it is found that Check No. 2025 in payment of rent is correctly drawn for $1,000 but is erroneously entered in the accounting records as $880.

d. The November 30 deposit of $17,150 was placed in the night depository after banking hours on that date, and this amount does not appear on the bank statement.

e. In reviewing the bank statement, a check written by Jumbo Enterprises in the amount of $160 was erroneously drawn against Jamboree's account.

f. A credit memorandum enclosed with the bank statement indicates that the bank collected a $30,000 note and $900 of related interest on Jamboree's behalf. This transaction was not recorded by Jamboree prior to receiving the statement.

g. A debit memorandum for $1,100 lists a $1,100 NSF check received from a customer, Marilyn Welch. Jamboree had not recorded the return of this check before receiving the statement.

h. Bank service charges for November total $40. These charges were not recorded by Jamboree before receiving the statement.

PLANNING THE SOLUTION

- Set up a bank reconciliation with a bank side and a book side (as in Exhibit 8.7). Leave room to both add and deduct items. Each column will result in a reconciled, equal balance.
- Examine each item *a* through *h* to determine whether it affects the book or the bank balance and whether it should be added or deducted from the bank or book balance.
- After all items are analyzed, complete the reconciliation and arrive at a reconciled balance between the bank side and the book side.
- For each reconciling item on the book side, prepare an adjusting entry. Additions to the book side require an adjusting entry that debits Cash. Deductions on the book side require an adjusting entry that credits Cash.

SOLUTION TO DEMONSTRATION PROBLEM 1

JAMBOREE ENTERPRISES
Bank Reconciliation
November 30, 2011

Bank statement balance		$ 38,520	Book balance		$ 16,380
Add			Add		
Deposit of Nov. 30	$17,150		Collection of note	$30,000	
Bank error (Jumbo)	160	17,310	Interest earned	900	30,900
		55,830			47,280
Deduct			Deduct		
Outstanding checks			NSF check (M. Welch)	1,100	
No. 2024	4,810		Recording error (# 2025) ...	120	
No. 2026	5,000	9,810	Service charge	40	1,260
Adjusted bank balance ...		$46,020	Adjusted book balance		$46,020

Required Adjusting Entries for Jamboree

Nov. 30	Cash	30,900	
	Notes Receivable		30,000
	Interest Earned		900
	To record collection of note with interest.		
Nov. 30	Accounts Receivable—M. Welch	1,100	
	Cash		1,100
	To reinstate account due from an NSF check.		
Nov. 30	Rent Expense	120	
	Cash		120
	To correct recording error on check no. 2025.		
Nov. 30	Bank Service Charges	40	
	Cash		40
	To record bank service charges.		

Point: Error correction can alternatively involve (1) reversing the error entry, and (2) recording the correct entry.

DEMONSTRATION PROBLEM 2

Bacardi Company established a $150 petty cash fund with Dean Martin as the petty cashier. When the fund balance reached $19 cash, Martin prepared a petty cash payment report, which follows.

Petty Cash Payments Report

Receipt No.	Account Charged		Approved by	Received by
12	Delivery Expense	$ 29	Martin	A. Smirnoff
13	Merchandise Inventory	18	Martin	J. Daniels
15	(Omitted)	32	Martin	C. Carlsberg
16	Miscellaneous Expense	41	(Omitted)	J. Walker
	Total	$120		

Required

1. Identify four internal control weaknesses from the payment report.
2. Prepare general journal entries to record:
   a. Establishment of the petty cash fund.
   b. Reimbursement of the fund. (Assume for this part only that petty cash receipt no. 15 was issued for miscellaneous expenses.)
3. What is the Petty Cash account balance immediately before reimbursement? Immediately after reimbursement?

SOLUTION TO DEMONSTRATION PROBLEM 2

1. Four internal control weaknesses are
   a. Petty cash ticket no. 14 is missing. Its omission raises questions about the petty cashier's management of the fund.
   b. The $19 cash balance means that $131 has been withdrawn ($150 − $19 = $131). However, the total amount of the petty cash receipts is only $120 ($29 + $18 + $32 + $41). The fund is $11 short of cash ($131 − $120 = $11). Was petty cash receipt no. 14 issued for $11? Management should investigate.
   c. The petty cashier (Martin) did not sign petty cash receipt no. 16. This omission could have been an oversight on his part or he might not have authorized the payment. Management should investigate.
   d. Petty cash receipt no. 15 does not indicate which account to charge. This omission could have been an oversight on the petty cashier's part. Management could check with C. Carlsberg and the petty cashier (Martin) about the transaction. Without further information, debit Miscellaneous Expense.

2. Petty cash general journal entries.

a. Entry to establish the petty cash fund.

Petty Cash	150	
Cash		150

b. Entry to reimburse the fund.

Delivery Expense	29	
Merchandise Inventory	18	
Miscellaneous Expense ($41 + $32)	73	
Cash Over and Short	11	
Cash		131

3. The Petty Cash account balance *always* equals its fund balance, in this case $150. This account balance does not change unless the fund is increased or decreased.

APPENDIX

8A Documentation and Verification

This appendix describes the important business documents of a voucher system of control.

P4 Describe the use of documentation and verification to control cash disbursements.

Purchase Requisition Department managers are usually not allowed to place orders directly with suppliers for control purposes. Instead, a department manager must inform the purchasing department of its needs by preparing and signing a **purchase requisition,** which lists the merchandise needed and requests that it be purchased—see Exhibit 8A.1. Two copies of the purchase requisition are sent to the purchasing department, which then sends one copy to the accounting department. When the accounting department receives a purchase requisition, it creates and maintains a voucher for this transaction. The requesting department keeps the third copy.

EXHIBIT 8A.1

Purchase Requisition

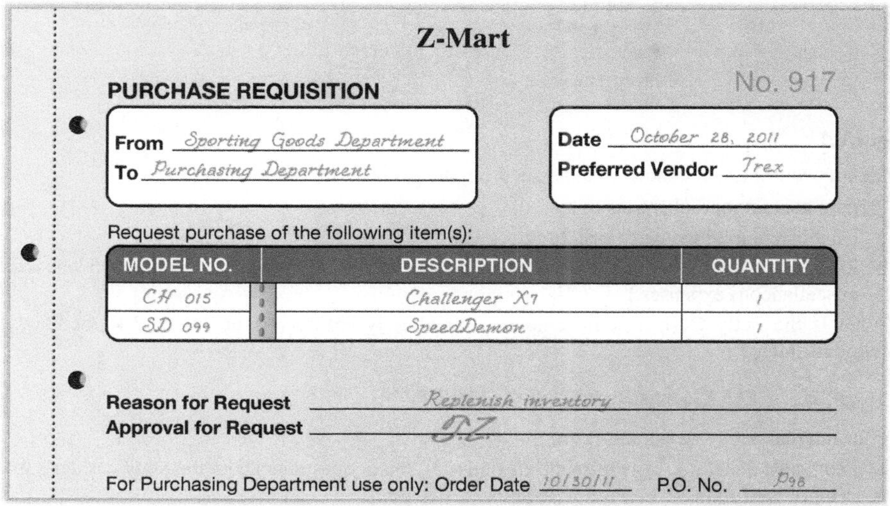

Z-Mart

PURCHASE REQUISITION No. 917

From Sporting Goods Department
To Purchasing Department

Date October 28, 2011
Preferred Vendor Trex

Request purchase of the following item(s):

MODEL NO.	DESCRIPTION	QUANTITY
CH 015	Challenger X7	1
SD 099	SpeedDemon	1

Reason for Request Replenish inventory
Approval for Request J.Z.

For Purchasing Department use only: Order Date 10/30/11 P.O. No. P98

Point: A voucher system is designed to uniquely meet the needs of a specific business. Thus, we should read this appendix as one example of a common voucher system design, but *not* the only design.

Purchase Order A **purchase order** is a document the purchasing department uses to place an order with a **vendor** (seller or supplier). A purchase order authorizes a vendor to ship ordered merchandise at the stated price and terms—see Exhibit 8A.2. When the purchasing department receives a purchase requisition, it prepares at least five copies of a purchase order. The copies are distributed as follows: *copy 1* to the vendor as a purchase request and as authority to ship merchandise; *copy 2,* along with a copy of the purchase requisition, to the accounting department, where it is entered in the voucher and used in approving payment of the invoice; *copy 3* to the requesting department to inform its manager that action is being taken; *copy 4* to the receiving department without order quantity so it can compare with goods received and provide independent count of goods received; and *copy 5* retained on file by the purchasing department.

EXHIBIT 8A.2
Purchase Order

Z-Mart
10 Michigan Street
Chicago, Illinois 60521

PURCHASE ORDER

No. P98

To: Trex
W9797 Cherry Road
Antigo, Wisconsin 54409

Date	10/30/11
FOB	Destination
Ship by	As soon as possible
Terms	2/15, n/30

Request shipment of the following item(s):

Model No.	Description	Quantity	Price	Amount
CH 015	Challenger X7	1	490	490
SD 099	SpeedDemon	1	710	710

All shipments and invoices must include purchase order number

J.W.
ORDERED BY

Invoice An **invoice** is an itemized statement of goods prepared by the vendor listing the customer's name, items sold, sales prices, and terms of sale. An invoice is also a bill sent to the buyer from the supplier. From the vendor's point of view, it is a *sales invoice*. The buyer, or **vendee,** treats it as a *purchase invoice*. When receiving a purchase order, the vendor ships the ordered merchandise to the buyer and includes or mails a copy of the invoice covering the shipment to the buyer. The invoice is sent to the buyer's accounting department where it is placed in the voucher. (Refer back to Exhibit 5.5, which shows Z-Mart's purchase invoice.)

Receiving Report Many companies maintain a separate department to receive all merchandise and purchased assets. When each shipment arrives, this receiving department counts the goods and checks them for damage and agreement with the purchase order. It then prepares four or more copies of a **receiving report,** which is used within the company to notify the appropriate persons that ordered goods have been received and to describe the quantities and condition of the goods. One copy is sent to accounting and placed in the voucher. Copies are also sent to the requesting department and the purchasing department to notify them that the goods have arrived. The receiving department retains a copy in its files.

Invoice Approval When a receiving report arrives, the accounting department should have copies of the following documents in the voucher: purchase requisition, purchase order, and invoice. With the information in these documents, the accounting department can record the purchase and approve its payment. In approving an invoice for payment, it checks and compares information across all documents. To facilitate this checking and to ensure that no step is omitted, it often uses an **invoice approval,** also called *check authorization*—see Exhibit 8A.3. An invoice approval is a checklist of steps necessary for approving an invoice for recording and payment. It is a separate document either filed in the voucher or preprinted (or stamped) on the voucher.

EXHIBIT 8A.3
Invoice Approval

INVOICE APPROVAL

DOCUMENT		BY	DATE
Purchase requisition	917	TZ	10/28/11
Purchase order	P98	JW	10/30/11
Receiving report	R85	SK	11/03/11
Invoice:	4657		11/12/11
Price		JK	11/12/11
Calculations		JK	11/12/11
Terms		JK	11/12/11
Approved for payment		BC	

Point: Recording a purchase is initiated by an invoice approval, not an invoice. An invoice approval verifies that the amount is consistent with that requested, ordered, and received. This controls and verifies purchases and related liabilities.

As each step in the checklist is approved, the person initials the invoice approval and records the current date. Final approval implies the following steps have occurred:

1. **Requisition check:** Items on invoice are requested per purchase requisition.
2. **Purchase order check:** Items on invoice are ordered per purchase order.
3. **Receiving report check:** Items on invoice are received per receiving report.
4. **Invoice check:** **Price:** Invoice prices are as agreed with the vendor.
   Calculations: Invoice has no mathematical errors.
   Terms: Terms are as agreed with the vendor.

Voucher Once an invoice has been checked and approved, the voucher is complete. A complete voucher is a record summarizing a transaction. Once the voucher certifies a transaction, it authorizes recording an obligation. A voucher also contains approval for paying the obligation on an appropriate date. The physical form of a voucher varies across companies. Many are designed so that the invoice and other related source documents are placed inside the voucher, which can be a folder.

Completion of a voucher usually requires a person to enter certain information on both the inside and outside of the voucher. Typical information required on the inside of a voucher is shown in Exhibit 8A.4, and that for the outside is shown in Exhibit 8A.5. This information is taken from the invoice and the supporting documents filed in the voucher. A complete voucher is sent to an authorized individual (often called an *auditor*). This person performs a final review, approves the accounts and amounts for debiting (called the *accounting distribution*), and authorizes recording of the voucher.

EXHIBIT 8A.4
Inside of a Voucher

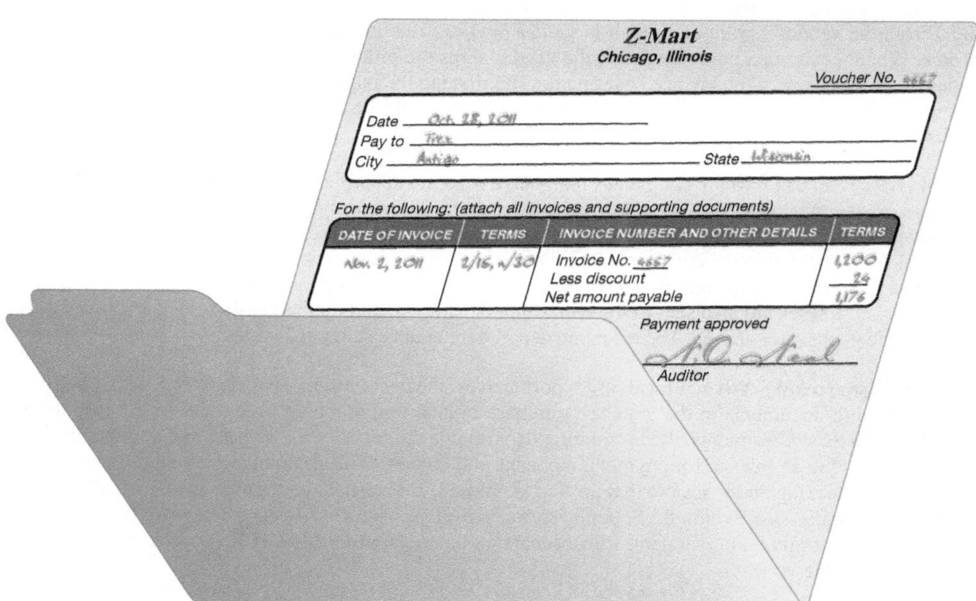

Z-Mart
Chicago, Illinois

Voucher No. 4657

Date Oct. 28, 2011
Pay to Trex
City Antigo State Wisconsin

For the following: (attach all invoices and supporting documents)

DATE OF INVOICE	TERMS	INVOICE NUMBER AND OTHER DETAILS	TERMS
Nov. 2, 2011	2/15, n/30	Invoice No. 4657	1,200
		Less discount	24
		Net amount payable	1,176

Payment approved
N.O. Steal
Auditor

After a voucher is approved and recorded (in a journal called a **voucher register**), it is filed by its due date. A check is then sent on the payment date from the cashier, the voucher is marked "paid," and the voucher is sent to the accounting department and recorded (in a journal called the **check register**). The person issuing checks relies on the approved voucher and its signed supporting documents as proof that an obligation has been incurred and must be paid. The purchase requisition and purchase order confirm the purchase was authorized. The receiving report shows that items have been received, and the invoice approval form verifies that the invoice has been checked for errors. There is little chance for error and even less chance for fraud without collusion unless all the documents and signatures are forged.

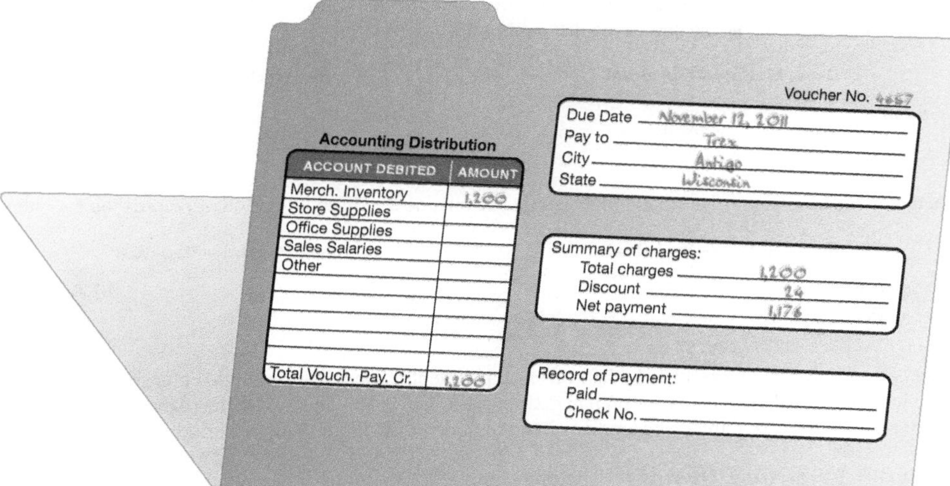

Voucher No. 4657

Due Date November 12, 2011
Pay to Trex
City Antigo
State Wisconsin

Accounting Distribution

ACCOUNT DEBITED	AMOUNT
Merch. Inventory	1,200
Store Supplies	
Office Supplies	
Sales Salaries	
Other	
Total Vouch. Pay. Cr.	1,200

Summary of charges:
Total charges 1,200
Discount 24
Net payment 1,176

Record of payment:
Paid
Check No.

EXHIBIT 8A.5

Outside of a Voucher

APPENDIX

Control of Purchase Discounts 8B

This appendix explains how a company can better control its cash *disbursements* to take advantage of favorable purchases discounts. Chapter 5 described the entries to record the receipt and payment of an invoice for a merchandise purchase with and without discount terms. Those entries were prepared under what is called the **gross method** of recording purchases, which initially records the invoice at its *gross* amount ignoring any cash discount.

P5 Apply the net method to control purchase discounts.

The **net method** is another means of recording purchases, which initially records the invoice at its *net* amount of any cash discount. The net method gives management an advantage in controlling and monitoring cash payments involving purchase discounts.

To explain, when invoices are recorded at *gross* amounts, the amount of any discounts taken is deducted from the balance of the Merchandise Inventory account when cash payment is made. This means that the amount of any discounts lost is not reported in any account or on the income statement. Lost discounts recorded in this way are unlikely to come to the attention of management. When purchases are recorded at *net* amounts, a **Discounts Lost** expense account is recorded and brought to management's attention. Management can then seek to identify the reason for discounts lost such as oversight, carelessness, or unfavorable terms. (Chapter 5 explains how managers assess whether a discount is favorable or not.)

Perpetual Inventory System To illustrate, assume that a company purchases merchandise on November 2 at a $1,200 invoice price with terms of 2/10, n/30. Its November 2 entries under the gross and net methods are

Gross Method—Perpetual

Merchandise Inventory	1,200	
Accounts Payable		1,200

Net Method—Perpetual

Merchandise Inventory	1,176	
Accounts Payable		1,176

If the invoice is paid on November 12 within the discount period, it records the following:

Gross Method—Perpetual

Accounts Payable	1,200	
Merchandise Inventory		24
Cash		1,176

Net Method—Perpetual

Accounts Payable	1,176	
Cash		1,176

If the invoice is *not* paid within the discount period, it records the following November 12 entry (which is the date corresponding to the end of the discount period):

Gross Method—Perpetual			Net Method—Perpetual		
No entry			Discounts Lost	24	
			Accounts Payable		24

Then, when the invoice is later paid on December 2, outside the discount period, it records the following:

Gross Method—Perpetual			Net Method—Perpetual		
Accounts Payable	1,200		Accounts Payable	1,200	
Cash		1,200	Cash		1,200

(The discount lost can be recorded when the cash payment is made with a single entry. However, in this case, when financial statements are prepared after a discount is lost and before the cash payment is made, an adjusting entry is required to recognize any unrecorded discount lost in the period when incurred.)

Periodic Inventory System The preceding entries assume a perpetual inventory system. If a company is using a periodic system, its November 2 entries under the gross and net methods are

Gross Method—Periodic			Net Method—Periodic		
Purchases	1,200		Purchases	1,176	
Accounts Payable		1,200	Accounts Payable		1,176

If the invoice is paid on November 12 within the discount period, it records the following:

Gross Method—Periodic			Net Method—Periodic		
Accounts Payable	1,200		Accounts Payable	1,176	
Purchases Discounts		24	Cash		1,176
Cash		1,176			

If the invoice is *not* paid within the discount period, it records the following November 12 entry:

Gross Method—Periodic			Net Method—Periodic		
No entry			Discounts Lost	24	
			Accounts Payable		24

Then, when the invoice is later paid on December 2, outside the discount period, it records the following:

Gross Method—Periodic			Net Method—Periodic		
Accounts Payable	1,200		Accounts Payable	1,200	
Cash		1,200	Cash		1,200

Summary

C1 Define internal control and identify its purpose and principles. An internal control system consists of the policies and procedures managers use to protect assets, ensure reliable accounting, promote efficient operations, and urge adherence to company policies. It can prevent avoidable losses and help managers both plan operations and monitor company and human performance. Principles of good internal control include establishing responsibilities, maintaining adequate records, insuring assets and bonding employees, separating recordkeeping from custody of assets, dividing responsibilities for related transactions, applying technological controls, and performing regular independent reviews.

C2 Define cash and cash equivalents and explain how to report them. Cash includes currency, coins, and amounts on (or acceptable for) deposit in checking and savings accounts. Cash equivalents are short-term, highly liquid investment assets readily convertible to a known cash amount and sufficiently close to their maturity date so that market value is not sensitive to interest rate changes. Cash and cash equivalents are liquid assets because they are readily converted into other assets or can be used to pay for goods, services, or liabilities.

A1 Compute the days' sales uncollected ratio and use it to assess liquidity. Many companies attract customers by selling to them on credit. This means that cash receipts from customers are delayed until accounts receivable are collected. Users want to know how quickly a company can convert its accounts receivable into cash. The days' sales uncollected ratio, one measure reflecting company liquidity, is computed by dividing the ending balance of receivables by annual net sales, and then multiplying by 365.

P1 Apply internal control to cash receipts and disbursements. Internal control of cash receipts ensures that all cash received is properly recorded and deposited. Attention focuses on two important types of cash receipts: over-the-counter and by mail. Good internal control for over-the-counter cash receipts includes use of a cash register, customer review, use of receipts, a permanent transaction record, and separation of the custody of cash from its recordkeeping. Good internal control for cash receipts by mail includes at least two people assigned to open mail and a listing of each sender's name, amount, and explanation. (Banks offer several services that promote the control and safeguarding of cash.)

P2 Explain and record petty cash fund transactions. Petty cash disbursements are payments of small amounts for items such as postage, courier fees, minor repairs, and supplies. A company usually sets up one or more petty cash funds. A petty cash fund cashier is responsible for safekeeping the cash, making payments from this fund, and keeping receipts and records. A Petty Cash account is debited only when the fund is established or increased in amount. When the fund is replenished, petty cash disbursements are recorded with debits to expense (or asset) accounts and a credit to cash.

P3 Prepare a bank reconciliation. A bank reconciliation proves the accuracy of the depositor's and the bank's records. The bank statement balance is adjusted for items such as outstanding checks and unrecorded deposits made on or before the bank statement date but not reflected on the statement. The book balance is adjusted for items such as service charges, bank collections for the depositor, and interest earned on the account.

P4A Describe the use of documentation and verification to control cash disbursements. A voucher system is a set of procedures and approvals designed to control cash disbursements and acceptance of obligations. The voucher system of control relies on several important documents, including the voucher and its supporting files. A key factor in this system is that only approved departments and individuals are authorized to incur certain obligations.

P5B Apply the net method to control purchase discounts. The net method aids management in monitoring and controlling purchase discounts. When invoices are recorded at gross amounts, the amount of discounts taken is deducted from the balance of the Inventory account. This means that the amount of any discounts lost is not reported in any account and is unlikely to come to the attention of management. When purchases are recorded at net amounts, a Discounts Lost account is brought to management's attention as an operating expense. Management can then seek to identify the reason for discounts lost, such as oversight, carelessness, or unfavorable terms.

Guidance Answers to Decision Maker and Decision Ethics

Entrepreneur A forced vacation policy is part of a good system of internal controls. When employees are forced to take vacations, their ability to hide any fraudulent behavior decreases because others must perform the vacationers' duties. A replacement employee potentially can uncover fraudulent behavior or falsified records. A forced vacation policy is especially important for employees in sensitive positions of handling money or in control of easily transferable assets.

Sales Representative A salesperson can take several steps to reduce days' sales uncollected. These include (1) decreasing the ratio of sales on account to total sales by encouraging more cash sales, (2) identifying customers most delayed in their payments and encouraging earlier payments or cash sales, and (3) applying stricter credit policies to eliminate credit sales to customers that never pay.

Guidance Answers to Quick Checks

1. (*c*)
2. Technology reduces processing errors. It also allows more extensive testing of records, limits the amount of hard evidence, and highlights the importance of separation of duties.
3. A company holds liquid assets so that it can purchase other assets, buy services, and pay obligations.
4. It owns cash equivalents because they yield a return greater than what cash earns (and are readily exchanged for cash).
5. Examples of cash equivalents are 90-day (or less) U.S. Treasury bills, money market funds, and commercial paper (notes).
6. (*a*)
7. A voucher system is used when an owner/manager can no longer control purchasing procedures through personal supervision and direct participation.
8. If all cash payments are made by check, numerous checks for small amounts must be written. Since this practice is expensive and time-consuming, a petty cash fund is often established for making small (immaterial) cash payments.
9. If the petty cash fund is not reimbursed at the end of an accounting period, the transactions involving petty cash are not yet recorded and the petty cash asset is overstated.
10. First, petty cash transactions are recorded when the petty cash fund is reimbursed. Second, reimbursement provides cash to allow the fund to continue being used. Third, reimbursement identifies any cash shortage or overage in the fund.
11. A bank statement is a report prepared by the bank describing the activities in a depositor's account.

12. To reconcile a bank balance means to explain the difference between the cash balance in the depositor's accounting records and the cash balance on the bank statement.
13. The purpose of the bank reconciliation is to determine whether the bank or the depositor has made any errors and whether the bank has entered any transactions affecting the account that the depositor has not recorded.
14. Unrecorded deposits—added
    Outstanding checks—subtracted
15. Interest earned—added
    Credit memos—added
    Debit memos—subtracted
    NSF checks—subtracted
    Bank service charges—subtracted

Key Terms

mhhe.com/wildFAP20e

Bank reconciliation (p. 331)
Bank statement (p. 330)
Canceled checks (p. 331)
Cash (p. 321)
Cash equivalents (p. 321)
Cash Over and Short (p. 323)
Check (p. 328)
Check register (p. 340)
Committee of Sponsoring Organizations (COSO) (p. 317)
Days' sales uncollected (p. 335)
Deposit ticket (p. 328)
Deposits in transit (p. 331)
Discounts lost (p. 341)
Electronic funds transfer (EFT) (p. 329)
Gross method (p. 341)
Internal control system (p. 316)
Invoice (p. 339)
Invoice approval (p. 339)
Liquid assets (p. 321)
Liquidity (p. 321)
Net method (p. 341)
Outstanding checks (p. 331)
Petty cash (p. 326)
Principles of internal control (p. 317)
Purchase order (p. 338)
Purchase requisition (p. 338)
Receiving report (p. 339)
Sarbanes-Oxley Act (p. 316)
Section 404 (of SOX) (p. 317)
Signature card (p. 328)
Vendee (p. 339)
Vendor (p. 338)
Voucher (p. 325)
Voucher register (p. 340)
Voucher system (p. 324)

Multiple Choice Quiz

Answers on p. 391

mhhe.com/wildFAP20e

Additional Quiz Questions are available at the book's Website.

1. A company needs to replenish its $500 petty cash fund. Its petty cash box has $75 cash and petty cash receipts of $420. The journal entry to replenish the fund includes
   a. A debit to Cash for $75.
   b. A credit to Cash for $75.
   c. A credit to Petty Cash for $420.
   d. A credit to Cash Over and Short for $5.
   e. A debit to Cash Over and Short for $5.
2. The following information is available for Hapley Company:
   - The November 30 bank statement shows a $1,895 balance.
   - The general ledger shows a $1,742 balance at November 30.
   - A $795 deposit placed in the bank's night depository on November 30 does not appear on the November 30 bank statement.
   - Outstanding checks amount to $638 at November 30.
   - A customer's $335 note was collected by the bank in November. A collection fee of $15 was deducted by the bank and the difference deposited in Hapley's account.
   - A bank service charge of $10 is deducted by the bank and appears on the November 30 bank statement.

   How will the customer's note appear on Hapley's November 30 bank reconciliation?
   a. $320 appears as an addition to the book balance of cash.
   b. $320 appears as a deduction from the book balance of cash.
   c. $320 appears as an addition to the bank balance of cash.
   d. $320 appears as a deduction from the bank balance of cash.
   e. $335 appears as an addition to the bank balance of cash.
3. Using the information from question 2, what is the reconciled balance on Hapley's November 30 bank reconciliation?
   a. $2,052
   b. $1,895
   c. $1,742
   d. $2,201
   e. $1,184
4. A company had net sales of $84,000 and accounts receivable of $6,720. Its days' sales uncollected is
   a. 3.2 days
   b. 18.4 days
   c. 230.0 days
   d. 29.2 days
   e. 12.5 days
5.[B] A company records its purchases using the net method. On August 1, it purchases merchandise on account for $6,000 with terms of 2/10, n/30. The August 1 journal entry to record this transaction includes a
   a. Debit to Merchandise Inventory for $6,000.
   b. Debit to Merchandise Inventory for $5,880.
   c. Debit to Merchandise Inventory for $120.
   d. Debit to Accounts Payable for $5,880.
   e. Credit to Accounts Payable for $6,000.

A(B) *Superscript letter A(B) denotes assignments based on Appendix 8A (8B).*

Icon denotes assignments that involve decision making.

Discussion Questions

1. List the seven broad principles of internal control.
2. Internal control procedures are important in every business, but at what stage in the development of a business do they become especially critical?
3. Why should responsibility for related transactions be divided among different departments or individuals?
4. Why should the person who keeps the records of an asset not be the person responsible for its custody?
5. When a store purchases merchandise, why are individual departments not allowed to directly deal with suppliers?
6. What are the limitations of internal controls?
7. Which of the following assets is most liquid? Which is least liquid? Inventory, building, accounts receivable, or cash.
8. What is a petty cash receipt? Who should sign it?
9. Why should cash receipts be deposited on the day of receipt?
10. Research In Motion's statement of cash flows in Appendix A describes changes in cash and cash equivalents for the year ended February 27, 2010. What total amount is provided (used) by investing activities? What amount is provided (used) by financing activities? RIM
11. Refer to Apple's financial statements in Appendix A. Identify Apple's net income for the year ended December 31, 2009. Is its net income equal to the increase in cash and cash equivalents for the year? Explain the difference between net income and the increase in cash and cash equivalents. Apple
12. Refer to Nokia's balance sheet in Appendix A. How does its cash (titled "bank and cash") compare with its other current assets (both in amount and percent) as of December 31, 2009? Compare and assess its cash at December 31, 2009, with its cash at December 31, 2008. NOKIA
13. Palm's balance sheet in Appendix A reports that cash and equivalents decreased during the fiscal year ended May, 31, 2009. Identify the cash generated (or used) by operating activities, by investing activities, and by financing activities. Palm

connect

QUICK STUDY

QS 8-1
Internal control objectives
C1 

An internal control system consists of all policies and procedures used to protect assets, ensure reliable accounting, promote efficient operations, and urge adherence to company policies.

1. What is the main objective of internal control procedures? How is that objective achieved?
2. Why should recordkeeping for assets be separated from custody over those assets?
3. Why should the responsibility for a transaction be divided between two or more individuals or departments?

QS 8-2
Internal control for cash
P1  

A good system of internal control for cash provides adequate procedures for protecting both cash receipts and cash disbursements.

1. What are three basic guidelines that help achieve this protection?
2. Identify two control systems or procedures for cash disbursements.

QS 8-3
Cash and equivalents
C2

Good accounting systems help in managing cash and controlling who has access to it.

1. What items are included in the category of cash?
2. What items are included in the category of cash equivalents?
3. What does the term *liquidity* refer to?

QS 8-4
Petty cash accounting
P2

1. The petty cash fund of the Rio Agency is established at $75. At the end of the current period, the fund contained $14 and had the following receipts: film rentals, $19, refreshments for meetings, $23 (both expenditures to be classified as Entertainment Expense); postage, $6; and printing, $13. Prepare journal entries to record (*a*) establishment of the fund and (*b*) reimbursement of the fund at the end of the current period.
2. Identify the two events that cause a Petty Cash account to be credited in a journal entry.

QS 8-5
Bank reconciliation
P3

1. For each of the following items, indicate whether its amount (i) affects the bank or book side of a bank reconciliation and (ii) represents an addition or a subtraction in a bank reconciliation.
   - **a.** Outstanding checks
   - **b.** Debit memos
   - **c.** NSF checks
   - **d.** Unrecorded deposits
   - **e.** Interest on cash balance
   - **f.** Credit memos
   - **g.** Bank service charges
2. Which of the items in part 1 require an adjusting journal entry?

QS 8-6
Bank reconciliation
P3

Cruz Company deposits all cash receipts on the day when they are received and it makes all cash payments by check. At the close of business on June 30, 2011, its Cash account shows an $11,352 debit balance. Cruz's June 30 bank statement shows $10,332 on deposit in the bank. Prepare a bank reconciliation for Cruz Company using the following information.

a. Outstanding checks as of June 30 total $1,713.

b. The June 30 bank statement included a $23 debit memorandum for bank services; Cruz has not yet recorded the cost of these services.

c. In reviewing the bank statement, a $90 check written by Cruz Company was mistakenly recorded in Cruz Company's books at $99.

d. June 30 cash receipts of $2,724 were placed in the bank's night depository after banking hours and were not recorded on the June 30 bank statement.

e. The bank statement included a $5 credit for interest earned on the cash in the bank.

QS 8-7
Days' sales uncollected
A1 

The following annual account balances are taken from ProTeam Sports at December 31.

	2011	2010
Accounts receivable	$ 75,692	$ 70,484
Net sales	2,591,933	2,296,673

What is the change in the number of days' sales uncollected between years 2010 and 2011? According to this analysis, is the company's collection of receivables improving? Explain.

QS 8-8A
Documents in a voucher system
P4

Management uses a voucher system to help control and monitor cash disbursements. Identify and describe at least four key documents that are part of a voucher system of control.

QS 8-9B
Purchase discounts P5 

An important part of cash management is knowing when, and if, to take purchase discounts.

a. Which accounting method uses a Discounts Lost account?

b. What is the advantage of this method for management?

QS 8-10
International accounting and internal controls

Answer each of the following related to international accounting standards.

a. Explain how the purposes and principles of internal controls are different between accounting systems reporting under IFRS versus U.S. GAAP.

b. Cash presents special internal control challenges. How do internal controls for cash differ for accounting systems reporting under IFRS versus U.S. GAAP? How do the procedures applied differ across those two accounting systems?

QS 8-11
Reviewing bank statements
P3

An entrepreneur commented that a bank reconciliation may not be necessary as she regularly reviews her online bank statement for any unusual items and errors.

a. Describe how a bank reconciliation and an online review (or reading) of the bank statement are not equivalent.

b. Identify and explain at least two frauds or errors that would be uncovered through a bank reconciliation and that would *not* be uncovered through an online review of the bank statement.

EXERCISES

Exercise 8-1
Internal control recommendations
C1 

What internal control procedures would you recommend in each of the following situations?

1. A concession company has one employee who sells towels, coolers, and sunglasses at the beach. Each day, the employee is given enough towels, coolers, and sunglasses to last through the day and enough cash to make change. The money is kept in a box at the stand.
2. An antique store has one employee who is given cash and sent to garage sales each weekend. The employee pays cash for any merchandise acquired that the antique store resells.

Exercise 8-2
Analyzing internal control
C1 

Cantu Company is a rapidly growing start-up business. Its recordkeeper, who was hired nine months ago, left town after the company's manager discovered that a large sum of money had disappeared over the past three months. An audit disclosed that the recordkeeper had written and signed several checks made payable to her fiancé and then recorded the checks as salaries expense. The fiancé, who cashed the checks but never worked for the company, left town with the recordkeeper. As a result, the company incurred an uninsured loss of $84,000. Evaluate Cantu's internal control system and indicate which principles of internal control appear to have been ignored.

Exercise 8-3
Control of cash receipts by mail
P1 

Some of Chester Company's cash receipts from customers are received by the company with the regular mail. Chester's recordkeeper opens these letters and deposits the cash received each day. (*a*) Identify any internal control problem(s) in this arrangement. (*b*) What changes to its internal control system do you recommend?

Exercise 8-4
Cash, liquidity, and return
C2

Good accounting systems help with the management and control of cash and cash equivalents.

1. Define and contrast the terms *liquid asset* and *cash equivalent.*
2. Why would companies invest their idle cash in cash equivalents?
3. Identify five principles of effective cash management.

Exercise 8-5
Petty cash fund with a shortage
P2

Hawk Company establishes a $400 petty cash fund on September 9. On September 30, the fund shows $166 in cash along with receipts for the following expenditures: transportation-in, $32; postage expenses, $113; and miscellaneous expenses, $87. The petty cashier could not account for a $2 shortage in the fund. Hawk uses the perpetual system in accounting for merchandise inventory. Prepare (1) the September 9 entry to establish the fund, (2) the September 30 entry to reimburse the fund, and (3) an October 1 entry to decrease the fund to $300.

Check (2) Cr. Cash $234 and (3) Dr. Cash $100

Exercise 8-6
Petty cash fund accounting
P2

NetPerks Co. establishes a $200 petty cash fund on January 1. On January 8, the fund shows $28 in cash along with receipts for the following expenditures: postage, $64; transportation-in, $19; delivery expenses, $36; and miscellaneous expenses, $53. NetPerks uses the perpetual system in accounting for merchandise inventory. Prepare journal entries to (1) establish the fund on January 1, (2) reimburse it on January 8, and (3) both reimburse the fund and increase it to $500 on January 8, assuming no entry in part 2. (*Hint*: Make two separate entries for part 3.)

Check (3) Cr. Cash $472 (total)

Exercise 8-7
Bank reconciliation and adjusting entries
P3

Prepare a table with the following headings for a monthly bank reconciliation dated September 30.

Bank Balance		Book Balance			Not Shown on the Reconciliation
Add	Deduct	Add	Deduct	Adjust	

For each item 1 through 12, place an *x* in the appropriate column to indicate whether the item should be added to or deducted from the book or bank balance, or whether it should not appear on the reconciliation. If the book balance is to be adjusted, place a *Dr.* or *Cr.* in the Adjust column to indicate whether the Cash balance should be debited or credited. At the left side of your table, number the items to correspond to the following list.

1. Bank service charge for September.
2. Checks written and mailed to payees on October 2.
3. Checks written by another depositor but charged against this company's account.
4. Principal and interest on a note receivable to this company is collected by the bank but not yet recorded by the company.
5. Special bank charge for collection of note in part 4 on this company's behalf.
6. Check written against the company's account and cleared by the bank; erroneously not recorded by the company's recordkeeper.
7. Interest earned on the September cash balance in the bank.
8. Night deposit made on September 30 after the bank closed.
9. Checks outstanding on August 31 that cleared the bank in September.
10. NSF check from customer is returned on September 25 but not yet recorded by this company.
11. Checks written by the company and mailed to payees on September 30.
12. Deposit made on September 5 and processed by the bank on September 6.

Exercise 8-8
Voucher system
P1

The voucher system of control is designed to control cash disbursements and the acceptance of obligations.

1. The voucher system of control establishes procedures for what two processes?
2. What types of expenditures should be overseen by a voucher system of control?
3. When is the voucher initially prepared? Explain.

Exercise 8-9
Bank reconciliation
P3

Frederick Clinic deposits all cash receipts on the day when they are received and it makes all cash payments by check. At the close of business on June 30, 2011, its Cash account shows a $15,141 debit balance. Frederick Clinic's June 30 bank statement shows $14,275 on deposit in the bank. Prepare a bank reconciliation for Frederick Clinic using the following information:

a. Outstanding checks as of June 30 total $2,500.
b. The June 30 bank statement included a $125 debit memorandum for bank services.
c. Check No. 919, listed with the canceled checks, was correctly drawn for $645 in payment of a utility bill on June 15. Frederick Clinic mistakenly recorded it with a debit to Utilities Expense and a credit to Cash in the amount of $654.
d. The June 30 cash receipts of $3,250 were placed in the bank's night depository after banking hours and were not recorded on the June 30 bank statement.

Check Reconciled bal., $15,025

Exercise 8-10
Adjusting entries from bank reconciliation P3

Prepare the adjusting journal entries that Frederick Clinic must record as a result of preparing the bank reconciliation in Exercise 8-9.

Exercise 8-11
Bank reconciliation
P3

Chung Company deposits all cash receipts on the day when they are received and it makes all cash payments by check. At the close of business on May 31, 2011, its Cash account shows a $15,500 debit balance. Chung's May 31 bank statement shows $13,800 on deposit in the bank. Prepare a bank reconciliation for Chung Company using the following information.

a. May 31 cash receipts of $2,200 were placed in the bank's night depository after banking hours and were not recorded on the May 31 bank statement.
b. Outstanding checks as of May 31 total $1,600.
c. The May 31 bank statement included a $100 debit memorandum for bank services; Chung has not yet recorded the cost of these services.
d. In reviewing the bank statement, a $400 check written by Wald Company was mistakenly drawn against Chung's account.
e. A debit memorandum for $600 refers to a $600 NSF check from a customer; Chung has not yet recorded this NSF check.

Check Reconciled bal., $14,800

Exercise 8-12
Liquid assets and accounts receivable
A1 

Deacon Co. reported annual net sales for 2010 and 2011 of $565,000 and $647,000, respectively. Its year-end balances of accounts receivable follow: December 31, 2010, $51,000; and December 31, 2011, $83,000. (*a*) Calculate its days' sales uncollected at the end of each year. (*b*) Evaluate and comment on any changes in the amount of liquid assets tied up in receivables.

Exercise 8-13[A]
Documents in a voucher system
P4

Match each document in a voucher system in column one with its description in column two.

Document	Description
1. Voucher	A. A document used to notify the appropriate persons that ordered goods have arrived, including a description of the quantities and condition of goods.
2. Invoice approval	B. An internal file used to store documents and information to control cash disbursements and to ensure that a transaction is properly authorized and recorded.
3. Receiving report	C. A document used to place an order with a vendor that authorizes the vendor to ship ordered merchandise at the stated price and terms.
4. Invoice	D. A checklist of steps necessary for the approval of an invoice for recording and payment; also known as a check authorization.
5. Purchase order	E. A document used by department managers to inform the purchasing department to place an order with a vendor.
6. Purchase requisition	F. An itemized statement of goods prepared by the vendor listing the customer's name, items sold, sales prices, and terms of sale.

Exercise 8-14[B]
Record invoices at gross or net amounts
P5

USA Imports uses the perpetual system in accounting for merchandise inventory and had the following transactions during the month of October. Prepare entries to record these transactions assuming that USA Imports records invoices (*a*) at gross amounts and (*b*) at net amounts.

Oct. 2 Purchased merchandise at a $4,000 price, invoice dated October 2, terms 2/10, n/30.
10 Received a $400 credit memorandum (at full invoice price) for the return of merchandise that it purchased on October 2.
17 Purchased merchandise at a $4,400 price, invoice dated October 16, terms 2/10, n/30.
26 Paid for the merchandise purchased on October 17, less the discount.
31 Paid for the merchandise purchased on October 2. Payment was delayed because the invoice was mistakenly filed for payment today. This error caused the discount to be lost.

connect

PROBLEM SET A

Problem 8-1A
Analyzing internal control
C1 

For each of these five separate cases, identify the principle(s) of internal control that is violated. Recommend what the business should do to ensure adherence to principles of internal control.

1. Heather Flat records all incoming customer cash receipts for her employer and posts the customer payments to their respective accounts.
2. At Netco Company, Jeff and Jose alternate lunch hours. Jeff is the petty cash custodian, but if someone needs petty cash when he is at lunch, Jose fills in as custodian.
3. Nadine Cox posts all patient charges and payments at the Dole Medical Clinic. Each night Nadine backs up the computerized accounting system to a tape and stores the tape in a locked file at her desk.
4. Barto Sayles prides himself on hiring quality workers who require little supervision. As office manager, Barto gives his employees full discretion over their tasks and for years has seen no reason to perform independent reviews of their work.
5. Desi West's manager has told her to reduce costs. Desi decides to raise the deductible on the plant's property insurance from $5,000 to $10,000. This cuts the property insurance premium in half. In a related move, she decides that bonding the plant's employees is a waste of money since the company has not experienced any losses due to employee theft. Desi saves the entire amount of the bonding insurance premium by dropping the bonding insurance.

Problem 8-2A
Establish, reimburse, and adjust petty cash
P2

GL QB

Shawnee Co. set up a petty cash fund for payments of small amounts. The following transactions involving the petty cash fund occurred in May (the last month of the company's fiscal year).

May 1 Prepared a company check for $250 to establish the petty cash fund.
15 Prepared a company check to replenish the fund for the following expenditures made since May1.
- *a.* Paid $78 for janitorial services.
- *b.* Paid $63.68 for miscellaneous expenses.
- *c.* Paid postage expenses of $43.50.
- *d.* Paid $57.15 to *The County Gazette* (the local newspaper) for an advertisement.
- *e.* Counted $11.15 remaining in the petty cash box.

16 Prepared a company check for $200 to increase the fund to $450.
31 The petty cashier reports that $293.39 cash remains in the fund. A company check is drawn to replenish the fund for the following expenditures made since May 15.
- *f.* Paid postage expenses of $48.36.
- *g.* Reimbursed the office manager for business mileage, $38.50.
- *h.* Paid $39.75 to deliver merchandise to a customer, terms FOB destination.

31 The company decides that the May 16 increase in the fund was too large. It reduces the fund by $50, leaving a total of $400.

Required

1. Prepare journal entries to establish the fund on May 1, to replenish it on May 15 and on May 31, and to reflect any increase or decrease in the fund balance on May 16 and May 31.

Check (1) Cr. to Cash: May 15, $238.85; May 16, $200.00

Analysis Component

2. Explain how the company's financial statements are affected if the petty cash fund is not replenished and no entry is made on May 31.

Problem 8-3A
Establish, reimburse, and increase petty cash
P2

Shelton Gallery had the following petty cash transactions in February of the current year.

Feb. 2 Wrote a $300 check, cashed it, and gave the proceeds and the petty cashbox to Bo Brown, the petty cashier.
5 Purchased bond paper for the copier for $10.13 that is immediately used.
9 Paid $22.50 COD shipping charges on merchandise purchased for resale, terms FOB shipping point. Shelton uses the perpetual system to account for merchandise inventory.
12 Paid $9.95 postage to express mail a contract to a client.
14 Reimbursed Alli Buck, the manager, $58 for business mileage on her car.
20 Purchased stationery for $77.76 that is immediately used.
23 Paid a courier $18 to deliver merchandise sold to a customer, terms FOB destination.
25 Paid $15.10 COD shipping charges on merchandise purchased for resale, terms FOB shipping point.
27 Paid $64 for postage expenses.
28 The fund had $21.23 remaining in the petty cash box. Sorted the petty cash receipts by accounts affected and exchanged them for a check to reimburse the fund for expenditures.
28 The petty cash fund amount is increased by $100 to a total of $400.

Required

1. Prepare the journal entry to establish the petty cash fund.
2. Prepare a petty cash payments report for February with these categories: delivery expense, mileage expense, postage expense, merchandise inventory (for transportation-in), and office supplies expense. Sort the payments into the appropriate categories and total the expenditures in each category.
3. Prepare the journal entries for part 2 to both (*a*) reimburse and (*b*) increase the fund amount.

Check (3a & 3b) Total Cr. to Cash $378.77

Problem 8-4A
Prepare a bank reconciliation and record adjustments
P3  
mhhe.com/wildFAP20e

The following information is available to reconcile Clark Company's book balance of cash with its bank statement cash balance as of July 31, 2011.

a. On July 31, the company's Cash account has a $26,193 debit balance, but its July bank statement shows a $28,020 cash balance.

b. Check No. 3031 for $1,380 and Check No. 3040 for $552 were outstanding on the June 30 bank reconciliation. Check No. 3040 is listed with the July canceled checks, but Check No. 3031 is not. Also, Check No. 3065 for $336 and Check No. 3069 for $2,148, both written in July, are not among the canceled checks on the July 31 statement.

c. In comparing the canceled checks on the bank statement with the entries in the accounting records, it is found that Check No. 3056 for July rent was correctly written and drawn for $1,250 but was erroneously entered in the accounting records as $1,230.

d. A credit memorandum enclosed with the July bank statement indicates the bank collected $9,000 cash on a non-interest-bearing note for Clark, deducted a $45 collection fee, and credited the remainder to its account. Clark had not recorded this event before receiving the statement.

e. A debit memorandum for $805 lists a $795 NSF check plus a $10 NSF charge. The check had been received from a customer, Jim Shaw. Clark has not yet recorded this check as NSF.

f. Enclosed with the July statement is a $15 debit memorandum for bank services. It has not yet been recorded because no previous notification had been received.

g. Clark's July 31 daily cash receipts of $10,152 were placed in the bank's night depository on that date, but do not appear on the July 31 bank statement.

Required

1. Prepare the bank reconciliation for this company as of July 31, 2011.
2. Prepare the journal entries necessary to bring the company's book balance of cash into conformity with the reconciled cash balance as of July 31, 2011.

Check (1) Reconciled balance, $34,308; (2) Cr. Note Receivable $9,000

Analysis Component

3. Assume that the July 31, 2011, bank reconciliation for this company is prepared and some items are treated incorrectly. For each of the following errors, explain the effect of the error on (i) the adjusted bank statement cash balance and (ii) the adjusted cash account book balance.
   a. The company's unadjusted cash account balance of $26,193 is listed on the reconciliation as $26,139.
   b. The bank's collection of the $9,000 note less the $45 collection fee is added to the bank statement cash balance on the reconciliation.

Els Company most recently reconciled its bank statement and book balances of cash on August 31 and it reported two checks outstanding, No. 5888 for $1,038.05 and No. 5893 for $484.25. The following information is available for its September 30, 2011, reconciliation.

Problem 8-5A
Prepare a bank reconciliation and record adjustments
P3

From the September 30 Bank Statement

PREVIOUS BALANCE	TOTAL CHECKS AND DEBITS	TOTAL DEPOSITS AND CREDITS	CURRENT BALANCE
16,800.45	9,620.05	11,182.85	18,363.25

CHECKS AND DEBITS			DEPOSITS AND CREDITS		DAILY BALANCE	
Date	No.	Amount	Date	Amount	Date	Amount
09/03	5888	1,038.05	09/05	1,103.75	08/31	16,800.45
09/04	5902	731.90	09/12	2,226.90	09/03	15,762.40
09/07	5901	1,824.25	09/21	4,093.00	09/04	15,030.50
09/17		588.25 NSF	09/25	2,351.70	09/05	16,134.25
09/20	5905	937.00	09/30	22.50 IN	09/07	14,310.00
09/22	5903	399.10	09/30	1,385.00 CM	09/12	16,536.90
09/22	5904	2,080.00			09/17	15,948.65
09/28	5907	213.85			09/20	15,011.65
09/29	5909	1,807.65			09/21	19,104.65
					09/22	16,625.55
					09/25	18,977.25
					09/28	18,763.40
					09/29	16,955.75
					09/30	18,363.25

From Els Company's Accounting Records

Cash Receipts Deposited

Date			Cash Debit
Sept.	5		1,103.75
	12		2,226.90
	21		4,093.00
	25		2,351.70
	30		1,582.75
			11,358.10

Cash Disbursements

Check No.		Cash Credit
5901		1,824.25
5902		731.90
5903		399.10
5904		2,050.00
5905		937.00
5906		859.30
5907		213.85
5908		276.00
5909		1,807.65
		9,099.05

Cash — Acct. No. 101

Date		Explanation	PR	Debit	Credit	Balance
Aug.	31	Balance				15,278.15
Sept.	30	Total receipts	R12	11,358.10		26,636.25
	30	Total disbursements	D23		9,099.05	17,537.20

Additional Information

Check No. 5904 is correctly drawn for $2,080 to pay for computer equipment; however, the recordkeeper misread the amount and entered it in the accounting records with a debit to Computer Equipment and a credit to Cash of $2,050. The NSF check shown in the statement was originally received from a customer, S. Nilson, in payment of her account. Its return has not yet been recorded by the company. The credit memorandum is from the collection of a $1,400 note for Els Company by the bank. The bank deducted a $15 collection fee. The collection and fee are not yet recorded.

Required

Check (1) Reconciled balance, $18,326.45 (2) Cr. Note Receivable $1,400

1. Prepare the September 30, 2011, bank reconciliation for this company.
2. Prepare the journal entries to adjust the book balance of cash to the reconciled balance.

Analysis Component

3. The bank statement reveals that some of the prenumbered checks in the sequence are missing. Describe three situations that could explain this.

PROBLEM SET B

Problem 8-1B
Analyzing internal control
C1 

For each of these five separate cases, identify the principle(s) of internal control that is violated. Recommend what the business should do to ensure adherence to principles of internal control.

1. Latoya Tally is the company's computer specialist and oversees its computerized payroll system. Her boss recently asked her to put password protection on all office computers. Latoya has put a password in place that allows only the boss access to the file where pay rates are changed and personnel are added or deleted from the payroll.
2. Lake Theater has a computerized order-taking system for its tickets. The system is active all week and backed up every Friday night.
3. X2U Company has two employees handling acquisitions of inventory. One employee places purchase orders and pays vendors. The second employee receives the merchandise.
4. The owner of Super-Aid Pharmacy uses a check protector to perforate checks, making it difficult for anyone to alter the amount of the check. The check protector is on the owner's desk in an office that contains company checks and is normally unlocked.
5. LeAnn Company is a small business that has separated the duties of cash receipts and cash disbursements. The employee responsible for cash disbursements reconciles the bank account monthly.

Problem 8-2B
Establishing, reimbursing, and adjusting petty cash
P2

Pepco Co. establishes a petty cash fund for payments of small amounts. The following transactions involving the petty cash fund occurred in January (the last month of the company's fiscal year).

Jan. 3 A company check for $150 is written and made payable to the petty cashier to establish the petty cash fund.

14 A company check is written to replenish the fund for the following expenditures made since January 3.
- *a.* Purchased office supplies for $16.29 that are immediately used up.
- *b.* Paid $17.60 COD shipping charges on merchandise purchased for resale, terms FOB shipping point. Pepco uses the perpetual system to account for inventory.
- *c.* Paid $36.57 to All-Tech for minor repairs to a computer.
- *d.* Paid $14.82 for items classified as miscellaneous expenses.
- *e.* Counted $62.28 remaining in the petty cash box.

15 Prepared a company check for $25 to increase the fund to $175.

31 The petty cashier reports that $17.35 remains in the fund. A company check is written to replenish the fund for the following expenditures made since January 14.
- *f.* Paid $40 to *The Smart Shopper* for an advertisement in January's newsletter.
- *g.* Paid $38.19 for postage expenses.
- *h.* Paid $58 to Take-You-There for delivery of merchandise, terms FOB destination.

31 The company decides that the January 15 increase in the fund was too little. It increases the fund by another $75, leaving a total of $250.

Required

Check (1) Cr. to Cash: Jan. 14, $87.72; Jan. 31 (total), $232.65

1. Prepare journal entries to establish the fund on January 3, to replenish it on January 14 and January 31, and to reflect any increase or decrease in the fund balance on January 15 and 31.

Analysis Component

2. Explain how the company's financial statements are affected if the petty cash fund is not replenished and no entry is made on January 31.

Problem 8-3B
Establish, reimburse, and increase petty cash
P2

RPM Music Center had the following petty cash transactions in March of the current year.

March	5	Wrote a $200 check, cashed it, and gave the proceeds and the petty cashbox to Liz Buck, the petty cashier.
	6	Paid $14.50 COD shipping charges on merchandise purchased for resale, terms FOB shipping point. RPM uses the perpetual system to account for merchandise inventory.
	11	Paid $8.75 delivery charges on merchandise sold to a customer, terms FOB destination.
	12	Purchased file folders for $12.13 that are immediately used.
	14	Reimbursed Will Nelson, the manager, $9.65 for office supplies purchased and used.
	18	Purchased printer paper for $22.54 that is immediately used.
	27	Paid $47.10 COD shipping charges on merchandise purchased for resale, terms FOB shipping point.
	28	Paid postage expenses of $16.
	30	Reimbursed Nelson $58.80 for business car mileage.
	31	Cash of $11.53 remained in the fund. Sorted the petty cash receipts by accounts affected and exchanged them for a check to reimburse the fund for expenditures.
	31	The petty cash fund amount is increased by $50 to a total of $250.

Required

1. Prepare the journal entry to establish the petty cash fund.
2. Prepare a petty cash payments report for March with these categories: delivery expense, mileage expense, postage expense, merchandise inventory (for transportation-in), and office supplies expense. Sort the payments into the appropriate categories and total the expenses in each category.
3. Prepare the journal entries for part 2 to both (*a*) reimburse and (*b*) increase the fund amount.

Check (2) Total expenses $189.47

(3a & 3b) Total Cr. to Cash $238.47

Problem 8-4B
Prepare a bank reconciliation and record adjustments
P3

The following information is available to reconcile Style Co.'s book balance of cash with its bank statement cash balance as of December 31, 2011.

a. The December 31 cash balance according to the accounting records is $31,743.70, and the bank statement cash balance for that date is $45,091.80.

b. Check No. 1273 for $1,084.20 and Check No. 1282 for $390, both written and entered in the accounting records in December, are not among the canceled checks. Two checks, No. 1231 for $2,289 and No. 1242 for $370.50, were outstanding on the most recent November 30 reconciliation. Check No. 1231 is listed with the December canceled checks, but Check No. 1242 is not.

c. When the December checks are compared with entries in the accounting records, it is found that Check No. 1267 had been correctly drawn for $2,435 to pay for office supplies but was erroneously entered in the accounting records as $2,453.

d. Two debit memoranda are enclosed with the statement and are unrecorded at the time of the reconciliation. One debit memorandum is for $749.50 and dealt with an NSF check for $732 received from a customer, Titus Industries, in payment of its account. The bank assessed a $17.50 fee for processing it. The second debit memorandum is a $79 charge for check printing. Style did not record these transactions before receiving the statement.

e. A credit memorandum indicates that the bank collected $20,000 cash on a note receivable for the company, deducted a $20 collection fee, and credited the balance to the company's Cash account. Style did not record this transaction before receiving the statement.

f. Style's December 31 daily cash receipts of $7,666.10 were placed in the bank's night depository on that date, but do not appear on the December 31 bank statement.

Required

1. Prepare the bank reconciliation for this company as of December 31, 2011.
2. Prepare the journal entries necessary to bring the company's book balance of cash into conformity with the reconciled cash balance as of December 31, 2011.

Check (1) Reconciled balance, $50,913.20; (2) Cr. Note Receivable $20,000

Analysis Component

3. Explain the nature of the communications conveyed by a bank when the bank sends the depositor (*a*) a debit memorandum and (*b*) a credit memorandum.

Problem 8-5B
Prepare a bank reconciliation and record adjustments
P3

Safe Systems most recently reconciled its bank balance on April 30 and reported two checks outstanding at that time, No. 1771 for $781 and No. 1780 for $1,325.90. The following information is available for its May 31, 2011, reconciliation.

From the May 31 Bank Statement

PREVIOUS BALANCE	TOTAL CHECKS AND DEBITS	TOTAL DEPOSITS AND CREDITS	CURRENT BALANCE
18,290.70	12,898.90	16,416.80	21,808.60

CHECKS AND DEBITS			DEPOSITS AND CREDITS		DAILY BALANCE	
Date	No.	Amount	Date	Amount	Date	Amount
05/01	1771	781.00	05/04	2,438.00	04/30	18,290.70
05/02	1783	195.30	05/14	2,898.00	05/01	17,509.70
05/04	1782	1,285.50	05/22	1,801.80	05/02	17,314.40
05/11	1784	1,449.60	05/25	7,200.00 CM	05/04	18,466.90
05/18		431.80 NSF	05/26	2,079.00	05/11	17,017.30
05/25	1787	8,032.50			05/14	19,915.30
05/26	1785	157.20			05/18	19,483.50
05/29	1788	554.00			05/22	21,285.30
05/31		12.00 SC			05/25	20,452.80
					05/26	22,374.60
					05/29	21,820.60
					05/31	21,808.60

From Safe Systems' Accounting Records

Cash Receipts Deposited

Date			Cash Debit
May	4		2,438.00
	14		2,898.00
	22		1,801.80
	26		2,079.00
	31		2,526.30
			11,743.10

Cash Disbursements

Check No.		Cash Credit
1782		1,285.50
1783		195.30
1784		1,449.60
1785		157.20
1786		353.10
1787		8,032.50
1788		544.00
1789		639.50
		12,656.70

Cash Acct. No. 101

Date		Explanation	PR	Debit	Credit	Balance
Apr.	30	Balance				16,183.80
May	31	Total receipts	R7	11,743.10		27,926.90
	31	Total disbursements	D8		12,656.70	15,270.20

Additional Information

Check No. 1788 is correctly drawn for $554 to pay for May utilities; however, the recordkeeper misread the amount and entered it in the accounting records with a debit to Utilities Expense and a credit to Cash for $544. The bank paid and deducted the correct amount. The NSF check shown in the statement was originally received from a customer, S. Bax, in payment of her account. The company has not yet recorded its return. The credit memorandum is from a $7,300 note that the bank collected for the company. The bank deducted a $100 collection fee and deposited the remainder in the company's account. The collection and fee have not yet been recorded.

Required

1. Prepare the May 31, 2011, bank reconciliation for Safe Systems.
2. Prepare the journal entries to adjust the book balance of cash to the reconciled balance.

Check (1) Reconciled balance, $22,016.40; (2) Cr. Note Receivable $7,300

Analysis Component

3. The bank statement reveals that some of the prenumbered checks in the sequence are missing. Describe three possible situations to explain this.

SERIAL PROBLEM

Business Solutions

P3

(This serial problem began in Chapter 1 and continues through most of the book. If previous chapter segments were not completed, the serial problem can begin at this point. It is helpful, but not necessary, to use the Working Papers that accompany the book.)

SP 8 Santana Rey receives the March bank statement for Business Solutions on April 11, 2012. The March 31 bank statement shows an ending cash balance of $67,566. A comparison of the bank statement with the general ledger Cash account, No. 101, reveals the following.

a. S. Rey notices that the bank erroneously cleared a $500 check against her account in March that she did not issue. The check documentation included with the bank statement shows that this check was actually issued by a company named Business Systems.
b. On March 25, the bank issued a $50 debit memorandum for the safety deposit box that Business Solutions agreed to rent from the bank beginning March 25.
c. On March 26, the bank issued a $102 debit memorandum for printed checks that Business Solutions ordered from the bank.
d. On March 31, the bank issued a credit memorandum for $33 interest earned on Business Solutions' checking account for the month of March.
e. S. Rey notices that the check she issued for $128 on March 31, 2012, has not yet cleared the bank.
f. S. Rey verifies that all deposits made in March do appear on the March bank statement.
g. The general ledger Cash account, No. 101, shows an ending cash balance per books of $68,057 as of March 31 (prior to any reconciliation).

Required

1. Prepare a bank reconciliation for Business Solutions for the month ended March 31, 2012.
2. Prepare any necessary adjusting entries. Use Miscellaneous Expenses, No. 677, for any bank charges. Use Interest Revenue, No. 404, for any interest earned on the checking account for the month of March.

Check (1) Adj. bank bal. $67,938

Beyond the Numbers

REPORTING IN ACTION

C2 A1

RIM

BTN 8-1 Refer to Research In Motion's financial statements in Appendix A to answer the following.

1. For both fiscal year-ends February 27, 2010, and February 28, 2009, identify the total amount of cash and cash equivalents. Determine the percent this amount represents of total current assets, total current liabilities, total shareholders' equity, and total assets for both years. Comment on any trends.
2. For fiscal years ended February 27, 2010, and February 28, 2009, use the information in the statement of cash flows to determine the percent change between the beginning and ending year amounts of cash and cash equivalents.
3. Compute the days' sales uncollected as of February 27, 2010, and February 28, 2009. Has the collection of receivables improved? Are accounts receivable an important asset for Research In Motion? Explain.

Fast Forward

4. Access Research In Motion's financial statements for fiscal years ending after February 27, 2010, from its Website (RIM.com) or the SEC's EDGAR database (www.SEC.gov). Recompute its days' sales uncollected for fiscal years ending after February 27, 2010. Compare this to the days' sales uncollected for 2010 and 2009.

COMPARATIVE ANALYSIS

A1 

RIM
Apple

BTN 8-2 Key comparative figures for **Research In Motion** and **Apple** follow.

($ millions)	Research In Motion Current Year	Research In Motion Prior Year	Apple Current Year	Apple Prior Year
Accounts receivable	$ 2,594	$ 2,112	$ 3,361	$ 2,422
Net sales	14,953	11,065	42,905	37,491

Required

Compute days' sales uncollected for these companies for each of the two years shown. Comment on any trends for the companies. Which company has the largest percent change in days' sales uncollected?

ETHICS CHALLENGE

C1  

BTN 8-3 Carol Benton, Sue Knox, and Marcia Diamond work for a family physician, Dr. Gwen Conrad, who is in private practice. Dr. Conrad is knowledgeable about office management practices and has segregated the cash receipt duties as follows. Benton opens the mail and prepares a triplicate list of money received. She sends one copy of the list to Knox, the cashier, who deposits the receipts daily in the bank. Diamond, the recordkeeper, receives a copy of the list and posts payments to patients' accounts. About once a month the office clerks have an expensive lunch they pay for as follows. First, Knox endorses a patient's check in Dr. Conrad's name and cashes it at the bank. Benton then destroys the remittance advice accompanying the check. Finally, Diamond posts payment to the customer's account as a miscellaneous credit. The three justify their actions by their relatively low pay and knowledge that Dr. Conrad will likely never miss the money.

Required

1. Who is the best person in Dr. Conrad's office to reconcile the bank statement?
2. Would a bank reconciliation uncover this office fraud?
3. What are some procedures to detect this type of fraud?
4. Suggest additional internal controls that Dr. Conrad could implement.

COMMUNICATING IN PRACTICE

BTN 8-4[B] Assume you are a business consultant. The owner of a company sends you an e-mail expressing concern that the company is not taking advantage of its discounts offered by vendors. The company currently uses the gross method of recording purchases. The owner is considering a review of all invoices and payments from the previous period. Due to the volume of purchases, however, the owner recognizes that this is time-consuming and costly. The owner seeks your advice about monitoring purchase discounts in the future. Provide a response in memorandum form.

TAKING IT TO THE NET

C1 P1  

BTN 8-5 Visit the Association of Certified Fraud Examiners Website at cfenet.com. Find and open the file "2008 Report to the Nation." Read the two-page Executive Summary and fill in the following blanks. (The report is under its *Fraud Resources* tab or under its *About the ACFE* tab [under Press Room]; we can also use the *Search* tab.)

1. The median loss caused by occupational frauds was $_______.
2. More than __________ of fraud cases caused at least $1 million in losses.
3. Companies lose ___% of their annual revenues to fraud; this figure translates to $_____ billion in fraud losses.
4. The typical length of fraud schemes was ____ years from the time the fraud began until it was detected.
5. Companies that conducted surprise audits suffered a median loss of $______, whereas those without surprise audits had a median loss of $______.
6. The median loss suffered by companies with fewer than 100 employees was $______ per scheme.
7. ____________ and ____________ were the most common small business fraud schemes.
8. ___% of respondents cited inadequate internal controls as the primary contributing factor in the frauds investigated.
9. Only ___% of the perpetrators had convictions prior to committing their frauds.

BTN 8-6 Organize the class into teams. Each team must prepare a list of 10 internal controls a consumer could observe in a typical retail department store. When called upon, the team's spokesperson must be prepared to share controls identified by the team that have not been shared by another team's spokesperson.

TEAMWORK IN ACTION
C1

BTN 8-7 Review the opening feature of this chapter that highlights Dylan Lauren and her company Dylan's Candy Bar.

ENTREPRENEURIAL DECISION
C1 P1  

Required

1. List the seven principles of internal control and explain how Dylan could implement each of them in her retail stores.
2. Do you believe that Dylan will need to add controls as her business expands? Explain.

BTN 8-8 Visit an area of your college that serves the student community with either products or services. Some examples are food services, libraries, and bookstores. Identify and describe between four and eight internal controls being implemented.

HITTING THE ROAD
C1 

BTN 8-9 The following information is from Nokia (www.Nokia.com), which is a leading global manufacturer of mobile devices and services.

GLOBAL DECISION
C2 A1 

EUR millions	Current Year	Prior Year
Cash	1,142	1,706
Accounts receivable	7,981	9,444
Current assets	23,613	24,470
Total assets	35,738	39,582
Current liabilities	15,188	20,355
Shareholders' equity	14,749	16,510
Net sales	40,984	50,710

Required

1. For each year, compute the percentage that cash represents of current assets, total assets, current liabilities, and shareholders' equity. Comment on any trends in these percentages.
2. Determine the percentage change between the current and prior year cash balances.
3. Compute the days' sales uncollected at the end of both the current year and the prior year. Has the collection of receivables improved? Explain.

ANSWERS TO MULTIPLE CHOICE QUIZ

1. e; The entry follows.

Debits to expenses (or assets)	420	
Cash Over and Short	5	
Cash		425

2. a; recognizes cash collection of note by bank.
3. a; the bank reconciliation follows.

Bank Reconciliation November 30			
Balance per bank statement	$1,895	Balance per books	$1,742
Add: Deposit in transit	795	Add: Note collected less fee	320
Deduct: Outstanding checks	(638)	Deduct: Service charge	(10)
Reconciled balance	$2,052	Reconciled balance	$2,052

4. d; ($6,720/$84,000) × 365 = 29.2 days
5. b; The entry follows.

Merchandise Inventory*	5,880	
Accounts Payable		5,880

*$6,000 × 98%

Accounting for Receivables

A Look Back

Chapter 8 focused on internal control and reporting for cash. We described internal control procedures and the accounting for and management of cash.

A Look at This Chapter

This chapter emphasizes receivables. We explain that they are liquid assets and describe how companies account for and report them. We also discuss the importance of estimating uncollectibles.

A Look Ahead

Chapter 10 focuses on plant assets, natural resources, and intangible assets. We explain how to account for, report, and analyze these long-term assets.

Learning Objectives

CAP

CONCEPTUAL

C1 Describe accounts receivable and how they occur and are recorded. (p. 360)

C2 Describe a note receivable, the computation of its maturity date, and the recording of its existence. (p. 370)

C3 Explain how receivables can be converted to cash before maturity. (p. 373)

ANALYTICAL

A1 Compute accounts receivable turnover and use it to help assess financial condition. (p. 375)

LP9

PROCEDURAL

P1 Apply the direct write-off method to account for accounts receivable. (p. 363)

P2 Apply the allowance method and estimate uncollectibles based on sales and accounts receivable. (p. 366)

P3 Record the honoring and dishonoring of a note and adjustments for interest. (p. 372)

Decision Insight

Monk E-Business

"We are not wearing bling . . . I mean, we are still monks"
—BROTHER BERNARD MCCOY

SPARTA, WI—"My printer ran out of toner," recalls Brother Bernard McCoy. "I was just appalled at the cost of the black dust . . . the markup on toner is sinfully high!" So, Bernard, who is part of a handful of monks living at and trying to keep a remote monastery in rural Wisconsin going, started thinking. "Nine hundred years ago, my brothers were copying manuscripts and making their own paper and ink," explains Bernard. His response was to launch LaserMonks **(LaserMonks.com)**, a supplier of toner and ink products (and other goods).

Sales quickly soared, and Bernard, along with what he calls his monk-helper angels, had to contend with accounting activities, receivables management, and other day-to-day recordkeeping needs. Special attention was focused on monitoring receivables. Decisions on credit sales and policies for extending credit can make or break a start-up, and Bernard was determined to succeed in spite of the demands of a monk's life. "We spend about five hours a day in Gregorian chant, and another couple of hours in prayers," explains Bernard. "We're monks . . . we do monk things!"

Nevertheless, Bernard and his angels ensured that credit sales were extended to customers in good credit standing. Further, his team knows their customers, including who pays and when. Explains Bernard, we understand our customers—inside and out—including cash payment patterns that allow them to estimate uncollectibles and minimize bad debts. Bernard points out, however, that "we use the money for good works and to support monks who dedicate their lives to serving God and neighbor."

A commitment to quality customers and products is propelling LaserMonks' sales and shattering Bernard's most optimistic goals. "The results have been beyond anything we could imagine," affirms Bernard. Both accounts and notes receivables receive his attention. Bernard and his team's financial focus includes reviewing the allowance for doubtful accounts monthly. "We're scrambling to keep up with growth," adds Bernard. "[We're] continuing to negotiate with suppliers . . . processing orders between our times of prayer."

Bernard's focus on serving people is unwavering. "Our customer service is following our order's tradition of hospitality," explains Bernard. "We try to transfer monastic hospitality into commerce hospitality . . . we try to treat every single customer with kid gloves." Bernard says he wishes that all customers "be abundantly blessed with prosperity of soul."

[Sources: *LaserMonks Website*, January 2011; *Entrepreneur*, September 2009; *CBS Broadcasting*, August 2006; *Religion & Ethics Newsweekly*, September 2009; *Consumer Reports*, February 2010]

Chapter Preview

This chapter focuses on accounts receivable and short-term notes receivable. We describe each of these assets, their uses, and how they are accounted for and reported in financial statements. This knowledge helps us use accounting information to make better business decisions. It can also help in predicting future company performance and financial condition as well as in managing one's own business.

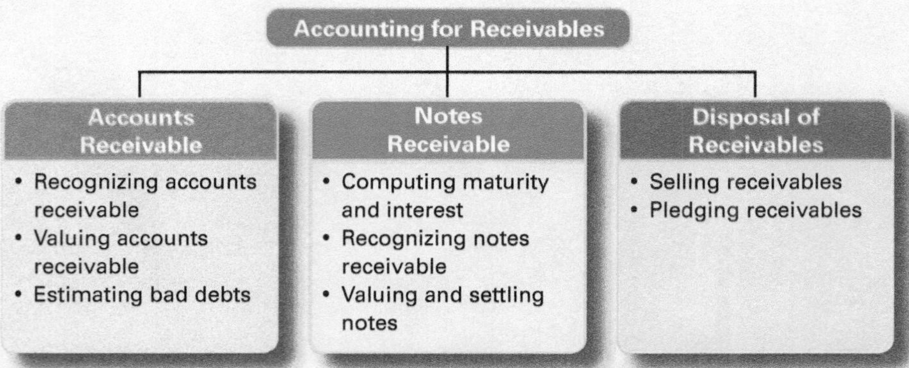

ACCOUNTS RECEIVABLE

A *receivable* is an amount due from another party. The two most common receivables are accounts receivable and notes receivable. Other receivables include interest receivable, rent receivable, tax refund receivable, and receivables from employees. **Accounts receivable** are amounts due from customers for credit sales. This section begins by describing how accounts receivable occur. It includes receivables that occur when customers use credit cards issued by third parties and when a company gives credit directly to customers. When a company does extend credit directly to customers, it (1) maintains a separate account receivable for each customer and (2) accounts for bad debts from credit sales.

Recognizing Accounts Receivable

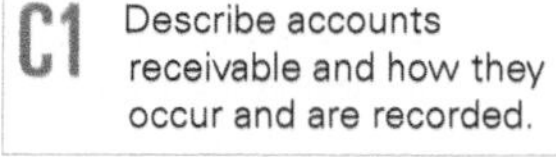

Accounts receivable occur from credit sales to customers. The amount of credit sales has increased in recent years, reflecting several factors including an efficient financial system. Retailers such as Costco and Best Buy hold millions of dollars in accounts receivable. Similar amounts are held by wholesalers such as SUPERVALU and SYSCO. Exhibit 9.1 shows recent dollar amounts of receivables and their percent of total assets for four well-known companies.

EXHIBIT 9.1

Accounts Receivable for Selected Companies

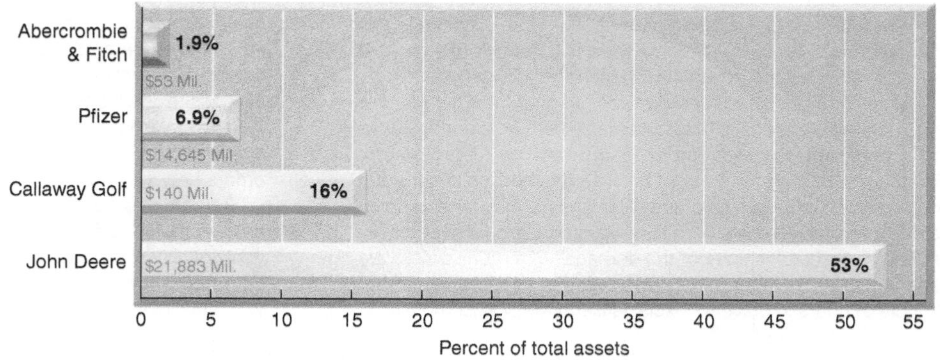

Sales on Credit Credit sales are recorded by increasing (debiting) Accounts Receivable. A company must also maintain a separate account for each customer that tracks how much that customer purchases, has already paid, and still owes. This information provides the basis for sending bills to customers and for other business analyses. To maintain this information, companies that extend credit directly to their customers keep a separate account receivable for each one of them. The general ledger continues to have a single Accounts Receivable account along with the other financial statement accounts, but a supplementary record is created to maintain a separate account for each customer. This supplementary record is called the *accounts receivable ledger.*

Exhibit 9.2 shows the relation between the Accounts Receivable account in the general ledger and its individual customer accounts in the accounts receivable ledger for TechCom, a small electronics wholesaler. This exhibit reports a $3,000 ending balance of TechCom's accounts receivable for June 30. TechCom's transactions are mainly in cash, but it has two major credit customers: CompStore and RDA Electronics. Its *schedule of accounts receivable* shows that the $3,000 balance of the Accounts Receivable account in the general ledger equals the total of its two customers' balances in the accounts receivable ledger.

EXHIBIT 9.2

General Ledger and the Accounts Receivable Ledger (before July 1 transactions)

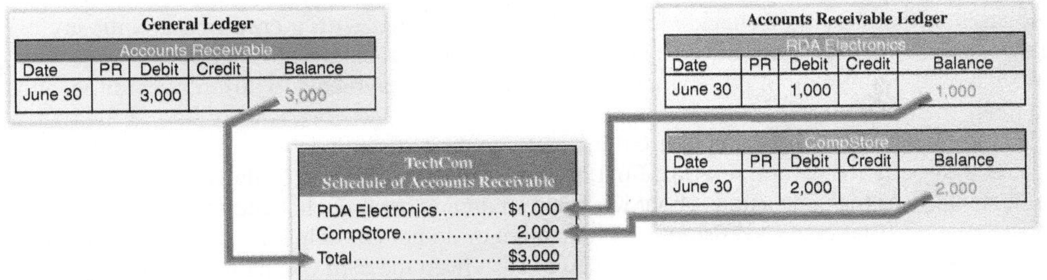

General Ledger — Accounts Receivable

Date	PR	Debit	Credit	Balance
June 30		3,000		3,000

Accounts Receivable Ledger — RDA Electronics

Date	PR	Debit	Credit	Balance
June 30		1,000		1,000

Accounts Receivable Ledger — CompStore

Date	PR	Debit	Credit	Balance
June 30		2,000		2,000

TechCom Schedule of Accounts Receivable

RDA Electronics	$1,000
CompStore	2,000
Total	$3,000

To see how accounts receivable from credit sales are recognized in the accounting records, we look at two transactions on July 1 between TechCom and its credit customers—see Exhibit 9.3. The first is a credit sale of $950 to CompStore. A credit sale is posted with both a debit to the Accounts Receivable account in the general ledger and a debit to the customer account in the accounts receivable ledger. The second transaction is a collection of $720 from RDA Electronics from a prior credit sale. Cash receipts from a credit customer are posted with a credit to the Accounts Receivable account in the general ledger and flow through to credit the customer account in the accounts receivable ledger. (Posting debits or credits to Accounts Receivable in two separate ledgers does not violate the requirement that debits equal credits. The equality of debits and credits is maintained in the general ledger. The accounts receivable ledger is a *supplementary* record providing information on each customer.)

EXHIBIT 9.3

Accounts Receivable Transactions

July 1	Accounts Receivable—CompStore	950	
	Sales		950
	*To record credit sales**		
July 1	Cash	720	
	Accounts Receivable—RDA Electronics		720
	To record collection of credit sales.		

Assets = Liabilities + Equity
+950 +950

Assets = Liabilities + Equity
+720
−720

* We omit the entry to Dr. Cost of Sales and Cr. Merchandise Inventory to focus on sales and receivables.

Exhibit 9.4 shows the general ledger and the accounts receivable ledger after recording the two July 1 transactions. The general ledger shows the effects of the sale, the collection, and the resulting balance of $3,230. These events are also reflected in the individual customer accounts: RDA Electronics has an ending balance of $280, and CompStore's ending balance is $2,950.

EXHIBIT 9.4

General Ledger and the Accounts Receivable Ledger (after July 1 transactions)

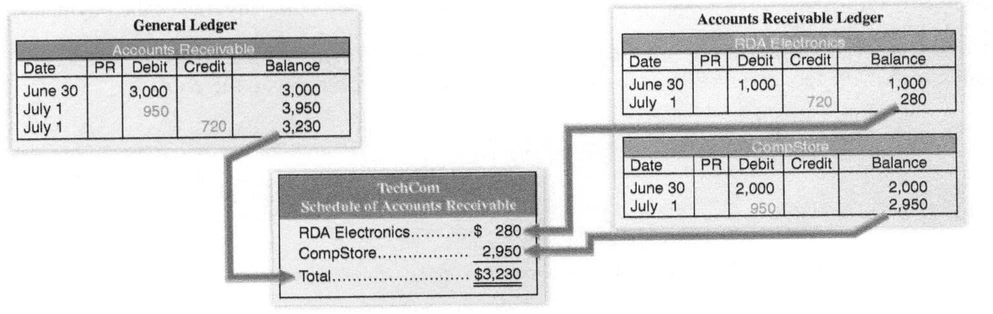

General Ledger — Accounts Receivable

Date	PR	Debit	Credit	Balance
June 30		3,000		3,000
July 1		950		3,950
July 1			720	3,230

Accounts Receivable Ledger — RDA Electronics

Date	PR	Debit	Credit	Balance
June 30		1,000		1,000
July 1			720	280

Accounts Receivable Ledger — CompStore

Date	PR	Debit	Credit	Balance
June 30		2,000		2,000
July 1		950		2,950

TechCom Schedule of Accounts Receivable

RDA Electronics	$ 280
CompStore	2,950
Total	$3,230

The $3,230 sum of the individual accounts equals the debit balance of the Accounts Receivable account in the general ledger.

Like TechCom, many large retailers such as Sears and JCPenney sell on credit. Many also maintain their own credit cards to grant credit to approved customers and to earn interest on any balance not paid within a specified period of time. This allows them to avoid the fee charged by credit card companies. The entries in this case are the same as those for TechCom except for the possibility of added interest revenue. If a customer owes interest on a bill, we debit Interest Receivable and credit Interest Revenue for that amount.

Credit Card Sales Many companies allow their customers to pay for products and services using third-party credit cards such as Visa, MasterCard, or American Express, and debit cards (also called ATM or bank cards). This practice gives customers the ability to make purchases without cash or checks. Once credit is established with a credit card company or bank, the customer does not have to open an account with each store. Customers using these cards can make single monthly payments instead of several payments to different creditors and can defer their payments.

Many sellers allow customers to use third-party credit cards and debit cards instead of granting credit directly for several reasons. First, the seller does not have to evaluate each customer's credit standing or make decisions about who gets credit and how much. Second, the seller avoids the risk of extending credit to customers who cannot or do not pay. This risk is transferred to the card company. Third, the seller typically receives cash from the card company sooner than had it granted credit directly to customers. Fourth, a variety of credit options for customers offers a potential increase in sales volume. Sears historically offered credit only to customers using a Sears card but later changed its policy to permit customers to charge purchases to third-party credit card companies in a desire to increase sales. It reported: "SearsCharge increased its share of Sears retail sales even as the company expanded the payment options available to its customers with the acceptance . . . of Visa, MasterCard, and American Express in addition to the [Sears] Card."

Point: Visa USA now transacts more than $1 trillion from its credit, debit, and prepaid cards.

There are guidelines in how companies account for credit card and debit card sales. Some credit cards, but nearly all debit cards, credit a seller's Cash account immediately upon deposit. In this case the seller deposits a copy of each card sales receipt in its bank account just as it deposits a customer's check. The majority of credit cards, however, require the seller to remit a copy (often electronically) of each receipt to the card company. Until payment is received, the seller has an account receivable from the card company. In both cases, the seller pays a fee for services provided by the card company, often ranging from 1% to 5% of card sales. This charge is deducted from the credit to the seller's account or the cash payment to the seller.

Decision Insight

Debit Card vs. Credit Card A buyer's debit card purchase reduces the buyer's cash account balance at the card company, which is often a bank. Since the buyer's cash account balance is a liability (with a credit balance) for the card company to the buyer, the card company would debit that account for a buyer's purchase—hence, the term *debit card.* A credit card reflects authorization by the card company of a line of credit for the buyer with preset interest rates and payment terms—hence, the term *credit card.* Most card companies waive interest charges if the buyer pays its balance each month. ■

Point: Web merchants pay twice as much in credit card association fees as other retailers because they suffer 10 times as much fraud.

The procedures used in accounting for credit card sales depend on whether cash is received immediately on deposit or cash receipt is delayed until the credit card company makes the payment.

Cash Received Immediately on Deposit To illustrate, if TechCom has $100 of credit card sales with a 4% fee, and its $96 cash is received immediately on deposit, the entry is

Assets	=	Liabilities	+	Equity
+96				+100
				−4

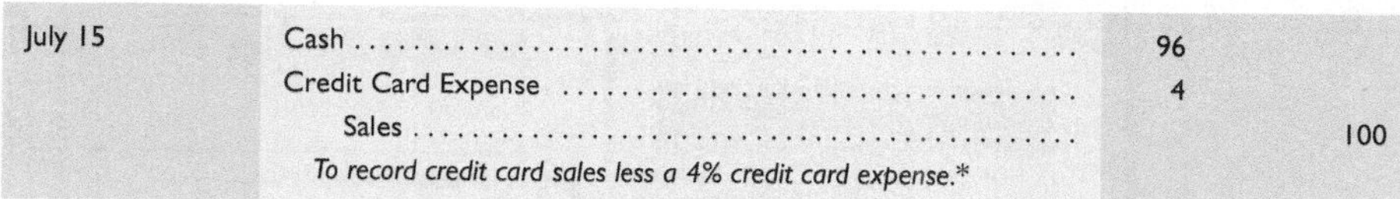

July 15	Cash	96	
	Credit Card Expense	4	
	Sales		100
	*To record credit card sales less a 4% credit card expense.**		

* We omit the entry to Dr. Cost of Sales and Cr. Merchandise Inventory to focus on credit card expense.

Cash Received Some Time after Deposit However, if instead TechCom must remit electronically the credit card sales receipts to the credit card company and wait for the $96 cash payment, the entry on the date of sale is

July 15	Accounts Receivable—Credit Card Co.	96	
	Credit Card Expense	4	
	Sales		100
	*To record credit card sales less 4% credit card expense.**		

Assets = Liabilities + Equity
+96 +100
−4

* We omit the entry to Dr. Cost of Sales and Cr. Merchandise Inventory to focus on credit card expense.

When cash is later received from the credit card company, usually through electronic funds transfer, the entry is

July 20	Cash	96	
	Accounts Receivable—Credit Card Co.		96
	To record cash receipt.		

Assets = Liabilities + Equity
+96
−96

Some firms report credit card expense in the income statement as a type of discount deducted from sales to get net sales. Other companies classify it as a selling expense or even as an administrative expense. Arguments can be made for each approach.

Point: Third-party credit card costs can be large. JCPenney reported third-party credit card costs exceeding $10 million.

Installment Sales and Receivables Many companies allow their credit customers to make periodic payments over several months. For example, **Ford Motor Company** reports more than $75 billion in installment receivables. The seller refers to such assets as *installment accounts* (or *finance*) *receivable,* which are amounts owed by customers from credit sales for which payment is required in periodic amounts over an extended time period. Source documents for installment accounts receivable include sales slips or invoices describing the sales transactions. The customer is usually charged interest. Although installment accounts receivable can have credit periods of more than one year, they are classified as current assets if the seller regularly offers customers such terms.

Decision Maker Answer — p. 378

Entrepreneur As a small retailer, you are considering allowing customers to buy merchandise using credit cards. Until now, your store accepted only cash and checks. What analysis do you use to make this decision? ■

Quick Check Answers — p. 379

1. In recording credit card sales, when do you debit Accounts Receivable and when do you debit Cash?
2. A company accumulates sales receipts and remits them to the credit card company for payment. When are the credit card expenses recorded? When are these expenses incurred?

Valuing Accounts Receivable—Direct Write-Off Method

P1 Apply the direct write-off method to account for accounts receivable.

When a company directly grants credit to its customers, it expects that some customers will not pay what they promised. The accounts of these customers are *uncollectible accounts,* commonly called **bad debts.** The total amount of uncollectible accounts is an expense of selling on credit. Why do companies sell on credit if they expect some accounts to be uncollectible? The answer is that companies believe that granting credit will increase total sales and net income enough to offset bad debts. Companies use two methods to account for uncollectible accounts: (1) direct write-off method and (2) allowance method. We describe both.

Point: Managers realize that some portion of credit sales will be uncollectible, but which credit sales are uncollectible is unknown.

Recording and Writing Off Bad Debts The **direct write-off method** of accounting for bad debts records the loss from an uncollectible account receivable when it is determined to be uncollectible. No attempt is made to predict bad debts expense. To illustrate, if TechCom determines on January 23 that it cannot collect $520 owed to it by its customer J. Kent, it recognizes the loss using the direct write-off method as follows:

Assets = Liabilities + Equity
−520 −520

Jan. 23	Bad Debts Expense	520	
	Accounts Receivable—J. Kent		520
	To write off an uncollectible account.		

The debit in this entry charges the uncollectible amount directly to the current period's Bad Debts Expense account. The credit removes its balance from the Accounts Receivable account in the general ledger (and its subsidiary ledger).

Point: If a customer fails to pay within the credit period, most companies send out repeated billings and make other efforts to collect.

Recovering a Bad Debt Although uncommon, sometimes an account written off is later collected. This can be due to factors such as continual collection efforts or a customer's good fortune. If the account of J. Kent that was written off directly to Bad Debts Expense is later collected in full, the following two entries record this recovery.

Assets = Liabilities + Equity
+520 +520

Assets = Liabilities + Equity
+520
−520

Mar. 11	Accounts Receivable—J. Kent....................	520	
	Bad Debts Expense		520
	To reinstate account previously written off.		
Mar. 11	Cash	520	
	Accounts Receivable—J. Kent		520
	To record full payment of account.		

Assessing the Direct Write-Off Method Examples of companies that use the direct write-off method include Rand Medical Billing, Gateway Distributors, Microwave Satellite Technologies, First Industrial Realty, New Frontier Energy, and Sub Surface Waste Management. The following disclosure by Pharma-Bio Serv is typical of the justification for this method: Bad debts are accounted for using the direct write-off method whereby an expense is recognized only when a specific account is determined to be uncollectible. The effect of using this method approximates that of the allowance method. Companies must weigh at least two accounting concepts when considering the use of the direct write-off method: the (1) matching principle and (2) materiality constraint.

Matching principle applied to bad debts. The **matching (expense recognition) principle** requires expenses to be reported in the same accounting period as the sales they helped produce. This means that if extending credit to customers helped produce sales, the bad debts expense linked to those sales is matched and reported in the same period. The direct write-off method usually does *not* best match sales and expenses because bad debts expense is not recorded until an account becomes uncollectible, which often occurs in a period after that of the credit sale. To match bad debts expense with the sales it produces therefore requires a company to estimate future uncollectibles.

Point: Harley-Davidson reports $169 million of credit losses matched against $4,782 million of total revenues.

Materiality constraint applied to bad debts. The **materiality constraint** states that an amount can be ignored if its effect on the financial statements is unimportant to users' business decisions. The materiality constraint permits the use of the direct write-off method when bad debts expenses are very small in relation to a company's other financial statement items such as sales and net income.

Valuing Accounts Receivable—Allowance Method

The **allowance method** of accounting for bad debts matches the *estimated* loss from uncollectible accounts receivable against the sales they helped produce. We must use estimated losses because when sales occur, management does not know which customers will not pay their bills. This means that at the end of each period, the allowance method requires an estimate of the total bad debts expected to result from that period's sales. This method has two advantages over the direct write-off method: (1) it records estimated bad debts expense in the period when the related sales are recorded and (2) it reports accounts receivable on the balance sheet at the estimated amount of cash to be collected.

Point: Under direct write-off, expense is recorded each time an account is written off. Under the allowance method, expense is recorded with an adjusting entry equal to the total estimated uncollectibles for that period's sales.

Recording Bad Debts Expense The allowance method estimates bad debts expense at the end of each accounting period and records it with an adjusting entry. TechCom, for instance, had credit sales of $300,000 during its first year of operations. At the end of the first year, $20,000 of credit sales remained uncollected. Based on the experience of similar businesses, TechCom estimated that $1,500 of its accounts receivable would be uncollectible. This estimated expense is recorded with the following adjusting entry.

Dec. 31	Bad Debts Expense	1,500	
	Allowance for Doubtful Accounts		1,500
	To record estimated bad debts.		

Assets = Liabilities + Equity
−1,500 −1,500

The estimated Bad Debts Expense of $1,500 is reported on the income statement (as either a selling expense or an administrative expense) and offsets the $300,000 credit sales it helped produce. The **Allowance for Doubtful Accounts** is a contra asset account. A contra account is used instead of reducing accounts receivable directly because at the time of the adjusting entry, the company does not know which customers will not pay. After the bad debts adjusting entry is posted, TechCom's account balances (in T-account form) for Accounts Receivable and its Allowance for Doubtful Accounts are as shown in Exhibit 9.5.

Point: Credit approval is usually not assigned to the selling dept. because its goal is to increase sales, and it may approve customers at the cost of increased bad debts. Instead, approval is assigned to a separate credit-granting or administrative dept.

EXHIBIT 9.5

General Ledger Entries after Bad Debts Adjusting Entry

Accounts Receivable			
Dec. 31	20,000		

Allowance for Doubtful Accounts			
		Dec. 31	1,500

The Allowance for Doubtful Accounts credit balance of $1,500 has the effect of reducing accounts receivable to its estimated realizable value. **Realizable value** refers to the expected proceeds from converting an asset into cash. Although credit customers owe $20,000 to TechCom, only $18,500 is expected to be realized in cash collections from these customers. In the balance sheet, the Allowance for Doubtful Accounts is subtracted from Accounts Receivable and is often reported as shown in Exhibit 9.6.

Point: Bad Debts Expense is also called *Uncollectible Accounts Expense*. The Allowance for Doubtful Accounts is also called *Allowance for Uncollectible Accounts*.

EXHIBIT 9.6

Balance Sheet Presentation of the Allowance for Doubtful Accounts

Current assets		
Accounts receivable	$20,000	
Less allowance for doubtful accounts	1,500	$18,500

Sometimes the Allowance for Doubtful Accounts is not reported separately. This alternative presentation is shown in Exhibit 9.7 (also see Appendix A).

EXHIBIT 9.7

Alternative Presentation of the Allowance for Doubtful Accounts

Current assets	
Accounts receivable (net of $1,500 doubtful accounts)	$18,500

Writing Off a Bad Debt When specific accounts are identified as uncollectible, they are written off against the Allowance for Doubtful Accounts. To illustrate, TechCom decides that J. Kent's $520 account is uncollectible and makes the following entry to write it off.

Jan. 23	Allowance for Doubtful Accounts	520	
	Accounts Receivable—J. Kent		520
	To write off an uncollectible account.		

Assets = Liabilities + Equity
+520
−520

Posting this write-off entry to the Accounts Receivable account removes the amount of the bad debt from the general ledger (it is also posted to the accounts receivable subsidiary ledger). The general ledger accounts now appear as in Exhibit 9.8 (assuming no other transactions affecting these accounts).

Point: The Bad Debts Expense account is not debited in the write-off entry because it was recorded in the period when sales occurred.

EXHIBIT 9.8

General Ledger Entries after Write-Off

Accounts Receivable			
Dec. 31	20,000		
		Jan. 23	520

Allowance for Doubtful Accounts			
		Dec. 31	1,500
Jan. 23	520		

Point: In posting a write-off, the ledger's Explanation column indicates the reason for this credit so it is not misinterpreted as payment in full.

The write-off does *not* affect the realizable value of accounts receivable as shown in Exhibit 9.9. Neither total assets nor net income is affected by the write-off of a specific account. Instead, both assets and net income are affected in the period when bad debts expense is predicted and recorded with an adjusting entry.

EXHIBIT 9.9

Realizable Value before and after Write-Off of a Bad Debt

	Before Write-Off	After Write-Off
Accounts receivable	$ 20,000	$ 19,480
Less allowance for doubtful accounts	1,500	980
Estimated realizable accounts receivable	$18,500	$18,500

Recovering a Bad Debt When a customer fails to pay and the account is written off as uncollectible, his or her credit standing is jeopardized. To help restore credit standing, a customer sometimes volunteers to pay all or part of the amount owed. A company makes two entries when collecting an account previously written off by the allowance method. The first is to reverse the write-off and reinstate the customer's account. The second entry records the collection of the reinstated account. To illustrate, if on March 11 Kent pays in full his account previously written off, the entries are

Assets = Liabilities + Equity
+520
−520

Assets = Liabilities + Equity
+520
−520

Mar. 11	Accounts Receivable—J. Kent	520	
	Allowance for Doubtful Accounts		520
	To reinstate account previously written off.		
Mar. 11	Cash	520	
	Accounts Receivable—J. Kent		520
	To record full payment of account.		

Example: If TechCom used a collection agency and paid a 35% commission on $520 collected from Kent, how is this recorded? *Answer:*
Cash 338
Collection Expense 182
Accts. Recble.—J. Kent 520

In this illustration, Kent paid the entire amount previously written off, but sometimes a customer pays only a portion of the amount owed. A question then arises as to whether the entire balance of the account or just the amount paid is returned to accounts receivable. This is a matter of judgment. If we believe this customer will later pay in full, we return the entire amount owed to accounts receivable, but if we expect no further collection, we return only the amount paid.

Decision Insight

PayPal PayPal is legally just a money transfer agent, but it is increasingly challenging big credit card brands—see chart. PayPal is successful because: (1) online credit card processing fees often exceed $0.15 per dollar, but PayPal's fees are under $0.10 per dollar. (2) PayPal's merchant fraud losses are under 0.2% of revenues, which compares to nearly 2% for online merchants using credit cards.

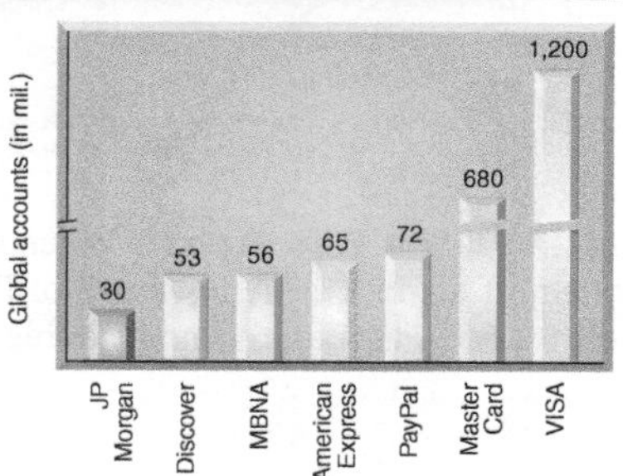

Estimating Bad Debts—Percent of Sales Method

P2 Apply the allowance method and estimate uncollectibles based on sales and accounts receivable.

The allowance method requires an estimate of bad debts expense to prepare an adjusting entry at the end of each accounting period. There are two common methods. One is based on the income statement relation between bad debts expense and sales. The second is based on the balance sheet relation between accounts receivable and the allowance for doubtful accounts.

The *percent of sales method,* also referred to as the *income statement method,* is based on the idea that a given percent of a company's credit sales for the period is uncollectible. To illustrate, assume that Musicland has credit sales of $400,000 in year 2011. Based on past experience,

Musicland estimates 0.6% of credit sales to be uncollectible. This implies that Musicland expects $2,400 of bad debts expense from its sales (computed as $400,000 × 0.006). The adjusting entry to record this estimated expense is

Point: Focus is on *credit* sales because cash sales do not produce bad debts. If cash sales are a small or stable percent of credit sales, total sales can be used.

Dec. 31	Bad Debts Expense	2,400	
	Allowance for Doubtful Accounts		2,400
	To record estimated bad debts.		

Assets = Liabilities + Equity
−2,400 −2,400

The allowance account ending balance on the balance sheet for this method would rarely equal the bad debts expense on the income statement. This is so because unless a company is in its first period of operations, its allowance account has a zero balance only if the prior amounts written off as uncollectible *exactly* equal the prior estimated bad debts expenses. (When computing bad debts expense as a percent of sales, managers monitor and adjust the percent so it is not too high or too low.)

Point: When using the *percent of sales method* for estimating uncollectibles, the estimate of bad debts is the number used in the adjusting entry.

Estimating Bad Debts—Percent of Receivables Method

The *accounts receivable methods,* also referred to as *balance sheet methods,* use balance sheet relations to estimate bad debts—mainly the relation between accounts receivable and the allowance amount. The goal of the bad debts adjusting entry for these methods is to make the Allowance for Doubtful Accounts balance equal to the portion of accounts receivable that is estimated to be uncollectible. The estimated balance for the allowance account is obtained in one of two ways: (1) computing the percent uncollectible from the total accounts receivable or (2) aging accounts receivable.

The *percent of accounts receivable method* assumes that a given percent of a company's receivables is uncollectible. This percent is based on past experience and is impacted by current conditions such as economic trends and customer difficulties. The total dollar amount of all receivables is multiplied by this percent to get the estimated dollar amount of uncollectible accounts—reported in the balance sheet as the Allowance for Doubtful Accounts.

To illustrate, assume that Musicland has $50,000 of accounts receivable on December 31, 2011. Experience suggests 5% of its receivables is uncollectible. This means that *after* the adjusting entry is posted, we want the Allowance for Doubtful Accounts to show a $2,500 credit balance (5% of $50,000). We are also told that its beginning balance is $2,200, which is 5% of the $44,000 accounts receivable on December 31, 2010—see Exhibit 9.10.

Point: When using an accounts receivable method for estimating uncollectibles, the allowance account balance is adjusted to equal the estimate of uncollectibles.

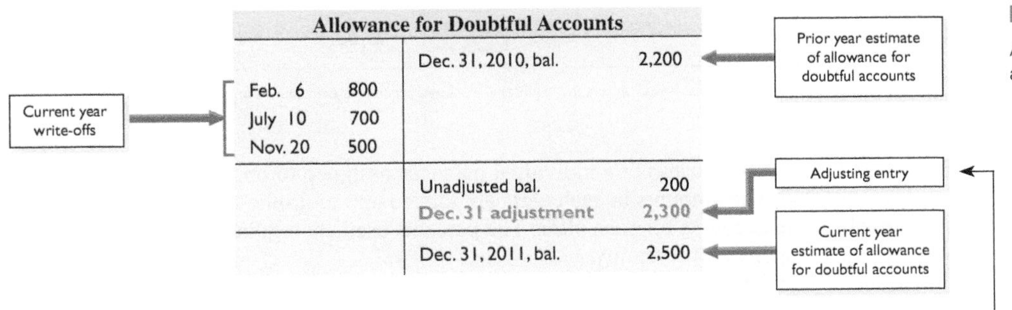

EXHIBIT 9.10

Allowance for Doubtful Accounts after Bad Debts Adjusting Entry

During 2011, accounts of customers are written off on February 6, July 10, and November 20. Thus, the account has a $200 credit balance *before* the December 31, 2011, adjustment. The adjusting entry to give the allowance account the estimated $2,500 balance is

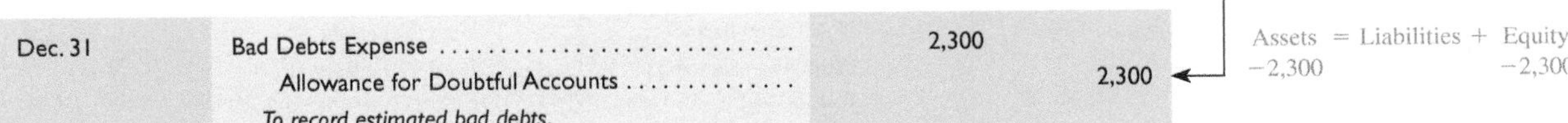

Dec. 31	Bad Debts Expense	2,300	
	Allowance for Doubtful Accounts		2,300
	To record estimated bad debts.		

Assets = Liabilities + Equity
−2,300 −2,300

Decision Insight

Aging Pains Experience shows that the longer a receivable is past due, the lower is the likelihood of its collection. An *aging schedule* uses this knowledge to estimate bad debts. The chart here is from a survey that reported estimates of bad debts for receivables grouped by how long they were past their due dates. Each company sets its own estimates based on its customers and its experiences with those customers' payment patterns. ■

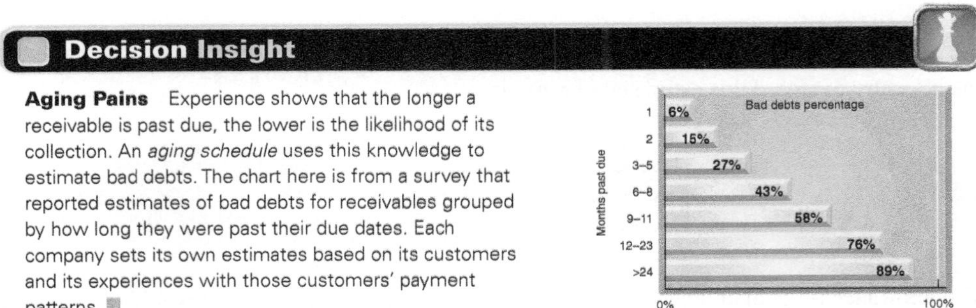

Estimating Bad Debts—Aging of Receivables Method

The **aging of accounts receivable** method uses both past and current receivables information to estimate the allowance amount. Specifically, each receivable is classified by how long it is past its due date. Then estimates of uncollectible amounts are made assuming that the longer an amount is past due, the more likely it is to be uncollectible. Classifications are often based on 30-day periods. After the amounts are classified (or aged), experience is used to estimate the percent of each uncollectible class. These percents are applied to the amounts in each class and then totaled to get the estimated balance of the Allowance for Doubtful Accounts. This computation is performed by setting up a schedule such as Exhibit 9.11.

EXHIBIT 9.11

Aging of Accounts Receivable

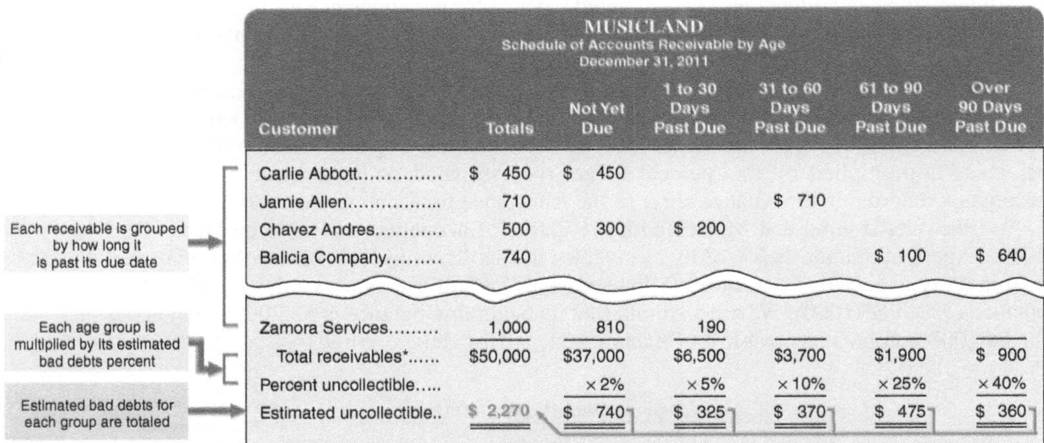

MUSICLAND
Schedule of Accounts Receivable by Age
December 31, 2011

Customer	Totals	Not Yet Due	1 to 30 Days Past Due	31 to 60 Days Past Due	61 to 90 Days Past Due	Over 90 Days Past Due
Carlie Abbott..............	$ 450	$ 450				
Jamie Allen................	710			$ 710		
Chavez Andres...........	500	300	$ 200			
Balicia Company..........	740				$ 100	$ 640
Zamora Services.........	1,000	810	190			
Total receivables*......	$50,000	$37,000	$6,500	$3,700	$1,900	$ 900
Percent uncollectible.....		× 2%	× 5%	× 10%	× 25%	× 40%
Estimated uncollectible..	$ 2,270	$ 740	$ 325	$ 370	$ 475	$ 360

*The "white line break" means that additional customer accounts are not shown in the table but are included in each column's total.

Exhibit 9.11 lists each customer's individual balances assigned to one of five classes based on its days past due. The amounts in each class are totaled and multiplied by the estimated percent of uncollectible accounts for each class. The percents used are regularly reviewed to reflect changes in the company and economy.

To explain, Musicland has \$3,700 in accounts receivable that are 31 to 60 days past due. Its management estimates 10% of the amounts in this age class are uncollectible, or a total of \$370 (computed as \$3,700 × 10%). Similar analysis is done for each of the other four classes. The final total of \$2,270 (\$740 + \$325 + 370 + \$475 + \$360) shown in the first column is the estimated balance for the Allowance for Doubtful Accounts. Exhibit 9.12 shows that since the allowance

EXHIBIT 9.12

Computation of the Required Adjustment for the Accounts Receivable Method

Unadjusted balance	$ 200 credit
Estimated balance	2,270 credit
Required adjustment	$2,070 credit

account has an unadjusted credit balance of $200, the required adjustment to the Allowance for Doubtful Accounts is $2,070. (We could also use a T-account for this analysis as shown in the margin.) This yields the following end-of-period adjusting entry.

Allowance for Doubtful Accounts	
	Unadj. bal. 200
	Req. adj. 2,070
	Estim. bal. 2,270

Dec. 31	Bad Debts Expense	2,070	
	Allowance for Doubtful Accounts		2,070
	To record estimated bad debts.		

Assets = Liabilities + Equity
−2,070 −2,070

Point: A debit balance implies that write-offs for that period exceed the total allowance.

Alternatively, if the allowance account had an unadjusted *debit* balance of $500 (instead of the $200 credit balance), its required adjustment would be computed as follows. (Again, a T-account can be used for this analysis as shown in the margin.)

Allowance for Doubtful Accounts	
Unadj. bal. 500	
	Req. adj. 2,770
	Estim. bal. 2,270

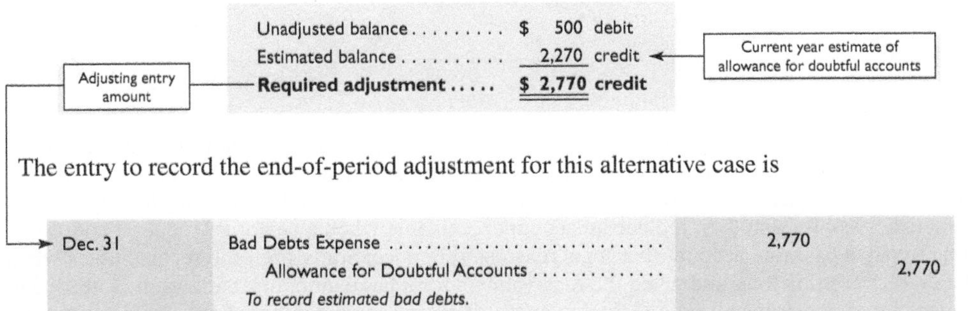

Unadjusted balance	$ 500	debit
Estimated balance	2,270	credit
Required adjustment	**$ 2,770**	**credit**

The entry to record the end-of-period adjustment for this alternative case is

Dec. 31	Bad Debts Expense	2,770	
	Allowance for Doubtful Accounts		2,770
	To record estimated bad debts.		

Assets = Liabilities + Equity
−2,770 −2,770

The aging of accounts receivable method is an examination of specific accounts and is usually the most reliable of the estimation methods.

Estimating Bad Debts—Summary of Methods Exhibit 9.13 summarizes the principles guiding all three estimation methods and their focus of analysis. Percent of sales, with its income statement focus, does a good job at matching bad debts expense with sales. The accounts receivable methods, with their balance sheet focus, do a better job at reporting accounts receivable at realizable value.

EXHIBIT 9.13

Methods to Estimate Bad Debts

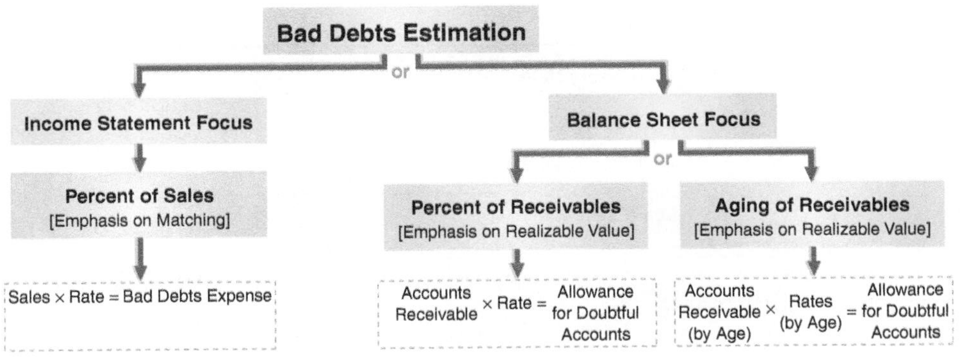

Answer — p. 379

Labor Union Chief One week prior to labor contract negotiations, financial statements are released showing no income growth. A 10% growth was predicted. Your analysis finds that the company increased its allowance for uncollectibles from 1.5% to 4.5% of receivables. Without this change, income would show a 9% growth. Does this analysis impact negotiations?

Quick Check Answers – p. 379 

3. Why must bad debts expense be estimated if such an estimate is possible?
4. What term describes the balance sheet valuation of Accounts Receivable less the Allowance for Doubtful Accounts?
5. Why is estimated bad debts expense credited to a contra account (Allowance for Doubtful Accounts) rather than to the Accounts Receivable account?
6. SnoBoard Company's year-end balance in its Allowance for Doubtful Accounts is a credit of $440. By aging accounts receivable, it estimates that $6,142 is uncollectible. Prepare SnoBoard's year-end adjusting entry for bad debts.
7. Record entries for these transactions assuming the allowance method is used:
   Jan. 10 The $300 account of customer Cool Jam is determined uncollectible.
   April 12 Cool Jam unexpectedly pays in full the account deemed uncollectible on Jan. 10.

NOTES RECEIVABLE

C2 Describe a note receivable, the computation of its maturity date, and the recording of its existence.

A **promissory note** is a written promise to pay a specified amount of money, usually with interest, either on demand or at a definite future date. Promissory notes are used in many transactions, including paying for products and services, and lending and borrowing money. Sellers sometimes ask for a note to replace an account receivable when a customer requests additional time to pay a past-due account. For legal reasons, sellers generally prefer to receive notes when the credit period is long and when the receivable is for a large amount. If a lawsuit is needed to collect from a customer, a note is the buyer's written acknowledgment of the debt, its amount, and its terms.

Exhibit 9.14 shows a simple promissory note dated July 10, 2011. For this note, Julia Browne promises to pay TechCom or to its order (according to TechCom's instructions) a specified amount of money ($1,000), called the **principal of a note,** at a definite future date (October 8, 2011). As the one who signed the note and promised to pay it at maturity, Browne is the **maker of the note.** As the person to whom the note is payable, TechCom is the **payee of the note.** To Browne, the note is a liability called a *note payable*. To TechCom, the same note is an asset called a *note receivable*. This note bears interest at 12%, as written on the note. **Interest** is the charge for using the money until its due date. To a borrower, interest is an expense. To a lender, it is revenue.

EXHIBIT 9.14

Promissory Note

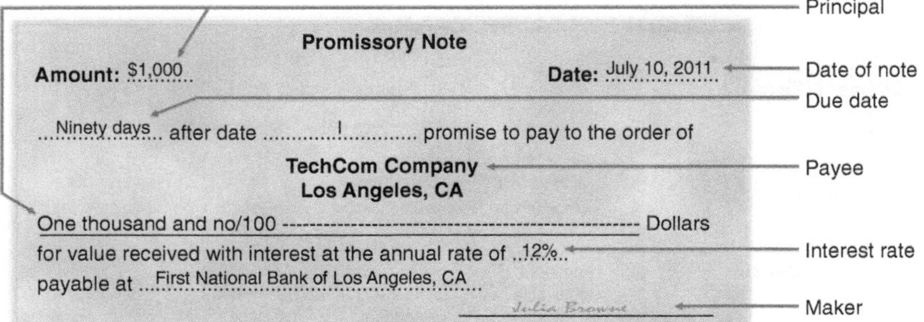

Computing Maturity and Interest

This section describes key computations for notes including the determination of maturity date, period covered, and interest computation.

Maturity Date and Period The **maturity date of a note** is the day the note (principal and interest) must be repaid. The *period* of a note is the time from the note's (contract) date to its maturity date. Many notes mature in less than a full year, and the period they cover is often expressed in days. When the time of a note is expressed in days, its maturity date is the specified number of days after the note's date. As an example, a five-day note dated June 15 matures and is due on June 20. A 90-day note dated July 10 matures on October 8. This October 8 due date is computed as shown in Exhibit 9.15. The period of a note is sometimes expressed in months or years. When months are used, the note matures and is payable in the month of its maturity on the *same day of the month* as its original date. A nine-month note dated July 10, for instance, is payable on April 10. The same analysis applies when years are used.

EXHIBIT 9.15

Maturity Date Computation

Days in July	31		
Minus the date of the note	10		
Days remaining in July		21	← July 11–31
Add days in August		31	← Aug. 1–31
Add days in September		30	← Sept. 1–30
Days to equal 90 days, or maturity date of October 8		8	← Oct. 1–8
Period of the note in days		90	

Interest Computation *Interest* is the cost of borrowing money for the borrower or, alternatively, the profit from lending money for the lender. Unless otherwise stated, the rate of interest on a note is the rate charged for the use of the principal for one year. The formula for computing interest on a note is shown in Exhibit 9.16.

EXHIBIT 9.16

Computation of Interest Formula

$$\text{Principal of the note} \times \text{Annual interest rate} \times \text{Time expressed in fraction of year} = \text{Interest}$$

To simplify interest computations, a year is commonly treated as having 360 days (called the *banker's rule* in the business world and widely used in commercial transactions). **We treat a year as having 360 days for interest computations in the examples and assignments.** Using the promissory note in Exhibit 9.14 where we have a 90-day, 12%, $1,000 note, the total interest is computed as follows.

$$\$1{,}000 \times 12\% \times \frac{90}{360} = \$1{,}000 \times 0.12 \times 0.25 = \$30$$

Recognizing Notes Receivable

Notes receivable are usually recorded in a single Notes Receivable account to simplify recordkeeping. The original notes are kept on file, including information on the maker, rate of interest, and due date. (When a company holds a large number of notes, it sometimes sets up a controlling account and a subsidiary ledger for notes. This is similar to the handling of accounts receivable.) To illustrate the recording for the receipt of a note, we use the $1,000, 90-day, 12% promissory note in Exhibit 9.14. TechCom received this note at the time of a product sale to Julia Browne. This transaction is recorded as follows.

July 10*	Notes Receivable	1,000	
	Sales		1,000
	Sold goods in exchange for a 90-day, 12% note.		

Assets = Liabilities + Equity
+1,000 +1,000

* We omit the entry to Dr. Cost of Sales and Cr. Merchandise Inventory to focus on sales and receivables.

When a seller accepts a note from an overdue customer as a way to grant a time extension on a past-due account receivable, it will often collect part of the past-due balance in cash. This partial payment forces a concession from the customer, reduces the customer's debt (and the seller's risk), and produces a note for a smaller amount. To illustrate, assume that TechCom agreed to accept $232 in cash along with a $600, 60-day, 15% note from Jo Cook to

Point: Notes receivable often are a major part of a company's assets. Likewise, notes payable often are a large part of a company's liabilities.

settle her $832 past-due account. TechCom made the following entry to record receipt of this cash and note.

Assets = Liabilities + Equity
+232
+600
−832

Oct. 5	Cash	232	
	Notes Receivable	600	
	Accounts Receivable—J. Cook		832
	Received cash and note to settle account.		

Valuing and Settling Notes

P3 Record the honoring and dishonoring of a note and adjustments for interest.

Recording an Honored Note The principal and interest of a note are due on its maturity date. The maker of the note usually *honors* the note and pays it in full. To illustrate, when J. Cook pays the note above on its due date, TechCom records it as follows.

Assets = Liabilities + Equity
+615 +15
−600

Dec. 4	Cash	615	
	Notes Receivable		600
	Interest Revenue		15
	Collect note with interest of $600 × 15% × 60/360.		

Interest Revenue, also called *Interest Earned,* is reported on the income statement.

Recording a Dishonored Note When a note's maker is unable or refuses to pay at maturity, the note is *dishonored.* The act of dishonoring a note does not relieve the maker of the obligation to pay. The payee should use every legitimate means to collect. How do companies report this event? The balance of the Notes Receivable account should include only those notes that have not matured. Thus, when a note is dishonored, we remove the amount of this note from the Notes Receivable account and charge it back to an account receivable from its maker. To illustrate, TechCom holds an $800, 12%, 60-day note of Greg Hart. At maturity, Hart dishonors the note. TechCom records this dishonoring of the note as follows.

Point: When posting a dishonored note to a customer's account, an explanation is included so as not to misinterpret the debit as a sale on account.

Assets = Liabilities + Equity
+816 +16
−800

Oct. 14	Accounts Receivable—G. Hart	816	
	Interest Revenue		16
	Notes Receivable		800
	To charge account of G. Hart for a dishonored note and interest of $800 × 12% × 60/360.		

Charging a dishonored note back to the account of its maker serves two purposes. First, it removes the amount of the note from the Notes Receivable account and records the dishonored note in the maker's account. Second, and more important, if the maker of the dishonored note applies for credit in the future, his or her account will reveal all past dealings, including the dishonored note. Restoring the account also reminds the company to continue collection efforts from Hart for both principal and interest. The entry records the full amount, including interest, to ensure that it is included in collection efforts.

Point: Reporting the details of notes is consistent with the **full disclosure principle,** which requires financial statements (including footnotes) to report all relevant information.

Recording End-of-Period Interest Adjustment When notes receivable are outstanding at the end of a period, any accrued interest earned is computed and recorded. To illustrate, on December 16, TechCom accepts a $3,000, 60-day, 12% note from a customer in granting an extension on a past-due account. When TechCom's accounting period ends on December 31, $15 of interest has accrued on this note ($3,000 × 12% × 15/360). The following adjusting entry records this revenue.

Assets = Liabilities + Equity
+15 +15

Dec. 31	Interest Receivable	15	
	Interest Revenue		15
	To record accrued interest earned.		

Interest Revenue appears on the income statement, and Interest Receivable appears on the balance sheet as a current asset. When the December 16 note is collected on February 14, TechCom's entry to record the cash receipt is

Feb. 14	Cash	3,060	
	Interest Revenue		45
	Interest Receivable		15
	Notes Receivable		3,000
	Received payment of note and its interest.		

Assets	=	Liabilities	+	Equity
+3,060				+45
−15				
−3,000				

Total interest earned on the 60-day note is $60. The $15 credit to Interest Receivable on February 14 reflects the collection of the interest accrued from the December 31 adjusting entry. The $45 interest earned reflects TechCom's revenue from holding the note from January 1 to February 14 of the current period.

Quick Check Answers — p. 379

8. Irwin purchases $7,000 of merchandise from Stamford on December 16, 2011. Stamford accepts Irwin's $7,000, 90-day, 12% note as payment. Stamford's accounting period ends on December 31, and it does not make reversing entries. Prepare entries for Stamford on December 16, 2011, and December 31, 2011.
9. Using the information in Quick Check 8, prepare Stamford's March 16, 2012, entry if Irwin dishonors the note.

DISPOSAL OF RECEIVABLES

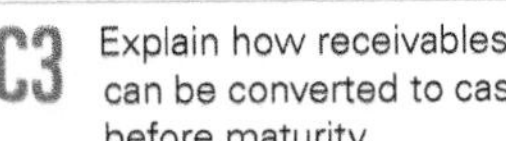

Companies can convert receivables to cash before they are due. Reasons for this include the need for cash or the desire not to be involved in collection activities. Converting receivables is usually done either by (1) selling them or (2) using them as security for a loan. A recent survey shows that about 20% of companies obtain cash from either selling receivables or pledging them as security. In some industries such as textiles, apparel and furniture, this is common practice.

Selling Receivables

A company can sell all or a portion of its receivables to a finance company or bank. The buyer, called a *factor*, charges the seller a *factoring fee* and then the buyer takes ownership of the receivables and receives cash when they come due. By incurring a factoring fee, the seller receives cash earlier and can pass the risk of bad debts to the factor. The seller can also choose to avoid costs of billing and accounting for the receivables. To illustrate, if TechCom sells $20,000 of its accounts receivable and is charged a 4% factoring fee, it records this sale as follows.

Global: Firms in export sales increasingly sell their receivables to factors.

Aug. 15	Cash	19,200	
	Factoring Fee Expense	800	
	Accounts Receivable		20,000
	Sold accounts receivable for cash, less 4% fee.		

Assets	=	Liabilities	+	Equity
+19,200				−800
−20,000				

The accounting for sales of notes receivable is similar to that for accounts receivable. The detailed entries are covered in advanced courses.

Pledging Receivables

A company can raise cash by borrowing money and *pledging* its receivables as security for the loan. Pledging receivables does not transfer the risk of bad debts to the lender because the borrower retains ownership of the receivables. If the borrower defaults on the loan, the lender has a right to be paid from the cash receipts of the receivable when collected. To illustrate, when TechCom borrows $35,000 and pledges its receivables as security, it records this transaction as follows.

Assets	= Liabilities	+ Equity
+35,000	+35,000	

Aug. 20	Cash	35,000	
	Notes Payable		35,000
	Borrowed money with a note secured by pledging receivables.		

Since pledged receivables are committed as security for a specific loan, the borrower's financial statements disclose the pledging of them. TechCom, for instance, includes the following note with its statements: Accounts receivable of $40,000 are pledged as security for a $35,000 note payable.

Decision Insight

What's the Proper Allowance? How can we assess whether a company has properly estimated its allowance for uncollectibles? One way is to compute the ratio of the allowance account to the gross accounts receivable. When this ratio is analyzed over several consecutive periods, trends often emerge that reflect on the adequacy of the allowance amount.

GLOBAL VIEW

This section discusses similarities and differences between U.S. GAAP and IFRS regarding the recognition, measurement, and disposition of receivables.

Recognition of Receivables Both U.S. GAAP and IFRS have similar asset criteria that apply to recognition of receivables. Further, receivables that arise from revenue-generating activities are subject to broadly similar criteria for U.S. GAAP and IFRS. Specifically, both refer to the realization principle and an earnings process. The realization principle under U.S. GAAP implies an *arm's-length transaction* occurs, whereas under IFRS this notion is applied in terms of reliable measurement and likelihood of economic benefits. Regarding U.S. GAAP's reference to an earnings process, IFRS instead refers to risk transfer and ownership reward. While these criteria are broadly similar, differences do exist, and they arise mainly from industry-specific guidance under U.S. GAAP, which is very limited under IFRS.

Valuation of Receivables Both U.S. GAAP and IFRS require that receivables be reported net of estimated uncollectibles. Further, both systems require that the expense for estimated uncollectibles be recorded in the same period when any revenues from those receivables are recorded. This means that for accounts receivable, both U.S. GAAP and IFRS require the allowance method for uncollectibles (unless uncollectibles are immaterial). The allowance method using percent of sales, percent of receivables, and aging was explained in this chapter. Nokia reports the following for its allowance for uncollectibles:

NOKIA

> Management specifically analyzes accounts receivables and historical bad debt, customer concentrations, customer creditworthiness, current economic trends and changes in our customer payment terms when evaluating the adequacy of the allowance.

Disposition of Receivables Both U.S. GAAP and IFRS apply broadly similar rules in recording dispositions of receivables. Those rules are discussed in this chapter. We should be aware of an important difference in terminology. Companies reporting under U.S. GAAP disclose Bad Debts Expense, which is also referred to as Provision for Bad Debts or the Provision for Uncollectible Accounts. For U.S. GAAP, *provision* here refers to expense. Under IFRS, the term *provision* usually refers to a liability whose amount or timing (or both) is uncertain.

Accounts Receivable Turnover

Decision Analysis

A1 Compute accounts receivable turnover and use it to help assess financial condition.

For a company selling on credit, we want to assess both the quality and liquidity of its accounts receivable. *Quality* of receivables refers to the likelihood of collection without loss. Experience shows that the longer receivables are outstanding beyond their due date, the lower the likelihood of collection. *Liquidity* of receivables refers to the speed of collection. **Accounts receivable turnover** is a measure of both the quality and liquidity of accounts receivable. It indicates how often, on average, receivables are received and collected during the period. The formula for this ratio is shown in Exhibit 9.17.

EXHIBIT 9.17

Accounts Receivable Turnover

$$\textbf{Accounts receivable turnover} = \frac{\textbf{Net sales}}{\textbf{Average accounts receivable, net}}$$

We prefer to use net *credit* sales in the numerator because cash sales do not create receivables. However, since financial statements rarely report net credit sales, our analysis uses net sales. The denominator is the *average* accounts receivable balance, computed as (Beginning balance + Ending balance) ÷ 2. TechCom has an accounts receivable turnover of 5.1. This indicates its average accounts receivable balance is converted into cash 5.1 times during the period. Exhibit 9.18 shows graphically this turnover activity for TechCom.

EXHIBIT 9.18

Rate of Accounts Receivable Turnover for TechCom

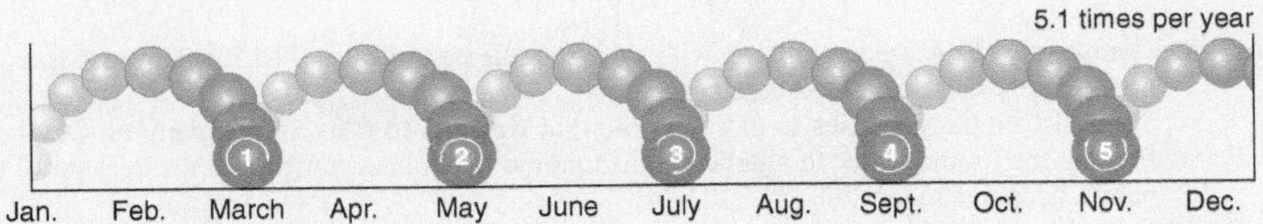

Accounts receivable turnover also reflects how well management is doing in granting credit to customers in a desire to increase sales. A high turnover in comparison with competitors suggests that management should consider using more liberal credit terms to increase sales. A low turnover suggests management should consider stricter credit terms and more aggressive collection efforts to avoid having its resources tied up in accounts receivable.

Point: Credit risk ratio is computed by dividing the Allowance for Doubtful Accounts by Accounts Receivable. The higher this ratio, the higher is credit risk.

To illustrate, we take fiscal year data from two competitors: **Dell** and **Apple**. Exhibit 9.19 shows accounts receivable turnover for both companies.

EXHIBIT 9.19

Analysis Using Accounts Receivable Turnover

Company	Figure ($ millions)	2008	2007	2006	2005
Dell	Net sales	$61,101	$61,133	$57,420	$55,788
	Average accounts receivable, net	$ 5,346	$ 5,292	$ 4,352	$ 3,826
	Accounts receivable turnover	11.4	11.6	13.2	14.6
Apple	Net sales	$32,479	$24,006	$19,315	$13,931
	Average accounts receivable, net	$ 2,030	$ 1,445	$ 1,074	$ 835
	Accounts receivable turnover	16.0	16.6	18.0	16.7

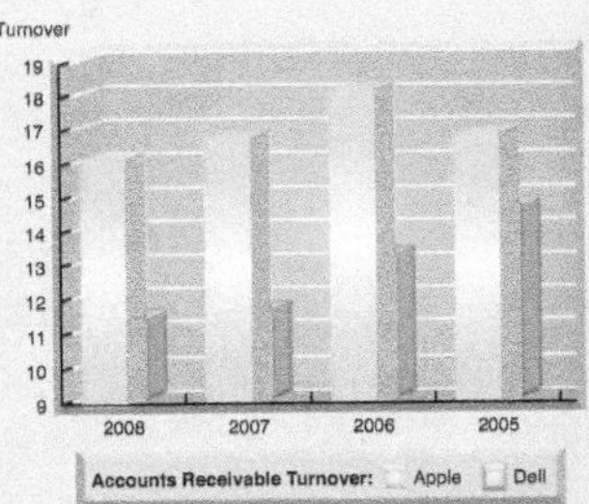

Dell's 2008 turnover is 11.4, computed as $61,101/$5,346 ($ millions). This means that Dell's average accounts receivable balance was converted into cash 11.4 times in 2008. Its turnover declined in 2008, as it has for each of the past 3 years. Apple's turnover exceeds that for Dell in each of the past 4 years. Is either company's turnover too high? Since sales are stable or markedly growing over this time period, each company's turnover rate does not appear to be too high. Instead, both Dell and Apple seem to be doing well in managing receivables. This is especially true given the recessionary period of 2008 and 2009. Turnover for competitors is generally in the range of 7 to 12 for this same period.[1]

Decision Maker Answer — p. 379

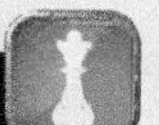

Family Physician Your medical practice is barely profitable, so you hire a health care analyst. The analyst highlights several points including the following: *"Accounts receivable turnover is too low. Tighter credit policies are recommended along with discontinuing service to those most delayed in payments."* How do you interpret these recommendations? What actions do you take?

DEMONSTRATION PROBLEM

Clayco Company completes the following selected transactions during year 2011.

July 14 Writes off a $750 account receivable arising from a sale to Briggs Company that dates to 10 months ago. (Clayco Company uses the allowance method.)

30 Clayco Company receives a $1,000, 90-day, 10% note in exchange for merchandise sold to Sumrell Company (the merchandise cost $600).

Aug. 15 Receives $2,000 cash plus a $10,000 note from JT Co. in exchange for merchandise that sells for $12,000 (its cost is $8,000). The note is dated August 15, bears 12% interest, and matures in 120 days.

Nov. 1 Completed a $200 credit card sale with a 4% fee (the cost of sales is $150). The cash is received immediately from the credit card company.

3 Sumrell Company refuses to pay the note that was due to Clayco Company on October 28. Prepare the journal entry to charge the dishonored note plus accrued interest to Sumrell Company's accounts receivable.

5 Completed a $500 credit card sale with a 5% fee (the cost of sales is $300). The payment from the credit card company is received on Nov. 9.

15 Received the full amount of $750 from Briggs Company that was previously written off on July 14. Record the bad debts recovery.

Dec. 13 Received payment of principal plus interest from JT for the August 15 note.

Required

1. Prepare journal entries to record these transactions on Clayco Company's books.
2. Prepare an adjusting journal entry as of December 31, 2011, assuming the following:
   a. Bad debts are estimated to be $20,400 by aging accounts receivable. The unadjusted balance of the Allowance for Doubtful Accounts is $1,000 debit.
   b. Alternatively, assume that bad debts are estimated using the percent of sales method. The Allowance for Doubtful Accounts had a $1,000 debit balance before adjustment, and the company estimates bad debts to be 1% of its credit sales of $2,000,000.

PLANNING THE SOLUTION

- Examine each transaction to determine the accounts affected, and then record the entries.
- For the year-end adjustment, record the bad debts expense for the two approaches.

[1] As an estimate of *average days' sales uncollected,* we compute how many days (*on average*) it takes to collect receivables as follows: 365 days ÷ accounts receivable turnover. An increase in this *average collection period* can signal a decline in customers' financial condition.

SOLUTION TO DEMONSTRATION PROBLEM

1.

Date	Account	Debit	Credit
July 14	Allowance for Doubtful Accounts	750	
	Accounts Receivable—Briggs Co.		750
	Wrote off an uncollectible account.		
July 30	Notes Receivable—Sumrell Co.	1,000	
	Sales		1,000
	Sold merchandise for a 90-day, 10% note.		
July 30	Cost of Goods Sold	600	
	Merchandise Inventory		600
	To record the cost of July 30 sale.		
Aug. 15	Cash	2,000	
	Notes Receivable—JT Co.	10,000	
	Sales		12,000
	Sold merchandise to customer for $2,000 cash and $10,000 note.		
Aug. 15	Cost of Goods Sold	8,000	
	Merchandise Inventory		8,000
	To record the cost of Aug. 15 sale.		
Nov. 1	Cash	192	
	Credit Card Expense	8	
	Sales		200
	To record credit card sale less a 4% credit card expense.		
Nov. 1	Cost of Goods Sold	150	
	Merchandise Inventory		150
	To record the cost of Nov. 1 sale.		
Nov. 3	Accounts Receivable—Sumrell Co.	1,025	
	Interest Revenue		25
	Notes Receivable—Sumrell Co.		1,000
	To charge account of Sumrell Company for a $1,000 dishonored note and interest of $1,000 × 10% × 90/360.		
Nov. 5	Accounts Receivable—Credit Card Co.	475	
	Credit Card Expense	25	
	Sales		500
	To record credit card sale less a 5% credit card expense.		
Nov. 5	Cost of Goods Sold	300	
	Merchandise Inventory		300
	To record the cost of Nov. 5 sale.		
Nov. 9	Cash	475	
	Accounts Receivable—Credit Card Co.		475
	To record cash receipt from Nov. 5 sale.		
Nov. 15	Accounts Receivable—Briggs Co.	750	
	Allowance for Doubtful Accounts		750
	To reinstate the account of Briggs Company previously written off.		
Nov. 15	Cash	750	
	Accounts Receivable—Briggs Co.		750
	Cash received in full payment of account.		
Dec. 13	Cash	10,400	
	Interest Revenue		400
	Note Receivable—JT Co.		10,000
	Collect note with interest of $10,000 × 12% × 120/360.		

2a. Aging of accounts receivable method.

Dec. 31	Bad Debts Expense	21,400	
	Allowance for Doubtful Accounts		21,400
	To adjust allowance account from a $1,000 debit balance to a $20,400 credit balance.		

2b. Percent of sales method.*

Dec. 31	Bad Debts Expense	20,000	
	Allowance for Doubtful Accounts		20,000
	To provide for bad debts as 1% × $2,000,000 in credit sales.		

* For the income statement approach, which requires estimating bad debts as a percent of sales or credit sales, the Allowance account balance is *not* considered when making the adjusting entry.

Summary

C1 Describe accounts receivable and how they occur and are recorded. Accounts receivable are amounts due from customers for credit sales. A subsidiary ledger lists amounts owed by each customer. Credit sales arise from at least two sources: (1) sales on credit and (2) credit card sales. *Sales on credit* refers to a company's granting credit directly to customers. Credit card sales involve customers' use of third-party credit cards.

C2 Describe a note receivable, the computation of its maturity date, and the recording of its existence. A note receivable is a written promise to pay a specified amount of money at a definite future date. The maturity date is the day the note (principal and interest) must be repaid. Interest rates are normally stated in annual terms. The amount of interest on the note is computed by expressing time as a fraction of one year and multiplying the note's principal by this fraction and the annual interest rate. A note received is recorded at its principal amount by debiting the Notes Receivable account. The credit amount is to the asset, product, or service provided in return for the note.

C3 Explain how receivables can be converted to cash before maturity. Receivables can be converted to cash before maturity in three ways. First, a company can sell accounts receivable to a factor, who charges a factoring fee. Second, a company can borrow money by signing a note payable that is secured by pledging the accounts receivable. Third, notes receivable can be discounted at (sold to) a financial institution.

A1 Compute accounts receivable turnover and use it to help assess financial condition. Accounts receivable turnover is a measure of both the quality and liquidity of accounts receivable. The accounts receivable turnover measure indicates how often, on average, receivables are received and collected during the period. Accounts receivable turnover is computed as net sales divided by average accounts receivable.

P1 Apply the direct write-off method to account for accounts receivable. The direct write-off method charges Bad Debts Expense when accounts are written off as uncollectible. This method is acceptable only when the amount of bad debts expense is immaterial.

P2 Apply the allowance method and estimate uncollectibles based on sales and accounts receivable. Under the allowance method, bad debts expense is recorded with an adjustment at the end of each accounting period that debits the Bad Debts Expense account and credits the Allowance for Doubtful Accounts. The uncollectible accounts are later written off with a debit to the Allowance for Doubtful Accounts. Uncollectibles are estimated by focusing on either (1) the income statement relation between bad debts expense and credit sales or (2) the balance sheet relation between accounts receivable and the allowance for doubtful accounts. The first approach emphasizes the matching principle using the income statement. The second approach emphasizes realizable value of accounts receivable using the balance sheet.

P3 Record the honoring and dishonoring of a note and adjustments for interest. When a note is honored, the payee debits the money received and credits both Notes Receivable and Interest Revenue. Dishonored notes are credited to Notes Receivable and debited to Accounts Receivable (to the account of the maker in an attempt to collect), and Interest Revenue is recorded for interest earned for the time the note is held.

Guidance Answers to Decision Maker and Decision Ethics

Entrepreneur Analysis of credit card sales should weigh the benefits against the costs. The primary benefit is the potential to increase sales by attracting customers who prefer the convenience of credit cards. The primary cost is the fee charged by the credit card company for providing this service. Analysis should therefore estimate the expected increase in dollar sales from allowing credit card sales and then subtract (1) the normal costs and expenses and (2) the credit card fees associated with this expected increase in dollar sales. If your analysis shows an increase in profit from allowing credit card sales, your store should probably accept them.

Labor Union Chief Yes, this information is likely to impact your negotiations. The obvious question is why the company markedly increased this allowance. The large increase in this allowance means a substantial increase in bad debts expense *and* a decrease in earnings. This change (coming immediately prior to labor contract discussions) also raises concerns since it reduces the union's bargaining power for increased compensation. You want to ask management for supporting documentation justifying this increase. You also want data for two or three prior years and similar data from competitors. These data should give you some sense of whether the change in the allowance for uncollectibles is justified.

Family Physician The recommendations are twofold. First, the analyst suggests more stringent screening of patients' credit standing. Second, the analyst suggests dropping patients who are most overdue in payments. You are likely bothered by both suggestions. They are probably financially wise recommendations, but you are troubled by eliminating services to those less able to pay. One alternative is to follow the recommendations while implementing a care program directed at patients less able to pay for services. This allows you to continue services to patients less able to pay and lets you discontinue services to patients able but unwilling to pay.

Guidance Answers to Quick Checks

1. If cash is immediately received when credit card sales receipts are deposited, the company debits Cash at the time of sale. If the company does not receive payment until after it submits receipts to the credit card company, it debits Accounts Receivable at the time of sale. (Cash is later debited when payment is received from the credit card company.)
2. Credit card expenses are usually *recorded* and *incurred* at the time of their related sales, not when cash is received from the credit card company.
3. If possible, bad debts expense must be matched with the sales that gave rise to the accounts receivable. This requires that companies estimate future bad debts at the end of each period before they learn which accounts are uncollectible.
4. Realizable value (also called *net realizable value*).
5. The estimated amount of bad debts expense cannot be credited to the Accounts Receivable account because the specific customer accounts that will prove uncollectible cannot yet be identified and removed from the accounts receivable subsidiary ledger. Moreover, if only the Accounts Receivable account is credited, its balance would not equal the sum of its subsidiary account balances.
6.

Date	Account	Debit	Credit
Dec. 31	Bad Debts Expense	5,702	
	Allowance for Doubtful Accounts		5,702

7.

Date	Account	Debit	Credit
Jan. 10	Allowance for Doubtful Accounts	300	
	Accounts Receivable—Cool Jam		300
Apr. 12	Accounts Receivable—Cool Jam	300	
	Allowance for Doubtful Accounts		300
Apr. 12	Cash	300	
	Accounts Receivable—Cool Jam		300

8.

Date	Account	Debit	Credit
Dec. 16	Note Receivable—Irwin	7,000	
	Sales		7,000
Dec. 31	Interest Receivable	35	
	Interest Revenue		35
	($7,000 × 12% × 15/360)		

9.

Date	Account	Debit	Credit
Mar. 16	Accounts Receivable—Irwin	7,210	
	Interest Revenue		175
	Interest Receivable		35
	Notes Receivable—Irwin		7,000

Key Terms

mhhe.com/wildFAP20e

Accounts receivable (p. 360)
Accounts receivable turnover (p. 375)
Aging of accounts receivable (p. 368)
Allowance for Doubtful Accounts (p. 365)
Allowance method (p. 364)
Bad debts (p. 363)
Direct write-off method (p. 363)
Interest (p. 370)
Maker of the note (p. 370)
Matching (expense recognition) principle (p. 364)
Materiality constraint (p. 364)
Maturity date of a note (p. 370)
Payee of the note (p. 370)
Principal of a note (p. 370)
Promissory note (or **note**) (p. 370)
Realizable value (p. 365)

Multiple Choice Quiz

Answers on p. 391 mhhe.com/wildFAP20e

Additional Quiz Questions are available at the book's Website.

1. A company's Accounts Receivable balance at its December 31 year-end is $125,650, and its Allowance for Doubtful Accounts has a credit balance of $328 before year-end adjustment. Its net sales are $572,300. It estimates that 4% of outstanding accounts receivable are uncollectible. What amount of Bad Debts Expense is recorded at December 31?
   a. $5,354
   b. $328
   c. $5,026
   d. $4,698
   e. $34,338
2. A company's Accounts Receivable balance at its December 31 year-end is $489,300, and its Allowance for Doubtful Accounts has a debit balance of $554 before year-end adjustment. Its net sales are $1,300,000. It estimates that 6% of outstanding accounts receivable are uncollectible. What amount of Bad Debts Expense is recorded at December 31?
   a. $29,912
   b. $28,804
   c. $78,000
   d. $29,358
   e. $554
3. Total interest to be earned on a $7,500, 5%, 90-day note is
   a. $93.75
   b. $375.00
   c. $1,125.00
   d. $31.25
   e. $125.00
4. A company receives a $9,000, 8%, 60-day note. The maturity value of the note is
   a. $120
   b. $9,000
   c. $9,120
   d. $720
   e. $9,720
5. A company has net sales of $489,600 and average accounts receivable of $40,800. What is its accounts receivable turnover?
   a. 0.08
   b. 30.41
   c. 1,341.00
   d. 12.00
   e. 111.78

[I] Icon denotes assignments that involve decision making.

Discussion Questions

1. [I] How do sellers benefit from allowing their customers to use credit cards?
2. [I] Why does the direct write-off method of accounting for bad debts usually fail to match revenues and expenses?
3. Explain the accounting constraint of materiality.
4. Explain why writing off a bad debt against the Allowance for Doubtful Accounts does not reduce the estimated realizable value of a company's accounts receivable.
5. [I] Why does the Bad Debts Expense account usually not have the same adjusted balance as the Allowance for Doubtful Accounts?
6. Why might a business prefer a note receivable to an account receivable?
7. [I] Refer to the financial statements and notes of Research In Motion in Appendix A. In its presentation of accounts receivable on the balance sheet, how does it title accounts receivable? What does it report for its allowance as of February 27, 2010? *RIM*
8. [I] Refer to the balance sheet of Apple in Appendix A. Does it use the direct write-off method or allowance method in accounting for its Accounts Receivable? What is the realizable value of its receivable's balance as of September 26, 2009? *Apple*
9. Refer to the financial statements of Palm in Appendix A. What are Palm's gross accounts receivable at May 31, 2009? What percentage of its accounts receivable does it believe to be uncollectible at this date? *Palm*
10. Refer to the December 31, 2009, financial statements of Nokia in Appendix A. What does it title its accounts receivable on its statement of financial position? What percent of its accounts receivable does it believe to be uncollectible? *NOKIA*

connect

QUICK STUDY

QS 9-1
Credit card sales
C1

Prepare journal entries for the following credit card sales transactions (the company uses the perpetual inventory system).

1. Sold $10,000 of merchandise, that cost $7,500, on MasterCard credit cards. The net cash receipts from sales are immediately deposited in the seller's bank account. MasterCard charges a 5% fee.
2. Sold $3,000 of merchandise, that cost $1,500, on an assortment of credit cards. Net cash receipts are received 7 days later, and a 4% fee is charged.

Milner Corp. uses the allowance method to account for uncollectibles. On October 31, it wrote off a $1,000 account of a customer, C. Schaub. On December 9, it receives a $200 payment from Schaub.

1. Prepare the journal entry or entries for October 31.

2. Prepare the journal entry or entries for December 9; assume no additional money is expected from Schaub.

QS 9-2
Allowance method for bad debts
P2

Wecker Company's year-end unadjusted trial balance shows accounts receivable of $89,000, allowance for doubtful accounts of $500 (credit), and sales of $270,000. Uncollectibles are estimated to be 1.5% of accounts receivable.

1. Prepare the December 31 year-end adjusting entry for uncollectibles.

2. What amount would have been used in the year-end adjusting entry if the allowance account had a year-end unadjusted debit balance of $200?

QS 9-3
Percent of accounts receivable method
P2

Assume the same facts as in QS 9-3, except that Wecker estimates uncollectibles as 1.0% of sales. Prepare the December 31 year-end adjusting entry for uncollectibles.

QS 9-4
Percent of sales method P2

On August 2, 2011, JLK Co. receives a $5,500, 90-day, 12% note from customer Tom Menke as payment on his $9,000 account. (1) Compute the maturity date for this note. (2) Prepare JLK's journal entry for August 2.

QS 9-5
Note receivable C2

Refer to the information in QS 9-5 and prepare the journal entry assuming the note is honored by the customer on October 31, 2011.

QS 9-6
Note receivable P3

Dekon Company's December 31 year-end unadjusted trial balance shows a $8,000 balance in Notes Receivable. This balance is from one 6% note dated December 1, with a period of 45 days. Prepare any necessary journal entries for December 31 and for the note's maturity date assuming it is honored.

QS 9-7
Note receivable P3

Record the sale by Kroll Company of $1,000 in accounts receivable on May 1. Kroll is charged a 3% factoring fee.

QS 9-8
Disposing receivables C3

Krugg Company determines on May 1 that it cannot collect $1,000 of its accounts receivable from its customer P. Carroll. Apply the direct write-off method to record this loss as of May 1.

QS 9-9
Direct write-off method P1

Refer to the information in QS 9-9. On May 30, P. Carroll unexpectedly paid his account in full to Krugg Company. Record Krugg's entry(ies) to reflect this recovery of this bad debt.

QS 9-10
Recovering a bad debt P1

The following data are taken from the comparative balance sheets of Fulton Company. Compute and interpret its accounts receivable turnover for year 2011 (competitors average a turnover of 7.5).

QS 9-11
Accounts receivable turnover
A1 

	2011	2010
Accounts receivable, net	$152,900	$133,700
Net sales	754,200	810,600

Answer each of the following related to international accounting standards.

a. Explain (in general terms) how the accounting for recognition of receivables is different between IFRS and U.S. GAAP.

b. Explain (in general terms) how the accounting for valuation of receivables is different between IFRS and U.S. GAAP.

QS 9-12
International accounting standards
C1 

connect

EXERCISES

Exercise 9-1
Accounting for credit card sales
C1

Petri Company uses the perpetual inventory system and allows customers to use two credit cards in charging purchases. With the Omni Bank Card, Petri receives an immediate credit to its account when it deposits sales receipts. Omni assesses a 4% service charge for credit card sales. The second credit card that Petri accepts is the Continental Card. Petri sends its accumulated receipts to Continental on a weekly basis and is paid by Continental about a week later. Continental assesses a 2.5% charge on sales for using its card. Prepare journal entries to record the following selected credit card transactions of Petri Company.

Apr. 8 Sold merchandise for $9,200 (that had cost $6,800) and accepted the customer's Omni Bank Card. The Omni receipts are immediately deposited in Petri's bank account.
12 Sold merchandise for $5,400 (that had cost $3,500) and accepted the customer's Continental Card. Transferred $5,400 of credit card receipts to Continental, requesting payment.
20 Received Continental's check for the April 12 billing, less the service charge.

Exercise 9-2
Accounts receivable subsidiary ledger; schedule of accounts receivable
C1

Sami Company recorded the following selected transactions during November 2011.

Date	Account	Debit	Credit
Nov. 5	Accounts Receivable—Surf Shop	4,417	
	Sales		4,417
10	Accounts Receivable—Yum Enterprises	1,250	
	Sales		1,250
13	Accounts Receivable—Matt Albin	733	
	Sales		733
21	Sales Returns and Allowances	189	
	Accounts Receivable—Matt Albin		189
30	Accounts Receivable—Surf Shop	2,606	
	Sales		2,606

1. Open a general ledger having T-accounts for Accounts Receivable, Sales, and Sales Returns and Allowances. Also open an accounts receivable subsidiary ledger having a T-account for each customer. Post these entries to both the general ledger and the accounts receivable ledger.
2. Prepare a schedule of accounts receivable (see Exhibit 9.4) and compare its total with the balance of the Accounts Receivable controlling account as of November 30.

Check Accounts Receivable ending balance, $8,817

Exercise 9-3
Direct write-off method
P1

Diablo Company applies the direct write-off method in accounting for uncollectible accounts. Prepare journal entries to record the following selected transactions of Diablo.

June 11 Diablo determines that it cannot collect $9,000 of its accounts receivable from its customer Chaffey Company.
29 Chaffey Company unexpectedly pays its account in full to Diablo Company. Diablo records its recovery of this bad debt.

Exercise 9-4
Percent of sales method; write-off
P2

At year-end (December 31), Alvare Company estimates its bad debts as 0.5% of its annual credit sales of $875,000. Alvare records its Bad Debts Expense for that estimate. On the following February 1, Alvare decides that the $420 account of P. Coble is uncollectible and writes it off as a bad debt. On June 5, Coble unexpectedly pays the amount previously written off. Prepare the journal entries of Alvare to record these transactions and events of December 31, February 1, and June 5.

Exercise 9-5
Percent of accounts receivable method
P2

At each calendar year-end, Cabool Supply Co. uses the percent of accounts receivable method to estimate bad debts. On December 31, 2011, it has outstanding accounts receivable of $53,000, and it estimates that 4% will be uncollectible. Prepare the adjusting entry to record bad debts expense for year 2011 under the assumption that the Allowance for Doubtful Accounts has (*a*) a $915 credit balance before the adjustment and (*b*) a $1,332 debit balance before the adjustment.

Exercise 9-6
Aging of receivables method
P2

Hecter Company estimates uncollectible accounts using the allowance method at December 31. It prepared the following aging of receivables analysis.

		Days Past Due				
	Total	0	1 to 30	31 to 60	61 to 90	Over 90
Accounts receivable	$190,000	$132,000	$30,000	$12,000	$6,000	$10,000
Percent uncollectible		1%	2%	4%	7%	12%

a. Estimate the balance of the Allowance for Doubtful Accounts using the aging of accounts receivable method.

b. Prepare the adjusting entry to record Bad Debts Expense using the estimate from part *a*. Assume the unadjusted balance in the Allowance for Doubtful Accounts is a $600 credit.

c. Prepare the adjusting entry to record Bad Debts Expense using the estimate from part *a*. Assume the unadjusted balance in the Allowance for Doubtful Accounts is a $400 debit.

Exercise 9-7
Percent of receivables method
P2

Refer to the information in Exercise 9-6 to complete the following requirements.

a. Estimate the balance of the Allowance for Doubtful Accounts assuming the company uses 3.5% of total accounts receivable to estimate uncollectibles, instead of the aging of receivables method.

b. Prepare the adjusting entry to record Bad Debts Expense using the estimate from part *a*. Assume the unadjusted balance in the Allowance for Doubtful Accounts is a $300 credit.

c. Prepare the adjusting entry to record Bad Debts Expense using the estimate from part *a*. Assume the unadjusted balance in the Allowance for Doubtful Accounts is a $200 debit.

Exercise 9-8
Writing off receivables
P2

Refer to the information in Exercise 9-6 to complete the following requirements.

a. On February 1 of the next period, the company determined that $1,900 in customer accounts is uncollectible; specifically, $400 for Oxford Co. and $1,500 for Brookes Co. Prepare the journal entry to write off those accounts.

b. On June 5 of that next period, the company unexpectedly received a $400 payment on a customer account, Oxford Company, that had previously been written off in part *a*. Prepare the entries necessary to reinstate the account and to record the cash received.

Exercise 9-9
Estimating bad debts
P2

At December 31, GreenTea Company reports the following results for its calendar-year.

Cash sales	$1,200,000
Credit sales	900,000

Its year-end unadjusted trial balance includes the following items.

Accounts receivable	$195,000 debit
Allowance for doubtful accounts	3,000 debit

a. Prepare the adjusting entry to record Bad Debts Expense assuming uncollectibles are estimated to be 1.5% of credit sales.

Check Dr. Bad Debts Expense: (*a*) $13,500

b. Prepare the adjusting entry to record Bad Debts Expense assuming uncollectibles are estimated to be 0.5% of total sales.

c. Prepare the adjusting entry to record Bad Debts Expense assuming uncollectibles are estimated to be 6% of year-end accounts receivable.

(*c*) $14,700

Exercise 9-10
Selling and pledging accounts receivable
C3

On June 30, Roman Co. has $125,900 of accounts receivable. Prepare journal entries to record the following selected July transactions. Also prepare any footnotes to the July 31 financial statements that result from these transactions. (The company uses the perpetual inventory system.)

July	4	Sold $6,295 of merchandise (that had cost $4,000) to customers on credit.
	9	Sold $18,000 of accounts receivable to Center Bank. Center charges a 4% factoring fee.
	17	Received $3,436 cash from customers in payment on their accounts.
	27	Borrowed $10,000 cash from Center Bank, pledging $13,000 of accounts receivable as security for the loan.

Exercise 9-11
Honoring a note
P3

Prepare journal entries to record these selected transactions for Eduardo Company.

Nov.	1	Accepted a $5,000, 180-day, 6% note dated November 1 from Melosa Allen in granting a time extension on her past-due account receivable.
Dec.	31	Adjusted the year-end accounts for the accrued interest earned on the Allen note.
Apr.	30	Allen honors her note when presented for payment; February has 28 days for the current year.

Exercise 9-12
Dishonoring a note
P3

Prepare journal entries to record the following selected transactions of Paloma Company.

Mar. 21 Accepted a $3,100, 180-day, 10% note dated March 21 from Salma Hernandez in granting a time extension on her past-due account receivable.
Sept. 17 Hernandez dishonors her note when it is presented for payment.
Dec. 31 After exhausting all legal means of collection, Paloma Company writes off Hernandez's account against the Allowance for Doubtful Accounts.

Exercise 9-13
Notes receivable transactions
C2

Check Dec. 31, Cr. Interest Revenue $40

Prepare journal entries for the following selected transactions of Deshawn Company for 2010.

2010

Dec. 13 Accepted a $10,000, 45-day, 8% note dated December 13 in granting Latisha Clark a time extension on her past-due account receivable.
31 Prepared an adjusting entry to record the accrued interest on the Clark note.

Exercise 9-14
Notes receivable transactions
P3

Check Jan. 27, Dr. Cash $10,100
June 1, Dr. Cash $4,100

Refer to the information in Exercise 9-13 and prepare the journal entries for the following selected transactions of Deshawn Company for 2011.

2011

Jan. 27 Received Clark's payment for principal and interest on the note dated December 13.
Mar. 3 Accepted a $4,000, 10%, 90-day note dated March 3 in granting a time extension on the past-due account receivable of Shandi Company.
17 Accepted a $2,000, 30-day, 9% note dated March 17 in granting Juan Torres a time extension on his past-due account receivable.
Apr. 16 Torres dishonors his note when presented for payment.
May 1 Wrote off the Torres account against the Allowance for Doubtful Accounts.
June 1 Received the Shandi payment for principal and interest on the note dated March 3.

Exercise 9-15
Accounts receivable turnover
A1 

The following information is from the annual financial statements of Waseem Company. Compute its accounts receivable turnover for 2010 and 2011. Compare the two years results and give a possible explanation for any change (competitors average a turnover of 11).

	2011	2010	2009
Net sales	$305,000	$236,000	$288,000
Accounts receivable, net (year-end)	22,900	20,700	17,400

Exercise 9-16
Accounting for bad debts following IFRS

Hitachi, Ltd., reports total revenues of ¥10,000,369 million for its fiscal year ending March 31, 2009, and its March 31, 2009, unadjusted trial balance reports a debit balance for trade receivables (gross) of ¥2,179,764 million.

a. Prepare the adjusting entry to record its Bad Debts Expense assuming uncollectibles are estimated to be 0.4% of total revenues and its unadjusted trial balance reports a credit balance of ¥10,000 million.

b. Prepare the adjusting entry to record Bad Debts Expense assuming uncollectibles are estimated to be 2.1% of year-end trade receivables (gross) and its unadjusted trial balance reports a credit balance of ¥10,000 million.

connect

PROBLEM SET A

Problem 9-1A
Sales on account and credit card sales

Atlas Co. allows select customers to make purchases on credit. Its other customers can use either of two credit cards: Zisa or Access. Zisa deducts a 3% service charge for sales on its credit card and credits the bank account of Atlas immediately when credit card receipts are deposited. Atlas deposits the Zisa credit card receipts each business day. When customers use Access credit cards, Atlas accumulates the receipts for several days before submitting them to Access for payment. Access deducts a 2% service charge and usually pays within one week of being billed. Atlas completes the following transactions in June. (The terms of all credit sales are 2/15, n/30, and all sales are recorded at the gross price.)

June 4 Sold $750 of merchandise (that had cost $500) on credit to Anne Cianci.
5 Sold $5,900 of merchandise (that had cost $3,200) to customers who used their Zisa cards.

6 Sold $4,800 of merchandise (that had cost $2,800) to customers who used their Access cards.
8 Sold $3,200 of merchandise (that had cost $1,900) to customers who used their Access cards.
10 Submitted Access card receipts accumulated since June 6 to the credit card company for payment.
13 Wrote off the account of Nakia Wells against the Allowance for Doubtful Accounts. The $329 balance in Wells's account stemmed from a credit sale in October of last year.
17 Received the amount due from Access.
18 Received Cianci's check in full payment for the purchase of June 4.

Check June 17, Dr. Cash $7,840

Required

Prepare journal entries to record the preceding transactions and events. (The company uses the perpetual inventory system. Round amounts to the nearest dollar.)

Problem 9-2A
Accounts receivable transactions and bad debts adjustments
C1 P2

Lopez Company began operations on January 1, 2010. During its first two years, the company completed a number of transactions involving sales on credit, accounts receivable collections, and bad debts. These transactions are summarized as follows.

2010

a. Sold $1,803,750 of merchandise (that had cost $1,475,000) on credit, terms n/30.
b. Wrote off $20,300 of uncollectible accounts receivable.
c. Received $789,200 cash in payment of accounts receivable.
d. In adjusting the accounts on December 31, the company estimated that 1.5% of accounts receivable will be uncollectible.

Check (*d*) Dr. Bad Debts Expense $35,214

2011

e. Sold $1,825,700 of merchandise (that had cost $1,450,000) on credit, terms n/30.
f. Wrote off $28,800 of uncollectible accounts receivable.
g. Received $1,304,800 cash in payment of accounts receivable.
h. In adjusting the accounts on December 31, the company estimated that 1.5% of accounts receivable will be uncollectible.

(*h*) Dr. Bad Debts Expense $36,181

Required

Prepare journal entries to record Lopez's 2010 and 2011 summarized transactions and its year-end adjustments to record bad debts expense. (The company uses the perpetual inventory system. Round amounts to the nearest dollar.)

Problem 9-3A
Estimating and reporting bad debts
P2 

At December 31, 2011, Ethan Company reports the following results for its calendar-year.

Cash sales	$1,803,750
Credit sales	3,534,000

In addition, its unadjusted trial balance includes the following items.

Accounts receivable	$1,070,100 debit
Allowance for doubtful accounts	15,750 debit

Required

1. Prepare the adjusting entry for this company to recognize bad debts under each of the following independent assumptions.
   a. Bad debts are estimated to be 2% of credit sales.
   b. Bad debts are estimated to be 1% of total sales.
   c. An aging analysis estimates that 5% of year-end accounts receivable are uncollectible.
2. Show how Accounts Receivable and the Allowance for Doubtful Accounts appear on its December 31, 2011, balance sheet given the facts in part 1*a*.
3. Show how Accounts Receivable and the Allowance for Doubtful Accounts appear on its December 31, 2011, balance sheet given the facts in part 1*c*.

Check Bad Debts Expense: (1*a*) $70,680, (1*c*) $69,255

Problem 9-4A
Aging accounts receivable and accounting for bad debts
P2  

Carmack Company has credit sales of $2.6 million for year 2011. On December 31, 2011, the company's Allowance for Doubtful Accounts has an unadjusted credit balance of $13,400. Carmack prepares a schedule of its December 31, 2011, accounts receivable by age. On the basis of past experience, it estimates the percent of receivables in each age category that will become uncollectible. This information is summarized here.

December 31, 2011 Accounts Receivable	Age of Accounts Receivable	Expected Percent Uncollectible
$730,000	Not yet due	1.25%
354,000	1 to 30 days past due	2.00
76,000	31 to 60 days past due	6.50
48,000	61 to 90 days past due	32.75
12,000	Over 90 days past due	68.00

Required

1. Estimate the required balance of the Allowance for Doubtful Accounts at December 31, 2011, using the aging of accounts receivable method.

2. Prepare the adjusting entry to record bad debts expense at December 31, 2011.

Check (2) Dr. Bad Debts Expense $31,625

Analysis Component

3. On June 30, 2012, Carmack Company concludes that a customer's $3,750 receivable (created in 2011) is uncollectible and that the account should be written off. What effect will this action have on Carmack's 2012 net income? Explain.

Problem 9-5A
Analyzing and journalizing notes receivable transactions
C2 C3 P3

The following selected transactions are from Ohlde Company.

2010

Dec. 16 Accepted a $9,600, 60-day, 9% note dated this day in granting Todd Duke a time extension on his past-due account receivable.
31 Made an adjusting entry to record the accrued interest on the Duke note.

2011

Feb. 14 Received Duke's payment of principal and interest on the note dated December 16.
Mar. 2 Accepted an $4,120, 8%, 90-day note dated this day in granting a time extension on the past-due account receivable from Mare Co.
17 Accepted a $2,400, 30-day, 7% note dated this day in granting Jolene Halaam a time extension on her past-due account receivable.
Apr. 16 Halaam dishonored her note when presented for payment.
June 2 Mare Co. refuses to pay the note that was due to Ohlde Co. on May 31. Prepare the journal entry to charge the dishonored note plus accrued interest to Mare Co.'s accounts receivable.
July 17 Received payment from Mare Co. for the maturity value of its dishonored note plus interest for 46 days beyond maturity at 8%.
Aug. 7 Accepted an $5,440, 90-day, 10% note dated this day in granting a time extension on the past-due account receivable of Birch and Byer Co.
Sept. 3 Accepted a $2,080, 60-day, 10% note dated this day in granting Kevin York a time extension on his past-due account receivable.
Nov. 2 Received payment of principal plus interest from York for the September 3 note.
Nov. 5 Received payment of principal plus interest from Birch and Byer for the August 7 note.
Dec. 1 Wrote off the Jolene Halaam account against Allowance for Doubtful Accounts.

Check Feb. 14, Cr. Interest Revenue $108

June 2, Cr. Interest Revenue $82

Nov. 2, Cr. Interest Revenue $35

Required

1. Prepare journal entries to record these transactions and events. (Round amounts to the nearest dollar.)

Analysis Component

2. What reporting is necessary when a business pledges receivables as security for a loan and the loan is still outstanding at the end of the period? Explain the reason for this requirement and the accounting principle being satisfied.

PROBLEM SET B

Problem 9-1B
Sales on account and credit card sales
C1

Able Co. allows select customers to make purchases on credit. Its other customers can use either of two credit cards: Commerce Bank or Aztec. Commerce Bank deducts a 3% service charge for sales on its credit card and immediately credits the bank account of Able when credit card receipts are deposited. Able deposits the Commerce Bank credit card receipts each business day. When customers use the Aztec card, Able accumulates the receipts for several days and then submits them to Aztec for payment. Aztec deducts a 2% service charge and usually pays within one week of being billed. Able completed the following transactions in August (terms of all credit sales are 2/10, n/30; and all sales are recorded at the gross price).

Aug. 4 Sold $2,780 of merchandise (that had cost $1,750) on credit to Stacy Dalton.
10 Sold $3,248 of merchandise (that had cost $2,456) to customers who used their Commerce Bank credit cards.
11 Sold $1,575 of merchandise (that had cost $1,150) to customers who used their Aztec cards.
14 Received Dalton's check in full payment for the purchase of August 4.
15 Sold $2,960 of merchandise (that had cost $1,758) to customers who used their Aztec cards.
18 Submitted Aztec card receipts accumulated since August 11 to the credit card company for payment.
22 Wrote off the account of Ness City against the Allowance for Doubtful Accounts. The $398 balance in Ness City's account stemmed from a credit sale in November of last year.
25 Received the amount due from Aztec.

Check Aug. 25, Dr. Cash $4,444

Required

Prepare journal entries to record the preceding transactions and events. (The company uses the perpetual inventory system. Round amounts to the nearest dollar.)

Problem 9-2B
Accounts receivable transactions and bad debts adjustments
C1 P2

Crist Co. began operations on January 1, 2010, and completed several transactions during 2010 and 2011 that involved sales on credit, accounts receivable collections, and bad debts. These transactions are summarized as follows.

2010

a. Sold $673,490 of merchandise (that had cost $500,000) on credit, terms n/30.
b. Received $437,250 cash in payment of accounts receivable.
c. Wrote off $8,330 of uncollectible accounts receivable.
d. In adjusting the accounts on December 31, the company estimated that 1% of accounts receivable will be uncollectible.

Check (*d*) Dr. Bad Debts Expense $10,609

2011

e. Sold $930,100 of merchandise (that had cost $650,000) on credit, terms n/30.
f. Received $890,220 cash in payment of accounts receivable.
g. Wrote off $10,090 of uncollectible accounts receivable.
h. In adjusting the accounts on December 31, the company estimated that 1% of accounts receivable will be uncollectible.

(*h*) Dr. Bad Debts Expense $10,388

Required

Prepare journal entries to record Crist's 2010 and 2011 summarized transactions and its year-end adjusting entry to record bad debts expense. (The company uses the perpetual inventory system. Round amounts to the nearest dollar.)

Problem 9-3B
Estimating and reporting bad debts
P2

At December 31, 2011, Klimek Company reports the following results for the year.

Cash sales	$1,015,000
Credit sales	1,241,000

In addition, its unadjusted trial balance includes the following items.

Accounts receivable	$475,000 debit
Allowance for doubtful accounts	5,200 credit

Required

1. Prepare the adjusting entry for Klimek Co. to recognize bad debts under each of the following independent assumptions.
   a. Bad debts are estimated to be 2.5% of credit sales.
   b. Bad debts are estimated to be 1.5% of total sales.
   c. An aging analysis estimates that 6% of year-end accounts receivable are uncollectible.
2. Show how Accounts Receivable and the Allowance for Doubtful Accounts appear on its December 31, 2011, balance sheet given the facts in part 1*a*.
3. Show how Accounts Receivable and the Allowance for Doubtful Accounts appear on its December 31, 2011, balance sheet given the facts in part 1*c*.

Check Bad debts expense: (1*b*) $33,840, (1*c*) $23,300

Problem 9-4B
Aging accounts receivable and accounting for bad debts
P2

Quisp Company has credit sales of $3.5 million for year 2011. At December 31, 2011, the company's Allowance for Doubtful Accounts has an unadjusted debit balance of $4,100. Quisp prepares a schedule of its December 31, 2011, accounts receivable by age. On the basis of past experience, it estimates the percent of receivables in each age category that will become uncollectible. This information is summarized here.

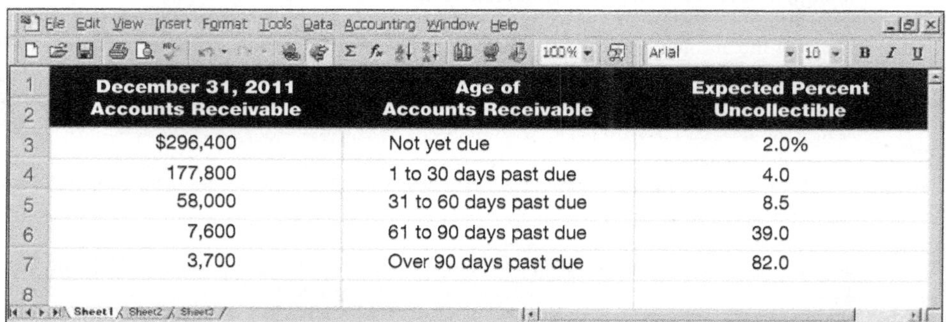

December 31, 2011 Accounts Receivable	Age of Accounts Receivable	Expected Percent Uncollectible
$296,400	Not yet due	2.0%
177,800	1 to 30 days past due	4.0
58,000	31 to 60 days past due	8.5
7,600	61 to 90 days past due	39.0
3,700	Over 90 days past due	82.0

Required

1. Compute the required balance of the Allowance for Doubtful Accounts at December 31, 2011, using the aging of accounts receivable method.
2. Prepare the adjusting entry to record bad debts expense at December 31, 2011.

Check (2) Dr. Bad Debts Expense $28,068

Analysis Component

3. On July 31, 2012, Quisp concludes that a customer's $2,345 receivable (created in 2011) is uncollectible and that the account should be written off. What effect will this action have on Quisp's 2012 net income? Explain.

Problem 9-5B
Analyzing and journalizing notes receivable transactions
C2 C3 P3 

The following selected transactions are from Seeker Company.

2010

Nov.	1	Accepted a $4,800, 90-day, 8% note dated this day in granting Julie Stephens a time extension on her past-due account receivable.
Dec.	31	Made an adjusting entry to record the accrued interest on the Stephens note.

2011

Jan.	30	Received Stephens's payment for principal and interest on the note dated November 1.
Feb.	28	Accepted a $12,600, 6%, 30-day note dated this day in granting a time extension on the past-due account receivable from Kramer Co.
Mar.	1	Accepted a $6,200, 60-day, 8% note dated this day in granting Shelly Myers a time extension on her past-due account receivable.
	30	The Kramer Co. dishonored its note when presented for payment.
April	30	Received payment of principal plus interest from Myers for the March 1 note.
June	15	Accepted a $2,000, 60-day, 10% note dated this day in granting a time extension on the past-due account receivable of Rhonda Rye.
	21	Accepted a $9,500, 90-day, 12% note dated this day in granting J. Striker a time extension on his past-due account receivable.
Aug.	14	Received payment of principal plus interest from R. Rye for the note of June 15.
Sep.	19	Received payment of principal plus interest from J. Striker for the June 21 note.
Nov.	30	Wrote off Kramer's account against Allowance for Doubtful Accounts.

Check Jan. 30, Cr. Interest Revenue $32

April 30, Cr. Interest Revenue $83

Sep. 19, Cr. Interest Revenue $285

Required

1. Prepare journal entries to record these transactions and events. (Round amounts to the nearest dollar.)

Analysis Component

2. What reporting is necessary when a business pledges receivables as security for a loan and the loan is still outstanding at the end of the period? Explain the reason for this requirement and the accounting principle being satisfied.

SERIAL PROBLEM
Business Solutions
P1 P2

(This serial problem began in Chapter 1 and continues through most of the book. If previous chapter segments were not completed, the serial problem can begin at this point. It is helpful, but not necessary, to use the Working Papers that accompany the book.)

SP 9 Santana Rey, owner of Business Solutions, realizes that she needs to begin accounting for bad debts expense. Assume that Business Solutions has total revenues of $44,000 during the first three months of 2012, and that the Accounts Receivable balance on March 31, 2012, is $22,867.

Required

1. Prepare the adjusting entry needed for Business Solutions to recognize bad debts expense on March 31, 2012, under each of the following independent assumptions (assume a zero unadjusted balance in the Allowance for Doubtful Accounts at March 31).

a. Bad debts are estimated to be 1% of total revenues. (Round amounts to the dollar.)

b. Bad debts are estimated to be 2% of accounts receivable. (Round amounts to the dollar.)

2. Assume that Business Solutions' Accounts Receivable balance at June 30, 2012, is $20,250 and that one account of $100 has been written off against the Allowance for Doubtful Accounts since March 31, 2012. If S. Rey uses the method prescribed in Part 1*b*, what adjusting journal entry must be made to recognize bad debts expense on June 30, 2012?

Check (2) Bad Debts Expense, $48

3. Should S. Rey consider adopting the direct write-off method of accounting for bad debts expense rather than one of the allowance methods considered in part 1? Explain.

Beyond the Numbers

REPORTING IN ACTION
A1
RIM

BTN 9-1 Refer to Research In Motion's financial statements in Appendix A to answer the following.

1. What is the amount of Research In Motion's accounts receivable as of February 27, 2010?

2. Compute Research In Motion's accounts receivable turnover as of February 27, 2010.

3. How long does it take, *on average*, for the company to collect receivables? Do you believe that customers actually pay the amounts due within this short period? Explain.

4. Research In Motion's most liquid assets include (*a*) cash and cash equivalents, (*b*) short-term investments, and (*c*) receivables. Compute the percentage that these liquid assets make up of current liabilities as of February 27, 2010. Do the same computations for February 28, 2009. Comment on the company's ability to satisfy its current liabilities as of its 2010 fiscal year-end compared to its 2009 fiscal year-end.

5. What criteria did Research In Motion use to classify items as cash equivalents?

Fast Forward

6. Access Research In Motion's financial statements for fiscal years after February 27, 2010, at its Website (www.RIM.com) or the SEC's EDGAR database (www.SEC.gov). Recompute parts 2 and 4 and comment on any changes since February 27, 2010.

COMPARATIVE ANALYSIS
A1 P2

RIM
Apple

BTN 9-2 Comparative figures for Research In Motion and Apple follow.

	Research In Motion			Apple		
($ millions)	Current Year	One Year Prior	Two Years Prior	Current Year	One Year Prior	Two Years Prior
Accounts receivable, net	$ 2,594	$ 2,112	$1,175	$ 3,361	$ 2,422	$ 1,637
Net sales	14,953	11,065	6,009	42,905	37,491	24,578

Required

1. Compute the accounts receivable turnover for Research In Motion and Apple for each of the two most recent years using the data shown.
2. Using results from part 1, compute how many days it takes each company, *on average,* to collect receivables. Compare the collection periods for RIM and Apple, and suggest at least one explanation for the difference.
3. Which company is more efficient in collecting its accounts receivable? Explain.

Hint: Average collection period equals 365 divided by the accounts receivable turnover.

ETHICS CHALLENGE

P2

BTN 9-3 Kelly Steinman is the manager of a medium-size company. A few years ago, Steinman persuaded the owner to base a part of her compensation on the net income the company earns each year. Each December she estimates year-end financial figures in anticipation of the bonus she will receive. If the bonus is not as high as she would like, she offers several recommendations to the accountant for year-end adjustments. One of her favorite recommendations is for the controller to reduce the estimate of doubtful accounts.

Required

1. What effect does lowering the estimate for doubtful accounts have on the income statement and balance sheet?
2. Do you believe Steinman's recommendation to adjust the allowance for doubtful accounts is within her right as manager, or do you believe this action is an ethics violation? Justify your response.
3. What type of internal control(s) might be useful for this company in overseeing the manager's recommendations for accounting changes?

COMMUNICATING IN PRACTICE

P2

BTN 9-4 As the accountant for Pure-Air Distributing, you attend a sales managers' meeting devoted to a discussion of credit policies. At the meeting, you report that bad debts expense is estimated to be $59,000 and accounts receivable at year-end amount to $1,750,000 less a $43,000 allowance for doubtful accounts. Sid Omar, a sales manager, expresses confusion over why bad debts expense and the allowance for doubtful accounts are different amounts. Write a one-page memorandum to him explaining why a difference in bad debts expense and the allowance for doubtful accounts is not unusual. The company estimates bad debts expense as 2% of sales.

TAKING IT TO THE NET

C1

BTN 9-5 Access eBay's, February 17, 2010, filing of its 10-K report for the year ended December 31, 2009, at www.SEC.gov.

Required

1. What is the amount of eBay's net accounts receivable at December 31, 2009, and at December 31, 2008?
2. "Financial Statement Schedule II" to its financial statements lists eBay's allowance for doubtful accounts (including authorized credits). For the two years ended December 31, 2009 and 2008, compute its allowance for doubtful accounts (including authorized credits) as a percent of gross accounts receivable.
3. Do you believe that these percentages are reasonable based on what you know about eBay? Explain.

TEAMWORK IN ACTION

P2

BTN 9-6 Each member of a team is to participate in estimating uncollectibles using the aging schedule and percents shown in Problem 9-4A. The division of labor is up to the team. Your goal is to accurately complete this task as soon as possible. After estimating uncollectibles, check your estimate with the instructor. If the estimate is correct, the team then should prepare the adjusting entry and the presentation of accounts receivable (net) for the December 31, 2011, balance sheet.

ENTREPRENEURIAL DECISION

C1

BTN 9-7 Bernard McCoy of LaserMonks is introduced in the chapter's opening feature. Bernard currently sells his products through multiple outlets. Assume that he is considering two new selling options.

Plan A. LaserMonks would begin selling additional products online directly to customers, which are only currently sold directly to outlet stores. These new online customers would use their credit cards. It currently has the capability of selling through its Website with no additional investment in hardware or software. Credit sales are expected to increase by $250,000 per year. Costs associated with this plan are: cost of these sales will be $135,500, credit card fees will be 4.75% of sales, and additional recordkeeping and shipping costs will be 6% of sales. These online sales will reduce the sales to stores by $35,000 because some customers will now purchase items online. Sales to stores have a 25% gross margin percentage.

Plan B. LaserMonks would expand its market to more outlet stores. It would make additional credit sales of $500,000 to those stores. Costs associated with those sales are: cost of sales will be $375,000, additional recordkeeping and shipping will be 4% of sales, and uncollectible accounts will be 6.2% of sales.

Required

1. Compute the additional annual net income or loss expected under (a) Plan A and (b) Plan B.
2. Should LaserMonks pursue either plan? Discuss both the financial and nonfinancial factors relevant to this decision.

Check (1*b*) Net income, $74,000

HITTING THE ROAD

C1  

BTN 9-8 Many commercials include comments similar to the following: "We accept **VISA**" or "We do not accept **American Express**." Conduct your own research by contacting at least five companies via interviews, phone calls, or the Internet to determine the reason(s) companies discriminate in their use of credit cards. Collect information on the fees charged by the different cards for the companies contacted. (The instructor can assign this as a team activity.)

GLOBAL DECISION

C1 P2

NOKIA

RIM

Apple

BTN 9-9 Key information from Nokia (www.Nokia.com), which is a leading global manufacturer of mobile devices and services, follows.

EUR millions	Current Year	Prior Year
Accounts receivable, net*	7,981	9,444
Sales	40,984	50,710

*Nokia refers to it as "Accounts receivable, net of allowance for doubtful accounts."

1. Compute the accounts receivable turnover for the current year.
2. How long does it take on average for Nokia to collect receivables?
3. Refer to BTN 9-2. How does Nokia compare to Research In Motion and Apple in terms of its accounts receivable turnover and its collection period?
4. Nokia reports an aging analysis of its receivables, based on due dates, as follows (in EUR millions) as of December 31, 2009. Compute the percent of receivables in each category.

EUR millions	Total Receivables
Current	7,302
Past due 1–30 days	393
Past due 31–180 days	170
More than 180 days	116

ANSWERS TO MULTIPLE CHOICE QUIZ

1. d; Desired balance in Allowance for Doubtful Accounts = $ 5,026 cr. ($125,650 × 0.04)
   Current balance in Allowance for Doubtful Accounts = (328) cr.
   Bad Debts Expense to be recorded = $ 4,698
2. a; Desired balance in Allowance for Doubtful Accounts = $29,358 cr. ($489,300 × 0.06)
   Current balance in Allowance for Doubtful Accounts = 554 dr.
   Bad Debts Expense to be recorded = $29,912
3. a; $7,500 × 0.05 × 90/360 = $93.75
4. c; Principal amount $9,000
   Interest accrued .... 120 ($9,000 × 0.08 × 60/360)
   Maturity value $9,120
5. d; $489,600/$40,800 = 12

11 Current Liabilities and Payroll Accounting

A Look Back

Chapter 10 focused on long-term assets including plant assets, natural resources, and intangibles. We showed how to account for and analyze those assets.

A Look at This Chapter

This chapter explains how to identify, compute, record, and report current liabilities in financial statements. We also analyze and interpret these liabilities, including those related to employee costs.

A Look Ahead

Chapter 12 explains the partnership form of organization. It also describes the accounting concepts and procedures for partnership transactions.

Learning Objectives

CONCEPTUAL

C1 Describe current and long-term liabilities and their characteristics. (p. 436)

C2 Identify and describe known current liabilities. (p. 438)

C3 Explain how to account for contingent liabilities. (p. 448)

ANALYTICAL

A1 Compute the times interest earned ratio and use it to analyze liabilities. (p. 450)

LP11

PROCEDURAL

P1 Prepare entries to account for short-term notes payable. (p. 439)

P2 Compute and record *employee* payroll deductions and liabilities. (p. 441)

P3 Compute and record *employer* payroll expenses and liabilities. (p. 443)

P4 Account for estimated liabilities, including warranties and bonuses. (p. 445)

P5 *Appendix 11A*—Identify and describe the details of payroll reports, records, and procedures. (p. 453)

Decision Insight

No Stuffed Shirts

"Part of the fun is the journey . . . working til 2 am every day"
—MATT WALLS

ATLANTA, GA—Brothers Matt and Bryan Walls never planned to be entrepreneurs in the T-shirt business. "[It was] an idea we had while hanging out in our parents' basement," explains Matt. "We were naive and, like many first-time entrepreneurs, just dove right in." Matt and Bryan's plans involved making T-shirts with visual humor and pop culture themes. Their company, SnorgTees **(SnorgTees.com),** had a shaky start but soon found its groove with best-selling T-shirts such as "With a shirt like this, who needs pants?" "Don't act like you're not impressed," and "I'm kind of a big deal."

"We dreamed it would be successful overnight," recalls Matt. "But when things first started we had a huge reality check, and at that point I don't know if I believed." Today their business is thriving. Their commitment to success carries over to the financial side. They especially focus on the important task of managing liabilities for payroll, supplies, employee wages, training, and taxes. Both insist that effective management of liabilities, especially payroll and employee benefits, is crucial. They stress that monitoring and controlling liabilities are a must.

To help control liabilities, Matt and Bryan describe how they began by working out of their parents' home to reduce liabilities. "Most people think all we do is sit around and think up funny ideas," explains Matt. "In reality most of the time is spent on executing projects and managing the business . . . [including] order fulfillment, supply chain management, marketing, and accounting." In short, creative reduction of liabilities can mean success or failure.

The two continue to monitor liabilities and their payment patterns. "I'm pretty conservative about spending money," admits Matt. "If you want to run a successful company, you can't forget all the details." The two insist that accounting for and monitoring liabilities are one key to a successful start-up. Their company now generates sufficient income to pay for liabilities and produces revenue growth for expansion. "We plan to keep having fun," insists Matt. "We do business with people all over the world."

Sources: *SnorgTees Website,* January 2011; *Entrepreneur,* September 2009; *RetireAt21.com,* October 2008; *Business to Business,* January 2008; *WannaBeMogul.com,* November 2007.

Chapter Preview

Previous chapters introduced liabilities such as accounts payable, notes payable, wages payable, and unearned revenues. This chapter further explains these liabilities and additional ones such as warranties, taxes, payroll, vacation pay, and bonuses. It also describes contingent liabilities and introduces long-term liabilities. The focus is on how to define, classify, measure, report, and analyze these liabilities so that this information is useful to business decision makers.

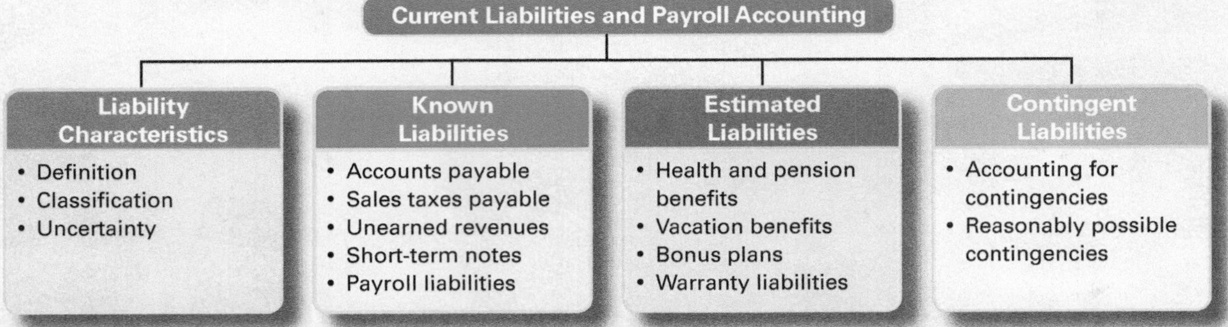

CHARACTERISTICS OF LIABILITIES

This section discusses important characteristics of liabilities and how liabilities are classified and reported.

Defining Liabilities

C1 Describe current and long-term liabilities and their characteristics.

A *liability* is a probable future payment of assets or services that a company is presently obligated to make as a result of past transactions or events. This definition includes three crucial factors:

1. A past transaction or event.
2. A present obligation.
3. A future payment of assets or services.

These three important elements are portrayed visually in Exhibit 11.1. Liabilities reported in financial statements exhibit those characteristics. No liability is reported when one or more of those characteristics is absent. For example, most companies expect to pay wages to their employees in upcoming months and years, but these future payments are *not* liabilities because no past event such as employee work resulted in a present obligation. Instead, such liabilities arise when employees perform their work and earn the wages.

EXHIBIT 11.1

Characteristics of a Liability

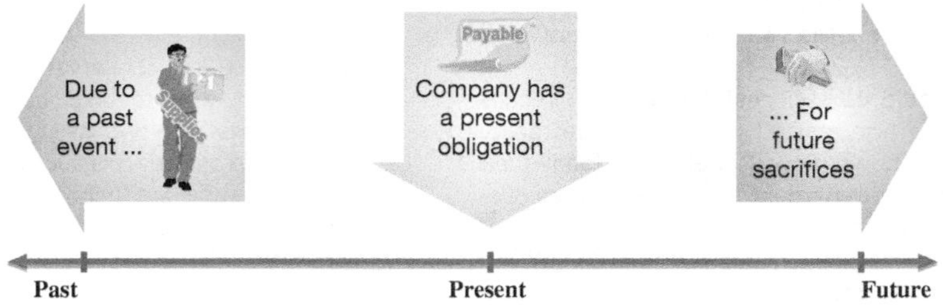

Classifying Liabilities

Information about liabilities is more useful when the balance sheet identifies them as either current or long term. Decision makers need to know when obligations are due so they can plan for them and take appropriate action.

Current Liabilities **Current liabilities,** also called *short-term liabilities,* are obligations due within one year or the company's operating cycle, whichever is longer. They are expected to be paid using current assets or by creating other current liabilities. Common examples of current liabilities are accounts payable, short-term notes payable, wages payable, warranty liabilities, lease liabilities, taxes payable, and unearned revenues.

Point: Improper classification of liabilities can distort ratios used in financial statement analysis and business decisions.

Current liabilities differ across companies because they depend on the type of company operations. MGM Mirage, for instance, included the following current liabilities related to its gaming, hospitality and entertainment operations ($000s):

Advance deposits and ticket sales	$104,911
Casino outstanding chip liability	83,957
Casino front money deposits	80,944

Harley-Davidson reports a much different set of current liabilities. It discloses current liabilities made up of items such as warranty, recall, and dealer incentive liabilities.

Long-Term Liabilities A company's obligations not expected to be paid within the longer of one year or the company's operating cycle are reported as **long-term liabilities.** They can include long-term notes payable, warranty liabilities, lease liabilities, and bonds payable. They are sometimes reported on the balance sheet in a single long-term liabilities total or in multiple categories. Domino's Pizza, for instance, reports long-term liabilities of $1,555 million. They are reported after current liabilities. A single liability also can be divided between the current and noncurrent sections if a company expects to make payments toward it in both the short and long term. Domino's reports ($ millions) long-term debt, $1,522; and current portion of long-term debt, $50. The second item is reported in current liabilities. We sometimes see liabilities that do not have a fixed due date but instead are payable on the creditor's demand. These are reported as current liabilities because of the possibility of payment in the near term. Exhibit 11.2 shows amounts of current liabilities and as a percent of total liabilities for selected companies.

Point: The current ratio is overstated if a company fails to classify any portion of long-term debt due next period as a current liability.

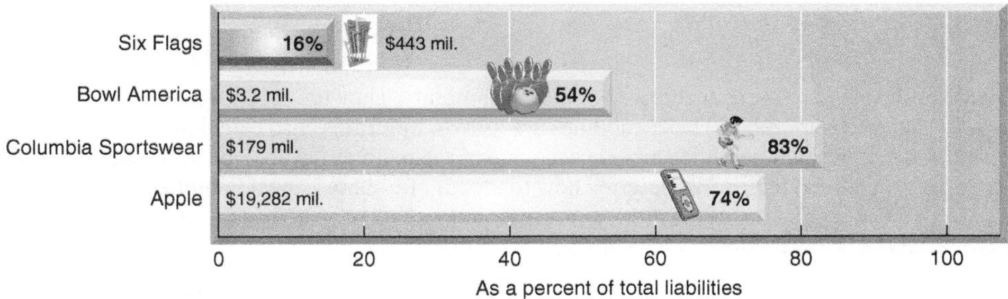

EXHIBIT 11.2

Current Liabilities of Selected Companies

Uncertainty in Liabilities

Accounting for liabilities involves addressing three important questions: Whom to pay? When to pay? How much to pay? Answers to these questions are often decided when a liability is incurred. For example, if a company has a $100 account payable to a specific individual, payable on March 15, the answers are clear. The company knows whom to pay, when to pay, and how much to pay. However, the answers to one or more of these questions are uncertain for some liabilities.

Uncertainty in Whom to Pay Liabilities can involve uncertainty in whom to pay. For instance, a company can create a liability with a known amount when issuing a note that is payable to its holder. In this case, a specific amount is payable to the note's holder at a specified date, but the company does not know who the holder is until that date. Despite this uncertainty, the company reports this liability on its balance sheet.

Point: An *accrued expense* is an unpaid expense, and is also called an *accrued liability*.

Uncertainty in When to Pay A company can have an obligation of a known amount to a known creditor but not know when it must be paid. For example, a legal services firm can accept fees in advance from a client who plans to use the firm's services in the future. This means that the firm has a liability that it settles by providing services at an unknown future date. Although this uncertainty exists, the legal firm's balance sheet must report this liability. These types of obligations are reported as current liabilities because they are likely to be settled in the short term.

Uncertainty in How Much to Pay A company can be aware of an obligation but not know how much will be required to settle it. For example, a company using electrical power is billed only after the meter has been read. This cost is incurred and the liability created before a bill is received. A liability to the power company is reported as an estimated amount if the balance sheet is prepared before a bill arrives.

IFRS

IFRS records a contingent liability when an obligation exists from a past event if there is a 'probable' outflow of resources and the amount can be estimated reliably. However, IFRS defines probable as 'more likely than not' while U.S. GAAP defines it as 'likely to occur.' ■

Quick Check Answers — p. 461

1. What is a liability? Identify its crucial characteristics.
2. Is every expected future payment a liability?
3. If a liability is payable in 15 months, is it classified as current or long term?

KNOWN LIABILITIES

C2 Identify and describe known current liabilities.

Most liabilities arise from situations with little uncertainty. They are set by agreements, contracts, or laws and are measurable. These liabilities are **known liabilities,** also called *definitely determinable liabilities.* Known liabilities include accounts payable, notes payable, payroll, sales taxes, unearned revenues, and leases. We describe how to account for these known liabilities in this section.

Accounts Payable

Accounts payable, or trade accounts payable, are amounts owed to suppliers for products or services purchased on credit. Accounting for accounts payable is primarily explained and illustrated in our discussion of merchandising activities in Chapters 5 and 6.

Sales Taxes Payable

Nearly all states and many cities levy taxes on retail sales. Sales taxes are stated as a percent of selling prices. The seller collects sales taxes from customers when sales occur and remits these collections (often monthly) to the proper government agency. Since sellers currently owe these collections to the government, this amount is a current liability. Home Depot, for instance, reports sales taxes payable of $362 million in its recent annual report. To illustrate, if Home Depot sells materials on August 31 for $6,000 cash that are subject to a 5% sales tax, the revenue portion of this transaction is recorded as follows:

Assets	=	Liabilities	+	Equity
+6,300		+300		+6,000

Aug. 31	Cash	6,300	
	Sales		6,000
	Sales Taxes Payable ($6,000 × 0.05)		300
	To record cash sales and 5% sales tax.		

Sales Taxes Payable is debited and Cash credited when it remits these collections to the government. Sales Taxes Payable is not an expense. It arises because laws require sellers to collect this cash from customers for the government.[1]

Unearned Revenues

Unearned revenues (also called *deferred revenues, collections in advance,* and *prepayments*) are amounts received in advance from customers for future products or services. Advance ticket sales for sporting events or music concerts are examples. Beyonce, for instance, has "deferred revenues" from advance ticket sales. To illustrate, assume that Beyonce sells $5 million in tickets for eight concerts; the entry is

Point: To *defer* a revenue means to postpone recognition of a revenue collected in advance until it is earned. Sport teams must defer recognition of ticket sales until games are played.

June 30	Cash	5,000,000	
	Unearned Ticket Revenue		5,000,000
	To record sale of concert tickets.		

Assets = Liabilities + Equity
+5,000,000 +5,000,000

When a concert is played, Beyonce would record revenue for the portion earned.

Oct. 31	Unearned Ticket Revenue	625,000	
	Ticket Revenue		625,000
	To record concert ticket revenues earned.		

Assets = Liabilities + Equity
−625,000 +625,000

Unearned Ticket Revenue is an unearned revenue account and is reported as a current liability. Unearned revenues also arise with airline ticket sales, magazine subscriptions, construction projects, hotel reservations, and custom orders.

Decision Insight

Reward Programs Gift card sales now exceed $100 billion annually, and reward (also called loyalty) programs are growing. There are no exact rules for how retailers account for rewards. When Best Buy launched its "Reward Zone," shoppers earned $5 on each $125 spent and had 90 days to spend it. Retailers make assumptions about how many reward program dollars will be spent and how to report it. Best Buy sets up a liability and reduces revenue by the same amount. Talbots does not reduce revenue but instead increases selling expense. Men's Wearhouse records rewards in cost of goods sold, whereas Neiman Marcus subtracts them from revenue. The FASB continues to review reward programs.

Short-Term Notes Payable

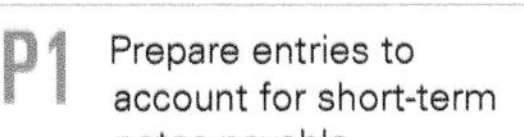

P1 Prepare entries to account for short-term notes payable.

A **short-term note payable** is a written promise to pay a specified amount on a definite future date within one year or the company's operating cycle, whichever is longer. These promissory notes are negotiable (as are checks), meaning they can be transferred from party to party by endorsement. The written documentation provided by notes is helpful in resolving disputes and for pursuing legal actions involving these liabilities. Most notes payable bear interest to compensate for use of the money until payment is made. Short-term notes payable can arise from many transactions. A company that purchases merchandise on credit can sometimes extend the credit period by signing a note to replace an account payable. Such notes also can arise when money is borrowed from a bank. We describe both of these cases.

Point: Required characteristics for negotiability of a note: (1) unconditional promise, (2) in writing, (3) specific amount, and (4) definite due date.

[1] Sales taxes can be computed from total sales receipts when sales taxes are not separately identified on the register. To illustrate, assume a 5% sales tax and $420 in total sales receipts (which includes sales taxes). Sales are computed as follows:

$$\text{Sales} = \text{Total sales receipts}/(1 + \text{Sales tax percentage}) = \$420/1.05 = \$400$$

Thus, the sales tax amount equals total sales receipts minus sales, or $420 − $400 = $20.

Note Given to Extend Credit Period A company can replace an account payable with a note payable. A common example is a creditor that requires the substitution of an interest-bearing note for an overdue account payable that does not bear interest. A less common situation occurs when a debtor's weak financial condition motivates the creditor to accept a note, sometimes for a lesser amount, and to close the account to ensure that this customer makes no additional credit purchases.

To illustrate, let's assume that on August 23, Brady Company asks to extend its past-due $600 account payable to McGraw. After some negotiations, McGraw agrees to accept $100 cash and a 60-day, 12%, $500 note payable to replace the account payable. Brady records the transaction with this entry:

Assets	=	Liabilities	+	Equity
−100		−600		
		+500		

Aug. 23	Accounts Payable—McGraw	600	
	Cash		100
	Notes Payable—McGraw		500
	Gave $100 cash and a 60-day, 12% note for payment on account.		

Point: Accounts payable are detailed in a subsidiary ledger, but notes payable are sometimes not. A file with copies of notes can serve as a subsidiary ledger.

Signing the note does not resolve Brady's debt. Instead, the form of debt is changed from an account payable to a note payable. McGraw prefers the note payable over the account payable because it earns interest and it is written documentation of the debt's existence, term, and amount. When the note comes due, Brady pays the note and interest by giving McGraw a check for $510. Brady records that payment with this entry:

Assets	=	Liabilities	+	Equity
−510		−500		−10

Oct. 22	Notes Payable—McGraw	500	
	Interest Expense	10	
	Cash		510
	Paid note with interest ($500 × 12% × 60/360).		

Point: Commercial companies commonly compute interest using a 360-day year. This is known as the *banker's rule*.

Interest expense is computed by multiplying the principal of the note ($500) by the annual interest rate (12%) for the fraction of the year the note is outstanding (60 days/360 days).

Note Given to Borrow from Bank A bank nearly always requires a borrower to sign a promissory note when making a loan. When the note matures, the borrower repays the note with an amount larger than the amount borrowed. The difference between the amount borrowed and the amount repaid is *interest*. This section considers a type of note whose signer promises to pay *principal* (the amount borrowed) plus interest. In this case, the *face value* of the note equals principal. Face value is the value shown on the face (front) of the note. To illustrate, assume that a company needs $2,000 for a project and borrows this money from a bank at 12% annual interest. The loan is made on September 30, 2011, and is due in 60 days. Specifically, the borrowing company signs a note with a face value equal to the amount borrowed. The note includes a statement similar to this: *"I promise to pay $2,000 plus interest at 12% within 60 days after September 30."* This simple note is shown in Exhibit 11.3.

Point: When money is borrowed from a bank, the loan is reported as an asset (receivable) on the bank's balance sheet.

EXHIBIT 11.3

Note with Face Value Equal to Amount Borrowed

Promissory Note

$2,000 — Face Value   Sept. 30, 2011 — Date

Sixty days after date, I promise to pay to the order of

National Bank
Boston, MA

Two thousand and no/100 ---------- Dollars

plus interest at the annual rate of 12%.

Janet Lee

The borrower records its receipt of cash and the new liability with this entry:

Sept. 30	Cash	2,000	
	Notes Payable		2,000
	Borrowed $2,000 cash with a 60-day, 12%, $2,000 note.		

Assets	=	Liabilities	+	Equity
+2,000		+2,000		

When principal and interest are paid, the borrower records payment with this entry:

Nov. 29	Notes Payable	2,000	
	Interest Expense	40	
	Cash		2,040
	Paid note with interest ($2,000 × 12% × 60/360).		

Assets	=	Liabilities	+	Equity
−2,040		−2,000		−40

End-of-period interest adjustment. When the end of an accounting period occurs between the signing of a note payable and its maturity date, the *matching principle* requires us to record the accrued but unpaid interest on the note. To illustrate, let's return to the note in Exhibit 11.3, but assume that the company borrows $2,000 cash on December 16, 2011, instead of September 30. This 60-day note matures on February 14, 2012, and the company's fiscal year ends on December 31. Thus, we need to record interest expense for the final 15 days in December. This means that one-fourth (15 days/60 days) of the $40 total interest is an expense of year 2011. The borrower records this expense with the following adjusting entry:

2011			
Dec. 31	Interest Expense	10	
	Interest Payable		10
	To record accrued interest on note ($2,000 × 12% × 15/360).		

Assets	=	Liabilities	+	Equity
		+10		−10

Example: If this note is dated Dec. 1 instead of Dec. 16, how much expense is recorded on Dec. 31? *Answer:* $2,000 × 12% × 30/360 = $20

When this note matures on February 14, the borrower must recognize 45 days of interest expense for year 2012 and remove the balances of the two liability accounts:

2012			
Feb. 14	Interest Expense*	30	
	Interest Payable	10	
	Notes Payable	2,000	
	Cash		2,040
	*Paid note with interest. *($2,000 × 12% × 45/360)*		

Assets	=	Liabilities	+	Equity
−2,040		−10		−30
		−2,000		

Decision Insight

Many franchisors such as **Baskin-Robbins**, **Dunkin' Donuts**, and **Cold Stone Creamery**, use notes to help entrepreneurs acquire their own franchises, including using notes to pay for the franchise fee and any equipment. Payments on these notes are usually collected monthly and often are secured by the franchisees' assets. ■

Payroll Liabilities

An employer incurs several expenses and liabilities from having employees. These expenses and liabilities are often large and arise from salaries and wages earned, from employee benefits, and from payroll taxes levied on the employer. **Boston Beer**, for instance, reports payroll-related current liabilities of more than $6.6 million from accrued "employee wages, benefits and reimbursements." We discuss payroll liabilities and related accounts in this section. Appendix 11A describes details about payroll reports, records, and procedures.

P2 Compute and record *employee* payroll deductions and liabilities.

Employee Payroll Deductions **Gross pay** is the total compensation an employee earns including wages, salaries, commissions, bonuses, and any compensation earned before deductions such as taxes. (*Wages* usually refer to payments to employees at an hourly rate. *Salaries* usually refer to payments to employees at a monthly or yearly rate.) **Net pay,** also called *take-home pay,* is gross pay less all deductions. **Payroll deductions,** commonly called *withholdings,* are amounts withheld from an employee's gross pay, either required or voluntary. Required deductions result from laws and include income taxes and Social Security taxes. Voluntary deductions, at an employee's option, include pension and health contributions, health and life insurance premiums, union dues, and charitable giving. Exhibit 11.4 shows the typical payroll deductions of an employee. The employer withholds payroll deductions from employees' pay and is obligated to transmit this money to the designated organization. The employer records payroll deductions as current liabilities until these amounts are transmitted. This section discusses the major payroll deductions.

Point: Deductions at some companies, such as those for insurance coverage, are "required" under its own labor contracts.

EXHIBIT 11.4

Payroll Deductions

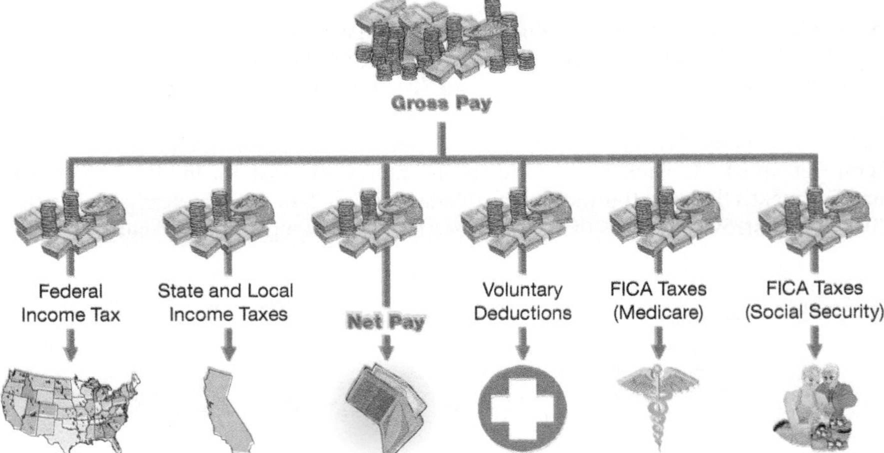

Employee FICA taxes. The federal Social Security system provides retirement, disability, survivorship, and medical benefits to qualified workers. Laws *require* employers to withhold **Federal Insurance Contributions Act (FICA) taxes** from employees' pay to cover costs of the system. Employers usually separate FICA taxes into two groups: (1) retirement, disability, and survivorship and (2) medical. For the first group, the Social Security system provides monthly cash payments to qualified retired workers for the rest of their lives. These payments are often called *Social Security benefits.* Taxes related to this group are often called *Social Security taxes.* For the second group, the system provides monthly payments to deceased workers' surviving families and to disabled workers who qualify for assistance. These payments are commonly called *Medicare benefits;* like those in the first group, they are paid with *Medicare taxes* (part of FICA taxes).

Law requires employers to withhold FICA taxes from each employee's salary or wages on each payday. The taxes for Social Security and Medicare are computed separately. For example, for the year 2010, the amount withheld from each employee's pay for Social Security tax was 6.2% of the first $106,800 the employee earns in the calendar year, or a maximum of $6,621.60. The Medicare tax was 1.45% of *all* amounts the employee earns; there is no maximum limit to Medicare tax.

Point: The sources of U.S. tax receipts are roughly as follows:
50% Personal income tax
35 FICA and FUTA taxes
10 Corporate income tax
5 Other taxes

Employers must pay withheld taxes to the Internal Revenue Service (IRS) on specific filing dates during the year. Employers who fail to send the withheld taxes to the IRS on time can be assessed substantial penalties. Until all the taxes are sent to the IRS, they are included in employers' current liabilities. For any changes in rates or with the maximum earnings level, check the IRS Website at www.IRS.gov or the SSA Website at www.SSA.gov.

Point: Part-time employees may claim "exempt from withholding" if they did not have any income tax liability in the prior year and do not expect any in the current year.

Employee income tax. Most employers are required to withhold federal income tax from each employee's paycheck. The amount withheld is computed using tables published by the IRS. The amount depends on the employee's annual earnings rate and the number of *withholding allowances* the employee claims. Allowances reduce the amount of taxes one owes the government. The more allowances one claims, the less tax the employer will withhold. Employees can claim allowances for themselves and their dependents. They also can claim additional allowances if they expect major declines in their taxable income for medical expenses. (An employee who claims more allowances than appropriate is subject to a fine.) Most states and many local governments require employers to withhold income taxes from employees' pay and to remit them promptly to the proper government agency. Until they are paid, withholdings are reported as a current liability on the employer's balance sheet.

Point: IRS withholding tables are based on projecting weekly (or other period) pay into an annual figure.

Employee voluntary deductions. Beyond Social Security, Medicare, and income taxes, employers often withhold other amounts from employees' earnings. These withholdings arise from employee requests, contracts, unions, or other agreements. They can include amounts for charitable giving, medical and life insurance premiums, pension contributions, and union dues. Until they are paid, such withholdings are reported as part of employers' current liabilities.

Recording employee payroll deductions. Employers must accrue payroll expenses and liabilities at the end of each pay period. To illustrate, assume that an employee earns a salary of $2,000 per month. At the end of January, the employer's entry to accrue payroll expenses and liabilities for this employee is

Jan. 31	Salaries Expense	2,000	
	FICA—Social Security Taxes Payable (6.2%)		124
	FICA—Medicare Taxes Payable (1.45%)		29
	Employee Federal Income Taxes Payable*		213
	Employee Medical Insurance Payable*		85
	Employee Union Dues Payable*		25
	Salaries Payable		1,524
	To record accrued payroll for January.		

Assets	=	Liabilities	+	Equity
		+124		−2,000
		+29		
		+213		
		+85		
		+25		
		+1,524		

* Amounts taken from employer's accounting records.

Salaries Expense (debit) shows that the employee earns a gross salary of $2,000. The first five payables (credits) show the liabilities the employer owes on behalf of this employee to cover FICA taxes, income taxes, medical insurance, and union dues. The Salaries Payable account (credit) records the $1,524 net pay the employee receives from the $2,000 gross pay earned. When the employee is paid, another entry (or a series of entries) is required to record the check written and distributed (or funds transferred). The entry to record cash payment to this employee is to debit Salaries Payable and credit Cash for $1,524.

Salaries Payable	1,524	
Cash		1,524

Decision Insight

A company's delay or failure to pay withholding taxes to the government has severe consequences. For example, a 100% penalty can be levied, with interest, on the unpaid balance. The government can even close a company, take its assets, and pursue legal actions against those involved.

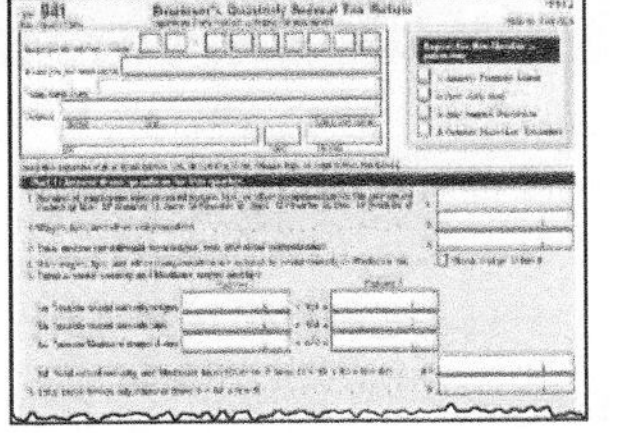

Employer Payroll Taxes Employers must pay payroll taxes in addition to those required of employees. Employer taxes include FICA and unemployment taxes.

P3 Compute and record *employer* payroll expenses and liabilities.

Employer FICA tax. Employers must pay FICA taxes *equal in amount to* the FICA taxes withheld from their employees. An employer's tax is credited to the same FICA Taxes Payable accounts used to record the Social Security and Medicare taxes withheld from employees. (A self-employed person must pay both the employee and employer FICA taxes.)

Federal and state unemployment taxes. The federal government participates with states in a joint federal and state unemployment insurance program. Each state administers its program. These programs provide unemployment benefits to qualified workers. The federal government approves state programs and pays a portion of their administrative expenses.

Federal Unemployment Taxes (FUTA). Employers are subject to a federal unemployment tax on wages and salaries paid to their employees. For the year 2010, employers were required to pay FUTA taxes of as much as 6.2% of the first $7,000 earned by each employee. This federal tax can be reduced by a credit of up to 5.4% for taxes paid to a state program. As a result, the net federal unemployment tax is often only 0.8%.

State Unemployment Taxes (SUTA). All states support their unemployment insurance programs by placing a payroll tax on employers. (A few states require employees to make a contribution. In the book's assignments, we assume that this tax is only on the employer.) In most states, the base rate for SUTA taxes is 5.4% of the first $7,000 paid each employee. This base rate is adjusted according to an employer's merit rating. The state assigns a **merit rating** that reflects a company's stability or instability in employing workers. A good rating reflects stability in employment and means an employer can pay less than the 5.4% base rate. A low rating reflects high turnover or seasonal hirings and layoffs. To illustrate, an employer with 50 employees each of whom earns $7,000 or more per year saves $15,400 annually if it has a merit rating of 1.0% versus 5.4%. This is computed by comparing taxes of $18,900 at the 5.4% rate to only $3,500 at the 1.0% rate.

Recording employer payroll taxes. Employer payroll taxes are an added expense beyond the wages and salaries earned by employees. These taxes are often recorded in an entry separate from the one recording payroll expenses and deductions. To illustrate, assume that the $2,000 recorded salaries expense from the previous example is earned by an employee whose earnings have not yet reached $5,000 for the year. This means the entire salaries expense for this period is subject to tax because year-to-date pay is under $7,000. Also assume that the federal unemployment tax rate is 0.8% and the state unemployment tax rate is 5.4%. Consequently, the FICA portion of the employer's tax is $153, computed by multiplying both the 6.2% and 1.45% by the $2,000 gross pay. Moreover, state unemployment (SUTA) taxes are $108 (5.4% of the $2,000 gross pay), and federal unemployment (FUTA) taxes are $16 (0.8% of $2,000). The entry to record the employer's payroll tax expense and related liabilities is

Example: If the employer's merit rating in this example reduces its SUTA rate to 2.9%, what is its SUTA liability? *Answer:* SUTA payable = $2,000 × 2.9% = $58

Assets	=	Liabilities	+	Equity
		+124		−277
		+29		
		+108		
		+16		

Jan. 31	Payroll Taxes Expense	277	
	FICA—Social Security Taxes Payable (6.2%)		124
	FICA—Medicare Taxes Payable (1.45%)		29
	State Unemployment Taxes Payable		108
	Federal Unemployment Taxes Payable		16
	To record employer payroll taxes.		

Point: Internal control is important for payroll accounting. Managers must monitor (1) employee hiring, (2) timekeeping, (3) payroll listings, and (4) payroll payments. Poor controls led the U.S. Army to pay nearly $10 million to deserters, fictitious soldiers, and other unauthorized entities.

Decision Ethics Answer — p. 460 

Web Designer You take a summer job working for a family friend who runs a small IT service. On your first payday, the owner slaps you on the back, gives you full payment in cash, winks, and adds: "No need to pay those high taxes, eh." What action, if any, do you take? ■

Multi-Period Known Liabilities

Many known liabilities extend over multiple periods. These often include unearned revenues and notes payable. For example, if Sports Illustrated sells a four-year magazine subscription, it records amounts received for this subscription in an Unearned Subscription Revenues account. Amounts in this account are liabilities, but are they current or long term? They are *both.* The portion of the Unearned Subscription Revenues account that will be fulfilled in the next year is reported as a current liability. The remaining portion is reported as a long-term liability.

The same analysis applies to notes payable. For example, a borrower reports a three-year note payable as a long-term liability in the first two years it is outstanding. In the third year, the borrower reclassifies this note as a current liability since it is due within one year or the operating cycle, whichever is longer. The **current portion of long-term debt** refers to that part of long-term debt due within one year or the operating cycle, whichever is longer. Long-term debt is reported under long-term liabilities, but the *current portion due* is reported under current liabilities. To illustrate, assume that a $7,500 debt is paid in installments of $1,500 per year for five years. The $1,500 due within the year is reported as a current liability. No journal entry is necessary for this reclassification. Instead, we simply classify the amounts for debt as either current or long term when the balance sheet is prepared.

Point: Some accounting systems do make an entry to transfer the current amount due out of Long-Term Debt and into the Current Portion of Long-Term Debt as follows:

Long-Term Debt	1,500
Current Portion of L-T Debt...	1,500

Some known liabilities are rarely reported in long-term liabilities. These include accounts payable, sales taxes, and wages and salaries.

Decision Insight

Liability Limits Probably the greatest number of frauds involve payroll. Companies must safeguard payroll activities. Controls include proper approvals and processes for employee additions, deletions, and pay rate changes. A common fraud is a manager adding a fictitious employee to the payroll and then cashing the fictitious employee's check. A study reports that 28% of employees in operations and service areas witnessed violations of employee wage, overtime, or benefit rules in the past year (KPMG 2009). Another 21% observed falsifying of time and expense reports.

Quick Check

Answers — p. 461

4. Why does a creditor prefer a note payable to a past-due account payable?
5. A company pays its one employee $3,000 per month. This company's FUTA rate is 0.8% on the first $7,000 earned; its SUTA rate is 4.0% on the first $7,000; its Social Security tax rate is 6.2% of the first $106,800; and its Medicare tax rate is 1.45% of all amounts earned. The entry to record this company's March payroll includes what amount for total payroll taxes expense?
6. Identify whether the employer or employee or both incurs each of the following: (*a*) FICA taxes, (*b*) FUTA taxes, (*c*) SUTA taxes, and (*d*) withheld income taxes.

ESTIMATED LIABILITIES

P4 Account for estimated liabilities, including warranties and bonuses.

An **estimated liability** is a known obligation that is of an uncertain amount but that can be reasonably estimated. Common examples are employee benefits such as pensions, health care and vacation pay, and warranties offered by a seller. We discuss each of these in this section. Other examples of estimated liabilities include property taxes and certain contracts to provide future services.

Health and Pension Benefits

Many companies provide **employee benefits** beyond salaries and wages. An employer often pays all or part of medical, dental, life, and disability insurance. Many employers also contribute to *pension plans,* which are agreements by employers to provide benefits (payments) to employees after retirement. Many companies also provide medical care and insurance benefits to their retirees. When payroll taxes and charges for employee benefits are totaled, payroll cost often exceeds employees' gross earnings by 25% or more.

To illustrate, assume that an employer agrees to (1) pay an amount for medical insurance equal to $8,000 and (2) contribute an additional 10% of the employees' $120,000 gross salary to a retirement program. The entry to record these accrued benefits is

Dec. 31	Employee Benefits Expense	20,000	
	Employee Medical Insurance Payable		8,000
	Employee Retirement Program Payable		12,000
	To record costs of employee benefits.		

Assets	=	Liabilities	+	Equity
		+8,000		−20,000
		+12,000		

Decision Insight

Postgame Spoils Baseball was the first pro sport to set up a pension, originally up to $100 per month depending on years played. Many former players now take home six-figure pensions. Cal Ripken Jr.'s pension when he reaches 62 is estimated at $160,000 per year (he played 21 seasons). The requirement is only 43 games for a full pension and just one game for full medical benefits. ■

Vacation Benefits

Many employers offer paid vacation benefits, also called *paid absences*. To illustrate, assume that salaried employees earn 2 weeks' vacation per year. This benefit increases employers' payroll expenses because employees are paid for 52 weeks but work for only 50 weeks. Total annual salary is the same, but the cost per week worked is greater than the amount paid per week. For example, if an employee is paid $20,800 for 52 weeks but works only 50 weeks, the total weekly expense to the employer is $416 ($20,800/50 weeks) instead of the $400 cash paid weekly to the employee ($20,800/52 weeks). The $16 difference between these two amounts is recorded weekly as follows:

Assets	=	Liabilities	+	Equity
		+16		−16

		Debit	Credit
	Vacation Benefits Expense	16	
	Vacation Benefits Payable		16
	To record vacation benefits accrued.		

Vacation Benefits Payable	#	
Cash		#

Vacation Benefits Expense is an operating expense, and Vacation Benefits Payable is a current liability. When the employee takes a vacation, the employer reduces (debits) the Vacation Benefits Payable and credits Cash (no additional expense is recorded).

Bonus Plans

Many companies offer bonuses to employees, and many of the bonuses depend on net income. To illustrate, assume that an employer offers a bonus to its employees equal to 5% of the company's annual net income (to be equally shared by all). The company's expected annual net income is $210,000. The year-end adjusting entry to record this benefit is

Assets	=	Liabilities	+	Equity
		+10,000		−10,000

		Debit	Credit
Dec. 31	Employee Bonus Expense*	10,000	
	Bonus Payable		10,000
	To record expected bonus costs.		

* Bonus Expense (B) equals 5% of net income, which equals $210,000 minus the bonus; this is computed as:

$$B = 0.05\ (\$210{,}000 - B)$$
$$B = \$10{,}500 - 0.05B$$
$$1.05B = \$10{,}500$$
$$\mathbf{B = \$10{,}500/1.05 = \$10{,}000}$$

When the bonus is paid, Bonus Payable is debited and Cash is credited for $10,000.

Warranty Liabilities

Point: Kodak recently reported $60 million in warranty obligations.

A **warranty** is a seller's obligation to replace or correct a product (or service) that fails to perform as expected within a specified period. Most new cars, for instance, are sold with a warranty covering parts for a specified period of time. Ford Motor Company reported more than $15 billion in "dealer and customer allowances and claims" in its annual report. To comply with the *full disclosure* and *matching principles,* the seller reports the expected warranty expense in the period when revenue from the sale of the product or service is reported. The seller reports this warranty obligation as a liability, although the existence, amount, payee, and date of future sacrifices are uncertain. This is because such warranty costs are probable and the amount can be estimated using, for instance, past experience with warranties.

To illustrate, a dealer sells a used car for $16,000 on December 1, 2011, with a maximum one-year or 12,000-mile warranty covering parts. This dealer's experience shows that warranty expense averages about 4% of a car's selling price, or $640 in this case ($16,000 × 4%). The dealer records the estimated expense and liability related to this sale with this entry:

2011			
Dec. 1	Warranty Expense	640	
	Estimated Warranty Liability		640
	To record estimated warranty expense.		

Assets = Liabilities + Equity
+640 −640

This entry alternatively could be made as part of end-of-period adjustments. Either way, the estimated warranty expense is reported on the 2011 income statement and the warranty liability on the 2011 balance sheet. To further extend this example, suppose the customer returns the car for warranty repairs on January 9, 2012. The dealer performs this work by replacing parts costing $200. The entry to record partial settlement of the estimated warranty liability is

Point: Recognition of warranty liabilities is necessary to comply with the matching and full disclosure principles.

2012			
Jan. 9	Estimated Warranty Liability	200	
	Auto Parts Inventory		200
	To record costs of warranty repairs.		

Assets = Liabilities + Equity
−200 −200

This entry reduces the balance of the estimated warranty liability. Warranty expense was previously recorded in 2011, the year the car was sold with the warranty. Finally, what happens if total warranty expenses are more or less than the estimated 4%, or $640? The answer is that management should monitor actual warranty expenses to see whether the 4% rate is accurate. If experience reveals a large difference from the estimate, the rate for current and future sales should be changed. Differences are expected, but they should be small.

Point: Both U.S. GAAP and IFRS account for restructuring costs in a manner similar to accounting for warranties.

Decision Insight

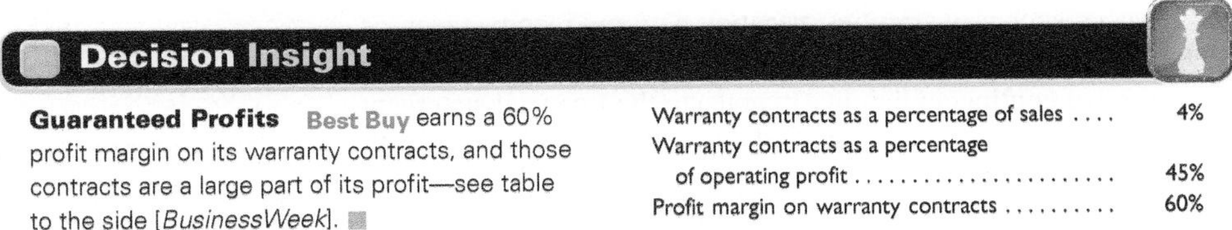

Guaranteed Profits Best Buy earns a 60% profit margin on its warranty contracts, and those contracts are a large part of its profit—see table to the side [*BusinessWeek*].

Warranty contracts as a percentage of sales	4%
Warranty contracts as a percentage of operating profit	45%
Profit margin on warranty contracts	60%

Multi-Period Estimated Liabilities

Estimated liabilities can be both current and long term. For example, pension liabilities to employees are long term to workers who will not retire within the next period. For employees who are retired or will retire within the next period, a portion of pension liabilities is current. Other examples include employee health benefits and warranties. Specifically, many warranties are for 30 or 60 days in length. Estimated costs under these warranties are properly reported in current liabilities. Many other automobile warranties are for three years or 36,000 miles. A portion of these warranties is reported as long term.

Quick Check Answers — p. 461

7. Estimated liabilities involve an obligation to pay which of these? (*a*) An uncertain but reasonably estimated amount owed on a known obligation or (*b*) A known amount to a specific entity on an uncertain due date.

8. A car is sold for $15,000 on June 1, 2011, with a one-year warranty on parts. Warranty expense is estimated at 1.5% of selling price at each calendar year-end. On March 1, 2012, the car is returned for warranty repairs costing $135. The amount recorded as warranty expense on March 1 is (*a*) $0; (*b*) $60; (*c*) $75; (*d*) $135; (*e*) $225.

CONTINGENT LIABILITIES

C3 Explain how to account for contingent liabilities.

A **contingent liability** is a potential obligation that depends on a future event arising from a past transaction or event. An example is a pending lawsuit. Here, a past transaction or event leads to a lawsuit whose result depends on the outcome of the suit. Future payment of a contingent liability depends on whether an uncertain future event occurs.

Accounting for Contingent Liabilities

Accounting for contingent liabilities depends on the likelihood that a future event will occur and the ability to estimate the future amount owed if this event occurs. Three different possibilities are identified in the following chart: record liability, disclose in notes, or no disclosure.

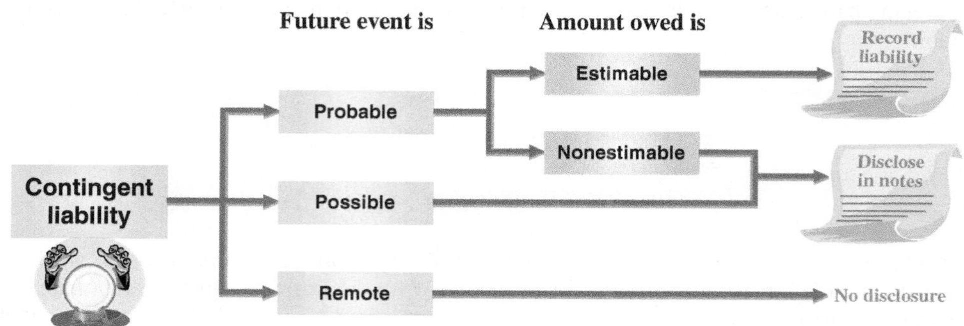

The conditions that determine each of these three possibilities follow:

1. The future event is *probable* (likely) and the amount owed can be *reasonably estimated.* We then record this amount as a liability. Examples are the estimated liabilities described earlier such as warranties, vacation pay, and income taxes.
2. The future event is *reasonably possible* (could occur). We disclose information about this type of contingent liability in notes to the financial statements.
3. The future event is *remote* (unlikely). We do not record or disclose information on remote contingent liabilities.

Point: A contingency is an *if*. Namely, if a future event occurs, then financial consequences are likely for the entity.

Reasonably Possible Contingent Liabilities

This section identifies and discusses contingent liabilities that commonly fall in the second category—when the future event is reasonably possible. Disclosing information about contingencies in this category is motivated by the *full-disclosure principle,* which requires information relevant to decision makers be reported and not ignored.

Potential Legal Claims Many companies are sued or at risk of being sued. The accounting issue is whether the defendant should recognize a liability on its balance sheet or disclose a contingent liability in its notes while a lawsuit is outstanding and not yet settled. The answer is that a potential claim is recorded in the accounts *only* if payment for damages is probable and the amount can be reasonably estimated. If the potential claim cannot be reasonably estimated or is less than probable but reasonably possible, it is disclosed. Ford Motor Company, for example, includes the following note in its annual report: "Various legal actions, governmental investigations and proceedings and claims are pending . . . arising out of alleged defects in our products."

Point: A sale of a note receivable is often a contingent liability. It becomes a liability if the original signer of the note fails to pay it at maturity.

Debt Guarantees Sometimes a company guarantees the payment of debt owed by a supplier, customer, or another company. The guarantor usually discloses the guarantee in its financial statement notes as a contingent liability. If it is probable that the debtor will default, the guarantor needs to record and report the guarantee in its financial statements as a liability. The Boston Celtics report a unique guarantee when it comes to coaches and players: "Certain of the contracts provide for guaranteed payments which must be paid even if the employee [player] is injured or terminated."

Other Contingencies Other examples of contingencies include environmental damages, possible tax assessments, insurance losses, and government investigations. Sunoco, for instance, reports that "federal, state and local laws . . . result in liabilities and loss contingencies. Sunoco accrues . . . cleanup costs [that] are probable and reasonably estimable. Management believes it is reasonably possible (i.e., less than probable but greater than remote) that additional . . . losses will be incurred." Many of Sunoco's contingencies are revealed only in notes.

Point: Auditors and managers often have different views about whether a contingency is recorded, disclosed, or omitted.

Decision Insight

Pricing Priceless What's it worth to see from one side of the Grand Canyon to the other? What's the cost when gulf coast beaches are closed due to an oil well disaster? A method to measure environmental liabilities is *contingent valuation,* by which people answer such questions. Regulators use their answers to levy fines and assess punitive damages.

Uncertainties that Are Not Contingencies

All organizations face uncertainties from future events such as natural disasters and the development of new competing products or services. These uncertainties are not contingent liabilities because they are future events *not* arising from past transactions. Accordingly, they are not disclosed.

Quick Check

Answers – p. 461

9. A future payment is reported as a liability on the balance sheet if payment is contingent on a future event that (*a*) is reasonably possible but the payment cannot be reasonably estimated; (*b*) is probable and the payment can be reasonably estimated; or (*c*) is not probable but the payment is known.

10. Under what circumstances is a future payment reported in the notes to the financial statements as a contingent liability?

GLOBAL VIEW

This section discusses similarities and differences between U.S. GAAP and IFRS in accounting and reporting for current liabilities.

Characteristics of Liabilities The definitions and characteristics of current liabilities are broadly similar for both U.S. GAAP and IFRS. Although differences exist, the similarities vastly outweigh any differences. Remembering that "provision" is typically used under IFRS to refer to what is titled "liability" under U.S. GAAP, Nokia describes its recognition of liabilities as follows:

NOKIA

> Provisions are recognized when the Group has a present legal or constructive obligation as a result of past events, it is probable that an outflow of resources will be required to settle the obligation and a reliable estimate of the amount can be made.

Known (Determinable) Liabilities When there is little uncertainty surrounding current liabilities, both U.S. GAAP and IFRS require companies to record them in a similar manner. This correspondence in accounting applies to accounts payable, sales taxes payable, unearned revenues, short-term notes, and payroll liabilities. Of course, tax regulatory systems of countries are different, which implies use of different rates and levels. Still, the basic approach is the same.

Estimated Liabilities When there is a known current obligation that involves an uncertain amount, but one that can be reasonably estimated, both U.S. GAAP and IFRS require similar treatment. This treatment extends to many obligations such as those arising from vacations, warranties, restructurings, pensions, and health care. Both accounting systems require that companies record estimated expenses related to these obligations when they can reasonably estimate the amounts. Nokia reports wages, salaries and bonuses of €5,658 million. It also reports pension expenses of €427 million.

Decision Analysis — Times Interest Earned Ratio

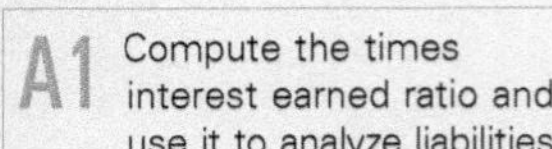

A1 Compute the times interest earned ratio and use it to analyze liabilities.

A company incurs interest expense on many of its current and long-term liabilities. Examples extend from its short-term notes and the current portion of long-term liabilities to its long-term notes and bonds. Interest expense is often viewed as a *fixed expense* because the amount of these liabilities is likely to remain in one form or another for a substantial period of time. This means that the amount of interest is unlikely to vary due to changes in sales or other operating activities. While fixed expenses can be advantageous when a company is growing, they create risk. This risk stems from the possibility that a company might be unable to pay fixed expenses if sales decline. To illustrate, consider Diego Co.'s results for 2011 and two possible outcomes for year 2012 in Exhibit 11.5.

EXHIBIT 11.5

Actual and Projected Results

		2012 Projections	
($ thousands)	2011	Sales Increase	Sales Decrease
Sales	$600	$900	$300
Expenses (75% of sales)	450	675	225
Income before interest	150	225	75
Interest expense (fixed)	60	60	60
Net income	$ 90	$165	$ 15

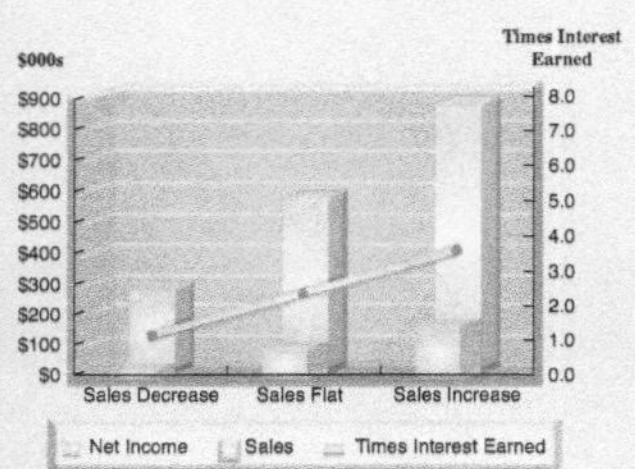

Expenses excluding interest are at, and expected to remain at, 75% of sales. Expenses such as these that change with sales volume are called *variable expenses*. However, interest expense is at, and expected to remain at, $60,000 per year due to its fixed nature.

The middle numerical column of Exhibit 11.5 shows that Diego's income increases by 83% to $165,000 if sales increase by 50% to $900,000. In contrast, the far right column shows that income decreases by 83% if sales decline by 50%. These results reveal that the amount of fixed interest expense affects a company's risk of its ability to pay interest, which is numerically reflected in the **times interest earned** ratio in Exhibit 11.6.

EXHIBIT 11.6

Times Interest Earned

$$\textbf{Times interest earned} = \frac{\textbf{Income before interest expense and income taxes}}{\textbf{Interest expense}}$$

For 2011, Diego's times interest earned is computed as $150,000/$60,000, or 2.5 times. This ratio suggests that Diego faces low to moderate risk because its sales must decline sharply before it would be unable to cover its interest expenses. (Diego is an LLC and does not pay income taxes.)

Experience shows that when times interest earned falls below 1.5 to 2.0 and remains at that level or lower for several periods, the default rate on liabilities increases sharply. This reflects increased risk for companies and their creditors. We also must interpret the times interest earned ratio in light of information about the variability of a company's income before interest. If income is stable from year to year or if it is growing, the company can afford to take on added risk by borrowing. If its income greatly varies from year to year, fixed interest expense can increase the risk that it will not earn enough income to pay interest.

Decision Maker Answer — p. 461

Entrepreneur You wish to invest in a franchise for either one of two national chains. Each franchise has an expected annual net income *after* interest and taxes of $100,000. Net income for the first franchise includes a regular fixed interest charge of $200,000. The fixed interest charge for the second franchise is $40,000. Which franchise is riskier to you if sales forecasts are not met? Does your decision change if the first franchise has more variability in its income stream? ■

DEMONSTRATION PROBLEM

The following transactions and events took place at Kern Company during its recent calendar-year reporting period (Kern does not use reversing entries).

a. In September 2011, Kern sold $140,000 of merchandise covered by a 180-day warranty. Prior experience shows that costs of the warranty equal 5% of sales. Compute September's warranty expense and prepare the adjusting journal entry for the warranty liability as recorded at September 30. Also prepare the journal entry on October 8 to record a $300 cash expenditure to provide warranty service on an item sold in September.

b. On October 12, 2011, Kern arranged with a supplier to replace Kern's overdue $10,000 account payable by paying $2,500 cash and signing a note for the remainder. The note matures in 90 days and has a 12% interest rate. Prepare the entries recorded on October 12, December 31, and January 10, 2012, related to this transaction.

c. In late December, Kern learns it is facing a product liability suit filed by an unhappy customer. Kern's lawyer advises that although it will probably suffer a loss from the lawsuit, it is not possible to estimate the amount of damages at this time.

d. Sally Bline works for Kern. For the pay period ended November 30, her gross earnings are $3,000. Bline has $800 deducted for federal income taxes and $200 for state income taxes from each paycheck. Additionally, a $35 premium for her health care insurance and a $10 donation for the United Way are deducted. Bline pays FICA Social Security taxes at a rate of 6.2% and FICA Medicare taxes at a rate of 1.45%. She has not earned enough this year to be exempt from any FICA taxes. Journalize the accrual of salaries expense of Bline's wages by Kern.

e. On November 1, Kern borrows $5,000 cash from a bank in return for a 60-day, 12%, $5,000 note. Record the note's issuance on November 1 and its repayment with interest on December 31.

f.[B] Kern has estimated and recorded its quarterly income tax payments. In reviewing its year-end tax adjustments, it identifies an additional $5,000 of income tax expense that should be recorded. A portion of this additional expense, $1,000, is deferrable to future years. Record this year-end income taxes expense adjusting entry.

g. For this calendar-year, Kern's net income is $1,000,000, its interest expense is $275,000, and its income taxes expense is $225,000. Calculate Kern's times interest earned ratio.

PLANNING THE SOLUTION

- For *a,* compute the warranty expense for September and record it with an estimated liability. Record the October expenditure as a decrease in the liability.
- For *b,* eliminate the liability for the account payable and create the liability for the note payable. Compute interest expense for the 80 days that the note is outstanding in 2011 and record it as an additional liability. Record the payment of the note, being sure to include the interest for the 10 days in 2012.
- For *c,* decide whether the company's contingent liability needs to be disclosed or accrued (recorded) according to the two necessary criteria: probable loss and reasonably estimable.
- For *d,* set up payable accounts for all items in Bline's paycheck that require deductions. After deducting all necessary items, credit the remaining amount to Salaries Payable.
- For *e,* record the issuance of the note. Calculate 60 days' interest due using the 360-day convention in the interest formula.
- For *f,* determine how much of the income taxes expense is payable in the current year and how much needs to be deferred.
- For *g,* apply and compute times interest earned.

SOLUTION TO DEMONSTRATION PROBLEM

a. Warranty expense = 5% × \$140,000 = \$7,000

Sept. 30	Warranty Expense	7,000	
	Estimated Warranty Liability		7,000
	To record warranty expense for the month.		
Oct. 8	Estimated Warranty Liability	300	
	Cash		300
	To record the cost of the warranty service.		

b. Interest expense for 2011 = 12% × \$7,500 × 80/360 = \$200
Interest expense for 2012 = 12% × \$7,500 × 10/360 = \$25

Oct. 12	Accounts Payable	10,000	
	Notes Payable		7,500
	Cash		2,500
	Paid \$2,500 cash and gave a 90-day, 12% note to extend the due date on the account.		
Dec. 31	Interest Expense	200	
	Interest Payable		200
	To accrue interest on note payable.		
Jan. 10	Interest Expense	25	
	Interest Payable	200	
	Notes Payable	7,500	
	Cash		7,725
	Paid note with interest, including the accrued interest payable.		

c. Disclose the pending lawsuit in the financial statement notes. Although the loss is probable, no liability can be accrued since the loss cannot be reasonably estimated.

d.

Nov. 30	Salaries Expense	3,000.00	
	FICA—Social Security Taxes Payable (6.2%)		186.00
	FICA—Medicare Taxes Payable (1.45%)		43.50
	Employee Federal Income Taxes Payable		800.00
	Employee State Income Taxes Payable		200.00
	Employee Medical Insurance Payable		35.00
	Employee United Way Payable		10.00
	Salaries Payable		1,725.50
	To record Bline's accrued payroll.		

e.

Nov. 1	Cash	5,000	
	Notes Payable		5,000
	Borrowed cash with a 60-day, 12% note.		

When the note and interest are paid 60 days later, Kern Company records this entry:

Dec. 31	Notes Payable	5,000	
	Interest Expense	100	
	Cash		5,100
	Paid note with interest (\$5,000 × 12% × 60/360).		

f.

Dec. 31	Income Taxes Expense	5,000	
	Income Taxes Payable		4,000
	Deferred Income Tax Liability		1,000
	To record added income taxes expense and the deferred tax liability.		

g. Times interest earned $= \frac{\$1{,}000{,}000 + \$275{,}000 + \$225{,}000}{\$275{,}000} = \underline{\underline{5.45 \text{ times}}}$

APPENDIX

Payroll Reports, Records, and Procedures 11A

Understanding payroll procedures and keeping adequate payroll reports and records are essential to a company's success. This appendix focuses on payroll accounting and its reports, records, and procedures.

P5 Identify and describe the details of payroll reports, records, and procedures.

Payroll Reports Most employees and employers are required to pay local, state, and federal payroll taxes. Payroll expenses involve liabilities to individual employees, to federal and state governments, and to other organizations such as insurance companies. Beyond paying these liabilities, employers are required to prepare and submit reports explaining how they computed these payments.

Reporting FICA Taxes and Income Taxes The Federal Insurance Contributions Act (FICA) requires each employer to file an Internal Revenue Service (IRS) **Form 941,** the *Employer's Quarterly Federal Tax Return,* within one month after the end of each calendar quarter. A sample Form 941 is shown in Exhibit 11A.1 for Phoenix Sales & Service, a landscape design company. Accounting information and software are helpful in tracking payroll transactions and reporting the accumulated information on Form 941. Specifically, the employer reports total wages subject to income tax withholding on line 2 of Form 941. (For simplicity, this appendix uses *wages* to refer to both wages and salaries.) The income tax withheld is reported on line 3. The combined amount of employee and employer FICA (Social Security) taxes for Phoenix Sales & Service is reported on line 5a (taxable Social Security wages, \$36,599 × 12.4% = \$4,538.28). The 12.4% is the sum of the Social Security tax withheld, computed as 6.2% tax withheld from the employee wages for the quarter plus the 6.2% tax levied on the employer. The combined amount of employee Medicare wages is reported on line 5c. The 2.9% is the sum of 1.45% withheld from employee wages for the quarter plus 1.45% tax levied on the employer. Total FICA taxes are reported on line 5d and are added to the total income taxes withheld of \$3,056.47 to yield a total of \$8,656.12. For this year, assume that income up to \$106,800 is subject to Social Security tax. There is no income limit on amounts subject to Medicare tax. Congress sets annual limits on the amount owed for Social Security tax.

Federal depository banks are authorized to accept deposits of amounts payable to the federal government. Deposit requirements depend on the amount of tax owed. For example, when the sum of FICA taxes plus the employee income taxes is less than \$2,500 for a quarter, the taxes can be paid when Form 941 is filed. Companies with large payrolls are often required to pay monthly or even semiweekly.

Reporting FUTA Taxes and SUTA Taxes An employer's federal unemployment taxes (FUTA) are reported on an annual basis by filing an *Annual Federal Unemployment Tax Return,* IRS **Form 940.** It must be mailed on or before January 31 following the end of each tax year. Ten more days are allowed if all required tax deposits are filed on a timely basis and the full amount of tax is paid on or before January 31. FUTA payments are made quarterly to a federal depository bank if the total amount due exceeds \$500. If \$500 or less is due, the taxes are remitted annually. Requirements for paying and reporting state unemployment taxes (SUTA) vary depending on the laws of each state. Most states require quarterly payments and reports.

EXHIBIT 11A.1

Form 941

Form **941** **Employer's QUARTERLY Federal Tax Return**

Department of the Treasury — Internal Revenue Service

(EIN) Employer identification number: 8 6 - 3 2 1 4 5 8 7

Name (not your trade name): Phoenix Sales & Service

Trade name (if any):

Address: 1214 (Number) Mill Road (Street) (Suite or room number)

Phoenix (City) AZ (State) 85621 (ZIP code)

Report for this Quarter ... (Check one.)

- ☐ 1: January, February, March
- ☐ 2: April, May, June
- ☐ 3: July, August, September
- ☒ 4: October, November, December

Part 1: Answer these questions for this quarter.

1 **Number of employees who received wages, tips, or other compensation for the pay period including:** ***Mar. 12*** **(Quarter 1),** ***June 12*** **(Quarter 2),** ***Sept. 12*** **(Quarter 3),** ***Dec. 12*** **(Quarter 4)**	1	1
2 **Wages, tips, and other compensation**	2	36,599.00
3 **Total income tax withheld from wages, tips, and other compensation**	3	3,056.47
4 **If no wages, tips, and other compensation are subject to social security or Medicare tax**		☐ Check and go to line 6.

5 **Taxable social security and Medicare wages and tips:**

	Column 1		Column 2
5a **Taxable social security wages**	36,599.00	× .124 =	4,538.28
5b **Taxable social security tips**	.	× .124 =	.
5c **Taxable Medicare wages & tips**	36,599.00	× .029 =	1,061.37

5d **Total social security and Medicare taxes** (*Column 2,* lines 5a + 5b + 5c = line 5d)		5d	5,599.65
6 **Total taxes before adjustments** (lines 3 + 5d = line 6)		6	8,656.12
7 **TAX ADJUSTMENTS** (Read the instructions for line 7 before completing lines 7a through 7h.):			
7a **Current quarter's fractions of cents**	.		
7b **Current quarter's sick pay**	.		
7c **Current quarter's adjustments for tips and group-term life insurance**	.		
7d **Current year's income tax withholding** (attach Form 941c)	.		
7e **Prior quarters' social security and Medicare taxes** (attach Form 941c)	.		
7f **Special additions to federal income tax** (attach Form 941c)	.		
7g **Special additions to social security and Medicare** (attach Form 941c)	.		
7h **TOTAL ADJUSTMENTS** (Combine all amounts: lines 7a through 7g.)		7h	0.00
8 **Total taxes after adjustments** (Combine lines 6 and 7h.)		8	8,656.12
9 **Advance earned income credit (EIC) payments made to employees**		9	.
10 **Total taxes after adjustment for advance EIC** (lines 8 – line 9 = line 10)		10	8,656.12
11 **Total deposits for this quarter, including overpayment applied from a prior quarter**		11	8,656.12
12 **Balance due** (If line 10 is more than line 11, write the difference here.) Make checks payable to *United States Treasury.*		12	0.00
13 **Overpayment** (If line 11 is more than line 10, write the difference here.)	0.00	Check one	☐ Apply to next return. ☐ Send a refund.

Part 2: Tell us about your deposit schedule and tax liability for this quarter.

If you are unsure about whether you are a monthly schedule depositor or a semiweekly schedule depositor, see ***Pub. 15 (Circular E),*** **section 11.**

14 A Z **Write the state abbreviation for the state where you made your deposits** OR **write "MU" if you made your deposits in** ***multiple*** **states.**

15 **Check one:** ☐ **Line 10 is less than $2,500.** Go to Part 3.

☒ **You were a monthly schedule depositor for the entire quarter. Fill out your tax liability for each month.** Then go to Part 3.

Tax liability:	**Month 1**	3,079.11
	Month 2	2,049.77
	Month 3	3,527.24
Total liability for quarter		8,656.12 **Total must equal line 10.**

☐ **You were a semiweekly schedule depositor for any part of this quarter.** Fill out *Schedule B (Form 941): Report of Tax Liability for Semiweekly Schedule Depositors,* and attach it to this form.

Part 3: Tell us about your business. If a question does NOT apply to your business, leave it blank.

16 **If your business has closed or you stopped paying wages** . ☐ Check here, and enter the final date you paid wages __/__/__ .

17 **If you are a seasonal employer and you do not have to file a return for every quarter of the year** . ☐ Check here.

Part 4: May we speak with your third-party designee?

Do you want to allow an employee, a paid tax preparer, or another person to discuss this return with the IRS? See the instructions for details.

☐ Yes. Designee's name

Phone ( ) – Personal Identification Number (PIN) ☐☐☐☐☐

☒ No.

Part 5: Sign here. You MUST fill out both sides of this form and SIGN it.

Under penalties of perjury, I declare that I have examined this return, including accompanying schedules and statements, and to the best of my knowledge and belief, it is true, correct, and complete.

X Sign your name here

Print name and title

Date / / Phone ( ) –

Reporting Wages and Salaries Employers are required to give each employee an annual report of his or her wages subject to FICA and federal income taxes along with the amounts of these taxes withheld. This report is called a *Wage and Tax Statement,* or **Form W-2.** It must be given to employees before January 31 following the year covered by the report. Exhibit 11A.2 shows Form W-2 for one of the employees at Phoenix Sales & Service. Copies of the W-2 Form must be sent to the Social Security Administration, where the amount of the employee's wages subject to FICA taxes and FICA taxes withheld are posted to each employee's Social Security account. These posted amounts become the basis for determining an employee's retirement and survivors' benefits. The Social Security Administration also transmits to the IRS the amount of each employee's wages subject to federal income taxes and the amount of taxes withheld.

EXHIBIT 11A.2

Form W-2

Form **W-2** Wage and Tax Statement — Copy 1—For State, City, or Local Tax Department — Department of Treasury—Internal Revenue Service

a Control number: AR101 — 22222	OMB No. 1545-0006	
b Employer identification number (EIN): 86-3214587	1 Wages, tips, other compensation: 4,910.00	2 Federal income tax withheld: 333.37
c Employer's name, address and ZIP code: Phoenix Sales & Service, 1214 Mill Road, Phoenix, AZ 85621	3 Social security wages: 4,910.00	4 Social security tax withheld: 304.42
	5 Medicare wages and tips: 4,910.00	6 Medicare tax withheld: 71.20
	7 Social security tips	8 Allocated tips
d Employee's social security number: 333-22-9999	9 Advance EIC payment	10 Dependent care benefits
e Employee's first name and initial: Robert J. — Last name: Austin	11 Nonqualified plans	12a Code
f Employee's address and ZIP code: 18 Roosevelt Blvd., Apt. C, Tempe, AZ 86322	13 Statutory employee / Retirement plan / Third-party sick pay	12b Code
	14 Other	12c Code
		12d Code

15 State	Employer's state ID number	16 State wages, tips, etc.	17 State income tax	18 Local wages, tips, etc.	19 Local income tax	20 Locality name
AZ	13-902319	4,910.00	26.68			

Payroll Records Employers must keep payroll records in addition to reporting and paying taxes. These records usually include a payroll register and an individual earnings report for each employee.

Payroll Register A **payroll register** usually shows the pay period dates, hours worked, gross pay, deductions, and net pay of each employee for each pay period. Exhibit 11A.3 shows a payroll register for Phoenix Sales & Service. It is organized into nine columns:

Col. 1 Employee identification (ID); Employee name; Social Security number (SS No.); Reference (check number); and Date (date check issued)
Col. 2 Pay Type (regular and overtime)
Col. 3 Pay Hours (number of hours worked as regular and overtime)
Col. 4 Gross Pay (amount of gross pay)[2]
Col. 5 FIT (federal income taxes withheld); FUTA (federal unemployment taxes)
Col. 6 SIT (state income taxes withheld); SUTA (state unemployment taxes)
Col. 7 FICA-SS_EE (social security taxes withheld, employee); FICA-SS_ER (social security taxes, employer)
Col. 8 FICA-Med_EE (medicare tax withheld, employee); FICA-Med_ER (medicare tax, employer)
Col. 9 Net pay (Gross pay less amounts withheld from employees)

[2] The Gross Pay column shows regular hours worked on the first line multiplied by the regular pay rate—this equals regular pay. Overtime hours multiplied by the overtime premium rate equals overtime premium pay reported on the second line. If employers are engaged in interstate commerce, federal law sets a minimum overtime rate of pay to employees. For this company, workers earn 150% of their regular rate for hours in excess of 40 per week.

EXHIBIT 11A.3
Payroll Register

Accounting System: Exhibit A.3

File Edit Maintain Tasks Analysis Options Reports Window Help

Phoenix Sales & Service
Payroll Register
For Week Ended Oct. 8, 2011

Employee ID Employee SS No. Refer., Date	Gross Pay Pay Type	 Pay Hours	 Gross Pay	FIT [blank] FUTA	SIT [blank] SUTA	FICA-SS_EE [blank] FICA-SS_ER	FICA-Med_EE [blank] FICA-Med_ER	Net Pay
AR101	Regular	40.00	400.00	−28.99	−2.32	−24.80	−5.80	338.09
Robert Austin	Overtime	0.00	0.00					
333-22-9999			400.00	−3.20	−10.80	−24.80	−5.80	
9001, 10/8/11								
CJ102	Regular	40.00	560.00	−52.97	−4.24	−36.02	−8.42	479.35
Judy Cross	Overtime	1.00	21.00					
299-11-9201			581.00	−4.65	−15.69	−36.02	−8.42	
9002, 10/8/11								
DJ103	Regular	40.00	560.00	−48.33	−3.87	−37.32	−8.73	503.75
John Diaz	Overtime	2.00	42.00					
444-11-9090			602.00	−4.82	−16.25	−37.32	−8.73	
9003, 10/8/11								
KK104	Regular	40.00	560.00	−68.57	−5.49	−34.72	−8.12	443.10
Kay Keife	Overtime	0.00	0.00					
909-11-3344			560.00	−4.48	−15.12	−34.72	−8.12	
9004, 10/8/11								
ML105	Regular	40.00	560.00	−34.24	−2.74	−34.72	−8.12	480.18
Lee Miller	Overtime	0.00	0.00					
444-56-3211			560.00	−4.48	−15.12	−34.72	−8.12	
9005, 10/8/11								
SD106	Regular	40.00	560.00	−68.57	−5.49	−34.72	−8.12	443.10
Dale Sears	Overtime	0.00	0.00					
909-33-1234			560.00	−4.48	−15.12	−34.72	−8.12	
9006, 10/8/11								
Totals	Regular	240.00	3,200.00	−301.67	−24.15	−202.30	−47.31	2,687.57
	Overtime	3.00	63.00					
			3,263.00	−26.11	−88.10	−202.30	−47.31	

Sales Purchases General Ledger Payroll Inventory Company Analysis

Net pay for each employee is computed as gross pay minus the items on the first line of columns 5–8. The employer's payroll tax for each employee is computed as the sum of items on the third line of columns 5–8. A payroll register includes all data necessary to record payroll. In some software programs the entries to record payroll are made in a special *payroll journal.*

Payroll Check Payment of payroll is usually done by check or electronic funds transfer. Exhibit 11A.4 shows a *payroll check* for a Phoenix employee. This check is accompanied with a detachable *statement of earnings* (at top) showing gross pay, deductions, and net pay.

Employee Earnings Report An **employee earnings report** is a cumulative record of an employee's hours worked, gross earnings, deductions, and net pay. Payroll information on this report is taken from the payroll register. The employee earnings report for R. Austin at Phoenix Sales & Service is shown in Exhibit 11A.5. An employee earnings report accumulates information that can show when an employee's earnings reach the tax-exempt points for FICA, FUTA, and SUTA taxes. It also gives data an employer needs to prepare Form W-2.

Payroll Procedures Employers must be able to compute federal income tax for payroll purposes. This section explains how we compute this tax and how to use a payroll bank account.

Computing Federal Income Taxes To compute the amount of taxes withheld from each employee's wages, we need to determine both the employee's wages earned and the employee's number of *withholding*

EMPLOYEE NO.	EMPLOYEE NAME	SOCIAL SECURITY NO.	PAY PERIOD END	CHECK DATE
AR101	Robert Austin	333-22-9999	10/8/11	10/8/11

ITEM	RATE	HOURS	TOTAL	ITEM	THIS CHECK	YEAR TO DATE
Regular	10.00	40.00	400.00	Gross	400.00	400.00
Overtime	15.00			Fed. Income tax	-28.99	-28.99
				FICA-Soc. Sec.	-24.80	-24.80
				FICA-Medicare	-5.80	-5.80
				State Income tax	-2.32	-2.32

HOURS WORKED	GROSS THIS PERIOD	GROSS YEAR TO DATE	NET CHECK	CHECK No.
40.00	400.00	400.00	$338.09	9001

(Detach and retain for your records)

PHOENIX SALES & SERVICE
1214 Mill Road
Phoenix, AZ 85621
602-555-8900

Phoenix Bank and Trust
Phoenix, AZ 85621
3312-87044

No. 9001

DATE October 8 20 11

Check No. 9001

Amount Three Hundred Thirty-Eight and 9/100 Dollars $ **************$338.09*

Pay to the order of Robert Austin
18 Roosevelt Blvd., Apt C
Tempe, AZ 86322

Mary Wills
AUTHORIZED SIGNATURE

EXHIBIT 11A.4

Check and Statement of Earnings

Accounting System: Exhibit A.5

File Edit Maintain Tasks Analysis Options Reports Window Help

Phoenix Sales & Service
Employee Earnings Report
For Month Ended Dec. 31, 2011

Employee ID Employee SS No.	Date Reference	Gross Pay	FIT [blank] FUTA	SIT [blank] SUTA	FICA-SS_EE [blank] FICA-SS_ER	FICA-Med_EE [blank] FICA-Med_ER	Net Pay
Beginning Balance for Robert Austin		2,910.00	−188.42	−15.08	−180.42	−42.20	2,483.88
			−23.28	−78.57	−180.42	−42.20	
AR101 Robert Austin 333-22-9999	12/03/11 9049	400.00	−28.99	−2.32	−24.80	−5.80	338.09
			−3.20	−10.80	−24.80	−5.80	
AR101 Robert Austin 333-22-9999	12/10/11 9055	400.00	−28.99	−2.32	−24.80	−5.80	338.09
			−3.20	−10.80	−24.80	−5.80	
AR101 Robert Austin 333-22-9999	12/17/11 9061	400.00	−28.99	−2.32	−24.80	−5.80	338.09
			−3.20	−10.80	−24.80	−5.80	
AR101 Robert Austin 333-22-9999	12/24/11 9067	400.00	−28.99	−2.32	−24.80	−5.80	338.09
			−3.20	−10.80	−24.80	−5.80	
AR101 Robert Austin 333-22-9999	12/31/11 9073	400.00	−28.99	−2.32	−24.80	−5.80	338.09
			−3.20	−10.80	−24.80	−5.80	
Total 12/01/11 thru 12/31/11		2,000.00	−144.95	−11.60	−124.00	−29.00	1,690.45
			−16.00	−54.00	−124.00	−29.00	
Year-to-date Total for Robert Austin		4,910.00	−333.37	−26.68	−304.42	−71.20	4,174.33
			−39.28	−132.57	−304.42	−71.20	

Sales | Purchases | General Ledger | Payroll | Inventory | Company | Analysis

EXHIBIT 11A.5

Employee Earnings Report

allowances. Each employee records the number of withholding allowances claimed on a withholding allowance certificate, **Form W-4,** filed with the employer. When the number of withholding allowances increases, the amount of income taxes withheld decreases.

Employers often use a **wage bracket withholding table** similar to the one shown in Exhibit 11A.6 to compute the federal income taxes withheld from each employee's gross pay. The table in Exhibit 11A.6 is for a single employee paid weekly. Tables are also provided for married employees and for biweekly, semimonthly, and monthly pay periods (most payroll software includes these tables). When using a wage bracket withholding table to compute federal income tax withheld from an employee's gross wages, we need to locate an employee's wage bracket within the first two columns. We then find the amount withheld by looking in the withholding allowance column for that employee.

EXHIBIT 11A.6

Wage Bracket Withholding Table

SINGLE Persons—WEEKLY Payroll Period

If the wages are—		And the number of withholding allowances claimed is—										
At least	But less than	0	1	2	3	4	5	6	7	8	9	10
		The amount of income tax to be withheld is—										
$600	$610	$76	$67	$58	$49	$39	$30	$21	$12	$6	$0	$0
610	620	79	69	59	50	41	32	22	13	7	1	0
620	630	81	70	61	52	42	33	24	15	8	2	0
630	640	84	72	62	53	44	35	25	16	9	3	0
640	650	86	73	64	55	45	36	27	18	10	4	0
650	660	89	75	65	56	47	38	28	19	11	5	0
660	670	91	76	67	58	48	39	30	21	12	6	0
670	680	94	78	68	59	50	41	31	22	13	7	1
680	690	96	81	70	61	51	42	33	24	14	8	2
690	700	99	83	71	62	53	44	34	25	16	9	3
700	710	101	86	73	64	54	45	35	27	17	10	4
710	720	104	88	74	65	56	47	37	28	19	11	5
720	730	106	91	76	67	57	48	39	30	20	12	6
730	740	109	93	78	68	59	50	40	31	22	13	7
740	750	111	96	80	70	60	51	42	33	23	14	8

Payroll Bank Account Companies with few employees often pay them with checks drawn on the company's regular bank account. Companies with many employees often use a special **payroll bank account** to pay employees. When this account is used, a company either (1) draws one check for total payroll on the regular bank account and deposits it in the payroll bank account or (2) executes an *electronic funds transfer* to the payroll bank account. Individual payroll checks are then drawn on this payroll bank account. Since only one check for the total payroll is drawn on the regular bank account each payday, use of a special payroll bank account helps with internal control. It also helps in reconciling the regular bank account. When companies use a payroll bank account, they usually include check numbers in the payroll register. The payroll register in Exhibit 11A.3 shows check numbers in column 1. For instance, Check No. 9001 is issued to Robert Austin. With this information, the payroll register serves as a supplementary record of wages earned by and paid to employees.

Who Pays What Payroll Taxes and Benefits We conclude this appendix with the following table identifying who pays which payroll taxes and which common employee benefits such as medical, disability, pension, charitable, and union costs. Who pays which employee benefits, and what portion, is subject to agreements between companies and their workers. Also, self-employed workers must pay both the employer and employee FICA taxes for Social Security and Medicare.

Employer Payroll Taxes and Costs	Employee Payroll Deductions
• FICA—Social Security Taxes	• FICA—Social Security taxes
• FICA—Medicare Taxes	• FICA—Medicare taxes
• FUTA (Federal Unemployment Taxes)	• Federal Income taxes
• SUTA (State Unemployment Taxes)	• State and local income taxes
• Share of medical coverage, if any	• Share of medical coverage, if any
• Share of pension coverage, if any	• Share of pension coverage, if any
• Share of other benefits, if any	• Share of other benefits, if any

Quick Check Answers — p. 461

11. What three items determine the amount deducted from an employee's wages for federal income taxes?
12. What amount of income tax is withheld from the salary of an employee who is single with three withholding allowances and earnings of $675 in a week? (*Hint:* Use the wage bracket withholding table in Exhibit 11A.6.)
13. Which of the following steps are executed when a company draws one check for total payroll and deposits it in a special payroll bank account? (*a*) Write a check to the payroll bank account for the total payroll and record it with a debit to Salaries Payable and a credit to Cash. (*b*) Deposit a check (or transfer funds) for the total payroll in the payroll bank account. (*c*) Issue individual payroll checks drawn on the payroll bank account. (*d*) All of the above.

APPENDIX 11B

Corporate Income Taxes

This appendix explains current liabilities involving income taxes for corporations.

Income Tax Liabilities Corporations are subject to income taxes and must estimate their income tax liability when preparing financial statements. Since income tax expense is created by earning income, a liability is incurred when income is earned. This tax must be paid quarterly under federal regulations. To illustrate, consider a corporation that prepares monthly financial statements. Based on its income in January 2011, this corporation estimates that it owes income taxes of $12,100. The following adjusting entry records this estimate:

Jan. 31	Income Taxes Expense	12,100	
	Income Taxes Payable		12,100
	To accrue January income taxes.		

Assets = Liabilities + Equity
+12,100 −12,100

The tax liability is recorded each month until the first quarterly payment is made. If the company's estimated taxes for this first quarter total $30,000, the entry to record its payment is

Apr. 10	Income Taxes Payable	30,000	
	Cash		30,000
	Paid estimated quarterly income taxes based on first quarter income.		

Assets = Liabilities + Equity
−30,000 −30,000

This process of accruing and then paying estimated income taxes continues through the year. When annual financial statements are prepared at year-end, the corporation knows its actual total income and the actual amount of income taxes it must pay. This information allows it to properly record income taxes expense for the fourth quarter so that the total of the four quarters' expense amounts equals the actual taxes paid to the government.

Deferred Income Tax Liabilities An income tax liability for corporations can arise when the amount of income before taxes that the corporation reports on its income statement is not the same as the amount of income reported on its income tax return. This difference occurs because income tax laws and GAAP measure income differently. (Differences between tax laws and GAAP arise because Congress uses tax laws to generate receipts, stimulate the economy, and influence behavior, whereas GAAP are intended to provide financial information useful for business decisions. Also, tax accounting often follows the cash basis, whereas GAAP follows the accrual basis.)

Some differences between tax laws and GAAP are temporary. *Temporary differences* arise when the tax return and the income statement report a revenue or expense in different years. As an example, companies are often able to deduct higher amounts of depreciation in the early years of an asset's life and smaller amounts in later years for tax reporting in comparison to GAAP. This means that in the early years, depreciation for tax reporting is often more than depreciation on the income statement. In later years, depreciation for tax reporting is often less than depreciation on the income statement. When temporary differences exist between taxable income on the tax return and the income before taxes on the income statement, corporations compute income taxes expense based on the income reported on the income statement. The result is that income taxes expense reported in the income statement is often different from the amount of income taxes payable to the government. This difference is the **deferred income tax liability.**

To illustrate, assume that in recording its usual quarterly income tax payments, a corporation computes $25,000 of income taxes expense. It also determines that only $21,000 is currently due and $4,000 is deferred to future years (a timing difference). The entry to record this end-of-period adjustment is

Assets	=	Liabilities	+	Equity
		+21,000		−25,000
		+4,000		

Dec. 31	Income Taxes Expense	25,000	
	Income Taxes Payable		21,000
	Deferred Income Tax Liability		4,000
	To record tax expense and deferred tax liability.		

The credit to Income Taxes Payable reflects the amount currently due to be paid. The credit to Deferred Income Tax Liability reflects tax payments deferred until future years when the temporary difference reverses.

Temporary differences also can cause a company to pay income taxes *before* they are reported on the income statement as expense. If so, the company reports a *Deferred Income Tax Asset* on its balance sheet.

Summary

C1 **Describe current and long-term liabilities and their characteristics.** Liabilities are probable future payments of assets or services that past transactions or events obligate an entity to make. Current liabilities are due within one year or the operating cycle, whichever is longer. All other liabilities are long term.

C2 **Identify and describe known current liabilities.** Known (determinable) current liabilities are set by agreements or laws and are measurable with little uncertainty. They include accounts payable, sales taxes payable, unearned revenues, notes payable, payroll liabilities, and the current portion of long-term debt.

C3 **Explain how to account for contingent liabilities.** If an uncertain future payment depends on a probable future event and the amount can be reasonably estimated, the payment is recorded as a liability. The uncertain future payment is reported as a contingent liability (in the notes) if (*a*) the future event is reasonably possible but not probable or (*b*) the event is probable but the payment amount cannot be reasonably estimated.

A1 **Compute the times interest earned ratio and use it to analyze liabilities.** Times interest earned is computed by dividing a company's net income before interest expense and income taxes by the amount of interest expense. The times interest earned ratio reflects a company's ability to pay interest obligations.

P1 **Prepare entries to account for short-term notes payable.** Short-term notes payable are current liabilities; most bear interest. When a short-term note's face value equals the amount borrowed, it identifies a rate of interest to be paid at maturity.

P2 **Compute and record *employee* payroll deductions and liabilities.** Employee payroll deductions include FICA taxes, income taxes, and voluntary deductions such as for pensions and charities. They make up the difference between gross and net pay.

P3 **Compute and record *employer* payroll expenses and liabilities.** An employer's payroll expenses include employees' gross earnings, any employee benefits, and the payroll taxes levied on the employer. Payroll liabilities include employees' net pay amounts, withholdings from employee wages, any employer-promised benefits, and the employer's payroll taxes.

P4 **Account for estimated liabilities, including warranties and bonuses.** Liabilities for health and pension benefits, warranties, and bonuses are recorded with estimated amounts. These items are recognized as expenses when incurred and matched with revenues generated.

P5A **Identify and describe the details of payroll reports, records, and procedures.** Employers report FICA taxes and federal income tax withholdings using Form 941. FUTA taxes are reported on Form 940. Earnings and deductions are reported to each employee and the federal government on Form W-2. An employer's payroll records often include a payroll register for each pay period, payroll checks and statements of earnings, and individual employee earnings reports.

Guidance Answers to Decision Maker and Decision Ethics

Web Designer You need to be concerned about being an accomplice to unlawful payroll activities. Not paying federal and state taxes on wages earned is illegal and unethical. Such payments also will not provide the employee with Social Security and some Medicare credits. The best course of action is to request payment by check. If this fails to change the owner's payment practices, you must consider quitting this job.

Entrepreneur Risk is partly reflected by the times interest earned ratio. This ratio for the first franchise is 1.5 [($100,000 + $200,000)/$200,000], whereas the ratio for the second franchise is 3.5 [($100,000 + $40,000)/$40,000]. This analysis shows that the first franchise is more at risk of incurring a loss if its sales decline. The second question asks about variability of income. If income greatly varies, this increases the risk an owner will not earn sufficient income to cover interest. Since the first franchise has the greater variability, it is a riskier investment.

Guidance Answers to Quick Checks

1. A liability involves a probable future payment of assets or services that an entity is presently obligated to make as a result of past transactions or events.
2. No, an expected future payment is not a liability unless an existing obligation was created by a past event or transaction.
3. In most cases, a liability due in 15 months is classified as long term. It is classified as a current liability if the company's operating cycle is 15 months or longer.
4. A creditor prefers a note payable instead of a past-due account payable so as to (*a*) charge interest and/or (*b*) have evidence of the debt and its terms for potential litigation or disputes.
5. $1,000* × (.008) + $1,000* × (.04) + $3,000 × (.062) + $3,000 × (.0145) = $277.50

* $1,000 of the $3,000 March pay is subject to FUTA and SUTA—the entire $6,000 pay from January and February was subject to them.

6. (*a*) FICA taxes are incurred by both employee and employer.
   (*b*) FUTA taxes are incurred by the employer.
   (*c*) SUTA taxes are incurred by the employer.
   (*d*) Withheld income taxes are incurred by the employee.
7. (*a*)
8. (*a*) Warranty expense was previously estimated and recorded.
9. (*b*)
10. A future payment is reported in the notes as a contingent liability if (*a*) the uncertain future event is probable but the amount of payment cannot be reasonably estimated or (*b*) the uncertain future event is not probable but has a reasonable possibility of occurring.
11. An employee's marital status, gross earnings and number of withholding allowances determine the deduction for federal income taxes.
12. $59
13. (*d*)

Key Terms

mhhe.com/wildFAP20e

Contingent liability (p. 448)
Current liabilities (p. 437)
Current portion of long-term debt (p. 445)
Deferred income tax liability (p. 460)
Employee benefits (p. 445)
Employee earnings report (p. 456)
Estimated liability (p. 445)
Federal depository bank (p. 453)
Federal Insurance Contributions Act (FICA) Taxes (p. 442)
Federal Unemployment Taxes (FUTA) (p. 444)
Form 940 (p. 453)
Form 941 (p. 453)
Form W-2 (p. 455)
Form W-4 (p. 458)
Gross pay (p. 442)
Known liabilities (p. 438)
Long-term liabilities (p. 437)
Merit rating (p. 444)
Net pay (p. 442)
Payroll bank account (p. 458)
Payroll deductions (p. 442)
Payroll register (p. 455)
Short-term note payable (p. 439)
State Unemployment Taxes (SUTA) (p. 444)
Times interest earned (p. 450)
Wage bracket withholding table (p. 458)
Warranty (p. 446)

Multiple Choice Quiz

Answers on p. 477

mhhe.com/wildFAP20e

Additional Quiz Questions are available at the book's Website.

1. On December 1, a company signed a $6,000, 90-day, 5% note payable, with principal plus interest due on March 1 of the following year. What amount of interest expense should be accrued at December 31 on the note?
   a. $300
   b. $25
   c. $100
   d. $75
   e. $0
2. An employee earned $50,000 during the year. FICA tax for social security is 6.2% and FICA tax for Medicare is 1.45%. The employer's share of FICA taxes is
   a. Zero, since the employee's pay exceeds the FICA limit.
   b. Zero, since FICA is not an employer tax.
   c. $3,100
   d. $725
   e. $3,825
3. Assume the FUTA tax rate is 0.8% and the SUTA tax rate is 5.4%. Both taxes are applied to the first $7,000 of an employee's pay. What is the total unemployment tax an employer must pay on an employee's annual wages of $40,000?
   a. $2,480
   b. $434
   c. $56
   d. $378
   e. Zero; the employee's wages exceed the $7,000 maximum.
4. A company sells big screen televisions for $3,000 each. Each television has a two-year warranty that covers the replacement of defective parts. It is estimated that 1% of all televisions sold will be returned under warranty at an average cost of $250 each. During July, the company sold 10,000 big screen televisions, and 80 were serviced under the warranty during July at a total cost of $18,000. The credit balance in the Estimated

Warranty Liability account at July 1 was $26,000. What is the company's warranty expense for the month of July?
a. $51,000
b. $1,000
c. $25,000
d. $33,000
e. $18,000

5. Employees earn vacation pay at the rate of 1 day per month. During October, 150 employees qualify for one vacation day each. Their average daily wage is $175 per day. What is the amount of vacation benefit expense for October?
a. $26,250
b. $175
c. $2,100
d. $63,875
e. $150

A(B) *Superscript letter A (B) denotes assignments based on Appendix 11A (11B).*
Icon denotes assignments that involve decision making.

Discussion Questions

1. What are the three important questions concerning the uncertainty of liabilities?
2. What is the difference between a current and a long-term liability?
3. What is an estimated liability?
4. If $988 is the total of a sale that includes its sales tax of 4%, what is the selling price of the item only?
5. What is the combined amount (in percent) of the employee and employer Social Security tax rate?
6. What is the current Medicare tax rate? This rate is applied to what maximum level of salary and wages?
7. What determines the amount deducted from an employee's wages for federal income taxes?
8. Which payroll taxes are the employee's responsibility and which are the employer's responsibility?
9. What is an employer's unemployment merit rating? How are these ratings assigned to employers?
10. Why are warranty liabilities usually recognized on the balance sheet as liabilities even when they are uncertain?
11. Suppose that a company has a facility located where disastrous weather conditions often occur. Should it report a probable loss from a future disaster as a liability on its balance sheet? Explain.
12. [A] What is a wage bracket withholding table?
13. [A] What amount of income tax is withheld from the salary of an employee who is single with two withholding allowances and earning $725 per week? What if the employee earned $625 and has no withholding allowances? (Use Exhibit 11A.6.)
14. Refer to Research In Motion's balance sheet in Appendix A. What revenue-related liability does Research In Motion report at February 27, 2010? RIM
15. Refer to Apple's balance sheet in Appendix A. What is the amount of Apple's accounts payable as of September 26, 2009? Apple
16. Refer to Nokia's balance sheet in Appendix A. List Nokia's current liabilities as of December 31, 2009. NOKIA
17. Refer to Palm's balance sheet in Appendix A. What current liabilities related to income taxes are on its balance sheet? Explain the meaning of each income tax account identified. Palm

connect

QUICK STUDY

QS 11-1
Classifying liabilities C1 

Which of the following items are normally classified as a current liability for a company that has a 15-month operating cycle?

1. Salaries payable.
2. Note payable due in 19 months.
3. FICA taxes payable.
4. Note payable maturing in 3 years.
5. Note payable due in 10 months.
6. Portion of long-term note due in 15 months.

QS 11-2
Accounting for sales taxes
C2

Wrecker Computing sells merchandise for $5,000 cash on September 30 (cost of merchandise is $2,900). The sales tax law requires Wrecker to collect 4% sales tax on every dollar of merchandise sold. Record the entry for the $5,000 sale and its applicable sales tax. Also record the entry that shows the remittance of the 4% tax on this sale to the state government on October 15.

QS 11-3
Unearned revenue 

Tickets, Inc., receives $5,500,000 cash in advance ticket sales for a four-date tour of Bruce Springsteen. Record the advance ticket sales on October 31. Record the revenue earned for the first concert date of November 8, assuming it represents one-fourth of the advance ticket sales.

QS 11-4
Accounting for contingent liabilities
C3 

The following legal claims exist for Kalamazoo Co. Identify the accounting treatment for each claim as either (*a*) a liability that is recorded or (*b*) an item described in notes to its financial statements.

1. Kalamazoo (defendant) estimates that a pending lawsuit could result in damages of $1,000,000; it is reasonably possible that the plaintiff will win the case.
2. Kalamazoo faces a probable loss on a pending lawsuit; the amount is not reasonably estimable.
3. Kalamazoo estimates damages in a case at $2,500,000 with a high probability of losing the case.

QS 11-5
Interest-bearing note transactions P1

On November 7, 2011, Ortez Company borrows $150,000 cash by signing a 90-day, 8% note payable with a face value of $150,000. (1) Compute the accrued interest payable on December 31, 2011, (2) prepare the journal entry to record the accrued interest expense at December 31, 2011, and (3) prepare the journal entry to record payment of the note at maturity.

QS 11-6
Record employee payroll taxes
P2

On January 14, the end of the first bi-weekly pay period of the year, Rockin Company's payroll register showed that its employees earned $14,000 of sales salaries. Withholdings from the employees' salaries include FICA Social Security taxes at the rate of 6.2%, FICA Medicare taxes at the rate of 1.45%, $2,600 of federal income taxes, $309 of medical insurance deductions, and $120 of union dues. No employee earned more than $7,000 in this first period. Prepare the journal entry to record Rockin Company's January 14 (employee) payroll expenses and liabilities.

QS 11-7
Record employer payroll taxes
P3

Merger Co. has ten employees, each of whom earns $2,000 per month and has been employed since January 1. FICA Social Security taxes are 6.2% of the first $106,800 paid to each employee, and FICA Medicare taxes are 1.45% of gross pay. FUTA taxes are 0.8% and SUTA taxes are 5.4% of the first $7,000 paid to each employee. Prepare the March 31 journal entry to record the March payroll taxes expense.

QS 11-8
Recording warranty repairs
P4

On September 11, 2010, Home Store sells a mower for $400 with a one-year warranty that covers parts. Warranty expense is estimated at 5% of sales. On July 24, 2011, the mower is brought in for repairs covered under the warranty requiring $35 in materials taken from the Repair Parts Inventory. Prepare the July 24, 2011, entry to record the warranty repairs.

QS 11-9
Accounting for bonuses P4

Paris Company offers an annual bonus to employees if the company meets certain net income goals. Prepare the journal entry to record a $10,000 bonus owed to its workers (to be shared equally) at calendar year-end.

QS 11-10
Accounting for vacations
P4

Chester Co.'s salaried employees earn four weeks vacation per year. It pays $192,000.12 in total employee salaries for 52 weeks but its employees work only 48 weeks. This means Chester's total weekly expense is $4,000 ($192,000/48 weeks) instead of the $3,692.31 cash paid weekly to the employees ($192,000/52 weeks). Record Chester's weekly vacation benefits expense.

QS 11-11
Times interest earned A1 

Compute the times interest earned for Weltin Company, which reports income before interest expense and income taxes of $2,044,000, and interest expense of $350,000. Interpret its times interest earned (assume that its competitors average a times interest earned of 4.0).

QS 11-12[A]
Net pay and tax computations
P5

The payroll records of Clix Software show the following information about Trish Farqua, an employee, for the weekly pay period ending September 30, 2011. Farqua is single and claims one allowance. Compute her Social Security tax (6.2%), Medicare tax (1.45%), federal income tax withholding, state income tax (1.0%), and net pay for the current pay period. (Use the withholding table in Exhibit 11A.6 and round tax amounts to the nearest cent.)

Total (gross) earnings for current pay period	$ 735
Cumulative earnings of previous pay periods	9,700

Check Net pay, $578.42

QS 11-13[B]
Record deferred income tax liability P4

Cather Corporation has made and recorded its quarterly income tax payments. After a final review of taxes for the year, the company identifies an additional $30,000 of income tax expense that should be recorded. A portion of this additional expense, $8,000, is deferred for payment in future years. Record Cather's year-end adjusting entry for income tax expense.

QS 11-14
International accounting standards
C1 C2 

Answer each of the following related to international accounting standards.

a. In general, how similar or different are the definitions and characteristics of current liabilities between IFRS and U.S. GAAP?

b. Companies reporting under IFRS often reference a set of current liabilities with the title *financial liabilities*. Identify two current liabilities that would be classified under financial liabilities per IFRS. (*Hint:* Nokia provides examples in this chapter and in Appendix A.)

connect

EXERCISES

Exercise 11-1
Classifying liabilities
C1 

The following items appear on the balance sheet of a company with a two-month operating cycle. Identify the proper classification of each item as follows: *C* if it is a current liability, *L* if it is a long-term liability, or *N* if it is not a liability.

_____ **1.** Sales taxes payable.
_____ **2.** FUTA taxes payable.
_____ **3.** Accounts receivable.
_____ **4.** Wages payable.
_____ **5.** Salaries payable.
_____ **6.** Notes payable (due in 6 to 12 months).
_____ **7.** Notes payable (due in 120 days).
_____ **8.** Current portion of long-term debt.
_____ **9.** Notes payable (mature in five years).
_____ **10.** Notes payable (due in 13 to 24 months).

Exercise 11-2
Recording known current liabilities
C2

Prepare any necessary adjusting entries at December 31, 2011, for Yacht Company's year-end financial statements for each of the following separate transactions and events.

1. Yacht Company records an adjusting entry for $2,000,000 of previously unrecorded cash sales (costing $1,000,000) and its sales taxes at a rate of 5%.
2. The company earned $40,000 of $100,000 previously received in advance for services.

Exercise 11-3
Accounting for contingent liabilities
C3

Prepare any necessary adjusting entries at December 31, 2011, for Moor Company's year-end financial statements for each of the following separate transactions and events.

1. A disgruntled employee is suing Moor Company. Legal advisers believe that the company will probably need to pay damages, but the amount cannot be reasonably estimated.
2. Moor Company guarantees the $5,000 debt of a supplier. The supplier will probably not default on the debt.

Exercise 11-4
Accounting for note payable
P1
Check (2b) Interest expense, $1,880

Perfect Systems borrows $94,000 cash on May 15, 2011, by signing a 60-day, 12% note.

1. On what date does this note mature?
2. Suppose the face value of the note equals $94,000, the principal of the loan. Prepare the journal entries to record (*a*) issuance of the note and (*b*) payment of the note at maturity.

Exercise 11-5
Interest-bearing notes payable with year-end adjustments
P1
Check (2) $2,250
(3) $1,125

Kwon Co. borrows $150,000 cash on November 1, 2011, by signing a 90-day, 9% note with a face value of $150,000.

1. On what date does this note mature? (Assume that February of 2011 has 28 days.)
2. How much interest expense results from this note in 2011? (Assume a 360-day year.)
3. How much interest expense results from this note in 2012? (Assume a 360-day year.)
4. Prepare journal entries to record (*a*) issuance of the note, (*b*) accrual of interest at the end of 2011, and (*c*) payment of the note at maturity.

Exercise 11-6
Computing payroll taxes
P2 P3
Check (*a*) FUTA, $4.80; SUTA, $17.40

MRI Company has one employee. FICA Social Security taxes are 6.2% of the first $106,800 paid to its employee, and FICA Medicare taxes are 1.45% of gross pay. For MRI, its FUTA taxes are 0.8% and SUTA taxes are 2.9% of the first $7,000 paid to its employee. Compute MRI's amounts for each of these four taxes as applied to the employee's gross earnings for September under each of three separate situations (*a*), (*b*), and (*c*).

	Gross Pay through August	Gross Pay for September
a.	$ 6,400	$ 800
b.	18,200	2,100
c.	100,500	8,000

Exercise 11-7
Payroll-related journal entries P2

Using the data in situation *a* of Exercise 11-6, prepare the employer's September 30 journal entries to record salary expense and its related payroll liabilities for this employee. The employee's federal income taxes withheld by the employer are $135 for this pay period.

Exercise 11-8
Payroll-related journal entries P3

Using the data in situation *a* of Exercise 11-6, prepare the employer's September 30 journal entries to record the *employer's* payroll taxes expense and its related liabilities.

Exercise 11-9
Computing and recording bonuses P4

For the year ended December 31, 2011, Winter Company has implemented an employee bonus program equal to 3% of Winter's net income, which employees will share equally. Winter's net income (prebonus) is expected to be $1,000,000, and bonus expense is deducted in computing net income.

1. Compute the amount of the bonus payable to the employees at year-end (use the method described in the chapter and round to the nearest dollar).
2. Prepare the journal entry at December 31, 2011, to record the bonus due the employees.
3. Prepare the journal entry at January 19, 2012, to record payment of the bonus to employees.

Check (1) $29,126

Exercise 11-10
Accounting for estimated liabilities
P4

Prepare any necessary adjusting entries at December 31, 2011, for Jester Company's year-end financial statements for each of the following separate transactions and events.

1. During December, Jester Company sold 3,000 units of a product that carries a 60-day warranty. December sales for this product total $120,000. The company expects 8% of the units to need warranty repairs, and it estimates the average repair cost per unit will be $15.
2. Employees earn vacation pay at a rate of one day per month. During December, 20 employees qualify for one vacation day each. Their average daily wage is $120 per employee.

Exercise 11-11
Warranty expense and liability computations and entries
P4

Chang Co. sold a copier costing $3,800 with a two-year parts warranty to a customer on August 16, 2011, for $5,500 cash. Chang uses the perpetual inventory system. On November 22, 2012, the copier requires on-site repairs that are completed the same day. The repairs cost $199 for materials taken from the Repair Parts Inventory. These are the only repairs required in 2012 for this copier. Based on experience, Chang expects to incur warranty costs equal to 4% of dollar sales. It records warranty expense with an adjusting entry at the end of each year.

1. How much warranty expense does the company report in 2011 for this copier?
2. How much is the estimated warranty liability for this copier as of December 31, 2011?
3. How much warranty expense does the company report in 2012 for this copier?
4. How much is the estimated warranty liability for this copier as of December 31, 2012?
5. Prepare journal entries to record (*a*) the copier's sale; (*b*) the adjustment on December 31, 2011, to recognize the warranty expense; and (*c*) the repairs that occur in November 2012.

Check (1) $220

(4) $21

Exercise 11-12
Computing and interpreting times interest earned
A1 

Use the following information from separate companies *a* through *f* to compute times interest earned. Which company indicates the strongest ability to pay interest expense as it comes due?

	Net Income (Loss)	Interest Expense	Income Taxes
a.	$140,000	$48,000	$ 35,000
b.	140,000	15,000	50,000
c.	140,000	8,000	70,000
d.	265,000	12,000	130,000
e.	79,000	12,000	30,000
f.	(4,000)	12,000	0

Check (b) 13.67

Exercise 11-13[A]
Gross and net pay computation
P5

Tony Newbern, an unmarried employee, works 48 hours in the week ended January 12. His pay rate is $12 per hour, and his wages are subject to no deductions other than FICA—Social Security, FICA— Medicare, and federal income taxes. He claims two withholding allowances. Compute his regular pay, overtime pay (for this company, workers earn 150% of their regular rate for hours in excess of 40 per week), and gross pay. Then compute his FICA tax deduction (use 6.2% for the Social Security portion and 1.45% for the Medicare portion), income tax deduction (use the wage bracket withholding table of Exhibit 11A.6), total deductions, and net pay. (Round tax amounts to the nearest cent.)

Check Net pay, $515.26

Exercise 11-14[B]
Accounting for income taxes
P4

Ming Corporation prepares financial statements for each month-end. As part of its accounting process, estimated income taxes are accrued each month for 30% of the current month's net income. The income taxes are paid in the first month of each quarter for the amount accrued for the prior quarter. The following information is available for the fourth quarter of year 2011. When tax computations are completed on January 20, 2012, Ming determines that the quarter's Income Taxes Payable account balance should be $29,100 on December 31, 2011 (its unadjusted balance is $23,640).

October 2011 net income	$27,900
November 2011 net income	18,200
December 2011 net income	32,700

Check (1) $5,460

1. Determine the amount of the accounting adjustment (dated as of December 31, 2011) to produce the proper ending balance in the Income Taxes Payable account.
2. Prepare journal entries to record (*a*) the December 31, 2011, adjustment to the Income Taxes Payable account and (*b*) the January 20, 2012, payment of the fourth-quarter taxes.

Exercise 11-15
Accounting for current liabilities under IFRS
P4

Volvo Group reports the following information for its product warranty costs as of December 31, 2008, along with provisions and utilizations of warranty liabilities for the year ended December 31, 2008 (SEK in millions).

Product warranty costs

Estimated costs for product warranties are charged to cost of sales when the products are sold. Estimated warranty costs include contractual warranty and goodwill warranty. Warranty provisions are estimated with consideration of historical claims statistics, the warranty period, the average time-lag between faults occurring and claims to the company, and anticipated changes in quality indexes. Differences between actual warranty claims and the estimated claims generally affect the recognized expense and provisions in future periods. At December 31, 2008, warranty cost provisions amounted to 10,354.

Product warranty liabilities, December 31, 2007	SEK 9,373
Additional provisions to product warranty liabilities	6,201
Utilizations and reductions of product warranty liabilities	(5,220)
Product warranty liabilities, December 31, 2008	10,354

1. Prepare Volvo's journal entry to record its estimated warranty liabilities (provisions) for 2008.
2. Prepare Volvo's journal entry to record its costs (utilizations) related to its warranty program for 2008. Assume those costs involve replacements taken out of Inventory, with no cash involved.
3. How much warranty expense does Volvo report for 2008?

Exercise 11-16
Recording payroll
P2 P3

The following monthly data are taken from Nunez Company at July 31: Sales salaries, $120,000; Office salaries, $60,000; Federal income taxes withheld, $45,000; State income taxes withheld, $10,000; Social security taxes withheld, $11,160; Medicare taxes withheld, $2,610; Medical insurance premiums, $7,000; Life insurance premiums, $4,000; Union dues deducted, $1,000; and Salaries subject to unemployment taxes, $50,000. The employee pays forty percent of medical and life insurance premiums.

Prepare journal entries to record: (1) accrued payroll, including employee deductions, for July; (2) cash payment of the net payroll (salaries payable) for July; (3) accrued employer payroll taxes, and other related employment expenses, for July—assume that FICA taxes are identical to those on employees and that SUTA taxes are 5.4% and FUTA taxes are 0.8%; and (4) cash payment of all liabilities related to the July payroll.

Exercise 11-17
Computing payroll taxes
P2 P3

Madison Company has nine employees. FICA Social Security taxes are 6.2% of the first $106,800 paid to each employee, and FICA Medicare taxes are 1.45% of gross pay. FUTA taxes are 0.8% and SUTA taxes are 5.4% of the first $7,000 paid to each employee. Cumulative pay for the current year for each of its employees follows.

Employee	Cumulative Pay	Employee	Cumulative Pay	Employee	Cumulative Pay
Steve S.	$ 6,000	Christina S.	$156,800	Dana W.	$116,800
Tim V.	60,000	Michelle H.	106,800	Stewart M.	36,800
Brent G.	87,000	Kathleen K.	110,000	Sankha B.	4,000

a. Prepare a table with the following column headings: Employee; Cumulative Pay; Pay Subject to FICA Social Security Taxes; Pay Subject to FICA Medicare Taxes; Pay Subject to FUTA Taxes; Pay Subject to SUTA Taxes. Compute the amounts in this table for each employee and total the columns.

b. For the company, compute each total for: FICA Social Security taxes, FICA Medicare taxes, FUTA taxes, and SUTA taxes. (*Hint:* Remember to include in those totals any employee share of taxes that the company must collect.)

Exercise 11-18
Preparing payroll register and related entries P5

SP Company has five employees. Employees paid by the hour receive a $10 per hour pay rate for the regular 40-hour work week plus one and one-half times the hourly rate for each overtime hour beyond the 40-hours per week. Hourly employees are paid every two weeks, but salaried employees are paid monthly on the last biweekly payday of each month. FICA Social Security taxes are 6.2% of the first $106,800 paid to each employee, and FICA Medicare taxes are 1.45% of gross pay. FUTA taxes are 0.8% and SUTA taxes are 5.4% of the first $7,000 paid to each employee. The company has a benefits plan that includes medical insurance, life insurance, and retirement funding for employees. Under this plan, employees must contribute 5 percent of their gross income as a payroll withholding, which the company matches with double the amount. Following is the partially completed payroll register for the biweekly period ending August 31, which is the last payday of August.

Employee	Cumulative Pay (Excludes Current Period)	Current Period Gross Pay: Pay Type	Pay Hours	Gross Pay	FIT / SIT	FUTA / SUTA	FICA-SS_EE / FICA-SS_ER	FICA-Med_EE / FICA-Med_ER	EE-Ben_Plan Withholding / ER-Ben_Plan Withholding	Employee Net Pay
Kathleen	$105,000.00	Salary	---	$7,000.00	$2,000.00					
					300.00					
Nichole	6,800.00	Salary	---	500.00	80.00					
					20.00					
Anthony	15,000.00	Regular	80		110.00					
		Overtime	8		25.00					
Zoey	6,500.00	Regular	80		100.00					
		Overtime	4		22.00					
Gracie	5,000.00	Regular	74	740.00	90.00					
		Overtime	0	0.00	21.00					
Totals	138,300.00				2,380.00					
					388.00					

* Table abbreviations follow those in Exhibit 11A.3 (see pages 455–456); and, "Ben_Plan" refers to employee (EE) or employer (ER) withholding for the benefits plan.

a. Complete this payroll register by filling in all cells for the pay period ended August 31. *Hint:* See Exhibit 11A.3 for guidance. (Round amounts to cents.)

b. Prepare the August 31 journal entry to record the accrued biweekly payroll and related liabilities for deductions.

c. Prepare the August 31 journal entry to record the employer's cash payment of the net payroll of part *b*.

d. Prepare the August 31 journal entry to record the employer's payroll taxes including the contribution to the benefits plan.

e. Prepare the August 31 journal entry to pay all liabilities (expect net payroll in part *c*) for this biweekly period.

connect

PROBLEM SET A

Problem 11-1A
Short-term notes payable transactions and entries
P1

mhhe.com/wildFAP20e

Tytus Co. entered into the following transactions involving short-term liabilities in 2010 and 2011.

2010

Apr. 20	Purchased $38,500 of merchandise on credit from Frier, terms are 1/10, n/30. Tytus uses the perpetual inventory system.
May 19	Replaced the April 20 account payable to Frier with a 90-day, $30,000 note bearing 9% annual interest along with paying $8,500 in cash.
July 8	Borrowed $60,000 cash from Community Bank by signing a 120-day, 10% interest-bearing note with a face value of $60,000.
___?___	Paid the amount due on the note to Frier at the maturity date.
___?___	Paid the amount due on the note to Community Bank at the maturity date.
Nov. 28	Borrowed $21,000 cash from UMB Bank by signing a 60-day, 8% interest-bearing note with a face value of $21,000.
Dec. 31	Recorded an adjusting entry for accrued interest on the note to UMB Bank.

2011

___?___	Paid the amount due on the note to UMB Bank at the maturity date.

Required

1. Determine the maturity date for each of the three notes described.

2. Determine the interest due at maturity for each of the three notes. (Assume a 360-day year.)

3. Determine the interest expense to be recorded in the adjusting entry at the end of 2010.

4. Determine the interest expense to be recorded in 2011.

5. Prepare journal entries for all the preceding transactions and events for years 2010 and 2011.

Check (2) Frier, $675
(3) $154
(4) $126

Problem 11-2A
Warranty expense and liability estimation
P4

On October 29, 2010, Lue Co. began operations by purchasing razors for resale. Lue uses the perpetual inventory method. The razors have a 90-day warranty that requires the company to replace any nonworking razor. When a razor is returned, the company discards it and mails a new one from Merchandise Inventory to the customer. The company's cost per new razor is $18 and its retail selling price is $80 in both 2010 and 2011. The manufacturer has advised the company to expect warranty costs to equal 7% of dollar sales. The following transactions and events occurred.

2010

Nov. 11 Sold 75 razors for $6,000 cash.
30 Recognized warranty expense related to November sales with an adjusting entry.
Dec. 9 Replaced 15 razors that were returned under the warranty.
16 Sold 210 razors for $16,800 cash.
29 Replaced 30 razors that were returned under the warranty.
31 Recognized warranty expense related to December sales with an adjusting entry.

2011

Jan. 5 Sold 130 razors for $10,400 cash.
17 Replaced 50 razors that were returned under the warranty.
31 Recognized warranty expense related to January sales with an adjusting entry.

Required

1. Prepare journal entries to record these transactions and adjustments for 2010 and 2011.
2. How much warranty expense is reported for November 2010 and for December 2010?
3. How much warranty expense is reported for January 2011?
4. What is the balance of the Estimated Warranty Liability account as of December 31, 2010?
5. What is the balance of the Estimated Warranty Liability account as of January 31, 2011?

Check (3) $728
(4) $786 Cr.
(5) $614 Cr.

Problem 11-3A
Computing and analyzing times interest earned
A1

Shown here are condensed income statements for two different companies (both are organized as LLCs and pay no income taxes).

Ace Company	
Sales	$500,000
Variable expenses (80%)	400,000
Income before interest	100,000
Interest expense (fixed)	30,000
Net income	$ 70,000

Deuce Company	
Sales	$500,000
Variable expenses (60%)	300,000
Income before interest	200,000
Interest expense (fixed)	130,000
Net income	$ 70,000

Required

1. Compute times interest earned for Ace Company.
2. Compute times interest earned for Deuce Company.
3. What happens to each company's net income if sales increase by 30%?
4. What happens to each company's net income if sales increase by 50%?
5. What happens to each company's net income if sales increase by 80%?
6. What happens to each company's net income if sales decrease by 10%?
7. What happens to each company's net income if sales decrease by 20%?
8. What happens to each company's net income if sales decrease by 40%?

Check (3) Ace net income, $100,000 (43% increase)

(6) Deuce net income, $50,000 (29% decrease)

Analysis Component

9. Comment on the results from parts 3 through 8 in relation to the fixed-cost strategies of the two companies and the ratio values you computed in parts 1 and 2.

Problem 11-4A
Payroll expenses, withholdings, and taxes
P2 P3

Legal Stars has four employees. FICA Social Security taxes are 6.2% of the first $106,800 paid to each employee, and FICA Medicare taxes are 1.45% of gross pay. Also, its FUTA taxes are 0.8% and SUTA taxes are 2.15% of the first $7,000 paid to each employee. The company is preparing its payroll calculations for the week ended August 25. Payroll records show the following information for the company's four employees.

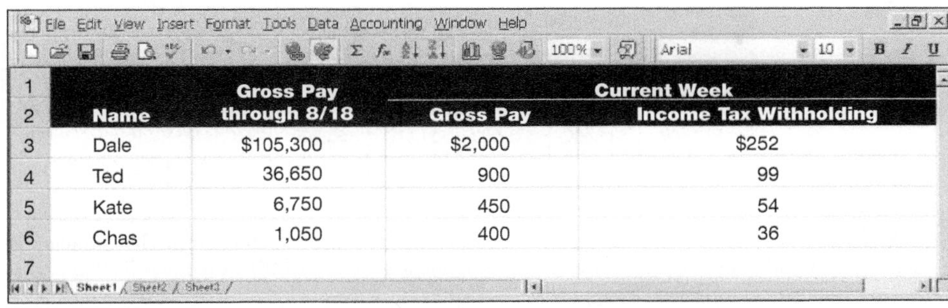

	Name	Gross Pay through 8/18	Gross Pay	Current Week Income Tax Withholding
3	Dale	$105,300	$2,000	$252
4	Ted	36,650	900	99
5	Kate	6,750	450	54
6	Chas	1,050	400	36

mhhe.com/wildFAP20e

In addition to gross pay, the company must pay one-half of the $32 per employee weekly health insurance; each employee pays the remaining one-half. The company also contributes an extra 8% of each employee's gross pay (at no cost to employees) to a pension fund.

Required

Compute the following for the week ended August 25 (round amounts to the nearest cent):

1. Each employee's FICA withholdings for Social Security.
2. Each employee's FICA withholdings for Medicare.
3. Employer's FICA taxes for Social Security.
4. Employer's FICA taxes for Medicare.
5. Employer's FUTA taxes.
6. Employer's SUTA taxes.
7. Each employee's net (take-home) pay.
8. Employer's total payroll-related expense for each employee.

Check (3) $201.50
(4) $54.38
(5) $5.20
(7) Total net pay, $2,989.12

Problem 11-5A
Entries for payroll transactions
P2 P3

On January 8, the end of the first weekly pay period of the year, Royal Company's payroll register showed that its employees earned $11,380 of office salaries and $32,920 of sales salaries. Withholdings from the employees' salaries include FICA Social Security taxes at the rate of 6.2%, FICA Medicare taxes at the rate of 1.45%, $6,340 of federal income taxes, $670 of medical insurance deductions, and $420 of union dues. No employee earned more than $7,000 in this first period.

Required

1. Calculate FICA Social Security taxes payable and FICA Medicare taxes payable. Prepare the journal entry to record Royal Company's January 8 (employee) payroll expenses and liabilities.
2. Prepare the journal entry to record Royal's (employer) payroll taxes resulting from the January 8 payroll. Royal's merit rating reduces its state unemployment tax rate to 4% of the first $7,000 paid each employee. The federal unemployment tax rate is 0.8%.

Check (1) Cr. Salaries Payable, $33,481.05
(2) Dr. Payroll Taxes Expense, $5,515.35

Problem 11-6A[A]
Entries for payroll transactions
P2 P3 P5

Polo Company has 10 employees, each of whom earns $2,600 per month and is paid on the last day of each month. All 10 have been employed continuously at this amount since January 1. Polo uses a payroll bank account and special payroll checks to pay its employees. On March 1, the following accounts and balances exist in its general ledger:

a. FICA—Social Security Taxes Payable, $3,224; FICA—Medicare Taxes Payable, $754. (The balances of these accounts represent total liabilities for *both* the employer's and employees' FICA taxes for the February payroll only.)
b. Employees' Federal Income Taxes Payable, $3,900 (liability for February only).
c. Federal Unemployment Taxes Payable, $416 (liability for January and February together).
d. State Unemployment Taxes Payable, $2,080 (liability for January and February together).

During March and April, the company had the following payroll transactions.

Mar. 15 Issued check payable to Fleet Bank, a federal depository bank authorized to accept employers' payments of FICA taxes and employee income tax withholdings. The $7,878 check is in payment of the February FICA and employee income taxes.

31 Recorded the March payroll and transferred funds from the regular bank account to the payroll bank account. Issued checks payable to each employee in payment of the March payroll. The payroll register shows the following summary totals for the March pay period.

Check March 31: Cr. Salaries Payable, $20,111

Salaries and Wages				Federal	
Office Salaries	Shop Wages	Gross Pay	FICA Taxes*	Income Taxes	Net Pay
$10,400	$15,600	$26,000	$1,612 $ 377	$3,900	$20,111

* FICA taxes are Social Security and Medicare, respectively.

March 31: Dr. Payroll Taxes Expenses, $2,853

April 15: Cr. Cash, $7,878 (Fleet Bank)

31 Recorded the employer's payroll taxes resulting from the March payroll. The company has a merit rating that reduces its state unemployment tax rate to 4.0% of the first $7,000 paid each employee. The federal rate is 0.8%.

Apr. 15 Issued check to Fleet Bank in payment of the March FICA and employee income taxes.

15 Issued check to the State Tax Commission for the January, February, and March state unemployment taxes. Mailed the check and the first quarter tax return to the Commission.

30 Issued check payable to Fleet Bank in payment of the employer's FUTA taxes for the first quarter of the year.

30 Mailed Form 941 to the IRS, reporting the FICA taxes and the employees' federal income tax withholdings for the first quarter.

Required

Prepare journal entries to record the transactions and events for both March and April.

PROBLEM SET B

Problem 11-1B
Short-term notes payable transactions and entries

P1

Bargen Co. entered into the following transactions involving short-term liabilities in 2010 and 2011.

2010

Apr. 22 Purchased $4,000 of merchandise on credit from Quinn Products, terms are 1/10, n/30. Bargen uses the perpetual inventory system.

May 23 Replaced the April 22 account payable to Quinn Products with a 60-day, $3,600 note bearing 15% annual interest along with paying $400 in cash.

July 15 Borrowed $9,000 cash from Blackhawk Bank by signing a 120-day, 10% interest-bearing note with a face value of $9,000.

__?__ Paid the amount due on the note to Quinn Products at maturity.

__?__ Paid the amount due on the note to Blackhawk Bank at maturity.

Dec. 6 Borrowed $16,000 cash from City Bank by signing a 45-day, 9% interest-bearing note with a face value of $16,000.

31 Recorded an adjusting entry for accrued interest on the note to City Bank.

2011

__?__ Paid the amount due on the note to City Bank at maturity.

Required

Check (2) Quinn, $90
(3) $100
(4) $80

1. Determine the maturity date for each of the three notes described.
2. Determine the interest due at maturity for each of the three notes. (Assume a 360-day year.)
3. Determine the interest expense to be recorded in the adjusting entry at the end of 2010.
4. Determine the interest expense to be recorded in 2011.
5. Prepare journal entries for all the preceding transactions and events for years 2010 and 2011.

Problem 11-2B
Warranty expense and liability estimation

P4

On November 10, 2011, Byung Co. began operations by purchasing coffee grinders for resale. Byung uses the perpetual inventory method. The grinders have a 60-day warranty that requires the company to replace any nonworking grinder. When a grinder is returned, the company discards it and mails a new one from Merchandise Inventory to the customer. The company's cost per new grinder is $14 and its retail selling price is $35 in both 2011 and 2012. The manufacturer has advised the company to expect warranty costs to equal 10% of dollar sales. The following transactions and events occurred.

2011

Nov. 16 Sold 50 grinders for $1,750 cash.

30 Recognized warranty expense related to November sales with an adjusting entry.

Dec. 12 Replaced six grinders that were returned under the warranty.

18 Sold 150 grinders for $5,250 cash.

28 Replaced 17 grinders that were returned under the warranty.

31 Recognized warranty expense related to December sales with an adjusting entry.

2012

Jan. 7 Sold 60 grinders for $2,100 cash.
21 Replaced 38 grinders that were returned under the warranty.
31 Recognized warranty expense related to January sales with an adjusting entry.

Required

1. Prepare journal entries to record these transactions and adjustments for 2011 and 2012.
2. How much warranty expense is reported for November 2011 and for December 2011?
3. How much warranty expense is reported for January 2012?
4. What is the balance of the Estimated Warranty Liability account as of December 31, 2011?
5. What is the balance of the Estimated Warranty Liability account as of January 31, 2012?

Check (3) $210
(4) $378 Cr.
(5) $56 Cr.

Problem 11-3B
Computing and analyzing times interest earned
A1 

Shown here are condensed income statements for two different companies (both are organized as LLCs and pay no income taxes).

Virgo Company	
Sales	$120,000
Variable expenses (50%)	60,000
Income before interest	60,000
Interest expense (fixed)	45,000
Net income	$ 15,000

Zodiac Company	
Sales	$120,000
Variable expenses (75%)	90,000
Income before interest	30,000
Interest expense (fixed)	15,000
Net income	$ 15,000

Required

1. Compute times interest earned for Virgo Company.
2. Compute times interest earned for Zodiac Company.
3. What happens to each company's net income if sales increase by 10%?
4. What happens to each company's net income if sales increase by 40%?
5. What happens to each company's net income if sales increase by 90%?
6. What happens to each company's net income if sales decrease by 20%?
7. What happens to each company's net income if sales decrease by 50%?
8. What happens to each company's net income if sales decrease by 80%?

Check (4) Virgo net income, $39,000 (160% increase)

(6) Zodiac net income, $9,000 (40% decrease)

Analysis Component

9. Comment on the results from parts 3 through 8 in relation to the fixed-cost strategies of the two companies and the ratio values you computed in parts 1 and 2.

Problem 11-4B
Payroll expenses, withholdings, and taxes
P2 P3

Sea Biz Co. has four employees. FICA Social Security taxes are 6.2% of the first $106,800 paid to each employee, and FICA Medicare taxes are 1.45% of gross pay. Also, its FUTA taxes are 0.8% and SUTA taxes are 1.75% of the first $7,000 paid to each employee. The company is preparing its payroll calculations for the week ended September 30. Payroll records show the following information for the company's four employees.

	Name	Gross Pay through 9/23	Gross Pay	Current Week Income Tax Withholding
3	Alli	$104,300	$2,500	$198
4	Eve	36,650	1,515	182
5	Hong	6,650	475	52
6	Juan	22,200	600	48

In addition to gross pay, the company must pay one-half of the $44 per employee weekly health insurance; each employee pays the remaining one-half. The company also contributes an extra 5% of each employee's gross pay (at no cost to employees) to a pension fund.

Required

Compute the following for the week ended September 30 (round amounts to the nearest cent):

1. Each employee's FICA withholdings for Social Security.
2. Each employee's FICA withholdings for Medicare.
3. Employer's FICA taxes for Social Security.
4. Employer's FICA taxes for Medicare.
5. Employer's FUTA taxes.
6. Employer's SUTA taxes.
7. Each employee's net (take-home) pay.
8. Employer's total payroll-related expense for each employee.

Check (3) $315.58 (4) $73.81 (5) $2.80 (7) Total net pay, $4,132.61

Problem 11-5B
Entries for payroll transactions
P2 P3

Palmer Company's first weekly pay period of the year ends on January 8. On that date, the column totals in Palmer's payroll register indicate its sales employees earned $69,490, its office employees earned $42,450, and its delivery employees earned $2,060. The employees are to have withheld from their wages FICA Social Security taxes at the rate of 6.2%, FICA Medicare taxes at the rate of 1.45%, $17,250 of federal income taxes, $2,320 of medical insurance deductions, and $275 of union dues. No employee earned more than $7,000 in the first pay period.

Required

1. Calculate FICA Social Security taxes payable and FICA Medicare taxes payable. Prepare the journal entry to record Palmer Company's January 8 (employee) payroll expenses and liabilities.
2. Prepare the journal entry to record Palmer's (employer) payroll taxes resulting from the January 8 payroll. Palmer's merit rating reduces its state unemployment tax rate to 3.4% of the first $7,000 paid each employee. The federal unemployment tax rate is 0.8%.

Check (1) Cr. Salaries Payable, $85,434

(2) Dr. Payroll Taxes Expense, $13,509

Problem 11-6B[A]
Entries for payroll transactions
P2 P3 P5

JLK Company has five employees, each of whom earns $1,200 per month and is paid on the last day of each month. All five have been employed continuously at this amount since January 1. JLK uses a payroll bank account and special payroll checks to pay its employees. On June 1, the following accounts and balances exist in its general ledger:

a. FICA—Social Security Taxes Payable, $744; FICA—Medicare Taxes Payable, $174. (The balances of these accounts represent total liabilities for *both* the employer's and employees' FICA taxes for the May payroll only.)
b. Employees' Federal Income Taxes Payable, $900 (liability for May only).
c. Federal Unemployment Taxes Payable, $96 (liability for April and May together).
d. State Unemployment Taxes Payable, $480 (liability for April and May together).

During June and July, the company had the following payroll transactions.

June 15 Issued check payable to Security Bank, a federal depository bank authorized to accept employers' payments of FICA taxes and employee income tax withholdings. The $1,818 check is in payment of the May FICA and employee income taxes.

30 Recorded the June payroll and transferred funds from the regular bank account to the payroll bank account. Issued checks payable to each employee in payment of the June payroll. The payroll register shows the following summary totals for the June pay period.

Check June 30: Cr. Salaries Payable, $4,641

Salaries and Wages					
Office Salaries	Shop Wages	Gross Pay	FICA Taxes*	Federal Income Taxes	Net Pay
$2,000	$4,000	$6,000	$372 $ 87	$900	$4,641

* FICA taxes are Social Security and Medicare, respectively.

30 Recorded the employer's payroll taxes resulting from the June payroll. The company has a merit rating that reduces its state unemployment tax rate to 4.0% of the first $7,000 paid each employee. The federal rate is 0.8%.

July 15 Issued check payable to Security Bank in payment of the June FICA and employee income taxes.

15 Issued check to the State Tax Commission for the April, May and June state unemployment taxes. Mailed the check and the second quarter tax return to the State Tax Commission.

31 Issued check payable to Security Bank in payment of the employer's FUTA taxes for the first quarter of the year.

31 Mailed Form 941 to the IRS, reporting the FICA taxes and the employees' federal income tax withholdings for the second quarter.

Check June 30: Dr. Payroll Taxes Expenses, $699

July 15: Cr. Cash $1,818 (Security Bank)

Required

Prepare journal entries to record the transactions and events for both June and July.

SERIAL PROBLEM

Business Solutions

P2 P3 C2

(This serial problem began in Chapter 1 and continues through most of the book. If previous chapter segments were not completed, the serial problem can begin at this point. It is helpful, but not necessary, to use the Working Papers that accompany the book.)

SP 11 Review the February 26 and March 25 transactions for Business Solutions (SP 5) from Chapter 5.

Required

1. Assume that Lyn Addie is an unmarried employee. Her $1,000 of wages are subject to no deductions other than FICA Social Security taxes, FICA Medicare taxes, and federal income taxes. Her federal income taxes for this pay period total $159. Compute her net pay for the eight days' work paid on February 26. (Round amounts to the nearest cent.)
2. Record the journal entry to reflect the payroll payment to Lyn Addie as computed in part 1.
3. Record the journal entry to reflect the (employer) payroll tax expenses for the February 26 payroll payment. Assume Lyn Addie has not met earnings limits for FUTA and SUTA—the FUTA rate is 0.8% and the SUTA rate is 4% for Business Solutions. (Round amounts to the nearest cent.)
4. Record the entry(ies) for the merchandise sold on March 25 if a 4% sales tax rate applies.

COMPREHENSIVE PROBLEM

Bug-Off Exterminators

(Review of Chapters 1–11)

CP 11 Bug-Off Exterminators provides pest control services and sells extermination products manufactured by other companies. The following six-column table contains the company's unadjusted trial balance as of December 31, 2011.

BUG-OFF EXTERMINATORS
December 31, 2011

	Unadjusted Trial Balance		Adjustments		Adjusted Trial Balance	
Cash	$ 17,000					
Accounts receivable	4,000					
Allowance for doubtful accounts		$ 828				
Merchandise inventory	11,700					
Trucks	32,000					
Accum. depreciation—Trucks		0				
Equipment	45,000					
Accum. depreciation—Equipment		12,200				
Accounts payable		5,000				
Estimated warranty liability		1,400				
Unearned services revenue		0				
Interest payable		0				
Long-term notes payable		15,000				
D. Buggs, Capital		59,700				
D. Buggs, Withdrawals	10,000					
Extermination services revenue		60,000				
Interest revenue		872				
Sales (of merchandise)		71,026				
Cost of goods sold	46,300					
Depreciation expense—Trucks	0					
Depreciation expense—Equipment	0					
Wages expense	35,000					
Interest expense	0					
Rent expense	9,000					
Bad debts expense	0					
Miscellaneous expense	1,226					
Repairs expense	8,000					
Utilities expense	6,800					
Warranty expense	0					
Totals	$226,026	$226,026				

The following information in *a* through *h* applies to the company at the end of the current year.

a. The bank reconciliation as of December 31, 2011, includes the following facts.

Cash balance per bank	$15,100
Cash balance per books	17,000
Outstanding checks	1,800
Deposit in transit	2,450
Interest earned (on bank account)	52
Bank service charges (miscellaneous expense)	15

Reported on the bank statement is a canceled check that the company failed to record. (Information from the bank reconciliation allows you to determine the amount of this check, which is a payment on an account payable.)

b. An examination of customers' accounts shows that accounts totaling $679 should be written off as uncollectible. Using an aging of receivables, the company determines that the ending balance of the Allowance for Doubtful Accounts should be $700.

c. A truck is purchased and placed in service on January 1, 2011. Its cost is being depreciated with the straight-line method using the following facts and estimates.

Original cost	$32,000
Expected salvage value	8,000
Useful life (years)	4

d. Two items of equipment (a sprayer and an injector) were purchased and put into service in early January 2009. They are being depreciated with the straight-line method using these facts and estimates.

	Sprayer	Injector
Original cost	$27,000	$18,000
Expected salvage value	3,000	2,500
Useful life (years)	8	5

e. On August 1, 2011, the company is paid $3,840 cash in advance to provide monthly service for an apartment complex for one year. The company began providing the services in August. When the cash was received, the full amount was credited to the Extermination Services Revenue account.

f. The company offers a warranty for the services it sells. The expected cost of providing warranty service is 2.5% of the extermination services revenue of $57,760 for 2011. No warranty expense has been recorded for 2011. All costs of servicing warranties in 2011 were properly debited to the Estimated Warranty Liability account.

g. The $15,000 long-term note is an 8%, five-year, interest-bearing note with interest payable annually on December 31. The note was signed with First National Bank on December 31, 2011.

h. The ending inventory of merchandise is counted and determined to have a cost of $11,700. Bug-Off uses a perpetual inventory system.

Required

Check (1*a*) Cash bal. $15,750
(1*b*) $551 credit

1. Use the preceding information to determine amounts for the following items.

a. Correct (reconciled) ending balance of Cash, and the amount of the omitted check.

b. Adjustment needed to obtain the correct ending balance of the Allowance for Doubtful Accounts.

c. Depreciation expense for the truck used during year 2011.

d. Depreciation expense for the two items of equipment used during year 2011.

e. The adjusted 2011 ending balances of the Extermination Services Revenue and Unearned Services Revenue accounts.

(1*f*) Estim. warranty liability, $2,844 Cr.

f. The adjusted 2011 ending balances of the accounts for Warranty Expense and Estimated Warranty Liability.

g. The adjusted 2011 ending balances of the accounts for Interest Expense and Interest Payable. (Round amounts to nearest whole dollar.)

2. Use the results of part 1 to complete the six-column table by first entering the appropriate adjustments for items *a* through *g* and then completing the adjusted trial balance columns. (*Hint:* Item *b* requires two adjustments.)
3. Prepare journal entries to record the adjustments entered on the six-column table. Assume Bug-Off's adjusted balance for Merchandise Inventory matches the year-end physical count.
4. Prepare a single-step income statement, a statement of owner's equity (cash withdrawals during 2011 were $10,000), and a classified balance sheet.

(2) Adjusted trial balance totals, $238,207

(4) Net income, $9,274; Total assets, $82,771

Beyond the Numbers

REPORTING IN ACTION
A1 P4
RIM

BTN 11-1 Refer to the financial statements of Research In Motion in Appendix A to answer the following.

1. Compute times interest earned for the fiscal years ended 2010, 2009, and 2008. Comment on RIM's ability to cover its interest expense for this period. Assume interest expense of $1, $502, and $31 for fiscal years ended 2010, 2009, and 2008 ($ thousands); and, assume an industry average of 18.1 for times interest earned.
2. RIM's current liabilities include "deferred revenue"; assume that this account reflects "Unredeemed gift card liabilities." Explain how this liability is created and how RIM satisfies this liability.
3. Does RIM have any commitments or contingencies? Briefly explain them.

Fast Forward

4. Access RIM's financial statements for fiscal years ending after February 27, 2010, at its Website (RIM.com) or the SEC's EDGAR database (www.sec.gov). Compute its times interest earned for years ending after February 27, 2010, and compare your results to those in part 1.

COMPARATIVE ANALYSIS
A1
RIM
Apple

BTN 11-2 Key figures for Research In Motion and Apple follow. (Interest expense figures for Apple are assumed as it has no interest expense for these years.)

	Research In Motion			Apple		
($ millions)	Current Year	One Year Prior	Two Years Prior	Current Year	One Year Prior	Two Years Prior
Net income	$2,457.144	$1,892.616	$1,293.867	$8,235	$6,119	$3,495
Income taxes	809.366	907.747	516.653	3,831	2,828	1,511
Interest expense	.001	.502	.031	3	2	1

Required

1. Compute times interest earned for the three years' data shown for each company.
2. Comment on which company appears stronger in its ability to pay interest obligations if income should decline. Assume an industry average of 18.1.

ETHICS CHALLENGE
P4

BTN 11-3 Connor Bly is a sales manager for an automobile dealership. He earns a bonus each year based on revenue from the number of autos sold in the year less related warranty expenses. Actual warranty expenses have varied over the prior 10 years from a low of 3% of an automobile's selling price to a high of 10%. In the past, Bly has tended to estimate warranty expenses on the high end to be conservative. He must work with the dealership's accountant at year-end to arrive at the warranty expense accrual for cars sold each year.

1. Does the warranty accrual decision create any ethical dilemma for Bly?
2. Since warranty expenses vary, what percent do you think Bly should choose for the current year? Justify your response.

COMMUNICATING IN PRACTICE
C3 

BTN 11-4 Dustin Clemens is the accounting and finance manager for a manufacturer. At year-end, he must determine how to account for the company's contingencies. His manager, Madeline Pretti, objects to Clemens's proposal to recognize an expense and a liability for warranty service on units of a new product introduced in the fourth quarter. Pretti comments, "There's no way we can estimate this warranty cost. We don't owe anyone anything until a product fails and it is returned. Let's report an expense if and when we do any warranty work."

Required

Prepare a one-page memorandum for Clemens to send to Pretti defending his proposal.

TAKING IT TO THE NET

C1 A1  

BTN 11-5 Access the February 26, 2010, filing of the December 31, 2009, annual 10-K report of McDonald's Corporation (Ticker: MCD), which is available from www.SEC.gov.

Required

1. Identify the current liabilities on McDonald's balance sheet as of December 31, 2009.
2. What portion (in percent) of McDonald's long-term debt matures within the next 12 months?
3. Use the consolidated statement of income for the year ended December 31, 2009, to compute McDonald's times interest earned ratio. Comment on the result. Assume an industry average of 12.0.

TEAMWORK IN ACTION

C2 P1

BTN 11-6 Assume that your team is in business and you must borrow $6,000 cash for short-term needs. You have been shopping banks for a loan, and you have the following two options.

A. Sign a $6,000, 90-day, 10% interest-bearing note dated June 1.
B. Sign a $6,000, 120-day, 8% interest-bearing note dated June 1.

Required

1. Discuss these two options and determine the best choice. Ensure that all teammates concur with the decision and understand the rationale.
2. Each member of the team is to prepare *one* of the following journal entries.
   a. Option A—at date of issuance.
   b. Option B—at date of issuance.
   c. Option A—at maturity date.
   d. Option B—at maturity date.
3. In rotation, each member is to explain the entry he or she prepared in part 2 to the team. Ensure that all team members concur with and understand the entries.
4. Assume that the funds are borrowed on December 1 (instead of June 1) and your business operates on a calendar-year reporting period. Each member of the team is to prepare *one* of the following entries.
   a. Option A—the year-end adjustment.
   b. Option B—the year-end adjustment.
   c. Option A—at maturity date.
   d. Option B—at maturity date.
5. In rotation, each member is to explain the entry he or she prepared in part 4 to the team. Ensure that all team members concur with and understand the entries.

ENTREPRENEURIAL DECISION

A1  

BTN 11-7 Review the chapter's opening feature about Matt and Bryan Walls, and their start-up company, SnorgTees. Assume that these young entrepreneurs are considering expanding their business to open an outlet in Europe. Assume their current income statement is as follows.

SNORGTEES Income Statement For Year Ended December 31, 2011	
Sales	$1,000,000
Cost of goods sold (30%)	300,000
Gross profit	700,000
Operating expenses (25%)	250,000
Net income	$ 450,000

SnorgTees currently has no interest-bearing debt. If it expands to open a European location, it will require a $300,000 loan. SnorgTees has found a bank that will loan it the money on a 7% note payable. The company believes that, at least for the first few years, sales at its European location will be $250,000, and that all expenses (including cost of goods sold) will follow the same patterns as its current locations.

Required

1. Prepare an income statement (showing three separate columns for current operations, European, and total) for SnorgTees assuming that it borrows the funds and expands to Europe. Annual revenues for current operations are expected to remain at $1,000,000.
2. Compute SnorgTees' times interest earned under the expansion assumptions in part 1.
3. Assume sales at its European location are $400,000. Prepare an income statement (with columns for current operations, European, and total) for the company and compute times interest earned.
4. Assume sales at its European location are $100,000. Prepare an income statement (with columns for current operations, European, and total) for the company and compute times interest earned.
5. Comment on your results from parts 1 through 4.

HITTING THE ROAD

P2

BTN 11-8 Check your phone book or the Social Security Administration Website (www.SSA.gov) to locate the Social Security office near you. Visit the office to request a personal earnings and estimate form. Fill out the form and mail according to the instructions. You will receive a statement from the Social Security Administration regarding your earnings history and future Social Security benefits you can receive. (Formerly the request could be made online. The online service has been discontinued and is now under review by the Social Security Administration due to security concerns.) It is good to request an earnings and benefit statement every 5 to 10 years to make sure you have received credit for all wages earned and for which you and your employer have paid taxes into the system.

GLOBAL DECISION

A1 

NOKIA

RIM

Apple

BTN 11-9 Nokia, Research In Motion, and Apple are all competitors in the global marketplace. Comparative figures for Nokia (www.Nokia.com), along with selected figures from Research In Motion and Apple, follow.

Key Figures	Nokia (EUR millions)		Research In Motion		Apple	
	Current Year	Prior Year	Current Year	Prior Year	Current Year	Prior Year
Net income	260	3,889	—	—	—	—
Income taxes	702	1,081	—	—	—	—
Interest expense	243	185	—	—	—	—
Times interest earned	?	?	3,267	5,579	4,023	4,475

Required

1. Compute the times interest earned ratio for the most recent two years for Nokia using the data shown.
2. Which company of the three presented provides the best coverage of interest expense? Explain.

ANSWERS TO MULTIPLE CHOICE QUIZ

1. b; $6,000 × 0.05 × 30/360 = $25
2. e; $50,000 × (.062 + .0145) = $3,825
3. b; $7,000 × (.008 + .054) = $434
4. c; 10,000 television sets × .01 × $250 = $25,000
5. a; 150 employees × $175 per day × 1 vacation day earned = $26,250

12 Accounting for Partnerships

A Look Back

Chapter 11 focused on how current liabilities are identified, computed, recorded, and reported. Attention was directed at notes, payroll, sales taxes, warranties, employee benefits, and contingencies.

A Look at This Chapter

This chapter explains the partnership form of organization. Important partnership characteristics are described along with the accounting concepts and procedures for its most fundamental transactions.

A Look Ahead

Chapter 13 extends our discussion to the corporate form of organization. We describe the accounting and reporting for stock issuances, dividends, and other equity transactions.

Learning Objectives

CONCEPTUAL

C1 Identify characteristics of partnerships and similar organizations. (p. 480)

ANALYTICAL

A1 Compute partner return on equity and use it to evaluate partnership performance. (p. 492)

LP12

PROCEDURAL

P1 Prepare entries for partnership formation. (p. 483)

P2 Allocate and record income and loss among partners. (p. 483)

P3 Account for the admission and withdrawal of partners. (p. 486)

P4 Prepare entries for partnership liquidation. (p. 490)

Decision Insight

Let's Do Eco-Lunch

"We are making a difference"

—CHANCE CLAXTON AND LYNN JULIAN

PHOENIX—Believe it or not, nearly 20,000 pounds of trash is generated annually from the typical elementary school. "When we researched it," explains Chance Claxton, "We discovered that 67 pounds of lunchtime trash is created by each schoolage child each school year." Armed with that evidence, and as mothers of young children, Chance, along with partner Lynn Julian, felt an urgent need to respond. The result is **Kids Konserve (KidsKonserve.com),** a start-up partnership that sells reusable and recycled food kits. "With waste from snack and lunch breaks at an all-time high," says Chance, "Kids Konserve is empowering parents and kids with information and a reusable product that will help . . . decrease waste in community landfills."

While Chance focuses on the design and sales side, Lynn's focus is on the accounting, marketing, and financial side of Kids Konserve. Her knowledge of partnerships and their financial implications are important to Kid Konserve's success. Lynn explains that she is working on a model for fund-raising opportunities to further expand their product opportunities. Both partners stress the importance of attending to partnership formation, partnership agreements, and financial reports to stay afloat. They refer to the partners' return on equity and establishing the proper organizational form as key inputs to partnership strategies and decisions.

Success is causing their partnership to evolve, but the partners adhere to an eco-focused mentality. "The best part of being a 'mompreneur' is that I am doing something for myself, for others, for my family, and for the earth," insists Chance. "It is a great feeling to have my children watch me work."

The partners continue to apply strict accounting fundamentals. Lynn explains that their partnership cannot survive unless the business is profitable, even with their noble agenda. To that end, both partners review their accounting results and regularly assess the partnership's costs and revenues. Nevertheless, Lynn emphasizes their greater goal: "We're delivering a program that reduces waste on campus. I'd say that deserves an A+."

[Sources: *Kids Konserve Website,* January 2011; *Entrepreneur,* October 2009; *MomBites.com,* September 2009; *Daily Grommet,* September 2009]

Chapter Preview

The three basic types of business organizations are proprietorships, partnerships, and corporations. Partnerships are similar to proprietorships, except they have more than one owner. This chapter explains partnerships and looks at several variations of them such as limited partnerships, limited liability partnerships, S corporations, and limited liability companies. Understanding the advantages and disadvantages of the partnership form of business organization is important for making informed business decisions.

Accounting for Partnerships

Partnership Organization	Basic Partnership Accounting	Partner Admission and Withdrawal	Partnership Liquidation
• Characteristics • Organizations with partnership characteristics • Choice of business form	• Organizing a partnership • Dividing income or loss • Partnership financial statements	• Admission of partner • Withdrawal of partner • Death of partner	• No capital deficiency • Capital deficiency

PARTNERSHIP FORM OF ORGANIZATION

C1 Identify characteristics of partnerships and similar organizations.

A **partnership** is an unincorporated association of two or more people to pursue a business for profit as co-owners. Many businesses are organized as partnerships. They are especially common in small retail and service businesses. Many professional practitioners, including physicians, lawyers, investors, and accountants, also organize their practices as partnerships.

Characteristics of Partnerships

Partnerships are an important type of organization because they offer certain advantages with their unique characteristics. We describe these characteristics in this section.

Voluntary Association A partnership is a voluntary association between partners. Joining a partnership increases the risk to one's personal financial position. Some courts have ruled that partnerships are created by the actions of individuals even when there is no *express agreement* to form one.

Partnership Agreement Forming a partnership requires that two or more legally competent people (who are of age and of sound mental capacity) agree to be partners. Their agreement becomes a **partnership contract,** also called *articles of copartnership.* Although it should be in writing, the contract is binding even if it is only expressed verbally. Partnership agreements normally include details of the partners' (1) names and contributions, (2) rights and duties, (3) sharing of income and losses, (4) withdrawal arrangement, (5) dispute procedures, (6) admission and withdrawal of partners, and (7) rights and duties in the event a partner dies.

Point: When a new partner is admitted, all parties usually must agree to the admission.

Limited Life The life of a partnership is limited. Death, bankruptcy, or any event taking away the ability of a partner to enter into or fulfill a contract ends a partnership. Any one of the partners can also terminate a partnership at will.

Point: The end of a partnership is referred to as its *dissolution.*

Taxation A partnership is not subject to taxes on its income. The income or loss of a partnership is allocated to the partners according to the partnership agreement, and it is included in determining the taxable income for each partner's tax return. Partnership income or loss is allocated each year whether or not cash is distributed to partners.

Point: Partners are taxed on their share of partnership income, not on their withdrawals.

Mutual Agency **Mutual agency** implies that each partner is a fully authorized agent of the partnership. As its agent, a partner can commit or bind the partnership to any contract within the scope of the partnership business. For instance, a partner in a merchandising business can sign contracts binding the partnership to buy merchandise, lease a store building, borrow money, or hire employees. These activities are all within the scope of a merchandising firm. A partner in a law firm, acting alone, however, cannot bind the other partners to a contract to buy snowboards for resale or rent an apartment for parties. These actions are outside the normal scope of a law firm's business. Partners also can agree to limit the power of any one or more of the partners to negotiate contracts for the partnership. This agreement is binding on the partners and on outsiders who know it exists. It is not binding on outsiders who do not know it exists. Outsiders unaware of the agreement have the right to assume each partner has normal agency powers for the partnership. Mutual agency exposes partners to the risk of unwise actions by any one partner.

Point: The majority of states adhere to the Uniform Partnership Act for the basic rules of partnership formation, operation, and dissolution.

Unlimited Liability **Unlimited liability** implies that each partner can be called on to pay a partnership's debts. When a partnership cannot pay its debts, creditors usually can apply their claims to partners' *personal* assets. If a partner does not have enough assets to meet his or her share of the partnership debt, the creditors can apply their claims to the assets of the other partners. A partnership in which all partners have *mutual agency* and *unlimited liability* is called a **general partnership.** Mutual agency and unlimited liability are two main reasons that most general partnerships have only a few members.

Point: Limited life, mutual agency, and unlimited liability are disadvantages of a partnership.

Co-Ownership of Property Partnership assets are owned jointly by all partners. Any investment by a partner becomes the joint property of all partners. Partners have a claim on partnership assets based on their capital account and the partnership contract.

Organizations with Partnership Characteristics

Organizations exist that combine certain characteristics of partnerships with other forms of organizations. We discuss several of these forms in this section.

Limited Partnerships Some individuals who want to invest in a partnership are unwilling to accept the risk of unlimited liability. Their needs can be met with a **limited partnership.** This type of organization is identified in its name with the words "Limited Partnership" or "Ltd." or "LP." A limited partnership has two classes of partners, general and limited. At least one partner must be a **general partner,** who assumes management duties and unlimited liability for the debts of the partnership. The **limited partners** have no personal liability beyond the amounts they invest in the partnership. Limited partners have no active role except as specified in the partnership agreement. A limited partnership agreement often specifies unique procedures for allocating income and losses between general and limited partners. The accounting procedures are similar for both limited and general partnerships.

Decision Insight

Nutty Partners The Hawaii-based ML Macadamia Orchards LP is one of the world's largest growers of macadamia nuts. It reported the following partners' capital balances ($ 000s) in its balance sheet: ■

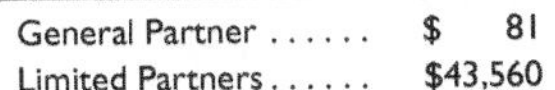

General Partner	$ 81
Limited Partners	$43,560

Limited Liability Partnerships Most states allow individuals to form a **limited liability partnership.** This is identified in its name with the words "Limited Liability Partnership" or by "LLP." This type of partnership is designed to protect innocent partners from malpractice or negligence claims resulting from the acts of another partner. When a partner provides service resulting in a malpractice claim, that partner has personal liability for the claim. The remaining partners who were not responsible for the actions resulting in the claim are not personally liable for it. However, most states hold all partners personally liable for other partnership debts. Accounting for a limited liability partnership is the same as for a general partnership.

Point: Many accounting services firms are set up as LLPs.

S Corporations Certain corporations with 100 or fewer stockholders can elect to be treated as a partnership for income tax purposes. These corporations are called *Sub-Chapter S* or simply **S corporations.** This distinguishes them from other corporations, called *Sub-Chapter C* or simply **C corporations.** S corporations provide stockholders the same limited liability feature that C corporations do. The advantage of an S corporation is that it does not pay income taxes. If stockholders work for an S corporation, their salaries are treated as expenses of the corporation. The remaining income or loss of the corporation is allocated to stockholders for inclusion on their personal tax returns. Except for C corporations having to account for income tax expenses and liabilities, the accounting procedures are the same for both S and C corporations.

Point: The majority of proprietorships and partnerships that are organized today are set up as LLCs.

Limited Liability Companies A relatively new form of business organization is the **limited liability company.** The names of these businesses usually include the words "Limited Liability Company" or an abbreviation such as "LLC" or "LC." This form of business has certain features similar to a corporation and others similar to a limited partnership. The owners, who are called *members,* are protected with the same limited liability feature as owners of corporations. While limited partners cannot actively participate in the management of a limited partnership, the members of a limited liability company can assume an active management role. A limited liability company usually has a limited life. For income tax purposes, a limited liability company is typically treated as a partnership. This treatment depends on factors such as whether the members' equity interests are freely transferable and whether the company has continuity of life. A limited liability company's accounting system is designed to help management comply with the dictates of the articles of organization and company regulations adopted by its members. The accounting system also must provide information to support the company's compliance with state and federal laws, including taxation.

Point: Accounting for LLCs is similar to that for partnerships (and proprietorships). One difference is that Owner (Partner), Capital is usually called *Members, Capital* for LLCs.

Choosing a Business Form

Choosing the proper business form is crucial. Many factors should be considered, including taxes, liability risk, tax and fiscal year-end, ownership structure, estate planning, business risks, and earnings and property distributions. The following table summarizes several important characteristics of business organizations:

	Proprietorship	Partnership	LLP	LLC	S Corp.	Corporation
Business entity	Yes	Yes	Yes	Yes	Yes	Yes
Legal entity	No	No	No	Yes	Yes	Yes
Limited liability	No	No	Limited*	Yes	Yes	Yes
Business taxed	No	No	No	No	No	Yes
One owner allowed	Yes	No	No	Yes	Yes	Yes

* A partner's personal liability for LLP debts is limited. Most LLPs carry insurance to protect against malpractice.

Point: The Small Business Administration provides suggestions and information on setting up the proper form for your organization—see SBA.gov.

We must remember that this table is a summary, not a detailed list. Many details underlie each of these business forms, and several details differ across states. Also, state and federal laws change, and a body of law is still developing around LLCs. Business owners should look at these details and consider unique business arrangements such as organizing various parts of their businesses in different forms.

Quick Check Answers — p. 495 

1. A partnership is terminated in the event (*a*) a partnership agreement is not in writing, (*b*) a partner dies, (*c*) a partner exercises mutual agency.
2. What does the term *unlimited liability* mean when applied to a general partnership?
3. Which of the following forms of organization do not provide limited liability to *all* of its owners? (*a*) S corporation, (*b*) limited liability company, (*c*) limited partnership.

BASIC PARTNERSHIP ACCOUNTING

Since ownership rights in a partnership are divided among partners, partnership accounting

- Uses a capital account for each partner.
- Uses a withdrawals account for each partner.
- Allocates net income or loss to partners according to the partnership agreement.

This section describes partnership accounting for organizing a partnership, distributing income and loss, and preparing financial statements.

Organizing a Partnership

P1 Prepare entries for partnership formation.

When partners invest in a partnership, their capital accounts are credited for the invested amounts. Partners can invest both assets and liabilities. Each partner's investment is recorded at an agreed-on value, normally the market values of the contributed assets and liabilities at the date of contribution. To illustrate, Kayla Zayn and Hector Perez organize a partnership on January 11 called BOARDS that offers year-round facilities for skateboarding and snowboarding. Zayn's initial net investment in BOARDS is $30,000, made up of cash ($7,000), boarding facilities ($33,000), and a note payable reflecting a bank loan for the new business ($10,000). Perez's initial investment is cash of $10,000. These amounts are the values agreed on by both partners. The entries to record these investments follow.

Zayn's Investment

Jan. 11	Cash	7,000	
	Boarding facilities	33,000	
	Note payable		10,000
	K. Zayn, Capital		30,000
	To record the investment of Zayn.		

Assets	=	Liabilities	+	Equity
+7,000		+10,000		+30,000
+33,000				

Perez's Investment

Jan. 11	Cash	10,000	
	H. Perez, Capital		10,000
	To record the investment of Perez.		

Assets	=	Liabilities	+	Equity
+10,000				+10,000

In accounting for a partnership, the following additional relations hold true: (1) Partners' withdrawals are debited to their own separate withdrawals accounts. (2) Partners' capital accounts are credited (or debited) for their shares of net income (or net loss) when closing the accounts at the end of a period. (3) Each partner's withdrawals account is closed to that partner's capital account. Separate capital and withdrawals accounts are kept for each partner.

Point: Both equity and cash are reduced when a partner withdraws cash from a partnership.

Decision Insight

Broadway Partners Big River Productions is a partnership that owns the rights to the play *Big River*. The play is performed on tour and periodically on Broadway. For a recent year-end, its Partners' Capital was approximately $300,000, and it was distributed in its entirety to the partners. ■

Dividing Income or Loss

P2 Allocate and record income and loss among partners.

Partners are not employees of the partnership but are its owners. If partners devote their time and services to their partnership, they are understood to do so for profit, not for salary. This means there are no salaries to partners that are reported as expenses on the partnership income statement. However, when net income or loss of a partnership is allocated among partners, the partners can agree to allocate "salary allowances" reflecting the relative value of services provided. Partners also can agree to allocate "interest allowances" based on the amount invested. For instance, since Zayn contributes three times the investment of Perez, it is only fair that this be considered when allocating income between them. Like salary allowances, these interest allowances are not expenses on the income statement.

Partners can agree to any method of dividing income or loss. In the absence of an agreement, the law says that the partners share income or loss of a partnership equally. If partners agree on how to share income but say nothing about losses, they share losses the same way they share income. Three common methods to divide income or loss use (1) a stated ratio basis, (2) the ratio of capital balances, or (3) salary and interest allowances and any remainder according to a fixed ratio. We explain each of these methods in this section.

Point: Partners can agree on a ratio to divide income and another ratio to divide a loss.

Allocation on Stated Ratios The *stated ratio* (also called the *income-and-loss-sharing ratio,* the *profit and loss ratio,* or the *P&L ratio*) method of allocating partnership income or loss gives each partner a fraction of the total. Partners must agree on the fractional share each receives. To illustrate, assume the partnership agreement of K. Zayn and H. Perez says Zayn receives two-thirds and Perez one-third of partnership income and loss. If their partnership's net income is $60,000, it is allocated to the partners when the Income Summary account is closed as follows.

Point: The fractional basis can be stated as a proportion, ratio, or percent. For example, a 3:2 basis is the same as ³⁄₅ and ²⁄₅, or 60% and 40%.

Assets = Liabilities + Equity
−60,000
+40,000
+20,000

Dec. 31	Income Summary	60,000	
	K. Zayn, Capital		40,000
	H. Perez, Capital		20,000
	To allocate income and close Income Summary.		

Allocation on Capital Balances The *capital balances* method of allocating partnership income or loss assigns an amount based on the ratio of each partner's relative capital balance. If Zayn and Perez agree to share income and loss on the ratio of their beginning capital balances—Zayn's $30,000 and Perez's $10,000—Zayn receives three-fourths of any income or loss ($30,000/$40,000) and Perez receives one-fourth ($10,000/$40,000). The journal entry follows the same format as that using stated ratios (see the preceding entries).

Point: To determine the percent of income received by each partner, divide an individual partner's share by total net income.

Allocation on Services, Capital, and Stated Ratios The *services, capital, and stated ratio* method of allocating partnership income or loss recognizes that service and capital contributions of partners often are not equal. Salary allowances can make up for differences in service contributions. Interest allowances can make up for unequal capital contributions. Also, the allocation of income and loss can include *both* salary and interest allowances. To illustrate, assume that the partnership agreement of K. Zayn and H. Perez reflects differences in service and capital contributions as follows: (1) annual salary allowances of $36,000 to Zayn and $24,000 to Perez, (2) annual interest allowances of 10% of a partner's beginning-year capital balance, and (3) equal share of any remaining balance of income or loss. These salaries and interest allowances are *not* reported as expenses on the income statement. They are simply a means of dividing partnership income or loss. The remainder of this section provides two illustrations using this three-point allocation agreement.

Illustration when income exceeds allowance. If BOARDS has first-year net income of $70,000, and Zayn and Perez apply the three-point partnership agreement described in the prior paragraph, income is allocated as shown in Exhibit 12.1. Zayn gets $42,000 and Perez gets $28,000 of the $70,000 total.

Illustration when allowances exceed income. The sharing agreement between Zayn and Perez must be followed even if net income is less than the total of the allowances. For example, if BOARDS' first-year net income is $50,000 instead of $70,000, it is allocated to the partners as shown in Exhibit 12.2. Computations for salaries and interest are identical to those in Exhibit 12.1. However, when we apply the total allowances against income, the balance of income is negative. This $(14,000) negative balance is allocated equally to the partners per their sharing agreement. This means that a negative $(7,000) is allocated to each partner. In this case, Zayn ends up with $32,000 and Perez with $18,000. If BOARDS had experienced a net loss, Zayn and Perez would share it in the same manner as the $50,000 income. The only difference is that they would have begun with a negative amount because of the loss. Specifically, the partners would still have been

Point: When allowances exceed income, the amount of this negative balance often is referred to as a *sharing agreement loss* or *deficit.*

Point: Check to make sure the sum of the dollar amounts allocated to each partner equals net income or loss.

EXHIBIT 12.1

Dividing Income When Income Exceeds Allowances

	Zayn	Perez	Total
Net income			$70,000
Salary allowances			
Zayn	$ 36,000		
Perez		$ 24,000	
Interest allowances			
Zayn (10% × $30,000)	3,000		
Perez (10% × $10,000)		1,000	
Total salaries and interest	39,000	25,000	64,000
Balance of income			6,000
Balance allocated equally			
Zayn	3,000		
Perez		3,000	
Total allocated			6,000
Balance of income			$ 0
Income of each partner	$42,000	$28,000	

EXHIBIT 12.2

Dividing Income When Allowances Exceed Income

	Zayn	Perez	Total
Net income			$50,000
Salary allowances			
Zayn	$ 36,000		
Perez		$ 24,000	
Interest allowances			
Zayn (10% × $30,000)	3,000		
Perez (10% × $10,000)		1,000	
Total salaries and interest	39,000	25,000	64,000
Balance of income			(14,000)
Balance allocated equally			
Zayn	(7,000)		
Perez		(7,000)	
Total allocated			(14,000)
Balance of income			$ 0
Income of each partner	$32,000	$18,000	

allocated their salary and interest allowances, further adding to the negative balance of the loss. This *total* negative balance *after* salary and interest allowances would have been allocated equally between the partners. These allocations would have been applied against the positive numbers from any allowances to determine each partner's share of the loss.

Point: When a loss occurs, it is possible for a specific partner's capital to increase (when closing income summary) if that partner's allowance is in excess of his or her share of the negative balance. This implies that decreases to the capital balances of other partners exceed the partnership's loss amount.

Quick Check Answer – p. 495

4. Denzel and Shantell form a partnership by contributing $70,000 and $35,000, respectively. They agree to an interest allowance equal to 10% of each partner's capital balance at the beginning of the year, with the remaining income shared equally. Allocate first-year income of $40,000 to each partner.

Partnership Financial Statements

Partnership financial statements are similar to those of other organizations. The **statement of partners' equity,** also called *statement of partners' capital,* is one exception. It shows *each* partner's beginning capital balance, additional investments, allocated income or loss, withdrawals, and ending capital balance. To illustrate, Exhibit 12.3 shows the statement of partners' equity for BOARDS prepared using the sharing agreement of Exhibit 12.1. Recall that BOARDS' income was $70,000; also, assume that Zayn withdrew $20,000 and Perez $12,000 at year-end.

EXHIBIT 12.3

Statement of Partners' Equity

BOARDS Statement of Partners' Equity For Year Ended December 31, 2011	Zayn		Perez		Total
Beginning capital balances		$ 0		$ 0	$ 0
Plus					
Investments by owners		30,000		10,000	40,000
Net income					
Salary allowances	$36,000		$24,000		
Interest allowances	3,000		1,000		
Balance allocated	3,000		3,000		
Total net income		42,000		28,000	70,000
		72,000		38,000	110,000
Less partners' withdrawals		(20,000)		(12,000)	(32,000)
Ending capital balances		$52,000		$26,000	$78,000

The equity section of the balance sheet of a partnership usually shows the separate capital account balance of each partner. In the case of BOARDS, both K. Zayn, Capital, and H. Perez, Capital, are listed in the equity section along with their balances of $52,000 and $26,000, respectively.

Decision Insight

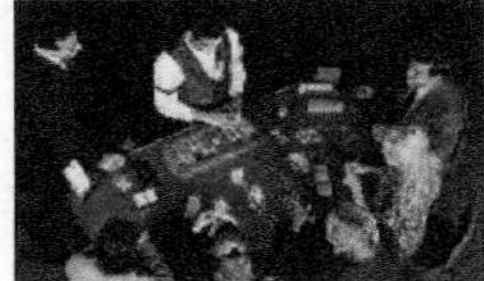

Gambling Partners Trump Entertainment Resorts LP and subsidiaries operate three casino hotel properties in Atlantic City: Trump Taj Mahal Casino Resort ("Trump Taj Mahal"), Trump Plaza Hotel and Casino ("Trump Plaza"), and Trump Marina Hotel Casino ("Trump Marina"). Its recent statement of partners' equity reports $1,020,000 in partners' withdrawals, leaving $605,314,000 in partners' capital balances.

ADMISSION AND WITHDRAWAL OF PARTNERS

P3 Account for the admission and withdrawal of partners.

A partnership is based on a contract between individuals. When a partner is admitted or withdraws, the present partnership ends. Still, the business can continue to operate as a new partnership consisting of the remaining partners. This section considers how to account for the admission and withdrawal of partners.

Admission of a Partner

A new partner is admitted in one of two ways: by purchasing an interest from one or more current partners or by investing cash or other assets in the partnership.

Purchase of Partnership Interest The purchase of partnership interest is a *personal transaction between one or more current partners and the new partner.* To become a partner, the current partners must accept the purchaser. Accounting for the purchase of partnership interest involves reallocating current partners' capital to reflect the transaction. To illustrate, at the end of BOARDS' first year, H. Perez sells one-half of his partnership interest to Tyrell Rasheed for $18,000. This means that Perez gives up a $13,000 recorded interest ($26,000 × 1/2) in the partnership (see the ending capital balance in Exhibit 12.3). The partnership records this January 4 transaction as follows.

Assets = Liabilities + Equity
−13,000
+13,000

Jan. 4	H. Perez, Capital	13,000	
	T. Rasheed, Capital		13,000
	To record admission of Rasheed by purchase.		

After this entry is posted, BOARDS' equity shows K. Zayn, Capital; H. Perez, Capital; and T. Rasheed, Capital, and their respective balances of $52,000, $13,000, and $13,000.

Two aspects of this transaction are important. First, the partnership does *not* record the $18,000 Rasheed paid Perez. The partnership's assets, liabilities, and *total equity* are unaffected by this transaction among partners. Second, Zayn and Perez must agree that Rasheed is to become a partner. If they agree to accept Rasheed, a new partnership is formed and a new contract with a new income-and-loss-sharing agreement is prepared. If Zayn or Perez refuses to accept Rasheed as a partner, then (under the Uniform Partnership Act) Rasheed gets Perez's sold share of partnership income and loss. If the partnership is liquidated, Rasheed gets Perez's sold share of partnership assets. Rasheed gets no voice in managing the company unless Rasheed is admitted as a partner.

Point: Partners' withdrawals are not constrained by the partnership's annual income or loss.

Investing Assets in a Partnership Admitting a partner by accepting assets is a *transaction between the new partner and the partnership.* The invested assets become partnership property. To illustrate, if Zayn (with a $52,000 interest) and Perez (with a $26,000 interest) agree to accept Rasheed as a partner in BOARDS after an investment of $22,000 cash, this is recorded as follows.

Jan. 4	Cash	22,000	
	T. Rasheed, Capital		22,000
	To record admission of Rasheed by investment.		

Assets	= Liabilities +	Equity
+22,000		+22,000

After this entry is posted, both assets (cash) and equity (T. Rasheed, Capital) increase by $22,000. Rasheed now has a 22% equity in the assets of the business, computed as $22,000 divided by the entire partnership equity ($52,000 + $26,000 + $22,000). Rasheed does not necessarily have a right to 22% of income. Dividing income and loss is a separate matter on which partners must agree.

Bonus to old partners. When the current value of a partnership is greater than the recorded amounts of equity, the partners usually require a new partner to pay a bonus for the privilege of joining. To illustrate, assume that Zayn and Perez agree to accept Rasheed as a partner with a 25% interest in BOARDS if Rasheed invests $42,000. Recall that the partnership's accounting records show that Zayn's recorded equity in the business is $52,000 and Perez's recorded equity is $26,000 (see Exhibit 12.3). Rasheed's equity is determined as follows.

Equities of existing partners ($52,000 + $26,000)	$ 78,000
Investment of new partner	42,000
Total partnership equity	$120,000
Equity of Rasheed (25% × $120,000)	$ 30,000

Although Rasheed invests $42,000, the equity attributed to Rasheed in the new partnership is only $30,000. The $12,000 difference is called a *bonus* and is allocated to existing partners (Zayn and Perez) according to their income-and-loss-sharing agreement. A bonus is shared in this way because it is viewed as reflecting a higher value of the partnership that is not yet reflected in income. The entry to record this transaction follows.

Jan. 4	Cash	42,000	
	T. Rasheed, Capital		30,000
	K. Zayn, Capital ($12,000 × ½)		6,000
	H. Perez, Capital ($12,000 × ½)		6,000
	To record admission of Rasheed and bonus.		

Assets	= Liabilities +	Equity
+42,000		+30,000
		+6,000
		+6,000

Bonus to new partner. Alternatively, existing partners can grant a bonus to a new partner. This usually occurs when they need additional cash or the new partner has exceptional talents. The bonus to the new partner is in the form of a larger share of equity than the amount invested. To illustrate, assume that Zayn and Perez agree to accept Rasheed as a partner with a

25% interest in the partnership, but they require Rasheed to invest only $18,000. Rasheed's equity is determined as follows.

Equities of existing partners ($52,000 + $26,000)	$78,000
Investment of new partner	18,000
Total partnership equity	$96,000
Equity of Rasheed (25% × $96,000)	$24,000

The old partners contribute the $6,000 bonus (computed as $24,000 minus $18,000) to Rasheed according to their income-and-loss-sharing ratio. Moreover, Rasheed's 25% equity does not necessarily entitle Rasheed to 25% of future income or loss. This is a separate matter for agreement by the partners. The entry to record the admission and investment of Rasheed is

Assets	= Liabilities +	Equity
+18,000		−3,000
		−3,000
		+24,000

Jan. 4	Cash	18,000	
	K. Zayn, Capital ($6,000 × ½)	3,000	
	H. Perez, Capital ($6,000 × ½)	3,000	
	T. Rasheed, Capital		24,000
	To record Rasheed's admission and bonus.		

Withdrawal of a Partner

A partner generally withdraws from a partnership in one of two ways. (1) First, the withdrawing partner can sell his or her interest to another person who pays for it in cash or other assets. For this, we need only debit the withdrawing partner's capital account and credit the new partner's capital account. (2) The second case is when cash or other assets of the partnership are distributed to the withdrawing partner in settlement of his or her interest. To illustrate these cases, assume that Perez withdraws from the partnership of BOARDS in some future period. The partnership shows the following capital balances at the date of Perez's withdrawal: K. Zayn, $84,000; H. Perez, $38,000; and T. Rasheed, $38,000. The partners (Zayn, Perez, and Rasheed) share income and loss equally. Accounting for Perez's withdrawal depends on whether a bonus is paid. We describe three possibilities.

No Bonus If Perez withdraws and takes cash equal to Perez's capital balance, the entry is

Assets	= Liabilities +	Equity
−38,000		−38,000

Oct. 31	H. Perez, Capital	38,000	
	Cash		38,000
	To record withdrawal of Perez from partnership with no bonus.		

Perez can take any combination of assets to which the partners agree to settle Perez's equity. Perez's withdrawal creates a new partnership between the remaining partners. A new partnership contract and a new income-and-loss-sharing agreement are required.

Bonus to Remaining Partners A withdrawing partner is sometimes willing to take less than the recorded value of his or her equity to get out of the partnership or because the recorded value is overstated. Whatever the reason, when this occurs, the withdrawing partner in effect gives the remaining partners a bonus equal to the equity left behind. The remaining partners share this unwithdrawn equity according to their income-and-loss-sharing ratio. To illustrate, if Perez withdraws and agrees to take $34,000 cash in settlement of Perez's capital balance, the entry is

Assets	= Liabilities +	Equity
−34,000		−38,000
		+2,000
		+2,000

Oct. 31	H. Perez, Capital	38,000	
	Cash		34,000
	K. Zayn, Capital		2,000
	T. Rasheed, Capital		2,000
	To record withdrawal of Perez and bonus to remaining partners.		

Perez withdrew $4,000 less than Perez's recorded equity of $38,000. This $4,000 is divided between Zayn and Rasheed according to their income-and-loss-sharing ratio.

Bonus to Withdrawing Partner A withdrawing partner may be able to receive more than his or her recorded equity for at least two reasons. First, the recorded equity may be understated. Second, the remaining partners may agree to remove this partner by giving assets of greater value than this partner's recorded equity. In either case, the withdrawing partner receives a bonus. The remaining partners reduce their equity by the amount of this bonus according to their income-and-loss-sharing ratio. To illustrate, if Perez withdraws and receives $40,000 cash in settlement of Perez's capital balance, the entry is

Oct. 31	H. Perez, Capital	38,000	
	K. Zayn, Capital	1,000	
	T. Rasheed, Capital	1,000	
	Cash		40,000
	To record Perez's withdrawal from partnership with a bonus to Perez.		

Assets	= Liabilities +	Equity
−40,000		−38,000
		−1,000
		−1,000

Falcon Cable Communications set up a partnership withdrawal agreement. Falcon owns and operates cable television systems and had two managing general partners. The partnership agreement stated that either partner "can offer to sell to the other partner the offering partner's entire partnership interest . . . for a negotiated price. If the partner receiving such an offer rejects it, the offering partner may elect to cause [the partnership] . . . to be liquidated and dissolved."

Death of a Partner

A partner's death dissolves a partnership. A deceased partner's estate is entitled to receive his or her equity. The partnership contract should contain provisions for settlement in this case. These provisions usually require (1) closing the books to determine income or loss since the end of the previous period and (2) determining and recording current market values for both assets and liabilities. The remaining partners and the deceased partner's estate then must agree to a settlement of the deceased partner's equity. This can involve selling the equity to remaining partners or to an outsider, or it can involve withdrawing assets.

Decision Ethics

Answer — p. 495

Financial Planner You are hired by the two remaining partners of a three-member partnership after the third partner's death. The partnership agreement states that a deceased partner's estate is entitled to a "share of partnership assets equal to the partner's relative equity balance" (partners' equity balances are equal). The estate argues that it is entitled to one-third of the current value of partnership assets. The remaining partners say the distribution should use asset book values, which are 75% of current value. They also point to partnership liabilities, which equal 40% of total asset book value and 30% of current value. How would you resolve this situation? ■

LIQUIDATION OF A PARTNERSHIP

P4 Prepare entries for partnership liquidation.

When a partnership is liquidated, its business ends and four concluding steps are required.

1. Record the sale of noncash assets for cash and any gain or loss from their liquidation.
2. Allocate any gain or loss from liquidation of the assets in step 1 to the partners *using their income-and-loss-sharing ratio.*
3. Pay or settle all partner liabilities.
4. Distribute any remaining cash to partners *based on their capital balances.*

Partnership liquidation usually falls into one of two cases, as described in this section.

No Capital Deficiency

No capital deficiency means that all partners have a zero or credit balance in their capital accounts for final distribution of cash. To illustrate, assume that Zayn, Perez, and Rasheed operate their partnership in BOARDS for several years, sharing income and loss equally. The partners then decide to liquidate. On the liquidation date, the current period's income or loss is transferred to the partners' capital accounts according to the sharing agreement. After that transfer, assume the partners' recorded account balances (immediately prior to liquidation) are:

Cash	$178,000	Accounts payable	$20,000	H. Perez, Capital	$66,000
Land	40,000	K. Zayn, Capital	70,000	T. Rasheed, Capital	62,000

We apply three steps for liquidation. ① *The partnership sells its noncash assets, and any losses or gains from liquidation are shared among partners according to their income-and-loss-sharing agreement* (equal for these partners). Assume that BOARDS sells its noncash assets consisting of $40,000 in land for $46,000 cash, yielding a net gain of $6,000. In a liquidation, gains or losses usually result from the sale of noncash assets, which are called *losses and gains from liquidation*. The entry to sell its assets for $46,000 follows.

Assets	= Liabilities +	Equity
−40,000		+6,000
+46,000		

Jan. 15	Cash	46,000	
	Land		40,000
	Gain from Liquidation		6,000
	Sold noncash assets at a gain.		

Allocation of the gain from liquidation per the partners' income-and-loss-sharing agreement follows.

Assets	= Liabilities +	Equity
		−6,000
		+2,000
		+2,000
		+2,000

Jan. 15	Gain from Liquidation	6,000	
	K. Zayn, Capital		2,000
	H. Perez, Capital		2,000
	T. Rasheed, Capital		2,000
	To allocate liquidation gain to partners.		

② *The partnership pays its liabilities, and any losses or gains from liquidation of liabilities are shared among partners according to their income-and-loss-sharing agreement.* BOARDS' only liability is $20,000 in accounts payable, and no gain or loss occurred.

Assets	= Liabilities +	Equity
−20,000	−20,000	

Jan. 15	Accounts Payable	20,000	
	Cash		20,000
	To pay claims of creditors.		

After step 2, we have the following capital balances along with the remaining cash balance.

K. Zayn		
	Bal.	70,000
	(2)	2,000
	Bal.	72,000

H. Perez, Capital		
	Bal.	66,000
	(2)	2,000
	Bal.	68,000

T. Rasheed, Capital		
	Bal.	62,000
	(2)	2,000
	Bal.	64,000

Cash			
Bal.	178,000	(3)	20,000
(1)	46,000		
Bal.	204,000		

③ *Any remaining cash is divided among the partners* ***according to their capital account balances.*** The entry to record the final distribution of cash to partners follows.

Assets	= Liabilities +	Equity
−204,000		−72,000
		−68,000
		−64,000

Jan. 15	K. Zayn, Capital	72,000	
	H. Perez, Capital	68,000	
	T. Rasheed, Capital	64,000	
	Cash		204,000
	To distribute remaining cash to partners.		

It is important to remember that the final cash payment is distributed to partners according to their capital account balances, whereas gains and losses from liquidation are allocated according to the income-and-loss-sharing ratio. The following *statement of liquidation* summarizes the three steps in this section.

Statement of Liquidation	Cash	Noncash Assets	=	Liabilities	K. Zayn, Capital	H. Perez, Capital	T. Rasheed, Capital
Balances prior to liquidation....	$178,000	$ 40,000		$ 20,000	$ 70,000	$66,000	$62,000
① Sale of noncash assets	46,000	(40,000)			2,000	2,000	2,000
② Payment of liabilities	(20,000)			(20,000)	0	0	0
Balances for distribution	204,000				72,000	68,000	64,000
③ Distribution of cash to partners	(204,000)				(72,000)	(68,000)	(64,000)

Capital Deficiency

Capital deficiency means that at least one partner has a debit balance in his or her capital account at the point of final cash distribution (during step ③ as explained in the prior section). This can arise from liquidation losses, excessive withdrawals before liquidation, or recurring losses in prior periods. A partner with a capital deficiency must, if possible, cover the deficit by paying cash into the partnership.

To illustrate, assume that Zayn, Perez, and Rasheed operate their partnership in BOARDS for several years, sharing income and losses equally. The partners then decide to liquidate. Immediately prior to the final distribution of cash, the partners' recorded capital balances are Zayn, $19,000; Perez, $8,000; and Rasheed, $(3,000). Rasheed's capital deficiency means that Rasheed owes the partnership $3,000. Both Zayn and Perez have a legal claim against Rasheed's personal assets. The final distribution of cash in this case depends on how this capital deficiency is handled. Two possibilities exist: the partner pays the deficiency or the partner cannot pay the deficiency.

Partner Pays Deficiency Rasheed is obligated to pay $3,000 into the partnership to cover the deficiency. If Rasheed is willing and able to pay, the entry to record receipt of payment from Rasheed follows.

Jan. 15	Cash	3,000	
	T. Rasheed, Capital		3,000
	To record payment of deficiency by Rasheed.		

Assets = Liabilities + Equity
+3,000 +3,000

After the $3,000 payment, the partners' capital balances are Zayn, $19,000; Perez, $8,000; and Rasheed, $0. The entry to record the final cash distributions to partners is

Jan. 15	K. Zayn, Capital	19,000	
	H. Perez, Capital	8,000	
	Cash		27,000
	To distribute remaining cash to partners.		

Assets = Liabilities + Equity
−27,000 −19,000
−8,000

Partner Cannot Pay Deficiency The remaining partners with credit balances absorb any partner's unpaid deficiency according to their income-and-loss-sharing ratio. To illustrate, if Rasheed is unable to pay the $3,000 deficiency, Zayn and Perez absorb it. Since they share income and loss equally, Zayn and Perez each absorb $1,500 of the deficiency. This is recorded as follows.

Jan. 15	K. Zayn, Capital	1,500	
	H. Perez, Capital	1,500	
	T. Rasheed, Capital		3,000
	To transfer Rasheed deficiency to Zayn and Perez.		

Assets = Liabilities + Equity
−1,500
−1,500
+3,000

After Zayn and Perez absorb Rasheed's deficiency, the capital accounts of the partners are Zayn, $17,500; Perez, $6,500; and Rasheed, $0. The entry to record the final cash distribution to the partners is

Jan. 15	K. Zayn, Capital	17,500	
	H. Perez, Capital	6,500	
	Cash		24,000
	To distribute remaining cash to partners.		

Assets = Liabilities + Equity
−24,000 −17,500
−6,500

Rasheed's inability to cover this deficiency does not relieve Rasheed of the liability. If Rasheed becomes able to pay at a future date, Zayn and Perez can each collect $1,500 from Rasheed.

GLOBAL VIEW

Partnership accounting according to U.S. GAAP is similar, but not identical, to that under IFRS. This section discusses broad differences in partnership accounting, organization, admission, withdrawal, and liquidation.

Both U.S. GAAP and IFRS include broad and similar guidance for partnership accounting. Further, partnership organization is similar worldwide; however, different legal and tax systems dictate different implications and motivations for how a partnership is effectively set up.

The accounting for partnership admission, withdrawal, and liquidation is likewise similar worldwide. Specifically, procedures for admission, withdrawal, and liquidation depend on the partnership agreements constructed by all parties involved. However, different legal and tax systems impact those agreements and their implications to the parties.

Decision Analysis — Partner Return on Equity

A1 Compute partner return on equity and use it to evaluate partnership performance.

An important role of partnership financial statements is to aid current and potential partners in evaluating partnership success compared with other opportunities. One measure of this success is the **partner return on equity** ratio:

$$\textbf{Partner return on equity} = \frac{\textbf{Partner net income}}{\textbf{Average partner equity}}$$

This measure is separately computed for each partner. To illustrate, Exhibit 12.4 reports selected data from the Boston Celtics LP. The return on equity for the *total* partnership is computed as \$216/[(\$85 + \$253)/2] = 127.8%. However, return on equity is quite different across the partners. For example, the Boston Celtics LP I partner return on equity is computed as \$44/[(\$122 + \$166)/2] = 30.6%, whereas the Celtics LP partner return on equity is computed as \$111/[(\$270 + \$333)/2] = 36.8%. Partner return on equity provides *each* partner an assessment of its return on its equity invested in the partnership. A specific partner often uses this return to decide whether additional investment or withdrawal of resources is best for that partner. Exhibit 12.4 reveals that the year shown produced good returns for all partners (the Boston Celtics LP II return is not computed because its average equity is negative due to an unusual and large distribution in the prior year).

EXHIBIT 12.4

Selected Data from Boston Celtics LP

($ thousands)	Total*	Boston Celtics LP I	Boston Celtics LP II	Celtics LP
Beginning-year balance	$ 85	$122	$(307)	$270
Net income (loss) for year	216	44	61	111
Cash distribution	(48)	—	—	(48)
Ending-year balance	$253	$166	$(246)	$333
Partner return on equity	127.8%	30.6%	n.a.	36.8%

* Totals may not add up due to rounding.

DEMONSTRATION PROBLEM

The following transactions and events affect the partners' capital accounts in several successive partnerships. Prepare a table with six columns, one for each of the five partners along with a total column to show the effects of the following events on the five partners' capital accounts.

Part 1

4/13/2009 Ries and Bax create R&B Company. Each invests \$10,000, and they agree to share income and losses equally.

12/31/2009 R&B Co. earns \$15,000 in income for its first year. Ries withdraws \$4,000 from the partnership, and Bax withdraws \$7,000.

1/1/2010 Royce is made a partner in RB&R Company after contributing \$12,000 cash. The partners agree that a 10% interest allowance will be given on each partner's beginning-year capital balance. In addition, Bax and Royce are to receive $5,000 salary allowances. The remainder of the income or loss is to be divided evenly.

12/31/2010 The partnership's income for the year is $40,000, and withdrawals at year-end are Ries, $5,000; Bax, $12,500; and Royce, $11,000.

1/1/2011 Ries sells her interest for $20,000 to Murdock, whom Bax and Royce accept as a partner in the new BR&M Co. Income or loss is to be shared equally after Bax and Royce receive $25,000 salary allowances.

12/31/2011 The partnership's income for the year is $35,000, and year-end withdrawals are Bax, $2,500, and Royce, $2,000.

1/1/2012 Elway is admitted as a partner after investing $60,000 cash in the new Elway & Associates partnership. He is given a 50% interest in capital after the other partners transfer $3,000 to his account from each of theirs. A 20% interest allowance (on the beginning-year capital balances) will be used in sharing any income or loss, there will be no salary allowances, and Elway will receive 40% of the remaining balance—the other three partners will each get 20%.

12/31/2012 Elway & Associates earns $127,600 in income for the year, and year-end withdrawals are Bax, $25,000; Royce, $27,000; Murdock, $15,000; and Elway, $40,000.

1/1/2013 Elway buys out Bax and Royce for the balances of their capital accounts after a revaluation of the partnership assets. The revaluation gain is $50,000, which is divided in using a 1:1:1:2 ratio (Bax:Royce:Murdock:Elway). Elway pays the others from personal funds. Murdock and Elway will share income on a 1:9 ratio.

2/28/2013 The partnership earns $10,000 of income since the beginning of the year. Murdock retires and receives partnership cash equal to her capital balance. Elway takes possession of the partnership assets in his own name, and the partnership is dissolved.

Part 2

Journalize the events affecting the partnership for the year ended December 31, 2010.

PLANNING THE SOLUTION

- Evaluate each transaction's effects on the capital accounts of the partners.
- Each time a new partner is admitted or a partner withdraws, allocate any bonus based on the income-or-loss-sharing agreement.
- Each time a new partner is admitted or a partner withdraws, allocate subsequent net income or loss in accordance with the new partnership agreement.
- Prepare entries to (1) record Royce's initial investment; (2) record the allocation of interest, salaries, and remainder; (3) show the cash withdrawals from the partnership; and (4) close the withdrawal accounts on December 31, 2010.

SOLUTION TO DEMONSTRATION PROBLEM

Part 1

Event	Ries	Bax	Royce	Murdock	Elway	Total
4/13/2009						
Initial investment	$10,000	$10,000				$ 20,000
12/31/2009						
Income (equal)	7,500	7,500				15,000
Withdrawals	(4,000)	(7,000)				(11,000)
Ending balance	$13,500	$10,500				$ 24,000
1/1/2010						
New investment			$12,000			$ 12,000
12/31/2010						
10% interest	1,350	1,050	1,200			3,600
Salaries		5,000	5,000			10,000
Remainder (equal)	8,800	8,800	8,800			26,400
Withdrawals	(5,000)	(12,500)	(11,000)			(28,500)
Ending balance	$18,650	$12,850	$16,000			$ 47,500

[continued on next page]

[continued from previous page]

Event	Ries	Bax	Royce	Murdock	Elway	Total
1/1/2011						
Transfer interest	(18,650)			$18,650		$ 0
12/31/2011						
Salaries		25,000	25,000			50,000
Remainder (equal)		(5,000)	(5,000)	(5,000)		(15,000)
Withdrawals		(2,500)	(2,000)			(4,500)
Ending balance	$ 0	$30,350	$34,000	$13,650		$ 78,000
1/1/2012						
New investment					$ 60,000	60,000
Bonuses to Elway		(3,000)	(3,000)	(3,000)	9,000	0
Adjusted balance		$27,350	$31,000	$10,650	$ 69,000	$138,000
12/31/2012						
20% interest		5,470	6,200	2,130	13,800	27,600
Remainder (1:1:1:2)		20,000	20,000	20,000	40,000	100,000
Withdrawals		(25,000)	(27,000)	(15,000)	(40,000)	(107,000)
Ending balance		$27,820	$30,200	$17,780	$ 82,800	$158,600
1/1/2013						
Gain (1:1:1:2)		10,000	10,000	10,000	20,000	50,000
Adjusted balance		$37,820	$40,200	$27,780	$102,800	$208,600
Transfer interests		(37,820)	(40,200)		78,020	0
Adjusted balance		$ 0	$ 0	$27,780	$180,820	$208,600
2/28/2013						
Income (1:9)				1,000	9,000	10,000
Adjusted balance				$28,780	$189,820	$218,600
Settlements				(28,780)	(189,820)	(218,600)
Final balance				$ 0	$ 0	$ 0

Part 2

Date	Account	Debit	Credit
2010			
Jan. 1	Cash	12,000	
	Royce, Capital		12,000
	To record investment of Royce.		
Dec. 31	Income Summary	40,000	
	Ries, Capital		10,150
	Bax, Capital		14,850
	Royce, Capital		15,000
	To allocate interest, salaries, and remainders.		
Dec. 31	Ries, Withdrawals	5,000	
	Bax, Withdrawals	12,500	
	Royce, Withdrawals	11,000	
	Cash		28,500
	To record cash withdrawals by partners.		
Dec. 31	Ries, Capital	5,000	
	Bax, Capital	12,500	
	Royce, Capital	11,000	
	Ries, Withdrawals		5,000
	Bax, Withdrawals		12,500
	Royce, Withdrawals		11,000
	To close withdrawal accounts.		

Summary

C1 Identify characteristics of partnerships and similar organizations. Partnerships are voluntary associations, involve partnership agreements, have limited life, are not subject to income tax, include mutual agency, and have unlimited liability. Organizations that combine selected characteristics of partnerships and corporations include limited partnerships, limited liability partnerships, S corporations, and limited liability companies.

A1 Compute partner return on equity and use it to evaluate partnership performance. Partner return on equity provides each partner an assessment of his or her return on equity invested in the partnership.

P1 Prepare entries for partnership formation. A partner's initial investment is recorded at the market value of the assets contributed to the partnership.

P2 Allocate and record income and loss among partners. A partnership agreement should specify how to allocate partnership income or loss among partners. Allocation can be based on a stated ratio, capital balances, or salary and interest allowances to compensate partners for differences in their service and capital contributions.

P3 Account for the admission and withdrawal of partners. When a new partner buys a partnership interest directly from one or more existing partners, the amount of cash paid from one partner to another does not affect the partnership total recorded equity. When a new partner purchases equity by investing additional assets in the partnership, the new partner's investment can yield a bonus either to existing partners or to the new partner. The entry to record a withdrawal can involve payment from either (1) the existing partners' personal assets or (2) partnership assets. The latter can yield a bonus to either the withdrawing or remaining partners.

P4 Prepare entries for partnership liquidation. When a partnership is liquidated, losses and gains from selling partnership assets are allocated to the partners according to their income-and-loss-sharing ratio. If a partner's capital account has a deficiency that the partner cannot pay, the other partners share the deficit according to their relative income-and-loss-sharing ratio.

Guidance Answers to Decision Ethics

Financial Planner The partnership agreement apparently fails to mention liabilities or use the term *net assets.* To give the estate one-third of total assets is not fair to the remaining partners because if the partner had lived and the partners had decided to liquidate, the liabilities would need to be paid out of assets before any liquidation. Also, a settlement based on the deceased partner's recorded equity would fail to recognize excess of current value over book value. This value increase would be realized if the partnership were liquidated. A fair settlement would seem to be a payment to the estate for the balance of the deceased partner's equity based on the *current value of net assets.*

Guidance Answers to Quick Checks

1. (*b*)
2. *Unlimited liability* means that the creditors of a partnership require each partner to be personally responsible for all partnership debts.
3. (*c*)
4.

	Denzel	Shantell	Total
Net income			$40,000
Interest allowance (10%)	$ 7,000	$ 3,500	10,500
Balance of income	↓	↓	$29,500
Balance allocated equally	14,750	14,750	29,500
Balance of income			$ 0
Income of partners	$21,750	$18,250	

Key Terms

mhhe.com/wildFAP20e

C corporation (p. 482)
General partner (p. 481)
General partnership (p. 481)
Limited liability company (LLC) (p. 482)
Limited liability partnership (p. 481)
Limited partners (p. 481)
Limited partnership (p. 481)
Mutual agency (p. 480)
Partner return on equity (p. 492)
Partnership (p. 480)
Partnership contract (p. 480)
Partnership liquidation (p. 489)
S corporation (p. 482)
Statement of partners' equity (p. 485)
Unlimited liability (p. 481)

Multiple Choice Quiz

Answers on p. 505 mhhe.com/wildFAP20e

Additional Quiz Questions are available at the book's Website.

1. Stokely and Leder are forming a partnership. Stokely invests a building that has a market value of $250,000; and the partnership assumes responsibility for a $50,000 note secured by a mortgage on that building. Leder invests $100,000 cash. For the partnership, the amounts recorded for the building and for Stokely's Capital account are these:
a. Building, $250,000; Stokely, Capital, $250,000.
b. Building, $200,000; Stokely, Capital, $200,000.
c. Building, $200,000; Stokely, Capital, $100,000.
d. Building, $200,000; Stokely, Capital, $250,000.
e. Building, $250,000; Stokely, Capital, $200,000.

2. Katherine, Alliah, and Paulina form a partnership. Katherine contributes $150,000, Alliah contributes $150,000, and Paulina contributes $100,000. Their partnership agreement calls for the income or loss division to be based on the ratio of capital invested. If the partnership reports income of $90,000 for its first year of operations, what amount of income is credited to Paulina's capital account?
a. $22,500
b. $25,000
c. $45,000
d. $30,000
e. $90,000

3. Jamison and Blue form a partnership with capital contributions of $600,000 and $800,000, respectively. Their partnership agreement calls for Jamison to receive $120,000 per year in salary. Also, each partner is to receive an interest allowance equal to 10% of the partner's beginning capital contributions, with any remaining income or loss divided equally. If net income for its initial year is $270,000, then Jamison's and Blue's respective shares are
a. $135,000; $135,000.
b. $154,286; $115,714.
c. $120,000; $150,000.
d. $185,000; $85,000.
e. $85,000; $185,000.

4. Hansen and Fleming are partners and share equally in income or loss. Hansen's current capital balance in the partnership is $125,000 and Fleming's is $124,000. Hansen and Fleming agree to accept Black with a 20% interest. Black invests $75,000 in the partnership. The bonus granted to Hansen and Fleming equals
a. $13,000 each.
b. $5,100 each.
c. $4,000 each.
d. $5,285 to Hansen; $4,915 to Fleming.
e. $0; Hansen and Fleming grant a bonus to Black.

5. Mee Su is a partner in Hartford Partners, LLC. Her partnership capital balance at the beginning of the current year was $110,000, and her ending balance was $124,000. Her share of the partnership income is $10,500. What is her partner return on equity?
a. 8.97%
b. 1060.00%
c. 9.54%
d. 1047.00%
e. 8.47%

Icon denotes assignments that involve decision making.

Discussion Questions

1. If a partnership contract does not state the period of time the partnership is to exist, when does the partnership end?

2. What does the term *mutual agency* mean when applied to a partnership?

3. Can partners limit the right of a partner to commit their partnership to contracts? Would such an agreement be binding (*a*) on the partners and (*b*) on outsiders?

4. Assume that Amey and Lacey are partners. Lacey dies, and her son claims the right to take his mother's place in the partnership. Does he have this right? Why or why not?

5. Assume that the Barnes and Ardmore partnership agreement provides for a two-third/one-third sharing of income but says nothing about losses. The first year of partnership operation resulted in a loss, and Barnes argues that the loss should be shared equally because the partnership agreement said nothing about sharing losses. Is Barnes correct? Explain.

6. Allocation of partnership income among the partners appears on what financial statement?

7. What does the term *unlimited liability* mean when it is applied to partnership members?

8. How does a general partnership differ from a limited partnership?

9. George, Burton, and Dillman have been partners for three years. The partnership is being dissolved. George is leaving the firm, but Burton and Dillman plan to carry on the business. In the final settlement, George places a $75,000 salary claim against the partnership. He contends that he has a claim for a salary of $25,000 for each year because he devoted all of his time for three years to the affairs of the partnership. Is his claim valid? Why or why not?

10. Kay, Kat, and Kim are partners. In a liquidation, Kay's share of partnership losses exceeds her capital account balance. Moreover, she is unable to meet the deficit from her personal assets, and her partners shared the excess losses. Does this relieve Kay of liability?

11. After all partnership assets have been converted to cash and all liabilities paid, the remaining cash should equal the sum of the balances of the partners' capital accounts. Why?

12. Assume a partner withdraws from a partnership and receives assets of greater value than the book value of his equity. Should the remaining partners share the resulting reduction in their equities in the ratio of their relative capital balances or according to their income-and-loss-sharing ratio?

connect

QUICK STUDY

Kent and Davis are partners in operating a store. Without consulting Kent, Davis enters into a contract to purchase merchandise for the store. Kent contends that he did not authorize the order and refuses to pay for it. The vendor sues the partners for the contract price of the merchandise. (*a*) Must the partnership pay for the merchandise? Why? (*b*) Does your answer differ if Kent and Davis are partners in a public accounting firm? Explain.

QS 12-1
Partnership liability
C1 

Lamb organized a limited partnership and is the only general partner. Maxi invested $20,000 in the partnership and was admitted as a limited partner with the understanding that she would receive 10% of the profits. After two unprofitable years, the partnership ceased doing business. At that point, partnership liabilities were $85,000 larger than partnership assets. How much money can the partnership's creditors obtain from Maxi's personal assets to satisfy the unpaid partnership debts?

QS 12-2
Liability in limited partnerships
P1 

Ann Keeley and Susie Norton are partners in a business they started two years ago. The partnership agreement states that Keeley should receive a salary allowance of $40,000 and that Norton should receive a $30,000 salary allowance. Any remaining income or loss is to be shared equally. Determine each partner's share of the current year's net income of $210,000.

QS 12-3
Partnership income allocation
P2

Jake and Ness are partners who agree that Jake will receive a $60,000 salary allowance and that any remaining income or loss will be shared equally. If Ness's capital account is credited for $1,000 as his share of the net income in a given period, how much net income did the partnership earn in that period?

QS 12-4
Partnership income allocation
P2 

Jones and Bordan are partners, each with $30,000 in their partnership capital accounts. Holly is admitted to the partnership by investing $30,000 cash. Make the entry to show Holly's admission to the partnership.

QS 12-5
Admission of a partner
P3

Mintz agrees to pay Bogg and Heyer $10,000 each for a one-third (33⅓%) interest in the Bogg and Heyer partnership. Immediately prior to Mintz's admission, each partner had a $30,000 capital balance. Make the journal entry to record Mintz's purchase of the partners' interest.

QS 12-6
Partner admission through purchase of interest
P3

The Red, White & Blue partnership was begun with investments by the partners as follows: Red, $175,000; White, $220,000; and Blue, $205,000. The operations did not go well, and the partners eventually decided to liquidate the partnership, sharing all losses equally. On August 31, after all assets were converted to cash and all creditors were paid, only $60,000 in partnership cash remained.

1. Compute the capital account balance of each partner after the liquidation of assets and the payment of creditors.
2. Assume that any partner with a deficit agrees to pay cash to the partnership to cover the deficit. Present the journal entries on August 31 to record (*a*) the cash receipt from the deficient partner(s) and (*b*) the final disbursement of cash to the partners.
3. Assume that any partner with a deficit is not able to reimburse the partnership. Present journal entries (*a*) to transfer the deficit of any deficient partners to the other partners and (*b*) to record the final disbursement of cash to the partners.

QS 12-7
Liquidation of partnership
P4

Check (1) Red, $(5,000)

Gilson and Lott's company is organized as a partnership. At the prior year-end, partnership equity totaled $300,000 ($200,000 from Gilson and $100,000 from Lott). For the current year, partnership net income is $50,000 ($40,000 allocated to Gilson and $10,000 allocated to Lott), and year-end total partnership equity is $400,000 ($280,000 from Gilson and $120,000 from Lott). Compute the total partnership return on equity *and* the individual partner return on equity ratios.

QS 12-8
Partner return on equity
A1 

EXERCISES

Exercise 12-1
Forms of organization
C1  

For each of the following separate cases, recommend a form of business organization. With each recommendation, explain how business income would be taxed if the owners adopt the form of organization recommended. Also list several advantages that the owners will enjoy from the form of business organization that you recommend.

a. Milan has been out of school for about six years and has become quite knowledgeable about the residential real estate market. He would like to organize a company that buys and sells real estate. Milan believes he has the expertise to manage the company but needs funds to invest in residential property.

b. Dr. Langholz and Dr. Clark are recent graduates from medical residency programs. Both are family practice physicians and would like to open a clinic in an underserved rural area. Although neither has any funds to bring to the new venture, an investor has expressed interest in making a loan to provide start-up funds for their practice.

c. Ross, Jenks and Keim are recent college graduates in computer science. They want to start a Website development company. They all have college debts and currently do not own any substantial computer equipment needed to get the company started.

Exercise 12-2
Characteristics of partnerships
C1

Next to the following list of eight characteristics of business organizations, enter a brief description of how each characteristic applies to general partnerships.

Characteristic	Application to General Partnerships
1. Ease of formation	
2. Transferability of ownership	
3. Ability to raise large amounts of capital	
4. Life	
5. Owners' liability	
6. Legal status	
7. Tax status of income	
8. Owners' authority	

Exercise 12-3
Journalizing partnership formation
P2

Anita Kroll and Aaron Rogers organize a partnership on January 1. Kroll's initial net investment is $60,000, consisting of cash ($14,000), equipment ($66,000), and a note payable reflecting a bank loan for the new business ($20,000). Rogers's initial investment is cash of $25,000. These amounts are the values agreed on by both partners. Prepare journal entries to record (1) Kroll's investment and (2) Rogers's investment.

Exercise 12-4
Journalizing partnership transactions
P2

On March 1, 2011, Abbey and Dames formed a partnership. Abbey contributed $88,000 cash and Dames contributed land valued at $70,000 and a building valued at $100,000. The partnership also assumed responsibility for Dames's $80,000 long-term note payable associated with the land and building. The partners agreed to share income as follows: Abbey is to receive an annual salary allowance of $30,000, both are to receive an annual interest allowance of 10% of their beginning-year capital investment, and any remaining income or loss is to be shared equally. On October 20, 2011, Abbey withdrew $32,000 cash and Dames withdrew $25,000 cash. After the adjusting and closing entries are made to the revenue and expense accounts at December 31, 2011, the Income Summary account had a credit balance of $79,000.

1. Prepare journal entries to record (*a*) the partners' initial capital investments, (*b*) their cash withdrawals, and (*c*) the December 31 closing of both the Withdrawals and Income Summary accounts.

2. Determine the balances of the partners' capital accounts as of December 31, 2011.

Check (2) Dames, $89,600

Exercise 12-5
Income allocation in a partnership
P2

Cosmo and Ellis began a partnership by investing $50,000 and $75,000, respectively. During its first year, the partnership earned $165,000. Prepare calculations showing how the $165,000 income should be allocated to the partners under each of the following three separate plans for sharing income and loss: (1) the partners failed to agree on a method to share income; (2) the partners agreed to share income and loss in proportion to their initial investments (round amounts to the nearest dollar); and (3) the partners agreed to share income by granting a $55,000 per year salary allowance to Cosmo, a $45,000 per year salary allowance to Ellis, 10% interest on their initial capital investments, and the remaining balance shared equally.

Check Plan 3, Cosmo, $86,250

Exercise 12-6
Income allocation in a partnership
P2

Assume that the partners of Exercise 12-5 agreed to share net income and loss by granting annual salary allowances of $55,000 to Cosmo and $45,000 to Ellis, 10% interest allowances on their investments, and any remaining balance shared equally.

1. Determine the partners' shares of Cosmo and Ellis given a first-year net income of $94,400.
2. Determine the partners' shares of Cosmo and Ellis given a first-year net loss of $15,700.

Check (2) Cosmo, $(4,100)

Exercise 12-7
Sale of partnership interest
P3

The partners in the Biz Partnership have agreed that partner Mona may sell her $90,000 equity in the partnership to Seal, for which Seal will pay Mona $75,000. Present the partnership's journal entry to record the sale of Mona's interest to Seal on September 30.

Exercise 12-8
Admission of new partner
P3

The Treed Partnership has total partners' equity of $510,000, which is made up of Elm, Capital, $400,000, and Oak, Capital, $110,000. The partners share net income and loss in a ratio of 80% to Elm and 20% to Oak. On November 1, Ash is admitted to the partnership and given a 15% interest in equity and a 15% share in any income and loss. Prepare the journal entry to record the admission of Ash under each of the following separate assumptions: Ash invests cash of (1) $90,000; (2) $125,000; and (3) $60,000.

Exercise 12-9
Retirement of partner
P3

Holland, Flowers, and Tulip have been partners while sharing net income and loss in a 5:3:2 ratio. On January 31, the date Tulip retires from the partnership, the equities of the partners are Holland, $350,000; Flowers, $240,000; and Tulip, $180,000. Present journal entries to record Tulip's retirement under each of the following separate assumptions: Tulip is paid for her equity using partnership cash of (1) $180,000; (2) $200,000; and (3) $150,000.

Exercise 12-10
Liquidation of partnership
P4

Tuttle, Ritter, and Lee are partners who share income and loss in a 1:4:5 ratio. After lengthy disagreements among the partners and several unprofitable periods, the partners decide to liquidate the partnership. Immediately before liquidation, the partnership balance sheet shows total assets, $116,000; total liabilities, $88,000; Tuttle, Capital, $1,200; Ritter, Capital, $11,700; and Lee, Capital, $15,100. The cash proceeds from selling the assets were sufficient to repay all but $24,000 to the creditors. (*a*) Calculate the loss from selling the assets. (*b*) Allocate the loss to the partners. (*c*) Determine how much of the remaining liability should be paid by each partner.

Check (b) Lee, Capital after allocation, $(10,900)

Exercise 12-11
Liquidation of limited partnership
P4

Assume that the Tuttle, Ritter, and Lee partnership of Exercise 12-10 is a limited partnership. Tuttle and Ritter are general partners and Lee is a limited partner. How much of the remaining $24,000 liability should be paid by each partner? (Round amounts to the nearest dollar.)

Exercise 12-12
Partner return on equity
A1 

Hunt Sports Enterprises LP is organized as a limited partnership consisting of two individual partners: Soccer LP and Football LP. Both partners separately operate a minor league soccer team and a semipro football team. Compute partner return on equity for each limited partnership (and the total) for the year ended June 30, 2011, using the following selected data on partner capital balances from Hunt Sports Enterprises LP.

	Soccer LP	Football LP	Total
Balance at 6/30/2010	$378,000	$1,516,000	$1,894,000
Annual net income	44,268	891,796	936,064
Cash distribution	—	(100,000)	(100,000)
Balance at 6/30/2011	$422,268	$2,307,796	$2,730,064

PROBLEM SET A

Problem 12-1A
Allocating partnership income
P2

Check (3) Thomas, Capital, $48,900

Kim Ries, Tere Bax, and Josh Thomas invested $40,000, $56,000, and $64,000, respectively, in a partnership. During its first calendar year, the firm earned $124,500.

Required

Prepare the entry to close the firm's Income Summary account as of its December 31 year-end and to allocate the $124,500 net income to the partners under each of the following separate assumptions: The partners (1) have no agreement on the method of sharing income and loss; (2) agreed to share income and loss in the ratio of their beginning capital investments; and (3) agreed to share income and loss by providing annual salary allowances of $33,000 to Ries, $28,000 to Bax, and $40,000 to Thomas; granting 10% interest on the partners' beginning capital investments; and sharing the remainder equally.

Problem 12-2A
Allocating partnership income and loss; sequential years
P2

mhhe.com/wildFAP20e

Rex Baker and Ty Farney are forming a partnership to which Baker will devote one-half time and Farney will devote full time. They have discussed the following alternative plans for sharing income and loss: (*a*) in the ratio of their initial capital investments, which they have agreed will be $21,000 for Baker and $31,500 for Farney; (*b*) in proportion to the time devoted to the business; (*c*) a salary allowance of $3,000 per month to Farney and the balance in accordance with the ratio of their initial capital investments; or (*d*) a salary allowance of $3,000 per month to Farney, 10% interest on their initial capital investments, and the balance shared equally. The partners expect the business to perform as follows: year 1, $18,000 net loss; year 2, $45,000 net income; and year 3, $75,000 net income.

Required

Prepare three tables with the following column headings.

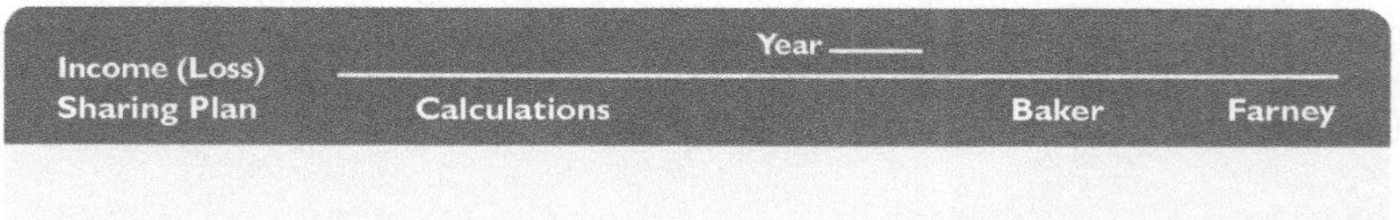

Income (Loss) Sharing Plan	Year ____ Calculations	Baker	Farney

Check Plan d, year 1, Farney's share, $9,525

Complete the tables, one for each of the first three years, by showing how to allocate partnership income or loss to the partners under each of the four plans being considered. (Round answers to the nearest whole dollar.)

Problem 12-3A
Partnership income allocation, statement of partners' equity, and closing entries
P2

mhhe.com/wildFAP20e

Will Beck, Ron Beck, and Barb Beck formed the BBB Partnership by making capital contributions of $183,750, $131,250, and $210,000, respectively. They predict annual partnership net income of $225,000 and are considering the following alternative plans of sharing income and loss: (*a*) equally; (*b*) in the ratio of their initial capital investments; or (*c*) salary allowances of $40,000 to Will, $30,000 to Ron, and $45,000 to Barb; interest allowances of 10% on their initial capital investments; and the balance shared equally.

Required

1. Prepare a table with the following column headings.

Income (Loss) Sharing Plan	Calculations	Will	Ron	Barb	Total

Use the table to show how to distribute net income of $225,000 for the calendar year under each of the alternative plans being considered. (Round answers to the nearest whole dollar.)

Check (2) Barb, Ending Capital, $223,000

2. Prepare a statement of partners' equity showing the allocation of income to the partners assuming they agree to use plan (*c*), that income earned is $104,500, and that Will, Ron, and Barb withdraw $17,000, $24,000, and $32,000, respectively, at year-end.
3. Prepare the December 31 journal entry to close Income Summary assuming they agree to use plan (*c*) and that net income is $104,500. Also close the withdrawals accounts.

Problem 12-4A
Partner withdrawal and admission
P3

Part 1. Goering, Zarcus, and Schmit are partners and share income and loss in a 3:2:5 ratio. The partnership's capital balances are as follows: Goering, $84,000; Zarcus, $69,000; and Schmit, $147,000. Zarcus decides to withdraw from the partnership, and the partners agree to not have the assets revalued upon Zarcus's retirement. Prepare journal entries to record Zarcus's February 1 withdrawal from the partnership under each of the following separate assumptions: Zarcus (*a*) sells her interest to Getz for $80,000 after Goering and Schmit approve the entry of Getz as a partner; (*b*) gives her interest to a son-in-law, Swanson, and thereafter Goering and Schmit accept Swanson as a partner; (*c*) is paid $69,000 in partnership cash for her equity; (*d*) is paid $107,000 in partnership cash for her equity; and (*e*) is paid $15,000 in partnership cash plus equipment recorded on the partnership books at $35,000 less its accumulated depreciation of $11,600.

Check (1*e*) Cr. Schmit, Capital, $19,125

Part 2. Assume that Zarcus does not retire from the partnership described in Part 1. Instead, Ford is admitted to the partnership on February 1 with a 25% equity. Prepare journal entries to record Ford's entry into the partnership under each of the following separate assumptions: Ford invests (*a*) $100,000; (*b*) $74,000; and (*c*) $131,000.

(2*c*) Cr. Zarcus, Capital, $4,650

Problem 12-5A
Liquidation of a partnership
P4

Quick, Drake, and Sage share income and loss in a 3:2:1 ratio. The partners have decided to liquidate their partnership. On the day of liquidation their balance sheet appears as follows.

QUICK, DRAKE, AND SAGE
Balance Sheet
May 31

Assets		**Liabilities and Equity**	
Cash	$ 90,400	Accounts payable	$122,750
Inventory	268,600	Quick, Capital	46,500
		Drake, Capital	106,250
		Sage, Capital	83,500
Total assets	$359,000	Total liabilities and equity	$359,000

Required

Prepare journal entries for (*a*) the sale of inventory, (*b*) the allocation of its gain or loss, (*c*) the payment of liabilities at book value, and (*d*) the distribution of cash in each of the following separate cases: Inventory is sold for (1) $300,000; (2) $250,000; (3) $160,000 and any partners with capital deficits pay in the amount of their deficits; and (4) $125,000 and the partners have no assets other than those invested in the partnership. (Round to the nearest dollar.)

Check (4) Cash distribution: Sage, $51,134

PROBLEM SET B

Problem 12-1B
Allocating partnership income
P2

Matt Albin, Ryan Peters and Seth Ramsey invested $82,000, $49,200 and $32,800, respectively, in a partnership. During its first calendar year, the firm earned $135,000.

Required

Prepare the entry to close the firm's Income Summary account as of its December 31 year-end and to allocate the $135,000 net income to the partners under each of the following separate assumptions. (Round answers to whole dollars.) The partners (1) have no agreement on the method of sharing income and loss; (2) agreed to share income and loss in the ratio of their beginning capital investments; and (3) agreed to share income and loss by providing annual salary allowances of $48,000 to Albin, $36,000 to Peters, and $25,000 to Ramsey; granting 10% interest on the partners' beginning capital investments; and sharing the remainder equally.

Check (3) Ramsey, Capital, $31,480

Problem 12-2B
Allocating partnership income and loss; sequential years
P2

Maria Karto and J.R. Black are forming a partnership to which Karto will devote one-third time and Black will devote full time. They have discussed the following alternative plans for sharing income and loss: (*a*) in the ratio of their initial capital investments, which they have agreed will be $52,000 for Karto and $78,000 for Black; (*b*) in proportion to the time devoted to the business; (*c*) a salary allowance of $2,000 per month to Black and the balance in accordance with the ratio of their initial capital investments; or (*d*) a salary allowance of $2,000 per month to Black, 10% interest on their initial capital investments, and the balance shared equally. The partners expect the business to perform as follows: year 1, $18,000 net loss; year 2, $38,000 net income; and year 3, $94,000 net income.

Required

Prepare three tables with the following column headings.

Income (Loss) Sharing Plan	Year ____ Calculations	Karto	Black

Check Plan d, year 1, Black's share, $4,300

Complete the tables, one for each of the first three years, by showing how to allocate partnership income or loss to the partners under each of the four plans being considered. (Round answers to the nearest whole dollar.)

Problem 12-3B
Partnership income allocation, statement of partners' equity, and closing entries
P2

Staci Cook, Lin Xi, and Kevin Schwartz formed the CXS Partnership by making capital contributions of $72,000, $108,000, and $60,000, respectively. They predict annual partnership net income of $120,000 and are considering the following alternative plans of sharing income and loss: (*a*) equally; (*b*) in the ratio of their initial capital investments; or (*c*) salary allowances of $20,000 to Cook, $15,000 to Xi, and $40,000 to Schwartz; interest allowances of 12% on their initial capital investments; and the balance shared equally.

Required

1. Prepare a table with the following column headings.

Income (Loss) Sharing Plan	Calculations	Cook	Xi	Schwartz	Total

Use the table to show how to distribute net income of $120,000 for the calendar year under each of the alternative plans being considered. (Round answers to the nearest whole dollar.)

Check (2) Schwartz, Ending Capital, $75,200

2. Prepare a statement of partners' equity showing the allocation of income to the partners assuming they agree to use plan (*c*), that income earned is $43,800, and that Cook, Xi, and Schwartz withdraw $9,000, $19,000, and $12,000, respectively, at year-end.

3. Prepare the December 31 journal entry to close Income Summary assuming they agree to use plan (*c*) and that net income is $43,800. Also close the withdrawals accounts.

Problem 12-4B
Partner withdrawal and admission
P3

Part 1. Gibbs, Mier, and Hill are partners and share income and loss in a 5:1:4 ratio. The partnership's capital balances are as follows: Gibbs, $303,000; Mier, $74,000; and Hill, $223,000. Gibbs decides to withdraw from the partnership, and the partners agree not to have the assets revalued upon Gibbs's retirement. Prepare journal entries to record Gibbs's April 30 withdrawal from the partnership under each of the following separate assumptions: Gibbs (*a*) sells her interest to Brady for $250,000 after Mier and Hill approve the entry of Brady as a partner; (*b*) gives her interest to a daughter-in-law, Cannon, and thereafter Mier and Hill accept Cannon as a partner; (*c*) is paid $303,000 in partnership cash for her equity; (*d*) is paid $175,000 in partnership cash for her equity; and (*e*) is paid $100,000 in partnership cash plus manufacturing equipment recorded on the partnership books at $269,000 less its accumulated depreciation of $168,000.

Check (1*e*) Cr. Hill, Capital, $81,600

Part 2. Assume that Gibbs does not retire from the partnership described in Part 1. Instead, Brise is admitted to the partnership on April 30 with a 20% equity. Prepare journal entries to record the entry of Brise under each of the following separate assumptions: Brise invests (*a*) $150,000; (*b*) $98,000; and (*c*) $213,000.

Check (2*c*) Cr. Mier, Capital, $5,040

Problem 12-5B
Liquidation of a partnership
P4

Asure, Ramirez, and Soney, who share income and loss in a 2:1:2 ratio, plan to liquidate their partnership. At liquidation, their balance sheet appears as follows.

ASURE, RAMIREZ, AND SONEY Balance Sheet January 18			
Assets		**Liabilities and Equity**	
Cash	$174,300	Accounts payable	$171,300
Equipment	308,600	Asure, Capital	150,200
		Ramirez, Capital	97,900
		Soney, Capital	63,500
Total assets	$482,900	Total liabilities and equity	$482,900

Required

Prepare journal entries for (*a*) the sale of equipment, (*b*) the allocation of its gain or loss, (*c*) the payment of liabilities at book value, and (*d*) the distribution of cash in each of the following separate cases: Equipment is sold for (1) $325,000; (2) $265,000; (3) $100,000 and any partners with capital deficits pay in the amount of their deficits; and (4) $75,000 and the partners have no assets other than those invested in the partnership. (Round amounts to the nearest dollar.)

Check (4) Cash distribution: Asure, $36,800

SERIAL PROBLEM
Business Solutions
P3

(This serial problem began in Chapter 1 and continues through most of the book. If previous chapter segments were not completed, the serial problem can begin at this point. It is helpful, but not necessary, to use the Working Papers that accompany the book.)

SP 12 At the start of 2012, Santana Rey is considering adding a partner to her business. She envisions the new partner taking the lead in generating sales of both services and merchandise for Business Solutions. S. Rey's equity in Business Solutions as of January 1, 2012, is reflected in the following capital balance.

S. Rey, Capital	$80,360

Required

1. S. Rey is evaluating whether the prospective partner should be an equal partner with respect to capital investment and profit sharing (1:1) or whether the agreement should be 4:1 with Rey retaining four-fifths interest with rights to four-fifths of the net income or loss. What factors should she consider in deciding which partnership agreement to offer?
2. Prepare the January 1, 2012, journal entry(ies) necessary to admit a new partner to Business Solutions through the purchase of a partnership interest for each of the following two separate cases: (*a*) 1:1 sharing agreement and (*b*) 4:1 sharing agreement.
3. Prepare the January 1, 2012, journal entry(ies) required to admit a new partner if the new partner invests cash of $20,090.
4. After posting the entry in part 3, what would be the new partner's equity percentage?

Beyond the Numbers

REPORTING IN ACTION
C1 
RIM

BTN 12-1 Take a step back in time and imagine Research In Motion in its infancy as a company. The year is 1984.

Required

1. Read the history of Research In Motion at www.RIM.com. Identify the two partners that founded the company.
2. Assume that Research In Motion was originally organized as a partnership. RIM's income statement in Appendix A varies in several key ways from what it would look like for a partnership. Identify at least two ways in which a corporate income statement differs from a partnership income statement.
3. Compare the Research In Motion balance sheet in Appendix A to what a partnership balance sheet would have shown. Identify and explain any account differences we would anticipate.

COMPARATIVE ANALYSIS

C1

RIM

Apple

BTN 12-2 Over the years Research In Motion and Apple have evolved into large corporations. Today it is difficult to imagine them as fledgling start-ups. Research each company's history online.

Required

1. Which company is older?
2. In what years did each company first achieve $1,000,000,000 in sales?
3. In what years did each company have its first public offering of stock?

ETHICS CHALLENGE

P2  

BTN 12-3 Doctors Maben, Orlando, and Clark have been in a group practice for several years. Maben and Orlando are family practice physicians, and Clark is a general surgeon. Clark receives many referrals for surgery from his family practice partners. Upon the partnership's original formation, the three doctors agreed to a two-part formula to share income. Every month each doctor receives a salary allowance of $3,000. Additional income is divided according to a percent of patient charges the doctors generate for the month. In the current month, Maben generated 10% of the billings, Orlando 30%, and Clark 60%. The group's income for this month is $50,000. Clark has expressed dissatisfaction with the income-sharing formula and asks that income be split entirely on patient charge percents.

Required

1. Compute the income allocation for the current month using the original agreement.
2. Compute the income allocation for the current month using Clark's proposed agreement.
3. Identify the ethical components of this partnership decision for the doctors.

COMMUNICATING IN PRACTICE

C1

BTN 12-4 Assume that you are studying for an upcoming accounting exam with a good friend. Your friend says that she has a solid understanding of general partnerships but is less sure that she understands organizations that combine certain characteristics of partnerships with other forms of business organization. You offer to make some study notes for your friend to help her learn about limited partnerships, limited liability partnerships, S corporations, and limited liability companies. Prepare a one-page set of well-organized, complete study notes on these four forms of business organization.

TAKING IT TO THE NET

P1 P2 

BTN 12-5 Access the March 29, 2010, filing of the December 31, 2009, 10-K of America First Tax Exempt Investors LP. This company deals with tax-exempt mortgage revenue bonds that, among other things, finance student housing properties.

1. Locate its December 31, 2009, balance sheet and list the account titles reported in the equity section of the balance sheet.
2. Locate its statement of partners' capital and comprehensive income (loss). How many units of limited partnership (known as "beneficial unit certificate holders") are outstanding at December 31, 2009?
3. What is the partnership's largest asset and its amount at December 31, 2009?

TEAMWORK IN ACTION

P2

BTN 12-6 This activity requires teamwork to reinforce understanding of accounting for partnerships.

Required

1. Assume that Baker, Warner, and Rice form the BWR Partnership by making capital contributions of $200,000, $300,000, and $500,000, respectively. BWR predicts annual partnership net income of $600,000. The partners are considering various plans for sharing income and loss. Assign a different team member to compute how the projected $600,000 income would be shared under each of the following separate plans:
   a. Shared equally.
   b. In the ratio of the partners' initial capital investments.
   c. Salary allowances of $50,000 to Baker, $60,000 to Warner, and $70,000 to Rice, with the remaining balance shared equally.
   d. Interest allowances of 10% on the partners' initial capital investments, with the remaining balance shared equally.

2. In sequence, each member is to present his or her income-sharing calculations with the team.
3. As a team, identify and discuss at least one other possible way that income could be shared.

ENTREPRENEURIAL DECISION

C1 

BTN 12-7 Recall the chapter's opening feature involving Chance Claxton and Lynn Julian, and their company, Kids Konserve. Assume that Chance and Lynn, partners in Kids Konserve, decide to expand their business with the help of general partners.

Required

1. What details should Chance, Lynn, and their future partners specify in the general partnership agreements?
2. What advantages should Chance, Lynn, and their future partners be aware of with respect to organizing as a general partnership?
3. What disadvantages should Chance, Lynn, and their future partners be aware of with respect to organizing as a general partnership?

GLOBAL DECISION

C1 

NOKIA

BTN 12-8 Access Nokia's Website (www.Nokia.com) and research the company's history.

1. When was the company founded?
2. What three companies merged to create Nokia Corporation?
3. What are some of the companies that are part of Nokia?

ANSWERS TO MULTIPLE CHOICE QUIZ

1. e; Capital = $250,000 − $50,000
2. a; $90,000 × [$100,000/($150,000 + $150,000 + $100,000)] = $22,500
3. d;

	Jamison	Blue	Total
Net income			$ 270,000
Salary allowance	$120,000		(120,000)
Interest allowance	60,000	$80,000	(140,000)
Balance of income			10,000
Balance divided equally	5,000	5,000	(10,000)
Totals	$185,000	$85,000	$ 0

4. b; Total partnership equity = $125,000 + $124,000 + $75,000 = $324,000
   Equity of Black = $324,000 × 20% = $64,800
   Bonus to old partners = $75,000 − $64,800 = $10,200, split equally
5. a; $10,500/[($110,000 + $124,000)/2] = 8.97%

13 Accounting for Corporations

A Look Back

Chapter 12 focused on the partnership form of organization. We described crucial characteristics of partnerships and the accounting and reporting of their important transactions.

A Look at This Chapter

This chapter emphasizes details of the corporate form of organization. The accounting concepts and procedures for equity transactions are explained. We also describe how to report and analyze income, earnings per share, and retained earnings.

A Look Ahead

Chapter 14 focuses on long-term liabilities. We explain how to value, record, amortize, and report these liabilities in financial statements.

Learning Objectives

CAP

CONCEPTUAL

C1 Identify characteristics of corporations and their organization. (p. 508)

C2 Explain characteristics of, and distribute dividends between, common and preferred stock. (p. 519)

C3 Explain the items reported in retained earnings. (p. 524)

ANALYTICAL

A1 Compute earnings per share and describe its use. (p. 527)

A2 Compute price-earnings ratio and describe its use in analysis. (p. 527)

A3 Compute dividend yield and explain its use in analysis. (p. 528)

A4 Compute book value and explain its use in analysis. (p. 528)

LP13

PROCEDURAL

P1 Record the issuance of corporate stock. (p. 512)

P2 Record transactions involving cash dividends, stock dividends, and stock splits. (p. 515)

P3 Record purchases and sales of treasury stock and the retirement of stock. (p. 522)

Decision Insight

Greener Lawns

"Every part of our business is . . . profitable"
—KELLY GIARD

FORT COLLINS, CO—According to the U.S. Environmental Protection Agency, a gas-powered lawn mower produces as much air pollution as 43 new cars each driven 12,000 miles. "At least 5 percent of pollution is caused by gas-powered maintenance equipment," explains Kelly Giard, owner of **Clean Air Lawn Care (CleanAirLawnCare.com).** "This is one of the last dirty frontiers in America that can be easily solved."

Kelly launched his business four years ago, which is a full-service sustainable lawn care company dedicated to using clean electrical and biodiesel powered equipment. His equipment is charged by solar panels during the day and by wind power overnight. "I started [it] out of my garage mostly for fun," says Kelly. "And business took off."

Kelly explains that his success would not have been possible without equity financing and knowledge of business operations. To make it happen, says Kelly, he studied corporate formation, equity issuance, stock types, retaining earnings, and dividend policies. After that analysis, Kelly set up Clean Air Lawn Care as a corporation, which had several benefits given his business goals and strategies. With his corporate structure in place, Kelly was ready to attack the market. "Only about 1% of the country uses an electrical mower," says Kelly. "That's awful, and that's something we're committed to changing."

The success of Kelly's corporate structure and his equity financing brings both opportunities and challenges. The positive is being part of the green movement, yielding "a ripple effect where there's profit, happy customers and an environmental benefit." The challenge is effectively using accounting for equity as a tool to achieve those objectives. That includes his knowledge of corporate formation, stock types, and equity transactions. "This is critical to us doing well in the long term," explains Kelly. Still, the focus remains on the environment. "We want [consumers] to have a choice when they hire a service: sustainable vs. dirty."

[Sources: *Clean Air Lawn Care Website,* January 2011; *Entrepreneur,* January 2010; *Lawn & Landscape,* April 2010; *Charles & Hudson Website,* 2010]

Chapter Preview

This chapter focuses on equity transactions. The first part of the chapter describes the basics of the corporate form of organization and explains the accounting for common and preferred stock. We then focus on several special financing transactions, including cash and stock dividends, stock splits, and treasury stock. The final section considers accounting for retained earnings, including prior period adjustments, retained earnings restrictions, and reporting guidelines.

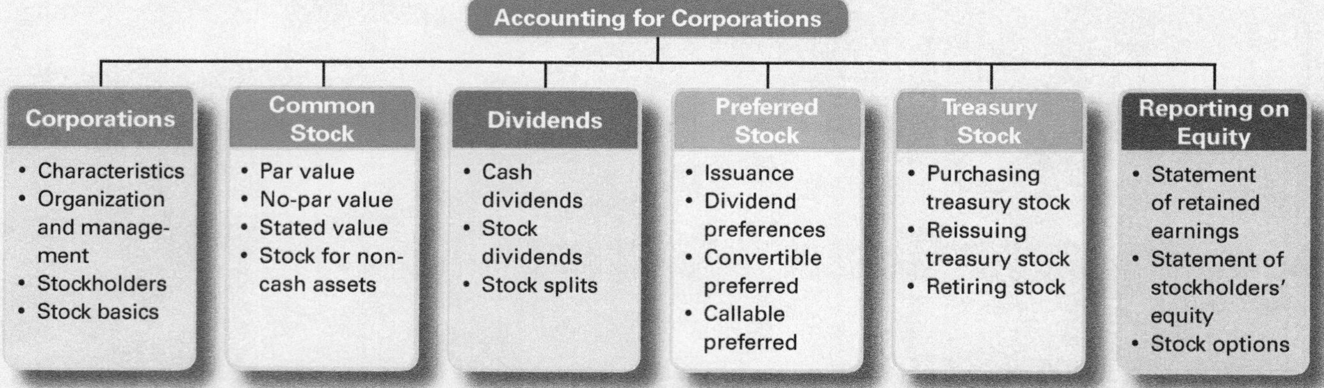

CORPORATE FORM OF ORGANIZATION

C1 Identify characteristics of corporations and their organization.

A **corporation** is an entity created by law that is separate from its owners. It has most of the rights and privileges granted to individuals. Owners of corporations are called *stockholders* or *shareholders.* Corporations can be separated into two types. A *privately held* (or *closely held*) corporation does not offer its stock for public sale and usually has few stockholders. A *publicly held* corporation offers its stock for public sale and can have thousands of stockholders. *Public sale* usually refers to issuance and trading on an organized stock market.

Characteristics of Corporations

Corporations represent an important type of organization. Their unique characteristics offer advantages and disadvantages.

Advantages of Corporate Characteristics

- **Separate legal entity:** A corporation conducts its affairs with the same rights, duties, and responsibilities of a person. It takes actions through its agents, who are its officers and managers.
- **Limited liability of stockholders:** Stockholders are liable for neither corporate acts nor corporate debt.
- **Transferable ownership rights:** The transfer of shares from one stockholder to another usually has no effect on the corporation or its operations except when this causes a change in the directors who control or manage the corporation.
- **Continuous life:** A corporation's life continues indefinitely because it is not tied to the physical lives of its owners.
- **Lack of mutual agency for stockholders:** A corporation acts through its agents, who are its officers and managers. Stockholders, who are not its officers and managers, do not have the power to bind the corporation to contracts—referred to as *lack of mutual agency.*
- **Ease of capital accumulation:** Buying stock is attractive to investors because (1) stockholders are not liable for the corporation's acts and debts, (2) stocks usually are transferred easily, (3) the life of the corporation is unlimited, and (4) stockholders are not corporate agents. These advantages enable corporations to accumulate large amounts of capital from the combined investments of many stockholders.

Point: The *business entity assumption* requires a corporation to be accounted for separately from its owners (shareholders).

Global: U.S., U.K., and Canadian corporations finance much of their operations with stock issuances, but companies in countries such as France, Germany, and Japan finance mainly with note and bond issuances.

Disadvantages of Corporate Characteristics

- **Government regulation:** A corporation must meet requirements of a state's incorporation laws, which subject the corporation to state regulation and control. Proprietorships and partnerships avoid many of these regulations and governmental reports.
- **Corporate taxation:** Corporations are subject to the same property and payroll taxes as proprietorships and partnerships plus *additional* taxes. The most burdensome of these are federal and state income taxes that together can take 40% or more of corporate pretax income. Moreover, corporate income is usually taxed a second time as part of stockholders' personal income when they receive cash distributed as dividends. This is called *double taxation.* (The usual dividend tax is 15%; however, it is less than 15% for lower income taxpayers, and in some cases zero.)

Point: Proprietorships and partnerships are not subject to income taxes. Their income is taxed as the personal income of their owners.

Point: Double taxation is less severe when a corporation's owner-manager collects a salary that is taxed only once as part of his or her personal income.

Decision Insight 

Stock Financing Marc Andreessen cofounded **Netscape** at age 22, only four months after earning his degree. One year later, he and friends issued Netscape shares to the public. The stock soared, making Andreessen a multimillionaire. ■

Corporate Organization and Management

This section describes the incorporation, costs, and management of corporate organizations.

Incorporation A corporation is created by obtaining a charter from a state government. A charter application usually must be signed by the prospective stockholders called *incorporators* or *promoters* and then filed with the proper state official. When the application process is complete and fees paid, the charter is issued and the corporation is formed. Investors then purchase the corporation's stock, meet as stockholders, and elect a board of directors. Directors oversee a corporation's affairs.

Point: A corporation is not required to have an office in its state of incorporation.

Organization Expenses **Organization expenses** (also called *organization costs*) are the costs to organize a corporation; they include legal fees, promoters' fees, and amounts paid to obtain a charter. The corporation records (debits) these costs to an expense account called *Organization Expenses.* Organization costs are expensed as incurred because it is difficult to determine the amount and timing of their future benefits.

Management of a Corporation The ultimate control of a corporation rests with stockholders who control a corporation by electing its *board of directors,* or simply, *directors.* Each stockholder usually has one vote for each share of stock owned. This control relation is shown in Exhibit 13.1. Directors are responsible for and have final authority for managing corporate activities. A board can act only as a collective body and usually limits its actions to setting general policy.

A corporation usually holds a stockholder meeting at least once a year to elect directors and transact business as its bylaws require. A group of stockholders owning or controlling votes of more than a 50% share of a corporation's stock can elect the board and control the corporation. Stockholders who do not attend stockholders' meetings must have an opportunity to delegate their voting rights to an agent by signing a **proxy,** a document that gives a designated agent the right to vote the stock.

EXHIBIT 13.1

Corporate Structure

Stockholders
Board of Directors
President, Vice President, and Other Officers
Employees of the Corporation

Day-to-day direction of corporate business is delegated to executive officers appointed by the board. A corporation's chief executive officer (CEO) is often its president. Several vice presidents, who report to the president, are commonly assigned specific areas of management responsibility such as finance, production, and marketing. One person often has the dual role

Point: *Bylaws* are guidelines that govern the behavior of individuals employed by and managing the corporation.

Global: Some corporate labels are:

Country	Label
United States	Inc.
France	SA
United Kingdom	
Public	PLC
Private	Ltd
Germany & Austria	
Public	AG
Private	GmbH
Sweden & Finland	AB
Italy	SpA
Netherlands	NV
Australia	AG
Mexico	SA
Bahamas	IBC

of chairperson of the board of directors and CEO. In this case, the president is usually designated the chief operating officer (COO).

Decision Insight

Seed Money Sources for start-up money include (1) "angel" investors such as family, friends, or anyone who believes in a company, (2) employees, investors, and even suppliers who can be paid with stock, and (3) venture capitalists (investors) who have a record of entrepreneurial success. See the National Venture Capital Association (NVCA.org) for information.

Stockholders of Corporations

This section explains stockholder rights, stock purchases and sales, and the role of registrar and transfer agents.

Rights of Stockholders When investors buy stock, they acquire all *specific* rights the corporation's charter grants to stockholders. They also acquire *general* rights granted stockholders by the laws of the state in which the company is incorporated. When a corporation has only one class of stock, it is identified as **common stock.** State laws vary, but common stockholders usually have the general right to

1. Vote at stockholders' meetings.
2. Sell or otherwise dispose of their stock.
3. Purchase their proportional share of any common stock later issued by the corporation. This **preemptive right** protects stockholders' proportionate interest in the corporation. For example, a stockholder who owns 25% of a corporation's common stock has the first opportunity to buy 25% of any new common stock issued.
4. Receive the same dividend, if any, on each common share of the corporation.
5. Share in any assets remaining after creditors and preferred stockholders are paid when, and if, the corporation is liquidated. Each common share receives the same amount.

Stockholders also have the right to receive timely financial reports.

Stock Certificates and Transfer Investors who buy a corporation's stock, sometimes receive a *stock certificate* as proof of share ownership. Many corporations issue only one certificate for each block of stock purchased. A certificate can be for any number of shares. Exhibit 13.2 shows a stock certificate of the Green Bay Packers. A certificate shows the company name, stockholder name, number of shares, and other crucial information. Issuance of certificates is becoming less common. Instead, many stockholders maintain accounts with the corporation or their stockbrokers and never receive actual certificates.

EXHIBIT 13.2

Stock Certificate

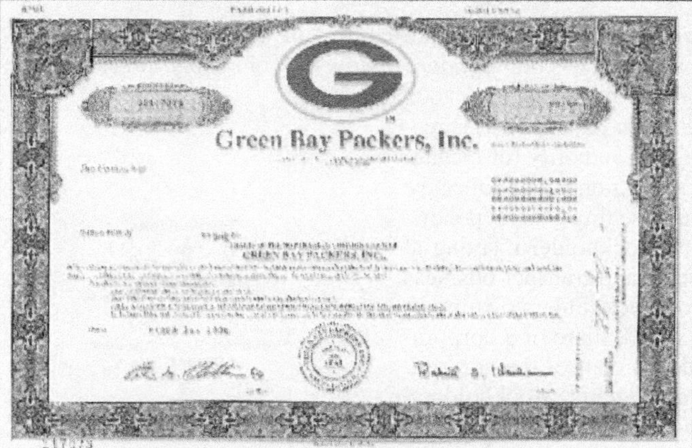

Registrar and Transfer Agents If a corporation's stock is traded on a major stock exchange, the corporation must have a registrar and a transfer agent. A *registrar* keeps stockholder records and prepares official lists of stockholders for stockholder meetings and dividend payments. A *transfer agent* assists with purchases and sales of shares by receiving and issuing certificates as necessary. Registrars and transfer agents are usually large banks or trust companies with computer facilities and staff to do this work.

Decision Insight

Pricing Stock A prospectus accompanies a stock's initial public offering (IPO), giving financial information about the company issuing the stock. A prospectus should help answer these questions to price an IPO: (1) Is the underwriter reliable? (2) Is there growth in revenues, profits, and cash flows? (3) What is management's view of operations? (4) Are current owners selling? (5) What are the risks?

Basics of Capital Stock

Capital stock is a general term that refers to any shares issued to obtain capital (owner financing). This section introduces terminology and accounting for capital stock.

Authorized Stock **Authorized stock** is the number of shares that a corporation's charter allows it to sell. The number of authorized shares usually exceeds the number of shares issued (and outstanding), often by a large amount. (*Outstanding stock* refers to issued stock held by stockholders.) No formal journal entry is required for stock authorization. A corporation must apply to the state for a change in its charter if it wishes to issue more shares than previously authorized. A corporation discloses the number of shares authorized in the equity section of its balance sheet or notes. Apple's balance sheet in Appendix A reports 1.8 billion common shares authorized as of the start of its 2010 fiscal year.

Subcategories of Authorized Stock

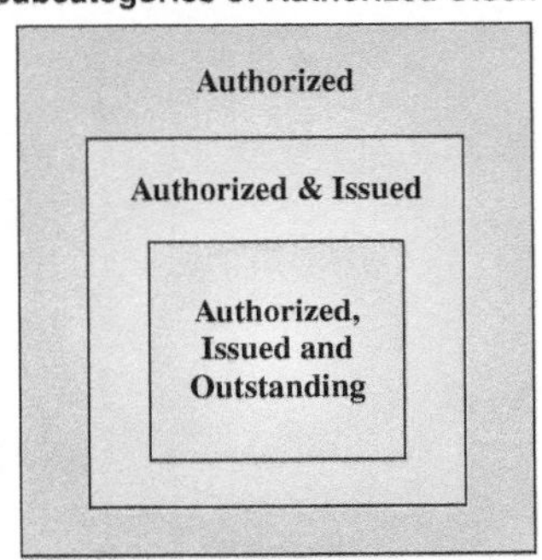

Selling (Issuing) Stock A corporation can sell stock directly or indirectly. To *sell directly,* it advertises its stock issuance to potential buyers. This type of issuance is most common with privately held corporations. To *sell indirectly,* a corporation pays a brokerage house (investment banker) to issue its stock. Some brokerage houses *underwrite* an indirect issuance of stock; that is, they buy the stock from the corporation and take all gains or losses from its resale.

Market Value of Stock **Market value per share** is the price at which a stock is bought and sold. Expected future earnings, dividends, growth, and other company and economic factors influence market value. Traded stocks' market values are available daily in newspapers such as *The Wall Street Journal* and online. The current market value of previously issued shares (for example, the price of stock in trades between investors) does not impact the issuing corporation's stockholders' equity.

Classes of Stock When all authorized shares have the same rights and characteristics, the stock is called *common stock.* A corporation is sometimes authorized to issue more than one class of stock, including preferred stock and different classes of common stock. American Greetings, for instance, has two types of common stock: Class A stock has 1 vote per share and Class B stock has 10 votes per share.

Par Value Stock **Par value stock** is stock that is assigned a **par value,** which is an amount assigned per share by the corporation in its charter. For example, Palm's common stock has a par value of $0.001. Other commonly assigned par values are $10, $5, $1 and $0.01. There is no restriction on the assigned par value. In many states, the par value of a stock establishes **minimum legal capital,** which refers to the least amount that the buyers of stock must contribute to the corporation or be subject to paying at a future date. For example, if a corporation issues 1,000 shares of $10 par value stock, the corporation's minimum legal capital in these states would be $10,000. Minimum legal capital is intended to protect a corporation's creditors. Since creditors cannot demand payment from stockholders' personal assets, their claims are limited to the corporation's assets and any minimum legal capital. At liquidation, creditor claims are paid before any amounts are distributed to stockholders.

Point: Managers are motivated to set a low par value when minimum legal capital or state issuance taxes are based on par value.

Point: Minimum legal capital was intended to protect creditors by requiring a minimum level of net assets.

No-Par Value Stock **No-par value stock,** or simply *no-par stock,* is stock *not* assigned a value per share by the corporate charter. Its advantage is that it can be issued at any price without the possibility of a minimum legal capital deficiency.

Point: Par, no-par, and stated value do *not* set the stock's market value.

EXHIBIT 13.3

Equity Composition

Corporation	
Common Stock — Normal bal.	Total Paid-In Capital
Paid-In Capital in Excess of Par — Normal bal.	
Retained Earnings — Normal bal.	

Point: Paid-in capital comes from stock-related transactions, whereas retained earnings comes from operations.

Stated Value Stock **Stated value stock** is no-par stock to which the directors assign a "stated" value per share. Stated value per share becomes the minimum legal capital per share in this case.

Stockholders' Equity A corporation's equity is known as **stockholders' equity,** also called *shareholders' equity* or *corporate capital.* Stockholders' equity consists of (1) paid-in (or contributed) capital and (2) retained earnings; see Exhibit 13.3. **Paid-in capital** is the total amount of cash and other assets the corporation receives from its stockholders in exchange for its stock. **Retained earnings** is the cumulative net income (and loss) not distributed as dividends to its stockholders.

Decision Insight

Stock Quote The **Best Buy** stock quote is interpreted as (left to right): **Hi,** highest price in past 52 weeks; **Lo,** lowest price in past 52 weeks; **Sym,** company exchange symbol; **Div,** dividends paid per share in past year; **Yld %,** dividend divided by closing price; **PE,** stock price per share divided by earnings per share; **Vol mil.,** number (in millions) of shares traded; **Hi,** highest price for the day; **Lo,** lowest price for the day; **Close,** closing price for the day; **Net Chg,** change in closing price from prior day. ■

52 Weeks				Yld		Vol				Net
Hi	Lo	Sym	Div	%	PE	mil.	Hi	Lo	Close	Chg
54.15	41.85	BBY	0.13	0.98	19	7.2	53.14	52.36	52.91	+0.20

Quick Check

Answers — p. 533

1. Which of the following is *not* a characteristic of the corporate form of business? (*a*) Ease of capital accumulation, (*b*) Stockholder responsibility for corporate debts, (*c*) Ease in transferability of ownership rights, or (*d*) Double taxation.
2. Why is a corporation's income said to be taxed twice?
3. What is a proxy?

COMMON STOCK

P1 Record the issuance of corporate stock.

Accounting for the issuance of common stock affects only paid-in (contributed) capital accounts; no retained earnings accounts are affected.

Issuing Par Value Stock

Par value stock can be issued at par, at a premium (above par), or at a discount (below par). In each case, stock can be exchanged for either cash or noncash assets.

Issuing Par Value Stock at Par When common stock is issued at par value, we record amounts for both the asset(s) received and the par value stock issued. To illustrate, the entry to record Dillon Snowboards' issuance of 30,000 shares of $10 par value stock for $300,000 cash on June 5, 2011, follows.

Assets = Liabilities + Equity
+300,000 +300,000

$10 par value × 30,000 shares

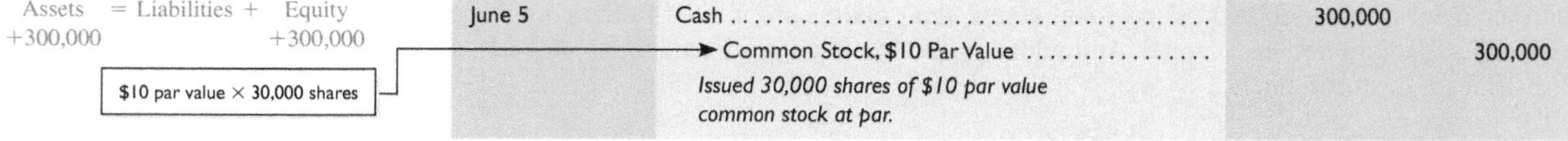

June 5	Cash	300,000	
	Common Stock, $10 Par Value		300,000
	Issued 30,000 shares of $10 par value common stock at par.		

Exhibit 13.4 shows the stockholders' equity of Dillon Snowboards at year-end 2011 (its first year of operations) after income of $65,000 and no dividend payments.

EXHIBIT 13.4

Stockholders' Equity for Stock Issued at Par

Stockholders' Equity	
Common Stock—$10 par value; 50,000 shares authorized; 30,000 shares issued and outstanding	$300,000
Retained earnings	65,000
Total stockholders' equity	$365,000

Issuing Par Value Stock at a Premium A **premium on stock** occurs when a corporation sells its stock for more than par (or stated) value. To illustrate, if Dillon Snowboards issues its $10 par value common stock at $12 per share, its stock is sold at a $2 per share premium. The premium, known as **paid-in capital in excess of par value,** is reported as part of equity; it is not revenue and is not listed on the income statement. The entry to record Dillon Snowboards' issuance of 30,000 shares of $10 par value stock for $12 per share on June 5, 2011, follows

Point: A *premium* is the amount by which issue price exceeds par (or stated) value. It is recorded in the "Paid-In Capital in Excess of Par Value, Common Stock" account; also called "Additional Paid-In Capital, Common Stock."

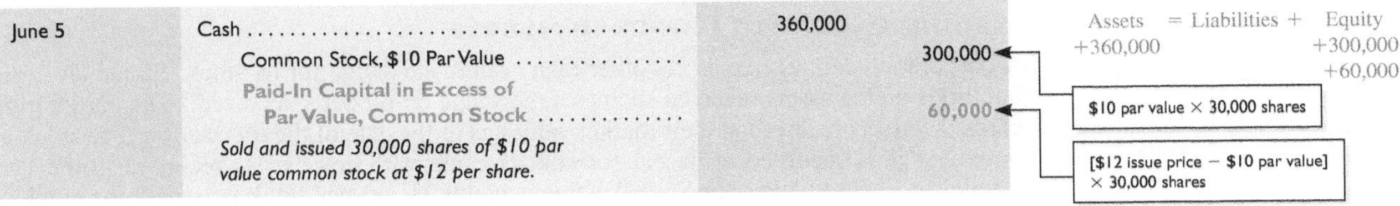

June 5	Cash	360,000	
	Common Stock, $10 Par Value		300,000
	Paid-In Capital in Excess of Par Value, Common Stock		60,000
	Sold and issued 30,000 shares of $10 par value common stock at $12 per share.		

The Paid-In Capital in Excess of Par Value account is added to the par value of the stock in the equity section of the balance sheet as shown in Exhibit 13.5.

Point: The *Paid-In Capital* terminology is interchangeable with *Contributed Capital.*

EXHIBIT 13.5

Stockholders' Equity for Stock Issued at a Premium

Stockholders' Equity	
Common Stock—$10 par value; 50,000 shares authorized; 30,000 shares issued and outstanding	$300,000
Paid-in capital in excess of par value, common stock	60,000
Retained earnings	65,000
Total stockholders' equity	$425,000

Issuing Par Value Stock at a Discount A **discount on stock** occurs when a corporation sells its stock for less than par (or stated) value. Most states prohibit the issuance of stock at a discount. In states that allow stock to be issued at a discount, its buyers usually become contingently liable to creditors for the discount. If stock is issued at a discount, the amount by which issue price is less than par is debited to a *Discount on Common Stock* account, a contra to the common stock account, and its balance is subtracted from the par value of stock in the equity section of the balance sheet. This discount is not an expense and does not appear on the income statement.

Point: Retained earnings can be negative, reflecting accumulated losses. Amazon.com had an accumulated deficit of $730 million at the start of 2009.

Issuing No-Par Value Stock

When no-par stock is issued and is not assigned a stated value, the amount the corporation receives becomes legal capital and is recorded as Common Stock. This means that the entire proceeds are credited to a no-par stock account. To illustrate, a corporation records its October 20 issuance of 1,000 shares of no-par stock for $40 cash per share as follows.

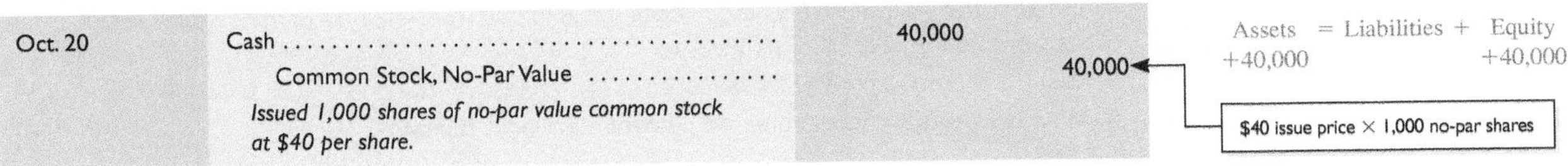

Oct. 20	Cash	40,000	
	Common Stock, No-Par Value		40,000
	Issued 1,000 shares of no-par value common stock at $40 per share.		

Frequency of Stock Types

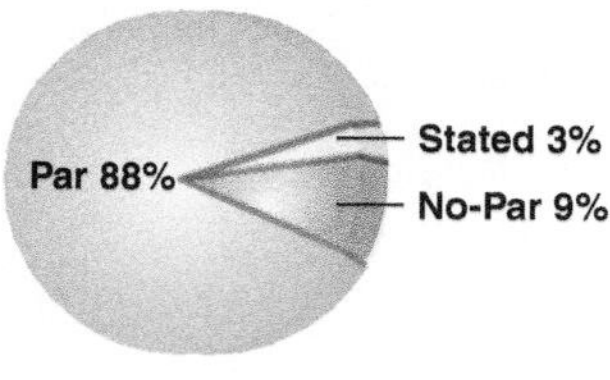

Issuing Stated Value Stock

When no-par stock is issued and assigned a stated value, its stated value becomes legal capital and is credited to a stated value stock account. Assuming that stated value stock is issued at an amount in excess of stated value (the usual case), the excess is credited to Paid-In Capital in Excess of Stated Value, Common Stock, which is reported in the stockholders' equity section. To illustrate, a corporation that issues 1,000 shares of no-par common stock having a stated value of $40 per share in return for $50 cash per share records this as follows.

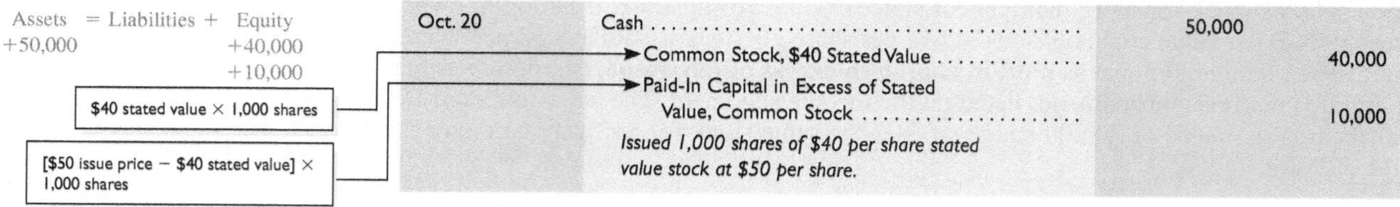

Assets	= Liabilities	+ Equity
+50,000		+40,000
		+10,000

Date	Account	Debit	Credit
Oct. 20	Cash	50,000	
	Common Stock, $40 Stated Value		40,000
	Paid-In Capital in Excess of Stated Value, Common Stock		10,000
	Issued 1,000 shares of $40 per share stated value stock at $50 per share.		

Issuing Stock for Noncash Assets

A corporation can receive assets other than cash in exchange for its stock. (It can also assume liabilities on the assets received such as a mortgage on property received.) The corporation records the assets received at their market values as of the date of the transaction. The stock given in exchange is recorded at its par (or stated) value with any excess recorded in the Paid-In Capital in Excess of Par (or Stated) Value account. (If no-par stock is issued, the stock is recorded at the assets' market value.) To illustrate, the entry to record receipt of land valued at $105,000 in return for issuance of 4,000 shares of $20 par value common stock on June 10 is

Point: Stock issued for noncash assets should be recorded at the market value of either the stock or the noncash asset, whichever is more clearly determinable.

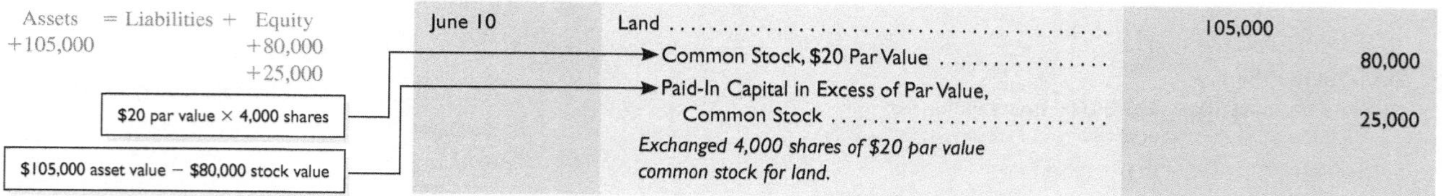

Assets	= Liabilities	+ Equity
+105,000		+80,000
		+25,000

Date	Account	Debit	Credit
June 10	Land	105,000	
	Common Stock, $20 Par Value		80,000
	Paid-In Capital in Excess of Par Value, Common Stock		25,000
	Exchanged 4,000 shares of $20 par value common stock for land.		

A corporation sometimes gives shares of its stock to promoters in exchange for their services in organizing the corporation, which the corporation records as **Organization Expenses.** The entry to record receipt of services valued at $12,000 in organizing the corporation in return for 600 shares of $15 par value common stock on June 5 is

Point: Any type of stock can be issued for noncash assets.

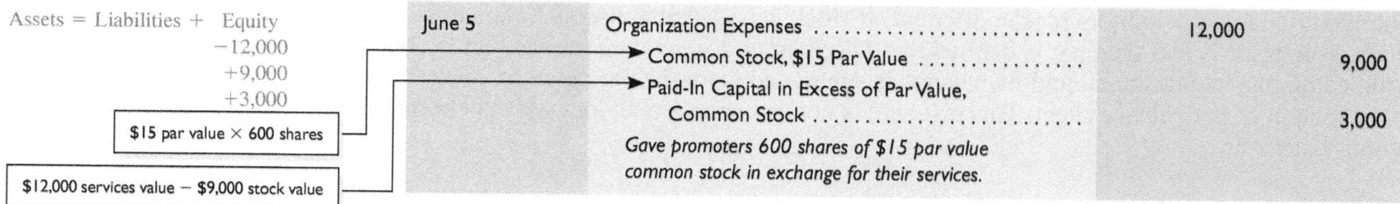

Assets	= Liabilities	+ Equity
		−12,000
		+9,000
		+3,000

Date	Account	Debit	Credit
June 5	Organization Expenses	12,000	
	Common Stock, $15 Par Value		9,000
	Paid-In Capital in Excess of Par Value, Common Stock		3,000
	Gave promoters 600 shares of $15 par value common stock in exchange for their services.		

Quick Check

Answers — p. 533

4. A company issues 7,000 shares of its $10 par value common stock in exchange for equipment valued at $105,000. The entry to record this transaction includes a credit to (*a*) Paid-In Capital in Excess of Par Value, Common Stock, for $35,000. (*b*) Retained Earnings for $35,000. (*c*) Common Stock, $10 Par Value, for $105,000.
5. What is a premium on stock issuance?
6. Who is intended to be protected by minimum legal capital?

DIVIDENDS

This section describes both cash and stock dividend transactions.

Cash Dividends

P2 Record transactions involving cash dividends, stock dividends, and stock splits.

The decision to pay cash dividends rests with the board of directors and involves more than evaluating the amounts of retained earnings and cash. The directors, for instance, may decide to keep the cash to invest in the corporation's growth, to meet emergencies, to take advantage of unexpected opportunities, or to pay off debt. Alternatively, many corporations pay cash dividends to their stockholders at regular dates. These cash flows provide a return to investors and almost always affect the stock's market value.

Percent of Corporations Paying Dividends

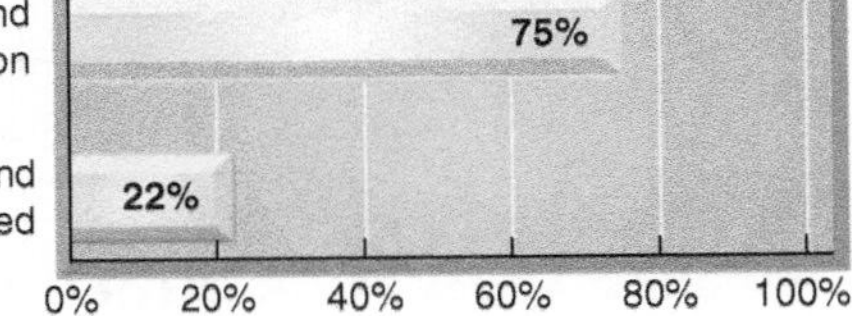

Accounting for Cash Dividends Dividend payment involves three important dates: declaration, record, and payment. **Date of declaration** is the date the directors vote to declare and pay a dividend. This creates a legal liability of the corporation to its stockholders. **Date of record** is the future date specified by the directors for identifying those stockholders listed in the corporation's records to receive dividends. The date of record usually follows the date of declaration by at least two weeks. Persons who own stock on the date of record receive dividends. **Date of payment** is the date when the corporation makes payment; it follows the date of record by enough time to allow the corporation to arrange checks, money transfers, or other means to pay dividends.

To illustrate, the entry to record a January 9 declaration of a $1 per share cash dividend by the directors of Z-Tech, Inc., with 5,000 outstanding shares is

Date of Declaration

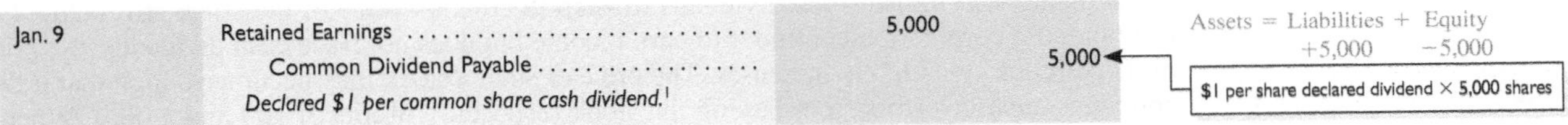

Date	Account	Debit	Credit
Jan. 9	Retained Earnings	5,000	
	Common Dividend Payable		5,000
	Declared $1 per common share cash dividend.[1]		

Assets = Liabilities + Equity
+5,000 −5,000

$1 per share declared dividend × 5,000 shares

Common Dividend Payable is a current liability. The date of record for the Z-Tech dividend is January 22. *No formal journal entry is needed on the date of record.* The February 1 date of payment requires an entry to record both the settlement of the liability and the reduction of the cash balance, as follows:

Date of Payment

Date	Account	Debit	Credit
Feb. 1	Common Dividend Payable	5,000	
	Cash		5,000
	Paid $1 per common share cash dividend.		

Assets = Liabilities + Equity
−5,000 −5,000

Deficits and Cash Dividends A corporation with a debit (abnormal) balance for retained earnings is said to have a **retained earnings deficit,** which arises when a company incurs cumulative losses and/or pays more dividends than total earnings from current and prior years. A deficit is reported as a deduction on the balance sheet, as shown in Exhibit 13.6. Most states prohibit a corporation with a deficit from paying a cash dividend to its stockholders. This legal restriction is designed to protect creditors by preventing distribution of assets to stockholders when the company may be in financial difficulty.

Point: It is often said a dividend is a distribution of retained earnings, but it is more precise to describe a dividend as a distribution of assets to satisfy stockholder claims.

Point: The Retained Earnings Deficit account is also called *Accumulated Deficit.*

[1] An alternative entry is to debit Dividends instead of Retained Earnings. The balance in Dividends is then closed to Retained Earnings at the end of the reporting period. The effect is the same: Retained Earnings is decreased and a Dividend Payable is increased. For simplicity, all assignments in this chapter use the Retained Earnings account to record dividend declarations.

EXHIBIT 13.6

Stockholders' Equity with a Deficit

Common stock—$10 par value, 5,000 shares authorized, issued, and outstanding	$50,000
Retained earnings deficit	(6,000)
Total stockholders' equity	$44,000

Some state laws allow cash dividends to be paid by returning a portion of the capital contributed by stockholders. This type of dividend is called a **liquidating cash dividend,** or simply *liquidating dividend,* because it returns a part of the original investment back to the stockholders. This requires a debit entry to one of the contributed capital accounts instead of Retained Earnings at the declaration date.

Point: Amazon.com has never declared a cash dividend.

Quick Check Answers — p. 534 

7. What type of an account is the Common Dividend Payable account?
8. What three crucial dates are involved in the process of paying a cash dividend?
9. When does a dividend become a company's legal obligation?

Stock Dividends

A **stock dividend,** declared by a corporation's directors, is a distribution of additional shares of the corporation's own stock to its stockholders without the receipt of any payment in return. Stock dividends and cash dividends are different. A stock dividend does not reduce assets and equity but instead transfers a portion of equity from retained earnings to contributed capital.

Reasons for Stock Dividends Stock dividends exist for at least two reasons. First, directors are said to use stock dividends to keep the market price of the stock affordable. For example, if a corporation continues to earn income but does not issue cash dividends, the price of its common stock likely increases. The price of such a stock may become so high that it discourages some investors from buying the stock (especially in lots of 100 and 1,000). When a corporation has a stock dividend, it increases the number of outstanding shares and lowers the per share stock price. Another reason for a stock dividend is to provide evidence of management's confidence that the company is doing well and will continue to do well.

Accounting for Stock Dividends A stock dividend affects the components of equity by transferring part of retained earnings to contributed capital accounts, sometimes described as *capitalizing* retained earnings. Accounting for a stock dividend depends on whether it is a small or large stock dividend. A **small stock dividend** is a distribution of 25% or less of previously outstanding shares. It is recorded by capitalizing retained earnings for an amount equal to the market value of the shares to be distributed. A **large stock dividend** is a distribution of more than 25% of previously outstanding shares. A large stock dividend is recorded by capitalizing retained earnings for the minimum amount required by state law governing the corporation. Most states require capitalizing retained earnings equal to the par or stated value of the stock.

To illustrate stock dividends, we use the equity section of Quest's balance sheet shown in Exhibit 13.7 just *before* its declaration of a stock dividend on December 31.

EXHIBIT 13.7

Stockholders' Equity *before* Declaring a Stock Dividend

Stockholders' Equity (before dividend)	
Common stock—$10 par value, 15,000 shares authorized, 10,000 shares issued and outstanding	$100,000
Paid-in capital in excess of par value, common stock	8,000
Retained earnings	35,000
Total stockholders' equity	$143,000

Recording a small stock dividend. Assume that Quest's directors declare a 10% stock dividend on December 31. This stock dividend of 1,000 shares, computed as 10% of its 10,000 issued and outstanding shares, is to be distributed on January 20 to the stockholders of record on January 15. Since the market price of Quest's stock on December 31 is $15 per share, this small stock dividend declaration is recorded as follows:

Point: Small stock dividends are recorded at market value.

Date of Declaration—Small Stock Dividend

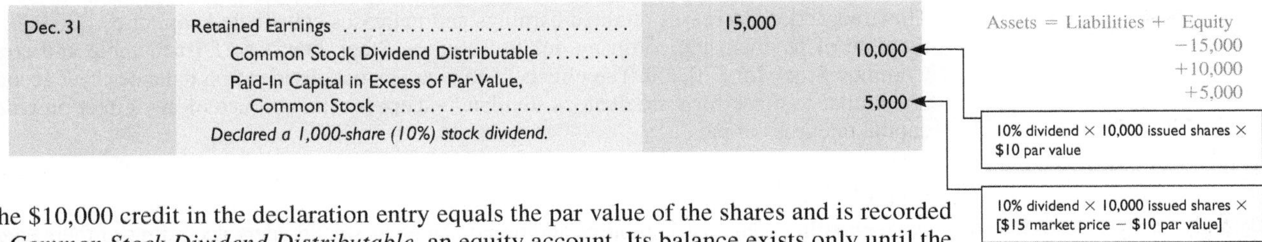

Dec. 31	Retained Earnings	15,000	
	Common Stock Dividend Distributable		10,000
	Paid-In Capital in Excess of Par Value, Common Stock		5,000
	Declared a 1,000-share (10%) stock dividend.		

The $10,000 credit in the declaration entry equals the par value of the shares and is recorded in *Common Stock Dividend Distributable,* an equity account. Its balance exists only until the shares are issued. The $5,000 credit equals the amount by which market value exceeds par value. This amount increases the Paid-In Capital in Excess of Par Value account in anticipation of the issuance of shares. In general, the balance sheet changes in three ways when a stock dividend is declared. First, the amount of equity attributed to common stock increases; for Quest, from $100,000 to $110,000 for 1,000 additional declared shares. Second, paid-in capital in excess of par increases by the excess of market value over par value for the declared shares. Third, retained earnings decreases, reflecting the transfer of amounts to both common stock and paid-in capital in excess of par. The stockholders' equity of Quest is shown in Exhibit 13.8 *after* its 10% stock dividend is declared on December 31—the items impacted are in bold.

Point: The term *Distributable* (not *Payable*) is used for stock dividends. A stock dividend is never a liability because it never reduces assets.

Point: The credit to Paid-In Capital in Excess of Par Value is recorded when the stock dividend is declared. This account is not affected when stock is later distributed.

EXHIBIT 13.8

Stockholders' Equity *after* Declaring a Stock Dividend

Stockholders' Equity (after dividend)	
Common stock—$10 par value, 15,000 shares authorized, 10,000 shares issued and outstanding	$100,000
Common stock dividend distributable—1,000 shares	**10,000**
Paid-in capital in excess of par value, common stock	**13,000**
Retained earnings	**20,000**
Total stockholders' equity	$143,000

No entry is made on the date of record for a stock dividend. On January 20, the date of payment, Quest distributes the new shares to stockholders and records this entry:

Date of Payment—Small Stock Dividend

Jan. 20	Common Stock Dividend Distributable	10,000	
	Common Stock, $10 Par Value		10,000
	To record issuance of common stock dividend.		

Assets = Liabilities + Equity
−10,000
+10,000

The combined effect of these stock dividend entries is to transfer (or capitalize) $15,000 of retained earnings to paid-in capital accounts. The amount of capitalized retained earnings equals the market value of the 1,000 issued shares ($15 × 1,000 shares). A stock dividend has no effect on the ownership percent of individual stockholders.

Point: A stock dividend does not affect assets.

Recording a large stock dividend. A corporation capitalizes retained earnings equal to the minimum amount required by state law for a large stock dividend. For most states, this amount is the par or stated value of the newly issued shares. To illustrate, suppose Quest's board declares a stock dividend of 30% instead of 10% on December 31. Since this dividend is more

Point: Large stock dividends are recorded at par or stated value.

than 25%, it is treated as a large stock dividend. Thus, the par value of the 3,000 dividend shares is capitalized at the date of declaration with this entry:

Date of Declaration—Large Stock Dividend

Dec. 31	Retained Earnings	30,000	
	→ Common Stock Dividend Distributable		30,000
	Declared a 3,000-share (30%) stock dividend.		

Assets = Liabilities + Equity
−30,000
+30,000

30% dividend × 10,000 issued shares × $10 par value

This transaction decreases retained earnings and increases contributed capital by $30,000. On the date of payment the company debits Common Stock Dividend Distributable and credits Common Stock for $30,000. The effects from a large stock dividend on balance sheet accounts are similar to those for a small stock dividend except for the absence of any effect on paid-in capital in excess of par.

Stock Splits

Before 5:1 Split: 1 share, $50 par

After 5:1 Split: 5 shares, $10 par

A **stock split** is the distribution of additional shares to stockholders according to their percent ownership. When a stock split occurs, the corporation "calls in" its outstanding shares and issues more than one new share in exchange for each old share. Splits can be done in any ratio, including 2-for-1, 3-for-1, or higher. Stock splits reduce the par or stated value per share. The reasons for stock splits are similar to those for stock dividends.

To illustrate, CompTec has 100,000 outstanding shares of $20 par value common stock with a current market value of $88 per share. A 2-for-1 stock split cuts par value in half as it replaces 100,000 shares of $20 par value stock with 200,000 shares of $10 par value stock. Market value is reduced from $88 per share to about $44 per share. The split does not affect any equity amounts reported on the balance sheet or any individual stockholder's percent ownership. Both the Paid-In Capital and Retained Earnings accounts are unchanged by a split, and *no journal entry is made.* The only effect on the accounts is a change in the stock account description. CompTec's 2-for-1 split on its $20 par value stock means that after the split, it changes its stock account title to Common Stock, $10 Par Value. This stock's description on the balance sheet also changes to reflect the additional authorized, issued, and outstanding shares and the new par value.

The difference between stock splits and large stock dividends is often blurred. Many companies report stock splits in their financial statements without calling in the original shares by simply changing their par value. This type of "split" is really a large stock dividend and results in additional shares issued to stockholders by capitalizing retained earnings or transferring other paid-in capital to Common Stock. This approach avoids administrative costs of splitting the stock. Harley-Davidson recently declared a 2-for-1 stock split executed in the form of a 100% stock dividend.

Point: Berkshire Hathaway has resisted a stock split. Its recent stock price was $150,000 per share.

Point: A **reverse stock split** is the opposite of a stock split. It increases both the market value per share and the par or stated value per share with a split ratio less than 1-for-1, such as 1-for-2. A reverse split results in fewer shares.

Decision Maker  Answer — p. 533 

Entrepreneur A company you cofounded and own stock in announces a 50% stock dividend. Has the value of your stock investment increased, decreased, or remained the same? Would it make a difference if it was a 3-for-2 stock split executed in the form of a dividend? ■

Quick Check Answers — p. 534 

10. How does a stock dividend impact assets and retained earnings?
11. What distinguishes a large stock dividend from a small stock dividend?
12. What amount of retained earnings is capitalized for a small stock dividend?

PREFERRED STOCK

C2 Explain characteristics of, and distribute dividends between, common and preferred stock.

A corporation can issue two basic kinds of stock, common and preferred. **Preferred stock** has special rights that give it priority (or senior status) over common stock in one or more areas. Special rights typically include a preference for receiving dividends and for the distribution of assets if the corporation is liquidated. Preferred stock carries all rights of common stock unless the corporate charter nullifies them. Most preferred stock, for instance, does not confer the right to vote. Exhibit 13.9 shows that preferred stock is issued by about one-fourth of corporations. All corporations issue common stock.

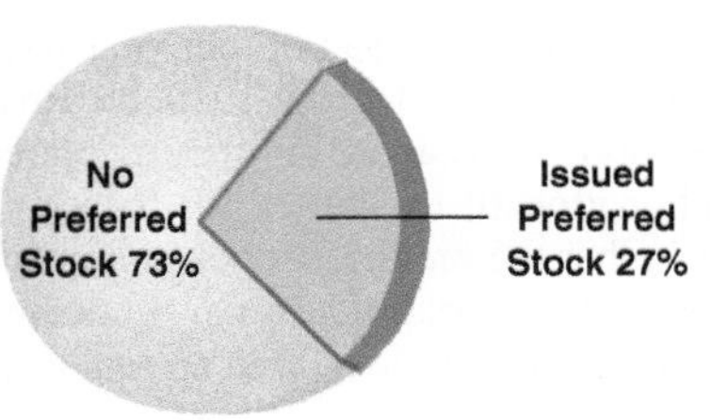

EXHIBIT 13.9

Corporations and Preferred Stock

Issuance of Preferred Stock

Preferred stock usually has a par value. Like common stock, it can be sold at a price different from par. Preferred stock is recorded in its own separate capital accounts. To illustrate, if Dillon Snowboards issues 50 shares of $100 par value preferred stock for $6,000 cash on July 1, 2011, the entry is

July 1	Cash	6,000	
	Preferred Stock, $100 Par Value		5,000
	Paid-In Capital in Excess of Par Value, Preferred Stock		1,000
	Issued preferred stock for cash.		

Assets = Liabilities + Equity
+6,000 +5,000
+1,000

$100 par value × 50 shares

$6,000 cash − [$100 par value × 50 shares]

The equity section of the year-end balance sheet for Dillon Snowboards, including preferred stock, is shown in Exhibit 13.10. (This exhibit assumes that common stock was issued at par.) Issuing no-par preferred stock is similar to issuing no-par common stock. Also, the entries for issuing preferred stock for noncash assets are similar to those for common stock.

Stockholders' Equity	
Common stock—$10 par value; 50,000 shares authorized; 30,000 shares issued and outstanding	$300,000
Preferred stock—$100 par value; 1,000 shares authorized; 50 shares issued and outstanding	5,000
Paid-in capital in excess of par value, preferred stock	1,000
Retained earnings	65,000
Total stockholders' equity	$371,000

EXHIBIT 13.10

Stockholders' Equity with Common and Preferred Stock

Dividend Preference of Preferred Stock

Preferred stock usually carries a preference for dividends, meaning that preferred stockholders are allocated their dividends before any dividends are allocated to common stockholders. The dividends allocated to preferred stockholders are usually expressed as a dollar amount per share or a percent applied to par value. A preference for dividends does *not* ensure dividends. If the directors do not declare a dividend, neither the preferred nor the common stockholders receive one.

Cumulative or Noncumulative Dividend Most preferred stocks carry a cumulative dividend right. **Cumulative preferred stock** has a right to be paid both the current and all prior periods' unpaid dividends before any dividend is paid to common stockholders. When preferred stock is cumulative and the directors either do not declare a dividend to preferred stockholders or declare one that does not cover the total amount of cumulative dividend, the unpaid dividend amount is called **dividend in arrears.** Accumulation of dividends in arrears on cumulative preferred stock does not guarantee they will be paid. **Noncumulative preferred stock** confers no right to prior periods' unpaid dividends if they were not declared in those prior periods.

Point: Dividend preference does not imply that preferred stockholders receive more dividends than common stockholders, nor does it guarantee a dividend.

To illustrate the difference between cumulative and noncumulative preferred stock, assume that a corporation's outstanding stock includes (1) 1,000 shares of $100 par, 9% preferred stock—yielding $9,000 per year in potential dividends, and (2) 4,000 shares of $50 par value common stock. During 2010, the first year of operations, the directors declare cash dividends of $5,000. In year 2011, they declare cash dividends of $42,000. See Exhibit 13.11 for the allocation of dividends for these two years. Allocation of year 2011 dividends depends on whether the preferred stock is noncumulative or cumulative. With noncumulative preferred, the preferred stockholders never receive the $4,000 skipped in 2010. If the preferred stock is cumulative, the $4,000 in arrears is paid in 2011 before any other dividends are paid.

EXHIBIT 13.11

Allocation of Dividends (noncumulative vs. cumulative preferred stock)

	Preferred	Common
Preferred Stock Is Noncumulative		
Year 2010	$ 5,000	$ 0
Year 2011		
Step 1: Current year's preferred dividend	$ 9,000	
Step 2: Remainder to common		$33,000
Preferred Stock Is Cumulative		
Year 2010	$ 5,000	$ 0
Year 2011		
Step 1: Dividend in arrears	$ 4,000	
Step 2: Current year's preferred dividend	9,000	
Step 3: Remainder to common		$29,000
Totals for year 2011	$13,000	$29,000

Example: What dividends do cumulative preferred stockholders receive in 2011 if the corporation paid only $2,000 of dividends in 2010? How does this affect dividends to common stockholders in 2011? *Answers:* $16,000 ($7,000 dividends in arrears, plus $9,000 current preferred dividends). Dividends to common stockholders decrease to $26,000.

A liability for a dividend does not exist until the directors declare a dividend. If a preferred dividend date passes and the corporation's board fails to declare the dividend on its cumulative preferred stock, the dividend in arrears is not a liability. The *full-disclosure principle* requires a corporation to report (usually in a note) the amount of preferred dividends in arrears as of the balance sheet date.

Participating or Nonparticipating Dividend **Nonparticipating preferred stock** has a feature that limits dividends to a maximum amount each year. This maximum is often stated as a percent of the stock's par value or as a specific dollar amount per share. Once preferred stockholders receive this amount, the common stockholders receive any and all additional dividends. **Participating preferred stock** has a feature allowing preferred stockholders to share with common stockholders in any dividends paid in excess of the percent or dollar amount stated on the preferred stock. This participation feature does not apply until common stockholders receive dividends equal to the preferred stock's dividend percent. Many corporations are authorized to issue participating preferred stock but rarely do, and most managers never expect to issue it.[2]

Convertible Preferred Stock

Preferred stock is more attractive to investors if it carries a right to exchange preferred shares for a fixed number of common shares. **Convertible preferred stock** gives holders the option to

[2] Participating preferred stock is usually authorized as a defense against a possible corporate *takeover* by an "unfriendly" investor (or a group of investors) who intends to buy enough voting common stock to gain control. Taking a term from spy novels, the financial world refers to this type of plan as a *poison pill* that a company swallows if enemy investors threaten its capture. A poison pill usually works as follows: A corporation's common stockholders on a given date are granted the right to purchase a large amount of participating preferred stock at a very low price. This right to purchase preferred shares is *not* transferable. If an unfriendly investor buys a large block of common shares (whose right to purchase participating preferred shares does *not* transfer to this buyer), the board can issue preferred shares at a low price to the remaining common shareholders who retained the right to purchase. Future dividends are then divided between the newly issued participating preferred shares and the common shares. This usually transfers value from common shares to preferred shares, causing the unfriendly investor's common stock to lose much of its value and reduces the potential benefit of a hostile takeover.

exchange their preferred shares for common shares at a specified rate. When a company prospers and its common stock increases in value, convertible preferred stockholders can share in this success by converting their preferred stock into more valuable common stock.

Callable Preferred Stock

Callable preferred stock gives the issuing corporation the right to purchase (retire) this stock from its holders at specified future prices and dates. The amount paid to call and retire a preferred share is its **call price,** or *redemption value,* and is set when the stock is issued. The call price normally includes the stock's par value plus a premium giving holders additional return on their investment. When the issuing corporation calls and retires a preferred stock, the terms of the agreement often require it to pay the call price *and* any dividends in arrears.

Point: The issuing corporation has the right, or option, to retire its callable preferred stock.

IFRS

Like U.S. GAAP, IFRS requires that preferred stocks be classified as debt or equity based on analysis of the stock's contractual terms. However, IFRS uses different criteria for such classification. ■

Reasons for Issuing Preferred Stock

Corporations issue preferred stock for several reasons. One is to raise capital without sacrificing control. For example, suppose a company's organizers have $100,000 cash to invest and organize a corporation that needs $200,000 of capital to start. If they sell $200,000 worth of common stock (with $100,000 to the organizers), they would have only 50% control and would need to negotiate extensively with other stockholders in making policy. However, if they issue $100,000 worth of common stock to themselves and sell outsiders $100,000 of 8%, cumulative preferred stock with no voting rights, they retain control.

A second reason to issue preferred stock is to boost the return earned by common stockholders. To illustrate, suppose a corporation's organizers expect to earn an annual after-tax income of $24,000 on an investment of $200,000. If they sell and issue $200,000 worth of common stock, the $24,000 income produces a 12% return on the $200,000 of common stockholders' equity. However, if they issue $100,000 of 8% preferred stock to outsiders and $100,000 of common stock to themselves, their own return increases to 16% per year, as shown in Exhibit 13.12.

EXHIBIT 13.12

Return to Common Stockholders When Preferred Stock Is Issued

Net (after-tax) income	$24,000
Less preferred dividends at 8%	(8,000)
Balance to common stockholders	$16,000
Return to common stockholders ($16,000/$100,000)	16%

Common stockholders earn 16% instead of 12% because assets contributed by preferred stockholders are invested to earn $12,000 while the preferred dividend is only $8,000. Use of preferred stock to increase return to common stockholders is an example of **financial leverage** (also called *trading on the equity*). As a general rule, when the dividend rate on preferred stock is less than the rate the corporation earns on its assets, the effect of issuing preferred stock is to increase (or *lever)* the rate earned by common stockholders.

Point: Financial leverage also occurs when debt is issued and the interest rate paid on it is less than the rate earned from using the assets the creditors lend the company.

Other reasons for issuing preferred stock include its appeal to some investors who believe that the corporation's common stock is too risky or that the expected return on common stock is too low.

Decision Maker Answer — p. 533

Concert Organizer Assume that you alter your business strategy from organizing concerts targeted at under 1,000 people to those targeted at between 5,000 to 20,000 people. You also incorporate because of increased risk of lawsuits and a desire to issue stock for financing. It is important that you control the company for decisions on whom to schedule. What types of stock do you offer? ■

Quick Check Answers — p. 534

13. In what ways does preferred stock often have priority over common stock?
14. Increasing the return to common stockholders by issuing preferred stock is an example of (*a*) Financial leverage. (*b*) Cumulative earnings. (*c*) Dividend in arrears.
15. A corporation has issued and outstanding (i) 9,000 shares of $50 par value, 10% cumulative, nonparticipating preferred stock and (ii) 27,000 shares of $10 par value common stock. No dividends have been declared for the two prior years. During the current year, the corporation declares $288,000 in dividends. The amount paid to common shareholders is (*a*) $243,000. (*b*) $153,000. (*c*) $135,000.

TREASURY STOCK

P3 Record purchases and sales of treasury stock and the retirement of stock.

Corporations acquire shares of their own stock for several reasons: (1) to use their shares to acquire another corporation, (2) to purchase shares to avoid a hostile takeover of the company, (3) to reissue them to employees as compensation, and (4) to maintain a strong market for their stock or to show management confidence in the current price.

A corporation's reacquired shares are called **treasury stock,** which is similar to unissued stock in several ways: (1) neither treasury stock nor unissued stock is an asset, (2) neither receives cash dividends or stock dividends, and (3) neither allows the exercise of voting rights. However, treasury stock does differ from unissued stock in one major way: The corporation can resell treasury stock at less than par without having the buyers incur a liability, provided it was originally issued at par value or higher. Treasury stock purchases also require management to exercise ethical sensitivity because funds are being paid to specific stockholders instead of all stockholders. Managers must be sure the purchase is in the best interest of all stockholders. These concerns cause companies to fully disclose treasury stock transactions.

Corporations and Treasury Stock

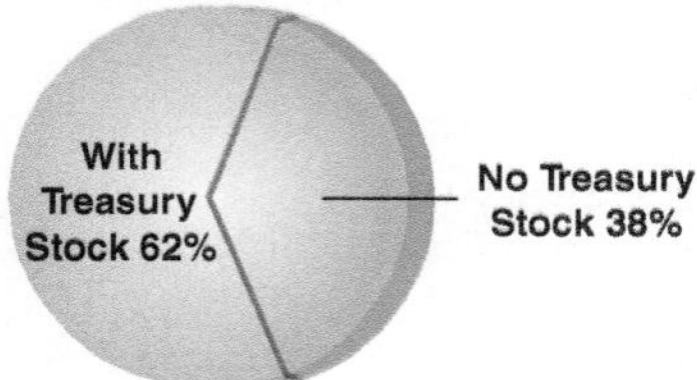

Purchasing Treasury Stock

Purchasing treasury stock reduces the corporation's assets and equity by equal amounts. (We describe the *cost method* of accounting for treasury stock, which is the most widely used method. The *par value* method is another method explained in advanced courses.) To illustrate, Exhibit 13.13 shows Cyber Corporation's account balances *before* any treasury stock purchase (Cyber has no liabilities).

EXHIBIT 13.13

Account Balances *before* Purchasing Treasury Stock

Assets		Stockholders' Equity	
Cash	$ 30,000	Common stock—$10 par; 10,000 shares authorized, issued, and outstanding	$100,000
Other assets	95,000	Retained earnings	25,000
Total assets	$125,000	Total stockholders' equity	$125,000

Cyber then purchases 1,000 of its own shares for $11,500 on May 1, which is recorded as follows.

Assets = Liabilities + Equity
−11,500 −11,500

$11.50 cost per share × 1,000 shares

May 1	Treasury Stock, Common	11,500	
	Cash		11,500
	Purchased 1,000 treasury shares at $11.50 per share.		

This entry reduces equity through the debit to the Treasury Stock account, which is a contra equity account. Exhibit 13.14 shows account balances *after* this transaction.

EXHIBIT 13.14

Account Balances *after* Purchasing Treasury Stock

Assets		Stockholders' Equity	
Cash	$ 18,500	Common stock—$10 par; 10,000 shares authorized and issued; 1,000 shares in treasury	$100,000
Other assets	95,000	Retained earnings, $11,500 restricted by treasury stock purchase	25,000
		Less cost of treasury stock	(11,500)
Total assets	$113,500	Total stockholders' equity	$113,500

The treasury stock purchase reduces Cyber's cash, total assets, and total equity by $11,500 but does not reduce the balance of either the Common Stock or the Retained Earnings account. The equity reduction is reported by deducting the cost of treasury stock in the equity section. Also, two disclosures are evident. First, the stock description reveals that 1,000 issued shares are in treasury, leaving only 9,000 shares still outstanding. Second, the description for retained earnings reveals that it is partly restricted.

Point: The Treasury Stock account is *not* an asset. Treasury stock does not carry voting or dividend rights.

Point: A treasury stock purchase is also called a *stock buyback*.

Reissuing Treasury Stock

Treasury stock can be reissued by selling it at cost, above cost, or below cost.

Selling Treasury Stock at Cost If treasury stock is reissued at cost, the entry is the reverse of the one made to record the purchase. For instance, if on May 21 Cyber reissues 100 of the treasury shares purchased on May 1 at the same $11.50 per share cost, the entry is

May 21	Cash	1,150	
	Treasury Stock, Common		1,150
	Received $11.50 per share for 100 treasury shares costing $11.50 per share.		

Assets = Liabilities + Equity
+1,150 +1,150

$11.50 cost per share × 100 shares

Selling Treasury Stock *above* Cost If treasury stock is sold for more than cost, the amount received in excess of cost is credited to the Paid-In Capital, Treasury Stock account. This account is reported as a separate item in the stockholders' equity section. No gain is ever reported from the sale of treasury stock. To illustrate, if Cyber receives $12 cash per share for 400 treasury shares costing $11.50 per share on June 3, the entry is

Point: Treasury stock does not represent ownership. A company cannot own a part of itself.

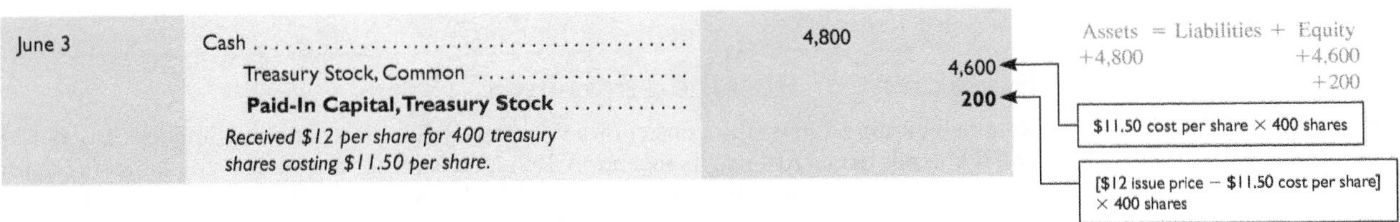

June 3	Cash	4,800	
	Treasury Stock, Common		4,600
	Paid-In Capital, Treasury Stock		**200**
	Received $12 per share for 400 treasury shares costing $11.50 per share.		

Assets = Liabilities + Equity
+4,800 +4,600
+200

$11.50 cost per share × 400 shares

[$12 issue price − $11.50 cost per share] × 400 shares

Selling Treasury Stock *below* Cost When treasury stock is sold below cost, the entry to record the sale depends on whether the Paid-In Capital, Treasury Stock account has a credit balance. If it has a zero balance, the excess of cost over the sales price is debited to Retained Earnings. If the Paid-In Capital, Treasury Stock account has a credit balance, it is debited for the excess of the cost over the selling price but not to exceed the balance in this account. When the credit balance in this paid-in capital account is eliminated, any remaining difference between the cost and selling price is debited to Retained Earnings. To illustrate, if Cyber sells its remaining 500 shares of treasury stock at $10 per share on July 10, equity is

Point: The phrase *treasury stock* is believed to arise from the fact that reacquired stock is held in a corporation's treasury.

Point: The Paid-In Capital, Treasury Stock account can have a zero or credit balance but never a debit balance.

reduced by $750 (500 shares × $1.50 per share excess of cost over selling price), as shown in this entry:

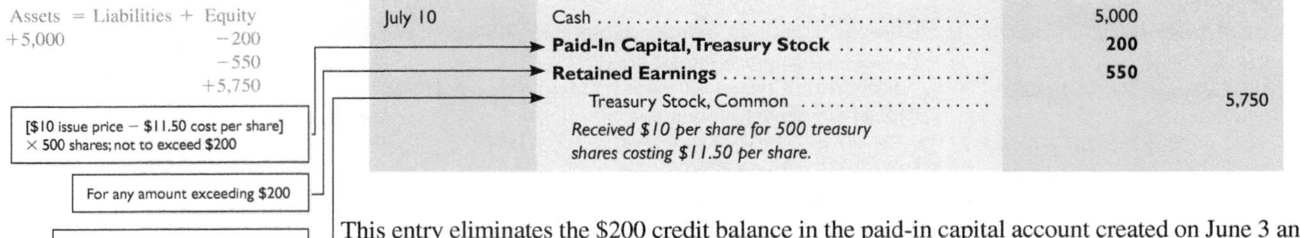

	Assets	=	Liabilities	+	Equity
	+5,000				−200
					−550
					+5,750

Date	Account	Debit	Credit
July 10	Cash	5,000	
	Paid-In Capital, Treasury Stock	**200**	
	Retained Earnings	**550**	
	Treasury Stock, Common		5,750
	Received $10 per share for 500 treasury shares costing $11.50 per share.		

[$10 issue price − $11.50 cost per share] × 500 shares; not to exceed $200

For any amount exceeding $200

$11.50 cost per share × 500 shares

This entry eliminates the $200 credit balance in the paid-in capital account created on June 3 and then reduces the Retained Earnings balance by the remaining $550 excess of cost over selling price. A company never reports a loss (or gain) from the sale of treasury stock.

Retiring Stock

A corporation can purchase its own stock and retire it. Retiring stock reduces the number of issued shares. Retired stock is the same as authorized and unissued shares. Purchases and retirements of stock are permissible under state law only if they do not jeopardize the interests of creditors and stockholders. When stock is purchased for retirement, we remove all capital amounts related to the retired shares. If the purchase price exceeds the net amount removed, this excess is debited to Retained Earnings. If the net amount removed from all capital accounts exceeds the purchase price, this excess is credited to the Paid-In Capital from Retirement of Stock account. A company's assets and equity are always reduced by the amount paid for the retiring stock.

Point: Recording stock retirement results in canceling the equity from the original issuance of the shares.

Quick Check

Answers — p. 534

16. Purchase of treasury stock *(a)* has no effect on assets; *(b)* reduces total assets and total equity by equal amounts; or *(c)* is recorded with a debit to Retained Earnings.

17. Southern Co. purchases shares of Northern Corp. Should either company classify these shares as treasury stock?

18. How does treasury stock affect the authorized, issued, and outstanding shares?

19. When a company purchases treasury stock, *(a)* retained earnings are restricted by the amount paid; *(b)* Retained Earnings is credited; or *(c)* it is retired.

REPORTING OF EQUITY

C3 Explain the items reported in retained earnings.

Statement of Retained Earnings

Retained earnings generally consist of a company's cumulative net income less any net losses and dividends declared since its inception. Retained earnings are part of stockholders' claims on the company's net assets, but this does *not* imply that a certain amount of cash or other assets is available to pay stockholders. For example, **Research In Motion** has $5,274,365 thousand in retained earnings, but only $1,550,861 thousand in cash. This section describes events and transactions affecting retained earnings and how retained earnings are reported.

Restrictions and Appropriations The term **restricted retained earnings** refers to both statutory and contractual restrictions. A common *statutory* (or *legal*) *restriction* is to limit treasury stock purchases to the amount of retained earnings. The balance sheet in Exhibit 13.14 provides an example. A common *contractual restriction* involves loan agreements that restrict paying dividends beyond a specified amount or percent of retained earnings. Restrictions are usually described in the notes. The term **appropriated retained earnings** refers to a voluntary transfer of amounts from the Retained Earnings account to the Appropriated Retained Earnings account to inform users of special activities that require funds.

Prior Period Adjustments **Prior period adjustments** are corrections of material errors in prior period financial statements. These errors include arithmetic mistakes, unacceptable accounting, and missed facts. Prior period adjustments are reported in the *statement of retained earnings* (or the statement of stockholders' equity), net of any income tax effects. Prior period adjustments result in changing the beginning balance of retained earnings for events occurring prior to the earliest period reported in the current set of financial statements. To illustrate, assume that ComUS makes an error in a 2009 journal entry for the purchase of land by incorrectly debiting an expense account. When this is discovered in 2011, the statement of retained earnings includes a prior period adjustment, as shown in Exhibit 13.15. This exhibit also shows the usual format of the statement of retained earnings.

Point: If a year 2009 error is discovered in 2010, the company records the adjustment in 2010. But if the financial statements include 2009 and 2010 figures, the statements report the correct amounts for 2009, and a note describes the correction.

EXHIBIT 13.15

Statement of Retained Earnings with a Prior Period Adjustment

ComUS
Statement of Retained Earnings
For Year Ended December 31, 2011

Retained earnings, Dec. 31, 2010, as previously reported	$4,745,000
Prior period adjustment	
Cost of land incorrectly expensed (net of $63,000 income taxes)	**147,000**
Retained earnings, Dec. 31, 2010, as adjusted	4,892,000
Plus net income	1,224,300
Less cash dividends declared	(301,800)
Retained earnings, Dec. 31, 2011	$5,814,500

Many items reported in financial statements are based on estimates. Future events are certain to reveal that some of these estimates were inaccurate even when based on the best data available at the time. These inaccuracies are *not* considered errors and are *not* reported as prior period adjustments. Instead, they are identified as **changes in accounting estimates** and are accounted for in current and future periods. To illustrate, we know that depreciation is based on estimated useful lives and salvage values. As time passes and new information becomes available, managers may need to change these estimates and the resulting depreciation expense for current and future periods.

Point: Accounting for changes in estimates is sometimes criticized as two wrongs to make a right. Consider a change in an asset's life. Depreciation neither before nor after the change is the amount computed if the revised estimate were originally selected. Regulators chose this approach to avoid restating prior period numbers.

Closing Process The closing process was explained earlier in the book as: (1) Close credit balances in revenue accounts to Income Summary, (2) Close debit balances in expense accounts to Income Summary, and (3) Close Income Summary to Retained Earnings. If dividends are recorded in a Dividends account, and not as an immediate reduction to Retained Earnings (as shown in this chapter), a fourth step is necessary to close the Dividends account to Retained Earnings.

Statement of Stockholders' Equity

Instead of a separate statement of retained earnings, companies commonly report a statement of stockholders' equity that includes changes in retained earnings. A **statement of stockholders' equity** lists the beginning and ending balances of key equity accounts and describes the changes that occur during the period. The companies in Appendix A report such a statement. The usual format is to provide a column for each component of equity and use the rows to describe events occurring in the period. Exhibit 13.16 shows a condensed statement for Apple.

Reporting Stock Options

The majority of corporations whose shares are publicly traded issue **stock options,** which are rights to purchase common stock at a fixed price over a specified period. As the stock's price rises, the option's value increases. Starbucks and Home Depot offer stock options to both full- and part-time employees. Stock options are said to motivate managers and employees to

EXHIBIT 13.16

Statement of Stockholders' Equity

Apple

APPLE Statement of Stockholders' Equity					
($ millions, shares in thousands)	Common Stock Shares	Common Stock Amount	Retained Earnings	Other	Total Equity
Balance, Sept. 27, 2008	**888,326**	**$7,177**	**$15,129**	**$(9)**	**$22,297**
Net income	—	—	8,235	—	8,235
Issuance of Common Stock	11,480	404	(11)	—	393
Other	—	629	—	86	715
Cash Dividends ($0.00 per share)	—	—	—	—	—
Balance, Sept. 26, 2009	**899,806**	**$8,210**	**$23,353**	**$77**	**$31,640**

(1) focus on company performance, (2) take a long-run perspective, and (3) remain with the company. A stock option is like having an investment with no risk ("a carrot with no stick").

To illustrate, Quantum grants each of its employees the option to purchase 100 shares of its $1 par value common stock at its current market price of $50 per share anytime within the next 10 years. If the stock price rises to $70 per share, an employee can exercise the option at a gain of $20 per share (acquire a $70 stock at the $50 option price). With 100 shares, a single employee would have a total gain of $2,000, computed as $20 × 100 shares. Companies report the cost of stock options in the income statement. Measurement of this cost is explained in advanced courses.

GLOBAL VIEW

This section discusses similarities and differences between U.S. GAAP and IFRS in accounting and reporting for equity.

NOKIA

Accounting for Common Stock The accounting for and reporting of common stock under U.S. GAAP and IFRS are similar. Specifically, procedures for issuing common stock at par, at a premium, at a discount, and for noncash assets are similar across the two systems. However, we must be aware of legal and cultural differences across the world that can impact the rights and responsibilities of common shareholders. Nokia's terminology is a bit different as it uses the phrase "share capital" in reference to what U.S. GAAP would title "common shares" (see Appendix A). It also discloses that it has issued (and outstanding) shares of 3,744,956,052.

Accounting for Dividends Accounting for and reporting of dividends under U.S. GAAP and IFRS are consistent. This applies to cash dividends, stock dividends, and stock splits. For Nokia, a "dividend of EUR 0.40 per share is to be paid out on the shares of the Company." Nokia, like many other companies, follows a dividend policy set by management and its board.

Accounting for Preferred Stock Accounting and reporting for preferred stock are similar for U.S. GAAP and IFRS, but there are some important differences. First, preferred stock that is redeemable at the option of the preferred stockholders is reported *between* liabilities and equity in U.S. GAAP balance sheets. However, that same stock is reported as a liability in IFRS balance sheets. Second, the issue price of convertible preferred stock (and bonds) is recorded entirely under preferred stock (or bonds) *and none is assigned to the conversion feature* under U.S. GAAP. However, IFRS requires that a portion of the issue price be allocated to the conversion feature when it exists. Nokia has no preferred stock.

Accounting for Treasury Stock Both U.S. GAAP and IFRS apply the principle that companies do not record gains or losses on transactions involving their own stock. This applies to purchases, reissuances, and retirements of treasury stock. Consequently, the accounting for treasury stock explained in this chapter is consistent with that under IFRS. However, IFRS in this area is less detailed than that of U.S. GAAP. Nokia's policy regarding treasury stock follows: "[It] recognizes acquired treasury shares as a deduction from equity at their acquisition cost."

Earnings per Share, Price-Earnings Ratio, Dividend Yield, and Book Value per Share

Decision Analysis

Earnings per Share

The income statement reports **earnings per share,** also called *EPS* or *net income per share,* which is the amount of income earned per each share of a company's outstanding common stock. The **basic earnings per share** formula is shown in Exhibit 13.17. When a company has no preferred stock, then preferred dividends are zero. The weighted-average common shares outstanding is measured over the income reporting period; its computation is explained in advanced courses.

A1 Compute earnings per share and describe its use.

EXHIBIT 13.17

Basic Earnings per Share

$$\textbf{Basic earnings per share} = \frac{\textbf{Net income} - \textbf{Preferred dividends}}{\textbf{Weighted-average common shares outstanding}}$$

To illustrate, assume that Quantum Co. earns $40,000 net income in 2011 and declares dividends of $7,500 on its noncumulative preferred stock. (If preferred stock is *non*cumulative, the income available [numerator] is the current period net income less any preferred dividends *declared* in that same period. If preferred stock is cumulative, the income available [numerator] is the current period net income less the preferred dividends whether declared or not.) Quantum has 5,000 weighted-average common shares outstanding during 2011. Its basic EPS[3] is

$$\text{Basic earnings per share} = \frac{\$40{,}000 - \$7{,}500}{5{,}000 \text{ shares}} = \$6.50$$

Price-Earnings Ratio

A stock's market value is determined by its *expected* future cash flows. A comparison of a company's EPS and its market value per share reveals information about market expectations. This comparison is traditionally made using a **price-earnings** (or **PE**) **ratio,** expressed also as *price earnings, price to earnings,* or *PE.* Some analysts interpret this ratio as what price the market is willing to pay for a company's current earnings stream. Price-earnings ratios can differ across companies that have similar earnings because of either higher or lower expectations of future earnings. The price-earnings ratio is defined in Exhibit 13.18.

A2 Compute price-earnings ratio and describe its use in analysis.

Point: The average PE ratio of stocks in the 1950–2010 period is about 14.

EXHIBIT 13.18

Price-Earnings Ratio

$$\textbf{Price-earnings ratio} = \frac{\textbf{Market value (price) per share}}{\textbf{Earnings per share}}$$

This ratio is often computed using EPS from the most recent period (for Amazon, its PE is 52; for Altria, its PE is 13). However, many users compute this ratio using *expected* EPS for the next period.

Some analysts view stocks with high PE ratios (higher than 20 to 25) as more likely to be overpriced and stocks with low PE ratios (less than 5 to 8) as more likely to be underpriced. These investors prefer to sell or avoid buying stocks with high PE ratios and to buy or hold stocks with low PE ratios. However, investment decision making is rarely so simple as to rely on a single ratio. For instance, a stock with a high PE ratio can prove to be a good investment if its earnings continue to increase beyond current expectations. Similarly, a stock with a low PE ratio can prove to be a poor investment if its earnings decline below expectations.

Point: Average PE ratios for U.S. stocks increased over the past two decades. Some analysts interpret this as a signal the market is overpriced. But higher ratios can at least partly reflect accounting changes that have reduced reported earnings.

[3] A corporation can be classified as having either a simple or complex capital structure. The term **simple capital structure** refers to a company with only common stock and nonconvertible preferred stock outstanding. The term **complex capital structure** refers to companies with dilutive securities. **Dilutive securities** include options, rights to purchase common stock, and any bonds or preferred stock that are convertible into common stock. A company with a complex capital structure must often report two EPS figures: basic and diluted. **Diluted earnings per share** is computed by adding all dilutive securities to the denominator of the basic EPS computation. It reflects the decrease in basic EPS *assuming* that all dilutive securities are converted into common shares.

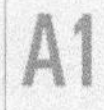

Decision Maker Answer — p. 533 

Money Manager You plan to invest in one of two companies identified as having identical future prospects. One has a PE of 19 and the other a PE of 25. Which do you invest in? Does it matter if your *estimate* of PE for these two companies is 29 as opposed to 22? ■

Dividend Yield

A3 Compute dividend yield and explain its use in analysis.

Investors buy shares of a company's stock in anticipation of receiving a return from either or both cash dividends and stock price increases. Stocks that pay large dividends on a regular basis, called *income stocks,* are attractive to investors who want recurring cash flows from their investments. In contrast, some stocks pay little or no dividends but are still attractive to investors because of their expected stock price increases. The stocks of companies that distribute little or no cash but use their cash to finance expansion are called *growth stocks*. One way to help identify whether a stock is an income stock or a growth stock is to analyze its dividend yield. **Dividend yield,** defined in Exhibit 13.19, shows the annual amount of cash dividends distributed to common shares relative to their market value.

EXHIBIT 13.19
Dividend Yield

$$\textbf{Dividend yield} = \frac{\textbf{Annual cash dividends per share}}{\textbf{Market value per share}}$$

Dividend yield can be computed for current and prior periods using actual dividends and stock prices and for future periods using expected values. Exhibit 13.20 shows recent dividend and stock price data for Amazon and Altria Group to compute dividend yield.

EXHIBIT 13.20
Dividend and Stock Price Information

Company	Cash Dividends per Share	Market Value per Share	Dividend Yield
Amazon	$0.00	$80	0.0%
Altria Group.........	1.68	20	8.4

Point: The *payout ratio* equals cash dividends declared on common stock divided by net income. A low payout ratio suggests that a company is retaining earnings for future growth.

Dividend yield is zero for Amazon, implying it is a growth stock. An investor in Amazon would look for increases in stock prices (and eventual cash from the sale of stock). Altria has a dividend yield of 8.4%, implying it is an income stock for which dividends are important in assessing its value.

Book Value per Share

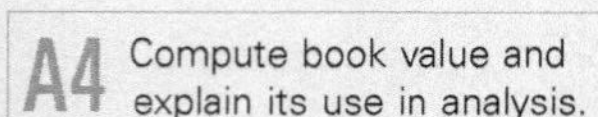
A4 Compute book value and explain its use in analysis.

Case 1: Common Stock (Only) Outstanding. **Book value per common share,** defined in Exhibit 13.21, reflects the amount of equity applicable to *common* shares on a per share basis. To illustrate, we use Dillon Snowboards' data from Exhibit 13.4. Dillon has 30,000 outstanding common shares, and the stockholders' equity applicable to common shares is $365,000. Dillon's book value per common share is $12.17, computed as $365,000 divided by 30,000 shares.

EXHIBIT 13.21
Book Value per Common Share

$$\textbf{Book value per common share} = \frac{\textbf{Stockholders' equity applicable to common shares}}{\textbf{Number of common shares outstanding}}$$

Point: Book value per share is also referred to as *stockholders' claim to assets on a per share basis.*

Case 2: Common and Preferred Stock Outstanding. To compute book value when both common and preferred shares are outstanding, we allocate total equity between the two types of shares. The **book value per preferred share** is computed first; its computation is shown in Exhibit 13.22.

EXHIBIT 13.22
Book Value per Preferred Share

$$\textbf{Book value per preferred share} = \frac{\textbf{Stockholders' equity applicable to preferred shares}}{\textbf{Number of preferred shares outstanding}}$$

The equity applicable to preferred shares equals the preferred share's call price (or par value if the preferred is not callable) plus any cumulative dividends in arrears. The remaining equity is the portion applicable to common shares. To illustrate, consider LTD's equity in Exhibit 13.23. Its preferred stock is callable at $108 per share, and two years of cumulative preferred dividends are in arrears.

EXHIBIT 13.23

Stockholders' Equity with Preferred and Common Stock

Stockholders' Equity	
Preferred stock—$100 par value, 7% cumulative, 2,000 shares authorized, 1,000 shares issued and outstanding	$100,000
Common stock—$25 par value, 12,000 shares authorized, 10,000 shares issued and outstanding	250,000
Paid-in capital in excess of par value, common stock	15,000
Retained earnings	82,000
Total stockholders' equity	$447,000

The book value computations are in Exhibit 13.24. Equity is first allocated to preferred shares before the book value of common shares is computed.

EXHIBIT 13.24

Computing Book Value per Preferred and Common Share

Total stockholders' equity		$447,000
Less equity applicable to preferred shares		
Call price (1,000 shares × $108)	$108,000	
Dividends in arrears ($100,000 × 7% × 2 years)	14,000	(122,000)
Equity applicable to common shares		$325,000
Book value per preferred share ($122,000/1,000 shares)		**$ 122.00**
Book value per common share ($325,000/10,000 shares)		**$ 32.50**

Book value per share reflects the value per share if a company is liquidated at balance sheet amounts. Book value is also the starting point in many stock valuation models, merger negotiations, price setting for public utilities, and loan contracts. The main limitation in using book value is the potential difference between recorded value and market value for assets and liabilities. Investors often adjust their analysis for estimates of these differences.

Decision Maker Answer — p. 533

Investor You are considering investing in BMX, whose book value per common share is $4 and price per common share on the stock exchange is $7. From this information, are BMX's net assets priced higher or lower than its recorded values? ■

DEMONSTRATION PROBLEM 1

Barton Corporation began operations on January 1, 2010. The following transactions relating to stockholders' equity occurred in the first two years of the company's operations.

2010

Jan. 1 Authorized the issuance of 2 million shares of $5 par value common stock and 100,000 shares of $100 par value, 10% cumulative, preferred stock.

Jan. 2 Issued 200,000 shares of common stock for $12 cash per share.

Jan. 3 Issued 100,000 shares of common stock in exchange for a building valued at $820,000 and merchandise inventory valued at $380,000.

Jan. 4 Paid $10,000 cash to the company's founders for organization activities.

Jan. 5 Issued 12,000 shares of preferred stock for $110 cash per share.

2011

June 4 Issued 100,000 shares of common stock for $15 cash per share.

Required

1. Prepare journal entries to record these transactions.
2. Prepare the stockholders' equity section of the balance sheet as of December 31, 2010, and December 31, 2011, based on these transactions.
3. Prepare a table showing dividend allocations and dividends per share for 2010 and 2011 assuming Barton declares the following cash dividends: 2010, $50,000, and 2011, $300,000.

4. Prepare the January 2, 2010, journal entry for Barton's issuance of 200,000 shares of common stock for $12 cash per share assuming
   a. Common stock is no-par stock without a stated value.
   b. Common stock is no-par stock with a stated value of $10 per share.

PLANNING THE SOLUTION

- Record journal entries for the transactions for 2010 and 2011.
- Determine the balances for the 2010 and 2011 equity accounts for the balance sheet.
- Prepare the contributed capital portion of the 2010 and 2011 balance sheets.
- Prepare a table similar to Exhibit 13.11 showing dividend allocations for 2010 and 2011.
- Record the issuance of common stock under both specifications of no-par stock.

SOLUTION TO DEMONSTRATION PROBLEM 1

1. Journal entries.

Date	Account	Debit	Credit
2010			
Jan. 2	Cash	2,400,000	
	Common Stock, $5 Par Value		1,000,000
	Paid-In Capital in Excess of Par Value, Common Stock		1,400,000
	Issued 200,000 shares of common stock.		
Jan. 3	Building	820,000	
	Merchandise Inventory	380,000	
	Common Stock, $5 Par Value		500,000
	Paid-In Capital in Excess of Par Value, Common Stock		700,000
	Issued 100,000 shares of common stock.		
Jan. 4	Organization Expenses	10,000	
	Cash		10,000
	Paid founders for organization costs.		
Jan. 5	Cash	1,320,000	
	Preferred Stock, $100 Par Value		1,200,000
	Paid-In Capital in Excess of Par Value, Preferred Stock		120,000
	Issued 12,000 shares of preferred stock.		
2011			
June 4	Cash	1,500,000	
	Common Stock, $5 Par Value		500,000
	Paid-In Capital in Excess of Par Value, Common Stock		1,000,000
	Issued 100,000 shares of common stock.		

2. Balance sheet presentations (at December 31 year-end).

	2011	2010
Stockholders' Equity		
Preferred stock—$100 par value, 10% cumulative, 100,000 shares authorized, 12,000 shares issued and outstanding	$1,200,000	$1,200,000
Paid-in capital in excess of par value, preferred stock	120,000	120,000
Total paid-in capital by preferred stockholders	1,320,000	1,320,000
Common stock—$5 par value, 2,000,000 shares authorized, 300,000 shares issued and outstanding in 2010, and 400,000 shares issued and outstanding in 2011	2,000,000	1,500,000
Paid-in capital in excess of par value, common stock	3,100,000	2,100,000
Total paid-in capital by common stockholders	5,100,000	3,600,000
Total paid-in capital	$6,420,000	$4,920,000

3. Dividend allocation table.

	Common	Preferred
2010 ($50,000)		
Preferred—current year (12,000 shares × $10 = $120,000)	$ 0	$ 50,000
Common—remainder (300,000 shares outstanding)	0	0
Total for the year	$ 0	$ 50,000
2011 ($300,000)		
Preferred—dividend in arrears from 2010 ($120,000 − $50,000)	$ 0	$ 70,000
Preferred—current year	0	120,000
Common—remainder (400,000 shares outstanding)	110,000	0
Total for the year	$110,000	$190,000
Dividends per share		
2010	$ 0.00	$ 4.17
2011	$ 0.28	$ 15.83

4. Journal entries.

a. For 2010 (no-par stock without a stated value):

Date	Account	Debit	Credit
Jan. 2	Cash	2,400,000	
	Common Stock, No-Par Value		2,400,000
	Issued 200,000 shares of no-par common stock at $12 per share.		

b. For 2010 (no-par stock with a stated value):

Date	Account	Debit	Credit
Jan. 2	Cash	2,400,000	
	Common Stock, $10 Stated Value		2,000,000
	Paid-In Capital in Excess of Stated Value, Common Stock		400,000
	Issued 200,000 shares of $10 stated value common stock at $12 per share.		

DEMONSTRATION PROBLEM 2

Precision Company began year 2011 with the following balances in its stockholders' equity accounts.

Common stock—$10 par, 500,000 shares authorized, 200,000 shares issued and outstanding	$2,000,000
Paid-in capital in excess of par, common stock	1,000,000
Retained earnings	5,000,000
Total	$8,000,000

All outstanding common stock was issued for $15 per share when the company was created. Prepare journal entries to account for the following transactions during year 2011.

Jan. 10	The board declared a $0.10 cash dividend per share to shareholders of record Jan. 28.
Feb. 15	Paid the cash dividend declared on January 10.
Mar. 31	Declared a 20% stock dividend. The market value of the stock is $18 per share.
May 1	Distributed the stock dividend declared on March 31.
July 1	Purchased 30,000 shares of treasury stock at $20 per share.
Sept. 1	Sold 20,000 treasury shares at $26 cash per share.
Dec. 1	Sold the remaining 10,000 shares of treasury stock at $7 cash per share.

PLANNING THE SOLUTION

- Calculate the total cash dividend to record by multiplying the cash dividend declared by the number of shares as of the date of record.
- Decide whether the stock dividend is a small or large dividend. Then analyze each event to determine the accounts affected and the appropriate amounts to be recorded.

SOLUTION TO DEMONSTRATION PROBLEM 2

Date	Account	Debit	Credit
Jan. 10	Retained Earnings	20,000	
	Common Dividend Payable		20,000
	Declared a $0.10 per share cash dividend.		
Feb. 15	Common Dividend Payable	20,000	
	Cash		20,000
	Paid $0.10 per share cash dividend.		
Mar. 31	Retained Earnings	720,000	
	Common Stock Dividend Distributable		400,000
	Paid-In Capital in Excess of Par Value, Common Stock		320,000
	Declared a small stock dividend of 20% or 40,000 shares; market value is $18 per share.		
May 1	Common Stock Dividend Distributable	400,000	
	Common Stock		400,000
	Distributed 40,000 shares of common stock.		
July 1	Treasury Stock, Common	600,000	
	Cash		600,000
	Purchased 30,000 common shares at $20 per share.		
Sept. 1	Cash	520,000	
	Treasury Stock, Common		400,000
	Paid-In Capital, Treasury Stock		120,000
	Sold 20,000 treasury shares at $26 per share.		
Dec. 1	Cash	70,000	
	Paid-In Capital, Treasury Stock	120,000	
	Retained Earnings	10,000	
	Treasury Stock, Common		200,000
	Sold 10,000 treasury shares at $7 per share.		

Summary

C1 Identify characteristics of corporations and their organization. Corporations are legal entities whose stockholders are not liable for its debts. Stock is easily transferred, and the life of a corporation does not end with the incapacity of a stockholder. A corporation acts through its agents, who are its officers and managers. Corporations are regulated and subject to income taxes. Authorized stock is the stock that a corporation's charter authorizes it to sell. Issued stock is the portion of authorized shares sold. Par value stock is a value per share assigned by the charter. No-par value stock is stock *not* assigned a value per share by the charter. Stated value stock is no-par stock to which the directors assign a value per share.

C2 Explain characteristics of, and distribute dividends between, common and preferred stock. Preferred stock has a priority (or senior status) relative to common stock in one or more areas, usually (1) dividends and (2) assets in case of liquidation. Preferred stock usually does not carry voting rights and can be convertible or callable. Convertibility permits the holder to convert preferred to common. Callability permits the issuer to buy back preferred stock under specified conditions. Preferred stockholders usually hold the right to dividend distributions before common stockholders. When preferred stock is cumulative and in arrears, the amount in arrears must be distributed to preferred before any dividends are distributed to common.

C3 Explain the items reported in retained earnings. Stockholders' equity is made up of (1) paid-in capital and (2) retained earnings. Paid-in capital consists of funds raised by stock issuances. Retained earnings consists of cumulative net income (losses) not distributed. Many companies face statutory and contractual restrictions on retained earnings. Corporations can voluntarily appropriate retained earnings to inform others about their disposition. Prior period adjustments are corrections of errors in prior financial statements.

A1 Compute earnings per share and describe its use. A company with a simple capital structure computes basic EPS by dividing net income less any preferred dividends by the weighted-average number of outstanding common shares. A company with a complex capital structure must usually report both basic and diluted EPS.

A2 Compute price-earnings ratio and describe its use in analysis. A common stock's price-earnings (PE) ratio is computed by dividing the stock's market value (price) per share by its EPS. A stock's PE is based on expectations that can prove to be better or worse than eventual performance.

A3 Compute dividend yield and explain its use in analysis. Dividend yield is the ratio of a stock's annual cash dividends per share to its market value (price) per share. Dividend yield can be compared with the yield of other companies to determine whether the stock is expected to be an income or growth stock.

A4 Compute book value and explain its use in analysis. Book value per common share is equity applicable to common shares divided by the number of outstanding common shares. Book value per preferred share is equity applicable to preferred shares divided by the number of outstanding preferred shares.

P1 Record the issuance of corporate stock. When stock is issued, its par or stated value is credited to the stock account and any excess is credited to a separate contributed capital account. If a stock has neither par nor stated value, the entire proceeds are credited to the stock account. Stockholders must contribute assets equal to minimum legal capital or be potentially liable for the deficiency.

P2 Record transactions involving cash dividends, stock dividends, and stock splits. Cash dividends involve three events. On the date of declaration, the directors bind the company to pay the dividend. A dividend declaration reduces retained earnings and creates a current liability. On the date of record, recipients of the dividend are identified. On the date of payment, cash is paid to stockholders and the current liability is removed. Neither a stock dividend nor a stock split alters the value of the company. However, the value of each share is less due to the distribution of additional shares. The distribution of additional shares is according to individual stockholders' ownership percent. Small stock dividends (≤25%) are recorded by capitalizing retained earnings equal to the market value of distributed shares. Large stock dividends (>25%) are recorded by capitalizing retained earnings equal to the par or stated value of distributed shares. Stock splits do not necessitate journal entries but do necessitate changes in the description of stock.

P3 Record purchases and sales of treasury stock and the retirement of stock. When a corporation purchases its own previously issued stock, it debits the cost of these shares to Treasury Stock. Treasury stock is subtracted from equity in the balance sheet. If treasury stock is reissued, any proceeds in excess of cost are credited to Paid-In Capital, Treasury Stock. If the proceeds are less than cost, they are debited to Paid-In Capital, Treasury Stock to the extent a credit balance exists. Any remaining amount is debited to Retained Earnings. When stock is retired, all accounts related to the stock are removed.

Guidance Answers to Decision Maker and Decision Ethics

Entrepreneur The 50% stock dividend provides you no direct income. A stock dividend often reveals management's optimistic expectations about the future and can improve a stock's marketability by making it affordable to more investors. Accordingly, a stock dividend usually reveals "good news" and because of this, it likely increases (slightly) the market value for your stock. The same conclusions apply to the 3-for-2 stock split.

Concert Organizer You have two basic options: (1) different classes of common stock or (2) common and preferred stock. Your objective is to issue to yourself stock that has all or a majority of the voting power. The other class of stock would carry limited or no voting rights. In this way, you maintain control and are able to raise the necessary funds.

Money Manager Since one company requires a payment of $19 for each $1 of earnings, and the other requires $25, you would prefer the stock with the PE of 19; it is a better deal given identical prospects. You should make sure these companies' earnings computations are roughly the same, for example, no extraordinary items, unusual events, and so forth. Also, your PE estimates for these companies do matter. If you are willing to pay $29 for each $1 of earnings for these companies, you obviously expect both to exceed current market expectations.

Investor Book value reflects recorded values. BMX's book value is $4 per common share. Stock price reflects the market's expectation of net asset value (both tangible and intangible items). BMX's market value is $7 per common share. Comparing these figures suggests BMX's market value of net assets is higher than its recorded values (by an amount of $7 versus $4 per share).

Guidance Answers to Quick Checks

1. (*b*)
2. A corporation pays taxes on its income, and its stockholders normally pay personal income taxes (at the 15% rate or lower) on any cash dividends received from the corporation.
3. A proxy is a legal document used to transfer a stockholder's right to vote to another person.
4. (*a*)
5. A stock premium is an amount in excess of par (or stated) value paid by purchasers of newly issued stock.
6. Minimum legal capital intends to protect creditors of a corporation by obligating stockholders to some minimum level of

equity financing and by constraining a corporation from excessive payments to stockholders.

7. Common Dividend Payable is a current liability account.
8. The date of declaration, date of record, and date of payment.
9. A dividend is a legal liability at the date of declaration, on which date it is recorded as a liability.
10. A stock dividend does not transfer assets to stockholders, but it does require an amount of retained earnings to be transferred to a contributed capital account(s).
11. A small stock dividend is 25% or less of the previous outstanding shares. A large stock dividend is more than 25%.
12. Retained earnings equal to the distributable shares' market value should be capitalized for a small stock dividend.
13. Typically, preferred stock has a preference in receipt of dividends and in distribution of assets.
14. (*a*)
15. (*b*)

Total cash dividend	$288,000
To preferred shareholders	135,000*
Remainder to common shareholders	$153,000

* 9,000 × $50 × 10% × 3 years = $135,000.

16. (*b*)
17. No. The shares are an investment for Southern Co. and are issued and outstanding shares for Northern Corp.
18. Treasury stock does not affect the number of authorized or issued shares, but it reduces the outstanding shares.
19. (*a*)

Key Terms

mhhe.com/wildFAP20e

Appropriated retained earnings (p. 525)
Authorized stock (p. 511)
Basic earnings per share (p. 527)
Book value per common share (p. 528)
Book value per preferred share (p. 528)
Call price (p. 521)
Callable preferred stock (p. 521)
Capital stock (p. 511)
Changes in accounting estimates (p. 525)
Common stock (p. 510)
Complex capital structure (p. 527)
Convertible preferred stock (p. 520)
Corporation (p. 508)
Cumulative preferred stock (p. 519)
Date of declaration (p. 515)
Date of payment (p. 515)
Date of record (p. 515)
Diluted earnings per share (p. 527)
Dilutive securities (p. 527)
Discount on stock (p. 513)
Dividend in arrears (p. 519)
Dividend yield (p. 528)
Earnings per share (EPS) (p. 527)
Financial leverage (p. 521)
Large stock dividend (p. 516)
Liquidating cash dividend (p. 516)
Market value per share (p. 511)
Minimum legal capital (p. 511)
Noncumulative preferred stock (p. 519)
Nonparticipating preferred stock (p. 520)
No-par value stock (p. 511)
Organization expenses (p. 509)
Paid-in capital (p. 512)
Paid-in capital in excess of par value (p. 513)
Participating preferred stock (p. 520)
Par value (p. 511)
Par value stock (p. 511)
Preemptive right (p. 510)
Preferred stock (p. 518)
Premium on stock (p. 513)
Price-earnings (PE) ratio (p. 527)
Prior period adjustments (p. 525)
Proxy (p. 509)
Restricted retained earnings (p. 524)
Retained earnings (p. 512)
Retained earnings deficit (p. 515)
Reverse stock split (p. 518)
Simple capital structure (p. 527)
Small stock dividend (p. 516)
Stated value stock (p. 512)
Statement of stockholders' equity (p. 525)
Stock dividend (p. 516)
Stock options (p. 525)
Stock split (p. 518)
Stockholders' equity (p. 512)
Treasury stock (p. 522)

Multiple Choice Quiz

Answers on p. 549

mhhe.com/wildFAP20e

Additional Quiz Questions are available at the book's Website.

1. A corporation issues 6,000 shares of $5 par value common stock for $8 cash per share. The entry to record this transaction includes:
   a. A debit to Paid-In Capital in Excess of Par Value for $18,000.
   b. A credit to Common Stock for $48,000.
   c. A credit to Paid-In Capital in Excess of Par Value for $30,000.
   d. A credit to Cash for $48,000.
   e. A credit to Common Stock for $30,000.
2. A company reports net income of $75,000. Its weighted-average common shares outstanding is 19,000. It has no other stock outstanding. Its earnings per share is:
   a. $4.69
   b. $3.95
   c. $3.75
   d. $2.08
   e. $4.41

3. A company has 5,000 shares of $100 par preferred stock and 50,000 shares of $10 par common stock outstanding. Its total stockholders' equity is $2,000,000. Its book value per common share is:
   a. $100.00
   b. $ 10.00
   c. $ 40.00
   d. $ 30.00
   e. $ 36.36
4. A company paid cash dividends of $0.81 per share. Its earnings per share is $6.95 and its market price per share is $45.00. Its dividend yield is:
   a. 1.8%
   b. 11.7%
   c. 15.4%
   d. 55.6%
   e. 8.6%
5. A company's shares have a market value of $85 per share. Its net income is $3,500,000, and its weighted-average common shares outstanding is 700,000. Its price-earnings ratio is:
   a. 5.9
   b. 425.0
   c. 17.0
   d. 10.4
   e. 41.2

Icon denotes assignments that involve decision making.

Discussion Questions

1. What are organization expenses? Provide examples.
2. How are organization expenses reported?
3. Who is responsible for directing a corporation's affairs?
4. What is the preemptive right of common stockholders?
5. List the general rights of common stockholders.
6. What is the difference between authorized shares and outstanding shares?
7. Why would an investor find convertible preferred stock attractive?
8. What is the difference between the market value per share and the par value per share?
9. What is the difference between the par value and the call price of a share of preferred stock?
10. Identify and explain the importance of the three dates relevant to corporate dividends.
11. Why is the term *liquidating dividend* used to describe cash dividends debited against paid-in capital accounts?
12. How does declaring a stock dividend affect the corporation's assets, liabilities, and total equity? What are the effects of the eventual distribution of that stock?
13. What is the difference between a stock dividend and a stock split?
14. Courts have ruled that a stock dividend is not taxable income to stockholders. What justifies this decision?
15. How does the purchase of treasury stock affect the purchaser's assets and total equity?
16. Why do laws place limits on treasury stock purchases?
17. How are EPS results computed for a corporation with a simple capital structure?
18. What is a stock option?
19. How is book value per share computed for a corporation with no preferred stock? What is the main limitation of using book value per share to value a corporation?
20. Review the 2009 balance sheet for Nokia in Appendix A and list the amounts for treasury shares and retained earnings. NOKIA
21. Refer to Research In Motion's 2010 balance sheet in Appendix A. How many shares of common stock are authorized? How many shares of voting common stock are issued? RIM
22. Refer to the 2009 balance sheet for Palm in Appendix A. What is the par value per share of its common stock? Suggest a rationale for the amount of par value it assigned. Palm
23. Refer to the financial statements for Apple in Appendix A. What are its cash proceeds from issuance of common stock *and* its cash repurchases of common stock for the year ended September 26, 2009? Explain. Apple

connect

QUICK STUDY

QS 13-1
Characteristics of corporations
C1

Of the following statements, which are true for the corporate form of organization?
1. Owners are not agents of the corporation.
2. It is a separate legal entity.
3. It has a limited life.
4. Capital is more easily accumulated than with most other forms of organization.
5. Corporate income that is distributed to shareholders is usually taxed twice.
6. Owners have unlimited liability for corporate debts.
7. Ownership rights cannot be easily transferred.

QS 13-2
Issuance of common stock
P1

Prepare the journal entry to record Channel One Company's issuance of 100,000 shares of $0.50 par value common stock assuming the shares sell for:

a. $0.50 cash per share.
b. $2 cash per share.

QS 13-3
Issuance of no-par common stock
P1

Prepare the journal entry to record Selectist Company's issuance of 104,000 shares of no-par value common stock assuming the shares:

a. Sell for $15 cash per share.
b. Are exchanged for land valued at $1,560,000.

QS 13-4
Issuance of par and stated value common stock
P1

Prepare the journal entry to record Typist Company's issuance of 250,000 shares of its common stock assuming the shares have a:

a. $1 par value and sell for $10 cash per share.
b. $1 stated value and sell for $10 cash per share.

QS 13-5
Issuance of common stock
P1

Prepare the issuer's journal entry for each separate transaction. (*a*) On March 1, Edgar Co. issues 44,500 shares of $4 par value common stock for $255,000 cash. (*b*) On April 1, GT Co. issues no-par value common stock for $50,000 cash. (*c*) On April 6, MTV issues 2,000 shares of $20 par value common stock for $35,000 of inventory, $135,000 of machinery, and acceptance of an $84,000 note payable.

QS 13-6
Issuance of preferred stock
P1 P2

a. Prepare the journal entry to record Stefan Company's issuance of 12,000 shares of $50 par value 6% cumulative preferred stock for $75 cash per share.
b. Assuming the facts in part 1, if Stefan declares a year-end cash dividend, what is the amount of dividend paid to preferred shareholders? (Assume no dividends in arrears.)

QS 13-7
Accounting for cash dividends
P2

Prepare journal entries to record the following transactions for Emerson Corporation.

April 15 Declared a cash dividend payable to common stockholders of $40,000.
May 15 Date of record is May 15 for the cash dividend declared on April 15.
May 31 Paid the dividend declared on April 15.

QS 13-8
Dividend allocation between classes of shareholders
C2  

Stockholders' equity of STIX Company consists of 75,000 shares of $5 par value, 8% cumulative preferred stock and 200,000 shares of $1 par value common stock. Both classes of stock have been outstanding since the company's inception. STIX did not declare any dividends in the prior year, but it now declares and pays a $108,000 cash dividend at the current year-end. Determine the amount distributed to each class of stockholders for this two-year-old company.

QS 13-9
Accounting for small stock dividend
P2

The stockholders' equity section of Zacman Company's balance sheet as of April 1 follows. On April 2, Zacman declares and distributes a 10% stock dividend. The stock's per share market value on April 2 is $25 (prior to the dividend). Prepare the stockholders' equity section immediately after the stock dividend.

Common stock—$5 par value, 375,000 shares authorized, 150,000 shares issued and outstanding	$ 750,000
Paid-in capital in excess of par value, common stock	352,500
Retained earnings	633,000
Total stockholders' equity	$1,735,500

QS 13-10
Accounting for changes in estimates; error adjustments
C3 

Answer the following questions related to a company's activities for the current year:

1. After using an expected useful life of 20 years and no salvage value to depreciate its office equipment over the preceding 15 years, the company decided early this year that the equipment will last only two more years. How should the effects of this decision be reported in the current year financial statements?
2. A review of the notes payable files discovers that two years ago the company reported the entire amount of a payment (principal and interest) on an installment note payable as interest expense. This mistake had a material effect on the amount of income in that year. How should the correction be reported in the current year financial statements?

On May 3, Lassman Corporation purchased 3,000 shares of its own stock for $27,000 cash. On November 4, Lassman reissued 750 shares of this treasury stock for $7,080. Prepare the May 3 and November 4 journal entries to record Lassman's purchase and reissuance of treasury stock.

QS 13-11
Purchase and sale of treasury stock P3

Barnes Company earned net income of $450,000 this year. The number of common shares outstanding during the entire year was 200,000, and preferred shareholders received a $10,000 cash dividend. Compute Barnes Company's basic earnings per share.

QS 13-12
Basic earnings per share A1

Campbell Company reports net income of $1,200,000 for the year. It has no preferred stock, and its weighted-average common shares outstanding is 300,000 shares. Compute its basic earnings per share.

QS 13-13
Basic earnings per share A1

Compute Fox Company's price-earnings ratio if its common stock has a market value of $30.75 per share and its EPS is $4.10. Would an analyst likely consider this stock potentially over- or underpriced? Explain.

QS 13-14
Price-earnings ratio A2

Fiona Company expects to pay a $2.10 per share cash dividend this year on its common stock. The current market value of Fiona stock is $28.50 per share. Compute the expected dividend yield on the Fiona stock. Would you classify the Fiona stock as a growth or an income stock? Explain.

QS 13-15
Dividend yield A3

The stockholders' equity section of Axel Company's balance sheet follows. The preferred stock's call price is $30. Determine the book value per share of the common stock.

QS 13-16
Book value per common share
A4

Preferred stock—5% cumulative, $10 par value, 10,000 shares authorized, issued and outstanding	$100,000
Common stock—$5 par value, 100,000 shares authorized, 75,000 shares issued and outstanding	375,000
Retained earnings	445,000
Total stockholders' equity	$920,000

Air France-KLM reports the following equity information for its fiscal year ended March 31, 2009 (euros in millions). Prepare its journal entry, using its account titles, to record the issuance of capital stock assuming that its entire par value stock was issued on March 31, 2009, for cash.

QS 13-17
International equity disclosures
P1

March 31	2009
Issued capital	€2,552
Additional paid-in capital	765

connect

EXERCISES

Describe how each of the following characteristics of organizations applies to corporations.

Exercise 13-1
Characteristics of corporations
C1

1. Duration of life	5. Owner authority and control
2. Owner liability	6. Ease of formation
3. Legal status	7. Transferability of ownership
4. Tax status of income	8. Ability to raise large capital amounts

Aloha Corporation issues 6,000 shares of its common stock for $144,000 cash on February 20. Prepare journal entries to record this event under each of the following separate situations.

1. The stock has neither par nor stated value.
2. The stock has a $20 par value.
3. The stock has an $8 stated value.

Exercise 13-2
Accounting for par, stated, and no-par stock issuances
P1

Exercise 13-3
Recording stock issuances
P1

Prepare journal entries to record the following four separate issuances of stock.

1. A corporation issued 2,000 shares of no-par common stock to its promoters in exchange for their efforts, estimated to be worth $30,000. The stock has no stated value.
2. A corporation issued 2,000 shares of no-par common stock to its promoters in exchange for their efforts, estimated to be worth $30,000. The stock has a $1 per share stated value.
3. A corporation issued 4,000 shares of $10 par value common stock for $70,000 cash.
4. A corporation issued 1,000 shares of $100 par value preferred stock for $120,000 cash.

Exercise 13-4
Stock issuance for noncash assets
P1

Soku Company issues 36,000 shares of $9 par value common stock in exchange for land and a building. The land is valued at $225,000 and the building at $360,000. Prepare the journal entry to record issuance of the stock in exchange for the land and building.

Exercise 13-5
Identifying characteristics of preferred stock
C2

Match each description 1 through 6 with the characteristic of preferred stock that it best describes by writing the letter of that characteristic in the blank next to each description.

A. Cumulative **B.** Noncumulative **C.** Convertible
D. Callable **E.** Nonparticipating **F.** Participating

_______ **1.** Holders of the stock lose any dividends that are not declared in the current year.
_______ **2.** The issuing corporation can retire the stock by paying a prespecified price.
_______ **3.** Holders of the stock can receive dividends exceeding the stated rate under certain conditions.
_______ **4.** Holders of the stock are not entitled to receive dividends in excess of the stated rate.
_______ **5.** Holders of this stock can exchange it for shares of common stock.
_______ **6.** Holders of the stock are entitled to receive current and all past dividends before common stockholders receive any dividends.

Exercise 13-6
Stock dividends and splits
P2  

On June 30, 2011, Quinn Corporation's common stock is priced at $31 per share before any stock dividend or split, and the stockholders' equity section of its balance sheet appears as follows.

Common stock—$10 par value, 60,000 shares authorized, 25,000 shares issued and outstanding	$250,000
Paid-in capital in excess of par value, common stock	100,000
Retained earnings	330,000
Total stockholders' equity	$680,000

1. Assume that the company declares and immediately distributes a 100% stock dividend. This event is recorded by capitalizing retained earnings equal to the stock's par value. Answer these questions about stockholders' equity as it exists *after* issuing the new shares.
   a. What is the retained earnings balance?
   b. What is the amount of total stockholders' equity?
   c. How many shares are outstanding?
2. Assume that the company implements a 2-for-1 stock split instead of the stock dividend in part 1. Answer these questions about stockholders' equity as it exists *after* issuing the new shares.
   a. What is the retained earnings balance?
   b. What is the amount of total stockholders' equity?
   c. How many shares are outstanding?
3. Explain the difference, if any, to a stockholder from receiving new shares distributed under a large stock dividend versus a stock split.

Check (1*b*) $680,000

(2*a*) $330,000

Exercise 13-7
Stock dividends and per share book values
P2 

The stockholders' equity of Whiz.com Company at the beginning of the day on February 5 follows.

Common stock—$25 par value, 150,000 shares authorized, 60,000 shares issued and outstanding	$1,500,000
Paid-in capital in excess of par value, common stock	525,000
Retained earnings	675,000
Total stockholders' equity	$2,700,000

On February 5, the directors declare a 20% stock dividend distributable on February 28 to the February 15 stockholders of record. The stock's market value is $40 per share on February 5 before the stock dividend. The stock's market value is $34 per share on February 28.

1. Prepare entries to record both the dividend declaration and its distribution.
2. One stockholder owned 750 shares on February 5 before the dividend. Compute the book value per share and total book value of this stockholder's shares immediately before *and* after the stock dividend of February 5.
3. Compute the total market value of the investor's shares in part 2 as of February 5 and February 28.

Check (2) Book value per share: before, $45; after, $37.50

Exercise 13-8
Dividends on common and noncumulative preferred stock
C2

Wade's outstanding stock consists of 40,000 shares of *noncumulative* 7.5% preferred stock with a $10 par value and also 100,000 shares of common stock with a $1 par value. During its first four years of operation, the corporation declared and paid the following total cash dividends.

2011	$ 10,000
2012	24,000
2013	100,000
2014	196,000

Determine the amount of dividends paid each year to each of the two classes of stockholders: preferred and common. Also compute the total dividends paid to each class for the four years combined.

Check 4-year total paid to preferred, $94,000

Exercise 13-9
Dividends on common and cumulative preferred stock C2

Use the data in Exercise 13-8 to determine the amount of dividends paid each year to each of the two classes of stockholders assuming that the preferred stock is *cumulative*. Also determine the total dividends paid to each class for the four years combined.

Exercise 13-10
Recording and reporting treasury stock transactions
P3 

On October 10, the stockholders' equity of Noble Systems appears as follows.

Common stock—$10 par value, 36,000 shares authorized, issued, and outstanding	$360,000
Paid-in capital in excess of par value, common stock	108,000
Retained earnings	432,000
Total stockholders' equity	$900,000

1. Prepare journal entries to record the following transactions for Noble Systems.
   a. Purchased 4,500 shares of its own common stock at $30 per share on October 11.
   b. Sold 1,200 treasury shares on November 1 for $36 cash per share.
   c. Sold all remaining treasury shares on November 25 for $25 cash per share.
2. Explain how the company's equity section changes after the October 11 treasury stock purchase, and prepare the revised equity section of its balance sheet at that date.

Check (1*c*) Dr. Retained Earnings, $9,300

Exercise 13-11
Preparing a statement of retained earnings
C3

The following information is available for Ballard Company for the year ended December 31, 2011.

a. Balance of retained earnings, December 31, 2010, prior to discovery of error, $850,000.
b. Cash dividends declared and paid during 2011, $15,000.
c. It neglected to record 2009 depreciation expense of $55,600, which is net of $5,500 in income taxes.
d. The company earned $205,000 in 2011 net income.

Prepare a 2011 statement of retained earnings for Ballard Company.

Exercise 13-12
Earnings per share
A1

Guess Company reports $648,500 of net income for 2011 and declares $102,500 of cash dividends on its preferred stock for 2011. At the end of 2011, the company had 260,000 weighted-average shares of common stock.

1. What amount of net income is available to common stockholders for 2011?
2. What is the company's basic EPS for 2011?

Check (2) $2.10

Exercise 13-13
Earnings per share
A1

Franklin Company reports $698,000 of net income for 2011 and declares $75,500 of cash dividends on its preferred stock for 2011. At the end of 2011, the company had 175,000 weighted-average shares of common stock.

Check (2) $3.56

1. What amount of net income is available to common stockholders for 2011?
2. What is the company's basic EPS for 2011? Round your answer to the nearest whole cent.

Exercise 13-14
Dividend yield computation and interpretation
A3 

Compute the dividend yield for each of these four separate companies. Which company's stock would probably *not* be classified as an income stock? Explain.

Company	Annual Cash Dividend per Share	Market Value per Share
1	$15.00	$216.00
2	12.00	128.00
3	6.00	61.00
4	1.20	86.00

Exercise 13-15
Price-earnings ratio computation and interpretation
A2 

Compute the price-earnings ratio for each of these four separate companies. Which stock might an analyst likely investigate as being potentially undervalued by the market? Explain.

Company	Earnings per Share	Market Value per Share
1	$10.00	$166.00
2	9.00	90.00
3	6.50	84.50
4	40.00	240.00

Exercise 13-16
Book value per share
A4 

The equity section of Webster Corporation's balance sheet shows the following.

Preferred stock—5% cumulative, $10 par value, $15 call price, 10,000 shares issued and outstanding	$100,000
Common stock—$10 par value, 55,000 shares issued and outstanding	550,000
Retained earnings	267,500
Total stockholders' equity	$917,500

Determine the book value per share of the preferred and common stock under two separate situations.

Check (1) Book value of common, $13.95

1. No preferred dividends are in arrears.
2. Three years of preferred dividends are in arrears.

Exercise 13-17
Accounting for equity under IFRS
C3 P1 

Unilever Group reports the following equity information for the years ended December 31, 2007 and 2008 (euros in millions).

December 31	2008	2007
Share capital	€ 484	€ 484
Share premium	121	153
Other reserves	(6,469)	(3,412)
Retained profit	15,812	15,162
Shareholders' equity	€ 9,948	€12,387

1. For each of the three account titles *share capital, share premium,* and *retained profit,* match it with the usual account title applied under U.S. GAAP from the following options:
   a. Paid-in capital in excess of par value, common stock
   b. Retained earnings
   c. Common stock, par value
2. Prepare Unilever's journal entry, using its account titles, to record the issuance of capital stock assuming that its entire par value stock was issued on December 31, 2007, for cash.
3. What were Unilever's 2008 dividends assuming that only dividends and income impacted retained profit for 2008 and that its 2008 income totaled €2,692?

Exercise 13-18
Cash dividends, treasury stock, and statement of retained earnings
C3 P2 P3

Kroll Corporation reports the following components of stockholders' equity on December 31, 2011.

Common stock—$25 par value, 40,000 shares authorized, 30,000 shares issued and outstanding	$ 750,000
Paid-in capital in excess of par value, common stock	50,000
Retained earnings	260,000
Total stockholders' equity	$1,060,000

In year 2012, the following transactions affected its stockholders' equity accounts.

Jan. 2	Purchased 2,000 shares of its own stock at $25 cash per share.
Jan. 7	Directors declared a $2 per share cash dividend payable on Feb. 28 to the Feb. 9 stockholders of record.
Feb. 28	Paid the dividend declared on January 7.
July 9	Sold 500 of its treasury shares at $30 cash per share.
Aug. 27	Sold 1,500 of its treasury shares at $23 cash per share.
Sept. 9	Directors declared a $2 per share cash dividend payable on October 22 to the September 23 stockholders of record.
Oct. 22	Paid the dividend declared on September 9.
Dec. 31	Closed the $8,000 credit balance (from net income) in the Income Summary account to Retained Earnings.

Required

1. Prepare journal entries to record each of these transactions for 2012.
2. Prepare a statement of retained earnings for the year ended December 31, 2012.
3. Prepare the stockholders' equity section of the company's balance sheet as of December 31, 2012.

connect

PROBLEM SET A

Problem 13-1A
Stockholders' equity transactions and analysis
C2 P1 

Oxygen Co. is incorporated at the beginning of this year and engages in a number of transactions. The following journal entries impacted its stockholders' equity during its first year of operations.

a.	Cash	150,000	
	Common Stock, $25 Par Value		125,000
	Paid-In Capital in Excess of Par Value, Common Stock		25,000
b.	Organization Expenses	75,000	
	Common Stock, $25 Par Value		62,500
	Paid-In Capital in Excess of Par Value, Common Stock		12,500
c.	Cash	21,500	
	Accounts Receivable	7,500	
	Building	30,000	
	Notes Payable		19,000
	Common Stock, $25 Par Value		25,000
	Paid-In Capital in Excess of Par Value, Common Stock		15,000

[continued on next page]

[continued from previous page]

d.	Cash	60,000	
	Common Stock, $25 Par Value		37,500
	Paid-In Capital in Excess of Par Value, Common Stock		22,500

Required

1. Explain the transaction(s) underlying each journal entry (*a*) through (*d*).
2. How many shares of common stock are outstanding at year-end?
3. What is the amount of minimum legal capital (based on par value) at year-end?
4. What is the total paid-in capital at year-end?
5. What is the book value per share of the common stock at year-end if total paid-in capital plus retained earnings equals $347,500?

Check (2) 10,000 shares (3) $250,000 (4) $325,000

Problem 13-2A
Cash dividends, treasury stock, and statement of retained earnings
C3 P2 P3

Context Corporation reports the following components of stockholders' equity on December 31, 2011.

Common stock—$10 par value, 50,000 shares authorized, 20,000 shares issued and outstanding	$200,000
Paid-in capital in excess of par value, common stock	30,000
Retained earnings	135,000
Total stockholders' equity	$365,000

In year 2012, the following transactions affected its stockholders' equity accounts.

Jan. 1	Purchased 2,000 shares of its own stock at $20 cash per share.
Jan. 5	Directors declared a $2 per share cash dividend payable on Feb. 28 to the Feb. 5 stockholders of record.
Feb. 28	Paid the dividend declared on January 5.
July 6	Sold 750 of its treasury shares at $24 cash per share.
Aug. 22	Sold 1,250 of its treasury shares at $17 cash per share.
Sept. 5	Directors declared a $2 per share cash dividend payable on October 28 to the September 25 stockholders of record.
Oct. 28	Paid the dividend declared on September 5.
Dec. 31	Closed the $194,000 credit balance (from net income) in the Income Summary account to Retained Earnings.

Required

1. Prepare journal entries to record each of these transactions for 2012.
2. Prepare a statement of retained earnings for the year ended December 31, 2012.
3. Prepare the stockholders' equity section of the company's balance sheet as of December 31, 2012.

Check (2) Retained earnings, Dec. 31, 2012, $252,250.

Problem 13-3A
Equity analysis—journal entries and account balances
P2

At September 30, the end of Excel Company's third quarter, the following stockholders' equity accounts are reported.

Common stock, $12 par value	$720,000
Paid-in capital in excess of par value, common stock	180,000
Retained earnings	640,000

In the fourth quarter, the following entries related to its equity are recorded.

Oct. 2	Retained Earnings	120,000	
	Common Dividend Payable		120,000
Oct. 25	Common Dividend Payable	120,000	
	Cash		120,000
Oct. 31	Retained Earnings	150,000	
	Common Stock Dividend Distributable		72,000
	Paid-In Capital in Excess of Par Value, Common Stock		78,000

[continued on next page]

[continued from previous page]

Nov. 5	Common Stock Dividend Distributable	72,000	
	Common Stock, $12 Par Value		72,000
Dec. 1	Memo—Change the title of the common stock account to reflect the new par value of $4.		
Dec. 31	Income Summary	420,000	
	Retained Earnings		420,000

Required

1. Explain the transaction(s) underlying each journal entry.

2. Complete the following table showing the equity account balances at each indicated date (include the balances from September 30).

	Oct. 2	Oct. 25	Oct. 31	Nov. 5	Dec. 1	Dec. 31
Common stock	$____	$____	$____	$____	$____	$____
Common stock dividend distributable	____	____	____	____	____	____
Paid-in capital in excess of par, common stock	____	____	____	____	____	____
Retained earnings	____	____	____	____	____	____
Total equity	$____	$____	$____	$____	$____	$____

Check Total equity: Oct. 2, $1,420,000; Dec. 31, $1,840,000

Problem 13-4A
Analysis of changes in stockholders' equity accounts

C3 P2 P3 

The equity sections from Salazar Group's 2011 and 2012 year-end balance sheets follow.

Stockholders' Equity (December 31, 2011)	
Common stock—$4 par value, 50,000 shares authorized, 20,000 shares issued and outstanding	$ 80,000
Paid-in capital in excess of par value, common stock	60,000
Retained earnings	160,000
Total stockholders' equity	$300,000

Stockholders' Equity (December 31, 2012)	
Common stock—$4 par value, 50,000 shares authorized, 23,700 shares issued, 1,500 shares in treasury	$ 94,800
Paid-in capital in excess of par value, common stock	89,600
Retained earnings ($15,000 restricted by treasury stock)	200,000
	384,400
Less cost of treasury stock	(15,000)
Total stockholders' equity	$369,400

The following transactions and events affected its equity during year 2012.

Jan. 5	Declared a $0.50 per share cash dividend, date of record January 10.
Mar. 20	Purchased treasury stock for cash.
Apr. 5	Declared a $0.50 per share cash dividend, date of record April 10.
July 5	Declared a $0.50 per share cash dividend, date of record July 10.
July 31	Declared a 20% stock dividend when the stock's market value is $12 per share.
Aug. 14	Issued the stock dividend that was declared on July 31.
Oct. 5	Declared a $0.50 per share cash dividend, date of record October 10.

Required

1. How many common shares are outstanding on each cash dividend date?

2. What is the total dollar amount for each of the four cash dividends?

3. What is the amount of the capitalization of retained earnings for the stock dividend?

4. What is the per share cost of the treasury stock purchased?

5. How much net income did the company earn during year 2012?

Check (3) $44,400
(4) $10
(5) $124,000

Problem 13-5A
Computation of book values and dividend allocations
C2 A4 

Razz Corporation's common stock is currently selling on a stock exchange at $170 per share, and its current balance sheet shows the following stockholders' equity section.

Preferred stock—5% cumulative, $___ par value, 1,000 shares authorized, issued, and outstanding	$100,000
Common stock—$___ par value, 4,000 shares authorized, issued, and outstanding	160,000
Retained earnings	300,000
Total stockholders' equity	$560,000

Required (Round per share amounts to cents.)

1. What is the current market value (price) of this corporation's common stock?
2. What are the par values of the corporation's preferred stock and its common stock?
3. If no dividends are in arrears, what are the book values per share of the preferred stock and the common stock?
4. If two years' preferred dividends are in arrears, what are the book values per share of the preferred stock and the common stock?
5. If two years' preferred dividends are in arrears and the preferred stock is callable at $110 per share, what are the book values per share of the preferred stock and the common stock?
6. If two years' preferred dividends are in arrears and the board of directors declares cash dividends of $20,000, what total amount will be paid to the preferred and to the common shareholders? What is the amount of dividends per share for the common stock?

Check (4) Book value of common, $112.50
(5) Book value of common, $110
(6) Dividends per common share, $1.25

Analysis Component

7. What are some factors that can contribute to a difference between the book value of common stock and its market value (price)?

PROBLEM SET B

Problem 13-1B
Stockholders' equity transactions and analysis
C2 P1 

Nilson Company is incorporated at the beginning of this year and engages in a number of transactions. The following journal entries impacted its stockholders' equity during its first year of operations.

a.	Cash	60,000	
	Common Stock, $1 Par Value		1,500
	Paid-In Capital in Excess of Par Value, Common Stock		58,500
b.	Organization Expenses	20,000	
	Common Stock, $1 Par Value		500
	Paid-In Capital in Excess of Par Value, Common Stock		19,500
c.	Cash	6,650	
	Accounts Receivable	4,000	
	Building	12,500	
	Notes Payable		3,150
	Common Stock, $1 Par Value		400
	Paid-In Capital in Excess of Par Value, Common Stock		19,600
d.	Cash	30,000	
	Common Stock, $1 Par Value		600
	Paid-In Capital in Excess of Par Value, Common Stock		29,400

Required

1. Explain the transaction(s) underlying each journal entry (*a*) through (*d*).
2. How many shares of common stock are outstanding at year-end?
3. What is the amount of minimum legal capital (based on par value) at year-end?

Check (2) 3,000 shares
(3) $3,000

4. What is the total paid-in capital at year-end?

(4) $130,000

5. What is the book value per share of the common stock at year-end if total paid-in capital plus retained earnings equals $141,500?

Problem 13-2B
Cash dividends, treasury stock, and statement of retained earnings
C3 P2 P3

Baycore Corp. reports the following components of stockholders' equity on December 31, 2011.

Common stock—$1 par value, 160,000 shares authorized, 100,000 shares issued and outstanding	$ 100,000
Paid-in capital in excess of par value, common stock	700,000
Retained earnings	1,080,000
Total stockholders' equity	$1,880,000

It completed the following transactions related to stockholders' equity in year 2012.

Jan. 10 Purchased 20,000 shares of its own stock at $12 cash per share.
Mar. 2 Directors declared a $1.50 per share cash dividend payable on March 31 to the March 15 stockholders of record.
Mar. 31 Paid the dividend declared on March 2.
Nov. 11 Sold 12,000 of its treasury shares at $13 cash per share.
Nov. 25 Sold 8,000 of its treasury shares at $9.50 cash per share.
Dec. 1 Directors declared a $2.50 per share cash dividend payable on January 2 to the December 10 stockholders of record.
Dec. 31 Closed the $536,000 credit balance (from net income) in the Income Summary account to Retained Earnings.

Required

1. Prepare journal entries to record each of these transactions for 2012.
2. Prepare a statement of retained earnings for the year ended December 31, 2012.
3. Prepare the stockholders' equity section of the company's balance sheet as of December 31, 2012.

Check (2) Retained earnings, Dec. 31, 2012, $1,238,000

Problem 13-3B
Equity analysis—journal entries and account balances
P2

At December 31, the end of Intertec Communication's third quarter, the following stockholders' equity accounts are reported.

Common stock, $10 par value	$480,000
Paid-in capital in excess of par value, common stock	192,000
Retained earnings	800,000

In the fourth quarter, the following entries related to its equity are recorded.

Jan. 17	Retained Earnings	48,000	
	Common Dividend Payable		48,000
Feb. 5	Common Dividend Payable	48,000	
	Cash		48,000
Feb. 28	Retained Earnings	126,000	
	Common Stock Dividend Distributable		60,000
	Paid-In Capital in Excess of Par Value, Common Stock		66,000
Mar. 14	Common Stock Dividend Distributable	60,000	
	Common Stock, $10 Par Value		60,000
Mar. 25	Memo—Change the title of the common stock account to reflect the new par value of $5.		
Mar. 31	Income Summary	360,000	
	Retained Earnings		360,000

Required

1. Explain the transaction(s) underlying each journal entry.
2. Complete the following table showing the equity account balances at each indicated date (include the balances from December 31).

	Jan. 17	Feb. 5	Feb. 28	Mar. 14	Mar. 25	Mar. 31
Common stock	$____	$____	$____	$____	$____	$____
Common stock dividend distributable	____	____	____	____	____	____
Paid-in capital in excess of par, common stock	____	____	____	____	____	____
Retained earnings	____	____	____	____	____	____
Total equity	$____	$____	$____	$____	$____	$____

Check Total equity: Jan. 17, $1,424,000; Mar. 31, $1,784,000

Problem 13-4B
Analysis of changes in stockholders' equity accounts
C3 P2 P3 

The equity sections from Jetta Corporation's 2011 and 2012 balance sheets follow.

Stockholders' Equity (December 31, 2011)	
Common stock—$20 par value, 15,000 shares authorized, 8,500 shares issued and outstanding	$170,000
Paid-in capital in excess of par value, common stock	30,000
Retained earnings	135,000
Total stockholders' equity	$335,000

Stockholders' Equity (December 31, 2012)	
Common stock—$20 par value, 15,000 shares authorized, 9,500 shares issued, 500 shares in treasury	$190,000
Paid-in capital in excess of par value, common stock	52,000
Retained earnings ($20,000 restricted by treasury stock)	147,600
	389,600
Less cost of treasury stock	(20,000)
Total stockholders' equity	$369,600

The following transactions and events affected its equity during year 2012.

Feb. 15 Declared a $0.40 per share cash dividend, date of record five days later.
Mar. 2 Purchased treasury stock for cash.
May 15 Declared a $0.40 per share cash dividend, date of record five days later.
Aug. 15 Declared a $0.40 per share cash dividend, date of record five days later.
Oct. 4 Declared a 12.5% stock dividend when the stock's market value is $42 per share.
Oct. 20 Issued the stock dividend that was declared on October 4.
Nov. 15 Declared a $0.40 per share cash dividend, date of record five days later.

Required

1. How many common shares are outstanding on each cash dividend date?
2. What is the total dollar amount for each of the four cash dividends?
3. What is the amount of the capitalization of retained earnings for the stock dividend?
4. What is the per share cost of the treasury stock purchased?
5. How much net income did the company earn during year 2012?

Check (3) $42,000
(4) $40
(5) $68,000

Problem 13-5B
Computation of book values and dividend allocations
C2 A4 

Scotch Company's common stock is currently selling on a stock exchange at $45 per share, and its current balance sheet shows the following stockholders' equity section.

Preferred stock—8% cumulative, $___ par value, 1,500 shares authorized, issued, and outstanding	$ 187,500
Common stock—$___ par value, 18,000 shares authorized, issued, and outstanding	450,000
Retained earnings	562,500
Total stockholders' equity	$1,200,000

Required (Round per share amounts to cents.)

1. What is the current market value (price) of this corporation's common stock?
2. What are the par values of the corporation's preferred stock and its common stock?
3. If no dividends are in arrears, what are the book values per share of the preferred stock and the common stock? (Round per share values to the nearest cent.)
4. If two years' preferred dividends are in arrears, what are the book values per share of the preferred stock and the common stock? (Round per share values to the nearest cent.)
5. If two years' preferred dividends are in arrears and the preferred stock is callable at $140 per share, what are the book values per share of the preferred stock and the common stock? (Round per share values to the nearest cent.)
6. If two years' preferred dividends are in arrears and the board of directors declares cash dividends of $50,000, what total amount will be paid to the preferred and to the common shareholders? What is the amount of dividends per share for the common stock? (Round per share values to the nearest cent.)

Check (4) Book value of common, $54.58

(5) Book value of common, $53.33

(6) Dividends per common share, $0.28

Analysis Component

7. Discuss why the book value of common stock is not always a good estimate of its market value.

SERIAL PROBLEM

Business Solutions

P1 C1 C2

(This serial problem began in Chapter 1 and continues through most of the book. If previous chapter segments were not completed, the serial problem can begin at this point. It is helpful, but not necessary, to use the Working Papers that accompany the book.)

SP 13 Santana Rey created Business Solutions on October 1, 2011. The company has been successful, and Santana plans to expand her business. She believes that an additional $86,000 is needed and is investigating three funding sources.

a. Santana's sister Cicely is willing to invest $86,000 in the business as a common shareholder. Since Santana currently has about $129,000 invested in the business, Cicely's investment will mean that Santana will maintain about 60% ownership, and Cicely will have 40% ownership of Business Solutions.
b. Santana's uncle Marcello is willing to invest $86,000 in the business as a preferred shareholder. Marcello would purchase 860 shares of $100 par value, 7% preferred stock.
c. Santana's banker is willing to lend her $86,000 on a 7%, 10-year note payable. She would make monthly payments of $1,000 per month for 10 years.

Required

1. Prepare the journal entry to reflect the initial $86,000 investment under each of the options (a), (b), and (c).
2. Evaluate the three proposals for expansion, providing the pros and cons of each option.
3. Which option do you recommend Santana adopt? Explain.

Beyond the Numbers

REPORTING IN ACTION

C2 A1 A4

RIM

BTN 13-1 Refer to Research In Motion's financial statements in Appendix A to answer the following.

1. How many shares of common stock are issued and outstanding at February 27, 2010, and February 28, 2009? How do these numbers compare with the basic weighted-average common shares outstanding at February 27, 2010, and February 28, 2009?
2. What is the book value of its entire common stock at February 27, 2010?
3. What is the total amount of cash dividends paid to common stockholders for the years ended February 27, 2010, and February 28, 2009?
4. Identify and compare basic EPS amounts across fiscal years 2010, 2009, and 2008. Identify and comment on any notable changes.
5. How many shares does Research In Motion hold in treasury stock, if any, as of February 27, 2010? As of February 28, 2009?

Fast Forward

6. Access Research In Motion's financial statements for fiscal years ending after February 27, 2010, from its Website (RIM.com) or the SEC's EDGAR database (www.SEC.gov). Has the number of common shares outstanding increased since that date? Has the company increased the total amount of cash dividends paid compared to the total amount for fiscal year 2010?

COMPARATIVE ANALYSIS

A1 A2 A3 A4 

RIM
Palm
Apple

BTN 13-2 Key comparative figures for Research In Motion, Palm, and Apple follow.

Key Figures	Research In Motion	Palm	Apple
Net income (in millions)	$2,457	$ (753)	$8,235
Cash dividends declared per common share	$ —	$ —	$ —
Common shares outstanding (in millions)	557	140	900
Weighted-average common shares outstanding (in mil.)	564	116	893
Market value (price) per share	$69.76	$12.19	$184.40
Equity applicable to common shares (in millions)	$7,603	$ (414)	$31,640

Required

1. Compute the book value per common share for each company using these data.
2. Compute the basic EPS for each company using these data.
3. Compute the dividend yield for each company using these data. Does the dividend yield of any of the companies characterize it as an income or growth stock? Explain.
4. Compute, compare, and interpret the price-earnings ratio for each company using these data.

ETHICS CHALLENGE

C3

BTN 13-3 Gianna Tuck is an accountant for Post Pharmaceuticals. Her duties include tracking research and development spending in the new product development division. Over the course of the past six months, Gianna notices that a great deal of funds have been spent on a particular project for a new drug. She hears "through the grapevine" that the company is about to patent the drug and expects it to be a major advance in antibiotics. Gianna believes that this new drug will greatly improve company performance and will cause the company's stock to increase in value. Gianna decides to purchase shares of Post in order to benefit from this expected increase.

Required

What are Gianna's ethical responsibilities, if any, with respect to the information she has learned through her duties as an accountant for Post Pharmaceuticals? What are the implications to her planned purchase of Post shares?

COMMUNICATING IN PRACTICE

A1 A2

BTN 13-4 Teams are to select an industry, and each team member is to select a different company in that industry. Each team member then is to acquire the selected company's financial statements (or Form 10-K) from the SEC site (www.SEC.gov). Use these data to identify basic EPS. Use the financial press (or finance.yahoo.com) to determine the market price of this stock, and then compute the price-earnings ratio. Communicate with teammates via a meeting, e-mail, or telephone to discuss the meaning of this ratio, how companies compare, and the industry norm. The team must prepare a single memorandum reporting the ratio for each company and identifying the team conclusions or consensus of opinion. The memorandum is to be duplicated and distributed to the instructor and teammates.

Hint: Make a transparency of each team's memo for a class discussion.

TAKING IT TO THE NET

C1 C3 

BTN 13-5 Access the February 26, 2010, filing of the 2009 calendar-year 10-K report of McDonald's, (ticker MCD) from www.SEC.gov.

Required

1. Review McDonald's balance sheet and identify how many classes of stock it has issued.
2. What are the par values, number of authorized shares, and issued shares of the classes of stock you identified in part 1?
3. Review its statement of cash flows and identify what total amount of cash it paid in 2009 to purchase treasury stock.
4. What amount did McDonald's pay out in common stock cash dividends for 2009?

TEAMWORK IN ACTION

P3

BTN 13-6 This activity requires teamwork to reinforce understanding of accounting for treasury stock.

1. Write a brief team statement (*a*) generalizing what happens to a corporation's financial position when it engages in a stock "buyback" and (*b*) identifying reasons why a corporation would engage in this activity.
2. Assume that an entity acquires 100 shares of its $100 par value common stock at a cost of $134 cash per share. Discuss the entry to record this acquisition. Next, assign *each* team member to prepare *one* of the following entries (assume each entry applies to all shares):
   a. Reissue treasury shares at cost.
   b. Reissue treasury shares at $150 per share.

Hint: Instructor should be sure each team accurately completes part 1 before proceeding.

c. Reissue treasury shares at $120 per share; assume the paid-in capital account from treasury shares has a $1,500 balance.

d. Reissue treasury shares at $120 per share; assume the paid-in capital account from treasury shares has a $1,000 balance.

e. Reissue treasury shares at $120 per share; assume the paid-in capital account from treasury shares has a zero balance.

3. In sequence, each member is to present his/her entry to the team and explain the *similarities* and *differences* between that entry and the previous entry.

ENTREPRENEURIAL DECISION

C2 P2

BTN 13-7 Assume that Kelly Giard of Clean Air Lawn Care decides to launch a new retail chain to market electrical mowers. This chain, named Mow Green, requires $500,000 of start-up capital. Kelly contributes $375,000 of personal assets in return for 15,000 shares of common stock, but he must raise another $125,000 in cash. There are two alternative plans for raising the additional cash. *Plan A* is to sell 3,750 shares of common stock to one or more investors for $125,000 cash. *Plan B* is to sell 1,250 shares of cumulative preferred stock to one or more investors for $125,000 cash (this preferred stock would have a $100 par value, an annual 8% dividend rate, and be issued at par).

1. If the new business is expected to earn $72,000 of after-tax net income in the first year, what rate of return on beginning equity will Kelly earn under each alternative plan? Which plan will provide the higher expected return?

2. If the new business is expected to earn $16,800 of after-tax net income in the first year, what rate of return on beginning equity will Kelly earn under each alternative plan? Which plan will provide the higher expected return?

3. Analyze and interpret the differences between the results for parts 1 and 2.

HITTING THE ROAD

A1 A2 A3

BTN 13-8 Review 30 to 60 minutes of financial news programming on television. Take notes on companies that are catching analysts' attention. You might hear reference to over- and undervaluation of firms and to reports about PE ratios, dividend yields, and earnings per share. Be prepared to give a brief description to the class of your observations.

GLOBAL DECISION

A1 C3

NOKIA

BTN 13-9 Financial information for Nokia Corporation (www.nokia.com) follows.

Net income (in millions)	€ 260
Cash dividends declared (in millions)	€ 1,481
Cash dividends declared per share	€ 0.40
Number of shares outstanding (in millions)*	3,708
Equity applicable to shares (in millions)	€14,749

* Assume that for Nokia the year-end number of shares outstanding approximates the weighted-average shares outstanding.

Required

1. Compute book value per share for Nokia.

2. Compute earnings per share (EPS) for Nokia.

3. Compare Nokia's dividends per share with its EPS. Is Nokia paying out a large or small amount of its income as dividends? Explain.

ANSWERS TO MULTIPLE CHOICE QUIZ

1. e; Entry to record this stock issuance is:

Cash (6,000 × $8)	48,000	
Common Stock (6,000 × $5)		30,000
Paid-In Capital in Excess of Par Value, Common Stock		18,000

2. b; $75,000/19,000 shares = $3.95 per share

3. d; Preferred stock = 5,000 × $100 = $500,000
Book value per share = ($2,000,000 − $500,000)/50,000 shares = $30 per common share

4. a; $0.81/$45.00 = 1.8%

5. c; Earnings per share = $3,500,000/700,000 shares = $5 per share
PE ratio = $85/$5 = 17.0

14 Long-Term Liabilities

A Look Back

Chapter 13 focused on corporate equity transactions, including stock issuances and dividends. We also explained how to report and analyze income, earnings per share, and retained earnings.

A Look at This Chapter

This chapter describes the accounting for and analysis of bonds and notes. We explain their characteristics, payment patterns, interest computations, retirement, and reporting requirements. An appendix to this chapter introduces leases and pensions.

A Look Ahead

Chapter 15 focuses on how to classify, account for, and report investments in both debt and equity securities. We also describe accounting for transactions listed in a foreign currency.

Learning Objectives

CAP

CONCEPTUAL

C1 Explain the types and payment patterns of notes. (p. 562)

C2 *Appendix 14A*—Explain and compute the present value of an amount(s) to be paid at a future date(s). (p. 570)

C3 *Appendix 14C*—Describe interest accrual when bond payment periods differ from accounting periods. (p. 574)

C4 *Appendix 14D*—Describe accounting for leases and pensions. (p. 576)

ANALYTICAL

A1 Compare bond financing with stock financing. (p. 552)

A2 Assess debt features and their implications. (p. 566)

A3 Compute the debt-to-equity ratio and explain its use. (p. 566)

LP14

PROCEDURAL

P1 Prepare entries to record bond issuance and interest expense. (p. 554)

P2 Compute and record amortization of bond discount. (p. 555)

P3 Compute and record amortization of bond premium. (p. 558)

P4 Record the retirement of bonds. (p. 561)

P5 Prepare entries to account for notes. (p. 564)

Decision Insight

Love At First Bite

"Each individual problem you face is totally surmountable"
—WARREN BROWN

WASHINGTON, DC—Warren Brown started baking cakes in his apartment after work each evening. He sold his sweet concoctions mostly to coworkers and friends, and even held a cake open house at the local art gallery. But Warren was determined to grow his business. He took a course in entrepreneurship at his local community college, and there he discovered the importance of financial reporting and accounting.

Launching his fledgling cake business presented Warren with many challenges. He needed to especially focus on the important task of managing liabilities for payroll, baking supplies, employee benefits, training, and taxes. Warren insists that effective management of liabilities, especially long-term financing from sources such as bonds and notes, is crucial to business success. "Everything feels like a disaster when it's right in your face," says Warren. "You just have to be calm, look at what you're doing, and fix the problem."

Warren fixed the problems and unveiled his business called Cake Love **(CakeLove.com),** funded with short- and long-term notes. "I opened up this tiny retail, walk-up bakery . . . [to sell] goodies that are baked from scratch," Warren explains. Today Cake Love entices the neighborhood with a gentle scent of fresh bakery and a sidewalk view into the kitchen. Warmly painted walls, comfy window seats, and free wireless Internet encourage customers to lounge for hours. "I want it to be relaxed and comfortable," says Warren. "People can bring their work, their kids, their friends, and just relax."

Warren continues to monitor liabilities and their payment patterns, and he is not shy about striving to better learn the accounting side. "I'm always getting better, improving my skills," he explains. Warren insists that accounting for and monitoring liabilities of long-term financing are important ingredients to a successful start-up. His company now generates sufficient income to pay for liabilities of interest and principal on long-term debt and still produces revenue growth for expansion. He shows a keen appetite for using accounting information to make good business decisions. "But," says Warren, "I love eating what I make more."

"The bigger message of Cake Love is finding your passion and working to reach your goals," explains Warren. That's a slice of advice worth more than any amount of dough.

[Sources: *Cake Love Website,* January 2011; *Black Enterprise,* September 2004; *Georgetown Voice,* March 2005; *National Public Radio (NPR) Website,* May 2005; *Inc.com,* April 2005]

Chapter Preview

Individuals, companies, and governments issue bonds to finance their activities. In return for financing, bonds promise to repay the lender with interest. This chapter explains the basics of bonds and the accounting for their issuance and retirement. The chapter also describes long-term notes as another financing source. We explain how present value concepts impact both the accounting for and reporting of bonds and notes. Appendixes to this chapter discuss present value concepts applicable to liabilities, effective interest amortization, and the accounting for leases and pensions.

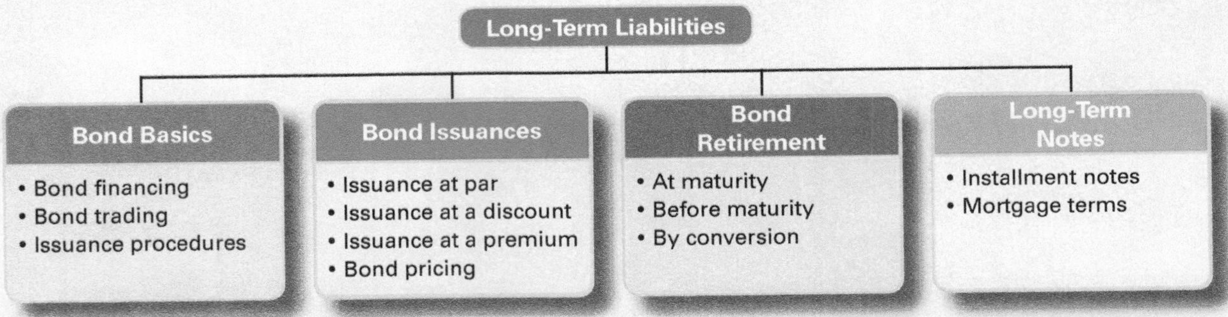

BASICS OF BONDS

This section explains the basics of bonds and a company's motivation for issuing them.

Bond Financing

Projects that demand large amounts of money often are funded from bond issuances. (Both for-profit and nonprofit companies, as well as governmental units, such as nations, states, cities, and school districts, issue bonds.) A **bond** is its issuer's written promise to pay an amount identified as the par value of the bond with interest. The **par value of a bond,** also called the *face amount* or *face value,* is paid at a specified future date known as the bond's *maturity date.* Most bonds also require the issuer to make semiannual interest payments. The amount of interest paid each period is determined by multiplying the par value of the bond by the bond's contract rate of interest for that same period. This section explains both advantages and disadvantages of bond financing.

Advantages of Bonds There are three main advantages of bond financing:

1. *Bonds do not affect owner control.* Equity financing reflects ownership in a company, whereas bond financing does not. A person who contributes $1,000 of a company's $10,000 equity financing typically controls one-tenth of all owner decisions. A person who owns a $1,000, 11%, 20-year bond has no ownership right. This person, or bondholder, is to receive from the bond issuer 11% interest, or $110, each year the bond is outstanding and $1,000 when it matures in 20 years.

2. *Interest on bonds is tax deductible.* Bond interest payments are tax deductible for the issuer, but equity payments (distributions) to owners are not. To illustrate, assume that a corporation with no bond financing earns $15,000 in income *before* paying taxes at a 40% tax rate, which amounts to $6,000 ($15,000 × 40%) in taxes. If a portion of its financing is in bonds, however, the resulting bond interest is deducted in computing taxable income. That is, if bond interest expense is $10,000, the taxes owed would be $2,000 ([$15,000 − $10,000] × 40%), which is less than the $6,000 owed with no bond financing.

3. *Bonds can increase return on equity.* A company that earns a higher return with borrowed funds than it pays in interest on those funds increases its return on equity. This process is called *financial leverage* or *trading on the equity.*

Point: Financial leverage reflects issuance of bonds, notes, or preferred stock.

To illustrate the third point, consider Magnum Co., which has $1 million in equity and is planning a $500,000 expansion to meet increasing demand for its product. Magnum predicts the

$500,000 expansion will yield $125,000 in additional income before paying any interest. It currently earns $100,000 per year and has no interest expense. Magnum is considering three plans. Plan A is to not expand. Plan B is to expand and raise $500,000 from equity financing. Plan C is to expand and issue $500,000 of bonds that pay 10% annual interest ($50,000). Exhibit 14.1 shows how these three plans affect Magnum's net income, equity, and return on equity (net income/equity). The owner(s) will earn a higher return on equity if expansion occurs. Moreover, the preferred expansion plan is to issue bonds. Projected net income under Plan C ($175,000) is smaller than under Plan B ($225,000), but the return on equity is larger because of less equity investment. Plan C has another advantage if income is taxable. This illustration reflects a general rule: *Return on equity increases when the expected rate of return from the new assets is higher than the rate of interest expense on the debt financing.*

Example: Compute return on equity for all three plans if Magnum currently earns $150,000 instead of $100,000.
Answer ($ 000s):
Plan A = 15% ($150/$1,000)
Plan B = 18.3% ($275/$1,500)
Plan C = 22.5% ($225/$1,000)

EXHIBIT 14.1

Financing with Bonds versus Equity

	Plan A: Do Not Expand	Plan B: Equity Financing	Plan C: Bond Financing
Income before interest expense	$ 100,000	$ 225,000	$ 225,000
Interest expense	—	—	(50,000)
Net income	**$ 100,000**	**$ 225,000**	**$ 175,000**
Equity	$1,000,000	$1,500,000	$1,000,000
Return on equity	**10.0%**	**15.0%**	**17.5%**

Disadvantages of Bonds The two main disadvantages of bond financing are these:

1. *Bonds can decrease return on equity.* When a company earns a lower return with the borrowed funds than it pays in interest, it decreases its return on equity. This downside risk of financial leverage is more likely to arise when a company has periods of low income or net losses.
2. *Bonds require payment of both periodic interest and the par value at maturity.* Bond payments can be especially burdensome when income and cash flow are low. Equity financing, in contrast, does not require any payments because cash withdrawals (dividends) are paid at the discretion of the owner (or board).

Point: Debt financing is desirable when interest is tax deductible, when owner control is preferred, and when return on equity exceeds the debt's interest rate.

A company must weigh the risks and returns of the disadvantages and advantages of bond financing when deciding whether to issue bonds to finance operations.

Bond Trading

Bonds are securities that can be readily bought and sold. A large number of bonds trade on both the New York Exchange and the American Exchange. A bond *issue* consists of a number of bonds, usually in denominations of $1,000 or $5,000, and is sold to many different lenders. After bonds are issued, they often are bought and sold by investors, meaning that any particular bond probably has a number of owners before it matures. Since bonds are exchanged (bought and sold) in the market, they have a market value (price). For convenience, bond market values are expressed as a percent of their par (face) value. For example, a company's bonds might be trading at 103½, meaning they can be bought or sold for 103.5% of their par value. Bonds can also trade below par value. For instance, if a company's bonds are trading at 95, they can be bought or sold at 95% of their par value.

Decision Insight

Bonds	Rate	Mat	Yld	Vol	Close	Chg
IBM	7	25	5.9	130	119¼	+1¼

Quotes The IBM bond quote here is interpreted (left to right) as **Bonds,** issuer name; **Rate,** contract interest rate (7%); **Mat,** matures in year 2025 when principal is paid; **Yld,** yield rate (5.9%) of bond at current price; **Vol,** daily dollar worth ($130,000) of trades (in 1,000s); **Close,** closing price (119.25) for the day as percentage of par value; **Chg,** change (+1.25) in closing price from prior day's close. ■

Bond-Issuing Procedures

State and federal laws govern bond issuances. Bond issuers also want to ensure that they do not violate any of their existing contractual agreements when issuing bonds. Authorization of bond issuances includes the number of bonds authorized, their par value, and the contract interest rate. The legal document identifying the rights and obligations of both the bondholders and the issuer is called the **bond indenture,** which is the legal contract between the issuer and the bondholders. A bondholder may also receive a bond certificate as evidence of the company's debt. A **bond certificate,** such as that shown in Exhibit 14.2, includes specifics such as the issuer's name, the par value, the contract interest rate, and the maturity date. Many companies reduce costs by not issuing paper certificates to bondholders.[1]

EXHIBIT 14.2

Bond Certificate

Point: *Indenture* refers to a bond's legal contract; *debenture* refers to an unsecured bond.

BOND ISSUANCES

This section explains accounting for bond issuances at par, below par (discount), and above par (premium). It also describes how to amortize a discount or premium and record bonds issued between interest payment dates.

Issuing Bonds at Par

P1 Prepare entries to record bond issuance and interest expense.

To illustrate an issuance of bonds at par value, suppose a company receives authorization to issue $800,000 of 9%, 20-year bonds dated January 1, 2011, that mature on December 31, 2030, and pay interest semiannually on each June 30 and December 31. After accepting the bond indenture on behalf of the bondholders, the trustee can sell all or a portion of the bonds to an underwriter. If all bonds are sold at par value, the issuer records the sale as follows.

Assets	=	Liabilities	+	Equity
+800,000		+800,000		

2011			
Jan. 1	Cash	800,000	
	Bonds Payable		800,000
	Sold bonds at par.		

This entry reflects increases in the issuer's cash *and* long-term liabilities.

The issuer records the first semiannual interest payment as follows.

Assets	=	Liabilities	+	Equity
−36,000				−36,000

2011			
June 30	Bond Interest Expense	36,000	
	Cash		36,000
	Paid semiannual interest (9% × $800,000 × ½ year).		

Point: The *spread* between the dealer's cost and what buyers pay can be huge. Dealers earn more than $25 billion in annual spread revenue.

Global: In the United Kingdom, government bonds are called *gilts*—short for gilt-edged investments.

[1] The issuing company normally sells its bonds to an investment firm called an *underwriter,* which resells them to the public. An issuing company can also sell bonds directly to investors. When an underwriter sells bonds to a large number of investors, a *trustee* represents and protects the bondholders' interests. The trustee monitors the issuer to ensure that it complies with the obligations in the bond indenture. Most trustees are large banks or trust companies. The trustee writes and accepts the terms of a bond indenture before it is issued. When bonds are offered to the public, called *floating an issue,* they must be registered with the Securities and Exchange Commission (SEC). SEC registration requires the issuer to file certain financial information. Most company bonds are issued in par value units of $1,000 or $5,000. *A baby bond* has a par value of less than $1,000, such as $100.

The issuer pays and records its semiannual interest obligation every six months until the bonds mature. When they mature, the issuer records its payment of principal as follows.

2030			
Dec. 31	Bonds Payable	800,000	
	Cash		800,000
	Paid bond principal at maturity.		

Assets	=	Liabilities	+	Equity
−800,000		−800,000		

Bond Discount or Premium

The bond issuer pays the interest rate specified in the indenture, the **contract rate,** also referred to as the *coupon rate, stated rate,* or *nominal rate.* The annual interest paid is determined by multiplying the bond par value by the contract rate. The contract rate is usually stated on an annual basis, even if interest is paid semiannually. For example, if a company issues a $1,000, 8% bond paying interest semiannually, it pays annual interest of $80 (8% × $1,000) in two semiannual payments of $40 each.

The contract rate sets the amount of interest the issuer pays in *cash,* which is not necessarily the *bond interest expense* actually incurred by the issuer. Bond interest expense depends on the bond's market value at issuance, which is determined by market expectations of the risk of lending to the issuer. The bond's **market rate** of interest is the rate that borrowers are willing to pay and lenders are willing to accept for a particular bond and its risk level. As the risk level increases, the rate increases to compensate purchasers for the bonds' increased risk. Also, the market rate is generally higher when the time period until the bond matures is longer due to the risk of adverse events occurring over a longer time period.

Many bond issuers try to set a contract rate of interest equal to the market rate they expect as of the bond issuance date. When the contract rate and market rate are equal, a bond sells at par value, but when they are not equal, a bond does not sell at par value. Instead, it is sold at a *premium* above par value or at a *discount* below par value. Exhibit 14.3 shows the relation between the contract rate, market rate, and a bond's issue price.

EXHIBIT 14.3

Relation between Bond Issue Price, Contract Rate, and Market Rate

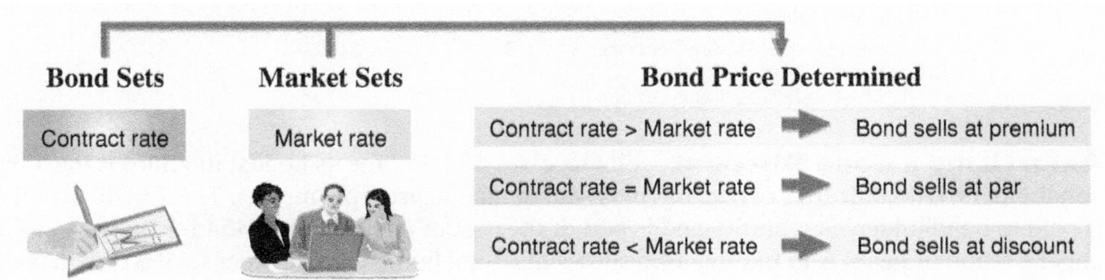

Quick Check Answers — p. 579 

1. A company issues $10,000 of 9%, 5-year bonds dated January 1, 2011, that mature on December 31, 2015, and pay interest semiannually on each June 30 and December 31. Prepare the entry to record this bond issuance and the first semiannual interest payment.
2. How do you compute the amount of interest a bond issuer pays in cash each year?
3. When the contract rate is above the market rate, do bonds sell at a premium or a discount? Do purchasers pay more or less than the par value of the bonds?

Issuing Bonds at a Discount

P2 Compute and record amortization of bond discount.

A **discount on bonds payable** occurs when a company issues bonds with a contract rate less than the market rate. This means that the issue price is less than par value. To illustrate, assume that Fila announces an offer to issue bonds with a $100,000 par value, an 8% annual contract rate (paid semiannually), and a two-year life. Also assume that the market rate for Fila bonds is

Point: The difference between the contract rate and the market rate of interest on a new bond issue is usually a fraction of a percent. We use a difference of 2% to emphasize the effects.

10%. These bonds then will sell at a discount since the contract rate is less than the market rate. The exact issue price for these bonds is stated as 96.454 (implying 96.454% of par value, or $96,454); we show how to compute this issue price later in the chapter. These bonds obligate the issuer to pay two separate types of future cash flows:

1. Par value of $100,000 cash at the end of the bonds' two-year life.
2. Cash interest payments of $4,000 (4% × $100,000) at the end of each semiannual period during the bonds' two-year life.

The exact pattern of cash flows for the Fila bonds is shown in Exhibit 14.4.

EXHIBIT 14.4

Cash Flows for Fila Bonds

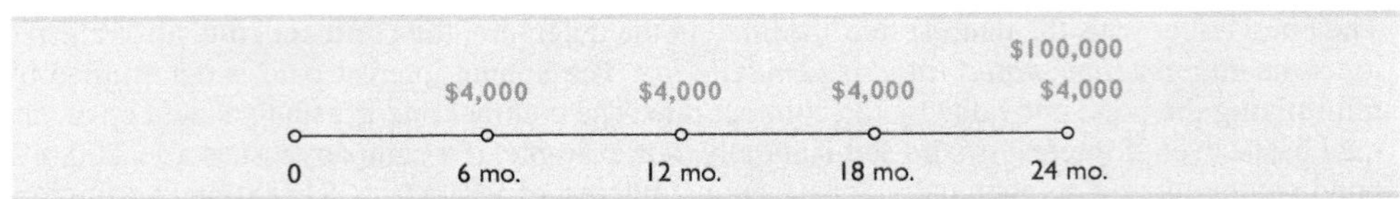

When Fila accepts $96,454 cash for its bonds on the issue date of December 31, 2011, it records the sale as follows.

Assets	=	Liabilities	+	Equity
+96,454		+100,000		
		−3,546		

Dec. 31	Cash	96,454	
	Discount on Bonds Payable	3,546	
	Bonds Payable		100,000
	Sold bonds at a discount on their issue date.		

Point: Book value at issuance always equals the issuer's cash borrowed.

These bonds are reported in the long-term liability section of the issuer's December 31, 2011, balance sheet as shown in Exhibit 14.5. A discount is deducted from the par value of bonds to yield the **carrying (book) value of bonds.** Discount on Bonds Payable is a contra liability account.

EXHIBIT 14.5

Balance Sheet Presentation of Bond Discount

Long-term liabilities		
Bonds payable, 8%, due December 31, 2013	$100,000	
Less discount on bonds payable	3,546	$96,454

Amortizing a Bond Discount Fila receives $96,454 for its bonds; in return it must pay bondholders $100,000 after two years (plus semiannual interest payments). The $3,546 discount is paid to bondholders at maturity and is part of the cost of using the $96,454 for two years. The upper portion of panel A in Exhibit 14.6 shows that total bond interest expense of $19,546 is the difference between the total amount repaid to bondholders ($116,000) and the amount borrowed from bondholders ($96,454). Alternatively, we can compute total bond interest expense as the sum of the four interest payments and the bond discount. This alternative computation is shown in the lower portion of panel A.

Point: *Zero-coupon bonds* do not pay periodic interest (contract rate is zero). These bonds always sell at a discount because their 0% contract rate is always below the market rate.

The total $19,546 bond interest expense must be allocated across the four semiannual periods in the bonds' life, and the bonds' carrying value must be updated at each balance sheet date. This is accomplished using the straight-line method (or the effective interest method in Appendix 14B). Both methods systematically reduce the bond discount to zero over the two-year life. This process is called *amortizing a bond discount.*

Straight-Line Method The **straight-line bond amortization** method allocates an equal portion of the total bond interest expense to each interest period. To apply the straight-line method to Fila's bonds, we divide the total bond interest expense of $19,546 by 4 (the number of semiannual periods in the bonds' life). This gives a bond interest expense of $4,887 per period, which is $4,886.5 rounded to the nearest dollar per period (all computations, including those for assignments, are rounded to the nearest whole dollar). Alternatively, we can find this number by first dividing the $3,546 discount by 4, which yields the $887 amount of discount to be amortized each interest period. When the $887 is added to the $4,000 cash payment, the bond

EXHIBIT 14.6

Interest Computation and Entry for Bonds Issued at a Discount

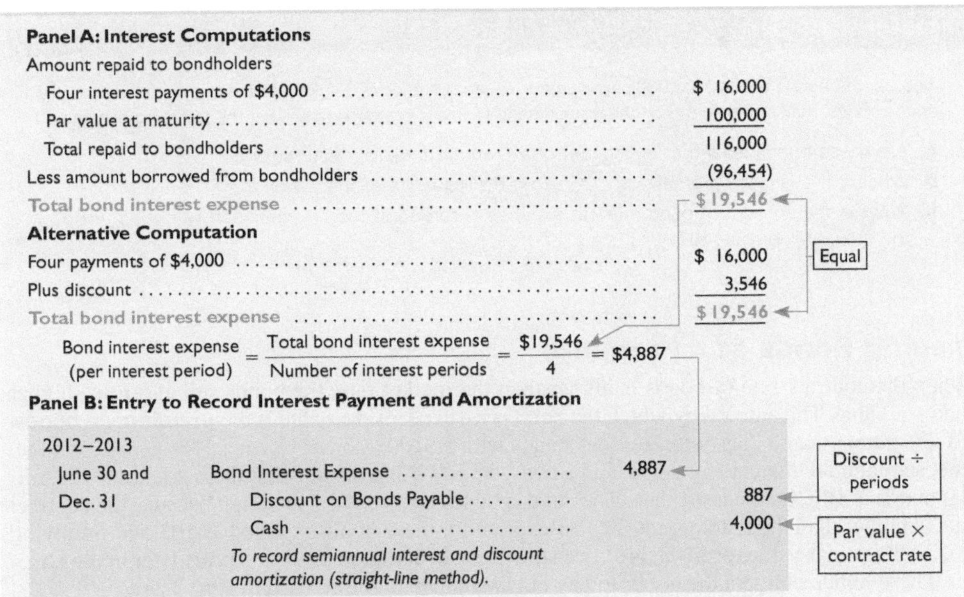

Panel A: Interest Computations

Amount repaid to bondholders	
Four interest payments of $4,000	$ 16,000
Par value at maturity	100,000
Total repaid to bondholders	116,000
Less amount borrowed from bondholders	(96,454)
Total bond interest expense	$ 19,546

Alternative Computation

Four payments of $4,000	$ 16,000
Plus discount	3,546
Total bond interest expense	$ 19,546

Equal

$$\frac{\text{Bond interest expense}}{\text{(per interest period)}} = \frac{\text{Total bond interest expense}}{\text{Number of interest periods}} = \frac{\$19,546}{4} = \$4,887$$

Panel B: Entry to Record Interest Payment and Amortization

2012–2013			
June 30 and Dec. 31	Bond Interest Expense	4,887	
	Discount on Bonds Payable		887
	Cash		4,000
	To record semiannual interest and discount amortization (straight-line method).		

Discount ÷ periods

Par value × contract rate

interest expense for each period is $4,887. Panel B of Exhibit 14.6 shows how the issuer records bond interest expense and updates the balance of the bond liability account at the end of *each* of the four semiannual interest periods (June 30, 2012, through December 31, 2013).

Exhibit 14.7 shows the pattern of decreases in the Discount on Bonds Payable account and the pattern of increases in the bonds' carrying value. The following points summarize the discount bonds' straight-line amortization:

EXHIBIT 14.7

Straight-Line Amortization of Bond Discount

Semiannual Period-End	Unamortized Discount*	Carrying Value†
(0) 12/31/2011	$3,546	$ 96,454
(1) 6/30/2012	2,659	97,341
(2) 12/31/2012	1,772	98,228
(3) 6/30/2013	885	99,115
(4) **12/31/2013**	**0‡**	**100,000**

* Total bond discount (of $3,546) less accumulated periodic amortization ($887 per semiannual interest period).

† Bond par value (of $100,000) less unamortized discount.

‡ Adjusted for rounding.

The two columns always sum to par value for a discount bond.

1. At issuance, the $100,000 par value consists of the $96,454 cash received by the issuer plus the $3,546 discount.
2. During the bonds' life, the (unamortized) discount decreases each period by the $887 amortization ($3,546/4), and the carrying value (par value less unamortized discount) increases each period by $887.
3. At maturity, the unamortized discount equals zero, and the carrying value equals the $100,000 par value that the issuer pays the holder.

We see that the issuer incurs a $4,887 bond interest expense each period but pays only $4,000 cash. The $887 unpaid portion of this expense is added to the bonds' carrying value. (The total $3,546 unamortized discount is "paid" when the bonds mature; $100,000 is paid at maturity but only $96,454 was received at issuance.)

Decision Insight

Ratings Game Many bond buyers rely on rating services to assess bond risk. The best known are Standard & Poor's, Moody's, and Fitch. These services focus on the issuer's financial statements and other factors in setting ratings. Standard & Poor's ratings, from best quality to default, are AAA, AA, A, BBB, BB, B, CCC, CC, C, and D. Ratings can include a plus (+) or minus (−) to show relative standing within a category.

Quick Check Answers — p. 579 

Five-year, 6% bonds with a $100,000 par value are issued at a price of $91,893. Interest is paid semiannually, and the bonds' market rate is 8% on the issue date. Use this information to answer the following questions:

4. Are these bonds issued at a discount or a premium? Explain your answer.
5. What is the issuer's journal entry to record the issuance of these bonds?
6. What is the amount of bond interest expense recorded at the first semiannual period using the straight-line method?

Issuing Bonds at a Premium

P3 Compute and record amortization of bond premium.

When the contract rate of bonds is higher than the market rate, the bonds sell at a price higher than par value. The amount by which the bond price exceeds par value is the **premium on bonds.** To illustrate, assume that Adidas issues bonds with a $100,000 par value, a 12% annual contract rate, semiannual interest payments, and a two-year life. Also assume that the market rate for Adidas bonds is 10% on the issue date. The Adidas bonds will sell at a premium because the contract rate is higher than the market rate. The issue price for these bonds is stated as 103.546 (implying 103.546% of par value, or $103,546); we show how to compute this issue price later in the chapter. These bonds obligate the issuer to pay out two separate future cash flows:

1. Par value of $100,000 cash at the end of the bonds' two-year life.
2. Cash interest payments of $6,000 (6% × $100,000) at the end of each semiannual period during the bonds' two-year life.

The exact pattern of cash flows for the Adidas bonds is shown in Exhibit 14.8.

EXHIBIT 14.8
Cash Flows for Adidas Bonds

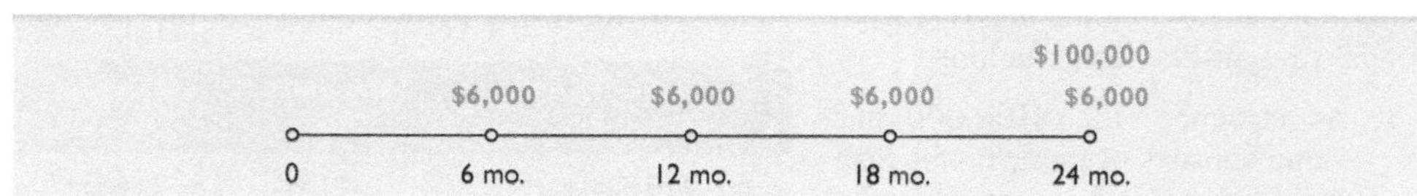

When Adidas accepts $103,546 cash for its bonds on the issue date of December 31, 2011, it records this transaction as follows.

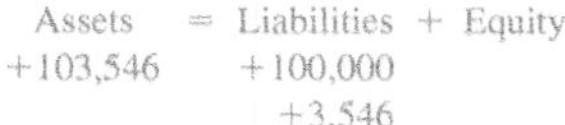

Dec. 31	Cash	103,546	
	Premium on Bonds Payable		3,546
	Bonds Payable		100,000
	Sold bonds at a premium on their issue date.		

These bonds are reported in the long-term liability section of the issuer's December 31, 2011, balance sheet as shown in Exhibit 14.9. A premium is added to par value to yield the carrying (book) value of bonds. Premium on Bonds Payable is an adjunct (also called *accretion*) liability account.

EXHIBIT 14.9
Balance Sheet Presentation of Bond Premium

Long-term liabilities		
Bonds payable, 12%, due December 31, 2013	$100,000	
Plus premium on bonds payable	3,546	$103,546

Amortizing a Bond Premium Adidas receives $103,546 for its bonds; in return, it pays bondholders $100,000 after two years (plus semiannual interest payments). The $3,546 premium not repaid to issuer's bondholders at maturity goes to reduce the issuer's expense of using the $103,546 for two years. The upper portion of panel A of Exhibit 14.10 shows that total bond interest expense of $20,454 is the difference between the total amount repaid to bondholders ($124,000) and the amount borrowed from bondholders ($103,546). Alternatively, we can compute total bond interest expense as the sum of the four interest payments less the bond premium. The premium is

EXHIBIT 14.10

Interest Computation and Entry for Bonds Issued at a Premium

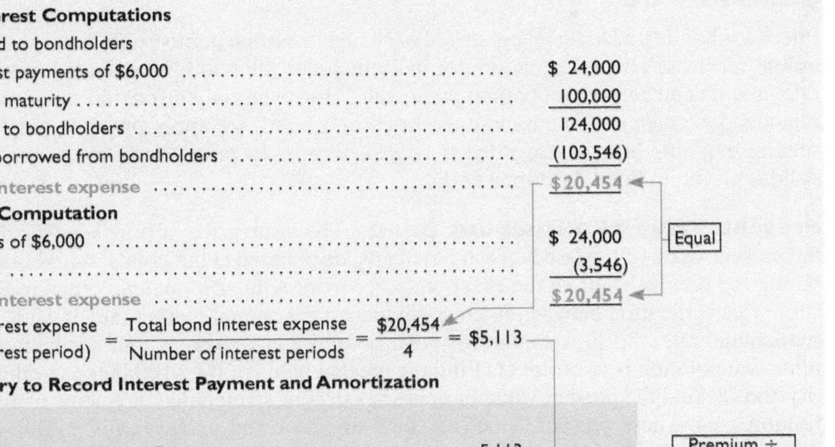

Panel A: Interest Computations

Amount repaid to bondholders	
Four interest payments of $6,000	$ 24,000
Par value at maturity	100,000
Total repaid to bondholders	124,000
Less amount borrowed from bondholders	(103,546)
Total bond interest expense	$20,454
Alternative Computation	
Four payments of $6,000	$ 24,000
Less premium	(3,546)
Total bond interest expense	$20,454

$$\frac{\text{Bond interest expense}}{\text{(per interest period)}} = \frac{\text{Total bond interest expense}}{\text{Number of interest periods}} = \frac{\$20{,}454}{4} = \$5{,}113$$

Panel B: Entry to Record Interest Payment and Amortization

2012–2013			
June 30 and Dec. 31	Bond Interest Expense	5,113	
	Premium on Bonds Payable	887	
	Cash		6,000
	To record semiannual interest and premium amortization (straight-line method).		

subtracted because it will not be paid to bondholders when the bonds mature; see the lower portion of panel A. Total bond interest expense must be allocated over the four semiannual periods using the straight-line method (or the effective interest method in Appendix 14B).

Straight-Line Method The straight-line method allocates an equal portion of total bond interest expense to each of the bonds' semiannual interest periods. To apply this method to Adidas bonds, we divide the two years' total bond interest expense of $20,454 by 4 (the number of semiannual periods in the bonds' life). This gives a total bond interest expense of $5,113 per period, which is $5,113.5 rounded down so that the journal entry balances and for simplicity in presentation (alternatively, one could carry cents). Panel B of Exhibit 14.10 shows how the issuer records bond interest expense and updates the balance of the bond liability account for *each* semiannual period (June 30, 2012, through December 31, 2013).

Point: A premium decreases Bond Interest Expense; a discount increases it.

EXHIBIT 14.11

Straight-Line Amortization of Bond Premium

Semiannual Period-End	Unamortized Premium*	Carrying Value†
(0) 12/31/2011	$3,546	$103,546
(1) 6/30/2012	2,659	102,659
(2) 12/31/2012	1,772	101,772
(3) 6/30/2013	885	100,885
(4) 12/31/2013	0‡	**100,000**

* Total bond premium (of $3,546) less accumulated periodic amortization ($887 per semiannual interest period).

† Bond par value (of $100,000) plus unamortized premium.

‡ Adjusted for rounding.

During the bond life, carrying value is adjusted to par and the amortized premium to zero.

Exhibit 14.11 shows the pattern of decreases in the unamortized Premium on Bonds Payable account and in the bonds' carrying value. The following points summarize straight-line amortization of the premium bonds:

1. At issuance, the $100,000 par value plus the $3,546 premium equals the $103,546 cash received by the issuer.
2. During the bonds' life, the (unamortized) premium decreases each period by the $887 amortization ($3,546/4), and the carrying value decreases each period by the same $887.
3. At maturity, the unamortized premium equals zero, and the carrying value equals the $100,000 par value that the issuer pays the holder.

The next section describes bond pricing. An instructor can choose to cover bond pricing or not. Assignments requiring the next section are Quick Study 14-5, and Exercises 14-9 & 14-10.

Bond Pricing

Prices for bonds traded on an organized exchange are often published in newspapers and through online services. This information normally includes the bond price (called *quote*), its contract rate, and its current market (called *yield*) rate. However, only a fraction of bonds are traded on organized exchanges. To compute the price of a bond, we apply present value concepts. This section explains how to use *present value concepts* to price the Fila discount bond and the Adidas premium bond described earlier.

Point: InvestingInBonds.com is a bond research and learning source.

Present Value of a Discount Bond The issue price of bonds is found by computing the present value of the bonds' cash payments, discounted at the bonds' market rate. When computing the present value of the Fila bonds, we work with *semiannual* compounding periods because this is the time between interest payments; the annual market rate of 10% is considered a semiannual rate of 5%. Also, the two-year bond life is viewed as four semiannual periods. The price computation is twofold: (1) Find the present value of the $100,000 par value paid at maturity and (2) find the present value of the series of four semiannual payments of $4,000 each; see Exhibit 14.4. These present values can be found by using *present value tables*. Appendix B at the end of this book shows present value tables and describes their use. Table B.1 at the end of Appendix B is used for the single $100,000 maturity payment, and Table B.3 in Appendix B is used for the $4,000 series of interest payments. Specifically, we go to Table B.1, row 4, and across to the 5% column to identify the present value factor of 0.8227 for the maturity payment. Next, we go to Table B.3, row 4, and across to the 5% column, where the present value factor is 3.5460 for the series of interest payments. We compute bond price by multiplying the cash flow payments by their corresponding present value factors and adding them together; see Exhibit 14.12.

Point: A bond's market value (price) at issuance equals the present value of its future cash payments, where the interest (discount) rate used is the bond's market rate.

Point: Many calculators have present value functions for computing bond prices.

EXHIBIT 14.12

Computing Issue Price for the Fila Discount Bonds

Cash Flow	Table	Present Value Factor		Amount		Present Value
$100,000 par (maturity) value	B.1	0.8227	×	$100,000	=	$ 82,270
$4,000 interest payments	B.3	3.5460	×	4,000	=	14,184
Price of bond						$96,454

Present Value of a Premium Bond We find the issue price of the Adidas bonds by using the market rate to compute the present value of the bonds' future cash flows. When computing the present value of these bonds, we again work with *semiannual* compounding periods because this is the time between interest payments. The annual 10% market rate is applied as a semiannual rate of 5%, and the two-year bond life is viewed as four semiannual periods. The computation is twofold: (1) Find the present value of the $100,000 par value paid at maturity and (2) find the present value of the series of four payments of $6,000 each; see Exhibit 14.8. These present values can be found by using present value tables. First, go to Table B.1, row 4, and across to the 5% column where the present value factor is 0.8227 for the maturity payment. Second, go to Table B.3, row 4, and across to the 5% column, where the present value factor is 3.5460 for the series of interest payments. The bonds' price is computed by multiplying the cash flow payments by their corresponding present value factors and adding them together; see Exhibit 14.13.

Point: There are nearly 5 million individual U.S. bond issues, ranging from huge treasuries to tiny municipalities. This compares to about 12,000 individual U.S. stocks that are traded.

EXHIBIT 14.13

Computing Issue Price for the Adidas Premium Bonds

Cash Flow	Table	Present Value Factor		Amount		Present Value
$100,000 par (maturity) value	B.1	0.8227	×	$100,000	=	$ 82,270
$6,000 interest payments	B.3	3.5460	×	6,000	=	21,276
Price of bond						$103,546

Quick Check Answers — p. 579 

On December 31, 2010, a company issues 16%, 10-year bonds with a par value of $100,000. Interest is paid on June 30 and December 31. The bonds are sold to yield a 14% annual market rate at an issue price of $110,592. Use this information to answer questions 7 through 9:

7. Are these bonds issued at a discount or a premium? Explain your answer.
8. Using the straight-line method to allocate bond interest expense, the issuer records the second interest payment (on December 31, 2011) with a debit to Premium on Bonds Payable in the amount of (*a*) $7,470, (*b*) $530, (*c*) $8,000, or (*d*) $400.
9. How are these bonds reported in the long-term liability section of the issuer's balance sheet as of December 31, 2011?

BOND RETIREMENT

This section describes the retirement of bonds (1) at maturity, (2) before maturity, and (3) by conversion to stock.

P4 Record the retirement of bonds.

Bond Retirement at Maturity

The carrying value of bonds at maturity always equals par value. For example, both Exhibits 14.7 (a discount) and 14.11 (a premium) show that the carrying value of bonds at the end of their lives equals par value ($100,000). The retirement of these bonds at maturity, assuming interest is already paid and entered, is recorded as follows:

2013			
Dec. 31	Bonds Payable	100,000	
	Cash		100,000
	To record retirement of bonds at maturity.		

Assets	=	Liabilities	+	Equity
−100,000		−100,000		

Bond Retirement before Maturity

Issuers sometimes wish to retire some or all of their bonds prior to maturity. For instance, if interest rates decline greatly, an issuer may wish to replace high-interest-paying bonds with new low-interest bonds. Two common ways to retire bonds before maturity are to (1) exercise a call option or (2) purchase them on the open market. In the first instance, an issuer can reserve the right to retire bonds early by issuing callable bonds. The bond indenture can give the issuer an option to *call* the bonds before they mature by paying the par value plus a *call premium* to bondholders. In the second case, the issuer retires bonds by repurchasing them on the open market at their current price. Whether bonds are called or repurchased, the issuer is unlikely to pay a price that exactly equals their carrying value. When a difference exists between the bonds' carrying value and the amount paid, the issuer records a gain or loss equal to the difference.

Point: Bond retirement is also referred to as *bond redemption*.

Point: Gains and losses from retiring bonds were *previously* reported as extraordinary items. New standards require that they now be judged by the "unusual and infrequent" criteria for reporting purposes.

To illustrate the accounting for retiring callable bonds, assume that a company issued callable bonds with a par value of $100,000. The call option requires the issuer to pay a call premium of $3,000 to bondholders in addition to the par value. Next, assume that after the June 30, 2011, interest payment, the bonds have a carrying value of $104,500. Then on July 1, 2011, the issuer calls these bonds and pays $103,000 to bondholders. The issuer recognizes a $1,500 gain from the difference between the bonds' carrying value of $104,500 and the retirement price of $103,000. The issuer records this bond retirement as follows.

July 1	Bonds Payable	100,000	
	Premium on Bonds Payable	4,500	
	Gain on Bond Retirement		1,500
	Cash		103,000
	To record retirement of bonds before maturity.		

Assets	=	Liabilities	+	Equity
−103,000		−100,000		+1,500
		−4,500		

An issuer usually must call all bonds when it exercises a call option. However, to retire as many or as few bonds as it desires, an issuer can purchase them on the open market. If it retires less than the entire class of bonds, it recognizes a gain or loss for the difference between the carrying value of those bonds retired and the amount paid to acquire them.

Bond Retirement by Conversion

Convertible Bond

Holders of convertible bonds have the right to convert their bonds to stock. When conversion occurs, the bonds' carrying value is transferred to equity accounts and no gain or loss is recorded. (We further describe convertible bonds in the Decision Analysis section of this chapter.)

To illustrate, assume that on January 1 the $100,000 par value bonds of Converse, with a carrying value of $100,000, are converted to 15,000 shares of $2 par value common stock. The entry to record this conversion follows (the market prices of the bonds and stock are *not* relevant to this entry; the material in Chapter 13 is helpful in understanding this transaction):

Assets	=	Liabilities	+	Equity
		−100,000		+30,000
				+70,000

Jan. 1	Bonds Payable	100,000	
	Common Stock		30,000
	Paid-In Capital in Excess of Par Value		70,000
	To record retirement of bonds by conversion.		

Decision Insight

Junk Bonds Junk bonds are company bonds with low credit ratings due to a higher than average likelihood of default. On the upside, the high risk of junk bonds can yield high returns if the issuer survives and repays its debt.

Quick Check

Answer — p. 579

10. Six years ago, a company issued $500,000 of 6%, eight-year bonds at a price of 95. The current carrying value is $493,750. The company decides to retire 50% of these bonds by buying them on the open market at a price of 102½. What is the amount of gain or loss on the retirement of these bonds?

LONG-TERM NOTES PAYABLE

C1 Explain the types and payment patterns of notes.

Like bonds, notes are issued to obtain assets such as cash. Unlike bonds, notes are typically transacted with a *single* lender such as a bank. An issuer initially records a note at its selling price—that is, the note's face value minus any discount or plus any premium. Over the note's life, the amount of interest expense allocated to each period is computed by multiplying the market rate (at issuance of the note) by the beginning-of-period note balance. The note's carrying (book) value at any time equals its face value minus any unamortized discount or plus any unamortized premium; carrying value is also computed as the present value of all remaining payments, discounted using the market rate at issuance.

Installment Notes

An **installment note** is an obligation requiring a series of payments to the lender. Installment notes are common for franchises and other businesses when lenders and borrowers agree to spread payments over several periods. To illustrate, assume that Foghog borrows $60,000 from a bank to purchase equipment. It signs an 8% installment note requiring six annual payments of principal plus interest and it records the note's issuance at January 1, 2011, as follows.

Jan. 1	Cash	60,000	
	Notes Payable		60,000
	Borrowed $60,000 by signing an 8%, six-year installment note.		

Assets	=	Liabilities	+	Equity
+60,000		+60,000		

Payments on an installment note normally include the accrued interest expense plus a portion of the amount borrowed (the *principal*). This section describes an installment note with equal payments.

The equal total payments pattern consists of changing amounts of both interest and principal. To illustrate, assume that Foghog borrows $60,000 by signing a $60,000 note that requires six *equal payments* of $12,979 at the end of each year. (The present value of an annuity of six annual payments of $12,979, discounted at 8%, equals $60,000; we show this computation in footnote 2 on the next page.) The $12,979 includes both interest and principal, the amounts of which change with each payment. Exhibit 14.14 shows the pattern of equal total payments and its two parts, interest and principal. Column A shows the note's beginning balance. Column B shows accrued interest for each year at 8% of the beginning note balance. Column C shows the impact on the note's principal, which equals the difference between the total payment in column D and the interest expense in column B. Column E shows the note's year-end balance.

Years

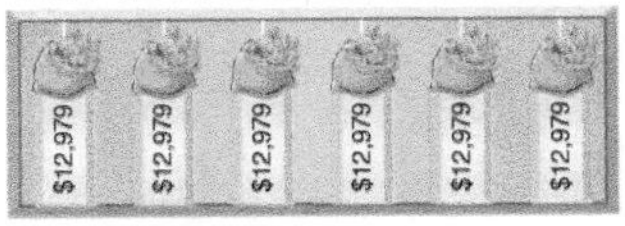

2011 2012 2013 2014 2015 2016

$12,979 $12,979 $12,979 $12,979 $12,979 $12,979

Point: Most consumer notes are installment notes that require equal total payments.

EXHIBIT 14.14

Installment Note: Equal Total Payments

		Payments			
Period Ending Date	(A) Beginning Balance	(B) *Debit* Interest Expense 8% × (A)	+ (C) *Debit* Notes Payable (D) − (B)	= (D) *Credit* Cash (computed)	(E) Ending Balance (A) − (C)
(1) **12/31/2011**	**$60,000**	**$ 4,800**	**$ 8,179**	**$12,979**	**$51,821**
(2) 12/31/2012	51,821	4,146	8,833	12,979	42,988
(3) 12/31/2013	42,988	3,439	9,540	12,979	33,448
(4) 12/31/2014	33,448	2,676	10,303	12,979	23,145
(5) 12/31/2015	23,145	1,852	11,127	12,979	12,018
(6) 12/31/2016	12,018	961	12,018	12,979	0
		$17,874	**$60,000**	**$77,874**	

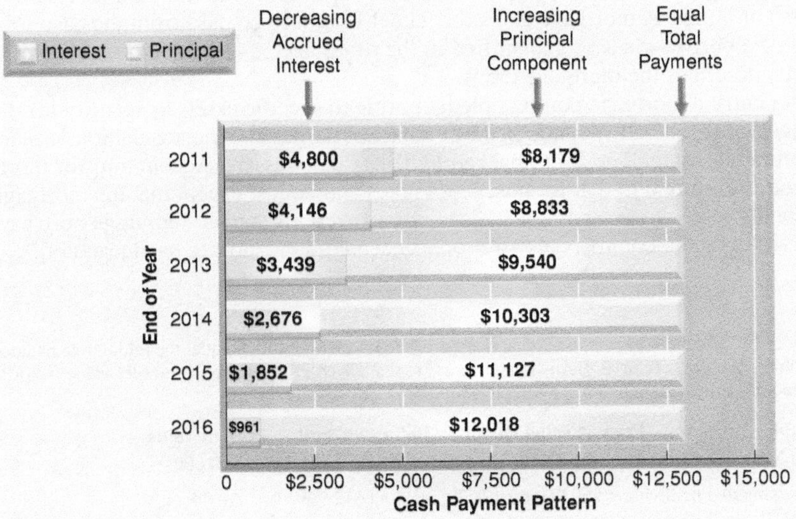

Decision Insight

Hidden Debt A study reports that 13% of employees in finance and accounting witnessed the falsifying or manipulating of accounting information in the past year (KPMG 2009). This is of special concern with long-term liabilities. For example, Enron violated GAAP to keep debt off its balance sheet. This concern extends to hidden environment liabilities. That same study reports 27% of employees in quality, safety, and environmental areas observed violations of environmental standards, which can yield massive liabilities.

P5 Prepare entries to account for notes.

Although the six cash payments are equal, accrued interest decreases each year because the principal balance of the note declines. As the amount of interest decreases each year, the portion of each payment applied to principal increases. This pattern is graphed in the lower part of Exhibit 14.14. Foghog uses the amounts in Exhibit 14.14 to record its first two payments (for years 2011 and 2012) as follows:

Assets	=	Liabilities	+	Equity
−12,979		−8,179		−4,800

Date	Account	Debit	Credit
2011			
Dec. 31	Interest Expense	4,800	
	Notes Payable	8,179	
	Cash		12,979
	To record first installment payment.		

Assets	=	Liabilities	+	Equity
−12,979		−8,833		−4,146

Date	Account	Debit	Credit
2012			
Dec. 31	Interest Expense	4,146	
	Notes Payable	8,833	
	Cash		12,979
	To record second installment payment.		

Foghog records similar entries but with different amounts for each of the remaining four payments. After six years, the Notes Payable account balance is zero.[2]

Mortgage Notes and Bonds

Point: The Truth-in-Lending Act requires lenders to provide information about loan costs including finance charges and interest rate.

A **mortgage** is a legal agreement that helps protect a lender if a borrower fails to make required payments on notes or bonds. A mortgage gives the lender a right to be paid from the cash proceeds of the sale of a borrower's assets identified in the mortgage. A legal document, called a *mortgage contract,* describes the mortgage terms.

Mortgage notes carry a mortgage contract pledging title to specific assets as security for the note. Mortgage notes are especially popular in the purchase of homes and the acquisition of plant assets. Less common *mortgage bonds* are backed by the issuer's assets. Accounting for mortgage notes and bonds is similar to that for unsecured notes and bonds, except that the mortgage agreement must be disclosed. For example, TIBCO Software reports that its "mortgage note payable . . . is collateralized by the commercial real property acquired [corporate headquarters]."

Global: Countries vary in the preference given to debtholders vs. stockholders when a company is in financial distress. Some countries such as Germany, France, and Japan give preference to stockholders over debtholders.

Example: Suppose the \$60,000 installment loan has an 8% interest rate with eight equal annual payments. What is the annual payment? *Answer* (using Table B.3): \$60,000/5.7466 = \$10,441

[2] Table B.3 in Appendix B is used to compute the dollar amount of the six payments that equal the initial note balance of \$60,000 at 8% interest. We go to Table B.3, row 6, and across to the 8% column, where the present value factor is 4.6229. The dollar amount is then computed by solving this relation:

Table	Present Value Factor		Dollar Amount		Present Value
B.3	4.6229	×	?	=	\$60,000

The dollar amount is computed by dividing \$60,000 by 4.6229, yielding \$12,979.

Decision Maker Answer — p. 579

Entrepreneur You are an electronics retailer planning a holiday sale on a custom stereo system that requires no payments for two years. At the end of two years, buyers must pay the full amount. The system's suggested retail price is $4,100, but you are willing to sell it today for $3,000 cash. What is your holiday sale price if payment will not occur for two years and the market interest rate is 10%? ■

Quick Check Answers — p. 579

11. Which of the following is true for an installment note requiring a series of equal total cash payments? (*a*) Payments consist of increasing interest and decreasing principal; (*b*) payments consist of changing amounts of principal but constant interest; or (*c*) payments consist of decreasing interest and increasing principal.

12. How is the interest portion of an installment note payment computed?

13. When a borrower records an interest payment on an installment note, how are the balance sheet and income statement affected?

GLOBAL VIEW

This section discusses similarities and differences between U.S. GAAP and IFRS in accounting and reporting for long-term liabilities such as bonds and notes.

Accounting for Bonds and Notes The definitions and characteristics of bonds and notes are broadly similar for both U.S. GAAP and IFRS. Although slight differences exist, accounting for bonds and notes under U.S. GAAP and IFRS is similar. Specifically, the accounting for issuances (including recording discounts and premiums), market pricing, and retirement of both bonds and notes follows the procedures in this chapter. Nokia describes its accounting for bonds, which follows the amortized cost approach explained in this chapter (and in Appendix 14B), as follows: Loans payable [bonds] are recognized initially at fair value, net of transaction costs incurred. In the subsequent periods, they are stated at amortized cost.

NOKIA

Both U.S. GAAP and IFRS allow companies to account for bonds and notes using fair value (different from the amortized value described in this chapter). This method is referred to as the **fair value option.** This method is similar to that applied in measuring and accounting for debt and equity securities. *Fair value* is the amount a company would receive if it settled a liability (or sold an asset) in an orderly transaction as of the balance sheet date. Companies can use several sources of inputs to determine fair value, and those inputs fall into three classes (ranked in order of preference):

Level 1: Observable quoted market prices in active markets for identical items.
Level 2: Observable inputs other than those in Level 1 such as prices from inactive markets or from similar, but not identical, items.
Level 3: Unobservable inputs reflecting a company's assumptions about value.

The exact procedures for marking liabilities to fair value at each balance sheet date are in advanced courses.

Accounting for Leases and Pensions Both U.S. GAAP and IFRS require companies to distinguish between operating leases and capital leases; the latter is referred to as *finance leases* under IFRS. The accounting and reporting for leases are broadly similar for both U.S. GAAP and IFRS. The main difference is the criteria for identifying a lease as a capital lease are more general under IFRS. However, the basic approach applies. Nokia describes its accounting for operating leases as follows: the payments . . . are treated as rentals and recognized in the profit and loss account.

For pensions, both U.S. GAAP and IFRS require companies to record costs of retirement benefits as employees work and earn them. The basic methods are similar in accounting and reporting for pensions.

Decision Analysis

Debt Features and the Debt-to-Equity Ratio

Collateral agreements can reduce the risk of loss for both bonds and notes. Unsecured bonds and notes are riskier because the issuer's obligation to pay interest and principal has the same priority as all other unsecured liabilities in the event of bankruptcy. If a company is unable to pay its debts in full, the unsecured creditors (including the holders of debentures) lose all or a portion of their balances. These types of legal agreements and other characteristics of long-term liabilities are crucial for effective business decisions. The first part of this section describes the different types of features sometimes included with bonds and notes. The second part explains and applies the debt-to-equity ratio.

A2 Assess debt features and their implications.

Features of Bonds and Notes

This section describes common features of debt securities.

Secured Debt

Unsecured Debt

Secured or Unsecured **Secured bonds** (and notes) have specific assets of the issuer pledged (or *mortgaged*) as collateral. This arrangement gives holders added protection against the issuer's default. If the issuer fails to pay interest or par value, the secured holders can demand that the collateral be sold and the proceeds used to pay the obligation. **Unsecured bonds** (and notes), also called *debentures,* are backed by the issuer's general credit standing. Unsecured debt is riskier than secured debt. *Subordinated debentures* are liabilities that are not repaid until the claims of the more senior, unsecured (and secured) liabilities are settled.

Term or Serial **Term bonds** (and notes) are scheduled for maturity on one specified date. **Serial bonds** (and notes) mature at more than one date (often in series) and thus are usually repaid over a number of periods. For instance, $100,000 of serial bonds might mature at the rate of $10,000 each year from 6 to 15 years after they are issued. Many bonds are **sinking fund bonds,** which to reduce the holder's risk require the issuer to create a *sinking fund* of assets set aside at specified amounts and dates to repay the bonds.

Registered or Bearer Bonds issued in the names and addresses of their holders are **registered bonds.** The issuer makes bond payments by sending checks (or cash transfers) to registered holders. A registered holder must notify the issuer of any ownership change. Registered bonds offer the issuer the practical advantage of not having to actually issue bond certificates. Bonds payable to whoever holds them (the *bearer*) are called **bearer bonds** or *unregistered bonds*. Sales or exchanges might not be recorded, so the holder of a bearer bond is presumed to be its rightful owner. As a result, lost bearer bonds are difficult to replace. Many bearer bonds are also **coupon bonds.** This term reflects interest coupons that are attached to the bonds. When each coupon matures, the holder presents it to a bank or broker for collection. At maturity, the holder follows the same process and presents the bond certificate for collection. Issuers of coupon bonds cannot deduct the related interest expense for taxable income. This is to prevent abuse by taxpayers who own coupon bonds but fail to report interest income on their tax returns.

Convertible Debt

Callable Debt

Convertible and/or Callable **Convertible bonds** (and notes) can be exchanged for a fixed number of shares of the issuing corporation's common stock. Convertible debt offers holders the potential to participate in future increases in stock price. Holders still receive periodic interest while the debt is held and the par value if they hold the debt to maturity. In most cases, the holders decide whether and when to convert debt to stock. **Callable bonds** (and notes) have an option exercisable by the issuer to retire them at a stated dollar amount before maturity.

Decision Insight

Munis More than a million municipal bonds, or "munis," exist, and many are tax exempt. Munis are issued by state, city, town, and county governments to pay for public projects including schools, libraries, roads, bridges, and stadiums. ■

A3 Compute the debt-to-equity ratio and explain its use.

Debt-to-Equity Ratio

Beyond assessing different characteristics of debt as just described, we want to know the level of debt, especially in relation to total equity. Such knowledge helps us assess the risk of a company's financing structure. A company financed mainly with debt is more risky because liabilities must be repaid—usually with periodic interest—whereas equity financing does not. A measure to assess the risk of a company's financing structure is the **debt-to-equity ratio** (see Exhibit 14.15).

$$\textbf{Debt-to-equity} = \frac{\textbf{Total liabilities}}{\textbf{Total equity}}$$

EXHIBIT 14.15

Debt-to-Equity Ratio

The debt-to-equity ratio varies across companies and industries. Industries that are more variable tend to have lower ratios, while more stable industries are less risky and tend to have higher ratios. To apply the debt-to-equity ratio, let's look at this measure for Cedar Fair in Exhibit 14.16.

($ millions)	2009	2008	2007	2006	2005
Total liabilities	$2,017.577	$2,079.297	$2,133.576	$2,100.306	$590.560
Total equity	$ 127.862	$ 106.786	$ 285.092	$ 410.615	$434.234
Debt-to-equity	15.8	19.5	7.5	5.1	1.4
Industry debt-to-equity	11.4	10.3	5.7	3.2	1.2

EXHIBIT 14.16

Cedar Fair's Debt-to-Equity Ratio

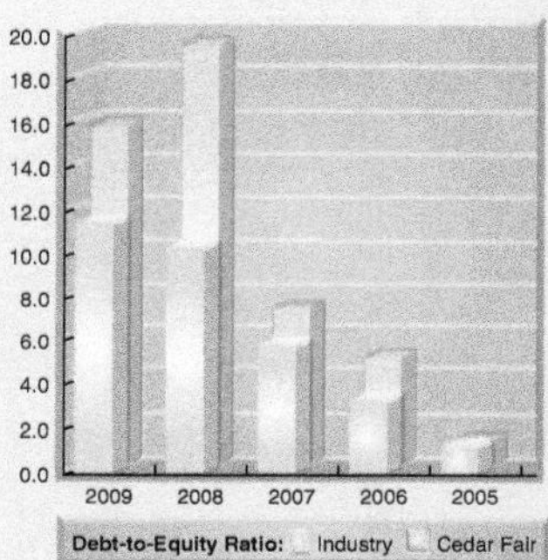

Cedar Fair's 2009 debt-to-equity ratio is 15.8, meaning that debtholders contributed $15.8 for each $1 contributed by equityholders. This implies a fairly risky financing structure for Cedar Fair. A similar concern is drawn from a comparison of Cedar Fair with its competitors, where the 2009 industry ratio is 11.4. Analysis across the years shows that Cedar Fair's financing structure has grown increasingly risky in recent years. Given its sluggish revenues and increasing operating expenses in recent years (see its annual report), Cedar Fair is increasingly at risk of financial distress.

Decision Maker Answer — p. 579

Bond Investor You plan to purchase debenture bonds from one of two companies in the same industry that are similar in size and performance. The first company has $350,000 in total liabilities, and $1,750,000 in equity. The second company has $1,200,000 in total liabilities, and $1,000,000 in equity. Which company's debenture bonds are less risky based on the debt-to-equity ratio? ■

DEMONSTRATION PROBLEM

Water Sports Company (WSC) patented and successfully test-marketed a new product. To expand its ability to produce and market the new product, WSC needs to raise $800,000 of financing. On January 1, 2011, the company obtained the money in two ways:

a. WSC signed a $400,000, 10% installment note to be repaid with five equal annual installments to be made on December 31 of 2011 through 2015.

b. WSC issued five-year bonds with a par value of $400,000. The bonds have a 12% annual contract rate and pay interest on June 30 and December 31. The bonds' annual market rate is 10% as of January 1, 2011.

Required

1. For the installment note, (*a*) compute the size of each annual payment, (*b*) prepare an amortization table such as Exhibit 14.14, and (*c*) prepare the journal entry for the first payment.

2. For the bonds, (*a*) compute their issue price; (*b*) prepare the January 1, 2011, journal entry to record their issuance; (*c*) prepare an amortization table using the straight-line method; (*d*) prepare the June 30, 2011, journal entry to record the first interest payment; and (*e*) prepare a journal entry to record retiring the bonds at a $416,000 call price on January 1, 2013.

3.[B] Redo parts 2(*c*), 2(*d*), and 2(*e*) assuming the bonds are amortized using the effective interest method.

PLANNING THE SOLUTION

- For the installment note, divide the borrowed amount by the annuity factor (from Table B.3) using the 10% rate and five payments to compute the amount of each payment. Prepare a table similar to Exhibit 14.14 and use the numbers in the table's first line for the journal entry.
- Compute the bonds' issue price by using the market rate to find the present value of their cash flows (use tables found in Appendix B). Then use this result to record the bonds' issuance. Next, prepare an amortization table like Exhibit 14.11 (and Exhibit 14B.2) and use it to get the numbers needed for the journal entry. Also use the table to find the carrying value as of the date of the bonds' retirement that you need for the journal entry.

SOLUTION TO DEMONSTRATION PROBLEM

Part 1: Installment Note

a. Annual payment = Note balance/Annuity factor = \$400,000/3.7908 = \$105,519 (The annuity factor is for five payments and a rate of 10%.)

b. An amortization table follows.

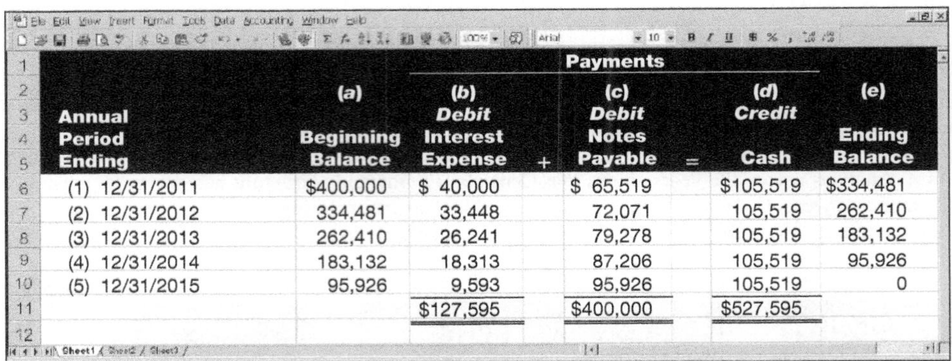

Annual Period Ending	(a) Beginning Balance	(b) Debit Interest Expense	+	(c) Debit Notes Payable	=	(d) Credit Cash	(e) Ending Balance
				Payments			
(1) 12/31/2011	\$400,000	\$ 40,000		\$ 65,519		\$105,519	\$334,481
(2) 12/31/2012	334,481	33,448		72,071		105,519	262,410
(3) 12/31/2013	262,410	26,241		79,278		105,519	183,132
(4) 12/31/2014	183,132	18,313		87,206		105,519	95,926
(5) 12/31/2015	95,926	9,593		95,926		105,519	0
		\$127,595		\$400,000		\$527,595	

c. Journal entry for December 31, 2011, payment.

Dec. 31	Interest Expense	40,000	
	Notes Payable	65,519	
	Cash		105,519
	To record first installment payment.		

Part 2: Bonds (Straight-Line Amortization)

a. Compute the bonds' issue price.

Cash Flow	Table	Present Value Factor*		Amount		Present Value
Par (maturity) value	B.1 in App. B (PV of 1)	0.6139	×	400,000	=	\$245,560
Interest payments	B.3 in App. B (PV of annuity)	7.7217	×	24,000	=	185,321
Price of bond						\$430,881

* Present value factors are for 10 payments using a semiannual market rate of 5%.

b. Journal entry for January 1, 2011, issuance.

Jan. 1	Cash	430,881	
	Premium on Bonds Payable		30,881
	Bonds Payable		400,000
	Sold bonds at a premium.		

c. Straight-line amortization table for premium bonds.

Semiannual Period-End	Unamortized Premium	Carrying Value
(0) 1/1/2011	$30,881	$430,881
(1) 6/30/2011	27,793	427,793
(2) 12/31/2011	24,705	424,705
(3) 6/30/2012	21,617	421,617
(4) 12/31/2012	18,529	418,529
(5) 6/30/2013	15,441	415,441
(6) 12/31/2013	12,353	412,353
(7) 6/30/2014	9,265	409,265
(8) 12/31/2014	6,177	406,177
(9) 6/30/2015	3,089	403,089
(10) 12/31/2015	0*	400,000

* Adjusted for rounding.

d. Journal entry for June 30, 2011, bond payment.

June 30	Bond Interest Expense	20,912	
	Premium on Bonds Payable	3,088	
	Cash		24,000
	Paid semiannual interest on bonds.		

e. Journal entry for January 1, 2013, bond retirement.

Jan. 1	Bonds Payable	400,000	
	Premium on Bonds Payable	18,529	
	Cash		416,000
	Gain on Retirement of Bonds		2,529
	To record bond retirement (carrying value as of Dec. 31, 2012).		

Part 3: Bonds (Effective Interest Amortization)[B]

c. The effective interest amortization table for premium bonds.

Semiannual Interest Period	(A) Cash Interest Paid 6% × $400,000	(B) Interest Expense 5% × Prior (E)	(C) Premium Amortization (A) − (B)	(D) Unamortized Premium Prior (D) − (C)	(E) Carrying Value $400,000 + (D)
(0) 1/1/2011				$30,881	$430,881
(1) 6/30/2011	$ 24,000	$ 21,544	$ 2,456	28,425	428,425
(2) 12/31/2011	24,000	21,421	2,579	25,846	425,846
(3) 6/30/2012	24,000	21,292	2,708	23,138	423,138
(4) 12/31/2012	24,000	21,157	2,843	20,295	420,295
(5) 6/30/2013	24,000	21,015	2,985	17,310	417,310
(6) 12/31/2013	24,000	20,866	3,134	14,176	414,176
(7) 6/30/2014	24,000	20,709	3,291	10,885	410,885
(8) 12/31/2014	24,000	20,544	3,456	7,429	407,429
(9) 6/30/2015	24,000	20,371	3,629	3,800	403,800
(10) 12/31/2015	24,000	20,200*	3,800	0	400,000
	$240,000	$209,119	$30,881		

* Adjusted for rounding

d. Journal entry for June 30, 2011, bond payment.

June 30	Bond Interest Expense	21,544	
	Premium on Bonds Payable	2,456	
	Cash		24,000
	Paid semiannual interest on bonds.		

e. Journal entry for January 1, 2013, bond retirement.

Jan. 1	Bonds Payable	400,000	
	Premium on Bonds Payable	20,295	
	Cash		416,000
	Gain on Retirement of Bonds		4,295
	To record bond retirement (carrying value as of December 31, 2012).		

APPENDIX

14A Present Values of Bonds and Notes

This appendix explains how to apply present value techniques to measure a long-term liability when it is created and to assign interest expense to the periods until it is settled. Appendix B at the end of the book provides additional discussion of present value concepts.

C2 Explain and compute the present value of an amount(s) to be paid at a future date(s).

Present Value Concepts The basic present value concept is that cash paid (or received) in the future has less value now than the same amount of cash paid (or received) today. To illustrate, if we must pay $1 one year from now, its present value is less than $1. To see this, assume that we borrow $0.9259 today that must be paid back in one year with 8% interest. Our interest expense for this loan is computed as $0.9259 × 8%, or $0.0741. When the $0.0741 interest is added to the $0.9259 borrowed, we get the $1 payment necessary to repay our loan with interest. This is formally computed in Exhibit 14A.1. The $0.9259 borrowed is the present value of the $1 future payment. More generally, an amount borrowed equals the present value of the future payment. (This same interpretation applies to an investment. If $0.9259 is invested at 8%, it yields $0.0741 in revenue after one year. This amounts to $1, made up of principal and interest.)

EXHIBIT 14A.1

Components of a One-Year Loan

Amount borrowed	**$0.9259**
Interest for one year at 8%	0.0741
Amount owed after 1 year	$ 1.0000

To extend this example, assume that we owe $1 two years from now instead of one year, and the 8% interest is compounded annually. *Compounded* means that interest during the second period is based on the total of the amount borrowed plus the interest accrued from the first period. The second period's interest is then computed as 8% multiplied by the sum of the amount borrowed plus interest earned in the first period. Exhibit 14A.2 shows how we compute the present value of $1 to be paid in two years. This amount is $0.8573. The first year's interest of $0.0686 is added to the principal so that the second year's interest is based on $0.9259. Total interest for this two-year period is $0.1427, computed as $0.0686 plus $0.0741.

Point: Benjamin Franklin is said to have described compounding as "the money, money makes, makes more money."

EXHIBIT 14A.2

Components of a Two-Year Loan

Amount borrowed	**$0.8573**
Interest for first year ($0.8573 × 8%)	0.0686
Amount owed after 1 year	0.9259
Interest for second year ($0.9259 × 8%)	0.0741
Amount owed after 2 years	$ 1.0000

Present Value Tables The present value of $1 that we must repay at some future date can be computed by using this formula: $1/(1 + i)^n$. The symbol i is the interest rate per period and n is the number of periods until the future payment must be made. Applying this formula to our two-year loan, we get $\$1/(1.08)^2$, or $0.8573. This is the same value shown in Exhibit 14A.2. We can use this formula to find any present value. However, a simpler method is to use a *present value table,* which lists present values computed with this formula for various interest rates and time periods. Many people find it helpful in learning present value concepts to first work with the table and then move to using a calculator.

Exhibit 14A.3 shows a present value table for a future payment of 1 for up to 10 periods at three different interest rates. Present values in this table are rounded to four decimal places. This table is drawn from the larger and more complete Table B.1 in Appendix B at the end of the book. Notice that the first value in the 8% column is 0.9259, the value we computed earlier for the present value of a $1 loan for one year at 8% (see Exhibit 14A.1). Go to the second row in the same 8% column and find the present value of 1 discounted at 8% for two years, or 0.8573. This $0.8573 is the present value of our obligation to repay $1 after two periods at 8% interest (see Exhibit 14A.2).

EXHIBIT 14A.3

Present Value of 1

	Rate		
Periods	6%	8%	10%
1	0.9434	**0.9259**	0.9091
2	0.8900	**0.8573**	0.8264
3	0.8396	0.7938	0.7513
4	0.7921	0.7350	0.6830
5	0.7473	0.6806	0.6209
6	0.7050	0.6302	0.5645
7	0.6651	0.5835	0.5132
8	0.6274	0.5403	0.4665
9	0.5919	0.5002	0.4241
10	0.5584	0.4632	0.3855

Example: Use Exhibit 14A.3 to find the present value of $1 discounted for 2 years at 6%. *Answer:* $0.8900

Applying a Present Value Table To illustrate how to measure a liability using a present value table, assume that a company plans to borrow cash and repay it as follows: $2,000 after one year, $3,000 after two years, and $5,000 after three years. How much does this company receive today if the interest rate on this loan is 10%? To answer, we need to compute the present value of the three future payments, discounted at 10%. This computation is shown in Exhibit 14A.4 using present values from Exhibit 14A.3. The company can borrow $8,054 today at 10% interest in exchange for its promise to make these three payments at the scheduled dates.

EXHIBIT 14A.4

Present Value of a Series of Unequal Payments

Periods	Payments	Present Value of 1 at 10%	Present Value of Payments
1	$2,000	0.9091	$ 1,818
2	3,000	0.8264	2,479
3	5,000	0.7513	3,757
Present value of all payments			$8,054

Present Value of an Annuity The $8,054 present value for the loan in Exhibit 14A.4 equals the sum of the present values of the three payments. When payments are not equal, their combined present value is best computed by adding the individual present values as shown in Exhibit 14A.4. Sometimes payments follow an **annuity,** which is a series of *equal* payments at equal time intervals. The present value of an annuity is readily computed.

To illustrate, assume that a company must repay a 6% loan with a $5,000 payment at each year-end for the next four years. This loan amount equals the present value of the four payments discounted at 6%. Exhibit 14A.5 shows how to compute this loan's present value of $17,326 by multiplying each payment by its matching present value factor taken from Exhibit 14A.3.

However, the series of $5,000 payments is an annuity, so we can compute its present value with either of two shortcuts. First, the third column of Exhibit 14A.5 shows that the sum of the present values of 1 at 6% for periods 1 through 4 equals 3.4651. One shortcut is to multiply this total of 3.4651 by the $5,000 annual payment to get the combined present value of $17,326. It requires one multiplication instead of four.

EXHIBIT 14A.5

Present Value of a Series of Equal Payments (Annuity) by Discounting Each Payment

Periods	Payments	Present Value of 1 at 6%	Present Value of Payments
1	$5,000	0.9434	$ 4,717
2	5,000	0.8900	4,450
3	5,000	0.8396	4,198
4	5,000	0.7921	3,961
Present value of all payments		3.4651	$17,326

EXHIBIT 14A.6

Present Value of an Annuity of 1

Periods	Rate 6%	8%	10%
1	0.9434	0.9259	0.9091
2	1.8334	1.7833	1.7355
3	2.6730	2.5771	2.4869
4	**3.4651**	3.3121	3.1699
5	4.2124	3.9927	3.7908
6	4.9173	4.6229	4.3553
7	5.5824	5.2064	4.8684
8	6.2098	5.7466	5.3349
9	6.8017	6.2469	5.7590
10	7.3601	6.7101	6.1446

The second shortcut uses an *annuity table* such as the one shown in Exhibit 14A.6, which is drawn from the more complete Table B.3 in Appendix B. We go directly to the annuity table to get the present value factor for a specific number of payments and interest rate. We then multiply this factor by the amount of the payment to find the present value of the annuity. Specifically, find the row for four periods and go across to the 6% column, where the factor is 3.4651. This factor equals the present value of an annuity with four payments of 1, discounted at 6%. We then multiply 3.4651 by $5,000 to get the $17,326 present value of the annuity.

Example: Use Exhibit 14A.6 to find the present value of an annuity of eight $15,000 payments with an 8% interest rate. *Answer:* $15,000 × 5.7466 = $86,199

Compounding Periods Shorter Than a Year The present value examples all involved periods of one year. In many situations, however, interest is compounded over shorter periods. For example, the interest rate on bonds is usually stated as an annual rate but interest is often paid every six months (semiannually). This means that the present value of interest payments from such bonds must be computed using interest periods of six months.

Assume that a borrower wants to know the present value of a series of 10 *semiannual payments* of $4,000 made over five years at an *annual interest rate* of 12%. The interest rate is stated as an annual rate of 12%, but it is actually a rate of 6% per semiannual interest period. To compute the present value of this series of $4,000 payments, go to row 10 of Exhibit 14A.6 and across to the 6% column to find the factor 7.3601. The present value of this annuity is $29,440 (7.3601 × $4,000).

Example: If this borrower makes five semiannual payments of $8,000, what is the present value of this annuity at a 12% rate? *Answer:* 4.2124 × $8,000 = $33,699

Appendix B further describes present value concepts and includes more complete present value tables and assignments.

Quick Check Answers — p. 579 

14. A company enters into an agreement to make four annual year-end payments of $1,000 each, starting one year from now. The annual interest rate is 8%. The present value of these four payments is (*a*) $2,923, (*b*) $2,940, or (*c*) $3,312.

15. Suppose a company has an option to pay either (*a*) $10,000 after one year or (*b*) $5,000 after six months and another $5,000 after one year. Which choice has the lower present value?

APPENDIX

14B Effective Interest Amortization

Effective Interest Amortization of a Discount Bond The straight-line method yields changes in the bonds' carrying value while the amount for bond interest expense remains constant. This gives the impression of a changing interest rate when users divide a constant bond interest expense over a changing carrying value. As a result, accounting standards allow use of the straight-line method only when its results do not differ materially from those obtained using the effective interest method. The **effective interest method,** or simply *interest method,* allocates total bond interest expense over the bonds' life in a way that yields a constant rate of interest. This constant rate of interest is the market rate at the issue date. Thus, bond interest expense for a period equals the carrying value of the bond at the beginning of that period multiplied by the market rate when issued.

Point: The effective interest method computes bond interest expense using the market rate at issuance. This rate is applied to a changing carrying value.

Exhibit 14B.1 shows an effective interest amortization table for the Fila bonds (as described in Exhibit 14.4). The key difference between the effective interest and straight-line methods lies in computing bond interest expense. Instead of assigning an equal amount of bond interest expense to each period, the effective interest method assigns a bond interest expense amount that increases over the life of a discount bond. **Both methods allocate the *same* $19,546 of total bond interest expense to the bonds' life, but in different patterns.** Specifically, the amortization table in Exhibit 14B.1 shows that the balance of the discount (column D) is amortized until it reaches zero. Also, the bonds' carrying value (column E) changes each period until it equals par value at maturity. Compare columns D and E to the corresponding columns in Exhibit 14.7 to see the amortization patterns. Total bond interest expense is $19,546, consisting of $16,000 of semiannual cash payments and $3,546 of the original bond discount, the same for both methods.

EXHIBIT 14B.1

Effective Interest Amortization of Bond Discount

Bonds: $100,000 Par Value, Semiannual Interest Payments, Two-Year Life, 4% Semiannual Contract Rate, 5% Semiannual Market Rate

Semiannual Interest Period-End	(A) Cash Interest Paid	(B) Bond Interest Expense	(C) Discount Amortization	(D) Unamortized Discount	(E) Carrying Value
(0) **12/31/2011**				**$3,546**	**$ 96,454**
(1) **6/30/2012**	**$4,000**	**$4,823**	**$ 823**	**2,723**	**97,277**
(2) 12/31/2012	4,000	4,864	864	1,859	98,141
(3) 6/30/2013	4,000	4,907	907	952	99,048
(4) 12/31/2013	4,000	4,952	952	**0**	**100,000**
	$16,000	$19,546	$3,546		

Column (**A**) is the par value ($100,000) multiplied by the semiannual contract rate (4%).
Column (**B**) is the prior period's carrying value multiplied by the semiannual market rate (5%).
Column (**C**) is the difference between interest paid and bond interest expense, or [(B) − (A)].
Column (**D**) is the prior period's unamortized discount less the current period's discount amortization.
Column (**E**) is the par value less unamortized discount, or [$100,000 − (D)].

Except for differences in amounts, journal entries recording the expense and updating the liability balance are the same under the effective interest method and the straight-line method. We can use the numbers in Exhibit 14B.1 to record each semiannual entry during the bonds' two-year life (June 30, 2012, through December 31, 2013). For instance, we record the interest payment at the end of the first semiannual period as follows:

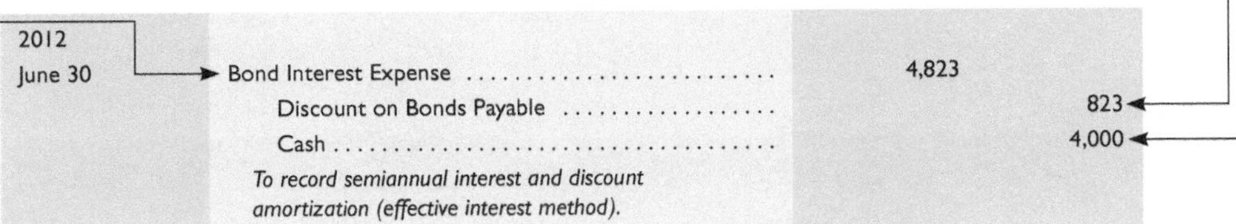

2012			
June 30	Bond Interest Expense	4,823	
	Discount on Bonds Payable		823
	Cash		4,000
	To record semiannual interest and discount amortization (effective interest method).		

Assets = Liabilities + Equity
−4,000 +823 −4,823

Effective Interest Amortization of a Premium Bond Exhibit 14B.2 shows the amortization table using the effective interest method for the Adidas bonds (as described in Exhibit 14.8). Column A lists the semiannual cash payments. Column B shows the amount of bond interest expense, computed as the 5% semiannual market rate at issuance multiplied by the beginning-of-period carrying value. The amount of cash paid in column A is larger than the bond interest expense because the cash payment is based on the higher 6% semiannual contract rate. The excess cash payment over the interest expense reduces the principal. These amounts are shown in column C. Column E shows the carrying value after

EXHIBIT 14B.2

Effective Interest Amortization of Bond Premium

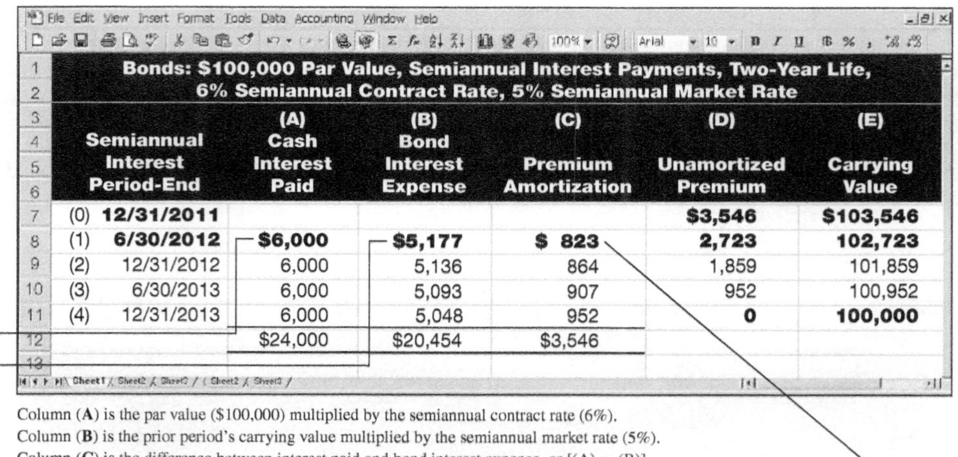

Bonds: $100,000 Par Value, Semiannual Interest Payments, Two-Year Life, 6% Semiannual Contract Rate, 5% Semiannual Market Rate

Semiannual Interest Period-End	(A) Cash Interest Paid	(B) Bond Interest Expense	(C) Premium Amortization	(D) Unamortized Premium	(E) Carrying Value
(0) **12/31/2011**				**$3,546**	**$103,546**
(1) **6/30/2012**	**$6,000**	**$5,177**	**$ 823**	**2,723**	**102,723**
(2) 12/31/2012	6,000	5,136	864	1,859	101,859
(3) 6/30/2013	6,000	5,093	907	952	100,952
(4) 12/31/2013	6,000	5,048	952	**0**	**100,000**
	$24,000	$20,454	$3,546		

Column (**A**) is the par value ($100,000) multiplied by the semiannual contract rate (6%).
Column (**B**) is the prior period's carrying value multiplied by the semiannual market rate (5%).
Column (**C**) is the difference between interest paid and bond interest expense, or [(A) − (B)].
Column (**D**) is the prior period's unamortized premium less the current period's premium amortization.
Column (**E**) is the par value plus unamortized premium, or [$100,000 + (D)].

deducting the amortized premium in column C from the prior period's carrying value. Column D shows the premium's reduction by periodic amortization. When the issuer makes the first semiannual interest payment, the effect of premium amortization on bond interest expense and bond liability is recorded as follows:

Assets = Liabilities + Equity
−6,000 −823 −5,177

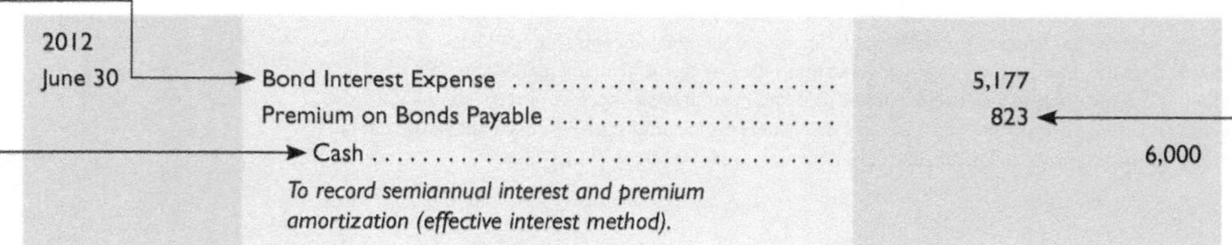

2012			
June 30	Bond Interest Expense	5,177	
	Premium on Bonds Payable	823	
	Cash		6,000
	To record semiannual interest and premium amortization (effective interest method).		

Similar entries with different amounts are recorded at each payment date until the bond matures at the end of 2013. The effective interest method yields decreasing amounts of bond interest expense and increasing amounts of premium amortization over the bonds' life.

IFRS

Unlike U.S. GAAP, IFRS requires that interest expense be computed using the effective interest method with *no exemptions.* ■

APPENDIX

14C Issuing Bonds between Interest Dates

C3 Describe interest accrual when bond payment periods differ from accounting periods.

An issuer can sell bonds at a date other than an interest payment date. When this occurs, the buyers normally pay the issuer the purchase price plus any interest accrued since the prior interest payment date. This accrued interest is then repaid to these buyers on the next interest payment date. To illustrate, suppose Avia sells $100,000 of its 9% bonds at par on March 1, 2011, 60 days after the stated issue date. The interest on Avia bonds is payable semiannually on each June 30 and December 31. Since 60 days have passed, the issuer collects accrued interest from the buyers at the time of issuance. This amount is $1,500 ($100,000 × 9% × 60/360 year). This case is reflected in Exhibit 14C.1.

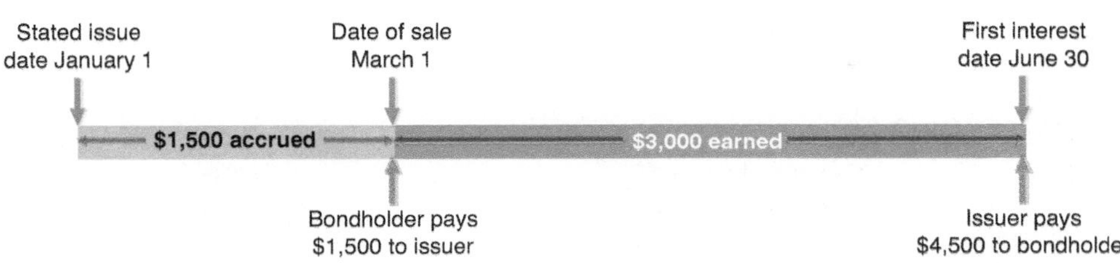

EXHIBIT 14C.1

Accruing Interest between Interest Payment Dates

Avia records the issuance of these bonds on March 1, 2011, as follows:

Mar. 1	Cash	101,500	
	Interest Payable		1,500
	Bonds Payable..........		100,000
	Sold bonds at par with accrued interest.		

Assets = Liabilities + Equity
+101,500 +100,000
+1,500

Liabilities for interest payable and bonds payable are recorded in separate accounts. When the June 30, 2011, semiannual interest date arrives, Avia pays the full semiannual interest of $4,500 ($100,000 × 9% × ½ year) to the bondholders. This payment includes the four months' interest of $3,000 earned by the bondholders from March 1 to June 30 *plus* the repayment of the 60 days' accrued interest collected by Avia when the bonds were sold. Avia records this first semiannual interest payment as follows:

Example: How much interest is collected from a buyer of $50,000 of Avia bonds sold at par 150 days after the contract issue date? *Answer:* $1,875 (computed as $50,000 × 9% × 150/360 year)

June 30	Interest Payable	1,500	
	Bond Interest Expense..........	3,000	
	Cash		4,500
	Paid semiannual interest on the bonds.		

Assets = Liabilities + Equity
−4,500 −1,500 −3,000

The practice of collecting and then repaying accrued interest with the next interest payment is to simplify the issuer's administrative efforts. To explain, suppose an issuer sells bonds on 15 or 20 different dates between the stated issue date and the first interest payment date. If the issuer does not collect accrued interest from buyers, it needs to pay different amounts of cash to each of them according to the time that passed after purchasing the bonds. The issuer needs to keep detailed records of buyers and the dates they bought bonds. Issuers avoid this recordkeeping by having each buyer pay accrued interest at purchase. Issuers then pay the full semiannual interest to all buyers, regardless of when they bought bonds.

Accruing Bond Interest Expense If a bond's interest period does not coincide with the issuer's accounting period, an adjusting entry is needed to recognize bond interest expense accrued since the most recent interest payment. To illustrate, assume that the stated issue date for Adidas bonds described in Exhibit 14.10 is September 1, 2011, instead of December 31, 2011, and that the bonds are sold on September 1, 2011. As a result, four months' interest (and premium amortization) accrue before the end of the 2011 calendar year. Interest for this period equals $3,409, or 4/6 of the first six months' interest of $5,113. Also, the premium amortization is $591, or 4/6 of the first six months' amortization of $887. The sum of the bond interest expense and the amortization is $4,000 ($3,409 + $591), which equals 4/6 of the $6,000 cash payment due on February 28, 2012. Adidas records these effects with an adjusting entry at December 31, 2011.

Point: Computation of accrued bond interest may use months instead of days for simplicity purposes. For example, the accrued interest computation for the Adidas bonds is based on months.

Dec. 31	Bond Interest Expense	3,409	
	Premium on Bonds Payable	591	
	Interest Payable		4,000
	To record four months' accrued interest and premium amortization.		

Assets = Liabilities + Equity
−591 −3,409
+4,000

Similar entries are made on each December 31 throughout the bonds' two-year life. When the $6,000 cash payment occurs on each February 28 interest payment date, Adidas must recognize bond interest expense and amortization for January and February. It must also eliminate the interest payable liability created by the December 31 adjusting entry. For example, Adidas records its payment on February 28, 2012, as follows:

Assets	=	Liabilities	+	Equity
−6,000		−4,000		−1,704
		−296		

Feb. 28	Interest Payable	4,000	
	Bond Interest Expense ($5,113 × 2/6)	1,704	
	Premium on Bonds Payable ($887 × 2/6)	296	
	Cash		6,000
	To record 2 months' interest and amortization, and eliminate accrued interest liability.		

The interest payments made each August 31 are recorded as usual because the entire six-month interest period is included within this company's calendar-year reporting period.

Decision Maker Answer — p. 579 

Bond Rater You must assign a rating to a bond that reflects its risk to bondholders. Identify factors you consider in assessing bond risk. Indicate the likely levels (relative to the norm) for the factors you identify for a bond that sells at a discount. ■

Quick Check Answer — p. 579 

16. On May 1, a company sells 9% bonds with a $500,000 par value that pay semiannual interest on each January 1 and July 1. The bonds are sold at par plus interest accrued since January 1. The issuer records the first semiannual interest payment on July 1 with (*a*) a debit to Interest Payable for $15,000, (*b*) a debit to Bond Interest Expense for $22,500, or (*c*) a credit to Interest Payable for $7,500.

APPENDIX

14D Leases and Pensions

This appendix briefly explains the accounting and analysis for both leases and pensions.

C4 Describe accounting for leases and pensions.

Lease Liabilities A **lease** is a contractual agreement between a *lessor* (asset owner) and a *lessee* (asset renter or tenant) that grants the lessee the right to use the asset for a period of time in return for cash (rent) payments. Nearly one-fourth of all equipment purchases are financed with leases. The advantages of lease financing include the lack of an immediate large cash payment and the potential to deduct rental payments in computing taxable income. From an accounting perspective, leases can be classified as either operating or capital leases.

Point: Home Depot reports that its rental expenses from operating leases total more than $900 million.

Operating Leases **Operating leases** are short-term (or cancelable) leases in which the lessor retains the risks and rewards of ownership. Examples include most car and apartment rental agreements. The lessee records such lease payments as expenses; the lessor records them as revenue. The lessee does not report the leased item as an asset or a liability (it is the lessor's asset). To illustrate, if an employee of Amazon leases a car for $300 at an airport while on company business, Amazon (lessee) records this cost as follows:

Assets	=	Liabilities	+	Equity
−300				−300

July 4	Rental Expense	300	
	Cash		300
	To record lease rental payment.		

Capital Leases **Capital leases** are long-term (or noncancelable) leases by which the lessor transfers substantially all risks and rewards of ownership to the lessee.[3] Examples include most leases of airplanes and department store buildings. The lessee records the leased item as its own asset along with a lease liability at the start of the lease term; the amount recorded equals the present value of all lease payments. To illustrate, assume that K2 Co. enters into a six-year lease of a building in which it will sell sporting equipment. The lease transfers all building ownership risks and rewards to K2 (the present value of its $12,979 annual lease payments is $60,000). K2 records this transaction as follows:

2011			
Jan. 1	Leased Asset—Building	60,000	
	Lease Liability		60,000
	To record leased asset and lease liability.		

Assets = Liabilities + Equity
+60,000 +60,000

K2 reports the leased asset as a plant asset and the lease liability as a long-term liability. The portion of the lease liability expected to be paid in the next year is reported as a current liability.[4] At each year-end, K2 records depreciation on the leased asset (assume straight-line depreciation, six-year lease term, and no salvage value) as follows:

Point: Home Depot reports *"certain locations . . . are leased under capital leases."* The net present value of this Lease Liability is about $400 million.

Dec. 31	Depreciation Expense—Building	10,000	
	Accumulated Depreciation—Building		10,000
	To record depreciation on leased asset.		

Assets = Liabilities + Equity
−10,000 −10,000

K2 also accrues interest on the lease liability at each year-end. Interest expense is computed by multiplying the remaining lease liability by the interest rate on the lease. Specifically, K2 records its annual interest expense as part of its annual lease payment ($12,979) as follows (for its first year):

2011			
Dec. 31	Interest Expense	4,800	
	Lease Liability	8,179	
	Cash		12,979
	*To record first annual lease payment.**		

Assets = Liabilities + Equity
−12,979 −8,179 −4,800

* These numbers are computed from a *lease payment schedule.* For simplicity, we use the same numbers from Exhibit 14.14 for this lease payment schedule—with different headings as follows:

		Payments			
	(A)	(B) *Debit*	(C) *Debit*	(D) *Credit*	(E)
Period Ending Date	**Beginning Balance of Lease Liability**	**Interest on Lease Liability 8% × (A)**	+ **Lease Liability (D) − (B)**	= **Cash Lease Payment**	**Ending Balance of Lease Liability (A) − (C)**
12/31/2011	**$60,000**	**$ 4,800**	**$ 8,179**	**$12,979**	**$51,821**
12/31/2012	51,821	4,146	8,833	12,979	42,988
12/31/2013	42,988	3,439	9,540	12,979	33,448
12/31/2014	33,448	2,676	10,303	12,979	23,145
12/31/2015	23,145	1,852	11,127	12,979	12,018
12/31/2016	12,018	961	12,018	12,979	0
		$17,874	**$60,000**	**$77,874**	

[3] A *capital lease* meets any one or more of four criteria: (1) transfers title of leased asset to lessee, (2) contains a bargain purchase option, (3) has a lease term that is 75% or more of the leased asset's useful life, or (4) has a present value of lease payments that is 90% or more of the leased asset's market value.

[4] Most lessees try to keep leased assets and lease liabilities off their balance sheets by failing to meet any one of the four criteria of a capital lease. This is because a lease liability increases a company's total liabilities, making it more difficult to obtain additional financing. The acquisition of assets without reporting any related liabilities (or other asset outflows) on the balance sheet is called **off-balance-sheet financing.**

Point: Fringe benefits are often 40% or more of salaries and wages, and pension benefits make up nearly 15% of fringe benefits.

Pension Liabilities A **pension plan** is a contractual agreement between an employer and its employees for the employer to provide benefits (payments) to employees after they retire. Most employers pay the full cost of the pension, but sometimes employees pay part of the cost. An employer records its payment into a pension plan with a debit to Pension Expense and a credit to Cash. A *plan administrator* receives payments from the employer, invests them in pension assets, and makes benefit payments to *pension recipients* (retired employees). Insurance and trust companies often serve as pension plan administrators.

Many pensions are known as *defined benefit plans* that define future benefits; the employer's contributions vary, depending on assumptions about future pension assets and liabilities. Several disclosures are necessary in this case. Specifically, a pension liability is reported when the accumulated benefit obligation is *more than* the plan assets, a so-called *underfunded plan.* The accumulated benefit obligation is the present value of promised future pension payments to retirees. *Plan assets* refer to the market value of assets the plan administrator holds. A pension asset is reported when the accumulated benefit obligation is *less than* the plan assets, a so-called *overfunded plan.* An employer reports pension expense when it receives the benefits from the employees' services, which is sometimes decades before it pays pension benefits to employees. (*Other Postretirement Benefits* refer to nonpension benefits such as health care and life insurance benefits. Similar to a pension, costs of these benefits are estimated and liabilities accrued when the employees earn them.)

Point: Two types of pension plans are (1) *defined benefit plan*—the retirement benefit is defined and the employer estimates the contribution necessary to pay these benefits—and (2) *defined contribution plan*—the pension contribution is defined and the employer and/or employee contributes amounts specified in the pension agreement.

Summary

C1 Explain the types and payment patterns of notes. Notes repaid over a period of time are called *installment notes* and usually follow one of two payment patterns: (1) decreasing payments of interest plus equal amounts of principal or (2) equal total payments. Mortgage notes also are common.

C2A Explain and compute the present value of an amount(s) to be paid at a future date(s). The basic concept of present value is that an amount of cash to be paid or received in the future is worth less than the same amount of cash to be paid or received today. Another important present value concept is that interest is compounded, meaning interest is added to the balance and used to determine interest for succeeding periods. An annuity is a series of equal payments occurring at equal time intervals. An annuity's present value can be computed using the present value table for an annuity (or a calculator).

C3C Describe interest accrual when bond payment periods differ from accounting periods. Issuers and buyers of debt record the interest accrued when issue dates or accounting periods do not coincide with debt payment dates.

C4D Describe accounting for leases and pensions. A lease is a rental agreement between the lessor and the lessee. When the lessor retains the risks and rewards of asset ownership (an *operating lease*), the lessee debits Rent Expense and credits Cash for its lease payments. When the lessor substantially transfers the risks and rewards of asset ownership to the lessee (a *capital lease*), the lessee capitalizes the leased asset and records a lease liability. Pension agreements can result in either pension assets or pension liabilities.

A1 Compare bond financing with stock financing. Bond financing is used to fund business activities. Advantages of bond financing versus stock include (1) no effect on owner control, (2) tax savings, and (3) increased earnings due to financial leverage. Disadvantages include (1) interest and principal payments and (2) amplification of poor performance.

A2 Assess debt features and their implications. Certain bonds are secured by the issuer's assets; other bonds, called *debentures,* are unsecured. Serial bonds mature at different points in time; term bonds mature at one time. Registered bonds have each bondholder's name recorded by the issuer; bearer bonds are payable to the holder. Convertible bonds are exchangeable for shares of the issuer's stock. Callable bonds can be retired by the issuer at a set price. Debt features alter the risk of loss for creditors.

A3 Compute the debt-to-equity ratio and explain its use. Both creditors and equity holders are concerned about the relation between the amount of liabilities and the amount of equity. A company's financing structure is at less risk when the debt-to-equity ratio is lower, as liabilities must be paid and usually with periodic interest.

P1 Prepare entries to record bond issuance and interest expense. When bonds are issued at par, Cash is debited and Bonds Payable is credited for the bonds' par value. At bond interest payment dates (usually semiannual), Bond Interest Expense is debited and Cash credited—the latter for an amount equal to the bond par value multiplied by the bond contract rate.

P2 Compute and record amortization of bond discount. Bonds are issued at a discount when the contract rate is less than the market rate, making the issue (selling) price less than par. When this occurs, the issuer records a credit to Bonds Payable (at par) and debits both Discount on Bonds Payable and Cash. The amount of bond interest expense assigned to each period is computed using either the straight-line or effective interest method.

P3 Compute and record amortization of bond premium. Bonds are issued at a premium when the contract rate is higher than the market rate, making the issue (selling) price greater than par. When this occurs, the issuer records a debit to Cash and credits both Premium on Bonds Payable and Bonds Payable (at par). The amount of bond interest expense assigned to each period is computed using either the straight-line or effective interest method. The Premium on Bonds Payable is allocated to reduce bond interest expense over the life of the bonds.

P4 Record the retirement of bonds. Bonds are retired at maturity with a debit to Bonds Payable and a credit to Cash at par value. The issuer can retire the bonds early by exercising a call option or purchasing them in the market. Bondholders can also retire bonds early by exercising a conversion feature on convertible bonds. The issuer recognizes a gain or loss for the difference between the amount paid and the bond carrying value.

P5 **Prepare entries to account for notes.** Interest is allocated to each period in a note's life by multiplying its beginning-period carrying value by its market rate at issuance. If a note is repaid with equal payments, the payment amount is computed by dividing the borrowed amount by the present value of an annuity factor (taken from a present value table) using the market rate and the number of payments.

Guidance Answers to Decision Maker

Entrepreneur This is a "present value" question. The market interest rate (10%) and present value ($3,000) are known, but the payment required two years later is unknown. This amount ($3,630) can be computed as $3,000 × 1.10 × 1.10. Thus, the sale price is $3,630 when no payments are received for two years. The $3,630 received two years from today is equivalent to $3,000 cash today.

Bond Investor The debt-to-equity ratio for the first company is 0.2 ($350,000/$1,750,000) and for the second company is 1.2 ($1,200,000/$1,000,000), suggesting that the financing structure of the second company is more risky than that of the first company. Consequently, as a buyer of unsecured debenture bonds, you prefer the first company (all else equal).

Bond Rater Bonds with longer repayment periods (life) have higher risk. Also, bonds issued by companies in financial difficulties or facing higher than normal uncertainties have higher risk. Moreover, companies with higher than normal debt and large fluctuations in earnings are considered of higher risk. Discount bonds are more risky on one or more of these factors.

Guidance Answers to Quick Checks

1.

2011			
Jan. 1	Cash	10,000	
	Bonds Payable		10,000
June 30	Bond Interest Expense	450	
	Cash		450

2. Multiply the bond's par value by its contract rate of interest.
3. Bonds sell at a premium when the contract rate exceeds the market rate and the purchasers pay more than their par value.
4. The bonds are issued at a discount, meaning that issue price is less than par value. A discount occurs because the bond contract rate (6%) is less than the market rate (8%).
5.

Cash	91,893	
Discount on Bonds Payable	8,107	
Bonds Payable		100,000

6. $3,811 (total bond interest expense of $38,107 divided by 10 periods; or the $3,000 semiannual cash payment plus the $8,107 discount divided by 10 periods).
7. The bonds are issued at a premium, meaning issue price is higher than par value. A premium occurs because the bonds' contract rate (16%) is higher than the market rate (14%).
8. (*b*) For each semiannual period: $10,592/20 periods = $530 premium amortization.
9.

Bonds payable, 16%, due 12/31/2020	$100,000	
Plus premium on bonds payable	9,532*	$109,532

* Original premium balance of $10,592 less $530 and $530 amortized on 6/30/2011 and 12/31/2011, respectively.

10. $9,375 loss, computed as the difference between the repurchase price of $256,250 [50% of ($500,000 × 102.5%)] and the carrying value of $246,875 (50% of $493,750).
11. (*c*)
12. The interest portion of an installment payment equals the period's beginning loan balance multiplied by the market interest rate at the time of the note's issuance.
13. On the balance sheet, the account balances of the related liability (note payable) and asset (cash) accounts are decreased. On the income statement, interest expense is recorded.
14. (*c*), computed as 3.3121 × $1,000 = $3,312.
15. The option of paying $10,000 after one year has a lower present value. It postpones paying the first $5,000 by six months. More generally, the present value of a further delayed payment is always lower than a less delayed payment.
16. (*a*) Reflects payment of accrued interest recorded back on May 1; $500,000 × 9% × 4/12 = $15,000.

Key Terms

mhhe.com/wildFAP20e

Annuity (p. 571)
Bearer bonds (p. 566)
Bond (p. 552)
Bond certificate (p. 554)
Bond indenture (p. 554)
Callable bonds (p. 566)
Capital leases (p. 577)
Carrying (book) value of bonds (p. 556)
Contract rate (p. 555)

Convertible bonds (p. 566)
Coupon bonds (p. 566)
Debt-to-equity ratio (p. 567)
Discount on bonds payable (p. 555)
Effective interest method (p. 572)
Fair value option (p. 565)
Installment note (p. 562)
Lease (p. 576)
Market rate (p. 555)
Mortgage (p. 564)
Off-balance-sheet financing (p. 577)
Operating leases (p. 576)
Par value of a bond (p. 552)
Pension plan (p. 578)
Premium on bonds (p. 558)
Registered bonds (p. 566)
Secured bonds (p. 566)
Serial bonds (p. 566)
Sinking fund bonds (p. 566)
Straight-line bond amortization (p. 556)
Term bonds (p. 566)
Unsecured bonds (p. 566)

Multiple Choice Quiz

Answers on p. 593

mhhe.com/wildFAP20e

Additional Quiz Questions are available at the book's Website.

1. A bond traded at 97½ means that
   - a. The bond pays 97½% interest.
   - b. The bond trades at $975 per $1,000 bond.
   - c. The market rate of interest is below the contract rate of interest for the bond.
   - d. The bonds can be retired at $975 each.
   - e. The bond's interest rate is 2½%.
2. A bondholder that owns a $1,000, 6%, 15-year bond has
   - a. The right to receive $1,000 at maturity.
   - b. Ownership rights in the bond issuing entity.
   - c. The right to receive $60 per month until maturity.
   - d. The right to receive $1,900 at maturity.
   - e. The right to receive $600 per year until maturity.
3. A company issues 8%, 20-year bonds with a par value of $500,000. The current market rate for the bonds is 8%. The amount of interest owed to the bondholders for each semiannual interest payment is
   - a. $40,000.
   - b. $0.
   - c. $20,000.
   - d. $800,000.
   - e. $400,000.
4. A company issued 5-year, 5% bonds with a par value of $100,000. The company received $95,735 for the bonds. Using the straight-line method, the company's interest expense for the first semiannual interest period is
   - a. $2,926.50.
   - b. $5,853.00.
   - c. $2,500.00.
   - d. $5,000.00.
   - e. $9,573.50.
5. A company issued 8-year, 5% bonds with a par value of $350,000. The company received proceeds of $373,745. Interest is payable semiannually. The amount of premium amortized for the first semiannual interest period, assuming straight-line bond amortization, is
   - a. $2,698.
   - b. $23,745.
   - c. $8,750.
   - d. $9,344.
   - e. $1,484.

B(C,D) *Superscript letter B(C, D) denotes assignments based on Appendix 14B (14C, 14D).*

Icon denotes assignments that involve decision making.

Discussion Questions

1. What is the main difference between a bond and a share of stock?
2. What is the main difference between notes payable and bonds payable?
3. What is the advantage of issuing bonds instead of obtaining financing from the company's owners?
4. What are the duties of a trustee for bondholders?
5. What is a bond indenture? What provisions are usually included in it?
6. What are the *contract* rate and the *market* rate for bonds?
7. What factors affect the market rates for bonds?
8. [B] Does the straight-line or effective interest method produce an interest expense allocation that yields a constant rate of interest over a bond's life? Explain.
9. [C] Why does a company that issues bonds between interest dates collect accrued interest from the bonds' purchasers?
10. If you know the par value of bonds, the contract rate, and the market rate, how do you compute the bonds' price?
11. What is the issue price of a $2,000 bond sold at 98¼? What is the issue price of a $6,000 bond sold at 101½?
12. Describe the debt-to-equity ratio and explain how creditors and owners would use this ratio to evaluate a company's risk.

13. What obligation does an entrepreneur (owner) have to investors that purchase bonds to finance the business?

14. Refer to Research In Motion's annual report in Appendix A. Is there any indication that RIM has issued bonds?

15. By what amount did Palm's long-term debt increase or decrease in 2009?

16. Refer to the statement of cash flows for Nokia in Appendix A. For the year ended December 31, 2009, what was the amount for repayment of bank loans?

17. Refer to the annual report for Apple in Appendix A. For the year ended September 26, 2009, what is its debt-to-equity ratio? What does this ratio tell us?

18.[D] When can a lease create both an asset and a liability for the lessee?

19.[D] Compare and contrast an operating lease with a capital lease.

20.[D] Describe the two basic types of pension plans.

connect

Round dollar amounts to the nearest whole dollar.

QUICK STUDY

QS 14-1
Bond features and terminology
A2

Enter the letter of the description *A* through *H* that best fits each term or phrase 1 through 8.

A. Records and tracks the bondholders' names.
B. Is unsecured; backed only by the issuer's credit standing.
C. Has varying maturity dates for amounts owed.
D. Identifies rights and responsibilities of the issuer and the bondholders.
E. Can be exchanged for shares of the issuer's stock.
F. Is unregistered; interest is paid to whoever possesses them.
G. Maintains a separate asset account from which bondholders are paid at maturity.
H. Pledges specific assets of the issuer as collateral.

1. ______ Debenture
2. ______ Bond indenture
3. ______ Bearer bond
4. ______ Registered bond
5. ______ Sinking fund bond
6. ______ Convertible bond
7. ______ Secured bond
8. ______ Serial bond

QS 14-2
Bond computations—straight-line
P1 P2

Alberto Company issues 8%, 10-year bonds with a par value of $350,000 and semiannual interest payments. On the issue date, the annual market rate for these bonds is 10%, which implies a selling price of 87½. The straight-line method is used to allocate interest expense.

1. What are the issuer's cash proceeds from issuance of these bonds?
2. What total amount of bond interest expense will be recognized over the life of these bonds?
3. What is the amount of bond interest expense recorded on the first interest payment date?

QS 14-3[B]
Bond computations—effective interest
P1 P3

Sanchez Company issues 10%, 15-year bonds with a par value of $120,000 and semiannual interest payments. On the issue date, the annual market rate for these bonds is 8%, which implies a selling price of 117¼. The effective interest method is used to allocate interest expense.

1. What are the issuer's cash proceeds from issuance of these bonds?
2. What total amount of bond interest expense will be recognized over the life of these bonds?
3. What amount of bond interest expense is recorded on the first interest payment date?

QS 14-4
Journalize bond issuance P1

Prepare the journal entries for the issuance of the bonds in both QS 14-2 and QS 14-3. Assume that both bonds are issued for cash on January 1, 2011.

QS 14-5
Computing bond price P2 P3

Using the bond details in both QS 14-2 and QS 14-3, confirm that the bonds' selling prices given in each problem are approximately correct. Use the present value tables B.1 and B.3 in Appendix B.

QS 14-6
Recording bond issuance and discount amortization P1 P2

Bellvue Company issues 10%, five-year bonds, on December 31, 2010, with a par value of $100,000 and semiannual interest payments. Use the following straight-line bond amortization table and prepare journal entries to record (*a*) the issuance of bonds on December 31, 2010; (*b*) the first interest payment on June 30, 2011; and (*c*) the second interest payment on December 31, 2011.

Semiannual Period-End	Unamortized Discount	Carrying Value
(0) 12/31/2010	$7,360	$92,640
(1) 6/30/2011	6,624	93,376
(2) 12/31/2011	5,888	94,112

QS 14-7
Bond retirement by call option P4

On July 1, 2011, Jackson Company exercises a $5,000 call option (plus par value) on its outstanding bonds that have a carrying value of $208,000 and par value of $200,000. The company exercises the call option after the semiannual interest is paid on June 30, 2011. Record the entry to retire the bonds.

QS 14-8
Bond retirement by stock conversion P4

On January 1, 2011, the $1,000,000 par value bonds of Gruden Company with a carrying value of $1,000,000 are converted to 500,000 shares of $0.50 par value common stock. Record the entry for the conversion of the bonds.

QS 14-9
Computing payments for an installment note C1

Valdez Company borrows $170,000 cash from a bank and in return signs an installment note for five annual payments of equal amount, with the first payment due one year after the note is signed. Use Table B.3 in Appendix B to compute the amount of the annual payment for each of the following annual market rates: (*a*) 4%, (*b*) 8%, and (*c*) 12%.

QS 14-10
Debt-to-equity ratio
A2

Compute the debt-to-equity ratio for each of the following companies. Which company appears to have a riskier financing structure? Explain.

	Canal Company	Sears Company
Total liabilities	$492,000	$ 384,000
Total equity	656,000	1,200,000

QS 14-11C
Issuing bonds between interest dates P1

Kemper Company plans to issue 6% bonds on January 1, 2011, with a par value of $1,000,000. The company sells $900,000 of the bonds on January 1, 2011. The remaining $100,000 sells at par on March 1, 2011. The bonds pay interest semiannually as of June 30 and December 31. Record the entry for the March 1 cash sale of bonds.

QS 14-12D
Recording operating leases C4

Lauren Wright, an employee of ETrain.com, leases a car at O'Hare airport for a three-day business trip. The rental cost is $350. Prepare the entry by ETrain.com to record Lauren's short-term car lease cost.

QS 14-13D
Recording capital leases C4

Juicyfruit, Inc., signs a five-year lease for office equipment with Office Solutions. The present value of the lease payments is $20,859. Prepare the journal entry that Juicyfruit records at the inception of this capital lease.

QS 14-14
International liabilities disclosures
P1 P2

Vodafone Group Plc reports the following information among its bonds payable as of March 31, 2009 (pounds in millions).

Financial Long-Term Liabilities Measured at Amortised Cost			
(£ millions)	Nominal (par) Value	Carrying Value	Fair Value
4.625% (US dollar 500 million) bond due July 2018	£350	£392	£315

a. What is the par value of the 4.625% bond issuance? What is its book (carrying) value?
b. Was the 4.625% bond sold at a discount or a premium? Explain.

QS 14-15
International liabilities disclosures and interpretations
P1 P2

Refer to the information in QS 14-14 for Vodafone Group Plc. The following price quotes (from Yahoo! Finance Bond Center) relate to its bonds payable as of late 2009. For example, the price quote indicates that the 4.625% bonds have a market price of 98.0 (98.0% of par value), resulting in a yield to maturity of 4.899%.

Price	Contract Rate (coupon)	Maturity Date	Market Rate (YTM)
98.0	4.625%	15-Jul-2018	4.899%

a. Assuming that the 4.625% bonds were originally issued at par value, what does the market price reveal about interest rate changes since bond issuance? (Assume that Vodafone's credit rating has remained the same.)
b. Does the change in market rates since the issuance of these bonds affect the amount of interest expense reported on Vodafone's income statement? Explain.
c. How much cash would Vodafone need to pay to repurchase the 4.625% bonds at the quoted market price of 98.0? (Assume no interest is owed when the bonds are repurchased.)
d. Assuming that the 4.625% bonds remain outstanding until maturity, at what market price will the bonds sell on the due date in 2018?

connect

EXERCISES

Round dollar amounts to the nearest whole dollar. Assume no reversing entries are used.

Exercise 14-1
Recording bond issuance and interest
P1

On January 1, 2011, Kidman Enterprises issues bonds that have a $1,700,000 par value, mature in 20 years, and pay 9% interest semiannually on June 30 and December 31. The bonds are sold at par.

1. How much interest will Kidman pay (in cash) to the bondholders every six months?
2. Prepare journal entries to record (*a*) the issuance of bonds on January 1, 2011; (*b*) the first interest payment on June 30, 2011; and (*c*) the second interest payment on December 31, 2011.
3. Prepare the journal entry for issuance assuming the bonds are issued at (*a*) 98 and (*b*) 102.

Exercise 14-2
Straight-line amortization of bond discount
P2

Moss issues bonds with a par value of $90,000 on January 1, 2011. The bonds' annual contract rate is 8%, and interest is paid semiannually on June 30 and December 31. The bonds mature in three years. The annual market rate at the date of issuance is 10%, and the bonds are sold for $85,431.

1. What is the amount of the discount on these bonds at issuance?
2. How much total bond interest expense will be recognized over the life of these bonds?
3. Prepare an amortization table like the one in Exhibit 14.7 for these bonds; use the straight-line method to amortize the discount.

Exercise 14-3[B]
Effective interest amortization of bond discount
P2

Welch issues bonds dated January 1, 2011, with a par value of $250,000. The bonds' annual contract rate is 9%, and interest is paid semiannually on June 30 and December 31. The bonds mature in three years. The annual market rate at the date of issuance is 12%, and the bonds are sold for $231,570.

1. What is the amount of the discount on these bonds at issuance?
2. How much total bond interest expense will be recognized over the life of these bonds?
3. Prepare an amortization table like the one in Exhibit 14B.1 for these bonds; use the effective interest method to amortize the discount.

Exercise 14-4
Straight-line amortization of bond premium
P3

Prairie Dunes Co. issues bonds dated January 1, 2011, with a par value of $800,000. The bonds' annual contract rate is 13%, and interest is paid semiannually on June 30 and December 31. The bonds mature in three years. The annual market rate at the date of issuance is 12%, and the bonds are sold for $819,700.

1. What is the amount of the premium on these bonds at issuance?
2. How much total bond interest expense will be recognized over the life of these bonds?
3. Prepare an amortization table like the one in Exhibit 14.11 for these bonds; use the straight-line method to amortize the premium.

Exercise 14-5[B]
Effective interest amortization of bond premium P3

Refer to the bond details in Exercise 14-4 and prepare an amortization table like the one in Exhibit 14B.2 for these bonds using the effective interest method to amortize the premium.

Exercise 14-6
Recording bond issuance and premium amortization
P1 P3

Jobbs Company issues 10%, five-year bonds, on December 31, 2010, with a par value of $100,000 and semiannual interest payments. Use the following straight-line bond amortization table and prepare journal entries to record (*a*) the issuance of bonds on December 31, 2010; (*b*) the first interest payment on June 30, 2011; and (*c*) the second interest payment on December 31, 2011.

Semiannual Period-End	Unamortized Premium	Carrying Value
(0) 12/31/2010	$8,111	$108,111
(1) 6/30/2011	7,300	107,300
(2) 12/31/2011	6,489	106,489

Exercise 14-7
Recording bond issuance and discount amortization
P1 P2

Matchbox Company issues 6%, four-year bonds, on December 31, 2011, with a par value of $100,000 and semiannual interest payments. Use the following straight-line bond amortization table and prepare journal entries to record (*a*) the issuance of bonds on December 31, 2011; (*b*) the first interest payment on June 30, 2012; and (*c*) the second interest payment on December 31, 2012.

Semiannual Period-End	Unamortized Discount	Carrying Value
(0) 12/31/2011	$6,733	$93,267
(1) 6/30/2012	5,891	94,109
(2) 12/31/2012	5,049	94,951

Exercise 14-8
Recording bond issuance and discount amortization
P1 P2

Oneil Company issues 5%, two-year bonds, on December 31, 2011, with a par value of $100,000 and semiannual interest payments. Use the following straight-line bond amortization table and prepare journal entries to record (*a*) the issuance of bonds on December 31, 2011; (*b*) the first through fourth interest payments on each June 30 and December 31; and (*c*) the maturity of the bond on December 31, 2013.

Semiannual Period-End	Unamortized Discount	Carrying Value
(0) 12/31/2011	$6,000	$ 94,000
(1) 6/30/2012	4,500	95,500
(2) 12/31/2012	3,000	97,000
(3) 6/30/2013	1,500	98,500
(4) 12/31/2013	0	100,000

Exercise 14-9
Computing bond interest and price; recording bond issuance
P2 

Jester Company issues bonds with a par value of $600,000 on their stated issue date. The bonds mature in 10 years and pay 6% annual interest in semiannual payments. On the issue date, the annual market rate for the bonds is 8%.

1. What is the amount of each semiannual interest payment for these bonds?
2. How many semiannual interest payments will be made on these bonds over their life?
3. Use the interest rates given to determine whether the bonds are issued at par, at a discount, or at a premium.
4. Compute the price of the bonds as of their issue date.
5. Prepare the journal entry to record the bonds' issuance.

Check (4) $518,465

Exercise 14-10
Computing bond interest and price; recording bond issuance
P3

Metro Company issues bonds with a par value of $75,000 on their stated issue date. The bonds mature in five years and pay 10% annual interest in semiannual payments. On the issue date, the annual market rate for the bonds is 8%.

1. What is the amount of each semiannual interest payment for these bonds?
2. How many semiannual interest payments will be made on these bonds over their life?
3. Use the interest rates given to determine whether the bonds are issued at par, at a discount, or at a premium.

4. Compute the price of the bonds as of their issue date.
5. Prepare the journal entry to record the bonds' issuance.

Check (4) $81,086

Exercise 14-11
Bond computations, straight-line amortization, and bond retirement
P2 P4

On January 1, 2011, Steadman issues $350,000 of 10%, 15-year bonds at a price of 97¾. Six years later, on January 1, 2017, Steadman retires 20% of these bonds by buying them on the open market at 104½. All interest is accounted for and paid through December 31, 2016, the day before the purchase. The straight-line method is used to amortize any bond discount.

1. How much does the company receive when it issues the bonds on January 1, 2011?
2. What is the amount of the discount on the bonds at January 1, 2011?
3. How much amortization of the discount is recorded on the bonds for the entire period from January 1, 2011, through December 31, 2016?
4. What is the carrying (book) value of the bonds as of the close of business on December 31, 2016? What is the carrying value of the 20% soon-to-be-retired bonds on this same date?
5. How much did the company pay on January 1, 2017, to purchase the bonds that it retired?
6. What is the amount of the recorded gain or loss from retiring the bonds?
7. Prepare the journal entry to record the bond retirement at January 1, 2017.

Check (6) $4,095 loss

Exercise 14-12[C]
Recording bond issuance with accrued interest
C4 P1

On May 1, 2011, Fellenger Enterprises issues bonds dated January 1, 2011, that have a $1,700,000 par value, mature in 20 years, and pay 9% interest semiannually on June 30 and December 31. The bonds are sold at par plus four months' accrued interest.

1. How much accrued interest do the bond purchasers pay Fellenger on May 1, 2011?
2. Prepare Fellenger's journal entries to record (*a*) the issuance of bonds on May 1, 2011; (*b*) the first interest payment on June 30, 2011; and (*c*) the second interest payment on December 31, 2011.

Check (1) $51,000

Exercise 14-13
Straight-line amortization and accrued bond interest expense
P1 P2

Simon issues four-year bonds with a $50,000 par value on June 1, 2011, at a price of $47,974. The annual contract rate is 7%, and interest is paid semiannually on November 30 and May 31.

1. Prepare an amortization table like the one in Exhibit 14.7 for these bonds. Use the straight-line method of interest amortization.
2. Prepare journal entries to record the first two interest payments and to accrue interest as of December 31, 2011.

Exercise 14-14
Installment note with equal total payments C1 P5

On January 1, 2011, Randa borrows $25,000 cash by signing a four-year, 7% installment note. The note requires four equal total payments of accrued interest and principal on December 31 of each year from 2011 through 2014.

1. Compute the amount of each of the four equal total payments.
2. Prepare an amortization table for this installment note like the one in Exhibit 14.14.

Check (1) $7,381

Exercise 14-15
Installment note entries P5

Use the information in Exercise 14-14 to prepare the journal entries for Randa to record the loan on January 1, 2011, and the four payments from December 31, 2011, through December 31, 2014.

Exercise 14-16
Applying debt-to-equity ratio
A3 

Ramirez Company is considering a project that will require a $500,000 loan. It presently has total liabilities of $220,000, and total assets of $620,000.

1. Compute Ramirez's (*a*) present debt-to-equity ratio and (*b*) the debt-to-equity ratio assuming it borrows $500,000 to fund the project.
2. Evaluate and discuss the level of risk involved if Ramirez borrows the funds to pursue the project.

Exercise 14-17[D]
Identifying capital and operating leases
C4

Indicate whether the company in each separate case 1 through 3 has entered into an operating lease or a capital lease.

1. The present value of the lease payments is 95% of the leased asset's market value, and the lease term is 70% of the leased asset's useful life.
2. The title is transferred to the lessee, the lessee can purchase the asset for $1 at the end of the lease, and the lease term is five years. The leased asset has an expected useful life of six years.
3. The lessor retains title to the asset, and the lease term is three years on an asset that has a five-year useful life.

Exercise 14-18[D]
Accounting for capital lease
C4

Flyer (lessee) signs a five-year capital lease for office equipment with a $20,000 annual lease payment. The present value of the five annual lease payments is $82,000, based on a 7% interest rate.

1. Prepare the journal entry Flyer will record at inception of the lease.
2. If the leased asset has a five-year useful life with no salvage value, prepare the journal entry Flyer will record each year to recognize depreciation expense related to the leased asset.

Exercise 14-19[D]
Analyzing lease options
C2 C3 C4

General Motors advertised three alternatives for a 25-month lease on a new Blazer: (1) zero dollars down and a lease payment of $1,750 per month for 25 months, (2) $5,000 down and $1,500 per month for 25 months, or (3) $38,500 down and no payments for 25 months. Use the present value Table B.3 in Appendix B to determine which is the best alternative (assume you have enough cash to accept any alternative and the annual interest rate is 12% compounded monthly).

Exercise 14-20
Accounting for long-term liabilities under IFRS
P1 P2 P3

Heineken N.V. reports the following information for its Loans and Borrowings as of December 31, 2008, including proceeds and repayments for the year ended December 31, 2008 (euros in millions).

Loans and borrowings (noncurrent liabilities)	
Loans and borrowings, December 31, 2008	€ 9,084
Proceeds (cash) from issuances of loans and borrowings	6,361
Repayments (in cash) of loans and borrowings	(2,532)

1. Prepare Heineken's journal entry to record its cash proceeds from issuances of its loans and borrowings for 2008. Assume that the par value of these issuances is €6,000.
2. Prepare Heineken's journal entry to record its cash repayments of its loans and borrowings for 2008. Assume that the par value of these issuances is €2,400, and the premium on them is €32.
3. Compute the discount or premium on its loans and borrowings as of December 31, 2008, assuming that the par value of these liabilities is €9,000.
4. Given the facts in part 3 and viewing the entirety of loans and borrowings as one issuance, was the contract rate on these loans and borrowings higher or lower than the market rate at the time of issuance? Explain. (Assume that Heineken's credit rating has remained the same.)

connect

PROBLEM SET A

Round dollar amounts to the nearest whole dollar. Assume no reversing entries are used.

Problem 14-1A
Computing bond price and recording issuance
P1 P2 P3

Stowers Research issues bonds dated January 1, 2011, that pay interest semiannually on June 30 and December 31. The bonds have a $20,000 par value and an annual contract rate of 10%, and they mature in 10 years.

Required

For each of the following three separate situations, (*a*) determine the bonds' issue price on January 1, 2011, and (*b*) prepare the journal entry to record their issuance.

1. The market rate at the date of issuance is 8%.
2. The market rate at the date of issuance is 10%.
3. The market rate at the date of issuance is 12%.

Check (1) Premium, $2,718

(3) Discount, $2,294

Problem 14-2A
Straight-line amortization of bond discount
P1 P2

mhhe.com/wildFAP20e

Heathrow issues $2,000,000 of 6%, 15-year bonds dated January 1, 2011, that pay interest semiannually on June 30 and December 31. The bonds are issued at a price of $1,728,224.

Required

1. Prepare the January 1, 2011, journal entry to record the bonds' issuance.
2. For each semiannual period, compute (*a*) the cash payment, (*b*) the straight-line discount amortization, and (*c*) the bond interest expense.
3. Determine the total bond interest expense to be recognized over the bonds' life.
4. Prepare the first two years of an amortization table like Exhibit 14.7 using the straight-line method.
5. Prepare the journal entries to record the first two interest payments.

Check (3) $2,071,776

(4) 12/31/2012 carrying value, $1,764,460

Problem 14-3A
Straight-line amortization of bond premium
P1 P3

Refer to the bond details in Problem 14-2A, *except* assume that the bonds are issued at a price of $2,447,990.

Required

1. Prepare the January 1, 2011, journal entry to record the bonds' issuance.
2. For each semiannual period, compute (*a*) the cash payment, (*b*) the straight-line premium amortization, and (*c*) the bond interest expense.
3. Determine the total bond interest expense to be recognized over the bonds' life.
4. Prepare the first two years of an amortization table like Exhibit 14.7 using the straight-line method.
5. Prepare the journal entries to record the first two interest payments.

Check (3) $1,352,010
(4) 12/31/2012 carrying value, $2,388,258

Problem 14-4A
Straight-line amortization of bond premium
P1 P3 eXcel
mhhe.com/wildFAP20e

Saturn issues 6.5%, five-year bonds dated January 1, 2011, with a $500,000 par value. The bonds pay interest on June 30 and December 31 and are issued at a price of $510,666. The annual market rate is 6% on the issue date.

Required

1. Calculate the total bond interest expense over the bonds' life.
2. Prepare a straight-line amortization table like Exhibit 14.11 for the bonds' life.
3. Prepare the journal entries to record the first two interest payments.

Check (2) 6/30/2013 carrying value, $505,331

Problem 14-5A[B]
Effective interest amortization of bond premium; computing bond price P1 P3

Refer to the bond details in Problem 14-4A.

Required

1. Compute the total bond interest expense over the bonds' life.
2. Prepare an effective interest amortization table like the one in Exhibit 14B.2 for the bonds' life.
3. Prepare the journal entries to record the first two interest payments.
4. Use the market rate at issuance to compute the present value of the remaining cash flows for these bonds as of December 31, 2013. Compare your answer with the amount shown on the amortization table as the balance for that date (from part 2) and explain your findings.

Check (2) 6/30/2013 carrying value, $505,728
(4) $504,653

Problem 14-6A
Straight-line amortization of bond discount
P1 P2

Patton issues $650,000 of 5%, four-year bonds dated January 1, 2011, that pay interest semiannually on June 30 and December 31. They are issued at $584,361 and their market rate is 8% at the issue date.

Required

1. Prepare the January 1, 2011, journal entry to record the bonds' issuance.
2. Determine the total bond interest expense to be recognized over the bonds' life.
3. Prepare a straight-line amortization table like the one in Exhibit 14.7 for the bonds' first two years.
4. Prepare the journal entries to record the first two interest payments.

Check (2) $195,639
(3) 12/31/2012 carrying value, $617,181

Analysis Component

5. Assume the market rate on January 1, 2011, is 4% instead of 8%. Without providing numbers, describe how this change affects the amounts reported on Patton's financial statements.

Problem 14-7A[B]
Effective interest amortization of bond discount P1 P2

Refer to the bond details in Problem 14-6A.

Required

1. Prepare the January 1, 2011, journal entry to record the bonds' issuance.
2. Determine the total bond interest expense to be recognized over the bonds' life.
3. Prepare an effective interest amortization table like the one in Exhibit 14B.1 for the bonds' first two years.
4. Prepare the journal entries to record the first two interest payments.

Check (2) $195,639
(3) 12/31/2012 carrying value, $614,614

mhhe.com/wildFAP20e

Problem 14-8A[B]
Effective interest amortization of bond premium; retiring bonds
P1 P3 P4 

Check (3) 6/30/2012 carrying value, $91,224

(5) $2,635 gain

mhhe.com/wildFAP20e

McFad issues $90,000 of 11%, three-year bonds dated January 1, 2011, that pay interest semiannually on June 30 and December 31. They are issued at $92,283. Their market rate is 10% at the issue date.

Required

1. Prepare the January 1, 2011, journal entry to record the bonds' issuance.
2. Determine the total bond interest expense to be recognized over the bonds' life.
3. Prepare an effective interest amortization table like Exhibit 14B.2 for the bonds' first two years.
4. Prepare the journal entries to record the first two interest payments.
5. Prepare the journal entry to record the bonds' retirement on January 1, 2013, at 98.

Analysis Component

6. Assume that the market rate on January 1, 2011, is 12% instead of 10%. Without presenting numbers, describe how this change affects the amounts reported on McFad's financial statements.

Problem 14-9A
Installment notes
C1 P5

Check (2) 10/31/2015 ending balance, $92,759

On November 1, 2011, Leetch Ltd. borrows $400,000 cash from a bank by signing a five-year installment note bearing 8% interest. The note requires equal total payments each year on October 31.

Required

1. Compute the total amount of each installment payment.
2. Complete an amortization table for this installment note similar to the one in Exhibit 14.14.
3. Prepare the journal entries in which Leetch records (*a*) accrued interest as of December 31, 2011 (the end of its annual reporting period), and (*b*) the first annual payment on the note.

Problem 14-10A
Applying the debt-to-equity ratio
A3 

At the end of the current year, the following information is available for both Kumar Company and Asher Company.

	Kumar Company	Asher Company
Total assets	$2,254,500	$1,123,500
Total liabilities	904,500	598,500
Total equity	1,350,000	525,000

Required

1. Compute the debt-to-equity ratios for both companies.
2. Comment on your results and discuss the riskiness of each company's financing structure.

Problem 14-11A[D]
Capital lease accounting
C4

Check (1) $79,854

(3) Year 3 ending balance, $35,664

Montana Company signs a five-year capital lease with Elway Company for office equipment. The annual lease payment is $20,000, and the interest rate is 8%.

Required

1. Compute the present value of Montana's five-year lease payments.
2. Prepare the journal entry to record Montana's capital lease at its inception.
3. Complete a lease payment schedule for the five years of the lease with the following headings. Assume that the beginning balance of the lease liability (present value of lease payments) is $79,854. (*Hint:* To find the amount allocated to interest in year 1, multiply the interest rate by the beginning-of-year lease liability. The amount of the annual lease payment not allocated to interest is allocated to principal. Reduce the lease liability by the amount allocated to principal to update the lease liability at each year-end.)

Period Ending Date	Beginning Balance of Lease Liability	Interest on Lease Liability	Reduction of Lease Liability	Cash Lease Payment	Ending Balance of Lease Liability

4. Use straight-line depreciation and prepare the journal entry to depreciate the leased asset at the end of year 1. Assume zero salvage value and a five-year life for the office equipment.

Round dollar amounts to the nearest whole dollar. Assume no reversing entries are used.

PROBLEM SET B

Problem 14-1B
Computing bond price and recording issuance
P1 P2 P3

Sedona Systems issues bonds dated January 1, 2011, that pay interest semiannually on June 30 and December 31. The bonds have a $45,000 par value and an annual contract rate of 12%, and they mature in five years.

Required

For each of the following three separate situations, (*a*) determine the bonds' issue price on January 1, 2011, and (*b*) prepare the journal entry to record their issuance.

1. The market rate at the date of issuance is 10%.
2. The market rate at the date of issuance is 12%.
3. The market rate at the date of issuance is 14%.

Check (1) Premium, $3,475

(3) Discount, $3,162

Problem 14-2B
Straight-line amortization of bond discount
P1 P2

ParFour issues $1,700,000 of 10%, 10-year bonds dated January 1, 2011, that pay interest semiannually on June 30 and December 31. The bonds are issued at a price of $1,505,001.

Required

1. Prepare the January 1, 2011, journal entry to record the bonds' issuance.
2. For each semiannual period, compute (*a*) the cash payment, (*b*) the straight-line discount amortization, and (*c*) the bond interest expense.
3. Determine the total bond interest expense to be recognized over the bonds' life.
4. Prepare the first two years of an amortization table like Exhibit 14.7 using the straight-line method.
5. Prepare the journal entries to record the first two interest payments.

Check (3) $1,894,999

(4) 6/30/2012 carrying value, $1,534,251

Problem 14-3B
Straight-line amortization of bond premium
P1 P3

Refer to the bond details in Problem 14-2B, *except* assume that the bonds are issued at a price of $2,096,466.

Required

1. Prepare the January 1, 2011, journal entry to record the bonds' issuance.
2. For each semiannual period, compute (*a*) the cash payment, (*b*) the straight-line premium amortization, and (*c*) the bond interest expense.
3. Determine the total bond interest expense to be recognized over the bonds' life.
4. Prepare the first two years of an amortization table like Exhibit 14.7 using the straight-line method.
5. Prepare the journal entries to record the first two interest payments.

Check (3) $1,303,534

(4) 6/30/2012 carrying value, $2,036,997

Problem 14-4B
Straight-line amortization of bond premium
P1 P3

Zooba Company issues 9%, five-year bonds dated January 1, 2011, with a $160,000 par value. The bonds pay interest on June 30 and December 31 and are issued at a price of $166,494. Their annual market rate is 8% on the issue date.

Required

1. Calculate the total bond interest expense over the bonds' life.
2. Prepare a straight-line amortization table like Exhibit 14.11 for the bonds' life.
3. Prepare the journal entries to record the first two interest payments.

Check (2) 6/30/2013 carrying value, $163,249

Problem 14-5B[B]
Effective interest amortization of bond premium; computing bond price P1 P3

Refer to the bond details in Problem 14-4B.

Required

1. Compute the total bond interest expense over the bonds' life.
2. Prepare an effective interest amortization table like the one in Exhibit 14B.2 for the bonds' life.
3. Prepare the journal entries to record the first two interest payments.
4. Use the market rate at issuance to compute the present value of the remaining cash flows for these bonds as of December 31, 2013. Compare your answer with the amount shown on the amortization table as the balance for that date (from part 2) and explain your findings.

Check (2) 6/30/2013 carrying value, $163,568

(4) $162,903

Problem 14-6B
Straight-line amortization of bond discount
P1 P2

Check (2) $128,753
(3) 6/30/2012 carrying value, $101,323

Roney issues $120,000 of 6%, 15-year bonds dated January 1, 2011, that pay interest semiannually on June 30 and December 31. They are issued at $99,247, and their market rate is 8% at the issue date.

Required

1. Prepare the January 1, 2011, journal entry to record the bonds' issuance.
2. Determine the total bond interest expense to be recognized over the life of the bonds.
3. Prepare a straight-line amortization table like the one in Exhibit 14.7 for the bonds' first two years.
4. Prepare the journal entries to record the first two interest payments.

Problem 14-7B[B]
Effective interest amortization of bond discount
P1 P2 

Check (2) $128,753;
(3) 6/30/2012 carrying value, $100,402

Refer to the bond details in Problem 14-6B.

Required

1. Prepare the January 1, 2011, journal entry to record the bonds' issuance.
2. Determine the total bond interest expense to be recognized over the bonds' life.
3. Prepare an effective interest amortization table like the one in Exhibit 14B.1 for the bonds' first two years.
4. Prepare the journal entries to record the first two interest payments.

Problem 14-8B[B]
Effective interest amortization of bond premium; retiring bonds
P1 P3 P4 

Check (3) 6/30/2012 carrying value, $958,406

(5) $6,174 loss

Hutton issues $900,000 of 13%, four-year bonds dated January 1, 2011, that pay interest semiannually on June 30 and December 31. They are issued at $987,217, and their market rate is 10% at the issue date.

Required

1. Prepare the January 1, 2011, journal entry to record the bonds' issuance.
2. Determine the total bond interest expense to be recognized over the bonds' life.
3. Prepare an effective interest amortization table like the one in Exhibit 14B.2 for the bonds' first two years.
4. Prepare the journal entries to record the first two interest payments.
5. Prepare the journal entry to record the bonds' retirement on January 1, 2013, at 106.

Analysis Component

6. Assume that the market rate on January 1, 2011, is 14% instead of 10%. Without presenting numbers, describe how this change affects the amounts reported on Hutton's financial statements.

Problem 14-9B
Installment notes
C1 P5

Check (2) 9/30/2013 ending balance, $109,673

On October 1, 2011, Milan Enterprises borrows $300,000 cash from a bank by signing a three-year installment note bearing 10% interest. The note requires equal total payments each year on September 30.

Required

1. Compute the total amount of each installment payment.
2. Complete an amortization table for this installment note similar to the one in Exhibit 14.14.
3. Prepare the journal entries to record (*a*) accrued interest as of December 31, 2011 (the end of its annual reporting period) and (*b*) the first annual payment on the note.

Problem 14-10B
Applying the debt-to-equity ratio
A3 

At the end of the current year, the following information is available for both West Elm Company and East Park Company.

	West Elm Company	East Park Company
Total assets	$396,396	$1,650,000
Total liabilities	178,596	1,237,500
Total equity	217,800	412,500

Required

1. Compute the debt-to-equity ratios for both companies.
2. Comment on your results and discuss what they imply about the relative riskiness of these companies.

Problem 14-11B[D]
Capital lease accounting
C4

Preston Company signs a five-year capital lease with Starbuck Company for office equipment. The annual lease payment is $10,000, and the interest rate is 10%.

Required

1. Compute the present value of Preston's lease payments.
2. Prepare the journal entry to record Preston's capital lease at its inception.
3. Complete a lease payment schedule for the five years of the lease with the following headings. Assume that the beginning balance of the lease liability (present value of lease payments) is $37,908. (*Hint:* To find the amount allocated to interest in year 1, multiply the interest rate by the beginning-of-year lease liability. The amount of the annual lease payment not allocated to interest is allocated to principal. Reduce the lease liability by the amount allocated to principal to update the lease liability at each year-end.)

Period Ending Date	Beginning Balance of Lease Liability	Interest on Lease Liability	Reduction of Lease Liability	Cash Lease Payment	Ending Balance of Lease Liability

4. Use straight-line depreciation and prepare the journal entry to depreciate the leased asset at the end of year 1. Assume zero salvage value and a five-year life for the office equipment.

Check (1) $37,908

(3) Year 3 ending balance, $17,356

SERIAL PROBLEM
Business Solutions
A1 A3

(This serial problem began in Chapter 1 and continues through most of the book. If previous chapter segments were not completed, the serial problem can begin at this point. It is helpful, but not necessary, to use the Working Papers that accompany the book.)

SP 14 Santana Rey has consulted with her local banker and is considering financing an expansion of her business by obtaining a long-term bank loan. Selected account balances at March 31, 2012, for Business Solutions follow.

Total assets	$120,268	Total liabilities	$875	Total equity	$119,393

Required

1. The bank has offered a long-term secured note to Business Solutions. The bank's loan procedures require that a client's debt-to-equity ratio not exceed 0.8. As of March 31, 2012, what is the maximum amount that Business Solutions could borrow from this bank (rounded to nearest dollar)?
2. If Business Solutions borrows the maximum amount allowed from the bank, what percentage of assets would be financed (*a*) by debt and (*b*) by equity?
3. What are some factors Santana Rey should consider before borrowing the funds?

Check (1) $94,639

Beyond the Numbers

REPORTING IN ACTION
A1 A2
RIM

BTN 14-1 Refer to Research In Motion's financial statements in Appendix A to answer the following.

1. Identify the items, if any, that make up RIM's long-term debt as reported on its balance sheet at February 27, 2010.
2. Assume that RIM has $402,000 thousand in convertible debentures that carry a 2.25% contract rate of interest. How much annual cash interest must be paid on those convertible debentures?
3. How much cash did it generate from issuance of debt for the year-ended February 27, 2010? How much cash did it use for repayments of debt for that same year?

Fast Forward

4. Access Research In Motion's financial statements for the years ending after February 27, 2010, from its Website (RIM.com) or the SEC's EDGAR database (www.SEC.gov). Has it issued additional long-term debt since the year-end February 27, 2010? If yes, identify the amount(s).

COMPARATIVE ANALYSIS

A3 

RIM

Apple

BTN 14-2 Key figures for Research In Motion and Apple follow.

($ millions)	Research In Motion Current Year	Research In Motion Prior Year	Apple Current Year	Apple Prior Year
Total assets	$10,204	$8,101	$47,501	$36,171
Total liabilities	2,602	2,227	15,861	13,874
Total equity	7,603	5,874	31,640	22,297

Required

1. Compute the debt-to-equity ratios for Research In Motion and Apple for both the current year and the prior year.
2. Use the ratios you computed in part 1 to determine which company's financing structure is least risky. Assume an industry average of 0.64 for debt-to-equity.

ETHICS CHALLENGE

C4 A1 

BTN 14-3 Holly County needs a new county government building that would cost $24 million. The politicians feel that voters will not approve a municipal bond issue to fund the building since it would increase taxes. They opt to have a state bank issue $24 million of tax-exempt securities to pay for the building construction. The county then will make yearly lease payments (of principal and interest) to repay the obligation. Unlike conventional municipal bonds, the lease payments are not binding obligations on the county and, therefore, require no voter approval.

Required

1. Do you think the actions of the politicians and the bankers in this situation are ethical?
2. How do the tax-exempt securities used to pay for the building compare in risk to a conventional municipal bond issued by Holly County?

COMMUNICATING IN PRACTICE

P3

BTN 14-4 Your business associate mentions that she is considering investing in corporate bonds currently selling at a premium. She says that since the bonds are selling at a premium, they are highly valued and her investment will yield more than the going rate of return for the risk involved. Reply with a memorandum to confirm or correct your associate's interpretation of premium bonds.

TAKING IT TO THE NET

A2

BTN 14-5 Access the March 25, 2010, filing of the 10-K report of Home Depot for the year ended January 31, 2010, from www.SEC.gov (Ticker: HD). Refer to Home Depot's balance sheet, including its note 4 (on debt).

Required

1. Identify Home Depot's long-term liabilities and the amounts for those liabilities from Home Depot's balance sheet at January 31, 2010.
2. Review Home Depot's note 5. The note reports that as of January 31, 2010, it had $2.96 billion of "5.875% Senior Notes; due December 16, 2036; interest payable semiannually on June 16 and December 16." These notes have a face value of $3.0 billion and were originally issued at $2.958 billion.
   a. Why would Home Depot issue $3.0 billion of its notes for only $2.958 billion?
   b. How much cash interest must Home Depot pay each June 16 and December 16 on these notes?

TEAMWORK IN ACTION

P2 P3 

BTN 14-6[B] Break into teams and complete the following requirements related to effective interest amortization for a premium bond.

1. Each team member is to independently prepare a blank table with proper headings for amortization of a bond premium. When all have finished, compare tables and ensure that all are in agreement.

Parts 2 and 3 require use of these facts: On January 1, 2010, Caleb issues $100,000, 9%, five-year bonds at 104.1. The market rate at issuance is 8%. Caleb pays interest semiannually on June 30 and December 31.

2. In rotation, *each* team member must explain how to complete *one* line of the bond amortization table, including all computations for his or her line. (Round amounts to the nearest dollar.) All members are to fill in their tables during this process. You need not finish the table; stop after all members have explained a line.

3. In rotation, *each* team member is to identify a separate column of the table and indicate what the final number in that column will be and explain the reasoning.
4. Reach a team consensus as to what the total bond interest expense on this bond issue will be if the bond is not retired before maturity.
5. As a team, prepare a list of similarities and differences between the amortization table just prepared and the amortization table if the bond had been issued at a discount.

Hint: Rotate teams to report on parts 4 and 5. Consider requiring entries for issuance and interest payments.

ENTREPRENEURIAL DECISION

A1  

BTN 14-7 Warren Brown is the founder of Cake Love. Assume that his company currently has $250,000 in equity, and he is considering a $100,000 expansion to meet increased demand. The $100,000 expansion would yield $16,000 in additional annual income before interest expense. Assume that the business currently earns $40,000 annual income before interest expense of $10,000, yielding a return on equity of 12% ($30,000/$250,000). To fund the expansion, he is considering the issuance of a 10-year, $100,000 note with annual interest payments (the principal due at the end of 10 years).

Required

1. Using return on equity as the decision criterion, show computations to support or reject the expansion if interest on the $100,000 note is (*a*) 10%, (*b*) 15%, (*c*) 16%, (*d*) 17%, and (*e*) 20%.
2. What general rule do the results in part 1 illustrate?

HITTING THE ROAD

A1

BTN 14-8 Visit your city or county library. Ask the librarian to help you locate the recent financial records of your city or county government. Examine those records.

Required

1. Determine the amount of long-term bonds and notes currently outstanding.
2. Read the supporting information to your municipality's financial statements and record
   a. The market interest rate(s) when the bonds and/or notes were issued.
   b. The date(s) when the bonds and/or notes will mature.
   c. Any rating(s) on the bonds and/or notes received from Moody's, Standard & Poor's, or another rating agency.

GLOBAL DECISION

A3  

NOKIA
RIM
Apple

BTN 14-9 Nokia (www.Nokia.com), Research In Motion, and Apple are competitors in the global marketplace. Selected results from these companies follow.

	Nokia (EURm)		Research In Motion ($ millions)		Apple ($ millions)	
Key Figures	Current Year	Prior Year	Current Year	Prior Year	Current Year	Prior Year
Total assets	€35,738	€39,582	$10,204	$8,101	$47,501	$36,171
Total liabilities	20,989	23,072	2,602	2,227	15,861	13,874
Total equity	14,749	16,510	7,603	5,874	31,640	22,297
Debt-to-equity ratio	?	?	0.34	0.38	0.50	0.62

Required

1. Compute Nokia's debt-to-equity ratios for the current year and the prior year.
2. Use the data provided and the ratios computed in part 1 to determine which company's financing structure is least risky.

ANSWERS TO MULTIPLE CHOICE QUIZ

1. b
2. a
3. c; $500,000 × 0.08 × ½ year = $20,000
4. a; Cash interest paid = $100,000 × 5% × ½ year = $2,500
   Discount amortization = ($100,000 − $95,735)/10 periods = $426.50
   Interest expense = $2,500.00 + $426.50 = $2,926.50
5. e; ($373,745 − $350,000)/16 periods = $1,484

16

Reporting the Statement of Cash Flows

A Look Back

Chapter 15 focused on how to identify, account for, and report investments in securities. We also accounted for transactions listed in a foreign currency.

A Look at This Chapter

This chapter focuses on reporting and analyzing cash inflows and cash outflows. We emphasize how to prepare and interpret the statement of cash flows.

A Look Ahead

Chapter 17 focuses on tools to help us analyze financial statements. We also describe comparative analysis and the application of ratios for financial analysis.

Learning Objectives

CAP

CONCEPTUAL

C1 Distinguish between operating, investing, and financing activities, and describe how noncash investing and financing activities are disclosed. (p. 633)

ANALYTICAL

A1 Analyze the statement of cash flows and apply the cash flow on total assets ratio. (p. 650)

LP16

PROCEDURAL

P1 Prepare a statement of cash flows. (p. 636)

P2 Compute cash flows from operating activities using the indirect method. (p. 639)

P3 Determine cash flows from both investing and financing activities. (p. 645)

P4 *Appendix 16A*—Illustrate use of a spreadsheet to prepare a statement of cash flows. (p. 654)

P5 *Appendix 16B*—Compute cash flows from operating activities using the direct method. (p. 657)

Decision Insight

Shape Up Your Images

"We feel like we have a great competitive advantage"
—BRAD JEFFERSON

NEW YORK—"I don't know about you, but I get shown so many boring slideshows of my friends' trips," admits Jason Hsiao. "It's like 20 minutes, and you're like, 'Kill me now.'" However, unlike the rest of us, Jason decided to do something about it. He, along with childhood buddies Brad Jefferson, Stevie Clifton, and Tom Clifton, launched Animoto **(Animoto.com).** Its Website describes their service as "a web application that automatically . . . analyzes and combines user-selected images, video clips, and music."

"We want to help users create professional-quality content," explains Jason. "So it doesn't matter what you give us, we'll take that and put it in our magic black box, and in a couple minutes, we'll deliver something that . . . you never could have dreamed of doing on your own." The owners point out that they can create a 30-second video for free. This has cash flow implications. "We decided that we would make a *freemium* model, which allows people to get a taste of the Animoto service for free," says Brad. However, longer videos and videos with more user-options require cash payments, which generate positive cash inflows.

User traffic at Animoto has grown to over 1 million per month. That type of growth has obvious cash implications for technology support, accounting, and other operating and investing cash outflows. The owners emphasize the importance of monitoring and tracking cash inflows and cash outflows. Jason admits, "There's no possible way we could handle [growth] . . . without quickly digging ourselves into a multimillion dollar hole!"

Accordingly, the young owners learned to monitor and control cash flows for each of their operating, investing, and financing activities. Their focus on controlling cash flows led them to apply *cloud computing,* which is a pay-as-you-go model. "[We] could not have existed . . . without cloud computing," admits Jason. A review of Animoto's statement of cash flows, and its individual cash inflows and outflows, led them to this cash flow model. Explains Brad, "We use Amazon . . . for all IT infrastructure . . . PayPal and Google . . . for billing/payment . . . SaaS for email and sales." This model highlights those activities that generate the most cash and those that are cash drains. Adds Jason, "The only real asset we have in our office [is] . . . a fancy espresso machine!"

Yet cash management has not curtailed the team's fun-loving approach. Their Website describes themselves as "a bunch of techies . . . who decided to lock themselves in a room together and nerd out!" Adds Brad, "We're going through the process of figuring out where we want the future to take us."

[Sources: *Animoto Website,* January 2011; *Entrepreneur,* January 2009; *Fast Company,* September 2008; *Bellevue Reporter,* May 2008]

Chapter Preview

A company cannot achieve or maintain profits without carefully managing cash. Managers and other users of information pay attention to a company's cash position and the events and transactions affecting cash. This chapter explains how we prepare, analyze, and interpret a statement of cash flows. It also discusses the importance of cash flow information for predicting future performance and making managerial decisions. More generally, effectively using the statement of cash flows is crucial for managing and analyzing the operating, investing, and financing activities of businesses.

Reporting the Statement of Cash Flows

Basics of Cash Flow Reporting
- Purpose
- Importance
- Measurement
- Classification
- Noncash activities
- Format and preparation

Cash Flows from Operating
- Indirect and direct methods of reporting
- Application of indirect method of reporting
- Summary of indirect method adjustments

Cash Flows from Investing
- Three-stage process of analysis
- Analysis of noncurrent assets
- Analysis of other assets

Cash Flows from Financing
- Three-stage process of analysis
- Analysis of noncurrent liabilities
- Analysis of equity

BASICS OF CASH FLOW REPORTING

This section describes the basics of cash flow reporting, including its purpose, measurement, classification, format, and preparation.

Purpose of the Statement of Cash Flows

The purpose of the **statement of cash flows** is to report cash receipts (inflows) and cash payments (outflows) during a period. This includes separately identifying the cash flows related to operating, investing, and financing activities. The statement of cash flows does more than simply report changes in cash. It is the detailed disclosure of individual cash flows that makes this statement useful to users. Information in this statement helps users answer questions such as these:

- How does a company obtain its cash?
- Where does a company spend its cash?
- What explains the change in the cash balance?

Point: Internal users rely on the statement of cash flows to make investing and financing decisions. External users rely on this statement to assess the amount and timing of a company's cash flows.

The statement of cash flows addresses important questions such as these by summarizing, classifying, and reporting a company's cash inflows and cash outflows for each period.

Importance of Cash Flows

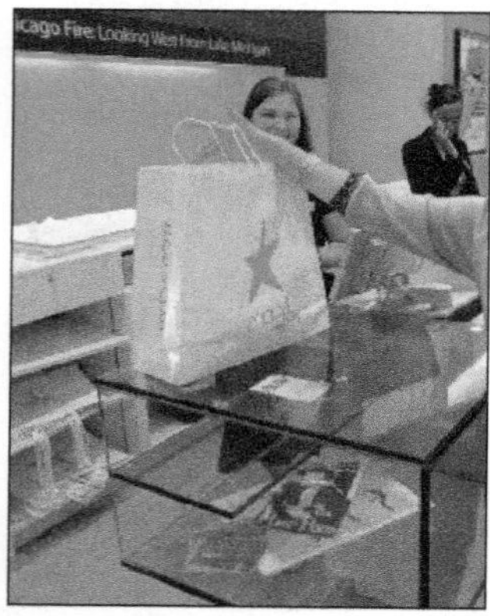

Information about cash flows can influence decision makers in important ways. For instance, we look more favorably at a company that is financing its expenditures with cash from operations than one that does it by selling its assets. Information about cash flows helps users decide whether a company has enough cash to pay its existing debts as they mature. It is also relied upon to evaluate a company's ability to meet unexpected obligations and pursue unexpected opportunities. External information users especially want to assess a company's ability to take advantage of new business opportunities. Internal users such as managers use cash flow information to plan day-to-day operating activities and make long-term investment decisions.

Macy's striking turnaround is an example of how analysis and management of cash flows can lead to improved financial stability. Several years ago Macy's obtained temporary protection from bankruptcy, at which time it desperately needed to improve its cash flows. It did so by engaging in aggressive cost-cutting measures. As a result, Macy's annual cash flow rose to \$210 million, up from a negative cash flow of \$38.9 million in the prior year. Macy's eventually met its financial obligations and then successfully merged with Federated Department Stores.

The case of W. T. Grant Co. is a classic example of the importance of cash flow information in predicting a company's future performance and financial strength. Grant reported net income of more than $40 million per year for three consecutive years. At that same time, it was experiencing an alarming decrease in cash provided by operations. For instance, net cash outflow was more than $90 million by the end of that three-year period. Grant soon went bankrupt. Users who relied solely on Grant's income numbers were unpleasantly surprised. This reminds us that cash flows as well as income statement and balance sheet information are crucial in making business decisions.

Decision Insight 

Cash Savvy "A lender must have a complete understanding of a borrower's cash flows to assess both the borrowing needs and repayment sources. This requires information about the major types of cash inflows and outflows. I have seen many companies, whose financial statements indicate good profitability, experience severe financial problems because the owners or managers lacked a good understanding of cash flows."—Mary E. Garza, Bank of America ■

Measurement of Cash Flows

Cash flows are defined to include both *cash* and *cash equivalents*. The statement of cash flows explains the difference between the beginning and ending balances of cash and cash equivalents. We continue to use the phrases *cash flows* and the *statement of cash flows,* but we must remember that both phrases refer to cash and cash equivalents. Recall that a cash equivalent must satisfy two criteria: (1) be readily convertible to a known amount of cash and (2) be sufficiently close to its maturity so its market value is unaffected by interest rate changes. In most cases, a debt security must be within three months of its maturity to satisfy these criteria. Companies must disclose and follow a clear policy for determining cash and cash equivalents and apply it consistently from period to period. American Express, for example, defines its cash equivalents as "time deposits and other highly liquid investments with original maturities of 90 days or less."

Classification of Cash Flows

C1 Distinguish between operating, investing, and financing activities, and describe how noncash investing and financing activities are disclosed.

Since cash and cash equivalents are combined, the statement of cash flows does not report transactions between cash and cash equivalents such as cash paid to purchase cash equivalents and cash received from selling cash equivalents. However, all other cash receipts and cash payments are classified and reported on the statement as operating, investing, or financing activities. Individual cash receipts and payments for each of these three categories are labeled to identify their originating transactions or events. A net cash inflow (source) occurs when the receipts in a category exceed the payments. A net cash outflow (use) occurs when the payments in a category exceed the receipts.

Operating Activities **Operating activities** include those transactions and events that determine net income. Examples are the production and purchase of merchandise, the sale of goods and services to customers, and the expenditures to administer the business. Not all items in income, such as unusual gains and losses, are operating activities (we discuss these exceptions later in the chapter). Exhibit 16.1 lists the more common cash inflows and outflows from operating activities. (Although cash receipts and cash payments from buying and selling trading

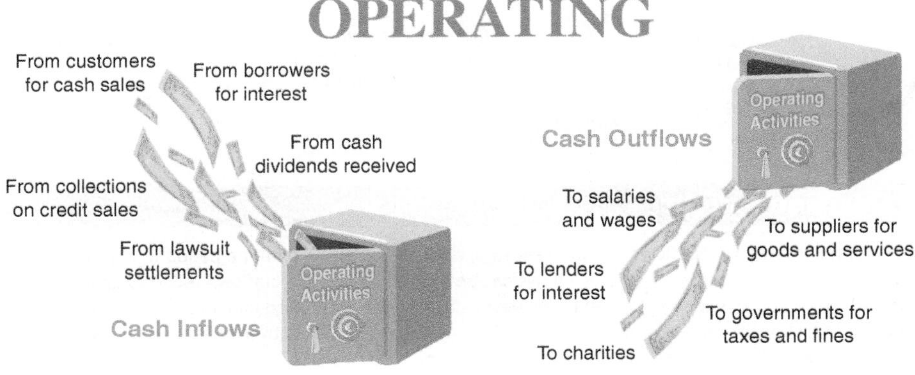

EXHIBIT 16.1

Cash Flows from Operating Activities

securities are often reported under operating activities, new standards require that these receipts and payments be classified based on the nature and purpose of those securities.)

Investing Activities **Investing activities** generally include those transactions and events that affect long-term assets—namely, the purchase and sale of long-term assets. They also include (1) the purchase and sale of short-term investments in the securities of other entities, other than cash equivalents and trading securities and (2) lending and collecting money for notes receivable. Exhibit 16.2 lists examples of cash flows from investing activities. Proceeds from collecting the principal amounts of notes deserve special mention. If the note results from sales to customers, its cash receipts are classed as operating activities whether short-term or long-term. If the note results from a loan to another party apart from sales, however, the cash receipts from collecting the note principal are classed as an investing activity. The FASB requires that the collection of interest on loans be reported as an operating activity.

Point: The FASB requires that *cash dividends received* and *cash interest received* be reported as operating activities.

EXHIBIT 16.2

Cash Flows from Investing Activities

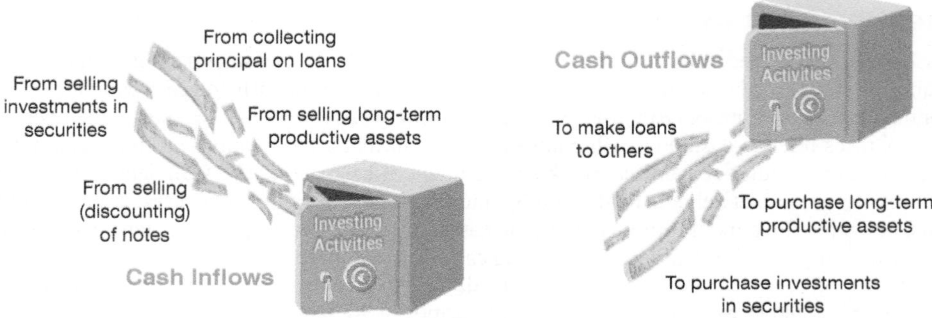

Financing Activities **Financing activities** include those transactions and events that affect long-term liabilities and equity. Examples are (1) obtaining cash from issuing debt and repaying the amounts borrowed and (2) receiving cash from or distributing cash to owners. These activities involve transactions with a company's owners and creditors. They also often involve borrowing and repaying principal amounts relating to both short- and long-term debt. GAAP requires that payments of interest expense be classified as operating activities. Also, cash payments to settle credit purchases of merchandise, whether on account or by note, are operating activities. Exhibit 16.3 lists examples of cash flows from financing activities.

EXHIBIT 16.3

Cash Flows from Financing Activities

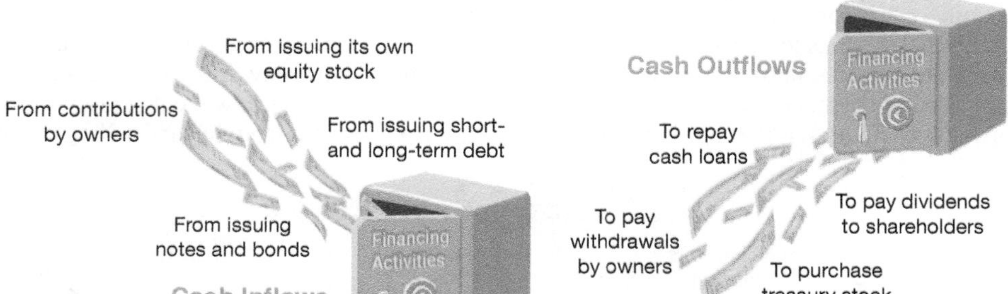

Point: Interest payments on a loan are classified as operating activities, but payments of loan principal are financing activities.

Decision Insight

Cash Monitoring Cash flows can be delayed or accelerated at the end of a period to improve or reduce current period cash flows. Also, cash flows can be misclassified. Cash outflows reported under operations are interpreted as expense payments. However, cash outflows reported under investing activities are interpreted as a positive sign of growth potential. Thus, managers face incentives to misclassify cash flows. For these reasons, cash flow reporting warrants our scrutiny. ■

Noncash Investing and Financing

When important investing and financing activities do not affect cash receipts or payments, they are still disclosed at the bottom of the statement of cash flows or in a note to the statement because of their importance and the *full-disclosure principle*. One example of such a transaction is the purchase of long-term assets using a long-term note payable (loan). This transaction involves both investing and financing activities but does not affect any cash inflow or outflow and is not reported in any of the three sections of the statement of cash flows. This disclosure rule also extends to transactions with partial cash receipts or payments.

To illustrate, assume that Goorin purchases land for $12,000 by paying $5,000 cash and trading in used equipment worth $7,000. The investing section of the statement of cash flows reports only the $5,000 cash outflow for the land purchase. The $12,000 investing transaction is only partially described in the body of the statement of cash flows, yet this information is potentially important to users because it changes the makeup of assets. Goorin could either describe the transaction in a footnote or include information at the bottom of its statement that lists the $12,000 land purchase along with the cash financing of $5,000 and a $7,000 trade-in of equipment. As another example, Borg Co. acquired $900,000 of assets in exchange for $200,000 cash and a $700,000 long-term note, which should be reported as follows:

Point: A stock dividend transaction involving a transfer from retained earnings to common stock or a credit to contributed capital is *not* considered a noncash investing and financing activity because the company receives no consideration for shares issued.

Fair value of assets acquired	$900,000
Less cash paid	200,000
Liabilities incurred or assumed	$700,000

Exhibit 16.4 lists transactions commonly disclosed as noncash investing and financing activities.

EXHIBIT 16.4

Examples of Noncash Investing and Financing Activities

- Retirement of debt by issuing equity stock.
- Conversion of preferred stock to common stock.
- Lease of assets in a capital lease transaction.
- Purchase of long-term assets by issuing a note or bond.
- Exchange of noncash assets for other noncash assets.
- Purchase of noncash assets by issuing equity or debt.

Format of the Statement of Cash Flows

Accounting standards require companies to include a statement of cash flows in a complete set of financial statements. This statement must report information about a company's cash receipts and cash payments during the period. Exhibit 16.5 shows the usual format. A company must report cash flows from three activities: operating, investing, and financing. The statement

EXHIBIT 16.5

Format of the Statement of Cash Flows

COMPANY NAME
Statement of Cash Flows
For period Ended date

Cash flows from operating activities	
[List of individual inflows and outflows]	
Net cash provided (used) by operating activities	$ #
Cash flows from investing activities	
[List of individual inflows and outflows]	
Net cash provided (used) by investing activities	#
Cash flows from financing activities	
[List of individual inflows and outflows]	
Net cash provided (used) by financing activities	#
Net increase (decrease) in cash	$ #
Cash (and equivalents) balance at prior period-end	#
Cash (and equivalents) balance at current period-end	$ #

Separate schedule or note disclosure of any "noncash investing and financing transactions" is required.

explains how transactions and events impact the prior period-end cash (and cash equivalents) balance to produce its current period-end balance.

Decision Maker Answer — p. 662

Entrepreneur You are considering purchasing a start-up business that recently reported a $110,000 annual net loss and a $225,000 annual net cash inflow. How are these results possible? ■

Quick Check Answers — p. 662

1. Does a statement of cash flows report the cash payments to purchase cash equivalents? Does it report the cash receipts from selling cash equivalents?
2. Identify the three categories of cash flows reported separately on the statement of cash flows.
3. Identify the cash activity category for each transaction: (*a*) purchase equipment for cash, (*b*) cash payment of wages, (*c*) sale of common stock for cash, (*d*) receipt of cash dividends from stock investment, (*e*) cash collection from customers, (*f*) notes issued for cash.

Preparing the Statement of Cash Flows

P1 Prepare a statement of cash flows.

Preparing a statement of cash flows involves five steps: [1] compute the net increase or decrease in cash; [2] compute and report the net cash provided or used by operating activities (using either the direct or indirect method; both are explained); [3] compute and report the net cash provided or used by investing activities; [4] compute and report the net cash provided or used by financing activities; and [5] compute the net cash flow by combining net cash provided or used by operating, investing, and financing activities and then *prove it* by adding it to the beginning cash balance to show that it equals the ending cash balance.

Step [1] Compute net increase or decrease in cash

Step [2] Compute net cash from operating activities

Step [3] Compute net cash from investing activities

Step [4] Compute net cash from financing activities

Step [5] Prove and report beginning and ending cash balances

Point: View the change in cash as a *target* number that we will fully explain and prove in the statement of cash flows.

Computing the net increase or net decrease in cash is a simple but crucial computation. It equals the current period's cash balance minus the prior period's cash balance. This is the *bottom-line* figure for the statement of cash flows and is a check on accuracy. The information we need to prepare a statement of cash flows comes from various sources including comparative balance sheets at the beginning and end of the period, and an income statement for the period. There are two alternative approaches to preparing the statement: (1) analyzing the Cash account and (2) analyzing noncash accounts.

Analyzing the Cash Account A company's cash receipts and cash payments are recorded in the Cash account in its general ledger. The Cash account is therefore a natural place to look for information about cash flows from operating, investing, and financing activities. To illustrate, review the summarized Cash T-account of Genesis, Inc., in Exhibit 16.6. Individual cash transactions are summarized in this Cash account according to the major types of cash receipts and cash payments. For instance, only the total of cash receipts from all customers is listed. Individual cash transactions underlying these totals can number in the thousands. Accounting software is available to provide summarized cash accounts.

Preparing a statement of cash flows from Exhibit 16.6 requires determining whether an individual cash inflow or outflow is an operating, investing, or financing activity, and then listing each by

EXHIBIT 16.6

Summarized Cash Account

Accounting System:

File Edit Maintain Tasks Analysis Options Reports Window Help

Cash			
Balance, Dec. 31, 2010	12,000		
Receipts from customers	570,000	Payments for merchandise	319,000
Receipts from asset sales	12,000	Payments for wages and operating expenses	218,000
Receipts from stock issuance	15,000	Payments for interest	8,000
		Payments for taxes	5,000
		Payments for assets	10,000
		Payments for notes retirement	18,000
		Payments for dividends	14,000
Balance, Dec. 31, 2011	17,000		

Sales Purchases General Ledger Payroll Inventory Company Analysis

1 Cash change

activity. This yields the statement shown in Exhibit 16.7. However, preparing the statement of cash flows from an analysis of the summarized Cash account has two limitations. First, most companies have many individual cash receipts and payments, making it difficult to review them all. Accounting software minimizes this burden, but it is still a task requiring professional judgment for many transactions. Second, the Cash account does not usually carry an adequate description of each cash transaction, making assignment of all cash transactions according to activity difficult.

EXHIBIT 16.7

Statement of Cash Flows—Direct Method

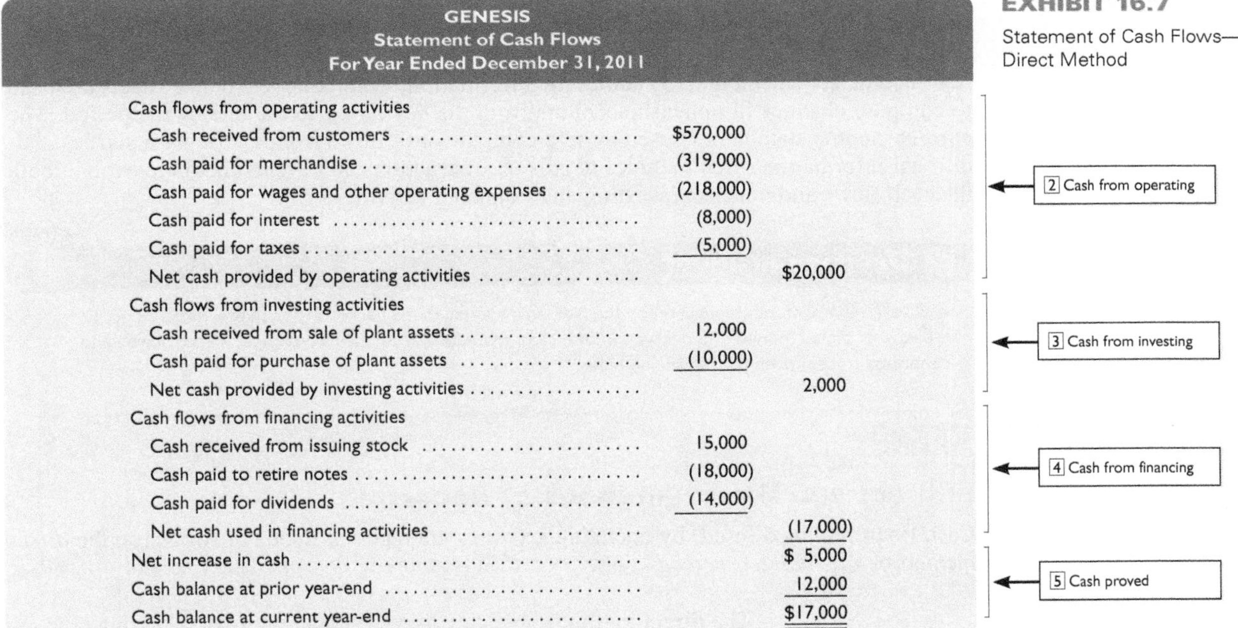

GENESIS
Statement of Cash Flows
For Year Ended December 31, 2011

Cash flows from operating activities		
Cash received from customers	$570,000	
Cash paid for merchandise	(319,000)	
Cash paid for wages and other operating expenses	(218,000)	
Cash paid for interest	(8,000)	
Cash paid for taxes	(5,000)	
Net cash provided by operating activities		$20,000
Cash flows from investing activities		
Cash received from sale of plant assets	12,000	
Cash paid for purchase of plant assets	(10,000)	
Net cash provided by investing activities		2,000
Cash flows from financing activities		
Cash received from issuing stock	15,000	
Cash paid to retire notes	(18,000)	
Cash paid for dividends	(14,000)	
Net cash used in financing activities		(17,000)
Net increase in cash		$ 5,000
Cash balance at prior year-end		12,000
Cash balance at current year-end		$17,000

2 Cash from operating

3 Cash from investing

4 Cash from financing

5 Cash proved

Analyzing Noncash Accounts A second approach to preparing the statement of cash flows is analyzing noncash accounts. This approach uses the fact that when a company records cash inflows and outflows with debits and credits to the Cash account (see Exhibit 16.6), it also records credits and debits in noncash accounts (reflecting double-entry accounting). Many of these noncash accounts are balance sheet accounts—for instance, from the sale of land for cash. Others are revenue and expense accounts that are closed to equity. For instance, the sale of services for cash yields a credit to Services Revenue that is closed to Retained Earnings for a corporation. In sum, *all cash transactions eventually affect noncash balance sheet accounts*. Thus, we can determine cash inflows and outflows by analyzing changes in noncash balance sheet accounts.

Exhibit 16.8 uses the accounting equation to show the relation between the Cash account and the noncash balance sheet accounts. This exhibit starts with the accounting equation at the

EXHIBIT 16.8

Relation between Cash and Noncash Accounts

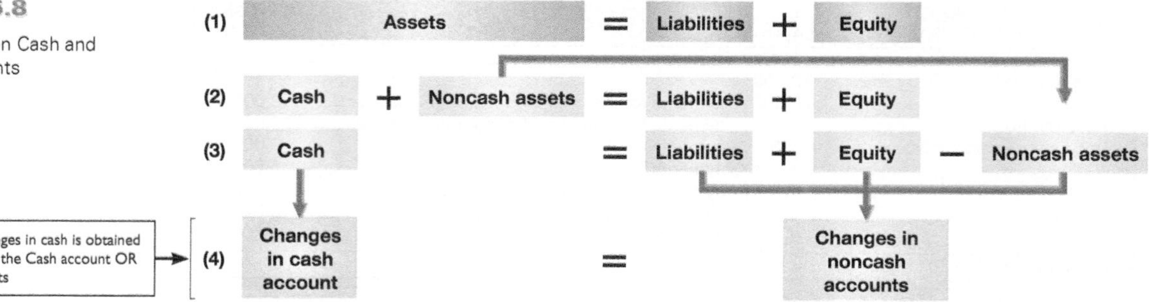

top. It is then expanded in line (2) to separate cash from noncash asset accounts. Line (3) moves noncash asset accounts to the right-hand side of the equality where they are subtracted. This shows that cash equals the sum of the liability and equity accounts *minus* the noncash asset accounts. Line (4) points out that *changes* on one side of the accounting equation equal *changes* on the other side. It shows that we can explain changes in cash by analyzing changes in the noncash accounts consisting of liability accounts, equity accounts, and noncash asset accounts. By analyzing noncash balance sheet accounts and any related income statement accounts, we can prepare a statement of cash flows.

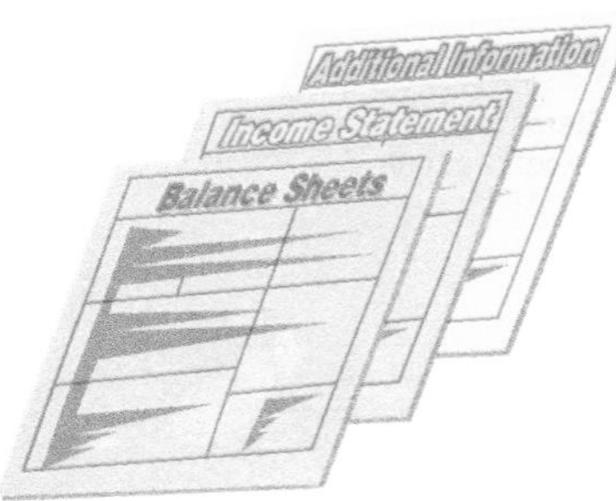

Information to Prepare the Statement Information to prepare the statement of cash flows usually comes from three sources: (1) comparative balance sheets, (2) the current income statement, and (3) additional information. Comparative balance sheets are used to compute changes in noncash accounts from the beginning to the end of the period. The current income statement is used to help compute cash flows from operating activities. Additional information often includes details on transactions and events that help explain both the cash flows and noncash investing and financing activities.

Decision Insight

e-Cash Every credit transaction on the Net leaves a trail that a hacker or a marketer can pick up. Enter e-cash—or digital money. The encryption of e-cash protects your money from snoops and thieves and cannot be traced, even by the issuing bank.

CASH FLOWS FROM OPERATING

Indirect and Direct Methods of Reporting

Cash flows provided (used) by operating activities are reported in one of two ways: the *direct method* or the *indirect method.* **These two different methods apply only to the operating activities section.**

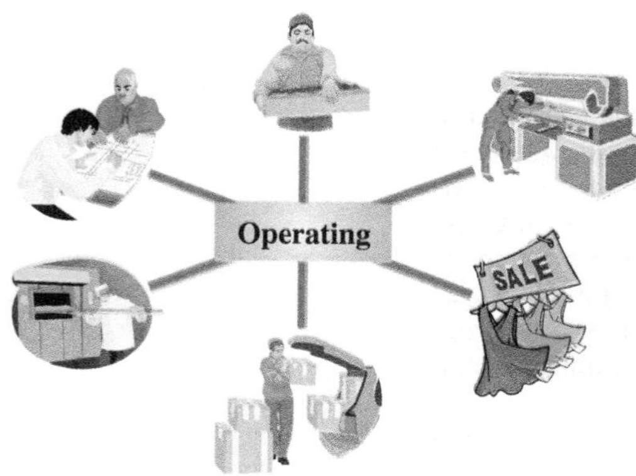

The **direct method** separately lists each major item of operating cash receipts (such as cash received from customers) and each major item of operating cash payments (such as cash paid for merchandise). The cash payments are subtracted from cash receipts to determine the net cash provided (used) by operating activities. The operating activities section of Exhibit 16.7 reflects the direct method of reporting operating cash flows.

The **indirect method** reports net income and then adjusts it for items necessary to obtain net cash provided or used by operating activities. It does *not* report individual items of cash inflows and cash outflows from operating activities. Instead, the indirect method reports the necessary adjustments to reconcile net income to net cash provided or used by operating activities. The operating activities section for Genesis prepared under the indirect method is shown in Exhibit 16.9. **The net cash amount provided by operating activities is *identical* under both the direct and indirect methods.**

EXHIBIT 16.9

Operating Activities Section—Indirect Method

Cash flows from operating activities		
Net income	$ 38,000	
Adjustments to reconcile net income to net cash provided by operating activities		
Increase in accounts receivable	(20,000)	
Increase in merchandise inventory	(14,000)	
Increase in prepaid expenses	(2,000)	
Decrease in accounts payable	(5,000)	
Decrease in interest payable	(1,000)	
Increase in income taxes payable	10,000	
Depreciation expense	24,000	
Loss on sale of plant assets	6,000	
Gain on retirement of notes	(16,000)	
Net cash provided by operating activities		**$20,000**

This equality always exists. The difference in these methods is with the computation and presentation of this amount. The FASB recommends the direct method, but because it is not required and the indirect method is arguably easier to compute, nearly all companies report operating cash flows using the indirect method.

Point: To better understand the direct and indirect methods of reporting operating cash flows, identify similarities and differences between Exhibits 16.7 and 16.11.

To illustrate, we prepare the operating activities section of the statement of cash flows for Genesis. Exhibit 16.10 shows the December 31, 2010 and 2011, balance sheets of Genesis along with its 2011 income statement. We use this information to prepare a statement of cash flows that explains the $5,000 increase in cash for 2011 as reflected in its balance sheets. This $5,000 is computed as Cash of $17,000 at the end of 2011 minus Cash of $12,000 at the end of 2010. Genesis discloses additional information on its 2011 transactions:

a. The accounts payable balances result from merchandise inventory purchases.
b. Purchased $70,000 in plant assets by paying $10,000 cash and issuing $60,000 of notes payable.
c. Sold plant assets with an original cost of $30,000 and accumulated depreciation of $12,000 for $12,000 cash, yielding a $6,000 loss.
d. Received $15,000 cash from issuing 3,000 shares of common stock.
e. Paid $18,000 cash to retire notes with a $34,000 book value, yielding a $16,000 gain.
f. Declared and paid cash dividends of $14,000.

The next section describes the indirect method. Appendix 16B describes the direct method. An instructor can choose to cover either one or both methods. Neither section depends on the other.

Application of the Indirect Method of Reporting

P2 Compute cash flows from operating activities using the indirect method.

Net income is computed using accrual accounting, which recognizes revenues when earned and expenses when incurred. Revenues and expenses do not necessarily reflect the receipt and payment of cash. The indirect method of computing and reporting net cash flows from operating activities involves adjusting the net income figure to obtain the net cash provided or used by operating activities. This includes subtracting noncash increases (credits) from net income and adding noncash charges (debits) back to net income.

To illustrate, the indirect method begins with Genesis's net income of $38,000 and adjusts it to obtain net cash provided by operating activities of $20,000. Exhibit 16.11 shows the results of the indirect method of reporting operating cash flows, which adjusts net income for three types of adjustments. There are adjustments ① to reflect changes in noncash current assets and current liabilities related to operating activities, ② to income statement items involving operating activities that do not affect cash inflows or outflows, and ③ to eliminate gains and losses resulting from investing and financing activities (not part of operating activities). This section describes each of these adjustments.

Point: *Noncash credits* refer to revenue amounts reported on the income statement that are *not collected in cash* this period. *Noncash charges* refer to expense amounts reported on the income statement that are *not paid* this period.

EXHIBIT 16.10

Financial Statements

GENESIS Income Statement For Year Ended December 31, 2011		
Sales		$590,000
Cost of goods sold	$300,000	
Wages and other operating expenses	216,000	
Interest expense	7,000	
Depreciation expense	24,000	(547,000)
		43,000
Other gains (losses)		
Gain on retirement of notes	16,000	
Loss on sale of plant assets	(6,000)	10,000
Income before taxes		53,000
Income taxes expense		(15,000)
Net income		$ 38,000

GENESIS Balance Sheets December 31, 2011 and 2010	2011	2010
Assets		
Current assets		
Cash	$ 17,000	$ 12,000
Accounts receivable	60,000	40,000
Merchandise inventory	84,000	70,000
Prepaid expenses	6,000	4,000
Total current assets	167,000	126,000
Long-term assets		
Plant assets	250,000	210,000
Accumulated depreciation	(60,000)	(48,000)
Total assets	$357,000	$288,000
Liabilities		
Current liabilities		
Accounts payable	$ 35,000	$ 40,000
Interest payable	3,000	4,000
Income taxes payable	22,000	12,000
Total current liabilities	60,000	56,000
Long-term notes payable	90,000	64,000
Total liabilities	150,000	120,000
Equity		
Common stock, $5 par	95,000	80,000
Retained earnings	112,000	88,000
Total equity	207,000	168,000
Total liabilities and equity	$357,000	$288,000

① **Adjustments for Changes in Current Assets and Current Liabilities** This section describes adjustments for changes in noncash current assets and current liabilities.

Point: Operating activities are typically those that determine income, which are often reflected in changes in current assets and current liabilities.

Adjustments for changes in noncash current assets. Changes in noncash current assets normally result from operating activities. Examples are sales affecting accounts receivable and building usage affecting prepaid rent. Decreases in noncash current assets yield the following adjustment:

Decreases in noncash current assets are added to net income.

To see the logic for this adjustment, consider that a decrease in a noncash current asset such as accounts receivable suggests more available cash at the end of the period compared to the beginning. This is so because a decrease in accounts receivable implies higher cash receipts than reflected in sales. We add these higher cash receipts (from decreases in noncash current assets) to net income when computing cash flow from operations.

In contrast, an increase in noncash current assets such as accounts receivable implies less cash receipts than reflected in sales. As another example, an increase in prepaid rent indicates that more cash is paid for rent than is deducted as rent expense. Increases in noncash current assets yield the following adjustment:

Increases in noncash current assets are subtracted from net income.

To illustrate, these adjustments are applied to the noncash current assets in Exhibit 16.10.

Accounts receivable. Accounts receivable *increase* $20,000, from a beginning balance of $40,000 to an ending balance of $60,000. This increase implies that Genesis collects less cash than is reported in sales. That is, some of these sales were in the form of accounts receivable and that amount increased during the period. To see this it is helpful to use *account analysis*. This usually involves setting up a T-account and reconstructing its major entries to compute cash receipts or payments. The following reconstructed Accounts Receivable T-account reveals that cash receipts are less than sales:

Numbers in black are taken from Exhibit 16.10. The red number is the computed (plug) figure.

Accounts Receivable			
Bal., Dec. 31, 2010	40,000		
Sales	590,000	Cash receipts =	570,000
Bal., Dec. 31, 2011	60,000		

We see that sales are $20,000 greater than cash receipts. This $20,000—as reflected in the $20,000 increase in Accounts Receivable—is subtracted from net income when computing cash provided by operating activities (see Exhibit 16.11).

Merchandise inventory. Merchandise inventory *increases* by $14,000, from a $70,000 beginning balance to an $84,000 ending balance. This increase implies that Genesis had greater cash purchases than cost of goods sold. This larger amount of cash purchases is in the form of inventory, as reflected in the following account analysis:

Merchandise Inventory			
Bal., Dec. 31, 2010	70,000		
Purchases =	314,000	Cost of goods sold	300,000
Bal., Dec. 31, 2011	84,000		

EXHIBIT 16.11

Statement of Cash Flows—Indirect Method

	GENESIS Statement of Cash Flows For Year Ended December 31, 2011		
	Cash flows from operating activities		
	Net income	$ 38,000	
	Adjustments to reconcile net income to net cash provided by operating activities		
①	Increase in accounts receivable	(20,000)	
①	Increase in merchandise inventory	(14,000)	
①	Increase in prepaid expenses	(2,000)	
①	Decrease in accounts payable	(5,000)	
①	Decrease in interest payable	(1,000)	
①	Increase in income taxes payable	10,000	
②	Depreciation expense	24,000	
③	Loss on sale of plant assets	6,000	
③	Gain on retirement of notes	(16,000)	
	Net cash provided by operating activities		$20,000
	Cash flows from investing activities		
	Cash received from sale of plant assets	12,000	
	Cash paid for purchase of plant assets	(10,000)	
	Net cash provided by investing activities		2,000
	Cash flows from financing activities		
	Cash received from issuing stock	15,000	
	Cash paid to retire notes	(18,000)	
	Cash paid for dividends	(14,000)	
	Net cash used in financing activities		(17,000)
	Net increase in cash		$ 5,000
	Cash balance at prior year-end		12,000
	Cash balance at current year-end		$17,000

Point: Refer to Exhibit 16.10 and identify the $5,000 change in cash. This change is what the statement of cash flows explains; it serves as a check.

The amount by which purchases exceed cost of goods sold—as reflected in the $14,000 increase in inventory—is subtracted from net income when computing cash provided by operating activities (see Exhibit 16.11).

Prepaid expenses. Prepaid Expenses *increase* $2,000, from a $4,000 beginning balance to a $6,000 ending balance, implying that Genesis's cash payments exceed its recorded prepaid expenses. These higher cash payments increase the amount of Prepaid Expenses, as reflected in its reconstructed T-account:

Prepaid Expenses			
Bal., Dec. 31, 2010	4,000		
Cash payments =	218,000	Wages and other operating exp.	216,000
Bal., Dec. 31, 2011	6,000		

The amount by which cash payments exceed the recorded operating expenses—as reflected in the $2,000 increase in Prepaid Expenses—is subtracted from net income when computing cash provided by operating activities (see Exhibit 16.11).

Adjustments for changes in current liabilities. Changes in current liabilities normally result from operating activities. An example is a purchase that affects accounts payable. Increases in current liabilities yield the following adjustment to net income when computing operating cash flows:

Increases in current liabilities are added to net income.

To see the logic for this adjustment, consider that an increase in the Accounts Payable account suggests that cash payments are less than the related (cost of goods sold) expense. As another example, an increase in wages payable implies that cash paid for wages is less than the recorded wages expense. Since the recorded expense is greater than the cash paid, we add the increase in wages payable to net income to compute net cash flow from operations.

Conversely, when current liabilities decrease, the following adjustment is required:

Decreases in current liabilities are subtracted from net income.

To illustrate, these adjustments are applied to the current liabilities in Exhibit 16.10.

Accounts payable. Accounts payable *decrease* $5,000, from a beginning balance of $40,000 to an ending balance of $35,000. This decrease implies that cash payments to suppliers exceed purchases by $5,000 for the period, which is reflected in the reconstructed Accounts Payable T-account:

Accounts Payable			
		Bal., Dec. 31, 2010	40,000
Cash payments =	319,000	Purchases	314,000
		Bal., Dec. 31, 2011	35,000

The amount by which cash payments exceed purchases—as reflected in the $5,000 decrease in Accounts Payable—is subtracted from net income when computing cash provided by operating activities (see Exhibit 16.11).

Interest payable. Interest payable *decreases* $1,000, from a $4,000 beginning balance to a $3,000 ending balance. This decrease indicates that cash paid for interest exceeds interest expense by $1,000, which is reflected in the Interest Payable T-account:

Interest Payable			
		Bal., Dec. 31, 2010	4,000
Cash paid for interest =	8,000	Interest expense	7,000
		Bal., Dec. 31, 2011	3,000

The amount by which cash paid exceeds recorded expense—as reflected in the $1,000 decrease in Interest Payable—is subtracted from net income (see Exhibit 16.11).

Income taxes payable. Income taxes payable *increase* $10,000, from a $12,000 beginning balance to a $22,000 ending balance. This increase implies that reported income taxes exceed the cash paid for taxes, which is reflected in the Income Taxes Payable T-account:

Income Taxes Payable			
		Bal., Dec. 31, 2010	12,000
Cash paid for taxes =	5,000	Income taxes expense	15,000
		Bal., Dec. 31, 2011	22,000

The amount by which cash paid falls short of the reported taxes expense—as reflected in the $10,000 increase in Income Taxes Payable—is added to net income when computing cash provided by operating activities (see Exhibit 16.11).

Summary Adjustments for Changes in Current Assets and Current Liabilities

Account	Increases	Decreases
Noncash current assets	Deduct from NI	Add to NI
Current liabilities......	Add to NI	Deduct from NI

② Adjustments for Operating Items Not Providing or Using Cash The income statement usually includes some expenses that do not reflect cash outflows in the period. Examples are depreciation, amortization, depletion, and bad debts expense. The indirect method for reporting operating cash flows requires that

Expenses with no cash outflows are added back to net income.

To see the logic of this adjustment, recall that items such as depreciation, amortization, depletion, and bad debts originate from debits to expense accounts and credits to noncash accounts. These entries have *no* cash effect, and we add them back to net income when computing net cash flows from operations. Adding them back cancels their deductions.

Similarly, when net income includes revenues that do not reflect cash inflows in the period, the indirect method for reporting operating cash flows requires that

Revenues with no cash inflows are subtracted from net income.

We apply these adjustments to the Genesis operating items that do not provide or use cash.

Depreciation. Depreciation expense is the only Genesis operating item that has no effect on cash flows in the period. We must add back the $24,000 depreciation expense to net income when computing cash provided by operating activities. (We later explain that any cash outflow to acquire a plant asset is reported as an investing activity.)

③ Adjustments for Nonoperating Items Net income often includes losses that are not part of operating activities but are part of either investing or financing activities. Examples are a loss from the sale of a plant asset and a loss from retirement of notes payable. The indirect method for reporting operating cash flows requires that

Nonoperating losses are added back to net income.

To see the logic, consider that items such as a plant asset sale and a notes retirement are normally recorded by recognizing the cash, removing all plant asset or notes accounts, and recognizing any loss or gain. The cash received or paid is not part of operating activities but is part of either investing or financing activities. *No* operating cash flow effect occurs. However, because the nonoperating loss is a deduction in computing net income, we need to add it back to net income when computing cash flow from operations. Adding it back cancels the deduction.

Point: An income statement reports revenues, gains, expenses, and losses on an accrual basis. The statement of cash flows reports cash received and cash paid for operating, financing, and investing activities.

Similarly, when net income includes gains not part of operating activities, the indirect method for reporting operating cash flows requires that

Nonoperating gains are subtracted from net income.

To illustrate these adjustments, we consider the nonoperating items of Genesis.

Loss on sale of plant assets. Genesis reports a $6,000 loss on sale of plant assets as part of net income. This loss is a proper deduction in computing income, but it is *not part of operating activities*. Instead, a sale of plant assets is part of investing activities. Thus, the $6,000 nonoperating loss is added back to net income (see Exhibit 16.11). Adding it back cancels the loss. We later explain how to report the cash inflow from the asset sale in investing activities.

Gain on retirement of debt. A $16,000 gain on retirement of debt is properly included in net income, but it is *not part of operating activities*. This means the $16,000 nonoperating gain must be subtracted from net income to obtain net cash provided by operating activities (see Exhibit 16.11). Subtracting it cancels the recorded gain. We later describe how to report the cash outflow to retire debt.

Summary of Adjustments for Indirect Method

Exhibit 16.12 summarizes the most common adjustments to net income when computing net cash provided or used by operating activities under the indirect method.

EXHIBIT 16.12

Summary of Selected Adjustments for Indirect Method

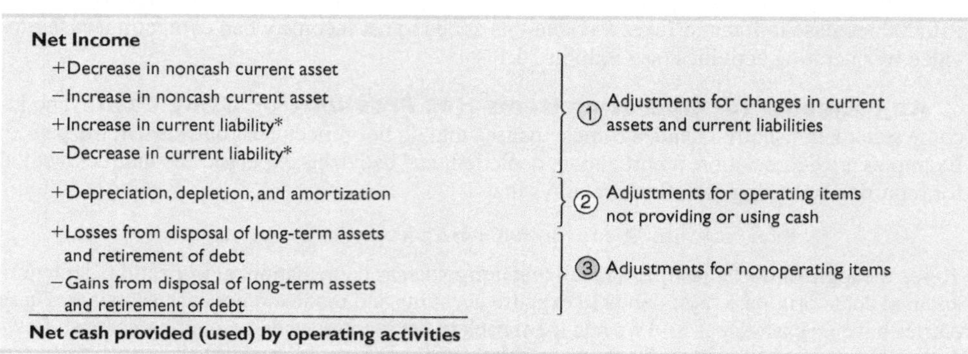

Net Income	
+Decrease in noncash current asset −Increase in noncash current asset +Increase in current liability* −Decrease in current liability*	① Adjustments for changes in current assets and current liabilities
+Depreciation, depletion, and amortization	② Adjustments for operating items not providing or using cash
+Losses from disposal of long-term assets and retirement of debt −Gains from disposal of long-term assets and retirement of debt	③ Adjustments for nonoperating items
Net cash provided (used) by operating activities	

* Excludes current portion of long-term debt and any (nonsales-related) short-term notes payable—both are financing activities.

The computations in determining cash provided or used by operating activities are different for the indirect and direct methods, but the result is identical. Both methods yield the same $20,000 figure for cash from operating activities for Genesis; see Exhibits 16.7 and 16.11.

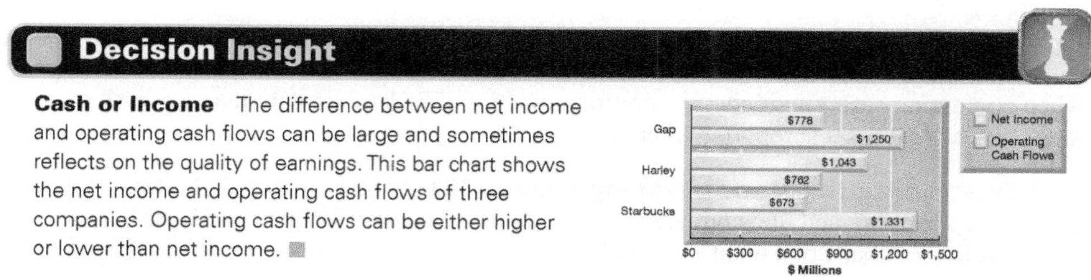

Decision Insight

Cash or Income The difference between net income and operating cash flows can be large and sometimes reflects on the quality of earnings. This bar chart shows the net income and operating cash flows of three companies. Operating cash flows can be either higher or lower than net income.

Quick Check Answers — p. 662

4. Determine the net cash provided or used by operating activities using the following data: net income, $74,900; decrease in accounts receivable, $4,600; increase in inventory, $11,700; decrease in accounts payable, $1,000; loss on sale of equipment, $3,400; payment of cash dividends, $21,500.
5. Why are expenses such as depreciation and amortization added to net income when cash flow from operating activities is computed by the indirect method?
6. A company reports net income of $15,000 that includes a $3,000 gain on the sale of plant assets. Why is this gain subtracted from net income in computing cash flow from operating activities using the indirect method?

CASH FLOWS FROM INVESTING

The third major step in preparing the statement of cash flows is to compute and report cash flows from investing activities. We normally do this by identifying changes in (1) all noncurrent asset accounts and (2) the current accounts for both notes receivable and investments in securities (excluding trading securities). We then analyze changes in these accounts to determine their effect, if any, on cash and report the cash flow effects in the investing activities section of the statement of cash flows. **Reporting of investing activities is identical under the direct method and indirect method.**

Three-Stage Process of Analysis

P3 Determine cash flows from both investing and financing activities.

Information to compute cash flows from investing activities is usually taken from beginning and ending balance sheets and the income statement. We use a three-stage process to determine cash provided or used by investing activities: (1) identify changes in investing-related accounts, (2) explain these changes using reconstruction analysis, and (3) report their cash flow effects.

Analysis of Noncurrent Assets

Information about the Genesis transactions provided earlier reveals that the company both purchased and sold plant assets during the period. Both transactions are investing activities and are analyzed for their cash flow effects in this section.

Plant Asset Transactions The first stage in analyzing the Plant Assets account and its related Accumulated Depreciation is to identify any changes in these accounts from comparative balance sheets in Exhibit 16.10. This analysis reveals a $40,000 increase in plant assets from $210,000 to $250,000 and a $12,000 increase in accumulated depreciation from $48,000 to $60,000.

Point: Investing activities include (1) purchasing and selling long-term assets, (2) lending and collecting on notes receivable, and (3) purchasing and selling short-term investments other than cash equivalents and trading securities.

The second stage is to explain these changes. Items *b* and *c* of the additional information for Genesis (page 639) are relevant in this case. Recall that the Plant Assets account is affected by both asset purchases and sales, while its Accumulated Depreciation account is normally increased from depreciation and decreased from the removal of accumulated depreciation in asset sales. To explain changes in these accounts and to identify their cash flow effects, we prepare *reconstructed entries* from prior transactions; *they are not the actual entries by the preparer.*

Point: Financing and investing info is available in ledger accounts to help explain changes in comparative balance sheets. Post references lead to relevant entries and explanations.

To illustrate, item *b* reports that Genesis purchased plant assets of $70,000 by issuing $60,000 in notes payable to the seller and paying $10,000 in cash. The reconstructed entry for analysis of item *b* follows:

Reconstruction	Plant Assets	70,000	
	Notes Payable		60,000
	Cash		**10,000**

This entry reveals a $10,000 cash outflow for plant assets and a $60,000 noncash investing and financing transaction involving notes exchanged for plant assets.

Next, item *c* reports that Genesis sold plant assets costing $30,000 (with $12,000 of accumulated depreciation) for $12,000 cash, resulting in a $6,000 loss. The reconstructed entry for analysis of item *c* follows:

Reconstruction	**Cash**	**12,000**	
	Accumulated Depreciation	12,000	
	Loss on Sale of Plant Assets	6,000	
	Plant Assets		30,000

This entry reveals a $12,000 cash inflow from assets sold. The $6,000 loss is computed by comparing the asset book value to the cash received and does not reflect any cash inflow or outflow. We also reconstruct the entry for Depreciation Expense using information from the income statement.

Reconstruction			
	Depreciation Expense	24,000	
	Accumulated Depreciation		24,000

This entry shows that Depreciation Expense results in no cash flow effect. These three reconstructed entries are reflected in the following plant asset and related T-accounts.

Plant Assets			
Bal., Dec. 31, 2010	210,000		
Purchase	**70,000**	**Sale**	**30,000**
Bal., Dec. 31, 2011	250,000		

Accumulated Depreciation—Plant Assets			
		Bal., Dec. 31, 2010	48,000
Sale	**12,000**	**Depr. expense**	**24,000**
		Bal., Dec. 31, 2011	60,000

Example: If a plant asset costing $40,000 with $37,000 of accumulated depreciation is sold at a $1,000 loss, what is the cash flow? What is the cash flow if this asset is sold at a gain of $3,000? *Answers:* +$2,000; +$6,000.

This reconstruction analysis is complete in that the change in plant assets from $210,000 to $250,000 is fully explained by the $70,000 purchase and the $30,000 sale. Also, the change in accumulated depreciation from $48,000 to $60,000 is fully explained by depreciation expense of $24,000 and the removal of $12,000 in accumulated depreciation from an asset sale. (Preparers of the statement of cash flows have the entire ledger and additional information at their disposal, but for brevity reasons only the information needed for reconstructing accounts is given.)

The third stage looks at the reconstructed entries for identification of cash flows. The two identified cash flow effects are reported in the investing section of the statement as follows (also see Exhibit 16.7 or 16.11):

Cash flows from investing activities	
Cash received from sale of plant assets	$12,000
Cash paid for purchase of plant assets	(10,000)

The $60,000 portion of the purchase described in item *b* and financed by issuing notes is a noncash investing and financing activity. It is reported in a note or in a separate schedule to the statement as follows:

Noncash investing and financing activity	
Purchased plant assets with issuance of notes	$60,000

Analysis of Other Assets

Many other asset transactions (including those involving current notes receivable and investments in certain securities) are considered investing activities and can affect a company's cash flows. Since Genesis did not enter into other investing activities impacting assets, we do not need to extend our analysis to these other assets. If such transactions did exist, we would analyze them using the same three-stage process illustrated for plant assets.

Quick Check

Answer – p. 662

7. Equipment costing $80,000 with accumulated depreciation of $30,000 is sold at a loss of $10,000. What is the cash receipt from this sale? In what section of the statement of cash flows is this transaction reported?

CASH FLOWS FROM FINANCING

The fourth major step in preparing the statement of cash flows is to compute and report cash flows from financing activities. We normally do this by identifying changes in all noncurrent liability accounts (including the current portion of any notes and bonds) and the equity accounts. These accounts include long-term debt, notes payable, bonds payable, common stock, and retained earnings. Changes in these accounts are then analyzed using available information to determine their effect, if any, on cash. Results are reported in the financing activities section of the statement. **Reporting of financing activities is identical under the direct method and indirect method.**

Three-Stage Process of Analysis

We again use a three-stage process to determine cash provided or used by financing activities: (1) identify changes in financing-related accounts, (2) explain these changes using reconstruction analysis, and (3) report their cash flow effects.

Analysis of Noncurrent Liabilities

Information about Genesis provided earlier reveals two transactions involving noncurrent liabilities. We analyzed one of those, the $60,000 issuance of notes payable to purchase plant assets. This transaction is reported as a significant noncash investing and financing activity in a footnote or a separate schedule to the statement of cash flows. The other remaining transaction involving noncurrent liabilities is the cash retirement of notes payable.

Point: Financing activities generally refer to changes in the noncurrent liability and the equity accounts. Examples are (1) receiving cash from issuing debt or repaying amounts borrowed and (2) receiving cash from or distributing cash to owners.

Notes Payable Transactions The first stage in analysis of notes is to review the comparative balance sheets from Exhibit 16.10. This analysis reveals an increase in notes payable from $64,000 to $90,000.

The second stage explains this change. Item *e* of the additional information for Genesis (page 639) reports that notes with a carrying value of $34,000 are retired for $18,000 cash, resulting in a $16,000 gain. The reconstructed entry for analysis of item *e* follows:

Reconstruction			
	Notes Payable	34,000	
	Gain on retirement of debt		16,000
	Cash		**18,000**

This entry reveals an $18,000 cash outflow for retirement of notes and a $16,000 gain from comparing the notes payable carrying value to the cash received. This gain does not reflect any cash inflow or outflow. Also, item *b* of the additional information reports that Genesis purchased plant assets costing $70,000 by issuing $60,000 in notes payable to the seller and paying $10,000 in cash. We reconstructed this entry when analyzing investing activities: It showed a $60,000 increase to notes payable that is reported as a noncash investing and financing transaction. The Notes Payable account reflects (and is fully explained by) these reconstructed entries as follows:

Notes Payable			
		Bal., Dec. 31, 2010	64,000
Retired notes	**34,000**	**Issued notes**	**60,000**
		Bal., Dec. 31, 2011	90,000

The third stage is to report the cash flow effect of the notes retirement in the financing section of the statement as follows (also see Exhibit 16.7 or 16.11):

Cash flows from financing activities	
Cash paid to retire notes	$(18,000)

Analysis of Equity

The Genesis information reveals two transactions involving equity accounts. The first is the issuance of common stock for cash. The second is the declaration and payment of cash dividends. We analyze both.

Common Stock Transactions The first stage in analyzing common stock is to review the comparative balance sheets from Exhibit 16.10, which reveal an increase in common stock from $80,000 to $95,000.

The second stage explains this change. Item *d* of the additional information (page 639) reports that 3,000 shares of common stock are issued at par for $5 per share. The reconstructed entry for analysis of item *d* follows:

Reconstruction			
	Cash	**15,000**	
	Common Stock		15,000

This entry reveals a $15,000 cash inflow from stock issuance and is reflected in (and explains) the Common Stock account as follows:

Common Stock			
		Bal., Dec. 31, 2010	80,000
		Issued stock	**15,000**
		Bal., Dec. 31, 2011	95,000

The third stage discloses the cash flow effect from stock issuance in the financing section of the statement as follows (also see Exhibit 16.7 or 16.11):

Cash flows from financing activities	
Cash received from issuing stock	$15,000

Retained Earnings Transactions The first stage in analyzing the Retained Earnings account is to review the comparative balance sheets from Exhibit 16.10. This reveals an increase in retained earnings from $88,000 to $112,000.

The second stage explains this change. Item *f* of the additional information (page 639) reports that cash dividends of $14,000 are paid. The reconstructed entry follows:

Reconstruction			
	Retained Earnings	14,000	
	Cash		**14,000**

This entry reveals a $14,000 cash outflow for cash dividends. Also see that the Retained Earnings account is impacted by net income of $38,000. (Net income was analyzed under the operating section of the statement of cash flows.) The reconstructed Retained Earnings account follows:

Retained Earnings			
		Bal., Dec. 31, 2010	88,000
Cash dividend	**14,000**	**Net income**	**38,000**
		Bal., Dec. 31, 2011	112,000

Point: Financing activities not affecting cash flow include *declaration* of a cash dividend, *declaration* of a stock dividend, payment of a stock dividend, and a stock split.

The third stage reports the cash flow effect from the cash dividend in the financing section of the statement as follows (also see Exhibit 16.7 or 16.11):

Cash flows from financing activities	
Cash paid for dividends....................	$(14,000)

Global: There are no requirements to separate domestic and international cash flows, leading some users to ask, "Where in the world is cash flow?"

We now have identified and explained all of the Genesis cash inflows and cash outflows and one noncash investing and financing transaction. Specifically, our analysis has reconciled changes in all noncash balance sheet accounts.

Proving Cash Balances

The fifth and final step in preparing the statement is to report the beginning and ending cash balances and prove that the *net change in cash* is explained by operating, investing, and financing cash flows. This step is shown here for Genesis.

Net cash provided by operating activities	$20,000
Net cash provided by investing activities	2,000
Net cash used in financing activities	(17,000)
Net increase in cash	**$ 5,000**
Cash balance at 2010 year-end	12,000
Cash balance at 2011 year-end	$17,000

The preceding table shows that the $5,000 net increase in cash, from $12,000 at the beginning of the period to $17,000 at the end, is reconciled by net cash flows from operating ($20,000 inflow), investing ($2,000 inflow), and financing ($17,000 outflow) activities. This is formally reported at the bottom of the statement of cash flows as shown in both Exhibits 16.7 and 16.11.

Decision Maker

Reporter Management is in labor contract negotiations and grants you an interview. It highlights a recent $600,000 net loss that involves a $930,000 extraordinary loss and a total net cash outflow of $550,000 (which includes net cash outflows of $850,000 for investing activities and $350,000 for financing activities). What is your assessment of this company? ■

GLOBAL VIEW

The statement of cash flows, which explains changes in cash (including cash equivalents) from period to period, is required under both U.S. GAAP and IFRS. This section discusses similarities and differences between U.S. GAAP and IFRS in reporting that statement.

Reporting Cash Flows from Operating Both U.S. GAAP and IFRS permit the reporting of cash flows from operating activities using either the direct or indirect method. Further, the basic requirements underlying the application of both methods are fairly consistent across these two accounting systems. Appendix A shows that Nokia reports its cash flows from operating activities using the indirect method, and in a manner similar to that explained in this chapter. Further, the definition of cash and cash equivalents is roughly similar for U.S. GAAP and IFRS.

NOKIA

There are, however, some differences between U.S. GAAP and IFRS in reporting operating cash flows. We mention two of the more notable. First, U.S. GAAP requires cash inflows from interest revenue and dividend revenue be classified as operating, whereas IFRS permits classification under operating or investing provided that this classification is consistently applied across periods. Nokia reports its cash from interest received under operating, consistent with U.S. GAAP (no mention is made of any dividends received). Second, U.S. GAAP requires cash outflows for interest expense be classified as operating, whereas IFRS again permits classification under operating or financing provided that it is consistently applied across periods. (Some believe that interest payments, like dividends payments, are better classified as financing because they represent payments to financiers.) Nokia reports cash outflows for interest under operating, which is consistent with U.S. GAAP and acceptable under IFRS.

Reporting Cash Flows from Investing and Financing U.S. GAAP and IFRS are broadly similar in computing and classifying cash flows from investing and financing activities. A quick review of these two sections for Nokia's statement of cash flows shows a structure similar to that explained in this chapter. One notable exception is that U.S. GAAP requires cash outflows for income tax be classified as operating, whereas IFRS permits the splitting of those cash flows among operating, investing, and financing depending on the sources of that tax. Nokia reports its cash outflows for income tax under operating, which is similar to U.S. GAAP.

Decision Analysis

Cash Flow Analysis

Analyzing Cash Sources and Uses

A1 Analyze the statement of cash flows and apply the cash flow on total assets ratio.

Most managers stress the importance of understanding and predicting cash flows for business decisions. Creditors evaluate a company's ability to generate cash before deciding whether to lend money. Investors also assess cash inflows and outflows before buying and selling stock. Information in the statement of cash flows helps address these and other questions such as (1) How much cash is generated from or used in operations? (2) What expenditures are made with cash from operations? (3) What is the source of cash for debt payments? (4) What is the source of cash for distributions to owners? (5) How is the increase in investing activities financed? (6) What is the source of cash for new plant assets? (7) Why is cash flow from operations different from income? (8) How is cash from financing used?

To effectively answer these questions, it is important to separately analyze investing, financing, and operating activities. To illustrate, consider data from three different companies in Exhibit 16.13. These companies operate in the same industry and have been in business for several years.

EXHIBIT 16.13

Cash Flows of Competing Companies

($ thousands)	BMX	ATV	Trex
Cash provided (used) by operating activities	$90,000	$40,000	$(24,000)
Cash provided (used) by investing activities			
Proceeds from sale of plant assets			26,000
Purchase of plant assets	(48,000)	(25,000)	
Cash provided (used) by financing activities			
Proceeds from issuance of debt			13,000
Repayment of debt	(27,000)		
Net increase (decrease) in cash	$15,000	$15,000	$ 15,000

Each company generates an identical $15,000 net increase in cash, but its sources and uses of cash flows are very different. BMX's operating activities provide net cash flows of $90,000, allowing it to purchase plant assets of $48,000 and repay $27,000 of its debt. ATV's operating activities provide $40,000 of cash flows, limiting its purchase of plant assets to $25,000. Trex's $15,000 net cash increase is due to selling plant assets and incurring additional debt. Its operating activities yield a net cash outflow of $24,000. Overall, analysis of these cash flows reveals that BMX is more capable of generating future cash flows than is ATV or Trex.

Decision Insight

Free Cash Flows Many investors use cash flows to value company stock. However, cash-based valuation models often yield different stock values due to differences in measurement of cash flows. Most models require cash flows that are "free" for distribution to shareholders. These *free cash flows* are defined as cash flows available to shareholders after operating asset reinvestments and debt payments. Knowledge of the statement of cash flows is key to proper computation of free cash flows. A company's growth and financial flexibility depend on adequate free cash flows. ■

Cash Flow on Total Assets

Cash flow information has limitations, but it can help measure a company's ability to meet its obligations, pay dividends, expand operations, and obtain financing. Users often compute and analyze a cash-based ratio similar to return on total assets except that its numerator is net cash flows from operating activities. The **cash flow on total assets** ratio is in Exhibit 16.14.

EXHIBIT 16.14

Cash Flow on Total Assets

$$\textbf{Cash flow on total assets} = \frac{\textbf{Cash flow from operations}}{\textbf{Average total assets}}$$

This ratio reflects actual cash flows and is not affected by accounting income recognition and measurement. It can help business decision makers estimate the amount and timing of cash flows when planning and analyzing operating activities.

To illustrate, the 2009 cash flow on total assets ratio for Nike is 13.5%—see Exhibit 16.15. Is a 13.5% ratio good or bad? To answer this question, we compare this ratio with the ratios of prior years (we could also compare its ratio with those of its competitors and the market). Nike's cash flow on total assets ratio for several prior years is in the second column of Exhibit 16.15. Results show that its 13.5% return is the lowest return over the past several years. This is probably reflective of the recent recessionary period.

Year	Cash Flow on Total Assets	Return on Total Assets
2009	13.5%	11.6%
2008	16.7	16.3
2007	18.3	14.5
2006	17.9	14.9
2005	18.8	14.5

EXHIBIT 16.15

Nike's Cash Flow on Total Assets

As an indicator of *earnings quality,* some analysts compare the cash flow on total assets ratio to the return on total assets ratio. Nike's return on total assets is provided in the third column of Exhibit 16.15. Nike's cash flow on total assets ratio exceeds its return on total assets in each of the five years, leading some analysts to infer that Nike's earnings quality is high for that period because more earnings are realized in the form of cash.

Decision Insight

Cash Flow Ratios Analysts use various other cash-based ratios, including the following two:

(1) $$\textbf{Cash coverage of growth} = \frac{\textbf{Operating cash flow}}{\textbf{Cash outflow for plant assets}}$$

where a low ratio (less than 1) implies cash inadequacy to meet asset growth, whereas a high ratio implies cash adequacy for asset growth.

(2) $$\textbf{Operating cash flow to sales} = \frac{\textbf{Operating cash flow}}{\textbf{Net sales}}$$

When this ratio substantially and consistently differs from the operating income to net sales ratio, the risk of accounting improprieties increases. ■

Point: The following ratio helps assess whether operating cash flow is adequate to meet long-term obligations: **Cash coverage of debt** = Cash flow from operations ÷ Noncurrent liabilities. A low ratio suggests a higher risk of insolvency; a high ratio suggests a greater ability to meet long-term obligations.

DEMONSTRATION PROBLEM

Umlauf's comparative balance sheets, income statement, and additional information follow.

UMLAUF COMPANY
Balance Sheets
December 31, 2011 and 2010

	2011	2010
Assets		
Cash	$ 43,050	$ 23,925
Accounts receivable	34,125	39,825
Merchandise inventory	156,000	146,475
Prepaid expenses	3,600	1,650
Equipment	135,825	146,700
Accum. depreciation—Equipment	(61,950)	(47,550)
Total assets	$310,650	$311,025
Liabilities and Equity		
Accounts payable	$ 28,800	$ 33,750
Income taxes payable	5,100	4,425
Dividends payable	0	4,500
Bonds payable	0	37,500
Common stock, $10 par	168,750	168,750
Retained earnings	108,000	62,100
Total liabilities and equity	$310,650	$311,025

UMLAUF COMPANY
Income Statement
For Year Ended December 31, 2011

Sales		$446,100
Cost of goods sold	$222,300	
Other operating expenses	120,300	
Depreciation expense	25,500	(368,100)
		78,000
Other gains (losses)		
Loss on sale of equipment	3,300	
Loss on retirement of bonds . .	825	(4,125)
Income before taxes		73,875
Income taxes expense		(13,725)
Net income		$ 60,150

Additional Information

a. Equipment costing $21,375 with accumulated depreciation of $11,100 is sold for cash.
b. Equipment purchases are for cash.
c. Accumulated Depreciation is affected by depreciation expense and the sale of equipment.
d. The balance of Retained Earnings is affected by dividend declarations and net income.
e. All sales are made on credit.
f. All merchandise inventory purchases are on credit.
g. Accounts Payable balances result from merchandise inventory purchases.
h. Prepaid expenses relate to "other operating expenses."

Required

1. Prepare a statement of cash flows using the indirect method for year 2011.
2.[B] Prepare a statement of cash flows using the direct method for year 2011.

PLANNING THE SOLUTION

- Prepare two blank statements of cash flows with sections for operating, investing, and financing activities using the (1) indirect method format and (2) direct method format.
- Compute the cash paid for equipment and the cash received from the sale of equipment using the additional information provided along with the amount for depreciation expense and the change in the balances of equipment and accumulated depreciation. Use T-accounts to help chart the effects of the sale and purchase of equipment on the balances of the Equipment account and the Accumulated Depreciation account.
- Compute the effect of net income on the change in the Retained Earnings account balance. Assign the difference between the change in retained earnings and the amount of net income to dividends declared. Adjust the dividends declared amount for the change in the Dividends Payable balance.
- Compute cash received from customers, cash paid for merchandise, cash paid for other operating expenses, and cash paid for taxes as illustrated in the chapter.
- Enter the cash effects of reconstruction entries to the appropriate section(s) of the statement.
- Total each section of the statement, determine the total net change in cash, and add it to the beginning balance to get the ending balance of cash.

SOLUTION TO DEMONSTRATION PROBLEM

Supporting computations for cash receipts and cash payments.

(1)	*Cost of equipment sold	$ 21,375
	Accumulated depreciation of equipment sold	(11,100)
	Book value of equipment sold	10,275
	Loss on sale of equipment	(3,300)
	Cash received from sale of equipment	$ 6,975
	Cost of equipment sold	$ 21,375
	Less decrease in the equipment account balance	(10,875)
	Cash paid for new equipment	$ 10,500
(2)	Loss on retirement of bonds	$ 825
	Carrying value of bonds retired	37,500
	Cash paid to retire bonds	$ 38,325
(3)	Net income	$ 60,150
	Less increase in retained earnings	45,900
	Dividends declared	14,250
	Plus decrease in dividends payable	4,500
	Cash paid for dividends	$ 18,750
(4)[B]	Sales	$ 446,100
	Add decrease in accounts receivable	5,700
	Cash received from customers	$451,800

[continued on next page]

[continued from previous page]

(5)[B] Cost of goods sold	$ 222,300
Plus increase in merchandise inventory	9,525
Purchases	231,825
Plus decrease in accounts payable	4,950
Cash paid for merchandise	$236,775
(6)[B] Other operating expenses	$ 120,300
Plus increase in prepaid expenses	1,950
Cash paid for other operating expenses	$122,250
(7)[B] Income taxes expense	$ 13,725
Less increase in income taxes payable	(675)
Cash paid for income taxes	$ 13,050

* Supporting T-account analysis for part 1 follows:

Equipment			
Bal., Dec. 31, 2010	146,700		
Cash purchase	10,500	Sale	21,375
Bal., Dec. 31, 2011	135,825		

Accumulated Depreciation—Equipment			
		Bal., Dec. 31, 2010	47,550
Sale	11,100	Depr. expense	25,500
		Bal., Dec. 31, 2011	61,950

UMLAUF COMPANY
Statement of Cash Flows (Indirect Method)
For Year Ended December 31, 2011

Cash flows from operating activities		
Net income	$60,150	
Adjustments to reconcile net income to net cash provided by operating activities		
Decrease in accounts receivable	5,700	
Increase in merchandise inventory	(9,525)	
Increase in prepaid expenses	(1,950)	
Decrease in accounts payable	(4,950)	
Increase in income taxes payable	675	
Depreciation expense	25,500	
Loss on sale of plant assets	3,300	
Loss on retirement of bonds	825	
Net cash provided by operating activities		$79,725
Cash flows from investing activities		
Cash received from sale of equipment	6,975	
Cash paid for equipment	(10,500)	
Net cash used in investing activities		(3,525)
Cash flows from financing activities		
Cash paid to retire bonds payable	(38,325)	
Cash paid for dividends	(18,750)	
Net cash used in financing activities		(57,075)
Net increase in cash		$19,125
Cash balance at prior year-end		23,925
Cash balance at current year-end		$43,050

UMLAUF COMPANY Statement of Cash Flows (Direct Method) For Year Ended December 31, 2011		
Cash flows from operating activities		
Cash received from customers	$451,800	
Cash paid for merchandise	(236,775)	
Cash paid for other operating expenses	(122,250)	
Cash paid for income taxes	(13,050)	
Net cash provided by operating activities		$79,725
Cash flows from investing activities		
Cash received from sale of equipment	6,975	
Cash paid for equipment	(10,500)	
Net cash used in investing activities		(3,525)
Cash flows from financing activities		
Cash paid to retire bonds payable	(38,325)	
Cash paid for dividends	(18,750)	
Net cash used in financing activities		(57,075)
Net increase in cash		$19,125
Cash balance at prior year-end		23,925
Cash balance at current year-end		$43,050

APPENDIX

16A Spreadsheet Preparation of the Statement of Cash Flows

This appendix explains how to use a spreadsheet to prepare the statement of cash flows under the indirect method.

P4 Illustrate use of a spreadsheet to prepare a statement of cash flows.

Preparing the Indirect Method Spreadsheet Analyzing noncash accounts can be challenging when a company has a large number of accounts and many operating, investing, and financing transactions. A *spreadsheet,* also called *work sheet* or *working paper,* can help us organize the information needed to prepare a statement of cash flows. A spreadsheet also makes it easier to check the accuracy of our work. To illustrate, we return to the comparative balance sheets and income statement shown in Exhibit 16.10. We use the following identifying letters *a* through *g* to code changes in accounts, and letters *h* through *m* for additional information, to prepare the statement of cash flows:

a. Net income is $38,000.

b. Accounts receivable increase by $20,000.

c. Merchandise inventory increases by $14,000.

d. Prepaid expenses increase by $2,000.

e. Accounts payable decrease by $5,000.

f. Interest payable decreases by $1,000.

g. Income taxes payable increase by $10,000.

h. Depreciation expense is $24,000.

i. Plant assets costing $30,000 with accumulated depreciation of $12,000 are sold for $12,000 cash. This yields a loss on sale of assets of $6,000.

j. Notes with a book value of $34,000 are retired with a cash payment of $18,000, yielding a $16,000 gain on retirement.

k. Plant assets costing $70,000 are purchased with a cash payment of $10,000 and an issuance of notes payable for $60,000.

l. Issued 3,000 shares of common stock for $15,000 cash.

m. Paid cash dividends of $14,000.

Exhibit 16A.1 shows the indirect method spreadsheet for Genesis. We enter both beginning and ending balance sheet amounts on the spreadsheet. We also enter information in the Analysis of Changes columns (keyed to the additional information items *a* through *m*) to explain changes in the accounts and determine the cash flows for operating, investing, and financing activities. Information about noncash investing and financing activities is reported near the bottom.

EXHIBIT 16A.1

Spreadsheet for Preparing Statement of Cash Flows—Indirect Method

GENESIS
Spreadsheet for Statement of Cash Flows—Indirect Method
For Year Ended December 31, 2011

	Dec. 31, 2010		Analysis of Changes Debit		Analysis of Changes Credit	Dec. 31, 2011
Balance Sheet—Debit Bal. Accounts						
Cash	$ 12,000					$ 17,000
Accounts receivable	40,000	(b)	$ 20,000			60,000
Merchandise inventory	70,000	(c)	14,000			84,000
Prepaid expenses	4,000	(d)	2,000			6,000
Plant assets	210,000	(k1)	70,000	(i)	$ 30,000	250,000
	$336,000					$417,000
Balance Sheet—Credit Bal. Accounts						
Accumulated depreciation	$ 48,000	(i)	12,000	(h)	24,000	$ 60,000
Accounts payable	40,000	(e)	5,000			35,000
Interest payable	4,000	(f)	1,000			3,000
Income taxes payable	12,000			(g)	10,000	22,000
Notes payable	64,000	(j)	34,000	(k2)	60,000	90,000
Common stock, $5 par value	80,000			(l)	15,000	95,000
Retained earnings	88,000	(m)	14,000	(a)	38,000	112,000
	$336,000					$417,000
Statement of Cash Flows						
Operating activities						
Net income		(a)	38,000			
Increase in accounts receivable				(b)	20,000	
Increase in merchandise inventory				(c)	14,000	
Increase in prepaid expenses				(d)	2,000	
Decrease in accounts payable				(e)	5,000	
Decrease in interest payable				(f)	1,000	
Increase in income taxes payable		(g)	10,000			
Depreciation expense		(h)	24,000			
Loss on sale of plant assets		(i)	6,000			
Gain on retirement of notes				(j)	16,000	
Investing activities						
Receipts from sale of plant assets		(i)	12,000			
Payment for purchase of plant assets				(k1)	10,000	
Financing activities						
Payment to retire notes				(j)	18,000	
Receipts from issuing stock		(l)	15,000			
Payment of cash dividends				(m)	14,000	
Noncash Investing and Financing Activities						
Purchase of plant assets with notes		(k2)	60,000	(k1)	60,000	
			$337,000		$337,000	

Entering the Analysis of Changes on the Spreadsheet The following sequence of procedures is used to complete the spreadsheet after the beginning and ending balances of the balance sheet accounts are entered:

① Enter net income as the first item in the Statement of Cash Flows section for computing operating cash inflow (debit) and as a credit to Retained Earnings.

② In the Statement of Cash Flows section, adjustments to net income are entered as debits if they increase cash flows and as credits if they decrease cash flows. Applying this same rule, adjust net income for the change in each noncash current asset and current liability account related to operating activities. For each adjustment to net income, the offsetting debit or credit must help reconcile the beginning and ending balances of a current asset or current liability account.

③ Enter adjustments to net income for income statement items not providing or using cash in the period. For each adjustment, the offsetting debit or credit must help reconcile a noncash balance sheet account.

④ Adjust net income to eliminate any gains or losses from investing and financing activities. Because the cash from a gain must be excluded from operating activities, the gain is entered as a credit in the operating activities section. Losses are entered as debits. For each adjustment, the related debit and/or credit must help reconcile balance sheet accounts and involve reconstructed entries to show the cash flow from investing or financing activities.

⑤ After reviewing any unreconciled balance sheet accounts and related information, enter the remaining reconciling entries for investing and financing activities. Examples are purchases of plant assets, issuances of long-term debt, stock issuances, and dividend payments. Some of these may require entries in the noncash investing and financing section of the spreadsheet (reconciled).

⑥ Check accuracy by totaling the Analysis of Changes columns and by determining that the change in each balance sheet account has been explained (reconciled).

Point: Analysis of the changes on the spreadsheet are summarized here:
1. Cash flows from operating activities generally affect net income, current assets, and current liabilities.
2. Cash flows from investing activities generally affect noncurrent asset accounts.
3. Cash flows from financing activities generally affect noncurrent liability and equity accounts.

We illustrate these steps in Exhibit 16A.1 for Genesis:

Step	Entries
①.........	*(a)*
②.........	*(b)* through *(g)*
③.........	*(h)*
④.........	*(i)* through *(j)*
⑤.........	*(k)* through *(m)*

Since adjustments *i*, *j*, and *k* are more challenging, we show them in the following debit and credit format. These entries are for purposes of our understanding; they are *not* the entries actually made in the journals. Changes in the Cash account are identified as sources or uses of cash.

i.	Loss from sale of plant assets	6,000	
	Accumulated depreciation	12,000	
	Receipt from sale of plant assets **(source of cash)**	12,000	
	Plant assets		30,000
	To describe sale of plant assets.		
j.	Notes payable	34,000	
	Payments to retire notes **(use of cash)**		18,000
	Gain on retirement of notes		16,000
	To describe retirement of notes.		
k1.	Plant assets	70,000	
	Payment to purchase plant assets **(use of cash)**		10,000
	Purchase of plant assets financed by notes		60,000
	To describe purchase of plant assets.		
k2.	Purchase of plant assets financed by notes	60,000	
	Notes payable		60,000
	To issue notes for purchase of assets.		

APPENDIX

Direct Method of Reporting Operating Cash Flows 16B

P5 Compute cash flows from operating activities using the direct method.

We compute cash flows from operating activities under the direct method by adjusting accrual-based income statement items to the cash basis. The usual approach is to adjust income statement accounts related to operating activities for changes in their related balance sheet accounts as follows:

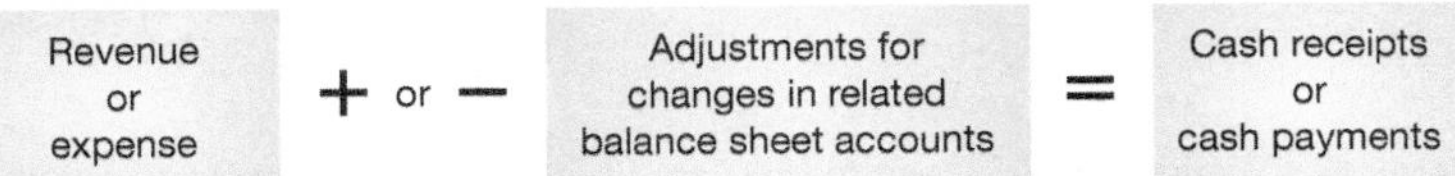

The framework for reporting cash receipts and cash payments for the operating section of the cash flow statement under the direct method is shown in Exhibit 16B.1. We consider cash receipts first and then cash payments.

EXHIBIT 16B.1
Major Classes of Operating Cash Flows

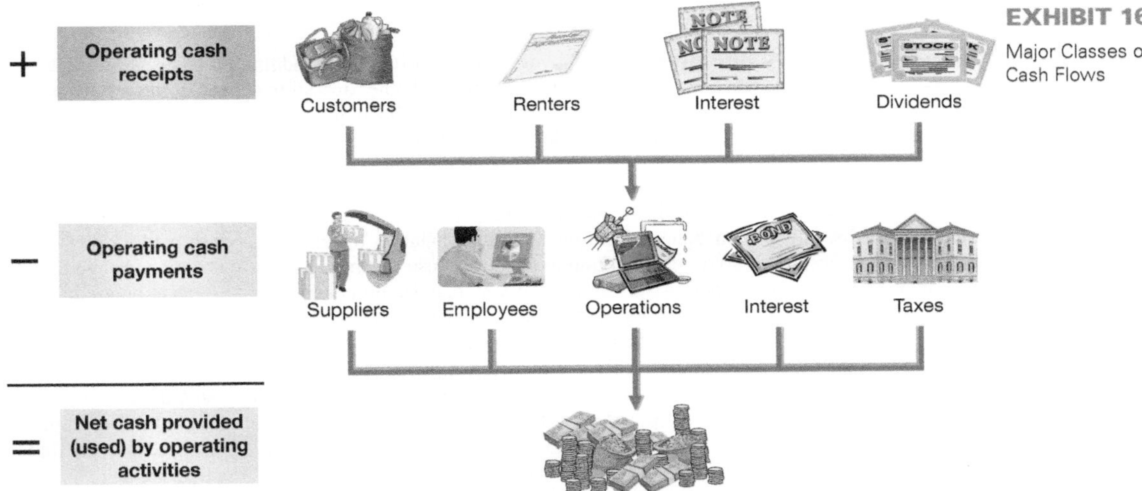

Operating Cash Receipts A review of Exhibit 16.10 and the additional information reported by Genesis suggests only one potential cash receipt: sales to customers. This section, therefore, starts with sales to customers as reported on the income statement and then adjusts it as necessary to obtain cash received from customers to report on the statement of cash flows.

Cash Received from Customers If all sales are for cash, the amount received from customers equals the sales reported on the income statement. When some or all sales are on account, however, we must adjust the amount of sales for the change in Accounts Receivable. It is often helpful to use *account analysis* to do this. This usually involves setting up a T-account and reconstructing its major entries, with emphasis on cash receipts and payments. To illustrate, we use a T-account that includes accounts receivable balances for Genesis on December 31, 2010 and 2011. The beginning balance is $40,000 and the ending balance is $60,000. Next, the income statement shows sales of $590,000, which we enter on the debit side of this account. We now can reconstruct the Accounts Receivable account to determine the amount of cash received from customers as follows:

Point: An accounts receivable increase implies that cash received from customers is less than sales (the converse is also true).

Accounts Receivable			
Bal., Dec. 31, 2010	40,000		
Sales	590,000	Cash receipts =	570,000
Bal., Dec. 31, 2011	60,000		

Example: If the ending balance of accounts receivable is $20,000 (instead of $60,000), what is cash received from customers? *Answer:* $610,000

This T-account shows that the Accounts Receivable balance begins at $40,000 and increases to $630,000 from sales of $590,000, yet its ending balance is only $60,000. This implies that cash receipts from customers are $570,000, computed as $40,000 + $590,000 − [?] = $60,000. This computation can be rearranged to express cash received as equal to sales of $590,000 minus a $20,000 increase in accounts receivable. This computation is summarized as a general rule in Exhibit 16B.2. The statement of cash flows in Exhibit 16.7 reports the $570,000 cash received from customers as a cash inflow from operating activities.

EXHIBIT 16B.2

Formula to Compute Cash Received from Customers—Direct Method

$$\text{Cash received from customers} = \text{Sales} \begin{cases} + \text{ Decrease in accounts receivable} \\ \text{or} \\ - \text{ Increase in accounts receivable} \end{cases}$$

Point: Net income is measured using accrual accounting. Cash flows from operations are measured using cash basis accounting.

Other Cash Receipts While Genesis's cash receipts are limited to collections from customers, we often see other types of cash receipts, most commonly cash receipts involving rent, interest, and dividends. We compute cash received from these items by subtracting an increase in their respective receivable or adding a decrease. For instance, if rent receivable increases in the period, cash received from renters is less than rent revenue reported on the income statement. If rent receivable decreases, cash received is more than reported rent revenue. The same logic applies to interest and dividends. The formulas for these computations are summarized later in this appendix.

Operating Cash Payments A review of Exhibit 16.10 and the additional Genesis information shows four operating expenses: cost of goods sold; wages and other operating expenses; interest expense; and taxes expense. We analyze each expense to compute its cash amounts for the statement of cash flows. (We then examine depreciation and the other losses and gains.)

Cash Paid for Merchandise We compute cash paid for merchandise by analyzing both cost of goods sold and merchandise inventory. If all merchandise purchases are for cash and the ending balance of Merchandise Inventory is unchanged from the beginning balance, the amount of cash paid for merchandise equals cost of goods sold—an uncommon situation. Instead, there normally is some change in the Merchandise Inventory balance. Also, some or all merchandise purchases are often made on credit, and this yields changes in the Accounts Payable balance. When the balances of both Merchandise Inventory and Accounts Payable change, we must adjust the cost of goods sold for changes in both accounts to compute cash paid for merchandise. This is a two-step adjustment.

First, we use the change in the account balance of Merchandise Inventory, along with the cost of goods sold amount, to compute cost of purchases for the period. An increase in merchandise inventory implies that we bought more than we sold, and we add this inventory increase to cost of goods sold to compute cost of purchases. A decrease in merchandise inventory implies that we bought less than we sold, and we subtract the inventory decrease from cost of goods sold to compute purchases. We illustrate the *first step* by reconstructing the Merchandise Inventory account of Genesis:

Merchandise Inventory			
Bal., Dec. 31, 2010	70,000		
Purchases =	314,000	Cost of goods sold	300,000
Bal., Dec. 31, 2011	84,000		

The beginning balance is $70,000, and the ending balance is $84,000. The income statement shows that cost of goods sold is $300,000, which we enter on the credit side of this account. With this information, we determine the amount for cost of purchases to be $314,000. This computation can be rearranged to express cost of purchases as equal to cost of goods sold of $300,000 plus the $14,000 increase in inventory.

The second step uses the change in the balance of Accounts Payable, and the amount of cost of purchases, to compute cash paid for merchandise. A decrease in accounts payable implies that we paid for more goods than we acquired this period, and we would then add the accounts payable decrease to cost of purchases to compute cash paid for merchandise. An increase in accounts payable implies that we paid for less than the amount of goods acquired, and we would subtract the accounts payable increase from purchases to compute cash paid for merchandise. The *second step* is applied to Genesis by reconstructing its Accounts Payable account:

Accounts Payable			
		Bal., Dec. 31, 2010	40,000
Cash payments =	319,000	Purchases	314,000
		Bal., Dec. 31, 2011	35,000

Its beginning balance of $40,000 plus purchases of $314,000 minus an ending balance of $35,000 yields cash paid of $319,000 (or $40,000 + $314,000 − [?] = $35,000). Alternatively, we can express cash paid for merchandise as equal to purchases of $314,000 plus the $5,000 decrease in accounts payable. The $319,000 cash paid for merchandise is reported on the statement of cash flows in Exhibit 16.7 as a cash outflow under operating activities.

We summarize this two-step adjustment to cost of goods sold to compute cash paid for merchandise inventory in Exhibit 16B.3.

Example: If the ending balances of Inventory and Accounts Payable are $60,000 and $50,000, respectively (instead of $84,000 and $35,000), what is cash paid for merchandise? *Answer:* $280,000

EXHIBIT 16B.3

Two Steps to Compute Cash Paid for Merchandise—Direct Method

Step 1

Purchases = Cost of goods sold [+ Increase in merchandise inventory or − Decrease in merchandise inventory]

Step 2

Cash paid for merchandise = Purchases [+ Decrease in accounts payable or − Increase in accounts payable]

Cash Paid for Wages and Operating Expenses (Excluding Depreciation) The income statement of Genesis shows wages and other operating expenses of $216,000 (see Exhibit 16.10). To compute cash paid for wages and other operating expenses, we adjust this amount for any changes in their related balance sheet accounts. We begin by looking for any prepaid expenses and accrued liabilities related to wages and other operating expenses in the balance sheets of Genesis in Exhibit 16.10. The balance sheets show prepaid expenses but no accrued liabilities. Thus, the adjustment is limited to the change in prepaid expenses. The amount of adjustment is computed by assuming that all cash paid for wages and other operating expenses is initially debited to Prepaid Expenses. This assumption allows us to reconstruct the Prepaid Expenses account:

Prepaid Expenses			
Bal., Dec. 31, 2010	4,000		
Cash payments =	218,000	Wages and other operating exp.	216,000
Bal., Dec. 31, 2011	6,000		

Prepaid Expenses increase by $2,000 in the period, meaning that cash paid for wages and other operating expenses exceeds the reported expense by $2,000. Alternatively, we can express cash paid for wages and other operating expenses as equal to its reported expenses of $216,000 plus the $2,000 increase in prepaid expenses.[1]

Point: A decrease in prepaid expenses implies that reported expenses include an amount(s) that did not require a cash outflow in the period.

Exhibit 16B.4 summarizes the adjustments to wages (including salaries) and other operating expenses. The Genesis balance sheet did not report accrued liabilities, but we include them in the formula to explain the adjustment to cash when they do exist. A decrease in accrued liabilities implies that we paid cash for more goods or services than received this period, so we add the decrease in accrued liabilities to the expense amount to obtain cash paid for these goods or services. An increase in accrued liabilities implies that we paid cash for less than what was acquired, so we subtract this increase in accrued liabilities from the expense amount to get cash paid.

[1] The assumption that all cash payments for wages and operating expenses are initially debited to Prepaid Expenses is not necessary for our analysis to hold. If cash payments are debited directly to the expense account, the total amount of cash paid for wages and other operating expenses still equals the $216,000 expense plus the $2,000 increase in Prepaid Expenses (which arise from end-of-period adjusting entries).

EXHIBIT 16B.4

Formula to Compute Cash Paid for Wages and Operating Expenses—Direct Method

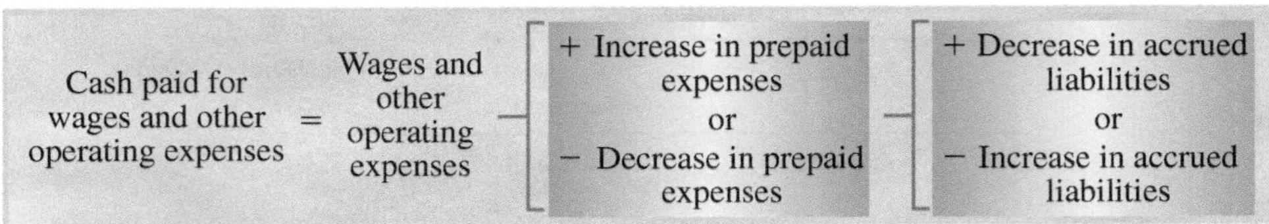

Cash paid for interest and income taxes Computing operating cash flows for interest and taxes is similar to that for operating expenses. Both require adjustments to their amounts reported on the income statement for changes in their related balance sheet accounts. We begin with the Genesis income statement showing interest expense of $7,000 and income taxes expense of $15,000. To compute the cash paid, we adjust interest expense for the change in interest payable and then the income taxes expense for the change in income taxes payable. These computations involve reconstructing both liability accounts:

Interest Payable			
		Bal., Dec. 31, 2010	4,000
Cash paid for interest =	8,000	Interest expense	7,000
		Bal., Dec. 31, 2011	3,000

Income Taxes Payable			
		Bal., Dec. 31, 2010	12,000
Cash paid for taxes =	5,000	Income taxes expense	15,000
		Bal., Dec. 31, 2011	22,000

These accounts reveal cash paid for interest of $8,000 and cash paid for income taxes of $5,000. The formulas to compute these amounts are in Exhibit 16B.5. Both of these cash payments are reported as operating cash outflows on the statement of cash flows in Exhibit 16.7.

EXHIBIT 16B.5

Formulas to Compute Cash Paid for Both Interest and Taxes—Direct Method

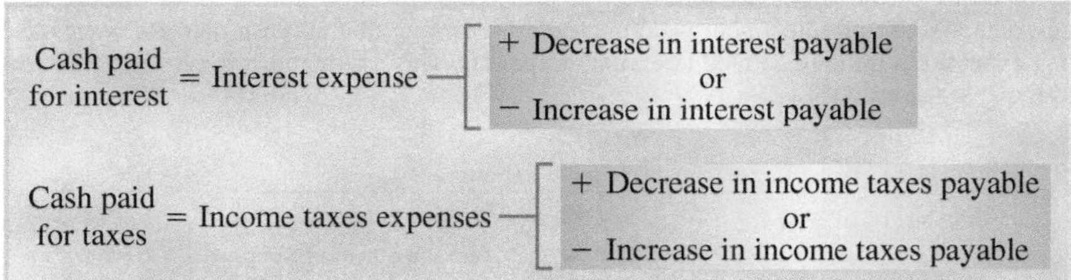

Analysis of Additional Expenses, Gains, and Losses Genesis has three additional items reported on its income statement: depreciation, loss on sale of assets, and gain on retirement of debt. We must consider each for its potential cash effects.

Depreciation Expense Depreciation expense is $24,000. It is often called a *noncash expense* because depreciation has no cash flows. Depreciation expense is an allocation of an asset's depreciable cost. The cash outflow with a plant asset is reported as part of investing activities when it is paid for. Thus, depreciation expense is *never* reported on a statement of cash flows using the direct method; nor is depletion or amortization expense.

Loss on Sale of Assets Sales of assets frequently result in gains and losses reported as part of net income, but the amount of recorded gain or loss does *not* reflect any cash flows in these transactions. Asset sales result in cash inflow equal to the cash amount received, regardless of whether the asset was sold at a gain or a loss. This cash inflow is reported under investing activities. Thus, the loss or gain on a sale of assets is *never* reported on a statement of cash flows using the direct method.

Point: The direct method is usually viewed as *user friendly* because less accounting knowledge is required to understand and use it.

Gain on Retirement of Debt Retirement of debt usually yields a gain or loss reported as part of net income, but that gain or loss does *not* reflect cash flow in this transaction. Debt retirement results in cash outflow equal to the cash paid to settle the debt, regardless of whether the debt is retired at a gain or loss.

This cash outflow is reported under financing activities; the loss or gain from retirement of debt is *never* reported on a statement of cash flows using the direct method.

Summary of Adjustments for Direct Method Exhibit 16B.6 summarizes common adjustments for net income to yield net cash provided (used) by operating activities under the direct method.

EXHIBIT 16B.6

Summary of Selected Adjustments for Direct Method

Item	From Income Statement	Adjustments to Obtain Cash Flow Numbers	
Receipts			
From sales	Sales Revenue	+Decrease in Accounts Receivable −Increase in Accounts Receivable	
From rent	Rent Revenue	+Decrease in Rent Receivable −Increase in Rent Receivable	
From interest	Interest Revenue	+Decrease in Interest Receivable −Increase in Interest Receivable	
From dividends	Dividend Revenue	+Decrease in Dividends Receivable −Increase in Dividends Receivable	
Payments			
To suppliers	Cost of Goods Sold	+Increase in Inventory −Decrease in Inventory	+Decrease in Accounts Payable −Increase in Accounts Payable
For operations	Operating Expense	+Increase in Prepaids −Decrease in Prepaids	+Decrease in Accrued Liabilities −Increase in Accrued Liabilities
To employees	Wages (Salaries) Expense	+Decrease in Wages (Salaries) Payable −Increase in Wages (Salaries) Payable	
For interest	Interest Expense	+Decrease in Interest Payable −Increase in Interest Payable	
For taxes	Income Tax Expense	+Decrease in Income Tax Payable −Increase in Income Tax Payable	

Direct Method Format of Operating Activities Section Exhibit 16.7 shows the Genesis statement of cash flows using the direct method. Major items of cash inflows and cash outflows are listed separately in the operating activities section. The format requires that operating cash outflows be subtracted from operating cash inflows to get net cash provided (used) by operating activities. The FASB recommends that the operating activities section of the statement of cash flows be reported using the direct method, which is considered more useful to financial statement users. *However, the FASB requires a reconciliation of net income to net cash provided (used) by operating activities when the direct method is used* (which can be reported in the notes). This reconciliation is similar to preparation of the operating activities section of the statement of cash flows using the indirect method.

Point: Some preparers argue that it is easier to prepare a statement of cash flows using the indirect method. This likely explains its greater frequency in financial statements.

IFRS

Like U.S. GAAP, IFRS allows cash flows from operating activities to be reported using either the indirect method or the direct method. ■

Quick Check

Answers — p. 662

8. Net sales in a period are $590,000, beginning accounts receivable are $120,000, and ending accounts receivable are $90,000. What cash amount is collected from customers in the period?
9. The Merchandise Inventory account balance decreases in the period from a beginning balance of $32,000 to an ending balance of $28,000. Cost of goods sold for the period is $168,000. If the Accounts Payable balance increases $2,400 in the period, what is the cash amount paid for merchandise inventory?
10. This period's wages and other operating expenses total $112,000. Beginning-of-period prepaid expenses totaled $1,200, and its ending balance is $4,200. There were no beginning-of-period accrued liabilities, but end-of-period wages payable equal $5,600. How much cash is paid for wages and other operating expenses?

Summary

C1 Distinguish between operating, investing, and financing activities, and describe how noncash investing and financing activities are disclosed. The purpose of the statement of cash flows is to report major cash receipts and cash payments relating to operating, investing, or financing activities. Operating activities include transactions and events that determine net income. Investing activities include transactions and events that mainly affect long-term assets. Financing activities include transactions and events that mainly affect long-term liabilities and equity. Noncash investing and financing activities must be disclosed in either a note or a separate schedule to the statement of cash flows. Examples are the retirement of debt by issuing equity and the exchange of a note payable for plant assets.

A1 Analyze the statement of cash flows and apply the cash flow on total assets ratio. To understand and predict cash flows, users stress identification of the sources and uses of cash flows by operating, investing, and financing activities. Emphasis is on operating cash flows since they derive from continuing operations. The cash flow on total assets ratio is defined as operating cash flows divided by average total assets. Analysis of current and past values for this ratio can reflect a company's ability to yield regular and positive cash flows. It is also viewed as a measure of earnings quality.

P1 Prepare a statement of cash flows. Preparation of a statement of cash flows involves five steps: (1) Compute the net increase or decrease in cash; (2) compute net cash provided or used by operating activities (*using either the direct or indirect method*); (3) compute net cash provided or used by investing activities; (4) compute net cash provided or used by financing activities; and (5) report the beginning and ending cash balance and prove that it is explained by net cash flows. Noncash investing and financing activities are also disclosed.

P2 Compute cash flows from operating activities using the indirect method. The indirect method for reporting net cash provided or used by operating activities starts with net income and then adjusts it for three items: (1) changes in noncash current assets and current liabilities related to operating activities, (2) revenues and expenses not providing or using cash, and (3) gains and losses from investing and financing activities.

P3 Determine cash flows from both investing and financing activities. Cash flows from both investing and financing activities are determined by identifying the cash flow effects of transactions and events affecting each balance sheet account related to these activities. All cash flows from these activities are identified when we can explain changes in these accounts from the beginning to the end of the period.

P4[A] Illustrate use of a spreadsheet to prepare a statement of cash flows. A spreadsheet is a useful tool in preparing a statement of cash flows. Six key steps (see Appendix 16A) are applied when using the spreadsheet to prepare the statement.

P5[B] Compute cash flows from operating activities using the direct method. The direct method for reporting net cash provided or used by operating activities lists major operating cash inflows less cash outflows to yield net cash inflow or outflow from operations.

Guidance Answers to Decision Maker

Entrepreneur Several factors might explain an increase in net cash flows when a net loss is reported, including (1) early recognition of expenses relative to revenues generated (such as research and development), (2) cash advances on long-term sales contracts not yet recognized in income, (3) issuances of debt or equity for cash to finance expansion, (4) cash sale of assets, (5) delay of cash payments, and (6) cash prepayment on sales. Analysis needs to focus on the components of both the net loss and the net cash flows and their implications for future performance.

Reporter Your initial reaction based on the company's $600,000 loss with a $550,000 decrease in net cash flows is not positive. However, closer scrutiny reveals a more positive picture of this company's performance. Cash flow from operating activities is $650,000, computed as [?] − $850,000 − $350,000 = $(550,000). You also note that net income *before* the extraordinary loss is $330,000, computed as [?] − $930,000 = $(600,000).

Guidance Answers to Quick Checks

1. No to both. The statement of cash flows reports changes in the sum of cash plus cash equivalents. It does not report transfers between cash and cash equivalents.
2. The three categories of cash inflows and outflows are operating activities, investing activities, and financing activities.
3. **a.** Investing **b.** Operating **c.** Financing **d.** Operating **e.** Operating **f.** Financing
4. $74,900 + $4,600 − $11,700 − $1,000 + $3,400 = $70,200
5. Expenses such as depreciation and amortization do not require current cash outflows. Therefore, adding these expenses back to net income eliminates these noncash items from the net income number, converting it to a cash basis.
6. A gain on the sale of plant assets is subtracted from net income because a sale of plant assets is not an operating activity; it is an investing activity for the amount of cash received from its sale. Also, such a gain yields no cash effects.
7. $80,000 − $30,000 − $10,000 = $40,000 cash receipt. The $40,000 cash receipt is reported as an investing activity.
8. $590,000 + ($120,000 − $90,000) = $620,000
9. $168,000 − ($32,000 − $28,000) − $2,400 = $161,600
10. $112,000 + ($4,200 − $1,200) − $5,600 = $109,400

Key Terms

mhhe.com/wildFAP20e

Cash flow on total assets (p. 650)
Direct method (p. 638)
Financing activities (p. 634)
Indirect method (p. 638)
Investing activities (p. 634)
Operating activities (p. 633)
Statement of cash flows (p. 632)

Multiple Choice Quiz

Answers on p. 683

mhhe.com/wildFAP20e

Additional Quiz Questions are available at the book's Website.

1. A company uses the indirect method to determine its cash flows from operating activities. Use the following information to determine its net cash provided or used by operating activities.

Net income	$15,200
Depreciation expense	10,000
Cash payment on note payable	8,000
Gain on sale of land	3,000
Increase in inventory	1,500
Increase in accounts payable	2,850

a. $23,550 used by operating activities
b. $23,550 provided by operating activities
c. $15,550 provided by operating activities
d. $42,400 provided by operating activities
e. $20,850 provided by operating activities

2. A machine with a cost of $175,000 and accumulated depreciation of $94,000 is sold for $87,000 cash. The amount reported as a source of cash under cash flows from investing activities is
a. $81,000.
b. $6,000.
c. $87,000.
d. Zero; this is a financing activity.
e. Zero; this is an operating activity.

3. A company settles a long-term note payable plus interest by paying $68,000 cash toward the principal amount and $5,440 cash for interest. The amount reported as a use of cash under cash flows from financing activities is
a. Zero; this is an investing activity.
b. Zero; this is an operating activity.
c. $73,440.
d. $68,000.
e. $5,440.

4. The following information is available regarding a company's annual salaries and wages. What amount of cash is paid for salaries and wages?

Salaries and wages expense	$255,000
Salaries and wages payable, prior year-end	8,200
Salaries and wages payable, current year-end	10,900

a. $252,300
b. $257,700
c. $255,000
d. $274,100
e. $235,900

5. The following information is available for a company. What amount of cash is paid for merchandise for the current year?

Cost of goods sold	$545,000
Merchandise inventory, prior year-end	105,000
Merchandise inventory, current year-end	112,000
Accounts payable, prior year-end	98,500
Accounts payable, current year-end	101,300

a. $545,000
b. $554,800
c. $540,800
d. $535,200
e. $549,200

A(B) *Superscript letter A (B) denotes assignments based on Appendix 16A (16B).*
Icon denotes assignments that involve decision making.

Discussion Questions

1. What is the reporting purpose of the statement of cash flows? Identify at least two questions that this statement can answer.
2. Describe the direct method of reporting cash flows from operating activities.
3. When a statement of cash flows is prepared using the direct method, what are some of the operating cash flows?
4. Describe the indirect method of reporting cash flows from operating activities.
5. What are some investing activities reported on the statement of cash flows?
6. What are some financing activities reported on the statement of cash flows?

7. Where on the statement of cash flows is the payment of cash dividends reported?
8. Assume that a company purchases land for $100,000, paying $20,000 cash and borrowing the remainder with a long-term note payable. How should this transaction be reported on a statement of cash flows?
9. On June 3, a company borrows $50,000 cash by giving its bank a 160-day, interest-bearing note. On the statement of cash flows, where should this be reported?
10. If a company reports positive net income for the year, can it also show a net cash outflow from operating activities? Explain.
11. Is depreciation a source of cash flow?
12. Refer to Research In Motion's statement of cash flows in Appendix A. (*a*) Which method is used to compute its net cash provided by operating activities? (*b*) While its balance sheet shows an increase in working capital (current assets less current liabilities) from fiscal years 2009 to 2010, why is this increase in working capital subtracted when computing net cash provided by operating activities for the year ended February 27, 2010?

RIM

13. Refer to Palm's statement of cash flows in Appendix A. What are its cash flows from financing activities for the year ended May 31, 2009? List items and amounts.

Palm

14. Refer to Nokia's statement of cash flows in Appendix A. List its cash flows from operating activities, investing activities, and financing activities.

NOKIA

15. Refer to Apple's statement of cash flows in Appendix A. What investing activities result in cash outflows for the year ended September 26, 2009? List items and amounts.

Apple

connect

QUICK STUDY

QS 16-1
Transaction classification by activity
C1 

Classify the following cash flows as operating, investing, or financing activities.

1. Paid cash for property taxes on building.
2. Paid cash dividends.
3. Paid cash for wages and salaries.
4. Purchased inventories for cash.
5. Received cash payments from customers.
6. Received cash from sale of land at a loss.
7. Received cash interest on a note.
8. Paid cash interest on outstanding notes.
9. Issued common stock for cash.
10. Sold long-term investments for cash.

QS 16-2
Statement of cash flows

The statement of cash flows is one of the four primary financial statements.

1. Describe the content and layout of a statement of cash flows, including its three sections.
2. List at least three transactions classified as significant noncash financing and investing activities in the statement of cash flows.
3. List at least three transactions classified as financing activities in a statement of cash flows.
4. List at least three transactions classified as investing activities in a statement of cash flows.

QS 16-3
Computing cash from operations (indirect)
P2

Use the following information to determine this company's cash flows from operating activities using the indirect method.

LING COMPANY
Selected Balance Sheet Information
December 31, 2011 and 2010

	2011	2010
Current assets		
Cash	$338,600	$107,200
Accounts receivable	100,000	128,000
Inventory	240,000	216,400
Current liabilities		
Accounts payable	121,600	102,800
Income taxes payable	8,200	8,800

LING COMPANY
Income Statement
For Year Ended December 31, 2011

Sales		$2,060,000
Cost of goods sold		1,326,400
Gross profit		733,600
Operating expenses		
Depreciation expense	$144,000	
Other expenses	486,000	630,000
Income before taxes		103,600
Income taxes expense		30,800
Net income		$ 72,800

QS 16-4
Computing cash from asset sales
P3

The following selected information is from Mooney Company's comparative balance sheets.

At December 31	2011	2010
Furniture	$155,000	$ 260,000
Accumulated depreciation—Furniture	(74,400)	(121,400)

The income statement reports depreciation expense for the year of $36,000. Also, furniture costing $105,000 was sold for its book value. Compute the cash received from the sale of furniture.

QS 16-5
Computing financing cash flows
P3

The following selected information is from the Teeter Company's comparative balance sheets.

At December 31	2011	2010
Common stock, $10 par value	$ 310,000	$300,000
Paid-in capital in excess of par	1,134,000	684,000
Retained earnings	627,000	575,000

The company's net income for the year ended December 31, 2011, was $196,000.

1. Compute the cash received from the sale of its common stock during 2011.

2. Compute the cash paid for dividends during 2011.

QS 16-6
Computing cash flows from operations (indirect)
P2

For each of the following separate cases, compute cash flows from operations. The list includes all balance sheet accounts related to operating activities.

	Case A	Case B	Case C
Net income	$ 20,000	$125,000	$105,000
Depreciation expense	60,000	16,000	48,000
Accounts receivable increase (decrease)	80,000	40,000	(8,000)
Inventory increase (decrease)	(40,000)	(20,000)	21,000
Accounts payable increase (decrease)	28,000	(44,000)	16,000
Accrued liabilities increase (decrease)	(88,000)	10,000	(16,000)

QS 16-7
Computing cash flows from investing
P3

Compute cash flows from investing activities using the following company information.

Sale of short-term investments	$16,000
Cash collections from customers	44,000
Purchase of used equipment	10,000
Depreciation expense	6,000

QS 16-8
Computing cash flows from financing
P3

Compute cash flows from financing activities using the following company information.

Additional short-term borrowings	$88,000
Purchase of short-term investments	25,000
Cash dividends paid	32,000
Interest paid	17,000

QS 16-9
Computing cash from operations (indirect) P2 

Use the following balance sheets and income statement to answer QS 16-9 through QS 16-14.

Use the indirect method to prepare the cash provided or used from operating activities section only of the statement of cash flows for this company.

ORWELL, INC.
Comparative Balance Sheets
December 31, 2011

	2011	2010
Assets		
Cash	$ 95,800	$ 25,000
Accounts receivable, net	42,000	52,000
Inventory	86,800	96,800
Prepaid expenses	6,400	5,200
Furniture	110,000	120,000
Accum. depreciation—Furniture	(18,000)	(10,000)
Total assets	$323,000	$289,000
Liabilities and Equity		
Accounts payable	$ 16,000	$ 22,000
Wages payable	10,000	6,000
Income taxes payable	2,400	3,600
Notes payable (long-term)	30,000	70,000
Common stock, $5 par value	230,000	180,000
Retained earnings	34,600	7,400
Total liabilities and equity	$323,000	$289,000

ORWELL, INC.
Income Statement
For Year Ended December 31, 2011

Sales		$468,000
Cost of goods sold		312,000
Gross profit		156,000
Operating expenses		
Depreciation expense	$38,600	
Other expenses	57,000	95,600
Income before taxes		60,400
Income taxes expense		24,600
Net income		$ 35,800

QS 16-10
Computing cash from asset sales P3 

Refer to the data in QS 16-9.
Furniture costing $54,000 is sold at its book value in 2011. Acquisitions of furniture total $44,000 cash, on which no depreciation is necessary because it is acquired at year-end. What is the cash inflow related to the sale of furniture?

QS 16-11
Computing financing cash outflows P3

Refer to the data in QS 16-9.

1. Assume that all common stock is issued for cash. What amount of cash dividends is paid during 2011?
2. Assume that no additional notes payable are issued in 2011. What cash amount is paid to reduce the notes payable balance in 2011?

QS 16-12[B]
Computing cash received from customers P5

Refer to the data in QS 16-9.

1. How much cash is received from sales to customers for year 2011?
2. What is the net increase or decrease in cash for year 2011?

QS 16-13[B]
Computing operating cash outflows P5

Refer to the data in QS 16-9.

1. How much cash is paid to acquire merchandise inventory during year 2011?
2. How much cash is paid for operating expenses during year 2011?

QS 16-14[B]
Computing cash from operations (direct) P5

Refer to the data in QS 16-9.
Use the direct method to prepare the cash provided or used from operating activities section only of the statement of cash flows for this company.

QS 16-15
Analyses of sources and uses of cash A1

Financial data from three competitors in the same industry follow.

1. Which of the three competitors is in the strongest position as shown by its statement of cash flows?
2. Analyze and compare the strength of Z-Best's cash flow on total assets ratio to that of Lopez.

($ thousands)	Z-Best	Lopez	Ahmed
Cash provided (used) by operating activities	$ 80,000	$ 70,000	$ (34,000)
Cash provided (used) by investing activities			
Proceeds from sale of operating assets			36,000
Purchase of operating assets	(38,000)	(35,000)	
Cash provided (used) by financing activities			
Proceeds from issuance of debt			33,000
Repayment of debt	(7,000)		
Net increase (decrease) in cash	$ 35,000	$ 35,000	$ 35,000
Average total assets	$ 800,000	$ 650,000	$ 400,000

QS 16-16[A] Noncash accounts on a spreadsheet P4

When a spreadsheet for a statement of cash flows is prepared, all changes in noncash balance sheet accounts are fully explained on the spreadsheet. Explain how these noncash balance sheet accounts are used to fully account for cash flows on a spreadsheet.

QS 16-17 Preparation of statement of cash flows (indirect) P1

Use the following financial statements and additional information to (1) prepare a statement of cash flows for the year ended December 31, 2012, using the *indirect method,* and (2) analyze and briefly discuss the statement prepared in part 1 with special attention to operating activities and to the company's cash level.

KRUG INC.
Comparative Balance Sheets
December 31, 2012 and 2011

	2012	2011
Assets		
Cash	$ 26,400	$ 30,550
Accounts receivable, net	14,050	12,150
Inventory	90,100	70,150
Equipment	49,900	44,500
Accum. depreciation—Equipment	(22,500)	(18,300)
Total assets	$157,950	$139,050
Liabilities and Equity		
Accounts payable	$ 23,350	$ 25,400
Salaries payable	1,050	600
Common stock, no par value	107,000	100,000
Retained earnings	26,550	13,050
Total liabilities and equity	$157,950	$139,050

KRUG INC.
Income Statement
For Year Ended December 31, 2012

Sales		$47,575
Cost of goods sold		(17,950)
Gross profit		29,625
Operating expenses		
Depreciation expense	$4,200	
Other expenses	8,550	
Total operating expense		12,750
Income before taxes		16,875
Income tax expense		3,375
Net income		$13,500

Additional Information

a. No dividends are declared or paid in 2012.
b. Issued additional stock for $7,000 cash in 2012.
c. Purchased equipment for cash in 2012; no equipment was sold in 2012.

QS 16-18 International cash flow disclosures C1 

Answer each of the following related to international accounting standards.

1. Which method, indirect or direct, is acceptable for reporting operating cash flows under IFRS?
2. For each of the following four cash flows, identify whether it is reported under the operating, investing, or financing section (or some combination) within the indirect format of the statement of cash flows reported under IFRS and under U.S. GAAP.

Cash Flow Source	US GAAP Reporting	IFRS Reporting
a. Interest paid		
b. Dividends paid		
c. Interest received		
d. Dividends received		

EXERCISES

Exercise 16-1
Cash flow from operations (indirect)
P2

Rasheed Company reports net income of $390,000 for the year ended December 31, 2011. It also reports $70,000 depreciation expense and a $10,000 gain on the sale of machinery. Its comparative balance sheets reveal a $30,000 increase in accounts receivable, $16,000 increase in accounts payable, $8,000 decrease in prepaid expenses, and $12,000 decrease in wages payable.

Required

Prepare only the operating activities section of the statement of cash flows for 2011 using the *indirect method.*

Exercise 16-2
Cash flow classification (indirect)
C1 

The following transactions and events occurred during the year. Assuming that this company uses the *indirect method* to report cash provided by operating activities, indicate where each item would appear on its statement of cash flows by placing an *x* in the appropriate column.

	Statement of Cash Flows			Noncash Investing and Financing Activities	Not Reported on Statement or in Notes
	Operating Activities	Investing Activities	Financing Activities		
a. Accounts receivable decreased in the year					
b. Purchased land by issuing common stock					
c. Paid cash to purchase inventory					
d. Sold equipment for cash, yielding a loss					
e. Accounts payable decreased in the year					
f. Income taxes payable increased in the year					
g. Declared and paid a cash dividend					
h. Recorded depreciation expense					
i. Paid cash to settle long-term note payable					
j. Prepaid expenses increased in the year					

Exercise 16-3[B]
Cash flow classification (direct)
C1 P5 

The following transactions and events occurred during the year. Assuming that this company uses the *direct method* to report cash provided by operating activities, indicate where each item would appear on the statement of cash flows by placing an *x* in the appropriate column.

	Statement of Cash Flows			Noncash Investing and Financing Activities	Not Reported on Statement or in Notes
	Operating Activities	Investing Activities	Financing Activities		
a. Accepted six-month note receivable in exchange for plant assets					
b. Recorded depreciation expense					
c. Paid cash to acquire treasury stock					
d. Collected cash from sales					
e. Borrowed cash from bank by signing a nine-month note payable					
f. Paid cash to purchase a patent					
g. Retired long-term notes payable by issuing common stock					
h. Paid cash toward accounts payable					
i. Sold inventory for cash					
j. Paid cash dividend that was declared in a prior period					

Exercise 16-4
Cash flows from operating activities (indirect)
P2

Roney Company's calendar-year 2011 income statement shows the following: Net Income, $364,000; Depreciation Expense, $45,000; Amortization Expense, $8,200; Gain on Sale of Plant Assets, $7,000. An examination of the company's current assets and current liabilities reveals the following changes (all from operating activities): Accounts Receivable decrease, $18,100; Merchandise Inventory decrease, $52,000; Prepaid Expenses increase, $3,700; Accounts Payable decrease, $9,200; Other Payables increase, $1,400. Use the *indirect method* to compute cash flow from operating activities.

Exercise 16-5B
Computation of cash flows (direct)
P5

For each of the following three separate cases, use the information provided about the calendar-year 2012 operations of Sahim Company to compute the required cash flow information.

Case A: Compute cash received from customers:	
Sales	$510,000
Accounts receivable, December 31, 2011	25,200
Accounts receivable, December 31, 2012	34,800
Case B: Compute cash paid for rent:	
Rent expense	$140,800
Rent payable, December 31, 2011	8,800
Rent payable, December 31, 2012	7,200
Case C: Compute cash paid for merchandise:	
Cost of goods sold	$528,000
Merchandise inventory, December 31, 2011	159,600
Accounts payable, December 31, 2011	67,800
Merchandise inventory, December 31, 2012	131,400
Accounts payable, December 31, 2012	84,000

Exercise 16-6
Cash flows from operating activities (indirect)
P2

Use the following income statement and information about changes in noncash current assets and current liabilities to prepare only the cash flows from operating activities section of the statement of cash flows using the *indirect* method.

BEKHAM COMPANY
Income Statement
For Year Ended December 31, 2011

Sales		$1,818,000
Cost of goods sold		891,000
Gross profit		927,000
Operating expenses		
Salaries expense	$248,535	
Depreciation expense	43,200	
Rent expense	48,600	
Amortization expenses—Patents	5,400	
Utilities expense	19,125	364,860
		562,140
Gain on sale of equipment		7,200
Net income		$ 569,340

Changes in current asset and current liability accounts for the year that relate to operations follow.

Accounts receivable	$40,500 increase	Accounts payable	$13,500 decrease
Merchandise inventory	27,000 increase	Salaries payable	4,500 decrease

Exercise 16-7B
Cash flows from operating activities (direct) P5

Refer to the information about Bekham Company in Exercise 16-6.
Use the *direct method* to prepare only the cash provided or used by operating activities section of the statement of cash flows for this company.

Exercise 16-8
Cash flows from investing activities
P3

Use the following information to determine this company's cash flows from investing activities.

a. Sold land costing $315,000 for $400,000 cash, yielding a gain of $15,000.
b. Paid $106,000 cash for a new truck.
c. Equipment with a book value of $80,500 and an original cost of $165,000 was sold at a loss of $34,000.
d. Long-term investments in stock were sold for $94,700 cash, yielding a gain of $15,750.

Exercise 16-9
Cash flows from financing activities
P3

Use the following information to determine this company's cash flows from financing activities.

a. Net income was $472,000.
b. Issued common stock for $75,000 cash.
c. Paid cash dividend of $13,000.
d. Paid $120,000 cash to settle a note payable at its $120,000 maturity value.
e. Paid $118,000 cash to acquire its treasury stock.
f. Purchased equipment for $92,000 cash.

Exercise 16-10
Preparation of statement of cash flows (indirect) P1 

Use the following financial statements and additional information to (1) prepare a statement of cash flows for the year ended June 30, 2011, using the *indirect method,* and (2) compute the company's cash flow on total assets ratio for its fiscal year 2011.

GECKO INC.
Income Statement
For Year Ended June 30, 2011

Sales		$668,000
Cost of goods sold		412,000
Gross profit		256,000
Operating expenses		
Depreciation expense	$58,600	
Other expenses	67,000	
Total operating expenses		125,600
		130,400
Other gains (losses)		
Gain on sale of equipment		2,000
Income before taxes		132,400
Income taxes expense		45,640
Net income		$ 86,760

GECKO INC.
Comparative Balance Sheets
June 30, 2011 and 2010

	2011	2010
Assets		
Cash	$ 85,800	$ 45,000
Accounts receivable, net	70,000	52,000
Inventory	66,800	96,800
Prepaid expenses	5,400	5,200
Equipment	130,000	120,000
Accum. depreciation—Equipment	(28,000)	(10,000)
Total assets	$330,000	$309,000
Liabilities and Equity		
Accounts payable	$ 26,000	$ 32,000
Wages payable	7,000	16,000
Income taxes payable	2,400	3,600
Notes payable (long term)	40,000	70,000
Common stock, $5 par value	230,000	180,000
Retained earnings	24,600	7,400
Total liabilities and equity	$330,000	$309,000

Additional Information

a. A $30,000 note payable is retired at its $30,000 carrying (book) value in exchange for cash.
b. The only changes affecting retained earnings are net income and cash dividends paid.
c. New equipment is acquired for $58,600 cash.
d. Received cash for the sale of equipment that had cost $48,600, yielding a $2,000 gain.
e. Prepaid Expenses and Wages Payable relate to Other Expenses on the income statement.
f. All purchases and sales of merchandise inventory are on credit.

Check (b) Cash dividends, $69,560

(d) Cash from equip. sale, $10,000

Exercise 16-11[B]
Preparation of statement of cash flows (direct)
P1

Refer to the data in Exercise 16-10.
Using the *direct method,* prepare the statement of cash flows for the year ended June 30, 2011.

Exercise 16-12[B]
Preparation of statement of cash flows (direct) and supporting note
P1

Use the following information about the cash flows of Kansas Company to prepare a complete statement of cash flows (*direct method*) for the year ended December 31, 2011. Use a note disclosure for any noncash investing and financing activities.

Cash and cash equivalents balance, December 31, 2010	$ 25,000
Cash and cash equivalents balance, December 31, 2011	70,000
Cash received as interest	2,500
Cash paid for salaries	72,500
Bonds payable retired by issuing common stock (no gain or loss on retirement)	187,500
Cash paid to retire long-term notes payable	125,000
Cash received from sale of equipment	61,250
Cash received in exchange for six-month note payable	25,000
Land purchased by issuing long-term note payable	106,250
Cash paid for store equipment	23,750
Cash dividends paid	15,000
Cash paid for other expenses	40,000
Cash received from customers	485,000
Cash paid for merchandise	252,500

Exercise 16-13[B]
Preparation of statement of cash flows (direct) from Cash T-account
P1 

The following summarized Cash T-account reflects the total debits and total credits to the Cash account of Texas Corporation for calendar year 2011.

(1) Use this information to prepare a complete statement of cash flows for year 2011. The cash provided or used by operating activities should be reported using the *direct method.*

(2) Refer to the statement of cash flows prepared for part 1 to answer the following questions *a* through *d*: (*a*) Which section—operating, investing, or financing—shows the largest cash (i) inflow and (ii) outflow? (*b*) What is the largest individual item among the investing cash outflows? (*c*) Are the cash proceeds larger from issuing notes or issuing stock? (*d*) Does the company have a net cash inflow or outflow from borrowing activities?

Accounting System:
File Edit Maintain Tasks Analysis Options Reports Window Help

Cash			
Balance, Dec. 31, 2010	135,200		
Receipts from customers	6,000,000	Payments for merchandise	1,590,000
Receipts from dividends	208,400	Payments for wages	550,000
Receipts from land sale	220,000	Payments for rent	320,000
Receipts from machinery sale	710,000	Payments for interest	218,000
Receipts from issuing stock	1,540,000	Payments for taxes	450,000
Receipts from borrowing	2,600,000	Payments for machinery	2,236,000
		Payments for long-term investments	2,260,000
		Payments for note payable	386,000
		Payments for dividends	500,000
		Payments for treasury stock	218,000
Balance, Dec. 31, 2011	$?		

Sales Purchases General Ledger Payroll Inventory Company Analysis

Exercise 16-14
Reporting cash flows from operations (indirect)
P2

Harold Company reports the following information for its recent calendar year.

Sales	$70,000
Expenses	
Cost of goods sold	40,000
Salaries expense	12,000
Depreciation expense	6,000
Net income	$12,000
Accounts receivable increase	$ 9,000
Inventory decrease	3,000
Salaries payable increase	800

Required

Prepare the operating activities section of the statement of cash flows for Harold Company using the indirect method.

Exercise 16-15
Reporting and interpreting cash flows from operations (indirect)
P2 

Oregon Company disclosed the following information for its recent calendar year.

Revenues	$100,000
Expenses	
Salaries expense	68,000
Utilities expense	28,000
Depreciation expense	29,200
Other expenses	6,800
Net loss	$ (32,000)
Accounts receivable decrease	$ 28,000
Purchased a machine	20,000
Salaries payable increase	26,000
Other accrued liabilities decrease	16,000

Required

1. Prepare the operating activities section of the statement of cash flows using the indirect method.
2. What were the major reasons that this company was able to report a net loss but positive cash flow from operations?
3. Of the potential causes of differences between cash flow from operations and net income, which are the most important to investors?

Exercise 16-16
Analyses of cash flow on total assets A1

A company reported average total assets of $248,000 in 2010 and $302,000 in 2011. Its net operating cash flow in 2010 was $20,575 and $27,750 in 2011. Calculate its cash flow on total assets ratio for both years. Comment on the results and any change in performance.

Exercise 16-17
Cash flows spreadsheet (indirect method)
P4

Complete the following spreadsheet in preparation of the statement of cash flows. (The statement of cash flows is not required.) Prepare the spreadsheet as in Exhibit 16A.1; report operating activities under the indirect method. Identify the debits and credits in the Analysis of Changes columns with letters that correspond to the following transactions *a* through *e*.

a. Net income for the year was $30,000.
b. Dividends of $10,000 cash were declared and paid.
c. Stylish's only noncash expense was $50,000 of depreciation.
d. The company purchased plant assets for $70,000 cash.
e. Notes payable of $40,000 were issued for $40,000 cash.

		STYLISH CORPORATION Spreadsheet for Statement of Cash Flows—Indirect Method For Year Ended December 31, 2011			
		Dec. 31, 2010	Analysis of Changes		Dec. 31, 2011
			Debit	Credit	
8	**Balance Sheet—Debit Bal. Accounts**				
9	Cash	$ 70,000			$ 60,000
10	Accounts receivable	180,000			190,000
11	Merchandise inventory	200,000			230,000
12	Plant assets	500,000			570,000
13		$950,000			$1,050,000
15	**Balance Sheet—Credit Bal. Accounts**				
16	Accumulated depreciation	$100,000			$ 150,000
17	Accounts payable	170,000			160,000
18	Notes payable	350,000			390,000
19	Common stock	200,000			200,000
20	Retained earnings	130,000			150,000
21		$950,000			$1,050,000
23	**Statement of Cash Flows**				
24	Operating activities				
25	Net income				
26	Increase in accounts receivable				
27	Increase in merchandise inventory				
28	Decrease in accounts payable				
29	Depreciation expense				
30	Investing activities				
31	Cash paid to purchase plant assets				
32	Financing activities				
33	Cash paid for dividends				
34	Cash received from note payable				

Exercise 16-18
Statement of cash flows under IFRS (indirect)
P1

Peugeot S.A. reports the following financial information for the year ended December 31, 2008 (euros in millions). Prepare its statement of cash flows under the indirect method.

Net loss	€ 500	Cash from sales of treasury stock and other	€ 812
Depreciation and amortization	3,679	Cash paid for dividends	361
Gains on disposals and other	(362)	Cash from disposal of plant assets and intangibles	88
Net increase in current assets	(417)	Cash paid for plant assets and intangibles	(3,331)
Net decrease in current liabilities	(2,338)	Cash and cash equivalents, December 31, 2007	5,937

connect

PROBLEM SET A

Problem 16-1A
Statement of cash flows (indirect method)
A1 P1 P2 P3

Kazaam Company, a merchandiser, recently completed its calendar-year 2011 operations. For the year, (1) all sales are credit sales, (2) all credits to Accounts Receivable reflect cash receipts from customers, (3) all purchases of inventory are on credit, (4) all debits to Accounts Payable reflect cash payments for inventory, and (5) Other Expenses are paid in advance and are initially debited to Prepaid Expenses. The company's balance sheets and income statement follow.

KAZAAM COMPANY
Comparative Balance Sheets
December 31, 2011 and 2010

	2011	2010
Assets		
Cash	$ 53,875	$ 76,625
Accounts receivable	65,000	49,625
Merchandise inventory	273,750	252,500
Prepaid expenses	5,375	6,250
Equipment	159,500	110,000
Accum. depreciation—Equipment	(34,625)	(44,000)
Total assets	$522,875	$451,000
Liabilities and Equity		
Accounts payable	$ 88,125	$116,625
Short-term notes payable	10,000	6,250
Long-term notes payable	93,750	53,750
Common stock, $5 par value	168,750	156,250
Paid-in capital in excess of par, common stock	32,500	0
Retained earnings	129,750	118,125
Total liabilities and equity	$522,875	$451,000

KAZAAM COMPANY
Income Statement
For Year Ended December 31, 2011

Sales		$496,250
Cost of goods sold		250,000
Gross profit		246,250
Operating expenses		
Depreciation expense	$ 18,750	
Other expenses	136,500	155,250
Other gains (losses)		
Loss on sale of equipment		5,125
Income before taxes		85,875
Income taxes expense		12,125
Net income		$ 73,750

Additional Information on Year 2011 Transactions

a. The loss on the cash sale of equipment was $5,125 (details in *b*).

b. Sold equipment costing $46,875, with accumulated depreciation of $28,125, for $13,625 cash.

c. Purchased equipment costing $96,375 by paying $25,000 cash and signing a long-term note payable for the balance.

d. Borrowed $3,750 cash by signing a short-term note payable.

e. Paid $31,375 cash to reduce the long-term notes payable.

f. Issued 2,500 shares of common stock for $18 cash per share.

g. Declared and paid cash dividends of $62,125.

Required

Check Cash from operating activities, $33,375

1. Prepare a complete statement of cash flows; report its operating activities using the *indirect method.* Disclose any noncash investing and financing activities in a note.

Analysis Component

2. Analyze and discuss the statement of cash flows prepared in part 1, giving special attention to the wisdom of the cash dividend payment.

Problem 16-2A[B]
Statement of cash flows (direct method) P1 P3 P5

Check Cash used in financing activities, $(44,750)

Refer to Kazaam Company's financial statements and related information in Problem 16-1A.

Required

Prepare a complete statement of cash flows; report its operating activities according to the *direct method.* Disclose any noncash investing and financing activities in a note.

Problem 16-3A[A]
Cash flows spreadsheet (indirect method)
P1 P2 P3 P4

Refer to the information reported about Kazaam Company in Problem 16-1A.

Required

Prepare a complete statement of cash flows using a spreadsheet as in Exhibit 16A.1; report its operating activities using the indirect method. Identify the debits and credits in the Analysis of Changes columns with letters that correspond to the following list of transactions and events.

a. Net income was $73,750.

b. Accounts receivable increased.

c. Merchandise inventory increased.

d. Prepaid expenses decreased.
e. Accounts payable decreased.
f. Depreciation expense was $18,750.
g. Sold equipment costing $46,875, with accumulated depreciation of $28,125, for $13,625 cash. This yielded a loss of $5,125.
h. Purchased equipment costing $96,375 by paying $25,000 cash and **(i.)** by signing a long-term note payable for the balance.
j. Borrowed $3,750 cash by signing a short-term note payable.
k. Paid $31,375 cash to reduce the long-term notes payable.
l. Issued 2,500 shares of common stock for $18 cash per share.
m. Declared and paid cash dividends of $62,125.

Check Analysis of Changes column totals, $515,375

Problem 16-4A
Statement of cash flows (indirect method)
P1 P2 P3

mhhe.com/wildFAP20e

Galley Corp., a merchandiser, recently completed its 2011 operations. For the year, (1) all sales are credit sales, (2) all credits to Accounts Receivable reflect cash receipts from customers, (3) all purchases of inventory are on credit, (4) all debits to Accounts Payable reflect cash payments for inventory, (5) Other Expenses are all cash expenses, and (6) any change in Income Taxes Payable reflects the accrual and cash payment of taxes. The company's balance sheets and income statement follow.

GALLEY CORPORATION
Comparative Balance Sheets
December 31, 2011 and 2010

	2011	2010
Assets		
Cash	$ 174,000	$117,000
Accounts receivable	93,000	81,000
Merchandise inventory	609,000	534,000
Equipment	333,000	297,000
Accum. depreciation—Equipment	(156,000)	(102,000)
Total assets	$1,053,000	$927,000
Liabilities and Equity		
Accounts payable	$ 69,000	$ 96,000
Income taxes payable	27,000	24,000
Common stock, $2 par value	582,000	558,000
Paid-in capital in excess of par value, common stock	198,000	162,000
Retained earnings	177,000	87,000
Total liabilities and equity	$1,053,000	$927,000

GALLEY CORPORATION
Income Statement
For Year Ended December 31, 2011

Sales		$1,992,000
Cost of goods sold		1,194,000
Gross profit		798,000
Operating expenses		
Depreciation expense	$ 54,000	
Other expenses	501,000	555,000
Income before taxes		243,000
Income taxes expense		42,000
Net income		$ 201,000

Additional Information on Year 2011 Transactions

a. Purchased equipment for $36,000 cash.
b. Issued 12,000 shares of common stock for $5 cash per share.
c. Declared and paid $111,000 in cash dividends.

Required

Prepare a complete statement of cash flows; report its cash inflows and cash outflows from operating activities according to the *indirect method.*

Check Cash from operating activities, $144,000

Problem 16-5A[B]
Statement of cash flows (direct method) P1 P3 P5

mhhe.com/wildFAP20e

Refer to Galley Corporation's financial statements and related information in Problem 16-4A.

Required

Prepare a complete statement of cash flows; report its cash flows from operating activities according to the *direct method.*

Check Cash used in financing activities, $(51,000)

Problem 16-6A[A]
Cash flows spreadsheet (indirect method)
P1 P2 P3 P4

mhhe.com/wildFAP20e

Refer to the information reported about Galley Corporation in Problem 16-4A.

Required

Prepare a complete statement of cash flows using a spreadsheet as in Exhibit 16A.1; report operating activities under the indirect method. Identify the debits and credits in the Analysis of Changes columns with letters that correspond to the following list of transactions and events.

a. Net income was $201,000.
b. Accounts receivable increased.
c. Merchandise inventory increased.
d. Accounts payable decreased.
e. Income taxes payable increased.
f. Depreciation expense was $54,000.
g. Purchased equipment for $36,000 cash.
h. Issued 12,000 shares at $5 cash per share.
i. Declared and paid $111,000 of cash dividends.

Check Analysis of Changes column totals, $579,000

Problem 16-7A
Computing cash flows from operations (indirect)
P2

Rapture Company's 2011 income statement and selected balance sheet data at December 31, 2010 and 2011, follow ($ thousands).

RAPTURE COMPANY
Income Statement
For Year Ended December 31, 2011

Sales revenue	$58,600
Expenses	
Cost of goods sold	21,000
Depreciation expense	6,000
Salaries expense	11,000
Rent expense	2,500
Insurance expense	1,900
Interest expense	1,800
Utilities expense	1,400
Net income	$13,000

RAPTURE COMPANY
Selected Balance Sheet Accounts

At December 31	2011	2010
Accounts receivable	$380	$390
Inventory	99	77
Accounts payable	120	130
Salaries payable	44	35
Utilities payable	11	8
Prepaid insurance	13	14
Prepaid rent	11	9

Required

Prepare the cash flows from operating activities section only of the company's 2011 statement of cash flows using the indirect method.

Check Cash from operating activities, $18,989

Problem 16-8A[B]
Computing cash flows from operations (direct)
P5

Refer to the information in Problem 16-7A.

Required

Prepare the cash flows from operating activities section only of the company's 2011 statement of cash flows using the direct method.

PROBLEM SET B

Problem 16-1B
Statement of cash flows (indirect method)
A1 P1 P2 P3

Kite Corporation, a merchandiser, recently completed its calendar-year 2011 operations. For the year, (1) all sales are credit sales, (2) all credits to Accounts Receivable reflect cash receipts from customers, (3) all purchases of inventory are on credit, (4) all debits to Accounts Payable reflect cash payments for inventory, and (5) Other Expenses are paid in advance and are initially debited to Prepaid Expenses. The company's balance sheets and income statement follow.

KITE CORPORATION
Comparative Balance Sheets
December 31, 2011 and 2010

	2011	2010
Assets		
Cash	$136,500	$ 71,550
Accounts receivable	74,100	90,750
Merchandise inventory	454,500	490,200
Prepaid expenses	17,100	19,200
Equipment	278,250	216,000
Accum. depreciation—Equipment	(108,750)	(93,000)
Total assets	$851,700	$794,700
Liabilities and Equity		
Accounts payable	$117,450	$123,450
Short-term notes payable	17,250	11,250
Long-term notes payable	112,500	82,500
Common stock, $5 par	465,000	450,000
Paid-in capital in excess of par, common stock	18,000	0
Retained earnings	121,500	127,500
Total liabilities and equity	$851,700	$794,700

KITE CORPORATION
Income Statement
For Year Ended December 31, 2011

Sales		$1,083,000
Cost of goods sold		585,000
Gross profit		498,000
Operating expenses		
Depreciation expense	$ 36,600	
Other expenses	392,850	
Total operating expenses		429,450
		68,550
Other gains (losses)		
Loss on sale of equipment		2,100
Income before taxes		66,450
Income taxes expense		9,450
Net income		$ 57,000

Additional Information on Year 2011 Transactions

a. The loss on the cash sale of equipment was $2,100 (details in *b*).

b. Sold equipment costing $51,000, with accumulated depreciation of $20,850, for $28,050 cash.

c. Purchased equipment costing $113,250 by paying $38,250 cash and signing a long-term note payable for the balance.

d. Borrowed $6,000 cash by signing a short-term note payable.

e. Paid $45,000 cash to reduce the long-term notes payable.

f. Issued 3,000 shares of common stock for $11 cash per share.

g. Declared and paid cash dividends of $63,000.

Required

1. Prepare a complete statement of cash flows; report its operating activities using the *indirect method.* Disclose any noncash investing and financing activities in a note.

Check Cash from operating activities, $144,150

Analysis Component

2. Analyze and discuss the statement of cash flows prepared in part 1, giving special attention to the wisdom of the cash dividend payment.

Problem 16-2B[B]
Statement of cash flows (direct method) P1 P3 P5

Refer to Kite Corporation's financial statements and related information in Problem 16-1B.

Required

Prepare a complete statement of cash flows; report its operating activities according to the *direct method.* Disclose any noncash investing and financing activities in a note.

Check Cash used in financing activities, $(69,000)

Problem 16-3B[A]
Cash flows spreadsheet (indirect method)
P1 P2 P3 P4

Refer to the information reported about Kite Corporation in Problem 16-1B.

Required

Prepare a complete statement of cash flows using a spreadsheet as in Exhibit 16A.1; report its operating activities using the *indirect method.* Identify the debits and credits in the Analysis of Changes columns with letters that correspond to the following list of transactions and events.

a. Net income was $57,000.
b. Accounts receivable decreased.
c. Merchandise inventory decreased.
d. Prepaid expenses decreased.
e. Accounts payable decreased.
f. Depreciation expense was $36,600.
g. Sold equipment costing $51,000, with accumulated depreciation of $20,850, for $28,050 cash. This yielded a loss of $2,100.
h. Purchased equipment costing $113,250 by paying $38,250 cash and **(i.)** by signing a long-term note payable for the balance.
j. Borrowed $6,000 cash by signing a short-term note payable.
k. Paid $45,000 cash to reduce the long-term notes payable.
l. Issued 3,000 shares of common stock for $11 cash per share.
m. Declared and paid cash dividends of $63,000.

Check Analysis of Changes column totals, $540,300

Problem 16-4B
Statement of cash flows (indirect method)
P1 P2 P3

Taurasi Company, a merchandiser, recently completed its 2011 operations. For the year, (1) all sales are credit sales, (2) all credits to Accounts Receivable reflect cash receipts from customers, (3) all purchases of inventory are on credit, (4) all debits to Accounts Payable reflect cash payments for inventory, (5) Other Expenses are cash expenses, and (6) any change in Income Taxes Payable reflects the accrual and cash payment of taxes. The company's balance sheets and income statement follow.

TAURASI COMPANY
Comparative Balance Sheets
December 31, 2011 and 2010

	2011	2010
Assets		
Cash	$ 53,925	$ 31,800
Accounts receivable	19,425	23,250
Merchandise inventory	175,350	139,875
Equipment	105,450	76,500
Accum. depreciation—Equipment	(48,300)	(30,600)
Total assets	$305,850	$240,825
Liabilities and Equity		
Accounts payable	$ 38,475	$ 35,625
Income taxes payable	4,500	6,750
Common stock, $2 par value	165,000	150,000
Paid-in capital in excess of par, common stock	42,000	15,000
Retained earnings	55,875	33,450
Total liabilities and equity	$305,850	$240,825

TAURASI COMPANY
Income Statement
For Year Ended December 31, 2011

Sales		$609,750
Cost of goods sold		279,000
Gross profit		330,750
Operating expenses		
Depreciation expense	$ 17,700	
Other expenses	179,775	197,475
Income before taxes		133,275
Income taxes expense		44,850
Net income		$ 88,425

Additional Information on Year 2011 Transactions

a. Purchased equipment for $28,950 cash.
b. Issued 3,000 shares of common stock for $14 cash per share.
c. Declared and paid $66,000 of cash dividends.

Required

Prepare a complete statement of cash flows; report its cash inflows and cash outflows from operating activities according to the *indirect method.*

Check Cash from operating activities, $75,075

Problem 16-5B[B]
Statement of cash flows (direct method) P1 P3 P5

Refer to Taurasi Company's financial statements and related information in Problem 16-4B.

Required

Prepare a complete statement of cash flows; report its cash flows from operating activities according to the *direct method.*

Check Cash used by financing activities, $(24,000)

Problem 16-6B^A
Cash flows spreadsheet (indirect method)
P1 P2 P3 P4

Refer to the information reported about Taurasi Company in Problem 16-4B.

Required

Prepare a complete statement of cash flows using a spreadsheet as in Exhibit 16A.1; report operating activities under the *indirect method.* Identify the debits and credits in the Analysis of Changes columns with letters that correspond to the following list of transactions and events.

a. Net income was $88,425.
b. Accounts receivable decreased.
c. Merchandise inventory increased.
d. Accounts payable increased.
e. Income taxes payable decreased.
f. Depreciation expense was $17,700.
g. Purchased equipment for $28,950 cash.
h. Issued 3,000 shares at $14 cash per share.
i. Declared and paid $66,000 of cash dividends.

Check Analysis of Changes column totals, $287,475

Problem 16-7B
Computing cash flows from operations (indirect)
P2

Tyra Company's 2011 income statement and selected balance sheet data at December 31, 2010 and 2011, follow ($ thousands).

TYRA COMPANY
Income Statement
For Year Ended December 31, 2011

Sales revenue	$412,000
Expenses	
Cost of goods sold	244,000
Depreciation expense	64,000
Salaries expense	30,000
Rent expense	20,000
Insurance expense	5,200
Interest expense	4,800
Utilities expense	4,000
Net income	$ 40,000

TYRA COMPANY
Selected Balance Sheet Accounts

At December 31	2011	2010
Accounts receivable	$820	$700
Inventory	272	296
Accounts payable	480	520
Salaries payable	280	220
Utilities payable	40	0
Prepaid insurance	28	36
Prepaid rent	40	60

Required

Prepare the cash flows from operating activities section only of the company's 2011 statement of cash flows using the indirect method.

Check Cash from operating activities, $103,992

Problem 16-8B^B
Computing cash flows from operations (direct)
P5

Refer to the information in Problem 16-7B.

Required

Prepare the cash flows from operating activities section only of the company's 2011 statement of cash flows using the direct method.

SERIAL PROBLEM
Business Solutions
P1 P2 P3

(This serial problem began in Chapter 1 and continues through most of the book. If previous chapter segments were not completed, the serial problem can begin at this point. It is helpful, but not necessary, to use the Working Papers that accompany the book.)

SP 16 Santana Rey, owner of Business Solutions, decides to prepare a statement of cash flows for her business. (Although the serial problem allowed for various ownership changes in earlier chapters, we will prepare the statement of cash flows using the following financial data.)

BUSINESS SOLUTIONS
Income Statement
For Three Months Ended March 31, 2012

Computer services revenue		$25,307
Net sales		18,693
Total revenue		44,000
Cost of goods sold	$14,052	
Depreciation expense—Office equipment	400	
Depreciation expense—Computer equipment	1,250	
Wages expense	3,250	
Insurance expense	555	
Rent expense	2,475	
Computer supplies expense	1,305	
Advertising expense	600	
Mileage expense	320	
Repairs expense—Computer	960	
Total expenses		25,167
Net income		$18,833

BUSINESS SOLUTIONS
Comparative Balance Sheets
December 31, 2011, and March 31, 2012

	2012	2011
Assets		
Cash	$ 68,057	$48,372
Accounts receivable	22,867	5,668
Merchandise inventory	704	0
Computer supplies	2,005	580
Prepaid insurance	1,110	1,665
Prepaid rent	825	825
Office equipment	8,000	8,000
Accumulated depreciation—Office equipment	(800)	(400)
Computer equipment	20,000	20,000
Accumulated depreciation—Computer equipment	(2,500)	(1,250)
Total assets	$120,268	$83,460
Liabilities and Equity		
Accounts payable	$ 0	$ 1,100
Wages payable	875	500
Unearned computer service revenue	0	1,500
Common stock	98,000	73,000
Retained earnings	21,393	7,360
Total liabilities and equity	$120,268	$83,460

Required

Prepare a statement of cash flows for Business Solutions using the *indirect method* for the three months ended March 31, 2012. Recall that the owner Santana Rey contributed $25,000 to the business in exchange for additional stock in the first quarter of 2012 and has received $4,800 in cash dividends.

Check Cash flows used by operations: $(515)

Beyond the Numbers

REPORTING IN ACTION
A1 
RIM

BTN 16-1 Refer to Research In Motion's financial statements in Appendix A to answer the following.

1. Is Research In Motion's statement of cash flows prepared under the direct method or the indirect method? How do you know?
2. For each fiscal year 2010, 2009, and 2008, is the amount of cash provided by operating activities more or less than the cash paid for dividends?
3. What is the largest amount in reconciling the difference between net income and cash flow from operating activities in 2010? In 2009? In 2008?
4. Identify the largest cash inflow and outflow for investing *and* for financing activities in 2010 and in 2009.

Fast Forward

5. Obtain Research In Motion's financial statements for a fiscal year ending after February 27, 2010, from either its Website (RIM.com) or the SEC's database (www.SEC.gov). Since February 27, 2010, what are Research In Motion's largest cash outflows and cash inflows in the investing and in the financing sections of its statement of cash flows?

COMPARATIVE ANALYSIS

A1

BTN 16-2 Key figures for Research In Motion and Apple follow.

RIM

Apple

($ millions)	Research In Motion Current Year	1 Year Prior	2 Years Prior	Apple Current Year	1 Year Prior	2 Years Prior
Operating cash flows	$ 3,035	$1,452	$1,577	$10,159	$ 9,596	$ 5,470
Total assets	10,204	8,101	5,511	47,501	36,171	25,347

Required

1. Compute the recent two years' cash flow on total assets ratios for Research In Motion and Apple.
2. What does the cash flow on total assets ratio measure?
3. Which company has the highest cash flow on total assets ratio for the periods shown?
4. Does the cash flow on total assets ratio reflect on the quality of earnings? Explain.

ETHICS CHALLENGE

C1 A1

BTN 16-3 Lisa Gish is preparing for a meeting with her banker. Her business is finishing its fourth year of operations. In the first year, it had negative cash flows from operations. In the second and third years, cash flows from operations were positive. However, inventory costs rose significantly in year 4, and cash flows from operations will probably be down 25%. Gish wants to secure a line of credit from her banker as a financing buffer. From experience, she knows the banker will scrutinize operating cash flows for years 1 through 4 and will want a projected number for year 5. Gish knows that a steady progression upward in operating cash flows for years 1 through 4 will help her case. She decides to use her discretion as owner and considers several business actions that will turn her operating cash flow in year 4 from a decrease to an increase.

Required

1. Identify two business actions Gish might take to improve cash flows from operations.
2. Comment on the ethics and possible consequences of Gish's decision to pursue these actions.

COMMUNICATING IN PRACTICE

C1

BTN 16-4 Your friend, Jessica Willard, recently completed the second year of her business and just received annual financial statements from her accountant. Willard finds the income statement and balance sheet informative but does not understand the statement of cash flows. She says the first section is especially confusing because it contains a lot of additions and subtractions that do not make sense to her. Willard adds, "The income statement tells me the business is more profitable than last year and that's most important. If I want to know how cash changes, I can look at comparative balance sheets."

Required

Write a half-page memorandum to your friend explaining the purpose of the statement of cash flows. Speculate as to why the first section is so confusing and how it might be rectified.

TAKING IT TO THE NET

A1

BTN 16-5 Access the March 19, 2010, filing of the 10-K report (for fiscal year ending January 30, 2010) of J. Crew Group, Inc. (ticker JCG), at www.SEC.gov.

Required

1. Does J. Crew use the direct or indirect method to construct its consolidated statement of cash flows?
2. For the fiscal year ended January 30, 2010, what is the largest item in reconciling the net income to net cash provided by operating activities?
3. In the recent three years, has the company been more successful in generating operating cash flows or in generating net income? Identify the figures to support the answer.
4. In the year ended January 30, 2010, what was the largest cash outflow for investing activities *and* for financing activities?
5. What item(s) does J. Crew report as supplementary cash flow information?
6. Does J. Crew report any noncash financing activities for fiscal year 2010? Identify them, if any.

TEAMWORK IN ACTION

C1 A1 P2 P5

BTN 16-6 Team members are to coordinate and independently answer one question within each of the following three sections. Team members should then report to the team and confirm or correct teammates' answers.

1. Answer *one* of the following questions about the statement of cash flows.
   a. What are this statement's reporting objectives?
   b. What two methods are used to prepare it? Identify similarities and differences between them.
   c. What steps are followed to prepare the statement?
   d. What types of analyses are often made from this statement's information?

2. Identify and explain the adjustment from net income to obtain cash flows from operating activities using the indirect method for *one* of the following items.
   a. Noncash operating revenues and expenses.
   b. Nonoperating gains and losses.
   c. Increases and decreases in noncash current assets.
   d. Increases and decreases in current liabilities.

3.[B] Identify and explain the formula for computing cash flows from operating activities using the direct method for *one* of the following items.
   a. Cash receipts from sales to customers.
   b. Cash paid for merchandise inventory.
   c. Cash paid for wages and operating expenses.
   d. Cash paid for interest and taxes.

Note: For teams of more than four, some pairing within teams is necessary. Use as an in-class activity or as an assignment. If used in class, specify a time limit on each part. Conclude with reports to the entire class, using team rotation. Each team can prepare responses on a transparency.

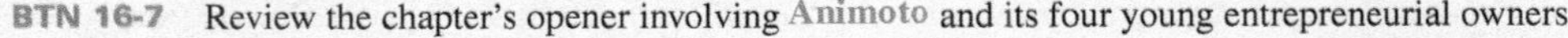

ENTREPRENEURIAL DECISION

C1 A1  

BTN 16-7 Review the chapter's opener involving Animoto and its four young entrepreneurial owners.

Required

1. In a business such as Animoto, monitoring cash flow is always a priority. Even though Animoto now has thousands in annual sales and earns a positive net income, explain how cash flow can lag behind earnings.

2. Animoto is a closely held corporation. What are potential sources of financing for its future expansion?

C1 A1  

BTN 16-8 Jenna and Matt Wilder are completing their second year operating Mountain High, a downhill ski area and resort. Mountain High reports a net loss of $(10,000) for its second year, which includes an $85,000 extraordinary loss from fire. This past year also involved major purchases of plant assets for renovation and expansion, yielding a year-end total asset amount of $800,000. Mountain High's net cash outflow for its second year is $(5,000); a summarized version of its statement of cash flows follows:

Net cash flow provided by operating activities	$295,000
Net cash flow used by investing activities	(310,000)
Net cash flow provided by financing activities	10,000

Required

Write a one-page memorandum to the Wilders evaluating Mountain High's current performance and assessing its future. Give special emphasis to cash flow data and their interpretation.

HITTING THE ROAD

C1

BTN 16-9 Visit The Motley Fool's Website (Fool.com). Enter the *Fool's School* (at *Fool.com/School*). Identify and select the link *How to Value Stocks*.

Required

1. Click on *Introduction to Valuation Methods,* and then *Cash-Flow-Based Valuations.* How does the Fool's school define cash flow? What is the school's reasoning for this definition?

2. Per the school's instruction, why do analysts focus on earnings before interest and taxes (EBIT)?

3. Visit other links at this Website that interest you such as "How to Read a Balance Sheet," or find out what the "Fool's Ratio" is. Write a half-page report on what you find.

BTN 16-10 Key comparative information for Nokia (www.Nokia.com), which is a leading global manufacturer of mobile devices and services, follows (in EUR).

GLOBAL DECISION

C1

NOKIA

RIM

Apple

(Euro millions)	Current Year	1 Year Prior	2 Years Prior
Operating cash flows	3,247	3,197	7,882
Total assets	35,738	39,582	37,599

Required

1. Compute the recent two years' cash flow on total assets ratio for Nokia.
2. How does Nokia's ratio compare to Research In Motion's and Apple's ratios from BTN 16-2?

ANSWERS TO MULTIPLE CHOICE QUIZ

1. b;

Net income	$15,200
Depreciation expense	10,000
Gain on sale of land	(3,000)
Increase in inventory	(1,500)
Increase in accounts payable	2,850
Net cash provided by operations	$23,550

2. c; cash received from sale of machine is reported as an investing activity.
3. d; FASB requires cash interest paid to be reported under operating.
4. a; Cash paid for salaries and wages = $255,000 + $8,200 − $10,900 = $252,300
5. e; Increase in inventory = $112,000 − $105,000 = $7,000
   Increase in accounts payable = $101,300 − $98,500 = $2,800
   Cash paid for merchandise = $545,000 + $7,000 − $2,800 = $549,200

Analysis of Financial Statements

A Look Back

Chapter 16 focused on reporting and analyzing cash inflows and cash outflows. We explained how to prepare, analyze, and interpret the statement of cash flows.

A Look at This Chapter

This chapter emphasizes the analysis and interpretation of financial statement information. We learn to apply horizontal, vertical, and ratio analyses to better understand company performance and financial condition.

A Look Ahead

Chapter 18 introduces us to managerial accounting. We discuss its purposes, concepts, and roles in helping managers gather and organize information for decisions. We also explain basic management principles.

Learning Objectives

CAP

CONCEPTUAL

C1 Explain the purpose and identify the building blocks of analysis. (p. 686)

C2 Describe standards for comparisons in analysis. (p. 688)

ANALYTICAL

A1 Summarize and report results of analysis. (p. 706)

A2 *Appendix 17A*—Explain the form and assess the content of a complete income statement. (p. 710)

LP17

PROCEDURAL

P1 Explain and apply methods of horizontal analysis. (p. 688)

P2 Describe and apply methods of vertical analysis. (p. 693)

P3 Define and apply ratio analysis. (p. 696)

Decision Insight

Motley Fool

"What goes on at The Motley Fool . . . is similar to what goes on in a library"

—**TOM GARDNER** (DAVID GARDNER ON LEFT)

ALEXANDRIA, VA—In Shakespeare's Elizabethan comedy *As You Like It,* only the fool could speak truthfully to the King without getting his head lopped off. Inspired by Shakespeare's stage character, Tom and David Gardner vowed to become modern-day fools who tell it like it is. With under $10,000 in start-up money, the brothers launched **The Motley Fool (Fool.com).** And befitting of a Shakespearean play, the two say they are "dedicated to educating, amusing, and enriching individuals in search of the truth."

The Gardners do not fear the wrath of any King, real or fictional. They are intent on exposing the truth, as they see it, "that the financial world preys on ignorance and fear." As Tom explains, "There is such a great need in the general populace for financial information." Who can argue, given their brilliant success through practically every medium, including their Website, radio shows, newspaper columns, online store, investment newsletters, and global expansion.

Despite the brothers' best efforts, however, ordinary people still do not fully use information contained in financial statements. For instance, discussions keep appearing on The Motley Fool's online bulletin board that can be easily resolved using reliable and available accounting data. So, it would seem that the Fools must continue their work of "educating and enriching" individuals and showing them the advantages of financial statement analysis.

Following The Motley Fool's objectives, this chapter introduces horizontal and vertical analyses—tools used to reveal crucial trends and insights from financial information. It also expands on ratio analysis, which gives insight into a company's financial condition and performance. By arming ourselves with the information contained in this chapter and the investment advice of The Motley Fool, *we* can be sure to not play the fool in today's financial world.

[Sources: *Motley Fool Website,* January 2011; *Entrepreneur,* July 1997; *What to Do with Your Money Now,* June 2002; *USA Weekend,* July 2004; *Washington Post,* November 2007; *Money after 40,* April 2007]

Chapter Preview

This chapter shows how we use financial statements to evaluate a company's financial performance and condition. We explain financial statement analysis, its basic building blocks, the information available, standards for comparisons, and tools of analysis. Three major analysis tools are presented: horizontal analysis, vertical analysis, and ratio analysis. We apply each of these tools using Research In Motion's financial statements, and we introduce comparative analysis using Apple and Nokia (and sometimes Palm). This chapter expands and organizes the ratio analyses introduced at the end of each chapter.

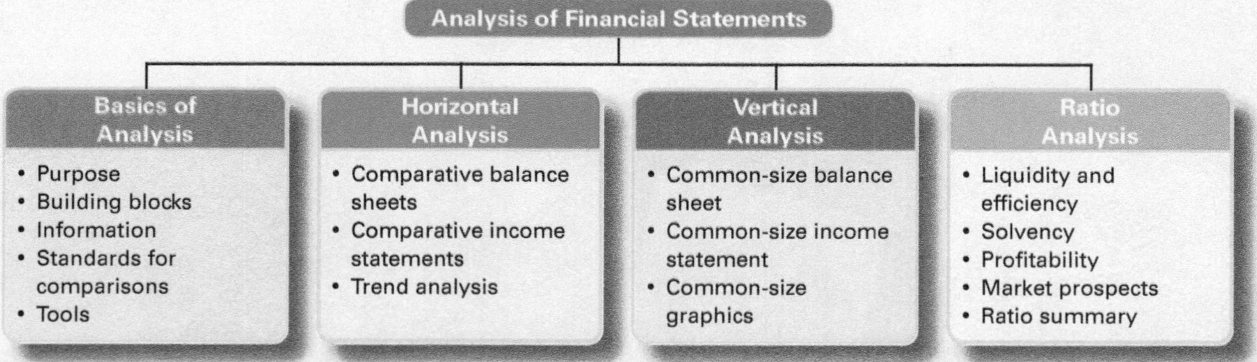

BASICS OF ANALYSIS

C1 Explain the purpose and identify the building blocks of analysis.

Financial statement analysis applies analytical tools to general-purpose financial statements and related data for making business decisions. It involves transforming accounting data into more useful information. Financial statement analysis reduces our reliance on hunches, guesses, and intuition as well as our uncertainty in decision making. It does not lessen the need for expert judgment; instead, it provides us an effective and systematic basis for making business decisions. This section describes the purpose of financial statement analysis, its information sources, the use of comparisons, and some issues in computations.

Purpose of Analysis

Internal users of accounting information are those involved in strategically managing and operating the company. They include managers, officers, internal auditors, consultants, budget directors, and market researchers. The purpose of financial statement analysis for these users is to provide strategic information to improve company efficiency and effectiveness in providing products and services.

External users of accounting information are *not* directly involved in running the company. They include shareholders, lenders, directors, customers, suppliers, regulators, lawyers, brokers, and the press. External users rely on financial statement analysis to make better and more informed decisions in pursuing their own goals.

Point: Financial statement analysis tools are also used for personal financial investment decisions.

We can identify other uses of financial statement analysis. Shareholders and creditors assess company prospects to make investing and lending decisions. A board of directors analyzes financial statements in monitoring management's decisions. Employees and unions use financial statements in labor negotiations. Suppliers use financial statement information in establishing credit terms. Customers analyze financial statements in deciding whether to establish supply relationships. Public utilities set customer rates by analyzing financial statements. Auditors use financial statements in assessing the "fair presentation" of their clients' financial results. Analyst services such as Dun & Bradstreet, Moody's, and Standard & Poor's use financial statements in making buy-sell recommendations and in setting credit ratings. The common goal of these users is to evaluate company performance and financial condition. This includes evaluating (1) past and current performance, (2) current financial position, and (3) future performance and risk.

Point: Financial statement analysis is a topic on the CPA, CMA, CIA, and CFA exams.

Building Blocks of Analysis

Financial statement analysis focuses on one or more elements of a company's financial condition or performance. Our analysis emphasizes four areas of inquiry—with varying degrees of importance. These four areas are described and illustrated in this chapter and are considered the *building blocks* of financial statement analysis:

- **Liquidity** and **efficiency**—ability to meet short-term obligations and to efficiently generate revenues.
- **Solvency**—ability to generate future revenues and meet long-term obligations.
- **Profitability**—ability to provide financial rewards sufficient to attract and retain financing.
- **Market prospects**—ability to generate positive market expectations.

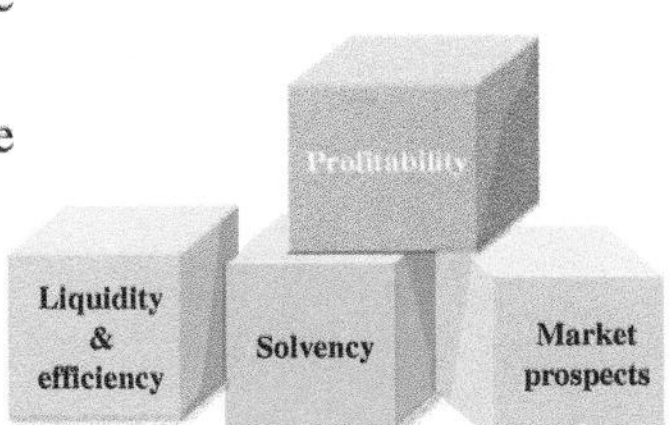

Applying the building blocks of financial statement analysis involves determining (1) the objectives of analysis and (2) the relative emphasis among the building blocks. We distinguish among these four building blocks to emphasize the different aspects of a company's financial condition or performance, yet we must remember that these areas of analysis are interrelated. For instance, a company's operating performance is affected by the availability of financing and short-term liquidity conditions. Similarly, a company's credit standing is not limited to satisfactory short-term liquidity but depends also on its profitability and efficiency in using assets. Early in our analysis, we need to determine the relative emphasis of each building block. Emphasis and analysis can later change as a result of evidence collected.

Decision Insight

Chips and Brokers The phrase *blue chips* refers to stock of big, profitable companies. The phrase comes from poker; where the most valuable chips are blue. The term *brokers* refers to those who execute orders to buy or sell stock. The term comes from wine retailers—individuals who broach (break) wine casks.

Information for Analysis

Some users, such as managers and regulatory authorities, are able to receive special financial reports prepared to meet their analysis needs. However, most users must rely on **general-purpose financial statements** that include the (1) income statement, (2) balance sheet, (3) statement of stockholders' equity (or statement of retained earnings), (4) statement of cash flows, and (5) notes to these statements.

Financial reporting refers to the communication of financial information useful for making investment, credit, and other business decisions. Financial reporting includes not only general-purpose financial statements but also information from SEC 10-K or other filings, press releases, shareholders' meetings, forecasts, management letters, auditors' reports, and Webcasts.

Management's Discussion and Analysis (MD&A) is one example of useful information outside traditional financial statements. Research In Motion's MD&A (available at RIM.com), for example, begins with an overview, followed by critical accounting policies and restatements of previous statements. It then discusses operating results followed by financial condition (liquidity, capital resources, and cash flows). The final few parts discuss legal proceedings, market risk of financial instruments, disclosure controls, and internal controls. The MD&A is an excellent starting point in understanding a company's business activities.

Decision Insight

Analysis Online Many Websites offer free access and screening of companies by key numbers such as earnings, sales, and book value. For instance, Standard & Poor's has information for more than 10,000 stocks (www.standardandpoors.com).

Standards for Comparisons

C2 Describe standards for comparisons in analysis.

When interpreting measures from financial statement analysis, we need to decide whether the measures indicate good, bad, or average performance. To make such judgments, we need standards (benchmarks) for comparisons that include the following:

- *Intracompany*—The company under analysis can provide standards for comparisons based on its own prior performance and relations between its financial items. Research In Motion's current net income, for instance, can be compared with its prior years' net income and in relation to its revenues or total assets.
- *Competitor*—One or more direct competitors of the company being analyzed can provide standards for comparisons. Coca-Cola's profit margin, for instance, can be compared with PepsiCo's profit margin.
- *Industry*—Industry statistics can provide standards of comparisons. Such statistics are available from services such as Dun & Bradstreet, Standard & Poor's, and Moody's.
- *Guidelines (rules of thumb)*—General standards of comparisons can develop from experience. Examples are the 2:1 level for the current ratio or 1:1 level for the acid-test ratio. Guidelines, or rules of thumb, must be carefully applied because context is crucial.

Point: Each chapter's *Reporting in Action* problems engage students in *intracompany* analysis, whereas *Comparative Analysis* problems require competitor analysis (RIM vs. Apple and often vs. Palm).

All of these comparison standards are useful when properly applied, yet measures taken from a selected competitor or group of competitors are often best. Intracompany and industry measures are also important. Guidelines or rules of thumb should be applied with care, and then only if they seem reasonable given past experience and industry norms.

Tools of Analysis

Three of the most common tools of financial statement analysis are

1. **Horizontal analysis**—Comparison of a company's financial condition and performance across time.
2. **Vertical analysis**—Comparison of a company's financial condition and performance to a base amount.
3. **Ratio analysis**—Measurement of key relations between financial statement items.

The remainder of this chapter describes these analysis tools and how to apply them.

Quick Check Answers – p. 713 

1. Who are the intended users of general-purpose financial statements?
2. General-purpose financial statements consist of what information?
3. Which of the following is *least* useful as a basis for comparison when analyzing ratios? (*a*) Company results from a different economic setting. (*b*) Standards from past experience. (*c*) Rule-of-thumb standards. (*d*) Industry averages.
4. What is the preferred basis of comparison for ratio analysis?

HORIZONTAL ANALYSIS

Analysis of any single financial number is of limited value. Instead, much of financial statement analysis involves identifying and describing relations between numbers, groups of numbers, and changes in those numbers. Horizontal analysis refers to examination of financial statement data *across time*. [The term *horizontal analysis* arises from the left-to-right (or right-to-left) movement of our eyes as we review comparative financial statements across time.]

Comparative Statements

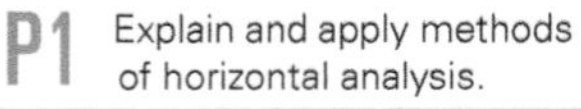

P1 Explain and apply methods of horizontal analysis.

Comparing amounts for two or more successive periods often helps in analyzing financial statements. **Comparative financial statements** facilitate this comparison by showing financial amounts in side-by-side columns on a single statement, called a *comparative format*. Using figures from Research In Motion's financial statements, this section explains how to compute dollar changes and percent changes for comparative statements.

Computation of Dollar Changes and Percent Changes Comparing financial statements over relatively short time periods—two to three years—is often done by analyzing changes in line items. A change analysis usually includes analyzing absolute dollar amount changes and percent changes. Both analyses are relevant because dollar changes can yield large percent changes inconsistent with their importance. For instance, a 50% change from a base figure of $100 is less important than the same percent change from a base amount of $100,000 in the same statement. Reference to dollar amounts is necessary to retain a proper perspective and to assess the importance of changes. We compute the *dollar change* for a financial statement item as follows:

Example: What is a more significant change, a 70% increase on a $1,000 expense or a 30% increase on a $400,000 expense? *Answer:* The 30% increase.

Dollar change = Analysis period amount − Base period amount

Analysis period is the point or period of time for the financial statements under analysis, and *base period* is the point or period of time for the financial statements used for comparison purposes. The prior year is commonly used as a base period. We compute the *percent change* by dividing the dollar change by the base period amount and then multiplying this quantity by 100 as follows:

$$\text{Percent change (\%)} = \frac{\text{Analysis period amount} - \text{Base period amount}}{\text{Base period amount}} \times 100$$

We can always compute a dollar change, but we must be aware of a few rules in working with percent changes. To illustrate, look at four separate cases in this chart:

Case	Analysis Period	Base Period	Change Analysis: Dollar	Change Analysis: Percent
A	$ 1,500	$(4,500)	$ 6,000	—
B	(1,000)	2,000	(3,000)	—
C	8,000	—	8,000	—
D	0	10,000	(10,000)	(100%)

When a negative amount appears in the base period and a positive amount in the analysis period (or vice versa), we cannot compute a meaningful percent change; see cases A and B. Also, when no value is in the base period, no percent change is computable; see case C. Finally, when an item has a value in the base period and zero in the analysis period, the decrease is 100 percent; see case D.

Example: When there is a value in the base period and zero in the analysis period, the decrease is 100%. Why isn't the reverse situation an increase of 100%? *Answer:* A 100% increase of zero is still zero.

It is common when using horizontal analysis to compare amounts to either average or median values from prior periods (average and median values smooth out erratic or unusual fluctuations).[1] We also commonly round percents and ratios to one or two decimal places, but practice on this matter is not uniform. Computations are as detailed as necessary, which is judged by whether rounding potentially affects users' decisions. Computations should not be excessively detailed so that important relations are lost among a mountain of decimal points and digits.

Comparative Balance Sheets Comparative balance sheets consist of balance sheet amounts from two or more balance sheet dates arranged side by side. Its usefulness is often improved by showing each item's dollar change and percent change to highlight large changes.

Analysis of comparative financial statements begins by focusing on items that show large dollar or percent changes. We then try to identify the reasons for these changes and, if possible, determine whether they are favorable or unfavorable. We also follow up on items with small changes when we expected the changes to be large.

Point: Spreadsheet programs can help with horizontal, vertical, and ratio analyses, including graphical depictions of financial relations.

[1] *Median* is the middle value in a group of numbers. For instance, if five prior years' incomes are (in 000s) $15, $19, $18, $20, and $22, the median value is $19. When there are two middle numbers, we can take their average. For instance, if four prior years' sales are (in 000s) $84, $91, $96, and $93, the median is $92 (computed as the average of $91 and $93).

EXHIBIT 17.1
Comparative Balance Sheets
RIM

RESEARCH IN MOTION Comparative Balance Sheets February 27, 2010 and February 28, 2009 ($ thousands)	2010	2009	Dollar Change	Percent Change
Assets				
Cash and cash equivalents	$ 1,550,861	$ 835,546	$ 715,315	85.6%
Short-term investments	360,614	682,666	(322,052)	(47.2)
Accounts receivable, net	2,593,742	2,112,117	481,625	22.8
Other receivables	206,373	157,728	48,645	30.8
Inventories	621,611	682,400	(60,789)	(8.9)
Other current assets	285,539	187,257	98,282	52.5
Deferred income tax asset	193,916	183,872	10,044	5.5
Total current assets	5,812,656	4,841,586	971,070	20.1
Long-term investments	958,248	720,635	237,613	33.0
Property, plant and equipment, net	1,956,581	1,334,648	621,933	46.6
Intangible assets, net	1,326,363	1,066,527	259,836	24.4
Goodwill	150,561	137,572	12,989	9.4
Deferred income tax asset	0	404	(404)	(100.0)
Total assets	$10,204,409	$8,101,372	$2,103,037	26.0
Liabilities				
Accounts payable	$ 615,620	$ 448,339	$ 167,281	37.3%
Accrued liabilities	1,638,260	1,238,602	399,658	32.3
Income taxes payable	95,650	361,460	(265,810)	(73.5)
Deferred revenue	67,573	53,834	13,739	25.5
Deferred income tax liability	14,674	13,116	1,558	11.9
Total current liabilities	2,431,777	2,115,351	316,426	15.0
Deferred income tax liability	141,382	87,917	53,465	60.8
Income taxes payable	28,587	23,976	4,611	19.2
Total liabilities	2,601,746	2,227,244	374,502	16.8
Shareholders' Equity				
Capital stock	2,207,609	2,208,235	(626)	0.0
Treasury stock	(94,463)	0	(94,463)	—
Retained earnings	5,274,365	3,545,710	1,728,655	48.8
Additional paid-in capital	164,060	119,726	44,334	37.0
Accumulated other comprehensive income	51,092	457	50,635	11,079
Total stockholders' equity	7,602,663	5,874,128	1,728,535	29.4
Total liabilities and stockholders' equity	$10,204,409	$8,101,372	$2,103,037	26.0

Point: Business consultants use comparative statement analysis to provide management advice.

Exhibit 17.1 shows comparative balance sheets for Research In Motion (RIM). A few items stand out. Many asset categories substantially increase, which is probably not surprising because RIM is a growth company. Much of the increase in current assets is from the 85.6% increase in cash and equivalents and the 22.8% increase in accounts receivable; although the 47.2% decline in short-term investments dampened this growth. The long-term assets of property, plant and equipment, intangible assets, and long-term investments also markedly increased. Of course, its sizeable total asset growth of 26.0% must be accompanied by future income to validate RIM's growth strategy.

We likewise see substantial increases on the financing side, the most notable ones (in amount) being accounts payable and accrued liabilities totaling $566,939 thousand. The increase in these items is probably related to the recessionary period covering this report. RIM also reinvested much of its income as reflected in the $1,728,655 thousand increase in retained earnings. Again, we must monitor these increases in investing and financing activities to be sure they are reflected in increased operating performance.

Comparative Income Statements Comparative income statements are prepared similarly to comparative balance sheets. Amounts for two or more periods are placed side by side, with additional columns for dollar and percent changes. Exhibit 17.2 shows Research In Motion's comparative income statements.

EXHIBIT 17.2

Comparative Income Statements

RIM

RESEARCH IN MOTION
Comparative Income Statements
For Years Ended February 27, 2010 and February 28, 2009

($ thousands, except per share data)	2010	2009	Dollar Change	Percent Change
Revenue	$14,953,224	$11,065,186	$3,888,038	35.1%
Cost of sales	8,368,958	5,967,888	2,401,070	40.2
Gross profit	6,584,266	5,097,298	1,486,968	29.2
Research and development	964,841	684,702	280,139	40.9
Selling, marketing, and administration	1,907,398	1,495,697	411,701	27.5
Amortization	310,357	194,803	115,554	59.3
Litigation	163,800	—	163,800	—
Income from operations	3,237,870	2,722,096	515,774	18.9
Investment income	28,640	78,267	(49,627)	(63.4)
Income before income taxes	3,266,510	2,800,363	466,147	16.6
Provision for income taxes	809,366	907,747	(98,381)	(10.8)
Net income	$ 2,457,144	$ 1,892,616	564,528	29.8
Basic earnings per share	$ 4.35	$ 3.35	$ 1.00	29.9
Diluted earnings per share	$ 4.31	$ 3.30	$ 1.01	30.6

RIM has substantial revenue growth of 35.1% in 2010. This finding helps support management's growth strategy as reflected in the comparative balance sheets. RIM evidences some ability to control costs of selling, marketing, and administration, which increased 27.5% (versus the 35.1% revenue increase). However, cost of sales increased 40.2% and other expenses also increased at a rate more than that for sales. RIM's net income growth of 29.8% on revenue growth of 35.1% is still good.

Point: Percent change can also be computed by dividing the current period by the prior period and subtracting 1.0. For example, the 35.1% revenue increase of Exhibit 17.2 is computed as: ($14,953,224/$11,065,186) − 1.

Trend Analysis

Trend analysis, also called *trend percent analysis* or *index number trend analysis,* is a form of horizontal analysis that can reveal patterns in data across successive periods. It involves computing trend percents for a series of financial numbers and is a variation on the use of percent changes. The difference is that trend analysis does not subtract the base period amount in the numerator. To compute trend percents, we do the following:

1. Select a *base period* and assign each item in the base period a weight of 100%.
2. Express financial numbers as a percent of their base period number.

Specifically, a *trend percent,* also called an *index number,* is computed as follows:

$$\textbf{Trend percent (\%)} = \frac{\textbf{Analysis period amount}}{\textbf{Base period amount}} \times 100$$

Point: *Index* refers to the comparison of the analysis period to the base period. Percents determined for each period are called *index numbers.*

To illustrate trend analysis, we use the Research In Motion data shown in Exhibit 17.3.

EXHIBIT 17.3

Revenue and Expenses

(in thousands)	2010	2009	2008	2007	2006
Revenue	$14,953,224	$11,065,186	$6,009,395	$3,037,103	$2,065,845
Cost of sales	8,368,958	5,967,888	2,928,814	1,379,301	925,598
Operating expenses	3,346,396	2,375,202	1,349,422	850,974	523,155

These data are from RIM's current and prior financial statements. The base period is 2006 and the trend percent is computed in each subsequent year by dividing that year's amount by its 2006 amount. For instance, the revenue trend percent for 2010 is 723.8%, computed as $14,953,224/$2,065,845. The trend percents—using the data from Exhibit 17.3—are shown in Exhibit 17.4.

EXHIBIT 17.4

Trend Percents for Revenue and Expenses

	2010	2009	2008	2007	2006
Revenue	723.8%	535.6%	290.9%	147.0%	100.0%
Cost of sales	904.2	644.8	316.4	149.0	100.0
Operating expenses	639.7	454.0	257.9	162.7	100.0

Point: Trend analysis expresses a percent of base, not a percent of change.

Graphical depictions often aid analysis of trend percents. Exhibit 17.5 shows the trend percents from Exhibit 17.4 in a *line graph,* which can help us identify trends and detect changes in direction or magnitude. It reveals that the trend line for revenue consistently falls short of that for cost of sales. Moreover, the magnitude of that difference has slightly grown. This result does not bode well for RIM because its cost of sales are by far its largest cost, and the company fails to show an ability to control these expenses as it expands. The line graph also reveals a consistent increase in each of these accounts, which is typical of growth companies. The trend line for operating expenses is more encouraging because it falls short of the revenue trend line in 2008, 2009 and 2010. Still, the bad news is that much of the shift in cost of sales occurred in the most recent two years. Management must try to better control those costs in future years.

EXHIBIT 17.5

Trend Percent Lines for Revenue and Expenses of Research In Motion

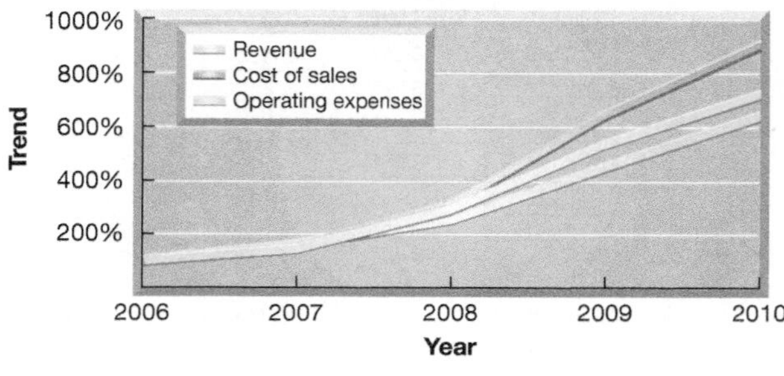

Exhibit 17.6 compares RIM's revenue trend line to that of Apple and Palm for this same period. RIM's revenues sharply increased over this time period while those of Apple exhibited less growth, and those for Palm were declining. These data indicate that RIM's products and services have met with considerable consumer acceptance.

EXHIBIT 17.6

Trend Percent Lines—Research In Motion, Apple and Palm

RIM

Apple

Palm

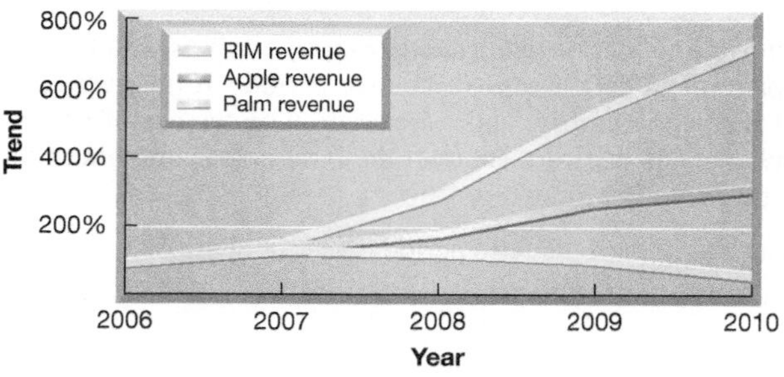

Trend analysis of financial statement items can include comparisons of relations between items on different financial statements. For instance, Exhibit 17.7 compares RIM's revenue and total assets. The rate of increase in total assets (440.9%) is less than the increase in revenues (723.8%) since 2006. Is this result favorable or not? The answer is that RIM was *more* efficient in using its assets in 2010. Management has generated revenues sufficient to compensate for this asset growth.

EXHIBIT 17.7

Revenue and Asset Data for Research In Motion

($ thousands)	2010	2006	Trend Percent (2010 vs. 2006)
Revenue	$14,953,224	$2,065,845	723.8%
Total assets	10,204,409	2,314,349	440.9

Overall we must remember that an important role of financial statement analysis is identifying questions and areas of interest, which often direct us to important factors bearing on a company's future. Accordingly, financial statement analysis should be seen as a continuous process of refining our understanding and expectations of company performance and financial condition.

Decision Maker Answer — p. 712

Auditor Your tests reveal a 3% increase in sales from $200,000 to $206,000 and a 4% decrease in expenses from $190,000 to $182,400. Both changes are within your "reasonableness" criterion of ±5%, and thus you don't pursue additional tests. The audit partner in charge questions your lack of follow-up and mentions the *joint relation* between sales and expenses. To what is the partner referring? ■

VERTICAL ANALYSIS

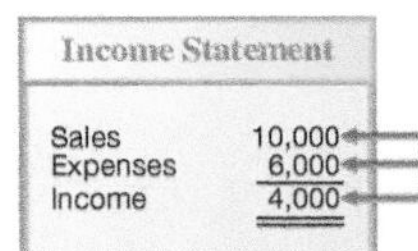

Vertical analysis is a tool to evaluate individual financial statement items or a group of items in terms of a specific base amount. We usually define a key aggregate figure as the base, which for an income statement is usually revenue and for a balance sheet is usually total assets. This section explains vertical analysis and applies it to Research In Motion. [The term *vertical analysis* arises from the up-down (or down-up) movement of our eyes as we review common-size financial statements. Vertical analysis is also called *common-size analysis*.]

Common-Size Statements

P2 Describe and apply methods of vertical analysis.

The comparative statements in Exhibits 17.1 and 17.2 show the change in each item over time, but they do not emphasize the relative importance of each item. We use **common-size financial statements** to reveal changes in the relative importance of each financial statement item. All individual amounts in common-size statements are redefined in terms of common-size percents. A *common-size percent* is measured by dividing each individual financial statement amount under analysis by its base amount:

$$\textbf{Common-size percent (\%)} = \frac{\textbf{Analysis amount}}{\textbf{Base amount}} \times \textbf{100}$$

Common-Size Balance Sheets Common-size statements express each item as a percent of a *base amount,* which for a common-size balance sheet is usually total assets. The base amount is assigned a value of 100%. (This implies that the total amount of liabilities plus equity equals 100% since this amount equals total assets.) We then compute a common-size percent for each asset, liability, and equity item using total assets as the base amount. When we present a company's successive balance sheets in this way, changes in the mixture of assets, liabilities, and equity are apparent.

Point: The *base* amount in common-size analysis is an *aggregate* amount from that period's financial statement.

Exhibit 17.8 shows common-size comparative balance sheets for RIM. Some relations that stand out on both a magnitude and percentage basis include (1) a 4.9% point increase in cash and equivalents, which is likely balanced with a 4.9% point decline in short-term investments, (2) a 2.3% point decline in inventories, (3) a 2.7% point increase in net property, plant and equipment, (4) a 3.6% point decline in taxes payable, and (5) a marked increase in retained earnings. Many of these changes are characteristic of a growth/stable company. The concern, if any, is whether RIM can continue to generate sufficient revenue and income to support its asset buildup within a very competitive industry.

Point: Common-size statements often are used to compare two or more companies in the same industry.

Point: Common-size statements are also useful in comparing firms that report in different currencies.

Common-Size Income Statements Analysis also benefits from use of a common-size income statement. Revenue is usually the base amount, which is assigned a value of 100%. Each common-size income statement item appears as a percent of revenue. If we think of the 100%

EXHIBIT 17.8

Common-Size Comparative Balance Sheets

RIM

RESEARCH IN MOTION Common-Size Comparative Balance Sheets February 27, 2010 and February 28, 2009			Common-Size Percents*	
(in thousands)	2010	2009	2010	2009
Assets				
Cash and cash equivalents	$ 1,550,861	$ 835,546	15.2%	10.3%
Short-term investments	360,614	682,666	3.5	8.4
Accounts receivable, net	2,593,742	2,112,117	25.4	26.1
Other receivables	206,373	157,728	2.0	1.9
Inventories	621,611	682,400	6.1	8.4
Other current assets	285,539	187,257	2.8	2.3
Deferred income tax asset	193,916	183,872	1.9	2.3
Total current assets	5,812,656	4,841,586	57.0	59.8
Long-term investments	958,248	720,635	9.4	8.9
Property, plant and equipment, net	1,956,581	1,334,648	19.2	16.5
Intangible assets, net	1,326,363	1,066,527	13.0	13.2
Goodwill	150,561	137,572	1.5	1.7
Deferred income tax asset	0	404	0.0	0.0
Total assets	$10,204,409	$8,101,372	100.0%	100.0%
Liabilities				
Accounts payable	$ 615,620	$ 448,339	6.0%	5.5%
Accrued liabilities	1,638,260	1,238,602	16.1	15.3
Income taxes payable	95,650	361,460	0.9	4.5
Deferred revenue	67,573	53,834	0.7	0.7
Deferred income tax liability	14,674	13,116	0.1	0.2
Total current liabilities	2,431,777	2,115,351	23.8	26.1
Deferred income tax liability	141,382	87,917	1.4	1.1
Income taxes payable	28,587	23,976	0.3	0.3
Total liabilities	2,601,746	2,227,244	25.5	27.5
Shareholders' Equity				
Capital stock	2,207,609	2,208,235	21.6	27.3
Treasury stock	(94,463)	0	(0.9)	0.0
Retained earnings	5,274,365	3,545,710	51.7	43.8
Additional paid-in capital	164,060	119,726	1.6	1.5
Accumulated other comprehensive income	51,092	457	0.5	0.0
Total stockholders' equity	7,602,663	5,874,128	74.5	72.5
Total liabilities and stockholders' equity	$10,204,409	$8,101,372	100.0%	100.0%

* Percents are rounded to tenths and thus may not exactly sum to totals and subtotals.

revenue amount as representing one sales dollar, the remaining items show how each revenue dollar is distributed among costs, expenses, and income.

Exhibit 17.9 shows common-size comparative income statements for each dollar of RIM's revenue. The past two years' common-size numbers are similar with a few exceptions. The bad news is that RIM has given up 0.7 cent in earnings per revenue dollar—evidenced by the 17.1% to 16.4% decline in earnings as a percentage of revenue. This implies that management is not effectively controlling costs. Much of this is attributed to the rise in cost of sales from 53.9% to 56.0% as a percentage of revenue. This is a concern given the price-competitive smartphone market. Some good news is apparent with the decline in selling, marketing, and administration expenses as a percentage of revenue. Analysis here shows that common-size percents for successive income statements can uncover potentially important changes in a company's expenses. Evidence of no changes, especially when changes are expected, is also informative.

Global: International companies sometimes disclose "convenience" financial statements, which are statements translated in other languages and currencies. However, these statements rarely adjust for differences in accounting principles across countries.

EXHIBIT 17.9

Common-Size Comparative Income Statements

RIM

RESEARCH IN MOTION
Common-Size Comparative Income Statements
For Years Ended February 27, 2010 and February 28, 2009

			Common-Size Percents*	
($ thousands)	2010	2009	2010	2009
Revenue	$14,953,224	$11,065,186	100.0%	100.0%
Cost of sales	8,368,958	5,967,888	56.0	53.9
Gross margin	6,584,266	5,097,298	44.0	46.1
Research and development	964,841	684,702	6.5	6.2
Selling, marketing, and administration	1,907,398	1,495,697	12.8	13.5
Amortization	310,357	194,803	2.1	1.8
Litigation	163,800	—	1.1	0.0
Income from operations	3,237,870	2,722,096	21.7	24.6
Investment income	28,640	78,267	0.2	0.7
Income before income taxes	3,266,510	2,800,363	21.8	25.3
Provision for income taxes	809,366	907,747	5.4	8.2
Net income	$ 2,457,144	$ 1,892,616	16.4%	17.1%

* Percents are rounded to tenths and thus may not exactly sum to totals and subtotals.

Common-Size Graphics

Two of the most common tools of common-size analysis are trend analysis of common-size statements and graphical analysis. The trend analysis of common-size statements is similar to that of comparative statements discussed under vertical analysis. It is not illustrated here because the only difference is the substitution of common-size percents for trend percents. Instead, this section discusses graphical analysis of common-size statements.

An income statement readily lends itself to common-size graphical analysis. This is so because revenues affect nearly every item in an income statement. Exhibit 17.10 shows RIM's 2010 common-size income statement in graphical form. This pie chart highlights the contribution of each cost component of revenue for net income, excluding investment income.

EXHIBIT 17.10

Common-Size Graphic of Income Statement

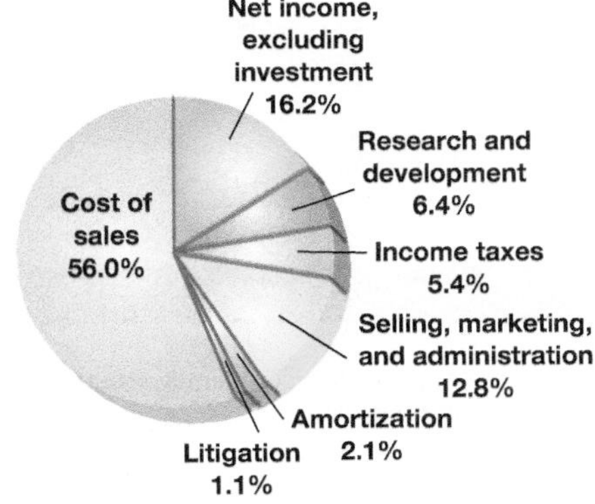

Exhibit 17.11 previews more complex graphical analyses available and the insights they provide. The data for this exhibit are taken from RIM's *Segments* footnote. RIM has at least two reportable segments: (1) United States, and (2) outside the United States (titled Non-U.S.).

EXHIBIT 17.11

Revenue and Total Asset Breakdown by Segment

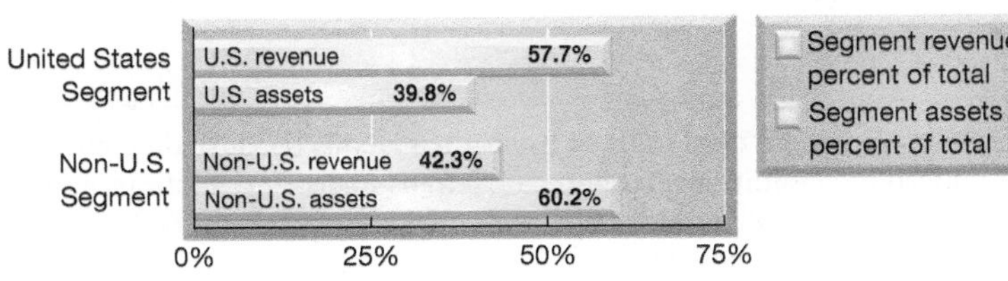

EXHIBIT 17.12

Common-Size Graphic of Asset Components

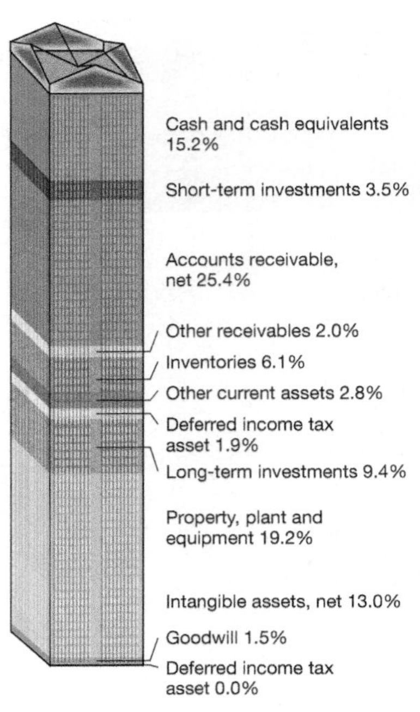

The upper set of bars in Exhibit 17.11 shows the percent of revenues from, and the assets invested in, its U.S. segment. Its U.S. segment generates 57.7% of its revenue, while only 39.8% of its assets are in the United States. The lower set of bars shows that 42.3% of its revenue is generated outside the United States, while 60.2% of its assets are outside the United States. This can lead to questions about the revenue generated per assets invested across different countries. This type of information can help users in determining strategic analyses and actions.

Graphical analysis is also useful in identifying (1) sources of financing including the distribution among current liabilities, noncurrent liabilities, and equity capital and (2) focuses of investing activities, including the distribution among current and noncurrent assets. To illustrate, Exhibit 17.12 shows a common-size graphical display of RIM's assets. Common-size balance sheet analysis can be extended to examine the composition of these subgroups. For instance, in assessing liquidity of current assets, knowing what proportion of *current* assets consists of inventories is usually important, and not simply what proportion inventories are of *total* assets.

Common-size financial statements are also useful in comparing different companies. Exhibit 17.13 shows common-size graphics of RIM, Apple and Nokia on financing sources. This graphic highlights the larger percent of equity financing for RIM and Apple than for Nokia. It also highlights the much larger noncurrent (debt) financing of Nokia and Apple versus RIM. Comparison of a company's common-size statements with competitors' or industry common-size statistics alerts us to differences in the structure or distribution of its financial statements but not to their dollar magnitude.

EXHIBIT 17.13

Common-Size Graphic of Financing Sources—Competitor Analysis

RIM
Apple
NOKIA

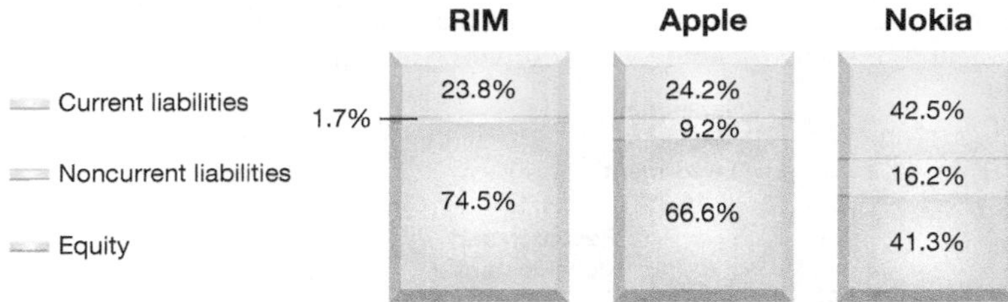

Quick Check

Answers — p. 713

5. Which of the following is true for common-size comparative statements? (*a*) Each item is expressed as a percent of a base amount. (*b*) Total assets often are assigned a value of 100%. (*c*) Amounts from successive periods are placed side by side. (*d*) All are true. (*e*) None is true.
6. What is the difference between the percents shown on a comparative income statement and those shown on a common-size comparative income statement?
7. Trend percents are (*a*) shown on comparative income statements and balance sheets, (*b*) shown on common-size comparative statements, or (*c*) also called *index numbers.*

RATIO ANALYSIS

P3 Define and apply ratio analysis.

Ratios are among the more widely used tools of financial analysis because they provide clues to and symptoms of underlying conditions. A ratio can help us uncover conditions and trends difficult to detect by inspecting individual components making up the ratio. Ratios, like other analysis tools, are usually future oriented; that is, they are often adjusted for their probable future trend and magnitude, and their usefulness depends on skillful interpretation.

A ratio expresses a mathematical relation between two quantities. It can be expressed as a percent, rate, or proportion. For instance, a change in an account balance from $100 to $250 can be expressed as (1) 150% increase, (2) 2.5 times, or (3) 2.5 to 1 (or 2.5:1). Computation of a ratio is a simple arithmetic operation, but its interpretation is not. To be meaningful, a ratio must refer to an economically important relation. For example, a direct and crucial relation exists between an item's sales price and its cost. Accordingly, the ratio of cost of goods sold to sales is meaningful. In contrast, no obvious relation exists between freight costs and the balance of long-term investments.

This section describes an important set of financial ratios and its application. The selected ratios are organized into the four building blocks of financial statement analysis: (1) liquidity and efficiency, (2) solvency, (3) profitability, and (4) market prospects. All of these ratios were explained at relevant points in prior chapters. The purpose here is to organize and apply them under a summary framework. We use four common standards, in varying degrees, for comparisons: intracompany, competitor, industry, and guidelines.

Point: Some sources for industry norms are *Annual Statement Studies* by Robert Morris Associates, *Industry Norms & Key Business Ratios* by Dun & Bradstreet, *Standard & Poor's Industry Surveys*, and Reuters.com/finance.

Liquidity and Efficiency

Liquidity refers to the availability of resources to meet short-term cash requirements. It is affected by the timing of cash inflows and outflows along with prospects for future performance. Analysis of liquidity is aimed at a company's funding requirements. *Efficiency* refers to how productive a company is in using its assets. Efficiency is usually measured relative to how much revenue is generated from a certain level of assets.

Both liquidity and efficiency are important and complementary. If a company fails to meet its current obligations, its continued existence is doubtful. Viewed in this light, all other measures of analysis are of secondary importance. Although accounting measurements assume the company's continued existence, our analysis must always assess the validity of this assumption using liquidity measures. Moreover, inefficient use of assets can cause liquidity problems. A lack of liquidity often precedes lower profitability and fewer opportunities. It can foretell a loss of owner control. To a company's creditors, lack of liquidity can yield delays in collecting interest and principal payments or the loss of amounts due them. A company's customers and suppliers of goods and services also are affected by short-term liquidity problems. Implications include a company's inability to execute contracts and potential damage to important customer and supplier relationships. This section describes and illustrates key ratios relevant to assessing liquidity and efficiency.

Working Capital and Current Ratio The amount of current assets less current liabilities is called **working capital,** or *net working capital.* A company needs adequate working capital to meet current debts, to carry sufficient inventories, and to take advantage of cash discounts. A company that runs low on working capital is less likely to meet current obligations or to continue operating. When evaluating a company's working capital, we must not only look at the dollar amount of current assets less current liabilities, but also at their ratio. The *current ratio* is defined as follows (see Chapter 3 for additional explanation):

$$\textbf{Current ratio} = \frac{\textbf{Current assets}}{\textbf{Current liabilities}}$$

Drawing on information in Exhibit 17.1, RIM's working capital and current ratio for both 2010 and 2009 are shown in Exhibit 17.14. Also, Apple (2.74), Palm (1.03), and the Industry's current ratio (2.4) are shown in the margin. RIM's 2010 ratio (2.39) is between the competitors' ratios, and it does not appear in danger of defaulting on loan payments. A high current ratio suggests a strong liquidity position and an ability to meet current obligations. A company can, however, have a current ratio that is too high. An excessively high current ratio means that the company has invested too much in current assets compared to its current obligations.

EXHIBIT 17.14

RIM's Working Capital and Current Ratio

($ thousands)	2010	2009
Current assets	$ 5,812,656	$ 4,841,586
Current liabilities	2,431,777	2,115,351
Working capital	$3,380,879	$2,726,235
Current ratio		
$5,812,656/$2,431,777 =	2.39 to 1	
$4,841,586/$2,115,351 =		2.29 to 1

Current ratio
Apple = 2.74
Palm = 1.03
Industry = 2.4

An excessive investment in current assets is not an efficient use of funds because current assets normally generate a low return on investment (compared with long-term assets).

Many users apply a guideline of 2:1 (or 1.5:1) for the current ratio in helping evaluate a company's debt-paying ability. A company with a 2:1 or higher current ratio is generally thought to be a good credit risk in the short run. Such a guideline or any analysis of the current ratio must recognize at least three additional factors: (1) type of business, (2) composition of current assets, and (3) turnover rate of current asset components.

Type of business. A service company that grants little or no credit and carries few inventories can probably operate on a current ratio of less than 1:1 if its revenues generate enough cash to pay its current liabilities. On the other hand, a company selling high-priced clothing or furniture requires a higher ratio because of difficulties in judging customer demand and cash receipts. For instance, if demand falls, inventory may not generate as much cash as expected. Accordingly, analysis of the current ratio should include a comparison with ratios from successful companies in the same industry and from prior periods. We must also recognize that a company's accounting methods, especially choice of inventory method, affect the current ratio. For instance, when costs are rising, a company using LIFO tends to report a smaller amount of current assets than when using FIFO.

Point: When a firm uses LIFO in a period of rising costs, the standard for an adequate current ratio usually is lower than if it used FIFO.

Composition of current assets. The composition of a company's current assets is important to an evaluation of short-term liquidity. For instance, cash, cash equivalents, and short-term investments are more liquid than accounts and notes receivable. Also, short-term receivables normally are more liquid than inventory. Cash, of course, can be used to immediately pay current debts. Items such as accounts receivable and inventory, however, normally must be converted into cash before payment is made. An excessive amount of receivables and inventory weakens a company's ability to pay current liabilities. The acid-test ratio (see below) can help with this assessment.

Turnover rate of assets. Asset turnover measures a company's efficiency in using its assets. One relevant measure of asset efficiency is the revenue generated. A measure of total asset turnover is revenues divided by total assets, but evaluation of turnover for individual assets is also useful. We discuss both receivables turnover and inventory turnover on the next page.

Decision Maker Answer — p. 713

Banker A company requests a one-year, $200,000 loan for expansion. This company's current ratio is 4:1, with current assets of $160,000. Key competitors carry a current ratio of about 1.9:1. Using this information, do you approve the loan application? Does your decision change if the application is for a 10-year loan? ■

Acid-Test Ratio Quick assets are cash, short-term investments, and current receivables. These are the most liquid types of current assets. The *acid-test ratio,* also called *quick ratio,* and introduced in Chapter 5, reflects on a company's short-term liquidity.

$$\text{Acid-test ratio} = \frac{\textbf{Cash + Short-term investments + Current receivables}}{\textbf{Current liabilities}}$$

RIM's acid-test ratio is computed in Exhibit 17.15. RIM's 2010 acid-test ratio (1.94) is between that for Apple (2.33) and Palm (0.94), and greater than the 1:1 common guideline for an

EXHIBIT 17.15

Acid-Test Ratio

($ thousands)	2010	2009
Cash and equivalents	$1,550,861	$ 835,546
Short-term investments	360,614	682,666
Current receivables	2,800,115	2,269,845
Total quick assets	$4,711,590	$3,788,057
Current liabilities	$2,431,777	$2,115,351
Acid-test ratio		
$4,711,590/$2,431,777	1.94 to 1	
$3,788,057/$2,115,351		1.79 to 1

Acid-test ratio
Apple = 2.33
Palm = 0.94
Industry = 1.5

acceptable acid-test ratio. The ratios for both RIM and Apple exceed the 1.5 industry norm. As with analysis of the current ratio, we need to consider other factors. For instance, the frequency with which a company converts its current assets into cash affects its working capital requirements. This implies that analysis of short-term liquidity should also include an analysis of receivables and inventories, which we consider next.

Global: Ratio analysis helps overcome currency translation problems, but it does *not* overcome differences in accounting principles.

Accounts Receivable Turnover We can measure how frequently a company converts its receivables into cash by computing the *accounts receivable turnover*. This ratio is defined as follows (see Chapter 9 for additional explanation):

$$\textbf{Accounts receivable turnover} = \frac{\textbf{Net sales}}{\textbf{Average accounts receivable, net}}$$

Short-term receivables from customers are often included in the denominator along with accounts receivable. Also, accounts receivable turnover is more precise if credit sales are used for the numerator, but external users generally use net sales (or net revenues) because information about credit sales is typically not reported. RIM's 2010 accounts receivable turnover is computed as follows ($ millions).

Point: Some users prefer using gross accounts receivable (before subtracting the allowance for doubtful accounts) to avoid the influence of a manager's bad debts estimate.

$$\frac{14,953,224}{(\$2,593,742 + \$2,112,117)/2} = 6.4 \text{ times}$$

Accounts receivable turnover
Apple = 14.8
Palm = 8.0
Industry = 6.6

RIM's value of 6.4 is between that of Apple's 14.8 and Palm's 8.0. Accounts receivable turnover is high when accounts receivable are quickly collected. A high turnover is favorable because it means the company need not commit large amounts of funds to accounts receivable. However, an accounts receivable turnover can be too high; this can occur when credit terms are so restrictive that they negatively affect sales volume.

Point: Ending accounts receivable can be substituted for the average balance in computing accounts receivable turnover if the difference between ending and average receivables is small.

Inventory Turnover How long a company holds inventory before selling it will affect working capital requirements. One measure of this effect is *inventory turnover,* also called *merchandise turnover* or *merchandise inventory turnover,* which is defined as follows (see Chapter 6 for additional explanation):

$$\textbf{Inventory turnover} = \frac{\textbf{Cost of goods sold}}{\textbf{Average inventory}}$$

Using RIM's cost of goods sold and inventories information, we compute its inventory turnover for 2010 as follows (if the beginning and ending inventories for the year do not represent the usual inventory amount, an average of quarterly or monthly inventories can be used).

Inventory turnover
Apple = 53.28
Palm = 13.22
Industry = 10.1

$$\frac{\$8,368,958}{(\$621,611 + \$682,400)/2} = 12.84 \text{ times}$$

RIM's inventory turnover of 12.84 is less than Apple's 53.28, but similar to Palm's 13.22, and the industry's 10.1. A company with a high turnover requires a smaller investment in inventory than one producing the same sales with a lower turnover. Inventory turnover can be too high, however, if the inventory a company keeps is so small that it restricts sales volume.

Days' Sales Uncollected Accounts receivable turnover provides insight into how frequently a company collects its accounts. Days' sales uncollected is one measure of this activity, which is defined as follows (Chapter 8 provides additional explanation):

$$\textbf{Days' sales uncollected} = \frac{\textbf{Accounts receivable, net}}{\textbf{Net sales}} \times \textbf{365}$$

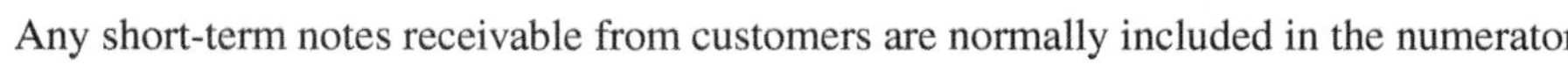

Any short-term notes receivable from customers are normally included in the numerator.

RIM's 2010 days' sales uncollected follows.

Day's sales uncollected
Apple = 28.59
Palm = 32.96

$$\frac{\$2,593,742}{\$14,953,224} \times 365 = 63.31 \text{ days}$$

Both Apple's days' sales uncollected of 28.59 days and Palm's 32.96 days are less than the 63.31 days for RIM. Days' sales uncollected is more meaningful if we know company credit terms. A rough guideline states that days' sales uncollected should not exceed $1\frac{1}{3}$ times the days in its (1) credit period, *if* discounts are not offered or (2) discount period, *if* favorable discounts are offered.

Days' Sales in Inventory *Days' sales in inventory* is a useful measure in evaluating inventory liquidity. Days' sales in inventory is linked to inventory in a way that days' sales uncollected is linked to receivables. We compute days' sales in inventory as follows (Chapter 6 provides additional explanation).

$$\textbf{Days' sales in inventory} = \frac{\textbf{Ending inventory}}{\textbf{Cost of goods sold}} \times \textbf{365}$$

RIM's days' sales in inventory for 2010 follows.

Days' sales in inventory
Apple = 6.5
Palm = 12.5
Industry = 25

$$\frac{\$621,611}{\$8,368,958} \times 365 = 27.1 \text{ days}$$

Point: Average collection period is estimated by dividing 365 by the accounts receivable turnover ratio. For example, 365 divided by an accounts receivable turnover of 6.1 indicates a 60-day average collection period.

If the products in RIM's inventory are in demand by customers, this formula estimates that its inventory will be converted into receivables (or cash) in 27.1 days. If all of RIM's sales were credit sales, the conversion of inventory to receivables in 27.1 days *plus* the conversion of receivables to cash in 63.31 days implies that inventory will be converted to cash in about 90.41 days (27.1 + 63.31).

Total Asset Turnover *Total asset turnover* reflects a company's ability to use its assets to generate sales and is an important indication of operating efficiency. The definition of this ratio follows (Chapter 10 offers additional explanation).

$$\textbf{Total asset turnover} = \frac{\textbf{Net sales}}{\textbf{Average total assets}}$$

RIM's total asset turnover for 2010 follows and is greater than that for both Apple (1.03) and Palm (0.81).

Total asset turnover
Apple = 1.03
Palm = 0.81
Industry = 1.0

$$\frac{\$14,953,224}{(\$10,204,409 + \$8,101,372)/2} = 1.63 \text{ times}$$

Quick Check Answers — p. 713 

8. Information from Paff Co. at Dec. 31, 2010, follows: cash, $820,000; accounts receivable, $240,000; inventories, $470,000; plant assets, $910,000; accounts payable, $350,000; and income taxes payable, $180,000. Compute its (*a*) current ratio and (*b*) acid-test ratio.
9. On Dec. 31, 2011, Paff Company (see question 8) had accounts receivable of $290,000 and inventories of $530,000. During 2011, net sales amounted to $2,500,000 and cost of goods sold was $750,000. Compute (*a*) accounts receivable turnover, (*b*) days' sales uncollected, (*c*) inventory turnover, and (*d*) days' sales in inventory.

Solvency

Solvency refers to a company's long-run financial viability and its ability to cover long-term obligations. All of a company's business activities—financing, investing, and operating—affect its solvency. Analysis of solvency is long term and uses less precise but more encompassing measures than liquidity. One of the most important components of solvency analysis is the composition of a company's capital structure. *Capital structure* refers to a company's financing sources. It ranges from relatively permanent equity financing to riskier or more temporary short-term financing. Assets represent security for financiers, ranging from loans secured by specific assets to the assets available as general security to unsecured creditors. This section describes the tools of solvency analysis. Our analysis focuses on a company's ability to both meet its obligations and provide security to its creditors *over the long run*. Indicators of this ability include *debt* and *equity* ratios, the relation between *pledged assets and secured liabilities,* and the company's capacity to earn sufficient income to *pay fixed interest charges*.

Debt and Equity Ratios One element of solvency analysis is to assess the portion of a company's assets contributed by its owners and the portion contributed by creditors. This relation is reflected in the debt ratio (also described in Chapter 2). The *debt ratio* expresses total liabilities as a percent of total assets. The **equity ratio** provides complementary information by expressing total equity as a percent of total assets. RIM's debt and equity ratios follow.

Point: For analysis purposes, Minority Interest is usually included in equity.

($ thousands)	2010	Ratios	
Total liabilities	$ 2,601,746	25.5%	[Debt ratio]
Total equity	7,602,663	74.5	[Equity ratio]
Total liabilities and equity	$10,204,409	100.0%	

Debt ratio :: Equity ratio
Apple = 33.4% :: 66.6%
Industry = 40% :: 60%

RIM's financial statements reveal more equity than debt. A company is considered less risky if its capital structure (equity and long-term debt) contains more equity. One risk factor is the required payment for interest and principal when debt is outstanding. Another factor is the greater the stockholder financing, the more losses a company can absorb through equity before the assets become inadequate to satisfy creditors' claims. From the stockholders' point of view, if a company earns a return on borrowed capital that is higher than the cost of borrowing, the difference represents increased income to stockholders. The inclusion of debt is described as *financial leverage* because debt can have the effect of increasing the return to stockholders. Companies are said to be highly leveraged if a large portion of their assets is financed by debt.

Point: Bank examiners from the FDIC and other regulatory agencies use debt and equity ratios to monitor compliance with regulatory capital requirements imposed on banks and S&Ls.

Debt-to-Equity Ratio The ratio of total liabilities to equity is another measure of solvency. We compute the ratio as follows (Chapter 14 offers additional explanation).

$$\text{Debt-to-equity ratio} = \frac{\text{Total liabilities}}{\text{Total equity}}$$

RIM's debt-to-equity ratio for 2010 is

$$\$2{,}601{,}746/\$7{,}602{,}663 = 0.34$$

Debt-to-equity
Apple = 0.50
Industry = 0.7

RIM's 0.34 debt-to-equity ratio is less than the 0.50 ratio for Apple, and less than the industry ratio of 0.7. Consistent with our inferences from the debt ratio, RIM's capital structure has more equity than debt, which decreases risk. Recall that debt must be repaid with interest, while equity does not. These debt requirements can be burdensome when the industry and/or the economy experience a downturn. A larger debt-to-equity ratio also implies less opportunity to expand through use of debt financing.

Times Interest Earned The amount of income before deductions for interest expense and income taxes is the amount available to pay interest expense. The following

Point: The times interest earned ratio and the debt and equity ratios are of special interest to bank lending officers.

times interest earned ratio reflects the creditors' risk of loan repayments with interest (see Chapter 11 for additional explanation).

$$\textbf{Times interest earned} = \frac{\textbf{Income before interest expense and income taxes}}{\textbf{Interest expense}}$$

The larger this ratio, the less risky is the company for creditors. One guideline says that creditors are reasonably safe if the company earns its fixed interest expense two or more times each year. RIM's times interest earned ratio follows; its value suggests that its creditors have little risk of nonrepayment.

Times interest earned
Apple = n.a.

$$\frac{\$2{,}457{,}144 + \sim\$0 \text{ (see RIM note \#16)} + \$809{,}366}{\sim\$0} = \text{"infinite" (not applicable)}$$

Decision Insight

Bears and Bulls A *bear market* is a declining market. The phrase comes from bear-skin jobbers who often sold the skins before the bears were caught. The term *bear* was then used to describe investors who sold shares they did not own in anticipation of a price decline. A *bull market* is a rising market. This phrase comes from the once popular sport of bear and bull baiting. The term *bull* came to mean the opposite of *bear*. ■

Profitability

We are especially interested in a company's ability to use its assets efficiently to produce profits (and positive cash flows). *Profitability* refers to a company's ability to generate an adequate return on invested capital. Return is judged by assessing earnings relative to the level and sources of financing. Profitability is also relevant to solvency. This section describes key profitability measures and their importance to financial statement analysis.

Profit Margin A company's operating efficiency and profitability can be expressed by two components. The first is *profit margin,* which reflects a company's ability to earn net income from sales (Chapter 3 offers additional explanation). It is measured by expressing net income as a percent of sales (*sales* and *revenues* are similar terms). RIM's profit margin follows.

Profit margin
Apple = 19.2%
Industry = 3%

$$\textbf{Profit margin} = \frac{\textbf{Net income}}{\textbf{Net sales}} = \frac{\$2{,}457{,}144}{\$14{,}953{,}224} = 16.4\%$$

To evaluate profit margin, we must consider the industry. For instance, an appliance company might require a profit margin between 10% and 15%; whereas a retail supermarket might require a profit margin of 1% or 2%. Both profit margin and *total asset turnover* make up the two basic components of operating efficiency. These ratios reflect on management because managers are ultimately responsible for operating efficiency. The next section explains how we use both measures to analyze return on total assets.

Return on Total Assets *Return on total assets* is defined as follows.

$$\textbf{Return on total assets} = \frac{\textbf{Net income}}{\textbf{Average total assets}}$$

RIM's 2010 return on total assets is

Return on total assets
Apple = 19.7%
Industry = 4%

$$\frac{\$2{,}457{,}144}{(\$10{,}204{,}409 + \$8{,}101{,}372)/2} = 26.8\%$$

RIM's 26.8% return on total assets is higher than that for many businesses and is higher than Apple's return of 19.7% and the industry's 4% return. We also should evaluate any trend in the rate of return.

Point: Many analysts add back *Interest expense* × *(1 − Tax rate)* to net income in computing return on total assets.

The following equation shows the important relation between profit margin, total asset turnover, and return on total assets.

$$\textbf{Profit margin} \times \textbf{Total asset turnover} = \textbf{Return on total assets}$$

or

$$\frac{\textbf{Net income}}{\textbf{Net sales}} \times \frac{\textbf{Net sales}}{\textbf{Average total assets}} = \frac{\textbf{Net income}}{\textbf{Average total assets}}$$

Both profit margin and total asset turnover contribute to overall operating efficiency, as measured by return on total assets. If we apply this formula to RIM, we get

$$16.4\% \times 1.63 = 26.8\% \text{ (with rounding error)}$$

Apple: 19.2% × 1.03 = 19.7% (with rounding)

This analysis shows that RIM's superior return on assets versus that of Apple is driven mainly by its higher total asset turnover.

Return on Common Stockholders' Equity Perhaps the most important goal in operating a company is to earn net income for its owner(s). *Return on common stockholders' equity* measures a company's success in reaching this goal and is defined as follows.

$$\textbf{Return on common stockholders' equity} = \frac{\textbf{Net income} - \textbf{Preferred dividends}}{\textbf{Average common stockholders' equity}}$$

RIM's 2010 return on common stockholders' equity is computed as follows:

$$\frac{\$2,457,144 - \$0}{(\$5,874,128 + \$7,602,663)/2} = 36.5\%$$

Return on common equity
Apple = 30.5%
Industry = 6%

The denominator in this computation is the book value of common equity (minority interest is often included in common equity for this ratio). In the numerator, the dividends on cumulative preferred stock are subtracted whether they are declared or are in arrears. If preferred stock is noncumulative, its dividends are subtracted only if declared.

Decision Insight

Wall Street *Wall Street* is synonymous with financial markets, but its name comes from the street location of the original New York Stock Exchange. The street's name derives from stockades built by early settlers to protect New York from pirate attacks. ■

Market Prospects

Market measures are useful for analyzing corporations with publicly traded stock. These market measures use stock price, which reflects the market's (public's) expectations for the company. This includes expectations of both company return and risk—as the market perceives it.

Price-Earnings Ratio Computation of the *price-earnings ratio* follows (Chapter 13 provides additional explanation).

$$\textbf{Price-earnings ratio} = \frac{\textbf{Market price per common share}}{\textbf{Earnings per share}}$$

Point: PE ratio can be viewed as an indicator of the market's expected growth and risk for a stock. High expected risk suggests a low PE ratio. High expected growth suggests a high PE ratio.

Predicted earnings per share for the next period is often used in the denominator of this computation. Reported earnings per share for the most recent period is also commonly used. In both cases, the ratio is used as an indicator of the future growth and risk of a company's earnings as perceived by the stock's buyers and sellers.

The market price of RIM's common stock at the start of fiscal year 2010 was \$50.84. Using RIM's \$4.35 basic earnings per share, we compute its price-earnings ratio as follows (some analysts compute this ratio using the median of the low and high stock price).

PE (year-end)
Apple = 13.9

$$\frac{\$50.84}{\$4.35} = 11.7$$

Point: Some investors avoid stocks with high PE ratios under the belief they are "overpriced." Alternatively, some investors *sell these stocks short*—hoping for price declines.

RIM's price-earnings ratio is less than that for Apple, but is slightly higher than the norm for the recessionary period 2009–2010. (Palm's ratio is negative due to its abnormally low earnings.) RIM's middle-of-the-pack ratio likely reflects investors' expectations of stagnant growth but normal earnings.

Dividend Yield *Dividend yield* is used to compare the dividend-paying performance of different investment alternatives. We compute dividend yield as follows (Chapter 13 offers additional explanation).

$$\textbf{Dividend yield} = \frac{\textbf{Annual cash dividends per share}}{\textbf{Market price per share}}$$

RIM's dividend yield, based on its fiscal year-end market price per share of \$50.84 and its policy of \$0.00 cash dividends per share, is computed as follows.

Dividend yield
Apple = 0.0%
Palm = 0.0%

$$\frac{\$0.00}{\$50.84} = 0.0\%$$

Some companies do not declare and pay dividends because they wish to reinvest the cash.

Summary of Ratios

Point: Corporate PE ratios and dividend yields are found in daily stock market quotations listed in *The Wall Street Journal*, *Investor's Business Daily*, or other publications and Web services.

Exhibit 17.16 summarizes the major financial statement analysis ratios illustrated in this chapter and throughout the book. This summary includes each ratio's title, its formula, and the purpose for which it is commonly used.

Decision Insight

Ticker Prices *Ticker prices* refer to a band of moving data on a monitor carrying up-to-the-minute stock prices. The phrase comes from *ticker tape*, a 1-inch-wide strip of paper spewing stock prices from a printer that ticked as it ran. Most of today's investors have never seen actual ticker tape, but the phrase survives. ■

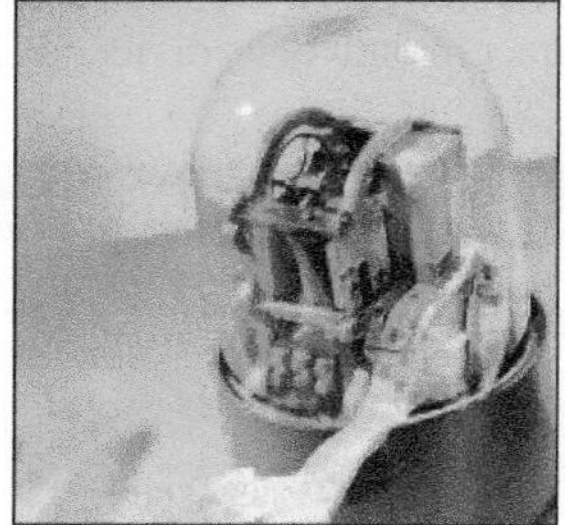

Quick Check

Answers – p. 713

10. Which ratio best reflects a company's ability to meet immediate interest payments? *(a)* Debt ratio. *(b)* Equity ratio. *(c)* Times interest earned.

11. Which ratio best measures a company's success in earning net income for its owner(s)? *(a)* Profit margin. *(b)* Return on common stockholders' equity. *(c)* Price-earnings ratio. *(d)* Dividend yield.

12. If a company has net sales of \$8,500,000, net income of \$945,000, and total asset turnover of 1.8 times, what is its return on total assets?

EXHIBIT 17.16

Financial Statement Analysis Ratios*

Ratio	Formula	Measure of
Liquidity and Efficiency		
Current ratio	$= \frac{\text{Current assets}}{\text{Current liabilities}}$	Short-term debt-paying ability
Acid-test ratio	$= \frac{\text{Cash + Short-term investments + Current receivables}}{\text{Current liabilities}}$	Immediate short-term debt-paying ability
Accounts receivable turnover	$= \frac{\text{Net sales}}{\text{Average accounts receivable, net}}$	Efficiency of collection
Inventory turnover	$= \frac{\text{Cost of goods sold}}{\text{Average inventory}}$	Efficiency of inventory management
Days' sales uncollected	$= \frac{\text{Accounts receivable, net}}{\text{Net sales}} \times 365$	Liquidity of receivables
Days' sales in inventory	$= \frac{\text{Ending inventory}}{\text{Cost of goods sold}} \times 365$	Liquidity of inventory
Total asset turnover	$= \frac{\text{Net sales}}{\text{Average total assets}}$	Efficiency of assets in producing sales
Solvency		
Debt ratio	$= \frac{\text{Total liabilities}}{\text{Total assets}}$	Creditor financing and leverage
Equity ratio	$= \frac{\text{Total equity}}{\text{Total assets}}$	Owner financing
Debt-to-equity ratio	$= \frac{\text{Total liabilities}}{\text{Total equity}}$	Debt versus equity financing
Times interest earned	$= \frac{\text{Income before interest expense and income taxes}}{\text{Interest expense}}$	Protection in meeting interest payments
Profitability		
Profit margin ratio	$= \frac{\text{Net income}}{\text{Net sales}}$	Net income in each sales dollar
Gross margin ratio	$= \frac{\text{Net sales} - \text{Cost of goods sold}}{\text{Net sales}}$	Gross margin in each sales dollar
Return on total assets	$= \frac{\text{Net income}}{\text{Average total assets}}$	Overall profitability of assets
Return on common stockholders' equity	$= \frac{\text{Net income} - \text{Preferred dividends}}{\text{Average common stockholders' equity}}$	Profitability of owner investment
Book value per common share	$= \frac{\text{Shareholders' equity applicable to common shares}}{\text{Number of common shares outstanding}}$	Liquidation at reported amounts
Basic earnings per share	$= \frac{\text{Net income} - \text{Preferred dividends}}{\text{Weighted-average common shares outstanding}}$	Net income per common share
Market Prospects		
Price-earnings ratio	$= \frac{\text{Market price per common share}}{\text{Earnings per share}}$	Market value relative to earnings
Dividend yield	$= \frac{\text{Annual cash dividends per share}}{\text{Market price per share}}$	Cash return per common share

* Additional ratios also examined in previous chapters included credit risk ratio; plant asset useful life; plant asset age; days' cash expense coverage; cash coverage of growth; cash coverage of debt; free cash flow; cash flow on total assets; and payout ratio.

GLOBAL VIEW

The analysis and interpretation of financial statements is, of course, impacted by the accounting system in effect. This section discusses similarities and differences for analysis of financial statements when prepared under U.S. GAAP vis-à-vis IFRS.

Horizontal and Vertical Analyses Horizontal and vertical analyses help eliminate many differences between U.S. GAAP and IFRS when analyzing and interpreting financial statements. Financial numbers are converted to percentages that are, in the best case scenario, consistently applied across and within periods. This enables users to effectively compare companies across reporting regimes. However, when fundamental differences in reporting regimes impact financial statements, such as with certain recognition rule differences, the user must exercise caution when drawing conclusions. Some users will reformulate one set of numbers to be more consistent with the other system to enable comparative analysis. This reformulation process is covered in advanced courses. The important point is that horizontal and vertical analyses help strip away differences between the reporting regimes, but several key differences sometimes remain and require adjustment of the numbers. Nokia reports the following partial vertical analysis to its shareholders as part of its MD&A report.

NOKIA

As a Percentage of Revenue	2010
Research and development	6.5%
Selling, marketing and administration	12.8
Amortization	2.1
Litigation	1.1
Total operating expenses	22.5%

Ratio Analysis Ratio analysis of financial statement numbers has many of the advantages and disadvantages of horizontal and vertical analyses discussed above. Importantly, ratio analysis is useful for business decisions, with some possible changes in interpretation depending on what is and what is not included in accounting measures across U.S. GAAP and IFRS. Still, we must take care in drawing inferences from a comparison of ratios across reporting regimes because what a number measures can differ across regimes. Nokia offers the following example of its own ratio analysis applied to gross margin: "Consolidated gross margin increased by $1.48 billion, or 29.2%, to $6.58 billion, or 44.0% of revenue, in fiscal 2010, compared to $5.10 billion, or 46.1% of revenue, in fiscal 2009. The decrease of 2.1% in consolidated gross margin percentage was primarily due to a decrease in the blended device margins."

Decision Insight

Not Created Equal Financial regulation has several goals. Two of them are to ensure adequate accounting disclosure and to strengthen corporate governance. For disclosure purposes, companies must now provide details of related-party transactions and material off-balance-sheet agreements. This is motivated by several major frauds. For corporate governance, the CEO and CFO must now certify the fairness of financial statements and the effectiveness of internal controls. Yet, concerns remain. A study reports that 23% of management and administrative employees observed activities that posed a conflict of interest in the past year (KPMG 2009). Another 12% witnessed the falsifying or manipulating of accounting information. The bottom line: All financial statements are not of equal quality. ■

Decision Analysis

Analysis Reporting

A1 Summarize and report results of analysis.

Understanding the purpose of financial statement analysis is crucial to the usefulness of any analysis. This understanding leads to efficiency of effort, effectiveness in application, and relevance in focus. The purpose of most financial statement analyses is to reduce uncertainty in business decisions through a rigorous and sound evaluation. A *financial statement analysis report* helps by directly addressing the building blocks of analysis and by identifying weaknesses in inference by requiring explanation: It forces us to organize our reasoning and to verify its flow and logic. A report also serves as a communication link with readers, and the writing process reinforces our judgments and vice versa. Finally, the report helps us (re)evaluate evidence and refine conclusions on key building blocks. A good analysis report usually consists of six sections:

1. **Executive summary**—brief focus on important analysis results and conclusions.
2. **Analysis overview**—background on the company, its industry, and its economic setting.
3. **Evidential matter**—financial statements and information used in the analysis, including ratios, trends, comparisons, statistics, and all analytical measures assembled; often organized under the building blocks of analysis.
4. **Assumptions**—identification of important assumptions regarding a company's industry and economic environment, and other important assumptions for estimates.
5. **Key factors**—list of important favorable and unfavorable factors, both quantitative and qualitative, for company performance; usually organized by areas of analysis.
6. **Inferences**—forecasts, estimates, interpretations, and conclusions drawing on all sections of the report.

We must remember that the user dictates relevance, meaning that the analysis report should include a brief table of contents to help readers focus on those areas most relevant to their decisions. All irrelevant matter must be eliminated. For example, decades-old details of obscure transactions and detailed miscues of the analysis are irrelevant. Ambiguities and qualifications to avoid responsibility or hedging inferences must be eliminated. Finally, writing is important. Mistakes in grammar and errors of fact compromise the report's credibility.

Decision Insight

Short Selling *Short selling* refers to selling stock before you buy it. Here's an example: You borrow 100 shares of Nike stock, sell them at $40 each, and receive money from their sale. You then wait. You hope that Nike's stock price falls to, say, $35 each and you can replace the borrowed stock for less than you sold it for, reaping a profit of $5 each less any transaction costs. ■

DEMONSTRATION PROBLEM

Use the following financial statements of Precision Co. to complete these requirements.

1. Prepare comparative income statements showing the percent increase or decrease for year 2011 in comparison to year 2010.
2. Prepare common-size comparative balance sheets for years 2011 and 2010.
3. Compute the following ratios as of December 31, 2011, or for the year ended December 31, 2011, and identify its building block category for financial statement analysis.
   a. Current ratio
   b. Acid-test ratio
   c. Accounts receivable turnover
   d. Days' sales uncollected
   e. Inventory turnover
   f. Debt ratio
   g. Debt-to-equity ratio
   h. Times interest earned
   i. Profit margin ratio
   j. Total asset turnover
   k. Return on total assets
   l. Return on common stockholders' equity

PRECISION COMPANY
Comparative Income Statements
For Years Ended December 31, 2011 and 2010

	2011	2010
Sales	$2,486,000	$2,075,000
Cost of goods sold	1,523,000	1,222,000
Gross profit	963,000	853,000
Operating expenses		
Advertising expense	145,000	100,000
Sales salaries expense	240,000	280,000
Office salaries expense	165,000	200,000
Insurance expense	100,000	45,000
Supplies expense	26,000	35,000
Depreciation expense	85,000	75,000
Miscellaneous expenses	17,000	15,000
Total operating expenses	778,000	750,000
Operating income	185,000	103,000
Interest expense	44,000	46,000
Income before taxes	141,000	57,000
Income taxes	47,000	19,000
Net income	$ 94,000	$ 38,000
Earnings per share	$ 0.99	$ 0.40

PRECISION COMPANY
Comparative Balance Sheets
December 31, 2011 and 2010

	2011	2010
Assets		
Current assets		
Cash	$ 79,000	$ 42,000
Short-term investments	65,000	96,000
Accounts receivable, net	120,000	100,000
Merchandise inventory	250,000	265,000
Total current assets	514,000	503,000
Plant assets		
Store equipment, net	400,000	350,000
Office equipment, net	45,000	50,000
Buildings, net	625,000	675,000
Land	100,000	100,000
Total plant assets	1,170,000	1,175,000
Total assets	$1,684,000	$1,678,000
Liabilities		
Current liabilities		
Accounts payable	$ 164,000	$ 190,000
Short-term notes payable	75,000	90,000
Taxes payable	26,000	12,000
Total current liabilities	265,000	292,000
Long-term liabilities		
Notes payable (secured by mortgage on buildings)	400,000	420,000
Total liabilities	665,000	712,000
Stockholders' Equity		
Common stock, $5 par value	475,000	475,000
Retained earnings	544,000	491,000
Total stockholders' equity	1,019,000	966,000
Total liabilities and equity	$1,684,000	$1,678,000

PLANNING THE SOLUTION

- Set up a four-column income statement; enter the 2011 and 2010 amounts in the first two columns and then enter the dollar change in the third column and the percent change from 2010 in the fourth column.
- Set up a four-column balance sheet; enter the 2011 and 2010 year-end amounts in the first two columns and then compute and enter the amount of each item as a percent of total assets.
- Compute the required ratios using the data provided. Use the average of beginning and ending amounts when appropriate (see Exhibit 17.16 for definitions).

SOLUTION TO DEMONSTRATION PROBLEM

1.

PRECISION COMPANY
Comparative Income Statements
For Years Ended December 31, 2011 and 2010

			Increase (Decrease) in 2011	
	2011	2010	Amount	Percent
Sales	$2,486,000	$2,075,000	$411,000	19.8%
Cost of goods sold	1,523,000	1,222,000	301,000	24.6
Gross profit	963,000	853,000	110,000	12.9

[continued on next page]

[continued from previous page]

Operating expenses				
Advertising expense	145,000	100,000	45,000	45.0
Sales salaries expense	240,000	280,000	(40,000)	(14.3)
Office salaries expense	165,000	200,000	(35,000)	(17.5)
Insurance expense	100,000	45,000	55,000	122.2
Supplies expense	26,000	35,000	(9,000)	(25.7)
Depreciation expense	85,000	75,000	10,000	13.3
Miscellaneous expenses	17,000	15,000	2,000	13.3
Total operating expenses	778,000	750,000	28,000	3.7
Operating income	185,000	103,000	82,000	79.6
Interest expense	44,000	46,000	(2,000)	(4.3)
Income before taxes	141,000	57,000	84,000	147.4
Income taxes	47,000	19,000	28,000	147.4
Net income	$ 94,000	$ 38,000	$ 56,000	147.4
Earnings per share	$ 0.99	$ 0.40	$ 0.59	147.5

2.

PRECISION COMPANY
Common-Size Comparative Balance Sheets
December 31, 2011 and 2010

	December 31		Common-Size Percents	
	2011	2010	2011*	2010*
Assets				
Current assets				
Cash	$ 79,000	$ 42,000	4.7%	2.5%
Short-term investments	65,000	96,000	3.9	5.7
Accounts receivable, net	120,000	100,000	7.1	6.0
Merchandise inventory	250,000	265,000	14.8	15.8
Total current assets	514,000	503,000	30.5	30.0
Plant assets				
Store equipment, net	400,000	350,000	23.8	20.9
Office equipment, net	45,000	50,000	2.7	3.0
Buildings, net	625,000	675,000	37.1	40.2
Land	100,000	100,000	5.9	6.0
Total plant assets	1,170,000	1,175,000	69.5	70.0
Total assets	$1,684,000	$1,678,000	100.0	100.0
Liabilities				
Current liabilities				
Accounts payable	$ 164,000	$ 190,000	9.7%	11.3%
Short-term notes payable	75,000	90,000	4.5	5.4
Taxes payable	26,000	12,000	1.5	0.7
Total current liabilities	265,000	292,000	15.7	17.4
Long-term liabilities				
Notes payable (secured by mortgage on buildings)	400,000	420,000	23.8	25.0
Total liabilities	665,000	712,000	39.5	42.4
Stockholders' equity				
Common stock, $5 par value	475,000	475,000	28.2	28.3
Retained earnings	544,000	491,000	32.3	29.3
Total stockholders' equity	1,019,000	966,000	60.5	57.6
Total liabilities and equity	$1,684,000	$1,678,000	100.0	100.0

* Columns do not always exactly add to 100 due to rounding.

3. Ratios for 2011:

a. Current ratio: $514,000/$265,000 = 1.9:1 (liquidity and efficiency)
b. Acid-test ratio: ($79,000 + $65,000 + $120,000)/$265,000 = 1.0:1 (liquidity and efficiency)
c. Average receivables: ($120,000 + $100,000)/2 = $110,000
Accounts receivable turnover: $2,486,000/$110,000 = 22.6 times (liquidity and efficiency)
d. Days' sales uncollected: ($120,000/$2,486,000) × 365 = 17.6 days (liquidity and efficiency)
e. Average inventory: ($250,000 + $265,000)/2 = $257,500
Inventory turnover: $1,523,000/$257,500 = 5.9 times (liquidity and efficiency)
f. Debt ratio: $665,000/$1,684,000 = 39.5% (solvency)
g. Debt-to-equity ratio: $665,000/$1,019,000 = 0.65 (solvency)
h. Times interest earned: $185,000/$44,000 = 4.2 times (solvency)
i. Profit margin ratio: $94,000/$2,486,000 = 3.8% (profitability)
j. Average total assets: ($1,684,000 + $1,678,000)/2 = $1,681,000
Total asset turnover: $2,486,000/$1,681,000 = 1.48 times (liquidity and efficiency)
k. Return on total assets: $94,000/$1,681,000 = 5.6% or 3.8% × 1.48 = 5.6% (profitability)
l. Average total common equity: ($1,019,000 + $966,000)/2 = $992,500
Return on common stockholders' equity: $94,000/$992,500 = 9.5% (profitability)

APPENDIX 17A Sustainable Income

A2 Explain the form and assess the content of a complete income statement.

When a company's revenue and expense transactions are from normal, continuing operations, a simple income statement is usually adequate. When a company's activities include income-related events not part of its normal, continuing operations, it must disclose information to help users understand these events and predict future performance. To meet these objectives, companies separate the income statement into continuing operations, discontinued segments, extraordinary items, comprehensive income, and earnings per share. For illustration, Exhibit 17A.1 shows such an income statement for ComUS. These separate distinctions help us measure *sustainable income,* which is the income level most likely to continue into the future. Sustainable income is commonly used in PE ratios and other market-based measures of performance.

Continuing Operations The first major section (①) shows the revenues, expenses, and income from continuing operations. Users especially rely on this information to predict future operations. Many users view this section as the most important. Earlier chapters explained the items comprising income from continuing operations.

Discontinued Segments A **business segment** is a part of a company's operations that serves a particular line of business or class of customers. A segment has assets, liabilities, and financial results of operations that can be distinguished from those of other parts of the company. A company's gain or loss from selling or closing down a segment is separately reported. Section ② of Exhibit 17A.1 reports both (1) income from operating the discontinued segment for the current period prior to its disposal and (2) the loss from disposing of the segment's net assets. The income tax effects of each are reported separately from the income taxes expense in section ①.

Extraordinary Items Section ③ reports **extraordinary gains and losses,** which are those that are *both unusual* and *infrequent.* An **unusual gain or loss** is abnormal or otherwise unrelated to the company's regular activities and environment. An **infrequent gain or loss** is not expected to recur given the company's operating environment. Reporting extraordinary items in a separate category helps users predict future performance, absent the effects of extraordinary items. Items usually considered extraordinary include (1) expropriation (taking away) of property by a foreign government, (2) condemning of property by a domestic government body, (3) prohibition against using an asset by a newly enacted law, and (4) losses and gains from an unusual and infrequent calamity ("act of God"). Items *not* considered extraordinary include (1) write-downs of inventories and write-offs of receivables, (2) gains and losses from disposing of segments, and (3) financial effects of labor strikes.

EXHIBIT 17A.1

Income Statement (all-inclusive) for a Corporation

ComUS
Income Statement
For Year Ended December 31, 2011

①	Net sales		$8,478,000
	Operating expenses		
	Cost of goods sold	$5,950,000	
	Depreciation expense	35,000	
	Other selling, general, and administrative expenses	515,000	
	Interest expense	20,000	
	Total operating expenses		(6,520,000)
	Other gains (losses)		
	Loss on plant relocation		(45,000)
	Gain on sale of surplus land		72,000
	Income from continuing operations before taxes		1,985,000
	Income taxes expense		(595,500)
	Income from continuing operations		1,389,500
②	**Discontinued segment**		
	Income from operating Division A (net of $180,000 taxes)	420,000	
	Loss on disposal of Division A (net of $66,000 tax benefit)	(154,000)	266,000
	Income before extraordinary items		1,655,500
③	**Extraordinary items**		
	Gain on land expropriated by state (net of $85,200 taxes)	198,800	
	Loss from earthquake damage (net of $270,000 tax benefit)	(630,000)	(431,200)
	Net income		$1,224,300
④	**Earnings per common share (200,000 outstanding shares)**		
	Income from continuing operations		$ 6.95
	Discontinued operations		1.33
	Income before extraordinary items		8.28
	Extraordinary items		(2.16)
	Net income (basic earnings per share)		$ 6.12

Gains and losses that are neither unusual nor infrequent are reported as part of continuing operations. Gains and losses that are *either* unusual *or* infrequent, but *not* both, are reported as part of continuing operations *but* after the normal revenues and expenses.

Decision Maker Answer — p. 713 

Small Business Owner You own an orange grove near Jacksonville, Florida. A bad frost destroys about one-half of your oranges. You are currently preparing an income statement for a bank loan. Can you claim the loss of oranges as extraordinary? ■

Earnings per Share The final section ④ of the income statement in Exhibit 17A.1 reports earnings per share for each of the three subcategories of income (continuing operations, discontinued segments, and extraordinary items) when they exist. Earnings per share is discussed in Chapter 13.

Changes in Accounting Principles The *consistency concept* directs a company to apply the same accounting principles across periods. Yet a company can change from one acceptable accounting principle (such as FIFO, LIFO, or weighted-average) to another as long as the change improves the usefulness of information in its financial statements. A footnote would describe the accounting change and why it is an improvement.

Point: Changes in principles are sometimes required when new accounting standards are issued.

Changes in accounting principles require retrospective application to prior periods' financial statements. *Retrospective application* involves applying a different accounting principle to prior periods as if that principle had always been used. Retrospective application enhances the consistency of financial information between periods, which improves the usefulness of information, especially with comparative analyses. (Prior to 2005, the cumulative effect of changes in accounting principles was recognized in net income in the period of the change.) Accounting standards also require that *a change in depreciation, amortization, or depletion method for long-term operating assets is accounted for as a change in accounting estimate*—that is, prospectively over current and future periods. This reflects the notion that an entity should change its depreciation, amortization, or depletion method only with changes in estimated asset benefits, the pattern of benefit usage, or information about those benefits.

Quick Check Answers — p. 713 

13. Which of the following is an extraordinary item? (*a*) a settlement paid to a customer injured while using the company's product, (*b*) a loss to a plant from damages caused by a meteorite, or (*c*) a loss from selling old equipment.

14. Identify the four major sections of an income statement that are potentially reportable.

15. A company using FIFO for the past 15 years decides to switch to LIFO. The effect of this event on prior years' net income is (*a*) reported as if the new method had always been used; (*b*) ignored because it is a change in an accounting estimate; or (*c*) reported on the current year income statement.

Summary

C1 Explain the purpose and identify the building blocks of analysis. The purpose of financial statement analysis is to help users make better business decisions. Internal users want information to improve company efficiency and effectiveness in providing products and services. External users want information to make better and more informed decisions in pursuing their goals. The common goals of all users are to evaluate a company's (1) past and current performance, (2) current financial position, and (3) future performance and risk. Financial statement analysis focuses on four "building blocks" of analysis: (1) liquidity and efficiency—ability to meet short-term obligations and efficiently generate revenues; (2) solvency—ability to generate future revenues and meet long-term obligations; (3) profitability—ability to provide financial rewards sufficient to attract and retain financing; and (4) market prospects—ability to generate positive market expectations.

C2 Describe standards for comparisons in analysis. Standards for comparisons include (1) intracompany—prior performance and relations between financial items for the company under analysis; (2) competitor—one or more direct competitors of the company; (3) industry—industry statistics; and (4) guidelines (rules of thumb)—general standards developed from past experiences and personal judgments.

A1 Summarize and report results of analysis. A financial statement analysis report is often organized around the building blocks of analysis. A good report separates interpretations and conclusions of analysis from the information underlying them. An analysis report often consists of six sections: (1) executive summary, (2) analysis overview, (3) evidential matter, (4) assumptions, (5) key factors, and (6) inferences.

A2[A] Explain the form and assess the content of a complete income statement. An income statement has four *potential* sections: (1) continuing operations, (2) discontinued segments, (3) extraordinary items, and (4) earnings per share.

P1 Explain and apply methods of horizontal analysis. Horizontal analysis is a tool to evaluate changes in data across time. Two important tools of horizontal analysis are comparative statements and trend analysis. Comparative statements show amounts for two or more successive periods, often with changes disclosed in both absolute and percent terms. Trend analysis is used to reveal important changes occurring from one period to the next.

P2 Describe and apply methods of vertical analysis. Vertical analysis is a tool to evaluate each financial statement item or group of items in terms of a base amount. Two tools of vertical analysis are common-size statements and graphical analyses. Each item in common-size statements is expressed as a percent of a base amount. For the balance sheet, the base amount is usually total assets, and for the income statement, it is usually sales.

P3 Define and apply ratio analysis. Ratio analysis provides clues to and symptoms of underlying conditions. Ratios, properly interpreted, identify areas requiring further investigation. A ratio expresses a mathematical relation between two quantities such as a percent, rate, or proportion. Ratios can be organized into the building blocks of analysis: (1) liquidity and efficiency, (2) solvency, (3) profitability, and (4) market prospects.

Guidance Answers to Decision Maker

Auditor The *joint relation* referred to is the combined increase in sales and the decrease in expenses yielding more than a 5% increase in income. Both *individual* accounts (sales and expenses) yield percent changes within the ±5% acceptable range. However, a joint analysis suggests a different picture. For example, consider a joint analysis using the profit margin ratio. The client's profit margin is 11.46% ($206,000 − $182,400/$206,000) for the current year compared with 5.0% ($200,000 − $190,000/$200,000) for the prior year—yielding a 129% increase in profit margin! This is what concerns the partner, and it suggests expanding audit tests to verify or refute the client's figures.

Banker Your decision on the loan application is positive for at least two reasons. First, the current ratio suggests a strong ability to meet short-term obligations. Second, current assets of $160,000 and a current ratio of 4:1 imply current liabilities of $40,000 (one-fourth of current assets) and a working capital excess of $120,000. This working capital excess is 60% of the loan amount. However, if the application is for a 10-year loan, our decision is less optimistic. The current ratio and working capital suggest a good safety margin, but indications of inefficiency in operations exist. In particular, a 4:1 current ratio is more than double its key competitors' ratio. This is characteristic of inefficient asset use.

Small Business Owner The frost loss is probably not extraordinary. Jacksonville experiences enough recurring frost damage to make it difficult to argue this event is both unusual and infrequent. Still, you want to highlight the frost loss and hope the bank views this uncommon event separately from continuing operations.

Guidance Answers to Quick Checks

1. General-purpose financial statements are intended for a variety of users interested in a company's financial condition and performance—users without the power to require specialized financial reports to meet their specific needs.
2. General-purpose financial statements include the income statement, balance sheet, statement of stockholders' (owners') equity, and statement of cash flows plus the notes related to these statements.
3. *a*
4. Data from one or more direct competitors are usually preferred for comparative purposes.
5. *d*
6. Percents on comparative income statements show the increase or decrease in each item from one period to the next. On common-size comparative income statements, each item is shown as a percent of net sales for that period.
7. *c*
8. (*a*) ($820,000 + $240,000 + $470,000)/($350,000 + $180,000) = 2.9 to 1.
   (*b*) ($820,000 + $240,000)/($350,000 + $180,000) = 2:1.
9. (*a*) $2,500,000/[($290,000 + $240,000)/2] = 9.43 times.
   (*b*) ($290,000/$2,500,000) × 365 = 42 days.
   (*c*) $750,000/[($530,000 + $470,000)/2] = 1.5 times.
   (*d*) ($530,000/$750,000) × 365 = 258 days.
10. *c*
11. *b*
12. $$\text{Profit margin} \times \frac{\text{Total asset}}{\text{turnover}} = \frac{\text{Return on}}{\text{total assets}}$$
    $$\frac{\$945{,}000}{\$8{,}500{,}000} \times 1.8 = 20\%$$
13. (*b*)
14. The four (potentially reportable) major sections are income from continuing operations, discontinued segments, extraordinary items, and earnings per share.
15. (*a*); known as retrospective application.

Key Terms

mhhe.com/wildFAP20e

Business segment (p. 710)
Common-size financial statement (p. 693)
Comparative financial statements (p. 688)
Efficiency (p. 687)
Equity ratio (p. 701)
Extraordinary gains and losses (p. 710)
Financial reporting (p. 687)
Financial statement analysis (p. 686)
General-purpose financial statements (p. 687)
Horizontal analysis (p. 688)
Infrequent gain or loss (p. 710)
Liquidity (p. 687)
Market prospects (p. 687)
Profitability (p. 687)
Ratio analysis (p. 688)
Solvency (p. 687)
Unusual gain or loss (p. 710)
Vertical analysis (p. 688)
Working capital (p. 697)

Multiple Choice Quiz

Answers on p. 729

mhhe.com/wildFAP20e

Additional Quiz Questions are available at the book's Website.

1. A company's sales in 2010 were $300,000 and in 2011 were $351,000. Using 2010 as the base year, the sales trend percent for 2011 is:
   a. 17%
   b. 85%
   c. 100%
   d. 117%
   e. 48%

Use the following information for questions 2 through 5.

GALLOWAY COMPANY Balance Sheet December 31, 2011	
Assets	
Cash	$ 86,000
Accounts receivable	76,000
Merchandise inventory	122,000
Prepaid insurance	12,000
Long-term investments	98,000
Plant assets, net	436,000
Total assets	$830,000
Liabilities and Equity	
Current liabilities	$124,000
Long-term liabilities	90,000
Common stock	300,000
Retained earnings	316,000
Total liabilities and equity	$830,000

2. What is Galloway Company's current ratio?
a. 0.69
b. 1.31
c. 3.88
d. 6.69
e. 2.39

3. What is Galloway Company's acid-test ratio?
a. 2.39
b. 0.69
c. 1.31
d. 6.69
e. 3.88

4. What is Galloway Company's debt ratio?
a. 25.78%
b. 100.00%
c. 74.22%
d. 137.78%
e. 34.74%

5. What is Galloway Company's equity ratio?
a. 25.78%
b. 100.00%
c. 34.74%
d. 74.22%
e. 137.78%

A *Superscript letter A denotes assignments based on Appendix 17A.*
Icon denotes assignments that involve decision making.

Discussion Questions

1. What is the difference between comparative financial statements and common-size comparative statements?

2. Which items are usually assigned a 100% value on (*a*) a common-size balance sheet and (*b*) a common-size income statement?

3. Explain the difference between financial reporting and financial statements.

4. What three factors would influence your evaluation as to whether a company's current ratio is good or bad?

5. Suggest several reasons why a 2:1 current ratio might not be adequate for a particular company.

6. Why is working capital given special attention in the process of analyzing balance sheets?

7. What does the number of days' sales uncollected indicate?

8. What does a relatively high accounts receivable turnover indicate about a company's short-term liquidity?

9. Why is a company's capital structure, as measured by debt and equity ratios, important to financial statement analysts?

10. How does inventory turnover provide information about a company's short-term liquidity?

11. What ratios would you compute to evaluate management performance?

12. Why would a company's return on total assets be different from its return on common stockholders' equity?

13. Where on the income statement does a company report an unusual gain not expected to occur more often than once every two years or so?

14. Use Research In Motion's financial statements in Appendix A to compute its return on total assets for fiscal years ended February 27, 2010, and February 28, 2009. Total assets at March 1, 2008, were $5,511,187 (in thousands). RIM

15. Refer to Palm's financial statements in Appendix A to compute its equity ratio as of May 31, 2009 and May 31, 2008. Palm

16. Refer to Nokia's financial statements in Appendix A. Compute its debt ratio as of December 31, 2009, and December 31, 2008. NOKIA

17. Refer to Apple's financial statements in Appendix A. Compute its profit margin for the fiscal year ended September 26, 2009. Apple

connect

QUICK STUDY

QS 17-1
Financial reporting C1

Which of the following items (1) through (9) are part of financial reporting but are *not* included as part of general-purpose financial statements? (1) stock price information and analysis, (2) statement of cash flows, (3) management discussion and analysis of financial performance, (4) income statement, (5) company news releases, (6) balance sheet, (7) financial statement notes, (8) statement of shareholders' equity, (9) prospectus.

QS 17-2
Standard of comparison C2

What are four possible standards of comparison used to analyze financial statement ratios? Which of these is generally considered to be the most useful? Which one is least likely to provide a good basis for comparison?

QS 17-3
Trend percents
P1

Use the following information for Tipster Corporation to determine the 2010 and 2011 trend percents for net sales using 2010 as the base year.

($ thousands)	2011	2010
Net sales	$201,600	$114,800
Cost of goods sold	109,200	60,200

QS 17-4
Common-size analysis P2

Refer to the information in QS 17-3. Use that information for Tipster Corporation to determine the 2010 and 2011 common-size percents for cost of goods sold using net sales as the base.

QS 17-5
Horizontal analysis
P1

Compute the annual dollar changes and percent changes for each of the following accounts.

	2011	2010
Short-term investments	$217,800	$165,000
Accounts receivable	42,120	48,000
Notes payable	57,000	0

QS 17-6
Ratio interpretation
P3

For each ratio listed, identify whether the change in ratio value from 2010 to 2011 is usually regarded as favorable or unfavorable.

Ratio	2011	2010	Ratio	2011	2010
1. Profit margin	8%	6%	5. Accounts receivable turnover	5.4	6.6
2. Debt ratio	45%	40%	6. Basic earnings per share	$1.24	$1.20
3. Gross margin	33%	45%	7. Inventory turnover	3.5	3.3
4. Acid-test ratio	0.99	1.10	8. Dividend yield	1%	0.8%

QS 17-7
Analysis of short-term financial condition
A1 

The following information is available for Silverado Company and Titan Company, similar firms operating in the same industry. Write a half-page report comparing Silverado and Titan using the available information. Your discussion should include their ability to meet current obligations and to use current assets efficiently.

	Silverado			Titan		
	2012	2011	2010	2012	2011	2010
Current ratio	1.6	1.7	2.0	3.1	2.6	1.8
Acid-test ratio	0.9	1.0	1.1	2.7	2.4	1.5
Accounts receivable turnover	29.5	24.2	28.2	15.4	14.2	15.0
Merchandise inventory turnover	23.2	20.9	16.1	13.5	12.0	11.6
Working capital	$60,000	$48,000	$42,000	$121,000	$93,000	$68,000

Team Project: Assume that the two companies apply for a one-year loan from the team. Identify additional information the companies must provide before the team can make a loan decision.

QS 17-8[A]
Error adjustments
A2  

A review of the notes payable files discovers that three years ago the company reported the entire amount of a payment (principal and interest) on an installment note payable as interest expense. This mistake had a material effect on the amount of income in that year. How should the correction be reported in the current year financial statements?

QS 17-9
International ratio analysis
C2 

Answer each of the following related to international accounting and analysis.

a. Identify an advantage to using horizontal and vertical analyses when examining companies reporting under different currencies.

b. Identify a limitation to using ratio analysis when examining companies reporting under different accounting systems such as IFRS versus U.S. GAAP.

connect

EXERCISES

Exercise 17-1
Building blocks of analysis
C1

Match the ratio to the building block of financial statement analysis to which it best relates.

A. Liquidity and efficiency **C.** Profitability
B. Solvency **D.** Market prospects

1. ______ Book value per common share
2. ______ Days' sales in inventory
3. ______ Accounts receivable turnover
4. ______ Debt-to-equity
5. ______ Times interest earned
6. ______ Gross margin ratio
7. ______ Acid-test ratio
8. ______ Equity ratio
9. ______ Return on total assets
10. ______ Dividend yield

Exercise 17-2
Identifying financial ratios
C2 

1. Which two short-term liquidity ratios measure how frequently a company collects its accounts?

2. What measure reflects the difference between current assets and current liabilities?

3. Which two ratios are key components in measuring a company's operating efficiency? Which ratio summarizes these two components?

Exercise 17-3
Computation and analysis of trend percents
P1

Compute trend percents for the following accounts, using 2009 as the base year. State whether the situation as revealed by the trends appears to be favorable or unfavorable for each account.

	2013	2012	2011	2010	2009
Sales	$283,880	$271,800	$253,680	$235,560	$151,000
Cost of goods sold	129,200	123,080	116,280	107,440	68,000
Accounts receivable	19,100	18,300	17,400	16,200	10,000

Exercise 17-4
Determination of income effects from common-size and trend percents
P1 P2

Common-size and trend percents for Aziz Company's sales, cost of goods sold, and expenses follow. Determine whether net income increased, decreased, or remained unchanged in this three-year period.

	Common-Size Percents			Trend Percents		
	2012	2011	2010	2012	2011	2010
Sales	100.0%	100.0%	100.0%	104.4%	103.2%	100.0%
Cost of goods sold	62.4	60.9	58.1	102.0	108.1	100.0
Total expenses	14.3	13.8	14.1	105.9	101.0	100.0

Exercise 17-5
Common-size percent computation and interpretation
P2 

Express the following comparative income statements in common-size percents and assess whether or not this company's situation has improved in the most recent year.

GERALDO CORPORATION Comparative Income Statements For Years Ended December 31, 2011 and 2010	2011	2010
Sales	$720,000	$535,000
Cost of goods sold	475,200	280,340
Gross profit	244,800	254,660
Operating expenses	151,200	103,790
Net income	$ 93,600	$150,870

Exercise 17-6
Analysis of efficiency and financial leverage
A1 

Rolf Company and Kent Company are similar firms that operate in the same industry. Kent began operations in 2011 and Rolf in 2008. In 2013, both companies pay 7% interest on their debt to creditors. The following additional information is available.

	Rolf Company			Kent Company		
	2013	2012	2011	2013	2012	2011
Total asset turnover	3.0	2.7	2.9	1.6	1.4	1.1
Return on total assets	8.9%	9.5%	8.7%	5.8%	5.5%	5.2%
Profit margin ratio	2.3%	2.4%	2.2%	2.7%	2.9%	2.8%
Sales	$400,000	$370,000	$386,000	$200,000	$160,000	$100,000

Write a half-page report comparing Rolf and Kent using the available information. Your analysis should include their ability to use assets efficiently to produce profits. Also comment on their success in employing financial leverage in 2013.

Exercise 17-7
Common-size percents
P2  

Sanderson Company's year-end balance sheets follow. Express the balance sheets in common-size percents. Round amounts to the nearest one-tenth of a percent. Analyze and comment on the results.

At December 31	2012	2011	2010
Assets			
Cash	$ 30,800	$ 35,625	$ 36,800
Accounts receivable, net	88,500	62,500	49,200
Merchandise inventory	111,500	82,500	53,000
Prepaid expenses	9,700	9,375	4,000
Plant assets, net	277,500	255,000	229,500
Total assets	$518,000	$445,000	$372,500
Liabilities and Equity			
Accounts payable	$128,900	$ 75,250	$ 49,250
Long-term notes payable secured by mortgages on plant assets	97,500	102,500	82,500
Common stock, $10 par value	162,500	162,500	162,500
Retained earnings	129,100	104,750	78,250
Total liabilities and equity	$518,000	$445,000	$372,500

Exercise 17-8
Liquidity analysis
P3 

Refer to Sanderson Company's balance sheets in Exercise 17-7. Analyze its year-end short-term liquidity position at the end of 2012, 2011, and 2010 by computing (1) the current ratio and (2) the acid-test ratio. Comment on the ratio results. (Round ratio amounts to two decimals.)

Exercise 17-9
Liquidity analysis and interpretation
P3  

Refer to the Sanderson Company information in Exercise 17-7. The company's income statements for the years ended December 31, 2012 and 2011, follow. Assume that all sales are on credit and then compute: (1) days' sales uncollected, (2) accounts receivable turnover, (3) inventory turnover, and (4) days' sales in inventory. Comment on the changes in the ratios from 2011 to 2012. (Round amounts to one decimal.)

For Year Ended December 31	2012		2011	
Sales		$672,500		$530,000
Cost of goods sold	$410,225		$344,500	
Other operating expenses	208,550		133,980	
Interest expense	11,100		12,300	
Income taxes	8,525		7,845	
Total costs and expenses		638,400		498,625
Net income		$ 34,100		$ 31,375
Earnings per share		$ 2.10		$ 1.93

Exercise 17-10
Risk and capital structure analysis P3

Refer to the Sanderson Company information in Exercises 17-7 and 17-9. Compare the company's long-term risk and capital structure positions at the end of 2012 and 2011 by computing these ratios: (1) debt and equity ratios, (2) debt-to-equity ratio, and (3) times interest earned. Comment on these ratio results.

Exercise 17-11
Efficiency and profitability analysis P3 

Refer to Sanderson Company's financial information in Exercises 17-7 and 17-9. Evaluate the company's efficiency and profitability by computing the following for 2012 and 2011: (1) profit margin ratio, (2) total asset turnover, and (3) return on total assets. Comment on these ratio results.

Exercise 17-12
Profitability analysis
P3 

Refer to Sanderson Company's financial information in Exercises 17-7 and 17-9. Additional information about the company follows. To help evaluate the company's profitability, compute and interpret the following ratios for 2012 and 2011: (1) return on common stockholders' equity, (2) price-earnings ratio on December 31, and (3) dividend yield.

Common stock market price, December 31, 2012	$15.00
Common stock market price, December 31, 2011	14.00
Annual cash dividends per share in 2012	0.30
Annual cash dividends per share in 2011	0.15

Exercise 17-13[A]
Income statement categories
A2

In 2011, Jin Merchandising, Inc., sold its interest in a chain of retail outlets, taking the company completely out of the retailing business. The company still operates its wholesale outlets. A listing of the major sections of an income statement follows:

A. Income (loss) from continuing operations
B. Income (loss) from operating, or gain (loss) from disposing, a discontinued segment
C. Extraordinary gain (loss)

Indicate where each of the following income-related items for this company appears on its 2011 income statement by writing the letter of the appropriate section in the blank beside each item.

Section	Item	Debit	Credit
______	1. Net sales		$3,000,000
______	2. Gain on state's condemnation of company property (net of tax)		330,000
______	3. Salaries expense	$ 640,000	
______	4. Income taxes expense	117,000	
______	5. Depreciation expense	432,500	
______	6. Gain on sale of retail business segment (net of tax)		875,000
______	7. Loss from operating retail business segment (net of tax)	544,000	
______	8. Cost of goods sold	1,580,000	

Use the financial data for Jin Merchandising, Inc., in Exercise 17-13 to prepare its income statement for calendar year 2011. (Ignore the earnings per share section.)

Exercise 17-14[A]
Income statement presentation
A2

Nintendo Company, Ltd., reports the following financial information as of, or for the year ended, March 31, 2008. Nintendo reports its financial statements in both Japanese yen and U.S. dollars as shown (amounts in millions).

Exercise 17-15
Ratio analysis under different currencies
P3 

Current assets	¥1,646,834	$16,468.348
Total assets	1,802,490	18,024.903
Current liabilities	567,222	5,672.229
Net sales	1,672,423	16,724.230
Net income	257,342	2,573.426

1. Compute Nintendo's current ratio, net profit margin, and sales-to-total-assets using the financial information reported in (a) yen and (b) dollars.
2. What can we conclude from a review of the results for part 1?

connect

PROBLEM SET A

Problem 17-1A
Ratios, common-size statements, and trend percents
P1 P2 P3 

mhhe.com/wildFAP20e

Selected comparative financial statements of Bennington Company follow.

BENNINGTON COMPANY
Comparative Income Statements
For Years Ended December 31, 2012, 2011, and 2010

	2012	2011	2010
Sales	$444,000	$340,000	$236,000
Cost of goods sold	267,288	212,500	151,040
Gross profit	176,712	127,500	84,960
Selling expenses	62,694	46,920	31,152
Administrative expenses	40,137	29,920	19,470
Total expenses	102,831	76,840	50,622
Income before taxes	73,881	50,660	34,338
Income taxes	13,764	10,370	6,962
Net income	$ 60,117	$ 40,290	$ 27,376

BENNINGTON COMPANY
Comparative Balance Sheets
December 31, 2012, 2011, and 2010

	2012	2011	2010
Assets			
Current assets	$ 48,480	$ 37,924	$ 50,648
Long-term investments	0	500	3,720
Plant assets, net	90,000	96,000	57,000
Total assets	$138,480	$134,424	$111,368
Liabilities and Equity			
Current liabilities	$ 20,200	$ 19,960	$ 19,480
Common stock	72,000	72,000	54,000
Other paid-in capital	9,000	9,000	6,000
Retained earnings	37,280	33,464	31,888
Total liabilities and equity	$138,480	$134,424	$111,368

Required

1. Compute each year's current ratio. (Round ratio amounts to one decimal.)
2. Express the income statement data in common-size percents. (Round percents to two decimals.)

Check (3) 2012, Total assets trend, 124.34%

3. Express the balance sheet data in trend percents with 2010 as the base year. (Round percents to two decimals.)

Analysis Component

4. Comment on any significant relations revealed by the ratios and percents computed.

Problem 17-2A
Calculation and analysis of trend percents
A1 P1 

Selected comparative financial statements of Sugo Company follow.

SUGO COMPANY
Comparative Income Statements
For Years Ended December 31, 2012–2006

($ thousands)	2012	2011	2010	2009	2008	2007	2006
Sales	$1,594	$1,396	$1,270	$1,164	$1,086	$1,010	$828
Cost of goods sold	1,146	932	802	702	652	610	486
Gross profit	448	464	468	462	434	400	342
Operating expenses	340	266	244	180	156	154	128
Net income	$ 108	$ 198	$ 224	$ 282	$ 278	$ 246	$214

SUGO COMPANY
Comparative Balance Sheets
December 31, 2012–2006

($ thousands)	2012	2011	2010	2009	2008	2007	2006
Assets							
Cash	$ 68	$ 88	$ 92	$ 94	$ 98	$ 96	$ 99
Accounts receivable, net	480	504	456	350	308	292	206
Merchandise inventory	1,738	1,264	1,104	932	836	710	515
Other current assets	46	42	24	44	38	38	19
Long-term investments	0	0	0	136	136	136	136
Plant assets, net	2,120	2,114	1,852	1,044	1,078	960	825
Total assets	$4,452	$4,012	$3,528	$2,600	$2,494	$2,232	$1,800
Liabilities and Equity							
Current liabilities	$1,120	$ 942	$ 618	$ 514	$ 446	$ 422	$ 272
Long-term liabilities	1,194	1,040	1,012	470	480	520	390
Common stock	1,000	1,000	1,000	840	840	640	640
Other paid-in capital	250	250	250	180	180	160	160
Retained earnings	888	780	648	596	548	490	338
Total liabilities and equity	$4,452	$4,012	$3,528	$2,600	$2,494	$2,232	$1,800

Required

Check (1) 2012, Total assets trend, 247.3%

1. Compute trend percents for all components of both statements using 2006 as the base year. (Round percents to one decimal.)

Analysis Component

2. Analyze and comment on the financial statements and trend percents from part 1.

Problem 17-3A
Transactions, working capital, and liquidity ratios
P3

mhhe.com/wildFAP20e

Park Corporation began the month of May with $650,000 of current assets, a current ratio of 2.50:1, and an acid-test ratio of 1.10:1. During the month, it completed the following transactions (the company uses a perpetual inventory system).

May 2 Purchased $75,000 of merchandise inventory on credit.
8 Sold merchandise inventory that cost $58,000 for $103,000 cash.
10 Collected $19,000 cash on an account receivable.
15 Paid $21,000 cash to settle an account payable.

17 Wrote off a $3,000 bad debt against the Allowance for Doubtful Accounts account.
22 Declared a $1 per share cash dividend on its 40,000 shares of outstanding common stock.
26 Paid the dividend declared on May 22.
27 Borrowed $75,000 cash by giving the bank a 30-day, 10% note.
28 Borrowed $90,000 cash by signing a long-term secured note.
29 Used the $165,000 cash proceeds from the notes to buy new machinery.

Check May 22: Current ratio, 2.12; Acid-test ratio, 1.04

May 29: Current ratio, 1.82; Working capital, $320,000

Required

Prepare a table showing Park's (1) current ratio, (2) acid-test ratio, and (3) working capital, after each transaction. Round ratios to two decimals.

Problem 17-4A
Calculation of financial statement ratios
P3

mhhe.com/wildFAP20e

Selected year-end financial statements of McCord Corporation follow. (All sales were on credit; selected balance sheet amounts at December 31, 2010, were inventory, $32,400; total assets, $182,400; common stock, $90,000; and retained earnings, $31,300.)

McCORD CORPORATION
Income Statement
For Year Ended December 31, 2011

Sales	$348,600
Cost of goods sold	229,150
Gross profit	119,450
Operating expenses	52,500
Interest expense	3,100
Income before taxes	63,850
Income taxes	15,800
Net income	$ 48,050

McCORD CORPORATION
Balance Sheet
December 31, 2011

Assets		**Liabilities and Equity**	
Cash	$ 9,000	Accounts payable	$ 16,500
Short-term investments	7,400	Accrued wages payable	2,200
Accounts receivable, net	28,200	Income taxes payable	2,300
Notes receivable (trade)*	3,500	Long-term note payable, secured by mortgage on plant assets	62,400
Merchandise inventory	31,150	Common stock	90,000
Prepaid expenses	1,650	Retained earnings	59,800
Plant assets, net	152,300		
Total assets	$233,200	Total liabilities and equity	$233,200

* These are short-term notes receivable arising from customer (trade) sales.

Required

Compute the following: (1) current ratio, (2) acid-test ratio, (3) days' sales uncollected, (4) inventory turnover, (5) days' sales in inventory, (6) debt-to-equity ratio, (7) times interest earned, (8) profit margin ratio, (9) total asset turnover, (10) return on total assets, and (11) return on common stockholders' equity.

Check Acid-test ratio, 2.3 to 1; Inventory turnover, 7.2

Problem 17-5A
Comparative ratio analysis
A1 P3  

Summary information from the financial statements of two companies competing in the same industry follows.

	Ryan Company	Priest Company
Data from the current year-end balance sheets		
Assets		
Cash	$ 18,500	$ 33,000
Accounts receivable, net	36,400	56,400
Current notes receivable (trade)	8,100	6,200
Merchandise inventory	83,440	131,500
Prepaid expenses	4,000	5,950
Plant assets, net	284,000	303,400
Total assets	$434,440	$536,450
Liabilities and Equity		
Current liabilities	$ 60,340	$ 92,300
Long-term notes payable	79,800	100,000
Common stock, $5 par value	175,000	205,000
Retained earnings	119,300	139,150
Total liabilities and equity	$434,440	$536,450

	Ryan Company	Priest Company
Data from the current year's income statement		
Sales	$660,000	$780,200
Cost of goods sold	485,100	532,500
Interest expense	6,900	11,000
Income tax expense	12,800	19,300
Net income	67,770	105,000
Basic earnings per share	1.94	2.56
Beginning-of-year balance sheet data		
Accounts receivable, net	$ 28,800	$ 53,200
Current notes receivable (trade)	0	0
Merchandise inventory	54,600	106,400
Total assets	388,000	372,500
Common stock, $5 par value	175,000	205,000
Retained earnings	94,300	90,600

Required

Check (1) Priest: Accounts receivable turnover, 13.5; Inventory turnover, 4.5

(2) Ryan: Profit margin, 10.3%; PE, 12.9

1. For both companies compute the (*a*) current ratio, (*b*) acid-test ratio, (*c*) accounts (including notes) receivable turnover, (*d*) inventory turnover, (*e*) days' sales in inventory, and (*f*) days' sales uncollected. Identify the company you consider to be the better short-term credit risk and explain why.

2. For both companies compute the (*a*) profit margin ratio, (*b*) total asset turnover, (*c*) return on total assets, and (*d*) return on common stockholders' equity. Assuming that each company paid cash dividends of $1.50 per share and each company's stock can be purchased at $25 per share, compute their (*e*) price-earnings ratios and (*f*) dividend yields. Identify which company's stock you would recommend as the better investment and explain why.

Problem 17-6A[A]
Income statement computations and format

A2 

Selected account balances from the adjusted trial balance for Zen Corporation as of its calendar year-end December 31, 2011, follow.

	Debit	Credit
a. Income taxes expense	$?	
b. Correction of overstatement of prior year's sales (pretax)	17,000	
c. Loss on sale of machinery	26,850	
d. Loss from settlement of lawsuit	24,750	
e. Other operating expenses	107,400	
f. Accumulated depreciation—Machinery		$ 72,600
g. Gain from settlement of lawsuit		45,000
h. Accumulated depreciation—Buildings		175,500
i. Loss from operating a discontinued segment (pretax)	19,250	
j. Gain on insurance recovery of tornado damage (pretax and extraordinary)		30,120
k. Net sales		999,500
l. Depreciation expense—Buildings	53,000	
m. Depreciation expense—Machinery	35,000	
n. Gain on sale of discontinued segment's assets (pretax)		35,000
o. Accounts payable		45,000
p. Interest revenue		15,000
q. Cost of goods sold	483,500	

Required

Answer each of the following questions by providing supporting computations.

1. Assume that the company's income tax rate is 30% for all items. Identify the tax effects and after-tax amounts of the four items labeled pretax.
2. What is the amount of income from continuing operations before income taxes? What is the amount of the income taxes expense? What is the amount of income from continuing operations?
3. What is the total amount of after-tax income (loss) associated with the discontinued segment?
4. What is the amount of income (loss) before the extraordinary items?
5. What is the amount of net income for the year?

Check (3) $11,025
(4) $241,325
(5) $262,409

PROBLEM SET B

Problem 17-1B
Ratios, common-size statements, and trend percents
P1 P2 P3 

Selected comparative financial statement information of Sawgrass Corporation follows.

SAWGRASS CORPORATION
Comparative Income Statements
For Years Ended December 31, 2012, 2011, and 2010

	2012	2011	2010
Sales	$199,800	$167,000	$144,800
Cost of goods sold	109,890	87,175	67,200
Gross profit	89,910	79,825	77,600
Selling expenses	23,680	20,790	19,000
Administrative expenses	17,760	15,610	16,700
Total expenses	41,440	36,400	35,700
Income before taxes	48,470	43,425	41,900
Income taxes	5,050	4,910	4,300
Net income	$ 43,420	$ 38,515	$ 37,600

SAWGRASS CORPORATION
Comparative Balance Sheets
December 31, 2012, 2011, and 2010

	2012	2011	2010
Assets			
Current assets	$ 55,860	$ 33,660	$ 37,300
Long-term investments	0	2,700	11,600
Plant assets, net	113,810	114,660	80,000
Total assets	$169,670	$151,020	$128,900
Liabilities and Equity			
Current liabilities	$ 23,370	$ 20,180	$ 17,500
Common stock	47,500	47,500	38,000
Other paid-in capital	14,850	14,850	12,300
Retained earnings	83,950	68,490	61,100
Total liabilities and equity	$169,670	$151,020	$128,900

Required

1. Compute each year's current ratio. (Round ratio amounts to one decimal.)
2. Express the income statement data in common-size percents. (Round percents to two decimals.)
3. Express the balance sheet data in trend percents with 2010 as the base year. (Round percents to two decimals.)

Check (3) 2012, Total assets trend, 131.63%

Analysis Component

4. Comment on any significant relations revealed by the ratios and percents computed.

Problem 17-2B
Calculation and analysis of trend percents
A1 P1 

Selected comparative financial statements of Deuce Company follow.

DEUCE COMPANY
Comparative Income Statements
For Years Ended December 31, 2012–2006

($ thousands)	2012	2011	2010	2009	2008	2007	2006
Sales	$660	$710	$730	$780	$840	$870	$960
Cost of goods sold	376	390	394	414	440	450	480
Gross profit	284	320	336	366	400	420	480
Operating expenses	184	204	212	226	240	244	250
Net income	$100	$116	$124	$140	$160	$176	$230

DEUCE COMPANY
Comparative Balance Sheets
December 31, 2012–2006

($ thousands)	2012	2011	2010	2009	2008	2007	2006
Assets							
Cash	$ 34	$ 36	$ 42	$ 44	$ 50	$ 52	$ 58
Accounts receivable, net	120	126	130	134	140	144	150
Merchandise inventory	156	162	168	170	176	180	198
Other current assets	24	24	26	28	28	30	30
Long-term investments	26	20	16	100	100	100	100
Plant assets, net	410	414	420	312	320	328	354
Total assets	$770	$782	$802	$788	$814	$834	$890
Liabilities and Equity							
Current liabilities	$138	$146	$176	$180	$200	$250	$270
Long-term liabilities	82	110	132	138	184	204	250
Common stock	150	150	150	150	150	150	150
Other paid-in capital	60	60	60	60	60	60	60
Retained earnings	340	316	284	260	220	170	160
Total liabilities and equity	$770	$782	$802	$788	$814	$834	$890

Required

Check (1) 2012, Total assets trend, 86.5%

1. Compute trend percents for all components of both statements using 2006 as the base year. (Round percents to one decimal.)

Analysis Component

2. Analyze and comment on the financial statements and trend percents from part 1.

Problem 17-3B
Transactions, working capital, and liquidity ratios P3

Ready Corporation began the month of June with $280,000 of current assets, a current ratio of 2.8:1, and an acid-test ratio of 1.2:1. During the month, it completed the following transactions (the company uses a perpetual inventory system).

Check June 1: Current ratio, 3.19; Acid-test ratio, 2.21

June 1 Sold merchandise inventory that cost $62,000 for $101,000 cash.
3 Collected $78,000 cash on an account receivable.
5 Purchased $130,000 of merchandise inventory on credit.
7 Borrowed $90,000 cash by giving the bank a 60-day, 10% note.
10 Borrowed $180,000 cash by signing a long-term secured note.
12 Purchased machinery for $280,000 cash.
15 Declared a $1 per share cash dividend on its 60,000 shares of outstanding common stock.
19 Wrote off a $7,000 bad debt against the Allowance for Doubtful Accounts account.
22 Paid $11,000 cash to settle an account payable.
30 Paid the dividend declared on June 15.

June 30: Working capital, $59,000; Current ratio, 1.19

Required

Prepare a table showing the company's (1) current ratio, (2) acid-test ratio, and (3) working capital after each transaction. Round ratios to two decimals.

Selected year-end financial statements of Overland Corporation follow. (All sales were on credit; selected balance sheet amounts at December 31, 2010, were inventory, $16,400; total assets, $95,900; common stock, $41,500; and retained earnings, $19,800.)

Problem 17-4B
Calculation of financial statement ratios
P3

OVERLAND CORPORATION Income Statement For Year Ended December 31, 2011	
Sales	$215,500
Cost of goods sold	136,100
Gross profit	79,400
Operating expenses	50,200
Interest expense	1,200
Income before taxes	28,000
Income taxes	2,200
Net income	$ 25,800

OVERLAND CORPORATION Balance Sheet December 31, 2011			
Assets		**Liabilities and Equity**	
Cash	$ 5,100	Accounts payable	$ 10,500
Short-term investments	5,900	Accrued wages payable	2,300
Accounts receivable, net	11,100	Income taxes payable	1,600
Notes receivable (trade)*	2,000	Long-term note payable, secured by mortgage on plant assets	25,000
Merchandise inventory	12,500	Common stock, $5 par value	41,000
Prepaid expenses	1,000	Retained earnings	30,100
Plant assets, net	72,900	Total liabilities and equity	$110,500
Total assets	$110,500		

* These are short-term notes receivable arising from customer (trade) sales.

Required

Compute the following: (1) current ratio, (2) acid-test ratio, (3) days' sales uncollected, (4) inventory turnover, (5) days' sales in inventory, (6) debt-to-equity ratio, (7) times interest earned, (8) profit margin ratio, (9) total asset turnover, (10) return on total assets, and (11) return on common stockholders' equity.

Check Acid-test ratio, 1.7 to 1; Inventory turnover, 9.4

Summary information from the financial statements of two companies competing in the same industry follows.

Problem 17-5B
Comparative ratio analysis
A1 P3

	Loud Company	Clear Company
Data from the current year-end balance sheets		
Assets		
Cash	$ 22,000	$ 38,500
Accounts receivable, net	79,100	72,500
Current notes receivable (trade)	13,600	11,000
Merchandise inventory	88,800	84,000
Prepaid expenses	11,700	12,100
Plant assets, net	178,900	254,300
Total assets	$394,100	$472,400
Liabilities and Equity		
Current liabilities	$ 92,500	$ 99,000
Long-term notes payable	95,000	95,300
Common stock, $5 par value	135,000	143,000
Retained earnings	71,600	135,100
Total liabilities and equity	$394,100	$472,400

	Loud Company	Clear Company
Data from the current year's income statement		
Sales	$395,600	$669,500
Cost of goods sold	292,600	482,000
Interest expense	7,900	12,400
Income tax expense	7,700	14,300
Net income	35,850	63,700
Basic earnings per share	1.33	2.23
Beginning-of-year balance sheet data		
Accounts receivable, net	$ 74,200	$ 75,300
Current notes receivable (trade)	0	0
Merchandise inventory	107,100	82,500
Total assets	385,400	445,000
Common stock, $5 par value	135,000	143,000
Retained earnings	51,100	111,700

Required

Check (1) Loud: Accounts receivable turnover, 4.7; Inventory turnover, 3.0

(2) Clear: Profit margin, 9.5%; PE, 11.2

1. For both companies compute the (*a*) current ratio, (*b*) acid-test ratio, (*c*) accounts (including notes) receivable turnover, (*d*) inventory turnover, (*e*) days' sales in inventory, and (*f*) days' sales uncollected. Identify the company you consider to be the better short-term credit risk and explain why.
2. For both companies compute the (*a*) profit margin ratio, (*b*) total asset turnover, (*c*) return on total assets, and (*d*) return on common stockholders' equity. Assuming that each company paid cash dividends of $3.00 per share and each company's stock can be purchased at $25 per share, compute their (*e*) price-earnings ratios and (*f*) dividend yields. Identify which company's stock you would recommend as the better investment and explain why.

Problem 17-6B[A]
Income statement computations and format

A2 

Selected account balances from the adjusted trial balance for Halogen Corp. as of its calendar year-end December 31, 2011, follow.

	Debit	Credit
a. Other operating expenses	$ 338,000	
b. Depreciation expense—Buildings	110,000	
c. Loss from settlement of lawsuit	46,000	
d. Income taxes expense	?	
e. Loss on hurricane damage (pretax and extraordinary)	74,000	
f. Accumulated depreciation—Buildings		$ 230,000
g. Accumulated depreciation—Equipment		410,000
h. Interest revenue		30,000
i. Net sales		2,650,000
j. Gain from settlement of lawsuit		78,000
k. Loss on sale of building	34,000	
l. Loss from operating a discontinued segment (pretax)	130,000	
m. Accounts payable		142,000
n. Correction of overstatement of prior year's expense (pretax)		58,000
o. Cost of goods sold	1,050,000	
p. Loss on sale of discontinued segment's assets (pretax)	190,000	
q. Depreciation expense—Equipment	166,000	

Required

Answer each of the following questions by providing supporting computations.

1. Assume that the company's income tax rate is 25% for all items. Identify the tax effects and after-tax amounts of the four items labeled pretax.
2. What is the amount of income from continuing operations before income taxes? What is the amount of income taxes expense? What is the amount of income from continuing operations?
3. What is the total amount of after-tax income (loss) associated with the discontinued segment?
4. What is the amount of income (loss) before the extraordinary items?
5. What is the amount of net income for the year?

Check (3) $(240,000)

(4) $520,500

(5) $465,000

SERIAL PROBLEM
Business Solutions

P3

(This serial problem began in Chapter 1 and continues through most of the book. If previous chapter segments were not completed, the serial problem can begin at this point. It is helpful, but not necessary, to use the Working Papers that accompany the book.)

SP 17 Use the following selected data from Business Solutions' income statement for the three months ended March 31, 2012, and from its March 31, 2012, balance sheet to complete the requirements below: computer services revenue, $25,307; net sales (of goods), $18,693; total sales and revenue, $44,000; cost of goods sold, $14,052; net income, $18,833; quick assets, $90,924; current assets, $95,568; total assets, $120,268; current liabilities, $875; total liabilities, $875; and total equity, $119,393.

Required

1. Compute the gross margin ratio (both with and without services revenue) and net profit margin ratio.
2. Compute the current ratio and acid-test ratio.
3. Compute the debt ratio and equity ratio.
4. What percent of its assets are current? What percent are long term?

Beyond the Numbers

REPORTING IN ACTION
A1 P1 P2 
RIM

BTN 17-1 Refer to Research In Motion financial statements in Appendix A to answer the following.

1. Using fiscal 2008 as the base year, compute trend percents for fiscal years 2008, 2009, and 2010 for revenues, cost of sales, operating expenses, income taxes, and net income. (Round percents to one decimal.)
2. Compute common-size percents for fiscal years 2009 and 2010 for the following categories of assets: (*a*) total current assets, (*b*) property and equipment, net, and (*c*) intangible assets. (Round to the nearest tenth of a percent.)
3. Comment on any notable changes across the years for the income statement trends computed in part 1 and the balance sheet percents computed in part 2.

Fast Forward

4. Access Research In Motion's financial statements for fiscal years ending after February 27, 2010, from its Website (RIM.com) or the SEC database (www.SEC.gov). Update your work for parts 1, 2, and 3 using the new information accessed.

COMPARATIVE ANALYSIS
C2 P2
RIM
Apple

BTN 17-2 Key figures for Research In Motion and Apple follow.

($ millions)	Research In Motion	Apple
Cash and equivalents	$ 1,551	$ 5,263
Accounts receivable, net	2,594	3,361
Inventories	622	455
Retained earnings	5,274	23,353
Cost of sales	8,369	25,683
Revenues	14,953	42,905
Total assets	10,204	47,501

Required

1. Compute common-size percents for each of the companies using the data provided. (Round percents to one decimal.)
2. Which company retains a higher portion of cumulative net income in the company?
3. Which company has a higher gross margin ratio on sales?
4. Which company holds a higher percent of its total assets as inventory?

ETHICS CHALLENGE
A1 

BTN 17-3 As Baldwin Company controller, you are responsible for informing the board of directors about its financial activities. At the board meeting, you present the following information.

	2011	2010	2009
Sales trend percent	147.0%	135.0%	100.0%
Selling expenses to sales	10.1%	14.0%	15.6%
Sales to plant assets ratio	3.8 to 1	3.6 to 1	3.3 to 1
Current ratio	2.9 to 1	2.7 to 1	2.4 to 1
Acid-test ratio	1.1 to 1	1.4 to 1	1.5 to 1
Inventory turnover	7.8 times	9.0 times	10.2 times
Accounts receivable turnover	7.0 times	7.7 times	8.5 times
Total asset turnover	2.9 times	2.9 times	3.3 times
Return on total assets	10.4%	11.0%	13.2%
Return on stockholders' equity	10.7%	11.5%	14.1%
Profit margin ratio	3.6%	3.8%	4.0%

After the meeting, the company's CEO holds a press conference with analysts in which she mentions the following ratios.

	2011	2010	2009
Sales trend percent	147.0%	135.0%	100.0%
Selling expenses to sales	10.1%	14.0%	15.6%
Sales to plant assets ratio	3.8 to 1	3.6 to 1	3.3 to 1
Current ratio	2.9 to 1	2.7 to 1	2.4 to 1

Required

1. Why do you think the CEO decided to report 4 ratios instead of the 11 prepared?
2. Comment on the possible consequences of the CEO's reporting of the ratios selected.

COMMUNICATING IN PRACTICE

A1 P3

BTN 17-4 Each team is to select a different industry, and each team member is to select a different company in that industry and acquire its financial statements. Use those statements to analyze the company, including at least one ratio from each of the four building blocks of analysis. When necessary, use the financial press to determine the market price of its stock. Communicate with teammates via a meeting, e-mail, or telephone to discuss how different companies compare to each other and to industry norms. The team is to prepare a single one-page memorandum reporting on its analysis and the conclusions reached.

TAKING IT TO THE NET

P3

BTN 17-5 Access the February 19, 2010, filing of the December 31, 2009, 10-K report of The Hershey Company (ticker HSY) at www.SEC.gov and complete the following requirements.

Required

Compute or identify the following profitability ratios of Hershey for its years ending December 31, 2009, *and* December 31, 2008. Interpret its profitability using the results obtained for these two years.

1. Profit margin ratio.
2. Gross profit ratio.
3. Return on total assets. (Total assets at year-end 2007 were $4,247,113,000.)
4. Return on common stockholders' equity. (Total shareholders' equity at year-end 2007 was $592,922,000.)
5. Basic net income per common share.

TEAMWORK IN ACTION

P1 P2 P3

BTN 17-6 A team approach to learning financial statement analysis is often useful.

Required

1. Each team should write a description of horizontal and vertical analysis that all team members agree with and understand. Illustrate each description with an example.
2. *Each* member of the team is to select *one* of the following categories of ratio analysis. Explain what the ratios in that category measure. Choose one ratio from the category selected, present its formula, and explain what it measures.
   a. Liquidity and efficiency
   b. Solvency
   c. Profitability
   d. Market prospects
3. Each team member is to present his or her notes from part 2 to teammates. Team members are to confirm or correct other teammates' presentation.

Hint: Pairing within teams may be necessary for part 2. Use as an in-class activity or as an assignment. Consider presentations to the entire class using team rotation with transparencies.

ENTREPRENEURIAL DECISION

A1 P1 P2 P3

BTN 17-7 Assume that David and Tom Gardner of The Motley Fool (Fool.com) have impressed you since you first heard of their rather improbable rise to prominence in financial circles. You learn of a staff opening at The Motley Fool and decide to apply for it. Your resume is successfully screened from the thousands received and you advance to the interview process. You learn that the interview consists of analyzing the following financial facts and answering analysis questions. (*Note:* The data are taken from a small merchandiser in outdoor recreational equipment.)

	2010	2009	2008
Sales trend percents	137.0%	125.0%	100.0%
Selling expenses to sales	9.8%	13.7%	15.3%
Sales to plant assets ratio	3.5 to 1	3.3 to 1	3.0 to 1
Current ratio	2.6 to 1	2.4 to 1	2.1 to 1
Acid-test ratio	0.8 to 1	1.1 to 1	1.2 to 1
Merchandise inventory turnover	7.5 times	8.7 times	9.9 times
Accounts receivable turnover	6.7 times	7.4 times	8.2 times
Total asset turnover	2.6 times	2.6 times	3.0 times
Return on total assets	8.8%	9.4%	11.1%
Return on equity	9.75%	11.50%	12.25%
Profit margin ratio	3.3%	3.5%	3.7%

Required

Use these data to answer each of the following questions with explanations.

1. Is it becoming easier for the company to meet its current liabilities on time and to take advantage of any available cash discounts? Explain.
2. Is the company collecting its accounts receivable more rapidly? Explain.
3. Is the company's investment in accounts receivable decreasing? Explain.
4. Is the company's investment in plant assets increasing? Explain.
5. Is the owner's investment becoming more profitable? Explain.
6. Did the dollar amount of selling expenses decrease during the three-year period? Explain.

HITTING THE ROAD
C1 P3

BTN 17-8 You are to devise an investment strategy to enable you to accumulate $1,000,000 by age 65. Start by making some assumptions about your salary. Next compute the percent of your salary that you will be able to save each year. If you will receive any lump-sum monies, include those amounts in your calculations. Historically, stocks have delivered average annual returns of 10–11%. Given this history, you should probably not assume that you will earn above 10% on the money you invest. It is not necessary to specify exactly what types of assets you will buy for your investments; just assume a rate you expect to earn. Use the future value tables in Appendix B to calculate how your savings will grow. Experiment a bit with your figures to see how much less you have to save if you start at, for example, age 25 versus age 35 or 40. (For this assignment, do not include inflation in your calculations.)

GLOBAL DECISION
A1 

NOKIA
RIM
Apple

BTN 17-9 Nokia (www.Nokia.com), which is a leading manufacturer of mobile devices and services, along with Research In Motion and Apple are competitors in the global marketplace. Key figures for Nokia follow (in Euro millions).

Cash and equivalents	1,142
Accounts receivable, net	7,981
Inventories	1,865
Retained earnings	10,132
Cost of sales	27,720
Revenues	40,984
Total assets	35,738

Required

1. Compute common-size percents for Nokia using the data provided. (Round percents to one decimal.)
2. Compare the results with Research In Motion and Apple from BTN 17-2.

ANSWERS TO MULTIPLE CHOICE QUIZ

1. d; ($351,000/$300,000) × 100 = 117%
2. e; ($86,000 + $76,000 + $122,000 + $12,000)/$124,000 = 2.39
3. c; ($86,000 + $76,000)/$124,000 = 1.31
4. a; ($124,000 + $90,000)/$830,000 = 25.78%
5. d; ($300,000 + $316,000)/$830,000 = 74.22%

Glossary

Absorption costing Costing method that assigns both variable and fixed costs to products. *(p. 915)*

Accelerated depreciation method Method that produces larger depreciation charges in the early years of an asset's life and smaller charges in its later years. *(p. 400)*

Account Record within an accounting system in which increases and decreases are entered and stored in a specific asset, liability, equity, revenue, or expense. *(p. 51)*

Account balance Difference between total debits and total credits (including the beginning balance) for an account. *(p. 55)*

Account form balance sheet Balance sheet that lists assets on the left side and liabilities and equity on the right. *(p. 18)*

Account payable Liability created by buying goods or services on credit; backed by the buyer's general credit standing. *(p. 50)*

Accounting Information and measurement system that identifies, records, and communicates relevant information about a company's business activities. *(p. 4)*

Accounting cycle Recurring steps performed each accounting period, starting with analyzing transactions and continuing through the post-closing trial balance (or reversing entries). *(p. 146)*

Accounting equation Equality involving a company's assets, liabilities, and equity; Assets = Liabilities + Equity; also called *balance sheet equation*. *(p. 14)*

Accounting information system People, records, and methods that collect and process data from transactions and events, organize them in useful forms, and communicate results to decision makers. *(p. 272)*

Accounting period Length of time covered by financial statements; also called *reporting period*. *(p. 94)*

Accounting rate of return Rate used to evaluate the acceptability of an investment; equals the after-tax periodic income from a project divided by the average investment in the asset; also called *rate of return on average investment*. *(p. 1039)*

Accounts payable ledger Subsidiary ledger listing individual creditor (supplier) accounts. *(p. 277)*

Accounts receivable Amounts due from customers for credit sales; backed by the customer's general credit standing. *(p. 360)*

Accounts receivable ledger Subsidiary ledger listing individual customer accounts. *(p. 277)*

Accounts receivable turnover Measure of both the quality and liquidity of accounts receivable; indicates how often receivables are received and collected during the period; computed by dividing net sales by average accounts receivable. *(p. 375)*

Accrual basis accounting Accounting system that recognizes revenues when earned and expenses when incurred; the basis for GAAP. *(p. 95)*

Accrued expenses Costs incurred in a period that are both unpaid and unrecorded; adjusting entries for recording accrued expenses involve increasing expenses and increasing liabilities. *(p. 101)*

Accrued revenues Revenues earned in a period that are both unrecorded and not yet received in cash (or other assets); adjusting entries for recording accrued revenues involve increasing assets and increasing revenues. *(pp. 103 & 960)*

Accumulated depreciation Cumulative sum of all depreciation expense recorded for an asset. *(p. 97)*

Acid-test ratio Ratio used to assess a company's ability to settle its current debts with its most liquid assets; defined as quick assets (cash, short-term investments, and current receivables) divided by current liabilities. *(p. 196)*

Activity-based budgeting (ABB) Budget system based on expected activities. *(p. 960)*

Activity-based costing (ABC) Cost allocation method that focuses on activities performed; traces costs to activities and then assigns them to cost objects. *(p. 861)*

Activity cost driver Variable that causes an activity's cost to go up or down; a causal factor. *(p. 861)*

Activity cost pool Temporary account that accumulates costs a company incurs to support an activity. *(p. 861)*

Adjusted trial balance List of accounts and balances prepared after period-end adjustments are recorded and posted. *(p. 106)*

Adjusting entry Journal entry at the end of an accounting period to bring an asset or liability account to its proper amount and update the related expense or revenue account. *(p. 96)*

Aging of accounts receivable Process of classifying accounts receivable by how long they are past due for purposes of estimating uncollectible accounts. *(p. 368)*

Allowance for Doubtful Accounts Contra asset account with a balance approximating uncollectible accounts receivable; also called *Allowance for Uncollectible Accounts*. *(p. 365)*

Allowance method Procedure that (a) estimates and matches bad debts expense with its sales for the period and/or (b) reports accounts receivable at estimated realizable value. *(p. 364)*

Amortization Process of allocating the cost of an intangible asset to expense over its estimated useful life. *(p. 409)*

Annual financial statements Financial statements covering a one-year period; often based on a calendar year, but any consecutive 12-month (or 52-week) period is acceptable. *(p. 94)*

Annual report Summary of a company's financial results for the year with its current financial condition and future plans; directed to external users of financial information. *(p. A-1)*

Annuity Series of equal payments at equal intervals. *(p. 571)*

Appropriated retained earnings Retained earnings separately reported to inform stockholders of funding needs. *(p. 525)*

Asset book value (See *book value.*)

Assets Resources a business owns or controls that are expected to provide current and future benefits to the business. *(p. 14)*

Audit Analysis and report of an organization's accounting system, its records, and its reports using various tests. *(p. 12)*

Auditors Individuals hired to review financial reports and information systems. *Internal auditors* of a company are employed to assess and evaluate its system of internal controls, including the resulting reports. *External auditors* are independent of a company and are hired to assess and evaluate the "fairness" of financial statements (or to perform other contracted financial services) *(p. 13).*

Authorized stock Total amount of stock that a corporation's charter authorizes it to issue. *(p. 511)*

Available-for-sale (AFS) securities Investments in debt and equity securities that are not classified as trading securities or held-to-maturity securities. *(p. 600)*

Average cost See *weighted average.*

Avoidable expense Expense (or cost) that is relevant for decision making; expense that is not incurred if a department, product, or service is eliminated. *(p. 1053)*

Bad debts Accounts of customers who do not pay what they have promised to pay; an expense of selling on credit; also called *uncollectible accounts. (p. 363)*

Balance column account Account with debit and credit columns for recording entries and another column for showing the balance of the account after each entry. *(p. 58)*

Balance sheet Financial statement that lists types and dollar amounts of assets, liabilities, and equity at a specific date. *(p. 19)*

Balance sheet equation (See *accounting equation.*)

Balanced scorecard A system of performance measurement that collects information on several key performance indicators within each of four perspectives: customer, internal processes, innovation and learning, and financial. *(p. 874)*

Bank reconciliation Report that explains the difference between the book (company) balance of cash and the cash balance reported on the bank statement. *(p. 331)*

Bank statement Bank report on the depositor's beginning and ending cash balances, and a listing of its changes, for a period. *(p. 330)*

Basic earnings per share Net income less any preferred dividends and then divided by weighted-average common shares outstanding. *(p. 527)*

Batch processing Accumulating source documents for a period of time and then processing them all at once such as once a day, week, or month. *(p. 286)*

Bearer bonds Bonds made payable to whoever holds them (the *bearer*); also called *unregistered bonds. (p. 566)*

Benchmarking Practice of comparing and analyzing company financial performance or position with other companies or standards. *(p. 1002)*

Betterments Expenditures to make a plant asset more efficient or productive; also called *improvements. (p. 405)*

Bond Written promise to pay the bond's par (or face) value and interest at a stated contract rate; often issued in denominations of $1,000. *(p. 552)*

Bond certificate Document containing bond specifics such as issuer's name, bond par value, contract interest rate, and maturity date. *(p. 554)*

Bond indenture Contract between the bond issuer and the bondholders; identifies the parties' rights and obligations. *(p. 554)*

Book value Asset's acquisition costs less its accumulated depreciation (or depletion, or amortization); also sometimes used synonymously as the *carrying value* of an account. *(p. 100)*

Book value per common share Recorded amount of equity applicable to common shares divided by the number of common shares outstanding. *(p. 528)*

Book value per preferred share Equity applicable to preferred shares (equals its call price [or par value if it is not callable] plus any cumulative dividends in arrears) divided by the number of preferred shares outstanding. *(p. 528)*

Bookkeeping (See *recordkeeping.*)

Break-even point Output level at which sales equals fixed plus variable costs; where income equals zero. *(p. 915)*

Break-even time (BET) Time-based measurement used to evaluate the acceptability of an investment; equals the time expected to pass before the present value of the net cash flows from an investment equals its initial cost. *(p. 1055)*

Budget Formal statement of future plans, usually expressed in monetary terms. *(p. 946)*

Budget report Report comparing actual results to planned objectives; sometimes used as a progress report. *(p. 990)*

Budgetary control Management use of budgets to monitor and control company operations. *(p. 990)*

Budgeted balance sheet Accounting report that presents predicted amounts of the company's assets, liabilities, and equity balances as of the end of the budget period. *(p. 958)*

Budgeted income statement Accounting report that presents predicted amounts of the company's revenues and expenses for the budget period. *(p. 958)*

Budgeting Process of planning future business actions and expressing them as formal plans. *(p. 946)*

Business An organization of one or more individuals selling products and/or services for profit. *(p. 10)*

Business entity assumption Principle that requires a business to be accounted for separately from its owner(s) and from any other entity. *(p. 11)*

Business segment Part of a company that can be separately identified by the products or services that it provides or by the geographic markets that it serves; also called *segment*. *(p. 710)*

C corporation Corporation that does not qualify for nor elect to be treated as a proprietorship or partnership for income tax purposes and therefore is subject to income taxes; also called *C corp*. *(p. 482)*

Call price Amount that must be paid to call and retire a callable preferred stock or a callable bond. *(p. 521)*

Callable bonds Bonds that give the issuer the option to retire them at a stated amount prior to maturity. *(p. 566)*

Callable preferred stock Preferred stock that the issuing corporation, at its option, may retire by paying the call price plus any dividends in arrears. *(p. 521)*

Canceled checks Checks that the bank has paid and deducted from the depositor's account. *(p. 331)*

Capital budgeting Process of analyzing alternative investments and deciding which assets to acquire or sell. *(p. 1036)*

Capital expenditures Additional costs of plant assets that provide material benefits extending beyond the current period; also called *balance sheet expenditures*. *(p. 404)*

Capital expenditures budget Plan that lists dollar amounts to be both received from disposal of plant assets and spent to purchase plant assets. *(p. 956)*

Capital leases Long-term leases in which the lessor transfers substantially all risk and rewards of ownership to the lessee. *(p. 577)*

Capital stock General term referring to a corporation's stock used in obtaining capital (owner financing). *(p. 511)*

Capitalize Record the cost as part of a permanent account and allocate it over later periods.

Carrying (book) value of bonds Net amount at which bonds are reported on the balance sheet; equals the par value of the bonds less any unamortized discount or plus any unamortized premium; also called *carrying amount or book value*. *(p. 556)*

Cash Includes currency, coins, and amounts on deposit in bank checking or savings accounts. *(p. 321)*

Cash basis accounting Accounting system that recognizes revenues when cash is received and records expenses when cash is paid. *(p. 95)*

Cash budget Plan that shows expected cash inflows and outflows during the budget period, including receipts from loans needed to maintain a minimum cash balance and repayments of such loans. *(p. 956)*

Cash disbursements journal Special journal normally used to record all payments of cash; also called *cash payments journal*. *(p. 284)*

Cash discount Reduction in the price of merchandise granted by a seller to a buyer when payment is made within the discount period. *(p. 183)*

Cash equivalents Short-term, investment assets that are readily convertible to a known cash amount or sufficiently close to their maturity date (usually within 90 days) so that market value is not sensitive to interest rate changes. *(p. 321)*

Cash flow on total assets Ratio of operating cash flows to average total assets; not sensitive to income recognition and measurement; partly reflects earnings quality. *(p. 650)*

Cash Over and Short Income statement account used to record cash overages and cash shortages arising from errors in cash receipts or payments. *(p. 323)*

Cash receipts journal Special journal normally used to record all receipts of cash. *(p. 281)*

Change in an accounting estimate Change in an accounting estimate that results from new information, subsequent developments, or improved judgment that impacts current and future periods. *(pp. 403 & 525)*

Chart of accounts List of accounts used by a company; includes an identification number for each account. *(p. 54)*

Check Document signed by a depositor instructing the bank to pay a specified amount to a designated recipient. *(p. 328)*

Check register Another name for a cash disbursements journal when the journal has a column for check numbers. *(pp. 284 & 340)*

Classified balance sheet Balance sheet that presents assets and liabilities in relevant subgroups, including current and noncurrent classifications. *(p. 147)*

Clock card Source document used to record the number of hours an employee works and to determine the total labor cost for each pay period. *(p. 782)*

Closing entries Entries recorded at the end of each accounting period to transfer end-of-period balances in revenue, gain, expense, loss, and withdrawal (dividend for a corporation) accounts to the capital account (to retained earnings for a corporation). *(p. 143)*

Closing process Necessary end-of-period steps to prepare the accounts for recording the transactions of the next period. *(p. 142)*

Columnar journal Journal with more than one column. *(p. 278)*

Committee on Sponsoring Organizations (COSO) Committee devoted to improving the quality of financial reporting through effective internal controls, consisting of five interrelated components, along with other mechanisms (www.COSO.org). *(p. 315)*

Common stock Corporation's basic ownership share; also generically called *capital stock*. *(pp. 12 & 510)*

Common-size financial statement Statement that expresses each amount as a percent of a base amount. In the balance sheet, total assets is usually the base and is expressed as 100%. In the income statement, net sales is usually the base. *(p. 693)*

Comparative financial statement Statement with data for two or more successive periods placed in side-by-side columns, often with changes shown in dollar amounts and percents. *(p. 688)*

Compatibility principle Information system principle that prescribes an accounting system to conform with a company's activities, personnel, and structure. *(p. 273)*

Complex capital structure Capital structure that includes outstanding rights or options to purchase common stock, or securities that are convertible into common stock. *(p. 527)*

Components of accounting systems Five basic components of accounting systems are source documents, input devices, information processors, information storage, and output devices. *(p. 273)*

Composite unit Generic unit consisting of a specific number of units of each product; unit comprised in proportion to the expected sales mix of its products. *(p. 922)*

Compound journal entry Journal entry that affects at least three accounts. *(p. 61)*

Comprehensive income Net change in equity for a period, excluding owner investments and distributions. *(p. 604)*

Computer hardware Physical equipment in a computerized accounting information system.

Computer network Linkage giving different users and different computers access to common databases and programs. *(p. 286)*

Computer software Programs that direct operations of computer hardware.

Conceptual framework A written framework to guide the development, preparation, and interpretation of financial accounting information. *(p. 9)*

Conservatism constraint Principle that prescribes the less optimistic estimate when two estimates are about equally likely. *(p. 238)*

Consignee Receiver of goods owned by another who holds them for purposes of selling them for the owner. *(p. 228)*

Consignor Owner of goods who ships them to another party who will sell them for the owner. *(p. 228)*

Consistency concept Principle that prescribes use of the same accounting method(s) over time so that financial statements are comparable across periods. *(p. 237)*

Consolidated financial statements Financial statements that show all (combined) activities under the parent's control, including those of any subsidiaries. *(p. 603)*

Contingent liability Obligation to make a future payment if, and only if, an uncertain future event occurs. *(p. 448)*

Continuous budgeting Practice of preparing budgets for a selected number of future periods and revising those budgets as each period is completed. *(p. 949)*

Continuous improvement Concept requiring every manager and employee continually to look to improve operations. *(p. 748)*

Contra account Account linked with another account and having an opposite normal balance; reported as a subtraction from the other account's balance. *(p. 99)*

Contract rate Interest rate specified in a bond indenture (or note); multiplied by the par value to determine the interest paid each period; also called *coupon rate, stated rate,* or *nominal rate. (p. 555)*

Contributed capital Total amount of cash and other assets received from stockholders in exchange for stock; also called *paid-in capital. (p. 13)*

Contributed capital in excess of par value Difference between the par value of stock and its issue price when issued at a price above par.

Contribution margin Sales revenue less total variable costs.

Contribution margin income statement Income statement that separates variable and fixed costs; highlights the contribution margin, which is sales less variable expenses.

Contribution margin per unit Amount that the sale of one unit contributes toward recovering fixed costs and earning profit; defined as sales price per unit minus variable expense per unit. *(p. 914)*

Contribution margin ratio Product's contribution margin divided by its sale price. *(p. 914)*

Control Process of monitoring planning decisions and evaluating the organization's activities and employees. *(p. 733)*

Control principle Information system principle that prescribes an accounting system to aid managers in controlling and monitoring business activities. *(p. 272)*

Controllable costs Costs that a manager has the power to control or at least strongly influence. *(pp. 737 & 875)*

Controllable variance Combination of both overhead spending variances (variable and fixed) and the variable overhead efficiency variance. *(p. 1003)*

Controlling account General ledger account, the balance of which (after posting) equals the sum of the balances in its related subsidiary ledger. *(p. 277)*

Conversion costs Expenditures incurred in converting raw materials to finished goods; includes direct labor costs and overhead costs. *(p. 743)*

Conversion costs per equivalent unit The combined costs of direct labor and factory overhead per equivalent unit. *(p. 829)*

Convertible bonds Bonds that bondholders can exchange for a set number of the issuer's shares. *(p. 566)*

Convertible preferred stock Preferred stock with an option to exchange it for common stock at a specified rate. *(p. 520)*

Copyright Right giving the owner the exclusive privilege to publish and sell musical, literary, or artistic work during the creator's life plus 70 years. *(p. 410)*

Corporation Business that is a separate legal entity under state or federal laws with owners called *shareholders* or *stockholders. (pp. 12 & 508)*

Cost All normal and reasonable expenditures necessary to get an asset in place and ready for its intended use. *(p. 395)*

Cost accounting system Accounting system for manufacturing activities based on the perpetual inventory system. *(p. 776)*

Cost-based transfer pricing A form of pricing transfers between divisions of the same company based on costs to the transferring division; typically used when the transferring division has excess capacity. *(p. 883)*

Cost-benefit constraint Notion that only information with benefits of disclosure greater than the costs of disclosure need be disclosed. *(p. 12)*

Cost-benefit principle Information system principle that prescribes the benefits from an activity in an accounting system to outweigh the costs of that activity. *(p. 273)*

Cost center Department that incurs costs but generates no revenues; common example is the accounting or legal department. *(p. 865)*

Cost object Product, process, department, or customer to which costs are assigned. *(p. 737)*

Cost of capital Rate the company must pay to its long-term creditors and shareholders; also called *hurdle rate. (p. 1041)*

Cost of goods available for sale Consists of beginning inventory plus net purchases of a period.

Cost of goods manufactured Total manufacturing costs (direct materials, direct labor, and factory overhead) for the period plus beginning goods in process less ending goods in process; also called *net cost of goods manufactured* and *cost of goods completed. (p. 827)*

Cost of goods sold Cost of inventory sold to customers during a period; also called *cost of sales. (p. 180)*

Cost principle Accounting principle that prescribes financial statement information to be based on actual costs incurred in business transactions. *(p. 10)*

Cost variance Difference between the actual incurred cost and the standard cost. *(p. 997)*

Cost-volume-profit (CVP) analysis Planning method that includes predicting the volume of activity, the costs incurred, sales earned, and profits received. *(p. 908)*

Cost-volume-profit (CVP) chart Graphic representation of cost-volume-profit relations. *(p. 916)*

Coupon bonds Bonds with interest coupons attached to their certificates; bondholders detach coupons when they mature and present them to a bank or broker for collection. *(p. 566)*

Credit Recorded on the right side; an entry that decreases asset and expense accounts, and increases liability, revenue, and most equity accounts; abbreviated Cr. *(p. 55)*

Credit memorandum Notification that the sender has credited the recipient's account in the sender's records. *(p. 189)*

Credit period Time period that can pass before a customer's payment is due. *(p. 183)*

Credit terms Description of the amounts and timing of payments that a buyer (debtor) agrees to make in the future. *(p. 183)*

Creditors Individuals or organizations entitled to receive payments. *(p. 52)*

Cumulative preferred stock Preferred stock on which undeclared dividends accumulate until paid; common stockholders cannot receive dividends until cumulative dividends are paid. *(p. 519)*

Current assets Cash and other assets expected to be sold, collected, or used within one year or the company's operating cycle, whichever is longer. *(p. 148)*

Current liabilities Obligations due to be paid or settled within one year or the company's operating cycle, whichever is longer. *(p. 149 & 437)*

Current portion of long-term debt Portion of long-term debt due within one year or the operating cycle, whichever is longer; reported under current liabilities. *(p. 445)*

Current ratio Ratio used to evaluate a company's ability to pay its short-term obligations, calculated by dividing current assets by current liabilities. *(p. 150)*

Curvilinear cost Cost that changes with volume but not at a constant rate. *(p. 910)*

Customer orientation Company position that its managers and employees be in tune with the changing wants and needs of consumers. *(p. 747)*

Cycle efficiency (CE) A measure of production efficiency, which is defined as value-added (process) time divided by total cycle time. *(p. 750)*

Cycle time (CT) A measure of the time to produce a product or service, which is the sum of process time, inspection time, move time, and wait time; also called *throughput time*. *(p. 749)*

Date of declaration Date the directors vote to pay a dividend. *(p. 515)*

Date of payment Date the corporation makes the dividend payment. *(p. 515)*

Date of record Date directors specify for identifying stockholders to receive dividends. *(p. 515)*

Days' sales in inventory Estimate of number of days needed to convert inventory into receivables or cash; equals ending inventory divided by cost of goods sold and then multiplied by 365; also called days' *stock on hand.* *(p. 241)*

Days' sales uncollected Measure of the liquidity of receivables computed by dividing the current balance of receivables by the annual credit (or net) sales and then multiplying by 365; also called *days' sales in receivables.* *(p. 335)*

Debit Recorded on the left side; an entry that increases asset and expense accounts, and decreases liability, revenue, and most equity accounts; abbreviated Dr. *(p. 55)*

Debit memorandum Notification that the sender has debited the recipient's account in the sender's records. *(p. 184)*

Debt ratio Ratio of total liabilities to total assets; used to reflect risk associated with a company's debts. *(p. 69)*

Debt-to-equity ratio Defined as total liabilities divided by total equity; shows the proportion of a company financed by non-owners (creditors) in comparison with that financed by owners. *(p. 567)*

Debtors Individuals or organizations that owe money. *(p. 51)*

Declining-balance method Method that determines depreciation charge for the period by multiplying a depreciation rate (often twice the straight-line rate) by the asset's beginning-period book value. *(p. 400)*

Deferred income tax liability Corporation income taxes that are deferred until future years because of temporary differences between GAAP and tax rules. *(p. 460)*

Degree of operating leverage (DOL) Ratio of contribution margin divided by pretax income; used to assess the effect on income of changes in sales. *(p. 924)*

Departmental accounting system Accounting system that provides information useful in evaluating the profitability or cost effectiveness of a department. *(p. 864)*

Departmental contribution to overhead Amount by which a department's revenues exceed its direct expenses. *(p. 871)*

Depletion Process of allocating the cost of natural resources to periods when they are consumed and sold. *(p. 408)*

Deposit ticket Lists items such as currency, coins, and checks deposited and their corresponding dollar amounts. *(p. 328)*

Deposits in transit Deposits recorded by the company but not yet recorded by its bank. *(p. 331)*

Depreciable cost Cost of a plant asset less its salvage value.

Depreciation Expense created by allocating the cost of plant and equipment to periods in which they are used; represents the expense of using the asset. *(pp. 99 & 397)*

Diluted earnings per share Earnings per share calculation that requires dilutive securities be added to the denominator of the basic EPS calculation. *(p. 527)*

Dilutive securities Securities having the potential to increase common shares outstanding; examples are options, rights, convertible bonds, and convertible preferred stock. *(p. 527)*

Direct costs Costs incurred for the benefit of one specific cost object. *(p. 737)*

Direct expenses Expenses traced to a specific department (object) that are incurred for the sole benefit of that department. *(p. 865)*

Direct labor Efforts of employees who physically convert materials to finished product. *(p. 742)*

Direct labor costs Wages and salaries for direct labor that are separately and readily traced through the production process to finished goods. *(p. 742)*

Direct material Raw material that physically becomes part of the product and is clearly identified with specific products or batches of product. *(p. 742)*

Direct material costs Expenditures for direct material that are separately and readily traced through the production process to finished goods. *(p. 742)*

Direct method Presentation of net cash from operating activities for the statement of cash flows that lists major operating cash receipts less major operating cash payments. *(p. 638)*

Direct write-off method Method that records the loss from an uncollectible account receivable at the time it is determined to be uncollectible; no attempt is made to estimate bad debts. *(p. 363)*

Discount on bonds payable Difference between a bond's par value and its lower issue price or carrying value; occurs when the contract rate is less than the market rate. *(p. 555)*

Discount on note payable Difference between the face value of a note payable and the (lesser) amount borrowed; reflects the added interest to be paid on the note over its life.

Discount on stock Difference between the par value of stock and its issue price when issued at a price below par value. *(p. 513)*

Discount period Time period in which a cash discount is available and the buyer can make a reduced payment. *(p. 183)*

Discount rate Expected rate of return on investments; also called *cost of capital, hurdle rate,* or *required rate of return. (p. B-2)*

Discounts lost Expenses resulting from not taking advantage of cash discounts on purchases. *(p. 341)*

Dividend in arrears Unpaid dividend on cumulative preferred stock; must be paid before any regular dividends on preferred stock and before any dividends on common stock. *(p. 519)*

Dividends Corporation's distributions of assets to its owners.

Dividend yield Ratio of the annual amount of cash dividends distributed to common shareholders relative to the common stock's market value (price). *(p. 528)*

Double-declining-balance (DDB) depreciation Depreciation equals beginning book value multiplied by 2 times the straight-line rate.

Double taxation Corporate income is taxed and then its later distribution through dividends is normally taxed again for shareholders.

Double-entry accounting Accounting system in which each transaction affects at least two accounts and has at least one debit and one credit. *(p. 55)*

Earnings (See *net income.*)

Earnings per share (EPS) Amount of income earned by each share of a company's outstanding common stock; also called *net income per share. (p. 527)*

Effective interest method Allocates interest expense over the bond life to yield a constant rate of interest; interest expense for a period is found by multiplying the balance of the liability at the beginning of the period by the bond market rate at issuance; also called *interest method. (p. 572)*

Efficiency Company's productivity in using its assets; usually measured relative to how much revenue a certain level of assets generates. *(p. 687)*

Efficiency variance Difference between the actual quantity of an input and the standard quantity of that input. *(p. 1010)*

Electronic funds transfer (EFT) Use of electronic communication to transfer cash from one party to another. *(p. 329)*

Employee benefits Additional compensation paid to or on behalf of employees, such as premiums for medical, dental, life, and disability insurance, and contributions to pension plans. *(p. 445)*

Employee earnings report Record of an employee's net pay, gross pay, deductions, and year-to-date payroll information. *(p. 456)*

Enterprise resource planning (ERP) software Programs that manage a company's vital operations, which range from order taking to production to accounting. *(p. 287)*

Entity Organization that, for accounting purposes, is separate from other organizations and individuals.

EOM Abbreviation for *end of month;* used to describe credit terms for credit transactions. *(p. 183)*

Equity Owner's claim on the assets of a business; equals the residual interest in an entity's assets after deducting liabilities; also called *net assets. (p. 14)*

Equity method Accounting method used for long-term investments when the investor has "significant influence" over the investee. *(p. 602)*

Equity ratio Portion of total assets provided by equity, computed as total equity divided by total assets. *(p. 701)*

Equity securities with controlling influence Long-term investment when the investor is able to exert controlling influence over the investee; investors owning 50% or more of voting stock are presumed to exert controlling influence. *(p. 603)*

Equity securities with significant influence Long-term investment when the investor is able to exert significant influence over the investee; investors owning 20 percent or more (but less than 50 percent) of voting stock are presumed to exert significant influence. *(p. 602)*

Equivalent units of production (EUP) Number of units that would be completed if all effort during a period had been applied to units that were started and finished. *(p. 821)*

Estimated liability Obligation of an uncertain amount that can be reasonably estimated. *(p. 445)*

Estimated line of cost behavior Line drawn on a graph to visually fit the relation between cost and sales. *(p. 912)*

Ethics Codes of conduct by which actions are judged as right or wrong, fair or unfair, honest or dishonest. *(pp. 8 & 736)*

Events Happenings that both affect an organization's financial position and can be reliably measured. *(p. 15)*

Expanded accounting equation Assets = Liabilities + Equity; Equity equals [Owner capital − Owner withdrawals + Revenues − Expenses] for a noncorporation; Equity equals [Contributed capital + Retained earnings + Revenues − Expenses] for a corporation where dividends are subtracted from retained earnings. *(p. 14)*

Expense recognition (or **matching) principle** (See *matching principle.) (pp. 11 & 96)*

Expenses Outflows or using up of assets as part of operations of a business to generate sales. *(p. 14)*

External transactions Exchanges of economic value between one entity and another entity. *(p. 15)*

External users Persons using accounting information who are not directly involved in running the organization. *(p. 5)*

Extraordinary gains or losses Gains or losses reported separately from continuing operations because they are both unusual and infrequent. *(p. 710)*

Extraordinary repairs Major repairs that extend the useful life of a plant asset beyond prior expectations; treated as a capital expenditure. *(p. 405)*

Factory overhead Factory activities supporting the production process that are not direct material or direct labor; also called *overhead and manufacturing overhead. (p. 742)*

Factory overhead costs Expenditures for factory overhead that cannot be separately or readily traced to finished goods; also called *overhead costs. (p. 742)*

Fair value option Reporting option that permits a company to use fair value in reporting certain assets and liabilities, which is presently based on a 3-level system to determine fair value. *(p. 565)*

Favorable variance Difference in actual revenues or expenses from the budgeted amount that contributes to a higher income. *(p. 991)*

Federal depository bank Bank authorized to accept deposits of amounts payable to the federal government. *(p. 453)*

Federal Insurance Contributions Act (FICA) Taxes Taxes assessed on both employers and employees; for Social Security and Medicare programs. *(p. 442)*

Federal Unemployment Taxes (FUTA) Payroll taxes on employers assessed by the federal government to support its unemployment insurance program. *(p. 444)*

FIFO method (See *first-in, first-out.*) *(pp. 233 & 833)*

Financial accounting Area of accounting aimed mainly at serving external users. *(p. 5)*

Financial Accounting Standards Board (FASB) Independent group of full-time members responsible for setting accounting rules. *(p. 9)*

Financial leverage Earning a higher return on equity by paying dividends on preferred stock or interest on debt at a rate lower than the return earned with the assets from issuing preferred stock or debt; also called *trading on the equity. (p. 521)*

Financial reporting Process of communicating information relevant to investors, creditors, and others in making investment, credit, and business decisions. *(p. 687)*

Financial statement analysis Application of analytical tools to general-purpose financial statements and related data for making business decisions. *(p. 686)*

Financial statements Includes the balance sheet, income statement, statement of owner's (or stockholders') equity, and statement of cash flows.

Financing activities Transactions with owners and creditors that include obtaining cash from issuing debt, repaying amounts borrowed, and obtaining cash from or distributing cash to owners. *(p. 634)*

Finished goods inventory Account that controls the finished goods files, which acts as a subsidiary ledger (of the Inventory account) in which the costs of finished goods that are ready for sale are recorded. *(pp. 741 & 779)*

First-in, first-out (FIFO) Method to assign cost to inventory that assumes items are sold in the order acquired; earliest items purchased are the first sold. *(p. 233)*

Fiscal year Consecutive 12-month (or 52-week) period chosen as the organization's annual accounting period. *(p. 95)*

Fixed budget Planning budget based on a single predicted amount of volume; unsuitable for evaluations if the actual volume differs from predicted volume. *(p. 991)*

Fixed budget performance report Report that compares actual revenues and costs with fixed budgeted amounts and identifies the differences as favorable or unfavorable variances. *(p. 991)*

Fixed cost Cost that does not change with changes in the volume of activity. *(p. 736)*

Flexibility principle Information system principle that prescribes an accounting system be able to adapt to changes in the company, its operations, and needs of decision makers. *(p. 273)*

Flexible budget Budget prepared (using actual volume) once a period is complete that helps managers evaluate past performance; uses fixed and variable costs in determining total costs. *(p. 992)*

Flexible budget performance report Report that compares actual revenues and costs with their variable budgeted amounts based on actual sales volume (or other level of activity) and identifies the differences as variances. *(p. 994)*

FOB Abbreviation for *free on board;* the point when ownership of goods passes to the buyer; *FOB shipping point* (or *factory*) means the buyer pays shipping costs and accepts ownership of goods when the seller transfers goods to carrier; *FOB destination* means the seller pays shipping costs and buyer accepts ownership of goods at the buyer's place of business. *(p. 185)*

Foreign exchange rate Price of one currency stated in terms of another currency. *(p. 610)*

Form 940 IRS form used to report an employer's federal unemployment taxes (FUTA) on an annual filing basis. *(p. 453)*

Form 941 IRS form filed to report FICA taxes owed and remitted. *(p. 453)*

Form 10-K (or 10-KSB) Annual report form filed with SEC by businesses (small businesses) with publicly traded securities. *(p. A-1)*

Form W-2 Annual report by an employer to each employee showing the employee's wages subject to FICA and federal income taxes along with amounts withheld. *(p. 455)*

Form W-4 Withholding allowance certificate, filed with the employer, identifying the number of withholding allowances claimed. *(p. 458)*

Franchises Privileges granted by a company or government to sell a product or service under specified conditions. *(p. 410)*

Full disclosure principle Principle that prescribes financial statements (including notes) to report all relevant information about an entity's operations and financial condition. *(p. 11)*

GAAP (See *generally accepted accounting principles.*)

General accounting system Accounting system for manufacturing activities based on the *periodic* inventory system. *(p. 776)*

General and administrative expenses Expenses that support the operating activities of a business. *(p. 193)*

General and administrative expense budget Plan that shows predicted operating expenses not included in the selling expenses budget. *(p. 955)*

General journal All-purpose journal for recording the debits and credits of transactions and events. *(pp. 56 & 276)*

General ledger (See *ledger*.) *(p. 51)*

General partner Partner who assumes unlimited liability for the debts of the partnership; responsible for partnership management. *(p. 481)*

General partnership Partnership in which all partners have mutual agency and unlimited liability for partnership debts. *(p. 481)*

Generally accepted accounting principles (GAAP) Rules that specify acceptable accounting practices. *(p. 8)*

Generally accepted auditing standards (GAAS) Rules that specify auditing practices.

General-purpose financial statements Statements published periodically for use by a variety of interested parties; includes the income statement, balance sheet, statement of owner's equity (or statement of retained earnings for a corporation), statement of cash flows, and notes to these statements. *(p. 687)*

Going-concern assumption Principle that prescribes financial statements to reflect the assumption that the business will continue operating. *(p. 11)*

Goods in process inventory Account in which costs are accumulated for products that are in the process of being produced but are not yet complete; also called *work in process inventory*. *(pp. 741 & 778)*

Goodwill Amount by which a company's (or a segment's) value exceeds the value of its individual assets less its liabilities. *(p. 411)*

Gross margin (See *gross profit*.)

Gross margin ratio Gross margin (net sales minus cost of goods sold) divided by net sales; also called *gross profit ratio*. *(p. 196)*

Gross method Method of recording purchases at the full invoice price without deducting any cash discounts. *(p. 341)*

Gross pay Total compensation earned by an employee. *(p. 442)*

Gross profit Net sales minus cost of goods sold; also called *gross margin*. *(p. 180)*

Gross profit method Procedure to estimate inventory when the past gross profit rate is used to estimate cost of goods sold, which is then subtracted from the cost of goods available for sale. *(p. 252)*

Held-to-maturity (HTM) securities Debt securities that a company has the intent and ability to hold until they mature. *(p. 600)*

High-low method Procedure that yields an estimated line of cost behavior by graphically connecting costs associated with the highest and lowest sales volume. *(p. 912)*

Horizontal analysis Comparison of a company's financial condition and performance across time. *(p. 688)*

Hurdle rate Minimum acceptable rate of return (set by management) for an investment. *(pp. 873 & 1045)*

Impairment Diminishment of an asset value. *(pp. 404 & 410)*

Imprest system Method to account for petty cash; maintains a constant balance in the fund, which equals cash plus petty cash receipts.

Inadequacy Condition in which the capacity of plant assets is too small to meet the company's production demands. *(p. 397)*

Income (See *net income*.)

Income statement Financial statement that subtracts expenses from revenues to yield a net income or loss over a specified period of time; also includes any gains or losses. *(p. 19)*

Income Summary Temporary account used only in the closing process to which the balances of revenue and expense accounts (including any gains or losses) are transferred; its balance is transferred to the capital account (or retained earnings for a corporation). *(p. 143)*

Incremental cost Additional cost incurred only if a company pursues a specific course of action. *(p. 1048)*

Indefinite life Asset life that is not limited by legal, regulatory, contractual, competitive, economic, or other factors. *(p. 409)*

Indirect costs Costs incurred for the benefit of more than one cost object. *(p. 737)*

Indirect expenses Expenses incurred for the joint benefit of more than one department (or cost object). *(p. 865)*

Indirect labor Efforts of production employees who do not work specifically on converting direct materials into finished products and who are not clearly identified with specific units or batches of product. *(p. 742)*

Indirect labor costs Labor costs that cannot be physically traced to production of a product or service; included as part of overhead. *(p. 742)*

Indirect material Material used to support the production process but not clearly identified with products or batches of product. *(p. 740)*

Indirect method Presentation that reports net income and then adjusts it by adding and subtracting items to yield net cash from operating activities on the statement of cash flows. *(p. 638)*

Information processor Component of an accounting system that interprets, transforms, and summarizes information for use in analysis and reporting. *(p. 274)*

Information storage Component of an accounting system that keeps data in a form accessible to information processors. *(p. 274)*

Infrequent gain or loss Gain or loss not expected to recur given the operating environment of the business. *(p. 710)*

Input device Means of capturing information from source documents that enables its transfer to information processors. *(p. 274)*

Installment note Liability requiring a series of periodic payments to the lender. *(p. 562)*

Institute of Management Accountants (IMA) A professional association of management accountants. *(p. 736)*

Intangible assets Long-term assets (resources) used to produce or sell products or services; usually lack physical form and have uncertain benefits. *(pp. 149 & 409)*

Interest Charge for using money (or other assets) loaned from one entity to another. *(p. 370)*

Interim financial statements Financial statements covering periods of less than one year; usually based on one-, three-, or six-month periods. *(pp. 94 & 251)*

Internal controls or **Internal control system** All policies and procedures used to protect assets, ensure reliable accounting, promote efficient operations, and urge adherence to company policies. *(pp. 272 & 736)*

Internal rate of return (IRR) Rate used to evaluate the acceptability of an investment; equals the rate that yields a net present value of zero for an investment. *(p. 1043)*

Internal transactions Activities within an organization that can affect the accounting equation. *(p. 15)*

Internal users Persons using accounting information who are directly involved in managing the organization. *(p. 6)*

International Accounting Standards Board (IASB) Group that identifies preferred accounting practices and encourages global acceptance; issues International Financial Reporting Standards (IFRS). *(p. 9)*

International Financial Reporting Standards (IFRS) International Financial Reporting Standards (IFRS) are required or allowed by over 100 countries; IFRS is set by the International Accounting Standards Board (IASB), which aims to develop a single set of global standards, to promote those standards, and to converge national and international standards globally. *(p. 9)*

Inventory Goods a company owns and expects to sell in its normal operations. *(p. 181)*

Inventory turnover Number of times a company's average inventory is sold during a period; computed by dividing cost of goods sold by average inventory; also called *merchandise turnover*. *(p. 241)*

Investing activities Transactions that involve purchasing and selling of long-term assets, includes making and collecting notes receivable and investments in other than cash equivalents. *(p. 634)*

Investment center Center of which a manager is responsible for revenues, costs, and asset investments. *(p. 865)*

Investment center residual income The net income an investment center earns above a target return on average invested assets. *(p. 873)*

Investment center return on total assets Center net income divided by average total assets for the center. *(p. 873)*

Investment turnover The efficiency with which a company generates sales from its available assets; computed as sales divided by average invested assets. *(p. 878)*

Invoice Itemized record of goods prepared by the vendor that lists the customer's name, items sold, sales prices, and terms of sale. *(p. 339)*

Invoice approval Document containing a checklist of steps necessary for approving the recording and payment of an invoice; also called *check authorization*. *(p. 339)*

Job Production of a customized product or service. *(p. 776)*

Job cost sheet Separate record maintained for each job. *(p. 778)*

Job lot Production of more than one unit of a customized product or service. *(p. 777)*

Job order cost accounting system Cost accounting system to determine the cost of producing each job or job lot. *(pp. 778 & 817)*

Job order production Production of special-order products; also called *customized production*. *(p. 776)*

Joint cost Cost incurred to produce or purchase two or more products at the same time. *(p. 883)*

Journal Record in which transactions are entered before they are posted to ledger accounts; also called *book of original entry*. *(p. 56)*

Journalizing Process of recording transactions in a journal. *(p. 56)*

Just-in-time (JIT) manufacturing Process of acquiring or producing inventory only when needed. *(p. 748)*

Known liabilities Obligations of a company with little uncertainty; set by agreements, contracts, or laws; also called *definitely determinable liabilities*. *(p. 438)*

Land improvements Assets that increase the benefits of land, have a limited useful life, and are depreciated. *(p. 396)*

Large stock dividend Stock dividend that is more than 25% of the previously outstanding shares. *(p. 516)*

Last-in, first-out (LIFO) Method to assign cost to inventory that assumes costs for the most recent items purchased are sold first and charged to cost of goods sold. *(p. 233)*

Lean business model Practice of eliminating waste while meeting customer needs and yielding positive company returns. *(p. 747)*

Lease Contract specifying the rental of property. *(pp. 411 & 576)*

Leasehold Rights the lessor grants to the lessee under the terms of a lease. *(p. 411)*

Leasehold improvements Alterations or improvements to leased property such as partitions and storefronts. *(p. 411)*

Least-squares regression Statistical method for deriving an estimated line of cost behavior that is more precise than the high-low method and the scatter diagram. *(p. 913)*

Ledger Record containing all accounts (with amounts) for a business; also called *general ledger*. *(p. 51)*

Lessee Party to a lease who secures the right to possess and use the property from another party (the lessor). *(p. 411)*

Lessor Party to a lease who grants another party (the lessee) the right to possess and use its property. *(p. 411)*

Liabilities Creditors' claims on an organization's assets; involves a probable future payment of assets, products, or services that a company is obligated to make due to past transactions or events. *(p. 14)*

Licenses (See *franchises.*) *(p. 410)*

Limited liability Owner can lose no more than the amount invested. *(p. 11)*

Limited liability company Organization form that combines select features of a corporation and a limited partnership; provides limited liability to its members (owners), is free of business tax, and allows members to actively participate in management. *(p. 482)*

Limited liability partnership Partnership in which a partner is not personally liable for malpractice or negligence unless that partner is responsible for providing the service that resulted in the claim. *(p. 481)*

Limited life (See *useful life.*)

Limited partners Partners who have no personal liability for partnership debts beyond the amounts they invested in the partnership. *(p. 481)*

Limited partnership Partnership that has two classes of partners, limited partners and general partners. *(p. 481)*

Liquid assets Resources such as cash that are easily converted into other assets or used to pay for goods, services, or liabilities. *(p. 321)*

Liquidating cash dividend Distribution of assets that returns part of the original investment to stockholders; deducted from contributed capital accounts. *(p. 516)*

Liquidation Process of going out of business; involves selling assets, paying liabilities, and distributing remainder to owners.

Liquidity Availability of resources to meet short-term cash requirements. *(pp. 321 & 687)*

List price Catalog (full) price of an item before any trade discount is deducted. *(p. 182)*

Long-term investments Long-term assets not used in operating activities such as notes receivable and investments in stocks and bonds. *(pp. 149 & 596)*

Long-term liabilities Obligations not due to be paid within one year or the operating cycle, whichever is longer. *(pp. 149 & 437)*

Lower of cost or market (LCM) Required method to report inventory at market replacement cost when that market cost is lower than recorded cost. *(p. 237)*

Maker of the note Entity who signs a note and promises to pay it at maturity. *(p. 370)*

Management by exception Management process to focus on significant variances and give less attention to areas where performance is close to the standard. *(p. 995)*

Managerial accounting Area of accounting aimed mainly at serving the decision-making needs of internal users; also called *management accounting*. *(pp. 6 & 732)*

Manufacturer Company that uses labor and operating assets to convert raw materials to finished goods.

Manufacturing budget Plan that shows the predicted costs for direct materials, direct labor, and overhead to be incurred in manufacturing units in the production budget. *(p. 966)*

Manufacturing statement Report that summarizes the types and amounts of costs incurred in a company's production process for a period; also called *cost of goods manufacturing statement*. *(p. 745)*

Margin of safety Excess of expected sales over the level of break-even sales. *(p. 920)*

Market-based transfer price The market price of a good or service being transferred between divisions within a company; typically used when the transferring division does not have excess capacity. *(p. 883)*

Market prospects Expectations (both good and bad) about a company's future performance as assessed by users and other interested parties. *(p. 687)*

Market rate Interest rate that borrowers are willing to pay and lenders are willing to accept for a specific lending agreement given the borrowers' risk level. *(p. 555)*

Market value per share Price at which stock is bought or sold. *(p. 511)*

Master budget Comprehensive business plan that includes specific plans for expected sales, product units to be produced, merchandise (or materials) to be purchased, expenses to be incurred, plant assets to be purchased, and amounts of cash to be borrowed or loans to be repaid, as well as a budgeted income statement and balance sheet. *(p. 950)*

Matching (or expense recognition) principle Prescribes expenses to be reported in the same period as the revenues that were earned as a result of the expenses. *(pp. 11 & 364)*

Materiality constraint Prescribes that accounting for items that significantly impact financial statement and any inferences from them adhere strictly to GAAP. *(pp. 12 & 364)*

Materials consumption report Document that summarizes the materials a department uses during a reporting period; replaces materials requisitions. *(p. 818)*

Materials ledger card Perpetual record updated each time units are purchased or issued for production use. *(p. 780)*

Materials requisition Source document production managers use to request materials for production; used to assign materials costs to specific jobs or overhead. *(p. 781)*

Maturity date of a note Date when a note's principal and interest are due. *(p. 370)*

Measurement principle Accounting information is based on cost with potential subsequent adjustments to fair value; see also *cost principle*. *(p. 10)*

Merchandise (See *merchandise inventory*.) *(p. 180)*

Merchandise inventory Goods that a company owns and expects to sell to customers; also called *merchandise* or *inventory*. *(p. 181)*

Merchandise purchases budget Plan that shows the units or costs of merchandise to be purchased by a merchandising company during the budget period. *(p. 953)*

Merchandiser Entity that earns net income by buying and selling merchandise. *(p. 180)*

Merit rating Rating assigned to an employer by a state based on the employer's record of employment. *(p. 444)*

Minimum legal capital Amount of assets defined by law that stockholders must (potentially) invest in a corporation; usually defined as par value of the stock; intended to protect creditors. *(p. 511)*

Mixed cost Cost that behaves like a combination of fixed and variable costs. *(p. 909)*

Modified Accelerated Cost Recovery System (MACRS) Depreciation system required by federal income tax law. *(p. 402)*

Monetary unit assumption Principle that assumes transactions and events can be expressed in money units. *(p. 11)*

Mortgage Legal loan agreement that protects a lender by giving the lender the right to be paid from the cash proceeds from the sale of a borrower's assets identified in the mortgage. *(p. 564)*

Multinational Company that operates in several countries. *(p. 610)*

Multiple-step income statement Income statement format that shows subtotals between sales and net income, categorizes expenses, and often reports the details of net sales and expenses. *(p. 192)*

Mutual agency Legal relationship among partners whereby each partner is an agent of the partnership and is able to bind the partnership to contracts within the scope of the partnership's business. *(p. 480)*

Natural business year Twelve-month period that ends when a company's sales activities are at their lowest point. *(p. 95)*

Natural resources Assets physically consumed when used; examples are timber, mineral deposits, and oil and gas fields; also called *wasting assets*. *(p. 408)*

Negotiated transfer price A price, determined by negotiation between division managers, to record transfers between divisions; typically lies between the variable cost and the market price of the item transferred. *(p. 883)*

Net assets (See *equity*.)

Net income Amount earned after subtracting all expenses necessary for and matched with sales for a period; also called *income, profit,* or *earnings*. *(p. 14)*

Net loss Excess of expenses over revenues for a period. *(p. 14)*

Net method Method of recording purchases at the full invoice price less any cash discounts. *(p. 341)*

Net pay Gross pay less all deductions; also called *take-home pay*. *(p. 442)*

Net present value (NPV) Dollar estimate of an asset's value that is used to evaluate the acceptability of an investment; computed by discounting future cash flows from the investment at a satisfactory rate and then subtracting the initial cost of the investment. *(p. 1041)*

Net realizable value Expected selling price (value) of an item minus the cost of making the sale. *(p. 228)*

Noncumulative preferred stock Preferred stock on which the right to receive dividends is lost for any period when dividends are not declared. *(p. 519)*

Noninterest-bearing note Note with no stated (contract) rate of interest; interest is implicitly included in the note's face value.

Nonparticipating preferred stock Preferred stock on which dividends are limited to a maximum amount each year. *(p. 520)*

Nonsufficient funds (NSF) check Maker's bank account has insufficient money to pay the check; also called *hot check*.

Non-value-added time The portion of cycle time that is not directed at producing a product or service; equals the sum of inspection time, move time, and wait time. *(p. 750)*

No-par value stock Stock class that has not been assigned a par (or stated) value by the corporate charter. *(p. 511)*

Not controllable costs Costs that a manager does not have the power to control or strongly influence. *(p. 737)*

Note (See *promissory note*.)

Note payable Liability expressed by a written promise to pay a definite sum of money on demand or on a specific future date(s).

Note receivable Asset consisting of a written promise to receive a definite sum of money on demand or on a specific future date(s).

Objectivity principle Principle that prescribes independent, unbiased evidence to support financial statement information. *(p. 9)*

Obsolescence Condition in which, because of new inventions and improvements, a plant asset can no longer be used to produce goods or services with a competitive advantage. *(p. 397)*

Off-balance-sheet financing Acquisition of assets by agreeing to liabilities not reported on the balance sheet. *(p. 577)*

Online processing Approach to inputting data from source documents as soon as the information is available. *(p. 286)*

Operating activities Activities that involve the production or purchase of merchandise and the sale of goods or services to customers, including expenditures related to administering the business. *(p. 633)*

Operating cycle Normal time between paying cash for merchandise or employee services and receiving cash from customers. *(p. 147)*

Operating leases Short-term (or cancelable) leases in which the lessor retains risks and rewards of ownership. *(p. 576)*

Operating leverage Extent, or relative size, of fixed costs in the total cost structure. *(p. 924)*

Opportunity cost Potential benefit lost by choosing a specific action from two or more alternatives. *(p. 738)*

Ordinary repairs Repairs to keep a plant asset in normal, good operating condition; treated as a revenue expenditure and immediately expensed. *(p. 404)*

Organization expenses (costs) Costs such as legal fees and promoter fees to bring an entity into existence. *(pp. 509 & 514)*

Other comprehensive income Equals net income less comprehensive income; includes unrealized gains and losses on available-for-sale securities, foreign currency adjustments, and pension adjustments. *(p. 604)*

Out-of-pocket cost Cost incurred or avoided as a result of management's decisions. *(p. 738)*

Output devices Means by which information is taken out of the accounting system and made available for use. *(p. 275)*

Outsourcing Manager decision to buy a product or service from another part of a *make-or-buy* decision; also called *make or buy*.

Outstanding checks Checks written and recorded by the depositor but not yet paid by the bank at the bank statement date. *(p. 331)*

Outstanding stock Corporation's stock held by its shareholders.

Overapplied overhead Amount by which the overhead applied to production in a period using the predetermined overhead rate exceeds the actual overhead incurred in a period. *(p. 787)*

Overhead cost variance Difference between the total overhead cost applied to products and the total overhead cost actually incurred. *(p. 1002)*

Owner, Capital Account showing the owner's claim on company assets; equals owner investments plus net income (or less net losses) minus owner withdrawals since the company's inception; also referred to as *equity*. *(p. 14)*

Owner investment Assets put into the business by the owner. *(p. 14)*

Owner's equity (See *equity*.)

Owner, withdrawals Account used to record asset distributions to the owner. (See also *withdrawals*.) *(p. 14)*

Paid-in capital (See *contributed capital*.) *(p. 512)*

Paid-in capital in excess of par value Amount received from issuance of stock that is in excess of the stock's par value. *(p. 513)*

Par value Value assigned a share of stock by the corporate charter when the stock is authorized. *(p. 511)*

Par value of a bond Amount the bond issuer agrees to pay at maturity and the amount on which cash interest payments are based; also called *face amount* or *face value* of a bond. *(p. 552)*

Par value stock Class of stock assigned a par value by the corporate charter. *(p. 511)*

Parent Company that owns a controlling interest in a corporation (requires more than 50% of voting stock). *(p. 603)*

Participating preferred stock Preferred stock that shares with common stockholders any dividends paid in excess of the percent stated on preferred stock. *(p. 520)*

Partner return on equity Partner net income divided by average partner equity for the period. *(p. 492)*

Partnership Unincorporated association of two or more persons to pursue a business for profit as co-owners. *(pp. 11 & 480)*

Partnership contract Agreement among partners that sets terms under which the affairs of the partnership are conducted; also called *articles of partnership*. *(p. 480)*

Partnership liquidation Dissolution of a partnership by (1) selling noncash assets and allocating any gain or loss according to partners' income-and-loss ratio, (2) paying liabilities, and (3) distributing any remaining cash according to partners' capital balances. *(p. 489)*

Patent Exclusive right granted to its owner to produce and sell an item or to use a process for 20 years. *(p. 410)*

Payback period (PBP) Time-based measurement used to evaluate the acceptability of an investment; equals the time expected to pass before an investment's net cash flows equal its initial cost. *(p. 1037)*

Payee of the note Entity to whom a note is made payable. *(p. 370)*

Payroll bank account Bank account used solely for paying employees; each pay period an amount equal to the total employees' net pay is deposited in it and the payroll checks are drawn on it. *(p. 458)*

Payroll deductions Amounts withheld from an employee's gross pay; also called *withholdings*. *(p. 442)*

Payroll register Record for a pay period that shows the pay period dates, regular and overtime hours worked, gross pay, net pay, and deductions. *(p. 455)*

Pension plan Contractual agreement between an employer and its employees for the employer to provide benefits to employees after they retire; expensed when incurred. *(p. 578)*

Period costs Expenditures identified more with a time period than with finished products costs; includes selling and general administrative expenses. *(p. 738)*

Periodic inventory system Method that records the cost of inventory purchased but does not continuously track the quantity available or sold to customers; records are updated at the end of each period to reflect the physical count and costs of goods available. *(p. 182)*

Permanent accounts Accounts that reflect activities related to one or more future periods; balance sheet accounts whose balances are not closed; also called *real accounts*. *(p. 142)*

Perpetual inventory system Method that maintains continuous records of the cost of inventory available and the cost of goods sold. *(p. 182)*

Petty cash Small amount of cash in a fund to pay minor expenses; accounted for using an imprest system. *(p. 326)*

Planning Process of setting goals and preparing to achieve them. *(p. 732)*

Plant asset age Estimate of the age of a company's plant assets, computed by dividing accumulated depreciation by depreciation expense. *(p. 413)*

Plant assets Tangible long-lived assets used to produce or sell products and services; also called *property, plant and equipment (PP&E)* or *fixed assets*. *(pp. 99 & 394)*

Pledged assets to secured liabilities Ratio of the book value of a company's pledged assets to the book value of its secured liabilities.

Post-closing trial balance List of permanent accounts and their balances from the ledger after all closing entries are journalized and posted. *(p. 146)*

Posting Process of transferring journal entry information to the ledger; computerized systems automate this process. *(p. 56)*

Posting reference (PR) column A column in journals in which individual ledger account numbers are entered when entries are posted to those ledger accounts. *(p. 58)*

Predetermined overhead rate Rate established prior to the beginning of a period that relates estimated overhead to another variable, such as estimated direct labor, and is used to assign overhead cost to production. *(p. 784)*

Preemptive right Stockholders' right to maintain their proportionate interest in a corporation with any additional shares issued. *(p. 510)*

Preferred stock Stock with a priority status over common stockholders in one or more ways, such as paying dividends or distributing assets. *(p. 518)*

Premium on bonds Difference between a bond's par value and its higher carrying value; occurs when the contract rate is higher than the market rate; also called *bond premium*. *(p. 558)*

Premium on stock (See *contributed capital in excess of par value*.) *(p. 513)*

Prepaid expenses Items paid for in advance of receiving their benefits; classified as assets. *(p. 97)*

Price-earnings (PE) ratio Ratio of a company's current market value per share to its earnings per share; also called *price-to-earnings*. *(p. 527)*

Price variance Difference between actual and budgeted revenue or cost caused by the difference between the actual price per unit and the budgeted price per unit. *(p. 995)*

Prime costs Expenditures directly identified with the production of finished goods; include direct materials costs and direct labor costs. *(p. 743)*

Principal of a note Amount that the signer of a note agrees to pay back when it matures, not including interest. *(p. 370)*

Principles of internal control Principles prescribing management to establish responsibility, maintain records, insure assets, separate recordkeeping from custody of assets, divide responsibility for related transactions, apply technological controls, and perform reviews. *(p. 317)*

Prior period adjustment Correction of an error in a prior year that is reported in the statement of retained earnings (or statement of stockholders' equity) net of any income tax effects. *(p. 525)*

Pro forma financial statements Statements that show the effects of proposed transactions and events as if they had occurred. *(p. 142)*

Process cost accounting system System of assigning direct materials, direct labor, and overhead to specific processes; total costs associated with each process are then divided by the number of units passing through that process to determine the cost per equivalent unit. *(p. 817)*

Process cost summary Report of costs charged to a department, its equivalent units of production achieved, and the costs assigned to its output. *(p. 826)*

Process operations Processing of products in a continuous (sequential) flow of steps; also called *process manufacturing* or *process production. (p. 814)*

Product costs Costs that are capitalized as inventory because they produce benefits expected to have future value; include direct materials, direct labor, and overhead. *(p. 738)*

Production budget Plan that shows the units to be produced each period. *(p. 966)*

Profit (See *net income.*)

Profit center Business unit that incurs costs and generates revenues. *(p. 865)*

Profit margin Ratio of a company's net income to its net sales; the percent of income in each dollar of revenue; also called *net profit margin. (pp. 109 & 878)*

Profitability Company's ability to generate an adequate return on invested capital. *(p. 687)*

Profitability index A measure of the relation between the expected benefits of a project and its investment, computed as the present value of expected future cash flows from the investment divided by the cost of the investment; a higher value indicates a more desirable investment, and a value below 1 indicates an unacceptable project. *(p. 1043)*

Promissory note (or **note**) Written promise to pay a specified amount either on demand or at a definite future date; is a *note receivable* for the lender but a *note payable* for the lendee. *(p. 370)*

Proprietorship (See *sole proprietorship.*) *(p. 11)*

Proxy Legal document giving a stockholder's agent the power to exercise the stockholder's voting rights. *(p. 509)*

Purchase discount Term used by a purchaser to describe a cash discount granted to the purchaser for paying within the discount period. *(p. 183)*

Purchase order Document used by the purchasing department to place an order with a seller (vendor). *(p. 338)*

Purchase requisition Document listing merchandise needed by a department and requesting it be purchased. *(p. 338)*

Purchases journal Journal normally used to record all purchases on credit. *(p. 283)*

Quantity variance Difference between actual and budgeted revenue or cost caused by the difference between the actual number of units and the budgeted number of units. *(p. 995)*

Ratio analysis Determination of key relations between financial statement items as reflected in numerical measures. *(p. 688)*

Raw materials inventory Goods a company acquires to use in making products. *(p. 740)*

Realizable value Expected proceeds from converting an asset into cash. *(p. 365)*

Receiving report Form used to report that ordered goods are received and to describe their quantity and condition. *(p. 339)*

Recordkeeping Part of accounting that involves recording transactions and events, either manually or electronically; also called *bookkeeping. (p. 4)*

Registered bonds Bonds owned by investors whose names and addresses are recorded by the issuer; interest payments are made to the registered owners. *(p. 566)*

Relevance principle Information system principle prescribing that its reports be useful, understandable, timely, and pertinent for decision making. *(p. 272)*

Relevant benefits Additional or incremental revenue generated by selecting a particular course of action over another. *(p. 1047)*

Relevant range of operations Company's normal operating range; excludes extremely high and low volumes not likely to occur. *(p. 917)*

Report form balance sheet Balance sheet that lists accounts vertically in the order of assets, liabilities, and equity.

Responsibility accounting budget Report of expected costs and expenses under a manager's control. *(p. 876)*

Responsibility accounting performance report Responsibility report that compares actual costs and expenses for a department with budgeted amounts. *(p. 876)*

Responsibility accounting system System that provides information that management can use to evaluate the performance of a department's manager. *(p. 864)*

Restricted retained earnings Retained earnings not available for dividends because of legal or contractual limitations. *(p. 524)*

Retail inventory method Method to estimate ending inventory based on the ratio of the amount of goods for sale at cost to the amount of goods for sale at retail. *(p. 251)*

Retailer Intermediary that buys products from manufacturers or wholesalers and sells them to consumers. *(p. 180)*

Retained earnings Cumulative income less cumulative losses and dividends. *(p. 512)*

Retained earnings deficit Debit (abnormal) balance in Retained Earnings; occurs when cumulative losses and dividends exceed cumulative income; also called *accumulated deficit. (p. 515)*

Return Monies received from an investment; often in percent form. *(p. 26)*

Return on assets (See *return on total assets*) *(p. 22)*

Return on equity Ratio of net income to average equity for the period.

Return on total assets Ratio reflecting operating efficiency; defined as net income divided by average total assets for the period; also called *return on assets* or *return on investment. (p. 605)*

Revenue expenditures Expenditures reported on the current income statement as an expense because they do not provide benefits in future periods. *(p. 404)*

Revenue recognition principle The principle prescribing that revenue is recognized when earned. *(p. 10)*

Revenues Gross increase in equity from a company's business activities that earn income; also called *sales. (p. 14)*

Reverse stock split Occurs when a corporation calls in its stock and replaces each share with less than one new share; increases both market value per share and any par or stated value per share. *(p. 518)*

Reversing entries Optional entries recorded at the beginning of a period that prepare the accounts for the usual journal entries as if adjusting entries had not occurred in the prior period. *(p. 154)*

Risk Uncertainty about an expected return. *(p. 26)*

Rolling budget New set of budgets a firm adds for the next period (with revisions) to replace the ones that have lapsed. *(p. 949)*

S corporation Corporation that meets special tax qualifications so as to be treated like a partnership for income tax purposes. *(p. 482)*

Safety stock Quantity of inventory or materials over the minimum needed to satisfy budgeted demand. *(p. 953)*

Sales (See *revenues.*)

Sales budget Plan showing the units of goods to be sold or services to be provided; the starting point in the budgeting process for most departments. *(p. 952)*

Sales discount Term used by a seller to describe a cash discount granted to buyers who pay within the discount period. *(p. 183)*

Sales journal Journal normally used to record sales of goods on credit. *(p. 278)*

Sales mix Ratio of sales volumes for the various products sold by a company. *(p. 921)*

Salvage value Estimate of amount to be recovered at the end of an asset's useful life; also called *residual value* or *scrap value*. *(p. 397)*

Sarbanes-Oxley Act (SOX) Created the *Public Company Accounting Oversight Board,* regulates analyst conflicts, imposes corporate governance requirements, enhances accounting and control disclosures, impacts insider transactions and executive loans, establishes new types of criminal conduct, and expands penalties for violations of federal securities laws. *(pp. 12 & 316)*

Scatter diagram Graph used to display data about past cost behavior and sales as points on a diagram. *(p. 911)*

Schedule of accounts payable List of the balances of all accounts in the accounts payable ledger and their totals. *(p. 284)*

Schedule of accounts receivable List of the balances of all accounts in the accounts receivable ledger and their totals. *(p. 279)*

Section 404 (of SOX) Section 404 of SOX requires that company management document and assess the effectiveness of all internal control processes that can affect financial reporting; company auditors express an opinion on whether management's assessment of the effectiveness of internal controls is fairly stated. *(p. 317)*

Secured bonds Bonds that have specific assets of the issuer pledged as collateral. *(p. 566)*

Securities and Exchange Commission (SEC) Federal agency Congress has charged to set reporting rules for organizations that sell ownership shares to the public. *(p. 9)*

Segment return on assets Segment operating income divided by segment average (identifiable) assets for the period. *(p. 288)*

Selling expense budget Plan that lists the types and amounts of selling expenses expected in the budget period. *(p. 954)*

Selling expenses Expenses of promoting sales, such as displaying and advertising merchandise, making sales, and delivering goods to customers. *(p. 193)*

Serial bonds Bonds consisting of separate amounts that mature at different dates. *(p. 566)*

Service company Organization that provides services instead of tangible products.

Shareholders Owners of a corporation; also called *stockholders*. *(p. 12)*

Shares Equity of a corporation divided into ownership units; also called *stock*. *(p. 12)*

Short-term investments Debt and equity securities that management expects to convert to cash within the next 3 to 12 months (or the operating cycle if longer); also called *temporary investments* or *marketable securities*. *(p. 596)*

Short-term note payable Current obligation in the form of a written promissory note. *(p. 439)*

Shrinkage Inventory losses that occur as a result of theft or deterioration. *(p. 190)*

Signature card Includes the signatures of each person authorized to sign checks on the bank account. *(p. 328)*

Simple capital structure Capital structure that consists of only common stock and nonconvertible preferred stock; consists of no dilutive securities. *(p. 527)*

Single-step income statement Income statement format that includes cost of goods sold as an expense and shows only one subtotal for total expenses. *(p. 193)*

Sinking fund bonds Bonds that require the issuer to make deposits to a separate account; bondholders are repaid at maturity from that account. *(p. 566)*

Small stock dividend Stock dividend that is 25% or less of a corporation's previously outstanding shares. *(p. 516)*

Social responsibility Being accountable for the impact that one's actions might have on society. *(p. 8)*

Sole proprietorship Business owned by one person that is not organized as a corporation; also called *proprietorship*. *(p. 11)*

Solvency Company's long-run financial viability and its ability to cover long-term obligations. *(p. 687)*

Source documents Source of information for accounting entries that can be in either paper or electronic form; also called *business papers*. *(p. 50)*

Special journal Any journal used for recording and posting transactions of a similar type. *(p. 276)*

Specific identification Method to assign cost to inventory when the purchase cost of each item in inventory is identified and used to compute cost of inventory. *(p. 231)*

Spending variance Difference between the actual price of an item and its standard price. *(p. 1010)*

Spreadsheet Computer program that organizes data by means of formulas and format; also called *electronic work sheet*.

Standard costs Costs that should be incurred under normal conditions to produce a product or component or to perform a service. *(p. 995)*

State Unemployment Taxes (SUTA) State payroll taxes on employers to support its unemployment programs. *(p. 444)*

Stated value stock No-par stock assigned a stated value per share; this amount is recorded in the stock account when the stock is issued. *(p. 512)*

Statement of cash flows A financial statement that lists cash inflows (receipts) and cash outflows (payments) during a period; arranged by operating, investing, and financing. *(pp. 19 & 632)*

Statement of owner's equity Report of changes in equity over a period; adjusted for increases (owner investment and net income) and for decreases (withdrawals and net loss). *(p. 19)*

Statement of partners' equity Financial statement that shows total capital balances at the beginning of the period, any additional investment by partners, the income or loss of the period, the partners' withdrawals, and the partners' ending capital balances; also called *statement of partners' capital. (p. 485)*

Statement of retained earnings Report of changes in retained earnings over a period; adjusted for increases (net income), for decreases (dividends and net loss), and for any prior period adjustment.

Statement of stockholders' equity Financial statement that lists the beginning and ending balances of each major equity account and describes all changes in those accounts. *(p. 525)*

Statements of Financial Accounting Standards (SFAS) FASB publications that establish U.S. GAAP.

Step-wise cost Cost that remains fixed over limited ranges of volumes but changes by a lump sum when volume changes occur outside these limited ranges. *(p. 910).*

Stock (See *shares.*) *(p. 12)*

Stock dividend Corporation's distribution of its own stock to its stockholders without the receipt of any payment. *(p. 516)*

Stock options Rights to purchase common stock at a fixed price over a specified period of time. *(p. 525)*

Stock split Occurs when a corporation calls in its stock and replaces each share with more than one new share; decreases both the market value per share and any par or stated value per share. *(p. 518)*

Stock subscription Investor's contractual commitment to purchase unissued shares at future dates and prices.

Stockholders (See *shareholders.*) *(p. 12)*

Stockholders' equity A corporation's equity; also called *shareholders' equity* or *corporate capital. (p. 512)*

Straight-line depreciation Method that allocates an equal portion of the depreciable cost of plant asset (cost minus salvage) to each accounting period in its useful life. *(pp. 99 & 398)*

Straight-line bond amortization Method allocating an equal amount of bond interest expense to each period of the bond life. *(p. 556)*

Subsidiary Entity controlled by another entity (parent) in which the parent owns more than 50% of the subsidiary's voting stock. *(p. 603)*

Subsidiary ledger List of individual subaccounts and amounts with a common characteristic; linked to a controlling account in the general ledger. *(p. 276)*

Sunk cost Cost already incurred and cannot be avoided or changed. *(p. 738)*

Supplementary records Information outside the usual accounting records; also called *supplemental records. (p. 186)*

Supply chain Linkages of services or goods extending from suppliers, to the company itself, and on to customers.

T-account Tool used to show the effects of transactions and events on individual accounts. *(p. 55)*

Target cost Maximum allowable cost for a product or service; defined as expected selling price less the desired profit. *(p. 777)*

Temporary accounts Accounts used to record revenues, expenses, and withdrawals (dividends for a corporation); they are closed at the end of each period; also called *nominal accounts. (p. 142)*

Term bonds Bonds scheduled for payment (maturity) at a single specified date. *(p. 566)*

Throughput time (See *cycle time.*)

Time period assumption Assumption that an organization's activities can be divided into specific time periods such as months, quarters, or years. *(pp. 11 & 94)*

Time ticket Source document used to report the time an employee spent working on a job or on overhead activities and then to determine the amount of direct labor to charge to the job or the amount of indirect labor to charge to overhead. *(p. 782)*

Times interest earned Ratio of income before interest expense (and any income taxes) divided by interest expense; reflects risk of covering interest commitments when income varies. *(p. 450)*

Total asset turnover Measure of a company's ability to use its assets to generate sales; computed by dividing net sales by average total assets. *(p. 413)*

Total quality management (TQM) Concept calling for all managers and employees at all stages of operations to strive toward higher standards and reduce number of defects. *(p. 748)*

Trade discount Reduction from a list or catalog price that can vary for wholesalers, retailers, and consumers. *(p. 182)*

Trademark or **trade (brand) name** Symbol, name, phrase, or jingle identified with a company, product, or service. *(p. 411)*

Trading on the equity (See *financial leverage.*)

Trading securities Investments in debt and equity securities that the company intends to actively trade for profit. *(p. 599)*

Transfer price The price used to record transfers of goods or services between divisions in the same company. *(p. 882)*

Transaction Exchange of economic consideration affecting an entity's financial position that can be reliably measured.

Treasury stock Corporation's own stock that it reacquired and still holds. *(p. 522)*

Trial balance List of accounts and their balances at a point in time; total debit balances equal total credit balances. *(p. 65)*

Unadjusted trial balance List of accounts and balances prepared before accounting adjustments are recorded and posted. *(p. 106)*

Unavoidable expense Expense (or cost) that is not relevant for business decisions; an expense that would continue even if a department, product, or service is eliminated. *(p. 1053)*

Unclassified balance sheet Balance sheet that broadly groups assets, liabilities, and equity accounts. *(p. 147)*

Uncontrollable costs Costs that a manager does not have the power to determine or strongly influence. *(p. 875)*

Underapplied overhead Amount by which overhead incurred in a period exceeds the overhead applied to that period's production using the predetermined overhead rate. *(p. 787)*

Unearned revenue Liability created when customers pay in advance for products or services; earned when the products or services are later delivered. *(pp. 52 & 100)*

Unfavorable variance Difference in revenues or costs, when the actual amount is compared to the budgeted amount, that contributes to a lower income.

Unit contribution margin Amount a product's unit selling price exceeds its total unit variable cost.

Units-of-production depreciation Method that charges a varying amount to depreciation expense for each period of an asset's useful life depending on its usage. *(p. 399)*

Unlimited liability Legal relationship among general partners that makes each of them responsible for partnership debts if the other partners are unable to pay their shares. *(p. 481)*

Unrealized gain (loss) Gain (loss) not yet realized by an actual transaction or event such as a sale. *(p. 599)*

Unsecured bonds Bonds backed only by the issuer's credit standing; almost always riskier than secured bonds; also called *debentures*. *(p. 566)*

Unusual gain or loss Gain or loss that is abnormal or unrelated to the company's ordinary activities and environment. *(p. 710)*

Useful life Length of time an asset will be productively used in the operations of a business; also called *service life* or *limited life*. *(p. 397)*

Value-added time The portion of cycle time that is directed at producing a product or service; equals process time. *(p. 750)*

Value chain Sequential activities that add value to an entity's products or services; includes design, production, marketing, distribution, and service. *(p. 748)*

Variable cost Cost that changes in proportion to changes in the activity output volume. *(p. 736)*

Variable costing income statement An income statement which reports variable costs and fixed costs separately; also called a *contribution margin income statement*. *(p. 915)*

Variance analysis Process of examining differences between actual and budgeted revenues or costs and describing them in terms of price and quantity differences. *(p. 995)*

Vendee Buyer of goods or services. *(p. 339)*

Vendor Seller of goods or services. *(p. 338)*

Vertical analysis Evaluation of each financial statement item or group of items in terms of a specific base amount. *(p. 688)*

Volume variance Difference between two dollar amounts of fixed overhead cost; one amount is the total budgeted overhead cost, and the other is the overhead cost allocated to products using the predetermined fixed overhead rate. *(p. 1003)*

Voucher Internal file used to store documents and information to control cash disbursements and to ensure that a transaction is properly authorized and recorded. *(p. 325)*

Voucher register Journal (referred to as *book of original entry*) in which all vouchers are recorded after they have been approved. *(p. 340)*

Voucher system Procedures and approvals designed to control cash disbursements and acceptance of obligations. *(p. 324)*

Wage bracket withholding table Table of the amounts of income tax withheld from employees' wages. *(p. 458)*

Warranty Agreement that obligates the seller to correct or replace a product or service when it fails to perform properly within a specified period. *(p. 446)*

Weighted average Method to assign inventory cost to sales; the cost of available-for-sale units is divided by the number of units available to determine per unit cost prior to each sale that is then multiplied by the units sold to yield the cost of that sale. *(pp. 234 & 824)*

Weighted-average contribution margin Contribution margin for a multiproduct company; computed based on each products' percentage of the company's sales mix. *(p. 922)*

Weighted-average method (See *weighted average*.)

Wholesaler Intermediary that buys products from manufacturers or other wholesalers and sells them to retailers or other wholesalers. *(p. 180)*

Withdrawals Payment of cash or other assets from a proprietorship or partnership to its owner or owners. *(p. 14)*

Work sheet Spreadsheet used to draft an unadjusted trial balance, adjusting entries, adjusted trial balance, and financial statements. *(p. 138)*

Working capital Current assets minus current liabilities at a point in time. *(p. 697)*

Working papers Analyses and other informal reports prepared by accountants and managers when organizing information for formal reports and financial statements. *(p. 138)*

Credits

Chapter 1
Page 3 AP Images/Paul Sakuma
Page 8 ©Mario Tama/Getty Images
Page 10 ©Martin Shields/Getty Images/Photographer's Choice
Page 11 ©Scott Boehm/Getty Images
Page 15 ©PAUL J. RICHARDS/AFP/Getty Images

Chapter 2
Page 49 Laura Boyd/ Courtesy of CitySlips
Page 52 Laura Boyd/ Courtesy of CitySlips
Page 53 ©Sports Illustrated/Getty Images
Page 54 ©Jed Jacobsohn/Getty Images

Chapter 3
Page 93 AP Images/Jason DeCrow
Page 95 EZIO PETERSEN/UPI/Landov

Chapter 4
Page 137 Courtesy of Gamer Grub
Page 147 ©Cameron Spencer/Getty Images

Chapter 5
Page 179 ©Asia Kepka Photography
Page 185 ©Christie & Cole/photolibrary
Page 189 ©Michael Newman/PhotoEdit

Chapter 6
Page 227 ©2010 Fitness Anywhere, Inc. Used under license
Page 229 © Blend Images/Alamy

Chapter 7
Page 271 Courtesy of New Belgium Brewing Company
Page 274 AP Images/Eric Risberg
Page 275 ©Royalty-Free/CORBIS
Page 277 ©Jody Dole/Getty Images/The Image Bank
Page 286 ©Nick Koudis/Getty Images/PhotoDisc

Chapter 8
Page 315 Courtesy of Dylan's Candy Bar
Page 318 ©Lawrence Lawry/Getty Images/Photodisc

Chapter 9
Page 359 AP Images/Morry Gash
Page 362 ©Ken Reid/Getty Images/Photographer's Choice
Page 363 ©STAN HONDA/AFP/Getty Images

Chapter 10
Page 393 Courtesy Emily O'Brien/Games2U
Page 396 ©Getty Images
Page 398 ©Bradley C. Bower/Bloomberg via Getty Images
Page 403 ©Streeter Lecka/Getty Images
Page 408 ©Digital Vision/Getty Images
Page 410 ©Hunter Martin/Getty Images

Chapter 11
Page 435 Courtesy of Snorg Tees
Page 439 ©Dove Shore/Getty Images
Page 441 ©Adam Gault/Getty Images/OJO Images
Page 446 ©Jeff Zelevansky/Getty Images
Page 449 ©John Burcham/National Geographic/Getty Images

Chapter 12
Page 479 "images by Kay Photography"
Page 481 ©Martin Harvey/Getty Images/Photodisc
Page 483 AP Images/Frank Franklin II, f
Page 486 ©Royalty Free/Corbis

Chapter 13
Page 507 Courtesy of Clean Air Lawn Care
Page 510 Courtesy of Green Bay Packers, Inc.

Chapter 14
Page 551 ©Josh Cogan
Page 554 Courtesy of Dow Chemicals

Chapter 15
Page 595 Courtesy of Blackboard, Inc.
Page 597 Courtesy of Scripophily.com

Chapter 16
Page 631 ©David Johnson
Page 632 AP Images/Brian Kersey

Chapter 17
Page 685 Carrie Devorah/WENN.com/newscom
Page 699 STELIOS VARIAS/Reuters /Landov
Page 704 ©Comstock Images/Jupiter Images

Index

Note: Page numbers followed by *n* indicate information found in footnotes; **bold-face** entries indicate defined terms.

Chart of Accounts

Following is a typical chart of accounts, which is used in several assignments. Every company has its own unique accounts and numbering system.

Assets

Current Assets

101 Cash
102 Petty cash
103 Cash equivalents
104 Short-term investments
105 Fair value adjustment, _______ securities (S-T)
106 Accounts receivable
107 Allowance for doubtful accounts
108 Legal fees receivable
109 Interest receivable
110 Rent receivable
111 Notes receivable
119 Merchandise inventory
120 _________ inventory
121 _________ inventory
124 Office supplies
125 Store supplies
126 _______ supplies
128 Prepaid insurance
129 Prepaid interest
131 Prepaid rent
132 Raw materials inventory
133 Goods in process inventory, _______
134 Goods in process inventory, _______
135 Finished goods inventory

Long-Term Investments

141 Long-term investments
142 Fair value adjustment, _______ securities (L-T)
144 Investment in _______
145 Bond sinking fund

Plant Assets

151 Automobiles
152 Accumulated depreciation—Automobiles
153 Trucks
154 Accumulated depreciation—Trucks
155 Boats
156 Accumulated depreciation—Boats
157 Professional library
158 Accumulated depreciation—Professional library
159 Law library
160 Accumulated depreciation—Law library
161 Furniture
162 Accumulated depreciation—Furniture
163 Office equipment
164 Accumulated depreciation—Office equipment
165 Store equipment
166 Accumulated depreciation—Store equipment
167 _______ equipment
168 Accumulated depreciation—_______ equipment
169 Machinery
170 Accumulated depreciation—Machinery
173 Building _______
174 Accumulated depreciation—Building _______
175 Building _______
176 Accumulated depreciation—Building _______
179 Land improvements _______
180 Accumulated depreciation—Land improvements _______
181 Land improvements _______
182 Accumulated depreciation—Land improvements _______
183 Land

Natural Resources

185 Mineral deposit
186 Accumulated depletion—Mineral deposit

Intangible Assets

191 Patents
192 Leasehold
193 Franchise
194 Copyrights
195 Leasehold improvements
196 Licenses
197 Accumulated amortization—_______

Liabilities

Current Liabilities

201 Accounts payable
202 Insurance payable
203 Interest payable
204 Legal fees payable
207 Office salaries payable
208 Rent payable
209 Salaries payable
210 Wages payable
211 Accrued payroll payable
214 Estimated warranty liability
215 Income taxes payable
216 Common dividend payable
217 Preferred dividend payable
218 State unemployment taxes payable
219 Employee federal income taxes payable
221 Employee medical insurance payable
222 Employee retirement program payable
223 Employee union dues payable
224 Federal unemployment taxes payable
225 FICA taxes payable
226 Estimated vacation pay liability

Unearned Revenues

230 Unearned consulting fees
231 Unearned legal fees
232 Unearned property management fees
233 Unearned _______ fees
234 Unearned _______ fees
235 Unearned janitorial revenue
236 Unearned _______ revenue
238 Unearned rent

Notes Payable

240 Short-term notes payable
241 Discount on short-term notes payable
245 Notes payable
251 Long-term notes payable
252 Discount on long-term notes payable

Long-Term Liabilities

253 Long-term lease liability
255 Bonds payable
256 Discount on bonds payable
257 Premium on bonds payable
258 Deferred income tax liability

Equity

Owner's Equity

301 _____________, Capital
302 _____________, Withdrawals
303 _____________, Capital
304 _____________, Withdrawals
305 _____________, Capital
306 _____________, Withdrawals

Paid-In Capital

307 Common stock, $ _______ par value
308 Common stock, no-par value
309 Common stock, $ _______ stated value
310 Common stock dividend distributable
311 Paid-in capital in excess of par value, Common stock

312 Paid-in capital in excess of stated value, No-par common stock
313 Paid-in capital from retirement of common stock
314 Paid-in capital, Treasury stock
315 Preferred stock
316 Paid-in capital in excess of par value, Preferred stock

Retained Earnings

318 Retained earnings
319 Cash dividends (or Dividends)
320 Stock dividends

Other Equity Accounts

321 Treasury stock, Common
322 Unrealized gain—Equity
323 Unrealized loss—Equity

Revenues

401 ________ fees earned
402 ________ fees earned
403 ________ services revenue
404 ________ services revenue
405 Commissions earned
406 Rent revenue (or Rent earned)
407 Dividends revenue (or Dividend earned)
408 Earnings from investment in ________
409 Interest revenue (or Interest earned)
410 Sinking fund earnings
413 Sales
414 Sales returns and allowances
415 Sales discounts

Cost of Sales

Cost of Goods Sold

502 Cost of goods sold
505 Purchases
506 Purchases returns and allowances
507 Purchases discounts
508 Transportation-in

Manufacturing

520 Raw materials purchases
521 Freight-in on raw materials
530 Factory payroll
531 Direct labor
540 Factory overhead
541 Indirect materials
542 Indirect labor
543 Factory insurance expired
544 Factory supervision
545 Factory supplies used
546 Factory utilities
547 Miscellaneous production costs
548 Property taxes on factory building
549 Property taxes on factory equipment
550 Rent on factory building
551 Repairs, factory equipment
552 Small tools written off
560 Depreciation of factory equipment
561 Depreciation of factory building

Standard Cost Variance

580 Direct material quantity variance
581 Direct material price variance
582 Direct labor quantity variance
583 Direct labor price variance
584 Factory overhead volume variance
585 Factory overhead controllable variance

Expenses

Amortization, Depletion, and Depreciation

601 Amortization expense—________
602 Amortization expense—________
603 Depletion expense—________
604 Depreciation expense—Boats
605 Depreciation expense—Automobiles
606 Depreciation expense—Building ________
607 Depreciation expense—Building ________
608 Depreciation expense—Land improvements ________
609 Depreciation expense—Land improvements ________
610 Depreciation expense—Law library
611 Depreciation expense—Trucks
612 Depreciation expense—________ equipment
613 Depreciation expense—________ equipment
614 Depreciation expense—________
615 Depreciation expense—________

Employee-Related Expenses

620 Office salaries expense
621 Sales salaries expense
622 Salaries expense
623 ________ wages expense
624 Employees' benefits expense
625 Payroll taxes expense

Financial Expenses

630 Cash over and short
631 Discounts lost
632 Factoring fee expense
633 Interest expense

Insurance Expenses

635 Insurance expense—Delivery equipment
636 Insurance expense—Office equipment
637 Insurance expense—________

Rental Expenses

640 Rent expense
641 Rent expense—Office space
642 Rent expense—Selling space
643 Press rental expense
644 Truck rental expense
645 ________ rental expense

Supplies Expenses

650 Office supplies expense
651 Store supplies expense
652 ________ supplies expense
653 ________ supplies expense

Miscellaneous Expenses

655 Advertising expense
656 Bad debts expense
657 Blueprinting expense
658 Boat expense
659 Collection expense
661 Concessions expense
662 Credit card expense
663 Delivery expense
664 Dumping expense
667 Equipment expense
668 Food and drinks expense
671 Gas and oil expense
672 General and administrative expense
673 Janitorial expense
674 Legal fees expense
676 Mileage expense
677 Miscellaneous expenses
678 Mower and tools expense
679 Operating expense
680 Organization expense
681 Permits expense
682 Postage expense
683 Property taxes expense
684 Repairs expense—________
685 Repairs expense—________
687 Selling expense
688 Telephone expense
689 Travel and entertainment expense
690 Utilities expense
691 Warranty expense
695 Income taxes expense

Gains and Losses

701 Gain on retirement of bonds
702 Gain on sale of machinery
703 Gain on sale of investments
704 Gain on sale of trucks
705 Gain on ________
706 Foreign exchange gain or loss
801 Loss on disposal of machinery
802 Loss on exchange of equipment
803 Loss on exchange of ________
804 Loss on sale of notes
805 Loss on retirement of bonds
806 Loss on sale of investments
807 Loss on sale of machinery
808 Loss on ________
809 Unrealized gain—Income
810 Unrealized loss—Income
811 Impairment gain
812 Impairment loss

Clearing Accounts

901 Income summary
902 Manufacturing summary

A Rose by Any Other Name

The same financial statement sometimes receives different titles. Following are some of the more common aliases.*

Balance Sheet	Statement of Financial Position Statement of Financial Condition
Income Statement	Statement of Income Operating Statement Statement of Operations Statement of Operating Activity Earnings Statement Statement of Earnings Profit and Loss (P&L) Statement
Statement of Cash Flows	Statement of Cash Flow Cash Flows Statement Statement of Changes in Cash Position Statement of Changes in Financial Position
Statement of Owner's Equity	Statement of Changes in Owner's Equity Statement of Changes in Owner's Capital Statement of Shareholders' Equity† Statement of Changes in Shareholders' Equity† Statement of Stockholders' Equity and Comprehensive Income† Statement of Changes in Capital Accounts†

* The term **Consolidated** often precedes or follows these statement titles to reflect the combination of different entities, such as a parent company and its subsidiaries.
† For corporations only.

We thank Dr. Louella Moore from Arkansas State University for suggesting this listing.

MANAGERIAL ANALYSES AND REPORTS

① Cost Types

Variable costs: Total cost changes in proportion to volume of activity
Fixed costs: Total cost does not change in proportion to volume of activity
Mixed costs: Cost consists of both a variable and a fixed element

② Cost Sources

Direct materials: Raw materials costs directly linked to finished product
Direct labor: Employee costs directly linked to finished product
Overhead: Costs indirectly linked to finished product

③ Costing Systems

Job order costing: Costs assigned to each unique unit or batch of units
Process costing: Costs assigned to similar products that are mass-produced in a continuous manner

④ Costing Ratios

Contribution margin ratio = (Net sales − Variable costs)/Net sales
Predetermined overhead rate = Estimated overhead costs/Estimated activity base
Break-even point in units = Total fixed costs/Contribution margin per unit

⑤ Planning and Control Metrics

Cost variance = Actual cost − Standard (budgeted) cost
Sales (revenue) variance = Actual sales − Standard (budgeted) sales

⑥ Capital Budgeting

Payback period = Time expected to recover investment cost
Accounting rate of return = Expected annual net income/Average annual investment
Net present value (NPV) = Present value of future cash flows − Investment cost
NPV rule: 1. Compute net present value (NPV in $)
2. If NPV ≥ 0, then accept project; If NPV < 0, then reject project
Internal rate of return rule: 1. Compute internal rate of return (IRR in %)
2. If IRR ≥ hurdle rate, accept project; If IRR < hurdle rate, reject project

⑦ Costing Terminology

Relevant range: Organization's normal range of operating activity.
Direct cost: Cost incurred for the benefit of one cost object.
Indirect cost: Cost incurred for the benefit of more than one cost object.
Product cost: Cost that is necessary and integral to finished products.
Period cost: Cost identified more with a time period than with finished products.
Overhead cost: Cost not separately or directly traceable to a cost object.
Relevant cost: Cost that is pertinent to a decision.
Opportunity cost: Benefit lost by choosing an action from two or more alternatives.
Sunk cost: Cost already incurred that cannot be avoided or changed.
Standard cost: Cost computed using standard price and standard quantity.
Budget: Formal statement of an organization's future plans.
Break-even point: Sales level at which an organization earns zero profit.
Incremental cost: Cost incurred only if the organization undertakes a certain action.
Transfer price: Price on transactions between divisions within a company.

⑧ Standard Cost Variances

Total materials variance = Materials price variance + Materials quantity variance

Total labor variance = Labor (rate) variance + Labor efficiency (quantity) variance

Total overhead variance = Overhead controllable variance + Fixed overhead volume variance

Overhead controllable variance = Actual total overhead − Applied total overhead from flexible budget
Fixed overhead volume variance = Budgeted fixed overhead − Applied fixed overhead
Variable overhead variance = Variable overhead spending variance + Variable overhead efficiency variance
Fixed overhead variance = Fixed overhead spending variance + Fixed overhead volume variance
(Variable overhead variance + Fixed overhead variance = Total overhead variance)

Materials price variance = [AQ × AP] − [AQ × SP]
Materials quantity variance = [AQ × SP] − [SQ × SP]
Labor (rate) variance = [AH × AR] − [AH × SR]
Labor efficiency (quantity) variance = [AH × SR] − [SH × SR]

Variable overhead spending variance = [AH × AVR] − [AH × SVR]
Variable overhead efficiency variance = [AH × SVR] − [SH × SVR]
Fixed overhead spending variance = Actual fixed overhead − Budgeted fixed overhead

where AQ is actual quantity of materials; AP is actual price of materials; AH is actual hours of labor; AR is actual rate of wages; AVR is actual variable rate of overhead; SQ is standard quantity of materials; SP is standard price of materials; SH is standard hours of labor; SR is standard rate of wages; SVR is standard variable rate of overhead.

⑨ Sales Variances

Sales price variance = [AS × AP] − [AS × BP]
Sales volume variance = [AS × BP] − [BS × BP]

where AS = actual sales units; AP = actual sales price; BP = budgeted sales price; BS = budgeted sales units (fixed budget)

Manufacturing Statement
For _period_ Ended _date_

Direct materials		
Raw materials inventory, Beginning		$ #
Raw materials purchases		#
Raw materials available for use		#
Raw materials inventory, Ending		(#)
Direct materials used		#
Direct labor		#
Overhead costs		
Total overhead costs		#
Total manufacturing costs		#
Add goods in process inventory, Beginning		#
Total cost of goods in process		#
Deduct goods in process inventory, Ending		(#)
Cost of goods manufactured		$ #

Contribution Margin Income Statement
For _period_ Ended _date_

Net sales (revenues)	$ #
Total variable costs	#
Contribution margin	#
Total fixed costs	#
Net income	$ #

Flexible Budget
For _period_ Ended _date_

	Flexible Budget: Variable Amount per Unit	Flexible Budget: Fixed Cost	Flexible Budget for Unit Sales of #
Sales (revenues)	$ #		$ #
Variable costs			
Examples: Direct materials, Direct labor,			
Other variable costs	#		#
Total variable costs	#		#
Contribution margin	$ #		#
Fixed costs			
Examples: Depreciation, Manager		$ #	#
salaries, Administrative salaries		#	#
Total fixed costs		$ #	#
Income from operations			$ #

Fixed Budget Performance Report
For _period_ Ended _date_

	Fixed Budget	Actual Performance	Variances†
Sales: In units	#	#	
In dollars	$ #	$ #	$ # F or U
Cost of sales			
Direct costs	#	#	# F or U
Indirect costs	#	#	# F or U
Selling expenses			
Examples: Commissions,	#	#	# F or U
Shipping expenses	#	#	# F or U
General and administrative expenses			
Examples: Administrative salaries	#	#	# F or U
Total expenses	$ #	$ #	$ # F or U
Income from operations	$ #	$ #	$ # F or U

†F = Favorable variance; U = Unfavorable variance.

Master Budget Sequence

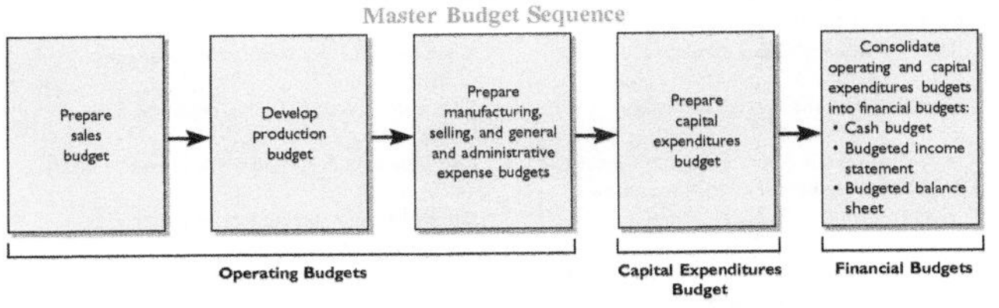

FUNDAMENTALS

① Accounting Equation

Assets		=	Liabilities		+	Equity	
↑ Debit for increases	↓ Credit for decreases		↓ Debit for decreases	↑ Credit for increases		↓ Debit for decreases	↑ Credit for increases

Owner's Capital*		−	Owner's Withdrawals*		+	Revenues		−	Expenses	
↓ Dr. for decreases	↑ Cr. for increases		↑ Dr. for increases	↓ Cr. for decreases		↓ Dr. for decreases	↑ Cr. for increases		↑ Dr. for increases	↓ Cr. for decreases

Indicates normal balance.

*Comparable corporate accounts are Common Stock (Paid-In Capital) and Dividends.

② Accounting Cycle

1. Analyze transactions → 2. Journalize → 3. Post → 4. Prepare unadjusted trial balance → 5. Adjust → 6. Prepare adjusted trial balance → 7. Prepare statements → 8. Close → 9. Prepare post-closing trial balance → 10. Reverse (Optional)

Accounting Cycle

③ Adjustments and Entries

Type	Adjusting Entry	
Prepaid Expenses	Dr. Expense	Cr. Asset*
Unearned Revenues	Dr. Liability	Cr. Revenue
Accrued Expenses	Dr. Expense	Cr. Liability
Accrued Revenues	Dr. Asset	Cr. Revenue

*For depreciation, credit Accumulated Depreciation (contra asset).

④ 4-Step Closing Process

1. Transfer revenue and gain account balances to Income Summary.
2. Transfer expense and loss account balances to Income Summary.
3. Transfer Income Summary balance to Owner's Capital.
4. Transfer Withdrawals balance to Owner's Capital.

⑤ Accounting Concepts

Characteristics	Assumptions	Principles	Constraints
Relevance	Business entity	Historical cost	Cost-benefit
Reliability	Going concern	Revenue recognition	Materiality
Comparability	Monetary unit	Expense recognition	Industry practice
Consistency	Periodicity	Full disclosure	Conservatism

⑥ Ownership of Inventory

	Ownership Transfers When Goods Passed To	Transportation Costs Paid By
FOB Shipping Point	Carrier	Buyer
FOB Destination	Buyer	Seller

⑦ Inventory Costing Methods

- Specific Identification
- First-In, First-Out (FIFO)
- Weighted-Average
- Last-In, First-Out (LIFO)

⑧ Depreciation and Depletion

Straight-Line: $\frac{\text{Cost} - \text{Salvage value}}{\text{Useful life in periods}} \times \text{Periods expired}$

Units-of-Production: $\frac{\text{Cost} - \text{Salvage value}}{\text{Useful life in units}} \times \text{Units produced}$

Declining-Balance: Rate* × Beginning-of-period book value

*Rate is often double the straight-line rate, or 2 × (1/Useful life)

Depletion: $\frac{\text{Cost} - \text{Salvage value}}{\text{Total capacity in units}} \times \text{Units extracted}$

⑨ Interest Computation

Interest = Principal (face) × Rate × Time

⑩ Accounting for Investment Securities

Classification*	Accounting
Short-Term Investment in Securities	
Held-to-maturity (debt) securities	**Cost** (without any discount or premium amortization)
Trading (debt and equity) securities	**Fair value** (with fair value adjustment to income)
Available-for-sale (debt and equity) securities	**Fair value** (with fair value adjustment to equity)
Long-Term Investment in Securities	
Held-to-maturity (debt) securities	**Cost** (with any discount or premium amortization)
Available-for-sale (debt and equity) securities	**Fair value** (with fair value adjustment to equity)
Equity securities with significant influence	Equity method
Equity securities with controlling influence	Equity method (with consolidation)

*A *fair value option* allows companies to report HTM and AFS securities much like trading securities.

ANALYSES

① Liquidity and Efficiency

Ratio	Formula	Page
Current ratio	$= \frac{\text{Current assets}}{\text{Current liabilities}}$	p. 148
Working capital	= Current assets − Current liabilities	p. 697
Acid-test ratio	$= \frac{\text{Cash} + \text{Short-term investments} + \text{Current receivables}}{\text{Current liabilities}}$	p. 196
Accounts receivable turnover	$= \frac{\text{Net sales}}{\text{Average accounts receivable, net}}$	p. 375
Credit risk ratio	$= \frac{\text{Allowance for doubtful accounts}}{\text{Accounts receivable, net}}$	p. 375
Inventory turnover	$= \frac{\text{Cost of goods sold}}{\text{Average inventory}}$	p. 241
Days' sales uncollected	$= \frac{\text{Accounts receivable, net}}{\text{Net sales}} \times 365^*$	p. 335
Days' sales in inventory	$= \frac{\text{Ending inventory}}{\text{Cost of goods sold}} \times 365^*$	p. 241
Total asset turnover	$= \frac{\text{Net sales}}{\text{Average total assets}}$	p. 413
Plant asset useful life	$= \frac{\text{Plant asset cost}}{\text{Depreciation expense}}$	p. 413
Plant asset age	$= \frac{\text{Accumulated depreciation}}{\text{Depreciation expense}}$	p. 413
Days' cash expense coverage	$= \frac{\text{Cash and cash equivalents}}{\text{Average daily cash expenses}}$	p. 322

*360 days is also commonly used.

② Solvency

Ratio	Formula	Page
Debt ratio	$= \frac{\text{Total liabilities}}{\text{Total assets}}$; Equity ratio $= \frac{\text{Total equity}}{\text{Total assets}}$	pp. 69 & 701
Debt-to-equity	$= \frac{\text{Total liabilities}}{\text{Total equity}}$	p. 567
Times interest earned	$= \frac{\text{Income before interest expense and income taxes}}{\text{Interest expense}}$	p. 450
Cash coverage of growth	$= \frac{\text{Cash flow from operations}}{\text{Cash outflow for plant assets}}$	p. 651
Cash coverage of debt	$= \frac{\text{Cash flow from operations}}{\text{Total noncurrent liabilities}}$	p. 646

③ Profitability

Ratio	Formula	Page
Profit margin ratio	$= \frac{\text{Net income}}{\text{Net sales}}$	p. 109
Gross margin ratio	$= \frac{\text{Net sales} - \text{Cost of goods sold}}{\text{Net sales}}$	p. 196
Return on total assets	$= \frac{\text{Net income}}{\text{Average total assets}}$	p. 22
	= Profit margin ratio × Total asset turnover	p. 703
Return on common stockholders' equity	$= \frac{\text{Net income} - \text{Preferred dividends}}{\text{Average common stockholders' equity}}$	p. 703
Book value per common share	$= \frac{\text{Stockholders' equity applicable to common shares}}{\text{Number of common shares outstanding}}$	p. 528
Basic earnings per share	$= \frac{\text{Net income} - \text{Preferred dividends}}{\text{Weighted-average common shares outstanding}}$	p. 527
Cash flow on total assets	$= \frac{\text{Cash flow from operations}}{\text{Average total assets}}$	p. 650
Payout ratio	$= \frac{\text{Cash dividends declared on common stock}}{\text{Net income}}$	p. 528

④ Market

Ratio	Formula	Page
Price-earnings ratio	$= \frac{\text{Market value (price) per share}}{\text{Earnings per share}}$	p. 527
Dividend yield	$= \frac{\text{Annual cash dividends per share}}{\text{Market price per share}}$	p. 528
Residual income	= Net income − Target net income	

FINANCIAL REPORTS

Income Statement*
For *period* Ended *date*

Net sales (revenues)		$ #
Cost of goods sold (cost of sales)		#
Gross margin (gross profit)		#
Operating expenses		
Examples: Depreciation, salaries,	$ #	
wages, rent, utilities, interest,	#	
amortization, advertising, taxes	#	
Total operating expenses		#
Nonoperating gains and losses		#
Net income (net profit or earnings)		$ #

* A typical chart of accounts is at the end of the book and classifies all accounts by financial statement categories.

Balance Sheet
Date

ASSETS		
Current assets		
Examples: Cash, Cash equivalents, Short-term investments,		
Accounts receivable, Current portion of notes	$ #	
receivable, Inventory, Prepaid expenses	#	
Total current assets		$ #
Long-term investments		
Examples: Investment in stock, Investment in bonds,	#	
Land for expansion	#	
Total long-term investments		#
Plant assets		
Examples: Equipment, Machinery, Buildings, Land	#	
Total plant assets, net of depreciation		#
Intangible assets		
Examples: Patent, Trademark, Copyright, License, Goodwill	#	
Total intangible assets, net of amortization		#
Total assets		$ #
LIABILITIES AND EQUITY		
Current liabilities		
Examples: Accounts payable, Wages payable, Salaries	$ #	
payable, Current notes payable, Taxes payable,	#	
Interest payable, Unearned revenues	#	
Total current liabilities		$ #
Long-term liabilities		
Examples: Notes payable, Bonds payable, Lease liability	#	
Total long-term liabilities		#
Total liabilities		#
Equity*		
Owner, Capital		#
Total liabilities and equity		$ #

* A corporation's equity consists of: Paid-In Capital and Retained Earnings (less any treasury stock).

Statement of Cash Flows
For *period* Ended *date*

Cash flows from operating activities	
[Prepared using the indirect (see below)† or direct method]	
Net cash provided (used) by operating activities	$ #
Cash flows from investing activities	
[List of individual investing inflows and outflows]	
Net cash provided (used) by investing activities	#
Cash flows from financing activities	
[List of individual financing inflows and outflows]	
Net cash provided (used) by financing activities	#
Net increase (decrease) in cash	$ #
Cash (and equivalents) balance at beginning of period	#
Cash (and equivalents) balance at end of period	$ #

Attach separate schedule or note disclosure of "Noncash investing and financing transactions."

†Indirect Method: Cash Flows from Operating Activities

Cash flows from operating activities		
Net income		$ #
Add: Decreases in noncash current assets	$ #	
Increases in current liabilities	#	
Expenses with no cash outflows (examples: depreciation, and amortization of both intangibles and bond discounts)	#	
Nonoperating losses (examples: losses from asset sales and from debt retirements)	#	#
Less: Increases in noncash current assets	#	
Decreases in current liabilities	#	
Revenues with no cash inflows (examples: amortization of bond premiums)	#	
Nonoperating gains (examples: gains from asset sales and from debt retirements)	#	#
Net cash provided (used) by operating activities		$ #

Statement of Owner's Equity*
For *period* Ended *date*

Owner, Capital, beginning		$ #
Add: Investments by owner	$ #	
Net income	#	#
		#
Less: Withdrawals by owner		#
Owner, Capital, ending		$ #

* For a corporation, statement of owner's equity becomes statement of retained earnings with these changes: "owner, capital" is retained earnings; "investments by owner" is deleted; and "withdrawals by owner" is dividends.

Premium Bond Amortization (Straight-Line) Table†

Semiannual Period-End	Unamortized Bond Premium*	Bond Carrying Value**
Bond life-start	$ #	$ #
⋮	⋮	⋮
Bond life-end	0	par

† Bond carrying value is adjusted to par and its amortized premium to zero over the bond life (note: carrying value less unamortized bond premium equals par).
* Equals total bond premium less its accumulated amortization.
** Equals bond par value plus its unamortized bond premium.

Discount Bond Amortization (Straight-Line) Table†

Semiannual Period-End	Unamortized Bond Discount*	Bond Carrying Value**
Bond life-start	$ #	$ #
⋮	⋮	⋮
Bond life-end	0	par

† Bond carrying value is adjusted to par and its amortized discount to zero over the bond life (note: unamortized bond discount plus carrying value equals par).
* Equals total bond discount less its accumulated amortization.
** Equals bond par value less its unamortized bond discount.

Effective Interest Amortization Table for Bonds with Semiannual Interest Payment

Semiannual Interest Period-End	Cash Interest Paid[A]	Bond Interest Expense[B]	Discount or Premium Amortization[C]	Unamortized Discount or Premium[D]	Carrying Value[E]
#	#	#	#	#	#
⋮	⋮	⋮	⋮	⋮	⋮

[A]Par value multiplied by the semiannual contract rate.
[B]Prior period's carrying value multiplied by the semiannual market rate.
[C]The difference between interest paid and bond interest expense.
[D]Prior period's unamortized discount or premium less the current period's discount or premium amortization.
[E]Par value less unamortized discount or plus unamortized premium.

Installment Notes Payment Table

Period Ending Date	Beginning Balance	Payments: Debit Interest Expense	+	Debit Notes Payable	=	Credit Cash	Ending Balance
#	#	#		#		#	#
⋮	⋮	⋮		⋮		⋮	⋮

Bank Reconciliation
Date

Bank statement balance	$#	Book balance	$#
Add: Unrecorded deposits	#	Add: Unrecorded bank credit memoranda	#
Bank errors understating the balance	#	Book errors understating the balance	#
	#		#
Less: Outstanding checks	#	Less: Unrecorded bank debit memoranda	#
Bank errors overstating the balance	#	Book errors overstating the balance	#
Adjusted bank balance	$#	**Adjusted book balance**	$#

Balances are equal (reconciled)

WORKING PAPERS

Chapter 1 Quick Study 1-1 ***Name*** ____________________

(a) & (b)

GAAP: ____________________

Importance: ____________________

SEC: ____________________

Importance: ____________________

FASB: ____________________

Importance: ____________________

IASB: ____________________

Importance: ____________________

IFRS: ____________________

Importance: ____________________

Quick Study 1-2

Chapter 1 **Quick Study 1-3** ***Name*** ______________________

(a)	(g)
(b)	(h)
(c)	(i)
(d)	(j)
(e)	(k)
(f)	(l)

Quick Study 1-4

(1)

(2)

(3)

(4)

Quick Study 1-5

Chapter 1 **Quick Study 1-6** ***Name*** ______________________

(a) ______________________

(b) ______________________

(c) ______________________

Quick Study 1-7

Assets	=	Liabilities	+	Equity
(a)				
(b)				

Quick Study 1-8

Assets	=	Liabilities	+	Equity
$ 30,000		(a) ________		$20,000
(b) ________		$50,000		$30,000
$ 90,000		$10,000		(c) ________

Chapter 1 Quick Study 1-9 ***Name*** ______________________

Business transactions:

Business events:

Quick Study 1-10

(a) (1)

(2)

(3)

(b)	Assets	=	Liabilities	+	Equity
		=		+	

Quick Study 1-11

Return on Assets:

Interpretation:

Quick Study 1-12

(a) ______ (d) ______ (g) ______
(b) ______ (e) ______ (h) ______
(c) ______ (f) ______ (i) ______

Quick Study 1-13

a.

b.

c.

Chapter 1 Exercise 1-1 *Name* ______________________

(1)	(5)
(2)	(6)
(3)	(7)
(4)	

Exercise 1-2

Part A

(1)	(5)
(2)	(6)
(3)	(7)
(4)	(8)

Part B

(1)	(5)
(2)	(6)
(3)	(7)
(4)	

Exercise 1-3

(1)	(5)
(2)	(6)
(3)	(7)
(4)	(8)

Chapter 1 **Exercise 1-4** ***Name*** ______________________

(a) ______________________

(b) ______________________

(c) ______________________

(d) ______________________

Exercise 1-5

(1) ______________________
(2) ______________________
(3) ______________________
(4) ______________________
(5) ______________________

Exercise 1-6

(1) ______________________
(2) ______________________
(3) ______________________
(4) ______________________
(5) ______________________
(6) ______________________
(7) ______________________
(8) ______________________

Exercise 1-7

(a) ______________________
(b) ______________________
(c) ______________________
(d) ______________________
(e) ______________________
(f) ______________________
(g) ______________________

Chapter 1 Exercise 1-8 ***Name*** ____________________

(a) ____________________

(b) ____________________

(c) ____________________

Exercise 1-9

Assets	=	Liabilities	+	Equity
(a)				
(b)				
(c)				

Chapter 1 Exercise 1-10 *Name* ______________________

(a) ______________________

(b) ______________________

(c) ______________________

(d) ______________________

(e) ______________________

(f) ______________________

(g) ______________________

Exercise 1-11

Cash	+ Accounts Receivable	+ Equipment	= Accounts Payable	+ L. Gold, Capital	- L. Gold, Withdrawals	+ Revenues	- Expenses
(a)							
Bal.							
(b)							
Bal.							
(c)							
Bal.							
(d)							
Bal.							
(e)							
Bal.							
(f)							
Bal.							
(g)							
Bal.							
(h)							
Bal.							
(i)							
Bal.							
(j)							
Bal.							

Chapter 1 Exercise 1-12 ***Name*** ______________________

(a) ______________________

(b) ______________________

(c) ______________________

(d) ______________________

(e) ______________________

Exercise 1-13

(a) ______________________

(b) ______________________

(c) ______________________

(d) ______________________

(e) ______________________

Chapter 1 **Exercise 1-14** ***Name*** ______________________

Income Statement

Exercise 1-15

Statement of Owner's Equity

Chapter 1 Exercise 1-16 *Name* ______

Balance Sheet

Exercise 1-17

Statement of Cash Flows

Chapter 1 Exercise 1-18 ***Name*** ______________________

Return on Assets:

Interpretation:

Exercise 1-19

(1)	(5)
(2)	(6)
(3)	(7)
(4)	(8)

Exercise 1-20[B]

(1)
(2)
(3)
(4)
(5)

Exercise 1-21

Income Statement

Chapter 1 **Problem 1-1A or 1-1B** ***Name*** ______________________

	Balance Sheet			Income Stmt.	Statement of Cash Flows		
TRANSACTION	TOTAL ASSETS	TOTAL LIABILITIES	TOTAL EQUITY	NET INCOME	OPERATING ACTIVITIES	FINANCING ACTIVITIES	INVESTING ACTIVITIES
1.							
2.							
3.							
4.							
5.							
6.							
7.							
8.							
9.							
10.							

Chapter 1 Problem 1-2A or 1-2B ***Name*** ______________________________

Part 1: Company______

(a)

(b)

(c)

Part 2: Company______

(a)

(b)

(c)

Chapter 1 **Problem 1-2A or 1-2B (Continued)** ***Name*** ____________________

Part 3: Company______

Chapter 1 **Problem 1-2A or 1-2B (Continued)** ***Name*** ______________________

Part 4: Company______

Part 5: Company______

Chapter 1 Problem 1-3A or 1-3B ***Name*** ______________________

Balance Sheet

Problem 1-4A or 1-4B

Income Statement

Problem 1-5A or 1-5B

Statement of Owner's Equity

Chapter 1 Problem 1-6A or 1-6B ***Name*** ______________________

Statement of Cash Flows

Chapter 1 Problem 1-7A or 1-7B

Name ____________________

Parts 1 & 2

	Assets					LIABILITIES		EQUITY			
	CASH	+ ACCOUNTS RECEIVABLE	+ OFFICE SUPPLIES	+ OFFICE EQUIPMENT	+ BUILDING	= ACCOUNTS PAYABLE	+ NOTES PAYABLE	+ ____, CAPITAL	- ____, WITHDRAWALS	+ REVENUES	- EXPENSES
a.											
b.											
Bal.											
c.											
Bal.											
d.											
Bal.											
e.											
Bal.											
f.											
Bal.											
g.											
Bal.											
h.											
Bal.											
i.											
Bal.											
j.											
Bal.											
k.											
Bal.											

Chapter 1 **Problem 1-7A or 1-7B (Continued)** ***Name*** ______________________

Part 3

____

____

____

Chapter 1 Problem 1-8A or 1-8B ***Name*** ____________________

Parts 1 & 2

	ASSETS			LIABILITIES	EQUITY			
		ACCOUNTS	________	ACCOUNTS	________,	________,		
DATE	CASH	+ RECEIVABLE	+ EQUIPMENT	= PAYABLE	+ CAPITAL	- WITHDRAWALS	+ REVENUES	- EXPENSES

Chapter 1 **Problem 1-8A or 1-8B (Continued)** *Name* ______________________

Part 3

Income Statement

Statement of Owner's Equity

Balance Sheet

Chapter 1 **Problem 1-8A or 1-8B** ***Name*** ____________________

Part 3 **(Continued)**

Statement of Cash Flows

Chapter 1 Problem 1-9A or 1-9B *Name* ____________

Parts 1 & 2

	ASSETS					LIABILITIES	EQUITY			
		ACCOUNTS	OFFICE	OFFICE	______	ACCOUNTS	______ ,	______ ,		
DATE	CASH	+ RECEIVABLE	+ SUPPLIES	+ EQUIPMENT	+ EQUIPMENT	= PAYABLE	+ CAPITAL	- WITHDRAWALS	+ REVENUES	- EXPENSES

Chapter 1 **Problem 1-9A or 1-9B (Continued)** ***Name*** ____________________

Part 3

Income Statement

Statement of Owner's Equity

Balance Sheet

Chapter 1 **Problem 1-9A or 1-9B** ***Name*** ______

Part 3 **(Continued)**

Statement of Cash Flows

Part 4

Chapter 1 Problem 1-10A or 1-10B *Name* ______

(1) ______

(2) ______

(3) ______

(4) ______

Problem 1-11A or 1-11B

(1a) ______

(1b) ______

(2) ______

(3) ______

(4) ______

Chapter 1 Problem 1-12A[A] or 1-12B[A] *Name* ______________________

(1) Return: ______________________

____

____

Risk: ______________________

____

____

(2) Return: ______________________

____

____

Risk: ______________________

____

____

(3) Return: ______________________

____

____

Risk: ______________________

____

____

(4) Return: ______________________

____

____

Risk: ______________________

____

____

Chapter 1 Problem 1-13A[B] *Name* ______________________

(1) Major Activity:

(2) Major Activity:

(3) Major Activity:

Problem 1-13B[B]

I.
A.
B.

II.
A.
B.

III.
A.
B.

Problem 1-14A[B] or 1-14B[B]

(1) (5)
(2) (6)
(3) (7)
(4) (8)

Chapter 1 **Serial Problem SP 1**
Business Solutions

Name ____________________

	ASSETS					LIABILITIES	EQUITY			
DATE	CASH	+ ACCOUNTS RECEIVABLE	+ COMPUTER SUPPLIES	+ COMPUTER SYSTEM	+ OFFICE EQUIPMENT	= ACCOUNTS PAYABLE	+ S. Rey, CAPITAL	- S. Rey, WITHDRAWALS	+ REVENUES	- EXPENSES
Oct. 1										
Oct. 3										
Bal.										
Oct. 6										
Bal.										
Oct. 8										
Bal.										
Oct. 12										
Bal.										
Oct. 15										
Bal.										
Oct. 17										
Bal.										
Oct. 20										
Bal.										
Oct. 22										
Bal.										
Oct. 28										
Bal.										
Oct. 31										
Bal.										
Oct. 31										
Bal.										

Chapter 1 **Reporting in Action** *Name* ____________________
BTN 1-1

(1) ____________________

(2) ____________________

(3) ____________________

(4) ____________________

(5) FastForward: ____________________

Chapter 1 **Comparative Analysis**
BTN 1-2

Name ______________________________

Research In Motion		Apple
(1)		
(2)		
(3)		
(4)		
(5)		

Ethics Challenge—BTN 1-3

(1)

(2)

(3)

(4)

Chapter 1 **Communicating in Practice** ***Name*** ______________________
BTN 1-4

(1) —*Request For Information*—

(2) ______________________

Chapter 1 **Taking It to the Net**
BTN 1-5

Name ______________________

1. ______________________

2. ______________________

Teamwork in Action—BTN 1-6

(1) Meeting Time and Place: ______________________

(2) Telephone and E-mail Addresses: ______________________

Instructor Notification: ☐ **YES** ______________________

Chapter 1 **Entrepreneurial Decision** ***Name*** ______________________
BTN 1-7

(1)(a)

(b)

(2)

Chapter 1 **Hitting the Road** *Name* ____________________

BTN 1-8

(1)

(2)

(3)

Global Decision—BTN 1-9

(1)

(2)

Chapter 2 Quick Study 2-1 *Name* ______________________

(a)	(f)
(b)	(g)
(c)	(h)
(d)	(i)
(e)	

Quick Study 2-2

Likely source documents are:

Quick Study 2-3

(a)	(f)
(b)	(g)
(c)	(h)
(d)	(i)
(e)	(j)

Quick Study 2-4

(a)	(f)
(b)	(g)
(c)	(h)
(d)	(i)
(e)	

Quick Study 2-5

(a)	(g)
(b)	(h)
(c)	(i)
(d)	(j)
(e)	(k)
(f)	(l)

Chapter 2 Quick Study 2-6 *Name* ______________________

GENERAL JOURNAL

Date		Account Titles and Explanation	PR	Debit	Credit

Quick Study 2-7

Answer: ______________________

Explanation: ______________________

Quick Study 2-8

(a) ______ (g) ______
(b) ______ (h) ______
(c) ______ (i) ______
(d) ______ (j) ______
(e) ______ (k) ______
(f) ______ (l) ______

Chapter 2 Quick Study 2-9 ***Name*** ________________

(a) ________________

____

(b) ________________

____

____

____

(c) ________________

____

____

____

____

Exercise 2-1

_______ a. Record relevant transactions in a journal
_______ b. Prepare and analyze the trial balance
_______ c. Analyze each transaction from source documents
_______ d. Post journal information to ledger accounts

Exercise 2-2

a. ________
b. ________
c. ________
d. ________
e. ________

Exercise 2-3

a. ________
b. ________

Chapter 2 Exercise 2-4 *Name* ____________________

ACCOUNT	TYPE OF ACCOUNT	NORMAL BALANCE	INCREASE (Dr. or Cr.)
a.			
b.			
c.			
d.			
e.			
f.			
g.			
h.			
i.			
j.			
k.			
l.			

Exercise 2-5

Chapter 2 Exercise 2-6 ***Name*** ______________________

(1)

(2)

(3)

Chapter 2 **Exercise 2-7** ***Name*** ______________________________

GENERAL JOURNAL

Date		Account Titles and Explanation	PR	Debit	Credit

Chapter 2 Exercise 2-8 ***Name*** ______________________

Cash	

Photography Equipment	

K. Madison, Capital	

Office Supplies	

Photography Fees Earned	

Prepaid Insurance	

Utilities Expense	

Trial Balance

Chapter 2 **Exercise 2-9** ***Name*** ______________________

GENERAL JOURNAL

Date		Account Titles and Explanation	PR	Debit	Credit

Chapter 2 **Exercise 2-9 (Continued)** ***Name*** ______________________

Cash	

Accounts Payable	

M. Dexter, Capital	

Accounts Receivable	

M. Dexter, Withdrawals	

Office Supplies	

Fees Earned	

Office Equipment	

Rent Expense	

Exercise 2-10

Trial Balance

Chapter 2 **Exercise 2-11** ***Name*** ______________________

Transactions creating revenues and their entries:

GENERAL JOURNAL

Date		Account Titles and Explanation	PR	Debit	Credit

Transactions not creating revenues and the reasons:

Chapter 2 Exercise 2-12 *Name* ______________________

Transactions creating expenses and their entries:

GENERAL JOURNAL

Date		Account Titles and Explanation	PR	Debit	Credit

Transactions not creating expenses and the reasons:

Chapter 2 **Exercise 2-13** ***Name*** ______________________

Income Statement

Exercise 2-14

Statement of Owner's Equity

Chapter 2 **Exercise 2-15** ***Name*** ______________________

Balance Sheet

Chapter 2 Exercise 2-16 ***Name*** ____________________

(a) Net Income (Loss) = [ ]
Supporting Computations:

(b) Net Income (Loss) = [ ]
Supporting Computations:

(c) Net Income (Loss) = [ ]
Supporting Computations:

(d) Net Income (Loss) = [ ]
Supporting Computations:

Chapter 2 Exercise 2-17 ***Name*** ______________________

	(a)	(b)	(c)	(d)

Exercise 2-18

(a) ______________________

(b) ______________________

(c) ______________________

(d) ______________________

(e) ______________________

(f) ______________________

(g) ______________________

Chapter 2 **Exercise 2-19** ***Name*** ______________________

GENERAL JOURNAL

Date		Account Titles and Explanation	PR	Debit	Credit
(a)					
(b)					
(c)					
(d)					
(e)					
(f)					
(g)					

Chapter 2 **Exercise 2-20** ***Name*** ______________________

	Description	(1) Difference between Debit and Credit Columns	(2) Column with the Larger Total	(3) Identify account(s) incorrectly stated	(4) Amount that account(s) is overstated or understated
(a)	$2,400 debit to Rent Expense is posted as a $1,590 debit.	$810	Credit	Rent Expense	Rent Expense is understated by $810
(b)					
(c)					
(d)					
(e)					
(f)					
(g)					

Chapter 2 **Exercise 2-21** ***Name*** ________________________

(a)

(b)

(c)

(d)

(e)

Chapter 2 Exercise 2-22 ***Name*** ______________________

Part 1

Co.	Debt Ratio	Return on Assets
(1)		
(2)		
(3)		
(4)		
(5)		
(6)		

Part 2

Part 3

Part 4

Part 5

Part 6

Chapter 2 **Exercise 2-23** ***Name*** ______________________

Balance Sheet

Chapter 2 **Problem 2-1A or 2-1B** ***Name*** ______________________________

Part 1

GENERAL JOURNAL

Date		Account Titles and Explanation	PR	Debit	Credit

Chapter 2 **Problem 2-1A or 2-1B** ***Name*** ______________________________

Part 1 **(Continued)**

Date		Account Titles and Explanation	PR	Debit	Credit

Chapter 2 **Problem 2-1A or 2-1B (Continued)** ***Name*** ____________________

Part 2

GENERAL LEDGER

Cash **ACCOUNT NO. 101**

Date	Explanation	PR	DEBIT	CREDIT	BALANCE

Accounts Receivable **ACCOUNT NO. 106**

Date	Explanation	PR	DEBIT	CREDIT	BALANCE

Office Supplies **ACCOUNT NO. 124**

Date	Explanation	PR	DEBIT	CREDIT	BALANCE

Prepaid Insurance **ACCOUNT NO. 128**

Date	Explanation	PR	DEBIT	CREDIT	BALANCE

Chapter 2 **Problem 2-1A or 2-1B** ***Name*** ____________________

Part 2 **(Continued)**

Prepaid Rent **ACCOUNT NO. 131**

Date	Explanation	PR	DEBIT	CREDIT	BALANCE

Office Equipment **ACCOUNT NO. 163**

Date	Explanation	PR	DEBIT	CREDIT	BALANCE

Accounts Payable **ACCOUNT NO. 201**

Date	Explanation	PR	DEBIT	CREDIT	BALANCE

____________, Capital **ACCOUNT NO. 301**

Date	Explanation	PR	DEBIT	CREDIT	BALANCE

____________, Withdrawals **ACCOUNT NO. 302**

Date	Explanation	PR	DEBIT	CREDIT	BALANCE

Chapter 2 Problem 2-1A or 2-1B *Name* ______________________

Part 2 (Continued)

Services Revenue ACCOUNT NO. 403

Date	Explanation	PR	DEBIT	CREDIT	BALANCE

Utilities Expense ACCOUNT NO. 690

Date	Explanation	PR	DEBIT	CREDIT	BALANCE

Part 3

Trial Balance

Chapter 2 **Problem 2-2A or 2-2B** ***Name*** ______________________

Part 1

GENERAL JOURNAL

Date		Account Titles and Explanation	PR	Debit	Credit

Chapter 2 **Problem 2-2A or 2-2B** ***Name*** ______________________

Part 1 **(Continued)**

GENERAL JOURNAL

Date		Account Titles and Explanation	PR	Debit	Credit

Chapter 2 Problem 2-2A or 2-2B (Continued) *Name* ______________________

Part 2

Cash No. 101

DATE	PR	Debit	Credit	Balance

Accounts Receivable No. 106

DATE	PR	Debit	Credit	Balance

Prepaid Insurance No. 108

DATE	PR	Debit	Credit	Balance

Office Equipment No. 163

DATE	PR	Debit	Credit	Balance

__________Equipment No. 164

DATE	PR	Debit	Credit	Balance

Building No. 170

DATE	PR	Debit	Credit	Balance

Land No. 172

DATE	PR	Debit	Credit	Balance

Accounts Payable No. 201

DATE	PR	Debit	Credit	Balance

Notes Payable No. 250

DATE	PR	Debit	Credit	Balance

__________, Capital No. 301

DATE	PR	Debit	Credit	Balance

__________, Withdrawals No. 302

DATE	PR	Debit	Credit	Balance

__________Fees Earned No. 402

DATE	PR	Debit	Credit	Balance

Wages Expense No. 601

DATE	PR	Debit	Credit	Balance

__________Rental Expense No. 602

DATE	PR	Debit	Credit	Balance

Advertising Expense No. 603

DATE	PR	Debit	Credit	Balance

Repairs Expense No. 604

DATE	PR	Debit	Credit	Balance

Chapter 2 **Problem 2-2A or 2-2B (Continued)** ***Name*** ______________________

Part 3

Trial Balance

Chapter 2 Problem 2-3A or 2-3B ***Name*** ______________________

Part 1

Balance Sheet

Balance Sheet

Chapter 2 Problem 2-3A or 2-3B (Continued) *Name* ______________________

Part 2

Net Income Computation:

Part 3

Debt Ratio:

Chapter 2 **Problem 2-4A or 2-4B** ***Name*** ______________________________

Part 1

GENERAL JOURNAL

Date		Account Titles and Explanation	PR	Debit	Credit

Chapter 2 **Problem 2-4A or 2-4B** ***Name*** ______________________________

Part 1 **(Continued)**

Date		Account Titles and Explanation	PR	Debit	Credit

Chapter 2 **Problem 2-4A or 2-4B (Continued)** ***Name*** ______________________

Part 2

GENERAL LEDGER

Cash **ACCOUNT NO. 101**

Date	Explanation	PR	DEBIT	CREDIT	BALANCE

Accounts Receivable **ACCOUNT NO. 106**

Date	Explanation	PR	DEBIT	CREDIT	BALANCE

Office Supplies **ACCOUNT NO. 124**

Date	Explanation	PR	DEBIT	CREDIT	BALANCE

Prepaid Insurance **ACCOUNT NO. 128**

Date	Explanation	PR	DEBIT	CREDIT	BALANCE

Chapter 2 **Problem 2-4A or 2-4B** ***Name*** ______________________

Part 2 **(Continued)**

Prepaid Rent **ACCOUNT NO. 131**

Date	Explanation	PR	DEBIT	CREDIT	BALANCE

Office Equipment **ACCOUNT NO. 163**

Date	Explanation	PR	DEBIT	CREDIT	BALANCE

Accounts Payable **ACCOUNT NO. 201**

Date	Explanation	PR	DEBIT	CREDIT	BALANCE

____________, Capital **ACCOUNT NO. 301**

Date	Explanation	PR	DEBIT	CREDIT	BALANCE

____________, Withdrawals **ACCOUNT NO. 302**

Date	Explanation	PR	DEBIT	CREDIT	BALANCE

Chapter 2 **Problem 2-4A or 2-4B** ***Name*** ____________________

Part 2 **(Continued)**

Service Fees Earned** **ACCOUNT NO. 401**

Date	Explanation	PR	DEBIT	CREDIT	BALANCE

Services Revenue* **ACCOUNT NO. 403**

Date	Explanation	PR	DEBIT	CREDIT	BALANCE

Utilities Expense **ACCOUNT NO. 690**

Date	Explanation	PR	DEBIT	CREDIT	BALANCE

* Problem 2-4A only.
** Problem 2-4B only.

Chapter 2 **Problem 2-4A or 2-4B (Continued)** ***Name*** ______________________

Part 3

Trial Balance

Chapter 2 **Problem 2-5A or 2-5B** ***Name*** ______________________________

Part 1

GENERAL JOURNAL

Date		Account Titles and Explanation	PR	Debit	Credit

Chapter 2 **Problem 2-5A or 2-5B** ***Name*** ________________________

Part 1 **(Continued)**

Date		Account Titles and Explanation	PR	Debit	Credit

Chapter 2 **Problem 2-5A or 2-5B (Continued)** ***Name*** ______________________

Part 2

Cash **No. 101**

DATE	PR	Debit	Credit	Balance

Accounts Receivable **No. 106**

DATE	PR	Debit	Credit	Balance

Office Supplies **No. 108**

DATE	PR	Debit	Credit	Balance

Office Equipment **No. 163**

DATE	PR	Debit	Credit	Balance

Automobiles **No. 164**

DATE	PR	Debit	Credit	Balance

Building **No. 170**

DATE	PR	Debit	Credit	Balance

Land **No. 172**

DATE	PR	Debit	Credit	Balance

Accounts Payable **No. 201**

DATE	PR	Debit	Credit	Balance

Notes Payable **No. 250**

DATE	PR	Debit	Credit	Balance

______________, Capital **No. 301**

DATE	PR	Debit	Credit	Balance

______________, Withdrawals **No. 302**

DATE	PR	Debit	Credit	Balance

Fees Earned **No. 402**

DATE	PR	Debit	Credit	Balance

Salaries Expense **No. 601**

DATE	PR	Debit	Credit	Balance

Utilities Expense **No. 602**

DATE	PR	Debit	Credit	Balance

Chapter 2 **Problem 2-5A or 2-5B (Continued)** ***Name*** ______________________

Part 3

Trial Balance

Chapter 2 **Problem 2-6A or 2-6B** ***Name*** ______________________

Part 1

Trial Balance

Part 2

Seven Most Likely Transactions (following order of trial balance):

(1)

(2)

(3)

(4)

(5)

(6)

(7)

Chapter 2 **Problem 2-6A or 2-6B (Continued)** ***Name*** ____________________

Part 3

Report of Cash Received and Cash Paid

Chapter 2 **Serial Problem, SP 2**
Business Solutions

Name ______________________________

Part 1

GENERAL JOURNAL

Date		Account Titles and Explanation	PR	Debit	Credit

Chapter 2 **Serial Problem, SP 2** ***Name*** ______________________________

Business Solutions

Part 1 **(Continued)**

Date		Account Titles and Explanation	PR	Debit	Credit

Chapter 2 **Serial Problem, SP 2** ***Name*** ______________________

Business Solutions

Part 1 **(Continued)**

Date		Account Titles and Explanation	PR	Debit	Credit

Chapter 2 **Serial Problem, SP 2**
Business Solutions
(Continued)

Name ______________________________

Part 2

GENERAL LEDGER

Cash **ACCOUNT NO. 101**

Date	Explanation	PR	DEBIT	CREDIT	BALANCE

Accounts Receivable **ACCOUNT NO. 106**

Date	Explanation	PR	DEBIT	CREDIT	BALANCE

Chapter 2 Serial Problem, SP 2 Business Solutions — Name ______________

Part 2 (Continued)

Computer Supplies ACCOUNT NO. 126

Date	Explanation	PR	DEBIT	CREDIT	BALANCE

Prepaid Insurance ACCOUNT NO. 128

Date	Explanation	PR	DEBIT	CREDIT	BALANCE

Prepaid Rent ACCOUNT NO. 131

Date	Explanation	PR	DEBIT	CREDIT	BALANCE

Office Equipment ACCOUNT NO. 163

Date	Explanation	PR	DEBIT	CREDIT	BALANCE

Computer Equipment ACCOUNT NO. 167

Date	Explanation	PR	DEBIT	CREDIT	BALANCE

Chapter 2 **Serial Problem, SP 2**
Business Solutions

Name ______________________

Part 2 **(Continued)**

Accounts Payable **ACCOUNT NO. 201**

Date	Explanation	PR	DEBIT	CREDIT	BALANCE

S. Rey, Capital **ACCOUNT NO. 301**

Date	Explanation	PR	DEBIT	CREDIT	BALANCE

S. Rey, Withdrawals **ACCOUNT NO. 302**

Date	Explanation	PR	DEBIT	CREDIT	BALANCE

Computer Services Revenue **ACCOUNT NO. 403**

Date	Explanation	PR	DEBIT	CREDIT	BALANCE

Chapter 2 **Serial Problem, SP 2** ***Name*** ______________________
Business Solutions

Part 2 **(Continued)**

Wages Expense **ACCOUNT NO. 623**

Date	Explanation	PR	DEBIT	CREDIT	BALANCE

Advertising Expense **ACCOUNT NO. 655**

Date	Explanation	PR	DEBIT	CREDIT	BALANCE

Mileage Expense **ACCOUNT NO. 676**

Date	Explanation	PR	DEBIT	CREDIT	BALANCE

Miscellaneous Expense **ACCOUNT NO. 677**

Date	Explanation	PR	DEBIT	CREDIT	BALANCE

Repairs Expense-Computer **ACCOUNT NO. 684**

Date	Explanation	PR	DEBIT	CREDIT	BALANCE

Chapter 2 **Serial Problem, SP 2**
Business Solutions
(Continued)

Name ______________________________

Part 3

Trial Balance

Chapter 2 **Reporting in Action** *Name* ____________________
BTN 2-1

(1)

(2)

(3)

(4)

(5) FastForward:

Chapter 2 **Comparative Analysis**
BTN 2-2

Name ______________________

(1) Current Year Debt Ratio:

Prior Year Debt Ratio:

(2) Current Year Debt Ratio:

Prior Year Debt Ratio:

(3)

Ethics Challenge—BTN 2-3

Chapter 2 Communicating in Practice—BTN 2-4

Name ______________________________

MEMORANDUM

TO:
FROM:
SUBJECT:
DATE:

Chapter 2 **Taking It to the Net**
BTN 2-5

Name ______________________

(1)

(2)

(3)

Chapter 2 **Teamwork in Action**
BTN 2-6

Name ______________________

(1) Component selected:

(2) (a)

(b)

(c)

(d)

(e)

(3) Presentation Notes:

Chapter 2 **Entrepreneurial Decision** ***Name*** ______________________
BTN 2-7

Chapter 2 **Entrepreneurial Decision BTN 2-8** ***Name*** ____________________

(1)

Balance Sheet

(2)

(3)

Chapter 2 **Hitting the Road** ***Name*** ______________________

BTN 2-9

(1)

(2)

(3)

(4)

Chapter 2 **Global Decision**
BTN 2-10

Name ______________________

(1)

(2)

(3)

Chapter 3 **Quick Study 3-1** ***Name*** ____________

(a) ____________

(b) ____________

(c) ____________

(d) ____________

(e) ____________

Quick Study 3-2

GENERAL JOURNAL

Date		Account Titles and Explanation	PR	Debit	Credit
(a)					
(b)					

Quick Study 3-3

GENERAL JOURNAL

Date		Account Titles and Explanation	PR	Debit	Credit
(a)					
(b)					

Chapter 3 Quick Study 3-4 *Name* ______________________

GENERAL JOURNAL

Date		Account Titles and Explanation	PR	Debit	Credit
(a)					
(b)					

Quick Study 3-5

GENERAL JOURNAL

Date		Account Titles and Explanation	PR	Debit	Credit

Chapter 3 Quick Study 3-6 ***Name*** ____________________

	Dr./Cr.	Account Titles	Financial Statement
(a)	Debit		
	Credit		
(b)			
	Debit		
	Credit		
(c)			
	Debit		
	Credit		
(d)			
	Debit		
	Credit		
(e)			
	Debit		
	Credit		

Quick Study 3-7

Cash Basis

Accrual Basis

Chapter 3 Quick Study 3-8 ***Name*** ______________________________

Answer is __________

Supporting work:

Quick Study 3-9

Answer is __________

Supporting work:

Quick Study 3-10

Adjustment	Debit	Credit
(1)		
(2)		
(3)		

Chapter 3 Quick Study 3-11 ***Name*** ______________________

Profit Margin:

Interpretation of Profit Margin:

Quick Study 3-12[A]

Answer is ____________

Supporting work:

Quick Study 3-13

a.

b.

Chapter 3 Exercise 3-1 ***Name*** ______________________

1.	4.
2.	5.
3.	6.

Exercise 3-2

GENERAL JOURNAL

Date		Account Titles and Explanation	PR	Debit	Credit
(a)					
(b)					
(c)					
(d)					
(e)					
(f)					
(g)					

Notes:

Chapter 3 **Exercise 3-3** ***Name*** ______________________

GENERAL JOURNAL

Date	Account Titles and Explanation	PR	Debit	Credit
(a)				
(b)				
(c)				
(d)				
(e)				
(f)				

Notes: ______________________

Chapter 3 Exercise 3-4 *Name* ______________________

(a)

GENERAL JOURNAL

Date		Account Titles and Explanation	PR	Debit	Credit
Adjusting Entry:					
Journal Entry (Next Period):					

(b)

GENERAL JOURNAL

Date		Account Titles and Explanation	PR	Debit	Credit
Adjusting Entry:					
Journal Entry (Next Period):					

(c)

GENERAL JOURNAL

Date		Account Titles and Explanation	PR	Debit	Credit
Adjusting Entry:					
Journal Entry (Next Period):					

Chapter 3 Exercise 3-5 *Name* ______________________

a. Answer:
Supporting Work:

b. Answer:
Supporting Work:

c. Answer:
Supporting Work:

d. Answer:
Supporting Work:

Exercise 3-6

GENERAL JOURNAL

Date		Account Titles and Explanation	PR	Debit	Credit
(a) Adjusting Entry:					
(b) Payday Entry:					

Chapter 3 Exercise 3-7 *Name* ______________________

GENERAL JOURNAL

Date		Account Titles and Explanation	PR	Debit	Credit

Chapter 3 Exercise 3-8 *Name* ______________________

Balance Sheet Prepaid Insurance Asset Using:			*Insurance Expense Using:*		
Date of:	***Accrual Basis***	***Cash Basis***	***Year***	***Accrual Basis***	***Cash Basis***
12/31/2009			**2009**		
12/31/2010			**2010**		
12/31/2011			**2011**		
12/31/2012			**2012**		
			Total		

Supporting work:

Chapter 3 Exercise 3-9 ***Name*** ______________________

Profit Margin Calculation:

(a) ______________________

____

(b) ______________________

____

(c) ______________________

____

(d) ______________________

____

(e) ______________________

____

Most Profitable: ______________________

____

Interpretation of Profit Margin: ______________________

____

____

Chapter 3 **Exercise 3-10[A]** ***Name*** ______________________________

GENERAL JOURNAL

Date		Account Titles and Explanation	PR	Debit	Credit
(a)					
(b)					

Chapter 3 **Exercise 3-10[A]** **Name** ______________________
(Continued)

(c)

Method in Part (a):

Unearned Fees = $ ______________

Fees Earned = $ ______________

Method in Part (b):

Unearned Fees = $ ______________

Fees Earned = $ ______________

Chapter 3 Exercise 3-11A *Name* ______________________

GENERAL JOURNAL

Date		Account Titles and Explanation	PR	Debit	Credit
(a)					
(b)					
(c)					
(d)					
(e)					
(f)					
(g)					

Chapter 3 Exercise 3-12 ***Name*** ____________________

Balance Sheet

Chapter 3 **Problem 3-1A or 3-1B** ***Name*** ____________________

Part 1

GENERAL JOURNAL

Date		Account Titles and Explanation	PR	Debit	Credit

Chapter 3 **Problem 3-1A or 3-1B** ***Name*** ______________________

Part 1 **(Continued)**

GENERAL JOURNAL

Date		Account Titles and Explanation	PR	Debit	Credit

Part 2

GENERAL JOURNAL

Date		Account Titles and Explanation	PR	Debit	Credit

Chapter 3 Problem 3-2A or 3-2B ***Name*** ______________________

(1)	**(7)**
(2)	**(8)**
(3)	**(9)**
(4)	**(10)**
(5)	**(11)**
(6)	**(12)**

Chapter 3 Problem 3-3A or 3-3B *Name* ______________________

Parts 1 & 2

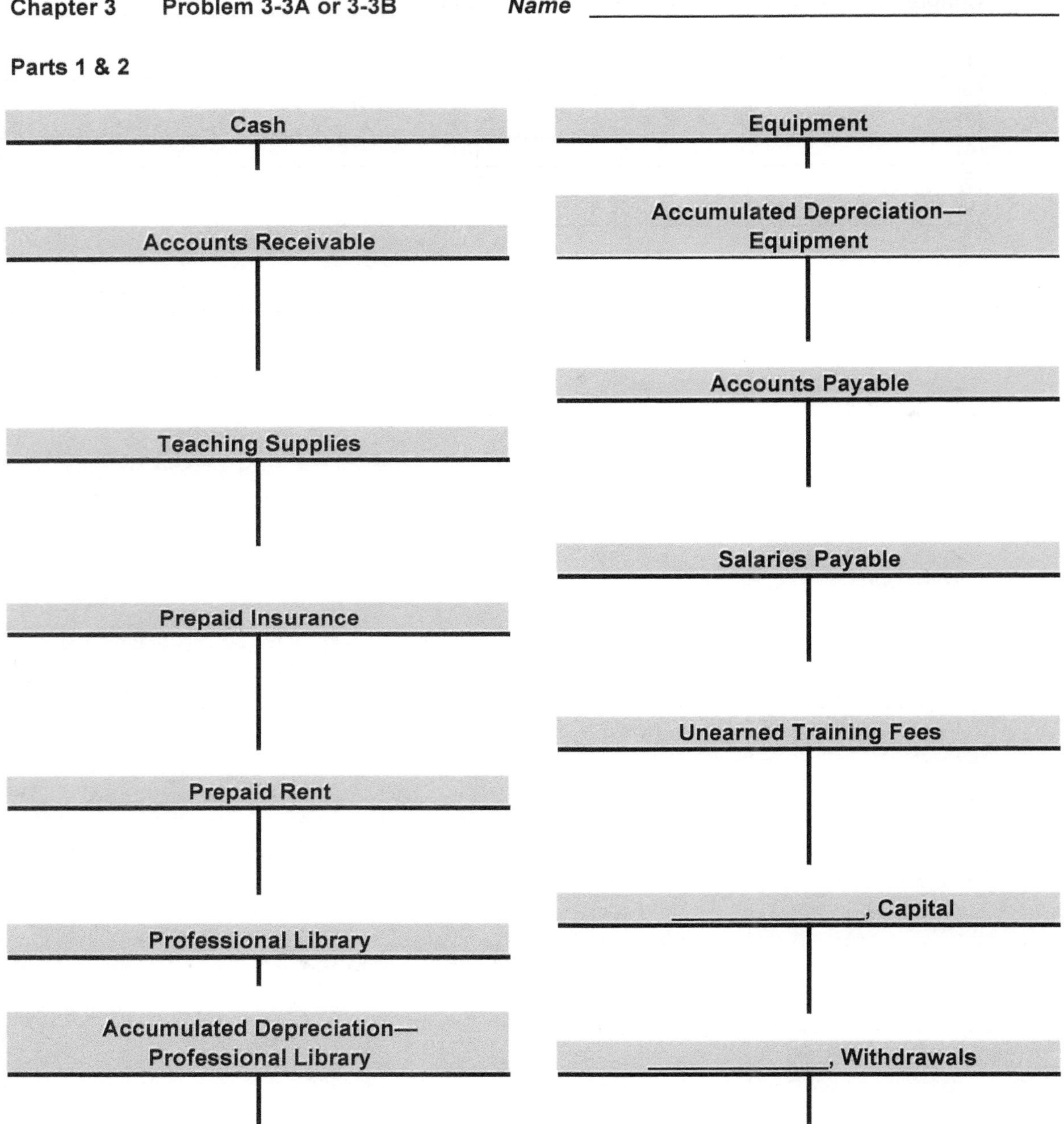

Chapter 3 Problem 3-3A or 3-3B *Name* ____________________

Parts 1 & 2 (Continued)

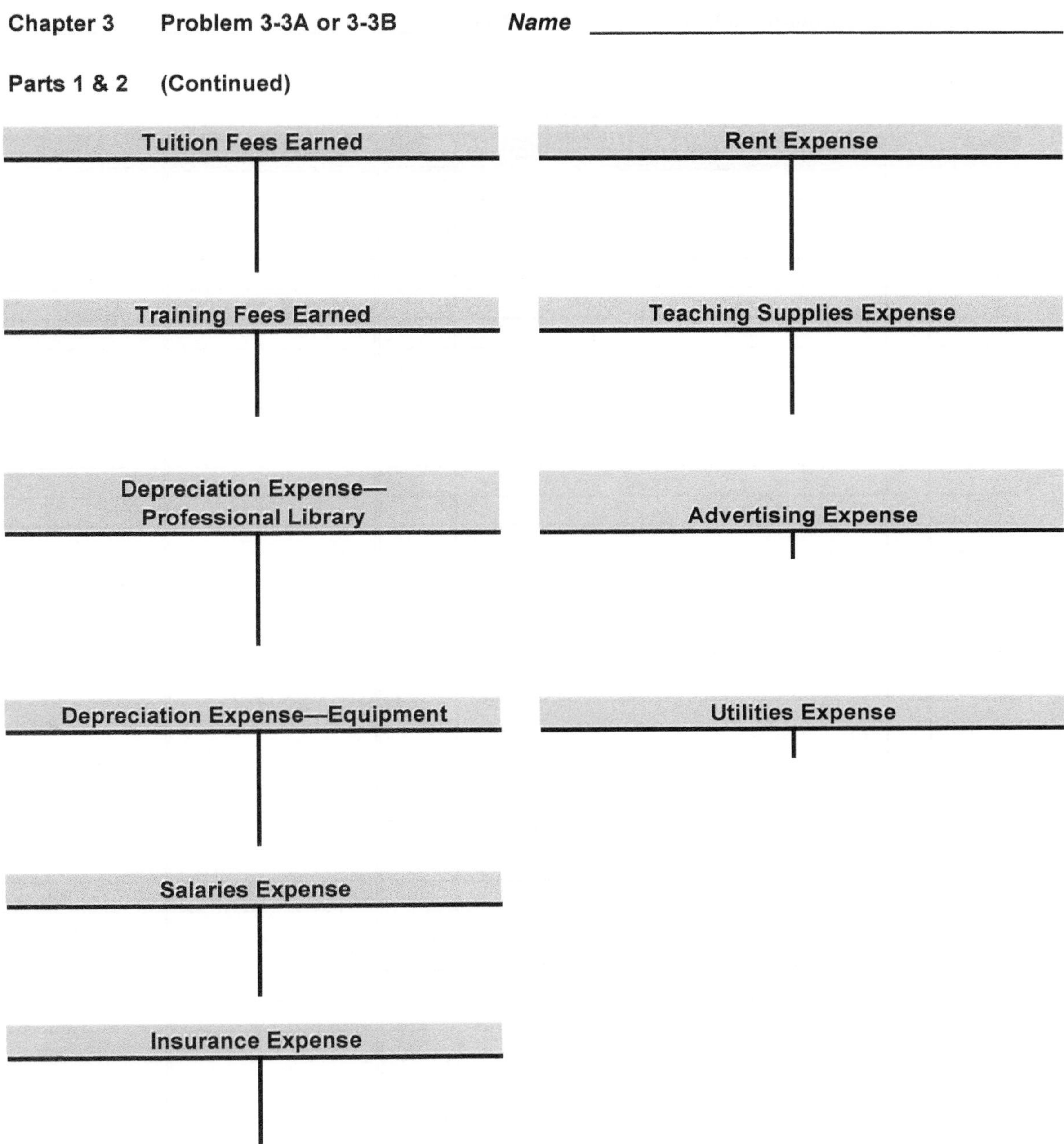

Chapter 3 **Problem 3-3A or 3-3B** ***Name*** ______________________

Part 2 **(Continued)**

GENERAL JOURNAL

Date		Account Titles and Explanation	PR	Debit	Credit

Chapter 3 Problem 3-3A or 3-3B (Continued) *Name* ____________________

Part 3

Adjusted Trial Balance

Chapter 3 **Problem 3-3A or 3-3B (Continued)** ***Name*** ______________________

Part 4

Income Statement

Statement of Owner's Equity

Chapter 3 **Problem 3-3A or 3-3B** ***Name*** ____________________

Part 4 **(Continued)**

Balance Sheet

Chapter 3 **Problem 3-4A or 3-4B** ***Name*** ______________________________

Part 1

ACCOUNT TITLES	UNADJUSTED TRIAL BALANCE		ADJUSTMENTS		ADJUSTED TRIAL BALANCE	
	DR	CR	DR	CR	DR	CR

Adjustment Descriptions

(a) ______________________________

(b) ______________________________

(c) ______________________________

(d) ______________________________

(e) ______________________________

(f) ______________________________

(g) ______________________________

(h) ______________________________

Chapter 3 **Problem 3-4A or 3-4B (Continued)** ***Name*** ____________________

Part 2

Income Statement

Statement of Owner's Equity

Chapter 3 Problem 3-4A or 3-4B **_Name_** ____________________

Part 2 (Continued)

Balance Sheet

Chapter 3 **Problem 3-5A or 3-5B** ***Name*** ______________________

Part 1

Income Statement

Statement of Owner's Equity

Chapter 3 **Problem 3-5A or 3-5B** ***Name*** ______________________

Part 1 **(Continued)**

Balance Sheet

Part 2

Profit Margin:

Chapter 3 Problem 3-6A[A] or 3-6B[A] Name ______________________

Part 1

GENERAL JOURNAL

Date		Account Titles and Explanation	PR	Debit	Credit

Chapter 3 **Problem 3-6A^A or 3-6B^A** ***Name*** ______________________________
(Continued)

Part 2

GENERAL JOURNAL

Date		Account Titles and Explanation	PR	Debit	Credit

Chapter 3 **Problem 3-6A[A] or 3-6B[A] (Continued)** ***Name*** ______________________

Part 3

Chapter 3 **Serial Problem, SP 3** *Name* ____________________

Business Solutions

Part 1

Journal Entries

GENERAL JOURNAL

Date		Account Titles and Explanation	PR	Debit	Credit

Chapter 3 **Serial Problem, SP 3**
Business Solutions

Name ____________________________

Part 2
Adjusting Entries

GENERAL JOURNAL

Date		Account Titles and Explanation	PR	Debit	Credit

Chapter 3 **Serial Problem, SP 3** *Name* ____________________

Business Solutions

Parts 1 & 2 (Continued)

GENERAL LEDGER

Cash **ACCOUNT NO. 101**

Date	Explanation	PR	DEBIT	CREDIT	BALANCE
2011 Nov. 30	Balance				38,264

Accounts Receivable **ACCOUNT NO. 106**

Date	Explanation	PR	DEBIT	CREDIT	BALANCE
2011 Nov. 30	Balance				12,618

Computer Supplies **ACCOUNT NO. 126**

Date	Explanation	PR	DEBIT	CREDIT	BALANCE
2011 Nov. 30	Balance				2,545

Chapter 3 **Serial Problem, SP 3** ***Name*** ______________________
Business Solutions

Parts 1 & 2 (Continued)

Prepaid Insurance **ACCOUNT NO. 128**

Date	Explanation	PR	DEBIT	CREDIT	BALANCE
2011 Nov. 30	Balance				2,220

Prepaid Rent **ACCOUNT NO. 131**

Date	Explanation	PR	DEBIT	CREDIT	BALANCE
2011 Nov. 30	Balance				3,300

Office Equipment **ACCOUNT NO. 163**

Date	Explanation	PR	DEBIT	CREDIT	BALANCE
2011 Nov. 30	Balance				8,000

Accumulated Depreciation-Office Equipment **ACCOUNT NO. 164**

Date	Explanation	PR	DEBIT	CREDIT	BALANCE

Computer Equipment **ACCOUNT NO. 167**

Date	Explanation	PR	DEBIT	CREDIT	BALANCE
2011 Nov. 30	Balance				20,000

Chapter 3 Serial Problem, SP 3 Business Solutions

Name ______________________

Parts 1 & 2 (Continued)

Accumulated Depreciation-Computer Equipment — ACCOUNT NO. 168

Date	Explanation	PR	DEBIT	CREDIT	BALANCE

Accounts Payable — ACCOUNT NO. 201

Date	Explanation	PR	DEBIT	CREDIT	BALANCE
2011 Nov. 30	Balance				0

Wages Payable — ACCOUNT NO. 210

Date	Explanation	PR	DEBIT	CREDIT	BALANCE

Unearned Computer Services Revenue — ACCOUNT NO. 236

Date	Explanation	PR	DEBIT	CREDIT	BALANCE

S. Rey, Capital — ACCOUNT NO. 301

Date	Explanation	PR	DEBIT	CREDIT	BALANCE
2011 Nov. 30	Balance				73,000

Chapter 3 **Serial Problem, SP 3** ***Name*** ______________________

Business Solutions

Parts 1 & 2 (Continued)

S. Rey, Withdrawals **ACCOUNT NO. 302**

Date	Explanation	PR	DEBIT	CREDIT	BALANCE
2011 Nov. 30	Balance				5,600

Computer Services Revenue **ACCOUNT NO. 403**

Date	Explanation	PR	DEBIT	CREDIT	BALANCE
2011 Nov. 30	Balance				25,659

Depreciation Expense-Office Equipment **ACCOUNT NO. 612**

Date	Explanation	PR	DEBIT	CREDIT	BALANCE

Depreciation Expense-Computer Equipment **ACCOUNT NO. 613**

Date	Explanation	PR	DEBIT	CREDIT	BALANCE

Wages Expense **ACCOUNT NO. 623**

Date	Explanation	PR	DEBIT	CREDIT	BALANCE
2011 Nov. 30	Balance				2,625

Chapter 3 **Serial Problem, SP 3**
Business Solutions

Name ______________________

Parts 1 & 2 **(Continued)**

Insurance Expense **ACCOUNT NO. 637**

Date	Explanation	PR	DEBIT	CREDIT	BALANCE

Rent Expense **ACCOUNT NO. 640**

Date	Explanation	PR	DEBIT	CREDIT	BALANCE

Computer Supplies Expense **ACCOUNT NO. 652**

Date	Explanation	PR	DEBIT	CREDIT	BALANCE

Advertising Expense **ACCOUNT NO. 655**

Date	Explanation	PR	DEBIT	CREDIT	BALANCE
2011 Nov. 30	Balance				1,728

Mileage Expense **ACCOUNT NO. 676**

Date	Explanation	PR	DEBIT	CREDIT	BALANCE
2011 Nov. 30	Balance				704

Chapter 3 **Serial Problem, SP 3** *Name* ______________________

Business Solutions

Parts 1 & 2 **(Continued)**

Miscellaneous Expense **ACCOUNT NO. 677**

Date	Explanation	PR	DEBIT	CREDIT	BALANCE
2011 Nov. 30	Balance				250

Repairs Expense-Computer **ACCOUNT NO. 684**

Date	Explanation	PR	DEBIT	CREDIT	BALANCE
2011 Nov. 30	Balance				805

Income Summary **ACCOUNT NO. 901**

Date	Explanation	PR	DEBIT	CREDIT	BALANCE

Chapter 3 **Serial Problem, SP 3**
Business Solutions
(Continued)

Name ______________________________

Part 3

BUSINESS SOLUTIONS
Adjusted Trial Balance

Chapter 3 **Serial Problem, SP 3** *Name* ______________________

Business Solutions

(Continued)

Part 4

BUSINESS SOLUTIONS

Income Statement

For Three Months Ended December 31, ____

Part 5

BUSINESS SOLUTIONS

Statement of Owner's Equity

For Three Months Ended December 31, ____

Chapter 3 **Serial Problem, SP 3** ***Name*** ______________________________
Business Solutions
(Continued)

Part 6

BUSINESS SOLUTIONS
Balance Sheet
December 31, ____

Chapter 3 Reporting in Action—BTN 3-1 ***Name*** ______________________

(1)

(2)

(3) 2010 Profit Margin:

2009 Profit Margin:

(4) FastForward:

Chapter 3 **Comparative Analysis** ***Name*** ______________________
BTN 3-2

(1) Research In Motion

Current Year Profit Margin:

Prior Year Profit Margin:

Apple

Current Year Profit Margin:

Prior Year Profit Margin:

(2) Analysis

Chapter 3 Ethics Challenge—BTN 3-3 *Name* ______________________

(1)

(2)

(3)

Chapter 3 **Communicating in Practice—BTN 3-4** ***Name*** ______________________

MEMORANDUM

TO:
FROM:
SUBJECT:
DATE:

Chapter 3 Taking It to the Net—BTN 3-5 ***Name*** ______

(1) ______

(2) ______

(3) ______

(4) ______

(5) ______

(6) ______

Chapter 3 Teamwork in Action—BTN 3-6 ***Name*** ______________________________

Chapter 3 **Entrepreneurial Decision**
BTN 3-7

Name ______________________________

(1)

GENERAL JOURNAL

Date		Account Titles and Explanation	PR	Debit	Credit
(a)					
(b)					

(2)

(3)

Chapter 3 **Hitting the Road—BTN 3-8** ***Name*** ______________________

Global Decision—BTN 3-9

(1)

(2) Profit Margin

Chapter 4 Quick Study 4-1 ***Name*** ____________________

Steps

1st

2nd

3rd

4th

5th

6th

7th

8th

9th

Quick Study 4-2

(1)

(2)

(3)

(4)

Quick Study 4-3

Current Ratio:

Quick Study 4-4

(1)	(5)
(2)	(6)
(3)	(7)
(4)	(8)

Chapter 4 Quick Study 4-5 *Name* ______________________

(a) ______________________ (d) ______________________
(b) ______________________ (e) ______________________
(c) ______________________ (f) ______________________

Quick Study 4-6

(a) ______________________ (d) ______________________
(b) ______________________ (e) ______________________
(c) ______________________

Quick Study 4-7

Chapter 4 Quick Study 4-8 *Name* ______________________

______Company
Work Sheet

ACCOUNT TITLE	Unadjusted Trial Balance		Adjustments		Adjusted Trial Balance		Income Statement		Balance Sheet and Statement of Owner's Equity	
	Dr.	Cr.	Dr.	Cr.	Dr.	Cr.	Dr.	Cr.	Dr.	Cr.
Prepaid rent										
Services revenue										
Wages expense										
Accounts receivable										
Wages payable										
Rent expense										

Chapter 4 **Quick Study 4-9** ***Name*** ______________________

GENERAL JOURNAL

Date		Account Titles and Explanation	PR	Debit	Credit

Quick Study 4-10

____

____

____

____

Quick Study 4-11[A]

GENERAL JOURNAL

Date		Account Titles and Explanation	PR	Debit	Credit

Chapter 4 **Quick Study 4-12** ***Name*** ______________________

a. ______________________

____

b. ______________________

____

Exercise 4-1
Closing Entries

GENERAL JOURNAL

Date		Account Titles and Explanation	PR	Debit	Credit

Chapter 4 **Exercise 4-1 (Continued)** *Name* ____________________

Posted accounts:

M. Mallon, Capital **No. 301**

DATE	PR	Debit	Credit	Balance
Mar. 31				42,000

Salaries Expense **No. 622**

DATE	PR	Debit	Credit	Balance
Mar. 31				21,000

M. Mallon, Withdrawals **No. 302**

DATE	PR	Debit	Credit	Balance
Mar. 31				25,000

Insurance Expense **No. 637**

DATE	PR	Debit	Credit	Balance
Mar. 31				4,500

Services Revenue **No. 401**

DATE	PR	Debit	Credit	Balance
Mar. 31				74,000

Rent Expense **No. 640**

DATE	PR	Debit	Credit	Balance
Mar. 31				9,600

Depreciation Expense **No. 603**

DATE	PR	Debit	Credit	Balance
Mar. 31				17,000

Income Summary **No. 901**

DATE	PR	Debit	Credit	Balance

Chapter 4 **Exercise 4-2** ***Name*** ______________________________

Work Sheet

NO.	ACCOUNT TITLE	ADJUSTED TRIAL BALANCE		CLOSING ENTRY INFORMATION		POST-CLOSING TRIAL BALANCE	
		DR	CR	DR	CR	DR	CR

Chapter 4 **Exercise 4-3** ***Name*** ______________________

1. Closing

GENERAL JOURNAL

Date		Account Titles and Explanation	PR	Debit	Credit

2. Post-Closing Trial Balance

Post-Closing Trial Balance

Chapter 4 **Exercise 4-4** ***Name*** ______________________

Income Statement

Statement of Owner's Equity

Chapter 4 **Exercise 4-5** ***Name*** ______________________

Balance Sheet

Chapter 4 **Exercise 4-6** ***Name*** ______________________

Current Ratio:

Interpretation:

Exercise 4-7

	Current Assets	Current Liabilities	Current Ratio
Case 1			
Case 2			
Case 3			
Case 4			
Case 5			

Analysis:

Chapter 4 **Exercise 4-8** ***Name*** ____________________

(1)	(5)	(9)	(13)
(2)	(6)	(10)	(14)
(3)	(7)	(11)	(15)
(4)	(8)	(12)	(16)

Exercise 4-9

GENERAL JOURNAL

Date		Account Titles and Explanation	PR	Debit	Credit
(a)					
(b)					
(c)					
(d)					
(e)					

Chapter 4 **Exercise 4-10** ***Name*** ______________________

Work Sheet

NO.	ACCOUNT TITLE	ADJUSTED TRIAL BALANCE		INCOME STATEMENT		BALANCE SHEET & STATEMENT OF OWNER'S EQUITY	
		DR	CR	DR	CR	DR	CR

Chapter 4 Exercise 4-11 *Name* ______________________

1. Work Sheet

Account Title	Debit	Credit
Rent earned		
Salaries expense		
Insurance expense		
Dock rental expense		
Boat supplies expense		
Depreciation expense—Boats		
Totals		
Net Income		
Totals		

2. Closing Entries

GENERAL JOURNAL

Date		Account Titles and Explanation	PR	Debit	Credit

Chapter 4 Exercise 4-12

Name ____________________

__________ Company

Work Sheet

ACCOUNT TITLE	Unadjusted Trial Balance		Adjustments		Adjusted Trial Balance		Income Statement		Balance Sheet and Statement of Owner's Equity	
	Dr.	Cr.	Dr.	Cr.	Dr.	Cr.	Dr.	Cr.	Dr.	Cr.

Chapter 4 **Exercise 4-12 (Continued)** *Name* ____________________

2. Closing Entries

GENERAL JOURNAL

Date		Account Titles and Explanation	PR	Debit	Credit

Capital on the Balance Sheet:

Chapter 4 Exercise 4-13[A] *Name* ______________________________

Part 1

GENERAL JOURNAL

Date		Account Titles and Explanation	PR	Debit	Credit

Part 2

GENERAL JOURNAL

Date		Account Titles and Explanation	PR	Debit	Credit

Part 3

GENERAL JOURNAL

Date		Account Titles and Explanation	PR	Debit	Credit

Chapter 4 Exercise 4-14[A] *Name* ______________________

GENERAL JOURNAL

Date		Account Titles and Explanation	PR	Debit	Credit

Exercise 4-15

Exercises 4-16

GENERAL JOURNAL

Date		Account Titles and Explanation	PR	Debit	Credit

Chapter 4 Exercise 4-17 ***Name*** ______________________________

______ Company
Work Sheet

ACCOUNT TITLE	Unadjusted Trial Balance		Adjustments		Adjusted Trial Balance	
	Dr.	Cr.	Dr.	Cr.	Dr.	Cr.

Chapter 4 Problem 4-1A or 4-1B *Name* ______________________

(1)	(6)	(11)	(16)
(2)	(7)	(12)	(17)
(3)	(8)	(13)	(18)
(4)	(9)	(14)	(19)
(5)	(10)	(15)	(20)

Chapter 4 **Problem 4-2A or 4-2B** ***Name*** ______________________

Part 1

GENERAL LEDGER

Cash **ACCOUNT NO. 101**

DATE	Explanation	PR	DEBIT	CREDIT	BALANCE

Accounts Receivable **ACCOUNT NO. 106**

DATE	Explanation	PR	DEBIT	CREDIT	BALANCE

Office Supplies **ACCOUNT NO. 124**

DATE	Explanation	PR	DEBIT	CREDIT	BALANCE

Prepaid Insurance **ACCOUNT NO. 128**

DATE	Explanation	PR	DEBIT	CREDIT	BALANCE

Chapter 4 **Problem 4-2A or 4-2B** ***Name*** ______________________________

Part 1 **(Continued)**

Computer Equipment* **ACCOUNT NO. 167**

DATE	Explanation	PR	DEBIT	CREDIT	BALANCE

Accumulated Depreciation-Computer Equipment* **ACCOUNT NO. 168**

DATE	Explanation	PR	DEBIT	CREDIT	BALANCE

Buildings** **ACCOUNT NO. 173**

DATE	Explanation	PR	DEBIT	CREDIT	BALANCE

Accumulated Depreciation-Buildings** **ACCOUNT NO. 174**

DATE	Explanation	PR	DEBIT	CREDIT	BALANCE

Salaries Payable **ACCOUNT NO. 209**

DATE	Explanation	PR	DEBIT	CREDIT	BALANCE

____________, Capital **ACCOUNT NO. 301**

DATE	Explanation	PR	DEBIT	CREDIT	BALANCE

* Problem 4-2A only.

** Problem 4-2B only.

Chapter 4 **Problem 4-2A or 4-2B** ***Name*** ____________________

Part 1 **(Continued)**

____________, Withdrawals — ACCOUNT NO. 302

DATE	Explanation	PR	DEBIT	CREDIT	BALANCE

Storage Fees Earned** — ACCOUNT NO. 401

DATE	Explanation	PR	DEBIT	CREDIT	BALANCE

Commissions Earned* — ACCOUNT NO. 405

DATE	Explanation	PR	DEBIT	CREDIT	BALANCE

Depreciation Expense-Buildings** — ACCOUNT NO. 606

DATE	Explanation	PR	DEBIT	CREDIT	BALANCE

Depreciation Expense-Computer Equipment* — ACCOUNT NO. 612

DATE	Explanation	PR	DEBIT	CREDIT	BALANCE

* Problem 4-2A only.

** Problem 4-2B only.

Chapter 4 Problem 4-2A or 4-2B **Name** ______________________

Part 1 (Continued)

Salaries Expense ACCOUNT NO. 622

DATE	Explanation	PR	DEBIT	CREDIT	BALANCE

Insurance Expense ACCOUNT NO. 637

DATE	Explanation	PR	DEBIT	CREDIT	BALANCE

Rent Expense ACCOUNT NO. 640

DATE	Explanation	PR	DEBIT	CREDIT	BALANCE

Office Supplies Expense ACCOUNT NO. 650

DATE	Explanation	PR	DEBIT	CREDIT	BALANCE

Repairs Expense ACCOUNT NO. 684

DATE	Explanation	PR	DEBIT	CREDIT	BALANCE

Telephone Expense ACCOUNT NO. 688

DATE	Explanation	PR	DEBIT	CREDIT	BALANCE

Chapter 4 **Problem 4-2A or 4-2B** ***Name*** ______________________

Part 1 **(Continued)**

		Income Summary			ACCOUNT NO. 901
DATE	Explanation	PR	DEBIT	CREDIT	BALANCE

Chapter 4 **Problem 4-2A or 4-2B (Continued)** ***Name*** ____________________

Part 2

GENERAL JOURNAL

Date		Account Titles and Explanation	PR	Debit	Credit

Chapter 4 Problem 4-2A or 4-2B (Continued) *Name* ______________________

Part 3

Unadjusted Trial Balance

Chapter 4 **Problem 4-2A or 4-2B (Continued)** ***Name*** ______________________

Part 4 **Adjusting Entries**

GENERAL JOURNAL

Date		Account Titles and Explanation	PR	Debit	Credit

Chapter 4 **Problem 4-2A or 4-2B (Continued)** ***Name*** ______________________

Part 5

Income Statement

Statement of Owner's Equity

Chapter 4 **Problem 4-2A or 4-2B** ***Name*** ______

Part 5 **(Continued)**

Balance Sheet

Chapter 4 **Problem 4-2A or 4-2B (Continued)** ***Name*** ______________________

Part 6
Closing Entries:

GENERAL JOURNAL

Date		Account Titles and Explanation	PR	Debit	Credit

Part 7

Post-Closing Trial Balance

Chapter 4 **Problem 4-3A or 4-3B** ***Name*** ______________________

Part 1

Income Statement

Statement of Owner's Equity

Chapter 4 **Problem 4-3A or 4-3B** ***Name*** ______________________

Part 1 **(Continued)**

Balance Sheet

Chapter 4 **Problem 4-3A or 4-3B** *Name* ______________________
(Continued)

Parts 2 & 3

Work Sheet

NO.	ACCOUNT TITLES	ADJUSTED TRIAL BALANCE		CLOSING ENTRY INFORMATION		POST-CLOSING TRIAL BALANCE	
		DR	CR	DR	CR	DR	CR

Chapter 4 **Problem 4-3A or 4-3B (Continued)** ***Name*** ______________________

Part 3
Closing Entries

GENERAL JOURNAL

Date		Account Titles and Explanation	PR	Debit	Credit

Chapter 4 **Problem 4-3A or 4-3B (Continued)** ***Name*** ______________________

Part 4

Financial Statement Changes:

Problem 4-4A or 4-4B

Part 1

Income Statement

Chapter 4 Problem 4-4A or 4-4B Name

Part 1 (Continued)

Statement of Owner's Equity

Balance Sheet

Chapter 4 **Problem 4-4A or 4-4B** ***Name*** ______________________________

(Continued)

Part 2
Closing Entries

GENERAL JOURNAL

Date		Account Titles and Explanation	PR	Debit	Credit

Chapter 4 Problem 4-4A or 4-4B (Continued) *Name* ____________________

Part 3

(a) ____________________

(b) ____________________

(c) ____________________

(d) ____________________

Chapter 4 Problem 4-5A or 4-5B *Name* ______________________

Part 1

Work Sheet											
		Unadjusted Trial Balance		Adjustments		Adjusted Trial Balance		Income Statement		Balance Sheet and Statement of Owner's Equity	
No.	Account Title	Dr.	Cr.	Dr.	Cr.	Dr.	Cr.	Dr.	Cr.	Dr.	Cr.

Chapter 4 **Problem 4-5A or 4-5B (Continued)** ***Name*** ______________________________

Part 2
Adjusting Entries

GENERAL JOURNAL

Date		Account Titles and Explanation	PR	Debit	Credit

Chapter 4 **Problem 4-5A or 4-5B** ***Name*** ______________________

Part 2 **(Continued)**

Closing Entries

GENERAL JOURNAL

Date		Account Titles and Explanation	PR	Debit	Credit

Chapter 4 **Problem 4-5A or 4-5B (Continued)** ***Name*** ____________________

Part 3

Income Statement

Statement of Owner's Equity

Chapter 4 **Problem 4-5A or 4-5B** ***Name*** ____________________

Part 3 **(Continued)**

Balance Sheet

Chapter 4 Problem 4-5A or 4-5B (Continued) *Name* ____________________

Part 4

(a)

(b)

Chapter 4 **Problem 4-6A[A] or 4-6B[A]** *Name* ______________________

Part 1

Work Sheet						
Account Title	Unadjusted Trial Balance		Adjustments		Adjusted Trial Balance	
	Dr.	Cr.	Dr.	Cr.	Dr.	Cr.

Chapter 4 **Problem 4-6A[A] or 4-6B[A] (Continued)** ***Name*** ______________________________

Part 2

GENERAL JOURNAL

Date		Account Titles and Explanation	PR	Debit	Credit

Chapter 4 **Problem 4-6A[A] or 4-6B[A] (Continued)** ***Name*** ______________________________

Part 3

GENERAL JOURNAL

Date		Account Titles and Explanation	PR	Debit	Credit

Part 4

GENERAL JOURNAL

Date		Account Titles and Explanation	PR	Debit	Credit

Chapter 4 **Serial Problem, SP 4** ***Name*** ______________________________

Business Solutions

Part 1 **Closing Entries**

GENERAL JOURNAL

Date		Account Titles and Explanation	PR	Debit	Credit

Chapter 4 **Serial Problem, SP 4** *Name* ______________________
Business Solutions

Part 1 **(Continued)**

GENERAL LEDGER

Cash — ACCOUNT NO. 101

Date	Explanation	PR	DEBIT	CREDIT	BALANCE
2011, Dec. 31	Balance				48,372

Accounts Receivable — ACCOUNT NO. 106

Date	Explanation	PR	DEBIT	CREDIT	BALANCE
2011, Dec. 31	Balance				5,668

Computer Supplies — ACCOUNT NO. 126

Date	Explanation	PR	DEBIT	CREDIT	BALANCE
2011, Dec. 31	Balance				580

Prepaid Insurance — ACCOUNT NO. 128

Date	Explanation	PR	DEBIT	CREDIT	BALANCE
2011, Dec. 31	Balance				1,665

Prepaid Rent — ACCOUNT NO. 131

Date	Explanation	PR	DEBIT	CREDIT	BALANCE
2011, Dec. 31	Balance				825

Chapter 4 Serial Problem, SP 4 Name ______________________
Business Solutions

Part 1 (Continued)

Office Equipment — ACCOUNT NO. 163

Date	Explanation	PR	DEBIT	CREDIT	BALANCE
2011, Dec. 31	Balance				8,000

Accumulated Depreciation-Office Equipment — ACCOUNT NO. 164

Date	Explanation	PR	DEBIT	CREDIT	BALANCE
2011, Dec. 31	Balance				400

Computer Equipment — ACCOUNT NO. 167

Date	Explanation	PR	DEBIT	CREDIT	BALANCE
2011, Dec. 31	Balance				20,000

Accumulated Depreciation-Computer Equipment — ACCOUNT NO. 168

Date	Explanation	PR	DEBIT	CREDIT	BALANCE
2011, Dec. 31	Balance				1,250

Accounts Payable — ACCOUNT NO. 201

Date	Explanation	PR	DEBIT	CREDIT	BALANCE
2011, Dec. 31	Balance				1,100

Wages Payable — ACCOUNT NO. 210

Date	Explanation	PR	DEBIT	CREDIT	BALANCE
2011, Dec. 31	Balance				500

Chapter 4 **Serial Problem, SP 4** ***Name*** ____________________
Business Solutions

Part 1 **(Continued)**

Unearned Computer Services Revenue **ACCOUNT NO. 236**

Date	Explanation	PR	DEBIT	CREDIT	BALANCE
2011, Dec. 31	Balance				1,500

A. Lopez, Capital **ACCOUNT NO. 301**

Date	Explanation	PR	DEBIT	CREDIT	BALANCE
2011, Dec. 31	Balance				73,000

A. Lopez, Withdrawals **ACCOUNT NO. 302**

Date	Explanation	PR	DEBIT	CREDIT	BALANCE
2011, Dec. 31	Balance				7,100

Computer Service Revenue **ACCOUNT NO. 403**

Date	Explanation	PR	DEBIT	CREDIT	BALANCE
2011, Dec. 31	Balance				31,284

Depreciation Expense-Office Equipment **ACCOUNT NO. 612**

Date	Explanation	PR	DEBIT	CREDIT	BALANCE
2011, Dec. 31	Balance				400

Depreciation Expense-Computer Equipment **ACCOUNT NO. 613**

Date	Explanation	PR	DEBIT	CREDIT	BALANCE
2011, Dec. 31	Balance				1,250

Chapter 4 Serial Problem, SP 4 Business Solutions Name ______________________

Part 1 (Continued)

Wages Expense ACCOUNT NO. 623

Date	Explanation	PR	DEBIT	CREDIT	BALANCE
2011, Dec. 31	Balance				3,875

Insurance Expense ACCOUNT NO. 637

Date	Explanation	PR	DEBIT	CREDIT	BALANCE
2011, Dec. 31	Balance				555

Rent Expense ACCOUNT NO. 640

Date	Explanation	PR	DEBIT	CREDIT	BALANCE
2011, Dec. 31	Balance				2,475

Computer Supplies Expense ACCOUNT NO. 652

Date	Explanation	PR	DEBIT	CREDIT	BALANCE
2011, Dec. 31	Balance				3,065

Advertising Expense ACCOUNT NO. 655

Date	Explanation	PR	DEBIT	CREDIT	BALANCE
2011, Dec. 31	Balance				2,753

Mileage Expense ACCOUNT NO. 676

Date	Explanation	PR	DEBIT	CREDIT	BALANCE
2011, Dec. 31	Balance				896

Chapter 4 **Serial Problem, SP 4** ***Name*** ______________________
Business Solutions

Part 1 **(Continued)**

Miscellaneous Expense **ACCOUNT NO. 677**

Date	Explanation	PR	DEBIT	CREDIT	BALANCE
2011, Dec. 31	Balance				250

Repairs Expense-Computer **ACCOUNT NO. 684**

Date	Explanation	PR	DEBIT	CREDIT	BALANCE
2011, Dec. 31	Balance				1,305

Income Summary **ACCOUNT NO. 901**

Date	Explanation	PR	DEBIT	CREDIT	BALANCE

Chapter 4 Serial Problem, SP 4
Business Solutions
(Continued)

Name ______________________________

Part 2

BUSINESS SOLUTIONS
Post-Closing Trial Balance
December 31, 2011

	Debit	Credit

Chapter 4 **Reporting in Action** ***Name*** ______________________
BTN 4-1

(1) ______________________

(2) ______________________

(3) ______________________

(4) ______________________

(5) FastForward: ______________________

Chapter 4 **Comparative Analysis** **BTN 4-2** ***Name*** ____________________

(1) **Research In Motion Current Ratio:**

Current Year

Prior Year

Apple Current Ratio:

Current Year

Prior Year

(2)

(3)

(4)

Chapter 4 **Ethics Challenge** ***Name*** ______________________

BTN 4-3

(1)

(2)

Chapter 4 Communicating in Practice—BTN 4-4

Name ______________________

MEMORANDUM

TO:
FROM:
DATE:
SUBJECT:

Chapter 4 **Taking It to the Net**
BTN 4-5

Name ______________________

(1) ______________________

(2) ______________________

(3) ______________________

Chapter 4 Teamwork in Action
BTN 4-6

Name ____________________

1.

Account Title	Trial Balance		Adjustments		Balance Sheet	
	Debit	Credit	Debit	Credit	Debit	Credit

2.

Account Title	Trial Balance		Adjustments		Income Statement	
	Debit	Credit	Debit	Credit	Debit	Credit

GENERAL JOURNAL

Date		Account Titles and Explanation	PR	Debit	Credit

Chapter 4 **Teamwork in Action** ***Name*** ______________________
BTN 4-6
(Continued)

3.

Account Title	Trial Balance		Adjustments		Income Statement	
	Debit	Credit	Debit	Credit	Debit	Credit

GENERAL JOURNAL

Date		Account Titles and Explanation	PR	Debit	Credit

Chapter 4 Teamwork in Action
BTN 4-6
(Continued)

Name ______________________

4.

D. Noseworthy, Capital	

Income Summary	

GENERAL JOURNAL

Date		Account Titles and Explanation	PR	Debit	Credit

5. Proving the Accounting Equation

Chapter 4 **Entrepreneurial Decision BTN 4-7** ***Name*** ____________________

(1)

(2)

(3)

Chapter 4 **Hitting the Road** ***Name*** ______________________
BTN 4-8

(1) ______________________

(2) ______________________

(3) ______________________

(4) ______________________

(5) ______________________

Global Decision—BTN 4-9

(1) Nokia Current Ratio:
Current Year

Prior Year

(2) ______________________

Chapter 7 Quick Study 7-1 *Name* ______

(1)	(7)
(2)	(8)
(3)	(9)
(4)	(10)
(5)	(11)
(6)	(12)

Quick Study 7-2

(1)
(2)
(3)
(4)
(5)

Quick Study 7-3

(1)
(2)
(3)
(4)

Quick Study 7-4

(a)
(b)
(c)
(d)
(e)
(f)
(g)
(h)

Chapter 7 Quick Study 7-5 *Name* ____________________

GENERAL JOURNAL

Date		Account Titles and Explanation	PR	Debit	Credit

Quick Study 7-6

(a)

ACCOUNTS RECEIVABLE LEDGER

Date	Explanation	PR	DEBIT	CREDIT	BALANCE

Date	Explanation	PR	DEBIT	CREDIT	BALANCE

Date	Explanation	PR	DEBIT	CREDIT	BALANCE

Chapter 7 Quick Study 7-6 (Continued) *Name* ______________________

(b)

GENERAL LEDGER

Accounts Receivable

Date	Explanation	PR	DEBIT	CREDIT	BALANCE

Quick Study 7-7

PURCHASES JOURNAL								
Date	Account	Date of Invoice	Terms	PR	Accts. Payable Cr.	Inventory Dr.	Office Supplies Dr.	Other Accts. Dr.

Quick Study 7-8

June 1 ______________________
8 ______________________
14 ______________________
17 ______________________
24 ______________________
28 ______________________
29 ______________________

Quick Study 7-9A

PURCHASES JOURNAL								
Date	Account	Date of Invoice	Terms	PR	Accts. Payable Cr.	Purchases Dr.	Office Supplies Dr.	Other Accts. Dr.

Chapter 7 **Quick Study 7-10** ***Name*** ______________________

Part 1

ACCOUNTS RECEIVABLE LEDGER

Eric Horner	

Hong Jiang	

Joe Mack	

Tess Wilson	

Part 2

GENERAL LEDGER

Accounts Receivable	

Sales	

Part 3

Schedule of Accounts Receivable

Chapter 7 Quick Study 7-11 *Name* ____________________

Segment	Segment Income	Average Segment Assets	Segment return on Assets

Interpretation:

Product	Product Sales	Percent of Total Sales

Interpretation:

Quick Study 7-12

GENERAL JOURNAL

Date		Account Titles and Explanation	PR	Debit	Credit
(1)					
(2)					
(3)					

Chapter 7 **Exercise 7-1** ***Name*** ______________________

SALES JOURNAL					
Date	Account Debited	Invoice Number	PR	Accts. Rec. Dr. Sales Cr.	Cost of Goods Sold Dr. Inventory Cr.

Exercise 7-2

March 2 ______________________

5 ______________________

7 ______________________

8 ______________________

12 ______________________

16 ______________________

19 ______________________

25 ______________________

Exercise 7-3[A]

SALES JOURNAL				
Date	Account Debited	Invoice Number	PR	Accts. Rec. Dr. Sales Cr.

Chapter 7 Exercise 7-4 *Name* ______________________

CASH RECEIPTS JOURNAL									
Date	Account Credited	Explanation	PR	Cash Dr.	Sales Discount Dr.	Accts. Rec. Cr.	Sales Cr.	Other Accts. Cr.	Cost of Goods Sold Dr. Inv. Cr.

Exercise 7-5

Nov. 3 ______________________

7 ______________________

9 ______________________

13 ______________________

18 ______________________

22 ______________________

27 ______________________

30 ______________________

Exercise 7-6[A]

CASH RECEIPTS JOURNAL								
Date	Account Credited	Explanation	PR	Cash Dr.	Sales Discount Dr.	Accts. Rec. Cr.	Sales Cr.	Other Accts. Cr.

Chapter 7 Exercise 7-7 ***Name*** ______________________

(a)

ACCOUNTS RECEIVABLE LEDGER

Date	Explanation	PR	DEBIT	CREDIT	BALANCE

Date	Explanation	PR	DEBIT	CREDIT	BALANCE

Date	Explanation	PR	DEBIT	CREDIT	BALANCE

(b)

Accounts Payable

Date	Explanation	PR	DEBIT	CREDIT	BALANCE

Chapter 7 Exercise 7-8 *Name* ______________________

CASH DISBURSEMENTS JOURNAL								
Date	Ck. No.	Payee	Account Debited	PR	Cash Cr.	Inventory Cr.	Other Accts. Dr.	Accts. Payable Dr.

Exercise 7-9

April 3 ______________________
9 ______________________
12 ______________________
17 ______________________
20 ______________________
28 ______________________
29 ______________________
30 ______________________

Exercise 7-10[A]

CASH DISBURSEMENTS JOURNAL								
Date	Ck. No.	Payee	Account Debited	PR	Cash Cr.	Purchases Discounts Cr.	Other Accts. Dr.	Accts. Payable Dr.

Chapter 7 **Exercise 7-11** ***Name*** ______________________

(a)

(b)

Chapter 7 **Exercise 7-12** ***Name*** ______________________________

Part 1

ACCOUNTS RECEIVABLE SUBSIDIARY LEDGER

Anna Page

Sara Reed

Aaron Reckers

Part 2

GENERAL LEDGER

Accounts Receivable

Sales

Sales Returns and Allowances

Inventory

Cost of Goods Sold

Chapter 7 **Exercise 7-12 (Continued)** ***Name*** ______________________

Part 3

Schedule of Accounts Receivable

Accounts Receivable Controlling Account

Chapter 7 Exercise 7-13 *Name* ______________________

(1) ______________________

(2) ______________________

(3) ______________________

(4) ______________________

(5) ______________________

Exercise 7-14

	Segment Income (in $ mil.)		Segment Assets (in $ mil.)		Segment Return on Assets
Segment	2011	2010	2011	2010	2011

Analysis and Interpretation:

Chapter 7 **Problem 7-1A or 7-1B** ***Name*** ____________________

Part 1

Sales Journal					Page 3
Date	Account Debited	Invoice Number	PR	Accts. Receivable Dr. Sales Cr.	Cost of Goods Sold Dr. Inventory Cr.

Cash Receipts Journal									Page 3
Date	Account Credited	Explanation	PR	Cash Dr.	Sales Disc. Dr.	Accts. Rec. Cr.	Sales Cr.	Other Accts. Cr.	Cost of Goods Sold Dr. Inv. Cr.

Chapter 7 **Problem 7-1A or 7-1B (Continued)** ***Name*** ______________________

Parts 2 & 3

GENERAL LEDGER

Cash **ACCOUNT NO. 101**

Date	Explanation	PR	DEBIT	CREDIT	BALANCE

Accounts Receivable **ACCOUNT NO. 106**

Date	Explanation	PR	DEBIT	CREDIT	BALANCE

Inventory **ACCOUNT NO. 119**

Date	Explanation	PR	DEBIT	CREDIT	BALANCE

Long-Term Notes Payable **ACCOUNT NO. 251**

Date	Explanation	PR	DEBIT	CREDIT	BALANCE

______________,Capital **ACCOUNT NO. 301**

Date	Explanation	PR	DEBIT	CREDIT	BALANCE

Sales **ACCOUNT NO. 413**

Date	Explanation	PR	DEBIT	CREDIT	BALANCE

Chapter 7 **Problem 7-1A or 7-1B** ***Name*** ______________________

Parts 2 & 3 **(Continued)**

Sales Discounts **ACCOUNT NO. 415**

Date	Explanation	PR	DEBIT	CREDIT	BALANCE

Cost of Goods Sold **ACCOUNT NO. 502**

Date	Explanation	PR	DEBIT	CREDIT	BALANCE

ACCOUNTS RECEIVABLE LEDGER

Date	Explanation	PR	DEBIT	CREDIT	BALANCE

Date	Explanation	PR	DEBIT	CREDIT	BALANCE

Date	Explanation	PR	DEBIT	CREDIT	BALANCE

Chapter 7 **Problem 7-1A or 7-1B (Continued)** ***Name*** ______________________

Part 4

Trial Balance

Schedule of Accounts Receivable

Part 5

Analysis:

Chapter 7 Problem 7-2A[A] or 7-2B[A] *Name* ______________________________

Parts 1 & 2

Sales Journal				Page 3
Date	Account Debited	Invoice Number	PR	Accts Receivable Dr. Sales Cr.

Cash Receipts Journal								Page 3
Date	Account Credited	Explanation	PR	Cash Dr.	Sales Discount Dr.	Accts. Rec. Cr.	Sales Cr.	Other Accts. Cr.

Chapter 7 **Problem 7-2A[A] or 7-2B[A]** *Name* ______________________________

Parts 2 & 3 **(Continued)**

GENERAL LEDGER

Cash **ACCOUNT NO. 101**

Date	Explanation	PR	DEBIT	CREDIT	BALANCE

Accounts Receivable **ACCOUNT NO. 106**

Date	Explanation	PR	DEBIT	CREDIT	BALANCE

Inventory **ACCOUNT NO. 119**

Date	Explanation	PR	DEBIT	CREDIT	BALANCE

Long-Term Notes Payable **ACCOUNT NO. 251**

Date	Explanation	PR	DEBIT	CREDIT	BALANCE

____________, Capital **ACCOUNT NO. 301**

Date	Explanation	PR	DEBIT	CREDIT	BALANCE

Sales **ACCOUNT NO. 413**

Date	Explanation	PR	DEBIT	CREDIT	BALANCE

Sales Discounts **ACCOUNT NO. 415**

Date	Explanation	PR	DEBIT	CREDIT	BALANCE

Chapter 7 **Problem 7-2A^A or 7-2B^A** ***Name*** ______________________

Parts 2 & 3 **(Continued)**

ACCOUNTS RECEIVABLE LEDGER

Date	Explanation	PR	DEBIT	CREDIT	BALANCE

Date	Explanation	PR	DEBIT	CREDIT	BALANCE

Date	Explanation	PR	DEBIT	CREDIT	BALANCE

Chapter 7 **Problem 7-2A[A] or 7-2B[A] (Continued)** ***Name*** ______________________

Part 4

Trial Balance

Schedule of Accounts Receivable

Part 5

Analysis Component:

Chapter 7 **Problem 7-3A or 7-3B** ***Name*** ____________________

Parts 1 & 2

Purchases Journal								Page 3
Date	Account	Date of Invoice	Terms	PR	Accts. Payable Cr.	Inventory Dr.	Office Supplies Dr.	Other Accts. Dr.

Cash Disbursements Journal								Page 3
Date	Ck. No.	Payee	Account Debited	PR	Cash Cr.	Inventory Cr.	Other Accts. Dr.	Accts. Payable Dr.

Chapter 7 **Problem 7-3A or 7-3B** ***Name*** ______________________

Parts 1 & 3 **(Continued)**

GENERAL JOURNAL **Page 3**

Date		Account Titles and Explanation	PR	Debit	Credit

Chapter 7 Problem 7-3A or 7-3B ***Name*** ______________________

Parts 2 & 3 (Continued)

GENERAL LEDGER

Cash **ACCOUNT NO. 101**

Date	Explanation	PR	DEBIT	CREDIT	BALANCE

Inventory **ACCOUNT NO. 119**

Date	Explanation	PR	DEBIT	CREDIT	BALANCE

Office Supplies **ACCOUNT NO. 124**

Date	Explanation	PR	DEBIT	CREDIT	BALANCE

Store Supplies **ACCOUNT NO. 125**

Date	Explanation	PR	DEBIT	CREDIT	BALANCE

Store Equipment **ACCOUNT NO. 165**

Date	Explanation	PR	DEBIT	CREDIT	BALANCE

Accounts Payable **ACCOUNT NO. 201**

Date	Explanation	PR	DEBIT	CREDIT	BALANCE

Chapter 7 **Problem 7-3A or 7-3B** ***Name*** ______________________

Parts 2 & 3 **(Continued)**

Long-Term Notes Payable **ACCOUNT NO. 251**

Date	Explanation	PR	DEBIT	CREDIT	BALANCE

______________,Capital **ACCOUNT NO. 301**

Date	Explanation	PR	DEBIT	CREDIT	BALANCE

Sales Salaries Expense **ACCOUNT NO. 621**

Date	Explanation	PR	DEBIT	CREDIT	BALANCE

Advertising Expense **ACCOUNT NO. 655**

Date	Explanation	PR	DEBIT	CREDIT	BALANCE

ACCOUNTS PAYABLE LEDGER

Date	Explanation	PR	DEBIT	CREDIT	BALANCE

Date	Explanation	PR	DEBIT	CREDIT	BALANCE

Date	Explanation	PR	DEBIT	CREDIT	BALANCE

Date	Explanation	PR	DEBIT	CREDIT	BALANCE

Chapter 7 **Problem 7-3A or 7-3B (Continued)** ***Name*** ____________________

Part 4

Trial Balance

Schedule of Accounts Payable

Chapter 7 **Problem 7-4A[A] or 7-4B[A]** ***Name*** ______________________

Parts 1 & 3

Purchases Journal								Page 3
Date	Account	Date of Invoice	Terms	PR	Accts. Payable Cr.	Purchases Dr.	Office Supplies Dr.	Other Accts. Dr.

Cash Disbursements Journal								Page 3
Date	Ck. No.	Payee	Account Debited	PR	Cash Cr.	Purchases Discount Cr.	Other Accts. Dr.	Accts. Payable Dr.

Chapter 7 **Problem 7-4A[A] or 7-4B[A]** ***Name*** ______________________________

Parts 1 & 3 **(Continued)**

GENERAL JOURNAL **Page 3**

Date		Account Titles and Explanation	PR	Debit	Credit

Chapter 7 Problem 7-4A[A] or 7-4B[A] *Name* ______________________

Parts 2 & 3 (Continued)

GENERAL LEDGER

Cash ACCOUNT NO. 101

Date	Explanation	PR	DEBIT	CREDIT	BALANCE

Inventory ACCOUNT NO. 119

Date	Explanation	PR	DEBIT	CREDIT	BALANCE

Office Supplies ACCOUNT NO. 124

Date	Explanation	PR	DEBIT	CREDIT	BALANCE

Store Supplies ACCOUNT NO. 125

Date	Explanation	PR	DEBIT	CREDIT	BALANCE

Store Equipment ACCOUNT NO. 165

Date	Explanation	PR	DEBIT	CREDIT	BALANCE

Accounts Payable ACCOUNT NO. 201

Date	Explanation	PR	DEBIT	CREDIT	BALANCE

Chapter 7 **Problem 7-4A[A] or 7-4B[A]** ***Name*** ______________________

Parts 2 & 3 **(Continued)**

Long-Term Notes Payable **ACCOUNT NO. 251**

Date	Explanation	PR	DEBIT	CREDIT	BALANCE

______________,Capital **ACCOUNT NO. 301**

Date	Explanation	PR	DEBIT	CREDIT	BALANCE

Purchases **ACCOUNT NO. 505**

Date	Explanation	PR	DEBIT	CREDIT	BALANCE

Purchase Returns and Allowances **ACCOUNT NO. 506**

Date	Explanation	PR	DEBIT	CREDIT	BALANCE

Purchase Discounts **ACCOUNT NO. 507**

Date	Explanation	PR	DEBIT	CREDIT	BALANCE

Sales Salaries Expense **ACCOUNT NO. 621**

Date	Explanation	PR	DEBIT	CREDIT	BALANCE

Advertising Expense **ACCOUNT NO. 655**

Date	Explanation	PR	DEBIT	CREDIT	BALANCE

Chapter 7 **Problem 7-4A[A] or 7-4B[A]** ***Name*** ______________________

Parts 2 & 3 **(Continued)**

ACCOUNTS PAYABLE LEDGER

____

Date	Explanation	PR	DEBIT	CREDIT	BALANCE

____

Date	Explanation	PR	DEBIT	CREDIT	BALANCE

____

Date	Explanation	PR	DEBIT	CREDIT	BALANCE

____

Date	Explanation	PR	DEBIT	CREDIT	BALANCE

Chapter 7 **Problem 7-4A[A] or 7-4B[A] (Continued)** ***Name*** ____________________

Part 4

Trial Balance

Schedule of Accounts Payable

Chapter 7 **Problem 7-5A or 7-5B** ***Name*** ______________________

Parts 1 & 2

Sales Journal					Page 2
Date	Account Debited	Invoice Number	PR	Accts. Rec. Dr. Sales Cr.	Cost of Goods Sold Dr. Inventory Cr.

Cash Receipts Journal									Page 2
Date	Account Credited	Explanation	PR	Cash Dr.	Sales Disc. Dr.	Accts. Rec. Cr.	Sales Cr.	Other Accts. Cr.	Cost of Goods Sold Dr. Inv. Cr.

Chapter 7 **Problem 7-5A or 7-5B** ***Name*** ______________________

Parts 1 & 2 **(Continued)**

Purchases Journal								Page 2
Date	Account	Date of Inv.	Terms	PR	Accts. Pay. Cr.	Inventory Dr.	Office Supplies Dr.	Other Accts. Dr.

Cash Disbursements Journal								Page 2
Date	Ck. No.	Payee	Account Debited	PR	Cash Cr.	Inventory Cr.	Other Accts. Dr.	Accts. Payable Dr.

GENERAL JOURNAL **Page 2**

Date		Account Titles and Explanation	PR	Debit	Credit

Chapter 7 **Problem 7-5A or 7-5B** ***Name*** ____________________

Parts 1 & 2 **(Continued)**

GENERAL LEDGER

Cash **ACCOUNT NO. 101**

Date	Explanation	PR	DEBIT	CREDIT	BALANCE

Accounts Receivable **ACCOUNT NO. 106**

Date	Explanation	PR	DEBIT	CREDIT	BALANCE

Inventory **ACCOUNT NO. 119**

Date	Explanation	PR	DEBIT	CREDIT	BALANCE

Office Supplies **ACCOUNT NO. 124**

Date	Explanation	PR	DEBIT	CREDIT	BALANCE

Store Supplies **ACCOUNT NO. 125**

Date	Explanation	PR	DEBIT	CREDIT	BALANCE

Office Equipment **ACCOUNT NO. 163**

Date	Explanation	PR	DEBIT	CREDIT	BALANCE

Chapter 7 **Problem 7-5A or 7-5B** ***Name*** ______________________

Parts 1 & 2 **(Continued)**

Accounts Payable **ACCOUNT NO. 201**

Date	Explanation	PR	DEBIT	CREDIT	BALANCE

Long-Term Notes Payable **ACCOUNT NO. 251**

Date	Explanation	PR	DEBIT	CREDIT	BALANCE

____________, Capital **ACCOUNT NO. 301**

Date	Explanation	PR	DEBIT	CREDIT	BALANCE

Sales **ACCOUNT NO. 413**

Date	Explanation	PR	DEBIT	CREDIT	BALANCE

Sales Discounts **ACCOUNT NO. 415**

Date	Explanation	PR	DEBIT	CREDIT	BALANCE

Cost of Goods Sold **ACCOUNT NO. 502**

Date	Explanation	PR	DEBIT	CREDIT	BALANCE

Sales Salaries Expense **ACCOUNT NO. 621**

Date	Explanation	PR	DEBIT	CREDIT	BALANCE

Chapter 7 **Problem 7-5A or 7-5B** ***Name*** ______________________

Parts 1 & 2 **(Continued)**

ACCOUNTS RECEIVABLE LEDGER

Date	Explanation	PR	DEBIT	CREDIT	BALANCE

Date	Explanation	PR	DEBIT	CREDIT	BALANCE

Date	Explanation	PR	DEBIT	CREDIT	BALANCE

Chapter 7 **Problem 7-5A or 7-5B** ***Name*** ______________________

Parts 1 & 2 **(Continued)**

ACCOUNTS RECEIVABLE LEDGER

Date	Explanation	PR	DEBIT	CREDIT	BALANCE

Date	Explanation	PR	DEBIT	CREDIT	BALANCE

Date	Explanation	PR	DEBIT	CREDIT	BALANCE

Date	Explanation	PR	DEBIT	CREDIT	BALANCE

Chapter 7 **Problem 7-5A or 7-5B (Continued)** ***Name*** ______________________

Part 3

Trial Balance

Schedule of Accounts Receivable

Schedule of Accounts Payable

Chapter 7 **Problem 7-6A[A] or 7-6B[A]** ***Name*** ____________________

Parts 1 & 2

Sales Journal				Page 2
Date	Account Debited	Invoice Number	PR	Accts. Receivable Dr. Sales Cr.

Cash Receipts Journal								Page 2
Date	Account Credited	Explanation	PR	Cash Dr.	Sales Disc. Dr.	Accts. Rec. Cr.	Sales Cr.	Other Accts. Cr.

Chapter 7 Problem 7-6A[A] or 7-6B[A] *Name* ____________________

Parts 1 & 2 (Continued)

Purchases Journal								Page 2
Date	Account	Date of Invoice	Terms	PR	Accts. Payable Cr.	Purchases Dr.	Office Supplies Dr.	Other Accts. Dr.

Cash Disbursements Journal								Page 2
Date	Ck. No.	Payee	Account Debited	PR	Cash Cr.	Purch. Disc. Cr.	Other Accts. Dr.	Accts. Payable Dr.

GENERAL JOURNAL Page 2

Date		Account Titles and Explanation	PR	Debit	Credit

Chapter 7 **Problem 7-6A[A] or 7-6B[A]** ***Name*** ____________________

Parts 1 & 2 **(Continued)**

GENERAL LEDGER

Cash **ACCOUNT NO. 101**

Date	Explanation	PR	DEBIT	CREDIT	BALANCE

Accounts Receivable **ACCOUNT NO. 106**

Date	Explanation	PR	DEBIT	CREDIT	BALANCE

Inventory **ACCOUNT NO. 119**

Date	Explanation	PR	DEBIT	CREDIT	BALANCE

Office Supplies **ACCOUNT NO. 124**

Date	Explanation	PR	DEBIT	CREDIT	BALANCE

Store Supplies **ACCOUNT NO. 125**

Date	Explanation	PR	DEBIT	CREDIT	BALANCE

Office Equipment **ACCOUNT NO. 163**

Date	Explanation	PR	DEBIT	CREDIT	BALANCE

Chapter 7 **Problem 7-6A[A] or 7-6B[A]** ***Name*** ____________________

Parts 1 & 2 **(Continued)**

Accounts Payable **ACCOUNT NO. 201**

Date	Explanation	PR	DEBIT	CREDIT	BALANCE

Long-Term Notes Payable **ACCOUNT NO. 251**

Date	Explanation	PR	DEBIT	CREDIT	BALANCE

____________, Capital **ACCOUNT NO. 301**

Date	Explanation	PR	DEBIT	CREDIT	BALANCE

Sales **ACCOUNT NO. 413**

Date	Explanation	PR	DEBIT	CREDIT	BALANCE

Sales Discounts **ACCOUNT NO. 415**

Date	Explanation	PR	DEBIT	CREDIT	BALANCE

Purchases **ACCOUNT NO. 505**

Date	Explanation	PR	DEBIT	CREDIT	BALANCE

Chapter 7 Problem 7-6A[A] or 7-6B[A] ***Name*** ______________________

Parts 1 & 2 (Continued)

Purchases Returns and Allowances **ACCOUNT NO. 506**

Date	Explanation	PR	DEBIT	CREDIT	BALANCE

Purchases Discounts **ACCOUNT NO. 507**

Date	Explanation	PR	DEBIT	CREDIT	BALANCE

Sales Salaries Expense **ACCOUNT NO. 621**

Date	Explanation	PR	DEBIT	CREDIT	BALANCE

ACCOUNTS RECEIVABLE LEDGER

Date	Explanation	PR	DEBIT	CREDIT	BALANCE

Date	Explanation	PR	DEBIT	CREDIT	BALANCE

Date	Explanation	PR	DEBIT	CREDIT	BALANCE

Chapter 7 **Problem 7-6A[A] or 7-6B[A]** ***Name*** ______________________________

Parts 1 & 2 **(Continued)**

ACCOUNTS PAYABLE LEDGER

Date	Explanation	PR	DEBIT	CREDIT	BALANCE

Date	Explanation	PR	DEBIT	CREDIT	BALANCE

Date	Explanation	PR	DEBIT	CREDIT	BALANCE

Date	Explanation	PR	DEBIT	CREDIT	BALANCE

Chapter 7 **Problem 7-6A[A] or 7-6B[A] (Continued)** ***Name*** ______________________

Part 3

Trial Balance

Schedule of Accounts Receivable

Schedule of Accounts Payable

Chapter 7 **Serial Problem, SP 7**
Business Solutions

Name ______________________________

Sales Journal					Page 2
Date	Account Debited	Invoice Number	PR	Accts. Rec. Dr. Sales Cr.	Cost of Goods Sold Dr. Inventory Cr.

Cash Receipts Journal									Page 2
Date	Account Credited	Explanation	PR	Cash Dr.	Sales Disc. Dr.	Accts. Rec. Cr.	Serv. Rev. Cr.	Other Accts. Cr.	Cost of Goods Sold Dr. Inv. Cr.

Purchases Journal								Page 2
Date	Account	Date of Invo.	Terms	PR	Accts. Pay. Cr.	Inventory Dr.	Computer Supplies Dr.	Other Accts. Dr.

Chapter 7 **Serial Problem, SP 7**
Business Solutions
(Continued)

Name ______________________________

Cash Disbursements Journal								Page 2
Date	Ck. No.	Payee	Account Debited	PR	Cash Cr.	Inventory Cr.	Other Accts. Dr.	Accts. Payable Dr.

Chapter 7 **Serial Problem, SP 7**
Business Solutions
(Continued)

Name ______________________________

Part 3

GENERAL JOURNAL **Page 2**

Date		Account Titles and Explanation	PR	Debit	Credit

Chapter 7 **Comprehensive Problem**
Colo Company

Name ______________________________

Sales Journal					Page 2
Date	Account Debited	Invoice Number	PR	Accts. Rec. Dr. Sales Cr.	Cost of Goods Sold Dr. Inventory Cr.

Cash Receipts Journal									Page 2
Date	Account Credited	Explanation	PR	Cash Dr.	Sales Disc. Dr.	Accts. Rec. Cr.	Sales Cr.	Other Accts. Cr.	Cost of Goods Sold Dr. Inv. Cr.

Purchases Journal								Page 2
Date	Account	Date of Invo.	Terms	PR	Accts. Pay. Cr.	Inventory Dr.	Office Supplies Dr.	Other Accts. Dr.

Chapter 7 **Comprehensive Problem**
Colo Company
(Continued)

Name ______________________________

Cash Disbursements Journal								Page 2
Date	Ck. No.	Payee	Account Debited	PR	Cash Cr.	Inventory Cr.	Other Accts. Dr.	Accts. Payable Dr.

Chapter 7 **Comprehensive Problem**
Colo Company
(Continued)

Name ______________________________

GENERAL JOURNAL **Page 2**

Date		Account Titles and Explanation	PR	Debit	Credit
		ADJUSTING ENTRIES (PART 2)			

Chapter 7 **Comprehensive Problem** ***Name*** ______________________
Colo Company
(Continued)

GENERAL JOURNAL **Page 2**

Date		Account Titles and Explanation	PR	Debit	Credit
		CLOSING ENTRIES			

Chapter 7 **Comprehensive Problem**
Colo Company
(Continued)

Name ______________________________

GENERAL LEDGER

Cash **ACCOUNT NO. 101**

Date	Explanation	PR	DEBIT	CREDIT	BALANCE
Apr. 30	Balance	√			50,247

Accounts Receivable **ACCOUNT NO. 106**

Date	Explanation	PR	DEBIT	CREDIT	BALANCE
Apr. 30	Balance	√			4,725

Merchandise Inventory **ACCOUNT NO. 119**

Date	Explanation	PR	DEBIT	CREDIT	BALANCE
Apr. 30	Balance	√			220,080

Office Supplies **ACCOUNT NO. 124**

Date	Explanation	PR	DEBIT	CREDIT	BALANCE
Apr. 30	Balance	√			430

Chapter 7 **Comprehensive Problem**
Colo Company
(Continued)

Name ______________________________

Store Supplies — **ACCOUNT NO. 125**

Date	Explanation	PR	DEBIT	CREDIT	BALANCE
Apr. 30	Balance	√			2,447

Prepaid Insurance — **ACCOUNT NO. 128**

Date	Explanation	PR	DEBIT	CREDIT	BALANCE
Apr. 30	Balance	√			3,318

Office Equipment — **ACCOUNT NO. 163**

Date	Explanation	PR	DEBIT	CREDIT	BALANCE
Apr. 30	Balance	√			22,470

Accumulated Depreciation-Office Equipment — **ACCOUNT NO. 164**

Date	Explanation	PR	DEBIT	CREDIT	BALANCE
Apr. 30	Balance	√			9,898

Store Equipment — **ACCOUNT NO. 165**

Date	Explanation	PR	DEBIT	CREDIT	BALANCE
Apr. 30	Balance	√			38,920

Accumulated Depreciation-Store Equipment — **ACCOUNT NO. 166**

Date	Explanation	PR	DEBIT	CREDIT	BALANCE
Apr. 30	Balance	√			17,556

Chapter 7 **Comprehensive Problem**
Colo Company
(Continued)

Name ______________________

Accounts Payable **ACCOUNT NO. 201**

Date	Explanation	PR	DEBIT	CREDIT	BALANCE
Apr. 30	Balance	√			7,098

Jenny Colo, Capital **ACCOUNT NO. 301**

Date	Explanation	PR	DEBIT	CREDIT	BALANCE
Apr. 30	Balance	√			308,085

Jenny Colo, Withdrawals **ACCOUNT NO. 302**

Date	Explanation	PR	DEBIT	CREDIT	BALANCE

Sales **ACCOUNT NO. 413**

Date	Explanation	PR	DEBIT	CREDIT	BALANCE

Sales Returns and Allowances **ACCOUNT NO. 414**

Date	Explanation	PR	DEBIT	CREDIT	BALANCE

Chapter 7 Comprehensive Problem Name ____________________
Colo Company
(Continued)

Sales Discounts ACCOUNT NO. 415

Date	Explanation	PR	DEBIT	CREDIT	BALANCE

Cost of Goods Sold ACCOUNT NO. 502

Date	Explanation	PR	DEBIT	CREDIT	BALANCE

Depreciation Expense-Office Equipment ACCOUNT NO. 612

Date	Explanation	PR	DEBIT	CREDIT	BALANCE

Depreciation Expense-Store Equipment ACCOUNT NO. 613

Date	Explanation	PR	DEBIT	CREDIT	BALANCE

Office Salaries Expense ACCOUNT NO. 620

Date	Explanation	PR	DEBIT	CREDIT	BALANCE

Sales Salaries Expense ACCOUNT NO. 621

Date	Explanation	PR	DEBIT	CREDIT	BALANCE

Chapter 7 **Comprehensive Problem** ***Name*** ____________________
Colo Company
(Continued)

Insurance Expense **ACCOUNT NO. 637**

Date	Explanation	PR	DEBIT	CREDIT	BALANCE

Rent Expense-Office Space **ACCOUNT NO. 641**

Date	Explanation	PR	DEBIT	CREDIT	BALANCE

Rent Expense-Selling Space **ACCOUNT NO. 642**

Date	Explanation	PR	DEBIT	CREDIT	BALANCE

Office Supplies Expense **ACCOUNT NO. 650**

Date	Explanation	PR	DEBIT	CREDIT	BALANCE

Store Supplies Expense **ACCOUNT NO. 651**

Date	Explanation	PR	DEBIT	CREDIT	BALANCE

Utilities Expense **ACCOUNT NO. 690**

Date	Explanation	PR	DEBIT	CREDIT	BALANCE

Chapter 7 **Comprehensive Problem**
Colo Company
(Continued)

Name ______________________

Income Summary **ACCOUNT NO. 901**

Date	Explanation	PR	DEBIT	CREDIT	BALANCE

ACCOUNTS RECEIVABLE LEDGER

Name Crane Corp.

Date	Explanation	PR	DEBIT	CREDIT	BALANCE

Name Hensel Company

Date	Explanation	PR	DEBIT	CREDIT	BALANCE

Name Knox, Inc.

Date	Explanation	PR	DEBIT	CREDIT	BALANCE
Apr. 30	Balance				4,725

Name Lee Services

Date	Explanation	PR	DEBIT	CREDIT	BALANCE

Chapter 7 **Comprehensive Problem**
Colo Company
(Continued)

Name ______________________________

ACCOUNTS PAYABLE LEDGER

Name **Fink Corp.**

Date	Explanation	PR	DEBIT	CREDIT	BALANCE

Name **Garcia Inc.**

Date	Explanation	PR	DEBIT	CREDIT	BALANCE

Name **Gear Supply Co.**

Date	Explanation	PR	DEBIT	CREDIT	BALANCE

Name **Peyton Products**

Date	Explanation	PR	DEBIT	CREDIT	BALANCE
Apr. 30	Balance				7,098

Chapter 7 Comprehensive Problem
Colo Company
(Continued)

Name ____________________

Colo Company
Work Sheet
For Month Ended May 31, 2011

Account Titles	Unadjusted Trial Balance		Adjustments		Adjusted Trial Balance		Income Statement		Balance Sheet & Statement of Owner's Equity	
	Dr.	Cr.	Dr.	Cr.	Dr.	Cr.	Dr.	Cr.	Dr.	Cr.

Chapter 7 **Comprehensive Problem** *Name* ______________________

Colo Company

(Continued)

Colo Company
Income Statement
For Month Ended May 31, 2011

Chapter 7 Comprehensive Problem Colo Company (Continued) *Name* ______________________

Colo Company Statement of Owner's Equity For Month Ended May 31, 2011

Colo Company Balance Sheet May 31, 2011

Chapter 7 **Comprehensive Problem** ***Name*** ______________________

Colo Company

(Continued)

Colo Company
Post-Closing Trial Balance
May 31, 2011

Colo Company
Schedule of Accounts Receivable
May 31, 2011

Colo Company
Schedule of Accounts Payable
May 31, 2011

Chapter 7 **Reporting in Action**
BTN 7-1

Name ______________________

(1) ______________________

(2) ______________________

(3) FastForward: ______________________

Chapter 7 **Comparative Analysis** **BTN 7-2** *Name* ______________________

Part 1

Research In Motion's Revenue on Segment Assets

Current Year—Domestic:

Current Year—International:

Prior Year—Domestic:

Prior Year—International:

Apple's Revenue on Segment Assets

Current Year—Domestic:

Current Year—International:

Prior Year—Domestic:

Prior Year—International:

Part 2—Analysis and Interpretation:

Chapter 7 **Ethics Challenge**
BTN 7-3

Name ______________________

(1)

(2)

(3)

Chapter 7 **Communicating in Practice—BTN 7-4** *Name* ______________________

MEMORANDUM

TO:
FROM:
SUBJECT:
DATE:

Chapter 7 **Taking It to the Net**
BTN 7-5

Name ____________________

(1)

(2)

(3)

(4)

Chapter 7 **Teamwork In Action** ***Name*** ______________________
BTN 7-6

Parts 1 & 2

SALES JOURNAL					Page 2
Date	Account Debited	Invoice Number	PR	Accts. Rec. Dr. Sales Cr.	Cost of Goods Sold Dr. Inventory Cr.

Cash Receipts Journal									Page 2
Date	Account Credited	Explanation	PR	Cash Dr.	Sales Disc. Dr.	Accts. Rec. Cr.	Sales Cr.	Other Accts. Cr.	Cost of Goods Sold Dr. Inv. Cr.

Chapter 7 Teamwork in Action
BTN 7-6

Name ______________________

Parts 1 & 2 (Continued)

Purchases Journal									Page 2
Date		Account	Date of Invoice	Terms	PR	Accts. Payable Cr.	Inventory Dr.	Office Supplies Dr.	Other Accts. Dr.

Cash Disbursements Journal								Page 2
Date	Ck. No.	Payee	Account Debited	PR	Cash Cr.	Inventory Cr.	Other Accts. Dr.	Accts. Payable Dr.

GENERAL JOURNAL Page 2

Date		Account Titles and Explanation	PR	Debit	Credit

Chapter 7 **Teamwork in Action** *Name* ______________________
BTN 7-6

Parts 1 & 2 **(Continued)**

GENERAL LEDGER

Cash **ACCOUNT NO. 101**

Date	Explanation	PR	DEBIT	CREDIT	BALANCE

Accounts Receivable **ACCOUNT NO. 106**

Date	Explanation	PR	DEBIT	CREDIT	BALANCE

Inventory **ACCOUNT NO. 119**

Date	Explanation	PR	DEBIT	CREDIT	BALANCE

Office Supplies **ACCOUNT NO. 124**

Date	Explanation	PR	DEBIT	CREDIT	BALANCE

Store Supplies **ACCOUNT NO. 125**

Date	Explanation	PR	DEBIT	CREDIT	BALANCE

Office Equipment **ACCOUNT NO. 163**

Date	Explanation	PR	DEBIT	CREDIT	BALANCE

Chapter 7 **Teamwork in Action**
BTN 7-6

Name ______________________________

Parts 1 & 2 **(Continued)**

Accounts Payable **ACCOUNT NO. 201**

Date	Explanation	PR	DEBIT	CREDIT	BALANCE

Long-Term Notes Payable **ACCOUNT NO. 251**

Date	Explanation	PR	DEBIT	CREDIT	BALANCE

____________, Capital **ACCOUNT NO. 301**

Date	Explanation	PR	DEBIT	CREDIT	BALANCE

Sales **ACCOUNT NO. 413**

Date	Explanation	PR	DEBIT	CREDIT	BALANCE

Sales Discounts **ACCOUNT NO. 415**

Date	Explanation	PR	DEBIT	CREDIT	BALANCE

Cost of Goods Sold **ACCOUNT NO. 502**

Date	Explanation	PR	DEBIT	CREDIT	BALANCE

Sales Salaries Expense **ACCOUNT NO. 621**

Date	Explanation	PR	DEBIT	CREDIT	BALANCE

Chapter 7 **Teamwork in Action** ***Name*** ______________________
BTN 7-6

Parts 1 & 2 **(Continued)**

ACCOUNTS RECEIVABLE LEDGER

Date	Explanation	PR	DEBIT	CREDIT	BALANCE

Date	Explanation	PR	DEBIT	CREDIT	BALANCE

Date	Explanation	PR	DEBIT	CREDIT	BALANCE

Chapter 7 **Teamwork in Action** *Name* ______________________
BTN 7-6

Parts 1 & 2 **(Continued)**

ACCOUNTS PAYABLE LEDGER

Date	Explanation	PR	DEBIT	CREDIT	BALANCE

Date	Explanation	PR	DEBIT	CREDIT	BALANCE

Date	Explanation	PR	DEBIT	CREDIT	BALANCE

Date	Explanation	PR	DEBIT	CREDIT	BALANCE

Chapter 7 **Teamwork in Action** *Name* ______________________

BTN 7-6

Parts 1 & 2 **(Continued)**

Trial Balance

Schedule of Accounts Receivable

Schedule of Accounts Payable

Chapter 7 **Entrepreneurial Decision** ***Name*** ______________________
BTN 7-7

(1)

(2)

Chapter 7 **Global Decision**
BTN 7-8

Name ______________________

(1)

(2)

(3)

Chapter 8 Quick Study 8-1 *Name* ______________________________

(1) ______________________________

(2) ______________________________

(3) ______________________________

Quick Study 8-2

(1) (a) ______________________________

(b) ______________________________

(c) ______________________________

(2) (a) ______________________________

(b) ______________________________

Quick Study 8-3

(1) ______________________________

(2) ______________________________

(3) ______________________________

Chapter 8 Quick Study 8-4 ***Name*** ______________________

(1)

GENERAL JOURNAL

Date		Account Titles and Explanation	PR	Debit	Credit
(a) Establishment of the Fund:					
(b) Reimbursement of the Fund:					

(2) ______________________

Chapter 8 Quick Study 8-5 ***Name*** ______________________

Parts 1 and 2

	(1)		(2)
	Bank or Book Effect	**Add or Subtract**	**Adjusting Entry Required or Not**
(a)			
(b)			
(c)			
(d)			
(e)			
(f)			
(g)			

Quick Study 8-6

Bank Reconciliation

Chapter 8 Quick Study 8-7 *Name* ______________________

Days' Sales Uncollected (2011):

Days' Sales Uncollected (2010):

Interpretation and Explanation:

Quick Study 8-8[A]

Quick Study 8-9[B]

(a)

(b)

Chapter 8 Quick Study 8-10 *Name* ____________________

a.

b.

Quick Study 8-11

a.

b. (1)

(2)

Chapter 8 Exercise 8-1 ***Name*** ____________________

(1)

(2)

Exercise 8-2

Evaluation:

Principles Ignored:

Exercise 8-3

(a) Internal Control Problems:

(b) Internal Control Recommendations:

Chapter 8 Exercise 8-4 *Name* ______________________

(1)

(2)

(3)

Chapter 8 **Exercise 8-5** ***Name*** ______________________

(1) Establish the Fund

GENERAL JOURNAL

Date		Account Titles and Explanation	PR	Debit	Credit

(2) Reimburse the Fund

GENERAL JOURNAL

Date		Account Titles and Explanation	PR	Debit	Credit

(3) Adjust the Fund Balance

GENERAL JOURNAL

Date		Account Titles and Explanation	PR	Debit	Credit

Chapter 8 Exercise 8-6 ***Name*** ______________________

(1) Establish the Fund

GENERAL JOURNAL

Date		Account Titles and Explanation	PR	Debit	Credit

(2) Reimburse the Fund

GENERAL JOURNAL

Date		Account Titles and Explanation	PR	Debit	Credit

(3) Reimburse and Increase the Fund

GENERAL JOURNAL

Date		Account Titles and Explanation	PR	Debit	Credit

Chapter 8 **Exercise 8-7** ***Name*** ________________________

		Bank Balance		Book Balance			Not Shown on
		Add	Deduct	Add	Deduct	Adjust	Reconciliation
1.	Bank service charge.						
2.	Checks written and mailed to payees on October 2.						
3.	Check written by another depositor but charged against this company's account.						
4.	Principal and interest on a note receivable to this company is collected by the bank but not yet recorded by the company.						
5.	Special bank charge for collection of note in No. 4 on company's behalf.						
6.	Check written against the company account and cleared by the bank; erroneously not recorded by the company recordkeeper.						
7.	Interest earned on the account.						
8.	Deposit made on September 30 after the bank closed.						
9.	Checks outstanding on August 31 that cleared the bank in September.						
10.	NSF check from customer returned on Sept. 25 but not recorded by this company.						
11.	Checks written by the company and mailed to payees on September 30.						
12.	Deposit made on September 5 and processed by bank on September 6.						

Chapter 8 **Exercise 8-8** ***Name*** ____________________

(1)

(2)

(3)

Exercise 8-9

Bank Reconciliation

Exercise 8-10

GENERAL JOURNAL

Date		Account Titles and Explanation	PR	Debit	Credit

Chapter 8 Exercise 8-11 ***Name*** ______________________

Bank Reconciliation

Exercise 8-12

(a)

Days' Sales Uncollected (2010):

Days' Sales Uncollected (2011):

(b) Interpretation of Change:

Exercise 8-13[A]

(1)	(3)	(5)
(2)	(4)	(6)

Chapter 8 Exercise 8-14[B] ***Name*** ______________________

(a) Recording Invoices at Gross Amounts—Gross Method

GENERAL JOURNAL

Date		Account Titles and Explanation	PR	Debit	Credit

Chapter 8 Exercise 8-14B (Continued) ***Name*** ______________________________

(b) Recording Invoices at Net Amounts—Net Method

GENERAL JOURNAL

Date		Account Titles and Explanation	PR	Debit	Credit

Chapter 8 **Problem 8-1A or 8-1B** ***Name*** ______________________

(1) Principle Violated:
Recommended

(2) Principle Violated:
Recommended

(3) Principle Violated:
Recommended

(4) Principle Violated:
Recommended

(5) Principle Violated:
Recommended

Chapter 8 **Problem 8-2A or 8-2B** ***Name*** ______________________

Part 1

GENERAL JOURNAL

Date		Account Titles and Explanation	PR	Debit	Credit

Part 2

Chapter 8 **Problem 8-3A or 8-3B** ***Name*** ______________________

Part 1

GENERAL JOURNAL

Date		Account Titles and Explanation	PR	Debit	Credit

Part 2

Petty Cash Payments Report

Part 3

GENERAL JOURNAL

Date		Account Titles and Explanation	PR	Debit	Credit

Chapter 8 **Problem 8-4A or 8-4B** ***Name*** ______________________

Part 1

Bank Reconciliation

Part 2

GENERAL JOURNAL

Date		Account Titles and Explanation	PR	Debit	Credit

Chapter 8 Problem 8-4A or 8-4B Name ______________________
(Continued)

Part 3

(a)

(b)

Problem 8-5A or 8-5B

Part 1

Bank Reconciliation

Chapter 8 **Problem 8-5A or 8-5B (Continued)** *Name* ______________________

Part 2

GENERAL JOURNAL

Date		Account Titles and Explanation	PR	Debit	Credit

Part 3

(1)

(2)

(3)

Chapter 8 Serial Problem, SP 8 Name ____________________

Business Solutions

Part 1

Bank Reconciliation

Part 2

GENERAL JOURNAL

Date		Account Titles and Explanation	PR	Debit	Credit

Chapter 8 Reporting in Action—BTN 8-1 ***Name*** ______________________

Part 1

	Fiscal Year 2010		Fiscal Year 2009	
Account	Balance ($)	Cash & Equiv. as % of Bal.	Balance ($)	Cash & Equiv. as % of Bal.

Interpretation:

Part 2

Chapter 8 Reporting in Action—BTN 8-1 (Continued) *Name* ____________________

Part 3

Days' Sales Uncollected (2010):

Days' Sales Uncollected (2009):

Interpretation:

Part 4

FastForward:

Chapter 8 **Comparative Analysis** ***Name*** ______________________
BTN 8-2

Research In Motion:
Days' Sales Uncollected (Current year):

Days' Sales Uncollected (Prior year):

Interpretation:

Apple:
Days' Sales Uncollected (Current year):

Days' Sales Uncollected (Prior year):

Interpretation:

Comparison—Research In Motion vs. Apple

Chapter 8 **Ethics Challenge**
BTN 8-3

Name ____________________

(1)

(2)

(3)

(4)

Chapter 8 Communicating in Practice—BTN 8-4

Name ______________________________

MEMORANDUM

TO:
FROM:
SUBJECT:
DATE:

Chapter 8 Taking It to the Net
BTN 8-5

Name ____________________

(1) ____________________

(2) ____________________

(3) ____________________

(4) ____________________

(5) ____________________

(6) ____________________

(7) ____________________

(8) ____________________

(9) ____________________

Chapter 8 Teamwork in Action—BTN 8-6 ***Name*** ______________________

(1) ______________________

(2) ______________________

(3) ______________________

(4) ______________________

(5) ______________________

(6) ______________________

(7) ______________________

(8) ______________________

(9) ______________________

(10) ______________________

Chapter 8 **Entrepreneurial Decision** ***Name*** ______________________
BTN 8-7

(1) (a) ______________________

(b) ______________________

(c) ______________________

(d) ______________________

(e) ______________________

(f) ______________________

(g) ______________________

(2) ______________________

Hitting the Road—BTN 8-8

____

Chapter 8 Global Decision—BTN 8-9 *Name* ______________________

1.

Accounts	Current Year Balance	Cash as % of Bal.:	Prior Year Balance	Cash as % of Bal.
Cash.........................				
Current assets.............				
Total assets................				
Current liabilities..........				
Stockholders' equity.....				

Analysis Comment:

2.

3.
Days' Sales Uncollected

Current Year:

Prior Year:

Assessment:

Chapter 9 Quick Study 9-1 *Name* ______________________

(1)

GENERAL JOURNAL

Date		Account Titles and Explanation	PR	Debit	Credit

(2)

GENERAL JOURNAL

Date		Account Titles and Explanation	PR	Debit	Credit

Chapter 9 Quick Study 9-2 ***Name*** ______________________

(1)

GENERAL JOURNAL

Date		Account Titles and Explanation	PR	Debit	Credit

(2)

GENERAL JOURNAL

Date		Account Titles and Explanation	PR	Debit	Credit

Chapter 9 Quick Study 9-3 *Name* ______________________

(1)

GENERAL JOURNAL

Date		Account Titles and Explanation	PR	Debit	Credit

(2) ______________________

Quick Study 9-4

GENERAL JOURNAL

Date		Account Titles and Explanation	PR	Debit	Credit

Quick Study 9-5

1. ______________________

2.

GENERAL JOURNAL

Date		Account Titles and Explanation	PR	Debit	Credit

Chapter 9 **Quick Study 9-6** ***Name*** ______________________

GENERAL JOURNAL

Date		Account Titles and Explanation	PR	Debit	Credit

Quick Study 9-7

GENERAL JOURNAL

Date		Account Titles and Explanation	PR	Debit	Credit

Quick Study 9-8

GENERAL JOURNAL

Date		Account Titles and Explanation	PR	Debit	Credit

Chapter 9 Quick Study 9-9 *Name* ______________________

GENERAL JOURNAL

Date		Account Titles and Explanation	PR	Debit	Credit

Quick Study 9-10

GENERAL JOURNAL

Date		Account Titles and Explanation	PR	Debit	Credit

Quick Study 9-11

Accounts Receivable Turnover:

Interpretation:

Chapter 9 Quick Study 9-12 *Name* ______________________________

a.

b.

Chapter 9 **Exercise 9-1** ***Name*** ____________________

GENERAL JOURNAL

Date		Account Titles and Explanation	PR	Debit	Credit

Chapter 9 Exercise 9-2 ***Name*** ____________________

Part 1

GENERAL LEDGER

Accounts Receivable		Sales		Sales Returns and Allowances	

ACCOUNTS RECEIVABLE LEDGER

Surf Shop		Yum Enterprises		Matt Albin	

Part 2

Schedule of Accounts Receivable

Comparison:

Chapter 9 **Exercise 9-3** ***Name*** ______________________

GENERAL JOURNAL

Date		Account Titles and Explanation	PR	Debit	Credit

Exercise 9-4

GENERAL JOURNAL

Date		Account Titles and Explanation	PR	Debit	Credit

Chapter 9 **Exercise 9-5** ***Name*** ______________________

(a)

GENERAL JOURNAL

Date		Account Titles and Explanation	PR	Debit	Credit

(b)

GENERAL JOURNAL

Date		Account Titles and Explanation	PR	Debit	Credit

Chapter 9 Exercise 9-6 *Name* ______________________

(a)

(b)

GENERAL JOURNAL

Date		Account Titles and Explanation	PR	Debit	Credit

(c)

GENERAL JOURNAL

Date		Account Titles and Explanation	PR	Debit	Credit

Exercise 9-7

(a)

Chapter 9 **Exercise 9-7 (Continued)** *Name* ______________________

(b)

GENERAL JOURNAL

Date		Account Titles and Explanation	PR	Debit	Credit

(c)

GENERAL JOURNAL

Date		Account Titles and Explanation	PR	Debit	Credit

Exercise 9-8

GENERAL JOURNAL

Date		Account Titles and Explanation	PR	Debit	Credit

Chapter 9 Exercise 9-9 *Name* ______________________________

(a)

GENERAL JOURNAL

Date		Account Titles and Explanation	PR	Debit	Credit

(b)

GENERAL JOURNAL

Date		Account Titles and Explanation	PR	Debit	Credit

(c)

GENERAL JOURNAL

Date		Account Titles and Explanation	PR	Debit	Credit

Chapter 9 **Exercise 9-10** ***Name*** ______________________

GENERAL JOURNAL

Date		Account Titles and Explanation	PR	Debit	Credit

Financial Statement Note(s):

Chapter 9 Exercise 9-11 *Name* ______________________

GENERAL JOURNAL

Date		Account Titles and Explanation	PR	Debit	Credit

Exercise 9-12

GENERAL JOURNAL

Date		Account Titles and Explanation	PR	Debit	Credit

Chapter 9 **Exercise 9-13** ***Name*** ______________________

GENERAL JOURNAL

Date		Account Titles and Explanation	PR	Debit	Credit

Exercise 9-14

GENERAL JOURNAL

Date		Account Titles and Explanation	PR	Debit	Credit

Chapter 9 Exercise 9-15 ***Name*** ______________________

Accounts Receivable Turnover (2010):

Accounts Receivable Turnover (2011):

Comparison and Interpretation:

Exercise 9-16

a.

GENERAL JOURNAL

Date		Account Titles and Explanation	PR	Debit	Credit

b.

GENERAL JOURNAL

Date		Account Titles and Explanation	PR	Debit	Credit

Chapter 9 Problem 9-1A or 9-1B *Name* ______________________

GENERAL JOURNAL

Date		Account Titles and Explanation	PR	Debit	Credit

Chapter 9 **Problem 9-2A or 9-2B** ***Name*** ________________

2010

GENERAL JOURNAL

Date		Account Titles and Explanation	PR	Debit	Credit

Supporting work:

Chapter 9 **Problem 9-2A or 9-2B (Continued)** ***Name*** ____________________

2011

GENERAL JOURNAL

Date		Account Titles and Explanation	PR	Debit	Credit

Supporting work:

Chapter 9 **Problem 9-3A or 9-3B** ***Name*** ____________________

Part 1

GENERAL JOURNAL

Date		Account Titles and Explanation	PR	Debit	Credit
(a)					
(b)					
(c)					

Part 2

Chapter 9 **Problem 9-3A or 9-3B (Continued)** ***Name*** ______________________

Part 3

Problem 9-4A or 9-4B

Part 1

Part 2

GENERAL JOURNAL

Date		Account Titles and Explanation	PR	Debit	Credit

Part 3

Chapter 9 **Problem 9-5A or 9-5B** ***Name*** ______________________

Part 1

Date		Account Titles and Explanation	PR	Debit	Credit
2010					
2011					

Chapter 9 **Problem 9-5A or 9-5B** ***Name*** ______________________

Part 1 **(Continued)**

Date		Account Titles and Explanation	PR	Debit	Credit
2011 Continued					

Part 2

Reporting:

Reasoning:

Principle:

Chapter 9 **Serial Problem, SP 9** ***Name*** ______________________

Business Solutions

Part 1

GENERAL JOURNAL

Date		Account Titles and Explanation	PR	Debit	Credit
(a)					
(b)					

Part 2

GENERAL JOURNAL

Date		Account Titles and Explanation	PR	Debit	Credit

Part 3

Chapter 9 Reporting in Action Name ______________________
BTN 9-1

(1)

(2) Accounts Receivable Turnover (2010):

(3) Average Collection Period:

Analysis:

(4) Liquid Assets as a percent of Current Liabilities (2010):

Liquid Assets as a percent of Current Liabilities (2009):

Comparison and Interpretation:

(5)

(6) FastForward:

Chapter 9 **Comparative Analysis** ***Name*** ________________

BTN 9-2

(1) RIM's Accounts Receivable Turnover (Current Year and Prior Year):

Apple's Accounts Receivable Turnover (Current Year and Prior Year):

(2) RIM's Average Collection Period (Current Year and Prior Year):

Apple's Average Collection Period (Current Year and Prior Year):

Interpretation:

(3) Efficiency Comparison:

Chapter 9 **Ethics Challenge**
BTN 9-3

Name ______________________________

(1)

(2)

(3)

Chapter 9 Communicating in Practice—BTN 9-4

Name ____________________

MEMORANDUM

TO:

FROM:

SUBJECT:

DATE:

Chapter 9 **Taking It to the Net** ***Name*** ______________________

BTN 9-5

(1)

(2)	Dec. 31, 2009	Dec. 31, 2008

(3)

Chapter 9 **Teamwork in Action**
BTN 9-6

Name ______________________

Estimate of Uncollectibles:

Adjusting Entry:

GENERAL JOURNAL

Date		Account Titles and Explanation	PR	Debit	Credit

Presentation of Net Realizable Accounts Receivable in Balance Sheet:

Chapter 9 **Entrepreneurial Decision** ***Name*** ______________________
BTN 9-7

Part 1

Added Monthly Net Income (Loss) under Plan A

Added Monthly Net Income (Loss) under Plan B

Part 2

Chapter 9 Hitting the Road
BTN 9-8

Name ____________________

Global Decision—BTN 9-9

(1) Accounts Receivable Turnover

(2) Average Collection Period

(3) Analysis

(4) Percent of Receivables per Category

Chapter 11 Quick Study 11-1 *Name* ______________________

Current Liabilities:

Quick Study 11-2

GENERAL JOURNAL

Date		Account Titles and Explanation	PR	Debit	Credit

Quick Study 11-3

GENERAL JOURNAL

Date		Account Titles and Explanation	PR	Debit	Credit

Chapter 11 Quick Study 11-4 ***Name*** ______________________

(1) ______________________

(2) ______________________

(3) ______________________

Quick Study 11-5

(1) Accrued Interest Payable: ______________________

(2) & (3)

GENERAL JOURNAL

Date		Account Titles and Explanation	PR	Debit	Credit

Quick Study 11-6

GENERAL JOURNAL

Date		Account Titles and Explanation	PR	Debit	Credit

Chapter 11 Quick Study 11-7 *Name* ______________________

GENERAL JOURNAL

Date		Account Titles and Explanation	PR	Debit	Credit

Quick Study 11-8

GENERAL JOURNAL

Date		Account Titles and Explanation	PR	Debit	Credit

Quick Study 11-9

GENERAL JOURNAL

Date		Account Titles and Explanation	PR	Debit	Credit

Quick Study 11-10

GENERAL JOURNAL

Date		Account Titles and Explanation	PR	Debit	Credit

Chapter 11 Quick Study 11-11 *Name* ______________________

Times Interest Earned:

Interpretation:

Quick Study 11-12[A]

Quick Study 11-13[B]

GENERAL JOURNAL

Date		Account Titles and Explanation	PR	Debit	Credit

Quick Study 11-14

a.

b.

Chapter 11 Exercise 11-1 *Name* ______________________

(1)	(6)
(2)	(7)
(3)	(8)
(4)	(9)
(5)	(10)

Exercise 11-2

GENERAL JOURNAL

Date		Account Titles and Explanation	PR	Debit	Credit
(1)					
(2)					

Chapter 11 Exercise 11-3 *Name* ______________________

GENERAL JOURNAL

Date		Account Titles and Explanation	PR	Debit	Credit
(1)					
(2)					

Exercise 11-4

(1) Maturity Date: ______________________

(2)

GENERAL JOURNAL

Date		Account Titles and Explanation	PR	Debit	Credit

Chapter 11 Exercise 11-5 ***Name*** ______________________

(1) Maturity Date:

(2) Interest Expense (2011):

(3) Interest Expense (2012):

(4)

GENERAL JOURNAL

Date		Account Titles and Explanation	PR	Debit	Credit

Chapter 11 Exercise 11-6 *Name* ____________________

	Subject to Tax	Rate	Tax
(a)			
FICA-Social Security.................	______	______	______
FICA-Medicare..........................	______	______	______
FUTA.......................................	______	______	______
SUTA.......................................	______	______	______
(b)			
FICA-Social Security.................	______	______	______
FICA-Medicare..........................	______	______	______
FUTA.......................................	______	______	______
SUTA.......................................	______	______	______
(c)			
FICA-Social Security.................	______	______	______
FICA-Medicare..........................	______	______	______
FUTA.......................................	______	______	______
SUTA.......................................	______	______	______

Chapter 11 Exercise 11-7 *Name* ______________________

GENERAL JOURNAL

Date		Account Titles and Explanation	PR	Debit	Credit

Exercise 11-8

GENERAL JOURNAL

Date		Account Titles and Explanation	PR	Debit	Credit

Chapter 11 Exercise 11-9 ***Name*** ______________________

1. ______________________

2.

GENERAL JOURNAL

Date		Account Titles and Explanation	PR	Debit	Credit

3.

GENERAL JOURNAL

Date		Account Titles and Explanation	PR	Debit	Credit

Exercise 11-10

GENERAL JOURNAL

Date		Account Titles and Explanation	PR	Debit	Credit
(1)					
(2)					

Chapter 11 Exercise 11-11 ***Name*** ____________________

(1) ____________________

(2) ____________________

(3) ____________________

(4) ____________________

(5)

GENERAL JOURNAL

Date		Account Titles and Explanation	PR	Debit	Credit

Chapter 11 Exercise 11-12 *Name* ______________________

(a) ______________________

(b) ______________________

(c) ______________________

(d) ______________________

(e) ______________________

(f) ______________________

Analysis: ______________________

Chapter 11 Exercise 11-13[A] ***Name*** ____________________

Exercise 11-14[B]

(1)

(2)

GENERAL JOURNAL

Date		Account Titles and Explanation	PR	Debit	Credit

Chapter 11 Exercise 11-15 ***Name*** ______________________

GENERAL JOURNAL

Date		Account Titles and Explanation	PR	Debit	Credit
(1)					
(2)					
(3)					

Chapter 11 Exercise 11-16 ***Name*** ____________________

GENERAL JOURNAL

Date		Account Titles and Explanation	PR	Debit	Credit
(1)					
(2)					
(3)					
(4)					

Chapter 11 Problem 11-1A or 11-1B *Name* ______________________

(1) Maturity Dates:

(2) Interest Due at Maturity:

(3) Accrued Interest at the End of 2010:

(4) Interest Expense in 2011:

Chapter 11 **Problem 11-1A or 11-1B (Continued)** ***Name*** ______________________

(5)

GENERAL JOURNAL

Date		Account Titles and Explanation	PR	Debit	Credit

Chapter 11 Problem 11-2A ***Name*** ______________________

(1)

GENERAL JOURNAL

Date		Account Titles and Explanation	PR	Debit	Credit
2010					

Chapter 11 Problem 11-2A *Name* ____________________

(1) (Continued from prior page)

GENERAL JOURNAL

Date		Account Titles and Explanation	PR	Debit	Credit
2011					

(2) Warranty Expense for November 2010 and December 2010:

(3) Warranty Expense for January 2011:

(4) Balance of the Estimated Warranty Liability as of December 31, 2010:

(5) Balance of the Estimated Warranty Liability as of January 31, 2011:

Chapter 11 Problem 11-2B ***Name*** ______________________

(1)

GENERAL JOURNAL

Date		Account Titles and Explanation	PR	Debit	Credit
2011					

Chapter 11 Problem 11-2B ***Name*** ______________________

(1) (Continued from prior page)

GENERAL JOURNAL

Date		Account Titles and Explanation	PR	Debit	Credit
2012					

(2) Warranty Expense for November 2011 and December 2011:

(3) Warranty Expense for January 2012:

(4) Balance of the Estimated Warranty Liability as of December 31, 2011:

(5) Balance of the Estimated Warranty Liability as of January 31, 2012:

Chapter 11 Problem 11-3A or 11-3B *Name* ______________________

(1) __________ Company:

Times Interest Earned:

(2) __________ Company:

Times Interest Earned:

(3) Sales Increase by ______ %

	________ Company	________ Company
Sales		
Variable expenses		
Income before interest		
Interest expense (fixed)		
Net Income		
Net income percent change		

(4) Sales Increase by ______ %

	________ Company	________ Company
Sales		
Variable expenses		
Income before interest		
Interest expense (fixed)		
Net Income		
Net income percent change		

Chapter 11 Problem 11-3A or 11-3B (Continued) ***Name*** ______________________

(5) Sales Increase by ______%

	____________ Company	____________ Company
Sales		
Variable expenses		
Income before interest		
Interest expense (fixed)		
Net Income		
Net income percent change		

(6) Sales Decrease by ______%

	____________ Company	____________ Company
Sales		
Variable expenses		
Income before interest		
Interest expense (fixed)		
Net Income		
Net income percent change		

(7) Sales Decrease by ______%

	____________ Company	____________ Company
Sales		
Variable expenses		
Income before interest		
Interest expense (fixed)		
Net Income		
Net income percent change		

Chapter 11 Problem 11-3A or 11-3B (Continued) ***Name*** ______________________

(8) Sales Decrease by ______%

	________ Company	________ Company
Sales		
Variable expenses		
Income before interest		
Interest expense (fixed)		
Net Income		
Net income percent change		

(9) Analysis:

Chapter 11 Problem 11-4A or 11-4B *Name* ______________________

(1) Each Employee's FICA Withholdings for Social Security:

Employee	______	______	______	______	Total
Maximum base					
Earned through ________					
Amount subject to tax					
Earned this week					
Pay subject to tax					
Tax rate					
Social Security tax					

(2) Each Employee's FICA Withholdings for Medicare:

Employee	______	______	______	______	Total
Earned this week					
Tax rate					
Medicare tax					

(3) Employer's FICA Taxes for Social Security:

Employee	______	______	______	______	Total

(4) Employer's FICA Taxes for Medicare:

Employee	______	______	______	______	Total

Chapter 11 Problem 11-4A or 11-4B (Continued) *Name* ______________________

(5) Employer's FUTA Taxes:

Employee	______	______	______	______	Total
Maximum base					
Earned through ________					
Amount subject to tax					
Earned this week					
Pay subject to tax					
Tax rate					
FUTA rate					

(6) Employer's SUTA Taxes:

Employee	______	______	______	______	Total
Subject to tax					
Tax rate					
SUTA tax					

(7) Each Employee's Net (Take-Home) Pay:

Employee	______	______	______	______	Total
Gross earnings					
Less:					
FICA Soc. Sec. tax					
FICA Medicare tax					
Withholding taxes					
Health Insurance					
Take-home pay					

(8) Employer's Total Payroll-Related Expense for Each Employee:

Employee	______	______	______	______	Total
Gross earnings					
Plus:					
FICA Soc. Sec. tax					
FICA Medicare tax					
FUTA tax					
SUTA tax					
Health Insurance					
Pension contrib.					
Total payroll exp.					

Chapter 11 Problem 11-5A or 11-5B ***Name*** ______________________

(1)

GENERAL JOURNAL

Date		Account Titles and Explanation	PR	Debit	Credit

(2)

GENERAL JOURNAL

Date		Account Titles and Explanation	PR	Debit	Credit

Chapter 11 Problem 11-6A[A] or 11-6B[A] ***Name*** ____________________

GENERAL JOURNAL

Date		Account Titles and Explanation	PR	Debit	Credit

Work Space:

Chapter 11 **Problem 11-6A[A] or 11-6B[A] (Continued)** ***Name*** ______________________

GENERAL JOURNAL

Date		Account Titles and Explanation	PR	Debit	Credit
Continued from prior page					

Work Space:

Chapter 11 **Serial Problem, SP 11** ***Name*** ______________________

Business Solutions

(1)

GENERAL JOURNAL

Date		Account Titles and Explanation	PR	Debit	Credit
(2)					
(3)					
(4)					

Work Space:

Chapter 11 Comprehensive Problem *Name* ______________________
Bug-Off Exterminators

Part 1

(a) Correct Ending Balance of Cash and the Amount of the Omitted Check:

(b) Allowance for Doubtful Accounts:

(c) Depreciation Expense on the Truck:

(d) Depreciation Expense on the Equipment:

Chapter 11 Comprehensive Problem
Bug-Off Exterminators

Name ______________________

Part 1 (Continued)

(e) Adjusted Revenue and Unearned Revenue Balances:

(f) Warranty Expense and Estimated Warranty Liability:

(g) Interest Payable and Interest Expense:

Chapter 11 **Comprehensive Problem**
Bug-Off Exterminators
(Continued)

Name ______________________________

Part 2

BUG-OFF EXTERMINATORS
December 31, 2011

	Unadjusted Trial Balance		Adjustments		Adjusted Trial Balance	
Account Titles	Dr.	Cr.	Dr.	Cr.	Dr.	Cr.
Cash						
Accounts Receivable						
Allowance for Doubtful Accounts						
Merchandise Inventory						
Trucks						
Accumulated Depreciation-Trucks						
Equipment						
Accum. Depreciation-Equipment						
Accounts Payable						
Estimated Warranty Liability						
Unearned Services Revenue						
Interest Payable						
Long-Term Notes Payable						
D. Buggs, Capital						
D. Buggs, Withdrawals						
Extermination Services Revenue						
Interest Revenue						
Sales						
Cost of Goods Sold						
Depreciation Expense-Trucks						
Depreciation Expense-Equipment						
Wages Expense						
Interest Expense						
Rent Expense						
Bad Debts Expense						
Miscellaneous Expense						
Repairs Expense						
Utilities Expense						
Warranty Expense						
Totals						

Chapter 11 **Comprehensive Problem**
Bug-Off Exterminators
(Continued)

Name ______________________________

Part 3

GENERAL JOURNAL

Date		Account Titles and Explanation	PR	Debit	Credit

Chapter 11 Comprehensive Problem
Bug-Off Exterminators
(Continued)

Name ______________________________

Part 4

BUG-OFF EXTERMINATORS Income Statement For Year Ended December 31, 2011

BUG-OFF EXTERMINATORS Statement of Owner's Equity For Year Ended December 31, 2011

Chapter 11 Comprehensive Problem
Bug-Off Exterminators

Name ______________________________

Part 4 (Continued)

BUG-OFF EXTERMINATORS
Balance Sheet
December 31, 2011

Chapter 11 **Reporting in Action**
BTN 11-1

Name ____________________

(1) Times Interest Earned (2010):

Times Interest Earned (2009):

Times Interest Earned (2008):

Interpretation:

(2)

(3)

(4) FastForward:

Chapter 11 Comparative Analysis Name ______________________
BTN 11-2

(1) RIM's Times Interest Earned (Current Year):

RIM's Times Interest Earned (One Year Prior):

RIM's Times Interest Earned (Two Years Prior):

Apple's Times Interest Earned (Current Year):

Apple's Times Interest Earned (One Year Prior):

Apple's Times Interest Earned (Two Years Prior):

(2) Interpretation:

Chapter 11 **Ethics Challenge**
BTN 11-3

Name ____________________

(1) ____________________

(2) ____________________

Chapter 11 Communicating in Practice—BTN 11-4 *Name* ________________________

MEMORANDUM

TO:
FROM:
SUBJECT:
DATE:

Chapter 11 **Taking It to the Net** ***Name*** ______________________________
BTN 11-5

(1)

(2)

(3)

Teamwork in Action—BTN 11-6

(1)

Chapter 11 **Teamwork in Action**
BTN 11-6
(Continued)

Name ______________________________

(2)

GENERAL JOURNAL

Date		Account Titles and Explanation	PR	Debit	Credit

(3) Team Discussion

(4)

GENERAL JOURNAL

Date		Account Titles and Explanation	PR	Debit	Credit

(5) Team Discussion

Chapter 11 **Entrepreneurial Decision BTN 11-7** ***Name*** ______________________

Part 1

	Income Statement (Prospective)		
	Current Operations	NEW	Total
Sales			
Cost of goods sold (30%)			
Gross profit			
Operating expenses (25%)			
Income before interest			
Interest expense			
Net income			

Part 2

Times Interest Earned: ______________________

____

____

____

Part 3

	Income Statement (Prospective)		
	Current Operations	NEW	Total
Sales			
Cost of Goods Sold (30%)			
Gross Profit			
Operating Expenses (25%)			
Income before interest			
Interest expense			
Net Income			

Times Interest Earned: ______________________

____

____

Chapter 11 Entrepreneurial Decision
BTN 11-7
(Continued)

Name ____________________

Part 4

	Income Statement (Prospective)		
	Current Operations	NEW	Total
Sales			
Cost of Goods Sold (30%)			
Gross Profit			
Operating Expenses (25%)			
Income before interest			
Interest expense			
Net Income			

Times Interest Earned: ____________________

Part 5

Chapter 11 **Hitting the Road** *Name* ______________________

BTN 11-8

Global Decision—BTN 11-9

(1) Times Interest Earned	**Current Year**	**One Year Prior**

(2)

Chapter 12 Quick Study 12-1 *Name* ______________________

(a) ______________________

(b) ______________________

Quick Study 12-2

Quick Study 12-3

	Share to ________	*Share to* ________	*Total*
Net income			
Salary allowance:			
________			
________			
Total salary allowances			
Balance of income			
Balance allocated:			
________			
________			
Total allocated			
Balance of income			
Shares of the partners			

Quick Study 12-4

Chapter 12 Quick Study 12-5 ***Name*** ______________________

GENERAL JOURNAL

Date		Account Titles and Explanation	PR	Debit	Credit

Quick Study 12-6

GENERAL JOURNAL

Date		Account Titles and Explanation	PR	Debit	Credit

Quick Study 12-7

(1)

	Red	*White*	*Blue*	*Total*
Initial investments				
Allocation of all losses				
Capital balances				

Chapter 12 Quick Study 12-7 (Continued) ***Name*** ______________________

(2)

GENERAL JOURNAL

Date		Account Titles and Explanation	PR	Debit	Credit

(3)

GENERAL JOURNAL

Date		Account Titles and Explanation	PR	Debit	Credit

Quick Study 12-8

Chapter 12 Exercise 12-1 ***Name*** ______________________

Part a

Recommended Organization:

Taxation Effects:

Advantages:

Part b

Recommended Organization:

Taxation Effects:

Advantages:

Chapter 12 Exercise 12-1 (Continued) ***Name*** ____________________

Part c

Recommended Organization:

Taxation Effects:

Advantages:

Exercise 12-2

	Characteristic	*General Partnerships*
1.	Ease of formation	
2.	Transferability of ownership	
3.	Ability to raise large amounts of capital	
4.	Life	
5.	Owners' liability	
6.	Legal status	
7.	Tax status of income	
8.	Owners' authority	

Chapter 12 Exercise 12-3 ***Name*** ______________________

GENERAL JOURNAL

Date		Account Titles and Explanation	PR	Debit	Credit
(1)					
(2)					

Chapter 12 Exercise 12-4 *Name* ____________________

(1)

GENERAL JOURNAL

Date		Account Titles and Explanation	PR	Debit	Credit
(a)					
(b)					
(c)					

(2)

Capital account balances:		
Initial investment		
Withdrawals		
Share of income		
Ending balances		

Chapter 12 Exercise 12-5 *Name* ______________________

	Share to ______	*Share to* ______	*Total*
(1)			
(2)			
(3)			

Chapter 12 Exercise 12-6 *Name* ______________________

	Share to ______	*Share to* ______	*Total*
(1)			
(2)			

Exercise 12-7

GENERAL JOURNAL

Date		Account Titles and Explanation	PR	Debit	Credit

Chapter 12 **Exercise 12-8** ***Name*** ______________________

(1)

GENERAL JOURNAL

Date		Account Titles and Explanation	PR	Debit	Credit

(2)

GENERAL JOURNAL

Date		Account Titles and Explanation	PR	Debit	Credit

(3)

GENERAL JOURNAL

Date		Account Titles and Explanation	PR	Debit	Credit

Chapter 12 Exercise 12-9 ***Name*** ____________________

(1)

GENERAL JOURNAL

Date		Account Titles and Explanation	PR	Debit	Credit

(2)

GENERAL JOURNAL

Date		Account Titles and Explanation	PR	Debit	Credit

(3)

GENERAL JOURNAL

Date		Account Titles and Explanation	PR	Debit	Credit

Chapter 12 Exercise 12-10 ***Name*** ______________________

(a) Loss computation from selling assets:

(b) Loss allocation

	________	________	________	***Total***
Capital balance before loss liquidation........................				
Allocation of loss:				
Capital balances after loss............				

(c) Liability to be paid:

Chapter 12 Exercise 12-11 *Name* ____________________

(a) Loss computation from selling assets:

(b) Loss and deficit allocation:

				Total
Capital balance before loss.........				
Allocation of loss:				
Capital balances after loss............				
Allocation of _______ deficit to:				
Cash paid by each partner............				

(c) Liability to be paid:

Exercise 12-12

Chapter 12 **Problem 12-1A or 12-1B** ***Name*** ____________________

GENERAL JOURNAL

Date		Account Titles and Explanation	PR	Debit	Credit
(1)					
(2)					
(3)					

Supporting calculations:

Chapter 12 Problem 12-2A or 12-2B *Name* ______________________

Inc./Loss Sharing Plan	YEAR 1 Calculations	Partner: ______	Partner: ______
(a)			
(b)			
(c)			
(d)			

Inc./Loss Sharing Plan	YEAR 2 Calculations	Partner: ______	Partner: ______
(a)			
(b)			
(c)			
(d)			

Chapter 12 Problem 12-2A or 12-2B ***Name*** ______________________
(Continued)

Inc./Loss Sharing Plan	YEAR 3 Calculations	*Partner:*	*Partner:*
(a)			
(b)			
(c)			
(d)			

Supporting Work Space:

Chapter 12 **Problem 12-3A or 12-3B** ***Name*** ______________________

Part 1

Inc./Loss Sharing Plan	Calculations	Partner:	Partner:	Partner:	Total for all Partners
(a)					
(b)					
(c)					

Chapter 12 **Problem 12-3A or 12-3B (Continued)** ***Name*** ____________________

Part 2

____________ PARTNERSHIP Statement of Partners' Equity For Year Ended December 31	Partner: ______	Partner: ______	Partner: ______	*Partners' Total*
Beg. capital balances				
Plus:				
Owner investments				
Net Income:				
Salary allowances				
Interest allowances				
Balance allocated				
Total net income				
Total				
Less partners' withdrawals				
End. capital balances				

Part 3

GENERAL JOURNAL

Date		Account Titles and Explanation	PR	Debit	Credit

Chapter 12 Problem 12-4A or 12-4B *Name* ____________________

Part 1

GENERAL JOURNAL

Date		Account Titles and Explanation	PR	Debit	Credit
(a)					
(b)					
(c)					
(d)					
(e)					

Chapter 12 **Problem 12-4A or 12-4B (Continued)** ***Name*** ______________________________

Part 2

GENERAL JOURNAL

Date		Account Titles and Explanation	PR	Debit	Credit
(a)					
(b)					
(c)					

Chapter 12 **Problem 12-5A or 12-5B** ***Name*** ______________________________

(1)

GENERAL JOURNAL

Date		Account Titles and Explanation	PR	Debit	Credit

Chapter 12 **Problem 12-5A or 12-5B** ***Name*** ______________________________
(Continued)

(2)

GENERAL JOURNAL

Date		Account Titles and Explanation	PR	Debit	Credit

Chapter 12 **Problem 12-5A or 12-5B** ***Name*** ______________________________

(Continued)

(3)

GENERAL JOURNAL

Date		Account Titles and Explanation	PR	Debit	Credit

Chapter 12 **Problem 12-5A or 12-5B (Continued)** ***Name*** ______________________________

(4)

GENERAL JOURNAL

Date		Account Titles and Explanation	PR	Debit	Credit

Chapter 12 **Serial Problem, SP 12** ***Name*** ______________________
Business Solutions

(1)

(2)

GENERAL JOURNAL

Date		Account Titles and Explanation	PR	Debit	Credit

(3)

GENERAL JOURNAL

Date		Account Titles and Explanation	PR	Debit	Credit

(4)

Chapter 12 Reporting in Action
BTN 12-1

Name ______________________

(1)

(2)

(3)

Comparative Analysis—BTN 12-2

(1)

(2)

(3)

Chapter 12 Ethics Challenge
BTN 12-3

Name ______________________________

(1) Income allocation per original agreement:

	Maben	Orlando	Clark	Total
Salary allowance				
Per patient charges				
Totals				

(2) Income allocation per Clark's proposal:

	Maben	Orlando	Clark	Total
Per patient charges				

(3)

Chapter 12 **Communicating in Practice** ***Name*** ______________________
BTN 12-4

STUDY NOTES
Organizations with Partnership Characteristics

Chapter 12 **Taking It to the Net** ***Name*** ______________________
BTN 12-5

(1) ______________________

(2) ______________________

(3) ______________________

Chapter 12 Teamwork in Action
BTN 12-6

Name ______________________

(1)

Income/Loss Sharing Plan	Calculations	Baker	Warner	Rice	Total
(a)					
(b)					
(c)					
(d)					

(2) Team members share solutions.

(3)

Chapter 12 Entrepreneurial Decision *Name* ____________________
BTN 12-7

(1)

(2)

(3)

Global Decision—BTN 12-8

(1)

(2)

(3)

Chapter 13 Quick Study 13-1 ***Name*** ______________________________

True Statements: ______________________________

____

____

Quick Study 13-2

GENERAL JOURNAL

Date		Account Titles and Explanation	PR	Debit	Credit
(a)					
(b)					

Quick Study 13-3

GENERAL JOURNAL

Date		Account Titles and Explanation	PR	Debit	Credit
(a)					
(b)					

Chapter 13 Quick Study 13-4 ***Name*** ______________________________

GENERAL JOURNAL

Date		Account Titles and Explanation	PR	Debit	Credit
(a)					
(b)					

Quick Study 13-5

GENERAL JOURNAL

Date		Account Titles and Explanation	PR	Debit	Credit
(a)					
(b)					
(c)					

Quick Study 13-6

(1)

GENERAL JOURNAL

Date		Account Titles and Explanation	PR	Debit	Credit

(2) ______________________________

Chapter 13 Quick Study 13-7 ***Name*** ____________________

GENERAL JOURNAL

Date		Account Titles and Explanation	PR	Debit	Credit

Quick Study 13-8

Cash Dividend to Common Shareholders

Quick Study 13-9

___________ Company

Stockholders' Equity

April 2 (after stock dividend)

Chapter 13 Quick Study 13-10 ***Name*** ______________________

(1)

(2)

Quick Study 13-11

GENERAL JOURNAL

Date		Account Titles and Explanation	PR	Debit	Credit

Quick Study 13-12

Basic Earnings Per Share

Quick Study 13-13

Basic Earnings Per Share

Chapter 13 Quick Study 13-14 ***Name*** ______________________

Price-Earnings Ratio

Analysis

Quick Study 13-15

Dividend Yield

Analysis

Quick Study 13-16

Quick Study 13-17

GENERAL JOURNAL

Date		Account Titles and Explanation	PR	Debit	Credit

Chapter 13 Exercise 13-1 *Name* ____________________

	Characteristic	Corporations
1	Duration of Life	
2	Owner liability	
3	Legal status	
4	Tax status of income	
5	Owner authority & control	
6	Ease of formation	
7	Transferability of ownership	
8	Ability to raise large amounts of capital	

Exercise 13-2

GENERAL JOURNAL

Date		Account Titles and Explanation	PR	Debit	Credit
(1)					
(2)					
(3)					

Chapter 13 Exercise 13-3 ***Name*** ______________________

GENERAL JOURNAL

Date		Account Titles and Explanation	PR	Debit	Credit
(1)					
(2)					
(3)					
(4)					

Chapter 13 Exercise 13-4 *Name* ______________________

GENERAL JOURNAL

Date		Account Titles and Explanation	PR	Debit	Credit

Exercise 13-5

(1) ______________________ (4) ______________________
(2) ______________________ (5) ______________________
(3) ______________________ (6) ______________________

Chapter 13 Exercise 13-6 ***Name*** ____________________

Part 1

(a) Retained Earnings:

(b) Total Stockholders' Equity:

(c) Number of Outstanding Shares:

Part 2

(a) Retained Earnings:

(b) Total Stockholders' Equity:

(c) Number of Outstanding Shares:

Part 3

Chapter 13 **Exercise 13-7** ***Name*** ______________________________

Part 1

GENERAL JOURNAL

Date		Account Titles and Explanation	PR	Debit	Credit

Part 2

	Before	After

Part 3

	Feb. 5	Feb. 28

Chapter 13 Exercise 13-8 *Name* ______________________

	Preferred	Common
2011:		
2012:		
2013:		
2014:		
Totals:		

Exercise 13-9

	Preferred	Common
2011:		
2012:		
2013:		
2014:		
Totals:		

Chapter 13 Exercise 13-10 *Name* ______________________

Part 1

GENERAL JOURNAL

Date		Account Titles and Explanation	PR	Debit	Credit

Chapter 13 Exercise 13-10 (Continued) ***Name*** ______________________

Part 2

Changes to the equity section include:

Revised Stockholders' Equity Section (for support of your part 2 solution):

Chapter 13 Exercise 13-11 *Name* ______________________

________ COMPANY
Statement of Retained Earnings
For Year Ended December 31, 2011

Exercise 13-12

(1) Net Income Available to Common Stockholders:

(2) Basic Earnings per Share:

Chapter 13 Exercise 13-13 *Name* ______________________

(1) Net Income Available to Common Stockholders:

(2) Basic Earnings per Share:

Exercise 13-14

Dividend Yield:

(1)

(2)

(3)

(4)

Analysis:

Exercise 13-15

Price-Earnings Ratio:

(1)

(2)

(3)

(4)

Analysis:

Chapter 13 Exercise 13-16 **Name** ______________________

(1)

(2)

Exercise 13-17

(1)

(2) GENERAL JOURNAL

Date		Account Titles and Explanation	PR	Debit	Credit

(3)

Chapter 13 Exercise 13-18 ***Name*** ______________________________

(1)

GENERAL JOURNAL

Date		Account Titles and Explanation	PR	Debit	Credit

Chapter 13 Exercise 13-18 *Name* ______________________

(2)

______ CORPORATION
Statement of Retained Earnings
For Year Ended December 31, 2012

(3)

______ CORPORATION
Stockholders' Equity Section of the Balance Sheet
December 31, 2012

Chapter 13 Problem 13-1A or 13-1B ***Name*** ______________________

Part 1

(a) ______________________

(b) ______________________

(c) ______________________

(d) ______________________

Part 2

Number of Outstanding Shares: ______________________

Part 3

Minimum Legal Capital: ______________________

Part 4

Total Paid-In Capital from Common Stockholders: ______________________

Part 5

Book Value Per Common Share: ______________________

Chapter 13 Problem 13-2A or 13-2B ***Name*** ______________________________

Part 1

GENERAL JOURNAL

Date		Account Titles and Explanation	PR	Debit	Credit

Chapter 13 **Problem 13-2A or 13-2B** ***Name*** ______________________
(Continued)

Part 2

______________________ CORPORATION
Statement of Retained Earnings
For Year Ended December 31, 2012

Part 3

______________________ CORPORATION
Stockholders' Equity Section of the Balance Sheet
December 31, 2012

Chapter 13 Problem 13-3A or 13-3B *Name* ______________________

Part 1

Explanations for each of the entries:
Oct. 2 (Jan.17)*
Oct 25 (Feb. 5)*
Oct. 31 (Feb. 28)*
Nov. 5 (Mar. 14)*
Dec. 1 (Mar. 25)*
Dec. 31 (Mar. 31)*

*Dates for Problem 13-3B are in parentheses.

Part 2

	Oct. 2 (Jan. 17)*	Oct. 25 (Feb. 5)*	Oct. 31 (Feb. 28)*	Nov. 5 (Mar. 14)*	Dec. 1 (Mar. 25)*	Dec. 31 (Mar. 31)*
Common stock..............						
Common stock dividend distributable..						
Paid-In capital in excess of par..............						
Retained earnings..........						
Total equity...................						

*Dates for Problem 13-3B are in parentheses.

Chapter 13 Problem 13-4A or 13-4B *Name* ______________________

Part 1
Outstanding Common Shares:

Part 2
Cash Dividend Amounts:

Part 3
Capitalization of Retained Earnings:

Part 4
Cost Per Share of Treasury Stock:

Part 5
Net Income Computation:

Chapter 13 Problem 13-5A or 13-5B **Name** ______________________

(1) Market Price Per Share:

(2) Computation of Stock Par Values:

(3) Book Value Per Preferred Share:

Book Value Per Common Share:

(4) Book Value Per Preferred Share:

Book Value Per Common Share:

Chapter 13 Problem 13-5A or 13-5B (Continued) ***Name*** ______________________

(5) Book Value Per Preferred Share:

Book Value Per Common Share:

(6)

(7)

Chapter 13 Serial Problem, SP 13 Business Solutions

Name ______________________

(1a) GENERAL JOURNAL

Date		Account Titles and Explanation	PR	Debit	Credit

(1b) GENERAL JOURNAL

Date		Account Titles and Explanation	PR	Debit	Credit

(1c) GENERAL JOURNAL

Date		Account Titles and Explanation	PR	Debit	Credit

(2) (a)

(b)

(c)

(3)

Chapter 13 Reporting in Action
BTN 13-1

Name ______________________

(1)

(2)

(3)

(4)

(5)

(6) FastForward:

Chapter 13 Comparative Analysis Name ______________________
BTN 13-2

(1)
RIM Book Value Per Common Share:

Palm Book Value Per Common Share:

Apple Book Value Per Common Share:

(2)
RIM Earnings Per Share:

Palm Earnings per Share:

Apple Earnings per Share:

(3)
RIM Dividend Yield:

Palm Dividend Yield:

Apple Dividend Yield:

Analysis:

Chapter 13 **Comparative Analysis** ***Name*** ______________________

BTN 13-2

(Continued)

(4)

RIM Price-Earnings Ratio:

Palm Price-Earnings Ratio:

Apple Price-Earnings Ratio:

Analysis & Interpretation:

Chapter 13 **Ethics Challenge**
BTN 13-3

Name ______________________

Chapter 13 Communicating in Practice
BTN 13-4

Name ______________________________

MEMORANDUM

TO:
FROM:
DATE:
SUBJECT:

Company	Earnings Per Share	Market Price of Stock	Price-Earnings Ratio

Industry Norm:

Meaning of Price-Earnings Ratio:

Comparison Across Companies:

Concluding Analysis:

Chapter 13 Taking It to the Net
BTN 13-5

Name ______________________

Part 1

Part 2

Part 3

Part 4

Teamwork in Action—BTN 13-6

Part 1

(a) Impact on Financial Position due to Stock Buyback:

(b) Reasons for Stock Buyback:

Chapter 13 **Teamwork in Action**
BTN 13-6 (Continued)

Name ______________________________

Part 2

GENERAL JOURNAL

Date	Account Titles and Explanation	PR	Debit	Credit
Reacquisition entry				
(a)				
(b)				
(c)				
(d)				
(e)				

Part 3
Similarities:

Differences:

Chapter 13 Entrepreneurial Decision Name ______________________
BTN 13-7

Part 1

	Plan A	Plan B

Part 2

	Plan A	Plan B

Part 3

Chapter 13 Hitting the Road—BTN 13-8 *Name* ______________________

Global Decision—BTN 13-9

(1) Book Value per Common Share

(2) Earnings per Share

(3) Analysis

Chapter 14 Quick Study 14-1 *Name* ____________________

1. ________ Debenture
2. ________ Bond indenture
3. ________ Bearer bond
4. ________ Registered bond
5. ________ Sinking fund bond
6. ________ Convertible bond
7. ________ Secured bond
8. ________ Serial bond

Quick Study 14-2

(1) Cash Proceeds:

(2) Total Bond Interest Expense:

(3) Bond Interest Expense on 1st Payment Date:

Quick Study 14-3[B]

(1) Cash Proceeds:

(2) Total Bond Interest Expense:

(3) Bond Interest Expense on 1st Payment Date:

Chapter 14 Quick Study 14-4 *Name* ______________________

GENERAL JOURNAL

Date		Account Titles and Explanation	PR	Debit	Credit

Quick Study 14-5

(a) ______________________

(b) ______________________

Chapter 14 Quick Study 14-6 *Name* ______________________

	Date		Account Titles and Explanation	PR	Debit	Credit
(a)						
(b)						
(c)						

Chapter 14 Quick Study 14-7 *Name* ______________________

GENERAL JOURNAL

Date		Account Titles and Explanation	PR	Debit	Credit

Quick Study 14-8

GENERAL JOURNAL

Date		Account Titles and Explanation	PR	Debit	Credit

Chapter 14 Quick Study 14-9 *Name* ______________________

(a)

(b)

(c)

Quick Study 14-10

Ratio Computations:

Analysis and Interpretation:

Quick Study 14-11[C]

GENERAL JOURNAL

Date		Account Titles and Explanation	PR	Debit	Credit

Chapter 14 Quick Study 14-12[D] *Name* ______________________

GENERAL JOURNAL

Date		Account Titles and Explanation	PR	Debit	Credit

Quick Study 14-13[D]

GENERAL JOURNAL

Date		Account Titles and Explanation	PR	Debit	Credit

Quick Study 14-14

(a) ______________________

(b) ______________________

Quick Study 14-15

(a) ______________________

(b) ______________________

(c) ______________________

(d) ______________________

Chapter 14 Exercise 14-1 ***Name*** ______________________

(1) ______________________

(2)

GENERAL JOURNAL

	Date		Account Titles and Explanation	PR	Debit	Credit
(a)						
(b)						
(c)						

(3)

GENERAL JOURNAL

	Date		Account Titles and Explanation	PR	Debit	Credit
(a)						
(b)						

Chapter 14 Exercise 14-2 *Name* ______________________

(1) ______________________

(2) Total Bond Interest Expense: ______________________

(3) Straight-Line Amortization Table

Semiannual Period-End	Unamortized Discount	Carrying Value
1/01/2011		
6/30/2011		
12/31/2011		
6/30/2012		
12/31/2012		
6/30/2013		
12/31/2013		

Chapter 14 Exercise 14-3[B] ***Name*** ______________________

(1) ______________________

(2) **Total Bond Interest Expense:** ______________________

(3) Effective Interest Amortization Table

Semiannual Interest Period-End	(A) Cash Interest Paid (4.5% x $250,000)	(B) Bond Interest Expense [6% x Prior (E)]	(C) Discount Amortization [(B) - (A)]	(D) Unamortized Discount [Prior (D) - (C)]	(E) Carrying Value [$250,000-(D)]
1/01/2011					
6/30/2011					
12/31/2011					
6/30/2012					
12/31/2012					
6/30/2013					
12/31/2013					

Chapter 14 Exercise 14-4 ***Name*** ______________________

(1) ______________________

(2) Total Bond Interest Expense: ______________________

(3) Straight-Line Amortization Table

Semiannual Period-End	Unamortized Premium	Carrying Value
1/01/2011		
6/30/2011		
12/31/2011		
6/30/2012		
12/31/2012		
6/30/2013		
12/31/2013		

Chapter 14 Exercise 14-5[B] ***Name*** ____________________

(1)

(2) Total Bond Interest Expense:

(3) Effective Interest Amortization Table

Semiannual Interest Period-End	(A) Cash Interest Paid [6.5% x $800,000]	(B) Bond Interest Expense [6% x Prior (E)]	(C) Premium Amortization [(A) - (B)]	(D) Unamortized Premium [Prior (D) - (C)]	(E) Carrying Value [$800,000+(D)]
1/01/2011					
6/30/2011					
12/31/2011					
6/30/2012					
12/31/2012					
6/30/2013					
12/31/2013					

Chapter 14 Exercise 14-6 ***Name*** ______________________________

	Date		Account Titles and Explanation	PR	Debit	Credit
(a)						
(b)						
(c)						

Exercise 14-7

	Date		Account Titles and Explanation	PR	Debit	Credit
(a)						
(b)						
(c)						

Chapter 14 Exercise 14-8 ***Name*** ____________________

	Date		Account Titles and Explanation	PR	Debit	Credit
(a)						
(b)						
(c)						

Chapter 14 Exercise 14-9 *Name* ______________________

(1) Semiannual Cash Interest Payment:

(2) Number of Payments:

(3)

(4) Market Price Computation:

(5)

GENERAL JOURNAL

Date		Account Titles and Explanation	PR	Debit	Credit

Chapter 14 Exercise 14-10 ***Name*** ______________________

(1) Semiannual Cash Interest Payment:

(2) Number of Payments:

(3)

(4) Market Price Computation:

(5)

GENERAL JOURNAL

Date		Account Titles and Explanation	PR	Debit	Credit

Chapter 14 Exercise 14-11 *Name* ______________________

(1) Cash proceeds from sale:

(2) Discount at issuance:

(3) Total Amortization for First 6 Years:

(4) Carrying value of the bonds at 12/31/2016:

(5) Purchase price:

(6) Loss on retirement:

(7)

GENERAL JOURNAL

Date		Account Titles and Explanation	PR	Debit	Credit

Chapter 14 Exercise 14-12C ***Name*** ______________________

(1)

____

____

____

____

____

(2)

GENERAL JOURNAL

Date		Account Titles and Explanation	PR	Debit	Credit

Chapter 14 Exercise 14-13 **Name** ______________________

(1) Straight-Line Amortization Table

Semiannual Period-End	Unamortized Discount	Carrying Value
6/01/2011		
11/30/2011		
5/31/2012		
11/30/2012		
5/31/2013		
11/30/2013		
5/31/2014		
11/30/2014		
5/31/2015		

Supporting computations:

Chapter 14 Exercise 14-13 (Continued) *Name* ______________________

(2)

GENERAL JOURNAL

Date		Account Titles and Explanation	PR	Debit	Credit

Chapter 14 Exercise 14-14 ***Name*** ______________________

(1) Amount of Each Payment:

(2)

		Payments			
	(A)	(B) Debit	(C) Debit	(D) Credit	(E)
Period Ending Date	Beginning Balance [Prior (E)]	Interest Expense + [7% x (A)]	Notes Payable = [(D) - (B)]	Cash [computed]	Ending Balance [(A) - (C)]
2011					
2012					
2013					
2014					

Chapter 14 Exercise 14-15 ***Name*** ______________________________

GENERAL JOURNAL

Date		Account Titles and Explanation	PR	Debit	Credit

Chapter 14 Exercise 14-16 *Name* ______________________

(1)(a) ______________________

(b) ______________________

(2) ______________________

Exercise 14-17[D]

(1) ______________________
(2) ______________________
(3) ______________________

Chapter 14 Exercise 14-18[D] *Name* ______________________

GENERAL JOURNAL

Date		Account Titles and Explanation	PR	Debit	Credit
(1)					
(2)					

Exercise 14-19[D]

Chapter 14 Exercise 14-20 **Name** ____________________

GENERAL JOURNAL

Date		Account Titles and Explanation	PR	Debit	Credit
(1)					
(2)					

(3) ____________________

(4) ____________________

Chapter 14 Problem 14-1A or 14-1B ***Name*** ____________________

Part 1

(a)

Cash Flow	PV Table Value	Amount	Present Value

(b)

GENERAL JOURNAL

Date		Account Titles and Explanation	PR	Debit	Credit

Part 2

(a)

Cash Flow	PV Table Value	Amount	Present Value

(b)

GENERAL JOURNAL

Date		Account Titles and Explanation	PR	Debit	Credit

Chapter 14 Problem 14-1A or 14-1B (Continued) **Name** ______________________

Part 3

(a)

Cash Flow	PV Table Value	Amount	Present Value

(b)

GENERAL JOURNAL

Date		Account Titles and Explanation	PR	Debit	Credit

Problem 14-2A or 14-2B

Part 1

GENERAL JOURNAL

Date		Account Titles and Explanation	PR	Debit	Credit

Chapter 14 Problem 14-2A or 14-2B (Continued) *Name* ______________________

Part 2

(a) Cash Payment:

(b) Semiannual Amortization:

(c) Bond Interest Expense:

Part 3

Total Bond Interest Expense:

Part 4 Straight-Line Amortization Table

Semiannual Period-End	Unamortized Discount	Carrying Value
1/01/2011		
6/30/2011		
12/31/2011		
6/30/2012		
12/31/2012		

Chapter 14 Problem 14-2A or 14-2B (Continued) *Name* ______________________

Part 5

GENERAL JOURNAL

Date		Account Titles and Explanation	PR	Debit	Credit

Problem 14-3A or 14-3B

Part 1

GENERAL JOURNAL

Date		Account Titles and Explanation	PR	Debit	Credit

Part 2

(a) Cash Payment: ______________________

(b) Semiannual Amortization: ______________________

(c) Bond Interest Expense: ______________________

Chapter 14 Problem 14-3A or 14-3B (Continued) *Name* ______________________

Part 3

Total Bond Interest Expense:

Part 4 Straight-Line Amortization Table

Semiannual Period-End	Unamortized Premium	Carrying Value
1/01/2011		
6/30/2011		
12/31/2011		
6/30/2012		
12/31/2012		

Part 5

GENERAL JOURNAL

Date		Account Titles and Explanation	PR	Debit	Credit

Chapter 14 Problem 14-4A or 14-4B *Name* ______________________

Part 1

Total Bond Interest Expense:

Part 2 Straight-Line Amortization Table

Semiannual Interest Period-End	Unamortized Premium	Carrying Value
1/01/2011		
6/30/2011		
12/31/2011		
6/30/2012		
12/31/2012		
6/30/2013		
12/31/2013		
6/30/2014		
12/31/2014		
6/30/2015		
12/31/2015		

Chapter 14 Problem 14-4A or 14-4B (Continued) *Name* ______________________

Part 3

GENERAL JOURNAL

Date		Account Titles and Explanation	PR	Debit	Credit

Chapter 14 Problem 14-5A[B] or 14-5B[B] ***Name*** ______________________

Part 1

Total Bond Interest Expense:

Part 2 Effective Interest Amortization Table

Semiannual Interest Period-End	(A) Cash Interest Paid [__% x $____]	(B) Bond Interest Expense [__% x Prior (E)]	(C) Premium Amortization [(A) - (B)]	(D) Unamortized Premium [Prior (D) - (C)]	(E) Carrying Value [$____ + (D)]
1/01/2011					
6/30/2011					
12/31/2011					
6/30/2012					
12/31/2012					
6/30/2013					
12/31/2013					
6/30/2014					
12/31/2014					
6/30/2015					
12/31/2015					

Chapter 14 Problem 14-5A[B] or 14-5B[B] (Continued) *Name* ______________________

Part 3

GENERAL JOURNAL

Date		Account Titles and Explanation	PR	Debit	Credit

Part 4

Cash Flow	PV Table Value	Amount	Present Value

Comparison to Part 2 Table:

Chapter 14 Problem 14-6A or 14-6B **Name** ______________________

Part 1

GENERAL JOURNAL

Date		Account Titles and Explanation	PR	Debit	Credit

Part 2

Total Bond Interest Expense: ______________________

Part 3 Straight-Line Amortization Table

Semiannual Interest Period-End	Unamortized Discount	Carrying Value
1/01/2011		
6/30/2011		
12/31/2011		
6/30/2012		
12/31/2012		

Chapter 14 **Problem 14-6A or 14-6B (Continued)** ***Name*** ______________________

Part 4

GENERAL JOURNAL

Date		Account Titles and Explanation	PR	Debit	Credit

Part 5 (for Problem 14-6A only)

Chapter 14 Problem 14-7A[B] or 14-7B[B] ***Name*** ______________________________

Part 1

GENERAL JOURNAL

Date		Account Titles and Explanation	PR	Debit	Credit

Part 2

Total Bond Interest Expense:

Part 3 Effective Interest Amortization Table

Semiannual Interest Period-End	(A) Cash Interest Paid [__% x $___]	(B) Bond Interest Expense [__% x Prior (E)]	(C) Discount Amortization [(B) - (A)]	(D) Unamortized Discount [Prior (D) - (C)]	(E) Carrying Value [$______ - (D)]
1/01/2011					
6/30/2011					
12/31/2011					
6/30/2012					
12/31/2012					

Chapter 14 **Problem 14-7A[B] or 14-7B[B] (Continued)** ***Name*** ______________________

Part 4

GENERAL JOURNAL

Date		Account Titles and Explanation	PR	Debit	Credit

Chapter 14 Problem 14-8A[B] or 14-8B[B] ***Name*** ________________________________

Part 1

GENERAL JOURNAL

Date		Account Titles and Explanation	PR	Debit	Credit

Part 2

Total Bond Interest Expense:

Part 3 Effective Interest Amortization Table

Semiannual Interest Period-End	(A) Cash Interest Paid [__% x $___]	(B) Bond Interest Expense [__% x Prior (E)]	(C) Premium Amortization [(A) - (B)]	(D) Unamortized Premium [Prior (D) - (C)]	(E) Carrying Value [$_____ + (D)]
1/01/2011					
6/30/2011					
12/31/2011					
6/30/2012					
12/31/2012					

Chapter 14 Problem 14-8A[B] or 14-8B[B] (Continued) ***Name*** ____________________

Part 4

GENERAL JOURNAL

Date		Account Titles and Explanation	PR	Debit	Credit

Part 5

GENERAL JOURNAL

Date		Account Titles and Explanation	PR	Debit	Credit

Part 6

Chapter 14 **Problem 14-9A or 14-9B** ***Name*** ______________________

Part 1

Amount of Each Payment:

Part 2

		Payments			
	(A)	(B)	(C)	(D)	(E)
		Debit	Debit		
Period	Beginning	Interest	Notes	Credit	Ending
Ending	Balance	Expense +	Payable =	Cash	Balance
Date	[Prior (E)]	[___% x (A)]	[(D) - (B)]	[computed]	[(A) - (C)]

Chapter 14 **Problem 14-9A or 14-9B (Continued)** ***Name*** ____________________

Part 3

GENERAL JOURNAL

Date		Account Titles and Explanation	PR	Debit	Credit

Problem 14-10A or 14-10B

Part 1

______________ **Company—Debt-to-Equity Ratio:**

______________ **Company—Debt-to-Equity Ratio:**

Part 2

Analysis and Interpretation:

Chapter 14 Problem 14-11A[D] or 14-11B[D] *Name* ____________________

Part 1

Present Value of the Lease Payments: ____________________

Part 2

GENERAL JOURNAL

Date		Account Titles and Explanation	PR	Debit	Credit

Part 3

Capital Lease Liability Payment (Amortization) Schedule:

Period Ending Date	Beginning Balance of Lease Liability	Interest on Lease Liability (__%)	Reduction of Lease Liability	Cash Lease Payment	Ending Balance of Lease Liability
Year 1					
Year 2					
Year 3					
Year 4					
Year 5					

Part 4

GENERAL JOURNAL

Date		Account Titles and Explanation	PR	Debit	Credit

Chapter 14 Serial Problem, SP 14
Business Solutions

Name ______________________

Part 1

Maximum Loan Allowed:

Part 2

(a) Percent of Assets Financed by Debt

(b) Percent of Assets Financed by Equity

Part 3

Chapter 14 **Reporting in Action**
BTN 14-1

Name ____________________

(1)

(2)

(3)

(4) Fast Forward:

Chapter 14 Comparative Analysis Name ______________________
BTN 14-2

(1) RIM

Current Year:

Prior Year:

Apple

Current Year:

Prior Year:

(2)

Chapter 14 **Ethics Challenge**
BTN 14-3

Name ______________________________

(1)

(2)

Chapter 14 Communicating in Practice *Name* ____________________
BTN 14-4

MEMORANDUM

TO:
FROM:
DATE:
SUBJECT:

Chapter 14 **Taking It to the Net** *Name* ______________________

BTN 14-5

(1) Long Term Liabilities:

(2a)

(2b)

Chapter 14 Teamwork in Action
BTN 14-6

Name ______________________

Parts 1 & 2

Part 3

Part 4

Chapter 14 **Teamwork in Action**
BTN 14-6 (Continued)

Name ______________________________

Part 5

Similarities	Differences

Chapter 14 Entrepreneurial Decision **Name** ____________________
BTN 14-7

Part 1

	Current	Alternative Notes for Expansion				
		10% Note	15% Note	16% Note	17% Note	20% Note
Income before interest..............						
Interest expense.						
Net income.........						
Equity................						
Return on equity.						

Work Space:

Part 2

Chapter 14 **Hitting the Road**
BTN 14-8

Name ______________________

Global Decision—BTN 14-9

(1) Current Year Ratio:

Prior Year Ratio:

(2)

Chapter 16 Quick Study 16-1 *Name* ________________

(1)	(6)
(2)	(7)
(3)	(8)
(4)	(9)
(5)	(10)

Quick Study 16-2

(1)

(2)

(3)

(4)

Quick Study 16-3

Cash Flows from Operating Activities

Chapter 16 Quick Study 16-4 *Name* ______________________

Quick Study 16-5

(1)

(2)

Quick Study 16-6

Cash Flows from Operating Activities	Case A	Case B	Case C

Chapter 16 Quick Study 16-7 ***Name*** ______________________

Investing Activities

Quick Study 16-8

Financing Activities

Quick Study 16-9[B]

Cash Flow from Operating Activities

Chapter 16 Quick Study 16-10 *Name* ____________________

Cash Inflow from Asset Sale:

Quick Study 16-11

(1) Cash Paid for Dividends:

(2) Cash Payments toward Notes:

Quick Study 16-12

(1) Cash Received from Customer:

(2) Net Increase or Decrease in Cash:

Chapter 16 Quick Study 16-13[B] *Name* ______

(1) Cash Paid for Merchandise:

(2) Cash Paid for Operating Expenses:

Quick Study 16-14[B]

Cash Flow from Operating Activities

Quick Study 16-15

(1)

(2)

Chapter 16 Quick Study 16-16[A] ***Name*** ______________________________

____
____
____
____
____
____
____
____

Chapter 16 Quick Study 16-17 ***Name*** ______________________

Krug, Inc.
Statement of Cash Flows (Indirect Method)
For Year Ended June 30, 20___

Supporting calculations:

(2)

Chapter 16 Quick Study 16-18 *Name* ______________________

(1) ______________________

	Cash Flow	U.S. GAAP	IFRS
(2)	a.		
	b.		
	c.		
	d.		

Exercise 16-1

Cash Flow from Operating Activities

Chapter 16 Exercise 16-2 *Name* ______________________

	Statement of Cash Flows				
	Operating Activities	*Investing Activities*	*Financing Activities*	*Noncash Investing & Financing Activities*	*Not Reported on Statement or in Note*
a. Accounts receivable decreased this year.					
b. Purchased land by issuing stock.					
c. Paid cash to purchase inventory.					
d. Sold equipment for cash, yielding a loss.					
e. Accounts payable decreased this year.					
f. Income taxes payable increased this year.					
g. Declared and paid a cash dividend.					
h. Recorded depreciation expense.					
i. Paid cash to settle long-term notes payable.					
j. Prepaid expenses increased this year.					

Chapter 16 Exercise 16-3[B] ***Name*** ______________________

		Statement of Cash Flows			Noncash Investing & Financing Activities	Not Reported on Statement or in Note
		Operating Activities	*Investing Activities*	*Financing Activities*		
a.	Accepted six-month note receivable in exchange for plant assets.					
b.	Recorded depreciation expense.					
c.	Paid cash to acquire treasury stock.					
d.	Collected cash from sales.					
e.	Borrowed cash from bank by signing a 9-month note payable.					
f.	Paid cash to purchase patent.					
g.	Retired long-term notes payable by issuing stock.					
h.	Paid cash toward accounts payable.					
i.	Sold inventory for cash.					
j.	Paid cash dividend that was declared in a prior period.					

Chapter 16 Exercise 16-4 *Name* ____________________

Cash Flows from Operating Activities

Exercise 16-5[B]

Case A

Case B

Case C

Chapter 16 Exercise 16-6 *Name* ______________________

Cash Flows from Operating Activities

Supporting computations:

Exercise 16-7[B]

Cash Flows from Operating Activities

Supporting computations:

Chapter 16 Exercise 16-8 ***Name*** ______________________

Cash Flows from Investing Activities

Exercise 16-9

Cash Flows for Financing Activities

Chapter 16 Exercise 16-10 *Name* ____________________

__________, Inc.
Statement of Cash Flows (Indirect Method)
For Year Ended June 30, 20____

Supporting Computations for:

(1) Cash received from sale of equipment:

Cash paid for new equipment:

Chapter 16 Exercise 16-10 (Continued) *Name* ______________________

Part 1

Supporting computations continued.

(2) Cash paid to retire notes:

(3) Cash paid for dividends:

Part 2

Cash Flow on Total Assets Ratio:

Interpretation:

Chapter 16 Exercise 16-11[B] ***Name*** ______________________

____________, Inc.

Statement of Cash Flows (Direct Method)

For Year Ended June 30, 20___

Supporting Computations for:

(1) Cash received from customers:

(2) Cash paid for merchandise inventory:

Chapter 16 Exercise 16-11[B] (Continued) *Name* ______________________

Part 1

Supporting Computations Continued.

(3) Cash paid for other operating expenses:

(4) Cash paid for income taxes:

(5) Cash received from sale of equipment:

Cash paid for new equipment:

(6) Cash paid to retire notes:

(7) Cash paid for dividends:

Chapter 16 **Exercise 16-12**[B] ***Name*** ______________________

__________ COMPANY
Statement of Cash Flows
For Year Ended December 31, 20___

Footnotes:

Chapter 16 Exercise 16-13[B] ***Name*** ______________________________

Part 1

__________ CORPORATION
Statement of Cash Flows
For Year Ended December 31, 20___

Part 2

(a)

(b)

(c)

(d)

Chapter 16 Exercise 16-14 *Name* ______________________

Cash Flows from Operating Activities

Exercise 16-15

(1) Cash Flows from Operating Activities

(2)

(3)

Chapter 16 Exercise 16-16 ***Name*** ______________________

2010

2011

Interpretation:

Chapter 16 Exercise 16-17 ***Name*** ______________________________

Spreadsheet for Statement of Cash Flows
For Year Ended December 31, 20___

		Analysis of changes		
	Dec. 31, 2010	***Debit***	***Credit***	***Dec. 31, 2011***
Balance sheet-debit bal. accounts:				
Cash...				
Accounts receivable......................				
Merchandise inventory..................				
Plant assets..................................				
Balance sheet-credit bal. accounts:				
Accum. depreciation-Plant assets				
Accounts payable....................				
Notes payable..........................				
Long-term notes payable..........				
Common Stock........................				
Retained earnings..................				
Statement of cash flows:				
Operating activities				
Net income..............................				
________ in accts. receivable...				
________ in merch. inventory...				
________ in accounts payable...				
Depreciation expense..............				
Investing activities				
Payment for plant assets.............				
Financing activities				
Payments of cash dividends.....				
Issued note payable..................				

Chapter 16 Exercise 16-18 ***Name*** ______________________

Statement of Cash Flows

For Year Ended December 31, 20___

Chapter 16 Problem 16-1A or 16-1B ***Name*** ______________________

Part 1

____

Statement of Cash Flows

For Year Ended December 31, 20___

Statement Footnotes:

Supporting calculations:

Chapter 16 **Problem 16-1A or 16-1B (Continued)** ***Name*** ______

Part 2

Chapter 16 Problem 16-2A[B] or 16-2B[B] ***Name*** ____________________

Statement of Cash Flows
For Year Ended December 31, 20___

Statement Footnotes:

Supporting calculations:

Chapter 16 Problem 16-3A[A] or 16-3B[A] *Name* ______________________

Spreadsheet for Statement of Cash Flows
For Year Ended December 31, 20___

	Dec. 31, 2010	Analysis of changes Debit	Credit	Dec. 31, 2011
Balance sheet-debit bal. accounts:				
Cash..				
Accounts receivable......................				
Merchandise inventory..................				
Prepaid expenses.........................				
Equipment....................................				
Balance sheet-credit bal. accounts:				
Accum. depreciation-Equip.......				
Accounts payable.....................				
Short-term notes payable.........				
Long-term notes payable..........				
Common Stock, $___par value...				
Paid-in capital in excess of par value, common stock.......				
Retained earnings..................				
Statement of cash flows:				
Operating activities				
Net income..............................				
________ in accts. receivable...				
________ in merch. inventory...				
________ in prepaid expenses...				
________ in accounts payable...				
Depreciation expense...............				
________ on sale of equipment..				
Investing activities				
Receipt from sale of equipment...				
Payment to purchase equipment..				
Financing activities				
Borrowed on short-term note....				
Payment on long-term note......				
Issued common stock for cash..				
Payments of cash dividends.....				
Noncash investing and financing activities:				
Purchase of equip. financed by long-term note payable.....				

Chapter 16 Problem 16-3A or 16-3B ***Name*** ______________________

____

Statement of Cash Flows

For Year Ended December 31, 20___

Statement Footnotes:

Supporting calculations:

Chapter 16 Problem 16-4A or 16-4B ***Name*** ______________________

Statement of Cash Flows
For Year Ended December 31, 20___

Supporting calculations:

Chapter 16 **Problem 16-5A[B] or 16-5B[B]** ***Name*** ______________________________

____

Statement of Cash Flows

For Year Ended December 31, 20___

Supporting calculations:

Chapter 16 Problem 16-6A[A] or 16-6B[A] *Name* ______________________

Spreadsheet for Statement of Cash Flows				
For Year Ended December 31, 20___				
		Analysis of changes		
	Dec. 31, 2010	*Debit*	*Credit*	*Dec. 31, 2011*
Balance sheet-debit bal. accounts:				
Cash				
Accounts receivable				
Merchandise inventory				
Equipment				
Balance sheet-credit bal. accounts:				
Accum. depreciation-Equip				
Accounts payable				
Income taxes payable				
Common stock, $___par value				
Paid-in capital in excess of par value, common stock				
Retained earnings				
Statement of cash flows:				
Operating activities				
Net income				
_________ in accts. receivable				
_________ in merch. inventory				
_________ in accounts payable				
_________ in income taxes payable				
Depreciation expense				
Investing activities				
Payment for equipment				
Financing activities				
Issued common stock for cash				
Paid cash dividends				

Chapter 16 Problem 16-6A[A] or 16-6B[A] *Name* ______________________

Statement of Cash Flows

For Year Ended December 31, 20__

Supporting calculations:

Chapter 16 Problem 16-7A or 16-7B *Name* ____________________

Cash Flows from Operating Activities—Indirect Method

Problem 16-8A[B] or 16-8B[B]

Cash Flows from Operating Activities—Direct Method

Chapter 16 **Serial Problem, SP 16** ***Name*** ______________________
Business Solutions

BUSINESS SOLUTIONS
Statement of Cash Flows
For Three Months Ended March 31, 20___

Supporting calculations:

Chapter 16 Reporting in Action ***Name*** ______

BTN 16-1

(1)

(2)

(3)

(4)

(5) FastForward:

Chapter 16 **Comparative Analysis** ***Name*** ____________________

BTN 16-2

(1) RIM's Cash Flow on Total Assets Ratio:

Current Year

Prior Year

Apple's Cash Flow on Total Assets Ratio:

Current Year

Prior Year

(2)

(3)

(4)

Chapter 16 **Ethics Challenge**
BTN 16-3

Name ______________________

(1) (a)

(b)

(2)

Chapter 16 **Communicating in Practice** ***Name*** ______________________
BTN 16-4

MEMORANDUM

TO:
FROM:
DATE:
SUBJECT:

Chapter 16 Taking It to the Net Name ______________________

BTN 16-5

(1)

(2)

(3)	2008	2009	2010
Net income (net loss)			
Cash flow from operations			

Analysis:

(4)

(5)

(6)

Teamwork in Action—BTN 16-6

Part 1

(a)

Chapter 16 **Teamwork in Action**
BTN 16-6
(Continued)

Name ______________________

Part 1

(b) Similarities	Differences

(c)

(d)

Part 2

Adjusting Net Income to Cash Flow from Operating Activities	
Items to Add	Items to Subtract
a.	
b.	
c.	
d.	

Chapter 16 Teamwork in Action
BTN 16-6
(Continued)

Name ______________________

Part 3

(a)

(b)

(c)

(d)

Chapter 16 Entrepreneurial Decision
BTN 16-7

Name ______________________________

(1) ______________________________

(2) ______________________________

Chapter 16 **Entrepreneurial Decision** ***Name*** ______________________
BTN 16-8

MEMORANDUM

TO:
FROM:
DATE:
SUBJECT:

Chapter 16 Hitting the Road *Name* ______________________

BTN 16-9

(1)

(2)

(3)

Global Decision—BTN 16-10

(1) Cash Flow on Total Assets Ratio

Current Year:

Prior Year:

(2) Comparative Analysis:

Chapter 17 Quick Study 17-1 ***Name*** ______________________

Not part of General-Purpose Statements:

Quick Study 17-2

Quick Study 17-3

Trend Percents

2011

2010

Quick Study 17-4

Common-Size Percents

2011

2010

Chapter 17 Quick Study 17-5 *Name* ____________________

Account	2011	2010	Dollar Change	Percent Change

Quick Study 17-6

Ratio	2011	2010	Change
1. Profit Margin Ratio	8%	6%	
2. Debt Ratio	45%	40%	
3. Gross Margin Ratio	33%	45%	
4. Acid-Test Ratio	0.99	1.10	
5. Accounts Receivable Turnover	5.4	6.6	
6. Basic Earnings Per Share	$1.24	$1.20	
7. Inventory Turnover	3.5	3.3	
8. Dividend Yield	1.0%	0.8%	

Chapter 17 Quick Study 17-7 *Name* ______________________

COMPARATIVE ANALYSIS REPORT

Quick Study 17-8[A]

Chapter 17 Quick Study 17-9 ***Name*** ____________________

(a)

(b)

Exercise 17-1

(1) (6)
(2) (7)
(3) (8)
(4) (9)
(5) (10)

Exercise 17-2

(1)

(2)

(3)

Chapter 17 Exercise 17-3 *Name* ______________________

Account	2013	2012	2011	2010	2009

Analysis:

Exercise 17-4

Answer:

Supporting Work:

Chapter 17 Exercise 17-5 **Name** ______________________

Account	2011	2010

Analysis:

Exercise 17-6

COMPARATIVE ANALYSIS REPORT

Chapter 17 Exercise 17-7 *Name* ______________________________

____________ Company Common-Size Comparative Balance Sheets December 31, 2010-2012	2012	2011	2010

Analysis and interpretation:

Chapter 17 Exercise 17-8 ***Name*** ______________________

(1) Current Ratio:

2012:

2011:

2010:

(2) Acid-test ratio:

2012:

2011:

2010:

Analysis and interpretation:

Chapter 17 Exercise 17-9 *Name* ____________________

1. Days' sales uncollected:

2012:

2011:

2. Accounts receivable turnover:

2012:

2011:

3. Inventory turnover:

2012:

2011:

4. Days' sales in inventory:

2012:

2011:

Analysis and interpretation:

Chapter 17 Exercise 17-10 **Name** ______________________

(1)

Debt Ratio and Equity Ratio	2012	2011

(2) Debt-to-Equity Ratio

(3) Times Interest Earned

Analysis and interpretation:

Chapter 17 Exercise 17-11 *Name* ______________________

(1) Profit margin:
2012:

2011:

(2) Total asset turnover:
2012:

2011:

(3) Return on total assets:
2012:

2011:

Analysis and interpretation:

Chapter 17 Exercise 17-12 **Name** ______________________

(1) Return on common stockholders' equity:

2012:

2011:

(2) Price-earnings ratio, December 31:

2012:

2011:

(3) Dividend yield:

2012:

2011:

Analysis and interpretation:

Chapter 17 Exercise 17-13[A] *Name* ____________________

(1)	(5)
(2)	(6)
(3)	(7)
(4)	(8)

Exercise 17-14[A]

____________ Merchandising
Income Statement
For Year Ended December 31, 20____

Exercise 17-15

1. Current ratio:

Net profit margin

Sales-to-assets:

2.

Chapter 17 Problem 17-1A or 17-1B **Name** ______________________

Part 1

Current Ratio:

2012: ______________________

2011: ______________________

2010: ______________________

Part 2

Common-Size Comparative Income Statements For Years Ended December 31, 2012, 2011, and 2010	2012	2011	2010

Chapter 17 Problem 17-1A or 17-1B (Continued) *Name* ______________________

Part 3

Balance Sheet Data in Trend Percents December 31, 2012, 2011, and 2010	2012	2011	2010

Part 4

Significant relations revealed:

Chapter 17 Problem 17-2A or 17-2B ***Name*** ______________________________

Part 1

	Income Statement Trends For Years Ended December 31, 2012-2006						
	2012	*2011*	*2010*	*2009*	*2008*	*2007*	*2006*

	Balance Sheet Trends December 31, 2012-2006						
	2012	*2011*	*2010*	*2009*	*2008*	*2007*	*2006*

Chapter 17 **Problem 17-2A or 17-2B** ***Name*** ______________________
(Continued)

Part 2

Analysis and interpretation:

Chapter 17 **Problem 17-3A or 17-3B** ***Name*** ______________________

Transaction	*Current Assets*	*Quick Assets*	*Current Liabilities*	*Current Ratio*	*Acid-Test Ratio*	*Working Capital*
Beg. Bal.						
End. Bal.						

Supporting computations:

Chapter 17 Problem 17-4A or 17-4B *Name* ____________________

(1) Current ratio:

(2) Acid-test ratio:

(3) Days' sales uncollected:

(4) Inventory turnover:

(5) Days' sales in inventory:

(6) Debt-to-equity ratio:

(7) Times interest earned:

(8) Profit margin ratio:

Chapter 17 Problem 17-4A or 17-4B (Continued) *Name* ______________________

(9) Total asset turnover:

(10) Return on total assets:

(11) Return on common stockholders' equity:

Chapter 17 Problem 17-5A or 17-5B *Name* ______________________

Part 1

	_______ *Company*	_______ *Company*
a. Current ratio:		
b. Acid-test ratio:		
c. Accounts (incl. notes) receivable turnover:		
d. Inventory turnover:		
e. Days' sales in inventory:		
f. Days' sales uncollected:		

Short-term credit risk analysis:

Chapter 17 **Problem 17-5A or 17-5B (Continued)** ***Name*** ______________________

Part 2

	______ ***Company***	______ ***Company***
a. Profit margin ratio:		
b. Total asset turnover:		
c. Return on total assets:		
d. Return on common stockholders' equity:		
e. Price-earnings ratio:		
f. Dividend yield:		

Investment analysis:

Chapter 17 Problem 17-6A[A] or 17-6B[A] ***Name*** ______________________

Part 1 Effect of Income Taxes:

Items	Pretax	___% Tax Effect	After-Tax

Part 2 Income from Continuing Operations (and its Components):

Chapter 17 Problem 17-6A[A] or 17-6B[A] *Name* ______________________
(Continued)

Part 3 Income from Discontinued Segment:

Part 4 Income before Extraordinary Items:

Part 5 Net Income:

Chapter 17 Serial Problem, SP 17 **Name** ______________________

Business Solutions

(1) Gross Margin Ratio (with services revenue):

Gross Margin Ratio (without services revenue):

Profit Margin Ratio:

(2) Current Ratio:

Acid-Test Ratio:

(3) Debt Ratio:

Equity Ratio:

(4) Current Assets as % of Total Assets:

Long-Term Assets as % of Total Assets:

Chapter 17 Reporting in Action
BTN 17-1

Name ______________________________

(1) Trend Percents for selected income statement accounts:

	2010	2009	2008
Revenues			
Cost of Goods Sold			
Operating expenses			
Income taxes			
Net income			

(2) Common-size percents for asset categories and accounts:

	2010	2009
Total current assets		
Property and equipment, net		
Intangible assets		

(3) Analysis and Interpretation:

(4) FastForward

Chapter 17 Comparative Analysis
BTN 17-2

Name ______________________________

(1)

Key figures	Research In Motion Percent	Apple Amount
Cash and cash equivalents		
Accounts receivable, net		
Inventories		
Retained earnings		
Cost of sales		
Revenues		
Total Assets		

(2)

(3)

(4)

Chapter 17 Ethics Challenge
BTN 17-3

Name ______________________

(1)

(2)

Chapter 17 Communicating in Practice *Name* ____________________
BTN 17-4

MEMORANDUM

TO:
FROM:
DATE:
SUBJECT:

Chapter 17 **Taking It to the Net**
BTN 17-5

Name ______________________

	2008	2009
1. Profit margin ratio		
2. Gross profit ratio		
3. Return on total assets		
4. Return on common stockholders' equity		
5. Basic earnings per share		

Analysis and Interpretation:

Chapter 17 Teamwork in Action
BTN 17-6

Name ______________________

Part 1

Part 2

Part 3

Chapter 17 **Entrepreneurial Decision** *Name* ____________________
BTN 17-7

(1)

(2)

(3)

(4)

(5)

(6)

Hitting the Road—BTN 17-8

Chapter 17 Global Decision—BTN 17-9 *Name* ______________________

Key Figures	Percent	Amount
Cash and equivalents..........................		
Accounts receivable, net......................		
Inventories..		
Retained earnings..............................		
Cost of Sales......................................		
Revenues..		
Total assets..		

(2) Comparisons and comments